PLATE 1 A sample plate from a color blindness test. Individuals with normal red-green vision will see the number 23.

PLATE 2 The "spreading effect": the same red is used throughout, but the white makes it look lighter and the black, darker.

PLATE 3 An afterimage experiment. Look steadily at the dot in the center of the blue circle for twenty seconds, then at the dot in the gray rectangle. Repeat with the yellow circle. What do you see?

THE ENCYCLOPEDIA OF
HUMAN BEHAVIOR

Other Books by Dr. Robert M. Goldenson

HELPING YOUR CHILD TO READ BETTER

UNDERSTANDING CHILDREN'S PLAY (co-author)

ALL ABOUT THE HUMAN MIND

THE COMPLETE BOOK OF CHILDREN'S PLAY (co-author)

THE
ENCYCLOPEDIA
OF
HUMAN BEHAVIOR

*Psychology, Psychiatry, and
Mental Health*

ROBERT M. GOLDENSON, Ph.D

Volume One

Garden City, New York
DOUBLEDAY & COMPANY, INC.
1970

Anatomical drawings by Howard S. Friedman.

Grateful acknowledgment is made to the authors and publishers for permission to reprint excerpts from the following material:

"Emotional Deprivation in Infants," H. Bakwin, *Journal of Pediatrics*, 35:512–21, 1949, The C. V. Mosby Company.

"Criminal Genesis and the Degrees of Responsibility in Epilepsies," R. S. Banay, *American Journal of Psychiatry*, Vol. 117, pages 875–76, 1961.

The Neglected/Battered Child Syndrome, G. J. Barbero et al., Child Welfare League of America, 1963.

A Mind That Found Itself, C. W. Beers. Copyright 1907, 1917, 1921, 1923, 1931, 1932, 1934, 1935, 1937, 1939, 1940, 1942, 1944, 1953, by the American Foundation for Mental Hygiene, Inc. Reprinted by permission of Doubleday & Company, Inc.

Clinical Psychology, L. E. Bisch, The Williams & Wilkins Company, 1925.

The Psychology of Behavior Disorders, N. Cameron, Houghton Mifflin Company, 1947.

Behavior Pathology, N. Cameron and A. Magaret, Houghton Mifflin Company, 1951.

Abnormal Psychology and Modern Life, J. C. Coleman. Copyright © 1964 by Scott, Foresman & Company.

Adapted from *The Great Imposter*. Copyright © 1959 by Robert Crichton. Reprinted by permission of Random House, Inc.

Textbook of Abnormal Psychology, R. M. Dorcus and G. W. Shaffer. Copyright © 1945, Williams and Wilkins Company.

Introduction to Psychiatry, O. Spurgeon English and Stuart M. Finch. Copyright 1964 by W. W. Norton & Company, Inc.

"Experimental Demonstrations of the Psychopathology of Everyday Life," M. H. Erickson, *The Psychoanalytic Quarterly*, VIII, 1939, pages 338–53.

"The Permanent Relief of an Obsessional Phobia by Means of Communications with an Unsuspected Dual Personality." M. H. Erickson and L. S. Kubie, *The Psychoanalytic Quarterly*, VIII, 1939, pages 471–509.

"The Use of Automatic Drawing in the Interpretation and Relief of a State of Acute Obsessional Depression," M. H. Erickson and L. S. Kubie. *The Psychoanalytic Quarterly*, VII, 1938, pages 449–50.

Practical Clinical Psychology, J. Ewalt, E. A. Strecker, and F. G. Ebaugh, McGraw-Hill Book Company, 1957.

"Developmental Evaluation and the Institution of Remedial Programs for Children with Learning Difficulties," M. Frostig, The Marianne Frostig Center of Educational Therapy, 1965.

"Exploring the World of the Insane," R. M. Goldenson, *Look* magazine, September 21, 1954, pages 30–32. By permission of the editors of *Look* magazine. Copyright © 1954, Cowles Communications, Inc.

"A Case Study of Fetishism," V. M. Grant, *Journal of Abnormal and Social Psychology*, 1953, 48, 142–49. Reprinted by permission of the American Psychological Association.

The Patient in the Mental Hospital, M. Greenblatt, The Macmillan Company, 1957.

Men Under Stress, R. R. Grinker and J. P. Spiegel, McGraw-Hill Book Company, Blakiston Division, 1945.

Condensed and adapted selection from *How to Increase Reading Ability*, A. J. Harris. 4th edition, 1961. By permission of David McKay Company, Inc.

"A Psychiatrist Listens to Dysphonia Syndromes," L. Heaver, *Talk* magazine, September–October 1957, Vol. 31, No. 3. Reprinted by permission of the Speech Rehabilitation Institute.

Henderson and Gillespie's Textbook of Psychiatry edited by D. Henderson and I. R. C. Batchelor, 9th edition, London, Oxford University Press, 1962.

"The Homosexual Community," Evelyn Hooker. From *Proceedings of the XIV International Congress of Applied Psychology*. Munksgaard Press, 1962.

The Lost Weekend by Charles Jackson. Copyright © 1944, 1960 by Charles R. Jackson. Reprinted by permission of Farrar, Straus & Giroux, Inc., and Brandt & Brandt.

Handbook of Pyschiatry, L. J. Karnosh and E. M. Zucker. The C. V. Mosby Company, 1945.

Mental Hygiene in Modern Living, B. Katz and G. Lehner. Copyright 1953, The Ronald Press Company.

"My Twelve Hours As a Madman," S. Katz, *Maclean's* magazine, October 1, 1953.

"Concepts of Normality and Abnormality in Sexual Behavior," by A. C. Kinsey, W. B. Pomeroy, C. E. Martin and P. H. Gebhard. From *Psychosexual Development in Health and Disease*, edited by P. H. Hoch and J. Zubin. Grune and Stratton, 1949. Used by permission.

The Disorganized Personality, G. W. Kisker. Copyright © 1964 by McGraw-Hill Book Company, Inc. Used by permission.

"The Character Structure of Sex Offenders," S. B. Kopp, *American Journal of Psychotherapy*, 1962, 16.

The Therapy of the Neuroses and Psychoses, S. H. Kraines, Lea & Febiger, 1948.

Mental Depressions and Their Treatment, S. H. Kraines. Copyright © 1957 by The Macmillan Company. Reprinted with permission.

Textbook of Abnormal Psychiatry, C. Landis and M. M. Bolles. Copyright 1946 by The Macmillan Company. Reprinted with permission.

"Narcolepsy as a Type of Response to Emotional Conflict," O. R. Langworthy and B. J. Betz. *Psychosomatic Medicine*, 6, 1944, 222–26.

"Primary Affect Hunger," D. M. Levy, *American Journal of Psychiatry*, Vol. 94, pages 644–45, 1937.

"Maternal Overprotection," D. M. Levy, *Psychiatry* (1938), 561–82. Reprinted by permission of the William Alanson White Psychiatric Foundation, Inc.

Research in Dementia Praecox, N. D. C. Lewis, 1936. Reprinted by permission of the Supreme Council, 33°, Ancient Accepted Scottish Rite of Freemasonry for the Northern Masonic Jurisdiction, U.S.A.

"Dissociated Personality: A Case Report," S. Lipton, *The Psychiatric Quarterly*, 17, 1943, pages 41–44.

Cases from *Principles of Abnormal Psychology*, revised edition by A. H. Maslow and B. Mittelmann. Copyright 1941, 1951 by Harper & Row, Publishers, Inc. Reprinted by permission of Harper & Row, Publishers.

The Practice of Dynamic Psychiatry, J. N. Masserman, W. B. Saunders Company, 1955.

Grateful acknowledgment is made to the following for permission to reproduce their material:

TEXT ILLUSTRATIONS

BLACK AND WHITE PLATES

COLOR PLATES

To Irene with love and gratitude

ACKNOWLEDGMENTS

The author gratefully acknowledges the invaluable contributions of Donald P. Kenefick, M.D., Director of Research and Professional Affairs, National Association for Mental Health, who reviewed the psychiatric and mental health articles; and of Sherman Ross, Ph.D., Executive Secretary, Education and Training Board, American Psychological Association, who reviewed the psychological topics. The author is deeply indebted to Robert Fudin, Ph.D., Assistant Professor of Psychology, Long Island University, for his careful and thorough research assistance. Philip S. Bergman, M.D., was kind enough to review the anatomical drawings skillfully executed by Howard S. Friedman. Special thanks are due Irene Goldenson, wife of the author, for her many helpful suggestions and her patience and fortitude in typing over 3000 pages of manuscript. Finally, an encyclopedia of this kind could not come into being without drawing, directly or indirectly, upon a vast number of sources—but here it is only possible to express blanket appreciation to the hundreds of authors listed in the References at the end of the book.

ROBERT M. GOLDENSON

HOW TO USE THIS BOOK

THE ENCYCLOPEDIA OF HUMAN BEHAVIOR is based on the need for a convenient yet comprehensive reference book covering all major phases of psychology, psychiatry, and mental health. Its purpose is to present essential information on what is surely the most important subject of all: man's knowledge of himself. There has probably never been a period when interest in human behavior was greater, nor a time when increased understanding was more urgently needed.

The book has been written with three principal objectives in mind. First, to offer a maximum amount of information within the scope of its two volumes. Second, to draw that information only from the most authoritative sources. And third, to present it in a form that will be readily understood by the student and the interested layman, yet useful to the professional worker.

The ENCYCLOPEDIA has been designed from the reader's point of view. Its over one thousand entries are arranged in alphabetical order for ready reference. Each article starts with a concise definition to establish an immediate frame of reference. All obscure or highly technical terms are briefly defined at the point of use. Illustrative cases, drawn from recognized sources, have been included in 165 articles on psychiatric disorders, to give them a personal as well as a clinical dimension. Nearly 100 other articles are illustrated with photographs and drawings.

The following suggestions are offered to enhance the usefulness of the book:

If a term or subject cannot be found among the alphabetical articles, consult the Index, which contains over 5000 entries.

If a fuller account of any topic is desired, follow the cross references from article to article.

If a comprehensive view of a major area or field is desired, make use of the Category Index, in which all topics are listed under broad headings.

CATEGORY INDEX

The following is a listing of all articles in the *Encyclopedia* grouped into related subject-matter categories.

FIELDS OF PSYCHOLOGY AND PSYCHIATRY

HISTORY OF PSYCHOLOGY

HISTORY OF PSYCHIATRY

THEORIES, SYSTEMS, SCHOOLS*

AREAS OF PSYCHOLOGY

CHILD DEVELOPMENT

* See History of Psychology and History of Psychiatry for other Theories.

EMOTIONS

INTELLIGENCE, MEMORY, THINKING

LEARNING

MOTIVATION

PERSONALITY AND INDIVIDUAL DIFFERENCES

PHYSICAL BASIS OF BEHAVIOR

PSYCHOLOGICAL TESTING

SENSATION AND PERCEPTION

SOCIAL BEHAVIOR

WORK AND EVERYDAY LIFE

MENTAL DISORDERS AND MENTAL HEALTH*

ORGANIC BRAIN DISORDERS

FUNCTIONAL DISORDERS

PSYCHOTIC DISORDERS

* Classification of mental disorders based on *Diagnostic and Statistical Manual: Mental Disorders,* American Psychiatric Association, 1952.

PSYCHOPHYSIOLOGIC AUTONOMIC AND VISCERAL DISORDERS

PSYCHONEUROTIC DISORDERS

SYMPTOMS AND REACTIONS

TREATMENT TECHNIQUES AND FACILITIES

MENTAL HEALTH

MISCELLANEOUS TERMS

ILLUSTRATIVE CASES

Cases will be found at the end of each of the following articles

LIST OF PLATES

THE ENCYCLOPEDIA OF
HUMAN BEHAVIOR

A

ABERRATION. A general term for any deviation from the normal or typical. In psychology and psychiatry aberration, or mental aberration, denotes any emotional or mental disorder without specifying its character. These terms may also be applied to individual symptoms, such as delusion of grandeur or hysterical paralysis. Though "aberration" is still in use, "mental aberration" appears to be obsolescent.

ABNORMAL PSYCHOLOGY. The study of disordered behavior; a specialized field of psychology in which scientific principles are sought to explain abnormal behavior and provide a sound psychological basis for diagnosis, treatment and prevention.

The fields of abnormal psychology and psychiatry show a considerable overlapping, since they are both concerned with the classification and elucidation of mental disorders of all kinds, as well as with problems of etiology (causation), personality development, methods of diagnosis, types of treatment, preventive measures, historical changes in the approach to mental disorder, and organized efforts for handling the problem of mental health. In psychiatry, however, the primary focus is on diagnosis and treatment, and there is greater emphasis on examination procedures, differential diagnosis, the physiological aspects of mental disorders, and the application of pharmacological and other medical therapies. Abnormal psychology, on the other hand, is not so clinically oriented, and there

is usually greater stress on the psychological, biological, and sociocultural determinants of different disorders; the psychological theories behind the various approaches to psychotherapy; and the experimental and statistical evidence for the success or failure of different types of treatment.

The systematic study of abnormal behavior is less than a hundred years old, although men have attempted to deal with this problem since the most primitive times. Many of the historical details are given in biographical form in this volume, but it might be useful to note here the major periods in the evolution of the field. There is evidence that Stone Age medicine men cut holes in the skulls of disordered individuals (trephining, trepanning) to permit the evil spirit which had invaded the organism to escape. Demonology was the prevailing view among the early Chinese, Egyptians, Hebrews, and Greeks as well, but instead of performing "brain surgery," they attempted to exorcize these spirits through incantations, purgatives and in some cases flogging or starvation.

During the Golden Age of Greece, Hippocrates and other physicians made the first classifications of mental disorders, viewing them as different forms of brain disease to be treated by diet, exercise and massage, as well as bleeding and purgation. Later Greeks and Romans added suggestion, hypnosis, musical and recreational therapy to this repertoire. One physician, Aretaeus, hinted that some mental disorders may simply be extensions of normal psychological processes due to emotional and personality factors; another, Galen, divided the causes of mental disorder into physical and mental. These advances, however, were soon lost in the resurgence of superstition and demonology that occurred in the Dark Ages and medieval times.

During the latter part of the Middle Ages, mental illness took the form of mass epidemics of dancing, raving, and biting, and treatment was largely a matter of driving the devil from the bodies of the "possessed" through every variety of torture. This practice reached a fiendish climax in the witch hunts of the fourteenth and fifteenth centuries, which took the lives of thousands of innocent women. A turning point was finally reached in the sixteenth century, when Paracelsus argued that the dancing manias were not due to possession but to disease, and Weyer dared to declare that most of the "witches" tortured and burned at the stake were actually sick people who needed medical treatment.

The modern era began when the mentally ill were placed in special "asylums," though at first many of these institutions were little better than prisons or concentration camps. The colony at Gheel, Belgium, where patients lived with families and were treated with love and kindness, pointed the way toward humanitarian reform; and by the end of the eighteenth century, under the influence of Philippe Pinel in France and William Tuke in England, the asylums began to change into modern hospitals and sanitariums. In America the care of the mentally ill was greatly advanced by the institutional reforms of Thomas Kirkbride and Benjamin Rush, the "moral treatment" of Isaac Ray, and the one-woman crusade of the remarkable Dorothea Dix. These advances were gradually matched by significant developments in psychiatric theory and practice. Toward the end of the nineteenth century Wilhelm Griesinger, Emil Kraepelin, John Hughlings Jackson, and others brought the findings of anatomy, physiology, and general medicine to bear on the problem of mental illness. This launched the organic viewpoint which traced mental disorders to brain pathology and classified them into separate and distinct disease entities.

At the turn of the century, however, a number of investigators began to recognize that many mentally ill people are not afflicted with organic disease of any kind. Through the work of Jean Charcot, Pierre Janet, Sigmund Freud, and others, the idea of functional mental disorder took hold, and the psychological approach to both etiology and therapy was developed. Psychoanalysis became the most influential theory of the time, giving rise to a new form of treatment directed to the patient's basic personality structure. A host of other approaches were soon proposed by theorists who could not accept Freud's formulations. These included other types of analytic approaches, such as those proposed by Carl Jung, Alfred Adler, and Wilhelm Stekel, as well as the theories of Karen Horney, Harry Stack Sullivan and Erich Fromm, who felt that Freud did not do justice to social and cultural factors. In recent years a number of quite different points of view have been introduced, such as the existentialism, client-centered therapy, and behavior or learning theory therapy.

These, then, are some of the highlights of the history of abnormal psychology. But what are the current trends in this ever-changing field? The following ten emphases, gathered from a variety of sources, appear to be fairly clear-cut, although no attempt has been made to place them in order of importance: (1) the holistic approach, integrating psychological, biological and sociocultural factors; (2) the team or staff approach to diagnosis and treatment, combining the services of psychiatrists, clinical psychologists, psychiatric social workers and other specialized personnel; (3) the development of community-centered treatment units, together with new facilities and techniques designed to prevent long-term disability, such as day care and night care centers, treatment in general hospitals, foster-family care, and halfway houses; (4) the interpretation of abnormal behavior as an extension or exaggeration of normal behavior tendencies; (5) a flexible and eclectic approach to psychotherapy, recognizing that different approaches may be advisable for different patients, different therapists, and different therapeutic aims; (6) a recognition of the urgent need for widespread public education on attitudes toward abnormal behavior and the importance of early detection and preventive measures; (7) emphasis on the importance of sound personal relationships, starting within the family and including relationships in the school, job, and community; (8) recognition of the social nature of mental disorders and emphasis on the importance of building a basically healthy society where people will not be subjected to excessive frustrations, tensions, or anxieties; (9) recognition that pharmacological therapy—the use of tranquilizers and energizers—is most effective when it is combined with psychotherapy; (10) growing realization that theories and therapies must be put to experimental test and judged by actual results. *See* CLINICAL PSYCHOLOGY, PSYCHIATRIST.

ABREACTION. The discharge of repressed emotions through reliving painful experiences which have been buried in the unconscious.

In psychoanalysis and other forms of psychotherapy, this process is used not only to drain off pent-up emotion, but to open the way toward increased insight and "desensitization"—that is, to reduce the emotional effect of the disturbing experiences through an understanding of their nature and origin. In the Freudian theory, the elimination of repressed emotions and resulting symptoms through abreaction is termed catharsis.

The abreaction technique was origi-nated by Freud's colleague, Josef Breuer, who used hypnotic suggestion to enable hysteria patients to recover repressed and apparently "forgotten" experiences which were instrumental in producing their physical symptoms. They were then encouraged to act out these disturbing events and express the long-suppressed emotions, or "strangulated affect," associated with them. This was followed in most cases by a disappearance of the symptoms. In reviewing a case of Breuer's in which a woman patient developed several physical symptoms after her father's death, Freud (1924) wrote:

"It is especially to be noted that Breuer's patient in almost all pathogenic situations had to suppress a strong excitement, instead of giving vent to it by appropriate words or deeds. While she was seated by her father's sickbed, she was careful to betray nothing of her anxiety and her painful depression to the patient. When later she reproduced the same scene before the physician, the emotion which she had suppressed on the occurrence of the scene burst out with a special strength, as though it had been pent up all along. We are forced to the conclusion that the patient fell ill because the emotion developed in the pathogenic situation was prevented from escaping normally, and that the essence of the sickness lies in the fact that these imprisoned emotions undergo a series of abnormal changes. In part they are preserved as a lasting charge and as a source of constant disturbance in psychical life; in part they undergo a change in unusual bodily innervations and inhibitions which present themselves as the physical symptoms of the case."

Breuer's approach led Freud to a psychological theory of hysteria which held that the physical symptoms are an expression of the patient's unconscious struggle with conflicting urges, as opposed to the prevailing theory that they were the result of nerve weakness. However, he soon abandoned hypnosis since many patients could not be hypnotized and symptoms often returned in another form. He then began using free association as a means of facilitating the revival of lost experiences. Later on, as the theory of psychoanalysis took final shape, less emphasis was placed on reliving and "abreacting" specific experiences and more on the internal process of recapturing and "working through" all types of unconscious wishes, feelings, and conflicts.

Today the abreactive technique is most frequently applied in the treatment of "gross stress reactions"—that is, reactions to traumatic experiences in military combat and civilian catastrophe. A number of special techniques are employed to recover repressed memories and emotions in such cases, and the effect is usually to shorten the therapeutic process. Hypnotic suggestion is sometimes used, but more frequently the abreaction is induced by injection of narcotic drugs such as pentothal sodium and sodium amytal. In addition, abreaction may play a part in psychodrama and play therapy. In psychodrama not only the patient but the auxiliary egos and the audience may release intense emotions associated with painful memories. A similar process often takes place during release, or play therapy with children, especially when their emotional difficulties have been caused by traumatic experiences. See NARCOTHERAPY, HYPNOTHERAPY, PSYCHOANALYSIS (THERAPY), PSYCHODRAMA, RELEASE THERAPY, NARCOSYNTHESIS, PLAY THERAPY, CATHARSIS, WORKING THROUGH.

ABSOLUTE THRESHOLD. The minimum level of stimulation that can be detected 50 per cent of the time; also called "detection threshold."

What is the finest line the human eye can see, the faintest sound the ear can hear, the slightest taste the tongue can detect? The questions are simple enough, but the answers are surprisingly difficult. The biggest problem is that there is no fixed level of stimulation that always activates a given sense organ. Sensitivity is not static; it changes from moment to moment due to changes in the receptor and the conditions under which it operates. This is why scientists have had to qualify the concept of absolute threshold by defining it as the level of stimulation the individual is able to detect 50 per cent of the time. It is actually a highly relative, statistical concept instead of an absolute quantity as the name might imply.

One method of determining the threshold for any sense modality is to present a series of stimuli in the neighborhood of the threshold, asking the subject whether he perceived each of them. The series is usually repeated in several different orders, and the stimulus of least intensity which is detected 50 per cent of the time is taken as the absolute threshold. The logic of this is clear enough, but complicating factors arise as soon as it is put in practice.

In vision, the threshold differs for different types of light, different areas of the retina, and especially the state of the eye at the time of the test. An extreme example will illustrate this last point: if a subject has been in darkness for twenty minutes, and is therefore dark-adapted, his eye is 100,000 times more sensitive than it is in bright sunlight. In hearing, the threshold has been found to vary according to the frequency and duration of the test tone, the use of one or two ears and so on. The condition of the organ is important here, too; the threshold is usually high after exposure to continuous loud noises, and the ears are most sensitive after a period of rest.

The skin senses show similar variations. The state of the superficial blood vessels affects the thresholds for warmth and cold, and the beat of the pulse radically affects pressure and pain sensitivity. Prior stimulation also has its effect: exposure to warm air lowers the threshold to cold, and exposure to cold lowers the heat threshold. In addition, the chemical senses, smell and taste, are particularly hard to investigate because in this case the stimuli alter the state of the receptors themselves.

In spite of these difficulties, threshold experiments have revealed some useful, and often astonishing, facts about human sensitivity. On a dark, clear night the human eye can detect the light of a single match at a distance of thirty miles. A person with normal hearing can detect the tick of a watch at twenty feet in a quiet room. It has been estimated that the auditory nerve cells can respond to vibrations of the bones in the middle ear that are less then 1 per cent of the diameter of a hydrogen molecule. These two senses appear to be very close to the useful limit of operation. If our eyes were any more sensitive, we would probably be able to see light particles (quanta) instead of a steady light; and if our ears were only slightly more sensitive, we would be continually bombarded by the noise of molecules colliding in the air around us!

Our other sense organs are also amazingly sensitive. Our sense of pressure (or touch) is so acute that we can feel the weight of a bee's wing dropped from a height of half an inch. We can smell certain substances, such as mercaptan, in a concentration of one part to 30 billion parts of air; and we can taste quinine sulphate when a single ounce is dissolved in 250 gallons of water. On the other hand our sensitivity to heat and cold is relatively low; it takes a temperature change of a full half degree Fahrenheit before we can feel the difference.

Studies of absolute threshold have led to a number of other findings. As we grow older we become progressively less sensitive in taste and smell as well as hearing and sight—but more sensitive to extremes of temperature. Certain illnesses and injuries play havoc with our threshold of sensitivity. The pressure of clothing becomes painful when we are sunburned, and a current of air can be excruciating to a person suffering from neuralgia. In hysteria (conversion reaction) certain types of sensitivity can be either raised or lowered far beyond normal limits. The threshold for pain can be so high that the skin will be completely anesthetic in certain areas, and the threshold for vision and sound can be so low that ordinary light and noise will be practically unbearable. These reactions can be matched to some degree in normal experience. Think how oversensitive we can be to the dentist's drill, and how insensitive we become to a cut or bruise received during an exciting basketball game. *See* SENSITIVITY DISTURBANCES.

ABULIA. Loss of the ability to perform voluntary actions and make decisions.

The term is usually reserved for extreme cases in which a patient manifests such a profound lack of initiative that he does not carry out the simplest actions such as walking or raising his arm to eat. He may also be unable to make up his mind about the simplest matters such as selecting his clothes or going to the dining room. His will appears to be completely paralyzed, probably by deep internal conflicts or despair.

Abulia is a rare condition most frequently found in schizophrenia, but also observed in some cases of profound depression. The more common disturbance of will is hypobulia, a reduction or impairment rather than a complete absence of initiative. A group of symptoms known as the akinetic-abulic syndrome sometimes appears in the course of treatment with tranquilizers. These symptoms include decreased mental drive, lack of interest, bradykinesia (slow movement), and tremor. For parabulia, or distortion of volition, *see* PARERGASIA.

ACATHISIA (AKATHISIA, AKATIZIA). While this term literally means "not sitting," and was originally applied to an impaired ability to sit down or sit still, it is now applied primarily to restlessness and jitteriness occasionally produced by tranquilizers of the phenothiazine type (Compazine, Trilafon, Stelazine). As Kalinowsky (1958) points out, the reaction is sometimes so intense that it becomes "impossible for the patients to sit still day or night, and is described by them as more difficult to endure than any of the symptoms for which they had been originally treated." The restlessness usually disappears, however, when the dosage is lowered.

The term is still used by some psychiatrists in the original sense. In the psychological form of acathisia, the patient experiences acute anxiety whenever he sits down or thinks of sitting down. One psychotic patient believed the world would be destroyed if he sat down. In such cases sitting has a symbolic meaning which frequently remains obscure.

An organic form of acathisia is also found in certain brain diseases which affect the striopallidal area (the basal ganglia deep within the cerebral hemispheres). Some of these patients cannot sit still, or do so only with an effort. They must get up, or move about, or shift the position of their limbs because inaction is unbearable. Typically, they rock back and forth incessantly, pace the floor, or kick in bicycling fashion while in bed. These reactions are accompanied by anxiety, irritability, and insomnia.

ACCIDENT-PRONENESS. A high susceptibility to accidents; the tendency to be an "accident repeater."

It is an accepted fact that there are wide variations in susceptibility to accidents. Some people seem practically immune, others become accident-prone under certain conditions, and a small minority are classed as repeaters or chronic offenders. Those who are relatively immune have received little systematic study, but the indications are that they have been brought up under conditions which foster attitudes and personality patterns leading to safe behavior. Their parents have satisfied their basic needs for affection, security, and self-esteem, have placed high value on foresight and intelligent action, have developed their basic skills, and have instilled attitudes of concern and regard for others. An upbringing of this kind increases their ability to cope with stress and danger, and reduces the likelihood of unthinking, irresponsible behavior that causes so many accidents.

The great majority of individuals, and possibly everyone, can be temporarily accident-prone—and these cases probably account for the majority of accidents that occur. Susceptibility is increased by physical illness, insomnia, hunger, boredom, "highway hypnosis," and alcohol. Just as significant are emotional disturbances arising out of health, job, or home situations, since they tend to increase an individual's distractibility and preoccupation. In many cases emotional problems give rise to feelings which interfere with the safe operation of machines, particularly when chance emergencies occur: feelings of hostility may make the car a handy weapon; apathy or depression may induce carelessness; and tension may interfere with co-ordination. Temporary susceptibility may also be due to lack of information or skill required to meet specific situations such as icy road conditions. *See* SAFETY PSYCHOLOGY.

Many accident-repeaters have been found to have basic traits that render them accident-prone. Although their "personality profile" is not so fixed as early studies seemed to indicate, the following cluster of characteristics is frequently found. They tend to be restless and distractible, highly impulsive, aggressive and intolerant of authority, emotionally unstable, and unable to tolerate tension and frustration. They are also inclined to trust to luck and take chances to prove their ability to handle any emergency. These people tend to develop an "accident habit" and often show a history of minor mishaps before a major accident is incurred. Safety devices cannot be counted on to protect them against themselves, and cautionary signs may actually serve as a challenge instead of a deterrent.

Psychoanalysts and other therapists have occasionally found evidence of suicidal impulses or a need for self-punishment in accident-prone patients. Their tendency to harm themselves has been described by Karl Menninger (1938) and others as unconsciously deliberate, "an addiction to accidental self-destruction." These are the people who have "purposive accidents"—who "carelessly" clean a loaded gun, fall into their own burglar traps, risk their lives in solitary mountain climbing, demand one unnecessary operation after another, or simply hurt themselves "accidentally on purpose" in order to escape an unpleasant situation or give vent to resentment. Here are some brief cases in which unconscious motives may be operating:

Illustrative Cases: ACCIDENT-PRONENESS

(1) In one of his earliest case histories, Freud reported that when a rejected lover of his patient Dora found himself suddenly face to face with her in a busy street, "as though in bewilderment and in his abstraction, he . . . allowed himself to be knocked down by a car." To Freud, this was "an interesting contribution to the problem of indirect attempt at suicide." (Freud, 1925)

(2) "In Detroit, Michigan, Mrs. John Kulcznski said to John Kulcznski: 'I wish you'd go out and have an accident.' He was run over, lost part of a foot. Then Mrs. John Kulcznski said to John Kulcznski: 'I wish you'd lose the other foot.' He did. To stop Mrs. John Kulcznski from wishing a third wish, John Kulcznski is seeking a divorce." (*Time,* March 26, 1934, cited by Menninger, 1938)

(3) "A twenty-year old girl suffered from fears so great that she had been unable to attend school since the age of ten. During analysis she mentioned one day the desire to exhibit herself nude and shortly afterwards the thought occurred to her that she would like to *cut off* her pubic hair. Then she confessed that the day before this she had used her finger to masturbate. The

analyst recalled that upon that same day she had reported having "accidentally" *cut her finger* with a razor blade. Here, then, were two sets of two associated events of precisely the same sort—a forbidden sexual act followed by cutting." (Menninger, 1938)

(4) The author of this book once asked a class of college students to describe any accidents they had recently had. One coed related that she hated to sew, but that during the past week her mother had tried to force her to repair a piece of clothing. In the girl's words, "I tried and tried to thread the needle, but I just couldn't do it. However, I kept on trying, and twisted it around until I finally succeeded in breaking it in two, jabbing one part right through my finger." "Succeeded" was the right word.

ACHIEVEMENT DRIVE. The motive, or need, to strive for high standards of performance in a wide range of situations.

It is an undeniable fact that success and accomplishment are among the major values of our culture—but it is equally apparent that the strength of the achievement drive varies greatly from individual to individual. Until recently, however, psychologists had no satisfactory way of measuring the strength of this drive, and little was known about the reasons for the wide variations not only within our own culture but between our society and others throughout the world. During the past fifteen years this situation has begun to change.

McClelland et al. (1953) have developed two techniques for measuring the achievement motive. One is a projective approach in which a subject tells stories suggested to him by four pictures designed to elicit different aspects of the drive: (1) two men working at a machine, (2) a boy seated at a desk with an open book in front of him, (3) a father and son picture, (4) a boy who appears to be daydreaming. The stories are analyzed from the standpoint of attitudes toward getting things done and emphasis on success or accomplishment, and the subjects are rated along an achievement-need continuum. The fact that this test actually measured achievement motivation was confirmed by having the same subjects work on a series of simple anagrams and additional problems. The output of the subjects who scored high in achievement motivation on the story test proved to be distinctly higher on the simple problem test as well.

Application of the McClelland test has led to the discovery that subjects who were encouraged to be independent and solve their own problems at an early age tend to develop a higher than average need for achievement (Winterbottom, 1953). Observations of childrearing practices in primitive cultures support this conclusion. The Navaho, who push their children toward independence at an early age, develop a much stronger drive for achievement than other Indians who adopt a more casual, easygoing attitude toward independence training. An earlier study by McClelland (1951) has shown that even when children resist or resent attempts to make them independent, they develop a high need for achievement.

In the second technique developed by McClelland and his associates, six groups of subjects were given a series of simple problems (anagrams, motor tests, etc). Different conditions were set for each group. The group working under "relaxed" conditions were told that they were merely helping to develop a test; the "failure" group were first warned that the tests were measures of intelligence and later told that they were below standard; the "neutral" group were informed that the tests were merely being used to set norms; the group subject to "success" conditions were told their scores were above standard; the "success-failure" group were informed that they were successful after taking the first test, but after the battery was finished were told that they did not come up to par; and an "achievement-oriented" situation was created for

the sixth group by telling them that the tests were designed to measure intelligence or other qualities. After the same battery was taken by each group, the subjects were given a so-called test of "creative imagination" in which they were asked to write stories about the pictures mentioned above.

The results of this complex experiment showed a clear difference between the sexes. When the test was given to college men, an analysis of the imagery used in the creative imagination test revealed that the group which had worked under relaxed conditions had the lowest achievement need, followed by the neutral, failure, and success-failure groups. This was the predictable order if these groups actually represented different degrees of arousal of the achievement need (McClelland et al., 1949). However, when the test was administered to high school and college women, the achievement-oriented conditions did not elicit higher achievement needs than the neutral conditions. On the other hand, when each of these female subjects was given a confidential rating of social acceptability (supposedly made by a committee), it was found that ratings of either acceptance or rejection increased their need-for-achievement scores as indicated by the imagery test. Significantly, neither of these social judgments had any effect on the males. (McClelland et al., 1953).

Some of the more indicative findings of other investigations will be briefly summarized. Morgan (1951) found that college students who make high scores on need-for-achievement tests make better grades than equally gifted students who have a weaker achievement drive. French and Thomas (1958) have shown that people with a strong achievement drive persist longer at problems than those with a weaker drive. McClelland and Liberman (1949) found that this need may have an effect on perception, since more high "achievers" recognized quickly exposed words relating to achievement than middle or low achievers. The middle achievers apparently showed the greatest fear of failure, since they did not recognize as many "failure" words as the other two groups. Ricciuti and Schultz (1958) have demonstrated that the strength of the achievement drive is usually closely related to level of aspiration, by showing that subjects with a high aspiration level expect to perform well on tasks presented to them—but they have also shown that this expectation does not necessarily indicate how well they will *actually* perform. All these findings must be qualified by the fact that arousal of the achievement motive is a complex affair depending on such factors as the type of task, the expectation of goal attainment, and the value of the incentive in the situation.

A few highly suggestive studies have been made of achievement motifs in different societies, notably by McClelland (1958, 1961). Analysis of the literature of Greece has indicated that achievement themes were most frequently expressed during the period when economic expansion was most rapid. A similar relationship was found in medieval Spain, in pre-Incan Peru, and in England from Tudor times to the Industrial Revolution. In addition, the amount of achievement imagery in children's literature was found to be directly related to the patent index in the United States between 1800 and 1950, and to economic growth in modern Russia, Hungary and Bulgaria. These findings indicate that the achievement drive tends to pervade the entire fabric of society.

McClelland (1961) has also discovered a relationship between the number of achievement themes in folk tales in preliterate cultures and the mean annual temperature. The optimal range was between forty and sixty degrees. This verifies the common observation of a loss of initiative in tropical climates, and suggests that in the colder regions an excessive amount of energy is dissipated in adapting to the elements. McClelland's studies have also indicated that the amount of *variation* in temperature is particularly significant. Twenty-four of twenty-six cultures in the high-achievement category showed at least a fifteen-degree daily or seasonal fluctuation, while the climate in only half of the low-achievement cultures showed this degree of variation.

ACHIEVEMENT TESTS. Tests designed to measure knowledge or skill attained through training in a specific subject or area.

Achievement tests are usually grouped into two categories: general batteries covering the major academic areas; and special instruments, including readiness tests, diagnostic tests, content-area tests, vocational achievement tests, and tests for the professions. The general batteries and content area tests will be briefly described below, and the special tests will be discussed under individual topics. For industrial achievement tests, or trade tests, *see* PERSONNEL TESTS.

Metropolitan Achievement Tests. A widely administered series consisting of five batteries, each available in three or four equivalent forms, and covering grades 1, 2, 3–4, 5–6, 7–9. The items deal with word knowledge, word discrimination, reading, arithmetic (concepts and skills, problem solving, computation), spelling, language (usage, pronunciation and capitalization, parts of speech and grammar, kinds of sentences), language-studies skills (use of dictionary and other references), social-studies skills (maps, tables, graphs), and science. Individual score profiles are constructed and converted into grade equivalents according to norms based on samples of the public school population.

Sequential Tests of Educational Progress (STEP). The following seven tests are available at each of four levels— grades 4–6, 7–9, 10–12, 13–14: Reading, Writing, Mathematics, Science, Social Studies, Language Comprehension, and Essay Writing. Parallel forms are provided at each level and all tests except the essays are of the multiple-choice variety. Though specific knowledge is often needed, the stress is on the application of learning to the solution of new, realistic problems. There is also special emphasis on the use of communication skills as in the essay test, listening and comprehension test, as well as the writing tests in which the subjects indicate how they would try to improve actual writing specimens.

Even though these tests are timed, like the Metropolitan Tests, they are essentially power rather than speed tests. The scoring methods also differ in that performance on any one of the STEP tests is expressed in terms of a single scale for all grades. All scores can be transformed into percentiles, and a profile is constructed for each student showing his relative standing on the different tests. In constructing these tests, committees of leading educators representing all school levels participated with specialists of the Educational Testing Service.

The two instruments just described illustrate two major types of general achievement tests. Other general batteries include the Stanford Achievement Test, which covers grades 1–3, 3–4, 5–6, 7–9, and consists of items on arithmetic, reading, science, study skills, and social studies; the Iowa Test of Basic Skills, for grades 3–9, offering tests of vocabulary, reading comprehension, language, arithmetical skills, and word-study skills; the California Achievement Test, which covers grades 1–2, 3–4, 4–6, 7–9, 9–14, and consists of tests of reading vocabulary, reading comprehension, arithmetic fundamentals, arithmetic reasoning, mechanics of English and spelling; the SRA Achievement Series, which includes forms for grades 2–4, 4–6, 6–9, and offers tests in reading, language perception, language arts,

arithmetic, and work-study skills; the Tests of Academic Promise; and the new Fundamental Achievement Series.

General batteries are also available for levels above grade school. The Essential High School Content Batteries, the Evaluation and Adjustment Series, and the Iowa Tests of Educational Development are all designed for the high school level and stress specific sciences, English and social studies, as well as the general application of thought processes and data in dealing with problematic situations. In addition, the Cooperative General Achievement Tests are designed for high school seniors and college freshmen; the Cooperative General Culture Test has been constructed for college use, particularly at the sophomore level; and the new Adult Basic Learning Examination (ABLE), consisting of practical problems in vocabulary, reading, spelling and arithmetic, has been specifically designed for undereducated adults, to assess their ability to participate in adult-education classes and programs conducted by penal institutions and special agencies such as the Job Corps.

Special and Content-Area Tests. A large number of specialized achievement tests have been devised for educational use. The Wide Range Achievement Test, revised in 1965, is an individual test used primarily for remedial and vocational purposes. It indicates level of skill in oral reading, spelling and computation, with the examiner adjusting the testing range to various levels from kindergarten to college. One of the most important tests of reading ability is the Davis Reading Test, which provides a continuous measure of level and speed of comprehension for grades eight to eleven and eleven to thirteen. A newly revised series of tests, the Gates-MacGinitie Reading Tests, based on a representative sample of 40,000 pupils in 38 communities, has recently replaced the widely used Gates Reading Tests.

Four tests in the field of science are Biology: BSCS Final Examination, for use at the end of a high school course; the Processes of Science Test, designed to measure understanding of scientific principles, reasoning and methods of inquiry; the Cooperative Science Tests; and the Test of Scientific Knowledge, measuring the student's background in general science through questions on factual information and principles.

The following is a list of other widely used achievement tests in special subjects: Anderson-Fiske Chemistry Test, Blyth Second-Year Algebra Test, Contemporary Mathematics Test, Cooperative Mathematics Tests, Crary American History Test, Cumming's World History Test, Dunning-Abeles Physics Test, Lankton First-Year Algebra Test, MLA Cooperative Foreign Language Tests, Modern Math Understanding Test, Nelson Biology Test, Pimsleur Modern Foreign Language Proficiency Tests (French, German, Spanish), Stanford Modern Mathematics Concepts Test, Wisconsin Contemporary Test of Elementary Mathematics.

ACROCEPHALY. A disorder characterized by an exceptionally high skull and severe mental retardation.

In one syndrome (Crouzon) these symptoms are associated with exophthalmos (protruding eyes), small orbital (eye) cavities, and increased intracranial pressure. This condition is believed to be due to a single dominant gene with "varying penetrance" (that is, not all who possess the gene are equally affected), since there are wide variations in the degree of skull deformity and exophthalmos. In the Apert syndrome, acrocephaly is combined with hypertelorism (eyes wide apart) and syndactylia (fingers grown together). In the Grieg syndrome (hypertelorism), the high skull is combined with a greater degree of telorism but without the defect in the fingers. There is evidence that these variations are also due to a dominant gene,

at least in some families. *See* MENTAL RETARDATION (CAUSES).

ACROMEGALY. A physical disorder caused by oversecretion of the anterior portion of the pituitary gland during adulthood. The outstanding symptoms are thickening and enlargement of the hands, feet, nose, and jaw, with increasing loss of vitality.

There may also be changes in personality resulting from a combination of causes: excessive endocrine secretion, social difficulties due to other people's reaction to the bodily deformities, and reactions of the patient himself to his new and disturbing body image. The "acromegaloid personality" is characterized by a lack of initiative and spontaneity, with frequent uncaused changes in mood. The individual may be cheerful and even elated at times, and at other times anxious, tense, and disagreeable. In advanced cases, the acromegalic patient is slow in both thought and action, and becomes increasingly egocentric, impatient, and oversensitive. Surgical or X-ray treatment may arrest the condition in its earlier stages.

ACTING-OUT. The tendency to express urges, conflicts, and fantasies in uncontrolled action.

In acting-out, the individual seeks to release impulses that are usually of a sexual or aggressive nature in order to gain relief from tension or anxiety. In doing so, he loses sight of consequences and frequently yields to an overwhelming desire to "get it over with." An acting-out pattern is characteristic of juvenile delinquent behavior.

Various forms of acting-out are used for psychotherapeutic purposes. Both children and adults may be encouraged to act out repressed feelings or re-enact traumatic experiences under controlled conditions. The release of tension usually has a salutary effect. *See* RELEASE THERAPY, HYPNOTHERAPY, NARCOSYNTHESIS, ABREACTION, PLAY THERAPY.

**ACTIVE ANALYTIC PSYCHOTHER-
APY.** The therapeutic approach of
Wilhelm Stekel in which the analyst
attempts to effect a cure as quickly as
possible by playing an active and often
directive role.

Stekel was one of Freud's original
associates, but left the fold largely because his primary concern was with
therapy, and he had become convinced
that Freud was more interested in
studying the psychology of his patients
than in curing them of their disorders.
In his own work he contributed both
to psychiatric theory and the practical
techniques of psychotherapy. His writings on the subject of sex, both normal
and pathological, hold up well today,
and his analysis of the use of symbols
is well accepted in dream interpretation
(1933). His view that there is a close
relationship between the patient's personality characteristics, or character
structure, and his psychoneurotic patterns has been emphasized in recent
psychoanalytic theory.

Stekel also helped to lay the basis
for the concept of "intrapsychic conflict" as a factor in anxiety and neurosis. He believed that conflicts arise because of antagonistic trends, or "bipo-
larity" in the personality—for example,
heterosexuality versus homosexuality, or
the id versus the superego. But though
he recognized that inner conflicts frequently stem from the past, he maintained that many patients could be
helped without delving into their early
childhood. He therefore disagreed with
Freud and his followers, who, he held,
were so preoccupied with the past that
they paid too little attention to conflicts in the present.

In his therapeutic approach, Stekel
(1950) put more emphasis on the personality of the therapist and his interaction with the patient than on specific
methodology. He viewed the therapist
as an active partner in the therapeutic
process—hence "active analytic therapy." This was particularly evident in

his approach to free association and
dream interpretation. Although he utilized the free-association method, he
held that the therapist should intervene
and direct the patient to discuss what
he considered an important point, or
suggest that a line of association be
dropped if it was unfruitful or produced
too much resistance. Likewise, he did
not hesitate to attack the patient's resistances in an authoritarian manner, and
occasionally offered direct advice and
exhortation—though he insisted that the
patient take full responsibility for making decisions. At the same time, he
felt that intervention by the therapist
should be carefully timed, and advised
his followers to develop intuition—a
mixture of sympathy and imaginative
insight—to help them to recognize the
most auspicious moment for taking action.

Stekel also viewed the interpretation
of dreams as a collaborative process.
Here, too, he stressed the importance
of intuition, and maintained that almost
any analyst could develop this skill
through special effort and training. He
was primarily concerned with dreams
that reflected the patient's current problems and attitudes, and was interested
in dreams that dealt with past events
only if they shed light on his basic
character and personality tendencies.
See DREAM INTERPRETATION (MODERN).

Stekel recognized that transference
(transfer of emotion to the therapist
as a parental figure) was bound to develop during this interaction between
patient and therapist, and realized its
positive value in the therapeutic process.
Nevertheless, he kept this relationship
on a limited level where it could be
easily handled. He insisted that while
the intense relationship which occurred
in classical analysis often helped to
bring to light the patient's early experiences and infantile attitudes, it was
not a necessary step in bringing about
improvement in his condition. Moreover. the analysis of the transference

itself extended the entire process by months, or even years, while his own approach usually shortened the therapy to six months or less. *See* TRANSFERENCE.

Stekel has had a number of followers in the United States, notably Emil A. Gutheil, who published an important volume on dream interpretation (1951). There is no Stekelian "school," but many psychiatrists have been influenced by his active, flexible approach. Most of them, however, do not put so much emphasis on intuition nor hold to the six months limitation which Stekel recommended.

ACTIVE PSYCHOTHERAPY. A treatment procedure in which the patient is directed to make a graduated series of changes in his behavior.

Active psychotherapy was developed by Alexander Herzberg (1945) as a means of breaking a neurotic behavior pattern and thereby speeding up the therapeutic process. The therapist assigns a progressive series of therapeutic tasks, first aimed at altering the more superficial expressions of the patient's neurosis, and later directed at his deeper problems. As White (1964) points out, the assigned behavior must not awaken too much anxiety and resistance, and "the strategy can succeed only when the proposed task is so nearly within the patient's present capacity that he needs only a little added impetus to carry it out . . . It is strong medicine, and the doses must be selected with the utmost skill."

In applying this treatment, the therapist takes a calculated risk, for the patient may not be able to carry out his first assignments, or may feel so anxious in carrying them out that he will break off treatment and perhaps be worse off than before. If he is able to get over the first hurdles, however, he will probably feel he can overcome his problems, and will "win at least a local victory over neurosis." To make the most of this local victory, the thera-

pist must go on to attack the patient's deeper problems—otherwise the behavioral changes will leave the basic neurosis untouched, and new symptoms may arise to replace the ones eliminated.

Illustrative Case: ACTIVE PSYCHOTHERAPY

The following summary of one of Herzberg's cases, quoted from White, represents a successful application of active therapy: "A wife felt strongly hostile toward her husband because of his lack of initiative and failure to earn well. At the same time she liked him for his kindness and consideration. For the sake of their children she wanted the marriage to continue, and her own hostility therefore filled her with self-reproach. Her aggressive feelings were thus constantly turned back on herself in the form of blame, and this finally resulted in depression with insomnia and various bodily symptoms. By concentrating fiercely on her symptoms she could now forget her aggression toward her husband. This neurotic solution of the main conflict, however, soon became exploited for secondary gain. By constant complaining about her illness she obtained increased attention from her husband, who took her out every day in order to make her feel better and who allowed her to keep a maid. Before long she was receiving presents and financial aid from her parents. Because of her condition she refused sexual intercourse, thus in effect punishing her husband. How can therapeutic tasks be used in treating this neurosis? Obviously it would be futile to direct them straight at the main emotional problem, telling her to stop hating her husband or punishing herself. Tasks were assigned instead which had the effect of removing the secondary gain. Progressively she was required to stop speaking of her symptoms at home, to discharge her maid and do her own housework, to resume sexual relations and discontinue her daily requests to be taken out, and to refuse all assistance from her parents. As these steps were successfully accomplished it became possible to go on to more nuclear problems." (White, 1964)

ACTIVITY DRIVE. The general drive for bodily activity, including restlessness, spontaneous exertion of energy, and movement in response to external stimuli.

Many investigators have observed that the activity level of animals increases when they are hungry, thirsty, or in heat. When rats, for example, are deprived of food or water, they continuously run about, sniffing and pawing everything within reach. This finding has been checked by putting them in special apparatus which records any movement they make. A similar increase in restlessness has been observed in human infants just before feeding time. For many years, the logical explanation for these facts seemed to be that the rise in activity level stemmed from the urge to find a way of satisfying their basic needs, and thereby reduce the discomfort caused by deprivation. In other words, activity was not viewed as an independent impulse, but only as a means of gratifying other drives.

More recently this interpretation has been challenged, and many psychologists now believe that activity is a basic, unlearned drive with satisfactions of its own quite separate from other physiological needs. A variety of observations and experiments have given at least limited support to this point of view. First, it has been found that short periods of activity deprivation increase running and restlessness in animals, although longer periods tend to reduce running behavior while slightly increasing restlessness. Second, rats that have been conditioned to press a bar in order to obtain a reward will continue to do so when their only reward is an opportunity to run. The satisfaction of the activity drive is apparently pleasurable in itself.

Finally, most human beings complain of a "pent-up feeling" if they are forced to be inactive for any length of time, and this feeling generates an overpowering urge to move about. One of the most difficult problems for the heart patient is to remain relatively inert for many weeks. And long ago it was discovered that one of the most severe forms of punishment was simply the restriction of movement; for this reason prisoners were put in chains or confined to a narrow dungeon. These facts argue strongly though not conclusively for the existence of a basic, independent drive for activity.

ACTIVITY GROUP THERAPY. A variation of group psychotherapy in which children revise their social and emotional patterns by participating in club activities. The technique was developed by S. R. Slavson, who described it as a form of situational therapy. Activity group therapists, or "group workers," may also work with adults.

Activity groups resemble ordinary hobby groups, but are composed of children who are so aggressive, isolated, timid, or willful that they cannot function in ordinary peer situations. The meetings are held in a room equipped with tools and materials for a variety of hobbies. The leader, technically termed a "group worker," does not attempt to engage them in specific activities, but busies himself with his own projects. However, he observes them unobtrusively and is ready to act in case of emergency. His primary purpose is to create a permissive atmosphere in which they can be free to release feelings of hostility, expend extra energy, test new ways of relating to others, and gradually discover for themselves the satisfactions to be gained from creative effort and normal give and take.

It may take six or eight months of weekly meetings to bring about significant changes, but in most cases the hyperactive child will gradually settle down, the aggressive child will grow more co-operative, and the social isolate will become involved with others. As they progress in their activities, the leader becomes less impersonal and rewards them with praise and encouragement; and as the group becomes more closely knit, the children receive recognition and approval from each other. In time, the group as a whole takes over the chores of cleaning up, serving refreshments and keeping order. When this point is reached, most of the members are ready to try their wings in more organized activities such as baseball or basketball. They then leave the activity group and transfer to the standard clubs of the neighborhood.

Illustrative Case: ACTIVITY GROUP THERAPY

Harris was referred to the agency at the age of eight, with problems of extreme rivalry with a younger brother, severe temper outbursts when frustrated, continual insistence upon new toys, and generally infantile adjustment, reflected in inability to dress himself and in asking to be fed. There was strong interest in fire making and a tendency toward compulsive masturbation. He had few friends and was withdrawn socially. . .

The mother was described as a tense, compulsive person who had great difficulty in accepting her role as a mother and who expressed strong disappointment for not having borne a girl. She was extremely rejecting and punitive—in fact both parents beat Harris severely in the belief that this was the only method of controlling him. . . . The parents showed open preference for the younger sibling, a passive and conforming child who presented no problems.

Deprived of the basic security of parental love, with his ego and sense of self-worth battered by rejection, beatings, and preference for his sibling, and thwarted in his expression of natural drives toward independence by a corrosive blend of punitive control and overprotection, Harris reacted with hostility, provocativeness, and infantile dependence. . . .

In the group, he immediately exhibited marked oral anxiety, continually asking about refreshments, grabbing at the food hungrily and at times sucking it in like an infant. He also displayed a readiness to regress at the slightest provocation. He spent considerable time in fire making and in smearing paints. At the treatment conference, held periodically on each child at the end of the first season, it was noted that Harris was blossoming out in the group, with increasing assertiveness and outgoing behavior.

One year later, continuing progress was indicated in his improved school adjustment, ability to dress and feed himself and to travel to the group alone. Several months later, in the group therapist's progress report, Harris was described as becoming "rough and tough" in his language, aggressive toward weaker children, and antagonistic toward new members. Thus we see him acting out against other children in his group the handling he received at the hands of his parents, and in his rejection of new members we see the expression of his own displacement by a younger sibling . . .

Periodic contacts with the mother by the follow-up caseworker indicated no insight into her own role in Harris' problems. . . . After considerable resistance on the part of the mother, the father was seen. He was given an opportunity to express his own anxieties about Harris and about his own problems in relation to his seasonal work and long hours. Interpretation was then given him on the harmful effects of physical punishment on the child's ego. Several months later the mother reported a "wonderful change" in the father: he had stopped hitting Harris, was spending time with the boy, playing ball and taking him bicycle riding. Though the mother's basic rejection of Harris could not be altered, she was guided, with the example of the father as an incentive, toward a less punitive handling of him.

After three seasons of treatment, significant changes in his personality had emerged. From the passive, suspicious, and inarticulate child who was referred initially, he had become open, assertive, eager to develop relationships. His strengthened ego structure was reflected in his whole carriage and in his forthrightness in self-expression. On his own initiative he had taken an after-school delivery job, thus paying his own recreational expenses. On Sunday mornings he traveled for an hour to attend his favorite skating rink . . .

A review of Harris' treatment may throw light on specific aspects of group structure which nurtured maturing development in this child. Initially withdrawn and fearful in the group, he discovered that there was no pressure to participate and no threat of competitive activity. . . . Initially, the adult's neutral attitude left him puzzled and suspicious and one may imagine that he suspected the therapist of "saving up" punishment for a sudden retributive onslaught; or perhaps he thought the therapist was extremely weak and therefore to be despised.

However, as the therapist continued to show calm acceptance, as he demonstrated in a variety of situations that there were neither favorites nor black sheep in the club-family, Harris came to perceive this attitude as indicative of strength and kindness . . . In a sense, having been accepted at his worst, he no longer needed to prolong the severe antisocial behavior. The permissiveness had diminished inner tensions, and the unqualified understanding of him by the adult and acceptance and recognition by fellow members helped to dissipate his inner feelings of worthlessness. In understanding the emergence of a new self-image, we can visualize Harris' inner voice saying "since he (the therapist) loves me, and they (the group) accept me, I cannot be as bad or as worthless as I thought I was." (Rosenthal, 1951)

ACT PSYCHOLOGY. Formulated by the German philosopher Franz Brentano (1838–1917) in 1874, this approach proposed to focus psychological investigation on psychic acts rather than psychic contents.

Act psychology was an attempt to establish the growing discipline of psychology as a science. In contrast to the structuralist, Wilhelm Wundt, who sought to dissect states of consciousness into their component parts and determine the laws of their synthesis, Brentano focused his study on mental processes and activities. He developed a theory concerning the relationship between acts and objects. In his view only the act can be called mental— that is, the act of seeing is mental, but not the color that is seen. But since the psychic act of seeing becomes meaningless unless something is seen, he concluded that an act always refers to a content and always implies or "intends" an object. The relationship is not mutually inclusive, however, for the act is related to a physical object, but the physical object is not part of the act. Rather, it is *contained* in the act by "intention." Brentano called this characteristic of psychic acts "immanent objectivity," to indicate that the object resides or "inexists" in the act. Through this theory he believed he distinguished between psychology and physics, between mental acts, such as feeling or seeing, and physical facts such as an object of a certain color or shape.

Brentano sought to understand experience by analyzing it into acts rather than by performing experiments. This approach led him to divide mental activities into three fundamental categories: (a) ideating (sensing, imagining), (b) judging (recalling, perceiving, acknowledging, rejecting), and (c) loving and hating (desiring, intending, feeling, wishing, resolving, etc.). Although the analytical approach enabled Brentano to make distinctions among psychological processes, it provided very few concrete facts. In contrast, the experimental psychologists of the time found it much easier to deal with mental contents, especially sensations, than with acts. The intensity, duration, and other qualities of sensations could be determined, even measured, but acts were impalpable and fleeting, and could only be studied in retrospect.

Historically, however, act psychology has led to at least one form of experimentation. It stimulated interest in the act of perceiving, and this eventually gave rise to the Gestalt school, which studies—often experimentally—the way perceptual experience organizes itself. Brentano's approach also had an influence on Edmund Husserl who systematized the doctrine of phenomenology, which focuses attention on immediate experience. *See* PHENOME-NOLOGY, GESTALT PSYCHOLOGY.

For a long time psychologists labeled themselves either act or content psychologists. The work of Külpe and the Würzburg school, however, helped to bring about a "bipartite" approach in which act and content were recognized as different but essential facets of mental life. Nevertheless, the emphasis on mental activity continued to exert an influence of its own, and is now regarded as a precursor of the purposive approach, which views the mind as an agent rather than a receptor. And from the purposive approach has developed the entire study of motivation and psychodynamics, which has contributed so much to both normal and abnormal psychology in the past two generations. *See* WUNDT, WÜRZBURG SCHOOL.

ACUTE ALCOHOLIC HALLUCINO-SIS. A psychotic disorder precipitated by prolonged, excessive drinking, and characterized primarily by auditory hallucinations.

The alcohol itself does not produce the symptoms, but the stress of continued drinking is believed to release psychotic tendencies which already exist. These tendencies determine the content of the hallucinations. In most cases male alcoholics hear voices that call them indecent names and accuse them of homosexual practices, while female alcoholics hear voices that accuse them of promiscuity and obscene acts. (The patients may have resorted to drinking in the first place as a defense against such behavior.) The accusations are often accompanied by threats: "We'll draw and quarter him tonight," "Let's stand him up and pump him full of lead." As they listen to these threats, the patients usually hear clanking chains or pistol shots in the distance, and in many cases scream out or appeal to the police for protection.

In contrast to delirium tremens, which is more common, the hallucina-

tions are usually confined to the auditory type, and visual hallucinations are rarely experienced. The patient's mind is also clearer, and he can later recollect most of the details of the episode. The disturbances are similar, however, in two principal ways: in both of them the patient is terror-stricken, and in both there is a danger of suicide.

Treatment for hallucinosis includes tranquilizing agents to relieve fear and anxiety, withdrawal of alcohol, abundant food, vitamin B complex, large quantities of orange juice, and in some cases hydrotherapy. Full recovery takes from five days to a month.

Illustrative Case: ACUTE ALCOHOLIC HALLUCINOSIS

The patient was hospitalized after a suicide attempt in which he slashed his wrists. He had been hospitalized once before after a similar incident in which he tried to hang himself with a bath towel. He was unmarried and lived alone.

The patient had been drinking excessively for a three-year period. He was not in the least particular about what he drank as long as it contained alcohol. For several days prior to his last suicidal attempt he had heard voices which accused him of all manner of "filthy sex acts." He was particularly outraged when they accused him of having committed homosexual acts with his mouth and of having had relations with animals. He complained of a terrible taste in his mouth and imagined that his food had been poisoned as a means of punishing him for his sins. He was generally fearful and apprehensive and slept poorly.

After a stay of two weeks in the hospital, the patient made a good recovery and was discharged. At this time he seemed to have some insight into his difficulties, stating that he felt that his sexual problems had something to do with his suicidal attempt. (Coleman, 1964)

ADDISON'S DISEASE. A disorder caused by undersecretion of the adrenal cortex; first described by Thomas Addison (1793–1860) in 1855.

Since the outer layer, or cortex, of the adrenal gland helps to regulate metabolism, pigmentation, and blood pressure, the resulting symptoms include a lowering of blood pressure, temperature, and basal metabolism, as well as a darkening of the skin. These symptoms are accompanied by bodily changes which have more direct psychological effects: lack of energy, headaches, irritability, reduced ambition and depressed sex functions. Patients may also show feelings of inadequacy and inferiority, and latent tendencies toward neurosis may come to the surface. In rare cases brain metabolism may be affected; this may precipitate a severe mental disturbance with hallucinations or delusions.

Hormone treatment usually has a dramatic effect on Addison's disease. In addition, psychotherapy may be needed to help the patient accommodate to the rapid physical changes produced by the hormone treatments, as well as to clear up residual psychiatric complications. See ADRENAL GLANDS.

Illustrative Case: ADDISON'S DISEASE

The patient was an eighteen-year-old male manifesting his first attack of mental illness. He was admitted to a mental hospital with complaints of tension, irritability, and the conviction that he was being doped. His illness had developed over a period of about five months without known precipitating events.

A psychological examination revealed psychomotor retardation, poverty of thought, and inappropriate smiling. Thought content centered about the notion that the lights outside the hospital were related to Sputnik and that the physicians were poisoning him with tablets. The patient was not hallucinated and was oriented as to time and also knew the year and month but not the exact date.

The medical examination was normal except that the EEG was slightly slow in the anterior and temporal lobes. The patient's personal history revealed that from the age of eight, he had had spells of nausea, vomiting, and extreme weakness accompanied by a "yellowing" of the skin. These spells lasted from two to seven days with spon-

taneous remission. The patient had received no medical treatment for them.

Because of gradual improvement following hospitalization, supportive psychotherapy was decided upon as the method of treatment. After the first week, however, the patient showed rapid deterioration with grimacing, muteness, and the maintenance of postures for hours when left alone. These symptoms were sometimes interrupted by outbursts of destructiveness and combativeness. As a consequence, electroshock treatments were given, and the patient showed marked improvement. Thorazine was prescribed but had to be discontinued as a consequence of undesirable side effects involving the swelling of the hands, wrists, and oropharynx. Eight days after the onset of the swelling, bronzing of the skin was noted and shortly thereafter the patient developed nausea, vomiting, abdominal pain, and hypotension. Laboratory findings proved consistent with hypoadrenalism.

As the signs and symptoms of Addison's disease progressed, the patient's condition again deteriorated—the patient becoming withdrawn and tense and demonstrating blocking of thought processes and strong emotional ambivalence. Cortisone treatment was instituted, and within forty-eight hours the symptom picture cleared up. The patient was placed on a maintenance dosage of 12.5 mg. of cortisone daily, and examination one year after discharge revealed no symptoms of either Addison's disease or schizophrenia.

The precise relation of Addison's disease to the mental reaction could not be ascertained, but the institution of hormonal therapy was closely followed by a remission of the schizophrenia symptoms. (Adapted from Wolff and Huston, 1959)

ADJUSTMENT. An individual's general adaptation to his environment and the demands of life—including the way he relates to other people, handles his responsibilities, deals with stress, and meets his own needs.

Adjustment is not a one-way process in which we conform to the requirements of others, for it includes the ability to be ourselves, hold our own, and make reality adapt itself to our requirements. Nor does it imply a static condition of contentment or peace of mind. Life is constantly changing, and the ability to revise our attitudes and behavior is an essential ingredient of adjustment.

There are several revealing ways of describing the kind of adjustment which any individual is making. We can consider every significant aspect of life—self-development, personal relationships, occupational effectiveness, etc.—and ask how well he is doing in each of them. We can view him as a growing person, and assess his effectiveness in meeting the "developmental tasks" or requirements of his stage in life as an infant, a school child, a mature or aging person. We can also look at him psychologically and ascertain the kind of defense reactions and other "adjustive behavior" he is in the habit of using, as well as his level of tolerance for stress and frustration, and the particular weaknesses he is likely to show when the going gets rough.

When adjustment breaks down and we cannot meet the demands of life without excessive strain or definite emotional symptoms, it is fairly certain that we need psychological aid. The major aim of psychotherapy is to enable the distressed individual to achieve a more adequate adjustment—that is, a more effective and satisfying way of living—by helping him to modify his behavior patterns and release his inner resources. For tests of adjustment *see* PERSONALITY INVENTORIES, MINNESOTA MULTIPHASIC PERSONALITY INVENTORY, FORCED CHOICE, PERSONOLOGY. *See also* MENTAL HEALTH, MENTAL HYGIENE.

ADLER, ALFRED (1870–1937) (Individual Psychology). Adler was born and educated in Vienna, receiving his medical degree from the University of Vienna in 1895. His first book, a treatise on the health and working conditions of tailors, foreshadowed his later emphasis on the total life and environment of the individual. In 1900 he wrote one of the few favorable reviews of Freud's book on dream interpretation, and as a result was invited to join his weekly discussion circle. Within a few years, however, he became the first disciple to break away, since he could not accept Freud's theory of early sexual trauma as the basis for neurosis.

In 1911 Adler and eight friends formed the Society for Free Psychoanalytic Research, renamed the Society for Individual Psychology the following year. In 1919 he organized the first child guidance clinic in Vienna. The demand for such clinics grew rapidly and soon spread to other countries. From 1926 on, when he accepted a visiting professorship at Columbia University, Adler spent the greater part of every year in the United States. His children, Kurt and Alexandra, both psychiatrists, have carried on his work in this country. His books include: *The Study of Organ Inferiority and Its Practical Compensation* (1917), *The Nervous Character* (1926), *Practice and Theory of Individual Psychology* (1927), *Understanding Human Nature* (1927), *The Education of Children* (1930), *What Life Should Mean to You* (1931), and *Social Interest: A Challenge to Mankind* (1938).

Adler's theories were in basic opposition to those of Freud in a number of ways. He held that human beings are not dominated by what he termed "blind" irrational instincts operating on an unconscious level, but are governed by a conscious drive to express and fulfill themselves as unique individuals. His psychology has a far more optimistic flavor than Freud's, for he believed that men can create their own destinies and change their own lives, and society as well, in accordance with basically humane needs and goals.

Adler characterized this general point of view as "fictional finalism," the belief that man is more strongly motivated by future possibilities than by events in the past. Freud tends to look behind to the childhood experiences that mold our personality; Adler looks ahead to the goals and expectations through which we realize ourselves. He describes these goals as ideals and, in that sense, "fictions," holding that the normal person can free himself from them when necessary while the neurotic person cannot.

Individual psychology is not a highly systematized structure; nevertheless it is based on six or seven related concepts. Chief among these is *the striving for superiority,* which Adler believes to be the essence of life itself. This is an innate drive for self-realization, an urge for completion and perfection rather than for superiority in the sense of social distinction or domination over others. All other drives and goals are conceived as components of this sovereign motive. Here again there is a difference between the normal and neurotic individual: the normal person sets his sights on social, co-operative goals; the neurotic only on selfish, egocentric aims.

The striving for perfection implies imperfection and *feelings of inferiority.* In its earliest form, inferiority feeling arises from the infant's sense of helplessness. It may also stem from any "organ inferiority" that afflicts the individual—that is, any structural defect or developmental abnormality, as well as from feelings of social inferiority. Early in his writings, Adler held that women experience particularly strong feelings of inferiority, and applied the term "masculine protest" to their tendency to imitate and compete with the dominant male in our society. Later he came to believe that *any* sense of incompletion gives rise to inferiority feelings, and in this way tied the concept to the general idea of self-realization.

Inferiority feelings generate a drive for *compensation.* To overcome his feelings of helplessness, the growing child tries to develop his skills and abilities. To counterbalance his "organ inferiority," the frail individual tries to strengthen his body, or concentrates on mental activity. To overcome their personal shortcomings or imperfections, men and women strive to improve themselves in accordance with their own individual goals and aspirations. In some cases, however, normal inferiority feelings may develop into an *inferiority complex* which dominates the individual's behavior and leads to *overcompensation.* This is an unhealthy neurotic trend that manifests itself in an extreme, egocentric drive for power and self-aggrandizement at the expense of others.

The strivings of the normal person, however, are not purely self-centered, for they are shaped and channeled by another powerful drive, that of *social interest.* Adler believed, optimistically, that human beings have a basic, innate urge to co-operate and work for the common good. Nevertheless this drive, like any other natural aptitude, must be nurtured and developed, and for this reason he devoted himself wholeheartedly to educational activities and the development of child guidance clinics.

Another key idea of Adler's is the *style of life:* each person develops his personality and expresses his striving for superiority in his own unique way. The individual's special style is basically set by the time he is four or five years of age, and stems from the particular inferiority that affects him most deeply. Once this style of life is set, it directs all his future experience, determining how he perceives his world, what he learns, and the way he seeks to attain his goals. A spoiled child, for example, will expect the world to conform to his fantasies and demands; a neglected child may become an enemy of society seeking revenge for the maltreatment he has received.

In his earlier statements, Adler stressed the fixed character of the individual's style of life, claiming that it was practically impossible to change. As he developed his theory, he became increasingly dissatisfied with this point of view, since it did not do justice to the dynamic aspects of human development. He therefore suggested another concept, that of the *creative self*, which he viewed as the "first cause" of all behavior. This idea was merely postulated, and no evidence was offered as to its nature. According to his own description, it appears to be the "active principle of life," comparable to the concept of soul. Its function is to guide each individual in his search for experiences that will enable him to develop to the fullest and thereby realize his unique style of life.

As a matter of fact, most of Adler's other concepts are also presented as postulates rather than as conclusions based on systematic observation or experimentation. Nevertheless they present an integrated approach to human nature which contrasts sharply with Freud's pessimistic conception of man's life as a continual battle with irrational, socially disapproved instincts. The effect of Adler's view was to assert man's sense of dignity and assure him that he is basically humane, social-minded, and capable of developing his own pattern of life.

Adler's point of view has exerted a lasting influence on psychology and psychiatry. His emphasis on the child's individual sense of inferiority led to many studies on birth order—that is, the effects of being the only child, middle child, or youngest child in the family. Many of these effects were suggested by Adler himself, though he offered little statistical evidence for his views. His concept that the style of life is largely determined by early experiences focused attention on the study of the handicapped child, the spoiled child and the neglected child, and this in turn spurred the search for the causes of emotional disturbance and delinquency. His recognition of the social aspects of experiences helped to stimulate interest in the field of social psychology. His insistence that the individual creates his own life

and is not merely driven by inborn instincts was an important step in the development of "ego psychology." His emphasis on personal and social goals offered an alternative to Freud's emphasis on the sexual drive, for in Adler's view an individual's style of life determines how his sexual needs will be expressed, not vice versa. Similarly, his belief that we are usually aware of the reasons for our behavior was a healthy antidote to Freud's stress on unconscious drives and repressed experiences, since it assured men that they could plan and guide their own lives.

The view that individuals can fashion their own lives became the central focus of Adlerian therapy, which is still practiced fairly widely. Basically, this process is an attempt to help the patient discover and develop his own individual life style and life plan. In doing so, the therapist establishes a close relationship with the patient (Adler was the first to emphasize this), and plays an essentially re-educative role in which he helps the patient substitute realistic for unrealistic goals and achieve more constructive relationships in the home and community.

Adlerian therapy does not emphasize free association, and face-to-face interviews are used instead of the couch technique. Through direct discussion, the therapist focuses the patient's attention on his neurotic attempts to cope with feelings of inferiority through aggressive striving for power or retreat into psychosomatic illness, fantasy, self-depreciation, or other defensive measures. Unconscious forces, sexual or otherwise, are not emphasized, and past events are explored only to throw initial light on the patient's basic life style. Dream analysis may also be used for this purpose, but the therapist is more active in offering interpretations than in the psychoanalytic approach. This active role characterizes the entire therapeutic process, for the therapist does not hesitate to interrupt the patient, point out self-deceptive tendencies, and suggest new interests or activities which are in line with his individual life style. Sessions are usually held three or four times a week rather than five or six, and the whole treatment process is usually shorter than in the Freudian approach. *See* COMPLEX, MASCULINE PROTEST, COMPENSATION, BIRTH ORDER.

ADOLESCENCE. The period of transition from the dependence and immaturity of childhood to the psychological, physical, and social maturity of adulthood; from approximately age twelve to age twenty-one in girls and thirteen to twenty-two in boys.

Nature of adolescence. Most psychologists in America view the behavior and problems of adolescents as the product of the interaction of cultural and biological factors, with cultural determinants playing the dominant role. Biological influences are especially important in producing the glandular and growth changes that determine whether the young person will be a "late bloomer" or an "early bloomer," and in determining his physical traits, temperament and basic intellectual capacity. Cultural influences determine whether society puts a premium on late or early blooming, whether particular physical and temperamental traits are or are not admired, whether the young person has opportunities to use and develop his intellectual capacities, and to a large extent whether the tensions accompanying physiological growth give rise to emotional disturbances. Society also determines the role which the teen-ager plays, his acceptance or rejection by adults, his opportunities for engaging in responsible activities, and his chances to explore life and develop his own values and goals.

The lot of the adolescent is vastly different in different societies. In simpler, more primitive cultures, where children actively contribute to the work of society, his task is mainly to broaden

his experience and increase his skill as steps toward taking on fuller responsibility. In such cases, assumption of responsibility is merely the continuation of a process begun early in life, and not an introduction of something new and different. Moreover, when puberty is reached, the child is at once inducted into adult society by means of elaborate initiation ceremonies which serve the important function of giving him status and a sense of security as he faces the heavier demands of the adult world. He knows at once where he stands and what is required of him; he is not left dangling in a no man's land between childhood and adulthood, nor is he treated as a marginal being floating on the fringe of society.

In contrast, the adolescent in Western culture is often (though not always) beset by problems and inner turmoil because he is accorded inferior status in society, is not encouraged to be emotionally and vocationally independent of his parents, is surrounded by restrictions, and in general has been given little opportunity to assume gradually the kind of responsibility that will ease the transition to adulthood. It is not surprising, then, that many young people, feeling that they have been rejected by established society, are making a desperate attempt to form a subculture of their own.

Physical adjustment. The beginning of adolescence is usually dated from the onset of puberty, which generally occurs from one to three years earlier in girls than boys. Since the basic physical changes are described under other topics we will confine ourselves here to their psychological effects on adolescents in our society. These effects are widespread, since increased glandular activity, under control of the anterior pituitary gland, stimulates growth and metabolic activity as well as primary sexual behavior and the bodily changes known as secondary sexual characteristics. Typically, the adolescent experiences an intense interest in the opposite sex and an insistent demand for sexual release, but frequently these new urges give rise to feelings of frustration, emotional upsets, and guilt reactions. As Horrocks (1962) points out, "the adolescent is a sexually mature individual who has all of the adult's biological sex drives, tensions, and needs for sexual release without any socially approved means of securing relief." See MEN-ARCHE.

The adolescent must also adapt to relatively rapid changes in metabolism, as manifested in frequent fluctuations in pulse rate, blood pressure and general energy. There is great individual variability in these changes, but in any case the maturing boy or girl must go through a continuous process of adjustment and readjustment, and this helps to account for his fluctuations in mood and activity level. In addition to all his other problems, the adolescent must therefore face a period of "physiological learning" before he reaches the relative stability of adulthood.

Another important problem is adaptation to an altered body image. In childhood, growth changes are gradually and readily absorbed; in adolescence, they are usually more rapid and more intimately related to emotional well-being. The adolescent feels he is "wearing" a different and strange kind of body, and since his body image is closely tied to his self-concept, he must go through a period of reconciling the new to the old. This is a complex process involving accentuated interest in the body, self-exploration, comparisons with others, preoccupation with personal appearance, concern over physical skill and health, and frequently conflict between a desire to display the body and an urge to conceal attributes that cause embarrassment. In our society, where so much attention is paid to "normality" and to specific body features, any apparent deviation (large ears, gangling limbs, flat chest) is likely to produce great anxiety

in the adolescent. This is frequently aggravated by the parents' own anxiety as well as by ridicule from relatives or contemporaries.

Social adjustment. One of the key features of adolescence is an expanding social interest. In our society this interest tends to revolve around the adolescent's own age group. Relationships with adults are frequently at a low ebb, and many teen-agers go to any length to win acceptance from their peers. In most—but not all—cases they adopt the prevailing fashions, pursue "in" activities and use the current teen-age vocabulary, partly because they do not have the courage to defy custom, partly because they are groping for the "right" way to behave, and partly because group approval gives them the security they need in facing a problematic world. Doubtless the need for group conformity during this transitional period is accentuated by the gap that exists in our society between the world of the child and the world of the adult.

The role of the adolescent in his peer group determines to a large extent his conception of himself as a member of society. He learns to see himself as a leader, a follower, a fringer, or an isolate—and this self-image tends to last throughout adulthood. If he is fully accepted in the group of his choice, he gains confidence and self-assurance. If he is only partially accepted, he suffers intense anxiety and self-doubt; if he is rejected, he may experience a genuine trauma and react by becoming hostile or by retreating into apathy or fantasy.

Many adults fail to give their sons and daughters the guidance they need in choosing groups in which they will not only be accepted for social reasons, but be able to make a genuine contribution. While it is useful to belong to a group only on the basis of friendship, it is often desirable to base group membership on common interests and constructive activities, particularly when these activities bring the members into contact with the adult world. Groups of this kind are likely to have the greatest maturing influence on the teen-ager.

Adolescent social groups are some-times classified into cliques, crowds, and gangs. Cliques are small, closely knit groups based primarily on clannishness and exclusion of outsiders rather than any specific purpose. Crowds appear somewhat later and often grow out of cliques. They are looser and less per-sonal groups, but as in cliques, this membership tends to be highly homo-geneous and restricted. Gangs are more highly organized than crowds and usu-ally arise out of conflict and outside pressures that bring the members to-gether for mutual assistance and sup-port. They are most frequently found among recent immigrant groups and in neighborhoods where there are racial or national tensions. Although some gangs are benign, the majority appear to be breeding grounds for juvenile delinquency. In addition to the group-ings just reviewed, many adolescents be-long to hobby groups, service groups, and study groups.

A number of authorities have pointed out that adolescents tend to form an entire subculture of their own, looking to each other for rewards and recogni-tion rather than to parents, teachers or adult society in general. On the basis of systematic investigation, Coleman (1961) concludes that adolescent society has not only created its own language, customs and value system but "main-tains only a few threads of connection with the outside adult society." He de-scribes the high school as a "cruel jungle of dating and rating" in which popu-larity among boys depends on athletic ability, ownership of a car, and family background, while popularity among girls depends largely on physical attrac-tiveness, enticing manners, and nice clothes.

Intellectual development. In general,

mental ability, or versatility—at least as measured by standard intelligence tests —continues to increase during the ad-olescent years, and is believed to reach its peak somewhere between the early and mid-twenties. This applies particu-larly to intellectual skills such as rea-soning, memory, and speed of response. It does not mean, however, that mental *growth* attains its highest point during this period, for knowledge, understand-ing, and wisdom continue to be acquired until late in life. Moreover, though some individuals have a high capacity for creativity before or during ado-lescence, the full expression of this capacity in the arts, sciences, industry, and business usually occurs well after adolescence.

In our society adolescence is generally a period of intellectual expansion and enrichment. During the high school years most young people are eager to explore new areas of knowledge, new occupa-tional possibilities, and new interests— although their opportunities to do so may be greatly restricted in the more rigid academic and vocational high schools. The broadening process con-tinues at an especially rapid rate for the 45 per cent who go to college, par-ticularly if they have stimulating in-structors and are not required to spe-cialize too early. Here again there are wide variations in opportunity both in and out of school. In some American families and communities the adolescent is encouraged to strike out for himself and test out many types of activities, but in many others this does not occur, due either to a limited environment or to parental overprotection.

A most important part of the ad-olescent's intellectual life, in the broad-est sense of the term, is development of a basic self-identity and personal philosophy. This period has long been recognized as one in which the young person asks profound questions about himself and life as a whole: Who am I? What am I here for? What is the point of it all? The thinking adolescent is constantly struggling to come to terms with himself and the world at large. These needs are particularly acute in a time like ours when the world is beset with unsolved problems and the older generation has appeared to fail on so many fronts.

There is undeniable value in the adolescent's struggle to find meaning and purpose: it broadens and deepens his attitudes, prevents complacent acceptance of conventional ideas and "time-honored" approaches. At the same time, however, many adolescents see only the failures and inadequacies in the world picture. This tendency, instead of arousing determination to set things right, has often led to a defeatist, "beat" attitude, retreat into a subculture of their own, and narcissistic experimentation with drugs and pseudoreligious cults. A peak was reached in the "hippie" movement, but fortunately there are signs of a reversal of the trend and a renewal of adolescent zest for life. But the problem of making the fullest use of the energies of youth and of helping young people find a "place in the sun" still remains.

ADOLESCENCE (Theories). Adolescence is probably the most controversial of all periods of human development. Since the beginning of this century literally dozens of theories have been suggested to explain this stage of growth, each professing to be based on careful observation and systematic investigation. This article will briefly review the eleven theories which appear to have had the greatest influence on American psychological thought, drawing largely from *Theories of Adolescence* by R. E. Muuss, 1962.

G. Stanley Hall. The first psychologist to make a scientific study of adolescence, Hall based his approach on an expansion of Darwin's theory of recapitulation. In his view, each individual relives the development of the human race from a primitive, animalistic stage to a civilized way of life. The entire process is guided by internal physiological and genetic forces, with little if any influence from the cultural environment. More specifically, infancy (the first four years of life) corresponds to the animal stage in which sensory-motor skills are developed; childhood (four to eight) represents the early human stage of hunting and fishing, and is characterized by such activities as cowboys and Indians, building of caves and tree houses; youth (eight to twelve) echoes the "humdrum life of savagery," and is the period in which the child learns the practical skills of reading and writing through drill and practice; while adolescence (puberty to adulthood) is a period of storm and stress corresponding to the turbulent transition from savagery to civilization.

Hall depicted the adolescent as oscillating between activity and lethargy, exuberance and apathy, euphoria and despondency, vanity and abasement, brashness and bashfulness, childish selfishness and idealistic altruism, longing for authority and rebellion against authority. The period of adolescence lasts almost ten years, but if it is allowed to take its natural course, and if adults are lenient and permissive, the conflict and turmoil will gradually give way to a state of civilized maturity by the time the age of twenty-two to twenty-five is reached.

Sigmund Freud. Freud's theory of psychosexual development, like Hall's, is based on a series of genetically determined stages which are relatively independent of environmental influence. In his original theory he put far more emphasis on infantile, pregenital sexuality and its effect on personality than on the adolescent years. According to his account, the libido is active at birth, directing itself to the child's own body during the oral and anal stages that occur in the first two or three years of life, followed by a phallic phase in which it becomes centered in the sex organs as a result of self-manipulation, and an Oedipus phase in which it is directed toward the parent of the opposite sex. These stages are followed by the latency period during which the libido and the "pleasure principle" are subordinated to the "reality principle" and development of the ego. When puberty is reached, the sex impulse again breaks through to produce "subordination of all sexual component-instincts under the primacy of the genital zone" (Freud, 1953). During this phase sexuality is expressed through psychological tension, external stimulation of the erogenous zones of the body, and the physiological need to release sexual products, all of which leads to a high rate of masturbation.

All through early adolescence the new awakening of sexuality is accompanied by nervous excitement, genital phobia, and personality turmoil "because of the outstanding power of the lust dynamism and the comparative hopelessness of learning how [to] do anything about it" (Sullivan, 1953). Like Hall, Freud felt that this conflict makes the adolescent especially vulnerable to emotional disturbances. In addition, increased sexual tension revives the incestuous drive of the earlier genital period, and he therefore spoke of a second Oedipal period. However, during the latency period the superego has erected an "incest barrier" which has resulted in repression of incestuous feelings toward the parents, and therefore during the Oedipal period of adolescence these feelings are displaced to mother and father figures— that is, the boy is likely to fall in love with a mature woman and the girl with an older man.

Though he devoted little space to adolescence, Freud did cite certain basic tasks to be accomplished during this period. First, the adolescent must further resolve the Oedipal situation by centering attention on his own peers rather than on an older man or woman; sec-

ond, he must face the problem of "not missing the opposite sex"—that is, he must not form such strong friendship ties to members of his own sex that he runs the risk of inversion (homosexuality); third, he must free himself from dependence on his parents even though this may lead for a time to feelings of resentment, hostility, or outright rejection toward them. All these tasks are subordinate to the main function of the adolescent period, which is "attainment of genital primacy and the definitive completion of the process of non-incestuous object finding" (finding a love object). See PSYCHOSEXUAL DEVELOPMENT.

Anna Freud describes the dynamics of adolescent development in more detail than her father. She also assigns greater importance to character formation during puberty, and puts more emphasis on the internal conflicts that take place between the ego and id during this period. In addition, she claims that the revival of the Oedipus complex during puberty reactivates earlier castration fears of boys and penis envy in girls. At this stage the child also defends himself against the anxieties which sexual impulses arouse by resorting to excessive fantasy, aggressive behavior, and asceticism. He may also lapse into pregenital (anal, oral) gratification. Ordinarily these conflicts resolve themselves as the young person goes through adolescence, until the "turmoil of boorishness, aggressiveness, and perverse behavior has vanished like a nightmare." In some cases, however, pathological trends may develop: (a) the id may dominate the ego, resulting in "a riot of uninhibited gratification of instincts"; (b) the ego may totally dominate the id, and the boy or girl may take refuge in overintellectualism or become completely inhibited and ascetic, not only in regard to sex but also in eating, sleeping, and dressing habits. The basic problem, then, is to maintain a balance between the id, ego, and super-ego during the adolescent period.

Otto Rank. Though psychoanalytic in approach, Rank (1945) was far more concerned with the conscious ego and the creative, productive development of the personality than with unconscious repressions, neurotic trends, and early experiences. In his approach the dominant force is not sexuality but will, with its emphasis on choice and activity. Though this faculty gradually develops during the early years of life, particularly in the Oedipus period, it does not begin to come into its own until early adolescence when young people assert their independence from parents and teachers and also from domination by biological, sexual needs. This striving for independence prevents the adolescent from forming strong emotional attachments, since they would lead him back to a dependency relationship. He therefore tends either toward promiscuity, in which sexual urges are satisfied without sacrificing independence; or toward asceticism, in which involvement of any kind is avoided—and in some cases he vacillates between the two.

Personality development, for Rank, is an evolutionary process which may go through three stages during the adolescent period. In the first stage the will is freed from external and internal forces (environmental and biological) that have dominated it. Most individuals do not go beyond this stage, and are content with adjusting to reality and carrying on ordinary responsibilities. In the second stage, the will actively struggles against the "counter-will" (parents, society, sex urges, unrealistic ideas), and the individual is at odds with both the internal and the external worlds. This struggle often leads to excessive self-criticism, feelings of inferiority and other neurotic symptoms—but some people respond to the conflict by leading creative, productive lives. The few who arrive at a successful integration between will and counter-will have reached the third stage and are able to free themselves from conflict and maintain a harmony between the internal and the external world. These individuals, characterized by Rank as geniuses, achieve a full and conscious realization of their potential. *See* RANK.

Erik Erikson. In his "Eight Stages of Man" (*Childhood and Society,* 1950), Erikson offers an account of personality growth that is reminiscent of Freud's theory of psychosexual development, but with three outstanding differences: (a) the core of the process is the gradual acquisition of "ego identity," a strong and healthy sense of personal worth and integrity; (b) at every stage, this process is rooted in social relationships as a whole, and not exclusively in sexual experiences; and (c) even though the general task of acquiring identity is the same for all societies, the specific way it is achieved varies widely from culture to culture. In a word, Erikson has modified the psychoanalytic theory in the light of cultural anthropology.

Each of the eight stages, which correspond roughly to Freud's, has its own positive goals and negative risks: (1) *oral sensory stage:* trust versus distrust; (2) *muscular anal:* autonomy versus shame and doubt; (3) *locomotor genital:* initiative versus guilt; (4) *latency:* industry versus inferiority; (5) *puberty and adolescence:* identity versus role diffusion; (6) *young adulthood:* intimacy versus isolation; (7) *adulthood:* generativity versus stagnation; (8) *maturity:* ego integrity versus disgust, despair.

In pubescence, the child experiences rapid growth and a "physiological revolution" which threatens his body image and sense of security. As a result he is excessively concerned with the way he appears to other people. In adolescence the primary concern is with the establishment of a dominant ego identity. This involves achieving sexual identity, forming values independent of parents, insistence on independence and privacy, and achievement of vocational identity. In this process the adolescent goes through a period of "role diffusion" in which he identifies with various heroes and leaders, and a period of identification with a gang or clique as a "defense against self-diffusion." The adolescent's frequent crushes and love affairs are not seen primarily as an expression of sexuality, but as an attempt to define the ego and prepare the way for the choice of a suitable mate, as well as a means of developing the capacity for a genuine love relationship in which he will be able to devote himself to another person without losing his own identity.

Edward Spranger. Spranger's approach, as expressed in his *Psychology of Adolescence* (1955) is an attempt to grasp the structure and meaning of adolescence in its totality. This stage of life is not pictured merely as a transition from childhood to physiological maturity, but as a period during which the psyche achieves full maturity and a "dominant value direction." This direction is the basic determiner of personality.

Spranger finds three characteristic patterns or rhythms during this period. In one of them, the adolescent goes through a rebirth in which he experiences the kind of storm, stress and personality change that Hall emphasized; the second is characterized by a slower process of growth, in which the cultural values and ideas of society are gradually acquired; in the third, the young person actively participates in his own growth through conscious attempts at changing and improving himself.

One or another of these patterns will usually be dominant in a given individual, but in any case adolescence is viewed as a period in which the psyche becomes organized through discovery of the ego or self, and through gradual formation of a life plan and personal value system. In this process, the young person challenges previously unquestioned ideas, mores and traditions; develops an increased need for social recognition and interpersonal relationships; begins to see how "sexuality" (sensuality) and "pure love" (empathy, devotion) can be merged in marriage; and also experiments with different aspects of his ego in order to answer the puzzling question, "Who am I?"

If all goes well, the adolescent develops a mature, harmonious ego with a unified philosophy of life centered about a major value which determines his type of personality. Spranger identifies the following eight personality types: (1) the person who is preoccupied with physical health, vitality and need for power; (2) the esthetic-enthusiastic type with a characteristic adolescent attitude toward life; (3) the theoretically oriented thinker who ponders about the meaning of existence; (4) the active person, interested in progress and success (the typical American, according to Spranger); (5) the adventurous type who yearns for fame; (6) the social, altruistic person, rare among adolescents, since adolescents tend to be egocentric; (7) the ethical enthusiast who defends rigorous principles; (8) the religious type, often found among adolescents. (Compare Spranger's six "Types of Men" which furnish the basis for the Allport-Vernon-Lindzey Study of Values. See this topic.)

Ruth Benedict and Margaret Mead. These anthropologists have contributed heavily to an understanding of adolescence through their recognition of the influence of cultural factors on development, and their descriptions of variations in adolescent behavior from society to society. Their views counterbalance the emphasis on biological constitution in Hall and Freud, and challenge the assumption that the adolescent in Western culture is characteristic of "human nature" as a whole. They point out that while development always proceeds from a state of infantile dependence to relative independence, the way this occurs differs widely from culture to culture. In American society, there is a sharp discontinuity between child and adult—for example, many children are spared household duties or other forms of work, and questions on sex are often discouraged, slurred over, or answered falsely. In Samoa, on the other hand, growth follows a continuous pattern, sexual activities are open and uninhibited, and what we consider perversions are characterized as "simply play." Similarly the Samoans make no sharp distinctions, as we do, between irresponsible youth and responsible adults, between submissiveness in childhood and dominance in maturity, or between work and play. The boys start to hunt and fish and the girls start to take care of the children as early as six or seven years of age. As a result, no basic change takes place during the adolescent period, there is no special conflict between generations, and young people are not suddenly required to assume responsibilities for which they are unprepared. For these reasons, storm and stress behavior is virtually unknown.

The views of the anthropologists, with their emphasis on cultural determinism, raise the question as to whether adolescence is a biological or a psychosocial phenomenon. In their earlier writings, Benedict and Mead do not actually deny the influence of biological factors; they are simply more concerned with cultural influences. Even when they discuss biological changes, they approach them from a cultural point of view—for example, they show that in primitive societies one tribe may regard menstruation as a danger and another as a blessing. However, in her later writings, especially in *Male and Female* (1949), Mead is less extreme in her emphasis on cultural relativism, and recognizes "basic regularities" such as the latency period and the trauma of menstruation as a transition to adulthood found in all cultures. In any case, however, she holds that cultural conditioning, usually in the form of child-rearing practices, determines whether development is a continuous affair, as in primitive societies, or a discontinuous set of stages, as it is in our own culture.

Kurt Lewin. In accordance with Lewin's field theory, the individual adolescent is to be understood in terms of the unique interactions between biological, sociological, environmental, and psychological factors that make up his "life space." The adolescent years are characterized by rapid changes in the structure of this space, or field, due to the young person's increased ability to distinguish between reality and "irreality" (fantasy, wishes, etc.), his thirst for new experiences and wider social contacts, and his urge to assert his independence. Of all these factors, Lewin believes that changes in group membership are most characteristic of this period: the adolescent is in a state of "social locomotion" between child groups and adult groups, and the boundaries of his life space are therefore uncertain. Typical reactions to this uncertainty and lack of "structure" are withdrawal, sensitivity, inhibition, aggressiveness, and radicalism.

Changes in the inner life space (the adolescent's self-image) are as drastic as those in the outer life space, and lead to doubt, instability and plasticity of personality. If this situation is prolonged, as it is in much of our society, the adolescent remains a "marginal man" for some time, torn between conflicting ideologies, values and styles of living. In other cultures this period may be much shorter and less turbulent—and even in our own culture some adolescents experience more conflict than others. The emphasis should therefore be on the individual's specific situation, not on statistical generalizations.

Following Lewin's lead, Robert G. Barker explains the American adolescent's major characteristics, as he sees them—instability, vacillating behavior, suggestibility and peer-group conformity

—in terms of the problem of dealing with his marginal situation and with the sharp differentiation between adult and child groups in our society. In addition, he stresses the further "somatopsychological" problem of adolescents who are physically adult but emotionally childlike, as well as the problems of adolescents who have difficulty adjusting different goals to each other, such as making friends and getting an education. *See* FIELD THEORY.

Allison Davis and *Robert Havighurst.* Davis views socialization as the crucial issue in adolescent development, defining it as a process of integrating the values, beliefs, and ways of the particular culture into the personality. The major motivating force toward mature, responsible, culturally acceptable behavior is "socialized anxiety" resulting from threats of punishment and withdrawal of love during childhood. The goals of socialization, however, differ not only from culture to culture but from class to class. He finds middle-class adolescents more socially anxious than lower-class adolescents, since the former are more concerned with success, status, and morality, and more sensitive toward social pressure. Lower-class adolescents are freer in expression of sex and aggression, less concerned about being "good," and more interested in immediate pleasure than in long-range goals and rewards that are available primarily to middle-class individuals.

Havighurst also sees socialization as a central issue, but places less emphasis on social anxiety and more on "developmental tasks" prescribed by both individual need and the demands of society. Successful mastery of the tasks at each stage results in good adjustment and adequate preparation for the harder tasks ahead. Here again there are class and cultural variations, and some tasks have a more biological basis while others have a more sociological basis. For adolescence, defined as the period from about twelve to eighteen, the developmental tasks are: (1) acceptance of one's physique and sex role; (2) new relations with agemates of both sexes; (3) emotional independence from parents and other adults; (4) selection and preparation for an occupation, to assure economic independence; (5) development of intellectual skills and concepts necessary for attaining independence; (6) achievement of socially responsible behavior; (7) preparation for marriage and family life; and (8) conscious adoption of values in keeping with the contemporary world. *See* DEVELOPMENTAL TASKS.

Arnold Gesell. Strongly influenced by Hall's biological and evolutionary theory, Gesell's emphasis was on an orderly sequence of growth determined by an "innate biological force." Maturation therefore initiates and governs the developmental process, while environmental influences (termed "acculturation") serve only to stimulate, modify and support it. Gesell makes the point, for example, that practice and exercise can take effect only if the "neural structures" are ripe and ready. The sequence of growth, however, is not described in terms of these structures, but in terms of characteristic behavior patterns on which he bases a flexible theory of age norms.

Gesell warns parents not to take these tables of norms too literally, and to "bear in mind the difference between an average and a baby." Nevertheless he is open to criticism for basing his developmental scales on a selected population in one section of the country—New Haven children in the high-average to superior ability range—and for considering them "more or less characteristic of the human species." He conceived the developmental process as oscillating along a spiral course toward maturity—that is, the child advances for a time, then regresses to earlier forms of behavior while he becomes inwardly prepared for further gains.

These "ups and downs" are found in adolescence as well as in earlier stages.

The adolescent period is viewed as a transition from childhood to adulthood in which the central task of the young person is to find himself. The following "maturity profiles" represent, for Gesell, the characteristic patterns during the years from ten to sixteen, when the most important changes are believed to take place:

The ten-year-old is in a state of "developmental balance," accepts life with ease and confidence, enjoys family activities, recognizes authority, denies any interest in the opposite sex, and engages in group activities with members of his own sex.

The eleven-year-old is in the foothills of adolescence where the terrain appears strange; his organism is in a state of change and his typical reactions are moodiness, impulsiveness, negativism, argumentativeness, and rebellion against parents.

The twelve-year-old swings away from emotional turmoil and becomes reasonable, tolerant and sociable; at the same time he strives for greater independence from home and wants to be treated as a grown-up. He is strongly influenced by his peer group in dress and interests, carries out self-chosen acts with enthusiasm, and likes to play kissing games at parties.

The thirteen-year-old turns inward and becomes withdrawn, reflective, self-critical, sensitive to outside criticism, and critical of parents. He has fewer friends than at twelve, choosing them more carefully on the basis of common interests. He experiences rapid changes in body structure and chemistry, affecting posture, voice, facial expression, and producing tensions, fluctuations of mood and awareness of growing up.

The fourteen-year-old again reverses the field and becomes extraversive, energetic, expansive, better integrated and more self-assured. He is friendly, interested in other people and particularly in their personalities; also interested in his own personality and identifies with a series of heroes and fictional characters, remarking again and again "That's me all over."

The fifteen-year-old cannot be reduced to a formula because of wide individual differences—but in general there is a strong trend toward a spirit of independence accompanied by tensions and conflicts with others; a demand for freedom from external control at school and home; increasing self-awareness, perfectionism, and self-criticism, with the beginnings of greater self-control; possibly rebellious behavior and delinquency, and an urge to leave school and home.

The sixteen-year-old, in mid-adolescence, is characterized as a "pre-adult," since he has usually achieved self-dependence, self-awareness, balanced social adjustment and good emotional control. He tends to be cheerful, friendly, outgoing, self-confident, and oriented toward the future. Boy-girl relationships are often still on a nonromantic basis, though many girls are beginning to think of marriage. The Gesell studies do not go beyond this age.

ADRENAL GLANDS. A pair of endocrine glands, located above the kidneys, which secrete hormones that control emotional reactions and basic life processes such as metabolism, blood pressure, and sexual development.

The adrenal cortex, or outer layer, of each gland is essential to life. It secretes at least thirty different hormones collectively known as cortin. Three of them are especially active: cortisol, a close relative of cortisone, is a primary regulator of carbohydrate metabolism and liver function; aldosterone governs the sodium level, water balance, and kidney functions of the body; and corticosterone is a participant in all these mechanisms. Complete destruction or removal of the cortex leads to increasing weakness, loss of appetite, and gradual death, although life can sometimes be prolonged by administering large quantities of salt. An undersecretion of cortin results in Addison's disease, which is characterized by low basal metabolism, reduced temperature and blood pressure, darkening of the skin, headaches, lassitude, and sexual inadequacy. On the other hand, a tumor or abnormal growth of the cortex sometimes leads to excessive secretion, and may produce a rare condition known as Cushing's syndrome. Typical symptoms of this disorder, which usually occurs in young women, are muscle weakness, excessive fatigue, reduced sex drive, headaches, skin disfigurement, spinal deformity, and obesity.

The cortex also produces the adrenal androgens and estrogens—male and female sex hormones which work with gonadal secretions in regulating such secondary sex characteristics as change of voice and pubic hair. An oversupply of androgens in the male may produce accelerated puberty in young boys (pubertas praecox), as well as a heavy beard and unusually deep voice. Similar changes may occur in the female (virilism). An undersecretion of androgens delays sexual maturity and may lead to feminine characteristics in the male, a condition known as feminism. An oversecretion of estrogens in the male may also bring about this condition.

The adrenal medulla, the inner core of the gland, secretes two similar hormones, epinephrine (adrenalin) and norepinephrine (noradrenalin). These are known as catechol amines, and are derived from phenylalanine, an amino acid which also metabolizes into thyroxin and phenylpyruvic acid. When these hormones are secreted into the bloodstream, they produce the physical changes associated with strong emotions such as anger and aggressiveness—that is, they release sugar into the bloodstream, increase the pulse rate, enlarge the air passages into the lungs, widen the pupils of the eye, and raise the

blood pressure. The combined effect of these changes is to mobilize energy and prepare the organism to meet an emergency. If the individual remains under stress for prolonged periods, and the physical changes persist, they may result in psychophysiologic (psychosomatic) disorders such as gastric ulcer, colitis, or hypertension. See PHENYLKETONURIA (PKU), PEPTIC ULCER, COLITIS, HYPERTENSION, ADDISON'S DISEASE, VIRILISM, CUSHING'S SYNDROME, BIOGENIC AMINES.

ADRENERGIC REACTION. A generalized reaction, produced or transmitted by adrenalin, which keys the organism up and prepares it to meet emergencies.

Adrenalin is a hormone secreted by the medulla, or inner core, of the adrenal gland during strong emotion or stress. It activates the sympathetic component of the autonomic nervous system, which rapidly mobilizes the resources of the organism when it faces a crisis. More specifically, it speeds up heart action, releases energy into the blood stream, and tenses muscles for action. Some authorities believe adrenalin (epinephrine) may act as a "chemical transmitter" by seeping across the synapses and exciting nerve fibers. Present evidence, however, seems to indicate that its close relative, noradrenalin (norepinephrine), usually if not always performs that function. The other known chemical transmitter is acetylcholine, which activates the parasympathetic system and portions of the brain. See CHOLINERGIC.

Recent studies have shown that adrenergic reactions may at times be more harmful than useful. In situations of great stress the organism may become "overmobilized" and the emergency responses may be so extreme that behavior becomes disorganized. Instead of being fully prepared for action, we may become confused, weak, and paralyzed by fright. This state is termed "autonomic disorganization."

Newer research also indicates that adrenergic secretions may not only call into action the autonomic nervous system but also brain centers involved in the control of emotions—particularly the hypothalamus and the reticular activating system. In addition, the secretions may help to release corticoids from the cortex or outer layer of the adrenal gland. The corticoids play a major role in the body's defense against stress and disease. *See* GENERAL ADAPTATION SYNDROME, RETICULAR FORMATION, HYPOTHALAMUS, ADRENAL GLANDS.

ADVERTISING RESEARCH. Psychologists have played a part in practically every phase of advertising research—the selection of appropriate appeals for specific commodities, the creation of product images and trade names, the development of techniques for measuring the effectiveness of different media and different types of ads. They have been especially involved with the human foundations on which advertising is built, including the behavior of individuals as consumers and the motives that prompt them to buy. *See* CONSUMER RESEARCH, MOTIVATION RESEARCH.

Appeals. Ever since the beginning of modern advertising it has been axiomatic that the advertiser must base his appeal on the needs and wants of the consumer. Since it seemed obvious that an appeal to strong needs would be most effective, psychologists used to construct lists of basic drives (hunger, sex, status, social approval, and so on) from which the advertiser might choose. While such lists might still be useful, they are too general and arbitrary to be of much value to the copywriter.

The newer approach is to base the appeal or message of a particular ad on the *specific* factors or combination of factors most likely to motivate the customer to buy a *specific* product. Opinion surveys and other techniques have been designed to reveal what people like or dislike about a product, the circumstances under which they buy it, what kind of people buy it, how they use it, and the special features that prompt them to change brands. Such studies often produce unexpected findings—for example, the ads for a certain household cleanser featured the idea that it "works faster," but a survey showed that only 2 per cent of the customers cited that reason for buying it, while 58 per cent said, "It's easy on the hands." (Hepner, 1956)

Although most ads concentrate on pleasant, positive appeals such as style and economy, research shows that the kind that remind the public about such negative, unpleasant conditions as halitosis, B.O., or tired blood may also be highly effective. However, if the situations depicted are revolting or frightening, the reader or hearer may be actively antagonized or simply ignore the ad. In some cases, as in ads on Sanforizing, it has proved effective to picture the positive effects of using the product as well as the negative effects of failing to use it. The reason for the success of such ads is that they do not merely focus on unpleasant situations but go beyond, to show how they can be avoided.

Feeling Tone. The direct appeals explicitly stated in an ad or sales talk can be greatly reinforced by indirect suggestion. Considerable attention has therefore been given to creating an effective "feeling tone," or mood, for a particular product, through the use of appropriate color, type, layout and language. Psychologists have done a good deal of research on all of these factors. In one study, a large group of subjects were shown eight colors and asked to name the one that best represented each of eleven moods, such as exciting and stimulating, tender and soothing, serene and peaceful. The results were definitive: to cite two examples, most subjects chose red for exciting and stimulating, and either blue or green for tender and soothing (Wexner, 1954). Such experiments have led advertisers to discard the old dictum "Any color is good so long as it's red." They now choose the color that appears to be most appropriate for the particular product—for instance, ads for menthol cigarettes frequently depict a green outdoor scene to reinforce the idea of a cool, soothing flavor. *See* COLOR REACTIONS, ESTHETICS.

Another consideration is legibility. Measurements made with such devices as eye cameras and tachistoscopes (rapid-exposure devices) have shown that reading speed is usually faster for black type on a white background, but green on white, blue on white and black on yellow are almost equally legible. Familiar layouts have proved more effective than unfamiliar ones, and bizarre arrangements frequently annoy the reader. Although preferences for different kinds of type change from one period to another, tests have shown that at any given time certain type faces are generally associated with specific kinds of products and evoke specific feeling tones. For this reason the advertising agency chooses one kind of type to convey dignity and elegance, another for practicality and economy. The choice of type for trade-marks, headlines, and letterheads is also given careful attention.

The language of the ad plays an important part in creating a desired feeling tone. The copy must be well suited to the product and the specific appeal. Technical terms are effective in ads for scientific instruments or construction materials, but the average buyer of cleansing materials is not interested in the chemistry of the product beyond the fact that it loosens dirt or dissolves grease. Sound and rhythm are also important factors. Short, lively sentences are appropriate for a product that "gives you a lift," but not for one associated with relaxation. Brand names must not

only be easy to pronounce and easy to remember, but should also convey the "atmosphere" of the product. The sharp, staccato sound of "Citgo" suggests the power of a gasoline; the soft, languorous sound of "Illusion" is more appropriate to a perfume. Tests have shown that we also associate certain sounds with certain types of shape. When subjects were shown a list of meaningless sounds and a group of forms, the word "Taratok" was matched with a drawing of a jagged figure, while "Lamolay" was applied to a smoothly curved shape (*Fig. 1*). In the

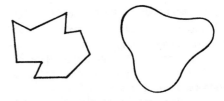

Fig. 1. Which of these shapes is Lamolay and which is Taratok? Brand names and symbols are frequently chosen with "feeling tone" in mind.

light of this finding it is interesting that the symbol chosen for Citgo is a triangle. *See* PHYSIOGNOMIC PERCEPTION.

Trademarks, trade names, and slogans. Trademarks and slogans are carefully devised to identify the product and stimulate recall, to prevent confusion with other products, to evoke a certain feeling tone, and in some cases to call attention to specific advantages of the product. One milk company prints a picture of a mother and child on every carton with the legend FROM DELLWOOD WITH LOVE; a cleanser package contains a picture of a newly hatched chick with the slogan HASN'T SCRATCHED YET; other companies use "trade characters" as associative devices—for example, the Campbell Kids or the man with an eyepatch in the Hathaway shirt ads. Sometimes brand names—Frigidaire, Kodak, Thermos—become so closely identified with a product that they are used as generic terms. In such cases the name ceases to serve its function of distinguishing the product from its competitors, and other devices such as special slogans or distinctive printing have to be used. In other cases confusion is created by similarity between trade names. Psychologists have devised experimental methods for testing such confusion, but so far very few courts have decided infringement cases on the basis of their research.

A number of procedures have also been created for testing the effectiveness of trademarks and trade names. In the free association technique, groups of subjects are shown trade names and asked to write down the first word that comes to mind. In one study it was found that when 100 subjects were shown the stimulus word Dixie Cola, twenty-nine of them wrote down Coca-Cola and twenty-two Pepsi-Cola (Foley, 1944). A second technique is the mock readership survey which tests the reaction of a cross-section of consumers to unpublished ads. In an investigation of this type, two groups of subjects were shown ads for television sets which were identical in all respects except that some of them used well known and others poorly known brand names. The experimenter (Koponen, 1956) found that the ads with the better known names were not only read more closely and recalled more fully than the others, but the sets themselves were rated higher on a number of characteristics! Other tests have shown that trademarks which are readily recognized and which create a positive feeling tone tend to be easily recalled.

Product Image Studies. Psychologists are frequently called upon to discover the "personality" of a given product— that is, the images, associations and feeling tone it evokes in the mind of the public. They also conduct studies on the images projected by corporations and other institutions. Practically all the techniques described under the topics Consumer Research and Motivation Research are used: opinion surveys, jury panels, depth interviews, projective techniques. When research revealed that Marlboro cigarettes had developed a highly feminine personality which discouraged male buyers, the company shifted to masculine themes. When a large bank discovered that its image was suffering from the "curse of bigness," it changed its advertising to put the emphasis on the neighborliness of its branches.

Two relatively objective procedures for assessing product image are coming into increasing use. One is the adjective checklist in which subjects are given a list of adjectives or descriptive phrases and asked to check any that apply to the product or company under study. To make this technique more intriguing, the words are sometimes arranged on a chessboard. In a study of the product personality of different automobiles, a large group of men were presented with a list of adjectives and asked to apply them to the owners of Ford, Plymouth, and Chevrolet. Among other things, the Plymouth owners were pictured as quiet, careful, and gentle. However, when the same test was applied a year later, the image of the Plymouth owner had shifted radically to "important, different, particular." The change was apparently due to the fact that new models had been introduced in the interim, and had been advertised as "dramatic, revolutionary, fabulous, with exhilarating sports car handling."

The second technique is the semantic differential (*Fig. 31*), developed originally for research on the psychology of meaning (Osgood, Suci and Tannenbaum, 1957). In this procedure the subject is asked to rate a product or company on a 7 point scale for each of a series of opposite qualities. In one study the comparative images of television and newspapers as a whole were determined by having subjects put an

X somewhere along a line drawn between such qualities as untruthful–truthful, fearful–courageous, aloof–friendly, unintelligent–intelligent. When the resulting images were assembled, the investigators found that television had a "warmer personality" than newspapers, but newspapers were considered more intelligent, credible, courageous, and reliable.

Physical Characteristics of Ads. If the message of an ad is to be communicated effectively, it must be presented in a form that will catch the eye, arouse interest, and impress the public. If it is to help sell the product, it must also be easily understood and remembered. For these reasons psychologists and their associates have made many studies of the effect of differences in size, position, color, illustration and repetition on attention and retention. Readership surveys conducted by Rudolph (1947) and Starch (1957) have shown that doubling the size of an ad will nearly double the readership, although a small ad with high attention value will show less gain when enlarged than one that is not so striking. Larger ads also have a tendency to attract more prospective users, while small ads attract more present users, who notice them because they are already interested in the product. When ads are enlarged, the additional space is usually devoted to more text or illustration, but sometimes it is more effective merely to add to the white space.

Studies by Starch (1960) and McGraw-Hill (1962) strongly support the policy of inserting the same ad unchanged in several different issues of the same magazine, for they found that the readership level remains approximately the same throughout. In another study, some subjects were exposed to certain magazine ads twice and others once. Later they were asked to name the first brand that came to mind for various products, and it was found that those who had seen the ads twice named

the products advertised in them twice as often as those who had seen them only once. They also named these brands twice as often when they were asked what brand they thought they would buy. (Politz, 1960)

As to position, Starch (1961a.b.) has shown that cover pages have an advantage of 30 to 64 per cent over inside pages in terms of attention, but there is little difference among the inside pages except when the ads are placed near relevant editorial material (for instance, book ads near book reviews). Controlled studies also show negligible differences between right and left pages and right and left halves of pages (Rudolph, 1947). The same investigator has also found that a two-color ad has practically no advantage (1 per cent) over black and white, certainly not enough to justify the extra cost of 17 per cent. On the other hand, four-color ads were found to increase readership 54 per cent with only a 44 per cent increase in cost. Starch has found that the readership increment was higher for half-page ads (85 per cent) than for full page ads (50 per cent). He also found that four-color ads were mentioned two and a half times as frequently as black and white ads by readers who were asked which ads impressed them most. However, color should not be used indiscriminately since it is more effective for some kinds of products than for others.

Illustrations must also be used selectively. A picture must be appropriate to the copy, the appeal and the feeling tone, and it must not simply attract attention to itself. In cases where the illustration lets the product speak for itself, very little copy is needed. Usually, however, ads that portray people make a greater impression than those showing only the product. Starch selected the fifty most widely read and the fifty least widely read ads from his records, and found that twenty-nine of the widely read group featured people, while nine of them showed the product alone. In the least widely read group, only ten featured people, and thirty-two showed the product alone. However, people do not need to be shown in ads that feature the various uses of a product, as in picturing various kinds of cakes baked with a certain flour.

Effectiveness of Advertising. There are two general approaches to testing the effectiveness of an ad. The first is to discover how the public reacts to it—whether it captures attention, evokes interest, and makes a lasting impression. The second and crucial test is whether they purchase the product.

The following are the most important methods of testing reactions to ads. In the *consumer jury technique,* a representative consumer panel is shown a series of ads (in person or through the mail) and asked to select the one that appears most interesting or the one most likely to induce them to buy. This technique has been found to work best when the jury consists of potential customers, and the results often agree quite closely with more objective methods.

A second technique is the *readership survey,* designed to measure the percentage of readers who actually remember the ads. There are several ways of doing this. In the "aided recall" method developed by Gallup and Robinson, Inc., the respondent is shown a list of brand or company names and asked whether he has seen an ad for any of them in a given issue of a magazine or newspaper. If he says yes, he is then asked to "play back" the ad's message and answer questions about it. In the "recognition" technique of Daniel Starch and Staff (1961), respondents who have seen the issue are shown several ads in turn and are asked three questions about each of them: whether they remember seeing it, whether they noted the name of the product or advertiser, and whether they read at least half of the copy. They then answer a series of questions de-

signed to explore their reactions to the ad and the product advertised. To correct for false recognition or falsification, ads that have not actually appeared are interspersed among the actual ads. Another promising technique, developed by the Advertising Research Foundation, is the "communiscope," a tachistoscopic, or exposure, device, which gives the subjects a momentary glimpse of ads, followed by questions about the material they contain.

A third general technique is the *controlled exposure* procedure in which ads are pretested by showing them in a dummy magazine or show window. Rough versions of radio and television commercials are also pretested on sample audiences. This technique enables the advertiser to bring ads which differ in size, position, color, and illustration to the attention of different subjects. Their reactions are determined by asking questions which reveal how much they noticed and remembered. Eye cameras, tachistoscopes, and the newly developed Visual Testing Apparatus (VISTA) are sometimes used to determine the way the subject looks at the ads and what "registers" most. R. R. Wells has recently developed an apparatus designed to determine the "subconscious response" of subjects to ads, television programs and other material by measuring fluctuations in skin resistance to an electric current. *See* GALVANIC SKIN RESPONSE.

While it is important to capture the attention and impress the memory of the public, the final test of advertising lies in its effect on sales. One important method of measuring the acceptance of the product is the *brand use survey* in which respondents are asked whether they are currently using a certain coffee, cleanser, or other product. (Sometimes this technique is supplemented by a "pantry check" of the kitchen shelves.) An extensive study by Starch (1961) involving an analysis of 400,000 interviews and 45,000 ads has indicated that about 13 per cent more ad readers than nonad readers bought the products advertised.

A second method is the analysis of *coupon returns,* but this applies of course only where the coupon is used for mail-order buying rather than merely for ordering a pamphlet or free sample. Advertisers frequently use a "split-run technique" (some readers see one ad, others another) to test the effectiveness of coupon ads of different size, position, and content. The split-run technique followed by a readership survey is sometimes used to test ads that do not carry coupons.

Finally, actual *sales surveys* are sometimes conducted to test the effectiveness of ads. To rule out extraneous factors such as the effects of weather on consumer purchasing, a number of typical but widely scattered cities are usually selected. The technique is complex and expensive, since cities in which the ad has run have to be compared with cities in which it has not, and the stores in both groups have to keep accurate sales records.

Various techniques have also been employed to test the effectiveness of the broadcast media. Telephone inquiries, Neilsen recorders, house-to-house surveys, mail questionnaires, and free offers are all used to estimate audience size and composition. Program preferences, on the other hand, are tested through personal interviews and the Program Analyzer, which automatically records the judgments of a sample audience, who press buttons to indicate likes and dislikes at various points in the presentation. There have also been a few notable brand use and sales tests. A survey reported by Stanton (1940) in which dealer inventories and sales records were checked, showed 88 per cent more sales of a certain product in an area reached by a radio commercial than in an area where it was not heard. Moreover, a telephone survey was made to determine which families actually listened to the particular program containing the commercial, and a field investigation of these families revealed that 81 per cent more of them were using the advertised brand than the next most popular brand, and that it was used by only 7 per cent more of the nonlisteners.

A field investigation of 7500 households in Fort Wayne conducted by NBC in 1953 and 1954 compared the sales of products before and after television was introduced in that city. The survey showed that the sale of twenty-four products advertised on TV grew 6 per cent in the TV households as compared with a rise of only 1.7 per cent in non-TV households. Sales differences are even more impressive when brands advertised on TV are compared with brands that are not so advertised. One study showed that a brand of tissues which was advertised on television rose 25 per cent in sales, while the sales of its competitor, which did not advertise on television, fell 3 per cent. (Coffin, Landes, and Baiman, 1955)

AEROPHAGIA (Aerophagy). This term means, literally, "air-eating," and applies to automatic swallowing or gulping of air as a psychiatric symptom.

Excessive swallowing of air is observed in the hyperventilation syndrome, a disorder characterized by rapid breathing attacks. During these attacks the stomach may become distended and uncomfortable due to the swallowed air. In some cases women (and occasionally men with feminine tendencies) swallow a great deal of air as the result of an unconscious association between pregnancy and eating stemming from a childhood misconception. These individuals eat air instead of excessive food and succeed in enlarging the abdomen to such an extent that they appear pregnant. It is believed that pregnancy is unconsciously desired in such cases. If, however, they fear pregnancy or rebel against it, they may express these feelings by rapidly expelling air instead of swallowing it. *See* HYPERVENTILATION SYNDROME, FALSE PREGNANCY.

AFFECT. A term used in psychology and psychiatry to denote any experience of feeling or emotion.

The expression "feeling tone" is probably the nearest equivalent of affect, although the word emotion is far more often used as a synonym. Affect includes an immense range of experience, from utmost pain to utmost pleasure, from the slightest feeling to the most intense emotion. The feeling tone produced by a pinprick is just as much an affect as the complex reaction to being jilted.

The term applies to both normal and pathological behavior. It would be hard to find any thought, attitude, or reaction that is not affectively toned. Affect gives body to our responses, and may at times distort our judgment, as in producing "halo" effects or biases. It helps to determine our values, aims, and aspirations, as well as the kind of energy we exert in attempting to fulfill them. In a word, affectivity colors our entire psychic life.

Affective factors operate on an unconscious as well as a conscious level, and for this reason we often experience aversion or attraction, discouragement or elation, without recognizing the source of our reaction. These factors influence physiological as well as psychological behavior, and may also be the hidden source behind such reactions as heart palpitation, tremor, and perspiring hands.

Affectivity plays a vital role in all psychologically caused (psychogenic) disorders and in most physiologically caused (organic) disorders as well. As Noyes and Kolb (1963) point out, "it is not ideas themselves which are the important factors in determining the patient's mental content or his forms of behavior but the affects that are attached to his ideas." This is a first principle of practically every form of psychotherapy in use today.

The evaluation of affect is an important feature of any psychiatric examination. The diagnostician looks for evidence of loss of affect (apathy, emotional flatness), inappropriate affect (reactions that are not in keeping with the situation), inadequate or "blunted" affect (insensitivity, indifference), ambivalence (contradictory feelings toward the same object), depersonalization (feelings of unreality), as well as manifestations of anxiety, depression, euphoria, or excitement.

An entire group of psychoses are classed as "affective reactions" since in these disorders distortions of mood and emotion are more conspicuous than disturbances of thought. They include manic-depressive reactions, psychotic depressive reaction, and involutional psychotic reaction. Affective factors may also be involved in psychotic disorders in which disturbances of intellect or consciousness are primary, such as paranoid or stuporous states. *See* HALO EFFECT, DEPERSONALIZATION, AFFECTIVE PSYCHOSIS.

AFFECTIONAL DRIVE. The urge to be close to and in contact with another living being; usually classified as a "general drive," that is, one that is unlearned and without a specific physiological basis.

The affectional drive can be expressed in many ways—through caressing, hugging and kissing as well as warm devotion and "tender loving care." It originates in the need for closeness and contact with others. Today, many psychologists believe this need to be innate since it is manifested soon after birth and does not appear to be basically dependent on any conditioning or other learning process. The best evidence for this lies in the fact that infants and young children experience undeniable satisfaction in being held, cuddled, and petted, and usually show signs of suffering if they are treated coldly and mechanically.

Although the need for affection is widely believed to be a fundamental component of human nature, some observers maintain that it is a by-product of other satisfactions. A few have suggested that it stems from a need for stimulation, or "stimulus hunger." Others, notably Freudians, claim that the young child becomes attached to the mother or other persons because of the role they play in gratifying his basic needs. As Jersild has expressed it, "Briefly put, he loves his mother because he loves his milk." This author goes on to point out: "In one sense, the question we have raised is academic, for whether the need for receiving and giving affection is original or acquired, it eventually plays a powerful role in the child's life. In another sense, however, it is not academic, for it touches on a basic issue in the philosophy of human growth. Our view of human potentialities is quite different if, for example, we assume that it is at least as natural for a child to love as to hate." (Jersild, 1960)

There are two aspects of the affectional drive: the need to receive affection and the need to bestow it. Craving for affection may be the more fundamental in the sense that it appears earlier in infancy. Yet the child makes affectionate responses as soon as he is capable of patting or stroking his mother. The more important point is that the two sides of the drive develop hand in hand, since careful observations show that children who receive a great deal of warmth always develop close attachments to other people, while those who are not loved and accepted tend to be cold and detached. There is further evidence in the fact that children raised in normal homes show more friendly than unfriendly responses toward both children and adults. Moreover, an intensive study of 261 well-adjusted children has shown that the most important single contributor to their good relationships was satisfaction of their need for love and acceptance. (Langdon and Stout, 1952)

Only a limited amount of experimental work has been done on the affectional drive in human beings, since it would be considered unethical to deprive children of affection for research purposes. But even if this were done, the experiments could not be adequately controlled since children develop slowly and come in contact with many outside influences. For these reasons, Harlow and his associates have experimented with baby monkeys, especially since these animals not only develop quickly, but resemble human infants in many ways, including the ability to manipulate objects and feed from a bottle. In one series of experiments, several baby monkeys were taken from their mothers shortly after birth and placed in cages which contained two types of artificial "mothers," one made of wire and the other of sponge rubber and terry cloth applied to a wire frame. Both of these "mother machines" or "mother surrogates" were heated from within, but there was no attempt to make them resemble monkeys other than giving them crude torsos, heads, and faces. When the baby monkeys were given a choice of "mothers," they almost completely ignored the wire mother but spent considerable time clinging to the cloth mother. This suggested that softness and "cuddliness" have a great deal to do with the infant's reactions (PLATE 1).

In a second series of experiments, feeding bottles were attached to some of the wire mothers and some of the cloth mothers. The baby monkeys that were given an opportunity to feed from the wire mother alone usually remained with it only long enough to satisfy their appetites, and then went over to the cloth mother for cuddling. On the other hand, the monkeys that were allowed to feed from the cloth figure spent both their feeding and cuddling time with this substitute mother. This finding lends support to the idea that the affectional drive is independent of the nutritional drive, although we have to be careful about transferring this idea from animal to human behavior.

A third series of experiments produced results that are even closer to human reactions. When baby monkeys were put in a strange but empty room, they invariably cowered in the corner. If the wire mother previously used for feeding was put in the room, this response did not change. If the cloth mother was there, however, the monkey rushed over and clung desperately to it. What is more, it soon gathered "confidence" enough to leave the cloth mother and explore its new surroundings. This experiment leaves little doubt that the cloth mother is more than a comfortable resting place. Like the human mother, it serves as a sanctuary and source of security when the infant is frightened and faced with danger. (Harlow and Zimmermann, 1959)

These early observations must be tempered by later findings. Even though the monkeys preferred the cloth mothers, they did not develop normally if they were raised completely on these mother substitutes. They became so aggressive that they were unable to play, and some failed to mate with other monkeys when they reached maturity. They also engaged in stereotyped behavior and in some cases inflicted wounds on themselves. Once they were grown, attempts to alter these disordered patterns were of no avail. However, when monkeys raised on substitute mothers were given an opportunity to play together during infancy, they later showed normal adult behavior. This finding points up the importance of "peer group relations." In fact, they were found to be essential even when the infants were raised with their natural mothers (Harlow, 1962). Apparently

close contact with living beings is required for normal development, but that contact must include peers as well as the mother—at least for monkeys.

Any attempt to apply these findings to human beings must be made with caution. Yet they do help to substantiate a basic drive for contact because of the continuity between animal and human behavior. The warmth of the mother's body is probably the fundamental source of comfort for the newborn infant, but within a few weeks her presence alone will give the child a sense of safety and security. His own affectionate responses are elicited not only by bodily contact, but by the loving care and attention he receives along with it, both from the father and the mother.

As the child's capacity to respond to affection grows, so does his capacity to express affection toward others. If he lives in a reasonably happy and accepting environment, and comes in contact with friendly playmates and devoted adults, this capacity continues to develop and extend itself. During adolescence it is further amplified—and complicated—by the addition of the sexual component, and the total drive reaches its highest and most productive expression in a good marriage and a warm family life. *See* MARITAL ADJUSTMENT, LOVE, MOTHERING, MATERNAL DEPRIVATION, SENSORY DEPRIVATION.

AFFECTIVE PSYCHOSIS. A functional psychotic reaction in which the predominant feature is a severe disturbance of mood or emotion.

The major subgroup of affective psychosis consists of manic-depressive reactions characterized by recurrent episodes of elation with increased thought and activity, or depression with decreased thought and activity, and sometimes by an alternation or mixture of the two. Another subgroup is psychotic depressive reaction, a depression that is usually precipitated by environmental factors. In this type of depression there is a gross distortion of reality, frequently with delusions and hallucinations. Involutional psychotic reactions (involutional melancholia) are also affective in nature, since their chief feature is depression—however, they are classified separately by the American Psychiatric Association. *See* MANIC-DEPRESSIVE REACTION, PSYCHOTIC DEPRESSIVE REACTION, INVOLUTIONAL PSYCHOTIC REACTION.

AFFILIATIVE DRIVE. The urge to associate, form friendships and attachments, and depend upon others.

Affiliation can be described as either a single drive with many manifestations, or as a group of closely related social motives. It is expressed in our tendency to seek the company of others, enjoy social gatherings and team sports, join clubs and organizations and derive a sense of security from group support. Practically all people feel frustrated and lost if these opportunities are lacking. If an individual is totally detached from other people or declares that he does not need anyone, it is usually a sign of emotional disturbance. Among normal people there is probably no more intensely unpleasant feeling than loneliness, and there are few if any punishments more severe than solitary confinement.

The tendency to affiliate is based on the fact that we grow up in a social context and come to depend on other people for support, guidance, and the satisfaction of our needs. This drive begins to develop at the very start of life, when the infant is totally dependent on another individual, usually the mother, for food, warmth, personal care, and comfort. The type of relationship between mother and child during the early years sets the framework within which later affiliative behavior develops. Sears et al. (1953, 1957) have shown that children who were made to feel helpless and frustrated in infancy

usually became overdependent in later life. Typical frustrating situations during infancy are rigid feeding schedules, abrupt and harsh weaning, and delayed gratification. Later on, some mothers force their children to beg or plead for things they should naturally receive, and they may also strike a bargain to make them do what they want: "If you do this for me, I'll do that for you." Others neglect their children or raise them in a frigid atmosphere. The child whose needs have not been gratified may come to feel that his wants are unnatural. Such a child may feel so anxious and guilt-ridden that he will become inhibited and withdrawn. If he has had to beg for everything he needed, he may become shy, ingratiating, and unsure of himself. Needless to say these reaction patterns interfere with later adjustment to other people.

Several studies have shown that the drive to affiliate is especially intense when we feel anxious. The reason for this reaction is that children have a tendency to feel anxious when they are hungry, thirsty, uncomfortable, or alone, and these needs are ordinarily satisfied by other people. In one indicative experiment, Schachter (1959) placed college girls in threatening situations to test their need for affiliation. The group subjected to "high anxiety" conditions were told that, as an experiment, they were to receive severe, painful but harmless electric shocks, and the "low anxiety" group was told that the shocks would only tickle them. While waiting for the experiment (which was not conducted), most of the girls in the high anxiety group indicated that they preferred to wait with other girls. One third of them chose not to participate in the experiment at all, even though they were to be given credit toward their final grade if they participated. Fewer of the low anxiety group indicated the need for other people, and none of them declined to participate.

In another study along these lines, the high anxiety group was given a choice of waiting with other girls who would also be shocked, or waiting with a professor or adviser who was not part of the experiment. Not all of the girls chose to wait with others, but those who did always chose to be with the girls who were involved in the experiment. This study therefore substantiated the old idea of "misery loves company," but it also showed that the company must be able to share our difficulties. Many good friends are chosen on this basis.

The relation between anxiety and affiliation has been analyzed further. When the subjects of Schachter's experiment were divided according to birth order, he found that the firstborns tended to have a greater need to affiliate under intense anxiety than the later-borns. A similar experiment carried out by Sarnoff and Zimbardo (1961) confirmed this result, although they found it applied primarily to firstborn males and only children. These findings were in line with expectation, since mothers are especially anxious with first-born and only children and frequently transfer their anxiety to their offspring. Also, they tend to shower them with care and attention, and therefore make them more dependent. It is interesting that later on in their lives these children are less likely to engage in isolated activities, such as chronic alcoholism, when they undergo stress. They have also been found to enter into psychotherapy more often and remain in it longer than the later-borns (Schachter, 1959). See BIRTH ORDER, ONLY CHILDREN.

Experimentation has also shown that not all types of unpleasant or "aversive" states lead to affiliation. Sarnoff and Zimbardo (1961) felt that Schachter's experiment with college girls involved more fear than anxiety, since it dealt with the direct physical threat of electric shock. They contended that genuine anxiety is aroused by repressed conflicts, and therefore set up a situation in which some subjects were told they were to engage in oral activities such as sucking their thumbs, using pacifiers, and drinking from bottles with nipples. These instructions were given to the high anxiety group. The low anxiety group, on the other hand, were told they would simply be asked to blow whistles and pipes or blow up balloons. In this case the high anxiety group showed less desire than the low anxiety group to affiliate during the waiting period before the experiment, probably because more shame or embarrassment was involved. Cofer and Appley (1965) suggest that people will affiliate only if they feel that this will help to relieve their unpleasant state, and that in some instances people have a need for solitude in order to get a grip on themselves.

There are still many unanswered questions in this field of investigation. We do not know, for example, exactly *how* affiliation reduces anxiety, nor the extent to which we use affiliative behavior to give vent to aggressive and destructive impulses, as opposed to the urge to co-operate or share experiences. But there is considerable evidence that the expression of this drive varies greatly from person to person, and that these individual differences are largely due to early experiences in the home. Although most people appear to seek the companionship of others when they are faced with difficulties, some prefer to go it alone.

AFTERIMAGE (Aftersensation). A sensation that arises out of another sensation immediately after the original stimulation ceases. A positive afterimage is a continuation of the original sensation. A negative afterimage is its opposite in hue or brightness. Negative afterimages are the more commonly observed type, since they are usually more intense and lasting than positive afterimages (COLOR PLATE 3).

Positive afterimages are most vividly experienced in a relatively dark surrounding after intense stimulation. One way to produce them is to look directly at the setting sun for a moment, then immediately close your eyes. Another way is to switch off a brightly lighted television program and keep looking at the tube. A positive afterimage is only fleetingly observed, and is automatically replaced by the comparatively long-lasting negative afterimage.

Negative color afterimages are the complementary of the original stimulus. If you stare at a small square of yellow paper until the borders take on a bluish tinge and the yellow begins to fade, then look at a sheet of white paper, a patch of blue color will be clearly visible, since blue is complementary to yellow. The duration and vividness of the afterimage depends on the intensity of the color and the area it covers as well as the time spent in viewing it. It is also affected by the illumination and composition of the second surface. If we quickly turn our eyes from one surface to another, the afterimage will move with our gaze. Its size will depend on the location of the surface we fixate. If the surface is nearby, the image will appear small; if it is at a distance, the image will be larger.

A negative afterimage will mix with color according to the regular laws of color mixture—for example, a blue afterimage projected onto orange paper will produce a red-purple hue. Moreover, if we look at a surface of a particular hue and then gaze at its complementary, this color will appear more saturated than it would normally be. In fact, this is believed to be the only way to obtain the fullest possible saturation.

Negative afterimages can sometimes have disturbing effects. If we look briefly at a brilliant light while driving a car, we may experience a distracting and dangerous blackout for a moment. If we wear a bright-hued sweater while reading, the book may take on an annoying complementary hue. Aftereffects can be so pronounced that artists, decorators, and house painters must be careful not to let them interfere with their judgment in selecting and mixing colors.

AGGRESSION. Violent, destructive behavior usually directed toward bringing suffering or death to other people, but sometimes displaced to objects or turned inward to the self.

The problem of aggression has been with us throughout history but is particularly relevant at a time when we possess instruments that could destroy all of civilization and possibly all life on this planet. The argument, however, that the aggressive impulse is innate and instinctive because it is so prevalent is not accepted today. In the first place, the universality of the drive is open to question. There are men, animals, and entire societies which display little or no aggression. As Konrad Lorenz (1966) has pointed out, even the wolf, which is accepted as the epitome of aggression, spares an enemy that bares his throat as a sign of surrender; and actually most animals will fight only for available food or mates and not as a matter of course.

The second reason for denying the instinctive character of aggression is that no specific physiological patterns of aggression, comparable, for example, to the nest-building instinct, have been found either in men or animals. While it is true that the autonomic nervous system puts the organism into a state of emergency when it is faced with a crisis, it is equally true that it may channel energy not merely into "fight" reactions, but into "flight" or into energetic attempts to deal with the problem. The fact that the organism is equipped for either constructive or destructive behavior argues not only against the instinct hypothesis, but indicates that learning and other environmental factors have a material effect on the way we meet situations. Dogs and even lions can be trained to fight or to play; children can be reared to be aggressive or non-aggressive; and whole societies, such as the Zuñi, can be organized on a co-operative rather than a competitive basis. (Benedict, 1934)

The view that aggression is a learned rather than an unlearned response is supported by a number of crucial experiments. Kuo (1930) has shown that if cats and rats are brought up together, these so-called "instinctive enemies" will not show the expected reactions to each other at maturity. The rats will not fear the cats, and the cats will not kill the rats even when they are hungry (though they may sometimes kill them by playing too roughly). On the other hand, if cats are allowed to watch their mothers kill a rodent regularly, most of them will kill when they grow up—but, interestingly, they will only kill the species they have seen the mother kill. The results of this experiment are supported by frequent reports of other "mortal enemies" brought up together in peace, as well as by the fact that mother animals sometimes "adopt" offspring of other species to which they tend to be antagonistic. Scott (1958) has surveyed the literature on aggression among animals as well as in human societies, and believes there is no conclusive evidence for an urge for aggression divorced from learning.

Basing their work on an idea derived from Freud, Dollard et al. (1939) have developed a "reactive theory," which holds that aggression occurs as a result of frustration, and that frustration always leads to aggression. Miller (1941) has offered a more limited version of this theory which accepts the idea that aggression always presupposes frustration, but that it is only one of several possible responses. The "frustration-aggression hypothesis" as it is called, holds that frustration occurs when a barrier of some type—psychological, physical, or symbolic—prevents a motivated individual from reaching his goal. If the barrier cannot be removed and/or the motivation increases in intensity, a state of frustration is produced and the attempts to overcome the barrier usually become less rational and adaptive than they were at first. A man may curse at, throw, or break a piece of equipment that does not perform as he wants; a child may attack a frustrating parent physically or verbally, or use less direct means such as negativism and tantrums.

In some cases, when aggression is denied outward expression, it may be directed inward, and the child hurts himself "accidentally on purpose." Miller, however, has pointed out that some individuals react to frustration in other ways. They may become passive, withdrawn, submissive, or they may seek to placate and appease the person who is thwarting them. Other investigators, notably Barker, Dembo, and Lewin (1941) have shown that some children respond to frustration with regressive rather than aggressive behavior. When they are repeatedly thwarted, these children become infantile, dependent, and unable to cope with problems on their own. See ACCIDENT-PRONENESS, SUICIDE.

Similar variations in response are found when a parent or other person in authority uses punishment or the threat of punishment to curb aggression. This technique may be effective for the immediate act, but the problem is that the punishment is itself felt as a frustration and will often provoke more aggression. Hostility breeds hostility. Sometimes it is expressed directly, but more often it takes indirect or delayed forms. Children who have been severely punished for aggressive behavior often displace their anger on younger or weaker children, or find ways of retaliating when they are older.

Sears et al. (1953, 1957) have shown a direct relation between aggression and severity of punishment in preschool children. Some severely punished children become bedwetters, a condition which is often interpreted by psychoanalysts as an aggressive, retaliatory act, but ascribed by others to tensions produced by resentful feelings. Again, some children react to punishment by becoming inhibited and fearful, but it has been shown that children who "contain" their anger will produce a tremendous amount of hostility when they can safely express it, as in a play therapy situation (Sears, 1951). In other cases it expresses itself in symbolic form, and the child (or adult) develops a phobia for knives or other instruments of aggression. See ANGER, HOSTILITY, PLAY THERAPY.

A number of studies have provided evidence that the expression of aggressive impulses is primarily a matter of social learning. Sears (1961) investigated the aggressive behavior of children at five and again at twelve, and found fairly sharp sex differences among them. At both ages, the boys were more aggressive and less anxious about their aggressive behavior than the girls. In most cases these boys had been encouraged by their parents to "fight it out," while the girls were not permitted to be aggressive because it was considered "unfeminine." Davis and Dollard (1940) found that parental attitudes differed on different social levels. In general they found more aggression among children from deprived homes than from more privileged homes. Nevertheless, even on a deprived level there was more aggression in families that approved and rewarded aggression than in families that did not condone it.

A study by Bandura, Ross, and Ross (1963) provides evidence that children may learn the actual *techniques* of aggression from adult models. A group of children were shown a film of an adult violently attacking an inflated plastic clown. Later on, when they were left alone with the clown, most of them closely emulated this behavior. Finally, the celebrated Lewin, Lippitt, and White (1939) study of hobby groups conducted under three types of leadership showed that, when left alone, the group which was used to authoritarian leadership often vented their pent-up hostility on a single victim, while the members of the group accustomed to a laissez-faire atmosphere tended to pick fights with each other or destroy objects in the room—apparently not only as a release of energy but as a response to frustration caused by the lack of guidance. Both of these groups exhibited far more aggression than the group which had worked with a democratic leader. See GROUP DYNAMICS.

It is doubtless true that aggressive impulses are inevitable in a competitive society, especially one that contains many social barriers, injustices, and frustrations. How can these impulses be handled? How can violent, destructive behavior be prevented? How can people be kept from displacing their aggressiveness on innocent parties? Many techniques have been suggested, though none applies in every case. First, in some instances the intensity of the frustration itself can be reduced by accepting it as inevitable (if it is), and by accommodating ourselves to it instead of allowing our anger to build up. Second, aggressive energies can be channeled into positive, constructive social action designed to root out the sources of frustration. Third, we can adopt congenial and socially acceptable ways of dissipating aggression before it builds up to overwhelming proportions: competitive sports (especially contact sports like basketball); hobbies that require physical activity, such as gardening or expeditions into the wilds; active but noncompetitive sports such as cycling and mountain-climbing; and vicarious release through identification with heroic figures in fiction or biography. (A study by Howard, 1957, has shown that novelists who have the least opportunity to release aggression in their daily lives are likely to depict the greatest amount of aggression in their books.) *See* SUBLIMATION, DISPLACEMENT.

In his recent book, *On Aggression* (1966), Konrad Lorenz suggests many of these ways of diverting conflict drives before they become lethal. He also adds others, such as personal intimacy across factions, opportunities for laughter, and "promotion of personal acquaintance and, if possible, friendship between individual members of different ideologies or nations." In an address given at Oxford University (1968), the Dutch ethologist, Nikolaas Tinbergen, has pointed out that man is the only animal who practices war and mass murder, and that the development of long-range weapons makes killing an "impersonal activity." Like Lorenz, he emphasizes the need for redirecting aggressive impulses into constructive channels, proposing a "crash program" to keep intergroup aggression in check and to find new outlets parallel to the perennial battle of the Dutch against the sea.

Finally, if the aggression has already built up to disturbing proportions, it is important to have a means of therapeutic release readily available: play therapy, ventilation of resentments in individual or group sessions, occupational and recreational therapy. It is interesting that one of the mental hospitals in Rotterdam provides a dummy of ambiguous shape against which the patients can vent their wrath. However, when the dummy is struck, it always bounces back to its original position, and in this way demonstrates to the patient that aggression is ultimately senseless since it does not change the situation itself. (Tolsma, 1953)

AGING (Geriatric Psychology and Psychiatry). One of the most basic changes that has occurred in this century is the enormous increase in the life-span of our population. Between 1900 and the present, the average life expectancy in this country has risen from less than fifty to more than seventy years, and the number of people over sixty-five has grown from 3½ million to 19 million. Of these, 3.4 million are 75 years of age or over, and 1.2 million are 85 or over.

The increase in the number of older people has been accompanied by an aggravation of the stresses to which they are subjected in our society, due to such factors as the generally negative attitude toward aging and the aged, the mandatory retirement age of sixty-five coupled with lack of preparation for retirement, and isolation of the aged due to the mobility and lack of cohesiveness of the modern family. The resulting inactivity, loneliness, and alienation from society frequently corrode the older person's self-esteem, intensify the effects of physical infirmity and illness, and accentuate hypochondriacal tendencies or other psychological reactions such as irritability, depression, brooding, nocturnal restlessness, loss of interest in the world, anxiety about the future, and dependence on memories of the past. All these factors, in combination with the sheer length of life, help to explain the fact that there is a peak suicide rate in late middle and old age —that between 1940 and 1960 the number of mental health patients sixty years and older increased about five times as fast as the over-all hospital population—and that psychoses associated with old age (especially those involving senile brain disease and cerebral arteriosclerosis) constituted over 16 per cent of all first admissions to mental hospitals in 1965 (second only to schizophrenia), not to mention those in nursing homes, homes for the aged, and in the community at large.

These are the negative aspects of the situation. There are also a number of positive developments. Many companies, taking the government's lead, are modifying the mandatory retirement age and adopting a more flexible policy. A total of about 3 million persons over 65 are still in the labor force, and senior citizen employment centers are cropping up throughout the country. Part-time service jobs, both paid and volunteer, and consultant positions for the highly experienced are becoming more available. Special housing arrangements and retirement villages are being developed for the elderly. Senior-citizen activities and Golden Age clubs are multiplying. A number of large companies are offering preretirement counseling, and various community and welfare organizations make a point of including the elderly in their family counseling programs. Older people in general are achieving greater security and independence as a result of Medicare, Social Security, Old Age Assistance, and industrial pensions. Special mental health education programs for the aging have also been put into operation, and greater attention is being paid to the development of psychotherapy and other treatment techniques for elderly people who become mentally ill. Many of these advances have been spurred by the findings of psychologists, psychiatrists, and other social scientists who have studied the personality characteristics and abilities of older people. Let us look briefly at the results of these studies.

The normal aging process involves both biological and psychological changes. The most prominent physical changes are: gradual decline in strength, co-ordination, sexual energy, perceptual acuity and sensitivity to taste and smell (food tastes flat); decreased ability to withstand physical stress, lower reserve energy, greater susceptibility to disease and slower recovery from illness—and in senility, some degree of impaired cerebral circulation and brain atrophy. The psychological changes include: longer reaction time, increasing memory loss for recent events, reduced ability to acquire new learning and solve problems imaginatively; tendency toward rigid thinking, and somewhat reduced capacity for coping with psychological stress. Many of these changes are hastened by the socio-economic situation of our aging population—for example, living alone makes for poor eating habits, insufficient exercise, and lack of stimulation; and reduction in income may lead to restriction of social activities as well as lack of medical care.

The changes just outlined are all in the downward direction—but again there is another side to the picture. The newer psychological studies have shown that a decline in over-all mental ability occurs at a slower rate and at a much later date than older studies indicated. The more superficial characteristics, such as quickness in thinking and ability to learn isolated details decline more rapidly than the intellectual abilities that really count. Accumulated wisdom and experience tend to offset changes in memory and flexibility, and frequently the ability to view problems in perspective and offer realistic solutions is maintained to an advanced age. The decrease in speed on psychomotor activities tends to be counterbalanced by greater care, resulting in a lower error rate and fewer accidents on the job. In spite of increased susceptibility to illness, the elderly worker usually has a better absenteeism record than his young associates, and is frequently more highly motivated. Finally, studies have shown that a far larger number of people than might be expected are capable of maintaining a high level of productivity and even creativity past the age of eighty. Among the more dramatic examples are Goethe, Oliver Wendell Holmes, Churchill, Picasso, Baruch, Adenauer, and Hoover.

The mental health aspects of aging

are being attacked on two fronts: prevention and treatment. An effective example of the preventive approach is a series of pamphlets published by the National Association for Mental Health entitled "Notes for After Fifty." Viewing mental health in its relation to physical, social and psychological well-being, the Notes emphasize such ideas as the need for making plans well in advance of retirement, realistic acceptance of inevitable limitations, regular and thorough physical checkups to catch disorders in their early stages, a balanced diet adapted to individual needs, full examination of all possible types of living arrangements, the need for mental stimulation and slower-paced hobbies, the advisability of a complete financial review well in advance of retirement, the importance of community service activities as a means of remaining useful and keeping in contact with other people, and learning to enjoy fully the new opportunity for leisure and freedom from regular responsibility.

If the aging individual is not able to avail himself of these protective measures, and if he is subjected to more than his share of frustrations and deprivations, he may eventually develop symptoms of disorder. In some cases the symptoms appear to be purely functional reactions; in others, they may be based on organic brain changes aggravated by faulty emotional patterns. While psychiatric disorders sometimes develop in previously stable and healthy individuals, often as a reaction to a particularly traumatic loss, they are far more likely to occur in people who have developed psychological weaknesses before reaching old age. As Rosen and Gregory (1965) point out, "The vicissitudes of aging tend to accentuate existing and latent psychological tendencies. The dependent individual may become wholly so and revert to infantilism; the compulsive individual may try to find in overt obsessions a means of holding onto the world he

once knew; the paranoiac may try to deny his inadequacies in self-aggrandizing delusions; and the schizoid may withdraw from unpleasant reality completely."

These authors report that in spite of the fact that Freud believed psychoanalysis was of no value beyond middle age because of lack of resiliency—and others have shied away from treating older persons possibly because of their own unconscious fears of aging—there is evidence that these patients often respond well to psychotherapy and other psychiatric treatments. Rechtschaffen (1959) has found that they profit most from supportive therapy consisting of active guidance, reassurance and readjustment of goals, but others (Alexander, 1944; Rosenthal, 1959) believe that insight therapy can also be applied in many cases. Goldfarb (1957) has reported that short psychotherapy sessions and other techniques were highly effective with eighty- to ninety-year-old residents of an old-age home who had become depressed, suicidal, querulous, abusive, or assaultive. Rosenthal suggests that serious disturbance can often be forestalled through psychotherapy applied in the early stages: "If psychologic treatment of the aged could be popularized and brought into the public eye, these people might find it worthwhile to seek such treatment for their depressive moods and their general feelings of inadequacy."

Illustrative Case: AGING

A seventy-two-year-old woman complained of weakness of her right arm, a weakness of a year's duration. Her physician at first believed that a cerebral vascular lesion was responsible for her symptoms, but he could not find substantiating evidence on physical or neurological examination.

He then recalled that her husband had suffered a right hemiplegia before his death, which had occurred a few weeks before the onset of the patient's symptoms. He discovered that she had not been on good terms with her husband at the time of his death, that she had not expressed much grief at that time, and that she had then moved in with her son and daughter-in-law. Her symptoms began when she had been frustrated in her attempts to take over their household. The physician noted that her weakness was not consistently present in the same degree and that it did not follow lines of anatomic distribution. In addition, she seemed somewhat indifferent to her disability.

From this evidence, the physician made a diagnosis of a concealed and prolonged grief reaction, manifested by conversion symptoms. He encouraged her to come to his office for a series of weekly half-hour interviews, and after an introductory phase, in which she found to her satisfaction that he was honestly interested in her personal life, they discussed her problems in her son's home, her feelings at the time of her husband's death, and, finally, her earlier marital problems.

As she began to face her feelings and share them with her doctor, she was able to free herself somewhat from her emotional bondage to her dead husband. She then took more interest in her appearance, her friends, and her former church and community activities. Meanwhile the physician had prescribed massage and exercises for her arm, both for their suggestive effect and to help her save face. He realized that as long as she was willing to talk about her emotional problems, he need not force her to acknowledge that her symptoms had no physical basis. After ten interviews, she had improved symptomatically and emotionally to the point where she took a part-time job at her church. As she found interests of her own, she no longer tried to run her daughter-in-law's household. (Aldrich, 1966)

AGITATION. A state of marked restlessness and anxiety.

The agitated person is emotionally overwrought, has a look of anguish on his face, and continually moves about in a tense manner. He gives psychomotor expression to his intense emotions through ceaseless activity and continuous talking during the day, and generally suffers from insomnia at night. States of agitation may be precipitated in relatively stable individuals by sudden loss of a loved one, severe failure or disappointment, or anticipation of disaster. They usually verbalize their anguish in such expressions as: "What am I going to do?" "How will I ever get out of this?" "What's going to happen to my family?"

The most severe and dangerous form of agitation occurs in agitated depression. Here the patient is assailed with the same thoughts of hopelessness and worthlessness that appear in the retarded type of depression, but instead of sitting in silent dejection, he paces up and down bemoaning his fate and wringing his hands. He is never still a moment, wears a look of unmistakable despair, and berates himself for exaggerated or fancied sins. Some of these patients feel so unworthy of care that they shrink from the nurse's hands. They may even refuse food on the grounds that they are unworthy of sustenance. They frequently talk about death, and many of them attempt suicide. *See* MANIC-DEPRESSIVE REACTION (CIRCULAR AND MIXED TYPES).

AGNOSIA. Loss or impairment of ability to recognize familiar objects, or to grasp the meaning of written or oral language, due to organic brain disorder; a form of aphasia.

Agnosia is an extremely varied condition, since lesions may occur in any part of the sensory cortex, and any type of sensory impression may be involved. Disturbances in visual perception (visual agnosia), for example, may result from lesions in the secondary visual areas of the occipital lobe. Typically, the patient can perceive the details of a figure but not recognize the object it represents. Luria (1965) gives these examples: "A picture of a divan may be identified as a briefcase (by the color of the leather) or as an automobile (the two arms ending in disks similar to headlights); a rooster may be identified as a bonfire (by the plumage of the tail, which is similar to tongues of flame)."

When both the occipital and parietal lobes of the brain are damaged, disturbances may occur in spatial perception, a condition sometimes termed visuospatial agnosia. In this disorder there is no noticeable difficulty in perceiving objects or pictures, but the patient cannot analyze the spatial relationships involved—for instance, he may be unable to identify the right and left sides of an object, locate points on a map, or recognize the positions of the hands on a clock, confusing IV with VI etc. Patients with lesions in the lower parts of these lobes are frequently unable to organize movements in space (spatial apractagnosia): they may go right instead of left, spread the blankets crosswise on a bed, or thrust their arm into the wrong sleeve in putting on a coat. Visuospatial agnosia may also affect reading and writing. In the condition known as "literal alexia," individual letters or numerals are not recognized, and letters like *d* and *b* are confused; in "verbal alexia" individual letters may be recognized but not whole words or combinations of letters, such as USA. Similar difficulties occur in writing, and are known as visual agraphia.

Damage to a portion (posterosuperior) of the left temporal lobe produces a disturbance in the auditory perception of language known as speech agnosia. This is a form of sensory or auditory aphasia and consists of the following symptoms: inability to distinguish different speech sounds and words; inability to repeat words (except motor stereotypes like "Well" or "You see," which do not require auditory feedback); difficulty in naming objects (usually resulting in substitution of an associated word for the correct name); and frequently a restriction of reading to simple words like New York or the patient's own name, as well as inability

to write any but highly familiar words. All these symptoms have one thing in common: they are disturbances in word comprehension. *See* ASTEREOGNOSIS, APHASIA, ALEXIA.

AIR HUNGER. The physiological need for air.

Our breathing is so regular and automatic that we usually take it for granted. Yet the effects of deprivation are more quickly felt than with any other drive. These effects occur on both a physical and a psychological level, as shown by the fact that when we swallow water while swimming we not only gasp for breath but feel terror-stricken. Moreover, although we have voluntary control over respiration, the physiological need for air is so great that most people cannot ordinarily hold their breath for more than forty seconds. It is possible to increase this interval somewhat by oxygenating the lungs beforehand. A world's record for staying under water was established by Robert Foster in 1960. After he had hyperventilated with oxygen for thirty minutes, he was able to remain below the surface for thirteen minutes and fifty-two seconds.

Our physiological processes are dependent on a continual supply of air, not only to burn the body's fuel and supply energy, but to flush out carbon dioxide collected in the lungs. When we engage in any strenuous physical activity such as climbing a hill or a long rally in tennis, metabolism may increase sixteen to twenty-four times its normal rate. As a result, we use up our available oxygen supply and our bloodstream does not get a sufficient amount to carry away the waste products that have accumulated during the activity. This creates an "oxygen debt" which we can usually pay back by breathing deeply or by taking a few minutes' rest. Sighing represents a similar need for air, since respiratory functions are at a low ebb during grief or depression.

There are many cases, however, when a shortage of oxygen cannot be so easily repaired. It is a well-known fact that nerve cells in the brain are more sensitive to oxygen lack than in the rest of the body, and complete anoxia (lack of oxygen) need be only brief to cause profound damage. Studies show that people who have been revived after being medically dead for a short period of time often suffer irreparable brain injury. Asphyxia occurring before, during, or just after birth is one of the causes of cerebral palsy, and may produce lifelong mental deficiency. Windle (1958) has demonstrated the effects of anoxia experimentally. He found that oxygen deprivation in adult guinea pigs produced changes in brain structure associated with impaired memory and learning ability, while asphyxia at birth caused changes in the nervous system of monkeys, accompanied by behavior deviations and neurological disorders such as epileptic seizures. See BIRTH ADJUSTMENTS, PREMATURITY.

The psychological effects of oxygen deprivation have been exhaustively investigated. Miners, balloonists, mountain climbers, and airplane pilots have provided considerable material from their own experiences, and a number of systematic studies have been undertaken in chambers that simulate atmospheric conditions at various altitudes. The reports of pilots flying before the days when oxygen masks and pressurized cabins were in full use are particularly illuminating. They show that when artificial oxygen is not used during a high-altitude climb, the first effect is one of stimulation and well-being—but this stage leads imperceptibly to a dulling of sensory, motor, and mental capacities. At sea level, air contains about 21 per cent oxygen. At 12,000 feet, where the oxygen content is only two thirds of that amount (14

per cent), there are marked changes in breathing rate. As the ascent continues, breathing becomes more labored and fatigue, drowsiness and headache set in. At an altitude where the oxygen content of the air is only 10 per cent, cyanosis (dusky blue skin, as in a "blue baby") occurs with a sharp decrease in mental ability. At altitudes above 15,000 feet there is increasing impairment of sight (for example, seeing double) followed by impairments in hearing, the sense of pain, time sense, memory, and judgment.

The most dangerous aspect of the situation is the fact that the pilot feels that his thinking is clear, his judgment sound, and his sensory abilities in good order (Carlson, 1960). For this reason he may perform irrational acts that endanger himself or others—for instance, one Air Force pilot felt that the horizon was out of place instead of realizing that he was viewing it from an angle; another merely waved at the enemy from an altitude of 19,000 feet; and a third, on a reconnaissance mission during World War I, took eighteen pictures on the same plate. Others were so unaware of their physiological and psychological changes that they continued their upward flight until they lost consciousness at around 25,000 feet. As a result of such experiences, it became common practice for Air Force pilots to hook up their oxygen masks before take-off, since they may not have the judgment or energy to put them on after anoxemia (lack of oxygen in the blood) sets in.

Studies of mountaineers who are not acclimated to high altitudes have confirmed these findings and added others. "Mountain sickness" starts as a feeling of exhilaration accompanied by excited talking, quarrelsomeness and generally unreasonable behavior. At around 15,000 feet many climbers feel lightheaded, become hypersensitive to cold, turn blue, and suffer from extreme weakness, nausea, vomiting, and chest discomfort. This may be followed by complete prostration. Emotional reactions that resemble alcoholic intoxication are frequently reported: the individual not only *is* high, but *feels* "high." He has little control over his emotions and may feel euphoric at one moment and depressed or apathetic at another. A study made by McFarland in 1932, in which a man was subjected to simulated altitude conditions, showed that his handwriting gradually deteriorated and became quite illegible at 23,000 feet. He also felt that his feet were a long way off and he could not orient other parts of his body, yet he was well satisfied with his performance and wanted to go much higher.

In another study by McFarland (1937), members of an Andean expedition were found to show marked impairment in ability to record words, as well as an increase in faulty associations even after they had been acclimatized. After spending six months in the Andes, ten subjects were found to be incapacitated in practically every type of function. When asked to check a list of possible psychological difficulties, they most often checked "great effort to carry out tasks," followed in order by "more critical attitudes toward others," "mental laziness," "heightened sensory irritability," "touchiness on various subjects," "dislike of being told how to do things," "difficulty in concentrating," "slowness in reasoning," "frequently recurring ideas," and "memory difficulty."

Certain generalizations can be derived from the various studies of oxygen deprivation. First, the critical point appears to be an oxygen concentration equivalent to an altitude of 15,000 feet. Second, both higher and lower mental processes are impaired—the higher probably because of impaired ability to attend, increased distractibility, and sensorimotor incapacity affecting finer coordination. Third, sensory modalities are affected in order, much as in general anesthesia, with vision going before hearing and paralysis occurring in the legs before the arms. Fourth, if the deprivation continues for a long period, as in mines, the effects may be cumulative and lead to permanent memory impairment, mania, and loss of general mental capacity. Fifth, there are large individual differences in reaction to oxygen deprivation.

Attempts have also been made to explore the relation between anoxemia and emotional disorder. There is evidence that people who are continually irritable may in some cases be suffering from a chronic oxygen insufficiency that does not allow an adequate interchange between the blood and the tissues. McFarland (1952) found that far more psychoneurotic patients than average individuals collapsed or approached collapse at a simulated altitude of 14,000 feet, indicating that their tolerance for biological stress was much lower than normal. It has also been found that many psychoneurotics show respiratory and water-balance disorders that may be a product of central nervous system disturbances. This suggests that subtle changes in activities like respiration, resulting from inner tension, may cause changes throughout the body. These physical changes may make the individual feel so badly that they affect his emotional well-being, and in this way a vicious cycle of mental illness may be set in motion. Finally, there is some evidence that people who live at higher altitudes tend to be more "temperamental," more restless and show a greater incidence of neurosis than similar groups living at lower altitudes. These findings are at present only straws in the wind, but they may eventually lead to greater knowledge of the relationship between physical and mental conditions.

ALCOHOLIC ADDICTION. Chronic dependence on the use of alcoholic beverages. In 1949 a committee of the

World Health Organization defined alcoholics as ". . . those excessive drinkers whose dependence upon alcohol has attained such a degree that it shows a noticeable mental disturbance or an interference with their bodily and mental health, their interpersonal relations, and their smooth social and economic functioning; or who show the prodromal [or first stage] signs of such development."

The alcoholic addict is a compulsive drinker, the victim of an insatiable, uncontrollable drive: "One drink is too many, a thousand are not enough." Although this drive is the primary characteristic of alcoholic addiction, there are other distinguishing marks. The alcoholic cannot face any trying situation without taking a drink; he secretly takes extra drinks when he is with other people; he drinks excessively when he is alone; and even if his drinking is successfully arrested by treatment, he will almost certainly have a latent tendency to alcoholism for the rest of his life.

Of the 70 million users of alcohol in this country, 5 million may be classed as addicts, and the number is increasing at the rate of 200,000 new cases each year. Alcoholism is the fourth most prevalent disease in America and a leading cause of death: 12,000 die of chronic alcoholism every year. It accounts for 15 per cent of first admissions to public mental hospitals; a loss to industry of one billion dollars a year due to absenteeism, reduced efficiency, and accidents; an annual cost of 1.25 billion dollars for care, treatment and financial support for alcoholics and their families; a large percentage of arrests (15 per cent of all murders involved drinking); as well as untold suffering and hardship for both the alcoholic and his family.

Four out of five alcoholics are men; their average age is forty-five years, and their life span is twelve years shorter than average. Contrary to common opinion only 5 per cent are the "Bowery bum" type; most alcoholics live on a middle or upper economic level. Some groups have been found to be more prone to alcoholism than others, probably for reasons of tradition: the incidence is high among the Irish and French, and low among Jews, Italians, and Chinese.

The amount of alcohol intake necessary to produce intoxication varies with body weight, personality factors, habitual consumption, and physical condition. A 0.1 per cent concentration in the blood is sufficient to produce intoxication, at 0.5 per cent consciousness is lost, and above 0.55 per cent death generally occurs. Recent studies indicate that while alcohol may drug the brain temporarily, it does not in itself cause damage to the brain or other organs—although non-alcoholic components of the beverages sometimes produce toxic effects. A diet that consists almost exclusively of alcohol, however, may result in vitamin and other nutritional deficiencies which lower resistance to disease. In addition, a whole set of psychotic and organic brain disorders is associated with alcoholism: pathological intoxication, delirium tremens, acute alcoholic hallucinosis, Korsakoff's syndrome, and Wernicke's syndrome. Alcoholism may also occur as a symptom in general paresis, manic-depressive psychosis, and epilepsy. *See* these topics.

The general reasons for the use of alcohol are reasonably clear. In our culture, consumption of alcohol is an acceptable accompaniment of social intercourse and an accepted technique for achieving a sense of well-being. Alcohol has a depressive effect on the higher brain centers, which enables the drinker to put aside both his troubles and his inhibitions. Even though most of his mental and physical abilities are dulled, he experiences an increased feeling of self-confidence and is enveloped by a warm, expansive, euphoric mood. Some drinkers become drowsy, others become lively; most drinkers become amiable; a few become pugnacious. These are the usual effects of alcohol taken in limited quantities.

The crucial question is why some individuals do not remain controlled, social drinkers but become alcoholic addicts. Although there does not seem to be a clear-cut "alcoholic personality," many studies indicate that alcoholics tend to be immature, passive-dependent persons who set unrealistic goals for themselves and cannot tolerate tension, failure, or criticism. Instead of protecting themselves against anxiety with the usual defense mechanisms such as overcompensation or displacement, they fall into the habit of seeking escape and relief in the bottle. In some instances they are following a pattern set by one or the other parent, and in some cases they may have a physiological make-up which makes alcohol particularly effective—although this has never been proven.

At any rate, they usually start by using alcohol as a means of alleviating loneliness, bolstering confidence, counteracting disappointment, gaining freedom from inhibitions, or narcotizing themselves against feelings of futility. They find that a few drinks are quite effective in achieving these ends, and at the same time give them a sense of pleasure and well-being. Though all these effects quickly wear off, the future alcoholics soon find that they can be regained at any time by the simple process of visiting the nearest bar or liquor store. This encourages them to use drinking as their *standard* technique of dealing with maladjustment and making themselves feel more comfortable.

The process by which addiction develops has been traced in great detail by Jellinek (1952). His study of over two thousand chronic alcoholics revealed four distinct stages in the process (*Fig. 2*). In the *prealcoholic symptomatic phase,* the prospective alcoholic

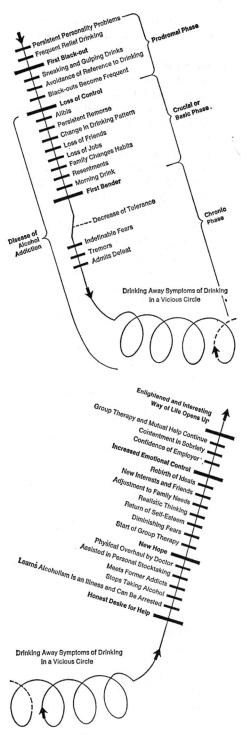

Fig. 2. Phases of alcoholic addiction and recovery.

finds special relief in the usual drinking situations, either because his tensions are greater than average or his ability to handle his problems is less than average. In a few months he progresses from occasional relief-drinking to constant relief-drinking. In the *prodromal phase,* he experiences occasional blackouts—that is, he carries on conversations and other activities while under the influence of alcohol but cannot remember a thing the next day. This tendency to amnesic episodes without loss of consciousness is a particularly clear danger signal. During this period, the future alcoholic starts his drinking with a few quick gulps to get ahead of the game, drinks surreptitiously, begins to feel guilty about his drinking, and tries to avoid reference to alcohol in his conversation.

The *crucial phase* is characterized by uncontrolled drinking leading to frequent intoxication. This is accompanied by "alcoholic alibis" devised to justify his drinking and answer the criticisms and warnings of others. He often feels remorseful about his drinking, but to alleviate this distressing feeling usually resorts to more drinking. He also has frequent hangovers, but the medicine he takes to ease the pain is a few drinks. He now begins to use many dodges to control his drinking, such as changing his beverage, or drinking only at certain hours. These devices are ineffective and he soon finds himself drinking in the afternoon as well as in the evening. As a result he loses one job after another, and one friend after another—although he sometimes tries to save face by quitting them before they quit him.

At this point the alcoholic's wife and children withdraw from social activities to avoid embarrassment, and his life becomes even more restricted. Improper nutrition begins to have an effect on his sexual drive, but as potency decreases, "alcoholic jealousy" increases, and he is likely to accuse his wife of infidelity. To all these mounting tensions there is but one answer for the alcoholic: more drinking. He now begins to hide liquor in unlikely places, and cannot face the day without a drink.

The *chronic phase* is ushered in with daily intoxication and frequent, prolonged "benders." The alcoholic will now drink anything any time and with anyone. His tolerance for alcohol starts to decrease, and half his usual intake will produce tremors, vague feelings of apprehension, and mental confusion—but again the only way he seeks relief is through more drinking. In about 10 per cent of these chronic cases, an out-and-out psychosis develops. Others drift into Skid Row until pneumonia or some other disease puts an end to their lives. The rest—at least some of them—finally admit defeat and accept treatment.

In acute intoxication cases, treatment must take place in a hospital where medical care, including the use of tranquilizing drugs, is given to alleviate nausea, encourage sleep, and prevent withdrawal symptoms. To reinforce the patient against future drinking, Antabuse or conditioned-response therapy may be used. These deterrent techniques prepare the way for psychotherapy and sociotherapy, which help the patient attain emotional insight and achieve more constructive patterns of adjustment.

Residential treatment is usually required for alcoholics, and the most successful results have been achieved by a combination of comfortable living, good food and congenial environment, with daily group psychotherapy and opportunities to do odd jobs and develop occupational skills. Social workers are usually called upon to reduce home stresses and prepare the way for the patient's return. A new trend is to use halfway houses as a transition back to community life. When the alcoholic is ready to attempt regular life again—

and even before that—he is frequently encouraged to become a member of an Alcoholics Anonymous group, so that he can benefit from the emotional and social support of others in his battle against addiction.

When full, intensive treatment is applied, between 60 and 80 per cent of alcoholics succeed in maintaining sobriety. However, they must recognize that they will be susceptible to alcohol for the rest of their lives and cannot become ordinary social drinkers.

If the alcoholic toll is to be reduced, a continuous educational program must be conducted on all economic levels and directed to older children as well as adults. Alcoholism should be presented as a psychiatric and social problem, and the alcoholic should be pictured as a sick person in desperate need of help rather than a moral degenerate. Above all, it is necessary to acquaint the entire public with the warning signals which can lead to early detection and preventive treatment. Among the most indicative are these four: (1) *increasing consumption,* even though it may be gradual; (2) *morning drinking,* to alleviate a hangover or face the day; (3) *uncontrolled behavior:* senseless, embarrassing, or violent actions while under the influence of alcohol; (4) *pulling blanks:* drinking enough to cause blackouts or amnesic episodes. Any one of these indicators is an ominous warning; and if all four apply, the individual is well on the way to chronic alcoholism. *See* ALCOHOLICS ANONYMOUS, ANTABUSE (DISULFIRAM) THERAPY, BEHAVIOR THERAPY, HALFWAY HOUSE.

Illustrative case: ALCOHOLIC ADDICTION, ACUTE TYPE

In his novel *The Lost Weekend,* Charles Jackson presents this classic description of the reactions of an acute alcoholic:

He had awakened fully dressed on the couch in the living room. His feet burned. He reached down and unlaced his shoes and kicked them off. He rose to a sitting posi-

tion and pulled off his coat and vest, untied his tie and loosened his collar. Automatically his hand groped beside the couch for the pint on the floor. His heart sank as he found it, and found it empty.

Had he been sleeping all night, or all night and all the next day? There was no way of telling till the light changed outside, for better or worse. If it were evening, thank Christ. He could go out and buy another, a dozen more. But if morning—he feared to find out; for if it were morning, dawn, he would be cut off till nine or after and so made to suffer the punishment he always promised himself to avoid. It would be like the dreaded Sunday, always (at these times) the day most abhorred of all the week; for on Sundays the bars did not open till two in the afternoon and the liquor stores did not open at all. Once again he had not been clever enough to provide a supply against this very thing; again he had lost all perspective and forgotten his inescapable desperation of the morning, so much more urgent and demanding than any need of the evening before. Last night it had been merely drink. It was medicine now . . .

Though he hated this need of his, hated his dependency on the pick-up, so often impossible to get—hated it for what it did to him till he got it—all the same he had a profound and superior contempt for those who spurned liquor on the morning after, whose stomachs, shaken as they were by the dissipation of the night, turned and retched at the very thought of it. How often he had been dumfounded—at first incredulous, then contemptuous—to hear someone say, after a night of drinking, "God, take it away, I don't want to smell it, I don't want to see it even, take it out of my sight!"—this at the very moment when he wanted and needed it most. How different that reaction was from his own, and how revealing. Clearly it was the difference between the alcoholic and the non-. He was angry to know this, but he knew it; he knew it far better than others; and he kept the knowledge to himself . . .

Thirst—there was a misnomer. He could honestly say he had never had a thirst for liquor or a craving for drink as such, no, not even in hangover. It wasn't because he was thirsty that he drank, and he didn't drink because he liked the taste (actually whisky was dreadful to the palate; he swallowed it at once to get it down as quickly as possible); he drank for what it did to him. As for quenching his thirst, liquor did exactly the opposite. To quench is to slake or to satisfy, to give you enough. Liquor couldn't do that. One drink led inevitably to the next, more demanded more, they became progressively easier and easier, culminating in the desperate need, no longer easy, that shook him on days such as these. His need to breathe was not more urgent. (Jackson, 1944)

Illustrative Case: ALCOHOLIC ADDICTION, CHRONIC TYPE

R.P., a married man of fifty years of age. He had always been of unusual temperament, having a difficulty in mixing with other people, so that even his own relatives did not visit him. He was always restless, never being able to enjoy a holiday because he wanted to get back to work. He owned a wine and spirit business, and had at one time a dozen retail shops of his own. Five years before his admission into hospital his disposition began to change. He commenced to grumble about everything at home, became irritable at trifles, swore volubly at his wife and children—a thing he had never done before. For some indefinite time he had been drinking secretly. Three years after this he fell into the hands of the police while drunk, and lost some of his licenses in consequence. His ordinary daily program at that time consisted in going out after breakfast, and returning drunk at midday, sleeping in the afternoon, going out again and returning drunk once more. He showed no care whatever for his family. His son, who was delicate, sometimes had to carry him home. While drunk he exposed himself to his family, including his daughter. During their convalescence from influenza he turned his children out of the house. He would send his wife on errands and refuse to readmit her till she had obtained what he happened to want—usually more alcohol. He took no interest in anything, neglected his business and threatened suicide but made no real attempt at it. In hospital he was antagonistic and resentful, saying that he was unjustly detained, refusing food at times, doing his best to find fault with the ward arrangements. Occa-

sionally, however, he was affable, making caustic jokes. He boasted of his athletic prowess (he was a puny, unpleasant-looking little man). He showed no shame at his conduct, denied most of it, and lied readily, often contradicting himself. A slight memory defect was revealed by the more difficult tests. He was persistently unco-operative and lacking in insight. (Henderson Gillespie, and Batchelor, 1962)

ALCOHOLICS ANONYMOUS (AA). A voluntary organization of alcoholics and ex-alcoholics which seeks to control the compulsive urge to drink through understanding, fellowship, and emotional support.

The first AA group was established in Akron, Ohio, in 1935 by a New York broker and an Ohio physician, both of whom had conquered alcoholism through a "fundamental spiritual change." Aided by publicity in a national magazine, the idea spread rapidly, and today there are said to be over 10,000 chapters throughout the world, with a membership variously estimated between 100,000 and 300,000. The names of the members are not revealed to the outside world, and only first names are used at meetings.

The organization describes its approach in terms of a series of steps which can be summarized as follows. To gain admission to an AA group, the alcoholic must admit from his own experience that he cannot control his drinking, and must recognize the existence of a supreme spiritual power which can give him the strength he needs. (Adherence to institutional religion or belief in God as such is not required.) With the aid of another member, he makes a searching inventory of his past errors, and undertakes to make amends. He then works out a simple code of living and pledges that he will follow it without depending on alcohol as a crutch. Finally, he shares his experiences and problems with other alcoholics, and maintains his morale by actively participating in meetings and social affairs, and by helping other alcoholics who are in need of support. The entire process can be characterized as a group approach with spiritual overtones.

An alcoholic usually attends his first AA meeting after he has reached the depths of despair. In most cases this follows a particularly frightening debauch, a long blackout, the loss of one job after another, or a breakdown in his family relations. During the meeting he hears vivid testimonials from other men and women who have had experiences as harrowing as his own, but who have been sustained and rehabilitated by the organization. He also listens to frank discussions of the problems of alcoholics, some of which he is bound to have faced himself. After the meeting is over, everyone is invited to stay for a social hour, in the course of which one of the members, an ex-alcoholic, engages him in conversation, befriends him, and offers him help.

In the days that follow, a close relationship is usually established between the alcoholic and his sponsor, who gives him support, assistance, and encouragement at any time, night or day, that he feels he is slipping. The sponsor also offers to interpret the alcoholic's problem to his family and enlist their co-operation. Even more important, he helps the new member rid himself of feelings of guilt, worthlessness, or fear of insanity, and encourages him to replace these negative feelings with self-understanding, hope for the future, and a more constructive way of life.

It is not possible to give an accurate appraisal of the effectiveness of the AA approach, since no records are kept by the organization. Claims have been made of 80 to 90 per cent success, but these must be tempered by the fact that the organization only accepts those who admit their failure and recognize a higher spiritual power. Moreover, the figures do not take into account the many alcoholics who attend a few meetings and then drop out. A more realistic estimate would be that something over 50 per cent of those who continue for a substantial period are able to control their drinking either completely or with occasional relapses. The chances of success, or at least some degree of effectiveness, are great enough for many therapists and organizations to urge alcoholics to attend AA meetings, often as an adjunct to individual psychotherapy or to various deterrent measures such as behavior therapy and Antabuse. See ALCOHOLIC ADDICTION, ANTABUSE, BEHAVIOR THERAPY.

ALEXIA. Inability to understand written language, a form of visual aphasia due to brain lesions; word-blindness.

The lesions occur in the parietal or occipital-parietal lobes of the brain, destroying associative fibers which make possible recognition and understanding of language. Some patients can read letters, syllables or even single words mechanically, but cannot comprehend their meaning. They may also be able to trace words and take dictation, but cannot understand what they write.

Alexia may be either a congenital or acquired condition. A small number of children are born with specific brain defects resulting from prenatal toxicity, injury or anoxia (lack of oxygen) during birth. Others may acquire these defects as a result of brain inflammation (encephalitis) or accidental head injury. In some cases the defect may make it hard or impossible for them to learn to read. At one time clear-cut brain damage was thought to be the major cause of severe reading disability; today it is considered only one of many possible causes.

Alexia may also occur in later life as a result of brain disease. It is most frequently observed in three degenerative psychoses in the presenile or senile period: Alzheimer's disease, Pick's disease, and psychosis with arteriosclerosis. *See* these topics; *also* READING DISABILITY, APHASIA, AGNOSIA, WORD BLINDNESS.

ALIENIST. A physician who is accepted as an expert witness on the mental competence of persons appearing before a court, either as parties to the legal action or as witnesses. The law does not always require that the alienist be a psychiatrist.

The term is still used in some jurisdictions, but many courts have discarded it. It dates back to an earlier view of mental disorder as a condition severe enough to require special legal provisions such as restraint or guardianship. The word itself derives from a Latin word meaning "other" or "stranger," and the implication is that the mentally unbalanced person is not himself, that is, he is a stranger or alien to himself. An alienist would therefore be an authority on strange behavior.

ALLOPSYCHIC. A general term characterizing the assignment or projection of one's own thoughts or ideas to people or events in the outside world.

In an allopsychic delusion or hallucination the patient projects his own feelings into other people (allo- means other, or different). If he is jealous, he believes his wife is jealous; if he is hostile, he believes other people are aggressive or conspiring against him; if he wishes to cheat others, he becomes convinced that they are out to cheat him. The term "allopsychosis" has been used by Wernicke to denote a psychosis marked by disorganization of the perceptive powers for the outside world (hallucinations and illusions) but without disorder of the motor powers such as speech or action. In this sense it contrasts with an autopsychosis in which the patient is afflicted with hallucinations or delusions about himself. *See* AUTOPSYCHIC, HALLUCINATION, PROJECTION.

ALL-OR-NONE LAW. The principle that a nerve fiber responds at full strength or not at all.

The basic function of the nervous system is to carry messages in the form of electrical impulses called spike potentials. These impulses supply the spinal cord and brain with information about external and internal events. The units of the system are nerve cells, or neurons, which react or "fire" when a certain level of stimulation is reached. This level, called threshold, varies considerably but is usually quite low—for example, our eyes can detect a single telephone wire at a distance of three miles. In 1912 E. D. Adrian and K. Lucas discovered the important fact that when a stimulus is above threshold intensity for a given nerve fiber, it fires at maximal strength.

The all-or-none law means that there are no gradations in the reactions of individual nerve fibers. In this respect they are like firecrackers, which fire with equal force whether they are lit by a match or a blowtorch. But if there is no correspondence between the strength of the stimulus and the strength of the response, how can we explain the obvious fact that our sensations vary widely in intensity? We experience mild pains and acute pains; we hear faint sounds and loud sounds; and the light of a match makes far less impression than the light of the sun. *See* NERVE CONDUCTION.

Physiologists have discovered two further facts that explain these gradations. First, since the thresholds of nerve fibers vary, a strong stimulus will fire more neurons than a weak stimulus. Second, nerve fibers must rest and recuperate for a short period following stimulation, but it has been found that this "refractory period" can be shortened by applying more intense stimulation. This serves to increase the rate of firing. A strong stimulus, then, will produce a strong response for two reasons: the frequency of impulses is great, and many neurons are activated.

The all-or-none principle has been revised in recent years. It still seems to hold most of the time for neurons that are not in contact with the environment, but receptor cells such as the rod and cone cells in the eye and the pressure cells in the skin seem to be capable of graded reactions that are roughly proportionate to the intensity of the stimulation (Gray, 1959). Unlike the spike potentials, these receptor potentials can only be evoked by certain kinds of stimulation, such as light energy, as well as by certain levels of stimulation. Graded potentials have also been found when an impulse jumps across the gap, or synapse, between one nerve fiber and another. These post-synaptic potentials, as well as the receptor potentials, help to explain the remarkable flexibility of the nervous system and the great variations in our sensitivity to stimuli. However, much additional research is needed before our understanding of these phenomena is complete. See NEURON, SYNAPSE.

ALLPORT - VERNON - LINDZEY STUDY OF VALUES. A personality test which attempts to uncover the individual's dominant and pervasive interests.

The study is in the form of a questionnaire designed to show the relative importance of six basic values in the subject's life. They are based on the following categories outlined in Edward Spranger's *Types of Men* (1928): (1) *theoretical:* seeks truth, follows rational and critical interests, attempts to systematize and order his knowledge; (2) *economic:* stresses the practical and useful, interested in accumulating wealth and in the marketing and production of goods—a typical businessman; (3) *esthetic:* values form and harmony above all things, enjoys each impression for its own sake, judges things and people according to fitness, symmetry, and grace; (4) *social:* loves people and views them as ends rather than means, values kindness, sympathy, and unselfishness; (5) *political:* stresses renown, influence, and personal power not only in the political arena but in his vocation; (6) *religious:* primarily interested in comprehending the cosmos as a whole, concerned with the unity of all experience. (A Pictorial Study of Values has also been developed for subjects with linguistic or reading difficulties, but it is not yet ready for general use.)

The authors of the test, as well as Spranger, recognize that these are six ideal types and that most people belong to more than one group. However, if an individual fits almost completely into one category, his outlook on other things will be colored by that dominant interest. Esthetic individuals, for example, may be sensitive to other people's feelings, but are not so vitally interested in their welfare as the individual with a dominant social interest. They might also interpret religious experience as an experience of beauty rather than spirituality. In other words, the "pure" types display dominant values which they use as a frame of reference in structuring their experiences.

The Study of Values presents questions and statements designed to evoke these six values in random order, with no hint as to the categories intended. On Part I of the test the subject is given two choices and three points to divide between them: 3–0, 2–1, 1–2, 0–3. This gives him some latitude in responding and also permits a rough estimate of the strength of his preferences. Thirty familiar ideas are presented on the test, such as "The main object of scientific research should be the discovery of pure truth rather than its practical application." An affirmative answer would score toward theoretical interest, a negative answer toward the economic.

Part II of the test consists of fifteen questions, each containing a series of alternatives which the subject is required to rank in order of preference. An example is: "Do you think a good government should aim chiefly at (a) more aid for the poor, sick and old? (b) the development of manufacturing and trade? (c) introducing more ethical principles into its policies and diplomacy? (d) establishing a position of prestige and respect among nations?"

The test is administered primarily to college students or adults with some college experience or its equivalent. The time required is about 20 minutes. The examiner tabulates the results and constructs a profile of the subject, showing the relative strength of his interests in the six areas. Norms have been established by testing college populations, but there are separate norms for each sex and for several different colleges. The test has been found to differentiate successfully between a number of different groups such as medical versus theological students, and its retest reliability is high. It has also revealed a number of sex differences: males generally score higher on theoretical, economic and political interests; females on esthetic, social, and religious values. These results undoubtedly reflect the influence of cultural factors on sex roles in American society. *See* SEX DIFFERENCES.

The authors of the test believe that one of the best ways to understand an individual is to ascertain his values. This point of view has been upheld by a number of investigations—for example, Postman, Bruner and McGinnis (1948) found that people recognize words in the area of their dominant interest more quickly than words from other areas, and Postman and Schneider (1951) found that ideas which are consistent with our values tend to be retained and organized better than other ideas. Studies of this kind indicate that we tend to construe our experience in terms of our value system.

The test has been criticized for apparently accepting the incomplete and frequently flattering personality portraits of Spranger. It does not seem to recognize that the social man may be selfish and egocentric, and it seems to ignore the fact that many people are motivated by purely sensual values. It also fails to recognize the existence of people who are almost totally devoid of values of any kind. But in spite of these limitations the test is considered an important contribution to the study of values, and an instrument that may be helpful in achieving self-understanding. *See* INTEREST TESTS.

ALTERNATION. A technique used in the study of thinking and problem solving; the subject is required to follow a sequence of activities such as turning right twice, then left twice (RRLL) in order to reach a goal.

The alternation method was devised as a means of testing the reasoning ability of lower animals and of comparing their thinking processes with those of human beings. It is also used in discovering exactly how language affects the ability to solve problems. The simplest alternation device is a maze in which an animal must make alternate left and right turns to reach a reward. This pattern is laid out in space, and the animal has a different set of cues to guide him at every turning point, or "choice point"—that is, the corridors and other features of the maze appear different when he is required to turn left and turn right, just as street corners look different when we are trying to follow directions through a town.

Simple alternation can readily be mastered by rats, but most investigators do not take this as evidence of reasoning ability. Rather they learn the maze by responding to visual, tactile, auditory, and olfactory cues, as well as to stimuli received from their own movements. These kinesthetic cues, as they are called, consist of one set of muscular tensions at a left turn and another set at a right turn, since each turn requires the contractions of different muscles. Experiments by Hunter (1940) have indicated that rats can be guided through a maze by these kinesthetic cues alone. He first let the rats run through a maze until they learned it perfectly. Then he eliminated all their outer senses by blinding and anesthetizing them, and even reoriented the maze. The rats were still able to get through with very few false moves, and Hunter concluded that they must have been responding to inner, kinesthetic cues.

The question then arises, What would happen if even the kinesthetic cues were removed? To answer this question, a *delayed* alternation problem was designed in which the animal was restrained for a period of time before making each turn. Many rats were able to solve this problem even with delays of fifteen seconds, which would be enough to dissipate the kinesthetic cues entirely. Some were even able to follow the right sequence when they were disoriented or anesthetized during the delay. These findings led to the hypothesis that an elementary "symbolic activity," or thinking process, enabled the rats to solve these problems.

This hypothesis has been reinforced by experiments with more complicated patterns of response. Rats can often master a double alternation problem (RRLL) and will even repeat the sequence two or three times in order to reach the reward. Some can succeed with triple (RRRLLL) or even quadruple (RRRRLLLL) alternation.

These successes, plus the difficulty in eliminating external cues, led Hunter to devise a double alternation problem utilizing a temporal rather than a spatial maze. Unlike the ordinary spatial maze, which requires the subject always to make the same turn at the same point, the temporal maze requires him to make different turns at the same point at different times. It also differs from the spatial maze in not providing different visual, auditory or other cues to which the subject can become conditioned. One form of the temporal maze resembles a letter T. The subject moves up the central alley to the end, where he must choose whether to go to the right or the left—but since this choice point always looks the same, he has no special cues to tell him which way to turn. To solve an RRLL problem under such conditions he must use at least a rudimentary reasoning process.

Repeated tests show that rats cannot solve the temporal maze even in a thousand trials. Raccoons, however, can learn one and one half sequences successfully, while monkeys can perform four correct sequences. This seems to be the limit of animal ability on this type of problem. Human adults can extend the sequence indefinitely by verbalizing right-right, left-left, etc. This clearly shows that our advantage over animals is due largely to our use of language.

Alternation problems of a somewhat different type are used with children. In a typical experiment, two boxes were placed in front of a child and controlled in such a way that he would have to lift them up in a double-alternation RRLL sequence before he could find a piece of candy. The full test required completion of three series of two sequences each. It was found that children below the age of three could not solve this problem; between three and four some solved it, and by four all solved it. Children under three were also unable to solve a temporal maze.

All these problems were so complex that the successful children undoubtedly "figured out" the solutions. From five years up they verbalized the problems and even devised rules, such as "It's in there (R) two times and in there (L) two times," or "I know now; two times and two times." Five-year-olds solved the problems in about half the number of trials required by three-year-olds. (Hunter and Bartlett, 1948)

The results of the various alternation tests indicate that (1) reasoning ability varies in proportion to the development of the cerebral cortex, since rats have relatively simple brains and show only rudimentary problem-solving ability while raccoons, monkeys and human beings manifest increasing capability in that order; and (2) reasoning is greatly influenced by the ability to use language. *See* THINKING, PROBLEM SOLVING, MAZE.

ALZHEIMER'S DISEASE. Presenile dementia due to widespread degeneration of brain cells into tangled, threadlike structures; first described by the German neurologist Alois Alzheimer (1864–1915) in 1907.

Unlike senile dementia, the cortical atrophy in this rare disease begins around fifty years of age, progresses rapidly, and often leads to severe language impairment. The behavioral and intellectual symptoms vary widely from case to case, but three general stages are frequently observed. Stage 1 involves gradual loss of memory, poor perception and reasoning, and inefficiency in everyday tasks. In stage 2, intellectual and emotional impairment become widespread, and confabulation, depression, and irritability are common symptoms. As the disease progresses, the patient begins to wander restlessly about, laughs and cries without apparent reason, frequently develops slurred speech and loses the ability to read and write (alexia, agraphia). In the third, or terminal, stage, the patient is increasingly disoriented and incoherent, cannot recognize relatives, and becomes so feeble and emaciated that he can only lead a vegetative existence.

Occasional remissions occur in the earlier stages of Alzheimer's disease, but in most instances the patient dies within four or five years. Treatment consists mainly of routine medical, nursing and custodial care. Although the cause of the disease is still unknown, research indicates that it might be due to a metabolic defect which may be either acquired or inherited. *See* SENILE PSYCHOSIS (GENERAL), BRAIN DISORDERS.

Illustrative Case: ALZHEIMER'S DISEASE

W.M. was admitted to the hospital at the age of fifty-two. The patient's early life, including medical history, does not appear to have been significant. The onset of his mental disorder was so insidious that his wife was able to give only an approximate date. About five or six years before his admission, he began to show less affection toward his family. His wife added that at about the same time "he grew lazy and his interests gradually dulled. He had a habit of just sitting around the house. For years he has not mentioned the payment of the interest on his mortgage or his taxes." About three years before admission his wife noticed that he could not tell time correctly and that he would make errors in writing a check. "He would set out for the store to buy feed for his cows and forget to do so. One time he wanted to walk to his father's place, thinking that it was just down the road, whereas it was a matter of sixty miles. He grew confused, and on one occasion he stopped the car in the middle of an intersection. He would put on his trousers backward and his overalls inside out. Sometimes, when a dish of food was put on the table for the whole family, he would eat the entire amount himself."

The preadmission history is obviously that of an insidiously developing and progressive dementia. On admission the patient appeared to be older than he actually was. He was completely disoriented for time and place. He did not know whether his home was in Pennsylvania or New Jersey. On the day of admission he said he was thirty-four years of age; on the following day he gave his age as twenty-five and a few weeks later, as eighty. He was careless and untidy in dress and wandered about the ward in a confused and bewildered manner, often mistaking the nurse for his wife.

On admission, general hyperreflexia (unusually active reflexes) was noted, but there were no other neurological abnormalities. Prior to his death his extremities showed spasticity. The patient became incontinent of urine; he gradually became weaker and even more demented. In August 1945, nearly two and one half years after admission, he suffered a rather typical epileptic seizure. About September 1, 1945 he became comatose and died nine days later. (Noyes and Kolb, 1963)

AMAUROSIS (literally, "dimming"). A partial or total loss of sight, especially when it is due to a defect in the optic nerve of the brain rather than to perceptible lesions in the eye itself. The term is also occasionally applied to functional, or hysterical, blindness, as in the following case excerpt from Masserman (1955): "An adolescent girl with intense sexual curiosity contrived, while unobserved, to witness intercourse between her parents. However, when she was discovered she developed intense guilts and fears and began to suffer attacks of functional blindness (hysterical amaurosis), as though in denial of, and expiation for, her forbidden act." *See* TAY-SACHS DISEASE, BLINDNESS, CONVERSION REACTION.

AMBIVALENCE. Contradictory feelings or attitudes toward the same person, event or goal.

Ambivalent attitudes may be either conscious or unconscious, or a mixture of the two. In cases where conflicting feelings are on the surface, as in hesitating to go on a trip or debating whether to buy a house, we may be able to postpone the decision long enough to weigh the alternatives. But if we cannot come to a decision, we may be sure that our ambivalence is due to feelings of which we are not fully aware. This is even more likely to be the case when we have to make highly personal decisions such as getting married.

In many cases we do not even realize that we have ambivalent feelings at all. In these instances we submerge, or "repress," one of the two components because it is painful or violates

our sense of decency. Many people, for example, have mixed feelings of acceptance and rejection, sympathy and annoyance toward aged members of their family, disfigured individuals, or invalids—but they are only aware of their more acceptable reactions. They frequently betray their negative feelings, however, by exaggerated expressions of sympathy and solicitude, or, in some cases, by projecting their own attitude of rejection onto the other person: "He really dislikes me and doesn't want my help."

The most common, and perhaps the most basic, expression of ambivalence is found in the mixture of love and hate which children feel toward their parents. These mixed feelings probably exist to some degree in all children. They originate from the fact that while parents are sources of satisfaction and affection, they are also the chief agents for restriction and discipline. According to psychoanalytic theory, this process starts in the first stage of development, the oral stage, when the child's (and the mother's) chief concern is with feeding. If parents recognize that some feelings of resentment are normal and healthy, and even reassure their children to this effect, no harm will result. But if they react with surprise and shock to a child's occasional outbursts of anger ("I'll kill you dead!"), they may unwittingly encourage him to suppress and feel guilty about these normal feelings. As a result, he may later feel anxious and hesitant about asserting himself—or, in some cases, the repressed anger may manifest itself in persistently over-aggressive behavior. *See* PSYCHOSEXUAL DEVELOPMENT.

Ambivalence may also take pathological forms in adults, particularly in schizophrenia, obsessive-compulsive reaction, and manic-depressive psychosis. The most extreme manifestations are found in schizophrenia, where it is one of the fundamental symptoms. Bleuler (1950) has described three forms in which it may appear. In *affective ambivalence* the same person, object, or event simultaneously arouses pleasant and unpleasant feelings—a patient may express great love for her nurse and in almost the same breath ask how to kill her. In *ambivalence of the will,* a patient may at the same time desire and not desire to do a certain thing—he may, for example, demand work or food but adamantly refuse it when it is offered. In *ambivalence of the intellect* ideas and counterideas conflict with each other—a patient may complain that his face is missing but ask for a razor to shave his beard, or he may vehemently deny that he hears voices, yet describe what they are saying.

AMENTIA (literally, lack of mind). An obsolescent term for mental retardation, particularly the severe, congenital type of defect in which the brain fails to develop. This type of mental retardation is also called primary mental deficiency.

The term has never been widely used in the United States, but in Britain it is applied to all grades of mental deficiency. In Germany, on the other hand, it is applied to the acute confusional state which occurs in delirium. American psychologists and psychiatrists usually avoid the term because of the confusion that surrounds its use, and because it implies a total lack of intellect, which is rarely found. *See* MENTAL RETARDATION (TYPES), PSEUDORETARDATION.

AMERICAN PSYCHIATRIC ASSOCIATION. The Association describes itself as "A society of medical specialists brought together by a common interest in the continuing study of psychiatry, in working together for more effective application of psychiatric knowledge to combat the mental illnesses, and in promoting mental health of all citizens." Its constitution enumerates the following specific objectives: "To further the study of the nature, treatment, and prevention of mental disorders and to promote mental health; to promote the care of the mentally ill; to further the interests, the maintenance, and the advancement of standards of all hospitals for mental disorders, of outpatient services, and of all other agencies concerned with the medical, social, and legal aspects of these disorders; to make available psychiatric knowledge to other branches of medicine, to other sciences, and to the public." *See* PSYCHIATRIST.

The American Psychiatric Association is the oldest national medical society in the United States. Founded in Philadelphia in 1844 by 13 hospital administrators, it was originally known as the Association of Medical Superintendents of American Institutions for the Insane. The major accomplishment of these early leaders was to bring about the transfer of the mentally ill from jails and almshouses to medical institutions that provided "moral treatment." In 1892 the name was changed to American Medical-Psychological Association, and in 1921, after a period of rapid growth in which the membership doubled every decade, the present name was adopted. In 1965 the number of members in all classes—primarily fellows, members, and associate members —totaled about 15,000, and included about 80 per cent of all psychiatrists and psychiatric residents in the United States, 12 per cent of whom were women. *See* MENTAL HOSPITAL.

The Association's members assemble during the annual meeting each May, and between these meetings the executive director, an elected Governing Council and the Executive Committee carry on its activities. There are district branches in nearly every state, which represent the profession and process most of the applications. The programs and policies of the Association originate in fifty committees, boards, commissions, and task forces dealing with such subjects as childhood, adolescence, aging, medical education, mental retardation, rehabilitation, research, therapy, hospitals, nomenclature, medical practice, nursing, law, federal health programs, disaster and civil defense, leisure time and its uses, occupational psychiatry, public information, religion, prevention, manpower, drug safety, and ethics. The central office of the Association is in Washington, D.C. Its periodicals include: *The American Journal of Psychiatry,* its official journal; *Psychiatric News,* its official newspaper; *Hospital and Community Psychiatry,* a staff magazine for non-medical service personnel; and *Psychiatric Research Reports.*

The Association serves as the profession's major channel for the exchange of scientific information through meetings, publications, institutes, and conferences. It has contributed directly and indirectly to the improvement of services for mental patients through the advancement of general hospital psychiatry, practitioner education, and the evolution of the new comprehensive community services. In its own terms, it has "always struggled, and with quickened success in recent years, to remove stigma and discrimination from the mentally ill, to safeguard their civil rights, to facilitate easy access to treatment, and to discourage judicial commitment in favor of voluntary procedures."

Other examples of public service cited by the Association are: the establishment of the American Board of Psychiatry and Neurology in 1939; establishment of the first standards for psychiatric hospitals and clinics in 1945; a program of public information on psychiatric and mental disorder; practical assistance to states in formulating long-range programs; initiative in organizing the Joint Commission on Mental Illness and Health in 1955, and the Joint Commission on Mental Health of Children in 1965; contributions to the development of psychiatric units in general hospitals; elimination of discrimination against the mentally ill in the Social Security program, and promotion of equal coverage for the mentally ill in all voluntary prepaid health insurance programs; promotion of the community mental health center program; and collaboration with other professional organizations including the American Medical Association, the National Association for Mental Health, the American Hospital Association, the National Association for Retarded Children, the American Psychological Association, the National Association for Social Workers, and the American Bar Association.

AMERICAN PSYCHOLOGICAL ASSOCIATION. Founded in 1892 and incorporated in 1925, the APA is the major psychological organization in the United States. Its membership, now numbering about 28,000, includes most of the qualified psychologists in the country. Its purpose is to advance psychology as a science, as a profession and as a means of promoting human welfare. These objectives are furthered through annual meetings; activities in support of improved standards for psychological training and service, and the publication of psychological journals, a monthly Employment Bulletin and an annual Directory of Members.

National headquarters for the APA are in Washington, D.C. Its chief governing body is the Council of Representatives, which includes representatives from affiliated state associations and its twenty-nine divisions. These divisions have their own membership requirements, officers and annual meetings, and include the following fields: General, Teaching, Experimental, Evaluation and Measurement, Physiological and Comparative, Developmental, Personality and Social, Society for the Psychological Study of Social Issues, Psychology and the Arts, Clinical, Consulting, Industrial, Educational, School, Counseling, Public Service, Military,

Maturity and Old Age, Society of Engineering Psychologists, Psychological Aspects of Disability, Consumer, Philosophical Psychology, Experimental Analysis of Behavior, History of Psychology, Community Psychology, Psychopharmacology, Pyschotherapy, Psychological Hypnosis and State Psychological Association Affairs.

The APA publishes the following journals: *American Psychologist,* containing official association papers and articles; *Contemporary Psychology,* containing critical reviews of books and other material; *Psychological Review,* containing original theoretical contributions; *Journal of Abnormal Psychology; Journal of Applied Psychology; Journal of Comparative and Physiological Psychology; Journal of Consulting and Clinical Psychology; Journal of Counseling Psychology; Journal of Educational Psychology; Journal of Experimental Psychology; Journal of Personality and Social Psychology; Psychological Abstracts,* summarizing the world's literature on psychology and related subjects; *Psychological Bulletin,* containing reviews of research literature and methodology. *See* PSYCHOLOGY, PSYCHOLOGIST.

AMNESIA (DISSOCIATIVE TYPE). Dissociative or psychogenic amnesia consists of a sudden failure to recall one's identity and past life.

The typical amnesic patient cannot remember his name, address, or age, nor can he recognize relatives and friends—yet his basic habits such as reading and writing are not lost. He usually seems quite normal apart from the amnesia, in contrast to some cases of organic amnesia. Morever, the memory process is not permanently damaged, since recollections usually return spontaneously or in response to psychological procedures.

In most psychogenic cases amnesia lasts for only a few hours. If it does not clear up spontaneously and remains untreated, it may persist for weeks or even years.

Psychogenic amnesia is an unconscious attempt to escape from distressing reality by blotting it out. Typical events that precipitate the disorder are family stresses, financial problems, and personal conflicts. In one case, a young girl had come to New York City in pursuit of a stage career in spite of the strong opposition of her parents. She was unsuccessful and finally her money ran out. As she was packing her bags to return home, she suddenly forgot who she was or where she was going. In many cases episodes of this sort are preceded by a conscious urge to "get away from it all," and some patients report a brief "twilight state" or stupor before the actual amnesia sets in.

Personality studies have shown that amnesics are usually immature, egocentric, highly suggestible individuals. In many patients there has been a long-term pattern of dodging problems, and in some cases episodes of absent-mindedness or forgetfulness have occurred in childhood. When the patient forgets who he is during the amnesic episode, he may also be responding to the wish to be a different person. Some amnesics respond to this desire by living a new life under a new name. *See* FUGUE STATE.

Loss of personal identity may serve another unconscious purpose as well. It may help the patient defend himself from feeling guilty, since no one can blame an individual who does not even know who he is. Significantly, many patients accept their amnesia in a rather matter-of-fact, unperturbed manner, indicating that it is the fulfillment of a wish. This attitude of "belle indifférence" is one of the reasons dissociative amnesia is often classified with the hysterical disorders. *See* BELLE INDIFFERENCE.

Many amnesics regain their memory after a short period of rest and relaxation. In more resistant cases a variety of techniques may be used. It is usually easy enough to find out who the person is, since most people carry some form of identification. The real problem is to unveil the patient's own memory. The most common method is to search for an associative thread that will lead the way back to his identity. This thread may be an occupational skill, an event in the newspaper, a familiar song, an area on the map. Word association is also of value in some cases. Once a clue is found, the individual's identity is gradually pieced together.

The above methods are sometimes slow and time-consuming and for this reason hypnosis and sodium amytal are frequently used as short cuts. Through these techniques, the patient is put into a suggestible state in which it is usually possible to break through his repressions. Automatic writing may also be tried, since, like amnesia itself, it is a dissociative phenomenon. In this technique the patient is distracted by reading a magazine while at the same time a pencil is placed in his hand. The therapist then whispers questions in his ear and, in some cases at least, the patient automatically writes the answers. As an example, one amnesic patient was tested for automatic writing and finally asked to write his name. After several false starts, the pencil slowly spelled out A-R-T-S-R. Since these letters did not make sense, he was asked to put aside his magazine and work on them. It finally dawned on him that by rearranging the letters, they spelled his own name, Starr. His unconscious resistance to revealing his identity had taken the form of an anagram.

The recovery of memory is usually followed by psychotherapy, for the amnesia is a signal that the patient needs to revise his reaction patterns and come to better terms with his life situation. The two cases that follow have some

similarity to each other, but the second is considerably more complex and represents a long-term tendency to dissociate. See NARCOTHERAPY, HYPNOSIS, HYPNOTHERAPY, AUTOMATIC WRITING AND DRAWING, AMNESIA (GENERAL) OR (GENERAL). (See below)

Illustrative Case: AMNESIA, DISSOCIATIVE TYPE (PANIC REACTION)

Miss B.Q., aged seventeen years, was brought to the clinic in a complete state of amnesia. She was found at a church, in a disheveled state, and could not tell who she was. She spoke coherently, but did not know her name, her address, who her relatives were, how old she was, where she went to school, or any other fact about her past life. Her mental processes were otherwise intact, and she could read, write, and discuss specific problems intelligently.

Under hypnosis, the essential history of her past was brought to light. She and her sister lived with her widowed father. He was a domineering, sadistic person who demanded implicit obedience and exact accounting of the household budget. On the day the amnesia developed, the patient was given the money for rent, and when she arrived at the agency discovered the money had been lost. The fear and panic that seized her was so great that rather than go back and face certain and severe punishment, she "forgot" all about herself. (Kraines, 1948)

Illustrative Case: AMNESIA, DISSOCIATIVE TYPE (REPEATED EPISODES)

An example is a patient who was brought to the hospital with a history of having had several attacks of amnesia. Usually the patient would arrive home from work or from visiting friends without being aware of how she arrived there or of the time intervening since her last recollection. The time was typically a period from one to three hours.

Admission was precipitated by awakening one morning in a strange hotel room with no recollection of how she got there or where she was. Checking with the manager of the hotel revealed that she had come by bus the night before and had checked into her room by herself. The hotel desk clerk had been a little concerned because he thought she probably was ill since she got off the bus in a small town without luggage. The patient's last recollection was that at 6:00 P.M. the evening before she was tired and lay down on the bed in her own room at home.

Therapy under hypnosis revealed that the first episode had been a very short one and occurred when the patient was at home in her room and had received notice that her husband, who was overseas, was divorcing her in order to marry a girl in that country. She states she recalled walking around in her room stating, "You are single and you don't like it." The next thing she remembered she was walking down the street not far from her home but with a complete change of clothing on and with no idea of where she was going. Other episodes were longer and were very frightening to her. The patient was able to discuss the loss of her husband which was a blow and also her tremendous need for love and affection.

Her mother, a dynamic, self-sufficient person whom the patient was fond of, had little time for affection or attention to the girl. The mother treated the patient as if she were still a child. The patient was anxious to have a home of her own. It also developed that the last episode had been preceded by a rather stormy discussion with her mother in which the mother advised her to rearrange her life and advised her to get out more with people of her own age and give up her circle of older and more intellectual friends. The patient's father died a few years before her marriage, and the patient had been very close to him. The patient stated that in her desire to establish a home and because of her great love for her husband, she had almost given up her own personality in an attempt to devote herself entirely to being a good wife to her husband.

She was able to see that the nature of her amnesia had been an attempt to run away from the overwhelming sense of loss of her husband's love and her own identity, because she had incorporated many of his qualities during the marital period. This identification seemed to be an attempt to gain some of the features of her greatly esteemed father. The episodes subsided rapidly; the patient gained at least a superficial insight from the therapy and returned to her responsible position. She subsequently

married another and more stable person and has continued to get along without further recurrence of her illness. (Ewalt, Strecker, and Ebaugh, 1957)

AMNESIA (GENERAL). A pathological loss of memory, either partial or complete, produced by either organic or psychogenic factors and occasionally by a combination of the two.

In *organic amnesia* a physiological disturbance in the nerve cells impairs the ability to register or retain experiences. In such cases events are completely forgotten and can rarely be recalled under any circumstances. The disturbances that cause organic amnesia are of several kinds: chemical changes produced by toxic conditions (lead or barbiturate poisoning, acute alcoholic intoxication, etc.); damage or destruction of nerve cells due to head injury or brain tumor; and degeneration of brain tissue as a result of cerebral arteriosclerosis or senile brain disease.

In *psychogenic amnesia* the memory "traces" are not passively lost but unconsciously repressed, and can in most cases be revived. In this type of case the inability to recollect is an active defense against experiences which have produced unbearable anxiety and distress. They are eliminated from memory because they are too painful to face. Psychogenic amnesia is usually more circumscribed and selective than organic amnesia, since it serves the purpose of providing escape from specific situations. A person may, for example, forget a distasteful appointment or an unpleasant task. Some individuals forget merely the name of a person associated with a distressing experience; their amnesia for the name symbolizes their desire to forget the person and the event. In rare cases a person may forget his entire past experience and his own identity along with it. During the period of amnesia he may take up another and more satisfying life in a new location.

It is important to distinguish between organic and psychogenic amnesia. The cause of an organic case is often obvious, but if it is not, a searching medical examination must be made. The major marks of organic amnesia are: disturbance of consciousness, impairment of other mental functions than memory, only gradual and incomplete recovery from amnesia, if recovery occurs at all, and maximal amnesia for events of the very recent past.

Different types of organic amnesia are found with different disorders. In general paralysis (paresis) and senile dementia there is frequently a fragmentary loss of memory for unrelated details. Degenerative brain disease is usually accompanied by a diffuse memory failure for both recent and remote events. Delirium is characterized by a period of confusion with patchy amnesia and recollection of isolated events during the period of confusion. The basic organic amnesia which follows head injuries may lead to or overlap with psychogenic memory loss—especially when the individual has had an urge to escape from the situation in which he got hurt, as in combat.

The major marks of psychogenic amnesia are a selective forgetting of distasteful experiences, an immature and suggestible personality, and frequently a sudden and complete recovery of memory. In general, a psychogenic diagnosis is not made until organic causes are ruled out and a positive emotional need for the amnesia is established.

It is also important to differentiate between malingering and genuine memory loss, since amnesia is sometimes feigned as a means of evading responsibility or escaping from unpleasant situations. In a study devoted primarily to military personnel, forty-one out of ninety-eight amnesic cases were found to be feigned. (Kiersch, 1962) See MALINGERING.

Amnesias are frequently classified into anterograde and retrograde types. In the *anterograde type* the memory loss is progressive, extending forward into the stream of experience. The boxer who continues fighting after receiving a heavy blow to the head may not remember that he finished the fight. The combat flyer whose plane has been shot from under him may not be able to recall parachuting to safety. In an unusual case cited by Ribot in his classic work, *Diseases of Memory* (1882), a woman patient appeared to be reading a book—but she did not get beyond the first page, since each time she came to the bottom of the page, she could not recall having read it and started again at the top. This went on for days because she was forgetting as she went along.

In *retrograde amnesia* loss of memory extends backward over a period of time just before the precipitating event. Soldiers thrown to the ground by a bursting shell frequently forget events that occurred during the preceding minutes. In cases where the shell killed a buddy, the soldier sometimes reacts to the memory gap by developing the guilty feeling that he did not do enough to save his friend. Retrograde amnesia may also follow other organic shocks such as suicide attempts by hanging or gas, epileptic convulsions, or electroshock therapy. It may also be psychogenic in nature, due to a traumatic emotional experience or an intense emotional conflict. Psychogenic amnesia frequently extends farther back than the organic type, since it may be rooted in long-term situations. Recovery for both types of retrograde amnesia is chronological, with memories nearest to the precipitating event the last to return.

See FUGUE STATE, DISSOCIATIVE REACTION, KORSAKOFF'S SYNDROME, TRANSIENT SITUATIONAL PERSONALITY DISORDERS, HEAD INJURY (ACUTE TRAUMATIC DISORDERS), AMNESIA (DISSOCIATIVE TYPE).

AMPHETAMINES. A group of chemically related antidepressant drugs which produce a temporary feeling of well-being through stimulation of the brain. The three most widely administered amphetamines are, in order of increasing potency, Benzedrine, Dexedrine, and methamphetamine (Desoxyn, Methedrine).

The amphetamines are the most common stimulants, or analeptics, in clinical use, and should only be taken on prescription. Recently huge numbers of tablets, popularly known as "pep pills," have fallen directly into the hands of the public, and an active trade has arisen in many parts of the country. Efforts are now being made to enforce the restrictions on the sale of these stimulants, since overdosage can have harmful effects and continued use can be habit-forming.

There are wide variations in the reactions to these drugs, but they usually have the following effects. Physiologically, they stimulate heart action, elevate blood pressure, relax the bronchial and intestinal muscles, and dilate the pupils of the eye. These physical changes are relatively insignificant in healthy individuals. The psychological effects are considerably more noticeable: the majority of individuals who take substantial therapeutic doses talk and move about more freely and feel more wakeful and alert. They also become optimistic and confident, and experience a feeling of euphoria and exhilaration which may mount to the level of elation. Everything that has a hampering effect drops away; aches, pains, fatigue, worry are replaced by enthusiasm, well-being, and a conviction of capability.

The drug has even more dramatic effects on those who take large doses or who are especially susceptible. These individuals are frequently thrown into a condition resembling hypomania, a state of excitement experienced by manic-depressive patients. They become so talkative that they are incoherent, so euphoric that they constantly giggle or shiver with joy, so confident that

they may believe they are supremely competent in every respect. This state may develop to a point where they lose their ability to concentrate and make an increasing number of errors in performance and judgment. In time, however, the feelings of euphoria subside, and they become tense, jumpy, restless, and unable to sleep. These reactions are often accompanied by disagreeable side effects, such as palpitation, headache, dizziness, dry mouth, weakness, and peculiar sensations in the stomach and chest.

There is growing evidence that uncontrolled doses of certain amphetamines may produce dangerous and lasting effects. Some long-term users appear to develop a "schizophreniform" psychosis in which thought processes become chronically impaired. Recently (1967) there have been a number of reports of young people who have reacted to massive, repeated doses of Methedrine (usually sniffed or injected into a vein) by developing paranoid delusions leading to violent, aggressive behavior. The drug has been nicknamed "speed" in the "hippie" groups because of its rapid effects on the system, and "speed demons" have been known to attack other people, including friends, who they feel are conspiring to turn them over to the police. Such reactions have prompted the "hippies" themselves to wear buttons reading "Speed Kills."

A substantial minority of individuals experience many of these side effects without the feelings of euphoria or the increase in mental and physical activity. Instead, they become drowsy, or more often despondent, apprehensive, and anxious. Individuals who have typical euphoric responses are also likely to feel somewhat let down and mildly depressive after the effects of the drug have worn off and they discover that their feelings of efficiency, including increased sexual potency, were largely illusory. It is probable that the drug merely made them less inhibited and temporarily mobilized their physical and psychological reserves through the reticular activating system. *See* RETICULAR FORMATION.

Amphetamines are used for a wide variety of purposes in psychiatry and general medicine. The psychiatrist administers this type of drug to bring symptomatic relief in some types of depression, to counteract drowsiness when tranquilizers are administered, to enhance the effect of sedatives in anxiety states, to treat organic narcolepsy, to combat behavior disorders (especially hyperactive and destructive tendencies) in children, to stimulate withdrawn and unproductive psychotic patients, and to facilitate psychotherapy by stimulating a flow of ideas. Amphetamines are also used as adjuncts in the symptomatic treatment of alcoholism, stuttering, enuresis, and some types of sexual impotence. The general practitioner uses the drug to counteract fatigue, lassitude, and mild melancholy; to diminish appetite during a reducing regimen; to improve the mood and facilitate the management of postoperative patients and victims of chronic disease.

The administration of these drugs requires careful prescription and supervision, not only because of the possibility of side effects, but because they are counter-indicated in many conditions such as hypertension, thyroid disorder, and certain types of depression. Moreover, there are vast individual differences in tolerance, and continued use can lead to dependency. Yet in spite of precautions an estimated ten million pills a year are being distributed through illegal channels. *See* EUPHORIA, ELATION, MANIC-DEPRESSIVE REACTION (MANIC PHASE), NARCOLEPSY.

AMUSIA. A loss or impairment of the ability to recognize or reproduce musical sounds.

The term amusic was at one time applied to all persons who were not only unmusical in the ordinary sense,

but who found every form and aspect of music strange and incomprehensible. It is still used occasionally to denote this extreme indifference and insensitivity. Technically, however, the term is now limited to lack of "musical perceptivity," that is, inability to recognize musical sounds. This disorder is a form of aphasia and is believed to be due to brain damage. The amusic individual, according to Révész (1954), "has lost a former musical ability, so that he is no longer capable of correctly perceiving or reproducing notes and musical patterns." Not only average but musically gifted individuals have been known to develop this disorder.

There are two principal types of amusia, corresponding to the two types of aphasia. With motor amusia, the patient loses the ability to reproduce and interpret melodies even though he grasps and understands music as well as before. He is aware that he is singing or playing incorrectly, but he cannot rectify his errors. There are many types of motor aphasia: a person may sing or play melodies but not in the proper rhythm, he may sing isolated notes correctly but not in melodic sequence, or he may sing after a fashion but lose his ability to play an instrument he has studied for years.

With the sensory type of amusia the patient's musical ear is intact and he can reproduce individual notes correctly. However, he cannot recognize even the most familiar tunes. A case in point is the opera singer who became afflicted with amusia while on stage and suddenly could not bring forth a single correct note because he could not understand what he was singing. Among the possible causes of such a condition are a tumor or blood clot (thrombosis) in the temporal lobe of the brain. *See* APHASIA.

AMYGDALA (Amygdaloid Complex). A brain structure located beneath the frontal lobe and involved in the control of emotion and motivation.

The amygdala is a part of the "old brain" or rhinencephalon, which is wholly devoted to the sense of smell in lower animals. But since this sense plays a smaller role in the behavior of human beings, the area has apparently become a center for dealing with emotional experience.

Research on the amygdala has been largely carried out on animals. It apparently has an excitatory effect on anger and an inhibitory effect on sexuality. When portions of the amygdala were cut, cats and monkeys became extremely placid and docile (Schreiner and Kling, 1956; Smith, 1950). After amygdalectomy (complete destruction) wild animals ceased to bite and scratch even when handled or pinched; a lynx, for example, became as tame as a kitten (Schreiner and Kling, 1953). Other experiments have shown that the relationship of animals to each other is also changed when lesions are made in this structure—for example, dominant male monkeys became extremely submissive after the operation. (Rosvold et al., 1954)

As expected, electrical stimulation of one part of the area produced rage, but stimulation of another part was found to elicit fearlike behavior. It is believed that the amygdala and the hypothalamus operate together in all these reactions, although the exact relationship between these structures is not wholly clear at present.

The inhibitory effect on sexuality was demonstrated by making lesions in parts of the amygdala. Eliminating these parts removed the inhibiting effect and as a result female cats were more easily aroused by the male, and male cats made advances not only to female cats but to males and to other animals such as hens (Schreiner and Kling, 1953, 1954). For reasons unknown, the same lesions made in immature animals did not affect sexual response when they

grew to adulthood (Kling, 1962). *See* LIMBIC SYSTEM.

ANACLITIC (literally, "leaning on"). Extreme dependence on another person or persons for emotional support. The model for an anaclitic relationship is the infant's dependence on the mother for his well-being and gratification. In psychoanalysis the term "anaclitic object choice" denotes selection of a mate or other love object who resembles the mother or other person who has provided comfort and support during early childhood. *See* ANACLITIC DEPRESSION, ANACLITIC THERAPY.

ANACLITIC DEPRESSION. An acute reaction of lethargy and apparent despair observed in some infants who are abruptly separated from the mother or mother figure. In psychiatry the term anaclitic is used to describe a relationship of extreme dependence. The paradigm for this relationship is the baby's dependence on his mother for the satisfaction of all his basic needs, both physical and emotional.

R. A. Spitz (1946) originated the term anaclitic depression after observing the acute reactions of children of six months to a year who were not only separated from their mothers but deprived of mothering care in impersonal institutions or foster homes. These infants began almost immediately to show signs of withdrawal, anxiety when approached, loss of appetite, and loss of weight. Somewhat later they became inactive and had trouble sleeping. Moreover, there were distinct signs that their development was impaired in all major areas, including the emotional, social, mental, and physical. Spitz attributed these effects to a loss of the "emotional supplies" which mothers or mother substitutes ordinarily provide—that is, warm and loving attention beyond the necessities of daily care. He found that if the emotional deprivation does not begin until after the first year, the depression and arrested development may be reversed, provided mothering is resumed within three months. However, if the child is deprived for a longer period, his deterioration continues.

The features of adult depression are frequently so similar to those of anaclitic depression that it has been suggested that many adult depressive reactions might have originated in infancy. Some investigators have also suggested that early emotional deprivation may account for some cases of mental retardation in view of the fact that the child's total development may be slowed if he is coldly treated during the crucial first year of life. *See* MATERNAL DEPRIVATION, MOTHERING.

Here is Spitz's original account of the depressive reactions of some infants to separation from the mother:

Illustrative Case: ANACLITIC DEPRESSION

The baby was one of the infants in the nursery previously mentioned, where the unmarried mothers took care of their children. The baby always greeted the observer with an immediate smile and gurgling pleasant sounds. She grasped toys offered to her and played happily with them.

"One day when we visited the baby—it was six months and two days old— . . . she was lying in a prone position in her cot, her head lifted, her eyes wide open as if looking for something. She gave the observer a long look at his approach and then the tears started to run down her cheeks. It was impossible to induce her either to a pleasant contact with the observer or to any play with toys. We learned from one of the institution's matrons that for unavoidable reasons the child's mother had been separated from her baby.

"Once aware of this reaction of babies toward separation from their mothers we focused our attention on any other separation of mothers from their children. When separations occurred a substitute mother was appointed for the child. In 45 out of 123 cases this choice was inadequate, the substitution not successful. In these cases the children developed a clinical picture, the inception of which we have described above and which I have called anaclitic depression.

"This depression starts with something that from the adult's point of view one would describe as a 'search for the mother.' Some babies weep with big tears, some babies cry violently, none of them can be quieted down by any intervention. In spite of their negative emotional attitude the babies at the initial stage of their depression cling to the adult. They 'weep on his shoulder.' This stage lasts for 3–4 weeks.

"If the mother does not return, the picture changes. The child lies quietly on its stomach, does not even look up if the observer enters the room, does not play with any toy, does not even grasp for it. It is passive and dejected, has eating difficulties, sleep disturbances, loses weight, and becomes more susceptible to colds and eczema . . . The whole developmental level drops. (Spitz, 1948)

ANACLITIC THERAPY. A form of psychiatric treatment in which the patient is encouraged to become as dependent as possible on the therapist, just as a baby is dependent on his mother for the gratification of his needs.

The object of anaclitic therapy is to create a situation that brings the patient back to infancy, and in this way to prompt him to relive early experiences that bring to the surface feelings and fixations now blocking normal adjustment. The term anaclitic was introduced by Freud, who applied it to the psychoanalytic process in which the patient lies on a couch like an infant, and establishes a close and dependent relationship to the therapist by meeting with him alone day after day.

Sensory deprivation techniques have recently been used in creating an anaclitic situation. The patient is confined to bed in a small dark hospital room, with goggles on his eyes, stiff gloves on his hands, and cardboard cuffs on his arms. To produce a state of dependency, and to quicken the return to infancy, only the therapist feeds and tends to the patient's needs. During interviews held at feeding time, he is encouraged to associate freely and re-create the scenes and reactions of early childhood. A case will illustrate:

Illustrative Case: ANACLITIC THERAPY

M was in a mixed borderline state of depression, anxiety, and obsessive behavior. She had always been inhibited and withdrawn, and her need for love had never been gratified. M's mother had died when she was an infant, and an aunt had taken care of M and her ten brothers and sisters (as well as three of her own) for the following five years, after which her father had remarried. This evidence of frustration during infancy made her a likely candidate for anaclitic therapy.

After twenty-four hours of anaclitic isolation, M began to relive childhood experiences in which she had conflicting feelings of being half good and half bad. These feelings came to the surface while she was being fed by the therapist. It became evident that she felt that she was responsible for her mother's death because she had been a bad girl. The feeding, however, made her feel more comfortable, and she remarked, "I have never been fed like this, somehow I've missed this. My mother left me when I was a year and a half old . . . and then my aunt and her children descended upon me."

As M gratified her frustrated infantile need for care and attention, she also succeeded in ridding herself of the guilt feelings associated with her mother's death—feelings which were at the root of her depression and anxiety. After four days of treatment, the procedure was discontinued, and she commented: "In isolation I felt plunged into my past, then suddenly I came to the surface stronger than ever."

As a result of this therapy, M became more outgoing and self-assertive, and was discharged within a month. (Adapted from Azima, Vispot, and Azima, 1961)

ANAL CHARACTER. A psychoanalytic term for a group of personality traits believed to stem from the anal stage of psychosexual development.

Between the ages of two and three, the child's libido is thought to be focused on defecation, and his process therefore provides him with a primary source of pleasure ("anal erotism"). Moreover, his response to his parents' requirements for bowel control are believed to determine many of his future character traits. But there are two aspects involved in the control of elimination—retention and expulsion—and according to the theory, the child's character may be influenced more by one than the other. The child who associates pleasure with expulsion tends to become ambitious, conceited, and generous. The ambitiousness and conceit are attributed to feelings of confidence generated by successful elimination, and the generosity is associated with willingness to "give" when he is expected to do so.

On the other hand, the child who derives particular satisfaction from retention tends to develop the more common "anal character," characterized by orderliness, frugality, and obstinacy, which are sometimes termed the "anal triad." The orderliness, which also includes punctuality and propriety, results from obedience to the mother's demand to be clean. The frugality is regarded as a continuation of anal retentiveness—just as the child cannot give up his feces, so the adult saves carefully, has a strong "collecting instinct," and may even become a miser or hoarder. The obstinacy is a carry-over of the child's rebellion against the mother's demand to eliminate. Adults who exhibit these traits in extreme degree are described by psychoanalysts as "fixated" at the anal stage. Compulsive characters are frequently termed anal characters, since they tend to be meticulous, controlled, rigid, overconscientious individuals. *See* OBSESSIVE-COMPULSIVE REACTION, PSYCHOSEXUAL DEVELOPMENT, COMPULSIVE PERSONALITY, HOARDING.

ANAL EROTISM (Anal Eroticism). A psychoanalytic term for pleasurable sensations associated with the anal region.

These sensations arise in infancy during the anal phase of psychosexual development when the child derives gratification from expulsion, retention, or observation of the feces. If the libido, or pleasure drive, is arrested or "fixated" at this stage, the individual will have a tendency to derive special pleasure from this region in later life. He may experience unusual gratification from elimination, manipulation of the anal region by himself or others, or may engage in anal intercourse. According to psychoanalytic theory, this drive may also be expressed in disguised or sublimated form in dreams, artistic productions, and humor. The individual who is fixated at the anal erotic stage is believed to develop anal character traits of obsessive orderliness, cleanliness, and miserliness. See ANAL CHARACTER, COPROPHILIA, PSYCHOSEXUAL DEVELOPMENT, HOARDING.

ANALYTIC GROUP THERAPY. The application of psychoanalytic principles to group therapy.

An experimental approach to group therapy was made by E. W. Lazell at St. Elizabeth's Hospital, Washington, D.C., in 1921. This technique was soon dropped, but was later revived by Louis Wender and Paul Schilder in the 1930s. Since then the most extensive use of psychoanalytic concepts in group therapy has been made by S. R. Slavson (1950), first president of the American Group Psychotherapy Association and editor of the *International Journal of Group Psychotherapy*.

Slavson first introduced this approach in a program for adolescents and adults at the Jewish Board of Guardians in 1943. In an article entitled "The Dynamics of Analytic Group Psychotherapy" (1951) he distinguishes between three different types: playgroup psychotherapy, for preschool children; activity-interview group psychotherapy, for children in the latency period; and interview group psychotherapy for adolescents and adults (PLATE 20).

Play is the basic technique in the first

of these therapies; hobbies and other recreational activities in the second. In both cases materials of various kinds are used to stimulate communication as well as expression of conflicts and fantasies. With young children, these materials consist of human and animal dolls, miniature toys, clay, water, and blocks; with older children, they include guns, soldiers, tools, arts, and crafts. In the analytic process, the therapist frequently asks questions which encourage the children to understand how their immediate problems are affecting their behavior and feelings. Interpretations are given not only by the therapist but by the children themselves, the members of the group commenting on each other's behavior as well as their own. As Slavson puts it, "Children hear talk about siblings, fears, enuresis, masturbation, anal and urethral interests, fears, inadequacies, hostilities and similar matters."

As an example of this process let us say that one of the children directs his anger against the therapist during the play period. To reduce the child's feelings of guilt and fear associated with prohibited feelings, the therapist refrains from punishing this display of hostility. Instead, he asks questions designed to make the child realize that his hostile feelings are really meant for a younger brother or sister, but are "displaced" from the real object. The child cannot be expected to understand this idea at once, and repeated incidents and explanations are usually required before he can arrive at the necessary insight.

In the third type of group psychotherapy—that is, interview group psychotherapy for adolescents and adults—the groups are carefully selected to reflect the best "therapeutic balance"—that is, the members must have common problems, similar motivation for treatment, and the same general level of intelligence. These conditions create a natural need for each other, and an atmosphere in which they will be most likely to reveal their attitudes, symptoms, and feelings. Each group operates on its own and the members are told that they can be helped by others only if they speak freely. They are also assured that everything they say will be strictly confidential. Slavson enumerates six basic principles of sound psychotherapy, and holds that they all apply in this process, though they may have to be somewhat modified to fit a particular group situation. First, *transference* takes place not only toward the therapist but toward the other members of the group. As in standard psychoanalysis, the therapist will usually come to represent a parent in the patient's eyes; but in addition, the other members of the group may represent either parents or siblings. In either case, these relationships are acted out in the group situation with revealing effect. Slavson holds that in many cases patients also experience an "identification transference" directed toward other members of the group who have similar problems, a process which creates empathy and promotes emotional growth.

The second aspect, *catharsis,* or release of pent-up emotion, takes place either through physical activity (especially in children's groups) or through verbalization. This process is accelerated by a number of factors. The group situation provides a greater opportunity for acting-out than individual therapy—for example, patients are more likely to mobilize their hostility by "ganging up" on the therapist. When this happens, the patients discover that other people have feelings and thoughts like their own, and this helps to alleviate their anxiety and guilt. Slavson terms this process "universalization." The group situation also provides the members with an opportunity to direct their sexual and aggressive drives toward a number of people in addition to the therapist. Slavson's term for this process, which also reduces the sense of guilt,

is "target multiplicity." In other words, the group situation stimulates the children to express their conflict-arousing feelings through both words and action. The effect is to hasten the cathartic process by allaying the anxiety which blocks it.

The third factor is *insight*. In children insight is achieved largely through "libido redistribution" rather than conscious realization. This occurs when the therapist, acting as a parent substitute, does not react to the child's overt acts or secret strivings with anger, fear, or anxiety, as the true parent does. This has the effect of diminishing and eventually dissipating the child's neurotic reactions. Slavson speaks of this process as a "devaluation" of these reactions through acceptance and understanding. The therapist's accepting attitude also helps the child to develop the ego strength he needs for handling his deviant impulses and urges by himself. Moreover, when he is freed from his intellectual conflicts, and therefore from his need to hold unconscious drives in check, he can use his energy in dealing constructively with his environment.

Among adults, insight cannot develop until the group member achieves some degree of emotional freedom and flexibility. Slavson describes two aspects of this process. "Derivative insight" is attained when the patient recognizes his own drives and conflicts in observing other people in the group; and "direct insight" comes about through actual experiences and interactions with the therapist and other group members.

The development of *ego strength* is the fourth phase of the group process. It is brought about by acting-out in an accepting atmosphere; by the process of universalization, which reduces guilt and reinforces the ego; and by testing one's self out in new relationships and interactions with the other group members. Children develop ego strength primarily through engaging in tasks and testing themselves in projects which bring them feelings of success and recognition not only from the group but from their parents and others in the family. *Reality testing,* the fifth factor, is closely allied to this process. Child patients, according to Slavson, need to be brought face to face with a graded set of situations which they can successfully meet. This helps them grow in both physical skill and emotional capacity. For adult patients, on the other hand, the group itself represents a segment of reality in which each member has an opportunity to test himself against both the therapist and the other members.

The last factor is *sublimation.* With children, opportunities for sublimation of basic drives are provided primarily by the use of play materials. Those who cannot sublimate are not accepted in group therapy, since they would disturb others. With adolescents and adults there are many opportunities for sublimation: talk, discussion of sexual problems, drawing, doodling, even giggling. It is sometimes advisable to supply additional opportunities outside the therapy situation, and in this case patients are referred to jobs, camps, music schools, and recreational centers.

Slavson has found that resistance plays an important role in group analytic therapy just as it does in individual psychoanalysis. Although many of the factors mentioned above—universalization, target multiplicity, sublimation, etc. —help to keep anxiety at a low level, certain subjects invoke defenses arising from deep-seated memories or from their reluctance to reveal themselves. These individuals tend to use many kinds of "escape": lateness, absenteeism, distraction, displacement (attacking or accusing another patient or the therapist in order to avoid discomfort), or deflection (changing the subject abruptly, or terminating the conversation altogether). They may also utilize general silence, in which they attend the sessions but do not talk; or selective silence, in which they "tune out" the group or refrain from communicating at certain points. As with individual analysis, these signs of resistance are viewed as highly indicative cues for the therapist to follow. *See* ACTIVITY GROUP THERAPY, CATHARSIS, EGO STRENGTH, REALITY TESTING, SUBLIMATION, INSIGHT, TRANSFERENCE.

ANAMNESIS. The developmental history of an individual in relation to his illness, particularly as given by the patient himself. The medical history following the illness (or following the initial examination) is termed the catamnesis.

The anamnestic approach was developed by Adolph Meyer and is now an integral part of the psychiatric examination. Its purpose is to assist the psychiatrist or clinical psychologist in making a diagnosis and discovering the causes and conditions (etiological factors) that produced the disorder. The more complete and accurate it is, the more helpful it will be. With children or acutely disturbed patients the data must be obtained from members of the family or from professional persons who have handled the case. But in most instances, the patient himself will provide a great many essential details if the proper questions are asked.

The anamnesis must comprise data about the patient's family as well as his own personal history. To uncover relevant information about environmental and familial factors, he is asked to give his impression of the personalities of his parents, siblings, and others who have lived in his home. He also describes the way he was reared and his relationship to each member of the family. Other important details might be the family's typical reactions to illness, the influence of a dominant grandparent, the patient's feelings of fear or jealousy toward one or another member, and his emotional response to the death or divorce of a parent. In addition, information is also obtained about the occurrence of mental illness, suicide, alcoholism, delinquency, or eccentricity in the family.

The personal history of the patient includes information on each stage of his development, with particular emphasis on critical experiences and interpersonal relationships. Many of the details about his infancy have to be provided by others, and should include facts about his origin (legitimate, adopted, etc.), the nature of his birth and his mother's reaction to it, whether he was a wanted child, any expectations his parents might have had for him, as well as data about his early development in terms of sitting, walking, talking, control of elimination, and patterns of eating, sleeping, and play. The account of his childhood should reveal early personality traits and relationships with parents and others, early dreams and fantasies, responses to discipline and to separation from parents, methods of coping with stress or frustration, first emotional disturbances, adjustment to school, and childhood illnesses.

The account of the patient's adolescent years should reveal the quality of his relations to peers and adults and any particularly disturbing events that may have occurred. It should also include details about his reactions to bodily changes during puberty, the kind of sex education he received, and his first experiences in this area. It is important, too, to find out about his struggles for independence, his attitudes toward authority, and his attempts to maintain self-esteem and elicit approval from others.

Information on the patient's adult life should include feelings toward the opposite sex, courtship, sex relations, attitudes toward children, relations with in-laws, as well as work experiences, attitudes toward money, and relationships with associates on the job or in the community. An account of the later years of life should focus on such questions as reactions to menopause, separation from children, retirement, loss of friends and family members, as well as the way he handles recreation, avocation, religious interests, and physical illness.

Full anamnestic data furnish clues to (a) the patient's general personality characteristics; (b) disturbing experiences that may have contributed to his illness; (c) predispostions due to familial patterns or early influences; and (d) long-standing personality weaknesses and faulty behavior patterns. As Adolf Meyer has pointed out, such clues are useful not only in diagnosing the disorder, but in formulating a treatment plan and appraising the possibilities for a successful outcome. *See* PSYCHIATRIC EXAMINATION, MEYER, PSYCHOBIOLOGY.

ANGER. A reaction of tension and hostility aroused by frustration of a desire or of other "goal directed behavior."

A number of physiological responses are involved in anger. They are governed by the activity of the sympathetic division of the autonomic nervous system and release of adrenalin into the blood stream. Among them are an increase of respiratory capacity, blood clotting, and blood pressure; release of blood sugar; and rapid elimination of waste through perspiration. All these responses put the organism on a "war footing" and enable it to respond aggressively to the frustration. Ordinarily situations that arouse anger pass over quickly, but if they do not, and the responses persist for a long period, they may produce psychosomatic symptoms. This is most likely to occur if they are denied overt expression and are "bottled up" or turned inward.

Anger reactions follow a fairly definite sequence in the course of the child's development. The first clear indications are found at about five months of age (Bridges, 1932), and take the form of thrashing, screaming, and stiffening of the body. The most frequent stimuli are physical restraint, minor physical discomforts, and being left alone. When the child begins to do things for himself, he may also be frustrated by his own inability to put on a piece of clothing, get food into his mouth with a spoon, or make himself understood. Preschool children are angered by interference with their possessions or activities, by frequent scolding and punishment, and by inability to gain the attention of adults. Their expressions of anger are usually directed at the source of the frustration, and take the form of hitting, kicking, spitting, biting, as well as crying and shouting. Between two and four years they are also subject to the more diffuse outbursts known as temper tantrums, which serve the double purpose of letting off steam and trying to get their own way. Stubbornness and spitefulness are other common expressions of anger during this period. *See* TEMPER TANTRUM, NEGATIVISM.

Between about six and ten years of age, children often express their anger through direct attempts to eliminate the source of the frustration, and by fighting, bullying, teasing, and surliness. In this period they also begin to depend upon verbal techniques, especially since words are more apt to be tolerated than overt attacks. These include name-calling, ridicule, sarcasm, threats, and rudeness. Other expressions also come to the fore in later elementary school years: excluding an enemy from group activities, refusing to speak to him, taking out anger against a younger child, against animals, or against children who are an object of prejudice. Some children learn to channel the energy generated by anger into activities that win them approval; others nurse their grievances, bottle up their feelings, become sullen, threaten to run away, or, in isolated cases, inflict physical pain on themselves. These more inhibited expressions of anger are most likely to occur at older ages.

The adolescent is primarily concerned with social and interpersonal relations, and therefore his anger tends to be directed at people rather than at things or events. Most typically, it is provoked by situations that play on his lack of security, his sensitivity to the opinions of his peers, his urge to rebel against authority, or his need for privacy. Gates (1926) asked a large number of college women to keep "anger diaries," in which they recorded all anger-provoking situations and all reactions to them for a period of a week. Of the 145 situations listed, 115 were found to be caused by other people—for example, bossing and teasing by parents, insulting or sarcastic remarks, or being scolded or contradicted. Following these incidents, fifty-three reported an impulse to make a verbal retort, forty to do some kind of physical damage to the offender, twenty to damage inanimate objects, twelve to leave the room or run away, and ten to swear, scream, or cry. In another study, conducted by Anastasi et al. (1948), college girls reported that the most frequent source of anger was interference with their plans, although feelings of intellectual or other inadequacy were also quite common. Meltzer (1933) found that college men were most often aroused to anger by frustration of their urge to assert themselves.

Adults, like younger people, react with anger when their activities are interfered with or when they are frustrated in the attainment of their goals. Typical incitements are an uncooperative neighbor, an unfair boss, an appliance that does not work, a discriminatory tax. In addition, adults respond to more abstract conditions—for example, they may show righteous indignation against social injustice. In all these situations the emotion is most frequently expressed in verbal form: criticizing, arguing, swearing, and in some cases gossiping and tale-telling. In old age, emotional responses in general tend to diminish in intensity, except for the violent outbursts of those who suffer from pathological conditions. Normally the elderly focus their anger on small, petty frustrations and tend to be cranky, petulant, and irritable rather than violent.

At all ages people differ greatly in their expressions of anger. Although these reactions are in some cases due to temporary conditions, such as fatigue, ill health, and stressful circumstances, most of them are based on tendencies developed in childhood. Among the most important formative factors are: (1) *methods of discipline:* excessive use of punishment arouses anger, which the child often displaces on others, while excessive leniency encourages the uninhibited expression of resentment; (2) *parental attitudes:* mothers may be intolerant of anger responses, especially among their daughters, and fathers may ignore or encourage these expressions by their sons because they consider them "manly," while both mothers and fathers may themselves set examples of intense, moderate, or mild anger responses; (3) *sex differences* are due not only to parental attitudes, but to peer influences which encourage the girl to express anger through scolding, ridiculing, tattling, or fantasy, and the boy to utilize physical attack; (4) *family status:* studies show that boys with girl siblings, only children and youngest children in large families tend to be most impulsive in their expressions of anger; (5) *socioeconomic level:* middle and upper level children are often taught to suppress their anger, while children from lower economic levels (especially boys) are often expected to express anger openly because it is a sign of strength—or, if they are subjected to authoritarian discipline, they tend to release their anger by fighting and bullying outside the home; (6) *personality characteristics:* all the above factors have an effect on personality, but in addition there are undoubtedly constitutional dif-

ferences in sensitivity to frustration and ease of arousal. It has also been found that better adjusted individuals do not let their anger "rankle" but tend to express it directly and in socially acceptable ways. *See* AGGRESSION, HOSTILITY, STRESS, ANNOYANCE.

ANHEDONIA. Chronic inability to derive pleasure from experiences that are normally pleasurable.

This is a functional symptom occurring primarily in the simple and pseudoneurotic forms of schizophrenia. The patient usually loses his capacity to experience any kind of pleasure, including the sexual. He is emotionally "flat," indifferent, and apathetic. If you tell him that his favorite ball team won the pennant, or that he has inherited a large sum of money, he will probably say, "Yes?" and go on talking about something else. Anhedonia is also observed in depressive patients.

ANNOYANCE. A mild form of anger which usually subsides quickly and rarely leads to energetic action. Occasionally, however, an inconsequential annoyance may trigger intense, pent-up emotions already in existence.

Annoyances differ widely from person to person, and probably from culture to culture. In a large-scale study conducted about forty years ago, 659 people were asked to list as many of their own annoyances and irritations as possible. The total list came to 18,000, about thirty per person, and included some 2600 different items. The investigator found that about 60 per cent of these annoyances had to do with human behavior, 12 per cent with people's clothes, and 10 per cent with their physical characteristics. Only a small minority were concerned with things rather than people—for example, a late bus—but even these usually involved frustration of personal drives. The five forms of behavior most often mentioned were: blowing the nose without a handkerchief, coughing in a person's face, cheating in a game, treating a child harshly, smelling dirty, and a woman spitting in public (Cason, 1930). Another study has shown that high-pitched sounds, such as screeching voices or strident musical notes, are particularly irritating to most people. (Kryter, 1950)

There is no question that our tolerance for annoyance varies considerably. Sensitivity seems to be greatest when we are fatigued, tense, or under emotional stress. If we are to get along with other people we have to learn to overlook petty annoyances and recognize that everyone has some slightly irritating habits. This is especially important in marital adjustment. Most minor annoyances can be handled by direct discussion, but if they tend to increase rather than diminish they may be a sign of deeper dissatisfaction. *See* ANGER.

ANOREXIA NERVOSA. Persistent lack of appetite and refusal of food resulting from emotional conflict; first described by William Gull in 1868.

The anorexic patient develops an active disgust for food, loses an alarming amount of weight, and may become emaciated to the point where life itself is threatened. The disorder is infrequent and is usually observed in young single women between twelve and twenty-one years of age, some of whom have had a previous history of obesity. It is often accompanied by such symptoms as menstrual disturbances, slow heart rate, low metabolism, and constipation.

Anorexia nervosa is sometimes classified as a hysterical reaction, but more often as a psychosomatic, or psychophysiologic, disorder of the gastrointestinal system. There is usually evidence that the loss of appetite serves such unconscious purposes as escape from problems or defense against dangerous impulses. Most patients show a history of early emotional problems and unhappy home life, often involving conflict between mother and daughter. They tend to be selfish, overly sensitive, and perfectionistic in personality.

The motivation behind this condition varies from case to case. Loss of appetite often gets its start as an unconscious expression of resentment against a mother who has overprotected the child, or who has rejected her by giving too little love or help in growing or by showing favoritism to another child. Refusal to eat is an ideal weapon in such cases, especially when the mother has made a great deal of fuss about eating. It is important to recognize that it not only causes great anxiety in parents but brings secondary gains to the child in the form of attention, solicitude, and control over others. Some young girls refuse to eat in response to an unconscious urge to make themselves unattractive or to remain as thin as a boy. Due largely to inner anxieties over sex and marriage, they feel threatened by the problems attendant on growing up and assuming their feminine role. Occasionally this anxiety is connected with a childhood misconception about oral impregnation, which establishes an association between eating and sex. In some cases, resistance to food is a form of punishment which the patient inflicts on herself for feelings of guilt associated with anger or sex— for example, it may be a defense against prostitution desires.

The treatment for anorexia is psychotherapy, with special attention to the patient's present adjustment to life situations. Behavior therapy has also been tried with considerable success, as in the case of a severely anorexic woman of thirty-seven reported by Bachrach, Erwin, and Mohr (1965). The patient's history showed that at age eleven she had been obese (120 pounds) and that she had been given daily thyroid with the warning never to let her weight get out of hand. She had also suffered from menorrhagia (profuse menstruation) and during marriage had experienced persistent dyspareunia (painful intercourse). She had ceased to menstruate and then steadily lost weight, especially during a period of loneliness and unhappiness when her husband was in military service.

The woman was later divorced, and by the age of thirty-seven her weight had dropped to an extremely dangerous forty-seven pounds, accompanied by such symptoms as purplish skin, gray and broken teeth, insomnia, nausea, headaches, high-pitched voice, body ulcers, and episodes of crying and screaming. In spite of these symptoms and her mummy-like appearance, she showed a surprising lack of concern. Tranquilizers, vitamins, and other measures failed to improve her condition or arouse her appetite.

In studying the case, Bachrach and his associates found that she derived her greatest enjoyment from visitors, television, and records, and therefore decided to use these pleasures as positive reinforcers in an operant conditioning procedure. Their first step was to remove the patient from her attractive hospital room to a barren room, and to have one of the experimenters present at each meal. A "schedule of reinforcement" was then set up, unknown to the patient, consisting of interesting talk each time she picked up a fork to take food, with rewards of television programs or phonograph music adjusted to the amount she ate. When these rewards proved effective, she was allowed the additional pleasures of dining with another patient of her own choice, walking with a nurse, receiving visits from family and friends, and special care for her hair. Within two months, her weight increased to sixty-four and she was discharged to her family, who were instructed to continue the reinforcement process by maintaining a pleasant social situation during meals. Her weight gradually rose to ninety, and she was able to engage in church work and later on to take a course in practical nursing, which resulted in a job in the hospital in which she had been treated. *See* BEHAVIOR THERAPY.

Illustrative Case: ANOREXIA NERVOSA

A socially immature adolescent schoolgirl had learned as a child to alarm and control her parents by rejecting food whenever she was crossed. The parents were mystified by her apparently occult ability to lose weight rapidly when punished, even though they forced her to remain facing her meal until she had eaten it. What they did not discover was that throughout her childhood the patient had practiced the common deception of concealing her food at the table and later flushing it down the toilet. Like many children of overprotective, domineering parents this girl did not welcome the approach of biosocial maturity with its anatomical and physiological changes, its new social responsibilities, and particularly the prospect of playing an adult sexual role.

She began her rebellion by attempting to delay her growth by drastically curtailing her food intake. This brought her immediately into sharp conflict with her oversolicitous parents, who made the mistake of using coercion and were rewarded by the paradox of increased eating with decreasing weight. Just as the eating had come to symbolize her growth into adulthood, so now the patient's contest with her parents represented for her the struggle, not only against her own approaching biosocial maturity, but against their whole domination of her. In public she appeared to accede to their demands that she build herself up, and then in private, like Penelope, she proceeded to undo her work. She went further than she had in childhood and not only concealed food to throw away but regurgitated much that she had swallowed. Eventually she reached a point where she could ingest only small amounts of food, with considerable coaxing, and even these she could seldom retain. She complained of inappetence and disgust with food, but not of hunger.

She was finally admitted in an emaciated condition to a general hospital and treated for the vomiting and malnutrition. It soon became obvious to the staff physicians, however, that she and her parents were primarily in need of psychiatric attention.

Through the coordinated efforts of internist and psychiatrist the vomiting was brought under control and normal feeding was reestablished. When the patient was given bathroom privileges she began again to conceal and dispose of food according to the old pattern, and expert psychiatric nursing had to be introduced to prevent her thus evading the fundamental issues which feeding symbolized for her. After three months she was discharged in good general health and without the symptoms for which her admission had been sought, but also without full acceptance of the role of an emancipated, biosocially mature adult. (Cameron, 1947)

ANOSOGNOSIA. Failure or refusal to recognize that one has a defect or disease.

Anosognosia is a form of the defense mechanism known as "denial of reality." The most common examples are probably a denial of deafness or poor vision, but any type of physical incapacity may be either unrecognized or actively denied, including aphasia, paraplegia, incontinence, disfigurement, or even loss of a limb or eye. Phantom limb reactions are considered a transitory form of anosognosia.

Some patients have been found to disclaim ownership of a paralyzed limb, asserting that it belongs to the nurse or that someone else in the family is paralyzed. Sometimes the denial is only partial, the patient claiming that he cannot move a paralyzed arm because it is sore from an injection. Other patients may deny or "forget" that they have had an accident, but will describe the identical event as having occurred to someone else. A person who has shot himself may deny it and also deny the problem that led to the shooting. Still others deny illness verbally but readily accept medication or submit to an operation.

Anosognosia is a mode of adaptation to stress, attributed by Weinstein and Kahn (1959) to "symbolic reorganization"—that is, a changed way of

thinking and speaking which enables the individual to cope with his problem. The patient's unspoken and usually unrecognized purpose in denying illness or defect is simply to make himself feel better. Studies have shown that most individuals who deny illness have long been concerned about their health and work, and have denied or minimized illnesses in the past. These people regard sickness as a weakness or failure, and as a consequence often postpone going to a doctor. They also tend to be extremely conscientious and worry if poor health interferes with their work. In some cases, however, distorted attitudes toward illness are associated with brain damage caused by cerebral arteriosclerosis, head injury, or metabolic disorders. *See* CONFABULATION, DENIAL OF REALITY, PHANTOM REACTION, BODY IMAGE.

ANTABUSE (DISULFIRAM) THERAPY. A form of deterrent therapy used in the treatment of alcoholism.

The drug disulfiram (trade name Antabuse) has been found to interfere with the metabolism of alcohol. If an individual drinks an alcoholic beverage within twelve hours after taking a prescribed dose of Antabuse, he feels intensely uncomfortable: his skin reddens, his face feels hot, his heart beats rapidly, and he soon begins to suffer from headache, shortness of breath, dizziness, chest pain, nausea, and vomiting. The initial treatment must be administered under supervision. The disagreeable effects of the drug do not diminish but actually increase with repeated doses, and in most cases a strong aversion to alcohol can be established in a relatively short time.

Although Antabuse induces the alcoholic to refrain from drinking for a time, it is rarely recommended as the sole approach to his problem. Its greatest value consists in interrupting the cycle of drinking long enough for psychotherapy and sociotherapy to be administered. The object of these therapies is to help the patient find constructive ways of meeting his problems, so that he will not be tempted to resort to alcohol as a crutch or an escape. See ALCOHOLIC ADDICTION, BEHAVIOR THERAPY, ALCOHOLICS ANONYMOUS.

ANTISOCIAL REACTION (Psychopathic Personality). A form of "sociopathic personality disturbance" characterized by impulsive, egocentric, unethical behavior.

The antisocial, or psychopathic, individual acts as if he has no conscience, no sense of responsibility, and no concern for the welfare of other people. He lives for the moment, fails to profit from experience, feels no genuine loyalty to any person, group, or code of behavior. He is clearly abnormal, yet he cannot be classified as neurotic, psychotic, or mentally retarded.

This type of personality occupies a twilight zone between the ordinary individual and the hardened criminal. The category includes a varied assortment of unscrupulous businessmen, confidence men, shyster lawyers, quack doctors, crooked politicians, prostitutes, and impostors. They are rarely committed to mental hospitals (and therefore constitute only .1 per cent of first admissions) but sometimes serve jail or prison sentences for their offenses. Most of them, however, manage to keep out of the hands of the law and talk their way out of conviction. Psychopathic behavior is believed to be considerably more common among males than females.

Psychiatrists have long had difficulty in interpreting and classifying this disorder. Prichard (1835) coined the phrase "moral insanity," applying it to an individual in whom "the moral and active principles of the mind are strongly perverted and depraved," making him "incapable . . . of conducting himself with decency and propriety in the business of life." The term "moral

imbecile" was also widely used in the nineteenth century to indicate that these individuals were intellectually sound but ethically defective. Many investigators felt this was a congenital condition, and the term "constitutional psychopath," or "constitutional psychopathic inferior" came into use. The inferiority was believed to consist primarily in insensitivity to moral distinctions and failure to develop warm and responsible personal relationships. This description seemed to apply to such a wide variety of personalities that many investigators sought to discard it as a catch-all, "wastebasket" concept, merely including individuals who could not be covered by the standard classifications.

The next step was to eliminate the idea of constitutionality from the title and substitute the more general term "psychopathic personality." The term "psychopathic" was then criticized as implying mental illness, and the American Psychiatric Association (1952) therefore renamed the disorder "antisocial personality," defining it in the following way:

"This term refers to chronically antisocial individuals who are always in trouble, profiting neither from experience or punishment, and maintaining no real loyalties to any person, group, or code. They are frequently calloused and hedonistic showing marked emotional immaturity, with lack of sense of responsibility, lack of judgment, and an ability to rationalize their behavior so that it appears warranted, reasonable, and justified."

This definition indicates that antisocial personalities may display a wide range of symptoms. Various recent writers (Cleckley, 1959; Heaton-Ward, 1963; Wirt et al. 1962) have attempted to list these symptoms in greater detail, although they recognize that they do not all apply to every case. The major features seem to be: (1) *defective conscience:* failure to understand, feel, and accept ethical standards in spite of glib assertions and pretensions; (2) *good intelligence:* used mainly to get around the law and rationalize immoral behavior, but without intellectual distortion in the form of delusions or hallucinations; (3) *absence of anxiety:* acts out tensions instead of transforming them into neurotic symptoms, and feels no sense of guilt for aggressive behavior; (4) *a good front:* an engaging, congenial manner which impresses others even while exploiting them; (5) *inability to form attachments:* a shallow emotional life with no sense of devotion, gratitude, or loyalty, usually accompanied by a promiscuous, irresponsible, and impersonal sex life; (6) *disregard for truth:* glibly makes promises he will never keep, often lies gratuitously, even when detection is certain, makes up stories to give his ego a lift ("pseudologia fantastica"); (7) *self-defeating behavior:* frustrates his own apparent aims by actions that bring on failure and disaster even at the height of success; (8) *rejection of authority and discipline:* hates to be held down and feels that ordinary social regulations do not apply to him; also feels hostile to constituted authority in school and society, and may engage in criminal activity without being a professional criminal; (9) *lack of foresight:* lives for the pleasures of the moment, disregards long-range goals; though he wants to "be somebody" and "have everything," he will not plan or work for these goals; (10) *extreme irresponsibility:* tries to give the impression of reliability, but actually shrugs off all responsibility to family and friends; (11) *failure to learn from experience:* shows poor judgment and does not profit from mistakes; blames others for disasters entirely due to him; persists in his bad conduct even when he promises to change.

There is little agreement about the origin of the antisocial personality pattern. Even though the term constitutional has been discarded from the title of this disorder, it is frequently pointed out that the general characteristics—particularly impulsive, egocentric, "acting out" behavior—appear early in life. Many authorities believe there is evidence of a hereditary neurologic disorder, but others have submitted contradictory reports.

Some investigators (Hill and Watterson, 1942; Silverman, 1944) have found abnormal electroencephalographs (EEG) patterns in 50 to 80 per cent of cases, but this finding has also been challenged. Others have pointed out that individuals whose brains have been damaged are not usually antisocial personalities, although epidemic encephalitis is sometimes followed by aggressive activity. A recent study by Stott (1962), however, has given the brain disorder theory some impetus. He found a positive relationship between congenital disorders and antisocial behavior, and attributed this behavior to impairment of higher control centers in the nervous system. Eysenck (1960) also argues that the psychopath lacks the ability to inhibit his impulses due to a basic defect, but he attributes the defect to a slower rate of conditioning than among normal individuals. More specifically, he believes that the psychopath does not develop an adequate conscience because he does not acquire the conditioned reactions that lead to normal social behavior. These investigations leave open the possibility that constitutional differences in the nervous system may be at least contributing factors in antisocial behavior.

Even if antisocial individuals have a constitutional tendency to act out their impulses, we still have to explain why these impulses tend to be aggressive and egocentric. Today's investigators are not satisfied with the simple assertion that they were "born that way." They have therefore attempted to search out psychological and environmental factors that might give rise to this particular "life style." Undoubtedly community influences play a role in some cases, since crowded conditions and deprivation create hostile attitudes, and delinquent gangs set a pattern for antisocial behavior. But these do not appear to be the key factors for two reasons: psychopathic tendencies frequently make their appearance early in life, before neighborhood influences could have much effect; and antisocial individuals are by no means concentrated at the lower socioeconomic levels—in fact, a high percentage come from middle- and upper-class families.

Investigators have therefore examined the home environment and parent-child relationships of psychopaths. Heaver (1943), Greenacre (1945), and others have found that in a large proportion of cases the mother was easygoing and overindulgent, and the father distant, stern, hard-driving, and highly successful. The child was not only caught between two conflicting sets of attitudes, but frequently the father was critical of the mother and the mother was contemptuous of her husband's desire to be an important man. The child therefore failed to develop a deep attachment to either parent, although he usually found it easier to adopt the easygoing attitudes of his mother than to live up to his father's expectations. In doing so, he developed a pattern of concealing and excusing himself for his inadequacies. These investigators also stress the fact that such families put on a good façade in order to conceal their inner conflicts from the world. This, too, contributes to the shallowness of the child's emotions and his feeling that he must put on an act to win social approval. It is not a far cry from such an attitude to the superficial charm and tendency to manipulate other people that characterize the antisocial personality. Nor is it hard to understand that a boy who has been rejected by a remote, fearsome father may become hostile and resentful toward all authority as he grows up. Although this family pattern seems

to occur in many cases, Cleckley and others have pointed out that other background factors may lead to antisocial tendencies. Some fathers—mothers, too—serve as direct models for their children's irresponsibility, egocentricity, and unethical behavior. Since they themselves have no regard for the rights of others and follow a policy of getting what they want by any means, the children follow suit.

In spite of the fact that feelings of anxiety and guilt are not apparent on the surface, some authorities believe they are nevertheless present. Franz Alexander (1930) concluded that most destructive individuals, including psychopaths, have a "neurotic character" due to severe, unconscious conflicts, and interpreted their tendency to act out their impulses as an attempt to ward off anxiety. Others have suggested that the self-defeating behavior of these individuals is due to feelings of guilt and an unconscious need for punishment. This might help to account for their tendency to bring on disaster even in the midst of success, as well as their need to continue their illegal behavior until they are caught and convicted.

In spite of these suggestions, a great many observers feel that the etiology of this disorder is still a mystery. Cleckley (1959), who has devoted a lifetime to the subject, states: "My own experience with psychopaths certainly does not suggest that they appear only in families of inferior moral or intellectual levels . . . I have not regularly encountered any specific type of error in parent-child relations in the early history of my cases . . . I do not believe that convincing evidence of the causal factors and developmental pattern of psychopathy has yet been established."

Successful treatment of the antisocial personality is largely a hope for the future. The behavior patterns of these individuals are so firmly established and they have so little self-understanding or genuine desire to change, that they are extremely resistant to therapy of any kind. Standard psychoanalysis cannot be used with them, although experience with hypnoanalysis—a combination of analytic and hypnotic techniques—has resulted in some success (Lindner, 1945). Intensive, long-range psychotherapy is sometimes effective, although it is hard to get the patient to stay with the treatment. (Thorne, 1959)

Milieu therapy, combining individual and group treatment with a warm and permissive environment, seems to be a promising approach. It has resulted in radical personality changes among many young boys at such residential treatment centers as the Wiltwyck School and the Hawthorne-Cedar Knolls School, both in New York. On the basis of experience in schools of this kind, as well as the experience of Maxwell Jones in his "therapeutic community" in England, it may be that the treatment of the future will take place in special institutions. Such institutions would utilize the total environment to encourage responsible behavior and redirection of the psychopath's superior intelligence into constructive channels. *See* MILIEU THERAPY, HYPNOTHERAPY.

The antisocial personality sometimes takes spectacular form, as illustrated in the account that follows:

Illustrative case: ANTISOCIAL REACTION

One of the boldest impostors of recent times was Ferdinand Waldo Demara, Jr. As an adolescent, he ran away from a rather tragic family situation and after unsuccessful attempts first to become a Trappist monk and then to teach school, he joined the army. Soon thereafter he went AWOL, joined the navy, and was assigned to duty on a destroyer during World War II. Here, by a ruse, he got hold of some navy stationery with which he managed to obtain the transcript of college grades of an officer who was on leave. He then "doctored" this transcript by substituting his own name and adding some courses; when photostated, it looked so impressive that he used it to

apply for a commission. While waiting for his commission to come through, he amused himself by obtaining other records, including the full credentials of a Dr. French, who had received a Ph.D. degree in psychology from Harvard. Informed during a visit to Norfolk that he could expect his commission as soon as a routine security check was completed, he realized that such a check would surely expose him. Under cover of darkness, he left his navy clothes on the end of a pier with a note that "this was the only way out."

Now that Demara was "dead"—drowned in the oily waters off Norfolk—he became Dr. French. He obtained an appointment as Dean of Philosophy in a small Canadian college and taught courses in general, industrial, and abnormal psychology. Eventually, however, he had a disagreement with his superior and reluctantly left.

During this period he had become friends with a physician by the name of Joseph Cyr and had learned a considerable amount about the practice of medicine from him during the cold winter months when neither man had much to occupy his time. Interested in the possibility of getting a license to practice in the States, the trusting doctor had given Demara a complete packet including baptism and confirmation certificates, school records, and his license to practice medicine in Canada.

Using these credentials, Demara now obtained a commission as lieutenant in the Royal Canadian Navy. His first assignment was to take sick call each morning at the base. To help solve his problem of lack of knowledge in the field, he went to his superior officer and told him that he needed material to prepare a thumb guide for people in lumber camps, where physicians are not usually immediately available. His superior cooperatively compiled a small booklet which Demara then used faithfully as his guide. He also studied medical books and evidently picked up considerable additional medical knowledge. In any event, when later assigned as medical officer aboard a destroyer in the combat zone in Korea, he successfully performed a number of difficult operations. When his ship was sent to Japan for refitting, an eager young press information officer seized on Dr. Cyr's exploits and gave them the full treatment. His copy was released to the civilian press and the "miracle doctor" became world famous. But the publicity proved to be his undoing, for it led to queries to the real Dr. Joseph Cyr as to whether the physician mentioned in the press release was a relative, and when Dr. Cyr saw the newspaper picture, he was shocked to find that it was his old friend.

Dropped from the Canadian Navy without fanfare—largely because he had managed to get a license to practice medicine in England and was now a licensed physician—Demara went through a difficult period. Wherever he went, he was soon recognized, and he lost job after job. He managed to work for a year at a state school for retarded children and did so well that he received a promotional transfer to a state hospital for the criminally insane. Here he found that the patients seemed to be attracted to him and that he was able to communicate with them. The experience began to bother him and he started to drink heavily and eventually resigned.

One morning after a prolonged drinking bout, he woke up in a Southern city and realized his drinking was getting out of hand. He joined the local chapter of Alcoholics Anonymous as Ben W. Jones, whose credentials he had acquired along the way. With the help of sympathetic friends in Alcoholics Anonymous and a few fraudulent references obtained by ingenious methods, he was hired as guard in a state penitentiary. Here he did a remarkable job, instituting a number of badly needed reforms in the maximal security block. Again he found himself able to communicate with the men, and he was promoted to assistant warden of maximal security. Ironically, one of his reform measures was to ask the townspeople to contribute old magazines, and before long one of the prisoners read the issue of *Life* which contained his picture and case history and recognized the new assistant warden.

Trying to get away lest he wind up as a prisoner in the same penitentiary, Demara was jailed in a nearby state and given considerable publicity but eventually released. Some time later he telephoned the author from whose book this material is adapted to say, "I'm on the biggest caper of them all. Oh, I wish I could tell you." (Adapted from Crichton, 1959)

ANXIETY. A diffuse feeling of dread, apprehension, and impending catastrophe.

Anxiety differs from fear on several counts. Although both are reactions to danger, in the case of fear the danger is external and directly perceived; in anxiety, its source is primarily internal and largely if not wholly unrecognized. Typically, fear is an intense response to a "clear and present danger," such as a mad dog or a combat situation. Anxiety, on the other hand, is a pervasive uneasiness experienced when we are threatened by unknown dangers from outside ourselves, or unconscious conflicts and impulses within ourselves.

In spite of these differences, fear and anxiety reactions tend to overlap. First, the physiological changes are similar in the two cases, since both involve accelerated heartbeat, rapid breathing, muscular tension, and other emergency responses. Second, many situations arouse mixed feelings of fear and anxiety—for example, a businessman who has encountered a series of reverses might fear the dangers he can anticipate and be anxious about those he cannot.

Most people develop a substantial capacity to bear anxiety—in fact, this is a necessary ingredient of mental health in a world that is full of danger and disturbance. The emotional support we receive from parents, as well as the mild doses of frustration and competition we experience in the course of growing up, help to increase our anxiety tolerance. We also learn to face our problems directly, and to recognize doubts and fears that make us feel uneasy. Likewise, we discover that everyone is subject to anxiety in one form or another, and that it is better to share our apprehensions with other people than to keep them entirely to ourselves. In these general ways we usually succeed in keeping anxiety under control.

Some people, however, develop persistent, painful feelings of anxiety which they cannot control with the ordinary techniques of adjustment. Anxiety of this kind stems from deeply embedded sources in the personality, such as dangerous impulses or severe emotional conflicts. A person may not even be aware that they exist; he only feels the distress of the anxiety they produce. As a result he may erect automatic, unconscious defenses to screen out or divert the anxiety—for example, he may insulate himself through apathy and indifference, or discharge his tensions through overactivity. These and other defense mechanisms may be partially successful, and in that case he merely remains mildly neurotic. But if they are inadequate and he is still threatened by anxiety, he may develop severe neurotic symptoms such as phobias, amnesia, or hysterical paralysis as a further attempt at self-protection. In one neurotic pattern, however, all defenses seem to be blocked or unused and the anxiety is experienced directly as the most prominent symptom. This condition is termed anxiety reaction, or anxiety neurosis. *See* ANXIETY REACTION, FREE-FLOATING ANXIETY, CASTRATION COMPLEX, SCHOOL PHOBIA.

ANXIETY HYSTERIA. A term applied by Freud to a neurosis characterized by anxiety and phobic reactions.

In this disorder the patient suffers from an irrational sense of dread arising from unconscious sources, and displaces this feeling onto specific objects or situations such as snakes, dirt, closed spaces, or crossing the street. Pierre Janet classified phobias with obsessions, since both reactions often occur in the same patient. He therefore used the term obsessive fear. Freud, however, felt that phobias are more akin to hysteria since the two conditions appeared to stem from similar basic conflicts, usually sexual in nature. He also found that phobia and hysteria sometimes occur together in patients who have anxiety attacks. For these two reasons he introduced the category of anxiety hysteria.

The term anxiety hysteria is still used by some psychoanalysts, but the American Psychiatric Association now classifies anxiety states separately under "anxiety reaction," and phobias under "phobic reaction." The term hysteria has largely been replaced by two categories: conversion reaction and dissociative reaction. *See* all these topics.

ANXIETY REACTION. A psychoneurotic disorder characterized by chronic anxiety and occasional eruptions of acute anxiety.

The chronic reaction is a persistent, distressing feeling of apprehensiveness and "catastrophic expectation," the feeling that something terrible is going to happen. Other prominent symptoms are general uneasiness, insomnia, difficulty in concentrating and making decisions, fear of making mistakes, together with loss of appetite, frequent nausea, heart palpitations, and raised blood pressure without apparent cause.

In acute attacks, the first symptoms are pounding of the heart, difficulty in breathing, excessive perspiration, trembling, and dizziness. At the peak of the reaction, the patient is thrown into a full-scale panic and experiences unbearable tension, fear of suffocation, and the feeling that he is going to die or that some horrible but unnamable disaster is going to descend upon him. He usually pleads for a doctor, who will probably give him reassurance and prescribe a sedative. The attack generally subsides in a few minutes but may recur without warning during the day or on waking from a sound sleep. Slight feelings of tension and apprehension are frequently experienced between attacks.

Anxiety reactions are responses to danger which the individual feels but does not recognize. These responses are out of proportion to any apparent cause. This is because they arise from situations touching sensitive areas deep within the personality—unresolved conflicts, forbidden impulses, disturbing memories—which threaten self-esteem and well-being. If the situations are sudden and overwhelming, the individual suffers acute anxiety attacks; if they are lower keyed but continuous, he finds himself in a chronic state of anxiety. In either case he does not consciously perceive the danger since it arises from below the level of consciousness. He therefore reacts only with the diffuse sense of dread and impending disaster that has aptly been termed "free-floating fear"—plus feelings of bodily tension which result from the fact that the organism automatically keys itself up to meet the threat.

Today most authorities believe that anxiety is at the root of all neurosis. The question then arises, why is the name anxiety reaction applied to only one of the many types of neurosis? The answer is that in anxiety reaction all the devices and defense mechanisms which are commonly used to ward off anxiety, such as compensation, projection, or rationalization, have failed or have never been utilized. Likewise, if the patient does not displace his anxiety upon specific fears (phobic reaction), transform it into bodily symptoms (conversion reaction), cut himself off from it through amnesia or dual personality (dissociative reaction), or screen it out by occupying himself with repetitious acts and ideas (obsessive-compulsive reaction), he is completely at the mercy of his anxiety.

It is not easy or even possible to explain why some individuals develop anxiety reactions rather than other types of neurosis. But numerous attempts have been made, since it is the most common psychoneurotic pattern, constituting 32 to 40 per cent of all these disorders. In general, it has been found that anxiety neurotics are hypersensitive, ineffectual individuals whose ability to withstand the usual stresses and demands of life has been impaired by faulty parental attitudes and disturbing experiences in childhood. In most cases their "ego strength" has been lowered, or has failed to develop, because they have been subjected to excessive and persistent criticism, or have been held to high and rigid standards which they could not possibly attain. As children, they were easily discouraged, overconcerned about making mistakes, continually upset by minor setbacks or vague fears and tensions. They usually show a history of disturbing dreams in which they are choked, shot at, or pursued by attackers who gradually catch up with them in spite of all efforts to escape.

As they grow older, these future anxiety neurotics become increasingly introverted, conscientious, and sensitive, and usually develop unrealistically high standards which lay them open to feelings of failure and guilt. As adults they tend to overreact to ordinary situations which other people can handle with a minimum of anxiety. Sudden changes in a routine, or moving from one area to another, are likely to "throw" them. A job promotion will produce a sense of dread and apprehension instead of happy excitement because it arouses latent feelings of anxiety or fears of failure. Difficult decisions and risky situations cause mild panic because of their sense of insecurity. Events that recall and reactivate the disturbing experiences of their childhood arouse uncontrollable anxiety.

Anxiety neurotics frequently endure their "psychic pain" for long periods with quiet courage—but always at great cost to happiness and effectiveness. They all need treatment. Tranquilizing drugs or other sedatives may be prescribed during acute attacks to make them feel more comfortable, but this is only symptomatic relief, and the only lasting remedy is insight therapy directed toward uncovering the sources of their feelings of dread. In some cases extended psychotherapy is needed to bring to the surface early experiences that have long been buried in the unconscious; in others short-term therapy may be sufficient to make the patient aware of his faulty behavior patterns and start him on the road to re-education. These techniques rarely eliminate the anxiety completely, but they often reduce it to a point where the patient can live with it. *See* ANXIETY.

The following is a particularly vivid first-person account of an anxiety attack:

Illustrative Case: ANXIETY REACTION

I had been feeling sort of tense all day—nothing out of the ordinary. My hands had been perspiring, and my head felt a little full and tight, and I didn't feel so comfortable and relaxed and in contact with people as I often do now.

I wasn't really prepared for what happened during the evening. I was sitting around with a small group of friends talking casually about this and that, when somebody mentioned something about homosexuality. Suddenly I began to sweat hard and my heart began to race; I could feel it pounding uncomfortably. I lost contact with everyone there and could pay attention only to myself and what I was feeling. I knew it was that homosexual business that had triggered it off, and I tried to get my mind off it, to tell myself not to be silly—there was nothing to be scared about.

By sheer will power I seemed to get control of myself, but I realized that I was more nervous now, even though I was talking with the group and trying to appear relaxed and at ease. I'm sure I looked relaxed enough and that no one knew what I was feeling inside. Somehow, I was afraid now of being afraid again; I was getting more and more anxious that someone was going to mention homosexuality again and set me off once more. To make a long story short, someone did and it really got me going. My heart began to race and pound; I began to sweat and felt as if I couldn't get enough air into my lungs. I can't quite describe that to you; it was as if something were expanding inside my chest and crowding everything else there out of the way; it made me want to take deep, rapid breaths—or to get to the window for fresh air. It was a feeling partly physical and partly of panic.

I don't know what I was afraid was going to happen. It was partly a fear that the other people there knew what was going on inside of me and that I'd make a fool of myself. But somehow during all of it I knew that people couldn't really know what I was feeling, and they really wouldn't care if they did. But that didn't help; this unnamable terror just seemed to take hold of me and I had the feeling I just *had* to get out of that room. I had to move; I had to do something; I just couldn't sit there any longer. I really can't tell you what I was scared of; not knowing was one of the worst parts of the whole thing. Well—I didn't move. I just sat there sweating it out, and pretty soon things began to quiet down. For the rest of the evening I was sort of tense, but I did not have any more of those terrible, panicky feelings. (Nemiah, 1961)

APHASIA. A loss or impairment of ability to communicate through language or speech due to brain injury or disease.

Aphasia takes two major forms. In *sensory, impressive, or receptive aphasia,* the ability to comprehend the meaning of words, signs, or gestures is impaired. In *motor or expressive aphasia,* understanding remains, but the ability to speak, write, or make meaningful gestures is lost. Although any form of aphasia is basically a neurological disorder, the problem comes within the province of psychology and psychiatry because of the vital importance of communication in mental health and human relationships.

Aphasia is one of the most varied disorders known. Any one or any combination of the many language functions can be affected, depending on the location and extent of the brain damage. The major causes of the damage are blocking of circulation by blood clots (thrombosis), brain tumors, inflammations due to infectious disease (encephalitis), or blows to the head. A large number of men suffered aphasic disorders during the world wars. The condition can occur at any age, but in the civilian population it is most frequent in the later decades when circulatory disease is most common.

The exact location of the brain damage which causes many types of aphasia is still in question, but most of the lesions are known to occur in the parietal and temporal lobes. Although in most instances only one or two speech functions are affected, there have been cases of massive lesions which disorganize both the receptive and expressive aspects of speech and produce total or "global" aphasia (Brain, 1951). In an extensive analysis of cases, Schuell et al. (1964), have recently challenged the idea that each type of aphasia results from injury to a specific part of the parieto-temporal area. They conclude that aphasia is "primarily a language deficit upon which various perceptual and sensory motor deficits concomitant with brain damage may or may not be superimposed." The patient, in their opinion, suffers from a generalized impairment in the ability to perceive and produce verbal messages. In many cases he does not understand words and sentences fully, and if asked to name an object such as a piece of furniture, he may not be able to say anything at all, or may say, after a long pause, "chair . . . no—bed, no—eat—no eat at the table—table—that's it, table."

Since a number of different kinds of aphasia are discussed under separate topics, we will merely list the major types here: (1) *alexia* or word blindness: inability to understand written language, inability to read; (2) *agraphia:* inability to translate verbal sounds into written symbols, inability to write; (3) *anomia* or *nominal aphasia:* difficulty in naming objects, conditions, and qualities; (4) *word deafness:* inability to understand spoken language, repeat spoken words, or write to dictation, although the ability to speak, write, and read spontaneously is preserved; (5) *central aphasia:* primarily a receptive aphasia characterized by defective appreciation of the meaning of words, both spoken and written, but also by inability to use the right words or grammar in speaking or writing; (6) *Broca's aphasia:* primarily an expressive aphasia in which the patient has difficulty uttering or writing words but may still be able to use gestures; (7) *word dumbness:* loss of voluntary speech even though inner speech is preserved—the patient cannot speak spontaneously, repeat words he hears, or read aloud, but all other speech functions such as silent reading and writing are normal; (8) *acalculia:* inability to use numbers in mathematical operations, although all other speech functions are intact; (9) *amimia:* inability to use or understand gestures, or to mimic the gestures of others; (10) *echolalia:* automatic, compulsive repetition of words uttered by others without understanding their meaning; like an infant learning to speak; (11) *amusia:* failure either to recognize familiar music (sensory amusia) or inability to sing, whistle, or hum a tune (motor amusia). *See* ALEXIA, ECHOLALIA, AMUSIA, ASTEREOGNOSIS, AGNOSIA, PARAPHASIA, JARGONAPHASIA, WORD BLINDNESS, MENTAL IMPAIRMENT TESTS.

APPARENT MOVEMENT. The perception of movement where no physical movement occurs.

A common example of apparent movement is the electrical advertising sign in which arrows seem to jump back and forth. The experienced movement is an illusion since there is no actual physical movement. This effect can be demonstrated by placing two lights of the right intensity at an appropriate distance from each other. If they are turned on and off at a certain time interval, a single light will be experienced as moving back and forth. This illusion of stroboscopic motion was termed "phi phenomenon" by the German psychologist Max Wertheimer in 1912.

Whenever the conditions for phi are set up, another type of apparent movement known as "gamma movement" may also be experienced. In this case a light apparently grows larger and approaches when its intensity is suddenly increased, and shrinks and recedes when its intensity is suddenly decreased. One way to produce these effects is to look fixedly at a light bulb as it is turned on or off.

Motion pictures are based on the illusion of apparent movement. Single still pictures are flashed on the screen in rapid succession, each registering a progressive step in the action being presented. If the succession of stills is exposed too slowly, the picture will flicker, but at the right speed flicker changes to fusion. This point is called "the critical flicker frequency," and is about fifteen to twenty frames per second for ordinary motion pictures. Early motion pictures were nicknamed "flickers" because film technology had not advanced far enough to produce a smooth fusion of frames.

Apparent movement can also be experienced in auditory and tactual sensation. If two similar tones, such as two shots or trumpet notes, are sounded in quick succession from slightly different directions, the first will appear to move toward the second. The same type of experience occurs when two spots on one's back, about two inches apart, are stimulated with a pointed object at an interval of about .1 second.

A pinpoint of light in a completely darkened room will also appear to move if we look at it fixedly. After a period of time it will seem to glide around, drift, or dart in sidewise and up-down gyrations. This illusion is called the autokinetic (self-movement) effect. If we watch a single star on a dark night,

we will usually have the same experience. Almost any small object, in fact, viewed against a homogeneous background will yield the same effect. This illusion can be a hazard in squadron flying at night, since steady fixation on the leader's wingtip may give rise to the faulty perception that he has changed his actual position. Pilots are therefore instructed to keep their eyes moving in order to prevent fixation on any single point.

The autokinetic effect has proved to be a valuable tool for investigating group dynamics. When individuals watch the light alone, there is considerable variation in the type and extent of movement they observe. But when the observations are made in groups, their reports tend to show increasing agreement. This demonstrates the influence of "normative" behavior in a social situation. Responses that might have deviated from the norm shift toward it due to the influence of the majority. If the group is told that words will be spelled out by the moving light, some subjects will even name a word they believe was traced.

Illusions of movement can also be produced by afterimages. The subject is first asked to stare at a drawing of a spiral that can be seen as either expanding or contracting. He will then find that the next object he looks at will appear to move in the direction opposite to the way he experienced the spiral. Watching a waterfall for a time will produce the same effect. At present there is no adequate explanation for these reactions. See AFTERIMAGE, SOCIAL NORM, GROUP DYNAMICS, WERTHEIMER.

APPLIED PSYCHOLOGY. A broad field of psychology covering the applications of psychological training and research to business and industry, diagnosis and therapy, counseling and guidance, education, medicine, law, and other areas of human behavior.

During the past two decades the

proportion of psychologists engaged in these areas has steadily increased, and today about two-thirds can be classed as applied psychologists, with the rest employed primarily in teaching and research. Of the twenty-nine divisions of the American Psychological Association, at least ten are largely concerned with applications, those having to do with clinical, consulting, and military psychology, industrial and business psychology, consumer psychology, engineering psychology, school psychology, public service, disability, and social issues. Members of these divisions work in a variety of locations: consulting firms advertising agencies, a wide range of business and industrial companies, state and Veterans Administration hospitals, outpatient clinics, counseling centers, schools, institutions for the mentally defective and the emotionally disturbed, training schools, prisons, military installations and civilian government agencies. Although they are likely to spend most of their time in service functions such as therapy, testing, and training, many of these psychologists are also engaged in applied research such as market surveys, evaluation of teaching methods, or studies of personnel selection procedures.

The first applications of psychology were made in business and industry, and the *Journal of Applied Psychology,* founded in 1917, is still concerned largely with these areas. Two of the early and most influential books on the subject were *Psychology of Advertising,* by Walter Dill Scott (1908) and *Psychology and Industrial Efficiency,* by Hugo Münsterberg (1913). Scott became interested in personnel selection and formed the first industrial consulting firm in this country; Munsterberg not only broadened the applications of psychology in business and industry, but also contributed to the psychology of law. *See* MÜNSTERBERG, LEGAL PSYCHOLOGY.

In its further development, industrial psychology was divided into two major areas: personnel psychology, which includes personnel selection, appraisal and training, and employee relations; and engineering psychology, which deals with work schedules, fatigue, work methods, the working environment, and the design of equipment. Advertising and consumer psychology have grown to a point where they have differentiated themselves from industrial psychology. They include such topics as the design and testing of ads, salesmanship, consumer surveys, motivation research, and studies of trade names and product images.

An entirely different area of applied psychology is clinical psychology, which grew out of mental testing and now includes diagnosis, treatment, and research in the field of emotional disorders. Counseling psychology includes not only personal counseling for relatively minor emotional difficulties, but also vocational, educational, employee, old age, and marital counseling.

In addition, the services of psychologists are utilized in three other professions: education, medicine, and law. Of the three, they are most heavily involved in the field of education, serving either as educational psychologists engaged in research and teacher training, or as school psychologists serving as counselors or as consultants to the administration of the school itself. Psychological contributions to medicine fall chiefly in the areas of psychodiagnosis, rehabilitation, psychosomatic studies, and preventive medicine, as well as research on psychotropic drugs, the nature of pain, and the psychological effects of illness and disability, an area sometimes called somatopsychology. The earliest application of psychology in the field of law dealt with the accuracy of testimony; more recently, psychologists have analyzed methods of detection, have developed lie detection apparatus, and have studied the factors that underlie crime and delinquency. Today they are serving in increasing numbers as expert witnesses, as diagnosticians and therapists in correctional institutions, and as consultants in the development of laws and legal policies. *See* SOMATOPSYCHOLOGY, EDUCATIONAL PSYCHOLOGY, CONSUMER PSYCHOLOGY, COUNSELING PSYCHOLOGY, MEDICAL PSYCHOLOGY, PERSONNEL SELECTION, ENGINEERING PSYCHOLOGY, CLINICAL PSYCHOLOGY, SCHOOL PSYCHOLOGY, ADVERTISING RESEARCH.

APRAXIA (literally, "inability to act or do"). Loss of ability to perform purposeful movements or manipulate common objects.

This disorder is caused by injury or disease which damages the parietal lobe of the brain. The injury does not produce paralysis or disturbances of sensation, but affects the memory for acts and skills. The apraxic individual cannot remember how to do things he has been doing all his life, such as tying his shoelaces, opening a door, driving a car, or eating with knife and fork. He can recognize objects and move his arms and legs but cannot put movements together into a useful pattern.

There are various types of apraxia, each tested by the types of activities mentioned in the following descriptions. In the *limb-kinetic type* the patient can appreciate and understand the kind of movement he wants to make, such as swinging a tennis racket, but cannot carry it out with accustomed skill. This disorder is usually limited to one limb or one side of the body, and results in extremely clumsy attempts at control. In the *idiokinetic type* the patient has no difficulty formulating the idea of the act he wishes to carry out, but finds that he is totally unable to execute it. His impulse simply will not translate itself into the appropriate movements. He may, for example, make a fist when he grasps objects automatically, but he cannot make a fist on command. The apraxia may be present on both sides or only on one side of the body. Sometimes the face is affected, and the individual cannot imitate a smile or any other expression at will.

Ideational apraxia consists in a failure to perform a complex series of actions because the patient has a distorted conception of the movement as a whole. In trying to light a cigar he might put the match in his mouth and rub the cigar against the matchbox. A person who is afflicted with the *constructive type* of apraxia, cannot reproduce simple patterns with matchsticks or blocks. An *apraxia for dressing* appears to be a separate category, sometimes occurring in isolation from the other types. The patient cannot choose or put on his clothes correctly because he is unable to relate the form of the garments to the shape of his body. (This is probably a blend of apraxia and agnosia, the inability to know or recognize objects or language.) *See* AGNOSIA.

APTITUDE TESTS (Multiple). A battery of separate tests designed to measure the basic components of intelligence.

Multiple aptitude tests are based on three observations. First, intelligence tests do not always measure the same abilities, and therefore an individual may score differently on different tests; second, some of the abilities measured on intelligence tests appear to be relatively independent aptitudes, since an individual might do consistently better on one part of the test than on another; and third, the usual intelligence tests do not cover every important intellectual function. As a result of these observations, psychologists have sought to identify all the basic abilities involved in intelligence. In so doing, they applied a procedure known as factor analysis, which consisted of three basic steps: (a) administration of tests on different functions to the same person; (b) a determination of the intercorrelations among the resulting scores; and (c) statistical analysis of the correlations to discover which abilities tended to cluster to-

SAMPLE ITEMS FROM MULTIPLE APTITUDE TESTS

PROBLEM FIGURES   ANSWER FIGURES

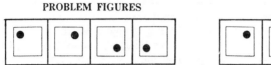 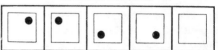

Fig. 3. Abstract Reasoning. The four "problem figures" make a series. Find the one among the "answer figures" which could be the next in the series.

gether and which were relatively independent.

When the basic abilities, or factors, were identified, aptitude tests were devised to measure them. Although different investigators have offered different combinations of tests, and different test items, the common purpose of multiple aptitude tests is to provide a more balanced and comprehensive measure of intelligence. To show the subject's strengths and weaknesses most graphically, a profile of scores rather than a single global I.Q. is computed.

The following batteries are in wide use today. (Sample items are not given here, since they are similar to those described under tests for intelligence and special aptitudes).

SRA Primary Mental Abilities (PMA) (Ages 5 to 7, 7 to 11, 11 to 17). These batteries are an outgrowth of Thurstone's Chicago PMA Tests (1941), which were based on his analysis of mental abilities into verbal comprehension, word fluency, number, space, as-

sociative memory, perceptual speed, and general reasoning. The SRA tests do not include all these factors in every battery. Research has shown that the tests for ages five to seven have little value since multiple aptitude batteries are ineffective in the primary level—in fact, differentiation of the child's abilities does not progress far enough to justify their use below the high school level. Critics find that the current batteries have a number of other serious weaknesses. They are oversimplified, depend excessively on speed, and do not present adequate normative or validity data. Their chief value is in illustrating Thurstone's factor theory.

Differential Aptitude Tests (DAT) (Ages 8 to 12, and unselected adults). Developed primarily for use in educational and vocational counseling, these tests yield scores for eight factors: verbal reasoning, numerical ability, abstract reasoning (*Fig. 3*), space relations (*Fig. 4*), mechanical reasoning (*Fig. 5*), clerical speed and accuracy, spelling,

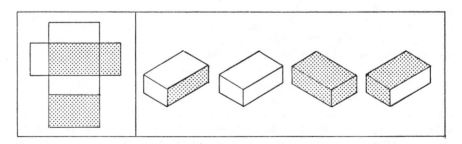

Fig. 4. Space Relations. Which of the figures on the right could be made by folding the given pattern?

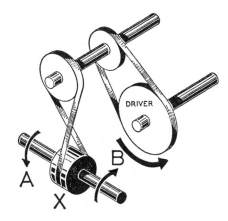

Fig. 5. Mechanical Reasoning. If the driver turns in the direction shown, which way will the pulley at "X" turn?

and sentence usage. Norms are based on a representative national sample, and reliability coefficients are high. A tremendous amount of validity data is available, most of which shows relatively high correlations with performance in high school and college. A combination of the scores on two of the tests, verbal reasoning and numerical ability, correlates so highly with grades that it may be effectively used as an intelligence (or at least a scholastic aptitude) test. The authors advocate a clinical rather than a statistical interpretation of scores, and in a case book, *Counseling From Profiles,* they show how they can be utilized in guiding students.

Flanagan Aptitude Classification Tests (FACT). Designed mainly for vocational counseling and employee selection, this battery is based on twenty-one "critical job elements" identified through job analysis. These elements were chosen because they differentiated successful

from unsuccessful workers on a variety of jobs. Tests were then created to measure each of the elements—for example, the "assembly" item shows parts of objects (*Fig 6*), and the subject selects one of five pictures in which they are correctly assembled. Some of the other elements are ingenuity, planning, carving, and tapping. *See* JOB ANALYSIS.

Norms have been established for grades nine to twelve, and the scores have been combined into thirty-eight occupational aptitude scores, including a score for general college aptitude, and scores for occupations ranging from plumber to humanities teacher. The reliabilities of the composite scores are higher than those for the individual tests, but they show considerable overlapping. This is to be expected for occupations as closely related as telephone operator and office clerk, which correlate .90, but not for airplane pilot and draftsman, which nevertheless have been found to correlate .95. The battery has proven effective in predicting success in occupational training, but there is as yet an insufficient amount of data on its ability to predict success on the job itself.

Guilford-Zimmerman Aptitude Survey. Constructed for counseling and personnel classification, this battery includes tests for (1) verbal comprehension, (2) general reasoning, (3) numerical operations, (4) perceptual speed, (5) spatial orientation, (6) spatial visualization, and (7) mechanical knowledge. Tests 1 and 2 can be combined to yield a score for abstract intelligence; 3 and 4 for clerical aptitude; and 5, 6, and 7 for mechanical aptitude. Two spatial tests are used because orientation is

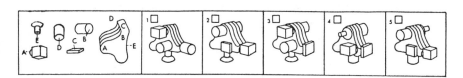

Fig. 6. Assembly. Which is the correct assembly of the parts at the left?

necessary for such operations as piloting a plane or running a machine, while visualization is involved in picturing objects as they would be when tilted or rotated. So far, validity studies show substantial correlations of tests 1 and 2 with grades in most courses, while scores on the numerical and space tests correlate with mechanical or scientific learning and with success in industrial training. Evidence of predictive validity for different occupations has not been offered.

Holzinger-Crowder Uni-Factor Tests. Based directly on factorial analysis, this battery provides tests for four sharply defined functions: verbal, spatial, numerical, and reasoning. The battery meets all technical requirements, and the norms are based on a large national sample of junior and senior high school students. The manual gives directions for combining the factor scores to predict general scholastic aptitude and performance in science, social studies, English, and mathematics. Evidence on differential validity is promising, and the tests are therefore considered useful in selecting educational and vocational areas.

Multiple Aptitude Tests (MAT). This battery presents nine well-constructed tests that yield scores in verbal comprehension, perceptual speed, numerical reasoning, and spatial visualization. The procedures for scoring and for evaluating resulting profiles are carefully handled. Like the DAT, the test is designed primarily for counseling, but there is as yet insufficient data on its effectiveness in predicting school grades or occupational performance.

General Aptitude Test Battery (GATB). Developed by the United States Employment Service for use by state employment counselors, this battery is the result of factorial analyses of preliminary tests given to large groups of trainees in vocational courses. After repeated revisions, the tests have been reduced to twelve, and the factors to

the following nine: intelligence (computed by adding the scores on the next three tests), verbal aptitude, numerical aptitude, spatial aptitude, form perception, clerical perception, motor co-ordination, finger dexterity, manual dexterity. The nine scores can be converted into standard scores, and can therefore be compared.

By testing large groups of employees and trainees, occupational ability patterns (OAP's) have been established, against which an individual's profile score can be matched. For instance, plumbing requires a minimum score of 85 for intelligence and 80 for numerical aptitude, spatial aptitude, and manual dexterity. The OAP's so far developed cover over five hundred occupations, and the test is now used in counseling about a half million applicants each year, not only in State Employment offices but in colleges, VA hospitals, prisons, and other nonprofit organizations. A huge amount of validity data has been reported in the Validity Information Exchange published in *Personnel Psychology*.

In general, the GATB is considered highly effective, although it has certain limitations: the tests are greatly speeded, mechanical comprehension is omitted, and reasoning and creativity do not receive sufficient attention.

Employee Aptitude Survey Test Series. This battery consists of ten brief, easily administered business and industry tests validated against performance on different jobs: the Verbal Comprehension Test, for executive and high-level office workers; the Numerical Ability Test, for supervisors, accountants, clerical workers; the Visual Pursuit Test (tracing lines), for draftsmen, checkers, technicians; the Visual Speed and Accuracy Test, for bookkeepers, stenographers, machine operators; the Space Visualization Test, for engineers, draftsmen, technicians; the Numerical Reasoning Test, for technical and supervisory positions; the Verbal Reasoning

Test, for administrative and technical decision-making positions; the Word Fluency Test of Oral and Written Expression, for journalists, salesmen, secretaries, executives; the Manual Speed and Accuracy Test, for clerical workers, technicians, and machine operators; and the Symbolic Reasoning Test, for data-programmers, accountants, engineers, and other high-level personnel.

APTITUDE TESTS (Professions). Tests designed for the selection of students for professional training in such fields as medicine, law, engineering, dentistry, teaching, accounting, nursing, and theology.

Some authors classify these instruments as aptitude tests, since they measure capacity for specialized training; others consider them achievement tests, since they are based largely on material and techniques learned in preprofessional courses. In general, these tests do not measure special abilities that are not covered by other tests. Instead, they measure general mental capacities needed for higher education and any professional work, plus the type of information, skill, and approach required for the particular profession involved. When possible they should be locally validated because of differences in curricula, standards, and student populations throughout the country.

Medical College Admissions Test (MCAT). The test consists of four separately scored parts: (1) *verbal:* including vocabulary and reading comprehension tests in science, social studies, and the humanities; (2) *quantitative:* mathematical problems involving numbers and symbols, requiring reasoning and utilization of given facts; (3) *understanding modern society:* multiple-choice questions on current economic, social, and political events; (4) *science:* information and interpretation questions on premedical courses in physics, chemistry, and biology. The tests on modern society are included because the MCAT is de-

signed to predict performance as a physician in our culture rather than merely to predict performance in medical school courses. This is probably one of the reasons why correlations between test scores and class rank have been under .40.

Iowa Legal Aptitude Test. The battery includes seven subtests: analogies, mixed relations, opposites, memory for the factual content of a judicial opinion read two hours earlier, judging relevancy of legal arguments, reasoning, and legal information (included on the assumption that students interested in law would have acquired common legal facts on their own). Three of these tests (reasoning, relevancy, and legal information) are now used as a short form, since they have been found to yield a slightly higher multiple correlation with law school grades than the entire battery.

Law School Admission Test (LSAT). This battery, constructed by the Educational Testing Service, has been administered to candidates on a national basis since 1948. A single score is computed from the following subtests: Principles and Cases (judging the relevance of given principles to described cases); Data Interpretation (through the use of charts, tables, and graphs); Reading Comprehension (answering questions on passages of general content); Reading Memory (answering questions without referring back to the passages); Writing Ability (recognizing errors in grammar, diction, etc.); Organization of Ideas (classifying sets of statements as central, main supporting, irrelevant, or illustrative fact); Finding Classification (a nonverbal perception and reasoning test); and General Background (questions on humanities, social studies, physical and biological sciences).

In contrast to the Iowa Test, the LSAT does not include any subtest on actual legal information. It is intended for predicting achievement in law school rather than in the profession itself. The test yields correlations of between .40 and .60 with first year law school grades in different institutions, and .55 to .75 when combined with undergraduate grades. Correlations with grades in the third year are about the same in spite of the greater homogeneity of the student groups in the later years.

Engineering and Physical Science Aptitude Test. A group of six previously developed and standardized tests is used: mathematics (algebra), algebraic formulation of scientific information, physical science information, arithmetical reasoning, scientific vocabulary, and comprehension of mechanical relationships and problems presented pictorially. Comparison of scores with college grades in introductory engineering subjects yields a reasonably high validity; correlations are higher with the more scientific subjects of physics and chemistry than with applied engineering.

The Pre-Engineering Ability Test contains two sections: (1) comprehension of scientific materials, consisting of reading and answering questions on scientific selections, tables, and graphs; and (2) general mathematical ability, including arithmetic, algebra, and geometry. The emphasis in the first section is on understanding rather than factual information, although familiarity with physical science concepts is an advantage.

The Minnesota Engineering Analogies Test (MEAT) is a more advanced test designed for candidates for jobs and admission to graduate schools, and is administered only at approved centers. It consists of analogies items dealing with scientific and mathematical material selected largely from engineering courses taken in the first two years of undergraduate work. Scores correlate .40 to .60 with grades and faculty ratings in undergraduate and graduate courses. Correlations are somewhat lower (about .30) with salaries and job ratings, since the test is limited to sci-

entific and mathematical reasoning, and additional abilities are needed in actual engineering practice.

Advanced Test in Engineering. This is one area of the Graduate Record Examinations, designed for testing graduate school candidates. It focuses on educational achievement, since it measures the information, principles, and problem-solving abilities acquired by the student in his high school and college courses. *See* below.

Dental Aptitude Testing Program. Developed by the American Dental Association in co-operation with the American Association of Dental Schools, this battery has been adopted by all dental schools. It includes measures of mechanical aptitude as well as academic material, since both are required for success in dental school training. One part of the battery consists of a spatial visualization test (similar to the Minnesota Paper Form Board; *see* SPECIAL APTITUDE TESTS), and a work sample test in which the candidate carves geometric patterns in chalk. Other parts include a reading comprehension test in the natural sciences, an achievement test measuring information and application of principles in biology and chemistry, and the ACE Psychological Examination, which yields separate linguistic and quantitative scores and permits comparison with other college and university students. Score profiles are constructed for each applicant, and different combinations of scores have yielded multiple correlations of .57 to .79 with grades in dental schools, and somewhat higher correlations when combined with previous grades. The test, however, should be validated for individual schools in view of the variations in students, graduating standards, and curricula throughout the country.

National Teacher Examinations. Developed and conducted by the Educational Testing Service, this program is used both in selecting teachers and in assessing the effectiveness of training programs. Two general types of tests are represented. The Common Examinations cover general competence for teaching and include tests on professional information, social studies, literature, fine arts, science and mathematics, English expression, and nonverbal reasoning. The Optional Examinations cover specialized areas, and are available in such fields as elementary school education, early childhood education, English language and literature, mathematics, physical sciences, biological sciences, social studies, art education, home economics, physical education, industrial arts, and music education. Both types emphasize understanding and application of knowledge rather than memory for facts.

Standard or "scaled" scores are computed, and compared with percentile norms on the basis of a nationwide sample tested each year. The major emphasis is on content validity (content analysis and internal consistency) but some data are available showing correlations in the fifties between test scores and ratings of effectiveness in teaching. Since the scores reflect only knowledge and understanding, they must be supplemented with information on attitudes, motivation, specific experience, emotional adjustment, and other factors which materially affect teacher effectiveness.

Teaching Aptitude Test. A test devised by F. A. Moss and others for counseling high school seniors, college, and education students. Its object is to measure judgment, reasoning, and information relative to teaching situations, as well as comprehension and retention of reading matter.

Graduate Record Examinations (*GRE*). This testing program is administered in two ways: as a national program for graduate school selection to be used for admissions as well as scholarships and fellowships; and as an institutional testing program to be applied by colleges and universities themselves for such purposes as student guidance, admission to candidacy for a degree, and evaluation of instruction. In both cases the tests are scored and retained by the Educational Testing Service.

Three types of tests are given. First, an aptitude test, which is basically a general intelligence or scholastic aptitude test, yielding separate verbal and quantitative scores. Second, area tests in social science, humanities, and natural science, and constituting a general achievement battery at the college level. Third, advanced tests in different fields of specialization, among them biology, chemistry, economics, education, engineering, French, geology, government, history, literature, mathematics, music, philosophy, physics, psychology, scholastic philosophy, sociology, Spanish, and speech.

GRE scores are all directly comparable, since they are based on a standard scale with a mean of 500. This scale has been "anchored" to aptitude test scores of a large group of seniors in eleven colleges. However, since there are consistent differences in the caliber of students majoring in different subjects, the percentiles for individual groups such as physics or English majors should be taken into account—and local norms would also be desirable. Reliability coefficients for different student samples are generally high. Many studies have been made in which scores are compared with grade school performance, instructor's ratings, and scores on Ph.D. qualifying examinations. In general, the validities are not much higher than for undergraduate grades taken alone; but when GRE scores and grades are combined, the multiple correlations are usually in the middle sixties, which is better than can be obtained by using the grades alone.

APTITUDE TESTS (Special). Tests designed to measure specific, concrete abilities, as contrasted with the more general and abstract capacities covered by standard intelligence tests.

The impetus to create special aptitude tests came from two major sources. First, the need for information on specific skills and abilities, to be used in vocational counseling and personnel selection and classification. Second, the development of factor analysis, which showed that intelligence itself comprises a broad range of relatively independent abilities, such as verbal comprehension, numerical reasoning, and spatial visualization. These two factors led to the development of tests which measure special capacities required for meeting practical situations.

Aptitude tests fall into the following three categories: (a) tests for business and industry, including sensory tests of vision and hearing, motor tests, mechanical aptitude tests, and clerical tests; (b) esthetic aptitude tests (music, art, literary appreciation); and (c) tests for the professions (medicine, law, teaching, and engineering). The first category will be discussed in this topic; for the others, see MUSIC TESTS, ART TESTS, APTITUDE TESTS (PROFESSIONS).

Sensory Tests. In testing vision, several different functions must be measured. Wall charts are most commonly used for testing far acuity: the Snellen Chart presents rows of letters gradually decreasing in size, and the subject reads as many as he can from a standard distance of twenty feet. Charts showing pictures, dots, or diagrams rather than letters are used with preschool children, older children with reading disability, and illiterate adults. As 20/20 vision is average, 20/100 means that the subject has to be as close as 20 feet to perceive material which the average person can identify at 100 feet. Another device for measuring acuity is the Landolt Ring, consisting of capital letter C's, with gaps of varying size placed in various orientations. The subject is required to indicate the position of the break from a standard distance. See VISUAL ACUITY.

Several instruments have been developed for large-scale testing of different visual functions: the Ortho-Rater (PLATE 39), the Sight-Screener, Protometer, and the Telebinocular. Each of these provides measures of near and far acuity, depth perception, lateral and vertical phoria (muscular balance), and color discrimination.

Tests conducted by the army have shown that the Snellen Chart is somewhat more reliable for far acuity, or "retinal resolution," than the machine tests; but the checkerboard pattern used on the Ortho-Rater is more effective than presentation of letters, since some letters are more readily identified than others. Also, the Snellen Chart is inadequate for detecting farsightedness or cases of muscular imbalance. (Tests for color blindness are discussed under that topic.)

The sense of hearing also includes several different functions. Acuity is again the most crucial, but tolerance for loud sounds and recognition of words against a noisy background are also important in certain situations. The simplest—and crudest—tests are the whispered speech and watch tick techniques, in which the examiner gradually increases or decreases his distance from the subject in order to determine his auditory threshold. The whispered speech test has the advantage of checking acuity in understanding words, and the watch tick test has the value of sampling the high frequencies where loss of hearing often starts. Such tests, however, lack uniformity and are affected by sounds in the background.

Far more effective are the electronic audiometer devices. The pure tone audiometer is generally used for individual testing, presenting tones of increasing and decreasing intensity to one ear at a time. The subject indicates when he can just barely hear or no longer hear the sound. Hearing levels can be read from a dial calibrated in decibels, and an audiogram chart is constructed for each ear. Because of the importance of understanding speech, there are also speech audiometers which present numbers, words, and sentences instead of pure tones. This technique is used in the "fading numbers test" for group administration via phonograph records. However, it has the distinct disadvantage of failing to explore differential hearing loss at different frequency levels. A child may therefore score in the normal range on the speech test, yet have a severe hearing loss at higher (or occasionally lower) frequencies. The present trend, therefore, is to adapt the pure tone audiometer to group administration by the use of headphones worn by each subject.

Motor Tests. These tests measure manipulative skills required primarily for industrial and military activities. Practically all of them involve the use of apparatus, and a few are of the "job miniature" type. In general, the correlations between the different tests are low, indicating that motor functions are highly specific. The following are some of the most widely used motor tests.

The O'Connor Finger Dexterity and Tweezer Dexterity Tests measure simple hand and finger movements by requiring the subject to insert pins into small holes by hand or with tweezers. Both tests are fairly valid for jobs demanding these specific manipulations. The Crawford Small Parts Dexterity Test covers several skills: use of tweezers in inserting pins and placing collars on them, and the use of a screw driver in tightening screws (PLATE 3). The Purdue Pegboard Tests involve, first, insertion of pins into holes with the right, left, and both hands in successive trials; and second, assembling pins, collars, and washers, using both hands simultaneously.

The Minnesota Rate of Manipulation Test requires, first, the insertion of sixty cylindrical blocks into sixty circular holes; and second, removal of each block and returning it to its hole with the other hand. In the Stromberg Dexterity Test, red, yellow, and blue blocks are arranged on a board in a standard order, and the subject inserts them into other sections of the board in a specified sequence. The Bennett Hand Tool Dexterity Test is designed to check proficiency in the use of ordinary mechanic's tools by having the subject remove a number of nuts and bolts from one upright piece of wood, and mount them on another upright in a prescribed sequence. In addition, a wide variety of tests have been devised primarily for research use, though they are occasionally incorporated into industrial batteries: speed of tapping, bodily sway, strength of grip, reaction time, steadiness.

Mechanical Aptitude Tests. These tests frequently overlap with motor tests, since many of them involve manipulation. However, the major emphasis is on perceptual and spatial aptitudes, and mechanical reasoning or information. Spatial and perceptual skills are stressed on tests of the formboard, puzzle, and paper-and-pencil variety; mechanical reasoning and information are the major abilities required on the assembly tests and on paper-and-pencil tests involving application of scientific principles. Here are some representative examples of each type:

The Minnesota Spatial Relations Test consists of four formboards into which variously shaped cutouts must be inserted. It is scored for both time and errors. The Minnesota Paper Form Board (*Fig. 7*) presents a series of

Fig. 7. Minnesota Paper Form Board, used in testing mechanical ability. Can the figures at the right be put together to form the square on the left?

figures cut into two or more parts, and in each item the subject must choose a drawing which could be made out of all the parts fitted together. Studies involving performance in shop and engineering courses, as well as production records in industry indicate that this test is particularly accurate in measuring the ability to visualize and manipulate objects in space. The Spatial Relations Test in the DAT battery has been found useful in gauging three-dimensional visualization. *See* APTITUDE TESTS (MULTIPLE).

The MacQuarrie Test for Mechanical Ability comprises seven subtests: Tracing, Tapping, Dotting (placing dots in circles), Copying (copying a given figure by joining dots), Location, Blocks (counting certain blocks in a pile), and Pursuit (following twisting lines with the eye). The test emphasizes spatial ability and manual dexterity, and validity studies for individual subtests or combinations of them indicate that they are fairly accurate in predicting different types of industrial performance.

The most widely applied test of the assembly variety is the Minnesota Mechanical Assembly Test, in which the subject is required to put together common objects, such as a bicycle bell. The full form of the test has yielded a high odd-even reliability (.94), and a correlation of .53 with performance in shopwork. Since it is not feasible to apply this test to a large number of subjects at one time, pictorial tests of mechanical comprehension have also been devised. The Mellenbruch Mechanical Motivation Test requires the subject to match pictures of mechanical objects, or parts of objects, that belong together.

The Bennett Test of Mechanical Comprehension puts more emphasis on the understanding of mechanical principles, and is offered in several forms—one for high school boys and unselected adults, another for engineering school applicants, another for women and still another for individuals at high ability levels. A sample item from the least difficult form shows two types of shears, and asks which would be better for cutting metal. The test has proved to be fairly valid in predicting success in training and performance on many mechanical jobs, and was one of the best predictors of pilot success in World War II.

The SRA Mechanical Aptitudes Test comprises three subtests; one measures mechanical knowledge by requiring the subject to identify different tools; the second uses the principle of fitting pieces together to test space relations; and the third measures shop arithmetic by presenting problems involving the use of tables and diagrams. The tests can be scored separately or combined into a single score. The shop arithmetic test has proved particularly valid in predicting success in trade and vocational schools.

Clerical Aptitude Tests. These are largely tests of perceptual speed. The Minnesota Clerical Test consists of two separately timed subtests. The Number Comparison Test presents two hundred pairs of numbers containing from three to twelve digits, and the subject places a checkmark between the pairs he judges to be identical. The Name Comparison Test is built on the same principle, but presents names instead of numbers. Speed is emphasized on both, but since deductions are made for errors, it has been found that some subjects tend to work more cautiously than others, and this must be taken into account in interpreting the scores. Correlations between scores and ratings by supervisors and teachers as well as performance records are moderately high. Even though clerical work involves far more functions than this test measures, studies have shown that a large proportion of time is spent on activities that require the kind of speed and accuracy for detail which the test emphasizes. The Minnesota test has also been found useful in predicting the performance of other employees such as inspectors, packers, and checkers, whose work requires similar perceptual skills.

Some clerical tests combine perceptual speed and accuracy with other functions required in clerical work. An example of a test that uses the work-sample principle is the Psychological Corporation General Clerical Test, which includes checking and alphabetizing, arithmetic, computation, error location, arithmetic reasoning, spelling, reading comprehension, vocabulary, and grammar. Other composite tests are the Turse Clerical Aptitude Test, the SRA Clerical Aptitude Test, Short Employment Tests, Short Tests of Clerical Ability, Purdue Clerical Adaptability Test, and the Clerical Speed and Accuracy Test of the DAT.

In addition, aptitude tests have been developed for predicting ability to learn typing and shorthand. Among them are the Turse Shorthand Aptitude Test, the E.R.C. Stenographic and Aptitude Test, the Typing Test for Business (typing copy, plus specialized tests involving correspondence, manuscript revision, editorial symbols, statistical tables), and Flanagan's Tapping Test for Predicting Performance in Typing Courses. In the last named test, the subject's fingers are assigned different letters, and each finger is covered with a felt dot which makes a differently colored mark on the answer sheet. The test involves the use of the fingers in tapping out words, just as the subject would do in actual typing. So far, predictions based on this test appear to be quite accurate.

Sales Aptitude Tests. Three tests have been developed by M. M. Bruce in the field of salesmanship. The brief, objective Aptitudes Associates Test of Sales Aptitude is widely used in selecting sales personnel. The Sales Comprehension Test is designed to assess ability to sell by measuring the subject's understanding and appreciation of sales principles. The easily administered and scored Sales Motivation Inventory focuses on appraisal of interests and drives related to sales work. *See* MUSIC TESTS, ART TESTS, CREATIVITY TESTS, SALESMANSHIP.

ARACHNODACTYLY (Marfan's syndrome). A rare inherited disorder characterized by long limbs and spidery hands and feet (the term means "spidery fingers"), and usually associated with mild mental deficiency. Other clinical manifestations are multiple skeletal anomalies, ocular anomalies such as dislocation of the lenses, and cardiac defects. The condition varies from case to case and is probably due to a dominant gene. *See* MENTAL RETARDATION (CAUSES).

ARETAEUS (c. A.D. 30–90). Little is known of the life of this great physician other than the fact that he was born in the small kingdom of Cappadocia in Asia Minor, and practiced medicine in Imperial Rome. We do know, however, that he was a penetrating and accurate observer of mental disorders and anticipated a number of the basic concepts of modern psychiatry.

Aretaeus' clinical accounts of mania and melancholia indicate that the disorder we now know as manic-depressive psychosis existed in essentially the same form in antiquity. His picture of the manic's overconfident, hyperactive behavior, and the melancholic's preoccupation with guilt feelings, self-sacrifice, and religious ideas would stand up well today. He recognized that there was a connection between these two states, and correctly observed that melancholia is not always followed by mania. He also noted that young people are more susceptible to mania and older people to melancholia, and that spontaneous recovery from these conditions is rarely lasting.

Aretaeus gave accurate descriptions of a number of other clinical entities and apparently followed up his cases in order to establish a prognosis for each type. He contributed to what would now be called differential diagnosis by presenting a clinical picture of agitated depression, senile disorders, and mental deterioration. He also distinguished between patients who were manic and melancholic and those who appeared "stupid, absent, and musing," a condition we now recognize as one type of schizophrenic reaction.

So far as we know, Aretaeus did not propose any new methods of treatment, but some of his ideas on etiology were distinctly in advance of his time. He apparently rejected the notion that mental illness is a sign of divine inspiration, and recognized both physical and psychological determinants. He attributed mania to hot, dry blood, and the "absent, musing condition" to refrigeration. Although these ideas are understandably crude, he adumbrated Galen's concept of "consensus," as well as the modern idea of the organism as a unitary system, by suggesting that a mental disease may originate in the abdomen and spread secondarily to the head.

Aretaeus' comments on the psychological factors underlying mental illness are even more impressive. He reported a severe case of melancholia in which the individual recovered fully after falling in love. He analyzed the ravings of manic patients and showed that they were not suddenly possessed of new, divinely inspired knowledge of poetry or geometry, but confined themselves to matters which they had already studied. And, more important, Aretaeus discovered that psychotic behavior of this kind is not a sudden metamorphosis but an extension of pre-existing tendencies—for example, he observed that people who develop mania are "naturally irritable, violent, easily given to joy, of a facile spirit for pleasant and childish things." Here was a clear and cogent anticipation of the modern concept of the premorbid personality.

ARISTOTLE (384–322 B.C.). Aristotle, whose work *De Anima* is considered the first treatise on psychology, was born in Stagira, Greece. As the son of a physician he acquired an early interest in zoology and physiology. Between the ages of seventeen and thirty-seven he studied at the philosophical school of Plato, the Academy, and probably remained to teach rhetoric and scientific subjects. Although chosen as Plato's successor, he refused this post and set up a small Platonic group on the island of Lesbos instead. From 343–336 he served as tutor to Alexander the Great, and from 335–323 he headed the Peripatetic School in Athens. When Alexander suddenly died in 323, he fled under political pressure to Chalcis on the island of Euboea, where he died the following year.

The scope of Aristotle's work is so immense that we can only indicate the major areas in which he influenced psychological thinking. One of the most important is the fact that he conceived of the psyche as part of the natural rather than the supernatural world: "The soul's study falls within the science of nature." For this reason his *De Anima,* though a work on the soul, was included among his physical rather than his metaphysical writings. In contrast to Plato, who viewed the soul only in its relation to the "Good" and "ideas," Aristotle considered it in some sense the "principle of animal life," and claimed that matter and form— the physical and mental—are always found together. He even described form as the actualization of matter. More specifically, he believed that the soul or psyche is the activity or functioning of the body: "The soul is to the body as cutting is to the axe." This concept was of great significance in later psychology, since it was based on an essential and functional relationship between mind and body.

Aristotle studied many of the activities of the soul, including the senses, learning, memory, emotion, imagination, and reasoning. He believed that these processes occupy positions on a single scale of nature in which plants are characterized by nutritive functions, animals by sensitive functions, and man by rational functions. In keeping with his view that matter is potentiality and form actuality, he claimed that the qualities inherent in objects became actualized as sensations of color, taste, smell, etc. There is therefore an integral relationship between the object's potential and the power of the sense organ. The sensory process itself was explained in somewhat mechanical terms, since he claimed that qualities are carried or communicated by the blood. Perception, too, was conceived as an activity of the soul carried out through the agency of the body. It consists in the communication of the form of the perceived object to the perceiving subject.

In addition to the particular qualities conveyed by the individual sense organs, Aristotle also claimed that certain qualities—unity, number, size, shape, time, rest, motion—are perceived through a "common sense" in which images produced by the individual sense organs are united. The organ of the common sense is the heart, and the medium through which the "motions" of the sense organs reach it is "pneuma" or breath. If the motion of the sense organ continues beyond the actual perception, it is called memory. Beyond these functions, man, and man alone, possesses "nous" or reason, which enables him to apprehend the highest truths. The connection between this activity and the animal soul, however, is not described.

In the light of the history of thought, Aristotle's account of the relation between body and soul has a double significance. First, he implied that the soul or psyche cannot be understood except by studying the physical functions, the body. And second, even though he did not actually perform experiments, his view that number, size, unity, etc., are "sensibles" made them at least theoretically amenable to experimental as well as physiological study. But it was not until the nineteenth century that men like Gustav Fechner and Ernst Weber actually engaged in this type of scientific research. See FECHNER.

ARTERIOSCLEROSIS. A thickening and hardening of the walls of the arteries, usually occurring in old age.

Arteriosclerosis interferes with the flow of blood, producing such physical symptoms as weakness, dizziness, syncope (fainting spells), cold extremities, high blood pressure, and in extreme cases apoplectic attacks and heart disease. Among the mental symptoms associated with hardening of the arteries of the brain (cerebral arteriosclerosis) are gradual loss of memory, difficulty in thinking, and when far advanced, general intellectual deterioration and confusion.

Cerebral arteriosclerosis is of particular interest to neurologists and psychiatrists, since it is associated with many cases of mental disorder in old age. It was long maintained that the seriousness of the mental disorder is directly related to the severity of the arteriosclerotic condition. However, recent studies indicate that in most cases there is very little relationship between the extent of the mental disorder and the degree of neurological damage. Some patients with slight damage become extremely ill; others with extensive damage show few signs of psychological impairment. Apparently the patient's personality and power of adjustment determine to a large extent how he reacts to the physical impairment.

Cerebral arteriosclerosis is one of the two conditions which account for the great majority of psychotic disorders of older people, the other being senile brain disease. See ARTERIOSCLEROTIC

BRAIN DISORDER, SENILE PSYCHOSIS (GENERAL), SYNCOPE, VERTIGO.

ARTERIOSCLEROTIC BRAIN DIS-ORDER.

A psychotic disorder caused by hardening of the arteries in the brain; classified by The American Psychiatric Association (1952) as "Chronic Brain Syndrome associated with cerebral arteriosclerosis."

A substantial percentage of psychosis occurring in later life is due to constriction or blocking of the cerebral arteries. This condition reduces the flow of blood which brings nutrition to the brain, resulting in damage to neural tissue and loss of mental functions. The term arteriosclerosis is somewhat loosely used in this connection to cover both the hardening of cerebral arteries and the narrowing of these blood vessels due to the formation of "plaques," or patches of fatty and calcified material on their inside walls. The latter condition is known specifically as atherosclerosis, and is believed to be more directly reponsible for the reduction of blood circulation than is a simple hardening of the arteries, since the deposits narrow the opening or "lumen" of the blood vessels. Brain circulation may be slowed by these deposits but also by blood clots clinging to the inside walls of the arteries (cerebral thrombosis), or by sloughed-off material carried to a narrow point in the arterial system (embolisms).

Blockage of the flow of blood may in some cases cause a rupture of blood vessels and consequent hemorrhage. If small blood vessels are involved, a "small stroke" occurs. A single stroke may lead to temporary mental and physical symptoms, but a series of these strokes may result in cumulative brain damage. If a large blood vessel is blocked or ruptured, a major stroke or "cerebral vascular accident" is suffered, leading not only to a confusional state or coma, but to serious and usually permanent loss of brain functions—if the patient survives at all.

These disorders are on the increase because of the lengthening span of life. The number of victims in this country is estimated at two million men and women at present. Not infrequently cerebrovascular disease leads to serious mental illness—"psychosis with cerebral arteriosclerosis"—and this disorder ranks second to schizophrenia, constituting about 12 per cent of all first admissions to mental hospitals in 1965. The onset of the psychosis usually occurs after fifty-five years of age, and the age at first admission is about seventy-four years for both sexes, with males slightly outnumbering females.

The clinical picture in these psychoses is greatly varied, since the symptoms depend on the nature and extent of brain damage as well as the pre-illness personality and life situation of the patient. Over half of all patients suffer a sudden attack as a result of a cerebral vascular accident, and are brought to the hospital in a state of acute confusion. They continue to show such symptoms as clouding of consciousness, disorientation, incoherence, excitement, and restlessness. About 50 per cent become temporarily paralyzed on one side of the body (hemiplegia). If these patients survive the acute attack, their symptoms usually subside in time but leave some residual mental and physical impairment.

Many patients, however, suffer from a series of small strokes instead of a large or apoplectic stroke and develop such physical symptoms as acute indigestion, unsteadiness in walking, aphasia, and changes in handwriting. Accompanying these effects are such psychological symptoms as irritability, intense concern with bodily functions, and general mental deterioration. Additional strokes may bring on periods of delirium, incoherence, paralysis, and convulsions. Their combined effect is to weaken the patient to a point where he has to remain in bed. He usually succumbs within three to five years as a result of pneumonia, heart attack, or another stroke.

Where onset is gradual, the initial symptoms are likely to be fatigue, headache, dizziness, memory defect, inability to concentrate, drowsiness late in the day, and reduced mental and physical efficiency. Some patients are subject to syncopal attacks (fainting spells). In most cases there is also a noticeable character change or exaggeration of previous personality tendencies. As the disease slowly progresses these patients may become irritable, jealous, suspicious, and flare up at the slightest provocation, after which they tearfully apologize. They also lose their initiative, neglect their appearance, and have a fixed expression on their faces. As mental deterioration sets in, they lose their power to concentrate, remember names, or do productive work of any kind. As in senile dementia, judgment is increasingly impaired, control of behavior is relaxed, and sexual indiscretions may be attempted, particularly with children. *See* SYNCOPE.

The general physical, mental, and moral decline of the advanced arteriosclerotic patient cannot be distinguished from the deterioration that occurs in senile dementia. Sometimes the two disorders may be present at once. In the less advanced stages, however, differential diagnosis is usually possible. Cerebral arteriosclerosis often sets in earlier in life and develops and runs its course more rapidly, especially when a vascular accident occurs. Intellectual impairment is less marked than in senile dementia. The patient usually has some recognition that he is failing both physically and mentally, and therefore is likely to develop depressive rather than paranoid reactions. Headaches, dizziness, convulsive seizures, and emotional lability are more common in arteriosclerotic patients, and there is usually greater fluctuation in the course of the disease.

This fluctuation is probably due to the fact that a series of minor hemorrhages frequently occurs, with relative absence of symptoms between attacks. If the course of the disorder is gradual, the patient may profit from rehabilitation procedures. Tranquilizing drugs are frequently administered to reduce insomnia, restlessness, and confusion. A balanced regimen of physical activity, good nutrition, recreation, and rest will help these patients maintain some sense of well-being as long as possible.

Illustrative Case: ARTERIOSCLEROTIC BRAIN DISORDER

L.A., white male, fifty-seven, admitted on court order for observation. Complained that, "I have weak spells, I've had them for four years. I get dizzy, sometimes I think it's my mind. My family upsets me all the time."

Developmental history is that of individual with sixth-grade education, no serious illnesses or accidents, outgoing social interests; marriage compatible until about four years ago. Farmed all his life.

Family history significant in that mother and one sister died of "apoplexy."

Examination upon admission showed neat, well-nourished male of stated age who displayed prominently emotional lability, weeping frequently but quickly shifting to different mood level. Talk coherent and relevant; displayed a defensive attitude with definite paranoid trends. Admitted increased irritability for four years and said he occasionally lost his temper. Was preoccupied with wife's supposed infidelity and accused children of wanting him "out of the way." Believed they purposely did things to antagonize and upset him. Hallucinations were not elicited. Orientation was satisfactory, but examination of remote memory was punctuated by such remarks as "I'm gonna guess," "Now let me see," and "Well, sir, I can't tell you." Recent memory intact. (Strecker and Ebaugh, 1940)

ARTHRITIS. An inflammation of the joints, often highly painful, associated with rheumatic disease.

Rheumatoid arthritis is included among the psychophysiologic or psychosomatic disorders as a "musculoskeletal reaction" for two reasons: many of the victims have similar personality patterns, and the illness often sets in or is exacerbated during a period of emotional stress.

Certain personality traits are frequently observed in arthritic patients. Many of them are emotionally controlled individuals who seem to enjoy being of service to others. They tend to be energetic, both physically and mentally, and their major outlet is often outdoor sports and other competitive activities. They generally come from families in which the mother is the dominant figure and the father gentle and passive. As a result the boys become dependent on the mother, and the girls compete with the father and brothers for her favor. Both the boys and the girls are afraid of the mother and seek approval by doing various chores that often involve some sacrifice on their part. At the same time they resent the demands of the mother but learn to suppress their anger because it arouses guilt feelings. They also find that they can control their feelings more successfully if they dominate others and engage in physical activities.

In keeping with this type of background, the events that appear to precipitate acute arthritis are frequently the kind that arouse unconscious feelings of resentment and rebellion heavily tinged with guilt. Such events might be the death of the mother with the threat of the father's remarrying, severe rejection or disappointment in an important relationship, miscarriage, or the birth of an unwanted child. In some cases the illness becomes aggravated on the anniversary of a disturbing event. Such "anniversary reactions" are quite common in psychophysiologic disorders and are frequently offered as evidence of an emotional basis for these conditions.

Psychiatric treatment is not usually undertaken during the acute phases of the illness. When the internist has brought the arthritis under control, supportive psychotherapy is often found to be helpful. Usually the patient is not amenable to classical psychoanalytic treatment, only responding to a direct, active approach which does not attempt to uncover the underlying source of his distress. *See* PSYCHOPHYSIOLOGIC DISORDERS (GENERAL).

ART TESTS. Tests designed to identify special talents required for painting, architecture, and other arts, or to reveal and appraise creative ability in the arts.

Work samples have long been used in assessing artistic ability. They are considered fairly effective as a means of comparing individuals who have had similar training, since their productions probably reflect creative ability as well as technical skill acquired through learning experiences. However, if the subjects are required to draw from the same model, there is little room for creativity, and if unselected individuals are asked to hand in a piece of work, there is no way of controlling the situation in which they have worked. For these reasons a number of standardized tests have been developed for measuring (a) art judgment and (b) art aptitude.

The Meier Art Judgment Test. This is a test of taste rather than execution. It does not stress specific principles such as balance or symmetry, but attempts a "global" evaluation based on the way the subject judges pictures as a whole. The materials consist of a hundred pairs of pictures, in which one of each pair is a recognized masterpiece and the other is an altered and inferior version of the original. The subject is required to indicate his preferences. His choices are then compared with the selections made by a group of art critics and other experts, and his score is calculated on this basis. The test is widely used but has not been adequately validated (PLATE 9).

The Graves Design Judgment Test. This test attempts to measure esthetic perception and judgment by requiring the subject to select from ninety pairs or triads of abstract designs. Representational art is not used since the author believes that judgment would be influenced by individual experiences, prejudices, and feelings rather than by purely esthetic considerations. One of the two or three pictures in each set is organized according to recognized principles of design—proportion, rhythm, balance, unity, variety, dominance, etc.—while the others violate one or more of these principles. The test, however, does not attempt to dissect the subject's esthetic perception but appraises his overall perceptual ability. It has an important weakness which it shares with the Meier Test: the subject may try to guess which rendering would be accepted by experts instead of giving his own opinion. One study showed that several additional points can be gained in this way. (Buros, 1953)

The Lewerenz Tests in Fundamental Abilities of Visual Art is designed for subjects without prior artistic training. It includes such tasks as locating the proper position of shadows, reproducing a form (a vase) from memory, color matching, and art vocabulary. The difficulty here as elsewhere is that there is no general agreement on the qualities needed for artistic talent. No validation information on this test has yet been published.

The Horn Art Aptitude Test is designed for art school candidates who usually have had previous training. It includes two major tasks: (1) arrangement of simple geometrical figures into balanced compositions, and sketching twenty familiar objects (fork, book, horse, etc.) on a small scale within a short time limit; and (2) an "imagery" test in which the subject incorporates printed lines into sketches of his own. Art instructors then judge these productions according to both imagination and technical drawing skill.

The Knauber Art Ability Test, for grades 7 to 16, includes such tasks as drawing figures from memory within space limitations, creating and completing designs from elements supplied, spotting errors in a drawing, and trying to represent a concept symbolically. The test basically measures mastery of traditional problems and tasks presented in art courses and is designed only for persons who have had formal instruction.

An unpublished test, known as the *Illinois Art Ability Test,* uses only one task from the Knauber test: drawing a table and other objects in perspective. The drawings are scored according to technical quality and the extent to which the subject has beautified or elaborated upon them—that is, it is a test of both artistic skill and creative ability. This test accurately predicted art course grades for a group of architecture students but failed to predict grades in engineering drawing.

On the whole the attempts to devise valid art tests have not been highly successful. There are several reasons for that: (1) there is too little agreement on the criteria to be used, since there are wide differences among critics and teachers in rating art productions; (2) there is no consensus on what skills and abilities are most important; (3) tests of esthetic judgment and of art aptitude seem to test different things, and the relationship between the two approaches has not been established; (4) due perhaps to the subjectivity of art, psychologists have not conducted the definitive research required to develop a test of general artistic capacity, one that could be applied to different types of art such as architecture, furniture design, clothing design, sculpture, and industrial design. It may be that such a test would have to combine the two general types of ability, art judgment, and artistic performance. This, however, remains to be seen.

ART THERAPY. The use of art activities, such as painting and clay modeling, as an adjunct in psychotherapy and rehabilitation.

Artistic expression has come to play an increasingly important role in the therapeutic process in recent years. It offers a wide variety of values applicable to many types of patients. In one form or another, it provides a nonthreatening form of emotional release; a helpful technique for assessing the progress of therapy; an avenue to renewed confidence and self-esteem; an opportunity to communicate without the use of words; a means of re-establishing social relationships; and a key to unconscious impulses and hidden sources of emotional problems (PLATE 5).

Art therapy is applicable on both a child and an adult level. It is a highly effective form of play therapy which can be used in treating disturbed children, and also in providing normal children with an opportunity to express their individual emotional needs. It is important to make available a wide variety of art materials and activities, and to allow the child freedom to find his own most satisfying medium. Studies have shown that each type of artistic expression has its own special values for different kinds of children (Hartley and Goldenson, 1963). A hostile child will usually obtain greater emotional release from kneading and pounding clay than from drawing a crayon picture. A small child who is having difficulty with toilet training may express himself most successfully by smearing fingerpaint. An inhibited child should be given a choice of bright and pastel colors, since he might begin with the softer shades and use intense reds and yellows only when he feels freer to express himself. A depressed child may pour out his sorrow in dark colors, and a fearful child might attempt to exorcise a "bogeyman" by putting him on paper. Many timid children confine themselves to a single color and make small, circumscribed pictures in one corner of the paper or surround them by a neat border. Hyperactive and aggressive children, on the other hand, are likely to paint bold strokes with the heel of the brush, and spread the paint over the entire easel instead of confining it to the paper. But as they "paint out" their feelings, they begin to exert more control over the brush and over themselves as well.

Painting and drawing are occasionally used in private therapy, but more often in an institutional setting. In his book *The Door to Serenity* (1958), Ainslie Meares has reproduced a remarkable series of paintings produced by a schizophrenic girl in the course of treatment. She began to bring bizarre productions to him at the beginning of the therapeutic process but had no idea what they meant. The psychiatrist, however, believed they contained a symbolic message and gradually learned to decipher them and used them as a means of establishing communication with his patient. He did not attempt to interpret them to her, since she was entirely withdrawn and terrified, and would not talk or even look at him. Instead, he used them as clues to her fears, conflicts, and emotional needs. Analysis of her first pictures (PLATE 6), which contained heavy black crosses, crawling objects, splashes of red, and a yellow square, indicated that she felt confined in a black prison, beset with fears of sex (the red splashes), but yearned to be free from her feelings of horror and live happily in a world of goodness (the yellow square). Though she could not talk about her fears, Meares was able to give the reassurance and friendship she needed by simple acts such as moving her chair closer to the fire and helping her light a cigarette. As she gradually improved and could talk about the childhood experiences that caused her fears, her paintings depicted her changing state of mind, and new symbols emerged; serene moon-lit mountains, red leaves falling from a tree, a bluebird flying freely (PLATE 31).

Art therapy is now a standard form of recreational therapy in mental institutions and rehabilitation centers. Some hospitals offer actual instruction in painting, sculpting, drawing, and other art forms; others do little more than provide the patients with a room and a variety of materials. Provision may also be made for exhibition of the patients' work, group discussions, classes and lectures given by visiting authorities, and visits to art galleries in a neighboring city. In most cases these art activities are regarded not merely as forms of emotional release, but as a means of remotivating and resocializing the patients. In a few hospitals the paintings and drawings are introduced in group therapy sessions and the patients are asked to interpret their meaning.

Art therapy has many applications outside the area of mental and emotional illness. It is a major instrument in schools for the physically handicapped, since it gives these children an opportunity to express themselves as individuals, experience the satisfaction of creation, and gain recognition and approval from others. As many art therapists and educators have pointed out, these aims can be achieved only if a wide range of materials and techniques is available so that each child can find his own most satisfying medium. In the past, the emphasis was on art as a form of "busywork," and upon highly patterned activity, such as the use of molds, which inhibited rather than encouraged free expression. Today the emphasis is on exploration, self-discovery, and perception of the kind of order which is implicit in the experience rather than imposed upon it.

The newer approach applies to the mentally retarded as well as to the physically handicapped. In their case,

however, simple and more repetitive tasks may be required to enhance visual-motor co-ordination or to enable the child to master a specific technique or tool. Even coloring books, which are ordinarily anathema to the art teacher, may have their value in helping the perceptually disturbed retardate see the organization and structure in the visual world. Although this type of activity is actually not a full art experience, it has therapeutic value since it may help to correct perceptual disorders.

On the other hand, there is a growing realization that most retarded children are capable of genuine artistic expression. Such expression, no matter how meager it may appear, can benefit them in many ways. It enables them to express themselves in a concrete, nonverbal manner, and thus compensates for their inability to deal with abstractions. It improves their self-image and makes them feel like real persons who can produce something of their own. It develops their visual and tactual abilities and helps them achieve greater confidence in dealing with the material world. It gives them courage and arouses interests that lead the way to more academic school experiences. "And primarily the art process stands as an end in itself as an esthetic experience for the retarded child. It is here that the retardate can establish an appreciation for the beauty in his otherwise frustrating world." (Semmel, 1961)

ASCLEPIADES (124 B.C.–?). This early physician, who anticipated many modern ideas on mental illness, was born in the Greek colony of Bithynia and migrated to Rome at a time when that city was replacing Alexandria as the medical center of the known world. At the start of his career he devoted himself to rhetoric, but he soon became interested in medicine, basing his theories on the views of Democritus who held that the body is made up of atoms and corpuscles in continual motion. Illness, according to Asclepiades, is brought about by restricting the harmonious motion of the atoms, and treatment consists of restoring the original harmony through change of diet, exercise, bathing, massage, and emetics. He strongly objected to many of the extreme and inhumane treatments, such as bleeding, which were widely applied at the time.

Asclepiades' approach to mental illness was remarkably similar to his approach to physical illness. Here too he advocated humane treatment, pointing out that confining a patient to a dungeon would fill him with terror and prevent his recovery. His aim was to provide comfort for the afflicted, and to restore mental balance through "musical harmony and a concert of voices," "a hundred kinds of baths," and the soothing effect of a gently swaying bed suspended in the air. He also advocated well-lighted rooms, ample fresh air and congenial activities.

Asclepiades was far in advance of his time not only in prescribing humane methods of treatment, but in his understanding of mental illness itself. He objected to the term "insanity," on the ground that it was based on the layman's reactions rather than on a clinical description of cases. He introduced the modern idea that emotional disturbances, which he called "passions of the sensations," are at the root of mental disorders, and he was the first to differentiate acute from chronic conditions. He also showed remarkable awareness of the nuances of behavior by distinguishing delusions from hallucinations, in spite of the fact that his Greek and Roman contemporaries believed them to be identical. It took nearly two thousand years for psychiatry to fully recognize this distinction. *See* ESQUIROL, MUSIC THERAPY, HYDROTHERAPY, RECREATIONAL THERAPY.

ASSERTION-STRUCTURED THERAPY. A systematic approach to psychotherapy developed by E. Lakin Phillips, based upon the theory that neurotic tendencies can be traced to faulty assumptions and expectations.

Phillips (1956) believes that the characteristic behavior of any individual can best be understood in terms of the implicit assertions he makes about the world of people and relationships. These assertions are not viewed as functions of the unconscious but as hypotheses used in meeting the situations of life. Some of them turn out well, others poorly; some lead to constructive relationships and effective action, others produce conflict and failure. The healthy individual governs his behavior by assertions that are "confirmed" by positive experiences. The neurotic, on the other hand, adopts assumptions which are "disconfirmed" by reality, but instead of discarding them as faulty he tends to repeat his behavior patterns in a circular, self-defeating manner.

The therapist's basic job is to "interfere" with what the patient is doing in order to make him aware of his faulty assumptions and teach him to "bet" on principles that have a greater probability of being confirmed. Phillips does not believe this process requires any long, complicated probing into the depths of the unconscious. Rather, he proposes a clear-cut procedure designed to rid the patient of inner tensions and outer conflicts, and to enable him to solve his own problems more satisfactorily. The following four steps show the way this procedure is applied to children's problems:

"1. *Assertion.* Child's expectations are for constant attention, accord, interest; he expects to get his own way; expects to have others give in to him in the interest of his comfort and his immediate demands.

"2. *Disconfirmation.* The school and other out-of-home environments cannot treat the child in this way; therefore they act to disconfirm the child's expectations. These social facts conflict with the expectations themselves.

"3. *Tension.* At school or in other atypical situations (i.e., not typically like the home setting) tensions develop from this conflict.

"4. *Redundancy.* Child redoubles his efforts to get attention, refuses to make academic effort, becomes a behavior problem owing to tension and partly to his fighting back at disconfirming experiences. The child now falls behind in school work in real and formidable ways; this failure, in turn, becomes more disconfirming to him and his original assertions. Thus the vicious circle proceeds and until it is entered into in effective ways, it continues."

To break through this vicious circle, the therapist attempts to get the child to abandon his rigid, defensive adherence to one mode of behavior. He tries to modify his hostile or egocentric attitudes, and reduce his fear of trying alternative solutions to his problems. Then he helps the child to see that he can make his way more effectively by adopting another pattern of behavior based on different assumptions—in this case, recognition that he cannot claim more than his share of attention, and that he will do better by cooperating with others.

ASSOCIATIONISM. The theory that explains complex mental processes, such as thinking, learning, and memory, in terms of associative links formed between one idea and another; "an explanation of all psychological events through the juxtaposition of sensory impressions" (Murphy, 1949).

Associationism has a long history which we will briefly review before giving the specific laws or principles advanced by associationist psychologists. The theory developed largely in opposition to the rationalistic philosophy of René Descartes (1596–1650), who held that the mind is inherently endowed with a set of axioms or innate ideas that determine the way we experience the world. Descartes' theory was challenged by Thomas Hobbes (1588–1679), who advanced the empirical view that all knowledge is derived from relatively simple sense impressions which are "compounded" into complex ideas through the process of association. Associative links are established when two individual sensations are experienced together, and as a result, when we later experience one of them, the other is called for—for example, rain and wetness are experienced together, and therefore when we think of rain we think of wetness. All the contents of memory and imagination, no matter how complex and interwoven, were believed to be attributable to associations of this kind.

The doctrine of association as expressed by Hobbes was solidified by John Locke and his successors in the empirical school of philosophy. Locke (1632–1704) described the mind of the newborn infant as a tabula rasa (blank paper) upon which sensory experiences are written—and these experiences, or simple ideas, are later combined into complex ideas through the process of association. Bishop Berkeley (1685–1753) applied the theory to visual perception; David Hume (1711–1776) described association as a "gentle force" or tendency which unites ideas with greater or lesser degree of firmness; and in 1749 David Hartley (1705–1757), a neurologist, systematized all previous ideas, plus many of his own, into a comprehensive theory. He is therefore considered the true founder of the movement, and was the first to suggest that association can take place not only between sensations and ideas, but between motions (movements) as well, thus anticipating the modern view of the conditioned reflex. He also pointed out that the principle of association explains not only the train or chain of thoughts, but a simultaneous fusion of ideas into a single complex— for example, a specific set of stars, stripes, colors, and national ideals fuse into the idea of the American flag. In addition, he extended the associationist concept to the area of dreams, imagination, memory, word meanings, and even morality, for he believed it to be a fundamental psychological law.

The next two figures in the development of the theory were James Mill (1773–1836) and his son John Stuart Mill (1806–1873). The elder Mill believed that all consciousness, all waking life, consists of a train of associations, and all objects as we know them are compounds of ideas. In his view, association was strictly a passive and mechanical process determined entirely by the fact that events (or "ideas") are experienced together. J. S. Mill, on the other hand, held that the mind actively associates elementary experiences into more complex ones. Moreover, we cannot always predict the properties of the complex from the simple—we would not know that a mixture (or "association") of red, green, and blue lights produces a white sensation unless we knew the laws of color mixture. This process of compounding ideas became known as "mental chemistry," and the view that the whole, or compound, is different from the sum of its parts is now considered an anticipation of the Gestalt theory. See GESTALT PSYCHOLOGY.

The work of Alexander Bain (1818–1903) represents a final attempt to cover all aspects of psychological functioning under the blanket of associationism. In his system of psychology he extended the doctrine to learning, habit, and various physiological functions. He worked out the associative process in greater detail than his predecessors, and was influential in popularizing the approach among the public.

In the course of this history, a number of "laws" or conditions of association were formulated. Hartley, for example, suggested that associations are formed because ideas (including sensations and movements) are experienced in close temporal contiguity—i.e., grass suggests green because the two are experienced at the same time. He added, however, that the experience has to be repeated a sufficient number of times before an association is formed. Hume applied this idea of repeated contiguity to the notion of causation. He also introduced the concept of resemblance as a source of associations—for example, we associate a zebra with a horse because of their similarity, even though we may never have seen them together.

Another investigator, Thomas Brown (1778–1820), added nine so-called "secondary laws of association," such as relative recency (associations recently formed tend to be easiest to remember), relative frequency (the more repetition, the stronger the association), relative duration (the longer the ideas are experienced together the easier it is to remember the association), and liveliness (the more vivid the experience, the stronger the bond). He also noted that the state of the organism influences the formation of associations, including not only temporary conditions like intoxication and emotional states, but lifetime habits and constitutional differences. Unfortunately Brown's recognition of these important factors was largely ignored by most associationists, since they viewed the process in a thoroughly mechanical way.

Associationism was doomed to fail as an explanatory doctrine for several reasons. It claimed too much, since it attempted to reduce all mental processes—perception, memory, thinking, reasoning—to a single function. It failed to do justice to the learning process because its exponents did not perform experiments on the way we actually learn and forget. And it ignored the effects which motivation and individual differences have on the formation of associations. Nevertheless, the movement has had a significant influence on many phases of modern psychology. Wilhelm Wundt used associative principles in attempting to reduce complex ideas to their simpler components. Free association became the prescribed procedure in Freudian analysis, and the word association test was adopted as an important tool by Carl Jung. Pavlov's principles of conditioning, with their emphasis on repetition and contiguity, are associative in nature. And the laws of association have been applied to stimulus-response theory as well. But most important, the doctrine helped to lay the groundwork and establish the need for an experimental attack on the higher mental functions, especially the learning process. As a result of this attack, the static character of traditional associationism has gradually been superseded by more dynamic concepts. *See* LEARNING (GENERAL), CONDITIONING, LOCKE, DESCARTES, STIMULUS-RESPONSE ASSOCIATION, STIMULUS-STIMULUS ASSOCIATION.

ASTASIA-ABASIA. A disturbance in the ability to stand and walk. Astasia means inability to stand; abasia, inability to walk.

While sitting or lying down, the astasic-abasic patient has normal control over his legs—but when on his feet his legs are wobbly and he walks with a grotesque, staggering gait. There is no organic pathology. The condition is a conversion (hysterical) symptom, unconsciously representing a desire to gain sympathy, attention, or control over others: "I am so weak I cannot even walk; you must *support* me by doing what I wish." The disorder was considerably more common in Victorian times than it is today, and was more often found in women than in men. *See* CONVERSION REACTION.

Illustrative Case: ASTASIA-ABASIA

Mr. D.W., aged sixty-three years, suddenly developed a paralysis of his legs which prevented him from walking. He had been perfectly well until four days before examination. He was in normal health in every other way, ate and slept well. Neurologic examination revealed no pathology. While in bed he could raise his knees and

flex all his joints even against great resistance.

Mr. D.W. lived with his daughter-in-law. He was a cranky old man who had retired and was tolerated only because he had some insurance which would eventually benefit the daughter-in-law. On the day of the development of the paralysis, his will and policy had been found, and it had been discovered that he was leaving some charities as beneficiaries. In great rage, the daughter-in-law ordered the old man from her home; and the paralysis promptly developed. It was a typical astasia-abasia. (Kraines, 1948)

ASTEREOGNOSIS. Loss or marked impairment of the capacity to identify objects by the sense of touch.

Astereognosis is a form of agnosia ("tactile agnosia"), which is the general term for inability to recognize stimuli. It is thought to be due to destruction of tissue in the parietal lobe, on the side of the brain, caused by either injury or disease. *See* AGNOSIA, APHASIA.

ASTHENIC REACTION (Neurasthenia). A neurotic reaction marked by persistent feelings of mental and physical fatigue, diffuse "nervousness," and vague aches and pains.

The asthenic patient feels that any exertion is too much for him, and finds it difficult to concentrate, make decisions, or carry any job through to completion. Minor problems or difficulties are magnified to major proportions, and any hint of criticism is likely to upset him completely. He spends an unusual amount of time sleeping but invariably awakens unrefreshed and out of sorts. Yet his fatigue and lassitude tend to be selective rather than total, for he may have ample energy for sports, recreation, or other activities that arouse his interest.

The asthenic individual is constantly worried about his physical condition. A chronic hypochondriac, he is always complaining about headaches, dizziness, back trouble, weakness, or vague discomfort in his stomach, head, chest, or genitals. In men potency is likely to be impaired, and in women menstruation is usually painful or irregular. Every upset, even the slightest, produces the same degree of distress and concern. Similarly an undue amount of attention is paid to digestion and elimination—and to the latest diets, laxatives, vitamins, and pills that are supposed to keep these processes in order.

Asthenic reactions are especially common among middle-aged persons, including the "nervous housewives" who feel trapped in their homes. The disorder seems to be most prevalent on the lower socioeconomic levels, and probably accounts for at least 10 per cent of all neurotic disorders.

The asthenic syndrome used to be ascribed to physical depletion of the nerve cells due to overwork and emotional burdens. The American psychiatrist George Miller Beard originated the name neurasthenia—literally, "nerve weakness"—but this term is falling into disuse today because the disorder is regarded as a psychological rather than a physical fatigue reaction. See NEURASTHENIA.

The dynamics of asthenic reaction are relatively clear since it is so closely related to everyday experience. We all know how readily we become tired and listless when we are disappointed or bored or torn by conflict—and how easy it is to concentrate on the slightest aches and pains at such times. It is not hard, then, to imagine how a person who feels chronically dissatisfied, discouraged, frustrated, or rejected would respond. In such a person the ordinary reactions might well be exaggerated and he would become exhausted instead of merely tired, inert and immobilized instead of merely sluggish, and prey to any number of physical complaints instead of just a few. This is actually what happens to the asthenic individual.

The life histories of asthenics may not reveal sufficient reason for their extreme reactions, but they usually show that they have experienced a fairly large amount of failure, monotony, lack of affection, sexual dissatisfaction, or social problems. In adult life asthenic wives may actually *be* trapped in the home and cheated by life (and sometimes by their husbands as well)—up to a point. But more important than these influences—which thousands of other people experience—are their own attitudes and reactions. Instead of "coming up fighting," they allow themselves to be consumed by resentment or numbed by feelings of hopelessness. Then, perhaps repeating a tendency which originated in childhood, they begin to exaggerate any physical complaints they happen to have, as a response to an unconscious urge to escape from responsibility. If this serves the purpose well and in addition brings them "secondary gains" in the form of attention and sympathy or control over others, the reaction may develop into a confirmed pattern.

As this pattern takes hold, the person with asthenic tendencies gradually becomes a chronic complainer and "wet blanket." Members of his family may try to excuse him because he suffers so much, but eventually they usually lose patience and find it hard to be sympathetic, especially since he may make them feel they are somehow responsible for his troubles. Moreover, it becomes increasingly hard to live with a person who is so lacking in confidence, independence, and ordinary cheerfulness. But any criticisms or suggestions they make fail to do any good since the asthenic is basically an immature individual who finds himself totally inadequate to face up to the problems of life. Instead, he falls back on illness, fatigue, and dependence as a way out.

It is not easy to change these personality patterns. The physical complaints are so real that the patient cannot believe that they have a psychological origin. Besides, organic disorders do develop in many cases because of lack of sleep and a generally run-down condition, and since these conditions have to be treated medically the patient feels that all his ailments must be purely physical. In many cases the frustrations of life are also so undeniable that it is hard to convince him that things are not as hopeless as they seem. Moreover, the benefits he derives from the attention and assistance of others make it even more difficult for him to give up his symptoms.

In spite of these obstacles it is often possible to treat the asthenic successfully, particularly if the reaction has not become too deeply ingrained. The object of therapy is to help him gain insight into the faulty techniques he has been using, and to grow to a point where he will no longer need to fall back on them. He must also learn to assess his life situation more accurately and become more and more confident that he has the ability to stand up and meet his problems. This is usually a step by step process in which he needs considerable support from the therapist. *See* HYPOCHONDRIASIS.

Illustrative Case: ASTHENIC REACTION

The following excerpts are taken from an interview with a middle-aged married woman who felt, and with good reason, that her husband was no longer interested in her. Often he failed to come home for several days at a time, and when he was home, he showed little evidence of interest or affection. Although the patient had completed high school, she had no occupational skills and felt completely dependent upon her husband for support and protection. She was self-pitying in her attitude, prone to relating her symptoms almost endlessly, and very demanding in her attitude toward the therapist.

PT: I used to talk rather fluently, but now I'm more nervous than I've ever been and my tongue seems to catch on my teeth so that I don't speak plainly. Everything seems such an effort . . . like I had an anchor tied to me or something. I no longer care to play cards or even talk to people any more. . . . Even the simplest things are too much for me.

DR: Even the simplest things . . .

PT: Ah, hm, I mean, the phone is there and I'm lonesome and yet I don't even phone. . . . I don't even talk to my neighbor much any more even though I know that I should be with people and I like people, but I've gotten so that . . . (long pause) . . . that . . . (sigh) . . . I feel too bad to even talk or do anything (voice breaks and tears).

I've tried so many things to get well, but it's just awful . . . I mean . . . sometimes I can just barely live . . . I mean just listen to the radio or read, or eat . . . I mean just like being in a daze or something . . . I don't know . . . I just feel so horribly tired and sick.

Two months ago I felt better than I had been. I mean I was able . . . well I went to several shows and I actually even went to a dance. Often I would begin to get tired, and I was very frightened that I would break down, but I would go on . . . I mean like some people would go to a battle or to a battlefront (proud tone of voice). But . . . now . . . well I am just so tired and run-down that I can't even go to the show . . . if I do go . . . I have to leave in the middle because I'm not strong enough . . . I mean I don't have enough strength to sit through it.

DR: Two months ago you felt better?

PT: Well, yes . . . you see my husband's brother came to visit us . . . and he would talk to me and he had such a way of diverting me and he was very interesting, and you'd be amazed, within a few minutes or a few hours I'd be just different . . . and he took me to several shows and to the dance. I felt so much better and I had a really good time. So I can see it isn't sleeping or eating. I mean . . . I need someone who'd give me something different to think about . . . someone who'd show you some affection . . . enough interest in you so that you would improve. But my husband . . . well, I just can't understand how he can treat a woman who is ill . . . and trying her best . . . well (tears) . . . I have just sort of withdrawn . . . he has really made me sick . . . (Coleman, 1964)

ASTHMA. A disorder characterized by painful wheezing and gasping due to blocking of the bronchial passages by spasmodic contractions and excessive secretion of mucus.

Ordinarily asthmatic reactions occur when certain substances such as dust or pollen are inhaled by individuals who have a constitutional sensitivity, or allergy, to them. Some surveys, however, indicate that psychological factors are also involved in as many as 75 per cent of cases, and for this reason asthma is included among the psychophysiologic disorders of the respiratory system. Since the respiratory system is so closely related to preservation of life, the attacks may be aggravated by the patient's own fear and apprehension, as well as by the overanxiety of parents or others. Moreover, it has long been observed that many people experience acute attacks during periods of emotional stress. In some cases, too, the reaction may be triggered by stimuli that are not physically allergenic: a papier-mâché rose, a sculptured cat, a particular song or story, or a visit to the grave of a parent. In such cases an emotional association can often be clearly established.

An experiment recently reported by McFadden et al. (1969) offers evidence that suggestion and expectation may sometimes precipitate an attack. Patients suffering from respiratory disease were asked to inhale air which they were told contained allergenic agents such as dust, pollen, and dander—although they were actually breathing air containing a non-irritating salt-water mist. Nineteen of the forty subjects developed typical asthmatic reactions, and the twelve who experienced the most severe attacks were treated successfully with a "remedy for asthma" which, unknown to them, was the same salt-water mist.

These findings have led to a close study of the personality of asthmatic individuals and the situations that seem to induce the attacks. A psychoanalytic study by Freud (1939) has indicated that the asthmatic tends to be insecure, anxious, and submissive, with a strong "maternal dependency" drive. According to this theory, the pattern originated in early childhood when his mother held him to rigid standards of behavior and made him feel rejected when he did not conform. As a result, he became dependent on the mother for approval, fearing that she might turn against him and deny her love if he became too independent. As to the asthmatic attacks themselves, Freud contended that they occurred when an individual of this kind contemplated or engaged in some independent activity, often of a sexual nature, that might "estrange him from a parental figure, usually the mother." These situations were felt as threats to the relationship with the mother, and the asthmatic attack was interpreted as a repressed cry, arising out of the patient's desire to confess and weep on her shoulder. The cry, however, was blocked by fear of her disapproval and rejection, and it was this blocking that was believed to precipitate the gasping and wheezing.

Other investigators have supported the idea that the chronic asthmatic is usually a dependent, passive personality who continues to seek the kind of care and protection his mother gave him —but many of them feel he harbors a good deal of repressed hostility and anger as well. On the other hand, an investigation by Knapp and Nemetz (1960) has challenged the whole idea of a single personality disturbance manifested by all asthmatic patients—but they did find that most of the severe cases showed *some* kind of personality defect.

Asthma always requires medical care, and in some cases removal to a pollen- and dust-free environment. Many patients profit from psychotherapy directed toward dependent tendencies or other emotional disturbances. With child asthmatics, lasting improvement is often contingent on counseling and psychotherapy with the parents as well as the patient. In cases where the asthma is not related to personality disturbance, it may still be affected by the attitudes of the patient and his family. The attacks may frequently be held in check by teaching the child to apply his own inhalant device and to look upon the condition as a transient nuisance rather than a chronic illness. *See* PSYCHOPHYSIOLOGIC DISORDERS (GENERAL).

In the case that follows, chronic asthma appears to be closely related to personality factors.

Illustrative Case: ASTHMA

John R. is a thirty-three-year-old married man who was referred for psychological treatment in connection with his asthma. The medical specialist who had been treating the patient came to the conclusion that an important component in the case was emotional. The patient gave a history of rather severe attacks of asthma from the time he was sixteen. The first attack occurred at a summer camp where the boy had been sent while his parents were traveling in Europe. The severity of the attack was such that the camp notified the parents, who cut their trip short and returned home. Another severe attack occurred while the patient was a freshman at a college in another part of the country. Once again, the attack was so serious that it was decided that it would be best if the patient were to attend the university in the city in which his parents lived. While it was not apparent at the time, the major attacks in this case occurred in connection with the stress of separation. The symptom which finally brought him to the medical specialist developed following his marriage. The attacks increased both in severity and frequency to the point that numerous medical consultations were held. The usual diagnostic and treatment procedures were of little effect, and the patient continued to suffer. It was at this time that the physician decided that psychological treatment was indicated. After a period of such treatment, the patient began to understand how his symptoms had become an effective way of protecting himself against separation from his family, particularly an overly affectionate and indulgent mother. The patient saw that prior to his marriage he was able to use the asthma attack as a device for keeping his mother near to him. He saw also that following his marriage, the device which had worked so successfully earlier in life was now of little use. The increased understanding made it possible to readjust his emotional attitudes toward his wife and his mother. From that time, the symptoms gradually disappeared. (Kisker, 1964)

ASYLUM (Insane Asylum) (literally, "refuge"). An obsolete term for a mental hospital or psychiatric institution.

The word has a long history. According to D. H. Tuke (1892) it is "a place safe from violence or pillage. The ancients set aside certain places of refuge where the vilest criminals were protected, and the name later on got to be applied especially to an institution which afforded a place of refuge or safety for the infirm or unsound of mind."

The term has been discarded because of its association with criminal behavior and its emphasis on refuge rather than treatment. *See* MENTAL HOSPITAL, BEDLAM, TUKE.

ATARACTIC (Ataraxic) (literally "undisturbed"). A drug used to control anxiety, tension, and overactivity without causing somnolence—a tranquilizer. *See* TRANQUILIZERS, CHEMOTHERAPY.

ATTENTION. The act of focusing on a specific portion of the total stimulation impinging on the organism.

Attention is probably the most common of all psychological functions. Whenever we engage in any activity, we focus on certain aspects of the situation and disregard all others. The student in a library directs his attention to the book in front of him and ignores (more or less) a host of other stimuli: tables, chairs, people, sounds from the room and the street outside, the pressure of his clothing, the kinesthetic sensations of sitting and crossing his legs.

All these, and more, are screened out and occupy the "margin" rather than the "focus" of attention. Reading a book is therefore a selective process which limits the student to certain aspects of his environment, but it is interesting that at any moment a change in the field of stimulation—a familiar voice, a sudden pain in the stomach —may cause a shift in attention, and what was marginal a moment ago will now be central. This brings up the question of identifying the variables or determinants involved in attention.

The internal determinants of attention include past experience, ongoing behavior, and the individual's physiological condition. First, *past experience and habitual attitudes* have a great deal to do with structuring our perceptual world. We notice things that have a meaning for us. The artist will approach a country scene with a different "internal context" from a farmer, and will "register" certain colors or shapes or patterns which the farmer completely overlooks. But the farmer, too, will see the scene in the light of his own experience.

Second, *ongoing behavior,* or "activity in progress," has a great effect on what we notice. As the runner poises himself to hear the starting gun and gets set for a fast takeoff, he shuts out the sights and sounds of the crowd. And as he runs the race, he may not attend to a cut or bruise he receives in jumping over a hurdle—but once the race is over he may realize that it is extremely painful. A special area of the brain, the reticular formation, appears to be involved in shunting aside stimulation which is not important for ongoing behavior. *See* RETICULAR FORMATION.

Third, the *physiological condition* of the organism has much to do with selective attention. The hungry man notices more restaurants than the man who has just eaten, and a person who is dying of thirst in the desert may even see a mirage. McClelland and At-

kinson (1948) kept groups of subjects hungry for one, four, and sixteen hours, respectively, then had them look at meaningless smudges on a dimly lighted screen. The subjects identified the smudges as articles of food in direct proportion to the time that had elapsed since they had last eaten.

The "external determinants" of attention can be dealt with summarily since most of them are illustrated under another topic. *See* ADVERTISING RESEARCH. First, *repetition* of a political slogan, trade name, or important point in a lesson usually captures attention, though it may defeat itself if it is overdone and becomes monotonous. Repetition with variation, or repetition in another sense modality, will often accomplish the purpose better. Second, sheer *size* may arrest attention, and is especially important in highway signs and advertisements. However, it does not operate by itself, since other factors such as clarity and color are usually involved. Third, *change and movement* have great attention value not only because we get bored with sameness, but because our sense organs actually fail to register when the level of stimulation remains the same. The changes may occur in place, color, speed of movement, or simply be an on-off affair as in some illuminated signs. *See* SENSORY ADAPTATION.

Fourth, *intensity* of the stimuli is an important factor, though this is a relative matter: a blowout occurring at Times Square will attract less attention than a blowout on a quiet street. Fifth, *novelty* is closely related to change but adds the dimension of the unusual—for example, "trick" photos, or animals appearing to mouth the words of a commercial. Sixth, *contrast:* the sharply contrasting color of the hunter's red shirt keeps others from shooting him; the high-pitched Navy whistle is designed to stand out from all other sounds on the ship. Camouflage, on the other hand, is designed to eliminate attention-getting contrasts in color and shape.

The postural adjustments involved in attention have been studied by many investigators. In general, their main purpose is to bring the receptors into maximal contact with the stimulus: we "sit up and take notice" or "sit on the edge of our seat." At the same time we may attempt to cut out competing stimuli, as in closing our eyes at a concert. The muscle tensions involved in attending can be measured, and it has been found that complex tasks which require precise attention use more energy than simple ones (Morgan, 1916).

Francis Galton was probably the first to record the muscular changes that take place in attention and other forms of mental activity. He devised an instrument called the automatograph consisting of a small plate which could be moved over a smooth glass surface with a minimum of friction. By this means he was able to record slight changes in the movement of the hands, showing, for example, that when a subject thought about a distant building, or added numbers, the hands involuntarily moved in the appropriate directions. This is the principle on which "hand readers" operate, and probably palmists as well, although palmists may also be sensitive to pulse and perspiration changes and more general behavioral reactions. *See* EXTRASENSORY PERCEPTION.

William James also made an interesting contribution to this subject. He suggested that the extraneous and highly individual motor activities that occur in attending—knitting the brows, pacing, etc.—help to dissipate incoming stimuli which might distract us from the task at hand. As evidence he cited the story that Walter Scott became the top student in his class by cutting off the jacket button the star student always played with as he recited. Deprived of this motor outlet the boy was distracted by irrelevant stimuli and could not maintain his intense concentration.

A number of studies have also been made of the fluctuation of attention. In an early experiment, Billings (1914) asked subjects to rivet their eyes on a specific visual object and report when they first noticed their attention wandering. The average time for this single act of attention was only two seconds, with a variation from .1 second to 5 seconds for different subjects. These results agree fairly well with measurements of the time taken by darting eye movements that occur when we explore a picture visually. Buswell (1935) showed that we make about four fixations per second when we observe a general visual field without any particular purpose in mind. Some psychologists believe the waxing and waning which occur when we listen to a ticking watch held at a distance from our ear is an example of fluctuation of attention, but others attribute it to changes in nerve activity.

How well can we attend to two or more things at once? Here again many of the important experiments were performed some time ago. Paulhan (1887) found it possible to write one familiar poem while reciting another or while performing simple multiplication. However, he found that even these simple and familiar operations would always interfere with the performance of tasks that involve any degree of difficulty. Mager (1920) and Pauli (1924) experimented with simultaneous tasks of an extremely simple nature, such as counting three to six short lines and telling which of two pressures applied to the fingers was the stronger. They found that both judgments were correct in only 12 per cent of cases, neither was correct in 28 per cent and one correct in 60 per cent. These and other experiments indicate that when two tasks are presented simultaneously, one or both will suffer in efficiency. Westphal (1911) and Schorn (1928) have shown that in general the best way to handle two simultaneous tasks is to combine them, if possible, into a single co-ordinated

126

ATTENTION SPAN

performance. There is wide individual variation in this ability, and for this reason people who are called upon to do many things at once—for example, telephone operators and pilots—are frequently given special tests to see if they can handle them. *See* ATTENTION SPAN.

ATTENTION SPAN (Span of Apprehension). The number of objects that can be distinctly perceived during a very brief presentation.

Early experiments on attention span have their roots in an ancient argument about the nature of the mind. Does it act as a unit, or is it possible to attend to two or more things at the same time? This philosophic problem is no longer a lively issue, but attention span is still an important question because of its bearing on such practical activities as reading, scanning, and detection of aircraft.

The problem was first attacked by William Hamilton in 1859. He repeatedly tossed black beans into a white tray, estimating the number as soon as they came to rest. The results showed he was 100 per cent correct with three or four beans, a little over 50 per cent with eight, and only 18 per cent with fifteen. In 1871 W. S. Jevons developed a way of statistically estimating the actual number of items from the subject's guesses. More recent experiments have employed a piece of apparatus known as a tachistoscope, which can be set, like the shutter of a camera, for a specific exposure of stimulus material. The usual setting is below .2 second, which allows one "act of attention," since it is about equal to the time it takes for the eyes to *start* to shift from one fixation point to another. When the stimulus consists of black dots scattered on a white card, and when the apparatus is set for .1 second exposure, alert adults average about eight objects correctly perceived, with an individual range of six to twelve. The span, however, is not constant for every subject, but varies by different amounts.

But how is the number of items actually ascertained? It appears that small numbers of items are perceived as a spontaneously formed group: two are seen as a pair, three as a trio, four as a quartet. However, larger numbers are usually estimated, although here too the subject may attempt to group them in some way. This tendency to group the items was demonstrated by Freeman (1916) when he showed that most subjects correctly reported twenty-five dots when they were arranged in five groups of five each, as they are on a playing card—but if one of these dots was omitted, the subjects rarely missed it. In a study by Oberly (1924) subjects reported that they perceived up to four dots without grouping, grouped together five and six dots, and both grouped and counted dots beyond that number. It appears, however, that the counting is not done in the usual way. Little is known about how it is actually accomplished, but it appears that the sensation remains about one quarter second beyond the presentation, like an after-image, and this allows the subject more time to "process" the data. Along this line, tests have shown that the greater the number of items presented, even within the person's normal span, the longer it takes him to "scan": .560 second for one dot, and 1.175 for six dots.

Rapid perception of the number of items up to the normal limit of attention span (six to eight items) is sometimes called subitizing (from the Latin word for sudden), and the term covert scanning has lately come into use for the rapid perception of any number of items momentarily presented. Studies of the process have turned up a number of revealing facts. First, any number of items up to six to eight are not only correctly perceived, but reported with almost perfect confidence; beyond that number confidence in judgment falls rapidly, as does the correctness of the estimate. Second, as a general rule the more intense the stimulus (clearly defined or brightly colored items), the easier it is to perceive, and for a small number of items such as seven the product of intensity multiplied by time is constant—that is, a short exposure at high intensity can be as readily perceived as a longer exposure at lower intensity (the Bunsen-Roscoe Law). Third, subjects can increase their attention span, up to a point, through practice in grouping the items. So-called "lightning calculators" develop this ability by themselves, but some experimentally trained subjects have equaled or even exceeded them. One such subject, for example, reduced the time he required to attend to a fifteen-digit number in order to recall it correctly from 20 to 1.45 seconds (Renshaw, 1945). Tachistoscopic practice of this kind has been successfully applied in remedial reading and speed reading programs, and has also been used in training members of the armed forces who serve as lookouts for enemy planes. *See* PRODIGY, SUBITIZING.

Attention span studies of letters and words have thrown considerable light on the basic reading process. The span for naming unconnected letters is shorter than for dots, because the letters have to be distinguished and identified while dots are all the same and rarely have to be subitized or counted. On the other hand, words are usually easier to report than either letters or dots. In one early study (Cattell, 1885), three to four unconnected letters, two unrelated short words, and four short words making up a phrase or sentence were correctly read at a glimpse. It has also been shown that familiar words and phrases containing as many as twelve to twenty letters can be perceived in the time it takes to read four to five unconnected letters (Erdmann and Dodge, 1898). The reason is that we correctly *perceive* these words even if we do not *see* them at all—for example, the phrase "Mary had a little lamb" can be correctly identified after a .15 to .20 second exposure, since we correctly perceive the first word plus fragments of the others, and fill in the gaps because we are dealing with a familiar "Gestalt." *See* INFORMATION THEORY.

These experiments have led to two other significant discoveries. First, we see more than we actually remember. There is evidence that we forget much of what is viewed in a tachistoscopic presentation before we can report it. This is particularly true of disconnected material which is hard to remember because it has no internal structure. We remember words better than dots because they make more sense. Second, the memory process is influenced by our interests, wants, and attitudes. A variety of experiments have proved this point, but one by Postman, Bruner, and McGinnis (1948) is particularly impressive. A number of subjects were given the Allport-Vernon-Lindzey Study of Values to test the relative strength of their interest in economic, theoretical, religious, political, esthetic, and social values. At another time the same subjects were briefly exposed to a large number of words, and it was found that they tended to identify words related to their dominant interest faster than those related to fields of lesser concern. *See* PERCEPTION, SUBLIMINAL PERCEPTION.

ATTITUDE. A response, favorable or unfavorable, to a person, group, idea, or situation.

Attitudes cannot be sharply distinguished from beliefs and opinions, but the latter tend to be more consciously held and more fully expressed in words. In contrast, attitudes frequently stem from unrecognized sources, operate partially on an unconscious level, and in most cases cannot be readily verbalized. They are complex psychological processes involving emotional, intellectual, and motivational components in varying proportions. Emotion usually plays a greater role than intellect in our prejudices and sympathies; intellect generally plays a greater part than emotion in determining our attitudes toward scientific theories and pursuits; and the two may contribute almost equally to our social and political views. The motivational, or dynamic, aspect of attitudes may also vary widely. Though all attitudes tend to have a drive quality, since they determine our positive and negative reactions to people and situations, their effect on actual behavior may be either great or small. Sympathy for the underprivileged may merely lead to kind words or righteous indignation, but it may also inspire a lifetime of service; prejudice may lead us to associate only with "our kind," but it can also be expressed in active discrimination, scapegoating, and even lynching.

We are not born with attitudes; they are acquired in the course of experience, and once acquired they tend to resist modification. Allport (1935) has described their development in terms of four processes. First, we gradually assimilate the ideas and reactions of people with whom we are closely identified —a child may develop a critical attitude toward the poor if he constantly hears his parents talk about how lazy and unambitious they are. Second, our attitudes may stem from dramatic or traumatic experiences, which frequently spread, or "generalize," to related situations—a gratifying experience with a summer job may establish a lasting inclination not only toward that particular job but also toward others like it; a single disturbing sexual experience in childhood may produce a negative attitude toward sex that can never be fully overcome. Third, a series of everyday experiences may shape and sharpen our attitudes toward specific objects or situations—for example, our preference or distaste for a particular kind of literature, architecture, or food. Fourth,

we may adopt ready-made attitudes of others with whom we associate, as in automatically echoing the likes and dislikes of the group to which we belong or aspire to belong.

Attitudes, then, consist of an enduring deposit of personal experience and a unique integration of feeling, thought, and drive. An individual's pattern of attitudes is considered one of the most characteristic expressions of his personality—in fact, one could go far toward making a "personality description" of any individual by determining his attitudes toward significant persons, events, situations, and ideas. A number of psychological tools can be used for this purpose—notably, scales that measure attitudes toward such subjects as capital punishment, race relations, and organized religion; interest tests that reveal patterns of likes and dislikes for various activities, types of people and occupations; self-report inventories and self-concept tests that disclose our appraisal of ourselves; and opinion surveys that sound out our attitudes on public issues. See ATTITUDE SCALES, INTEREST TESTS, PERSONALITY INVENTORIES, SELF-CONCEPT TESTS, PUBLIC OPINION SURVEYS.

Since many aspects of this subject are discussed under separate topics, such as PREJUDICE, STEREOTYPE, COGNITIVE DISSONANCE, MASS BEHAVIOR, BRAINWASHING, and ATTITUDES TOWARD MENTAL ILLNESS, we will confine ourselves here to a review of representative research on the formation and modification of attitudes.

Parental Influences. The influence of parents on the attitudes of their children has been investigated by a number of experimenters. Hirschberg and Gilliland (1942) found fairly substantial positive correlations (.29 to .58) between the attitudes of college students and of their parents toward God, economic depression, and the New Deal. On the basis of a review of various studies, Hyman (1959) found that, contrary to the common idea, children rarely rebel against the political attitudes of their parents. He found greater evidence of similarity in political party preference, however, than in specific political beliefs, and concluded that a child adopts the family political party almost to the same degree that he adopts the family religion. He also found that party affiliation was closely related to socioeconomic status. College graduates who earned considerably more than their parents tended to shift from Democrat to Republican, but those who earned less than their parents did not change from Republican to Democrat.

Peer Influences. In spite of the potency of parental influence, the effect of companions and acquaintances should not be underestimated. Peer influences are particularly effective during adolescence when young people feel socially and intellectually insecure and tend to rely heavily on other people for approval, acceptance and support. Research has shown, however, that changes in social attitudes are far less likely to occur in traditional and parochial colleges (which usually confirm their parents' attitudes) than in the more unconventional colleges. A study conducted by Newcomb at Bennington College in 1943 is particularly revealing. He found that most of the students came from the upper- and middle-class levels and shared the conservative views of their parents during their first year or so. During the junior and senior years, however, they tended to adopt the New Deal orientation of the closely knit college community. Analysis showed that the effect was far greater among those who became identified with the college than among those who did not enter fully into college life because of attachment to their family, personal insecurity, or failure to gain acceptance due to lack of social or intellectual skills.

Communication Influences. Which is more likely to be effective, an argument presenting one side of the case or an argument presenting both sides but favoring one side? Hovland, Lumsdaine, and Sheffield (1949) attempted to answer this question in an experiment on soldier attitudes near the end of World War II. They first asked a large group of men to estimate the probable length of the war, then divided them into two groups and played radio transcriptions designed to discourage the idea that the war with Japan would be over shortly after the war ended in Europe. One of the two groups heard only the arguments stating why the Pacific war would be a lengthy one, while the other group heard these arguments plus arguments which maintained that the United States might shorten the Pacific war by concentrating on the Japanese after ending the European conflict. When both groups were retested the overall effectiveness of the two presentations was about equal, with the percentage of soldiers who expected the war to last at least another year and a half increasing from 37 to 59 per cent. Further analysis, however, revealed an important difference. The "both sides" argument was especially effective with those who originally thought the war would be over soon, and the one-sided argument had a greater influence on those who originally thought it would last considerably longer. This result indicated that a one-sided presentation is most effective in reinforcing an original belief, while a two-sided argument is most effective in swaying individuals who are initially opposed to the point of view advocated. In explanation, the investigators suggested that the men who originally thought the war would be short already knew the arguments favoring their own side, but when they heard the speaker give these arguments, they acquired enough confidence in him to listen to the opposing arguments. It is also probable that confidence in the speaker was increased by his apparent objectivity in giving both sides of the case.

The importance of confidence in the speaker has been confirmed by an experiment by Kelman and Hovland (1953). These experimenters had a speaker give an identical talk strongly favoring extreme leniency toward juvenile delinquents to three audiences of high school students. In one group he was introduced as an authority (judge of a juvenile court), in the second he was presented as an ordinary individual (an unidentified member of the audience), and in the third he was introduced as a delinquent out on bail for dope peddling. The first group was considerably more influenced than the last, with the second in between. A retest three weeks later, however, produced a striking result: the effect on the first group had greatly diminished while the effect on the third group had increased. The experimenters concluded that high prestige has a greater *immediate* effect than low prestige, but in time, audiences tend to dissociate the message from its source, and remember the arguments alone without considering who presented them.

ATTITUDE SCALES. Psychological instruments designed to measure personal attitudes on a variety of topics and issues.

Typically, attitude scales contain a set of statements which represent different shades of opinion on a single issue. These statements range from the strongly positive to the strongly negative, and each of them is assigned a number, or "scale value," which expresses its position along this continuum. By noting his agreement or disagreement with each statement, the subject reveals the nature and relative strength of his attitudes on the subject in question.

The Thurstone Scales measure attitudes on about thirty subjects, including capital punishment, censorship, communism, Negroes, patriotism, Chinese, and the church. In constructing these scales, large numbers of statements were gathered from different groups of people and also from current literature. When it appeared that all grades of opinion were represented, the list was edited and reduced to about a hundred short statements. Next, about three hundred judges were asked to sort these statements into eleven categories, within which they were to represent "equal-appearing intervals" from most to least favorable. The scale values for each statement were then computed from the percentage of judges who placed each statement in the different categories. After this, the authors of the test selected statements whose scale values were equally spaced along the continuum. Ambiguous and irrelevant statements were then eliminated and a final group compiled.

The selected statements were usually divided into two parallel or equivalent forms, each containing about twenty items arranged in random order. The following are some samples from the Thurstone Scale on the subject of the church, with their scale values in parentheses: "I find the services of the church both restful and inspiring" (2.3) . . . "I think the teaching of the church is altogether too superficial to have much social significance" (8.3) . . . "I believe in religion but I seldom go to church" (5.4).

The subject who takes a Thurstone type of scale checks off all statements with which he agrees, and his score consists of their median scale value. The parallel forms of the test are usually used to determine attitudes before and after certain experiences, such as viewing a motion picture related to the topic.

The construction of this test was, of course, dependent on the attitudes of the judges who classified the statements. Thurstone maintained that this did not appreciably affect the scale values. However, he eliminated the records of judges who placed too many statements in a single pile, since he believed this indicated careless sorting, but in so doing he disregarded some of the more extreme views. Also, it must be recognized that attitudes on such subjects as Negroes and war shift materially with the times, and this would tend to alter the scale values originally assigned by the judges.

In spite of these limitations the Thurstone test has considerable value in making comparisons between groups and in determining shifts of opinion due to propaganda or changes in the individual's life situation, such as a shift from employment to unemployment. Special scales of this type have also been constructed for measuring the attitudes of employees toward their company.

Another method of constructing attitude scales has been developed by Likert. In his procedure the items are not classified by a group of judges but are selected on the basis of responses made by subjects to whom they are administered. This type of instrument is not limited to simple agreement or disagreement, for the responses are graded Strongly Agree, Agree, Undecided, Disagree, and Strongly Disagree. Each response is given an item credit from 1 to 5 according to strength of agreement or disagreement. The total score consists of the sum of these credits, and the author provides empirically established forms against which any given score can be compared.

An example of a scale of the Likert type is the Minnesota Personality Scale (for men), which presents such items as "On the whole lawyers are honest" and "Education only makes a person discontented." The Minnesota Teacher Attitude Survey also uses this technique. It consists of 150 items designed to assess pupil-teacher relations, chosen from over 700 statements administered to 100 teachers nominated by their principals as superior, and 100 as inferior in their relationships with pupils. The final items were validated against a criterion based upon ratings by the principal, pupils, and a visiting expert. A sample item is "A teacher should never acknowledge his ignorance of a topic in the presence of his pupils." *See* MORALE (INDUSTRIAL), SOCIAL DISTANCE, SOCIOMETRY.

ATTITUDES TOWARD MENTAL ILLNESS. Attitudes of the public toward mental illness are extremely important since they may spell the difference between accepting and refusing treatment, and between accepting and rejecting individuals who suffer from mental disorders. The success of new facilities such as halfway houses, day hospitals, and community mental health centers is also dependent to a large extent on public attitudes.

Many people are still influenced by misconceptions that have come down through the ages via legend and literature, hearsay and humor. Even though some of the blatant superstitions have been discarded—for example, that the mentally ill are possessed of the demon, or that sin produces insanity—a large number of people still feel that mental patients have been foredoomed by heredity and are basically incurable. And a great many still associate mental disorders with behavior that is repellent, terrifying, and even disgraceful. As Coleman (1964) has pointed out: "There is a popular notion that inmates of mental hospitals are a weird lot who spend their time cutting out paper dolls, posing as Napoleon, or ranting and raving. The majority of patients are well aware of what is going on around them and can discuss their condition in much the same way that we might tell our doctor about severe indigestion. Only a minority of patients present a picture of severely disturbed or deviant behavior."

In spite of lingering misconceptions,

scientific surveys carried out between 1948 and 1962 indicate that public opinion on mental illness is gradually becoming more enlightened. The most significant findings in the surveys in the earlier part of this period, between 1948 and 1954, are these: (1) the great majority of people viewed mental illness as a sickness, and over half felt that treatment would be at least moderately effective; (2) most people would seek help from a clergyman, general practitioner, or friend, and go to a psychiatrist only as a last resort; (3) younger respondents and those on higher educational and occupational levels were more optimistic about treatment, more scientifically oriented, and better informed than older and less educated people; (4) most people recognized the need for more doctors and facilities, but had little understanding of treatment methods, or mistrusted them; (5) there was little understanding of the origins of mental illness—the causes most frequently cited were poor living conditions, alcohol, money troubles, excessive brainwork, and unwillingness to face everyday problems; (6) when presented with case descriptions of actual mental illnesses, most people failed to recognize the seriousness of the disorders and recommended such measures as kindness, calming the patient by talking to him, or increased social contacts; (7) there was a widespread tendency to picture the mentally ill as irrational, queer, and unpredictable.

Two studies reported in 1960 indicate that progress is being made on many of these points (Halpert, 1963). A survey conducted in a relatively low socioeconomic neighborhood in Baltimore showed that a far higher percentage of people recognized serious disorders from case descriptions than a decade before, and these respondents were also more optimistic about chances of recovery. Only 15 per cent showed attitudes of rejection toward the mentally ill and the great majority showed positive attitudes—for example, 81 per cent were willing to work side by side with a recovered person. Similar results were obtained in a study conducted among civic leaders in a lower-middle-class district of New York City. This survey indicated that the educational leaders were best informed, then politico-legal leaders, religious leaders, and economic leaders, in that order.

In spite of this evidence of progress, the Joint Commission on Mental Illness and Health concluded in its 1962 report that a forceful educational program conducted on a national scale is urgently needed. Its objective would be to help the general public recognize mental illness, to convince them that treatment is both safe and effective, and to get them to adopt a more sympathetic attitude toward the mentally ill. The report states: "The National Mental Health Program should avoid the risk of false promise of 'public education for better mental health' and focus on the more modest goal of disseminating such information about mental illness as the public needs and wants in order to recognize psychological forms of sickness and to arrive at an informed opinion on its responsibility toward the mentally ill." See JOINT COMMISSION ON MENTAL ILLNESS AND HEALTH.

AUDIOGRAM. A graph representing the acuity of an individual's hearing; it records the lowest intensity of sound that can be heard by each ear throughout the entire range of frequencies.

Auditory acuity is measured by using an apparatus called an audiometer, which generates pure tones in octaves over the entire audible range. The examiner records the minimum intensity of sound, in decibels, the subject can hear at each frequency. The results are plotted on an audiogram chart which contains a line representing normal hearing. Hearing deviations at each frequency are represented by the distance between the graph line and the normal line.

Different types of deafness have been found to produce different audiograms. Conduction deafness is due to a stopped-up ear, a broken eardrum, or damaged bones in the middle ear. As a result there is difficulty in conducting the sound signal from the outer ear to the auditory nerve that leads to the brain. In these cases the audiogram shows a hearing loss at all frequencies, although it is somewhat greater at low frequencies since they demand relatively large movements of the eardrum and bones of the middle ear. Nerve deafness, on the other hand, is due to damage to the auditory nerve or the cochlea in the inner ear (see Fig. 28, p. 543). Here the audiogram indicates that the greatest loss is in the high-frequency range. This defect is commonly found in older persons, who have trouble understanding speech since it is largely made up of the higher frequencies. Another form of nerve deafness consists of a "tonal gap," in which a small range of frequencies is inaudible, and a third form is the "tonal island," in which the audiogram shows a large area of loss with a small area intact.

The audiometer often uncovers hearing losses among schoolchildren who are having difficulty in learning to read or in other classwork or social life. The device yields far more accurate results than the usual school tests in which the children respond to recordings played to an entire class. Audiometer tests are also administered where occupational hearing loss is suspected. After years of employment on noisy jobs, boilermakers, shipyard workers, and machinists often show marked high-tone loss, an affliction that is known as stimulation deafness or boilermaker's deafness. This condition is also a serious problem in modern warfare and rocketry. Earplugs called "ear wardens" are recommended to minimize the possibility of damage. See DEAFNESS, HEARING, APTITUDE TESTS (SPECIAL).

AUDITORY SPACE PERCEPTION. The perception of spatial qualities through the sense of hearing.

Space perception occurs in audition as well as vision since hearing gives us cues both to the direction and distance of the source of sound. It is of little use, however, in determining the size or exact position of objects.

There are three auditory cues to direction: time difference, phase difference, and intensity difference. We judge where a sound comes from partly by the fact that it usually reaches our two ears at different times. We know that a sound comes from our left because our left ear receives it a fraction of a second (about .0002 second) before our right. We can even tell, roughly, how far it is toward our left. When both ears hear the sound at the same time, we know it comes from a point midway between our two ears, but we cannot tell whether it is above or below, in front or behind us.

The second directional cue is intensity, or loudness. Intensity decreases as the square of the distance from the source. When one ear is closer to the source, it receives the sound at greater intensity than the farther ear. The farther ear is also in the "sound shadow" of the head, and consequently the sound waves it receives are weakened. Without realizing we are doing so, we learn to judge direction by these differences.

We are even less consciously aware of the third type of cue, phase difference. This is the difference in pressure (positive or negative) between two tones at any particular instant. If one ear faces the source of sound more directly than the other, the maximum positive pressure of the sound wave reaches this ear before it reaches the more distant ear. The tones received by the two ears are then out of phase, and the extent of the difference helps us determine the direction of the sound source.

Time, phase, and intensity differences provide a fairly good direction location when the head and source are stationary, but they are usually more accurate when the head and source are moving. The reason is that we can then perceive how these cues change with changes in the relative position of the head and the sound source. This is why we automatically move our heads in determining where a sound comes from.

In contrast to the perception of direction, auditory perception of distance requires the use of only one ear, since it depends wholly on the monaural cues of intensity, frequency, and complexity. If we are familiar with a sound we can usually judge its distance in terms of its loudness, for we know that the closer it is the louder it will be. A distant train whistle may sound no louder than a nearby clock chime, but we know from experience that train whistles are louder than chimes, and conclude that the train must therefore be far away.

We also base estimates of distance on the fact that low-frequency, low-pitched sounds can be heard much further than high sounds—even though we may not be consciously aware of this fact. This helps us recognize that a foghorn is actually far away even when the sound is loud. It also helps us know whether an orchestra is playing in the distance or nearby. If it is in the distance we will hear far more of the low notes than the high notes and this will alter the total effect, or composition, of the music being played. *See* DEPTH PERCEPTION.

AURA (literally, "air" or "atmosphere"). In psychiatry, subjective premonitory symptoms preceding an epileptic convulsion, and in some cases an acute migraine attack or other approaching disorder.

Sensations of all types (psychic, sensory, visceral, motor) may be experienced: peculiar odors, strange tastes, colored lights, feelings of numbness, crawling sensations, stomach discomfort, weird sounds, muffled voices, déjà vu, feelings of unreality, a compulsive desire to run. Each patient experiences his own typical aura and may learn to use it as a warning of an impending seizure. In some cases there is time to prepare for the attack; in others, the convulsion follows immediately.

The term aura is also used in parapsychology and psychical research to denote alleged emanations from the body. These emanations are believed to be visible to others who are sensitive to such phenomena. Some people claim to see halos surrounding the head or entire body of certain individuals, and even rank them in a spiritual hierarchy. A violet aura is thought to indicate a high degree of spirituality, a yellow aura a low degree.

AUTHORITARIAN PERSONALITY. A cluster of traits which includes "a high degree of conformity, dependence on authority, overcontrol of feelings and impulses, rigidity of thinking and ethnocentrism" (Krech, et al., 1962). Individuals possessing these traits adhere strictly to conventional values, are preoccupied with considerations of power and status, identify with authoritative figures, and are generally hostile to members of minority or other outgroups. As Secord and Backman (1964) point out, these traits belong together in such a way that a person who is high, low, or average in some of them tends to be high, low, or average in all of them.

The syndrome was first identified in 1950 in an extensive study conducted by Adorno, Frenkel-Brunswik, and others under the title *The Authoritarian Personality*. The purpose of the study was to expose the psychological roots of anti-Semitism: "The anti-Semite in America turned out to be generally ethnocentric, generally antagonistic to groups other than his own because he thought of these groups as having various disagreeable innate qualities. Politically the anti-Semite tended to be conservative, a firm believer in 'free enterprise,' nationalistic, a friend of business and an enemy of labor unions" (Brown, 1965). In view of these facts, the authors concluded that anti-Semitism, with its prejudicial, antidemocratic attitudes, was in many cases part of a well-organized and much larger personality structure which they termed authoritarian.

A study of the origins of this personality revealed that it tended to develop in persons who were subjected to very strict parental control early in life, and who had learned to bury their resentments and adopt an attitude of acquiescence. As a result, they remained overly obedient to strong authority in adulthood, while expressing their hidden hostilities toward weak individuals or groups who might be attacked without risk. Since minorities and foreign nations provided safe targets for these attacks, authoritarian individuals became particularly susceptible to prejudice against minorities and developed strong ethnocentric attitudes.

Adorno and his co-workers supported this analysis with both attitude tests and clinical studies. They discovered that authoritarian individuals scored high on attitude scales measuring Fascism, anti-Semitism and ethnocentrism. In addition, they also found that their description of the authoritarian personality was strikingly similar to the description of the ideal Nazi as given by E. R. Jaensch, a psychologist and a member of the Nazi party. A series of depth clinical interviews with various subjects who represented high and low points on the scales of anti-Semitism and ethnocentrism provided even more conclusive evidence that the acceptance or rejection of this cluster of prejudices was associated with the individual's over-all personality structure. In a word, people who were most apt to adopt antidemocratic attitudes were also found to exhibit an authoritarian personality structure. *See* PREJUDICE, GROUP DYNAMICS.

AUTISM (Autistic Thinking). Uncritical thinking dominated by fantasies that have little or no relation to reality; the gratification of wishes and desires in imagination.

Reverie, flights of fancy, and daydreams are normal forms of autistic thinking and may have positive value in arousing ambition and in enabling us to release emotions and temporarily escape everyday pressures. The boy who imagines himself a hero and the girl who sees herself as the belle of the ball are common examples. Drowsiness, sleep, fatigue, or monotonous tasks invite autistic thinking, particularly among those who have a store of unfulfilled wishes or frustrations within them.

In psychiatry, autism generally means loss of contact with reality and retreat into a private world of delusions, hallucinations, or disjointed ideas (PLATE 8). This kind of thinking appears in a variety of disorders, including senile psychoses, some forms of depression, and Kanner's syndrome (early infantile autism). It manifests itself most frequently in schizophrenic reactions and was at one time considered to be the major characteristic of this psychosis.

A distinction is sometimes made between an agitated autistic state in which the psychotic patient experiences terror, religious ecstasy, martyrdom, or messianic delusions; and a calm autistic state in which he believes he is receiving thoughts from another planet or from a divine being. Yet, as Maslow and Mittelmann (1951) point out, even in an outwardly calm condition, such as a state of stupor, a patient's fantasies may be "very vivid and often on a cosmic scale." They cite the case of a patient who "stated that a gigantic struggle was going on in the universe between good and evil and that he was the battleground. The forces of good and evil were so equally balanced that any movement on his part might have decided the struggle one way or another. He was afraid to make the wrong move, hence he lay still." *See* DEREISTIC THINKING, EARLY INFANTILE AUTISM, DAYDREAMING, SCHIZOPHRENIC REACTIONS (GENERAL), IMAGINARY COMPANION.

Illustrative Case: AUTISM

A young engineer, who had graduated creditably from an engineering school and landed a good job for himself, showed a gradual decline in his ability to do his work until he finally lost his job. At home he spent his days lying around the house; he had no complaints. After admission to a psychiatric clinic he said frankly that there was nothing anyone in the world could offer him as valuable as his daydreams.

This patient said that as a child he had always had an imaginary boy playmate who meant a great deal to him. In adolescence the imaginary playmate became a girl with whom he fell in love. He made strong attempts in college to get away from this autistic affair and managed to fall in love with a married woman who appears, from all the evidence available, to have considered him as no more than a good friend. He did well in his studies and went aggressively and successfully after a job, as we have said. But here the difficulties involved in getting started in a competitive field, where rewards were only in a vague and distant future, proved too much for him.

It was the imaginary playmate of his daydreams who rescued him from this situation. In his fantasy he courted and married her; and they lived a complete life together as man and wife in the autistic community of his own imagining. Thus, the satisfactions he had learned to find by this technique, throughout childhood and adolescence, now culminated fittingly in the perfect autistic union. To leave this fantasied world for the drab loneliness of the shared social community was to give up everything he valued in return for nothing. He said, "I know where this is leading me, but it doesn't matter." (Cameron, 1947)

AUTISTIC CHILD. A child who has lost or never achieved contact with other people and is totally preoccupied with his own fantasies, thoughts, and stereotyped behavior. Autistic children are so withdrawn that they are often thought to be mentally retarded, although actually they are immature and emotionally disturbed. The term autism is somewhat loosely used to cover both early infantile autism and childhood schizophrenia. *See* EARLY INFANTILE AUTISM, SCHIZOPHRENIA (CHILDHOOD TYPE).

AUTOCHTHONOUS IDEA. A delusion or other false idea which the individual feels is thrust upon him, even though it actually stems from his own unconscious.

The word autochthonous means, literally, "sprung from the soil" and is synonymous with native or indigenous. An autochthonous idea is therefore one that springs from within the region of the mind, just as certain plants or animals are indigenous to a given region of the earth. The reason the patient feels this idea comes from outside himself is that it appears so strange and foreign. He may therefore conclude that he is possessed by a demon or that his enemies are injecting thoughts into his mind. Delusions of this kind are characteristic of paranoia or the paranoid type of schizophrenia.

Less extreme autochthonous ideas are found in some obsessive-compulsive individuals. Such patients are at the mercy of repetitive thoughts which appear to be forced upon them. Even though they consider these ideas irrational, they cannot get them out of their minds. See PARANOIA, SCHIZOPHRENIA (PARANOID TYPE), OBSESSIVE-COMPULSIVE REACTION.

AUTOEROTISM. Sexual pleasure derived from one's own body.

The term was invented by Havelock Ellis and is most frequently used as a synonym for masturbation. However, it covers a wider range, including satisfaction from genital play, self-stimulation of the lips (as in smacking the lips or making sucking movements), and anal stimulation, as well as sexual pleasure from observing one's own masturbation and from fantasies involving self-gratification.

Psychoanalysts believe autoerotic tendencies make their first appearance in the earliest phase of psychosexual development, the oral sucking stage, before the child can distinguish between himself and the outer world. "The libido is directed along one main channel, namely toward the individual's own body at the time when there is no sensing of 'I' or 'it'" (Healy, Bronner, and Bowers, 1930). *See* EROTOGENIC ZONE, PSYCHOSEXUAL DEVELOPMENT, INCORPORATION.

AUTOMATIC WRITING AND DRAWING. The production of graphic material without conscious volition or control.

Psychiatrists and psychologists occasionally use automatic writing as a technique in exploring the unconscious. A common procedure is to engage the subject in conversation, or give him a book to read, and at the same time put a pencil in his hand. The paper is usually placed behind a pile of books to hide his hand from view as he writes. An apt subject will write revealing material or answer whispered questions which have nothing to do with the conversation or the book he is reading. Some hysteric patients write or draw automatically during a dissociated, trancelike state; other subjects are deliberately put into a trance through hypnosis and commanded to write.

Wolberg (1945) offers this assessment of the method: "Automatic writing is a splendid means of gaining access to unconscious material that lies beyond the grasp of conscious recall. The portion of the cerebrum that controls automatic writing seems to have access to material unavailable to centers that control speech. Consequently hypnotic verbalization of feelings and impulses may not yield information as vital as that brought up through automatic writing."

Automatic writing is used for many purposes: to elicit repressed and apparently forgotten memories; to help victims of amnesia regain their identity; to break through resistances encountered in the course of psychotherapy. In some cases unconscious material revealed in automatic writing is condensed or disguised, and has to be analyzed and interpreted in the light of the patient's experience. This is even more true of automatic drawing than of automatic writing, as illustrated by the case at the end of this article. *See* AMNESIA (DISSOCIATIVE TYPE).

In an article on automatic writing, Anita M. Mühl (1922) distinguishes between two types of subjects, those who can write only while they are being deliberately distracted and stimulated, and those who can write only while relaxed and with their attention fixed on what they are doing. She further subdivides these groups into subjects who have no idea what the hand is writing and those who are aware of what is being recorded, but who are "flooded with ideas without volition and without logical association toward the normal mental processes." She points out that "the writing is the manifestation of dissociated ideas of which the writer is not aware. Very frequently the subject has no idea what causes him to do the writing and he may be accredited with mediumistic possession and supernatural powers so that he may even be given to believe he has 'psychic tendencies.'" The writing, however, arises from unconscious sources, and may in some cases "masquerade" in the form of un-suspected secondary personalities.

In one of her examples, no less than seven distinct personalities appeared in the automatic writing of a demure young woman named Violet X—each with its own name, characteristics, and handwriting. These personalities in-cluded, among others, an irrepressible fallen woman, Annie McGinnis, who expressed her hatred of men in letters two inches high; a cosmopolitan lady named Mary Minnott, who drew pic-tures of fashionable gowns (though Miss X could not draw at all in her normal state); her own dead father, with writ-ing identical to his; the "Spirit of War and Desolation," who urged her to work for the Red Cross (World War I was in progress at the time); and Man, who carried on a running battle with Annie McGinnis, each "wresting" the pen from the other in an effort to gain dominance over Violet. The ex-periment was brought to a close when Man gained the upper hand and forced the timid Violet to engage in a violent frenzied dance.

Another of Mühl's subjects, a twenty-six-year-old girl whom she called Violet Z, had been in the habit of amusing herself and her friends by automatically writing imaginative crime stories. The psychiatrist decided to test the girl, and once again found that a number of conflicting personalities appeared and expressed themselves on paper. The ex-periment culminated in the following startling scene:

"Violet Z sat at the table and made some incoherent records with her right hand. The facility for smooth produc-tion seemed to have been lost. At last becoming impatient, I put the pencil in her left hand and said, "Let's see what that will do!" Almost immediately the left hand (which she ordinarily cannot use for writing) began to fly across the paper and the resulting records were perfectly coherent. Then I decided it would be fun to see what would happen

if I put a pencil in each of her hands. There seemed to be a momentary quiver of each arm and then both hands began writing simultaneously, each hand recording a different message and each denoting a different sex. The left hand wrote in small characters and claimed to be representing a girl by the name of Aneta Glane who expressed admira-tion for Violet Z. The right hand wrote in bold flourishing style under the name of Daniel Raun and was pompous and boastful. After some time the left hand wrote, "If you will help me I can write better," while *simultaneously* the right hand recorded, "I would like to let you but I am stronger and I hinder." The last thing written was, "I want to be strong, but I am weaker"—with the left hand—while the right hand pranced all over the page in huge letters saying, "Good, good—and Good Again—and Good Again!"

For an example of a psychiatric cure effected by a secondary personality through the use of automatic writing, *see* MULTIPLE PERSONALITY.

Illustrative Case: AUTOMATIC DRAWING

A college girl came to a psychiatrist with two complaints: an acute feeling of im-pending catastrophe; and a sudden mount-ing, inexplicable dislike for her best friend. During the interview, the doctor had occa-sion to glance through the girl's notebook, and noticed the drawings in Fig. 8, scat-tered in the margins of the pages. Sensing a possible clue, he questioned the girl about

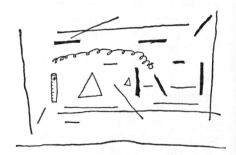

Fig. 8.

them. Although she commented that she had recently become interested in symbolism in her psychology course, she insisted that the drawings were only doodles.

In an attempt to probe more deeply, she was put into a trance and questioned about the figures. She immediately asked for a pencil and produced the drawing in Fig. 9.

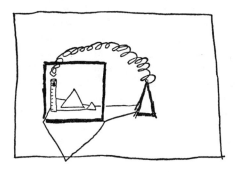

Fig. 9.

Under questioning, she interpreted its symbolism somewhat as follows: "My home—the rectangle—is going to pieces: see that break at the bottom? My dad, the cigarette—my mother, the larger triangle—and I, the smaller triangle—are still together. But see how the smoke—and the line, too—are moving out of the frame to that other triangle? That can mean only one thing . . . My dad is having an affair outside our home."

On further questioning, the girl became increasingly agitated but finally was able to name the third triangle: it was her best friend. The suspicion was confirmed the following day. The only possible clue to this "intuition" came out in a further session in which she recalled that her friend had recently visited their home, and her father had offered the girl a light, using a packet of matches from a hotel in the city. Questioned by his daughter, he admitted that he had been meeting her friend in secret at that hotel. (Adapted from Erickson and Kubie, 1938)

AUTOMATISM. This term is used in several senses. Basically, as English and English (1958) state, it is "an act performed without realization or intent, often without realizing that it is taking place." Examples are reflex responses, as in lifting our foot when we step on a tack, and thoroughly habitual acts such as repeatedly using the same linguistic expressions.

In a more specialized sense, the term is applied to certain acts performed in the absence of normal conscious awareness or attention—for example, automatic writing, sleepwalking, or behavior in a fugue state. Still more specialized is Janet's use of the term: "a system of psychological and physiological phenomena, arising from a traumatic experience that grows by annexing other phenomena, originally independent. These annexed behaviors are the secondary symptoms that mark the neurotic." An example would be feelings of anxiety and tension which some individuals experience in elevators or subways, and which may be traced to traumatic experiences such as being locked in a closet. In this usage, an automatism is similar to a complex, though more restricted. *See* JANET, SOMNAMBULISM, AUTOMATIC WRITING AND DRAWING.

Automatisms are found in a number of psychiatric and neurological conditions. In the early stages of senile psychosis, some patients mechanically perform certain activities which previously required an act of will—for example, they repeatedly make, unmake, and remake their bed. Such performance of habitual activities is probably associated with another characteristic of these patients, their "misoneism," or extreme intolerance of anything new or changed. In the senile disorder known as Pick's disease the ability to think abstractly is impaired, and the patient often falls back on "habitual automatisms or immediate concrete images; as a result, impulsive bizarre actions are performed. At times these automatic impulsive responses may be the expression of a cover-up on the part of the patients for their unwillingness to think, rather than of impairment of abstract attitudes" (Ferraro, 1959). If, for example, the patient is given a jigsaw puzzle, he will merely move the pieces about haphazardly instead of making a rational attack with the picture as a whole in mind. *See* PICK'S DISEASE, SENILE PSYCHOSIS.

In psychomotor epilepsy, or psychic seizures, the patient does not become unconscious, but he may be afflicted with an attack of "automatic thinking." After the episode he usually cannot remember much of the thought content but recalls its emotional tone. There is evidence that these patients occasionally experience "panoramic memories" similar to those experienced by a drowning person. In a psychic seizure, such memories tend to be accompanied by vivid sights and sounds as if the patient were actually going through the experience. *See* HYPERMNESIA.

In still other cases the patient goes through a five- or ten-minute "twilight state" during which he is disoriented as to time and place, and performs such automatic acts as mumbling unintelligible sounds, uttering a single word over and over, taking off his clothes, smacking his lips repeatedly, or walking about aimlessly. Other patients continue their normal activity, such as sewing, in a thoroughly mechanical way, or walk down the street until they suddenly "snap out of it." A few develop "epilepsia cursiva," a condition in which they run swiftly and automatically while in a state of disturbed consciousness. All these reactions tend to be of short duration, but in rare cases a condition known as "poriomanic fugue" may develop and last one or two days. In this state the patient sometimes has a bad accident or commits a crime but later has no memory at all or only a patchy recollection of what transpired. *See* FUGUE STATE, EPILEPSY (SYMPTOMS AND TYPES), TWILIGHT STATE.

AUTONOMIC NERVOUS SYSTEM.
A division of the nervous system which serves the endocrine glands and smooth muscles, and controls the internal activities of the body in both normal and emergency situations.

The autonomic system is divided into two parts, the sympathetic and parasympathetic systems (*Fig. 10*). These divisions maintain the stability of the internal environment of the body through antagonistic yet co-ordinated activities—for example, if one division stimulates stomach activity, the other retards it. In general, the sympathetic division mobilizes the resources of the organism when it is threatened with danger or involved in strenuous work, while the parasympathetic division conserves its energy and regulates the normal ongoing functions of the heart, stomach, and other visceral organs.

The nerve fibers of the sympathetic system stem from the thoracicolumbar region of the spine (the middle of the back), and gather together into twenty-two ganglia just outside the spinal cord. These ganglia are interconnected and form the so-called sympathetic chains, one on each side of the cord, which enable the system to act as a unit. Fibers extend from these chains to the iris of the eye, the salivary glands, the heart, lungs, liver, stomach, pancreas, intestines, adrenal glands, kidneys, bladder, colon, rectum, and genitals, as well as to the surface blood vessels, sweat glands, and hair follicles of the entire body. When the organism is faced with work that requires a heavy expenditure of energy or situations that arouse fear, rage, and other forms of emotional excitement, the typical sympathetic changes take place. The pupils widen to facilitate vision, the arteries constrict to supply more blood to the muscles and brain, the heart accelerates to pump extra blood, adrenalin is secreted to raise the blood sugar level and increase tissue metabolism. In addition, stomach and intestinal activities cease so that energy can be directed elsewhere, rectum and bladder action

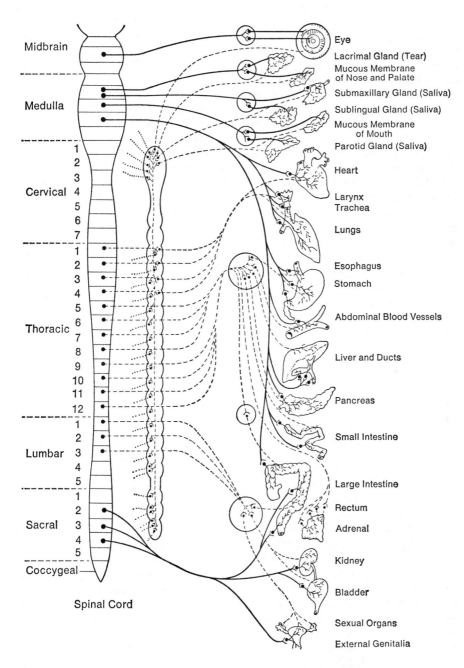

Fig. 10. A schematic diagram of the autonomic nervous system. Fibers of the sympathetic division are shown in broken lines, fibers of the parasympathetic division in solid lines.

are usually inhibited, the skin perspires to eliminate waste products and maintain a comfortable temperature for the overworked organism, and during sexual activity the male organ ejaculates. All these changes have the single effect of mobilizing the organism to meet the special situation.

The structure of the parasympathetic system differs from that of the sympathetic in two major ways: the ganglia lie close to the organs they innervate, and they do not form a chain. As a result they usually act in a more piecemeal fashion than the sympathetic nerves. The fibers of this system stem primarily from the cranial and sacral regions, at the top and bottom of the spinal cord. The cranial division serves the iris, salivary glands, heart, lungs, stomach, and other digestive organs; the sacral division serves the bladder, colon, rectum, and genitals. (Note that there is no connection to the adrenal gland, which is active during excitement.)

These fibers carry on functions that preserve and build up the body's resources, and most of them produce effects that are opposite to those produced by the sympathetic fibers. They constrict the pupil of the eye to protect it from excessive light, inhibit heartbeat, and dilate the arteries to lower the blood pressure and conserve fuel; facilitate digestion and build tissue by increasing the rate and amount of salivary secretion, by increasing stomach contractions, and by stimulating the flow of digestive juices; and rid the body of unwanted and harmful waste material by causing the bladder and colon to empty. Although most of these activities are in opposition to the sympathetic nervous system, it should be noted that the emptying of the bladder and colon can also occur in excitement. Also, the two work together in male sex activity, since the parasympathetic system controls erection while the sympathetic brings about orgasm.

Even though the various functions of the parasympathetic system are relatively independent of each other, their total effect is to maintain a balanced operation of the organism under quiescent conditions. That balance may be temporarily disturbed if the organism has to meet an emergency or adapt to conditions that drain its energy. When this happens, the sympathetic system takes over to key it up and call upon its reserves. But when the crisis has passed the parasympathetic again takes over and restores its equilibrium. *See* ADRENAL GLANDS, EMOTION (GENERAL), GENERAL ADAPTATION SYNDROME, DYSAUTONOMIA.

AUTOPSYCHIC. A general term characterizing impulses or ideas which originate from the self; also, pertaining to self-consciousness or ideas relating to the individual's own personality.

Autopsychic is the opposite of allopsychic, a term applied to projecting one's own ideas or feelings into other people. Autopsychic ideas may occur on either a normal or pathological level. An example of the former is the belief in our own competence as a reflection of inner wishes or convictions rather than of the opinions of others. The pathological type frequently occurs in paranoid disorders, which are sometimes termed autopsychoses. In these disorders the patient has distorted ideas about himself: he may think he is an undiscovered genius, a savior, or the devil incarnate. Such delusions are believed to result from unconscious needs, and are termed autopsychic because they pertain to the self and also because they arise from within the psyche. *See* ALLOPSYCHIC.

AUTOSCOPIC SYNDROME. A rare psychotic disorder in which the patient suffers from the delusion of seeing a "double" who looks, talks, dresses, and acts exactly like himself. (The term means "view one's self.")

The double usually appears suddenly and in colorless form, as in a dream.

In spite of the strange nature of the experience, the patient is more likely to react with indifference than with amazement. In some cases the double appears only once, lasting for a few seconds; in others it appears repeatedly, generally in the evening; in still others, the experience always follows disturbing incidents.

The term autoscopy was applied by Schilder (1950) to the process of projecting one's own body-image into the outside world—for example, a crippled person sees a crippled individual. The symptom is most often reported by patients suffering from migraine and epilepsy, though it occasionally occurs in schizophrenic and depressive reactions. Arieti and Meth (1959) suggest that it may be remotely related to such phenomena as eidetic imagery and imaginary companions in children, but that it bears a closer relation to "those conditions in which a psychological picture is superimposed on an original organic condition, such as symptomatic epilepsy, cases of phantom limb, duplication of parts of the body, and denial of illness." However, no satisfactory explanation for the symptom has yet been found. *See* EIDETIC IMAGERY, IMAGINARY COMPANION, ANOSOGNOSIA, PHANTOM REACTION.

AUTOSUGGESTION. The process of giving suggestions to one's self to improve morale or promote recovery from illness. Autosuggestion may be carried out either in a relaxed waking state or in a state of self-hypnosis.

Autosuggestion was originated, or at least popularized, by Émile Coué in his pamphlet "Self-Mastery Through Conscious Autosuggestion" (1922). Although he began his work by "putting his patients to sleep," Coué later abandoned this technique and advocated the use of suggestion in the normal state. His patients were simply told to repeat to themselves, twenty to thirty times a day, the sentence "Every day in every way I am getting better and better." Un-doubtedly there was a hypnotic element in this procedure (though he avoided the term), for he suggested that they fixate on the point of their nose or slip a knotted string through their hands as they repeated the formula. Brenman and Gill (1947) comment: "It was actually a crude attempt to deal with the dawning recognition that the forces both of illness and recovery lie essentially within the person and not in an external agent."

It is interesting, too, that Coué maintained that "all suggestion is autosuggestion," for a number of recent investigators, such as Moss (1958), insist that hypnotic suggestion takes effect only if the subject applies it to himself. In this view, the subject is not simply an automaton blindly responding to the hypnotist, but an active participant in the process.

There is little doubt that self-suggestion can play a part in rallying our physical and emotional resources. Many people find it helpful to give themselves a "pep talk" when they are faced with a crisis. Repeating "I won't give in" or "I am not going to let down" can sometimes spell the difference between a half-hearted approach and an all-out effort on the playing field—and in illness it may make the difference between a slow and a speedy recovery, or even, perhaps, between life and death.

Some popular books and articles go much further and recommend autosuggestion and autohypnosis as general techniques for self-improvement and keys to success in every area of life. One such book instructs the reader to fixate on an imaginary crystal ball and inwardly repeat the suggestions: "Keep your eyes focused on the ball . . . You are going to sink into deep relaxation . . . Your eyes will relax and all the rest of your body, etc. etc." When relaxation (actually light hypnosis) is achieved, the subject gives himself posthypnotic suggestions that are supposed to help him overcome whatever difficulty he is encountering—for example, if he has lost faith in himself, he is instructed to induce a state of self-hypnosis and tell himself that every time he feels self-contemptuous, words like the following will spring to mind: "You respect yourself! You believe in yourself! You will face your errors positively and constructively!" Similar suggestions are recommended for overcoming shyness, combating depression, stimulating creative thinking, improving concentration, getting rid of tension, and conquering grief—not to mention such small matters as achieving a better marriage, getting along with "everyone," and winning success in the competitive world of business.

Autosuggestion of this kind may give suggestible people a momentary lift, but it can hardly be taken seriously as a genuine attack on the problems of life. In fact, a short-cut approach of this type is likely to keep them from seeking rational and intelligent solutions to their difficulties.

This questionable use of suggestion should not, however, be confused with the legitimate application of autohypnosis as an adjunct to hypnotherapy. In this technique, a psychologist or other professionally qualified person (1) trains his patient to achieve an adequate hypnotic level; (2) gives him therapeutic suggestions; and (3) implants posthypnotic suggestions that will enable him to put himself into a light trance and renew the therapeutic suggestions by himself. This technique is used for a variety of specific purposes—for example, to induce relaxation, encourage sleep, eliminate the need for chemical anesthesia in dentistry, curb an asthmatic attack, control the tendency to overeat, and prevent excessive pain during childbirth. *See* HYPNOTHERAPY, SUGGESTION, SUGGESTION THERAPY.

AVOIDANCE LEARNING. Learning to avoid an unpleasant or painful stimulus by responding to a warning signal.

In the course of our lives we acquire many avoidance responses. Most of them, like keeping our hands away from fire or staying out of drafts, are highly useful. Others, such as running at the sight of a mouse, are unnecessary or exaggerated. Once they are learned, reactions of this kind tend to stay with us for the remainder of our lives. But the question is, how do we acquire them and why are they so persistent?

Psychologists have looked for answers to these questions primarily in experiments on animals. A typical laboratory apparatus consists of an enclosure with two compartments and a low fence between them. A dog is placed in one of the compartments and a buzzer is sounded for ten seconds. If the dog remains in the compartment for the full ten seconds, he receives an electric shock through a floor grill until he jumps over the fence to the other compartment. If he jumps during the ten seconds that the buzzer sounds, he does not receive the shock.

In one series of experiments, Solomon and Wynne (1954) found that the dog does not jump to avoid the shock during the early trials. However, he soon begins to yelp not only when he receives the shock, but as soon as he hears the buzzer sound. A little later he becomes increasingly agitated when he receives the shock, and scurries around in an apparently aimless way. Then, during his scurrying, he happens to jump over the barrier and gets away from the shock. This brings him to a stage of learning called *escape learning,* for it takes only about ten trials for him to learn to jump the fence within three seconds after the onset of the shock. Finally, he learns to jump while the buzzer is on and *before* the shock begins. This is termed *avoidance learning,* and once it is established, the animal rarely gets shocked again.

But why *are* avoidance responses so persistent? The experiment suggests three reasons. First, the dog has received shocks after hearing the buzzer sound, and he therefore associates the two and comes to fear the buzzer. Second, this tie is strengthened by the fact that he occasionally makes a mistake and receives a shock even when he is performing well—and it has been found that "partial reinforcement" of this kind makes a response particularly resistant to extinction. Third, each time he makes the correct response he obtains relief from his conditioned fear response set in motion by the buzzer, and this further reinforces the avoidance response. Tests have shown that when a dog learns an avoidance response in this way, he will react to the buzzer thousands of times even when the shock is never again administered. *See* REINFORCEMENT.

The key to this situation seems to be that the animal constantly relives his fear and makes his avoidance response before he has a chance to see if the situation is painful. In fact, by avoiding the response, he never permits himself to find out if it is still dangerous. This helps to explain why childhood fears are so lasting. The child who has had a frightening experience in a swimming pool or lake will associate water with fear, and each time someone suggests going swimming his fear reaction will be evoked and the strength of his avoidance response will increase. Therefore he never gives himself a chance to test out the situation to see if it is still dangerous. What is more, his fear may "generalize" and he may avoid anything that has to do with swimming, including beaches, bathing suits or even stories about swimmers. *See* PHOBIAS, BEHAVIOR THERAPY, GENERALIZATION.

B

BABINSKI REFLEX. When the sole of an infant is lightly stroked prior to the eighth month of age, there is an upward extension of the toes, especially the big toe. This reaction is called the sign of Babinski, or Babinski reflex, after the French neuropathologist Josef Babinski (1857–1932) who first described it. It is commonly tested by physicians to determine whether the motor area of the brain is intact.

As the child grows older, the same type of stimulation causes a flexion movement: the toes point in toward the sole of the foot as if to grasp the stimulating instrument. This "plantar reflex" depends upon motor tracts that mature after birth. It is also the normal adult reaction to stimulation of this type.

If damage to the pyramidal tract occurs—that is, the neurons in the brain and spinal cord that control movement

—the Babinski sign is again found. It is one of the reactions used by clinical neurologists to detect cerebrospinal disorder. If there is damage to the region just in front of the motor area in the brain, a so-called "fanning sign of Babinski" will be obtained. Here stimulation causes the toes to separate out from each other in a fanlike movement. *See* REFLEX.

BARBITURATE ADDICTION. Physical and psychological dependence on barbiturate drugs.

Barbiturate sedatives rank with the opiates and alcohol as the major addiction drugs in use today. Taken in small amounts and under the direction of a physician, they are not considered harmful; but if three average-dose pills are taken every day for three to six months, they are almost certain to lead to addiction.

The same type of individuals who drink excessively become barbiturate addicts, and for much the same reasons: to ease tension and escape into a state of carefree intoxication. During this state, they become drowsy, are unable to solve even simple problems, and lack motor coordination. They also show poor judgment and readily become depressed, irritable, and quarrelsome. As their tolerance for the drug increases, they take larger and larger doses and become confused and disoriented. Prolonged usage leads to brain damage and mental deterioration, and large amounts taken at one time may be fatal. *See* BARBITURATE INTOXICATION.

Withdrawal of barbiturates must be carried out with extreme care and under continuous supervision in a hospital. The process has to be gradual and extended over two to three weeks. During this period the patient becomes weak, anxious, and tremulous, and these reactions are usually followed by nausea, abdominal cramps, increased heart rate, and insomnia. Many patients develop convulsions and psychotic reactions resembling delirium tremens. These symptoms are often more severe, persistent, and dangerous than in withdrawal from opium. Where barbiturate users are basically narcotics addicts, as is often the case, the problem of withdrawal is a particularly difficult one. *See* DRUG ADDICTION.

After withdrawal has been accomplished, the patient should be given intensive psychotherapy to help him overcome the personality defects which have led to his addiction.

BARBITURATE INTOXICATION.

Barbiturate poisoning is the most common cause of brain disorder due to toxic conditions. It is also the toxic disorder which most frequently leads to death.

Excessive amounts of drugs are taken for many purposes: to relieve anxiety, induce sleep, reinforce or substitute for narcotics, reduce tension after alcoholic debauches, or simply for kicks. Death may occur from accidental as well as deliberate overdosage, since the person who takes one or two pills as a sedative may become so mentally confused that he will take several more without realizing it. Sudden withdrawal of the drug after long-continued use may also result in death.

Acute barbiturate intoxication may take a mild, moderate, or severe form. In the mild form respiration and blood pressure are unaffected, but the individual becomes mentally confused, loses emotional control and laughs or cries without provocation. In the moderate state reflexes and respiration are slowed, and he becomes sleepy and hard to arouse. The severe state is characterized by deep coma, absence of all reflexes, periodic respiration, and symptoms of shock.

Treatment of the first two stages of barbiturate intoxication is aimed at eliminating the drug from the system and keeping the patient from lapsing into sleep or coma. To keep him awake he is usually held up and walked about. If he falls into a deep stupor, emergency measures such as plasma expanders and artificial respiration will be required to maintain life. During recovery, the patient goes through a period of delirium which requires continuous nursing.

In contrast to these acute cases, chronic intoxication occurs in constant users of barbiturates. Here the symptoms are impaired thinking and judgment, general mental confusion, defective reflexes, and poor motor coordination. Sudden withdrawal of the drug may be dangerous to life, since it is followed by extreme weakness, delirium, severe tremors, and often convulsions. Gradual withdrawal requires constant supervision and nursing. *See* BARBITURATE ADDICTION.

Illustrative Case: BARBITURATE INTOXI-
CATION.

(On withdrawal) the patient developed
signs of an acute brain syndrome. She had
a marked tremor and was unsteady on her
feet. She hallucinated, thought she heard
the voice of her husband telling her that he
was coming to get her in a taxi and she
cried out to him. Soon she began seeing
people climbing trees and looking through
the windows at her. Even after receiving
sedative medication she remained restless,
muttering to herself incoherently. Her
tremor increased, her face became flushed,
and she began to perspire excessively. At
times she twitched convulsively. A little
later she began picking up imaginary objects
and muttering "thank you" as if someone
were handing them to her. Later she was
observed reaching for an imaginary glass
and drinking from it. She ate imaginary
food and picked imaginary cigarettes out
of the air; she heard nonexistent doorbells
and an ambulance siren. Following several
injections of a phenothiazine tranquilizer,
her hallucinations ceased and she again became rational. (Rosen and Gregory, 1965)

BEDLAM. A contraction of the name
of one of the first institutions for mental patients, St. Mary's of Bethlehem.

St. Mary's, located in London, was
founded as a monastery in 1247, became a mental hospital in 1402, and
was officially proclaimed a "lunatic asylum" by Henry VIII in 1547. The conditions in the institution were so de-
plorable that the term bedlam is now
a synonym for wild confusion. Patients
were shackled, starved, beaten, confined
to unlighted cells, and exhibited to the
public for a penny a look. The more
harmless inmates were forced to seek
charity on the streets of the city, and
were described by Shakespeare as:

"Bedlam beggars, who, with roaring
        voices . . .
Sometime with lunatic bans,
        sometime with prayers
Enforce their charity."
            —King Lear, Act II, Scene 3.

BEERS, CLIFFORD WHITTINGHAM
(1876–1943). The man who became
the founder of the mental hygiene
movement in America was born in Connecticut and attended Yale University.
Though haunted by a fear that he
would be afflicted with the same disease as his brother, a form of epilepsy,
he managed to struggle through his
studies and obtain his degree in 1897.
During the following three years he
worked in a tax collector's office and a
life insurance company, but in 1900
developed a severe depression with persecutory delusions. His despair became
so acute that he attempted suicide by
jumping from a fourth-floor bedroom
window. Though seriously injured, he
recovered from the fall within a few
months. His mental disorder persisted,
however, and he was placed in a mental hospital, with a diagnosis of manic-
depressive reaction.

During one of his hyperactive, manic
states, Beers directed his restless energies to reforming and improving conditions in the institution. His activities
were greatly resented by the hospital
authorities, and at one point he was
placed in a straitjacket for 15 hours.
Soon after, he was transferred to another hospital, where his attempts at
reform were rewarded with 14 weeks
of confinement in a violent ward. However, he continued his crusade, writing
letters to public officials on every scrap
of paper he could find, and arranging
to have them smuggled out of the institution. One of these letters reached the
governor of the state and actually
brought some improvements in the hospitals. Encouraged by this success, Beers
sought to gain his complete freedom so
that he could continue his efforts for
reform.

Beers was discharged from the hospital in 1903 and returned to his old
job in the insurance firm. He immediately took up his crusade again, un-
daunted by the dual handicap of having been a mental patient and of hav-

ing no influential friends. His first attempts actually landed him back in an institution, for when he told his friends that he planned to continue his campaign and was going to write to President Theodore Roosevelt himself, they concluded that he was headed for a relapse and persuaded him to "put himself away" for a time. He did so, but within a month was out again. In the summer of 1905 he wrote to a complete stranger, a prominent man named Joseph H. Choate, asking for an interview. When the two men saw each other, Beers outlined a plan to set up a national movement to bring about reform in the treatment of the mentally ill. Choate approved of his ideas and suggested that Beers write an outline of his plans which businessmen could read and consider at their leisure. He immediately set to work and within a year completed his remarkable volume *A Mind that Found Itself.*

This book presents, with rare insight, a clinical picture of Beers' mental state and emotional reactions during the various phases of his illness. But, more important, he offered dramatic, personal proof that a patient could recover from a serious mental disorder, and gave many suggestions for promoting other recoveries through "proper contextual support." He also insisted that mental disorder was not a sin, but an illness that is treatable, often curable, and even preventable; and he argued that individuals who authorize methods of physical punishment and restraint are themselves acting in an irrational manner. He sent his manuscript to Choate and also to William James, who wrote him a letter saying, "It is the best written out 'case' that I have seen; and you no doubt have put your finger on the weak spots of our treatment of the insane, and suggest the right line of remedy."

James' encouraging comments gave Beers the incentive to submit the work for publication. It appeared in 1908 and was widely read throughout the world. As a result, many distinguished individuals rallied to the support of his crusade, among them Adolf Meyer, who suggested the name "Mental Hygiene" for the new movement. Within a few months the Connecticut Society for Mental Hygiene, the first of its kind in the world, was established, with the objective of testing the feasibility of instituting reforms in standards of treatment, and of disseminating information on the nature and prevention of mental illness. One year later, in 1909, the National Committee for Mental Hygiene was founded, with Adolf Meyer and William James among its twelve charter members.

Beers continued his activities, serving as secretary of the National Committee until 1939. Branches were established in practically every state of the Union, and by 1930, when he helped to organize the first International Congress on Mental Health, thirty of the fifty nations represented had national committees of their own. In 1933 he received the highest award from the National Institute of Social Science for his outstanding humanitarian work.

Shortly after Clifford Beers' death in 1943, Dr. George Stevenson, medical director of the National Association for Mental Health, published an obituary in the American Journal of Psychiatry in which he stated, "He takes his place with Pinel and Dix in a triumvirate of immortals whose influence has been so deep that it continues to roll on and on, receiving a constant onward impulse from the rebound of the good that they do." *See* PINEL, DIX, MEYER, JAMES, MENTAL HYGIENE, NATIONAL ASSOCIATION FOR MENTAL HEALTH, MANIC-DEPRESSIVE REACTION (MANIC PHASE).

BEHAVIOR DISORDERS. A somewhat loose term with three major applications. First, it is occasionally applied to any type of abnormal behavior, or behavior pathology, and in this sense is roughly equivalent to "psychiatric disorder" or "mental disorder." Second, it is used as a synonym for "conduct disorder," referring to a pattern of impulsive antisocial behavior not accompanied by neurotic anxiety or psychotic misinterpretation of reality. In this sense the term is applied to many types of unacceptable behavior (stealing, assault, forgery, pathological lying, rape) when this behavior stems from a persistent personality disturbance whose major characteristic is failure to conform to social and ethical standards. See ANTISOCIAL REACTION, DYSSOCIAL REACTION, SEXUAL DEVIATIONS (GENERAL).

In its third application, the term behavior disorder, or "primary behavior disorder," partially overlaps with the second usage, but is applied specifically to a variety of psychiatric disorders of children and adolescents resulting from an unfavorable environment rather than from organic disease or defect. These disorders include the following major types: (a) undesirable traits and habit disturbances such as temper tantrums, nail biting, persistent thumb sucking, enuresis, and excessive masturbation; (b) conduct disorders such as cruelty, fire setting, continual lying, vandalism, sex offenses, glue sniffing, use of alcohol or drugs, stealing and other delinquencies; (c) certain neurotic symptoms such as tics, stuttering, somnambulism, and overactivity; (d) school difficulties such as disruptive behavior, school phobia, and truancy. See CHILD PHYCHIATRY, JUVENILE DELINQUENCY, TEMPER TANTRUM, NAIL BITING, THUMB SUCKING, ENURESIS, MASTURBATION, TIC, STUTTERING, SOMNAMBULISM, SCHOOL PHOBIA, PERSONALITY DISORDER.

BEHAVIORISM. A psychological approach in which investigation is limited to objective, observable phenomena and to the methods of natural science.

Behaviorism was first formulated by John Broadus Watson in 1913. It can be viewed both as a culmination of the movement toward objective psychology and as a revolt against functionalism and introspectionism. Watson equated science with the mechanistic, the materialistic, and the physical, labeling as "unscientific" or "supernatural" everything that could be classed as mental. He therefore conducted a veritable crusade against introspectionism because it not only accepted the concepts of mind and consciousness but concentrated entirely on subjective, qualitative experience. He was equally vehement in his denunciation of functionalism since it not only used introspection as a method, but based itself on "elusive" concepts that could not be anchored to observable fact—concepts like mental process, emotion, and volition.

In contrast to these subjective approaches, Watson proposed to make psychology scientific by utilizing only objective, naturalistic methods, including adaptations of Pavlov's conditioning techniques, investigations of human physiology, the study of animal behavior, and especially laboratory procedures in which experiments were repeated with different subjects until statistically significant results were obtained.

Watson defined behavior in completely naturalistic terms as movements in time and space. This immediately associated the field of psychology with the quantitative approach of the physical sciences, since all movements in time and space are theoretically measurable. Although he believed that psychology should investigate the activities of the total organism, Watson's own studies dealt primarily with the following aspects of behavior:

Stimulus-Response. All complex forms of behavior, including reasoning, habit, and emotional reactions are at bottom composed only of simple stimulus-response events which can be seen, measured, and therefore known. If we study a child's attitudes toward others, for example, we will find that they originated as responses to specific stimulus situations. Moreover, once we have isolated the stimuli that produce responses, whether normal or abnormal, we can use them to predict an individual's behavior and, if the stimuli are within our control, to control his behavior completely.

Conditioning. Most of our learning is the result of simple conditioning, a process that is so powerful and so pervasive that Watson believed it possible to mould any kind of child into any kind of man. He was an extreme environmentalist and, unlike most of his followers, almost completely ignored the contributions of heredity to human behavior. Conditioning applies not only to the stimuli and responses involved in common activities such as driving a car, but to the formation of our attitudes as well. He claimed that emotional reactions are learned in the same way as manual skills. If a child's conditioning experiences are favorable, he will be happy and well-adjusted. If they are unfavorable, his future life will be dominated by hostility and fear.

Watson used his experiment on Albert—a child who became afraid of all kinds of furry objects as a result of a conditioning—as paradigm for all conditioned fears. However, he also maintained that certain expressions of fear, rage, and love are natural and "visceral"; among these biologically based responses are the infant's fear of loss of support, high places and loud sounds. Yet even though these responses are basic, they, too, can be altered by later conditioning. *See* CONDITIONING.

Watson's emphasis on the "scientific" approach to behavior and his stress on observable, measurable phenomena led him to derogate such seeming imponderables as feeling, sympathy, and understanding. The best evidence of this lies in his oft-quoted comment: "Mother love is the most powerful poison that can be given to a child." Many parents took him at his word, and for an entire generation bought mechanical contrivances for conditioning their children. Among them were a flexible rod that could be attached to the crib to hold the baby's bottle, to eliminate the danger that he would be spoiled by his mother's caresses.

Thinking. The processes of thinking and reasoning are also explained in terms of conditioning and physiology. Unlike emotions, which are basically visceral, all forms of thought, including imagination, are described as "implicit speech," and are reduced to muscular movements acquired through conditioning. As evidence Watson cited the fact that action potentials can be recorded from the larynx of a person who is working on a problem of mental arithmetic, and the fact that deaf mutes make slight finger movements when they are thinking or dreaming. *See* SUB-VOCAL SPEECH.

Animal Studies. Watson believed the fundamental relationships between organisms and the environment are much the same for men and animals. For this reason he advocated an expansion of animal psychology as a means of discovering principles that would apply to human behavior. Such studies would allow more complete control over experimental conditions than is possible in human research—for example, we can perform operations on animals that we would not perform on men. Since he found that the results of such experiments can usually be applied to human beings, with allowances for the greater complexity of the human organism, Watson felt that this approach would bring a greater amount of our behavior within the realm of "real science." This point of view resulted in a tremendous increase in animal experimentation, particularly in the fields of physiological psychology and learning behavior. *See* SKINNER BOX, AVOIDANCE LEARNING, ESCAPE LEARNING.

The major criticisms of behaviorism can be briefly summarized. First, its claim to objectivity cannot be substantiated, for there is a private, subjective element in all experimentation and all knowledge that comes through our senses—at least, we have no guarantee that different observers see things in exactly the same way. Second, behaviorism makes the material world more real than the mental realm, yet it would be more scientific to include the mental within the laws of science instead of excluding it. Third, reducing thinking to laryngeal contractions, and feelings to organic changes, gives the illusion of "respectable" scientific fact, but such procedures actually fail to do justice to common sense experience. Fourth, reducing all learning and experience to a single stimulus-response model lends an air of false simplicity to extremely complex processes. Fifth, in his overemphasis on conditioning and the control of behavior and development, Watson conceives the human being as an automaton instead of a creature of will and purpose. Sixth, some bahaviorists (including Watson) exclude the whole idea of consciousness—yet this would lead to the absurd position that human beings, behaviorists included, are completely unaware of what they are doing. Other behaviorists merely say that the problem of consciousness must be bypassed for the present, but this means that their system is grossly incomplete since conscious activity is an undeniable and all-important fact of life.

The behavioristic approach has exerted a strong influence on American psychology. It has stimulated the development of carefully designed, highly objective, and rigidly controlled experimental investigation. It has led to the wider use of statistical procedures in basic research and applied psychology. And, in general, it has helped to turn the attention of psychologists to the task of applying scientific knowledge of human behavior to the solution of the real problems of life instead of devoting themselves to dissecting states of consciousness.

BEHAVIOR THERAPY. A form of psychotherapy employing conditioned response techniques.

Behavior therapy is based on the theory that emotional problems arise because the individual has either failed to learn effective responses or has acquired faulty behavior patterns. In any case the problem is one of learning and can be resolved by applying basic learning techniques. For this reason behavior therapy is often referred to as learning theory therapy. There is no attempt to probe the unconscious, evoke insight, or produce any basic change in the patient's personality. The only object is to revise current behavior patterns and alleviate symptoms: "Get rid of the symptom and you have eliminated the neurosis." (Eysenck, 1960)

Several techniques of conditioning may be used. *Simple classical conditioning* has been found effective in altering certain behavior patterns, such as those involved in enuresis. In one procedure, the child lies on an electrical device that activates a bell when he urinates in his sleep. After being awakened a number of times, his distended bladder takes over as the "conditioned stimulus" and wakes him up before he wets the bed. The apparatus can then be removed, since the enuresis has been eliminated. (Mowrer and Mowrer, 1938)

In the *operant conditioning* technique, rewards are used to reinforce the desired responses (PLATE 38). In one series of experiments, food was successfully employed with chronic, "unreachable" schizophrenic patients who had for years refused to eat unless fed by nurses. (Some of them were simply withdrawn and inactive; others had delusions that the food was poisoned or that God had forbidden them to eat.) Here the procedure was simply to announce the meal and open the dining-room door without escorting or coaxing them in. If they did not enter in a given time (at first thirty minutes, then twenty, fifteen, and five), the door was closed and they went hungry. In about three days they were all eating unassisted. The patients were later induced to respond in other ways. The experimenters succeeded in getting them to drop a penny in a can and to obey oral instructions to push certain buttons in order to be admitted to the dining room (Ayllon and Haughton, 1962). Experimenters have also used the hunger drive to alter other forms of psychotic behavior such as hoarding towels and wearing excess clothing. In these cases they were denied access to the dining room if they did not conform.

In *aversion conditioning,* a change in behavior is achieved through associating punishment with the undesirable behavior pattern—for example, by painting fingernails with a bitter substance to discourage nail biting, or by giving the alcoholic patient a drug that produces nausea whenever he takes a drink. Attitudes can also be modified by the process of *extinction*—that is, eliminating the reinforcement that is necessary to maintain a conditioned response. In one experiment, galvanic skin responses recorded during psychotherapy indicated that the patient reacted strongly to all references to sex. When the therapist did not show any disapproval but remained permissive, these signs of emotional disturbance gradually disappeared. The effects of both aversion conditioning and extinction can be enhanced by introducing the element of reward in the form of the therapist's interest and encouragement. *See* ANTABUSE (DISULFIRAM), THERAPY, HOMOSEXUALITY, CONDITIONING.

A more complex technique of reconditioning, called *reciprocal inhibition,* or systematic desensitization, has been successfully applied to anxiety states, phobias, sexual difficulties, and other neurotic disorders. Wolpe (1958) states the rationale of this procedure as follows:

". . . Neurotic behavior consists of persistent habits of learned (conditioned) adaptive behavior in anxiety-generating situations. If a response inconsistent with anxiety can be made to occur in the presence of anxiety-evoking stimuli so that it is accompanied by a complete or partial suppression of the anxiety-response, the bond between these stimuli and the anxiety-responses will be weakened." In the treatment of anxiety reaction, for example, the therapist first makes a list of the patient's anxieties, obtained through interviews and tests. Then he devotes several sessions to systematic training in muscle relaxation (the incompatible response). After this he arranges the list in a hierarchical order, and in succeeding sessions has the patient imagine situations that produce his anxiety, and at the same time practice muscle relaxation. Hypnosis may or may not be used to enhance this process.

To be more specific, the therapist starts by describing a scene that relates to the weakest item on the list, then works his way up to the strongest so that the patient will gradually become desensitized to his fears. Here is a brief example, condensed from a report by Wolpe:

A patient with a strong fear of death was found to feel anxious whenever she (1) saw an ambulance, (2) passed a hospital, (3) read an obituary notice, (4) witnessed a funeral, (5) heard of a young person dying of heart attack, (6) attended a burial, or (7) thought of her first husband in a coffin (arranged in order of increasing anxiety). In a typical session with this patient, the therapist first induced a state of relaxation by using suggestion, then asked her to imagine certain scenes, raising her left hand if they felt disturbing. To take No. 4 (above) as an example: "First I want you to imagine that you are standing at a street corner and a funeral procession passes you. You may have some feeling of sadness, but apart from this you are absolutely calm. (*Brief pause.*) Stop this scene. (*Pause of about four seconds.*) Now I want you to imagine the same scene of the funeral passing in the street before you, etc."

Each scene was repeated a number of times until the patient remained relaxed and did not experience any emotional disturbance when she saw it in her imagination. He then progressed to the next item on the list.

Highly successful results have been reported for this technique, particularly with phobic conditions. In some cases these results have proved to be relatively short-lived, but in others the alleviation of symptoms is more lasting and itself leads to personality improvement. This is most likely to occur when the disorder is not deep-rooted.

A simpler type of desensitization procedure is illustrated by the following case from Kraines (1948): "Mr. J.M., a freshman in medical school, wondered whether he should give up the study of medicine, for whenever he went into an operating room, he fainted at the sight of blood. In addition to the analysis of the causes and the changing of the boy's attitude toward his basic problems, desensitization was carried out. The student was told to walk into the operating room during an operation and immediately walk out. On the second day he was to walk into the room, count five, and walk out; on the third day he was to stay a full minute and walk out; and each day the length of time he stayed was increased. In two weeks the student reported that on the preceding day he was supposed to remain for ten minutes, 'but I got so interested in the operation that I forgot how long I was to stay.' In other words, this boy was desensitized to his fear by small but increasing doses of that which he feared. He had no trouble thereafter about witnessing blood."

Brief mention may also be made of Andrew Salter's controversial *conditioned reflex therapy* (1949). Basing his theory on Pavlov's distinction between excitatory and inhibitory impulses, Salter holds that the core of life is excitation and the core of neurosis is overinhibition. Emotional health, he believes, consists in behaving spontaneously, and the therapist therefore seeks to condition his client to act on the basis of feeling rather than thinking. This is done by encouraging him to say whatever he feels whenever he feels it ("feeling-talk"), by showing emotions on his face ("facial-talk"), by speaking up and expressing disagreement openly, by using the word "I" deliberately and without hesitation, by accepting the praise of others and returning the compliment, and by improvised living in the here and now instead of thinking and planning. Salter acknowledges that excitatory impulses can be carried too far, but feels that emotional release is a necessary first step in the achievement of healthy spontaneity. He has made extravagant claims for the effectiveness of his approach and has been severely criticized for oversimplifying the task of psychotherapy.

A recent compilation, *Case Studies in Behavior Modification,* edited by Ullmann and Krasner (1965), indicates that behavior therapy is increasing both in scope and acceptance as a treatment technique. It is being applied in various forms to a wide variety of disorders, including habit disturbance (tics, thumb sucking, stuttering, cigarette habit), personality disorders (homosexuality, transvestism, fetishism, exhibitionism, alcoholism, drug addiction), neurotic reactions (somnambulism, hysterical aphonia, hysterical blindness, phobias, frigidity, writer's cramp), psychophysiologic reactions (neurodermatitis, hypertension, duodenal ulcer, bronchial asthma), and occasionally to psychotic behavior. A few brief examples will be cited to illustrate some of the principles mentioned above and their variations.

During World War II cases of "combat fatigue" were successfully treated by Saul et al. (1946) by repeatedly showing combat films with the sound turned off. When the men became bored and satiated with the battle scenes, their panic reactions subsided and they were able to watch sound films of hand-to-hand combat with relative equanimity. Stuttering, which is usually highly resistant to therapy, has been alleviated or eliminated altogether through a variety of behavior procedures: subjecting the patient to a blast of noise each time he stutters (Flanagen, Goldiamond and Azrin, 1958); requiring the stutterer to repeat every stuttered word until it is spoken correctly (Sheehan, 1951); application of a technique known as "drive manipulation," in which the patient is prohibited to talk for two days, then allowed to talk only to people who do not arouse fear, after which he is gradually permitted to talk with feared individuals; and a procedure termed "shadowing" in which the stutterer must repeat every word the therapist utters, but always lagging two syllables behind—a method designed to prevent the patient from listening to his own speech. See STUTTERING, COMBAT REACTIONS.

Many tics have been effectively treated by "negative practice" and "massed practice"—that is, by forced repetition until the drive is fatigued or until it comes under voluntary control. As early as 1930, Hollingworth used this method to cure a persistent eyeblink that interfered with reading. The subject was required to lay a lead pencil across the frame of his glasses in light contact with his eyelids, and was then asked to lift and close the lids repeatedly. The motor coordination of many cerebral palsied and other brain-damaged children has been materially improved by giving them rewards (reinforcements) of tokens which could be exchanged for toys when they correctly assembled articles on a miniature factory assembly line—a technique

that was later extended to practice in standing and walking (Michael, 1963). See TIC.

Kushner (1965) has successfully applied the reciprocal inhibition technique in desensitizing a young man who was afraid to drive after a car accident. He was first taught how to relax by the Jacobson method, and was then asked to relax as fully as possible while imagining that he was looking at a car, then leaning on it, then sitting in it with the ignition off, and so on, until he was able to drive by himself. The same therapist applied aversive conditioning to a male patient who suffered from a long-standing fetish of masturbating while wearing women's panties stolen from clotheslines. The subject was shown pictures of scantily clad women while holding panties in his hand, and each picture was immediately followed by a light electric shock applied to his fingertips until it became uncomfortable. The shocks were also applied as he imagined himself wearing panties, observing a clothesline with panties on it, and standing in front of a lingerie shop. See RELAXATION THERAPY, KLEPTOMANIA, FETISHISM.

Positive reinforcements—rewards—have been found particularly effective with children's disturbances. As an example, Patterson (1965) used the technique of giving a seven-year-old boy a material reinforcer (M&M candy) plus a social reinforcer (praise) as a means of helping him overcome a school phobia. The experimenter arranged a structured doll play situation in which the boy doll, Henry, was taken by his mother to see the doctor. The actual mother was in the room at first, due to his "separation anxiety," and after each thirty second interval during which the boy did not look at his mother, he was given a candy (without telling him this was a reward). The same "contingency reinforcement" was applied each time he made "Henry" act independently—for example, when he had the doll stay at the doctor's office or remain at home by himself. Later, school sequences were introduced, such as saying goodbye to his mother, and getting on his bike, and each of these was followed by the candy reward and by praise if he had the doll act appropriately. The cooperation of the parents was elicited and they also rewarded the boy with praise at home each time he acted independently. Within a few weeks, during which ten fifteen-minute sessions were held and twenty bags of M&M's consumed, the boy was able to go to school without hesitation. *See* SCHOOL PHOBIA, RE-EDUCATION, ANOREXIA NERVOSA, REINFORCEMENT, PHOBIC REACTION.

BELLE INDIFFERENCE. A term originally used by Pierre Janet to characterize the air of unconcern manifested by hysteric patients toward their physical symptoms. Instead of arousing anxiety or distress, a paralyzed arm or loss of voice is accepted with an outward calm that seems to bespeak inner satisfaction. The reason for this reaction is probably that the disability actually does produce a measure of satisfaction, since it helps to resolve a conflict, relieve anxiety, and usually brings "secondary gains" in the form of sympathy, attention, and domination over others. *See* SECONDARY GAIN.

BENDER GESTALT TEST (Bender Visual-Motor Gestalt Test). A personality test based on the way a subject copies nine geometrical figures. It is designed to throw light not only on personality structure and dynamics, but also on perception, visual-motor coordination, and the way a subject attacks a problem. The test is an effective psychiatric instrument in diagnosing both functional and organic disorders.

Nine geometrical forms, printed in black on white paper, are presented to the subject, one at a time. They include, among others, a circle with a diamond touching it at one point, a row of twelve unequally spaced dots, and ten columns of three circles each placed at a slight slant from the vertical. The subject is asked to copy each figure on a plain piece of paper (*Fig. 15*). The examiner unobtrusively takes note of the order in which the various parts of each figure are drawn, as well as any questions, spontaneous comments, or evidence of blocking, resistance, or other significant behavior.

The interpretation of the drawings is based on a knowledge of personality dynamics, developmental factors relating to visual-motor activity, and Gestalt principles of perception. These principles indicate, for example, that the twelve dots are not normally seen as separate objects but as a single configuration or pattern (Gestalt). Such patterns are believed to be due to processes occurring in the brain, and any serious disturbance in the Gestalt is taken as evidence of a pathological condition or faulty maturation.

The test has been used in many areas of research. One important field is the investigation of visual-motor maturation. Examination of many records has shown that until the age of four the average child will draw only one figure, an enclosed loop, in attempting to reproduce all the designs. The seven year old can copy only two of the simpler figures with any degree of accuracy, but the ten year old can master all but the one that consists of two overlapping polygons. In contrast to these normal children, schizophrenic children continue to use spontaneous whirling strokes long after the normal child has advanced to a higher stage. The test is therefore useful in establishing developmental norms.

The second major application of the test is in personality diagnosis. There are many indicative signs of disorder, all of which must be checked against material gathered from other diagnostic procedures. Among the most important are:

Fragmentation: Seeing the figure, such as the circle and diamond, as separate elements instead of a unified whole. This may suggest either an "organization disturbance" as in schizophrenia, or certain diseases involving brain damage. It may also indicate inability to control the movements, suggesting organic involvement.

Inability to copy angles, dots, or curves accurately: This generally indicates a disturbance in visual-motor coordination, which may be due to an organic condition, but in some cases may reflect emotional instability. People who lack motor control make sweeping lines that do not stop where they should, or substitute dashes for lines or dots.

Interpreting the figures: Some subjects can handle the task only by giving the figures specific meanings—for example, the columns of dots are thought of as flocks of birds. Concrete thinking of this kind is usually pathological, suggesting schizophrenia or organic difficulty.

Rotation of figures, left for right: Very young children, children with reading difficulties, and left-handed people tend to reverse the figures. If literate adults do this, it may be a sign of deeper disturbance.

Repetition of the same pattern: This tendency is called perseveration, and is a possible indication of brain damage.

Primitivization: Childish oversimplification of the drawings, found in mental defectives and organic patients.

Impulsivity: A characteristic of psychopathic individuals, who tend to draw hastily, with as little exertion as possible, and produce oversize designs in which the lines do not meet. Bender believes their tendency to leave spaces indicates an inability to complete a task and the desire to leave themselves a way out of situations because of their anxieties and self-doubts.

The character of the lines is also thought to be significant—for instance, flattening of curves suggests a "flattening of affect," that is, shallowness of emotional reaction, while rounding of angles suggests impulsiveness; and sharpening shows an attempt to control underlying disturbances and conflicts. The paper itself is viewed as symbolic of the environment, and a heavy ripping line denotes aggressive tendencies toward other people, while faint, sketchy strokes suggest that the subject is anxious, timid, and lacking in confidence. In addition, tiny reproductions are characteristic of inhibited individuals; and if they draw a box around each figure, it is a fairly sure sign of an intense need for security due to feelings of anxiety. Many subjects also project their conflicts in pictorial form by vacillating between two or more of these tendencies.

The Bender-Gestalt test has been subjected to a great deal of study and research. Records made before and after brain injuries or traumatic experiences show clear and indicative differences. The test has also been shown to reflect changes due to a release of emotion after subjects have smoked marijuana. Even more important than these specific experiments is the widespread clinical experience gained over the years. The test has proved to be a valuable diagnostic tool in psychiatry, and appears to deserve its reputation as the most effective test of perceptual motor skills. *See* MENTAL IMPAIRMENT TESTS.

BENIGN. In psychiatry a benign disorder is one from which recovery is likely or possible. The condition may be mild or serious—for example, a stupor is a severe pathological state, but if it is of the benign type, the patient generally gets better. A malignant condition, on the other hand, is a progressive disorder which is highly resistant to treatment and may be irreversible.

BERI BERI. A vitamin deficiency disease which may have psychological as well as physical effects.

The disorder was prevalent at one time in the Far East, where a diet of polished rice caused a serious lack of vitamin B_1 (thiamine). The symptoms of beri beri are general weakness, lassitude, intestinal distress, lack of will, and sometimes Korsakoff's syndrome. The word beri beri, which means "I cannot," aptly describes the patient's total reaction. The disorder is seldom found in western countries, although it may sometimes be associated with Wernicke's syndrome.

The search for the cause of beri beri led Casimir Funk (1884–1967) to the discovery of vitamins in 1912. His experiments on pigeons revealed that the bran coating of rice contains an important nutritional substance later termed thiamine. This substance, which is eliminated if the rice is polished for human consumption, was found capable of curing a form of beri beri in these birds. The discovery was then successfully applied to the disease in humans, and led to the prevention or cure of other vitamin deficiency diseases such as scurvy, rickets and pellagra. See METABOLIC DISORDERS, WERNICKE'S SYNDROME, KORSAKOFF'S SYNDROME, PELLAGRINOUS PSYCHOSIS.

BESTIALITY (Zooerasty, Zoophilia). A sexual deviation in which excitement or gratification is achieved through relations with animals. The term includes actual intercourse as well as stimulation through friction against an animal, fellatio (mouth-genital contact), or masturbation of the animal.

Bestiality is most commonly practiced with large domesticated animals, such as sheep, goats or dogs, and less often with chickens, ducks, and geese. Kinsey (1948) has reported that about 8 per cent of all males, and 17 per cent in rural areas, admitted to at least one full sexual experience with animals. Bestiality is far less common among females, with whom it usually takes the masturbatory form of bodily friction.

Sexual contact with animals appears to be a universal phenomenon, since laws and taboos concerning bestiality are found in practically all societies. Most religious codes, including the Old Testament, condemn the practice, but it is permitted in a few societies, particularly during initiation ceremonies. In our culture the practice usually results from observing coitus between animals. Boys and young men find this form of voyeurism sexually stimulating, and some of them decide to experiment with animals themselves. If they do not have an adequate opportunity for heterosexual relations, or if others around them engage in this behavior, they may make a regular practice of bestiality.

Although all forms of bestiality are considered objectionable in our society, the practice is regarded as clearly pathological only where sexual relations with animals are preferred to contacts with humans of the opposite sex. As in other cases of sexual deviation, it may reflect a fear of inadequacy and rejection in approaching ordinary sexual relations. When this deviation is persistently practiced, it is often a sign of either psychosis or inferior intelligence. See SEXUAL DEVIATIONS (GENERAL).

Illustrative Case: BESTIALITY

A business man finally married a woman who had worked in his office for some years and who thought she knew him quite well. He had paid desultory court to her a year or so before proposing and seemed always to be in some perplexity about the matter of marriage, but they were finally married when he was twenty-eight.

They left immediately on a honeymoon and, as the matter was afterward explained to the physician, it was during this time that the wife discovered an extraordinary curious reaction on her newly acquired husband's part to sexual intercourse. He became increasingly disturbed as night approached, and highly nervous and apprehensive about the sexual act. He deferred intercourse for quite a while on various excuses and finally consummated the marriage, but seemed greatly disturbed afterward, wringing his hands and exclaiming that it was wrong of him to do so, and that he must not do it again. Later on in the marriage he was less indecisive, but after an act of intercourse with his wife he would jump up from the bed, dress, and leave the room, returning an hour or so later, apparently quiet and composed. . . .

One night, for reasons which she was unable clearly to explain, his wife resolved to follow him upon one of his mysterious disappearances from their bedroom. She trailed him to the stable where, to her utter amazement, she observed him in the act of cohabiting with his mare. She was most of all impressed by the fact that not only did the man show the utmost evidence of affection for the mare, kissing and fondling her as if she were a woman, but that the mare showed definite and unmistakable signs of responding to his maneuvers with sexual pleasure.

The wife was thunderstruck by her discovery, so much so that she confronted her husband with it immediately. He fell on his knees before her, broke into loud sobbing, confessed that his behavior had gone on since several years before their marriage, and that his great distress in marrying her was not his shame about it, but his feeling that he was being unfaithful to the various mares with whom he had love affairs and sexual relations. This the wife was quite unable to understand or believe, but subsequent developments bore out the probable truth of the story. He agreed, now, to get rid of the mare and break away from his perversion.

True to his word, he did so. He sold the mare and stayed at home religiously, persuading his wife that he was penitently attempting to conduct himself in a more normal and human fashion. For a time all was well. Then, contrary to his promise, he became interested in another mare and purchased her over his wife's protests. He assured his wife that he would not become involved in a sexual interest in this mare, that it was a good investment, that it looked silly for a man who had been a horse fancier as long as he had to refrain from as good a purchase as this was, etc. Ultimately, the same situation developed again. He became more and more passionately attached to the mare, petted and caressed her in a manner which his wife, in the light

of her knowledge, found unbearable. He then began disappearing at night for short periods in as surreptitious a way as possible to continue his affair with the mare. . . .

She continued to live with him until she discovered that he was clandestinely continuing to practice bestiality with various horses. Upon this discovery she left him flatly, arranging for separate maintenance. (Menninger, 1951)

BIBLIOTHERAPY. A form of supportive psychotherapy in which the patient is given carefully selected material to read.

During the era of "moral treatment" many physicians used a form of bibliotherapy in suggesting that their patients read the Bible. This practice is still advocated by pastoral counselors and chaplains in mental institutions. Usually the patient chooses his own passages to read, though sometimes the counselor makes suggestions. There is, however, another type of bibliotherapy which is occasionally used as an adjunct to individual psychotherapy. In this case the reading matter is selected by the therapist from mental health literature on the basis of the particular patient's age, emotional problems and personality needs. And instead of merely suggesting the reading, he assigns it as a medical prescription.

Bibliotherapy may be used with both young people and adults. In either case it is important to establish rapport before introducing the reading, otherwise it would probably be rejected. Books on sex education are often given to children and adolescents with sexual problems, and material on new hobbies and interests is recommended to those who are excessively preoccupied with other personal difficulties. Since children often resent assignments, it is advisable for the therapist to enlist their co-operation in choosing the reading material. With adults, the therapist must make an "educated guess" as to his patient's reactions to the books he prescribes, and be especially careful to avoid material that will threaten the therapeutic situation. This does not necessarily mean that the content must be bland and innocuous, since it may be useful to assign reading that will provoke specific reactions such as anger or aggression.

Gottschalk (1948) has enumerated the major ways in which selected reading material can advance the therapeutic process. First, it can relieve tensions resulting from misinformation, for example on sexual matters. Second, it can bring about insight into emotional dynamics, especially the use of defense mechanisms. Third, it can help the patient understand his physiological and psychological reactions to conflicts and frustrations. Fourth, it can facilitate communication between patient and therapist by giving them a common body of material to discuss. Fifth, reading about others who have similar problems will often alleviate the patient's feeling of guilt or fear, and also bolster his morale—especially if it shows that they have overcome their difficulties. Sixth, carefully chosen biographies of admirable individuals may be used to encourage the patient to test out more acceptable patterns of behavior.

Studies have shown that bibliotherapy is most effective when the patient himself asks for material to read, when he has adequate intellectual ability and good reading habits, and when his emotional disturbance is relatively mild. A number of therapists have compiled lists of books which have proved especially helpful, although the actual selection must always be made with the individual patient in mind. Here are some samples from a list recommended by English and Finch (1964): Clifford R. Adams, *Preparing for Marriage;* Dorothy W. Baruch, *New Ways in Discipline;* Carl Binger, *More About Psychiatry;* Oliver M. Butterfield, *Sex Life in Marriage;* Child Study Association of America, *A Reader for Parents;* Flanders Dunbar, *Mind and Body;* O. S. English and G. H. J. Pearson, *Emo-*tional *Problems of Living;* Marynia F. Farnham, *The Adolescent;* James F. Himes, *Understanding Your Child;* Karen Horney, *Self-Analysis;* George Lawton, *Aging Successfully;* John Levy and Ruth Monroe, *The Happy Family;* Joshua L. Liebman, *Peace of Mind;* Rollo May, *Man's Search for Himself;* Margaret Mead, *Male and Female;* Karl A. Menninger, *Love Against Hate;* William C. Menninger and Munro Leaf, *You and Psychiatry;* Emily Mudd and A. Krich, editors, *Man and Wife;* Harry A. Overstreet, *The Mature Mind;* Margaret Ribble, *The Rights of Infants;* Benjamin Spock, *Pocket Book of Baby and Child Care;* Edward Strecker and Kenneth Appel, *Discovering Ourselves;* Anna W. M. Wolf, *The Parent's Manual.*

BILIRUBIN ENCEPHALOPATHY (Kernicterus). A toxic brain disorder occurring in infants, due to accumulation in the gall bladder of bilirubin, a red breakdown product of hemoglobin. The condition is often associated with jaundice, and in some cases is due to blood incompatibility between mother and child.

Several types of blood incompatibility have been found to produce excessive bilirubin in the blood of infants, including a small percentage of Rh-positive children with Rh-negative mothers. The condition may also be associated with prematurity or with severe neonatal sepsis (blood poisoning). The result is an acute disease in the newborn child termed kernicterus, which is characterized by jaundice, anemia, a high-pitched cry, drowsiness, and unstable body temperature. A yellow staining occurs in structures at the base of the brain, particularly the basal ganglia, cerebellum, and hippocampus, with destruction of cells in severe cases. If the condition is not arrested it may lead to paralysis, convulsions, spasticity, deafness, and mental retardation.

The disorder, however, can be detected a few days after birth, and the danger of brain damage virtually eliminated by exchange blood transfusions. In addition, an effective preventive procedure has been recently developed. After the birth of her first child, the mother can be injected with a serum prepared by injection of laboratory animals with Rh cells. This serum contains an antibody which renders harmless the blood cells of the child that have leaked across the placental membranes during pregnancy and delivery—cells which would otherwise have initiated the production of maternal antibodies harmful to succeeding babies. In cases where the mother has not been treated with the anti-Rh serum, the treatment of choice for a jaundiced offspring is still exchange transfusions, which can now be performed while the child is still in the uterus, as well as after birth. See MENTAL RETARDATION (CAUSES).

BINET, ALFRED (1857–1911). Binet, originator of the first true intelligence test, was born in Nice, France. Though trained as a lawyer, he never practiced that profession but followed interests which grew out of his other studies, particularly medicine, biology, and abnormal psychology. These interests were reflected in his early works, which included a study of hypnosis entitled *Animal Magnetism,* with Féré as co-author (1886), and a volume on psychopathology entitled *Alternations of Personality* (1894). Between these dates, in 1889, Binet was instrumental in setting up his country's first psychology laboratory at the Sorbonne, and in 1895 he founded the first French psychological journal, *L'Année Psychologique.*

Emphasis on Binet's work in intelligence testing has tended to obscure his contributions to other fields of psychology. He performed pioneer experiments on handwriting abnormalities, suggestibility, and mental processes, using a number of original techniques. In one study, schoolboys were shown a number of lines, one at a time, and asked to estimate their length. The first five were progressively longer, but from there on they were exactly equal. Many of the children (particularly the younger ones) tended to overestimate the equal lines, and Binet concluded that they were especially suggestible. (Today this tendency would probably be attributed to set, or expectation, rather than suggestibility.) He also noted that subjects are frequently influenced by the judgments of people in authority and applied the term "prestige suggestion" to this phenomenon.

The study of thought processes was an early and lasting interest of Binet's. His first work on the subject, *The Psychology of Reasoning* (1886), was written from the associationist point of view. Later, however, he revised his views, largely on the basis of experiments conducted on his two daughters. The girls were given simple problems to solve, and then were asked to report on their methods of attack and their train of thought. To his surprise, Binet found that many of their reports conflicted with interpretations prevalent at the time, particularly the idea that all thought, no matter how complex, could be reduced to simple sensory experiences and simple laws of combination. He found, for example, that the girls often solved problems without using images at all, and concluded that these are not essential to the process. He also employed ink blots and pictures in testing his daughters' mental processes, and thereby foreshadowed their use in projective techniques.

Binet then turned his attention to the study of individuals whose thinking deviated from the average, notably mental defectives, lightning calculators, chess players, and multiple personalities. His study of chess players who played several games simultaneously suggested that attention cannot easily be divided, and he concluded that the players were therefore shifting their full attention from one game to the next. He also showed that interference ordinarily occurs when we try to do several things at once unless the tasks are very similar or very easy. Influenced by Galton's work, Binet also undertook the study of eminent artists, writers, and mathematicians. In his earlier studies he tried to relate their abilities to handwriting, head measurements, and body build, but later on he became interested in developing tests which would reveal complex mental processes.

In 1903 Binet presented the results of his investigations of intellectual ability in a book entitled *Experimental Studies of Intelligence.* This work offered a new concept of intelligence measurement which contrasted directly with the approach of the German school of psychology. James M. Cattell and others, believing that higher mental ability could be reduced to sensory capacities, had been exclusively concerned with tests of reaction time, discrimination and other relatively simple processes. In contrast, Binet claimed that these tests could not explain the higher functions of imagination, esthetic appreciation, comprehension, and memory. He believed that the higher abilities, which are so important for adaptation to life, would have to be approached directly on their own level instead of on the sensory level. He therefore abandoned the "brass instruments" approach in favor of devising a variety of intelligence test problems, including paper and pencil tests, pictorial items, and objects which could be handled by the subject.

It was soon recognized that problems of the Binet type might be more useful in predicting school success than the laboratory-inspired tests of Cattell. As a consequence, the French government asked Binet to construct a test that would differentiate between pupils who were mentally defective and those who had the ability to succeed in the usual curriculum but who were not applying

themselves. His first scales, developed in collaboration with a physician, Théophile Simon, were published in 1905, and later revised in 1908 and 1911, the year of Binet's death. The scales were all based on the ability of average children to solve different verbal and numerical problems at different ages. A child's "mental age" was determined by noting how many he was able to do correctly below, above, and at his own age level. The same scoring technique is used today in the Stanford-Binet intelligence scale, except for the addition of the I.Q., which is the ratio between the mental age and the chronological age. *See* INTELLIGENCE TESTS, STANFORD-BINET TEST, CATTELL, GALTON.

BIOGENIC AMINES. A group of amines (derivatives of amino acids), three of which are known to exert important influences on the nervous system: epinephrine, norepinephrine and serotonin.

Epinephrine (adrenalin) and norepinephrine (noradrenalin) are both secreted by the adrenal medulla, and are frequently described as neurohormones since they activate the sympathetic nervous system during emotional and physical stress. Their specific effects on heart rate, blood pressure, blood sugar level, etc., are described under ADRENAL GLANDS.

Serotonin is chemically related to these hormones, but is an indole amine rather than a catechol amine. It is produced in certain gastrointestinal cells and carried to the internal organs through the blood stream. One of its effects is to reduce hemorrhaging when the organism is damaged, since it lowers the blood pressure. It is also found in the brain and is believed to increase its metabolism and exert a stimulating effect on the activity of the nerve cells.

Recent investigations have shown that certain psychic energizers, the monoamine oxidase inhibitors (MAOI), cause the serotonin level to rise in the brain and liver, and this may be one reason for their antidepressant effect. It has also been found that the tranquilizing drug, Reserpine, causes a marked and persistent fall in the level of brain serotonin (Shore et al., 1957). Findings of this kind have led some investigators to believe that disturbances in the brain serotonin level might be a major causal factor in serious mental disturbance (Wooley and Shaw, 1954). So far, research has failed to confirm this hypothesis. See ADRENAL GLANDS, ADRENERGIC REACTION, ENERGIZERS, SCHIZOPHRENIC REACTION: (ETIOLOGY), TRANQUILIZERS.

BIRTH ADJUSTMENTS. When a baby is born he goes through the most abrupt, complete, and dramatic change of surroundings in his entire life. For nine months he has been living a parasitic existence within the warmth of the womb, but is suddenly thrust into a situation where he must behave as a separate, distinct individual capable of surviving under a wholly new set of conditions. This change requires a drastic adjustment, especially during the first fifteen to thirty minutes after birth (the partunate period), but extending well into the period of the neonate, or newborn, which covers the remainder of infancy.

The change actually begins during the birth process rather than after birth has occurred. There are four types of birth: the normal, spontaneous, headfirst birth; the breech, or buttocks-first, birth; the crosswise, or transverse, presentation; and the Caesarean section in which the infant emerges through a slit made in the abdominal wall in order to avoid a difficult birth. But whatever the type of birth, the newborn infant must make several major adjustments as soon as his new life begins. He must adapt to a temperature of 70 degrees instead of 100 degrees, obtain oxygen by inhalation, take nourishment through his mouth, and eliminate waste products through the proper organs instead of

through the cord and placenta. In view of these vast readjustments there is no wonder that the average baby loses weight and shows many signs of behavior disorganization for several days: he gasps, sneezes, coughs, and has trouble sucking and swallowing.

There is considerable variation from infant to infant during the early adjustment period. Studies show that when a mother has gone through persistent emotional disturbances and stresses during the last months of pregnancy, her infant will tend to have a variety of difficulties: feeding problems, gastrointestinal dysfunctions, sleep problems, hyperactivity, and general irritability. As Sontag (1944) has put it, such an infant "has not had to wait until childhood for a bad home situation or other cause to make him neurotic. It was done for him before he even saw the light of day."

The type of birth experience may also have specific effects on the child. In most cases, infants born spontaneously make a quicker and more successful adjustment to the new environment than infants who have gone through a long and difficult labor (especially transverse and breech births), or infants born by Caesarean section. If the mother receives heavy doses of certain types of medication during the birth process, the infant may have trouble breathing and feeding during the first days of life. In addition, emotional tension on the part of the mother, due to fear of childbirth or resistance to having a child, may complicate the birth process and also, as noted above, hinder the infant's adjustment to postnatal life.

Even though birth is an ordeal and an entirely new environment must be faced immediately afterward, the baby usually makes a remarkably successful adjustment during the first few weeks of his life. Some infants, however, fail to make the grade and are either stillborn or succumb during the period of postnatal adjustment. The most critical time is the day of birth itself, and the days that immediately follow; and the most common causes of death are prematurity, congenital debility, malformation, injury at birth, pneumonia, influenza, diabetes and anoxia (lack of oxygen due to excessive medication of the mother or strangulation by the umbilical cord during birth.)

Surveys show that the mortality rate among neonates is higher among boys than among girls, among nonwhites than whites, and among infants from deprived environments than among those from privileged homes (due largely to inadequate maternal nutrition and medical care). It is also higher than average in cases where the mother has gone through an emotionally stressful pregnancy leading to a difficult childbirth. *See* BIRTH TRAUMA.

BIRTH ORDER. The ordinal position of a child—first born, second born, middle, or youngest—particularly in relation to his personal adjustment and status in the family.

There is a vast psychological literature on birth order, but the findings can only be stated as tendencies rather than laws or principles, since the child's *psychological* position in the family—his relationships with parents, brothers, and sisters—may bear no relation to his ordinal position. In general, however, it may be said that there is no ideal position in the family; rather, every position has its special advantages and special problems. These can best be described by summarizing the results of investigations into the four family positions mentioned above.

A number of studies indicate that the average I.Q. of first-borns tends to be slightly lower than that of later children (Thurstone and Jenkins, 1931). There seem to be three possible reasons for this finding: absence of stimulation from brothers and sisters during their early development, higher rate of difficult births, and parental inexperience.

On the other hand, there are more gifted children and men of science among first-born than among later-born children (Terman et al., 1925). They are also likely to be more dependent, conservative, anxious, and suggestible, and in consequence of receiving exclusive attention, more selfish and spoiled than their siblings. In addition they also tend to become more aggressive and easily depressed by a change in status when other children arrive (Adler, 1930; Strauss, 1951). Some studies (for example, Rosenow, 1930) show a greater relative frequency of first-born children among delinquents and first admissions to child guidance clinics. They also tend to be conformist (Becker and Carroll, 1962) and to seek out the company of others in an anxiety situation (Schachter, 1959).

Second-born children are usually less dependent and anxious than first-borns because the parents have become less tense and overprotective. The mother-child relationship tends to be warmer, and this is reflected in their relationships with other children and adults. It may also account for the fact that they are likely to be more fun-loving, as well as less neurotic and introverted. They often suffer at the hands of the older children, but advance more quickly, especially if the first-born is a male: "It is not that the male has greater skill or knowledge but rather that he, by the challenge he presents, stimulates or alerts his sibling more than does a girl." (Koch, 1960)

The middle child tends to be somewhat neglected and lost in the shuffle. Studies show that he is likely to be less aggressive than the older and younger children, more easily distracted, and often more gregarious. Since he is more likely to be overlooked than the others, he may have a special craving for affection. He may also be a victim of family tensions, which might help to account for the fact that more extremely unpopular children have been found among those in the middle position than in other family positions. (Elkins, 1958)

The youngest child is apt to be pampered and remain spoiled longer than the oldest child because his position remains unchallenged. According to Alfred Adler, some of these children continue to expect attention and help, but others "fight for their place in the sun" and develop a strong impulse to surpass their peers. In some cases this competitive urge is tinctured with defiance, irritability, and a chip-on-the-shoulder attitude—especially when these children have been "bossed around" by the older children. In the long run they tend to be rather self-confident and optimistic, partly because their position has never been usurped by a newly arrived sibling, and partly because they develop a competitive spirit.

A number of the findings cited above have been corroborated by indirect studies. In one investigation mothers of pairs of children of the same sex were asked to compare their youngsters. On the whole they found their older child more fearful, dependent, and anxious, while the younger was more aggressive, stubborn, affectionate, happy, and good-natured (Dean, 1947). In a study of maternal attitudes, Lasko (1954) found that mothers were less warm and more restrictive and coercive toward the first child than the second. They also put greater pressure on the first child in an effort to speed up his development, and were less consistent in dealing with him. As a result, there was greater friction between the first child and the mother. These differences, plus the added difficulty of adjusting to a newcomer, help to explain the greater anxiety and dependence of the first-born. An experiment on college students carried out by Staples and Walters (1961) has indicated that these early tendencies tend to endure. These investigators found that first-borns were more suggestible in social situations and more apprehensive in anxiety-provoking situations than later-borns. *See* ONLY CHILDREN.

BIRTH TRAUMA. Psychological shock resulting from the birth process; the shock of being born.

The concept of birth trauma originated with Otto Rank in 1924. He believed that the birth experience is the crucial fact of life, and that reactions to this experience set the stage for both normal adjustment and neurosis. In his view, the painful experience (trauma) of birth creates a "primal anxiety" in every infant, and gives rise to a universal desire to forget the pain, a process he termed "primal repression." Through love and care, the normal mother seeks to allay her child's terror; but if she is unsuccessful and the child's own efforts at repression are ineffective, he develops an overpowering urge to return to the blissful security of the womb. This urge runs counter to the demands of life, which require increasing separation from the mother.

According to Rank, the struggle between these two forces—the need to be independent and the desire to return to the womb—comes to a peak at certain critical periods, such as weaning and entrance into school. At such times, the child may develop acute "separation anxiety" and have repeated dreams that symbolize a return to the womb. If he cannot work through these anxieties, a lasting predisposition to neurosis may be established. The desire to return to the womb is even more vividly exhibited by patients with catatonic schizophrenia who curl up into a fetal position.

The theory of the birth trauma has never gained wide acceptance because of Rank's overemphasis on this single event and because of insufficient evidence relating later neurosis to a severe birth experience. There is a possibility that the birth process may sometimes have lasting psychological effects, but the emphasis today is upon the child's feeling of helplessness and insecurity during the first weeks after birth rather than his reaction to the birth process itself. If he is treated coldly and mechanically at this time, or if feeding is forced, he is almost certain to develop some of the emotional symptoms which Rank attributes to the birth trauma. And if he is suddenly taken away from his mother and put into an institution, he may indeed experience "separation anxiety." He will want desperately to return to his mother and may feel lost and rejected if he cannot. See MATERNAL DEPRIVATION, MOTHERING, BIRTH ADJUSTMENTS, ANACLITIC DEPRESSION, SCHOOL PHOBIA.

BLEULER, EUGEN (1857–1939). One of the major contributors to dynamic psychiatry, Bleuler was born in Zürich, received his medical training at its university, and later became professor of psychiatry and director of the city's mental hospital. In the early 1900s he and his assistant, C. G. Jung, became interested in the work of Sigmund Freud, and in 1908 these three, with a number of other psychiatrists, held the first scientific conclave on psychoanalysis. This was followed by a second meeting two years later at which the group founded the International Psychoanalytic Association, which published the yearbook *Imago* under their editorship.

With the assistance of Jung, Bleuler made original and far-reaching contributions to psychoanalysis by showing how the various mechanisms which Freud had found in neurotic patients could also be applied to psychotic behavior. This new approach—later termed "interpretive psychiatry"—represented a radical departure from the classificatory approach of the time, since it was not limited to a mere description of symptoms, but sought to understand their etiology and dynamics. Moreover, this theory offered an alternative to the widely accepted view that attributed psychosis to organic brain damage and ruled out psychological causes entirely.

Bleuler formulated his new theory in a volume published in 1911, *Dementia Praecox or the Group of Schizophrenias,* a work which Zilboorg and Henry (1941) have called "the most important contribution to psychiatry made by the twentieth century." Prior to this publication the clinical picture of dementia praecox, as it was then called, was based on the work of Emil Kraepelin, who not only believed the disorder was caused by brain damage but that it inevitably led to progressive deterioration. In spite of statistics to the contrary, this negative conclusion became the "official" view in psychiatry, and, as Roback (1961) has pointed out, "it was because of Kraepelin's supposition that schizophrenia was incurable that so little was done in most institutions to find better treatment than the hospital routine."

Bleuler's work challenged the Kraepelin view at every point. He looked beneath the symptoms to find their hidden meaning; he insisted that the disorder could be effectively treated; and he even discarded the name dementia praecox because it not only failed to describe the disease but implied an early and irreversible deterioration. Bleuler renamed the illness "schizophrenia" (literally, split personality), pointing out that this label described a group of psychotic reactions rather than a single disease. The common denominator, however, was not a splitting into several personalities, but a loosening of associations that causes the personality to disintegrate. This internal splitting occurs because the patient develops patterns of thinking and reaction which are dictated by his own inner emotional life rather than by the laws of logic or the realities of the external world. To an outsider, however, his mental processes appear to be dissociated, his verbalizations disconnected, and his thoughts full of strange condensations and gross generalizations. He is also torn by contradictory feelings, which Bleuler called "ambivalences," a term quickly adopted into the vocabulary of psychoanalysis.

Bleuler placed special emphasis on schizophrenic delusions. He attributed them to what he called dereistic or autistic thinking, a form of fantasy which is controlled by unconscious dynamics rather than by objective reality. This concept, which probably stemmed in part from Freud's concept of narcissism, was a radical departure from the prevailing view that schizophrenics were emotionally "flat" and had no affective life at all. In contrast, Bleuler showed that they actually had an affective life, and, in fact, were creating an entire inner world of their own in response to their emotional needs. For the first time this suggested a rationale for their fantasies and delusions, for it meant that they were retreating from an outer reality with which they could not cope into an inner reality which they could master.

In Bleuler's view, then, schizophrenia was largely if not wholly a matter of faulty, inappropriate reactions adopted by the patient as a means of meeting inner needs. His interpretation suggested that analysis of unconscious mechanisms operating in the individual case might lead to successful treatment along psychological lines. This aroused new hope that psychiatry's greatest single problem was about to be solved, but unfortunately the hope has not been realized. There still remains a wide gap between understanding the dynamics of the disease and discovering its causes and its cure. See BRILL, KRAEPELIN, SCHIZOPHRENIC REACTIONS (GENERAL), NARCISSISM, AMBIVALENCE, DYNAMIC PSYCHIATRY, DEREISTIC THINKING, AUTISTIC THINKING.

BLINDNESS. The definition of legal blindness varies from country to country. In the United States an individual is rated blind if vision in his better eye does not exceed 20/200 when corrected by lenses, or if the widest diameter of his visual field is no greater than twenty degrees. People with this degree of defect are considered legally blind because they cannot perform work for which eyesight is essential. See VISUAL ACUITY.

There are about 100,000 blind people in the United States and 6,000,000 in the world. An estimated 20 per cent of cases are hereditary, 15 per cent due to accidents, and the rest caused by disease. Trachoma, a virus infection which scars the cornea, is a major factor in many parts of the world, particularly North Africa, but the disease is also prevalent in the Alleghenies and among American Indians. Ophthalmia neonatorum, or "babies' sore eyes," an inflammatory disease usually due to gonorrhea, was the largest single cause among children in the United States at the beginning of this century, but the incidence gradually dropped from 28.2 per cent to 1.2 per cent through administration of a silver nitrate solution soon after birth. A similar decrease has occurred in the incidence of blindness due to smallpox and syphilis. Many other cases are due to war injuries. *Seven* per cent of all Korean casualties lost their sight. Other causes are neglected or inoperable cataracts, especially in older people; and glaucoma, due to destruction of the optic nerve by internal pressure that may be aggravated by emotional stress. An estimated one half of all cases of blindness are considered preventable.

A number of psychological studies have been made of the blind. If they have been without sight from birth, their sensory experience consists wholly of sounds, tactile impressions, temperature changes, odors and tastes. Visual images are completely absent, even in dreams. Many, however, are capable of counterbalancing this loss by developing acuity in other senses, particularly when they are given special training. This compensatory development can reach remarkable proportions: in industry blind people have often been found superior to sighted people in detecting slight imperfections by the sense of touch.

Some blind persons can learn to get around without receiving help from other people, or even from guide dogs through training in "echo location"— that is, they learn to judge the direction and distance of large objects or obstacles by sensing the echoes made by their footsteps, the tapping of their cane, or even their breathing. It was suggested at one time that this ability was largely due to unusual sensitivity of their facial skin and nerves to air currents, and the term "facial vision" was coined. This theory has been disproved by experimental investigation. When heavy hoods were placed over the heads of blind subjects, and they were asked to walk toward large obstacles, they were completely unable to detect their presence. Their ears were then plugged, and again they ran into the obstacles. Further experiments indicated that the telltale cues were auditory, and that high-pitched sounds were particularly effective since they reflect more sharply from objects than low-pitched sounds (Cotzin and Dallenbach, 1950). These findings were supported by the fact that bats also use echo location, or "bat radar," by emitting high-pitched sounds that bounce back to them from walls and even wires (Griffin and Galambos, 1941). As a result of these experiments, technologists have developed an electrical "sound-thrower" which blind people can carry around with them.

Studies indicate that people who are born blind have, on the whole, more personality problems than those who have lost their sight later in life. A survey of 143 adolescents in a school for the blind (Sommers, 1949) has shown that these difficulties more often arise from the attitudes of other people than from their adjustment to the physical world. The children stated that they were particularly disturbed "When people pity me," "When I am treated like a baby," "When I went to a camp and was the only blind girl there," "When my seeing friends play games," "When I cannot find something I dropped," "When I want to go somewhere." In general, they felt that their social difficulties were primarily due to the fact that other people put too much emphasis on their limitations.

In an extensive review of research literature, other investigators (Baker et al., 1953) concluded that "probably the most impressive fact yet discovered about the psychology of the blind is the relatively small amount of personality disturbance that accompanies it." A number of other conclusions were also drawn from psychological studies: personality characteristics present before the disability tend to persist afterward; near blindness does not necessarily affect the personality; and there are wide variations in the way different people respond to the same degree of defect.

When efforts were first made to find employment for blind people, they were usually placed on jobs that required fine discrimination through the sense of touch or hearing—for example, basket weaving and piano tuning. More recently the New York State Employment Service has demonstrated that if the major criterion is simply the ability to do the job, the blind are found to be far more versatile than most employers realize. When the Service gave them brief orientation on the physical features of the job, they were found to be capable of working in all major fields, including clerical and agricultural occupations, dictaphone, switchboard and power-press operations, and even medical social work and selling securities on the outside (Altman and Baumann, 1955). *See* AMAUROSIS, VISUAL DEFECTS.

How does the world look to a person

who has been born blind but who later gains his sight? Psychologists have sought the answer to this question in order to solve the basic problem of how much of our perceptual experience is innate and how much acquired. In 1932, Senden made a careful study of a number of individuals who were seeing for the first time after surgical removal of cataracts which had obscured their vision from birth. At first these patients were confused and bewildered by the sudden flood of visual stimuli; nevertheless, they were able to distinguish vague figures and could follow moving objects with their eyes. These abilities were apparently innate. As expected, they were unable to recognize any colors, and they were also unable to distinguish different shapes, such as a triangle from a square, unless they traced their outline with their fingers or counted their corners. Familiar faces and objects which they had learned to recognize by touch could not be identified by sight alone. When they were shown two sticks, they could not tell which one was longer except by touching them, although they reported that they looked different. When these individuals were given special training, they learned to distinguish colors before they could distinguish shapes, but even after weeks of practice they had trouble recognizing a triangle when it was turned upside down or viewed under different illumination.

In experiments performed by Riesen (1950, 1961), chimpanzees were reared in total darkness, or wearing translucent goggles, until they were sixteen months of age. At that point tests showed that they could respond to light but were unable to perceive complex patterns. They also failed to blink at threatening objects and were poorly co-ordinated in visual-motor performance. The retinas of the animals reared in total darkness were found to be defective, since apparently light stimulation is necessary

for normal development of the eye. *See* SENSORY DEPRIVATION.

BLOCKING. An abrupt interruption in the flow of thought and speech; the individual cannot recall what he wanted to say or find words to express himself.

A transient form of blocking occurs in healthy individuals who are suddenly overwhelmed by strong emotion such as anger, terror, grief, or horror. In psychiatric cases it is believed that unconscious material of a distasteful or threatening nature exerts an inhibiting effect on the train of thought. When blocking of this kind first occurs, it is often associated with specific topics, but in some cases it becomes so pervasive that all thought and speech are obstructed for prolonged periods. Severe blocking of this kind seems to be confined to schizophrenia. Equivalent terms are "thought obstruction" and "thought deprivation."

BODY IMAGE. The mental image we form of our body as a whole, including both its physical characteristics (body percept), and our attitudes toward these characteristics (body concept).

Our body image is a basic component of our concept of self and our feeling of personal identity. It stems from both conscious and unconscious sources. If we succeed in separating the two factors, we are likely to find that the conscious picture differs materially from the unconscious picture—and both may be in sharp contrast to our actual characteristics. Psychological studies have indicated that while a few people (usually timid, insecure individuals) underrate their physical characteristics, most of us think we are slimmer, stronger, or more attractive than we actually are. Freud himself has given us a classic example of this tendency. In his *Psychopathology of Everyday Life* (1904) he mentions an experience of his own while traveling in an overnight train. He was sitting on the bed in his compartment when suddenly the door opened and a strange and ugly old man came lurching toward him. A moment later he realized that the mirrored door of the lavatory facing him had swung open!

The body image develops slowly and undergoes many changes in the course of growth. The body percept probably begins to take shape in the third or fourth months of life when the infant discovers his fingers and toes. He first explores them with his mouth, then with his hands, and a little later begins to get acquainted with the rest of his body through touch, sight, and kinesthetic (body movement) sensations. Experiences of warmth, cold, and pain, as well as sensations received through hearing, taste, and smell, also contribute to body awareness. Stomach distress and other internal pain produce at least a dim realization that the body has an inside as well as an outside. Through eating, eliminating, reaching, and playing, the growing child goes on to discover his body's abilities; and through encounters with play apparatus, games, sports, and other children, he gradually develops a vague idea of what his body can and cannot do. This is the beginning of the body *concept.*

As time goes on, other people play a major role in the formation of the child's attitudes and feelings about his body and its parts. Parents and relatives call him "big and strong," "chubby" or "wiry," and make comparisons, sometimes favorable and sometimes unfavorable, with other members of the family. Before the child is three, he is reminded in many ways that he is a boy or a girl, and may begin to identify masculinity with muscles and femininity with daintiness.

During the first few years many parents imply that some parts of the body are good, clean, and acceptable, while certain parts—particularly the organs of elimination and sex—are bad, dirty, and repulsive. Other parents, fortunately, are more sensible. Later on, when puberty is reached and the secondary sexual characteristics develop, the child is called upon to revise his body image. At this point cultural influences enter the picture to establish standards of bodily contours—for example, the American emphasis on tall men and "curvaceous" women. Such standards often exert a disproportionate effect on the development of feelings of self-esteem and self-acceptance. *See* ADOLESCENCE.

In recent years there have been a number of investigations of "body image disturbances"—that is, psychological maladjustments stemming from deformity, disfigurement, or dismemberment (Schilder, 1950). Reactions to conspicuous body defects vary from slight self-consciousness and anxiety to deep depression and even paranoid states. Many persons are still affected by superstitions, such as the idea that deformed children are a punishment for the sins of their parents. Common stereotypes and jokes about receding chins, large ears or noses, as well as terrifying characterizations of amputees in literature (Melville's Ahab and Stevenson's Long John Silver) also have their effect. But an individual's reactions to deformity or disfigurement depend primarily on the reactions of his family and associates. It has been found that almost any defect can be absorbed without serious harm to the personality if the family avoids oversolicitude, overprotection, concealment of the defect, and simply accepts the afflicted person for what he is. In most cases the family can also be of great help by encouraging him to develop skills and abilities that will offset his loss or defect.

Nevertheless, severe emotional disturbances do occur in some cases. They are less often observed in individuals who have congenital or early acquired defects than in those who suddenly lose their sense of sight or hearing, develop bodily disfigurement as a result of metabolic disorder, or undergo radical surgery or amputation of major parts of the body. The older defects are likely to be incorporated in the body image during the normal process of development, but later damage disrupts an already established concept. In these cases it is always advisable to anticipate a possible emotional disturbance and take preventive measures.

Some feelings of anxiety and dejection are to be expected when the body image is abruptly damaged. Perceptual distortions, nightmares, and wish-fulfilling dreams are common. More specific reactions occur in certain cases—for instance, women who lose a breast as a result of mastectomy before they are married are likely to react more acutely than those who have been married and have children. Many amputees mourn the loss of their severed member and become intensely concerned that it be accorded a decent burial. If these reactions are discussed openly with the patient and his family, and if a plan of readjustment or rehabilitation is fully outlined, pathological disturbances can usually be prevented.

Another form of body image disturbance is frequently encountered by plastic surgeons—the drive to undergo operation after operation to correct imagined deformities. An example is the man who came to Johns Hopkins Hospital seeking to have his nose remodeled for the thirteenth time. The doctor could find nothing wrong with his nose. Others request changes in chin, cheeks, lips, ears, eyelids, or a combination of features. Knorr et al. (1967) have made a special study of this disorder and have found that nearly all the patients are mentally disturbed unmarried males between the ages of twenty and thirty-five, most of whom appear to be latent schizophrenics. The typical patient displays grandiose ambition, low self-esteem, little heterosexual interest, and high anxiety. Some develop clearcut paranoid tendencies, particularly delusions of persecution centering around the refusal of surgeons to treat them. Knorr and his associates suggest that some of these "insatiable" patients can benefit from surgery coupled with psychiatric treatment since it is important for them to feel that the doctors are on their side.

When there is evidence that severe body image disturbances are developing, a psychiatrist or clinical psychologist should be called upon to examine the patient. He may use special questions and tests, such as the Word Association Test and the Draw a Person test, in order to determine the character and depth of the disorder. He will be on the lookout for such reactions as: denial of the loss of a body part, unwillingness to accept prosthetic devices, a conviction of loathsomeness, feelings of self-punishment, severe depression, expressions of intense hostility, paranoid reactions, and extreme discomfort or pain in the phantom limb in cases of amputation. Where these reactions occur, some form of psychotherapy is generally recommended. It may take the form of outpatient treatment with the tranquilizer chlorpromazine, or short-term psychotherapy in which hypnosis or narcosis are used. In cases where deeper neurotic conditions have developed, psychoanalysis may be recommended; and if psychotic reactions occur, electroshock therapy may be required. *See* PHANTOM REACTION, AUTOSCOPIC SYNDROME, SCHILDER, FIGURE DRAWING TEST, DYSAUTONOMIA.

BODY LANGUAGE (Organ Language). The expression of unconscious feelings, impulses, or conflicts through altered functioning of bodily organs; also, nonverbal communication through the body, as in posture, gesture, and facial expression.

The clearest examples of the language of the body are found in conversion hysteria, since this disorder consists of somatic expressions of emotional disturbance. In treating this condition, the therapist views the patient's symptoms as symbols which must be deciphered—and this can only be accomplished by a study of his emotional history and present reaction patterns. As Rosen and Gregory (1965) point out, "A chronically uncontrollable contraction of the hand into a clenched fist, for example, may symbolize hostility as much as angry words do. Hysterical seizures may, in a distorted fashion, express sexuality or tantrum-like hostility and anger. (A single symptom may simultaneously have several meanings.) Blurred vision and functional blindness have been interpreted in various cases as an expression of guilt consequent on real or fancied misdeeds, a fear of the outer world and a magical attempt to do away with it, or a reaction-formation to the unconscious wish to be a voyeur. A hand paralysis may symbolize masturbation guilt or a struggle to inhibit hostility." *See* SYMBOLIZATION, SYMPTOM.

Many therapists, particularly those of the psychoanalytic school, also explain psychophysiologic (psychosomatic) symptoms in terms of unconscious meanings. Thus, "difficulty in swallowing food has been interpreted by analysts as evidence of something 'unpalatable' in the person's life situation; nausea is inability to 'stomach' something unpleasant; vomiting is rejection; asthmatic difficulties symbolize the existence of a load on one's chest; pain in the shoulder or arm indicates an inhibited impulse to strike out aggressively; and neurodermatitic itching is a somatic expression of the saying, 'He gets under my skin'" (Rosen and Gregory, 1965). Some authors, including Ruesch et al. (1946), believe these disorders represent an infantile use of body language by individuals who are unable to express themselves effectively by verbal means. *See* CONVERSION REACTION, PSYCHOPHYSIOLOGIC DISORDERS (GENERAL).

The functional psychoses offer many illustrations of nonverbal communication through posture, gestures, and other bodily movements. Some of these appear to be on an intentional level; others seem to be completely unconscious. In retarded depression, for example, the facial expression is rigid, posture is slumped, and gesticulation is reduced or nonexistent. Some patients deliberately attempt to mask their despair by looking alert and assuming a particularly energetic posture; others try to show how helpless they are or how much they need affection by adopting a sad expression and a dejected air.

The reading of body language is particularly important—and particularly difficult—in schizophrenic patients. It may be the only way to penetrate their minds, and even then it is conjectural. As Spiegel (1959) points out, "Posture, stance, movement, muscle tension, and facial expression give a wide range of information of the patient's inner state of emotions and of communication, including the following: his emotional attitudes, such as rage, anxiety, beatitude; the age at which he is experiencing or fantasizing himself; often the thought-content he is symbolizing; the degree of withdrawnness from the environment in autism or in catatonic stupor; his inner communication with hallucinated figures; and the changeover to stereotyping of gesture and facial expression from spontaneous expressive movements."

As an example of the symbolic use of body language, Spiegel cites the case of the young girl who had made several suicidal attempts, and who later went into a catatonic stupor for eighteen hours. When she came out of it, she revealed that she had been overwhelmed by rage and the desire to destroy herself, and then said "Isn't it better to sleep for eighteen hours than to kill myself?" In another case, a male patient who had been hospitalized for ten years and who was practically nonverbal, expressed his longing for closeness by moving his chair nearer and nearer to the therapist until he was almost in physical contact with her.

Finally, in a discussion of language and pain, Szasz (1959) makes the comment that "the psychiatrist's role is like that of a translator and interpreter of a foreign language. He must translate the patient's body language (for example, 'I have pains in my chest') into the language of everyday speech (I am unhappy with my wife, husband, job, children, religion, etc.)" However, patients must be carefully prepared to accept these translations before they are introduced.

BORDERLINE DISORDERS. A group of psychological disturbances which exhibit various combinations of normality, neurosis, functional psychosis, and psychopathy.

Schmideberg (1959) believes these disorders comprise a distinct clinical entity, since borderline patients do not usually develop outright neuroses or psychoses: "The patient, as a rule, remains substantially the same throughout his life. He is stable in his instability, whatever ups and downs he has, and often even keeps constant his pattern of peculiarity." The category includes a number of different subgroups: "depressives, schizoids, paranoids, querulents, hypochondriacs, antisocials (representing attenuated forms of psychopathy), mixed cases etc."

The outstanding characteristic of the borderline patient is a severe personality disturbance that affects practically every aspect of his life—his attitudes, relationships, values, work habits, emotional responses, and sexual behavior. There is wide variation in the characteristic reactions of the different subgroups. The schizoids tend to be nonsocial and detached; psychopaths are more antisocial, tending to be aggressive and defiant; self-righteous querulents collect grievances and are overaware of social injustices; hypochondriacs suffer from a variety of physical complaints; depressives are pessimistic and unable to enjoy themselves; paranoids cannot get along with others due to mistrust, arrogance, and oversensitivity to criticism.

Beneath these differences are a number of basic similarities. Schmideberg stresses the following tendencies, noting that they may be more prominent in one patient than another: (1) lack of empathy, consideration, and deep feeling in their relations with other people; (2) low tolerance for frustration; inability to accept rules, routines, and a steady job; (3) poor judgment, lack of common sense, inability to concentrate and learn from experience; (4) general unhappiness and emptiness, leading to excessive need for money, sex, food, or thrills, but without a full capacity for enjoyment; (5) inability to establish healthy sexual and love relationships: promiscuity, impotence, frigidity, etc.; (6) inconsistency and changeability: obsessively clean at one time, utterly neglectful at another; (7) lack of repression: "The patient cannot forget and forgive, he cannot repress his hurts, the injustices he suffered, the little aches and pains he felt, as would the ordinary person and also the neurotic" (Schmideberg). In the light of these characteristics it is understandable that many borderline individuals do not have the drive or the ability to establish constructive work and personal relationships. They therefore give up one job after another, and some drift into unemployment, alcoholism, or crime.

Treatment of borderline patients is a difficult matter, not only because they often have no desire for therapy, but because the standard procedures such as suggestion, hypnosis, shock treatment, and orthodox psychoanalysis are ineffective. Experience has shown that the free association technique is likely to encourage them to think autistically and withdraw even further from reality; and release of repressed material may push them over the borderline into delinquency, addiction, or psychosis. Moreover, the detached, passive attitude of the classical analyst simply encourages them to express their impulses without helping them control their behavior. For these and other reasons, Schmideberg has developed a direct, active approach which aims to "improve the borderline's relationship to people, develop his reality sense, judgment, sense of continuity, foresight, and awareness of the consequences of his actions; in short, socialize him and develop control."

Schmideberg describes her therapy as a form of re-education in which the patient's healthy behavior is strengthened and his pathological reactions discouraged. The key element in the process is the establishment of a friendly, interested relationship so that the patient will openly discuss his immediate situations and needs and the way he is tackling his problems, and will accept direct, authoritative guidance which will show where he has gone astray and where he is on the right track.

The therapist does not attempt to make him aware of basic conflicts or repressed experiences that are influencing his behavior. However, "We can deal with the underlying conflict without revealing it to the patient; for example, if it concerns his unconscious hostility toward his father, we can find other acceptable outlets for his aggression, make him less sensitive to guilt, improve realistically his relation to his father and to father substitutes, make him more independent, and remove some of the causes of his resentment." As this statement indicates, each patient must be treated according to his own inner needs. Some need more freedom, others more control; some need higher standards, some greater flexibility; some need direct advice on finding a job or meeting eligible male or female friends; others need help with relationships within the immediate family.

In any case, the therapist proceeds step-by-step, utilizing the actual situations of the patient's present life—for instance, his need for a job or his desire to make a good impression on a probation officer—to "get him moving" in the direction of stronger motivation, better controlled behavior, and more constructive relationships. As the patient tests out new approaches and finds them to his advantage, he may be motivated to build on them. In this way, a short-term approach may achieve long-term results.

BRAIN DISORDERS. A group of disorders caused by or associated with impairment of brain tissue function, and characterized by impairment of (a) orientation, (b) memory, (c) judgment, (d) general intellectual functions such as comprehension, learning, and reasoning, and by (e) lability or shallowness of affect (emotional reactions). These symptoms may be mild, moderate, or severe, depending on the nature and extent of the brain damage. The individual's reaction to the impaired functioning depends not only on the severity of the precipitating organic disorder, but on his personality characteristics, current emotional conflicts, life situation, and relationships. For this reason, severe brain damage sometimes produces surprisingly slight effects on the personality; and, conversely, mild damage may lead to extreme and even psychotic reactions.

Approximately 15 million people in the United States suffer from brain disorders, though the great majority of cases do not involve serious mental disturbance. Nevertheless, disorders associated with brain pathology constitute over one third of all first admissions to mental hospitals. This percentage is constantly increasing due to the lengthening of the life span and the fact that brain disorders reach a peak in old age.

Organic brain disorders are classified as acute and chronic. The acute disorders result from temporary, reversible impairment; the chronic disorders involve permanent damage to the nervous system. However, a sharp line cannot be drawn between the two types, since some conditions, such as a blow on the head, may produce what appears to be a temporary disorder but actually cause permanent damage; while other conditions, such as pernicious anemia, may produce effects that last for weeks or months, yet the patient may recover fully in the long run.

Acute brain disorders produce symptoms ranging from mild changes in mood to acute delirium with delusions and hallucinations. In some cases the tissue impairment releases latent personality and behavior disturbances. The American Psychiatric Association (1952) classifies these acute disorders into syndromes associated with (1) intracranial infection (encephalitis, meningitis, brain abscess); (2) systemic infection (pneumonia, typhoid fever, acute rheumatic fever); (3) drug or poison intoxication (by bromides, barbiturates, opiates, and such poisons as lead and gas); (4) alcoholic intoxication (delirium tremens, acute alcoholic hallucinosis); (5) brain trauma (head injury due to accident); (6) circulatory disturbance (cerebral embolism, arteriosclerosis, hypertension, cardiac-renal disease, and cardiac disease); (7) convulsive disorder (idiopathic epilepsy); (8) metabolic disturbance (uremia, diabetes, hyperthyroidism, hypocalcemia, vitamin deficiency, hypoglycemic states, etc.; (9) intracranial neoplasm (brain tumor); (10) diseases or conditions of unknown cause (multiple sclerosis, etc.).

Chronic brain disorders involve disturbances of the higher functions—memory, judgment, reasoning, comprehension—and in general, the greater the amount of tissue loss, the greater the impairment of function. In some cases neuroses, psychoses, or character disorders are precipitated by the impairment, or superimposed upon it. These disorders are classified by The American Psychiatric Association into syndromes associated with (1) congenital cranial anomalies (congenital spastic paraplegia, mongolism, prenatal infectious disease, birth trauma—resulting in mild, moderate or severe mental deficiency); (2) central nervous system syphilis (meningoencephalitic type—general paresis); (3) central nervous system syphilis (meningovascular type); (4) central nervous system syphilis (other types); (5) cranial infections other than syphilis; (6) intoxication by lead, arsenic, mercury, carbon monoxide, illuminating gas, alcohol; (7) brain trauma (permanent head injury); (8) cerebral arteriosclerosis; (9) other circulatory disorders (due to cerebral embolism, hemorrhages, arterial hypertension); (10) convulsive disorder (idiopathic epilepsy); (11) senile brain disease; (12) other disturbances of metabolism, growth, or nutrition (glandular, pellagra, familial amaurosis, complications of diabetes, thyroid, pituitary, and adrenal disorders); (13) intracranial neoplasm; and (14) diseases and conditions of unknown or uncertain cause, such as multiple sclerosis, Pick's disease, or Huntington's chorea. For individual topics, see the listing Organic Brain Disorders in the Category Index.

BRAIN TUMOR DISORDERS. Acute and chronic brain syndromes due to intracranial neoplasms (tumors). These neoplasms, or "new growths," are of unknown origin and vary greatly in size. They may be either benign or malignant. Some tumors remain small and relatively harmless, depending on their location. Others may reach the size of an orange and do extensive damage by exerting pressure on brain tissue. Malignant tumors cause damage by direct destruction of cells.

Brain tumors occur most frequently

in adults between the ages of forty and sixty, but are also occasionally seen in children. Although about 1 per cent of the population are afflicted, brain tumor patients account for only about .1 per cent of first admissions to mental hospitals since they seldom develop serious and chronic mental symptoms.

The clinical picture in brain tumor disorders is a varied one since the symptoms are due not only to the size, location, and rapidity of growth of the tumor, but to the pre-illness personality and insight of the patient. There is probably no disorder in which the individual's reactions are so dependent on his degree of maturity, stability, and tolerance for stress. In fact, these factors frequently outweigh the physical effects of the tumor itself in determining the symptom picture. Some patients undergo noticeable changes in personality and attitude even when the physical symptoms are not severe. They may become easily upset, indifferent toward work, neglectful of personal appearance, or shameless in their behavior. Others are able to endure even the most intense suffering with courage, determination, and a refusal to admit defeat.

The most common early symptoms are absentmindedness, fatigability, drowsiness, and mild confusion. As the disorder advances, memory, concentration, reasoning, and sensation become increasingly affected. Patients who have some awareness of their condition often become depressed and apprehensive; those who do not understand what is wrong with them may become euphoric or jocular, in an unconscious effort to deny that it is anything serious.

The specific symptoms depend largely on the area affected. Temporal lobe tumors frequently produce disagreeable taste and smell sensations, strange dreamlike states, transient feelings of fear or dread, or "Lilliputian" hallucinations in which they see small animals crawling around. In some cases automatic, irrational actions are carried out suddenly and without recollection later on. Tumors of the frontal lobe lead to absentmindedness, memory impairment, and inability to concentrate. These patients also develop personality changes, often becoming apathetic about their personal appearance, indifferent toward their work, suspicious and uninhibited in their behavior. Occipital lobe tumors are most frequently associated with simple visual hallucinations such as flashes of colored light, or auditory hallucinations such as ringing, buzzing, or roaring sounds. Tumors of the corpus callosum (the tissue joining the two hemispheres of the brain) are accompanied by impairment of concentration and thinking processes. In general, mental symptoms are less likely to occur if the intracranial pressure builds up slowly than if it develops rapidly.

Brain tumor cases usually require surgery where this is feasible. Its success depends on the size and location of the tumor, the damage it has already done, and the amount of tissue that must be sacrificed in removing it. Early and accurate diagnosis is essential, although some tumors, particularly the benign type, grow so slowly that it is hard to discover them in their early stages. An estimated 40 per cent of cases are completely curable; 20 per cent can be relieved for five or more years, but may involve some impairment of physical or mental functions; the remainder are fatal within a relatively short period. There are no known methods of prevention.

Illustrative Case: BRAIN TUMOR DISORDERS

A twenty-five-year-old mechanic grew very dull mentally. His reactions slowed and his facial expression became dull and stupid. He was unable to grasp simple matters. For example, when he expected an out-of-town visitor, he would ask how the guest would travel and how long he would stay; he was unable to figure out where the visitor would sleep. He became more and more forgetful, even forgetting where he put his tools. He failed to complete jobs, and, when criticized for it, did not know what he had done wrong. A mental examination showed that he had memory disturbances and slight intellectual impairment. His physical examination showed neither general nor local symptoms of brain tumor, but the encephalogram showed partial obliteration of the ventricles. On the basis of this, a tumor in both frontal lobes was diagnosed. It was removed surgically, the patient recovered fully and has been well for ten years. (Maslow and Mittelmann, 1951)

BRAINWASHING. Intensive propaganda techniques applied under conditions of stress; coercive persuasion. In this process an individual is subjected to conditions deliberately designed to undermine morale and call in question accepted attitudes. This paves the way for indoctrination with a set of beliefs that may produce a change in behavior.

During the Korean War the Communists used many techniques to "soften up" prisoners in order to elicit "confessions" and useful information from them. At first the emphasis was largely on punitive measures such as forced death marches, vicious beatings, inadequate diet, exposure to freezing weather, and sleep deprivation. Later in the war the Chinese Communists developed more subtle and refined techniques for producing a state of DDD: "debility, dependence, and dread" (Farber et al., 1957). Among them were isolation, continuous interrogation, a system of rewards for giving information, and actual or implied threats of death, nonrepatriation, permanent disability, and harm to loved ones at home—all aimed at the one objective of inducing collaboration with the Communists. This general approach has been broken down into the following three phases, all of which were in operation at the same time:

Isolation. Prisoners were deprived of leadership by removing their officers to a separate location and silently banish-

ing emerging leaders to "reactionary" camps. Only complaining letters from home were delivered. Informers were used to cultivate attitudes of suspicion among the prisoners. These procedures lowered morale and destroyed *esprit de corps.* Isolation and absence of personal ties also prevented the men from checking their attitudes and values with others who could give them emotional support. As a result many of them lost their power to resist and became increasingly vulnerable to threats, bribes, and indoctrination.

Thought control. Prisoners were forced to choose between "co-operation" and starvation, torture, or death. Self-preservation could be achieved only by giving up loyalty, identity, and other ethical values. Resisters were punished and deprived of food and decent lodging; co-operators were rewarded with food, privileges, and promises of early repatriation. Compulsory "confessions" and self-criticism were required of the men in order to stimulate guilt feelings. They were confused and worn out by unpredictable treatment—now harsh, now friendly.

These techniques produced varying degrees of anxiety, dread, and guilt. Many men became confused about how to act, especially since they did not have leaders or friends to depend on. Others, however, successfully resisted the brainwashing by "playing it cool." They cultivated a noncommittal and indifferent air, guarded against becoming emotionally involved, and "co-operated" only in minor ways.

Political Conditioning. This consisted primarily of daily, repetitious "instruction" in Communist ideas and phrases, with constant appeals to fairness and open-mindedness. Reading was limited to books and magazines that stressed injustices in the United States and portrayed Communists as peace seekers. Every prisoner was offered an opportunity to "work for peace," and the more susceptible men were used to indoctrinate the others. This approach was reinforced by giving favors for co-operation and applying punishment for resistance.

The conditioning process fostered considerable doubt, confusion, and poor morale, but actual conversion was rare. In some cases "progressives" and "reactionaries" turned against each other. Studies indicate that 85 per cent succeeded in playing it cool, and 15 per cent were later judged to have complied unduly.

The brainwashing experience left its mark on the prisoners. When first released, most of them showed a "zombie reaction." They were apathetic, detached, dazed, tense, and suspicious, and many had large memory gaps, especially for the period of capture and the death marches. Some of them were ambivalent in their feelings toward the Chinese Communists, but were assailed with strong guilt feelings and were therefore not anxious to return to the United States. After three or four days of freedom practically all the men became more spontaneous and outgoing, although they still felt "suspended in time" and were confused and incapable of making decisions about their future. Most of them were apprehensive about homecoming, felt alienated from others who had not gone through the POW experience, and usually banded together in small, uneasy groups.

On returning home, some men got into trouble due to outbursts of pent-up hostility, and many were easily discouraged and disillusioned when they tried to re-establish relationships and adapt to economic or other changes. Adjustment problems were frequently complicated by physical disability, chronic fatigue, and confusion about themselves; as a result some men resorted to drinking and other forms of escape. The majority, however, regained their stability in time, and a few showed increased inner strength

and capacity. *See* PRISONER OF WAR REACTIONS.

BRAIN WAVES (Electroencephalogram, EEG). Electrical changes, or potentials, occurring during brain activity. The fluctuations are detected through electrodes placed on the skull, and are recorded on a machine known as an electroencephalograph.

It has been known for many years that electrical changes taken place in the brain, but it was not until 1929 that a German physiologist, Hans Berger, gave a substantial account of these changes. His original research arose out of an interest in the possibility of extrasensory perception and psychical phenomena, and led to the development of the electroencephalograph, which has enabled investigators to record many types of brain waves and relate them to many aspects of behavior. When electrodes are placed on various parts of the scalp, this sensitive instrument amplifies and registers the slight electrical activity that occurs under different conditions. Recordings from different locations provide a simultaneous comparison of activity in different regions of the brain.

Brain waves are analyzed into two components, amplitude and frequency. The amplitude, or height and depth of the wave, represents its electrical strength; its frequency, as expressed in cycles per second (cps) refers to the number of times per second the wave reaches its greatest height and depth. If you stand on the shore watching the ocean, amplitude corresponds to the height of the waves, and frequency to the number of times they strike the beach in a given time.

Analysis of EEG recordings indicates that there are several kinds of brain waves, or "Berger rhythms," although there is no distinct dividing line between the various types. Alpha waves have the largest amplitude and a frequency of about ten to twelve cps. They are typical of normal adults when awake and relaxed, and if they are missing or greatly reduced in number, it is usually a sign of brain dysfunction. Beta waves have a lower amplitude and a frequency of twenty to twenty-five cps at peak strength; if the frequency is slightly lower or slightly higher, they are called "slow beta waves" and "fast beta waves." Gamma waves have the highest frequency of any recorded on the EEG, reaching forty to fifty cps at peak amplitude. They appear to be part of the beta pattern. Both gamma and beta waves are found primarily in the forward part of the cortex and appear to reflect thinking and reasoning. The so-called "spindle waves" register twelve to fifteen cps and frequently appear during sleep.

Three other types of waves have also been discovered. Delta waves are extremely slow (one to two cps) with a wide amplitude, and appear at irregular intervals during sleep. They seem to arise from deeper regions of the brain, possibly the hypothalamus, and are also believed to stem from areas of the cortex in which there is a lesion or tumor. Theta, or "saw-tooth" waves, with a frequency of four to seven cps, are typically found in young children. The most recent finding is the kappa wave, with a frequency similar to that of alpha waves (ten cps) but a much weaker amplitude. These normally occur while the subject is reading, dreaming, or thinking, and since they are also found in electrical records of eye movements, they are believed to reflect motor activity during thought.

The differences between wave types has suggested that the EEG might be extremely useful in investigating both the normal and pathological functioning of the brain. Studies to date indicate that it is a valuable tool, but not so effective as it first appeared to be. Many difficulties have presented themselves. First, the origin of the waves is not always clear, since they seem to involve not only the cortex but deeper parts of the brain. Second, it is hard to pin-point them because they represent the additive effects of thousands and perhaps millions of neurons acting together. Third, it is not known whether they represent a simultaneous, quick burst of activity or a slow, continuous change in the electrical potential of brain cells. Fourth, scientists are not sure whether the brain waves produce changes in behavior or whether changes in behavior produce the brain changes. Nevertheless, research has led to a number of notable discoveries about the activity of the brain under both normal and abnormal conditions.

Recent applications of the EEG indicate that there is a wide difference between the wave patterns of different individuals. These patterns appear to be relatively stable for each person, a fact that implies that the EEG is a reliable measure, even though *what* it measures is not always clear. The patterns, however, change with age. Alpha rhythms are infrequent at birth, but slow seven cps waves coming from the central region of the skull are typical of the newborn child. This is an important fact because slow waves of this type indicate brain damage in an adult but not in children. The adult brain wave pattern is not reached until the child is about nine years old.

There are profound differences in the patterns for waking and sleeping, as well as special patterns for drowsiness, light sleep, deep slumber, and dreaming. Alpha waves predominate in waking life, and appear to stem largely from the occipital, or visual, area in the back of the head. When we are drowsy or asleep, trains of delta waves appear. Dreaming has been correlated not only with the return of alpha waves (probably because most dreams are visual), but with recordings of rapid eye movements (Dement and Kleitman, 1957). *See* DREAM-STATE.

Although a fairly large percentage

of alpha waves occur when a person is awake and relaxed, they disappear and are replaced by fast, low-voltage "activation patterns" when visual and other sensory stimulation occurs. This "alpha blocking" also takes place when changes in stimulation are constantly occurring, as in reading, talking, or watching a movie. If the stimulation continues without change, as with a persistent pain or the ticking of a clock, the alpha waves slowly return. This is believed to reflect the process of adaptation. Studies indicate that the blocking of the alpha waves is due to the reticular activation system, which seems to be the "waking center" of the brain, putting the cortex in a state of readiness for incoming stimulation. *See* RETICULAR FORMATION.

Although much of the research on brain waves is considered experimental and exploratory, some of the findings have been put to practical use in neurology and psychiatry. The EEG is particularly helpful in diagnosing brain lesions, tumors, and epilepsy. Slow alpha waves and saw-tooth theta waves of four to seven cps are indicative of lesions or tumors, and very slow waves of one to three cps are one of the surest signs of damaged tissue. The diagnosis of epilepsy is often difficult since the records of normal people and of epileptics may be almost identical. Nevertheless, certain telltale waves appear in the records of epileptics thirty times more often than in the normal records. Very large and very fast waves occurring in bursts are indicative of *grand mal* epilepsy; an alternating "spike and dome" pattern in the forward brain areas is symptomatic of *petit mal;* large, slow, three to six cps waves occur in the psychomotor type of epilepsy in which the patient is afflicted with dream states but has no convulsions. These patterns are most evident during seizures, but less dramatic EEG abnormalities are found between seizures and in individuals who have a predisposition to epilepsy (PLATES 9, 10, 11 AND 12) *See* EPILEPSY (SYMPTOMS AND TYPES).

Many attempts have been made to diagnose mental disorder through EEG records, but the results have not lived up to early expectations. Schizophrenic patients often show slightly faster, weaker, and more irregular waves than normal individuals, but these differences are not consistent. Records taken during the depressive stage of manic-depressive reaction are more normal than different types of personality and differences are not great enough to be indicative (Davis, 1941). Some investigators have found abnormal patterns in antisocial individuals (Hill and Watterson, 1942). The relationship between different types of personality and different kinds of wave patterns is not definite enough to be useful, although active, mentally awake, and "fidgety" people tend to show much less alpha activity than more relaxed and passive persons. This ties up with the findings on sensory stimulation and alpha blocking. The technique has been of even less value in measuring emotional behavior, reactions under stressful conditions, and changes in behavior produced by tranquilizers and other drugs. If the EEG is to be used with confidence as a tool for personality studies and psychiatric diagnosis, that time is still in the future.

BREATH-HOLDING. A behavior disturbance in which a child expresses anger by holding his breath; classified by the American Psychiatric Association (1952) as an "adjustive reaction of infancy," under "Transient Situational Personality Disorders."

Few experiences are more frightening to parents than watching their child hold his breath, especially if he turns blue. Yet "this common condition probably is more alarming than dangerous" (Wittkower and White, 1959). Nevertheless, repeated breath-holding should be diagnosed and dealt with at an early stage to prevent more serious behavior problems or possible brain damage from occurring.

Breath-holding attacks usually start within the first two years of life, and generally disappear spontaneously when the period of violent crying ends between the ages of four and six. This behavior pattern tends to occur in children who are tense and hyperactive; it affects both sexes equally. The attacks generally follow some disturbing or frustrating event, often minor in character, which precipitates disproportionate rage and uncontrolled crying. Sometimes the breath is held so long that the child turns blue (cyanosis) and becomes unconscious.

Breath-holding attacks are considered a sign of disturbance in parent-child relations. Investigators have often found that the parents are usually overprotective and at the same time tense in their insistence upon a rigid feeding schedule or premature toilet training. The attacks result from overwhelming rage and loss of control when the child feels he cannot cope with the situation.

Treatment of this condition requires a study of the child's relation to his family, and particularly situations in which conflict occurs and anger is aroused. Therapy directed at improving the parents' own emotional adjustment is usually recommended.

BRIGHAM, AMARIAH (1798–1849). Brigham was a distinguished physician, author and hospital administrator who exerted a widespread influence on the understanding and care of the mentally ill in the early days of American psychiatry. After teaching anatomy for several years at the College of Physicians and Surgeons in New York City, he became superintendent of the Hartford Retreat in 1840, and two years later was appointed to the same post at the New York State Lunatic Asylum in Ithaca. In 1844 he and twelve other superintendents, known as the "original thirteen," organized the Association of

Medical Superintendents of American Institutions for the Insane. This association was the first national society of physicians in this country, and later evolved into the American Psychiatric Association. In the year of its origin, Brigham became the founder and first editor of its official organ, the *American Journal of Insanity,* which changed its name to the *American Journal of Psychiatry* in 1921.

The asylum at Ithaca was the first New York State institution for mental illness, and under Brigham's leadership it became an outstanding training center for medical superintendents. He was a strong advocate of humane treatment, opposing blood-letting, and rarely recommending physical restraint. Along with other leading psychiatrists of his time, he accepted the idea that mental illness is basically curable, and claimed that "no fact relating to insanity appears better established than the general certainty of curing it in its early stages." However, he cautioned against undue optimism and was considerably more conservative than some of his colleagues, such as William Awl, the superintendent of the Ohio State Asylum for the Insane, who actually claimed a recovery rate of 100 per cent.

Brigham's writings include *A Treatise on Epidemic Cholera, Observations on the Influence of Religion on the Health of Mankind,* and *An Inquiry Concerning the Diseases and Functions of the Brain, the Spinal Cord and Nerves.* His major psychiatric work, *Remarks on the Influence of Mental Cultivation Upon Health* attained a remarkably wide distribution in Europe as well as America.

BRILL, ABRAHAM ARDEN (1874–1948). Brill, chiefly known as one of the first exponents of psychoanalysis in America, was born in Austria and came to the United States as a boy. After graduating from New York University and receiving his medical degree from Columbia College of Physicians and Surgeons, he served as assistant physician at the Central Islip State Hospital for four years, then went to Europe to study under Sigmund Freud. Following a period as chief of the psychiatric clinic at the University of Zürich, he studied under Eugen Bleuler. Returning to the United States, he became head of the Columbia University Clinic of Psychiatry in 1911, and in the same year founded the New York Psychoanalytic Society. In the years that followed he became a lecturer on psychoanalysis and abnormal psychology at Columbia, New York University and Postgraduate Medical Center. At the same time he devoted himself to the translation of Freud's works, and made many important contributions of his own through such books as *Psychoanalysis, Its Theories and Practical Applications* (1921) and *Fundamental Conceptions of Psychoanalysis* (1922).

Brill's studies in Europe had brought him into contact not only with Freud's theory of psychoanalysis but with Bleuler's views on the psychodynamics of psychoses. Although these developments were practically unknown in the United States, he recognized their significance and sought to introduce them into American psychiatry.

The Freudian theories, with their revolutionary emphasis on unconscious determinants of behavior, met with open hostility. The profession did not take kindly to the idea that men are not the masters of their fate and have little insight into their own motivations. Moreover, the treatment of the neurotic, which Freud stressed, had been largely neglected in America as well as Europe, since most psychiatrists were solely concerned with the more extreme disturbances. It was largely through Brill's translations of one after another of Freud's works, as well as his persistent and astute efforts to explain the theory, that the psychoanalytic approach gradually gained a foothold in this country. He was also instrumental in introducing the psychoanalytic treatment of neurotic disorders, and within the relatively short

span of two to three decades it had become the dominant technique in the field.

The second major approach which Brill brought to America resulted from the studies he made with Bleuler on patients with chronic dementia praecox (later termed schizophrenia). These studies suggested that even though the schizophrenic's behavior appeared bizarre, it nevertheless had an underlying meaning in terms of the patient's own life experiences. Brill therefore felt that if the therapist would establish a relationship with the patient and adopt a flexible approach which departed from the orthodox Freudian techniques, he might discover the hidden meaning of the patient's symptoms and help him gain insight into his reactions. In his own words, he attempted to treat the schizophrenic analytically in the hope that "an unknown something might change him to a normal human being." Like others who have made similar attempts, he had little success with this approach, but his work did give impetus to further experiments with psychotherapy for psychotic patients. *See* BLEULER.

BROMIDE INTOXICATION. A toxic disorder produced by excessive use of bromides, usually taken to relieve tension, alleviate physical discomfort or induce sleep.

Bromide poisoning is not so common today as it was when this drug was widely available in commercial preparations and used for self-medication. It is also less frequently prescribed by physicians for nervous and mental disorders. Yet there is still a problem, since bromides are still overused by many individuals to relieve tension or combat the aftereffects of alcohol. Elderly and arteriosclerotic individuals are particularly susceptible to bromide intoxication.

The first signs of bromide intoxication are weakness, irritability, drowsiness, inability to concentrate, and memory defect. If the drug continues to accumulate in the system, it may result in a psychotic reaction that is characterized by confusion, disorientation, clouding of consciousness, restlessness, excitement, apprehension, loss of memory, and hallucinations. These symptoms constitute a delirious state which may last for ten days to two months.

Treatment consists in the general elimination of the drug from the body by forcing of liquids and administration of sodium or ammonium chloride. *See* TOXIC PSYCHOSES.

BRUXISM. Persistent teeth-grinding, usually occurring at night during sleep.

Bruxism is generally regarded as a tension symptom and, in many cases, an unconscious expression of repressed anger or resentment. It occurs most frequently in older children and adolescents, but is also observed in alcoholics and other adults, particularly during periods of stress. In some instances the grinding or gnashing of the teeth is loud enough to disturb others, and if it continues for any length of time there is danger that the tooth surfaces will become worn, resulting in malocclusion.

Bruxism usually responds to brief psychotherapy aimed at releasing hostility or other pent-up feelings verbally, and reducing or helping the individual adjust to the pressures in his life situation. Hypnotic suggestion may also be effective, particularly when accompanied by psychotherapy.

BULIMIA (Hyperorexia, Polyphagia). Insatiable hunger; pathological overeating.

The psychological drive to overeat is usually classified as a psychophysiologic disorder of the gastrointestinal system, although some regard it as a hysterical, or conversion, symptom. Regardless of the classification, the important fact is that in most cases bulimia is believed to be due to emotional factors. It

may be a means of relieving stresses due to external situations or internal tensions, and is often interpreted as an unconscious attempt to recapture the feeling of security experienced early in life when food was received from the mother.

An insatiable appetite may also have a number of symbolic meanings arising from unconscious sources. It may represent a hunger for affection, since love is so closely associated with being fed in infancy. It may be a substitute or a compensation for satisfactions presently denied, such as tenderness, sex, or attention. It may express hostile wishes, since chewing and swallowing are, in a sense, acts of destruction. Moreover, the resulting obesity may be an unconscious attempt to seek security in size and to clothe one's self in an armor of fat against a threatening world.

In some cases, according to psychoanalytic theory, the compulsive drive to consume food may stem from unresolved problems, such as emotional starvation, during the oral phase of psychosexual development when the mouth and its functions were the child's basic source of satisfaction. Some analysts have also suggested that overeating may arise from an unconscious wish to become pregnant, a wish that may motivate men as well as women. In this view, eating and drinking are symbolic acts of fertilization, and obesity represents pregnancy.

Ravenous appetites are also found among psychotic patients, especially schizophrenics who have regressed to primitive, infantile behavior. On the other hand, bulimia may be due to a number of organic disorders involving endocrine disturbances; it may also be caused by an inflammation affecting the hunger center in the hypothalamic region of the brain. Only a small minority of cases, however, are believed to be due to organic conditions. *See* OBESITY, HYPOTHALAMUS.

C

CAFETERIA FEEDING. A technique used in studying the hunger drive. The subject is offered a variety of foods, with freedom to choose any kind or amount he wishes.

Cafeteria feeding was first employed in experiments conducted by Clara Davis in 1928. She offered twelve to twenty different foods in separate containers to infants between six and twelve months of age, and allowed them to select whatever they wanted. At any given meal some of the babies were found to eat all butter or all vegetables, but over a period of about six weeks they all tried different foods and ate a well-balanced diet. Tests showed that their growth rate was at least as good as that of infants fed according to a dietician's formula. Similar experiments performed on rats have produced the same general result (Pilgrim and Patton, 1947).

Cafeteria feeding experiments indicate that the organism possesses a basic physiological wisdom of its own. They also suggest some wisdom for parents to follow: "One implication here is that we do not have to worry ourselves sick about the eating habits of our children—provided we can (a) make available to them a wide choice of foods, (b) refrain from injecting psychological and emotional factors into the process of eating, and (c) tolerate the mess." (Sanford, 1965) *See* SPECIFIC HUNGER.

CANALIZATION. A tendency to channel needs into specific, fixed gratifications.

The hunger drive is unselective in the first few years. Young children attempt to eat practically anything. After a time, however, we limit ourselves to certain foods which have repeatedly given us satisfaction and are at the same time considered acceptable. Other articles of food, such as fried grasshoppers, appear unnatural and repulsive even though they may be regarded as delicacies in some cultures. Similarly, we gradually restrict our esthetic tastes, our friendships, our sex life, our work and recreational interests, to a relatively narrow range of satisfactions. In other words, we tend to fall into a pattern in the way we seek to gratify most of our needs.

Gardner Murphy (1946) has applied the term "canalization," borrowed from Pierre Janet, to this universal tendency. He believes these acquired wants can be distinguished from conditioned responses, since they can seldom if ever be eradicated completely, while conditioned responses can usually be extinguished. As evidence he offers the fact that although we may replace old canalizations with new ones, we have a tendency to revert to original satisfactions when we are under stress—that is, we derive a nostalgic pleasure from the music or the sweets or the mother love we enjoyed in childhood. There is further evidence in the hypnotic-regression technique, in which an individual is able to recapture the entire level of behavior which obtained at four or five years of age.

Murphy regards canalization as an important aspect of personality development. The child's own body is the first center for the process since it is a source of his early satisfactions. Within a few months the mother gradually emerges as the most intense satisfier in the outside world, and since the strongest and most lasting canalizations usually occur in the early years of childhood, she may remain the child's basic source of satisfaction in life—in other words the child may become "fixated" on her. As a result he may fail to respond adequately to other satisfiers, and in later life may seek a love mate who will be expected to provide everything, just as mother used to do.

Fortunately there is a countertendency which Murphy believes to be equally basic—the desire for novelty, variety and adventure. This helps to insure diversity in the canalization of our drives. At the beginning of life we are all basically similar, since we are endowed with similar physiological mechanisms—but as we grow and come in contact with different cultural and personal influences, we acquire more and more specific and divergent ways of satisfying our needs. In other words, identical drives become canalized in different ways, but our humanity remains essentially the same.

CANNON, WALTER BRADFORD
(1871–1945). Cannon, America's foremost physiologist, was associated with the Harvard Medical School during his entire career—first as student, then as instructor and professor. His professional contributions began when he became the first investigator to use X rays in the study of the gastric process. This technique enabled him to observe the motility function of the gastrointestinal tract, which he later described in a book entitled *The Mechanical Factors of Digestion* (1911). His studies of the digestive system, which he carried out with Anton J. Carlson, also led to the theory that hunger was due to contractions of an empty stomach. This so-called local theory of hunger was directly opposed to the prevailing theory which explained this sensation in terms of a response by brain mechanisms to nutritive deficiencies in the blood. He also advanced a local theory of thirst, which he attributed to a dry mouth

caused by lack of saliva flow. *See* HUNGER, THIRST.

Cannon's greatest contributions arose out of his studies of the bodily changes that take place in emotion. He showed that in fear, rage, and other intense emotional states respiration rate, blood pressure, and heartbeat are sharply increased, while the digestive processes are inhibited. He further demonstrated that these changes are mediated by the sympathetic nervous system through an increase in the secretion of adrenalin into the bloodstream. In a word, the two systems, sympathetic and adrenal, work together to put the organism on a "war footing" and prepare it for "fight or flight." This new theory was advanced in 1915 in a book entitled *Bodily Changes in Pain, Hunger, Fear and Rage*.

Further studies led to an elaboration of this theory of emotion. Cannon found that when he stimulated certain parts of the brains of animals, they responded with ragelike behavior; and extirpation experiments conducted by his pupil Philip Bard, indicated that the thalamus was the actual control center. From these and other experiments Cannon and Bard developed the theory that the thalamus directly affects the cortex and the muscles and, through the autonomic nervous system, the visceral organs as well. This center appeared to be implicated in the entire pattern of bodily changes in emotion, and for this reason the new concept became known as the thalamic theory. *See* EMOTION (THEORIES).

These early investigations led Cannon to a broader investigation of the body's reactions to stresses and disturbances. In a book published in 1932, *The Wisdom of the Body,* he documented the astounding number and complexity of physiological mechanisms that enable the organism to maintain a constant internal state even when it is subjected to radical changes in the external environment. He applied Claude Bernard's term "homeostasis" to the co-ordination of functions that makes this stability possible, and he demonstrated that the sympathico-adrenal system is of utmost importance in this process. This he did by showing that when this system is removed, animals will be able to maintain themselves only if the environment makes very few demands on them. *See* HOMEOSTASIS.

Cannon made many other major contributions, which he reported in a number of books and over 200 journal articles. His study of surgical shock, which he carried out in the laboratory and near the front lines, is credited with saving many lives during World War I. His new findings were later described in a book *Traumatic Shock* (1923). Another book, *Autonomic Neuro-Effector Systems,* written in collaboration with A. Rosenblueth (1937), added substantially to our knowledge of the autonomic nervous system and the way nerve impulses are transmitted to peripheral organs.

Cannon did not confine himself to the laboratory, but took a deep interest in social matters. Among his contributions in this sphere was his conception of a society that would provide an environment in which the individual could not only maintain himself but realize his fullest potential. He held that such a society must have built-in mechanisms for handling economic and natural calamities that threaten its "homeostasis." In a word, he believed that the principles he had discovered for the biological organism could also be applied to the social organism.

CAPGRAS SYNDROME. A rare psychotic disorder in which the patient insists that other individuals are not really themselves, but are "doubles" or impostors.

The reaction was first described in 1923 by the French psychiatrist J. Capgras, who termed it "L'illusion des sosies" (the illusion of doubles). His patients were all women, but more recently a few male cases have been reported in this country. French psychiatrists consider the condition a syndrome, or disease entity, in itself, but American and German authors generally view it as a special symptom of paranoid schizophrenia, paranoid state, or less often, manic-depressive reaction.

Davidson (1941) interprets the reaction as a form of magical thinking which serves the unconscious purpose of rejecting important persons in the patient's life. Arieti and Meth (1959) also believe it is a form of rejection, but make the further point that the double serves as a target for resentments felt against the person whose existence is being denied. If, for example, a female patient is confronted by her mother, but insists that she is an impostor, the reason is that "the patient rejects the mother, actually attributes very bad habits to her, but cannot allow herself to become conscious of this rejection because of concomitant feelings of guilt or other ambivalent attitudes. What the patient feels about the mother is thus displaced to the double or impostor who allegedly assumes her appearance." In other words, the patient can still maintain the fiction that her mother is a model of virtue, while giving vent to her true feelings against the double.

The following is an excerpt from the case of a seventy-three-year-old man who had been diagnosed as a schizophrenic, paranoid type, subject to auditory hallucinations of a persecutory and threatening character. These symptoms subsided during long hospitalization, but he developed a typical Capgras reaction toward his wife and others:

Illustrative Case: CAPGRAS SYNDROME

Since the writer has known the patient, the man always has made a good appearance, clean-shaven, very neat in dress, polite in conversation. He seems much younger than his age, shows remarkable preservation of personality; there are no defect symptoms. His memory is unusually good, with the exception of memory falsifications which are in harmony with his delusional content. As far as the problems studied here are concerned, he gave additional information. He said that he had never cared for his wife. For some three years before his admission, he asserted, he had noticed she was changing considerably. He recalled that one day when she was undressed her skin appeared to him gray and like a cow's udder. He thought that the power of the devil displaced her in the form of a double. Once this double came to the hospital and asked him what he did for sexual intercourse; and when he was horrified by the question, the double advised him to commit suicide. In response to this, he told her to run for her life, since he would kill and get away with it, being considered insane. A week later, he said, the "true" wife visited him. When he asked her about the conversation of the last visit, she denied any knowledge of it. Further "proof" for the existence of the double was his assertion that his wife, on the day of the visit of the double, was in Connecticut.

The man identified other doubles as well. One took the place of a male stenographer. Another displaced the physician in charge of the city psychopathic hospital; as proof of this, the patient had two photographs of the person in question cut out from newspapers. He declared that the true head of the hospital was a kindly man, while the double was cruel, committing people to state hospitals. Still another double replaced a hospital clergyman. The patient, therefore, stopped going to church, saying that after all he was a priest himself and was able to say mass daily himself." (Davidson, 1941)

CARBON DIOXIDE THERAPY. An inhalation treatment occasionally used with psychoneurotic patients, particularly in anxiety and conversion reactions and in certain psychosomatic syndromes. It may or may not be accompanied by psychotherapy.

The method was originated by the Hungarian psychiatrist, Ladislas J. Meduna in 1946, and usually consists of administering a 30 per cent carbon dioxide and 70 per cent oxygen mixture until the patient reaches a state of brief coma. Recovery is rapid, and treatments are generally given three times a week. Some specialists employ modifications of this treatment, with higher proportions of carbon dioxide or initial administration of nitrous oxide to bring on coma more rapidly and with less anxiety for the patient.

Several theories have been proposed to explain the effectiveness of the treatment. Meduna believed the carbon dioxide interrupts pathological brain circuits by raising the threshold of the higher nerve centers. Others attribute its effects entirely to suggestion, or to the gratification of masochistic or other unconscious needs. McGraw and Oliven (1959) evaluate the technique in these words: "It is physically harmless, easy to give, inexpensive, and occasionally highly effective. Improvement and marked improvement in well-selected cases has been reported to be 65 to 68 per cent. It deserves a continued place in treatment."

CARBON MONOXIDE POISONING. A toxic disorder produced by inhalation of carbon monoxide, a colorless, odorless gas.

Inhalation of carbon monoxide in the form of fumes from defective stoves or automobile exhausts deprives the blood, and consequently the brain, of sufficient oxygen. Severe exposure may bring on death by asphyxiation. Most victims, however, sink into a deep coma that is usually followed by confusion and delirium. This acute state generally clears up within a few days, and the patient recovers. A small number of victims, however, may suffer brain damage leading to such permanent symptoms as memory defect, apathy, bewilderment, and loss of initiative. Occasionally these symptoms are accompanied by convulsions and tremors, and a few patients ultimately sink to a vegetative level of existence. *See* TOXIC PSYCHOSES.

Illustrative Case: CARBON MONOXIDE POISONING

A woman of thirty-five became depressed after a disappointment in her husband and attempted suicide by turning on the gas. She remained unconscious for about twenty-four hours after discovery. She had a rise in temperature and pain in the abdomen for the next few days. After a period of time she developed some stiffness and tremor in her extremities, with excessive salivation. She was apathetic and neglectful of her appearance, was disoriented for time, and had memory defects. She would confabulate about having visited relatives or having gone shopping the previous day or in the morning when she actually had not left the house. She did not remember her suicidal attempt and attributed her physical symptoms to having fallen or to having overworked. (Maslow and Mittelmann, 1951)

CASTRATION COMPLEX. In psychoanalytic theory, the unconscious fear of being deprived—or the feeling that one has already been deprived—of the male genital organs.

According to classical Freudian theory, the castration complex is a universal phenomenon, occurring in normal and abnormal individuals of both sexes. It is believed to stem from the primary phallic stage of psychosexual development which occurs in late infancy, a time when large amounts of libido (sexual energy) converge on the genital area. During this period Freud believed the child tends to construe the slightest hints as threats to his genitals. This fear of castration is believed to be closely bound up with the Oedipus situation, and the way it is handled largely determines whether that situation is satisfactorily resolved.

More specifically, the theory holds that the castration complex arises from vague memories of unconscious fears and fantasies experienced early in life. First, by the end of infancy the boy has already lost contact with valued possessions in which his libido has been invested, namely the mother's nipple and his own feces. He then begins to fantasy the loss of another libidinal object, the phallus. Second, this fantasy is intensified when he discovers, through games like "Doctor," that girls do not possess a penis. This suggests that the organ can actually be taken away. (The theory assumes that children of both sexes believe that everyone is born with a penis.)

Third, at about the time when this fantasy arises—that is, at three to five years of age—the Oedipus complex is becoming stronger, and the boy experiences an intense sexual interest in his mother, regarding his father as his prime rival. It is then a small step to the fear that the father will cut off his penis out of anger, and thus deprive him of the organ through which his sexual interest in his mother is expressed. Moreover, the boy may have dreams or fantasies that his rival, the father, has lost his own penis, and guilt feelings aroused by these thoughts make him afraid that he will be deprived of his own penis in retaliation. *See* TALION LAW

Fourth, this fear is fed by threats, reproaches, or physical punishment for masturbation, which is ordinarily practiced during this period. This may have a particularly strong effect on boys who have incest fantasies involving the mother during the masturbation activity. It must be recognized, however, that outright castration threats are seldom made. However, because of his latent anxieties, the child transforms warnings against masturbation, such as "It will make you sick," into the fear that he will lose his penis. Furthermore, ideas about the genitals are often laden with guilt due to overemphasis on cleanliness and toilet training, and therefore any threatened punishment is attached to this area.

Ordinarily the boy resolves the Oedipus situation by identifying with the father. This alleviates his castration fear, and it therefore remains dormant during the latency period between the ages of six and eleven or twelve. However, the castration anxiety may be revived during puberty as a result of the upsurge of libido energy at that time.

Freud did not work out the details of the castration complex among girls. He did point out, however, that they often believe they have been deprived of a penis as punishment. In addition, the lack of a sexual organ equal to that of the male generates feelings of inferiority and "penis envy." Consequently many girls interpret the loss as an injury, and blame the mother for it. These reactions play an important part in the Electra complex. See PENIS ENVY, PSYCHOSEXUAL DEVELOPMENT, OEDIPUS COMPLEX, MASTURBATION.

CATALEPSY. A condition in which the muscles become semirigid and the patient maintains the same position for long periods of time. An arm may be raised or a leg held in an awkward position without any evidence of discomfort even though the limb may begin to turn blue. While this occurs the patient is usually in a trancelike or stuporous state, and if another person changes the position of his limbs, he usually holds that posture without objection. Cataleptic rigidity has been observed in some cases of cerebral arteriosclerosis, hysteria (conversion reaction) and disorders involving the cerebellum, but is most frequently found in catatonic schizophrenia. In the latter disorder it is believed to be due to a high degree of suggestibility, and is frequently associated with echolalia and echopraxia. It may also be induced by hypnosis and by certain drugs, such as bulbocapnine. See CEREA FLEXIBILITAS, ECHOLALIA, ECHOPRAXIA, AUTOMATISM.

CATAPLEXY. A sudden paralysis of all voluntary movement resulting in a collapse of the entire body.

Cataplectic attacks are provoked by emotional excitement—most often by an uncontrollable fit of laughter, but in some cases by overwhelming anxiety or anger. The victim usually sinks helplessly to the ground and cannot speak during the episode, although he is fully conscious. The reaction is probably related to narcolepsy—a sudden sleep attack—and some investigators regard it as a symptom of that disease. The two reactions are sometimes termed the narcolepsy-cataplexy syndrome. See NARCOLEPSY.

CATHARSIS. As a psychiatric term, catharsis refers to the therapeutic elimination, or release, of emotionally charged material which has been causing anxiety, tension or other symptoms.

The process of catharsis may operate on either of two levels: first, talking out conscious feelings and ideas that are emotionally disturbing to the patient; and second, bringing to the surface repressed or "forgotten" events that are instrumental in producing psychological symptoms. The first type of catharsis may bring some relief, but it is superficial as compared to the therapeutic effect of the second type, which leads to greater awareness and insight into the unconscious forces at the root of the disturbance. See ABREACTION, RELEASE THERAPY, PSYCHOANALYSIS (THERAPY), HYPNOTHERAPY, TALKING IT OUT.

CATHEXIS. The investment of an object, idea, or act with special emotional significance, or "affect." Positive cathexis denotes attraction; negative cathexis, repulsion.

The term is widely used in psychoanalysis and other personality theories. Psychoanalytic theory distinguishes three major types of cathexis: (1) ego-cathexis, as in narcissistic attachment to one's self; (2) fantasy-cathexis, a concentration of psychic energy on wishes fantasies or their sources in the unconscious; and (3) object-cathexis, an attachment to persons or things outside of the individual.

Many investigators, including not only Freud but H. A. Murray and H. S. Sullivan, describe parents and other family members as "significant cathectic objects" in the child's world, since relationships established with these figures have a profound influence on interpersonal relations throughout life. A simpler way of putting this would be that we attach a special value to our parents and other members of our family. Kurt Lewin's term "valence" also implies a positive or negative cathexis.

Disturbances in cathexis are found in many psychiatric conditions. In early infantile autism failure to establish a positive cathexis (or, warm attachment) with the mother prevents the child from establishing normal cathexes with other human beings; he therefore remains withdrawn, isolated and unresponsive to practically any form of communication. In body-image disturbances, such as those caused by disfigurement, the tendency is to invest excessive emotion in the affected part of the body. In such cases, the nose, breasts, skin, etc; become "overcathected." *See* VALENCE, EARLY INFANTILE AUTISM, BODY IMAGE.

CATTELL, JAMES McKEEN (1860–1944). Cattell did more than any psychologist of his time to advance the cause of experimental psychology in this country. He learned his basic techniques at the University of Leipzig, where he worked for years, first as a student and later as assistant in the celebrated laboratory of Wilhelm Wundt. He also worked with Francis Galton in England and was deeply influenced by his studies of individual differences. At the age of twenty-eight he was appointed professor of psychology at the University of Pennsylvania, this country's first chair in psychology as a distinct discipline. He held this post from 1888 to 1891, then transferred to Columbia University until 1917, when he was dismissed by President Nicholas Murray Butler for taking a pacifist stand during the war.

Cattell was extremely active and influential not only in psychology but in science as a whole. He founded and became the first president of the Psychological Corporation, an organization which provides psychological services to education and industry. He served as editor of a number of scientific publications, including *Science, Scientific Monthly, Psychological Review, Popular Science Monthly, American Men of Science,* and *American Naturalists.* He occupied a position of leadership in many professional organizations, serving as president of the American Psychological Association, the International Congress of Psychology at Yale in 1929, and the American Association for the Advancement of Science.

Cattell did much to shape the early character of American psychology, not only through his many articles and papers, but through his pupils as well. It is said that more students came into contact with him than with any psychologist of the time, and an impressive number of them became distinguished contributors to the field—among them Thorndike, Woodworth, Franz, Hollingsworth, Strong, Dashiell, and Gates.

Practically all of Cattell's major contributions stem from laboratory experiments involving measurement and control. Since most of them have been incorporated in the main body of modern psychology and are therefore represented in many of the topics of this book, they will be mentioned only briefly at this point. His studies of reaction time, begun at Leipzig, covered practically every phase of this subject including the effects of concentrating on the stimulus and on the response, and its use in investigating discrimination and the average speed of reaction to different stimuli, such as sound, light, touch, and electric shock. He made tachistoscopic measurements of the perception of colors, forms, letters, sentences, and objects, and showed that groups of words could be recognized in a fraction of a second if they formed a meaningful unit. These experiments, plus his work on the legibility of different letters and different type faces, contributed greatly to our knowledge of the dynamics of reading.

Cattell advanced the understanding of association by showing that free associations are generally slower than controlled associations (for instance, naming the state in which a given city is found), and he constructed the first tables showing frequency of response to various stimulus words. In the field of psychophysics he devised a formula for errors in observation that proved more accurate than Weber's Law. He invented the "order of merit" rating system and applied it to the study of eminent men of science, showing that personal attitudes that appear to be hard to measure in the laboratory can actually be handled quantitatively.

Finally, Cattell devised the first battery of psychological tests ever given to a large population. It included such items as rate of tapping, strength of grip, memory span for letters, reaction time to sound, free and controlled association. He began administering these tests to Columbia University students and others as early as 1894. Even though Cattell described the series as "mental tests," they could not be said to measure intelligence since, as Binet pointed out, complex intellectual processes can only be measured by complex tasks. However, they were the first valid tests made of specific abilities, and added considerably to our knowledge of the range and variability of human capacity. Through these tests and his experimental measurements of behavior, Cattell probably did more than any other psychologist with the exception of Galton to make individual differences an important field of scientific inquiry. *See* GALTON, INTELLIGENCE TESTS.

CAUSALGIA. An intense "burning pain" resulting from nerve injuries due to penetrating wounds.

The term causalgia was coined by Weir Mitchell, who described it as "the most terrible of the tortures which a nerve wound may inflict." At one time many cases of drug addiction and suicide resulted from this excruciating condition. The usual site of the pain is the hand or foot. The skin becomes glossy and purplish, and the palms or soles continually sweat. The entire extremity becomes so tender that the patient cannot tolerate clothing, direct rays of the sun, or even air drafts. "The sufferer becomes more and more a recluse and seeks to withdraw himself from the noise and activity of an open ward." (White and Sweet, 1955)

Treatment of causalgia is a difficult problem. Continual moistening of the skin brings temporary relief, but heat and massage cannot be tolerated. The condition may clear up in a few months, but if it persists, surgery is usually required to prevent atrophy of the bones and muscles, as well as to obtain relief from the unbearable pain. This may involve moving the damaged nerve to an area free from scar tissue, excision of the damaged portion of the nerve, or removal of the appropriate sympathetic ganglia (sympathectomy).

Causalgia comes within the province of the psychiatrist because of the severe reactions of its victims. In extreme cases they cannot tolerate physical contact of the slightest kind in any part of the body, and cannot even bear to listen to loud radio programs or watch exciting movies. Some specialists believe these reactions are at least partially due to psychological factors, but others argue against this view. After examining 600 cases during World War II, White and Sweet concluded, "Many aspects of the causalgic syndrome suggest that it is a form of psychoneurosis, and this diagnosis has often and most unfairly been applied to these victims. The fact that the whole pseudoneurotic picture so often clears immediately following suitable intervention, when the sufferer has lost his dread of pain, no longer requires sedatives, and can resume normal activities, indicates that the personality disturbance is a result rather than the cause of an unendurable condition. Psychological studies made after successful treatment have not brought to light any predisposing psychogenic factors."

CENSOR. In psychoanalytic theory, the name for the unconscious components of the personality which seek to repress unacceptable thoughts or impulses and thereby prevent them from entering consciousness.

The censor is a figurative concept, since there is no specific agent involved but rather a process of criticism and selection. The term censorship therefore seems preferable to censor, and was often used by Freud himself. In this process a barrier to unconscious memories and impulses is erected. It consists primarily of the rules and prohibitions adopted by the individual from his parents or other members of society. These constitute the superego, or conscience, and the ego-ideal, the image of what the individual aspires to be, based upon the picture of an idealized parent. These two components operate primarily on an unconscious level, and are responsible for the feelings of guilt which help to keep threatening urges out of consciousness. They are aided by a third component, the ego, which enters into the censorship process on a conscious level. The ego is the organized, self-aware portion of the personality, which enforces repression by directly controlling perception, thought, feeling and behavior in the interest of the reality principle—in other words, the demands of the external world.

The censor is one of the earliest psychoanalytic concepts of Freud, introduced in his epoch-making work, *The Interpretation of Dreams,* in 1900. He described it as a theoretical function, which not only excludes unconscious wishes during the daytime, but preserves some of its force even when we sleep. During our waking hours it keeps us from admitting our sexual and hostile desires to ourselves, especially those associated with infantile sexuality. It saves us from the discomfort, guilt, or shame which these unconscious strivings would produce if they reached the level of consciousness—for example, a boy's wish to kill his father in order to possess his mother. During sleep, when repressions are partially lifted, an impulse of this kind may gain some expression —but due to the fact that the censorship process is still in force to some extent, the wish is usually expressed in disguised or symbolic form and the boy might dream of killing a large animal.

In this early form of his theory, Freud distinguished between three levels or layers of the mind: conscious mental activity, unconscious processes, and the preconscious (or foreconscious) which is composed of psychological events outside of consciousness but readily available to it through the process of memory. He held that the censor operates at the preconscious level, serving to keep unconscious urges under control and out of consciousness. In his later theory he abandoned the concept of the preconscious and restated the censorship process in terms of the ego and superego, as outlined above. *See* PSYCHOANALYSIS (THEORY), DREAM INTERPRETATION (MODERN), PRECONSCIOUS.

CEREA FLEXIBILITAS (Waxy Flexibility). A common symptom of catatonic schizophrenia in which the limbs of the patient remain in any position in which they are placed, like the limbs of a jointed doll. It is a form of cataleptic immobility.

The catatonic patient can maintain an ordinarily uncomfortable position far longer than a normal individual. Some authorities believe that the symptom is due to a pathological suggestibility that stems, paradoxically, from the patient's desire to withdraw from a threatening world. Evidence for this theory lies in the fact that the catatonic becomes passive and immobile, and when the position of his arm or leg is changed by others, he apparently finds it less disturbing to comply with the suggestion and endure the discomfort than to question it or fight it. It is interesting that the same reaction can be induced in normal persons through hypnosis, in which a similar condition of withdrawal into a restricted environment ("Listen only to my voice!") is present. See CATALEPSY, SCHIZOPHRENIA (CATATONIC TYPE), AUTOMATISM.

CEREBELLUM. A roughly spherical part of the hindbrain, located beneath the cerebral hemispheres (PLATE 1). The structure gets its name, which means "little brain," from its resemblance to the cerebrum, since its outer surface consists of brain matter (cell bodies) and its inner core is largely made up of white matter (nerve fibers).

The cerebellum is primarily an organ of motor co-ordination. It receives impulses from all the senses, but particularly from the muscles and inner ear, and relays messages that regulate the movements involved in posture, walking, manipulation, and balance.

In the course of evolution the cerebellum was the first area of the nervous system which had the special function of co-ordinating sensory and motor impulses. It reached its greatest relative size in birds since it regulates the complex functions involved in flying. Its structure became differentiated in mammals, with a ventral or bottom portion receiving fibers from the sense organs for equilibrium in the inner ear, and anterior and posterior portions connecting with the spinal cord. In the higher mammals and especially in man, an additional structure called the neocerebellum developed in the rear or dorsal region. This area is primarily concerned with the co-ordination of impulses passing to and from the cerebral cortex. If the neocerebellum is damaged, the individual cannot properly put together the movements required for any complex activity, such as feeding himself or playing the piano. Other cerebellar disorders are cerebellar ataxia, a loss of muscular coordination which usually affects standing and walking (the wobbly "cerebellar gait"); intention tremor (a tremor occurring only in purposeful action, as in reaching for something); vertigo; and adiadochokinesis (inability to perform rapid alternating movements).

CEREBRAL CORTEX. The gray "bark," or surface layer of the cerebral hemispheres, containing the nerve cells involved in the higher mental processes. It is part of the telencephalon, or forebrain, and lies in folds near the inner surface of the skull.

Structurally speaking, the cerebral cortex looks like a large shelled walnut, covered with ridges known as gyri, and crevices called sulci or fissures (*Fig. 11*). One of these crevices, the longitudinal fissure, divides the brain into two symmetrical halves—the cerebral hemispheres—which are mirror images of each other in both structure and function. A second major groove, the fissure of Rolando or central sulcus, runs across the top and down the sides of each hemisphere (*Fig. 12*). In front of this fissure lies the frontal lobe, often described as the expressive part of the brain, since it contains the motor senses which control action and movement. Behind it lie the three lobes which comprise the receptive areas of the brain because they contain most of the centers for incoming sensory impulses. The third major crevice, known as the lateral

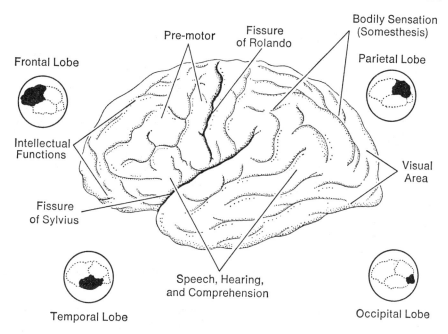

Frontal Lobe

Pre-motor

Fissure of Rolando

Bodily Sensation (Somesthesis)

Parietal Lobe

Intellectual Functions

Fissure of Sylvius

Visual Area

Speech, Hearing, and Comprehension

Temporal Lobe

Occipital Lobe

Fig. 11. The cerebral cortex. Localization of functions in the four lobes of the left hemisphere.

sulcus or fissure of Sylvius, serves as a dividing line between two of these lobes: the parietal lobe lies above this fissure, the temporal lobe lies below it, while the occipital lobe is situated at the rear of the brain.

The cortex contains an estimated ten billion cell bodies from which extend a mass of fibers of enormous complexity. These fibers fall into three categories. The commissural fibers connect the cortex of one hemisphere to the cortex of the other; the association fibers are found within each cortex, connecting one part to another; and the projection fibers carry the impulses to and from the cortex. Fibers carrying impulses upward are called afferent or corticopetal fibers and originate for the most part in the thalamus; those carrying impulses downward are called efferent or corticofugal fibers, and these end in the lower parts of the brain (the basal ganglia, thalamus, midbrain, hindbrain) or the spinal cord.

Many methods are used in exploring the "wiring diagram" of the cortex. Since the fibers can only be roughly traced by their natural white color, anatomists and physiologists—usually working with animals—resort to (1) staining them with various dyes; (2) cutting them and noting their degeneration and change of color; (3) studying the specific effects of injury or disease, such as tumor or gunshot wounds, in different regions; (4) extirpating specific fibers by surgery or electrolytic lesions and noting the effects on the behavior; (5) recording brain waves (EEG) from different areas during different activities; (6) inserting electrodes to determine which fibers or sets of fibers are active under different conditions; (7) stimulating different areas electrically or chemically in order to activate different parts of the body or different functions such as memory; and, most recently, (8) direct implantation of

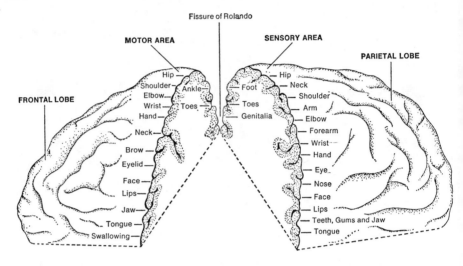

Fig. 12. A diagram of the upper half of the left hemisphere, opened up along the Fissure of Rolando to indicate the approximate location of sensory and motor functions.

electrodes to study the deeper functions of the brain.

Although the cerebral cortex is by no means fully "mapped" as yet, these techniques have succeeded in locating a great many functions. They are usually grouped into the following major areas:

First, the *motor area,* immediately in front of the fissure of Rolando, and next to it the premotor area. These frontal lobe areas control muscular movements throughout the body, but the specific locations are in reverse order: the right hemisphere controls the left half of the body and vice versa, while fibers at the top of the area control the toes and legs, and fibers at the bottom control the tongue and mouth movements. The motor area makes these movements possible while the premotor area is believed to make them function smoothly.

Second, the *somesthetic area,* which receives sensory experiences of movement, temperature, touch, and pain from different areas of the body—again in reverse order.

Third, the *visual area,* located in the parts of each occipital lobe known as the striate areas. Reversal occurs here, too, but it is somewhat more compli-

cated: the right striate area controls the right half of each retina, and the left controls the left half. This means that the right enables us to see the left half and left enables us to see the right half of the visual field. The fibers cross at a point below the cortex known as the optic chiasm. More specific correspondences between parts of the retina and parts of the visual areas have also been established.

Fourth, the *auditory area,* located on the surface of the temporal lobes. The general organization of these areas is unlike that of the visual areas in one major respect: both ears are totally represented on both sides, so that the loss of one temporal lobe has little effect on hearing, while loss of one striate area causes blindness in half of each eye. Some specific localizations have been determined—for example, different regions are sensitive to high and low tones.

Fifth, the *speech area.* Several regions appear to be involved in speech and language. This is not surprising because these functions include a wide variety of activities: speaking, writing, and understanding both oral and written language. There is considerable experimental evidence against the early theory of Broca (1861) that the control of the tongue, jaws, and vocal organs is centered in the left hemisphere in right-handed people and the right hemisphere in left-handed people (Humphrey and Zangwill, 1952). Studies of brain-injured people indicate that the sensory or receptive type of aphasia, in which the individual cannot recognize words or names, involves the temporal and perhaps the occipital lobes; while motor or expressive asphasia, in which the patient cannot speak or write even though he understands, is centered in the frontal lobes. Neurologists are beginning to localize these areas more precisely—for instance, there seems to be an area for speech in the lateral frontal lobe and one for writing and drawing farther up in the frontal lobe. Moreover, direct stimulation of an area in front of the fissure of Rolando produces long vowel-like sounds in conscious patients undergoing brain surgery, and counting is interrupted by the stimulation of certain areas on either side of this fissure (Penfield and Rasmussen, 1950).

Sixth, the *association areas*. The five general regions just described are all designated primary projection areas since they "project" sensory or motor fibers to parts of the body outside the brain. Another group of areas, association areas or "intrinsic systems," as Pribram calls them, (1960) contain a huge number of fibers that apparently integrate the different parts of the brain and the different aspects of behavior. These areas are practically nonexistent in the lower animals, such as the rabbit, and are far less extensive in apes than in men. They are believed to be responsible for the psychological abilities which are most distinctively human: learning, perception, memory, and thinking.

There are association areas near the primary cortical areas for each of the senses. The visual association area (or prestriate) is in the occipital lobe, the parietal association area occupies most of the parietal lobe, and the auditory association area is found in the temporal lobe. Each of these is concerned with complex sensory discriminations such as those involved in distinguishing between a circle and an ellipse, noting the difference between musical chords, judging heat or cold, or getting the "feel" of a golf swing.

Investigators have also begun to localize certain memory areas. In 1958, Penfield applied a small electrical current directly to the temporal lobe of a surgical patient. When one point was stimulated, the patient recalled a long-past experience, and when another point was stimulated, he heard a piece of music. Studies of apraxia cases have indicated that there are memory areas for sequential tasks, such as dressing one's self or driving a car, in the frontal lobe. Other investigations indicate that lesions in the parietal lobe produce agnosia—that is, the patient cannot remember what a fork or an automobile is used for. Finally, relatively large areas in the frontal lobe, called the prefrontal areas or frontal association areas, are concerned with more general intellectual processes. Destruction of these areas drastically reduces the individual's ability to concentrate, solve problems, take responsibility, and plan ahead. When two investigators, Freeman and Watts, noted that these patients often became relaxed and unworried, they began performing prefrontal lobotomies on deeply disturbed mental patients. *See* PSYCHOSURGERY, AGNOSIA, APHASIA, APRAXIA, MEMORY STORAGE, LASHLEY, FRANZ.

The cerebral cortex is the culmination of an evolutionary process that has spanned billions of years. This process began with the first nervous system, or "nerve net," in primitive organisms like the jellyfish, and progressed through three general stages. The first was ganglionic organization, in which nerve cells gathered into clusters or ganglia which controlled different segments of the body. In the second stage, encephalization, a major ganglion developed at the head end of the organism. In the third and final stage, corticalization took place—that is, a single brain center gradually took over control of all the major mental and physical functions of the organism. In the early vertebrates, the entire nervous system was devoted to routine activities such as breathing, digestion, moving, and mating; but as evolution went on, control centers for all sensory and motor functions "moved upstairs" to the forebrain.

Finally, the forebrain itself enlarged to a point where it could accommodate additional functions which are most characteristically human: thinking, learning, and language. This development can be graphically expressed by comparing the weight of the brain with the weight of the spinal cord in different species. The alligator's forebrain, which is only rudimentary, weighs just about the same as its spinal cord. The more highly developed brain of the chimpanzee is fifteen times as heavy as its spinal cord, and man's brain is fifty-five times the weight of his spinal cord.

In general, then, the cerebral cortex is not only the major center for sensory discrimination and motor functions, but the "control tower" for the elaborate associative processes that distinguish man from animal. Without it we would be unable to solve scientific problems, create works of art, organize a complex society, or preserve and extend our knowledge of the world in which we live.

CHARACTER DEVELOPMENT. As used here, character development refers to the development of conscience, moral concepts, religious values, and social attitudes in the child. Research on these interrelated subjects has been somewhat scattered and sporadic since many psy-

chologists have felt that this entire area does not lend itself to scientific investigation. Nevertheless there have been some revealing studies, and there is little doubt that the growth of standards and "inner controls" is "one of the most important problems facing students of personality development today." (Sears, 1960)

General trends. No child is born with a character or conscience. Moral concepts and moral behavior must be learned, and this is a gradual affair extending from the earliest years through adolescence. The learning process, however, is more than an intellectual matter, for in addition to learning the approved ways of behaving, the child must shift from an acceptance of specific rules to a general conception of right and wrong, and from external conformity to internal control. In so doing, he must develop his own standards and apply them voluntarily, thoughtfully, and self-critically. Put in another way, he must develop a conscience of his own, an inward voice which not only approves right behavior but makes him feel guilty when he turns in a wrong direction: "Guilt . . . constitutes a most efficient watchdog within each individual, serving to keep his behavior compatible with the moral values of the society in which he lives." (Ausubel, 1955)

Moral behavior. During the first few years of life the emphasis is on conduct rather than concept. The child develops social behavior in two principal ways. One is by direct training and teaching: parents and others show him what to do and what not to do in specific situations, reinforcing their efforts with discipline when he goes wrong and approval when he conforms. Studies however, show, that punishment and reproof are generally less effective than praise and reward (Eysenck, 1960). The other way is through identification with parents or other persons the child admires. In this process he adopts desirable (and sometimes undesirable) patterns of behavior through voluntary emulation and unconscious imitation rather than through pressure or teaching. See IDENTIFICATION.

Moral concepts. As the child grows older and more mature, he gradually learns to generalize from specific behavior, and forms abstract principles of right and wrong. A child of six or seven may say, "It's bad to steal a ball," but by eight or nine he will probably use the general concept, "Stealing is wrong," and within another three or four years will relate this concept to social justice.

The acquisition of mature concepts and values, however, is no simple cut-and-dried affair. Some children do not have the intelligence or attention span to understand moral reasoning, and in many instance they are confused by parental inconsistency, conflicts between moral codes and pressures both inside and outside the home, or by teaching that emphasizes what is wrong without showing or explaining what is right. Such confusions not only hamper the learning process but make it difficult for the child to make his own moral decisions. He may then take the simpler path of following his own social group, for good or ill, especially since this helps him win acceptance and approval.

Some specific values. Considerable light has been thrown on the development of character through studies of special moral concepts. Harrower (1934) found that ideas about cheating differed markedly on different socioeconomic and educational levels. School children from higher levels most frequently said, "It doesn't do any good," or "One can't learn that way," while those from poorer neighborhoods made such comments as, "Cheating is forbidden," "It's naughty," or "It's unfair." She also found a difference in ideas of punishment. When they were told a story in which one child took another child's toy, six to eight year olds from poor homes usually said the culprit should be "smacked," while children from more privileged homes said he should replace the toy (restitution). However, the majority of eight to eleven year olds in both groups advocated restitution rather than retaliation, indicating that the moral code becomes more standardized as children grow older and more thoughtful.

A study of honesty and deceit made by Hartshorne and May in 1928 is still cited as a landmark in the study of character development. These investigators had groups of children take a number of tests which were so devised that it was possible to detect whether they cheated. They found that (1) older children were slightly more deceptive than younger children, (2) there was no significant difference between boys and girls, (3) brighter children were on the whole more honest than duller children, (4) maladjusted children tended to be more deceptive than well-adjusted children, (5) children who had received poor marks in general deportment tended to cheat more than others, (6) there was a progressive increase in cheating from the top of the socioeconomic scale downward, (7) suggestible children deceived more than nonsuggestible children, (8) children whose teachers emphasized cooperation and good will cheated less than children whose teachers stressed rigid routines, and surprisingly, (9) children who were members of organizations that stressed the virtue of honesty cheated just about as much as others. Finally, the study revealed that cheating is a specific rather than a general and uniform trait —that is, it was not possible to make sharp divisions between honest and dishonest children because children who lie or cheat in one situation might be perfectly honorable in another. This points up the importance of looking inward to discover the child's motives as well as outward to assess the pressures acting on him in a particular situation.

Conscience development. Psychologists recognize that many factors contribute to the development of conscience: parents and home life, playmates and schoolmates, teachers, neighborhood, religion, as well as intellectual capacity. One of these, however, is outstanding, and that is the family. For this reason a number of investigators have attempted to determine what *kind* of family and what kind of child-rearing practices are most likely to foster a well-developed conscience. First, a widely accepted study by Sears, Maccoby, and Levin (1957) has shown that, on the whole, psychological and love-oriented techniques, such as praise or isolation of the child, are more effective than the materialistic or physical approach which stresses tangible rewards, deprivation, and physical punishment. Second, consistency and the combination of mutual trust and approval are extremely influential in conscience development. The child must know what is expected of him and must feel that his parents have faith in him and accept him even when they are rejecting his behavior. But third, a warm and loving relationship between parents and child is most essential, for it creates the kind of atmosphere that encourages the adoption of high standards of character and conduct.

Religious influences. The effects of church attendance and religious training are extremely hard to assess. Although it seems reasonable to suppose that contact with moral precepts, spiritual values, and religious sanctions would have a positive effect on character development, the few psychological investigations so far conducted have not offered direct and conclusive proof. In fact, as Jersild (1960) has pointed out, "Such studies do not, on the whole, show that youngsters who regularly receive religious instruction are significantly more honest or humane than those who do not." The Hartshorne and May study showed that children who regularly attended Sunday school cheated only slightly less than children who did not. Other research has indicated that people who were involved in church activities or whose parents had favorable attitudes toward religion tend to be more negative toward Negroes (Kelly et al., 1958), more anti-Semitic (Wilson, 1960), and more authoritarian in social attitudes (Jones, 1954) than people who were not associated with religious institutions. The implication is that membership in their own institution makes them more rigid and intolerant of nonmembers. On the other hand, studies show that most delinquents either have never attended Sunday school or have attended a school that stressed punishment after death (Watterberg, 1954), and there is evidence that good religious instruction leads to internal controls over conduct (Jones, 1954). The limited nature of these findings points up the need for more extensive and systematic investigations.

CHARCOT, JEAN-MARTIN (1825–93). Charcot, regarded as the founder of clinical neurology, was born in Paris and received his medical degree from that city's university. In 1860 he became professor of pathological medicine at the university's Faculty of Medicine, and in 1862 was appointed head of the Salpétrière Hospital, where he developed a world famous laboratory and clinic for the study of neurological diseases.

Between 1862 and 1870 Charcot successfully identified causes of cerebral hemorrhage, noted the effects of spinal cord injury, gave the first accurate description of multiple sclerosis, differentiated rheumatism from a disorder which became known as Charcot's joints (due to wasting of the spinal cord), and showed that poliomyelitis was related to other forms of muscular atrophy. Between 1870 and 1880 he concentrated on the functions of the cerebrum, and his findings greatly influenced Jackson, Horsley and other members of the English school of neurology. In 1882 the French government established the world's first Chair of Medical Diseases of the Nervous System specifically for Charcot.

In the later years of his career, Charcot entered upon a study of hypnosis and hysteria that eventually resulted in a fuller understanding of the psychoneuroses. He established what has become known as the Salpêtrière school of hypnosis, and sought to put this technique on a firm scientific footing by describing the successive stages of hypnosis (lethargy, catalepsy, somnambulism), and by showing that changes take place in the nervous system when an individual is hypnotized —for example, changes in reflex action, neuromuscular excitability, and sensory functions. After examining his experimental findings, Charcot concluded that hysteria and hypnosis are due to the same activities of the nervous system, and mistakenly claimed that only hysterics could be hypnotized.

Before Charcot, hypnosis was in disrepute due largely to the questionable practices of Mesmer and his followers. The Académie des Sciences had even condemned all research on "animal magnetism." But when Charcot presented his views "on diverse nervous states determined by the hypnotization of hysterics," the Académie felt his work was unrelated to animal magnetism and accepted his findings. In the words of Charcot's successor, Janet, the new interpretation "broke a dam and let in a tide which was ready to rush." Soon physicians from the world over came to Salpêtrière to hear Charcot's lectures on hysteria and to witness his demonstration of both the production and removal of hysterical symptoms by hypnosis. Among the most distinguished of these visitors was Sigmund Freud.

Though impressed by Charcot's demonstrations, Freud could not accept his emphasis on the neurological basis of hypnosis or his organic interpretation of hysteria. Charcot had noted that hysteria was often accompanied by convulsions, and harked back to the traditional theory that the ovaries were involved in the attack. He apparently did not believe that emotions had anything to do with these convulsive states. However, he was aware that external suggestion and autosuggestion could produce some hysterical symptoms, and he also spoke at times of the significance of postural changes as reflections of emotional states. Nevertheless, his neurological orientation prevented him from doing full justice to the psychological aspects of the disorder.

Another group of investigators, sometimes referred to as the Nancy School, did recognize these factors. A. A. Liébeault (1823–1904), a French country doctor, published a book in 1866 in which he reported that he could put 20 per cent of his patients under hypnosis simply through sleep suggestion. He converted Hippolyte Bernheim (1837–1919) to his point of view when he cured a hysterical patient of Bernheim's through this technique. Bernheim then proposed the theory that hypnosis was merely an intensification of normal suggestion, and that with rare exceptions anyone could be hypnotized. He pointed out that persuasion is actually a form of suggestion, and that various socializing agencies (mother, teacher, state) use suggestion as a means of education and control. In his view, hypnosis is simply a dramatic form of suggestion which utilizes rapport between the hypnotist and the subject in bringing about a restriction of attention and a limitation of the senses to the commands of the hypnotist. He also argued that the neuromuscular and other symptoms obtained at the Salpêtrière were actually a *product* of the suggestions made by the hypnotist. These observations helped to bridge the gap between abnormal conditions and normal behavior, and furthered the use of hypnotic suggestion as a therapeutic tool.

Even more important, Bernheim's emphasis on suggestion and his psychological interpretation of hysterical symptoms began to focus attention on a psychogenic approach to behavior, in contradistinction to the attempts of Charcot and others to explain all types of reactions in physiological and genetic terms. Bernheim himself contributed to this trend by making a special study of criminal behavior in which he presented the view that suggestion plays a role in almost every crime. He sagaciously pointed out that many ordinary acts are not of conscious origin, but are imposed in subtle and obscure ways because people are naturally suggestible and imitative. He therefore was on the brink of a recognition of unconscious factors and the complexity of man's hidden motivations. It should not be surprising, therefore, that Freud was far more influenced by Bernheim than by Charcot. *See* HYPNOSIS, CONVERSION REACTION.

CHEMOTHERAPY. The use of psychoactive (psychotropic) drugs in the treatment of mental disorder.

Chemotherapy is a branch of the larger field of psychopharmacology, which develops and investigates all types of drugs that produce changes in psychological processes. Today's psychotherapeutic drugs, sometimes termed psychochemicals, fall into two major categories: tranquilizers or ataractics, used to calm disturbed, excited, hyperactive or anxious patients; and antidepressants, or energizers, used as "mood elevators" in depressive reactions. Tranquilizers were developed first, but both types have come into widespread use only within the past ten to twelve years.

In this short period of time chemotherapy has created a revolution in modern psychiatry. Practically all phases of the care and treatment of psychotic patients have benefited. Carefully prescribed drugs have enabled thousands of patients to avoid hospitalization, and have brought earlier discharges to thousands of others. The use of maintenance doses has also prevented relapses and has enabled many patients to live useful lives in the community.

Thanks to these drugs the symptoms of overactive patients are now being controlled to a point where locked wards, isolation rooms and restraint are rarely needed. Depressed patients become less suicidal and more sociable; apathetic patients begin to take an interest in themselves and the world; and many deteriorated patients reach a point where they can care for their basic physical processes. The management of patients is therefore greatly facilitated, and the total climate of the hospital is greatly improved.

Due to their potentiating or reinforcing effects, tranquilizers and energizers frequently reduce the need for strong doses of other drugs. Unlike some of the more drastic techniques, they do not inspire fear or anxiety. They have helped materially to outmode psychosurgery and in many cases have shortened the course of electroshock therapy or have eliminated the need for it altogether. Moreover, it has been found that drug treatments not only alleviate the symptoms of the disorder, but usually render patients amenable to psychotherapy and sociotherapy. The milder tranquilizers have also proved helpful in relieving anxiety in psychoneurotics and in reducing the tensions of normal individuals; and the milder energizers have proved effective in cases of neurotic depression.

The effectiveness of these drugs is frequently increased by using them in combination. Stronger tranquilizers, such as chlorpromazine, or the milder meprobamates, may be combined with an energizer in treating depressive reactions or cases where acute anxiety is accompanied by depression. When acutely disturbed schizophrenics are relieved by tranquilizers, depressive symptoms sometimes develop, and in that case a combination of the two types of drugs may also be used. Tranquilizers are often combined with electroshock therapy in particularly resistant cases. In addition to increasing the rate of improvement, combination treatments often result in fewer side effects due to the fact that smaller doses of the drugs are required.

In spite of its pronounced benefits, chemotherapy cannot be considered a panacea. It must also be carried out with great caution and on a highly individual basis. For each patient the drug must be carefully selected, the proper dosage determined, and then administered under close supervision. The medication or dosages may have to be changed as the patient's reactions are observed. Some patients have physical disorders which contraindicate the use of psychotropic drugs altogether, while others suffer unpleasant or even dangerous side effects with certain drugs. Moreover, both the energizers and tranquilizers tend to mask symptoms and give the false impression that the patient is completely cured, and there may be a tendency to delay or avoid psychotherapy when it is vitally needed for full recovery. Finally, there is as yet too little information on the long-term effects of most of these drugs. What has been discovered so far, however, is reassuring. *See* TRANQUILIZERS, ENERGIZERS, ELECTROSHOCK THERAPY, NARCOSYNTHESIS, NARCOTHERAPY, COMBAT REACTIONS, HYPNOTHERAPY, LYSERGIC ACID, HALLUCINOGEN, DRUG ADDICTION, EPILEPSY (ETIOLOGY AND THERAPY).

CHILD ABUSE (The Battered-Child Syndrome). Maltreatment of children, especially by those entrusted with their care.

Child abuse has a long and sordid history, dating back to periods when the father had the power of life and death over his children and when children were sold into slavery or mutilated to make them objects of almsgiving. Though mistreatment of children is not a new problem, it has been recently brought to the fore by surveys which indicate that about 10,000 cases of child abuse are reported in this country every year. Unreported cases may be an even larger figure. Studies have also shown that very few communities now have organized facilities for dealing with this problem on a social welfare basis.

The nature of the problem has been indicated by a survey conducted by the American Humane Association in 1962. In this study, investigators sought to secure data on cases reported in the newspapers. Despite the acknowledged weaknesses of this procedure some revealing results were obtained. The survey showed that every conceivable type and degree of abuse is inflicted upon children. They are beaten with fists, hairbrushes, straps, bats; deliberately burned by open flames or lighted cigarettes; struck with pokers, irons, sticks; strangled, stabbed, suffocated, kicked, and shocked by electricity. One child of fifteen months was found to have 30 broken bones; others suffered severe head and internal injuries, including ruptured organs—not to mention innumerable welts, bruises and broken teeth.

The statistics of this study showed that over half of the victims were younger than four years of age, and only 10 per cent over 16. More than 25 per cent died of their injuries, and 81 per cent of these children were under four or five (a fact that directly implicates their parents). Fathers inflicted injuries in 38 per cent of the cases and were responsible for 22 per cent of the fatalities; mothers were the abusers in 28 per cent, but were responsible for 48 per cent of the deaths.

The remaining cases involved both father and mother, stepfathers, older siblings and other relatives, with the much-maligned stepmother responsible in less than 3 per cent of the cases.

Since this survey was confined to newspaper reports, the cases undoubtedly represent the most serious instances of child abuse rather than the totality of cases that occur. The preliminary phases of a study now being conducted by investigators from Brandeis University (Gil, 1966), who are using a broader base, indicate that the total percentage of deaths and serious injury may be somewhat lower than in the newspaper survey.

In another phase of the American Humane Association study, the investigators sought to obtain information about the families and communities in which the children lived. Their findings showed that surprisingly few homes of abused children were outwardly broken: in 80 per cent, two parental figures, usually the natural parents, were living at home. All economic and social levels were represented, and all occupational levels except the professional. The ages of the parents involved averaged twenty-six for mothers and thirty for fathers; very few were teen-agers.

The single most prominent causal factor appeared to be emotional immaturity. There were many cases of marital maladjustment, alcoholism, adult crime, and in some instances there was evidence of mental illness in the family background or in the immediate family. Though the survey did not attempt to discover the underlying motivations for the abuse, many of the situations appeared to fall into the following four categories: (a) sudden emotional explosions, particularly on the part of the fathers; (b) acute reactive depression, especially on the part of the mother, due to overwhelming circumstances that produced feelings of hopelessness and a desire to "get the child out of this cruel world"; (c) mercy killings in which the parent (usually the mother) sought to relieve a handicapped child of his burdens, or "return him to God"; and (d) disturbed parents prematurely discharged from mental institutions and unable to cope with the children.

The author of the survey, De Francis (1963), summarizes his findings in these words: "We recognize that destructive parental behavior of this type is usually symptomatic of deeper emotional problems. Rarely is child abuse the product of wanton, willful, or deliberate acts of cruelty. We see abuse to result from parental inadequacy, from immaturity and from lack of capacity for coping with the pressures and tensions which beset the modern family. . . . Parents who abuse children are parents who react violently to their own unmet needs which may be in conflict with needs of their children. They are people with a low level of frustration tolerance, with hair-trigger controls which any irritant can set off into emotional violence. With few exceptions, these parents are not sadists. They do not take cruel delight in mistreating their children. They can be described more accurately as people who cannot help themselves."

Far too little is being done at the present time to give such parents the kind of psychological and social assistance they need. The vast majority of child abuse cases that come to notice are reported to law-enforcement agencies but never reach a child welfare or social agency where they could be handled without recourse to criminal action. As De Francis concludes, "Should not the primary objective be, first, to remove children from hazardous situations and, second, to plan for their best care and supervision, preferably in their own homes? And should not services be extended to their parents to help them resolve problems leading to neglect and abuse, and to help build in them the emotional stability so necessary and important to good parenthood?" The answer seems to be that we need a network of child protection services which will have the double aim of maintaining a healthy family life and dealing constructively with the problem of child abuse when it does occur.

The solution to the urgent problem of child abuse, then, requires extensive social action. In recent years, one of the most noteworthy developments has been the enactment of reporting laws. In response to the shocking findings of the survey reported above, all fifty states enacted laws between the years 1963 and 1967, requiring doctors, teachers and other professional persons or organizations to report all cases of suspected child abuse. A common feature of these laws is that they grant immunity to the individual who makes the report, so that he will not be liable to criminal or civil action initiated by the parent of the reported child. Although some of the laws were hastily conceived and inadequate, taken as a whole they represent an unprecedented example of social action. It might be added that the new reporting laws make it even more imperative to develop special social services devoted to the protection of neglected and abused children.

CHILD PSYCHIATRY. The study, treatment, and prevention of psychiatric disorders of childhood—including transient reactions, habit disturbances, conduct disturbances, neurotic traits, neuroses, and psychoses.

The psychiatric disorders of children received little attention before the present century. In his long-accepted classification Kraepelin made no mention at all of children's disturbances, simply assuming that they belonged in the adult categories. Little if any treatment was given at his time or before, since, as Rosen and Gregory (1965) put it, these disorders were "regarded fatalistically as the irreversible results of hereditary degeneracy, excessive masturbation, overwork or religious preoccupation."

In the early 1900s several developments took place which focused attention on the child and his problems. Freud and Meyer began to emphasize the effect of childhood experiences on later adjustment, and as a result, the biographical history became an important part of every psychiatric examination. Groups of educators in Germany, Austria, and Switzerland, inspired by the early educators Pestalozzi and Von Fellenberg, established remedial programs dealing with learning and behavior problems. In France Binet advanced the study of the individual child by developing the first effective intelligence test. In the United States the first juvenile courts were established, and in 1909 the first systematic investigations of disturbed and delinquent children were made by William Healy.

At about the same time the mental-hygiene movement began to emphasize the prevention of mental illness during childhood, and by the early 1920s child guidance clinics had been established in a number of cities. However, it was not until the 1930s that the first modern book on child psychiatry was published by Leo Kanner. In the years that followed, increasing attention was given to child disorders, leading to the discovery of special reaction types, such as infantile autism; the development of special treatment techniques, such as activity group therapy and play therapy; the establishment of specialized treatment facilities, including residential centers and children's departments in mental hospitals; and attempts to create a milieu in the home, school and neighborhood that would foster mental health.

The classification of children's disorders remains a key problem. Many of these disturbances, such as symbiotic psychosis, enuresis and school phobia do not fall within the standard adult categories. Some psychiatrists have even abandoned formal diagnosis in favor of terms which describe outstanding symptoms, such as "hyperactive and impulsive." As Noyes and Kolb (1963) point out, "Since there is less fixity of patterns of disturbed behavior because of the plastic personality of the child, there is less unanimity in regard to the diagnostic schemata for the disorders of childhood than for those of adulthood." The American Psychiatric Association classifies the disorders that cannot be directly related to major adult syndromes as adjustment reactions of infancy, childhood, or adolescence and puts them under the general heading of "transient situational personality disorders." The infancy reactions include undue apathy, excitability, feeding difficulties, and sleeping difficulties resulting from emotional deprivation or other injurious conditions in the family. The childhood reactions include habit disturbances (thumbsucking, nail-biting, masturbation, temper tantrums, enuresis), conduct disturbances (truancy, lying, fire-setting, stealing, destructiveness, cruelty, sexual offenses, use of alcohol), and neurotic traits (tics, somnabulism, overactivity, stuttering, specific fears, school phobia). The adolescent reactions comprise rebellion, vacillation, moodswings and other emotional behavior.

The Group for the Advancement of Psychiatry (GAP) has recently (1966) proposed to replace the three broad groupings of the APA with the following descriptive categories: (1) healthy responses (normal variations in all areas; transient developmental and situational crises, such as separation anxiety and grief reaction); (2) reactive disorders (arising out of illness, accident, hospitalization, parental attitudes); (3) developmental deviations (lags, unevenness, or precocities; deviations in motor, sensory, speech, cognitive, psychosexual, affective, and social functions); (4) psychoneurotic disorders (anxiety, phobic, conversion, obsessive-compulsive, dissociative, depressive reaction types); (5)

personality disorders (compulsive, hysterical, anxious, overly dependent, oppositional, overly inhibited, overly independent, isolated, mistrustful, impulse-ridden, neurotic, antisocial); (6) psychotic disorders (early childhood: infantile autism, symbiotic psychosis; later childhood: schizophreniform reactions; adolescence: acute confusional states, schizophrenic reactions); (7) psychophysiologic disorders (covering all body systems, and including, among others: neurodermatitis, rheumatoid arthritis, bronchial asthma, migraine, ulcerative colitis, reactive obesity, dysmenorrhea, idiopathic epilepsy, vertigo); (8) brain syndromes (acute, due to infection, poison, trauma, and chronic, due to cerebral palsy, syphilis, convulsive disorder); (9) mental retardation (caused by biological defect or environmental and psychological conditions, or both). This classification and that of the APA indicate the wide variety among children's disorders. The major types are discussed in this volume under separate topics.

The lack of uniformity in identifying and classifying children's psychiatric disorders makes it extremely hard to estimate their incidence. Moreover, the statistics we have are largely confined to cases which the parents recognize and bring to the clinics. Nevertheless a few broad though tentative findings can be reported. In general, most clinics see two to three times as many boys as girls, possibly because boys exhibit more aggressive symptoms that disturb the parents or the school. Several studies have shown that more patients in child clinics come from middle and upper economic levels than from lower levels, although this may be a function of the ability to recognize psychiatric disorder. The over-all estimates of the number of children who need attention or care for emotional maladjustment, mild or severe, hover around 20 per cent. According to The National Committee against Mental Illness (1966), about four million children under fourteen need some kind of psychiatric help, and from one half to one million are so severely disturbed that they need immediate treatment.

The incidence of different disturbances, as well as the age at which they occur, varies widely. Persistent bed-wetting becomes a problem (enuresis) only after the age of four or five, but this difficulty may recur during a stressful adolescence. Restless sleep, disturbing dreams, physical timidity, and demanding of attention all tend to have two periods of high frequency, one in the pre-school years and the other in late pubescence. Speech difficulties, temper tantrums, and specific fears are most commonly reported at age three to three and a half; while overactivity and destructiveness reach their peak at about five. The normal "developmental stuttering" that occurs between two and four years of age must be sharply distinguished from the persistent, pathological form that reflects emotional tensions and conflicts in later childhood. Nail-biting is a problem among about 40 per cent of girls and 33 per cent of boys; it increases in frequency till about eleven in girls and somewhat later in boys.

There are two distinct forms of school phobia: the one occurring on entering school is considered a form of "separation anxiety"; the other, occurring in later childhood, is usually found in families with deeply disturbed parents who cannot handle their children. It is important to distinguish tics of psychogenic origin from those resulting from encephalitic disease; similarly, functional hyperactivity must be differentiated, if possible, from overactivity associated with brain damage, epilepsy, or mental retardation. Masturbation is practiced by over 90 per cent of children, but is a symptom of emotional disturbance in only a small number.

As indicated in the GAP classification cited above, all the major neurotic syndromes are found among children,

though they occur far less frequently than among adults. The same theory applies to child neurosis as to adult neurosis—that is, the symptoms are interpreted as defenses against anxiety. Many children have neurotic personalities but no full-blown neurosis. As a rule, these children tend to be shy, self-conscious, inhibited, conformist, and afflicted with feelings of insecurity and inadequacy, often as a result of excessively high standards imposed by the parents. Most forms of affective psychosis are rare before age fifteen, though psychotic depressions are sometimes observed in childhood and early adolescence. Psychoses resembling simple schizophrenia are more prevalent; the major symptoms are withdrawal, autistic thinking, and loss of affect. See SCHIZOPHRENIA (CHILDHOOD TYPE), EARLY INFANTILE AUTISM, SYMBIOTIC PSYCHOSIS.

The behavior disorders or conduct disturbances of childhood consist of various forms of persistent delinquency, sexual deviation, and addictions to glue-sniffing, kerosene or gasoline sniffing, codeine cough syrup, and benzedrine inhalers. The addictions of childhood do not usually have the permanence of addictions in adolescence and adulthood. Stealing, vandalism, fire-setting, and other conduct disorders are often interpreted as a way of acting out problems and bidding for attention and help. In some cases antisocial behavior may be associated with school failure caused by learning disturbances. See BEHAVIOR DISORDERS, JUVENILE DELINQUENCY.

Infancy and early childhood are a peak period for organic brain syndromes, which may produce either temporary or permanent damage to the central nervous system. Minimal brain injury, often of unknown origin, is believed to be one of the major causes of learning and behavior disorders; severe brain lesions of the congenital type may result in more obvious defects such as blindness, paralyses, cerebral palsy, or mental deficiency—all of which may have lasting effects on personality and behavior. Brain lesions occurring after birth may result in partial or complete arrest of intellectual development, loss of sensory or motor functions, and behavior disorders. Most of the acute brain syndromes are due to high fevers and convulsions associated with infectious diseases, but some cases may follow head injury, cerebral-vascular accidents, intracranial tumors, or toxic disorders such as lead poisoning, which may be associated with pica. Chronic brain syndromes, which may lead to mental deterioration, speech defects, and behavior problems, are largely the result of epidemic encephalitis, juvenile paresis, and epilepsy. The incidence of epilepsy among school-age children is estimated at seven per one thousand. The brief, mild attacks known as pyknolepsy may disappear spontaneously; other seizures may continue unless controlled by sedation. In a study of 1640 cases, Lennox (1949) found that 67 per cent were of normal intelligence, 23 per cent slightly subnormal, and only 10 per cent severely deteriorated. *See* MINIMAL BRAIN DYSFUNCTION, BRAIN DISORDERS, EPILEPSY, JUVENILE PARESIS, EPIDEMIC ENCEPHALITIS, PICA.

Since etiology and treatment are discussed under the separate disorders, we will give only a brief overview of these topics. As to the problem of causation, biological factors are most prominent in hereditary types of mental retardation, in brain disorders due to rubella (German measles) and other congenital conditions, in difficult births, in head injuries, and in brain inflammations that occur during infancy and early childhood. Some investigators (Bender, 1947; Goldfarb, 1961) suggest that brain abnormalities may underlie childhood schizophrenia, while others (for example, Rimland, 1964) also apply this theory to infantile autism, though

neurological tests have so far been inconclusive. Twin studies on preadolescent schizophrenia (Kallmann and Roth, 1956) suggest the possibility of hereditary influences, since the concordance rate between monozygotic twins is much higher than between dizygotic twins of the same sex. Others, such as Shields and Slater (1960), claim similar results in twin studies on children with juvenile delinquency, behavior disorders, and neurotic traits. Stott (1959, 1962) believes he has found evidence that "prenatal stress" can be a major factor in reading and learning disabilities which are accompanied by withdrawal, lack of confidence, and poor motivation; and Kawi and Pasamanick (1959) found a significant percentage of obstetrical complications among the mothers of boys afflicted with severe reading problems. As noted in our article on juvenile delinquency, Glueck and Glueck (1956) found a suggestive relationship between delinquency and an athletic, "mesomorphic" body build.

As to psychological factors, it seems true that only a minority of functional disorders are due to single traumatic events, such as the sudden death or desertion of a parent, sexual assault, or other intensely frightening experiences. Far more often the emotional disturbances of children appear to be associated with a progressive weakening of the personality by such long-term conditions as neglect, coldness, excessive criticism, maternal overprotection (especially when accompanied by feelings of rejection), and favoritism toward another sibling. This general finding is supported by the fact that a high percentage of children treated in child guidance and juvenile delinquency clinics come from broken homes. There is also evidence that a lack of "mothering" may be a major factor in schizoid and schizophrenic reactions. *See* MATERNAL DEPRIVATION.

Recent personality studies, using the MMPI, have indicated that parents of child patients show considerably more disturbances than parents of normal children, and presumably create an injurious psychological environment (Marks, 1961; Wolking et al., 1964). In cases of juvenile delinquency, the parents were often found to be outwardly conforming yet inwardly rebellious—which suggests that they may unconsciously encourage antisocial behavior in their children as a vicarious gratification of their own impulses (Johnson, 1959). Wolking et al. (1964) also found a possible relation between neurotic tendencies in parents and in their children—boys with conversion reactions tended to have hypochondriacal fathers, and girls and boys with psychosomatic symptoms were often found to have mothers with similar problems. All these studies, however, are still in their early stages. *See* MINNESOTA MULTIPHASIC PERSONALITY INVENTORY.

Sociocultural factors are even harder to assess. Far too little data is available on child disorders in different cultures and on different social levels. A few suggestive studies of child-rearing practices have been made, however. Davis and Havighurst (1946) found lower-class parents more permissive, relaxed, and undemanding than middle-class parents—but more recent studies (Klatskin, 1952; Sears et al., 1957) describe middle-class mothers as more gentle and less punitive than working-class mothers, especially on such matters as toilet training, dependency, sex training, and expression of aggressive impulses. The middle-class mothers were also somewhat warmer, more demonstrative and democratic toward their children, and less likely to reject them. A study by Kohn and Carroll (1960) showed that middle-class mothers expected their husbands to be more encouraging and supportive than disciplinarian toward their children; working-class mothers, on the other hand, wanted their husbands to be authoritarian and directive, though the men themselves often

avoided this role and left the child-rearing responsibilities entirely to their wives. Most important, from the point of view of delinquency, is the fact that lower-class boys usually found it much harder to identify with their fathers than middle-class boys.

Since the beginning of this century the field of child therapy has gradually broadened, and today it is possible to select the approach which seems most likely to meet the needs of the individual child. Among the many techniques are: (1) play therapy, in which the young child is encouraged to release his emotions and test out new ways of behaving through the use of play materials in a permissive and accepting environment; (2) activity group therapy, in which older children achieve self-understanding and develop constructive relationships through group activities; (3) environmental manipulation, such as sending the child to a boarding school, or placing the child in a carefully chosen foster home when the family situation is intolerable; (4) remedial work with children who have learning and reading problems, including those with brain dysfunction; (5) individual supportive therapy involving such techniques as persuasion, suggestion, and direct guidance; (6) individual nondirective therapy, in which a therapeutic relationship is established and the child is encouraged to draw on his own capacities and create a more satisfying self-image; (7) learning theory or behavior therapy, which reinforces healthy behavior and extinguishes unhealthy patterns, such as nail-biting or stuttering; (8) milieu therapy, which utilizes a total residential setting in the treatment of retarded, delinquent or emotionally disturbed children (Alt, 1960); (9) relationship therapy, in which maladjusted children are given an opportunity to develop warm and satisfying relationships with a therapist, houseparent, or other child-care worker; (10) team therapy in child guidance clinics, with a psychiatrist treating the child and a social worker counseling the parents; (11) family-centered therapy, in which the same therapist treats the child, his parents and his siblings. *See* RELEASE THERAPY, PLAY THERAPY, ACTIVITY GROUP THERAPY, FAMILY THERAPY, BEHAVIOR THERAPY, RELATIONSHIP THERAPY, MILIEU THERAPY, MINIMAL BRAIN DYSFUNCTION.

CHILD PSYCHOLOGY. The scientific study of the behavior and development of the child from the time of conception to the beginning of adolescence.

At the present time approximately 4 per cent of all psychologists classify themselves specifically as child psychologists, with slightly more women than men in the field. Many others, however, are working in this general area, particularly educational psychologists, school psychologists, and clinical psychologists. The American Psychological Association has separate divisions for developmental, educational, clinical, and school psychology.

Modern child psychology began with G. Stanley Hall's use of the questionnaire in investigating the interests and activities of children. His results were published in the *Pedagogical Seminary,* the first journal in the field (1891). Shortly afterward, Binet's work on mental testing stimulated great interest in child development. However, organized research did not gain a foothold until after World War I, when special centers devoted to the scientific study of children were established at the State University of Iowa (1917), Columbia University (1924), the University of Minnesota (1925), and the University of California (1925). By 1930 child psychology was a distinct discipline in this country and had developed research procedures which could be applied both in the child's own environment and in the laboratory. These procedures include carefully documented developmental data, full case histories, controlled observations of behavior with use of one-way screens and plastic domes, rating scales, standardized psychological tests, projective methods, and experimental situations.

Today the leading texts in child psychology cover every important phase of development and aspect of the child's life: the contributions of heredity, environment, maturation, and learning to growth and development; physical care (feeding, toilet training, sleeping); motor activities (locomotion, handedness, writing); the effects of parental attitudes (acceptance, rejection, overprotection, discipline); formation of the personality (self-awareness, self-image, general adjustment); family relationships (birth order, family size, sibling rivalry, cultural influences); social relationships (first responses to others, competition, co-operation, quarreling, boy-girl relations, social acceptance); emotional life (affection, pleasure, anger, fear, anxiety, hostility, humor); mental life (first awareness, language, make-believe, imaginary companions, dreams, questions, concept formation, reasoning, intellectual ability); attitudes and interests (play interests, reading interests, religious ideas, moral values, sympathy, prejudice).

The topics just listed are generally approached from a developmental point of view, since the best way to understand the child is to view him as a growing person. For this reason many texts and courses use the term child development instead of child psychology. (The older term "genetic psychology" has fallen into disuse). Some authors divide the child's life into the prenatal period, infancy, babyhood, childhood (some include adolescence), and report the results of observations, tests and experiments within this general framework. Others prefer to focus on the developmental changes that occur throughout childhood under such broad topics as physical development, motor development, speech development, emotional development, social development, intellectual development, moral development, and personality development. But in any case no sharp distinction can be made between child psychology and developmental psychology, except that some authors place more emphasis on the cross-sectional and others on the longitudinal, or life history, point of view. But both are necessary if we are to do justice to the total life of the child. (For separate topics, see the CATEGORY INDEX under CHILD DEVELOPMENT.)

CHILDREN'S QUESTIONS. As soon as the child can use language to express himself, he begins to ask questions. This is one of his major means of satisfying curiosity; but as he develops, other motives usually come into play. He may ask questions to maintain social contact, gain attention, obtain reassurance, practice language, and in some cases to express resentment by annoying others. But even though we might suspect that a child's questions arise from motives other than curiosity, it is best to answer them rather than put them off—otherwise we might discourage him from using this important way of learning.

The so-called "questioning age" begins at about three years and reaches a peak at around six. The sheer number of questions can be overwhelming, since they have been found to comprise as much as 20 to 25 per cent of the average youngster's speech. "What" and "who" questions usually precede questions about why and how, since the child wants to learn the names for things (and people) before he can ask how they operate. Until about twelve years of age, practically all questions (about 85 per cent) deal with immediate situations rather than remembered or remote events. Boys ask for causal explanations more frequently than girls, and girls ask more questions about social relations than boys (Davis, 1932).

All types of questions play an important role in the formation of concepts, and answers must be geared to the child's level of development. If a four year old asks "What's a year?" it is better to answer "A long time, the time from last Christmas to next Christmas (or between your last birthday and your next birthday)" rather than to say "365 days." Similarly, young children can be given the truth but not the whole truth in answer to the question, "Where do babies come from?" "From a special place in mommy's body," is usually enough for a three year old; but for a five year old the answer might be "From special seeds called cells"—and if the child asks where they come from, "From the father and the mother" would probably be sufficient.

It is best not to read too much into a child's queries about matters that are emotionally toned for adults—questions about babies, sickness, or death. Curiosity about these subjects is as normal as curiosity about what makes a car go, or where the people are in television programs, or who made God. Nevertheless, some children are prompted by more than idle curiosity when they ask these questions, especially if they ask them repeatedly. It may be that they are still puzzled by our inadequate answers, or they may be troubled by some hidden fear or worry. If we suspect this to be the case, we would do well to look behind the question for the real reason, and give the child the help and reassurance he needs while answering the question he asks. See CURIOSITY DRIVE, CONCEPT FORMATION.

CHOLINERGIC. Activated or transmitted by acetylcholine. Acetylcholine is one of the two types of "chemical transmitters" in the nervous system; the other type includes adrenalin and noradrenalin. See ADRENERGIC REACTION.

Recent investigations indicate that messages in the nervous system are transmitted electrically in the body of the nerve fiber, but chemically at the synapse or junction between fibers (see *Fig. 40*). The chemical, acetylcholine, is synthesized and stored in the terminals of the axon fibers and released by spike potentials, or nerve impulses (Von Euler, 1959, and De Robertis et al., 1963). Cholinergic transmission occurs primarily at the synapses of motor fibers and striped muscles, at synapses in the parasympathetic portion of the autonomic nervous system (controlling the smooth muscles), and in the central nervous system as well—for example, in the neural mechanisms for thirst (Grossman, 1960; Fisher and Coury, 1962). See SYNAPSE.

In view of the stimulating effects of acetylcholine on the brain and nervous system, a number of cholinergic drugs have been developed. These drugs are classified as activators or antidepressants, and one of them, Deaner, has been applied with some success to schizophrenic patients (Berger, 1960). In addition, acetylcholine has been employed in attempts to measure autonomic changes accompanying emotional disturbances. In the Funkenstein test (1952), originally developed to predict the outcome of electroshock treatment, Mecholyl (acetylcholine) is injected intramuscularly and its effect on blood pressure observed for several minutes. Some psychiatrists find that a drop in blood pressure indicates that the patient will benefit from electroshock treatments or from psychotherapy. There are also indications that this response occurs only when the subject is in an emotional state of fear or anxiety, and for this reason the test is sometimes used as a diagnostic indicator of neurotic reactions to stress.

CINGULATE GYRUS (Literally "ring-shaped ridge"). The cortical part of the limbic system of the brain, lying just above the corpus callosum (PLATE 1).

Although the functions of this structure are not yet fully determined, there are some promising leads. Monkeys have shown an increased urge to eat when this area was stimulated with an electrode; therefore it seems to play a role in hunger (Robinson and Mishkin, 1962). It also appears to be involved in certain types of avoidance conditioning. When lesions were made in the anterior portion of the gyrus, cats readily learned an active response in which they moved or jumped to avoid a shock area, but they had trouble learning a passive response—that is, withholding their approach to food in order to avoid a shock. Cats with posterior cingulate lesions showed the opposite pattern (McCleary, 1961). Further experiments with monkeys showed a reduced ability to retain already acquired active responses following a cingulate lesion (Pribram and Weiskrantz, 1957).

Apparently the cingulate gyrus plays a part not only in hunger, but in learning and retention. Though it appears that different parts are involved in different types of responses, both the structural and functional details have still to be discovered. See AVOIDANCE LEARNING, LIMBIC SYSTEM.

CIRCUMSTANTIALITY. Circuitous, "labyrinthine" speech; the inclusion of numerous trivial and often irrelevant details in relating an incident, explaining a point, or answering a question. The term overinclusion is sometimes applied to this tendency.

The concept has particular relevance to psychiatric examinations. In a diagnostic interview the examiner must distinguish between three different types of circumstantiality. One is the normal variety in which a literal or small-minded person insists on giving every tiresome detail. The second involves a conscious or unconscious attempt to conceal facts by talking around the point or diverting attention to unimportant details. The third results from a definite disturbance in the flow of thought.

Some individuals—usually the first type just mentioned—have never learned to focus their thoughts or to distinguish essentials from nonessentials. Others tell their story in exhaustive detail as a response to inner anxiety, or the need to evoke sympathy from the listener. Still others may be using a wealth of detail as a substitute for lapses in memory, or as a dodge to avoid ideas that are threatening to them. In examining for mental disorder, the psychiatrist must determine whether the circumstantiality is due to one of these factors, or to a disorganization of thought over which the patient has no control. The latter is frequently the case in schizophrenia, mental deficiency, some forms of epilepsy, and senile psychosis. The tendency may also be found in the manic phase of manic-depressive reaction. *See* HYPERMNESIA.

Illustrative Case: CIRCUMSTANTIALITY

A schizophrenic patient who was asked whether prior to hospitalization he had been living alone or had shared his apartment took over forty minutes to answer the question. He detailed to an absurd degree the layout and furnishings of the apartment, the reasons why it might or might not have been desirable to have a roommate, the step-by-step changes from his initial preference for sharing the apartment to a later preference for solitude, and so forth. (Rosen and Gregory, 1965)

CIVILIAN CATASTROPHE REACTIONS. Transient situational personality disorders resulting from severely traumatic experiences in civilian life, classified by the American Psychiatric Association (1952) under the subheading "Gross Stress Reactions." The other type of disorder included in this category is combat reaction. Among the civilian experiences are auto accidents. plane crashes, earthquakes, tornadoes, fires, and sexual assault. In addition to these catastrophes, a large number of disturbing situations such as financial failure, divorce proceedings, social disgrace, and the sudden death of a loved person may produce traumatic reactions. *See* COMBAT REACTIONS.

The key feature of all these reactions is a temporary personality disorganization. The individual is for the time being overwhelmed and incapable of gathering his resources together to cope with the situation. The most acute and disrupting reactions are likely to occur when the victims have had a history of instability or immaturity, when prior traumas have made them sensitive to anxiety-provoking experiences, or when catastrophe occurs with little or no warning or preparation.

Although the symptom picture may vary widely from case to case, Raker et al. (1956) have found significant common features among victims of tornadoes and other catastrophes. They have outlined the following three-stage "disaster syndrome":

(1) In the "shock stage" the victim is so dazed and stunned that he is unaware of the extent of his injuries and wanders aimlessly, making little effort to help himself or others—and in extreme cases he may become stuporous, disoriented and amnesic for the traumatic event. The reason for these intense reactions is that the victim is suddenly overpowered by anxiety. The threat to security is so great that he cannot meet it with his ordinary techniques of adjustment and therefore becomes totally disorganized.

(2) In the "suggestible stage" the victim passively accepts directions and is extremely concerned about other people involved in the disaster; but his efforts at assistance and even his performance of routine tasks are highly inefficient. This stage also results from temporary inability to deal with the situation, plus a tendency to regress to infantile, passive dependence on other people.

(3) In the "recovery stage" he gradually regains control. Nevertheless, he will probably remain somewhat tense and apprehensive, and constantly talk about the disaster or criticize the rescue

workers. About one half of the victims re-enact the experience in recurrent nightmares. In this stage the tension and apprehensiveness are residual effects of the shock reaction, and the nightmares and repetitious talk are an unconscious attempt to reduce anxiety and "get it out of the system."

The three stages are clearly illustrated in this account of the *Andrea Doria-Stockholm* disaster off Nantucket Island:

"During the phase of initial shock the survivors acted as if they had been sedated . . . as though nature provided a sedation mechanism which went into operation automatically." During the phase of suggestibility "the survivors presented themselves for the most part as an amorphous mass of people tending to act passively and compliantly. They displayed psychomotor retardation, flattening of affect, somnolence, and in some instances, amnesia for data of personal identification. They were nonchalant and easily suggestible." During the stage of recovery, after the initial shock had worn off and the survivors had received aid, "they showed . . . an apparently compulsive need to tell the story again and again, with identical detail and emphasis." (Friedman and Linn, 1957). *See* REPETITION-COMPULSION.

The disaster reaction is frequently intensified by grief and depression caused by the loss of loved ones. It may be further complicated by feelings of guilt and self-reproach. A man or woman may be haunted for months or years by the thought, "There must be something I could have done." Even totally unjustified feelings of guilt can cause extreme agitation, nightmares, tension symptoms, and a sense of impending doom. One of the survivors of the Cocoanut Grove fire, which took over 400 lives in Boston in 1943, developed such morbid guilt feelings for failing to save his wife that he finally committed suicide.

The Cocoanut Grove disaster can be used to illustrate another type of traumatic reaction to panic. In acute panic the individual is thoroughly demoralized and overwhelmed by fear. He "loses his head," acts in a completely irrational manner and tries to save himself without regard to others. This extreme reaction does not often occur in the usual disaster situation, such as a tornado, but tends to take place only where an unprepared group of people is suddenly threatened and opportunities for escape are extremely limited (Fritz, 1957). This was exactly the situation at the Cocoanut Grove night club, where over six hundred people tried to get through only two revolving doors, even though many of them could have escaped through the kitchen.

Another set of reactions may develop days or weeks after the catastrophe. This "post-traumatic syndrome" is characterized by mild to acute anxiety attacks; persistent tension with tremors, restlessness, and insomnia; recurrent nightmares directly or symbolically related to the traumatic event; irritability, often with startle reaction; avoidance of excitement of any kind, including sexual and social contacts or discussion of the incident. Post-traumatic reactions also develop after severe physical injuries, and the symptoms may be aggravated or prolonged by the possibility of compensation. *See* COMPENSATION NEUROSIS.

The disaster syndrome and other shock reactions usually clear up quite rapidly if supportive psychotherapy is given immediately after the incident. Extra rest and sleep, with or without sedation, are practically always helpful. If prompt therapy is not given, there is not only a danger that the symptoms will become fixed, but that a post-traumatic syndrome will develop. In accident cases, such as being thrown from a horse or nearly drowning, it is often advisable to continue the activity in order to prevent anxiety from crystallizing. Although the prognosis in all these cases is generally favorable, some patients do not respond to therapy because of basic maladjustment or immaturity. *See* EMERGENCY PSYCHOTHERAPY, PANIC.

CLANG ASSOCIATION. An association of words or ideas by similarity of sound.

Young children often use clang associations when they talk or sing to themselves. A typical example is "Pit, Pat, Putt, Puff, Muff, Tough". Many nonsense rhymes are based on clang associations: "Ana manna mona mike, Barcelona bona pike." Nonsensical talk of this kind is believed to provide valuable practice in the sound and rhythm of language.

Clang associations are also found in a number of psychiatric conditions, particularly in manic states and schizophrenia. In such cases they are part of a more general disturbance of thought termed "flight of ideas." Patients with this symptom talk in a rapid, disconnected manner, and frequently jump from one idea to another only on the basis of superficial sound associations. Noyes and Kolb (1963) cite a case in which a patient was asked, "Are you sad?" His immediate reply was, "Yes, you have to be quiet to be sad. Everything having to do with 's' is quiet—on the qt—sit, sob, sigh, sign, sorrow, surcease, sought, sand, sweet mother's love, and salvation. This is my first case —I am kind of a bum lawyer or liar— to demand honesty, to be a lawyer, so had to be a liar." Speech of this sort is sometimes attributed to a "loosening of associations," and is taken as evidence of psychotic disorganization of thought. *See* FLIGHT OF IDEAS, MANIC-DEPRESSIVE REACTION (MANIC PHASE).

CLIENT-CENTERED THERAPY. The nondirective approach developed by Carl Rogers, in which psychotherapy is viewed as an opportunity for the patient to grow and "become a person" by realizing his own inner potentialities.

The client-centered approach is based on the theory that human nature is fundamentally sound and that every individual has a capacity for self-actualization and healthy adjustment. However, that capacity may be blocked by emotional conflicts, distorted ideas, or a faulty self-image. In such cases, he is not regarded as a sick person who needs a doctor (hence the term client rather than patient), but as an individual who has rejected or lost touch with his true and unique self. In spite of this, his capacity for self-realization remains, and the object of therapy is to bring it to the fore so that he may resolve his own conflicts, correct his self-image, and reorganize his personality and approach to life.

The function of the therapist is to create a situation in which this process of self-correction and personality growth can occur. To accomplish this, he must be a warm person who feels an "unconditional personal regard" for his client; he must adopt a completely accepting attitude toward whatever is revealed; and he must be capable of "empathic understanding" of his client's inner life. Moreover, he must be able to *communicate* that understanding to the client through two processes, reflection and clarification. In reflection, he merely repeats what the client says, or part of what he says, in a tone that conveys understanding but neither approval nor disapproval. In clarification, he restates the kernel of what the client is trying to say. In either case the effect is to hold up a mirror to the client so that he will be able to see himself more clearly and recognize his feelings and attitudes for what they are.

Rogers (1942, 1951) has found that the nondirective process takes a fairly regular course. The first interview is considered a major step for the client, since in coming for help he is already taking the initiative toward his own recovery. The therapist explains that the client himself will lead the way throughout the entire process, because this will enable him to find an answer to his own problems. This, the therapist explains, is the only way it can be accomplished, since his problems are unique to himself and must be solved in the light of his own personality and not on anyone else's terms.

The therapist then immediately establishes a permissive atmosphere by encouraging his client to feel free to bring up any topic and say anything he likes. This usually opens the way to expressions of discouragement and negative feelings toward himself. The therapist responds by echoing and clarifying the client's comments, and this stimulates him to explore his attitudes further. In the course of this process, he gradually reveals that he has positive as well as negative feelings toward himself. The therapist subtly encourages him to express these feelings in the same way that he elaborated on his negative feelings. And by adopting an accepting attitude toward both sets of feelings, he helps his client accept himself as he is, contradictions and all.

Ideally, as the process continues, the client gradually drops his defenses and faulty assumptions about himself. Self-condemnation and self-approval both recede, and a more objective evaluation takes their place. He begins to see himself, his situation, and his relationship to others in better perspective. Moreover, as he releases his emotions and gains greater insight, his tensions subside and he feels he is becoming a real person. This gives him the courage to accept aspects of his personality that were formerly repressed or disowned. Finally, he begins to set up achievable goals, and to consider the steps he must take to reach them. He then makes tentative moves in the positive direction, and when these efforts bring increased feelings of adequacy and satisfaction, his need for help decreases. The

decision to terminate, like all other phases of the therapy, comes from the client, and represents a final step toward independence.

The distinguishing characteristics of client-centered therapy are these: the responsibility for the direction and pace of the therapy rests with the client; the therapist's role is restricted to accepting, reflecting, and clarifying the client's responses; transference between therapist and patient is minimized, making it unnecessary to work through this complex relationship; diagnostic and other psychological tests are eliminated; and the entire process is based on the view that the therapy will only be an effective growth experience if the client arrives at his own interpretations of his emotional patterns and his own realization of the need for changing his attitudes and behavior.

The nondirective approach has had widespread impact not only on individual verbal therapy, but on play therapy, group therapy and the training of counselors and psychotherapists, as well as on the fields of education, business and industrial administration, and religious activities. Rogersian therapists have carefully documented the changes that take place in the therapeutic process through the analysis of tape recordings and films, but definitive comparisons with other forms of therapy have yet to be made. *See* CLINICAL PSYCHOLOGY.

Illustrative   Case: CLIENT-CENTERED THERAPY

Excerpt from first transcribed interview:

S (subject): Well, it's just reached the point where it becomes unbearable. I'd rather be dead than live as I am now.

C (counselor): You'd rather be dead than live as you are now? Can you tell me a little more about that?

S: Well, I hope. Of course we always live on hope.

C: Yes.

S: But—No, I don't have any conscious suicidal urge or anything like that. It's just that—looking at it rationally, I feel that I'm—that I'm in the red now and I wouldn't want to keep on living in the red. (*Pause.*)

C: Well, can you tell me in any more detailed way what—in what way it blocks you so much that you really feel sometimes that you'd be better off dead?

S: Well, I don't know if I can any more accurately describe the sensation. It's just a —a very impressive and painful weight as if an ax were pressing on the whole abdomen, pressing down, I can almost—I can almost sense the position and I feel that it is oppressing me very radically, that is, that it goes right down to the roots of my dynamic energy, so that no matter in what field I assay any sort of effort, I find the blocking.

Excerpt from eighth and final interview:

S: Well, I've been noticing something decidedly new. Rather than having fluctuations, I've been noticing a very gradual steady improvement. It's just as if I had become more stabilized and my growth had been one of the hard way and the sure way rather than the wavering and fluctuating way.

C: M-mm.

S: I go into situations, and even though it's an effort, why I go ahead and make my progress, and I find that when you sort of seize the bull by the horns, as it were, why it isn't so bad as if you sort of deliberate and perhaps—well, think too long about it like I used to. I sort of say to myself, "Well, I know absolutely that avoiding the situation will leave me in the same old rut I've been taking," and I realize that I don't want to be in the same old rut, so I go ahead and go into the situation, and even when I have disappointments in the situation, I find that they don't bring me down as much as they used to.

C: That sounds like real progress.

S: And what pleases me is that my feelings are on an even keel, steadily improving, which gives me much more of a feeling of security than if I had fluctuations. You see, fluctuations lead you from the peaks to the valleys, and you can't get as much self-confidence as when you're having gradual improvement. (Rogers, 1942)

CLINICAL PSYCHOLOGY. A field of psychology devoted to psychological methods of diagnosing and treating mental and emotional disorders, as well as research into the causes of these disorders and the effects of therapy.

The first American psychological clinic was established by Lightner Witmer at the University of Pennsylvania in 1896. It was devoted largely to mental testing, and most of the clients were children. The growth of the field was slow until World War II, but from that time to the present it has rapidly expanded in scope and importance. Clinical psychologists now deal with adult as well as child clients, engage in psychotherapy as well as testing, and conduct research projects in the entire field of mental and emotional disorders.

According to the latest survey, published by the *American Psychologist* in March, 1966, approximately 37 per cent of all psychologists function in this general area, and it is therefore by far the largest single category in the field. Clinical psychologists occupy positions not only in mental institutions, out-patient clinics, and community mental health centers, but also in industry, schools, courts, correctional institutions, government agencies, and the armed forces, and approximately 14 per cent are in private practice. A growing number of clinical psychologists are engaged in all phases of community mental health, and the American Psychological Association now has a Division of Community Psychology. While many devote themselves to diagnosis, treatment and research, others are active in planning and administering community-based facilities such as the community mental health centers which are now in formation through the country. *See* COMMUNITY MENTAL HEALTH CENTERS.

The work of clinical psychologists requires a background in practically every branch of psychology, but draws most heavily on the study of abnormal psychology, personality theory, and psychological testing. Preparation must also include specialized courses and supervised training in the clinical field. A growing number are obtaining specialty certification through the American Board of Examiners in Professional Psychology. To receive the ABEPP diploma, the candidate must offer a Ph.D. and five years experience, and must pass intensive written and practical examinations.

The major activities of clinical psychologists fall into three related fields: diagnosis, therapy, and research. The rest of this topic will review some of their work in these areas with special emphasis on the techniques they employ and the problems they encounter.

Diagnosis. The object of diagnosis is to make a full evaluation of the invidual's personality and functioning, so that the most appropriate type of therapy can be applied. Although some classification of patients into categories of mental deficiency, neurosis, or psychosis is useful for screening purposes, there is less and less emphasis on specific diagnostic labels today. An increasing number of psychologists and psychiatrists have been pointing out, first, that the textbook cases are rarely found in clinical practice; and, second, that psychological disorders cannot be viewed as distinctive diseases like typhoid fever or diphtheria. Instead, they put the emphasis on specific behavior patterns, and construct a full and detailed personal description of each patient in terms of his particular defense and escape mechanisms. This approach gives the therapist leads for exploring the sources of maladjustment, and enables him to put his finger on ineffectual or distorted attitudes which need to be revised. In other words, diagnosis is aimed at treatment rather than at classification.

There are two other important objectives. One is that an evaluation of the patient is important in predicting the possibility of improvement as well as in selecting the type of treatment that is most likely to be effective. Studies have shown that evaluation and prognosis must take many factors into account, including the form of the disorder (reactive schizophrenia has a better prognosis than process schizophrenia), the post-hospital environment of the patient (an oversolicitous family is a handicap) and the ego-strength of the patient. The other goal of diagnosis is the attainment of insight. During the exploratory, fact-finding process a client often comes to know and understand himself better, especially if he is encouraged to verbalize his feelings and speak openly about his problems. This is most likely to occur in the client-centered and psychoanalytic approaches, which therefore do not draw a hard and fast line between diagnosis and therapy.

The clinical psychologist collects his diagnostic data in three principal ways: by compiling a case history, by interviewing the patient, and by administering psychological tests. In compiling the case history, or anamnesis, he gathers information on the client's family background; psychological and physical development; medical, educational, and vocational history; and his current situation. To assemble as complete a biography as possible, he not only interviews the client himself but may also consult members of the family, teachers, the family physician, employers, and social agencies. In the diagnostic interview, or series of interviews, the client is encouraged to describe his problem and talk freely about himself, and the clinician notes his characteristic ways of reacting to his experiences, as well as telltale behavioral clues such as blushing, grimaces, gestures, and changes in posture as he tells his story. He refrains from expressing any judgments of approval or disapproval, but maintains a warm, relaxed and interested attitude. Clinical psychologists have found that if they establish a good rapport with their clients during the diagnostic process, they will not only elicit a wealth of material but set the stage for effective therapy. *See* ANAMNESIS.

The clinician occasionally uses academic achievement, vocational and interest tests when they are relevant to specific problems; but his major instruments are intelligence tests and personality tests. Since the major tests in both of these categories are described under separate topics, they will receive a minimum of attention here. Individual intelligence tests, such as the Stanford-Binet and Wechsler, not only provide objective indexes of intellectual functioning, but give the clinician an opportunity to observe work habits, attitudes, problem-solving techniques, and emotional responses to the test situation. Performance tests usually reveal perceptual and spatial rather than numerical and verbal behavior, and are particularly useful in testing infants, preschool children, illiterates, foreigners, and clients with disabilities (dyslexia, cerebral palsy, etc.) which prevent the administration of verbal tests. A number of tests have also been constructed for assessing intellectual impairment due to brain damage, psychosis, senility, and certain types of mental defect. *See* MENTAL IMPAIRMENT TESTS.

In contrast to the tests of intellectual functioning, personality tests are designed to assess the client's emotional, social, and motivational patterns. Since these tests are of more debatable value than the intellectual tests, they are used primarily for exploratory purposes, and greater weight is usually given to the case history and interview data. The three major types of personality tests are self-report inventories, such as the MMPI in which the client responds to printed statements about feelings, attitudes, and behavior; the various projective techniques (Word Association Test, Sentence Completion Test, Rorschach, TAT) in which the individual responds in his own way to relatively unstructured material; and tests which reveal the way the client views himself and others (self-concept tests, attitude and interest tests).

Therapy. The involvement of the clinical psychologist in therapy has broadened in recent years, and now includes an immense variety of procedures. One indication of this expansion is the fact that this volume describes more than eighty different kinds of treatment, although some of them are of an auxiliary nature and others primarily experimental. The psychologist should be conversant with every type of therapeutic approach, even those he does not himself apply, since he is often called upon to participate in clinical conferences and to evaluate the procedures of others.

The psychologist does not administer somatic treatments—shock therapy, drugs, psychosurgery—since these require medical training. However, he may collaborate with physicians in determining which approach to use, in evaluating the progress of therapy, and in applying psychotherapy when the patient is amenable to it. In many instances, too, he is deeply involved in environmental therapy, which is now a major feature of the treatment program in mental institutions. The object of this approach is to make the hospital a "therapeutic community" by focusing the entire milieu on the single objective of bringing patients back to a normal life. Among the techniques used are occupational therapy, sheltered workshops, recreational and social activities, contacts with the community, and self-government by the patients. Clinical psychologists frequently act as advisers or administrators in these programs. *See* MILIEU THERAPY.

The clinical psychologist also serves as a psychotherapist in his own right, dealing primarily with cases of milder emotional disturbance, neurosis, and behavior disorders, and rarely with psychotic patients except when they are on the road to recovery.

Since the various types of psycho-therapy are described under individual topics, we will only stop to enumerate some of the major approaches at this point. Some therapists are nondirective and client-centered in their approach, others are more directive and serve as guides or counselors. Some put the emphasis on insight and interpretation; others stress learning processes and behavioral change. A few clinical psychologists utilize an analytic approach for some types of disorder and conditioning techniques for others. In addition, psychologists apply many varieties of group therapy in institutions and clinics, and may use play therapy and psychodrama when they appear most appropriate. Some specialize in briefer forms of therapy, including hypnoanalysis; others engage in more extended treatment, practicing either a Freudian or a neo-Freudian form of psychoanalysis. But, interestingly, a sizable number of psychotherapists do not confine themselves to a single procedure or school but adapt their approach to the particular needs of the patient. There is evidence for this trend in a 1960 survey conducted by the American Psychological Association's Division of Clinical Psychology which showed that 49 per cent of the respondents described their orientation as "eclectic."

Research. This is the area in which the clinical psychologist can probably make his most needed and distinctive contributions, for only through research can present mental health techniques be evaluated and new ones developed. Unfortunately there was little attempt to apply scientific methods to the study of clinical problems before World War II, and even now there are far more questions than answers. However, some promising approaches have been made in four areas—diagnosis, the process of therapy, the outcome of therapy, and causes of mental disorder. Some examples of significant research in each of these areas will now be given.

The validation of projective tests and other diagnostic techniques presents a particularly knotty problem. The difficulties arise from a variety of factors —for example, a TAT may provide different kinds of information about different individuals because of its unstructured nature, and much of this information is in the form of inner attitudes and reactions (such as unconscious feelings of inferiority) that cannot easily be translated into observable, verifiable patterns of behavior. Also, as Anastasi (1964) has pointed out, many of the attempts to evaluate diagnostic tests have been inconclusive because they have used questionable procedures or inappropriate statistical techniques. There have been, however, a few carefully constructed investigations, and she cites as an example a study conducted by Little and Shneidman (1959), in which four groups of subjects (neurotic, psychotic, psychosomatic, and normal) were administered the Rorschach, TAT, MAPS and MMPI, with a detailed case history compiled independently for each subject. A thoroughgoing blind analysis was performed by two sets of judges: forty-eight clinical psychologists analyzed the test results, and twenty-three psychiatrists and one psychologist evaluated the case studies. Analysis of their findings revealed little correspondence between the diagnostic labels assigned to the subjects and their previously established diagnoses. Moreover, the test judges disagreed widely among themselves, and there was a strong tendency to classify the normal subjects as neurotic or psychotic. There was a somewhat higher than chance agreement among their personality descriptions, but the correlation between the case studies and the test results , was low. Also, there was little agreement from one test to another and even among different judges using the same test. The findings, in other words, were not very promising.

Another area of research, which has

yielded happier results, is the study of the changes occurring during psychotherapy. Seeman (1949) analyzed client and therapist statements taken from sixty nondirective sessions with ten clients, and found that in the course of psychotherapy the percentage of statements dealing with problems or symptoms sharply declined, and statements that showed understanding or insight increased in number. Toward the end of the process, the clients also showed increased optimism and interest in future plans. Some studies using the Q sort technique have shown that the client's self-concept becomes more favorable as therapy progresses. Other studies have shown that defensiveness decreases and expressions of hostility tend to increase, indicating a growing ability to express feelings freely. Still another line of investigation has suggested that the personality characteristics of the therapist enable him to function more effectively with one type of therapy than another, and with one kind of patient as well. Snyder (1961) has found a close correspondence between the way a client feels toward the therapist and the way the therapist feels toward the client in the different therapeutic sessions. The importance of compatability between therapist and patient is now well recognized. See SELF-CONCEPT TESTS.

A third area of research—evaluation of the outcome of therapy—presents more problems than may be expected. First of all, what criteria should be used? The patient's own judgment is likely to be misleading because he may be defensive about admitting failure to improve, and may be influenced by the "hello, good-bye" effect—that is, the tendency to exaggerate his difficulties when seeking therapy and to minimize them at the end, out of courtesy or gratitude. The therapist's report may be influenced by expectation and belief in his procedures, and he may judge improvement more by changes in the patient's attitude during the process than by changes in behavior outside his office. The same may occur in the hospital, where apparent improvement may be due only to better adjustment toward life, not to the real world. It is even hard to judge changes in adaptation to the outside world because the experimenter has no control over the circumstances of the patient's life, which may be favorable in one case and highly unfavorable in another. In view of these difficulties it should not be surprising that the correlations between different criteria are rather low (Fulkerson and Barry, 1961), and that a patient may be judged to be greatly improved according to one criterion and unimproved according to another (Fairweather et al. 1960).

It is also extremely difficult to design conclusive experiments in this field. One method is to compare treated with untreated groups, yet it is hard to match them completely in all important variables such as age, sex, socioeconomic level, duration of illness, type of onset. In comparing different kinds of psychotherapy, different therapists are generally used, and variations in the results may be due to the therapists rather than the therapies. In evaluating drugs, a possible placebo effect must be taken into account. In a recent study hospitalized psychiatric patients were divided into an experimental group and a control group; the experimental group was given either "a new tranquilizer" or "a new energizer," and the control group received no tablet at all. After a six-week period the experimental group was evaluated by psychiatrists, nurses, and themselves, and from 53 per cent to 80 per cent appeared to have benefited. Yet the fact of the matter is that all the drugs administered were placebos, although neither the patients nor the staff were aware of this (Loranger, Prout, and White, 1961). See PLACEBO.

Research on the causes of mental disorder is even more tentative than research on the effects of treatment.

Since many of the theories and findings are reported under separate topics, such as schizophrenia and manic-depressive psychosis, we will confine ourselves here to enumerating some of the approaches currently under exploration. In attempting to assess hereditary factors, some specialists have investigated the incidence of a given disorder in closely intermarried families, in isolated inbred communities, and in different members of the same families. Others have studied the incidence of disorders that follow Mendelian ratios (phenylketonuria, amaurotic idiocy), and have attempted to trace the physiological mechanisms through which the defect manifests itself. Still others have explored the incidence of schizophrenia and other disorders among fraternal and identical twins, and the extent to which close association and similar environment may be an explanatory factor.

Two other sets of factors are receiving their share of attention today. Clinical psychologists are frequently concerned with assessing the effects of organic conditions on behavior—among them, birth injuries, minimal brain damage, disordered metabolism due to stress, endocrine dysfunctions, brain wave irregularities, and vitamin deficiencies. They are especially involved in the study of the relation between life experience and psychological disorder. Here, too, there are many avenues of inquiry: the effects of emotional deprivation, parent-child relations during the formative years, the "schizophreno-genic mother," cultural differences in child-rearing practices, characteristic symptom patterns, and disorders among different nationalities and other social groups.

These factors—hereditary, organic, environmental—are hard enough to investigate when attacked singly, but in many cases all three collaborate to produce a single disorder—which poses the further problem of appraising the interrelationships among them. This re-quires the collaboration of many specialists from many disciplines, which in itself can be a problem. See ETIOLOGY.

CLOUDING OF CONSCIOUSNESS.
A mental disturbance in which the individual is unable to perceive, understand, and think clearly.

When a patient's consciousness becomes clouded he appears to be in a "mental fog" and it is hard to "get through" to him. Every perceptual function—the entire "sensorium"—is impaired. Sights and sounds fail to register, and events that occur around him pass unnoticed. It may be necessary to shout, shake him or repeat questions several times in order to capture attention and get a response. Clouding may be relatively mild, or may occur in extreme degree as in states of somnolence, stupor or coma.

Clouding of consciousness may result from physical disturbances, such as infectious diseases or toxic conditions which affect brain functions. In epilepsy, clouded states may precede or follow a convulsive attack; in such cases the dazed reaction is accompanied by deep confusion or excitement, anxiety, and bewilderment. The symptom may also occur in psychogenic disorders. Patients suffering from acute anxiety and tension may become so preoccupied with inner turmoil that external reality cannot impress itself clearly upon them. In dissociative reactions, clouding may serve the unconscious purpose of self-defense against distressing or threatening events. It is a way of excluding these events from awareness and may be followed by complete amnesia for the clouded period. See SENSORIUM.

CLUTTERING   (Tachyphemia).
Excessively rapid, arhythmic speech with a tendency to stutter, jumble words, omit syllables, and reverse parts of words. According to Arnold (1960), cluttering differs from stuttering in a number of major respects. Unlike stut-

tering, it appears to be hereditary, comes on gradually, and is associated with severely delayed speech, poor academic ability in languages, almost total lack of musical ability, and diffuse dysrhythmia in EEG tracings.

Cluttering includes all degrees of articulatory disorder from poorly enunciated speech to almost total incomprehensibility. A common characteristic is the accidental transposition of initial sounds known as spoonerisms, named after a Rev. W. A. Spooner of New College, Oxford, who inadvertently made such mistakes as "Kelley and Sheets" (for Keats and Shelley) and "The Lord is a shoving leopard" (loving shepherd). It is frequently associated with language disorders including dysgrammatism (use of incorrect grammar), congenital dyslexia and dysgraphia (reading and writing words in the opposite direction, slips of the pen, skipping syllables or words in reading etc.), cluttered handwriting (stereotyped errors, careless spelling mistakes, almost illegible writing). In view of the presence of these defects, which are frequently found in aphasia, cluttering is viewed by Arnold, Bakwin, and others as a congenital and general language disability involving a mild but diffuse brain dysfunction. See APHASIA.

Arnold has found that clutterers show evidence of a "congenital peculiarity of the entire personality structure." The predominant characteristic is a hasty, untidy, erratic temperament; impulsiveness and hyperactivity, with rapid walking, restless sleep, and fidgetiness; interest in mathematical, mechanical, and scientific occupations rather than verbal vocations; generally normal intelligence, though thoughts tend to run ahead of words or sometimes vice versa; and excellent memory except for a short auditory memory span. The clutterer, unlike the stutterer, is usually unconscious of his defect and improves when attention is called to his speech. Therapy, therefore, consists largely of concentrated practice in speaking slowly and rhythmically, to help him become aware of his faulty patterns and establish smoother and clearer articulation. See STUTTERING.

COCAINE HABITUATION. Psychological dependence on cocaine resulting in habitual use.

Cocaine, a drug derived from the leaves of the coca plant and long used as a local anesthetic, is taken by some individuals for its stimulating and pleasurable effects. Though there are fewer cocaine users today than there were after World War I, the drug has its devotees and is sometimes taken by young people for kicks or by addicts as a substitute for morphine or heroin. Unlike these drugs, it does not produce actual addiction, since the user does not develop increasing tolerance or physical craving, nor is he afflicted with severe symptoms when it is withdrawn. Nevertheless the cocaine user may become psychologically dependent on the drug and it may therefore become a habit.

In contrast to the opiates, cocaine is not a narcotic but a stimulant. When sniffed or taken by hypodermic, it produces a slight dizziness or headache followed by a state of exhilaration, euphoria, and self-confidence that lasts for several hours. During this period the user becomes extremely active and loquacious and feels he can accomplish an. thing. He is constantly excited, easily aroused sexually, and finds sleep almost impossible. But as the effect wears off he becomes increasingly weak, depressed, and irritable; and these reactions are usually followed by digestive disturbances, tremors, palpitation, slight confusion, and impotence. If a cocaine habituate does not receive the drug, he may experience episodes of fear or panic which make his behavior dangerous and unpredictable.

If large doses of the drug are taken over a long period, acute psychotic reactions may occur. The most common symptoms are terrifying hallucinations, including formication, the conviction that insects are crawling beneath the skin (the "cocaine bug"). In some cases there are delusions of jealousy and persecution which may lead to acts of violence. The expression "dope fiend" was coined with cocaine users in mind. Studies have shown that, on the whole, they lose their self-respect and become morally deteriorated sooner than narcotic addicts, and the chances of rehabilitation are considerably more remote.

Illustrative Case: COCAINE HABITUATION

The patient was a strikingly pretty, intelligent girl of nineteen who had divorced her husband two years previously. She had married at the age of sixteen and stated that she was terribly in love with her husband but that he turned out to be cruel and brutal to her. He would frequently take her to bars, where he would force her to drink while he spent the evening criticizing and berating her for no apparent reason. On several occasions he tried to force her to have sexual relations with his acquaintances under threat of bodily injury.

After six months of marriage she became pregnant. Her husband, who did not wish to have any children, flew into a rage. He accused her of betraying him with other men, and hit her several times, finally knocking her into a stove with such force that she had a miscarriage.

The girl was too ashamed of her marriage failure (her parents had violently opposed the marriage and she had left home against their will) to return to her home. She moved away from her husband and got a job as a barmaid in the same bar where her husband had been accustomed to taking her. She was severely depressed, and several of his friends insisted on buying her drinks to cheer her up. This process continued for almost a year, during which she drank excessively but managed to hold her job.

Following this, she met a man in the bar where she worked who introduced her to cocaine, assuring her that it would cheer her up and get rid of her blues. At this time she was still feeling very depressed and sorry for herself and she thought she would try it out. She states that it both "hopped me up and gave me a feeling of peace and contentment." For a period of several months she purchased her supplies of cocaine from this same man until she became ill with appendicitis and was unable to pay the stiff price which he asked. Following an appendectomy, she was induced to share his apartment as a means of defraying her expenses and ensuring the supply of cocaine which she had now become heavily dependent upon psychologically. She stated that she felt she could not work without it. During this period she had sexual relations with the man although she considered it immoral and had severe guilt feelings about it.

This pattern continued for several months until her "roommate" upped his prices on the cocaine on the excuse that it was getting more difficult to obtain and suggested to her that she might be able to earn enough money to pay for it if she were not so prudish about whom she slept with. At this time the full significance of where her behavior was leading seems to have dawned upon her and she came voluntarily for psychiatric assistance. (Coleman, 1964)

COGNITIVE DISSONANCE (Dissonance Theory). A state of conflict occurring when beliefs or assumptions are contradicted by new information. Dissonance theory holds that the conflict produces feelings of discomfort which the individual seeks to relieve by reconciling the differences, by convincing himself they do not exist, or by adopting some other type of defensive maneuver.

An example of dissonance is the conflict that occurs when a habitual smoker encounters evidence that smoking is dangerous to health. Many techniques might be used to reduce the tension arising from dissonant ideas in this case. The smoker might eliminate the conflict by giving up smoking. He might refuse to accept the evidence that smoking is dangerous to health, or continually demand more conclusive evidence. He might, as Brown (1965) suggests, "control his flow of information, seeking out reports of reassuring research and avoiding the lung-cancer statistics. He might also seek out other smokers who would give him social support."

The theory of cognitive dissonance was introduced by Festinger in 1957, and since then has inspired a large number of theoretical discussions and empirical studies. A thorough review of the field was made by Brehm and Cohen in 1962 in their book *Studies in Cognitive Dissonance.* Brown, a strong supporter of the theory, considers it one of the most important ideas in social psychology today; others have found it applicable to the field of abnormal psychology and psychiatry as well as to certain aspects of animal behavior. A review of a few major experiments and theoretical interpretations will show how widely it has been employed.

Brown has applied the concept to the problem of revising social attitudes. He points out that we can accept a greater amount of dissonance when we do not act upon our beliefs than when we do. Our "pet hates," for instance, do not cause us much discomfort if we keep them to ourselves, even though we know they are irrational and unjustified, but if we voice them in public or express them in action we are likely to feel somewhat embarrassed and uncomfortable. This leads Brown to suggest that we might be able to change people's attitudes if we get them to change their actions first, for "if action cannot adequately be accounted for by factors other than a favorable judgment, then there is a very great need to make judgment favorable in order to motivate what has been done." This leads him to suggest, as an example, that if we are to reduce discrimination against Negroes, we must not concentrate on generating favorable attitudes directly, but on inducing a prejudiced person to take favorable action toward them. He may then change his attitude to account for his action, and thereby reduce the discomfort caused by conflicting attitudes toward the Negro. This, of course, still leaves the problem of how to convince prejudiced individuals to become involved in such action.

Another important point brought out by dissonance theory is the relation between commitment and attitude change. When we are committed to engage in behavior that arouses negative attitudes, a state of tension is set up, and we must make an effort to reduce the dissonance in one way or another. One way of doing this is to change our negative attitude and decide that the behavior is not so bad after all. Festinger and Carlsmith (1959) tested this hypothesis by having subjects perform a series of extremely tedious tasks and then paying some of them to lie and tell prospective subjects that they were a lot of fun. The investigators found that the subjects who committed themselves to making this false report, which required action dissonant with their beliefs, later rated the tasks more interesting than a control group who had not committed themselves to lie.

In another experiment on commitment, Aronson and Mills (1959) found that when people voluntarily choose to join a group (in this case, a sex discussion group), and the experience proves disappointing, there is a tendency to think that it has turned out well. In other words, dissonance is reduced by distorting the facts. Moreover, if the members have been initiated into the group, the more severe the initiation, the greater the commitment, and the more favorable the attitude toward the group and its activities. This is probably one of the reasons behind the solemn and complex initiations of members into the Ku Klux Klan and other secret organizations.

Research on cognitive dissonance has not been confined to the laboratory, but has also been carried out in actual social situations. In *When Prophecy*

Fails (1956) Festinger, Riecken, and Schachter report a study of a group that awaited the end of the world on an appointed day. It might be expected that after the fateful day had passed they would resolve their dissonance by losing faith in the prophet who had made the prediction. However, dissonance theory holds that when many people share a belief, or when commitment is so great that a reversal will involve severe hardship or embarrassment, the disconfirmation of the prophecy will probably be followed by increased proselytizing. This is actually what happened. The group that made the prophecy attempted to bolster their threatened belief by winning others to their cause, thereby increasing social support. The mechanism can be duplicated in many other situations—for example, the smoker's tendency to seek out others to support his view.

These examples indicate that the concept of cognitive dissonance can be employed to explain much of our self-protective behavior. Human beings seem to have a basic psychological need to maintain consistency, stability, and order in their perception of the world. When new information threatens their previous views or assumptions, they feel uneasy and resort to defensive maneuvers of one kind or another. Many neurotic or semineurotic activities can be explained in this way—for instance, the tendency to "screen out" upsetting experiences, to deny obvious facts, or to reinforce beliefs by making aggressive, belligerent assertions, and by desperately looking for justifications ("consonant cognitions") (Brehm and Cohen, 1962).

Carl Rogers, as Coleman (1964) points out, believes these defensive measures are particularly likely to be undertaken when the dissonant cognition "thwarts the adequacy and worth of the self." If that threat is great enough, "the individual's self-image becomes less congruent with realities and more defenses, accordingly, must be brought into operation to maintain it. The self thereby loses contact with large segments of inner and outer experience, and the increasing opposition between reality and self leads to tension, anxiety, and a lowered sense of self-identity and self-direction." As a consequence, the individual lives "in perpetual jeopardy" and resorts to greater and greater defensive maneuvers. In this way the concept of cognitive dissonance helps to account for the vicious circle that lies behind neurotic behavior. *See* CLIENT-CENTERED THERAPY, PREJUDICE.

COLITIS. There are two principal diseases of the colon, or large intestine: mucous colitis and ulcerative colitis. Since both may be produced or aggravated by emotional tension, they are included among the psychophysiologic (psychosomatic) disorders of the gastrointestinal system.

Mucous colitis is probably not due to an actual inflammation or infection, as the name implies, but the bowels become highly sensitive and irritable. Among the symptoms are constipation and mucus-containing stools, and the patient complains of indigestion, nausea, stomach distention, poor appetite, and general weakness. These reactions are often erroneously attributed to organic causes, such as gall-bladder disease, prostatitis, appendicitis, and consequently many unnecessary operations have been performed. Spasm-relieving drugs and irrigation of the colon are unlikely to bring lasting relief in persistent cases, since the underlying cause is usually emotional. Psychiatrists believe the condition is a physical reaction to situations that arouse feelings of guilt, anxiety, and resentment, particularly in individuals who tend to be oversensitive and overconscientious. Women are considerably more prone to mucous colitis than men.

Ulcerative colitis is a more serious disease, since there is an actual inflammation which produces lesions in the wall of the intestine. The symptoms are acute diarrhea, blood in the stool, intense abdominal pain, weakness, emaciation, and anemia. It is a stubborn disease that calls for close attention of an internist, since it requires a carefully prescribed diet and medications, and in some cases hospitalization and surgery. The patient also needs psychiatric help. During the acute phase of the illness, however, the psychiatrist may merely establish a supportive and protective role with the patient, or advise the internist to do so, since he has a need to be dependent on a strong, understanding person who will accept him as he is.

Case histories of patients with ulcerative colitis show that this dependency need was established early in life. Many of them had domineering, hostile, and cold mothers who frustrated their normal desire for protective care. As a result they often felt rejected and reacted with feelings of rage, hostility, and fear of retaliation—and these upsetting emotions disrupted their bowel functions.

The early frustrations and conflicting feelings of love and hate toward their mothers are believed to have had a double effect on these patients. First, it became hard for them to establish warm, dependent relationships with other people because they anticipated rejection—yet the need for these relationships remained. Second, they were highly sensitized to any events that threatened their security or self-esteem. In keeping with this tendency their history shows that the colitis attacks frequently set in a short time after a period of intense emotional stress caused by bereavement, disillusionment, rejection, graduation from school (with the necessity of facing a hostile world), or failure at school or at work.

The reassurance, support, and protection offered by the psychiatrist often brings about dramatic improvement by itself. Anaclitic therapy, in which the patient is encouraged to regress to helpless, dependent, infantile behavior, has also proved effective in some cases—although extended therapy of this type is often not feasible since the therapist cannot fulfill the patient's expectations of continuous emotional support. However, many patients respond favorably to intensive psychotherapy that does not attempt deep analysis. See ANACLITIC THERAPY.

Illustrative Case: COLITIS

A man of fifty-five, an efficient carpenter, had symptoms of colitis. He had always been headstrong, rather aggressive, and inclined always to dominate the situation. His wife was completely obedient to him and accepted his verdict in everything. His father's character had resembled his own, and his mother had accepted all his father's verdicts. The father was rather strict with the patient and punished him severely when he rebelled, as he often did. He finally left home, chiefly to get away from his father. He later became reconciled with his father, but he himself adopted a similar behavior. When he was about fifty, he found it difficult to maintain his earning capacity and his position in his trade. Although he was not hard up financially, the situation enraged him, and it was during this period that his bowel movements became too frequent and finally colitis developed.

This patient had felt dominated, insecure, and unfairly treated in his relationship with his parents. His relationship with everyone else had the same qualities as that with his parents. He solved his conflicts chiefly by assuming a dominant, overbearing, ambitious, superior, self-centered attitude. This carried him along fairly well until his age and the economic depression made it impossible for him to maintain such an attitude successfully. The preference for younger men threatened his whole security system, his method of solving life problems. It was the threat to his overvalued picture of himself that aroused his anger and his anxiety. (Maslow and Mittelmann, 1951)

COLLECTIVE UNCONSCIOUS. A Jungian term denoting the portion of the unconscious which is common to all mankind. It is also called the racial unconscious.

In the theory of Carl Jung there are two divisions of the unconscious, the personal and the collective. In his own language, the personal unconscious "embraces all the acquisitions of the personal existence—hence the forgotten, the repressed, the subliminal, perceived, thought, and felt. But in addition to these personal unconscious contents, there exist other contents which do not originate in personal acquisitions but in the inherited possibility of psychic functioning in general, viz., in the inherited brain-structure. These are the mythological associations—those motives and images which can spring anew in every age and clime, without historical tradition or migration. I term these contents the *collective unconscious*" (1928).

Jung had this to say about the contents of the collective unconscious: "All those psychic contents I term collective which are peculiar not to one individual, but to many at the same time, i.e. either to a society, a people, or to mankind in general. Such contents are the 'mystical collective ideas' . . . of the primitive; they include also the general concepts of right, the state, religion, science, etc., current among civilized men." *See* JUNG.

COLOR BLINDNESS. A defect in the ability to discriminate between simple colors. John Dalton, the British chemist, who was himself color blind, gave the first accurate description of this disorder in 1794. For about a hundred years afterward it was known as Daltonism.

Color blindness takes many forms, ranging from simple color weakness to the complete inability to detect color differences. Some people have normal color vision in one eye and have some form of defect in the other. These rare individuals are invaluable for scientific research since they can report and compare normal and defective color perception of the same object.

There are three major categories of color blindness. In *anomalous trichromatism* the individual can respond to all three of the primary colors in the spectrum (red, blue, and yellow), but only if they are bright and vivid. However, he has trouble distinguishing pale colors such as tan, pink, and light green. This is a fairly common defect and many authorities describe it as color weakness rather than color blindness.

In *dichromatism* the individual responds to only two of the primary colors. This defect takes two basic forms, red-green and blue-yellow blindness. In the red-green variety, red, green, blue, and violet are difficult to differentiate, and all colors are seen as the same shade of yellow or blue. Some people are more insensitive to red hues (protanopia), others to green hues (deuteranopia). These are often called red blindness and green blindness respectively.

Red-green color blindness is by far the most common form. Between 4 and 8 per cent of males are affected, but only about 0.5 per cent of females. The reason for the greater prevalence of this defect among males is that it is a sex-linked recessive trait, transmitted by the mother.

In blue-yellow blindness all colors are seen as either red or green. This is a rare defect which is usually congenital but may also be due to a disease of the retina or optic nerve tract or both.

In *monochromatism,* or achromatism, the individual is totally color blind and everything is seen in different shades of gray. This form of the defect is extremely rare, occurring once in about 40,000 persons. There seem to be two different causes. In the congenital variety the "cones," or color-sensitive cells of the retina do not develop. Since these cells are the only kind found in the fovea of the eye, the person is blind in this area. In order to see at all, he must make jerky eye movements called "miner's nystagmus." Monochromatic individuals are extremely sensitive to light and often go about with half-closed eyelids. The defect is most often found in albinism, an inherited condition in which there is an absence of pigment cells throughout the body.

Color blindness can also be brought about as a result of injury or disease such as optic neuritis, lead poisoning, and carbon disulfide poisoning. Recovery is possible in these cases, but no adequate treatment for congenital color blindness has been found. There is no scientific justification for the claim that vitamin A cures the condition. It may, however, improve visual acuity to a point where a partially color-blind person can pass a color-vision test.

Color-blind individuals are frequently unaware of the defect unless they are tested and informed of the results. They do not miss color simply because they have never experienced it. Moreover, if they become aware of the defect, they are often able to hide it by learning the colors of common objects from other people.

There are various tests for color blindness. In one test (the Holmgren Test) a subject is required to sort strands of yarn on the basis of color. Red-green blind individuals will sort red and green strands into the same pile. This test is open to question since the yarns differ in both color and brightness and a person might sort them on the basis of brightness alone. The widely used Ishihara test consists of a series of cards containing dots of various colors. They are so arranged that numbers are formed by dots of a given color. People with normal color vision immediately see the numbers, but individuals with color defects are unable to read some or all of the numbers because the dots appear to be the same color as the background. This general principle is also used in more recently developed tests, such as the Dvorine Pseudo-Isochromatic Plates and the Hardy-Rand-Rittler Pseudo-Isochromatic Plates. The latter test employs colored triangles, circles, and squares instead of numbers so that it will be applicable to illiterate persons and children who have not yet learned to read. *See* COLOR PLATE 1.

The short, quickly administered Farnsworth Dichotomous Test For Color Blindness is a particularly useful screening instrument for industry, military service and vocational guidance purposes. The subject arranges plastic caps in order according to color. Normal response patterns can be determined by immediate inspection, and errors can be quickly plotted on a diagnostic chart. The Farnsworth Munsell 100-Hue Test for Color Discrimination is widely used not only in measuring color discrimination of color blind persons, but also in carrying out research on vision, and in selecting color graders, dye and paint mixers, and inspectors for jobs requiring accurate color discrimination.

Most color-blind people do not feel they are greatly handicapped. They learn to compensate by becoming more aware of brightness differences, and by remembering which articles of clothing go together. Color weakness can sometimes be remedied by wearing glasses with special filters, and even people who are red-green blind can read the traffic lights because the "go" is usually a blue green. Only a small number of occupations require keen color discrimination; John Dalton's defect did not prevent him from becoming a renowned figure in the exacting science of chemistry.

COLOR CIRCLE. A circular arrangement of chromatic colors in the order in which they appear in the spectrum. The purpose of the arrangement is to show the relationship between different colors and the results of color mixture.

The color circle can be pictured by imagining the visible spectrum bent completely around so that the red is next to the violet. When set up in this way, complementary colors appear exactly opposite each other on the circumference. However, it has been found that colors in the green region have no single complementary in the visible spectrum, and therefore impure colors called extraspectral purples (mixtures of blue and red) have been added to the circle in order to fulfill the requirement that complementary colors be found at opposite points.

The circle is also used to indicate the results of any mixture of two or more colors. The center of a line drawn from red to yellow falls in the orange region; therefore an equal mixture of the two will produce orange. If the colors are mixed in different proportions, the new color will be found somewhere between them—for example, a mixture of two parts of yellow and one part of red would be found at a point closer to the yellow.

The circle also predicts the saturation or purity of color mixtures. The center of the circle represents a neutral gray, and the closeness of any line to this point indicates how saturated or unsaturated a color mixture will be. The line between two complementary colors always goes through the center of the circle and therefore they will produce gray when mixed in equal proportions. The red-yellow mixture yields a highly saturated orange because the two colors are close together on the circumference and the line drawn between them does not come near the center. Red and green, on the other hand, lie nearly opposite each other and a connecting line indicates a yellow of low saturation because it passes close to the center of the figure.

Color circle principles apply only where surfaces emit or reflect light, but cannot be used for mixing paints since pigments reflect some wave lengths and absorb others. Blue paint, for example, reflects yellow-green, green, blue, and violet, but absorbs red, orange, and

yellow. Yellow and blue are complementary on the color circle, and yield gray when mixed on a revolving color wheel, but when yellow and blue pigments are combined, they produce green. Therefore in mixing paints the important thing is to determine what colors finally reach the eye.

COLOR REACTIONS. The most important fact here is that the organism as a whole, and not just the visual system, is involved in our reactions to color. We respond in special ways to colors not only because of their physiological effects, but because of the emotions and associations they evoke.

The so-called "advancing" colors—yellow, orange, and red—appear to be nearer to the observer than the "receding" colors, green, blue, and blue-green. The advancing colors suggest warmth and the receding colors coolness—but this is probably due less to the suggestion of nearness than to the association of the red end of the spectrum with fire and sun, and the blue-green end with the coolness of a forest or a body of water. Psychological studies have supported the common observation that different colors suggest different moods. Wexner (1954) found that red is usually rated as exciting, stimulating, or hostile; blue as serene, tender, peaceful; orange as distressed, upset; black as either melancholy or powerful.

In view of such associations it is not surprising that our language uses various colors to express emotional states. A depressed person is "blue" and, as the song tells us, his mood is indigo. Red-haired girls are supposed to be fiery and passionate. Yellow is the mark of cowardice and green the color of envy. The explanation of these associations is often a matter of conjecture. Perhaps blue suggests depression because we tend to be dejected and lonely at night when the sky is indigo. The association of fiery hair with fiery temperament seems clear enough, though the facts do not bear it out. But what about cowardice and envy—are they yellow and green because in these emotional reactions the stomach is upset, excess yellow bile is secreted, and the natural color is drained from the cheeks? *See* DIFFERENTIAL PSYCHOLOGY.

Color preferences have been investigated from time to time, but few generalizations can be made. The idea that combinations of complementaries are particularly pleasing seems to stand up; so does the idea that colors next to each other on the spectrum (red and orange, for example) are often distasteful. For most people red and blue rank above orange and yellow, and men as a whole tend to prefer red more often than blue, and the other way around for women. However, these generalizations are frequently upset by two factors: the highly individual preferences that grow out of special associations and experiences; and the "decrees" of the prevailing fashion, which exert a strong suggestive effect on our preferences, however transient they may be.

People react differently under different kinds of illumination. When a person is asked to stretch his arms out in front of him, he will spread them farther apart under red light than under green light. Under red light he will also tend to overestimate time, judge weights to be heavier and lines to be longer than they actually are (Goldstein, 1942). Subjects have also been found to react more quickly than usual under red light, and slower than usual when the illumination is blue or green (Birren, 1961). These findings have been applied with some success to stimulating depressed patients and calming excited patients.

Recently investigators have uncovered what is called the color-stereo effect (Kohler, 1962). Various colored patches —red, blue, orange, green, yellow—are placed side by side at random in a rectangle. If this mosaic of colors is viewed with the outer half of each eye shielded with a card, the patches will appear to be at different depths. Blue and green squares seem to float above the others; red is farthest away (contrary to the view that red is an "advancing" color). Some people with prismatic defects of the eye can obtain this effect under normal viewing conditions. The reason is that it is produced by the lens, which bends light according to wave lengths, so that hues of different wave lengths may appear to be at different distances from the viewer. Investigators have speculated that early in the development of the vertebrate eye, colors may not have been associated with hue but with subtle differences in depths of images. This color-stereo ability may explain why a small percentage of certain animals known to be color blind—cats and mice, for example—can distinguish between strong colors on visual tests. *See* ESTHETICS, ADVERTISING RESEARCH.

COLOR SOLID. A three-dimensional figure representing all degrees and combinations of hue, saturation, and brightness in the perception of color; also called the color cone, color pyramid, and color spindle.

The color solid is an extension of the color circle to include the dimension of brightness. In the color circle all the hues in the spectrum (plus purple) are arranged around the circle according to wave length, and the degree of saturation or purity is indicated by distance from the center. The color solid adds a cone on the top side of the circle to show colors of increasing brightness, and another cone on the bottom side to represent colors of decreasing brightness. The distance from the basic circle shows the degree of brightness and darkness, with maximum brightness at the point of the top cone and maximum darkness at the peak of the bottom cone. The straight line between these two points, passing through the center of the circle, represents only varying degrees of brightness, that is, the black-white dimension, since hue and saturation are both lacking along this line.

To picture the color solid more vividly, imagine a series of color circles of increasing size piled above and below the basic color circle. Starting from the basic circle itself, these layers become lighter and lighter as you go up and darker and darker as you go down. Hues toward the outer rim of each circle are richer (more saturated), while those toward the center are paler (less saturated). But note that the layers also become smaller and smaller as they get farther away from the basic circle. The reason is that the greatest range of saturation is found in colors of medium brightness—that is, the point where the color solid is widest—and the range of saturation decreases as the hues approach pure white and pure black.

Color studies have shown that the color solid should not be perfectly symmetrical, since the relationships are not quite so uniform as it indicates—for example, a highly saturated yellow is much brighter than a well-saturated blue. Nevertheless every combination of hue, saturation, and brightness lies within its boundaries, and there is no better way to show the impressive array of colors that can be perceived by the human eye. If an accurate three-dimensional color solid were constructed, showing every gradation, it is estimated that the total number of distinguishable colors would come to no less than 7.5 million.

COLOR VISION THEORIES. Many theories of color vision have been offered by physicists and physiological psychologists, and at least five are in active competition today. No single theory appears to fit all the facts, and the issue will probably not be decided until we know more about the chemistry of the cells of the eye and the effect of light upon them.

The Young-Helmholtz theory, first advanced in the early eighteen hundreds and later revised by Hecht, holds that there are three kinds of cones in the retina, each sensitive to a different wave length of light. Stimulation of one kind of cone, or color-sensitive cell, yields red, another blue and another green. Yellow is believed to be produced by the simultaneous stimulation of red and green cones, and white by an equal stimulation of all three types. Supporters of the theory point out that all the colors in the visible spectrum can be produced by mixing the three basic colors. Critics, however, contend that yellow is actually a primary color and not secondary to red and green. They also claim that the theory does not explain the facts of color blindness— that is, color blindness usually runs in pairs (red-green, yellow-blue), and people who are red-green blind can still see yellow. Moreover, white-black vision is unimpaired in color-blind persons, in spite of the fact that in the theory white is supposed to be a combination of red, green, and blue.

The Hering Theory, first proposed in 1878 and now known as the opponent-colors theory, assumes that there are three *sets* of cones, all of which are able to function in opposing ways. One set is sensitive to white and black, another to red and green, and the third to yellow and blue. The breaking down, or catabolism, of these substances is supposed to yield one of these pairs (white, yellow, or red), while the building up, or anabolism, of the same substances yields the other (black, green, or blue). Some authorities believe this theory takes into account all the phenomena of color blindness, and also squares with the laws of color mixture and complementary colors. Critics point out that the nerve fibers leading from the cones to the brain must carry two different kinds of impulses, one for the anabolic and one for the catabolic activities, and this runs counter to the "law of specific energies" which states that any given nerve cell reacts in a particular way and only in one way. In answer to this criticism it has been proposed that there may be *four* color cones instead of only two, but they function in opponent-pairs. However, this revision is also considered questionable. *See* SPECIFIC ENERGIES.

In 1929, Christine Ladd-Franklin advanced the theory that red, green, blue, and yellow all have separate receptors. These receptors, however, evolved slowly from a first stage in which organisms possessed only achromatic, black-white sensitive rods through a stage of yellow-blue receptors, with red-green receptors later developing out of the yellow-sensitive cones. This theory seems to account for yellow as a basic color, and for the different types of color blindness. It also offers an explanation for the fact that red-green blindness is more prevalent than blue-yellow: it developed later in the course of evolution and is therefore less firmly grounded in the organism. Red-green blindness, then, is therefore a regression to a more primitive stage of development, while total color blindness, which may be genetic, is a still further throwback. The theory also seems to account for the fact that the blue-yellow zone of the retina extends farther toward the periphery than the red-green area, since it started earlier in the course of evolution and had a longer time to develop. Critics point out that this theory cannot explain the fact that red blindness and green blindness are sometimes two separate disorders. According to the theory, they should always be found together, since they would be caused by a defect in the splitting of the yellow into red and green. There is also evidence against the evolutionary theory of color zones in the fact that the red and green fields do not coincide in the retina, nor do the blue and

yellow. But the strongest evidence against the theory is the supposition that the same types of receptors respond to different kinds of color stimulation. It seems more reasonable to assume that cells containing different chemical substances are sensitive to different kinds of light.

Another theory has been developed by Ragnar Granit (1959) on the basis of experimentation involving electrical stimulation of extremely small areas of the retina. Granit claims he has found three different types of receptors, which he has termed (a) scotopic dominators, consisting of rods that are most sensitive at 500 millimicrons, (b) photopic dominators, certain cones that are most sensitive at 560 millimicrons, and (c) photopic modulators, other cones which are sensitive to very narrow frequency ranges. The sensation of hue is attributed to activity of the modulators, and brightness is due to stimulation of the dominators. Color blindness is explained as a defect of the particular modulator cells responsible for the missing color sensations, and dark adaptation is explained by the shift from the photopic to the scotopic dominators when illumination is low.

E. H. Land (1959), inventor of the Polaroid camera, offers still another approach, based on the idea that color registration is carried out in the brain rather than in the retina. His theory arose from experiments in which two black and white photographs (positive transparencies) were made of the same group of colored objects, one taken with a red filter and the other with a green filter placed over the shutter. The two pictures were slightly different, since the red filter only allows the long wave lengths to be registered and the green filter only the short wave lengths —in other words, the photos produced a "color separation" through selective filtering. Land found that when these two photos were projected on a screen by means of lights of different wave lengths—for example, a longer wave length yellow light for the red filter picture and a shorter wave length light for the green filter picture—an amazing thing happened. The resulting picture showed all the original colors as well as the blacks and whites!

This experiment and others of a similar nature suggested that the perception of color is not due to the stimulation of the visual receptors by different wave lengths, but results from the process of comparing longer and shorter wave lengths over the entire visual scene. More specifically, the various wave lengths register on the color-sensitive components of the retina as a large number color-separated "photographs." The visual mechanism in the brain then acts as a computer, averaging together and comparing the long wave photos with the average of the shorter wave photos, and assigning different colors to them according to the ratios between them.

This explanation is undoubtedly ingenious and revolutionary, but it has not gone unchallenged. G. L. Walls (1960) maintains that the effects obtained in the Land experiments could all be predicted from information already known, and that his work can be integrated into existing theories. The final decision, however, must be left to future research.

COMBAT REACTIONS. Traumatic reactions to the combat conditions of war. Typical symptoms are weariness, irritability, depression, tremors, and sleep disturbances.

The American Psychiatric Association now classifies combat reactions as "gross stress reactions," and places them under the general heading of "transient situational personality disorders." The term gross stress reactions is used because they involve a severe response to an overwhelming threat; and they are classified as transient disorders because they generally clear up rapidly when the combat situation is over or when short-term therapy is administered.

It is important, however, to recognize that some combat reactions result from deeply embedded personality disturbances which are aggravated by the war situation. These reactions are genuine neuroses (and in some cases psychoses), as opposed to transient situational disorders. Such reactions usually require long-term therapy.

During the Civil War the phrase "irritable heart of soldiers" was used to describe the typical reaction to combat. In World War I, when artillery fire reached high intensity, the term "shell shock" came into use. It was thought that tremors, confusion, paralysis, and other common battle symptoms were due to minor brain hemorrhages or other effects of concussion produced by exploding shells and bombs. Most soldiers accepted the idea of brain injury, especially since it meant that they would be evacuated from the front lines to base hospitals. However, it was gradually recognized that shell shock was primarily a psychological condition, and that prolonged hospitalization only served to fix the symptoms more firmly.

During World War II, psychiatrists discovered that the recovery rate was much higher if they treated these cases near the front lines and gave the men assurance that their condition was only temporary and did not involve organic damage. As a consequence new terms were applied to this reaction, among them "operational fatigue" and "war neurosis." Finally, the army adopted the classification "combat exhaustion" for nearly all the types of psychiatric casualties, since this term implied that the condition was the logical and "honorable" result of the strain of fighting, and would clear up after a short period of recuperation. The term was not, of course, fully accurate since it played down the factor of emotional stress and anxiety in battle reactions.

During World War II an estimated

10 per cent of men in combat developed severe enough combat-exhaustion symptoms to be evacuated from the front lines. Many others received help at battle-aid stations and were returned to combat within a few hours. Of the ten million men accepted for military service, 1,363,000 were given medical discharges, 39 per cent for neuropsychiatric disorders. This percentage was reduced to about 25 per cent in the Korean conflict as a result of improved psychiatric care, and also because of more effective screening procedures at the time of induction. Following World War II, over one half of all patients in Veterans Administration hospitals were psychiatric cases.

There is no universal set of symptoms in combat cases, since there is wide variation in both the traumatic experience and the personalities of servicemen. The branch of service may also make a difference. There is some evidence that dejection, hypersensitivity, sleep disturbances, tremors, and fatigue are most frequent among combat troops; while anxiety, depression, irritability, phobias, and startle reactions are most likely to be found among combat fliers. In spite of these differences there are many common features, particularly in the preliminary symptoms. The first evidence of combat exhaustion is usually increased irritability with angry flare-ups at slight frustrations; sensitivity to noise ("hyperacusis"), light, and sudden movement; and various sleep disturbances, including inability to fall asleep, battle dreams, and nightmares. These incipient symptoms were so common in World War II and the Korean conflict that psychiatric care could not be administered in all cases. In some instances, however, the incipient symptoms developed into acute reactions after particularly traumatic experiences or an accumulation of stress resulting from a prolonged campaign. William Menninger has given the following picture of typical psychological casualties treated at a battle aid station:

"In the majority of cases they followed a stereotyped pattern: 'I just can't take it any more'; 'I can't stand those shells'; 'I just couldn't control myself.' They varied little from patient to patient. Whether it was the soldier who had experienced his baptism of fire or the older veteran who had lost his comrades, the superficial result was very similar. Typically he appeared as a dejected, dirty, weary man. His facial expression was one of depression, sometimes of tearfulness. Frequently his hands were trembling or jerking. Occasionally he would display varying degrees of confusion, perhaps to the extent of being mute or staring into space. Very occasionally he might present classically hysterical symptoms." (Menninger, 1948)

Many men suffered severe and persistent psychological disturbances. Among these were repeated anxiety attacks, constant tension, and inability to relax, depression with acute guilt feelings, defensive rituals and ceremonials (for example, being able to sleep only if their clothing is arranged in a certain order), classic conversion symptoms (blindness, paralysis, deafness, camptocormia or "bent back"), stupor, amnesia with a loss of interest in the world, or phobias centering around guns or trenches or officers or almost anything else associated with the war situation. *See* SYNCOPE.

It is interesting that anxiety states and other combat symptoms were seldom found among severely wounded men (except where they were permanently maimed), since their injuries enabled them to escape from combat. It is interesting, too, that some soldiers who managed to hold up well under combat conditions developed delayed combat reactions after returning home. Apparently their psychological reserves had been depleted by the traumatic experiences of war.

The common source of these symptoms of combat neurosis is the continual, catastrophic threat of injury and loss of life that occurs in war. The soldier mobilizes all his emotional and physical resources but finds that the adjustive devices that work well enough in civilian life are inadequate to meet these threats. He then develops an overwhelming sense of anxiety that disorganizes his behavior and increases his feelings of tension and fatigue. As a consequence he reacts with irritability, tremors, or startle reactions, and may unconsciously seek relief and escape through such symptoms as stupor, amnesia, or hysterical paralysis.

Many men were able to endure almost unimaginable stress without breaking down; others became psychiatric casualties after relatively mild combat experience. What makes the difference? Biological factors are hard to assess, although it may be assumed that constitutional differences in emotional and physical make-up have a considerable effect. A somewhat lower incidence of mental illness has been found in the families of successful rather than unsuccessful soldiers, but the difference is not considered proof of hereditary predisposition. Moreover, mental illness has been found in the families of many stable servicemen. Most authorities, however, agree that severe biological factors such as extreme fatigue, insufficient food and sleep, debilitating climatic conditions, and constant emotional tension contribute materially to breakdown by lowering the fighting man's stress tolerance. This occurs most often in individuals who are psychologically vulnerable.

A large number of psychological factors, operating on different levels, pave the way for combat reactions. First, immature, overprotected individuals find it difficult to endure the stresses of war. Many of them develop symptoms long before they reach the combat zone, since they cannot tolerate separation from home and submission to discipline. Some authorities believe a faulty home background is the major predisposing factor. Second, special situations which put an emotional burden on the man may reduce his ability to withstand battle conditions. Two types of situations have been found particularly destructive: domestic difficulties, such as economic strains or the illness or infidelity of the wife; and the death of a buddy, which deprives the man of emotional support and in some cases arouses feelings of guilt for not having done more to save him. Third, the strangeness of the battle situation overwhelms many men, especially when new conditions arise for which they have not been prepared. Fourth, the necessity of killing the enemy arouses intense conflicts and guilt feelings in many men; in some cases these reactions are aggravated by an unconscious fear of retaliation and punishment. The resulting anxiety and depression are sometimes severe enough to incapacitate the man. See TALION LAW.

Fifth, many soldiers derive emotional support from the feeling "It can't happen to me"; but as time goes on and their buddies are killed, they begin to feel "My number is coming up." This conviction undermines their sense of security and leads to acute feelings of dread and apprehension. Sixth, conflicts between devotion to duty and the impulse to escape from combat have a weakening effect on some men, particularly after they have been through a long and debilitating period of combat. Finally, the emotional armor of many men is corroded by psychological factors of a social nature. Among these are lack of group solidarity and *esprit de corps* in their unit, disgruntlement over crowded or unfair conditions, ineffectual leadership or lack of confidence in leaders, and failure to understand the reason for fighting. Poor motivation and poor morale not only reduce the effectiveness of soldiers but weaken their resistance to battle stress.

It is a curious fact that although highly immature and severely maladjusted individuals do not fare well in the service, many genuinely neurotic men stand up far better than expected. Some of them have developed compensatory patterns of determination, perseverance, and attachment to comrades that serve them well; others have become so accustomed to anxiety that they are better able to cope with it than normal individuals who have little or no practice in enduring inner tension. In some cases both neurotics and antisocial individuals maintain their stability and become good soldiers because they are able to direct their aggressive drives against an external enemy.

The treatment of combat reactions underwent a drastic change during World War II and the Korean War. To forestall the development of persistent and incapacitating symptoms, treatment centers were set up as close to the front lines as possible. Psychological and medical "first aid" were given in the form of supportive psychotherapy, good food, and sedation that would counteract tension and ensure sleep. In most cases the men were able to return to combat within a day or two. See EMERGENCY PSYCHOTHERAPY.

In the Korean War special efforts were made to reduce the factor of gain from psychiatric illness by fostering a "duty-expectant" attitude—that is, the idea that every man is expected to perform his duty, and that feelings of anxiety and tension are not a sufficient reason for removal from the battle scene. This attitude, plus the presence of psychiatric personnel in the forward area, encouraged the idea that a serviceman must accept his symptoms as part of the situation. This approach was believed to be chiefly responsible for a 30 per cent reduction in the psychiatric casualty rate over that in World War II.

As for actual treatment, much of it was carried out in forward areas. Severe and disabling symptoms, such as mutism and amnesia, were frequently alleviated by psychotherapy administered under sodium pentothal. The drug paved the way for the release of repressed fears and guilt feelings, and enabled the patient to discharge tensions by reliving the traumatic event that brought them on. Discussion with the therapist then helped him accept and assimilate the experience. See NARCOSYNTHESIS.

Basically unstable and maladjusted individuals sometimes developed neurotic disturbances (usually paralyses or other hysterical or hypochondriacal symptoms) which had to be treated in rear-area hospitals. In such cases standard civilian methods were followed, except for the greater use of group therapy. The large majority were able to return to non-combat or even combat duty. Some men with psychotic symptoms were also successfully treated in these hospitals, but a few of the more resistant cases had to be evacuated to the United States.

Remarkable progress has been made in the treatment of combat neurosis. At the beginning of World War II, when these casualties were treated in base hospitals far behind the front lines, only 10 per cent were able to return to duty; in the Korean War the percentage increased to between 50 and 90 per cent depending on whether the men belonged to an old or new division. It must be recognized, however, that in some cases the symptoms of combat reaction, such as anxiety, depression, and tension may persist for years in spite of treatment. This is particularly likely to happen when the psychological condition is complicated by a permanent physical disability. See BEHAVIOR THERAPY.

COMMON COLD. Practically all recent research on the common cold has been devoted to finding the viruses which are believed to be responsible for this unpleasant condition. While considerable progress has been made in this direction, there is also increasing recognition that the state of the organism itself determines whether the virus will take hold and produce the usual symptoms. Evidence for this lies in the fact that some individuals are more susceptible to colds than others, and that the same person may have greater resistance at one time than at another. Studies have shown, for example, that if people are exposed to infected nasal secretions, only about one half of them will develop symptoms— and this apparently has nothing to do with the season of the year, the length of time since the last cold, or even drafty surroundings. While some of this susceptibility is probably due to physical conditions, such as fatigue or sensitivity of the nasal passages, there is a growing conviction that emotional factors "can also alter the permeability of the mucosa (mucous membranes) or modify immune responses" through the autonomic nervous system (Wittkower and White, 1959).

As these authors point out, there is at present only limited evidence for the effects of emotion on the common cold, but what there is, is highly suggestive. Despert (1944) carefully recorded the absences of children from nursery school which were attributed to colds, and found that they totaled twice as many for eight children from broken homes as for eight children from especially happy families. In a larger sample, she found a close though by no means perfect relationship between colds and emotional stress. Richter (1943) has observed that respiratory infections may be the *cause* as well as the effect of emotional disturbances in children, and are particularly likely to produce apathy and depression. Holmes et al. (1951) found evidence of repressed resentment in patients with repeated colds, and suggested that disturbances of the respiratory tract are attempts at ridding

the organism not only of physical irritants but of emotional irritants.

A number of psychoanalysts have reported that some patients develop colds, laryngitis, or other respiratory ailments while working through important conflicts, or while repressing feelings of rage. Alexander and Saul (1940) found that colds either disappeared entirely or became less frequent following successful psychoanalytic treatment for other complaints. One patient, for example, had colds whenever she became distressed or panicky as a result of being denied affection and attention. This is a reminder that colds often yield "secondary gains" in terms of sympathy and concern from others or temporary escape from unpleasant situations. Redlich and Freedman (1966) make this comment, "It is a common clinical observation that the common cold follows slights, humiliations, and disappointments in love," and quote Friedrich Nietzsche's remark, "Contentment preserves one even from catching cold. Has a woman who knew that she was well dressed ever caught cold? No, not even when she had scarcely a rag on her back."

At the present time there are not enough data on which to base any general conclusions on this or any other line, especially since there is always the possibility that a cold may be due to such physical factors as infection, allergens, or changes in temperature and humidity. But it also has to be borne in mind that emotional tension may render the organism more susceptible to these factors.

COMMUNITY MENTAL HEALTH CENTERS. In 1963 Congress passed the Community Mental Health Centers Act, authorizing an appropriation of 150 million dollars to finance up to two-thirds of the cost of construction of comprehensive treatment facilities in communities throughout the country. This act was the direct outcome of

President Kennedy's message to Congress asking for "a bold new approach," as well as recommendations made by the Joint Commission on Mental Illness and Health in 1961, and by the National Congress on Mental Illness and Health held by the American Medical Association in 1962.

The object of these centers is to offer a practical alternative to the inadequate and costly custodial care generally given mental patients: "The persons treated in these community centers need never leave home for the strange and lonely mental hospital which for years has been a world apart." The entire plan has been made possible by the development of new techniques, such as tranquilizing drugs, and by the growing evidence that many people who would ordinarily be "put away" can be treated through part-time hospitalization or outpatient care in their own communities. Experiments along these lines led to the idea of assembling all services into one community entity, so that treatment could be individually tailored to the patient's needs and given without having him leave his family or, in most cases, his job or school.

According to present proposals, the plan for each center must be an integral part of a comprehensive state plan, but it must at the same time reflect the special needs and resources of each community. In general, a comprehensive mental health center should offer these services, though not necessarily under one roof: (1) Inpatient treatment for emergency cases, or those needing twenty-four-hour care for a limited time; (2) outpatient programs offering individual and group treatment to adults, children, and families without a waiting period; (3) hospitalization on a day basis for patients able to return home at night and on weekends, and on a night basis for those who can work or attend school; (4) consultation to physicians, clergymen, schools, health departments, and welfare agencies concerning emotional problems of individuals; (5) full diagnostic services prior to admission; (6) rehabilitation through vocational, educational, and social programs for both current patients and former hospital patients; (7) pre-care and after-care, including foster homes or halfway houses, and home visiting; (8) training for all types of mental health personnel; (9) research and evaluation of results. Implementation of these services will require a full complement of psychiatrists, general practitioners, clinical psychologists, psychiatric social workers, mental health nurses, occupational therapists and counselors, research specialists, and volunteers from the community.

Although the federal government provides most of the funds for planning and building these centers, local communities must supply the leadership that will secure public acceptance, and the unified direction that is necessary to co-ordinate all services into one all-embracing agency. So far it has been found that a new center can best get its start through expanding the services of an existing agency, such as a general hospital which already provides inpatient, outpatient, day, night, and home care; a county health department already providing clinics, rehabilitation service and specialized treatment units for alcoholics, delinquents and disturbed children; or a community or county psychiatric center that offers emergency treatment, family therapy, and consultation to agencies, courts and schools. In some areas, however, a comprehensive center may have to start from scratch by developing a basic treatment program on an inpatient, outpatient, and day-care basis. In any case, it is hoped that the concept of community care will usher in a new era in dealing with the mental health problem. *See* JOINT COMMISSION ON MENTAL ILLNESS AND HEALTH.

COMMUNITY PSYCHIATRY. A recently developed specialty defined by

Hume (1966) as "the maximum utilization of community resources in the identification, treatment, or rehabilitation of the mentally ill or retarded." It is "simultaneously treatment-oriented, prevention-oriented, and community-oriented for the purpose of reducing to a minimum, by all discoverable means, the mental disorders of a given population."

Community psychiatry overlaps with both preventive psychiatry and social psychiatry. In common with preventive psychiatry (in the fullest sense of the term), it aims at primary prevention (promotion of conditions that forestall development of mental disorder), secondary prevention (early treatment to prevent further development of disorder), and tertiary prevention (application of rehabilitative measures to prevent or reduce handicaps resulting from disorder). In common with social psychiatry it is concerned with the impact of the social setting on mental health and psychiatric practice. The specialty has developed out of both of these areas, and has also been fed by the fields of school psychiatry, industrial psychiatry, military psychiatry, correctional psychiatry, and administrative psychiatry. Historically speaking, it has evolved from such sources as the mental hygiene movement originated by Beers, the child guidance clinics of the 20s and 30s, the National Mental Health Act of 1946, the creation of The National Institute for Mental Health in 1949, the report of the Joint Commission on Mental Illness, the development of the public health point of view, and the community mental health centers program.

The major areas and objectives of community psychiatry are: (1) the development of comprehensive clinical services in the community, with emphasis on outpatient and extramural services to keep as many people as possible out of mental institutions; (2) the development of a community program

uniting the efforts of all nonpsychiatric organizations and individuals whose work has a bearing on mental health, including general hospitals, health departments, schools, welfare and family agencies, churches, industries, labor unions, legislative bodies, courts and prisons, lay leaders, and volunteers; (3) the promotion of epidemiological research focused on the natural history, distribution, and incidence of mental disorders in the population in order to isolate social and environmental factors that contribute to these disorders (as in the case of pellagra and general paresis); and (4) the development of a corps of psychiatrists to serve as mental health consultants, or community mental health specialists, working on either a client-centered or a program-centered basis. In his client-centered activities, the psychiatrist is concerned with diagnostic evaluation and recommendation of treatment. In his program-centered activities, he serves as administrator (planning, organizing, and directing programs and services); research director (developing and supervising projects); educator (developing and teaching courses for various institutions); and consultant in preventive psychiatry to various community services as well as to lay leaders, health educators, legislators, and others outside the psychiatric and welfare agencies.

The field of community psychiatry is extremely complex. In her account, Hume lists a huge number of activities involved in carrying out a co-ordinated program. The following enumeration will aim only at indicating their variety: surveys and assessments of community organizations, leadership and public interest in mental health problems; collection of data on the character of the population, characteristics of the community, and specific local mental health problems; analysis of the administration of present programs; development of policies and standards for mental health jobs, staff training and development, managerial and supervisory functions, interagency co-ordination, informational and educational services, and financing; promotion of research, including experimental methods, case studies, surveys, biostatistical data-collection, epidemiological studies, and program evaluation; development of clinical methods and services aimed at maximum utilization of resources, including new techniques of consultation and collaborative treatment; primary prevention aimed at eradication of specific factors causing breakdowns, including harmful social policies, as well as positive measures for maintaining mental health, such as anticipatory guidance and counseling; development of services directed to early case-finding, handling of psychiatric emergencies, inpatient and outpatient treatment, vocational training, rehabilitation, re-education, home nursing, sheltered workshops, halfway houses, etc.; and indirect mental health services through education of nonpsychiatric personnel (public health nurses, teachers, supervisors, child-care workers), and general education of the public through films, lectures, discussion groups, television, etc.

Training for the field of community psychiatry is still available in only a few centers and is largely limited to psychiatrists, though it is now being broadened to include clinical psychologists, public health nurses, and psychiatric social workers. Leading institutions in the field are Johns Hopkins, Harvard, Columbia, University of California, Berkeley, and the Menninger Foundation.

COMPENSATION. The tendency to develop strength in one area to offset weakness in another.

Compensation may be a deliberate, conscious reaction, an unconscious defense mechanism, or a mixture of the two. Many people deliberately try to counterbalance their physical handicaps, deficiencies in skill, or even their personality defects by developing special abilities. The blind man concentrates on his senses of touch and hearing, the homely girl designs clothes for the social élite, the timid boy becomes a chess expert.

No sharp line can be drawn between compensation as an adjustment device and as a defense mechanism. Generally speaking, however, it is likely to be a defense mechanism if it is grossly exaggerated or unconsciously adopted as a protection against anxiety. The braggart, the show-off, the "Royal Imperial Potentate" of the lodge, are not aware that they are responding to feelings of inferiority. The small man who develops a pompous, overbearing manner, and the woman from a "lowly" background who strives for the social register usually do not realize that they are reacting to a sense of inadequacy.

Compensation may be a powerful motive for achievement and an effective force in adapting ourselves to handicaps that cannot be corrected. It may lead to increased emotional security and greater self-esteem, and in this way may contribute to sound mental health. But in some forms, such as intense competitiveness or tyrannical behavior, it does more harm than good. It may also be a factor in clearly neurotic or psychotic behavior. In fugue states, for example, the individual may not only unconsciously seek to escape from distressing situations, but to compensate for his deficiencies or frustrations by losing his identity and acting like a totally different person. In cases of brain impairment due to infection or injury, the patient sometimes develops grandiose delusions as a compensation for his reduced capacities. A similar reaction occurs in the paranoid type of schizophrenia in which the patient may become convinced that he is a great savior or a great sinner. See ADLER, SCHIZOPHRENIA (PARANOID TYPE), DEFENSE MECHANISM, FUGUE STATE, GRANDIOSE DELUSIONS.

COMPENSATION NEUROSIS (Accident Neurosis). A psychoneurotic reaction following a real or presumed disability which involves the question of financial compensation for injury or disease.

Compensation neurosis is a genuine disorder which usually falls into the category of conversion reaction. It may also take the form of anxiety reaction, hypochondriasis, or mixed neurosis. At one time it was thought that the desire for compensation was the principal if not the only factor in these reactions, but personality studies have indicated that suggestibility and the desire for attention or escape from a disagreeable work situation may also play a part. If someone in the family, or even the physician, remarks on how badly the individual looks after the accident, he may become convinced that he is going to be disabled. This conviction may actually aggravate his condition, and at the same time suggest that he has a perfect right to indemnification. At this point the lines between true neurosis, deliberate self-deception, and outright malingering (faking) begin to blur. *See* IATROGENIC ILLNESS, MALINGERING.

This problem becomes even harder to resolve when several further points are taken into consideration. First, compensation neuroses are more likely to develop after slight than after obvious and detectable injuries. Are they exaggerated consciously or unconsciously? Second, accident neuroses rarely occur when the victim must bear the financial responsibility. Third, there is often a considerable time gap between the accident and the appearance of the chronic disability, particularly when suggestion or other emotional factors are involved—and sometimes it does not make its appearance until after the patient returns to his job. Fourth, when the possibility of financial compensation is mentioned, the patient often vehemently denies that he wants it, but at

the same time he does not seem vitally concerned about getting rid of his symptoms. Fifth, certain disorders appear to be more prevalent in countries where they are compensable—for example, "writer's cramp" is compensable in England and seems to occur more often there than in the United States where it is not compensable.

Finally, there is little doubt that the present availability of industrial compensation has increased the number of compensation neuroses—that is, cases where no disabling physical injury can be found. These patients are not malingerers, but people who are predisposed to neurotic reactions—and it seems that they are unconsciously encouraged to develop these reactions by the benefits they might receive. On the other hand, it is often found that they recover with startling rapidity once they have received compensation! As a possible way of handling this problem, Dr. Howard Rusk has proposed that insurance carriers pay for rehabilitation and retraining instead of giving the claimant a lump sum.

It is hard to make black and white judgments on this whole question since there is undoubtedly a mixture of motives as well as a mingling of different levels of consciousness. This complexity is reflected in the oft-quoted statement that compensation neurosis is "a state of mind, born of fear, kept alive by avarice, stimulated by lawyers, and cured by verdict" (as stated in Hinsie and Campbell, 1960).

Illustrative Case: COMPENSATION NEUROSIS

A thirty-three-year-old married woman was referred by her family physician to a neurosurgical service because of severe pain in the back and legs. Her legs were weak and she had a pulling sensation in her toes. The neurological examination revealed no organic basis for her symptoms and she was referred to the psychiatric division.

In an evaluative interview she related without emotion that she had been in pain for eighteen months since an accident. It was striking that she remembered the exact date, and even the hour, of the accident. After a party she had been waiting for her husband to bring the car around when a man who had been drinking heavily came up to her and pushed her; she sat down sharply and felt pains going down both her legs. The next day the pains returned and she reported fainting twice. "I first started to feel pain when I was laying the table for breakfast," she said. Although X rays ordered by her physician were negative she continued to feel stiff and sore and her symptoms interfered with her ability to do housework, prepare meals for her family, or have sexual relations with her husband. She was very angry with the man who pushed her and felt that he should pay all medical expenses incurred as a result of the accident. Her lawyer advised her not to accept a final settlement of her claim until she was completely well.

Inquiry into her earlier history revealed that she was the third of four children and had two older sisters and a younger brother. The brother received a great deal of attention throughout their childhood. She grew up in a lower-middle-class family which emphasized comformity, did not permit the expression of anger and provided the girls with little sexual information. She married two years after graduation from high school. The following year, shortly after a child was born, her husband left her. She described him, in a somewhat whining voice, as an irresponsible man who slapped her and was "terribly mean" to her. She obtained a divorce and lived with her parents until a second marriage, at the age of twenty-two, to a considerably older man who was a law enforcement inspector and resembled her moralistic father in many ways. A child was born the following year. Her husband was considerate and a good provider and she maintained that her second marriage was satisfactory in every respect. She claimed that their sexual relationship had been satisfactory but she was noticeably untroubled by the cessation of sexual relations since the accident. The interviewer felt that she was narcissistic, with little feeling for other people and with a tendency to use the defense of denial. Her MMPI was marked by elevations on the hysteria and hypochondriasis scales.

The general symptomatic picture of a conversion reaction was consistent with this test pattern. A definite predisposition to neurosis seemed to be present. Following a strong childhood emphasis on conformity she had chosen an irresponsible husband for neurotic reasons, apparently in revolt against her parents. However, he frightened her and after her divorce she married a "safer" man with whom she could feel secure, but unconsciously she displaced her hostility from the first husband onto the second and punished him by withholding herself sexually. Since the latter resembled her father, she could also continue to lash back at parental values in her second marriage. Her conversion reaction was thus an expression of hostility whose roots lay in childhood, as well as an escape from the drudgery of housework and a way of obtaining medical attention and financial compensation. She was extremely reluctant to accept emotional disturbance as the basis for her symptoms and resisted the recommendation that she accept final settlement of her compensation claim and enter outpatient psychotherapy. (Rosen and Gregory, 1965)

COMPETITION. There is no more complex question in the field of psychology than that of competition. Early in the century this drive was labeled an instinct, an "explanation" that seemed to settle the problem entirely—that is, until social psychologists began to look closely at the behavior of groups, child development specialists focused their attention on the early years of life, students of animal behavior performed experiments on social relationships, cultural anthropologists investigated widely scattered societies, and sociologists joined hands with psychologists in studying behavior on different socioeconomic levels. The combined effect of all these assaults has been to show that the competitive drive is not only learned rather than instinctual, but that its expression is dependent on a large number of factors, including early upbringing, reinforcements and rewards, social pressures, and cultural values.

Comparative studies of society have indicated that competitive behavior can be dominant and pervasive in one culture and practically nonexistent in another. No more dramatic illustration can be given than Ruth Benedict's contrast between the Kwakiutl and Zuñi tribes (Benedict, 1934). Among the Kwakiutl the tribesmen use gifts as competitive weapons in the ceremonial feast called the potlatch. One man gives fifty blankets to another, but the recipient must give him, in turn, a larger number or else face humiliation. The competition goes back and forth until one of them is bankrupt and may even commit suicide. The Zuñi, on the other hand, frown upon any sort of competition. If any family loses its crops, others in the tribe automatically come to its assistance. Similar observations have been made among Hopi, Arapesh, and Pueblo Indians. Such examples argue strongly that the competitive drive is not inborn but learned.

We actually do not have to go beyond our own society to find evidence on this point. Middle-class upbringing often puts a heavy emphasis on goals that can be attained through cutthroat competition: status, power, money, prestige. Since members of the upper class have already "arrived," they do not have to strive for these goals and can spend their time in more friendly competition in which each "throws a little business" to the other. At the other extreme, people on the lower socio-economic levels are so likely to lose out due to lack of education or capital, that they have learned to avoid competition on tests and on the job because of its bitter consequences. Moreover, many of them have also learned the value of cooperation since they must come to each other's aid in order to survive.

Although these examples show the importance of cultural standards, they tend to oversimplify the picture. In his study of Hopi children, published in 1940, Klineberg found that they would not compete with each other—for example, when they were asked to complete a task as soon as possible, no child would signal that he had finished until all the rest had completed their work. But Dennis (1955) demonstrated that if these children were put in a situation in which it was easy for them to cheat without being caught, 40 per cent of the group cheated (a high figure, though lower than for a white control group). Further, more Hopi than white children gave answers indicating competitiveness when they were asked questions about winning a race or getting a good grade. This study suggests that individuals who do not manifest competitiveness because of cultural demands may still *feel* competitive. There may therefore be more to the question of the roots of competition than the cultural studies have fathomed.

A number of studies in comparative psychology indicate that the competitive behavior of animals can be modified. Crawford (1937) showed that pairs of chimps can learn to cooperate with each other in obtaining food which neither could obtain by itself. In one experiment he found that they would pull on two ropes at the same time to bring a heavy box of food within reach. He also found that a satiated chimp would sometimes help a hungry one obtain food. Similarly, Tsai (1950) showed that a kitten and a rat which had been raised together could learn to work jointly toward the acquisition of food. Moreover, Church (1961) has demonstrated that the "reinforcement schedule," or schedule of rewards, determined whether pairs of white rats would do well or poorly on a learning task. If the superior member was highly rewarded for his performance, *both* members made good responses; but if the inferior member was highly rewarded, they both significantly decreased their output. The implication for human beings is that the opportunity for reward rather than competition in itself determines output. In other words, people tend to accomplish less if they are given the same reward for good and for poor performance.

What are the effects of competition on performance? In 1924, Whittemore showed that in simple tasks a competitive situation resulted in greater quantity but poorer quality than a situation in which subjects worked by themselves. A number of other studies on children and college students have confirmed this finding (Dashiell, 1935; Young, 1936; Sherif and Sherif, 1956). Investigators do not agree, however, on the relative value of competition versus cooperation. Deutsch (1949) and French (1951), among others, found that competition leads to greater improvement in the classroom. On the other hand, studies by Hurlock (1927) and Leuba (1933) have indicated that the cooperative situation is more effective. The difference in results may be due to the nature of the tasks or to subtle differences in the situations which make competition (or cooperation) more effective in one case than another. Moreover, it is a well-known fact that some people respond well to competition while others do not, and the groups used in the experiments may have had a predominance of one or the other kind of person.

It is also impossible to make a general statement about the value of group vs. individual competition. Simms (1928) found that individuals performed better when they were pitted individually against each other than when they worked in competitive groups with their scores merely contributing to the group score. This finding probably applies rather widely since most individuals tend to depend upon the group, and poor performance is easier to mask in a group situation than an individual situation. Nevertheless there are many cases in which group competition brings better results than individual competition, es-

pecially where *esprit de corps* is high, where there is an effective division of labor, and where the group exerts the kind of pressure that brings out the best in the individual. But here again it is a question of the character of the group, the nature of the task, and the personalities of the members. *See* GROUP DYNAMICS, MORALE (INDUSTRIAL).

Many studies have been made of competition in childhood, and psychologists generally agree that it can have both beneficial and harmful effects. Competitive situations keep the child on the alert, challenge him to do well, and provide an opportunity to test his abilities and discover his resources. As Jersild (1960) points out, competition can add zest to many activities that would otherwise be boring or distasteful. "The pace and performance of others often set a standard which the youngster can achieve and enjoy. He may, for example, discover that he can get his homework out of the way more effectively than he thought, get dressed in less time than was his custom, endure and enjoy the water of a cold shower which otherwise he would not plunge into, draw upon reserves of strength in his work and play." On the other hand, competition becomes unhealthy when it is so intense that the child will act unscrupulously in order to win, when his self-esteem hinges on his ability to outdo others, when he plays a game only to prove he can win, or works at school only for the marks he receives. In commenting on the competitive struggle that goes on in some summer camps, Sidonie Gruenberg (1954) says, "The girl who stumbles in a relay race is made to fear that she has jeopardized the victory of her side. In such an atmosphere of juvenile hysteria, the losers are dejected beyond all reason, while the victors crow with the altogether unwarranted conviction that they are superior. . . . But the harm is not alone to the defeated. The child who always wins in one kind of activity may fear failure if he should try another, and so never come to experiment with his own potentialities in a field where he is not sure of beating his competitors."

Competition is a fact of life, particularly in our culture, and it is important to develop what might be called "competition tolerance" during the childhood years. How can this be done without incurring harmful effects? There are many ways—among them, by balancing individual competition with group competition that calls for a good deal of teamwork and cooperation; by encouraging children to compete against their own records, and praising them when they make progress; by matching groups or individuals so that competition will be among equals; and by giving individuals who continually lose in direct competition an opportunity to gain approval by making other contributions to the group, in this way preventing them from losing their confidence and self-esteem.

Finally, we can take the bitterness out of competition if we encourage our children to derive their major satisfaction not from outdoing others but from working for the group, improving their skills, overcoming their handicaps, and in general striving toward constructive goals and helping others to reach them. But adults must themselves accept these standards before they can expect the children to accept them.

COMPLEX. In psychiatry, a group or system of related ideas which have a strong common emotional tone. The term was introduced by Jung but is also found in Freud, Adler, and others.

Complexes operate largely if not wholly on an unconscious level; at least the "nuclear component" that brings the ideas together has been repressed. They have a significant effect on our attitudes and behavior, and are believed to be at the core of many of our fundamental drives and conflicts.

The most important of these complexes in modern psychiatry are the castration complex, the inferiority complex, and the Oedipus complex. Other complexes are occasionally found in psychiatric literature: the obscenity-purity complex (the "Puritan complex"), the power complex (in Jung), and in psychoanalytic theory, the small-penis complex (a variety of castration complex), the grandfather complex (the desire of small children to become their parents' parents), and the femininity complex (the small boy's dread of becoming female through castration). *See* CASTRATION COMPLEX, INFERIORITY COMPLEX, OEDIPUS COMPLEX, WORD ASSOCIATION TEST.

COMPULSIVE PERSONALITY. A personality trait disturbance characterized by an exaggerated sense of responsibility and an excessive need for perfection.

The compulsive personality tends to go over and over his work with meticulous care, and has difficulty making up his mind—but once he decides on a course of action, he holds stubbornly to it. He is almost totally incapable of relaxing and usually has an earnest, driven, humorless air. A compulsive officer worker always insists on a clean desk; a compulsive housewife spends her life dusting and picking up. Although some compulsives accomplish a great deal, they usually make unnecessary work for themselves or others, and show little imagination or verve in carrying out their duties.

Compulsive individuals may use their excessive drive for perfection as a means of expressing hostility by dominating others and holding them to lofty standards. At the same time they may hold *themselves* to high standards as a safeguard against aggressive impulses or feelings of guilt which often date back to childhood experiences with overcritical parents.

A certain amount of compulsiveness

may contribute to strength of character and solid achievement, and the compulsive personality may be well within the range of normality. However, the individual who keeps himself under constant tension and becomes increasingly anxious if he does not achieve his high goals leaves himself vulnerable to neurosis. Not surprisingly, if a psychological disorder does develop, it usually takes the form of obsessive-compulsive neurosis. *See* OBSESSIVE-COMPULSIVE REACTION.

Illustrative Case: COMPULSIVE PERSONALITY.

I am incessantly concerned over the fact that I am not going to get done all I want to. I always have several lists, some very extensive, and as I do the task I cross it off. I try to make a concise list of what I plan or want for the week. During the week I will add to it, but I never cross something off as being unnecessary. Even on my day off, I get up early to do something on my list. I only wish there were more than twenty-four hours in a day. (Kisker, 1964)

CONCEPT FORMATION. The development of concepts—that is, ideas based on the common properties of a group of objects, events, or qualities, and usually but not always represented by a word or other symbol.

Most words, other than proper names, are labels that refer to some common property of objects. Red, for example, is not the name for a single thing—rather, it is applied to anything that has the property of redness regardless of its other features. Any simple noun like dog, plant, table, chair, serves the same purpose. More abstract concepts, such as right, truth, or sincerity are more difficult to define and are subject to different interpretations. Nevertheless they refer to general qualities of experience and are therefore concepts.

Concepts are developed through observation and experience. Before he can associate the label "apple" with the fruit of that name, a child must notice that all apples are approximately round, have stems, can be eaten, etc. This application of a word label to the common properties of different objects is the essence of most concept formation. The process of acquiring these concepts, however, is a long, slow trial-and-error affair. The child's first concept of apple will probably be so general that it includes most fruits, since plums, peaches, oranges, etc., have many properties in common with apples. With more training and the opportunity to observe the difference between these fruits, the concept will gradually be applied in the more correct, delimited way. Thus concept formation involves learning both similarities and differences.

Since concepts develop through each individual's unique experiences, they often vary considerably from person to person. This is particularly the case with abstract concepts, and it frequently causes misunderstandings and difficulties in communication. Two people who have different concepts of God, happiness, or immortality can hardly arrive at a meeting of minds on these questions, although they may clarify their own concepts and know each other's thinking better by discussing them. Even concrete concepts can differ widely. The suburban child's concept of "house" includes appliances and comforts that the Kentucky mountain child would not think of including. *See* BODY IMAGE.

Not all concepts have to be expressed verbally. Young children, and even lower animals, can show by their actions that they are aware of distinguishing characteristics. By an ingenious use of reward and punishment rats can be trained to leap toward a triangular figure rather than a nontriangular one. Moreover, they will often continue to choose the triangle even if its specific features such as size, shape, and orientation have been somewhat altered. In other words, the rat responds to triangle-in-general, or triangularity, not merely to a specific triangle. Ducks, too, have been trained to distinguish between triangles and other figures (PLATE 13). See ODDITY METHOD.

The Swiss psychologist, Jean Piaget, has investigated the development of the child's concepts of causality, space, mass, weight, and time. He showed that conceptual knowledge of the physical world develops very slowly, after much trial-and-error interaction with the environment. The child's first concepts of space, for example, are centered on his own body and his manipulation of objects. He has also shown that it takes considerable time for external objects to attain permanence and continued existence when out of sight. A seven-month-old infant may reach for a partially hidden bottle, but will not do so when he has seen it placed completely out of sight. At eight months he may discover a ball hidden under a cloth to his right, but if it is transferred surreptitiously to his left, he will persist in looking only to his right.

When the child learns to use language, his concept of space becomes less dependent on sensori-motor operations, for he can perform internal, "mental experiments" instead of being limited to overt action. It takes several years, however, for the child to develop and utilize what Piaget calls logical addition and subtraction of classes, the two basic processes that enable him to grasp complex space concepts. Five- and six-year-olds have not yet mastered these concepts, and when water is poured from a wide beaker into a taller narrower one, they will say that there is more water in the second beaker because it is "taller" or "looks like much more." An eight-year-old, however, will recognize that the two quantities are the same, and will say that the second beaker is "taller but thinner." The more advanced concepts enable the older child to penetrate beneath the surface and grasp hidden relationships (Piaget, 1968).

Concepts of time also develop slowly. Most children understand the meaning of "tomorrow" by the time they are thirty months of age, but it takes them another six months to grasp the meaning of "yesterday." They usually cannot tell morning from afternoon until the age of four. They know the days of the week at five, the seasons at seven, and the day of the month at eight. These concepts, which adults take for granted, actually take a great deal of practice, experimentation, and inquiry to establish. Much of the characteristic questioning of children arises out of an attempt to form and sharpen concepts. See CHILDREN'S QUESTIONS.

Educational psychologists have identified four major methods of learning concepts. First, *discrimination learning:* the child or adult follows the lead of others in attaching a word label to an object or quality, and in the course of doing this notes similarities and differences between it and other things. The apple example, given above, illustrates this method. Concept formation of this type depends on the availability of a name. If a term is lacking, we may notice a class of things that are similar but we will not have the means of responding to it. For example, human beings can discriminate hundreds of thousands of colors, but we have only a few dozen color names. As a matter of fact, most of us utilize only a small number of the color concepts that *are* available. We are likely to apply the concept "red" to a wide variety of hues that include crimson, scarlet, magenta, and certain shades of pink.

This brings up another fact: discrimination is largely determined by need and use. If these more refined color concepts were essential for our activities, we would certainly utilize them. Artists would never call a crimson object red because the difference between the two hues is extremely important to them. Similarly, the nomadic Arab, whose economy is built around the camel, is said to utilize six thousand different concepts to describe that beast, and the Eskimo language contains over a dozen different terms for what we simply call snow.

Second, *context clues:* we often acquire a new word (concept) by seeing or hearing it in different contexts. Each sentence in which the word appears gives us some hint of its meaning. This process is something like the game of Twenty Questions, where each successive question is geared to finding out certain properties of the unknown.

Third, *definition:* most of the concepts we learn in later life are acquired by definition, which is simply a way of pointing out how the new concept resembles and differs from concepts we already know. Most six-year-olds know about horses but not about zebras. They also know what stripes are. They can then obtain a good idea about the concept zebra by putting these two ideas together.

Fourth, *classification:* many of our concepts are formed by grouping things according to their common elements. The zoologist does this by identifying organisms which have certain characteristics in common, applying labels like "insect" or "mammal" to these groups.

Several other methods can be used to facilitate concept formation. One of these is *transfer:* in explaining a new concept it is a good idea to look for a similar concept that is already known, but also to point out the differences between the two. A second is *analogy:* to make an abstract concept easier to grasp, it is usually helpful to draw an analogy with a concrete concept. Young children can often learn arithmetic more quickly by observing the relationships between things they can touch and manipulate than by studying symbols written on a blackboard. Experiments have demonstrated that even third-grade children can learn calculus and physics if concrete examples and analogies are used by the teacher.

Another method is *highlighting:* concept formation is easier if the common property is made to stand out from a varying background. Children quickly grasp the idea of "squareness" if square shapes are embedded in various drawings but outlined in red. Attention-getting devices used by advertisers are designed to emphasize the qualities of the product they want to impress on the public. The advertisement for a certain cigarette always contains a photograph of attractive people at leisure in a beautiful wooded scene. The object is to highlight the concepts of freshness, coolness, and relaxation, and associate them with the product. *See* LANGUAGE, THINKING, DISCRIMINATION LEARNING.

Finally, the ability to form and apply concepts is one of the prime indicators of intelligence and is therefore measured in all major intelligence tests. Moreover, the inability to use abstractions is one of the basic indicators of serious mental disorder of both the organic and the functional type. Concrete thinking is characteristic of many brain-damaged individuals and schizophrenic patients, and a number of special instruments, such as the Hanfmann-Kasanin Concept Formation Test (PLATE 31) are used in assessing the ability to form concepts. *See* MENTAL IMPAIRMENT TESTS, PARALOGICAL THINKING, MINIMAL BRAIN DYSFUNCTION, INTELLIGENCE TESTS.

CONDITIONING. A basic form of learning in which (1) an old response is evoked by a new stimulus, or (2) a new response is acquired as a result of satisfying a need. The first type is called classical or respondent conditioning; the second is termed instrumental or operant conditioning.

Both types of conditioning are found in animals as well as human beings. Here are some typical examples of classical conditioning: a dog gets excited as soon as he sees his leash, not merely when we actually take him out; a driver learns to respond to a red light by stopping his car, instead of waiting until he encounters an obstruction on the road. In instrumental conditioning, a rat learns to respond by turning a wheel to get some food, and a child learns to turn a key to get into his house.

The classical conditioning process was developed by Ivan Pavlov in about 1900 while studying digestion in animals. He observed that some of the dogs he was working with began to salivate before he gave them food. This observation suggested that they were responding to stimuli which were repeatedly associated with the food, such as the experimental apparatus. To test this hypothesis he set up an experiment in which a bell was sounded each time he showed the dog food. He then found that the repeated association or "pairing" of the two stimuli successfully linked the salivation response with the bell by itself. In other words, a formerly neutral stimulus (the bell) evoked the same response as the natural stimulus (food). Pavlov recognized this as an important form of learning and named it conditioning because the learned response was contingent (or conditional) upon the presentation of the unlearned stimulus. See PAVLOV.

Further studies showed that classical conditioning is not an experimental artifact but one of the most common forms of learning in animals and men. In animals it has great survival value—for example, the deer flees as soon as he scents a hunter, since the scent and the hunter have been associated in the past, and this conditions him to react to the scent alone as if it were the real danger. Similarly many animals learn to respond to other signals such as warning cries and love calls.

The conditioned responses of animals involve reflexes and physiological processes such as hunger, thirst, and sex. This type of conditioning is also found in human beings: our saliva begins to flow when we hear the dinner bell, and our sexual responses are greater to one individual than to another. But in man the range of conditioning is immensely widened by our ability to respond to any number of signals that the animal cannot respond to—including gestures, symbols, pictures, and words. The American flag is a "neutral stimulus" when we are two years of age, but it takes on great significance later because it is repeatedly associated with exciting experiences and important values. It therefore loses its neutrality and arouses emotions whenever we see it.

In 1920, Watson and Rayner showed that another kind of emotion, fear, can be aroused by conditioning. Albert, an eleven-month-old infant, showed no fear in the presence of a white rat, but he did react violently to loud noises. The experimenters then showed him a rat and at the same time sounded a loud bell—and soon the boy became frightened of the rat by itself. The experiment suggested that many of our so-called "instinctive fears" are actually acquired by the process of conditioning. See BEHAVIORISM.

It has been found that classical conditioning is most easily effected in the early years and diminishes as we grow older. The reason is probably that it is an automatic, mechanical affair, and we play a passive role in the process. However, in the course of our development we learn to use another form of conditioning—operant conditioning—in which we are more active; and we also learn by other means, such as research and scientific investigation.

The first systematic study of operant and instrumental conditioning was made by B. F. Skinner in 1938. He developed an apparatus which basically consisted of a small enclosure with a lever device and a food receptacle. A hungry rat was placed in the box and in time usually pressed the lever by chance and automatically received the small reward of food. After a period, most of the rats learned to make this lever-pressing response as soon as they were placed in the box. This type of learning was termed operant conditioning because the animal had to perform an operation to get a reward. It has also been described as instrumental conditioning since the operation was effective or instrumental in achieving the desired outcome. *See* SKINNER BOX.

Operant conditioning was not a new discovery; it has long been used in teaching animals to do tricks. The standard technique is to give repeated rewards for behavior that comes closer and closer to what we want the animal to do. Skinner and his associates refined this process, called "behavior shaping," and studied it in a psychological laboratory. The techniques they developed were put to use in many ways —for example, pigeons were trained to guide missiles by pecking at images on a radar screen, and chimps were trained to manipulate instruments in the first successful satellites.

When these studies were extended to human behavior, psychologists realized for the first time that far more of our learning is due to operant conditioning than to classical conditioning. Practically every detail of our behavior, and our children's behavior, is "shaped" by reward and punishment in one form or another. When we are thirsty, we try turning the faucet counterclockwise, and if the water flows, we are "rewarded" and will do it the same way next time —but if it does not turn in that direction, we are "punished" by our failure and thereby learn to turn it the other way. When our child reaches for forbidden cookies we shake a finger or say "No!" with a scowl on our face, and he will at least think twice before performing that "operation" again. The same type of process applies to such widely different activities as learning to drive a car, carrying on a conversation, writing a letter, or getting along with the boss. If we find that our behavior is rewarding, we tend to repeat it. If it is proves ineffective or leads to negative results, we drop it and try something else.

There have been a number of recent applications of operant conditioning. Two of these techniques are particularly relevant to the subject matter of this book, and are described elsewhere in some detail. One is programmed learning, in which subject matter is broken into small, understandable steps or "frames," each followed by a question which the student can almost always answer correctly. The object is to reinforce the learning process through (a) an immediate response, and (b) the reward of getting it right. The second application is more experimental. It has been found that isolated, withdrawn mental patients can sometimes be aroused to activity, and even cooperative activity, by giving them special rewards of food. *See* PROGRAMMED LEARNING, BEHAVIOR THERAPY.

Studies of both classical and operant conditioning have resulted in the discovery of a number of subsidiary processes. *See* GENERALIZATION, DISCRIMINATION, REINFORCEMENT, ESCAPE LEARNING, AVOIDANCE LEARNING, PSEUDOCONDITIONING.

CONFABULATION   (Pseudoreminiscence). A distortion of memory, or paramnesia, in which gaps in recall are filled by fictional events and experiences.

Confabulations can be differentiated from delusions by the fact that the fictional material refers to specific times, places, and people, whereas delusions tend to be more generalized. Though sometimes these fabrications are palpably fictitious and absurdly simple, they may also be elaborate, detailed, and plausible-sounding. In any case, the patient himself accepts them as fact.

Confabulation must also be distinguished from pseudologia fantastica, a clinical syndrome characterized by fantasies having no relation to reality. Typical examples are found among antisocial, or psychopathic, individuals who tell tall tales to give their ego a lift or to get out of a tight situation. In most cases these tales are believed only momentarily and are dropped as soon as they are contradicted by evidence. The confabulator, on the other hand, sticks steadfastly to his story. See ANTISOCIAL REACTION.

The motives behind confabulation are usually unconscious. The individual hides his embarrassment due to actual memory loss by inventing details. In some brain-injury cases, for example, the patient may deny that he is ill at all, or give a fictitious reason to explain why he is in the hospital: "I tripped over the cat and hit my head on a golf ball," "I was blown up by an atomic explosion." One indication of confabulation is that many irrelevant details are usually included in the fictitious stories. Another is that the patient may spontaneously change his story from moment to moment, or in response to questions or suggestions made by the therapist. See ANOSOGNOSIA.

Confabulation is found principally in Korsakoff's syndrome, and to a lesser extent in other organic psychoses, such as senile psychosis (senile dementia), lead poisoning, general paresis, Wernicke's syndrome, and cases of severe head injury. See these topics.

CONFUSION. A generalized disturbance of consciousness in which the patient is bewildered and disoriented. He looks and acts perplexed and distressed, does not know who or where he is, and cannot find words or ideas to express himself.

The most extreme form of mental confusion occurs in cases of extensive brain damage due to infection, injury, toxic agents, or senile brain disease. The condition is also found in epileptic dream states, hysteria with dissociation, and in some schizophrenic, depressive, and mentally retarded individuals. See PERPLEXITY STATE.

CONNECTOR. A nerve cell which connects a receptor with an effector. The term is sometimes applied to hormones and the blood stream as well.

Connector cells number in the millions and constitute the vast majority of neurons in the body. Connectors called interneurons are usually found between the sensory and motor fibers in the spinal cord (see *Fig. 45,* p. 1115), while other connector neurons go up to the brain and down to the rest of the body. These connections are usually rather simple. The cerebral cortex, on the other hand, contains an enormously complex network of connectors. In the early treatises on the nervous system, this network was compared to a telephone switchboard. Today scientists no longer picture it as a complicated relay system but compare it to an electronic computer, since the brain not only transmits impulses but also plays an active role in organizing and directing behavior (Hebb, 1949). See SPINAL CORD, CEREBRAL CORTEX.

The blood stream and hormones are known as connectors because they, too, take an active part in integrating the functions of the organism. An overfatigued muscle will affect muscles in other regions of the body because chemical substances resulting from fatigue are distributed through the blood stream. Coordination also occurs through the circulation of hormones. Adrenal secretions released in an emergency situation bring about an entire pattern of responses that includes heightened blood pressure, increased clotting of blood, dilation of pupils of the eye, and tensions in the skeletal muscles. These functions justify the application of the term connector to both the hormones and the blood stream.

CONSCIOUSNESS (States of Awareness). Consciousness may be defined as a state of direct, personal awareness, as in perception, dreaming, thinking, feeling, and sensation.

The nature of consciousness has long been a key problem in philosophy and is a major topic in philosophical psychology. In the early days of modern psychology, the structuralists and introspectionists set themselves the task of analyzing conscious experience into its components. The emphasis on the contents of consciousness has recently come to the fore again in new guises as a result of experimental research on dreaming, "psychedelic" experience, hypnosis, and the study of psychopathological states. This article will be confined to a brief statement of the controversy over consciousness in modern psychology, and an enumeration of some of the problems raised by the fields of experimental research just noted. No attempt will be made to present details, since individual topics are devoted to each of these areas of investigation. (See the topics listed in this article.)

The problem of consciousness raises two interrelated questions in psychology. One is the nature and subject matter of psychology itself, and the other is the mind-body problem. Until well into this century, most investigators defined psychology as the study of consciousness or conscious experience, and described their basic technique as immediate observation or introspection of its contents. Everything that occurred inside the mind—feelings, sensations, thought processes—was placed on the psychological plane; everything that took place in the body—glandular changes, nerve currents etc.—was conceived to occur on the physiological plane. This division inevitably brought up the perennial question of the relation between mind and body. Philosophically minded psychologists are still wrestling with that problem—in fact, an entire division of the American Psychological Association is devoted to

philosophical questions of this kind. *See* PSYCHOLOGY, INTROSPECTION, WUNDT, TITCHENER.

The major alternatives on the mind-body problem have been stated in theoretical terms by the classic philosophers. The dualistic approach is based on the view that mind and body are essentially distinct—but the modern tendency is to maintain that they interact with each other rather than run a parallel course, as was claimed by a few philosophers such as Leibnitz. The interactionist view holds that the mind can control the body (for example, in jumping), and that the body limits what the mind can accomplish (we cannot leap unaided over a ten-foot obstacle), and may also affect our conscious processes (it is hard to think of anything but our stomach when it is aching). This view is exemplified by the psychophysiological or psychosomatic approach that emphasizes the fact that emotions can produce bodily symptoms, and that our physical condition can also affect our state of mind. The philosophical theory on which this approach is based stems largely from Descartes, Locke and William James's functionalist point of view. It runs into the difficulty of explaining how mind and body actually influence each other if they are different in essence—that is, how physical energy can be translated into mental energy while still preserving the law of conservation of energy. *See* PSYCHOPHYSIOLOGIC DISORDERS, SOMATOPSYCHOLOGY, DESCARTES, LOCKE, JAMES.

The second general approach, monism, attempts to avoid the difficulties of the dualistic view by contending that the basic substance of the universe is of one kind—either mind, as in Berkeley's idealism; or matter, as in La Mettrie's materialism; or a neutral substance which appears to be mental from one point of view and material from another, as in Spinoza's double-aspect theory. The latter view has the advantage that it enables the investigator to bypass the metaphysical problem while still keeping the way open to both the physiological and experimental approaches to such activities as dreaming and thinking. This position, sometimes termed the double-language theory, appears to be highly favored in contemporary psychology, although there are still some extreme behaviorists who follow John B. Watson in denying the existence of consciousness altogether, as well as less extreme behaviorists who, following E. C. Tolman, do not deny introspective facts but rule them out as subject matter for scientific investigation. *See* BEHAVIORISM.

The study of consciousness has been greatly advanced in recent years by the application of scientific methods of observation, description, and measurement to states of awareness. Studies of normal waking consciousness indicate that this is not a single, clearly defined state, but varies greatly in complexity, especially when different kinds of stimuli are received at once or when we are trying to do several things at the same time. Experiments conducted by Broadbent (1958) show that under such circumstances (a) we can usually attend clearly to only one message at a time, (b) we are able to select that message from others while still remembering something from one or more simultaneous messages, and (c) we sometimes shift back and forth from one message to another and even fill in the gaps if the material is relatively easy to understand. Other experimenters have shown that (d) it is possible to listen and talk at the same time as is done in simultaneous translation (Cherry, 1953); (e) we carry out a form of planning while we are in the midst of listening or talking—while listening to a lecture we are at the same time deciding whether to make a note of one point or another (Miller, Galanter, Pribram, 1960)—and (f) when we have an intellectual task to perform we often tend to fall back into a state of "vacant staring" unless we use some device, such as chewing on a pencil, squirming, or reminding ourselves of how much time we have left, to keep ourselves on the alert and probably to keep the reticular formation active. (Mackworth, 1950)

There are also wide variations in states of awareness on the borderland between consciousness and unconsciousness. Freud's description of a preconscious or foreconscious level midway between consciousness and the unconscious is a recognition of such an in-between state; Jung's theory of intuition in which consciousness draws on the reservoir of the unconscious is another example; and perhaps our common experience of having an idea on the tip of our tongue is a third. *See* FORECONSCIOUS, JUNG, REMEMBERING.

The fact that there is no sharp line between sleeping and waking is demonstrated by a variety of experiences: the mother's tendency to awaken at the slightest sound of her baby's cry, our ability to recall dreams and to awaken at a given time, and the fact that we can distinguish between light and deep sleep or between restful and restless sleep. Many studies have been made of the drowsy condition between sleeping and waking known as the hypnagogic state, the state of delirium due to high fever or drugs, states of intoxication produced by alcohol or metallic poisoning, and states of hallucination and illusion associated with severe mental disorder. In addition, the ineffable states of ecstasy experienced by religious mystics have been vividly described by William James, and more recently similar states experienced by schizophrenic and manic patients have been studied by specialists in psychopathology. *See* SLEEP, HYPNAGOGIC STATE, HALLUCINATION, DELIRIUM, ALCOHOLIC HALLUCINOSIS, SOMNAMBULISM, ELATION, ECSTASY.

Three types of investigations into states of awareness have received special attention in recent years. First, a great deal of new light has been shed on sleeping and dreaming by the use of the EEG (electroencephalograph, or brain wave) technique and REM (rapid eye movement) research. These studies have expanded our knowledge of the stages and types of sleep, the length of dreams, the prevalence of dreaming, and reactions to stimuli during sleep. Second, there has been an upsurge of interest in drugs that produce alterations in consciousness—mescaline and psilocybin, which have long been known to produce hallucinations; and the more recent "psychotomimetic" drug, LSD. These so-called "mind-expanding" drugs have been used not only in studying variations in states of consciousness but in research on mental illness and therapy. Psychologists and psychiatrists, however, decry the uncontrolled self-administration of these powerful drugs because of their unpredictable effects. Finally, the scientific study of hypnosis has focused attention on still other aspects of consciousness: hypnotizability, levels of trance, post-hypnotic suggestion, and applications of hypnosis in medicine, psychiatry, and dentistry. *See* HYPNOSIS, HYPNOTHERAPY, HALLUCINOGEN, LYSERGIC ACID.

CONSTITUTION. The relatively enduring biological make-up of an individual, in part due to heredity and in part to life experience and environmental factors.

Some authors use the term constitution to indicate a fixed quantity or "endowment" that is present, at least in potential form, at birth. The more recent tendency is to regard the constitution as a set of fairly constant characteristics that can nevertheless change somewhat in the course of life: a robust constitution can be weakened, a constitutional predisposition to a certain type of disease might be overcome. In this view, any constitutional traits, such as sexual characteristics or energy

level, may change as the individual goes through the life cycle.

Among the constitutional factors that play a major role in psychiatry and psychology are the following: general body structure and physique, disharmonies of growth (dysplasia), the balance of masculine and feminine characteristics, nervous system functions, visceral functions (the internal organs), endocrine gland functions, and the temperament of the individual. The specific character of these factors is believed to determine in large part an individual's personality traits, his susceptibility to certain types of neurotic or psychotic disorder, and his predisposition to specific psychosomatic reactions. *See* CONSTITUTIONAL TYPES, TEMPERAMENT.

CONSTITUTIONAL TYPES. The classification of individuals into types on the basis of constitutional factors, particularly physique.

Type theories date back to antiquity. The ancient Hindus divided men into hares, bulls, and horses; and women into mares, elephants, and deer. Greek and Roman physicians believed there was a connection between body build and susceptibility to different diseases —Hippocrates, for example, made a distinction between the obese *homo apoplecticus* and the lean *homo phthisicus,* the apoplectic and tubercular types. In the nineteenth century Rostan distinguished four types, the digestive, respiratory, cerebral and muscular; and Carus distinguished five, the athletic, phlegmatic, phthisic, cerebral, and sterile. Modern investigators have been particularly concerned with finding relationships between physique, temperament and psychiatric disorders, on the assumption that the constitutional type characterizes the individual as a whole. The two most influential theories are those of Ernst Kretschmer and W. H. Sheldon. *See* HUMORAL THEORY.

Kretschmer's Typology. In a work entitled *Physique and Character* published in English translation in 1925 the German psychiatrist, Kretschmer, claimed to have found a "clear biological affinity" between specific personality tendencies and specific body builds. Basing his conclusions on a study of mental patients, he found that (1) the short, thick-set, stocky *pyknic* tends to be jovial, extraversive, and subject to mood swings; (2) the frail, long-limbed, narrow-chested *asthenic* (or leptosome) is likely to be shy, sensitive, cold, and introversive; (3) the muscular, broad-shouldered, well-proportioned *athletic* individual is usually energetic and aggressive; and (4) the disproportioned, "ugly" *dysplastic* presents a combination of traits which tend more toward the asthenic than toward the other types.

Kretschmer attributed these tendencies to endocrine secretions and believed there are continuous gradations from normal to psychotic behavior. When the pyknic characteristics are somewhat exaggerated, the individual develops a "cycloid" personality characterized by fluctuations from elation to dejection. In extreme cases these tendencies lead to manic-depressive psychosis. The asthenic, and to a lesser extent the athletic and dysplastic individuals, tend to be introversive, withdrawn, and "schizoid," and is vulnerable to schizophrenia. Kretschmer also applied the theory to individuals who manifest no personality disturbance, and devised the terms cyclothyme and schizothyme (roughly equivalent to Jung's introvert and extravert) for the two normal biotypes.

The theory has been attacked from a number of angles. First, an analysis of Kretschmer's original study has shown that he did not take the age of his subjects into consideration. This may be of great importance, since manic-depressive psychosis usually occurs later in life than schizophrenia, and older patients are more likely to show increased weight and therefore appear to be pyknic in physique. Later investigators have found that when the two groups are precisely measured and equated in age, there is a very considerable overlapping (Garvey, 1933; Burchard, 1936). Second, careful research has shown that there is no significant correlation between Kretschmer's personality and body types in normal individuals (Klineberg, Asch, Block, 1934); or, for that matter, between his biotypes and any characteristics measured by standard psychological tests (Klineberg, Fjeld, Foley, 1936). Third, no relationship can be demonstrated between the endocrine system and body build except in extreme cases, such as hypothyroidism. Fourth, the classifications are too rigid: there are several different types of schizophrenic reactions, and many of these patients are not introverted or have a pyknic rather than an asthenic body build (Eysenck, 1947). Finally, there is no evidence for pure biotypes associated with fixed psychological characteristics. Instead, as Sheldon has pointed out, most people are mixtures of many physical and psychological characteristics in various proportions. In view of these criticisms, it is generally agreed that the relationships Kretschmer claimed to have found are actually too tenuous to be of practical use.

Sheldon's Typology. In this system the individual is not simply placed in a category but rated along a seven-point scale for three dimensions of physique and three dimensions of temperament. The physical components were derived from detailed measurements of the photographs of 4000 college men. The temperamental components were condensed from a list of over 650 traits and further refined through intensive interviews and supplementary observations carried out with thirty-three young men. The final temperament scale consisted of a cluster of twenty traits for each dimension.

Sheldon's physical dimensions are

termed endomorphic (soft, round build; digestive visceral development), mesomorphic (hard, rectangular build; bone and muscle development) and ectomorphic (linear, fragile build; nervous system development). The individual's somatotype is represented by three numbers—for example, 2-6-2 would mean highly mesomorphic and 6-2-1 would mean highly endomorphic. The temperament dimensions are termed viscerotonic (tendency toward relaxation, physical comfort, pleasure in eating, sociability), somatotonic (tendency toward energetic activity, assertiveness, love of power, physical courage) and cerebrotonic (tendency toward introversion, restraint, inhibition, love of privacy and solitude).

A study of two hundred university men revealed remarkably high correlations—averaging .80—between endomorphic and viscerotonic, mesomorphic and somatotonic, and ectomorphic and cerebrotonic (Sheldon and Stevens, 1942). Other investigators have obtained significant but much lower correlations between physique and temperament scores. Sheldon has also applied his classification to psychiatric patients and delinquents. In a study conducted by Wittman, Sheldon, and Katz (1948) in which large numbers of male patients were rated on the basis of case-history files, impressive correlations were found between endomorphism and disturbed affective behavior (typical of manic-depressive psychosis), mesomorphism and paranoid behavior (as in paranoid psychosis), and ectomorphism and heboid behavior (as in hebephrenic schizophrenia). In a study of delinquent boys published in 1949, he found a predominance of endomorphic mesomorphs, although he pointed out that this body type is also characteristic of geniuses, statesmen, and business leaders. This finding was corroborated by Glueck and Glueck (1950) in their comparison of 500 delinquent with 500 nondelinquent boys from the same depressed neighborhood.

Sheldon's studies have been criticized on several counts. The photographic method of assessing body build is open to question, and is probably less reliable than direct measurement. Neither age nor nutritional status was taken sufficiently into account. The initial study of temperament, on which later studies were based, involved too small a number and too limited a group (thirty-three college men). But most important, Sheldon's results may have been contaminated by the "halo effect" and by social stereotypes, since the same observer usually assigned both physique and temperament ratings and one might have influenced his conception of the other, especially since the raters were acquainted with the Sheldon theory—i.e. a rater might *expect* a mesomorph to be energetic. It is interesting that when blind ratings of ectomorphs and endomorphs were made by other investigators, using the Minnesota Multiphasic Personality Inventory, the personality differences between these two groups were found to be relatively small, although consistent with the Sheldon hypothesis. (Hood, 1963)

In spite of these criticisms, "Evidence on both normal and abnormal cases suggests that some association between physique and personality exists along the lines specified by Kretschmer and Sheldon, although it is much weaker than was originally supposed" (Anastasi, 1958). It may be that other techniques, such as factor analysis, will give us more precise information on this relationship. But even though we may grant that some correlation exists between physique and temperament, we still have to discover its basis. First, there is a possibility—unproven as yet—that hereditary endowment may determine *both* physique and behavior, i.e., there may be "body-linked" personality traits. Second, environment may provide the common basis—for example, as Rosen and Gregory point out (1965), extreme economic deprivation may make a child seclusive and withdrawn, and poor diet in a deprived area may lead to an asthenic (ectomorphic) physique. Third, cultural expectation may determine how the individual expresses himself: the mesomorph may play a dominant social role because others prescribe that role for him due to his strong and energetic appearance. And fourth, the person with one physique may find that the balance of rewards versus costs is in his favor, while it militates against a person with another body build—for example, the mesomorph may develop an aggressive personality more readily than an ectomorph because his attempts at aggression meet with greater success. This may be the reason juvenile delinquents tend to be mesomorphic. *See* ETIOLOGY, JUVENILE DELINQUENCY.

CONSUMER PSYCHOLOGY. A psychological field dealing with the behavior of individuals as consumers; the systematic study of the relationship between organizations that provide goods and services and the persons who use them.

Consumer psychology started in the early 1900s with studies of advertising and selling conducted by Hollingworth and Scott. Their work focused primarily on advertising—that is, communication from producer to consumer—but during the 1920s the field broadened to include communications from consumer to producer as well. From that time to the present there has been an increasing concern with the wants, motivations, and preferences of consumers not merely as a means of preparing more effective advertisements, but to supply valuable information for designing products, packages, and displays that more fully meet the consumer's needs.

Modern consumer psychology covers a wide area and utilizes a broad range of research methods. The psychologist applies his knowledge of learning and habit formation to the buying behavior of people; he employs his understanding of drives and motives to develop advertising and sales techniques; and he uses his knowledge of statistics and other quantitative procedures to measure results. He draws upon his experience in the laboratory and the field in adapting interview, questionnaire, and projective methods to the practical problems of product and package testing, market research, brand identification, and readership studies. He plays an important role in media research, which determines the composition of audiences, and he is often active in estimating demand for specific goods and services, and in investigating the "images" of products. In a word, the psychologist brings the approach of the behavioral scientist to bear on the entire range of consumer behavior.

Consumer psychology is an expanding field which already employs the services of many psychologists. In 1960 it became one of the divisions of the American Psychological Association, with its own organization and officers. *See* ADVERTISING RESEARCH, CONSUMER RESEARCH, MOTIVATION RESEARCH.

CONSUMER RESEARCH (Market Research). A broad field of inquiry covering consumer reactions to advertisements, products, and packages—the value of trademarks and trade names, studies of consumer characteristics and personality traits, and the needs and motives that underlie buying behavior.

The phases of consumer research overlap considerably. The specific topics selected for this article are consumer surveys and other data-collection techniques, consumer characteristics, product testing, and package testing. The psychological approaches most directly related to advertising are considered in this volume under Advertising Research, and those most closely associated with the more personal drives and reactions of the consumer are described under Motivational Research. Other related subjects, such as Readability Studies, Salesmanship and Subliminal Perception are also covered under separate entries.

Consumer Surveys. The general purpose of these surveys is to establish two-way communication that will elicit reactions of the consumer to existing products, in order to provide data that will help in designing new products and packaging, preparing ads, choosing a trade name, or discovering new uses for present products. The procedures and the pitfalls are similar to those of public opinion surveys. It is important to select the most appropriate sampling method (random, stratified, or area sampling), to determine the most effective size of the sample, and to allow for sampling errors and possible biases. It is also essential to construct well-formulated questionnaires for the particular purpose in mind (telephone, mail, or house-to-house response), and to pre-test the questions and train the interviewers.

While opinion surveys can be extremely valuable, it must be recognized that they are sensitive to many influences. The respondents tend to give socially desirable answers in face-to-face interviews—for example, they often mention prestige magazines such as *Harper's* in magazine surveys (Longstaff and Laybourn, 1949). Some people tend to give favorable responses and others to give unfavorable responses whenever their opinions are asked, and a disproportionate number of "yea-sayers" or "nay-sayers" may seriously distort the findings (Wells, 1961). Results may also be influenced by the interviewer's own opinion or by the fact that he knows the respondent. One experiment even showed that the interviewer's appearance can have a significant effect: in a survey on beverages, two interviewers who fitted the common idea of a prohibitionist reported much less use of liquor than their colleagues! (Skelley, 1954).

The form of the questionnaire may also make a difference. Weitz (1950) found that preferences for cooking ranges differed widely for groups who were presented with pictorial alternatives and groups presented with verbal alternatives. In a test of TV viewing, Belson and Duncan (1962) found that respondents who were given a check list of programs claimed to have viewed 50 per cent more programs the previous day than respondents who were given a blank form on which to list the programs they watched. Interestingly, only 1 per cent of the check-list group listed newscasts while 25 per cent of the open-end group mentioned them. These examples indicate that consumer surveys must be carried out with extreme care. See PUBLIC OPINION SURVEYS.

Other data-collection techniques. Among these are: (a) consumer panels or juries either brought together as a group, or questioned individually by mail, telephone or in person; (b) rating and scaling methods, as in asking respondents to rate the performance of an appliance or rank the factors they consider important in selecting a house; (c) structured interviews, a flexible technique which starts with the purchase and proceeds to the advertising —for example, the respondent is asked to recall the circumstances leading to his purchase or give details about any ads that may have played a part in his decision; (d) other techniques described under Motivation Research: depth interviews, word association tests, sentence completion tests, cartoon tests; and (e) still others mentioned under Advertising Research: use of eye cameras, preference-recording devices, one-way mirrors, etc.

Product and Package Testing. Product testing may be carried out either before or after the product is on the market. It plays an essential part in developing new products that will be acceptable to the public, as well as in improving existing products. A study by Harris will illustrate the importance of pretesting: ten dinner plates of different patterns were placed on a table, and 140 women were asked to rank them and indicate the degree of preference on a twenty-one-point scale. A Preference Index was then computed for each pattern based on the percentage of respondents rating the plates in the top three positions. A subsequent study showed a correlation of .91 between these indices and actual sales. Later on, seventy new patterns were pretested on a national scale, and several of the patterns became top sellers in their grades (Harris, 1964). Other pretesting studies have shown, for example, that all-numeral telephone dialing is speedy, accurate, and acceptable to the public, and that civilian subjects can be effectively used in judging foods for the armed forces.

Testing procedures are also employed in studies of brand identification and brand preference. Some early blindfold tests seemed to show that subjects could not tell the difference between one brand of cigarette and another, but a recent investigation in which tactual and visual cues were carefully eliminated has shown that a significant number of habitual smokers were able to identify their own brand correctly, and also showed a preference for this brand (Littman and Manning, 1954). A field study of beer preferences has also been made. A consumer panel of twenty families was used, and the subjects were given a free choice of identical but unlabeled bottles over a period of time. Significant brand preferences were found both in the number of bottles consumed and in the pattern of preferences. (Fleishman, 1951)

Package Testing. This phase of market research is receiving a considerable amount of attention, since package design is not only important in protecting products but often has a substantial influence on consumer acceptance. The most common method of pretesting different designs is through interviews with representative samples of customers. One experimenter found that customers judged bread to be fresher when it was wrapped in cellophane than when it was wrapped in waxed paper, apparently because of the difference in touch when it was squeezed (Brown, 1958). A push-button machine is sometimes used for recording customer reactions on a mass scale. In a study involving a comparison between an old and a new package for Vicks Vaporub, 3000 votes were recorded in selected supermarkets within three days, and the results clearly indicated that the new design was more popular (*Modern Packaging,* March 1961).

Consumer Characteristics. Personality studies of consumers are usually made with advertising in mind, since they help the agency to select the most suitable medium for the product and are also useful in adapting the language, pictures, and appeals to the target audience. At one time these studies were confined to the more obvious human characteristics, such as age, sex, and economic levels, but they have recently been extended to personality traits as well. Depth interviews, projective tests, and personality inventories are the principal methods used, and a wide variety of characteristics have been investigated in relation to use of products for reducing cigarette smoking, automobile preferences, soap opera and motion picture tastes. In one study, Ford and Chevrolet owners were successfully differentiated on several characteristics: age of car they owned, smoking or not, renting or not, having three or more children at home—and administration of the Edwards Personal Preference Schedule indicated that for the group in question the Ford owners had a greater need for exhibition and dominance than the Chevrolet owners.

The Edwards personality test has also been administered to a nationwide panel of 8963 heads of households, and significant differences were found for many of the subgroups. For example, heavy smokers scored higher in expressed needs for success, aggression, and achievement, while nonsmokers scored higher in the needs for order and compliance. In still another investigation, the Gordon Personal Profile was administered to a large group of business college students, along with a disguised questionnaire on the use of various products such as deodorants, cigarettes, and headache remedies. Several low but indicative correlations were found between personality test scores and product use—for instance, the more the students used headache remedies the less likely they were to be ascendant and emotionally stable, and the more they accepted new fashions the more likely they were to be ascendant and sociable (Tucker and Painter, 1961). These and other studies indicate that personality characteristics play a part in buying behavior, at least for certain products. *See* MOTIVATION RESEARCH.

CONTRAST EFFECT. The influence of marked difference in color, brightness, size, or other qualities on perception. The effects occur when the two stimuli are juxtaposed, or when one immediately follows the other (simultaneous and successive contrast).

Contrast effect is an everyday occurrence. While watching a college basketball game you may be struck by the fact that one or two players look like midgets, and you may wonder how anyone that short could have made the team. The next day you pass a group of students, and the tallest, about six feet in height, seems familiar—and you suddenly realize that this is one of the "midgets." Among the very tall basketball players he seemed short, but his own above-average height is evident in

a group of normal-sized students. Similarly, a twenty degree drop in temperature after the mercury has been in the 90s for a week will make you wonder whether summer is coming to an end. It has also been shown that if we meet two people at once, one of whom we like and the other we dislike, our reactions will be more extreme than if we see them separately.

All these examples illustrate the fact that our perceptions are profoundly affected by contrasts. The same object or event can appear one way in a neutral context and quite different in a context that brings out these contrasts.

There are a number of special types of contrast effect. One is *brightness contrast:* a gray disk looks darker on a white background than on a black background. An unexplained exception is the "spreading effect" in which a dark area makes a neighboring light area look darker and a light area appears to lighten a dark area (COLOR PLATE 2). Another contrast effect is *color contrast:* in simultaneous contrast, a red patch on a background of its complementary green looks richer (more saturated) than the same red against a blue background. It has also been found that the borders between complementary colors, such as red and green or blue and yellow, will be highlighted by gray, since complementary colors mix and produce gray at the point where they meet. This principle has been utilized in designing pennants and banners. Another example: similar gray discs will look different when placed against differently colored backgrounds. In each case the gray is tinged with the complementary color of the background. This phenomenon is known as "color induction."

Successive color contrast obeys similar laws. If one color is immediately followed by another, as in a colored motion picture, our perception of the second will be affected by its contrast with the first. This also occurs in afterimages. If you stare at a small black square for about a minute, then project the afterimage on a colored wall, it will take on a color that is the complement of the wall.

These factors play an important role in advertising, decorating, and other artistic endeavors that utilize brightness and color. A rug or piece of furniture may look perfect in the room in which it is displayed, but at home, in a different context, its color may appear entirely wrong. The same is true of articles of clothing that are bought apart from the ensemble. Artists must master the principles of contrast if they are to deal effectively with the nuances of shading and composition.

The effects of contrasting sensations are far more prevalent than these examples indicate. Tastes affect tastes: an orange tastes sweeter after a lemon than after a piece of cake. Odors affect odors: sniffing one perfume after another gives a different impression from sniffing them with an interval between. Sound affects sound: the ticking of a grandfather clock sounds much louder at night than during the day because it contrasts more sharply with the softer sounds of the night. And if it should stop ticking we would probably become acutely aware of the sudden silence. This indicates that any change in STIMULATION, or any event that contrasts with what preceded it, is especially likely to be noticed. The word typed in capital letters above probably caught your eye as soon as you looked at this part of the page because it contrasts with the words in lower case.

Contrast has broader implications than its effects on perception or its use as an attention-getting device. Studies on sensory deprivation have shown that we need almost a continual change in stimulation if we are to function efficiently; behavior is greatly disrupted in a constant unchanging environment. Variety may therefore be much more

than "the spice of life"; without an adequate amount of it there may be no normal life at all. *See* SENSORY DEPRIVATION, METACONTRAST, AFTERIMAGE.

CONVERSION. An unconscious psychological process, or mental mechanism, in which repressed conflicts and impulses are expressed as somatic (bodily) symptoms.

There is an endless variety of conversion symptoms—anesthesia, paralysis, deafness, mutism—but all have the same purpose of providing self-protection against anxiety. This they accomplish either by preventing a direct, conscious expression of threatening impulses, or by providing an escape from disturbing situations.

Conversion symptoms usually take the form of a loss or inhibition of some bodily function which has either a direct or a symbolic relation to the person's problem. An example of the direct affect is the case of the singer who was acutely apprehensive about a certain concert performance. Just before she was to make her appearance, she suddenly developed such a severe case of hoarseness that a substitute had to be found. The symbolic type of reaction is illustrated by the man who developed a paralysis of his right leg. The psychiatrist discovered that the paralysis represented his attempt to keep deeply hostile impulses in check—impulses which were unconsciously symbolized by kicking. *See* CONVERSION REACTION.

CONVERSION REACTION (Hysteria). A neurotic reaction in which anxiety is unconsciously converted into physical symptoms such as blindness, paralysis, or loss of sensation.

Conversion symptoms are functional in nature; there is no underlying organic pathology. They serve a number of important psychological purposes. By focusing attention on these physical symptoms, the patient is able to screen out or dispel his feelings of anxiety. This is termed the "primary gain," or advantage, which the patient derives from his symptoms. But there are additional benefits, or "secondary gains," which accrue from the fact that the symptoms usually elicit attention and sympathy and enable the patient to exert control over others. In most cases conversion symptoms can be shown to be closely related to the underlying conflict or emotional problem that causes anxiety, yet the patient is completely unaware of this connection.

The older name for conversion reaction is hysteria, a term derived from Hippocrates' theory that the disorder occurs in women whose uterus (*hystera*) has wandered to different parts of the body in search of a child. He believed the symptoms were often due to sexual difficulties, and considered marriage the best remedy. In the seventeenth century anesthesias and other symptoms found in this disorder were considered signs of witchcraft or possession by demons. Two centuries later Jean Charcot showed that these symptoms could be both produced and relieved through hypnosis, but he ascribed them to organic defect rather than psychological causes. Near the end of the nineteenth century Pierre Janet advanced the thought that they originated in the weakening of "psychic tension" or energy as a result of emotional experiences, while Bernheim believed they were produced by suggestion. *See* HIPPOCRATES, DEMONOLOGY, CHARCOT, JANET.

This trend toward recognition of the psychogenic origin of hysterical symptoms reached a climax with Sigmund Freud, who used the term conversion hysteria and maintained that the manifestations are a release of repressed impulses in disguised form. He believed these impulses were wholly sexual in nature—for example, a boy's hand might become paralyzed as a means of repressing his guilty urge to masturbate.

Today the idea of repressed conflicts is well accepted, but they are not limited to sexual problems. Also, the present emphasis is on conversion symptoms as a means of defense against the anxiety produced by conflicts rather than as a direct result of the conflicts.

Cultural and historical influences play a large role in conversion reactions. Dramatic, histrionic symptoms such as fainting spells were common in Charcot's clinic, and difficulty in walking was often observed in Victorian women. Paralysis and mutism were among the most frequently observed psychiatric symptoms during World War I, but were far less common during World War II. Since then conversion reactions as a whole have declined, and they now comprise only about 5 per cent of neurotic disorders. The incidence is highest among young women of slightly lower than average intelligence, socioeconomic, and educational levels.

Hysterical symptoms have been found to simulate an astounding number of organic illnesses. They also account for many diffuse aches and pains which cannot be clearly identified. In general, these symptoms fall into two categories: sensory and motor. Among the sensory symptoms are blindness (hysterical amaurosis), narrowing of the visual field (tunnel vision), macropsia or micropsia (seeing objects too large or too small), impairment of taste (ageusia) or smell (anosmia), deafness, vertigo, loss of pain sensitivity (analgesia) and, less frequently, anesthesia (loss of sensitivity in the skin or other organs), hypesthesia (partial loss of sensitivity), and paresthesia (exceptional sensations, such as tingling). The anesthesias do not follow the anatomical distribution of a nerve but what the patient believes it to be —for example, in "glove" anesthesia the loss of sensation starts at a sharp line on the wrist even though the nerve fibers do not stop there. Similarly, hysterical blindness cannot be a simple neurological defect, since the pupils continue to react to light and the patient automatically avoids or dodges objects that would injure him. Moreover, these sensory symptoms appear to be selected for their special advantages—for example, anxious night pilots may develop night blindness, while day fliers develop defects of day vision. Significantly, too, the visual symptoms do not usually interfere with driving a car. See AMAUROSIS, SENSITIVITY DISTURBANCES.

Motor symptoms show a similar variety and selectivity. Paralyses usually affect only one limb (monoplegia). They may also affect only the lower half of the body (paraplegia), or one side of the body (hemiplegia). In contrast to organic paralysis, the deep reflexes are not lost and there is little or no wasting in these cases. In occupational disorders, such as writer's cramp, the patient cannot write but may be able to use the same muscles in shuffling cards.

Other motor symptoms are tics, tremors, bent back (camptocormia), concave or convex posture ("arc de cercle"), choreiform movements, contractures of fingers, toes, knees, or elbows, and jumping or skipping movements ("saltatory spasm"). Tics, such as eye blinking or body twitches, may dramatize stressful experiences. In one case a young boy who had been caught from behind while stealing apples developed a tic in which he repeatedly turned his head to one side. Some patients can control their leg movements while sitting or lying down but wobble about grotesquely when they walk (astasia-abasia). Speech disturbances are not uncommon, and sometimes set in after an emotional shock. Mutism is less common than aphonia, a condition in which the individual is unable to talk above a whisper. Hysterical convulsions occasionally occur. They can be differentiated from epileptic seizures by the fact that the patient does not injure himself, become incontinent, or lose his pupillary reflex during the attack. See OCCUPATIONAL NEUROSIS, COMPENSATION NEUROSIS, TIC, ASTASIA-ABASIA, DYSLALIA, MUTISM, VERTIGO, VOICE DISORDERS.

Although some authorities place most visceral symptoms, such as bulimia, in the psychophysiologic category, there are some that seem to belong with conversion reactions. Among them are certain types of headaches (such as clavus, the feeling that a nail is being driven into the head), choking sensations, raised temperature (thermoneurosis), coughing or sneezing spells, persistent blushing, breathing difficulties (for example, dyspnea, shortness of breath), clammy extremities, scanty urination (oliguresis), belching and nausea. Four others, globus hystericus (lump in the throat), syncope (fainting spells), anorexia nervosa (extreme loss of appetite or refusal of food), and false pregnancy are discussed in this book as separate topics. The aches and pains about which today's hysterics complain are sometimes mistaken for specific diseases, such as appendicitis and even malaria or tuberculosis. This has led to many unnecessary treatments and even operations. See BULIMIA.

It is important, then, to set up criteria to distinguish hysterical from organic disorder. First, conversion symptoms often do not follow neural pathways or square with other anatomical facts. Second, atrophy and changes in reflex action rarely occur. Third, the personality of the patient is usually immature, and the symptoms tend to set in after an emotional shock or other form of psychological stress. Fourth, the patient's complaints seem to bring him some special benefits in the form of sympathy or attention. Fifth, in spite of the fact that the symptoms would usually be upsetting, he appears surprisingly unconcerned about his condition. Sixth, the symptoms have a selective character that differentiates them from organic symptoms. And seventh, they can be readily induced, shifted, or eliminated through the use of direct suggestion, hypnosis, or narcosis. Frequently, too, the mute patient can be tricked into talking and the paralyzed patient into using his limb. For ways of distinguishing conversion reactions from faking, *see* MALINGERING. *See also* GANSER SYNDROME, PSEUDORETARDATION.

Illustrative Case: CONVERSION REACTION

Fred K. is a fifty-year-old married man who developed a marked contracture of his left hand, and a partial paralysis of his arm. He held his arm bent in front of him, as if it were in a sling, and his fingers were curled inward toward the palm of his hand. He could raise his arm to the level of his shoulder, and there was a slight movement in his fingers.

The symptoms came on suddenly, and before he was referred for psychological treatment, the patient had undergone medical and neurological work-ups by local physicians as well as by specialists at Rochester, Cleveland, Baltimore, and Boston. Various diagnoses were made, including vertebral dislocation, with the recommendation of surgery on the spine. One medical center placed the patient in an elaborate traction device "to take the pressure off a pinched nerve." Other medical treatments were tried, but the patient did not respond, and the symptoms remained unaltered.

The psychological evaluation of this patient revealed that he was a well-to-do executive, that he was married to an attractive and considerably younger wife, and that while he seemed anxious to be cured of his disorder, there was nevertheless a remarkable casualness about it, and one sensed that the patient took a certain pride in it. He displayed his hand and arm with some satisfaction, demonstrating the lack of feeling by touching his lit cigarette to the back of his hand to show he felt no pain. The attitude of the patient toward his symptom, combined with the lack of positive neurological findings, pointed to the possibility of a conversion reaction. Psychotherapy was recommended, and at the end of several treatment hours, the symptom was removed. While it returned a few days later, the psychological nature of the disorder had been proved, and psychotherapy was continued.

It was clear to the therapist that the patient had been using his neurotic symp-toms to solve his problems. His young and attractive wife was fond of parties and nightclubs, while the patient merely wanted to come home at night, have dinner, read his paper, and go to bed. The difference in age and interests resulted in serious conflict. Finally, the wife began to go out without her husband. It was at this point that the symptoms appeared.

The paralysis served a number of purposes. It gave the patient a good excuse for staying home at night. After all who would expect a man with a paralyzed arm to go to nightclubs? It also forced the patient's wife to spend more time with him at home in the evenings. Only the most callous wife would go out and leave her paralyzed husband at home alone. Moreover, the paralysis brought the patient the sympathy and attention of friends and relatives. Previously, being a rather colorless and uninteresting person, he had been overshadowed by his attractive and vivacious wife. Now he was the center of things. Finally, because the patient was jealous of his wife and suspected her infidelity, he used his symptom as an excuse to come home from his office at any hour of the day. Sometimes he would return home, complaining of his arm, an hour after leaving in the morning.

Interestingly enough, the eventual cure in this case was not brought about through the efforts of a psychotherapist, but rather by a policeman! The patient's suspicions about his wife had not been unfounded, and one day he awoke to find that his wife had run off with a police officer. Days later, when he was convinced that his wife would never return to him, his symptom disappeared spontaneously. It had served its unconscious purpose, and he no longer had need of it. Without his wife and the problems of living with her, the symptom was meaningless. (Kisker, 1964)

COOPERATION. Most of the early studies of cooperation were carried out with animals, in an effort to discover its general features, its nonhuman expressions, and the dividing line between animal and human forms. In a series of classic experiments, Crawford demonstrated that chimpanzees reached the highest level of cooperation of any animals. In 1937 he found that two chimpanzees would work together to draw a heavy food box into their cage, and would cooperate in this activity even when one of them was not hungry. In 1941 he trained a chimpanzee to press four colored plaques in a certain order to obtain a food reward. He then divided the cage in half, placing the first and third plaque on one side and the second and fourth on the other. Next, a trained subject was placed on one side and another chimpanzee which knew how to push plaques, but did not know the proper order was placed on the other. Crawford found that the trained subject not only observed the behavior of the untrained one, but even directed it to respond in the correct order.

In another revealing experiment, Tsai (1950) has shown that a cat and a rat reared together would perform a food-getting task that required cooperative activity. In their review of the experiments of Crawford, Tsai, and others, Hebb and Thompson (1954) point out that, phylogenetically speaking, the ability to communicate and to cooperate parallel each other so closely that they probably depend on the same level of intellectual development. They also distinguish between three forms of cooperative behavior: first, a nonpurposive type as exhibited by bees, ants, and other insects which engage in highly complicated behavior through purely physical, reflexive response to each other; second, purposive but "one-sided" cooperation, shown by the higher vertebrates and illustrated by an adult chimp rescuing an infant headed for trouble (Nissen, 1931); and third, "two-sided" cooperation, or teamwork, which is ordinarily found only in man.

The human being appears to repeat this phylogenetic order. The infant's first responses to the bottle or breast—opening his mouth, sucking, swallowing—are basically reflexive; but he soon learns the more purposive though somewhat one-sided act of holding still when he is being dressed. Studies show that the first phases of two-sided cooperation occur between two and a half and three years of age when the child begins to play with other youngsters. A rapid increase in cooperative activity occurs between three and four, especially if the child attends nursery school or participates in other play groups. Team play and group activity, however, do not develop until six or seven years of age.

The more opportunity the youngster has to learn work skills and to "help mother" at home, the sooner he learns cooperative behavior. Unfortunately some parents do not have the patience or interest to help their children develop these skills, and others feel that childhood should be a happy, carefree time in which the child should never be burdened with anything that looks like work. (The fact is, however, that the small child is usually happiest when he is allowed to help, and does not think of housekeeping activities as work.) Some parents go to the opposite extreme and try to force cooperation in an authoritarian manner. This usually arouses resistance and negativism, as well as a tendency to be uncooperative when adults are not at hand to tell them what to do. For the relation between competition and cooperation in the child's life, *see* COMPETITION.

Experimental studies of adults have led to a number of fairly definitive findings. Many investigators stress the fact that cooperation and competition can both take place in the same situation, as in team contests like football. In a summary of experimental work in this area, Dashiell (1935) states that more work is performed when one group competes with another than when individuals work by themselves under no special motivation. However, when group competition is compared to individual competition, the group situation is sometimes more and sometimes less productive, depending on whether the individuals are responding to drives that will be satisfied by the success of the group.

Lewis (1944) applied the Zeigarnik technique in studying this problem, showing that interrupted tasks were remembered better than completed ones in both isolated and cooperative work. This indicates that when we complete a task with the help of a partner we relieve our tension just as much as when we complete it by ourselves. The finding, however, applies to routine tasks, such as copying letters, more fully than it does to complex tasks such as solving a jigsaw puzzle. Another series of studies has revealed that when cooperative effort is rewarded, (a) constructive use is made of specialized efforts and division of labor; (b) highly effective communication is maintained; and (c) friendship between group members is enhanced. One of the basic values of cooperative effort is that one member of the group relieves others since they do not have to duplicate his work. See ZEIGARNIK EFFECT.

Finally, many studies suggest that both quantity and quality of output are increased when the members of a team or work group share the group goal and identify closely with the group. Industrial psychologists have shown that development of group goals is usually enhanced by having the workers themselves discuss them and participate in setting them up. See MORALE (INDUSTRIAL), GROUP DYNAMICS.

COPROPHILIA. Excessive or morbid preoccupation with excreta or filth, or with objects and words that represent feces.

Coprophiliac tendencies may be shown in many ways. The milder manifestations are constant talk and jokes about defecation, the urge to splash in mud and mire, and a special interest in animal dung. Obsessive-compulsive individuals, such as the Collyer brothers, sometimes hoard their feces as they hoard everything else. Some sexual deviants attain gratification only when they are thinking of feces. Hebephrenic patients sometimes smear themselves or the walls with their own excrement, and deteriorated schizophrenic patients have been known to eat their feces (coprophagia).

In psychoanalytic theory coprophilia represents a fixation at the anal stage of development, particularly at the phase of that stage in which the child takes pleasure in the product itself as opposed to the act of retention or expulsion. This interest is believed to be transferred unconsciously to other objects that resemble the feces. According to Sandor Ferenczi such objects include mud pies, sand, pebbles, marbles, buttons, jewels, and coins. Collecting or hoarding any of these objects is interpreted (at least partially) as an anal, or coprophiliac, interest. Some analysts go further and consider painting, sculpturing, and cooking as sublimations of this interest. They also claim that fingerpainting is a valuable psychiatric technique largely because it enables the child to gratify his urge to handle and smear the feces.

CORPUS CALLOSUM. The massive band of nerve fibers connecting the two hemispheres of the brain (*Fig. 11*). Thousands of these fibers fan out from this band to connect areas in the cortex of one hemisphere with corresponding areas in the other.

Until recently little was known about this connecting system, but experiments on "split-brain" animals (that is, animals in which the cerebral hemispheres have been surgically separated) are indicative. One investigator cut the fibers from the two eyes in the optic chiasma (the point in the brain where they cross) in such a way that the left eye could send messages only to the left hemisphere and the right only to the right. He then blindfolded the right eye and taught the animal to discriminate (with the left eye) between a square and a triangle by rewarding him with food when the square was presented, and by withholding the reward when the triangle was shown. After this he blindfolded the left eye and presented the problem to the right—and found that the correct form was selected at once. Half of the brain had evidently "taught" the other half by way of messages transferred through the corpus callosum —an example of "bilateral transfer." When the corpus callosum was cut through entirely, the transfer did not occur (Sperry, 1961).

Later experiments have shown that animals with split brains can learn two conflicting discriminations simultaneously. Such learning is impossible for normal animals; when it is tried, they react with signs of intense frustration (Trevarthen, 1962). Both types of experiment demonstrate that the corpus callosum is a transmission area which enables the two hemispheres to work together.

This finding has been supported by studies of human subjects who have had their corpus callosum severed as a means of treating intractable epileptic seizures (Gazzaniga, Bogen, and Sperry, 1965). In a recently reported experiment, Gazzaniga (1967) had one of these patients look directly at the center of a screen while a picture of a spoon was flashed to the left. He then found that the subject could not say what he had seen. The explanation is that information presented to the left side of the body is processed by the brain's right hemisphere (and vice versa), but since the operation had cut this hemisphere off from the left hemisphere, where the speech center is located, the subject could not say what he had seen. However, the subject demonstrated that he knew what was there even though he could not verbalize it, since he was able to pick out a spoon with his left hand from a group of objects as the one that matched the picture. On the basis of experiments of this type, Gazzaniga has speculated that the two halves of the brain might even have separate thoughts and separate emotions. See TRANSFER OF TRAINING.

CORPUS STRIATUM (Striped Body). A portion of the cerebral hemispheres, enveloped by the cortex, and consisting of projection fibers passing upward and downward between the cortex and the thalamus, interspersed among cell bodies of the basal ganglia. The white fibers and gray cells give the structure its striped appearance.

In the course of evolution, the corpus striatum became established as a motor center in fishes. Its importance continued in amphibia and reptiles, and reached its highest development in birds. In mammals, however, the cerebral cortex gradually took over its motor functions, and in man it is primarily a transmission area rather than a control center. However, some authorities believe it is still involved in motor control, since injuries located in it are associated with certain forms of chorea, a disorder characterized by spasmodic, involuntary movements of the limbs or facial muscles. This suggests that the corpus striatum may play a role in smoothing and integrating motor activities.

COTARD'S SYNDROME (Chronic Delusional State of Negation). A psychotic state characterized by anxious depression, suicidal tendencies, and nihilistic delusions in which the patient denies the existence of his body and in some cases believes the whole of reality has ceased to exist.

First reported by the French neurologist Jules Cotard in 1880 under the title *Délire de Négation,* this disorder is now recognized as a separate entity only in France and Italy, and even in those countries it is often considered a symptom rather than a syndrome.

It is rarely observed in the United States and would probably be classified as an involutional psychotic reaction of the paranoid type. Arieti and Meth (1959) describe it as follows: "After an interval of anxiety, the patient, generally a woman in the involutional age, but at times even men and younger or older women, denies any existence to the surrounding reality. Nothing exists; the world has disappeared. After the cosmic reality is denied, the physical reality of the patient himself is denied. At first the patient claims that he has lost all sensation throughout his body; in some cases, he later claims that he does not exist. Everything is denied in this overwhelming delusional state. At times even the possibility of death is denied—the patient considers himself immortal. Other symptoms resemble the picture of involutional psychosis: the patient is depressed, may refuse food, has ideas of having been condemned by God. He may also hallucinate. He retains, however, the capacity to talk freely in spite of the depression and often is given to philosophical contemplation about his own life, life in general, and the world." *See* NIHILISM, DELUSION, DENIAL OF REALITY.

COUNSELING PSYCHOLOGY. A psychological specialty in which trained psychologists, usually Ph.D.'s, engage professionally in one or more fields of counseling. Counseling psychologists are usually known as psychologists rather than counselors, since the latter term is often applied to individuals who have had less training and who function at a lower professional level.

Counseling psychology originated in the vocational guidance movement, but gradually spread to other areas because of the widespread and growing need for specialized assistance. By 1945 the field had grown to a point where it became a separate division of the American Psychological Association, and today approximately 11 per cent of all psychologists specialize in this field. They are concerned with a wide variety of human problems, as indicated by the number of different settings in which they operate: schools, colleges, industrial and business organizations, government agencies, the armed services, as well as rehabilitation centers, hospitals, vocational guidance bureaus, marriage clinics, and other community agencies. The specific types of counseling, however, fall into seven major categories:

Vocational Counseling is still the major concern of most men and women in this field, particularly those who are connected with schools and colleges. Their work requires a broad knowledge of occupational and employment trends, and specialized training and experience in interviewing and vocational testing. *See* VOCATIONAL COUNSELING.

Educational Counseling is closely related to vocational counseling, since it is usually necessary for the student to select a program that will implement his choice of a vocation. But apart from specific vocational guidance, the educational counselor deals with the choice of college or specialized school, the selection of courses and curricula, and such problems as study skills and reading disability. In addition, he may direct the counseling activities of teachers and participate in training programs conducted by schools of education or special training institutes. Some psychologists have also developed group counseling programs, and studies show that they may be as effective as individual counseling in some situations. *See* SCHOOL PSYCHOLOGY.

Employee Counseling is a growing field in business, industry, and governmental organizations because of the current emphasis on worker morale. Psychologists carry on a wide range of activities, some directly and some indirectly related to the employees' job. Among them are counseling on schools, housing, family problems, emotional difficulties, and preparation for retirement. The employee counselor may handle the more overt problems himself, but usually makes referrals to specialists when long-term psychotherapy or psychiatric care is needed. Counseling of executive personnel is often handled by independent consulting psychologists on a part-time basis. *See* MORALE (INDUSTRIAL).

Rehabilitation Counseling has expanded so rapidly over recent years that the American Psychological Association has formed a separate division called The National Council on Psychological Aspects of Disability. The rehabilitation counselor works directly with the physically handicapped, including the blind, deaf, cardiac, tubercular, cerebral palsied, and orthopedically handicapped; his activities are coordinated with the remedial and training programs carried out by other specialists. He deals with such problems as the handicapped child's need for special educational opportunities and normal social experiences, a disfigured person's emotional problems arising from a changed "self-concept," or a patient's adjustment to prosthetic devices or life in a wheelchair. Many individuals also need vocational testing and advisement to help them make new adjustments to their regular occupation, or to receive adequate training for a job that is within the limits set by their disability. Rehabilitation counseling has also been extended to mental patients in some institutions, and a few centers for the physically handicapped (such as the Institute for the Crippled and Disabled in New York City) have begun to include psychiatric patients in their program. *See* REHABILITATION.

Old-Age Counseling is another field that has grown large enough to be included in a separate division of the American Psychological Association, the Division on Maturity and Old Age. Many members of this division are primarily concerned with research on the aptitudes, interests and personality characteristics of older people, and a growing number are engaged in counseling activities which draw heavily on these investigations. The work of the old age or geriatrics counselor focuses on four areas in particular: vocational guidance, retirement problems, personal difficulties (living alone versus living with a family, adjusting to life in an institution etc.), and intellectual and emotional disorders brought on by the aging process. Psychologists who work with older people have found that counseling frequently turns up unsuspected usable skills, and psychotherapy often brings improvement even with those who show signs of deterioration. *See* AGING.

Marriage Counseling has attracted a relatively small number of psychologists. The field is one in which the psychologist could well play a more significant part, since he would emphasize the crucial interpersonal aspects of marriage, dealing with such questions as choice of a marital partner, prediction of success and failure, sexual behavior, the problem of ambivalence, techniques for resolving conflicts, and problems of child-rearing and parent-child relations. This does not mean that the psychologist should ignore the other considerations which so frequently figure in marital counseling—sexual physiology, change of life, genetics, religion, economic problems, and legal questions. These would all have their place, but the psychologically trained counselor would view them in the light of the fact that marriage is basically a relationship between people. *See* MARRIAGE COUNSELING, MARITAL ADJUSTMENT.

Personal Counseling, also known as adjustment counseling, is concerned with human relations and emotional difficulties. Since questions of adjustment arise in every other type of counseling, and are often at the root of the problems encountered by the client, every counselor has to be capable of handling them: "The counseling psychologist recognizes the close interrelationship of all adjustment problems and therefore functions at a broad level regardless of the type of counseling involved. His orientation tends to be toward counseling the whole individual." (Anastasi, 1964)

The nature of counseling psychology as a whole, and personal counseling in particular, can probably be best clarified by differentiating counseling psychology from clinical psychology. As Tyler (1961) and others have pointed out, the two fields are similar in their emphasis on rapport between psychologist and client, and their confidential, accepting approach. The prime difference, however, is that the aim of clinical psychology is to change the client's reaction patterns, while the aim of counseling psychology is to enable the client to make more effective use of his present resources. Tyler has aptly described this process "minimum-change therapy," with an emphasis on readjustment as contrasted with any therapy that deals with the deeper levels of the personality.

Counseling, then, concentrates on the solution of specific problems such as timidity or poor study habits, and specific decisions, such as those involved in the selection of courses or choice of an occupation. Such problems ordinarily take much less time than psychotherapy, since the focus of the counseling psychologist is on the client's available assets, and not on deeply concealed feelings, memories and deficiencies which have to be slowly and carefully brought to the surface. And since the level at which they work differs, so do their techniques. The counseling psychologist frequently gives factual information, or tells his client where to get it, and often uses relatively objective tests of interests and skills; the clinical psychologist, on the other hand, relies more completely on clinical judgment and projective tests. Finally, the two tend to work with different types of clients, the counseling psychologist with

more nearly normal individuals who have minor personal difficulties or practical decisions to make, and the clinical psychologist with individuals who have deeper and more incapacitating personality disturbances. *See* CLINICAL PSYCHOLOGY.

Just how effective is psychological counseling? Studies of the predictive value of tests used in vocational and educational counseling have yielded fairly indicative results. An extensive follow-up investigation of 17,000 Air Force men who received a comprehensive battery of tests (general intelligence, numerical fluency, visual perception, psychomotor skills, mechanical ability) showed a fairly close correspondence between test performance and the type of work they engaged in thirteen years later. However, there was little or no relationship between test performance and degree of success on the job. (Thorndike and Hagen, 1959)

Other studies, cited by Tyler (1961), obtained the same results. In addition, a close relationship has been found between the initial tests and future educational level, but not the degree of academic success which the subjects achieved. Apparently success on the job or in school and college depends on factors which the test scores do not reveal. Other investigations have clearly indicated that vocational counseling which includes tests is of greater value than counseling without tests. In a British study, for example, 1639 young people were divided into two groups, one counseled with and the other without tests; follow-up studies showed that, on the whole, the group which took the tests made better job adjustments than those who had not been counseled on the basis of tests (Hunt and Smith, 1945).

Attempts have been made to study the effects of counseling from the point of view of increased self-knowledge, but so far it has not been possible to construct rating scales or other tests that show changes in insight. However, there is evidence that a continuous guidance program generally has a favorable effect on the future vocational and educational adjustment of high school and college students (though the effect was greater among better than among poorer students). The Wisconsin Counseling Study (Rothney, 1958) divided 870 high school sophomores into two groups, half of them receiving no counseling and half counseling by the university staff. The counseled students as a whole made somewhat better academic records, were more realistic about their weaknesses, were less dissatisfied with high school, were more consistent about their vocational choices, made better progress on the job, and were more apt to continue their education through high school graduation and beyond.

There is additional evidence of the value of counseling in the long-range Demonstration Guidance Project conducted in New York City (Wrightstone, 1960, 1961). In this project special opportunities are given to promising but culturally deprived seventh to ninth grade students and their parents: an intensive counseling program; cultural enrichment through field trips, concerts, etc.; remedial instruction where needed; counseling and social work with parents. Surveys of the results so far show that these pupils have been encouraged to continue their education in high school and possibly college. There have been positive effects on their interests, participation in activities, self-esteem, and social adjustment. The drop-out rate for these students is half the average, their academic work has improved markedly, and their I.Q.'s have risen an average of nine points as compared with the decline which is usually found in underprivileged groups. The investigators attribute much of this improvement to their relationship with their guidance counselor.

Although many individuals attest to the value of personal counseling, ade-

quate techniques for measuring its effectiveness have not yet been developed.

COUNTERTRANSFERENCE. The conscious or unconscious emotional reaction of a therapist to his patient.

In psychoanalysis and other forms of psychotherapy the patient displaces, or "transfers," his own repressed thoughts and feelings to the therapist. At times he may be angry at the therapist, at times he may feel strong affection for him. The therapist's tendency to respond to these emotions in kind is termed the countertransference. The psychoanalytic theory holds that if the therapist reacts to the attitudes and emotional outbursts of the patient, it is because they arouse his own repressed impulses. Such reactions are believed to interfere with the progress of therapy. One of the major reasons why future analysts are required to go through analysis themselves is to make them aware of the countertransference and to enable them to adopt measures that will help them avoid becoming emotionally involved with their patients. In this so-called didactic analysis they become aware of their own sensitivities and reinforce themselves against reacting to displays of hostility, love, criticism, or anxiety on the part of the patient. In other words, they learn how to counter the countertransference. *See* TRANSFERENCE, PSYCHOANALYSIS (THERAPY).

CRANIAL NERVES. The twelve nerves of the somatic nervous system, some sensory and some motor, which connect directly to the brain.

The cranial nerves are known by both name and number. The olfactory nerve (I) which mediates the sense of smell, and the optic nerve (II) which mediates the sense of vision are not true nerves in that they are made up of brain tissue that has migrated from the central nervous system to form the retina of the eye and the olfactory membrane. The oculomotor (III), trochlear (IV) and abducens (VI) all consist of motor fibers controlling the muscles and movements of the eye. The trigeminal nerve (V) consists of sensory fibers which carry tactile sensations from the face, tongue, and mouth; and motor fibers which exert major control over chewing, tongue movements, and swallowing. The latter functions are also served by the glossopharyngeal (IX) and hypoglossal (XII). Several of the nerves are involved in the sense of taste: the sensory portion of the facial (VII) serves the front two-thirds of the tongue, but the glossopharyngeal (IX) and vagus (X) also play a part since they innervate the taste buds in the back of the tongue and throat. The motor portion of the facial (VII) controls facial movement. The auditory vestibular (VIII) carries impulses for both hearing and balance from the inner ear. The spinal accessory (XI) controls the neck muscles and viscera.

The vagus nerve (X) deserves special mention because of its importance in emotional reactions. It is the only one of the twelve that extends beyond the cranium, since it serves the heart, blood vessels, and viscera. It works closely with the autonomic system which controls the internal organs and is involved in psychophysiologic (psychosomatic) reactions. As one example of the latter reactions, studies have shown that the vagus nerve is responsible for the oversecretion of gastric fluids that produce ulcers in men and women who undergo prolonged stress (Gellhorn and Loofbourrow, 1963). When it is rendered inoperative, gastric secretion is reduced and the ulcers heal in 90 per cent of cases. *See* NERVOUS SYSTEM.

CREATIVE THINKING. A form of directed thinking applied to the discovery of new solutions to problems, new techniques and devices, or new artistic expressions.

Everyday thinking is largely devoted to problems that can be solved by assembling readily available information and applying established rules. This "closed system" approach is usually sufficient for most of our practical difficulties, such as repairing a lamp or marketing a product. But occasionally we are faced with problems that cannot be solved by conventional techniques—problems that require "open system" thinking, the kind that can best be termed adventurous or creative. We usually associate the scientist, the artist, and the inventor with this type of thinking, but in a world as complex and changing as ours, a high degree of creativity is demanded in every phase of life.

The psychological studies of creative thinking have focused largely on scientists. Although it is not easy to put their thinking processes into words, there appear to be four major steps in the germination of original ideas (Wallas, 1926):

Preparation. The scientist prepares himself for discovery by studying the work of his predecessors. In the process, he assembles pertinent facts, clarifies his thinking, raises meaningful questions, and finds promising leads. Thorough preparation frequently shortens the period of actual discovery. Einstein began thinking about the basic concepts of physics in their relation to the speed of light when he was a student of sixteen. It took seven more years of intensive study and fact-gathering before he realized that he could resolve the discrepancies in current theories by questioning the ordinary concept of time. After that, it took him only five weeks to write his revolutionary paper on relativity, even though he was employed as a full time clerk in a Swiss patent office.

The fact that many scientific discoveries are accidental seems to deny the importance of preparation. Alexander Fleming happened to place some staphylococci, a pus-forming bacteria, on a culture plate that contained penicillin mold, and found that the penicillin dissolved the bacteria. Here was a happy accident that led to a whole new chapter in medical science. And yet, was it completely accidental? It is highly unlikely that a person untrained in bacteriology would have noticed this effect or realized its importance, and he certainly would not have followed it up by performing a series of experiments. In other words, preparation is essential in transforming chance events into significant discoveries. Bread mold containing penicillin had been used by the German people for over a thousand years as a treatment for infection, yet none of them followed up this lead scientifically because they did not have the proper preparation.

There is so much emphasis on inspiration in art that the importance of preparation in this field is often overlooked. But biographies of great writers, musicians, and artists invariably reveal that they have gone through long years of self-training, practice, and experimentation before they were able to develop their own techniques. Child prodigies appear to start ahead of the game, and yet they must also go through this process if they are to develop mature creative ability. People who have been inadequately prepared occasionally produce a single good work more or less by chance, but they seldom repeat or build on their triumphs.

Incubation and Illumination. Overemphasis on sudden inspiration also makes us overlook another side of the process. Once we have adequately prepared ourselves to solve a problem, and are eager to find a solution, it takes time for creative ideas to ripen. During this so-called incubation period, our mind continues to mull over the problem on an unconscious or semiconscious level and, in some cases at least, a solution rises to the surface and dramatically presents itself in the form of sudden insight or illumination. In other words, we "see the light."

There is an air of mystery about creative thinking since the process of incubation is indescribable and the moment of illumination unpredictable. We do know that many solutions occur to us after a period of relaxation or sleep, but psychologists differ in their opinions about the process that produced them. Some claim that when we think about the same problem persistently we get into a rut, but after a rest period we are likely to approach it from a new angle. Others believe we actively work out the problem during the rest period itself. Descartes, for example, claimed that the basic idea of analytic geometry came to him in two dreams. Friedrich Kekule had a dream in which a snake seized its own tail, and this suggested the ring configuration of the benzine molecule. Hermann Hilprecht solved a Babylonian inscription in a dream, and Henri Poincaré claimed that the idea of the calculus suddenly popped into his mind as he put his foot on the step of a bus. The poet A. E. Housman insisted that his poems originated in the pit of his stomach and later rose into consciousness. Mozart claimed that he had a visual image of his melodies in the form of a wavy line which gradually and automatically congealed into notes, and finally presented itself to him as a completed work. These experiences are all on the descriptive level, but they argue strongly for the theory of unconscious thinking.

Verification. The process does not end with illumination, for no idea is genuinely creative until it is put to the test. The artist's vision must be expressed in stone or paint, and the scientist's hypothesis must be tested through observation and experimentation. There is less agreement on the standards on which artistic productions are judged than the standards for scientific discoveries, but the important fact is that each requires verification of some kind.

Even in science there is some variation in the process. An idea that is internally coherent requires less extensive testing than an idea that is more fragmentary. Observations made during one eclipse of the sun were enough to convince many physicists of the validity of Einstein's theories on light and mass, but thousands of trials were necessary before tranquilizers were accepted in psychiatry. Einstein's ideas were an integral part of the broader theory of relativity, but we do not know enough about the brain and nervous system to explain why tranquilizers act as they do.

What kinds of people are most likely to be creative? A number of personality studies have been made, but there are few if any consistent findings. In one piece of research, masculinity and social nonconformity were both found to be highly correlated with problem-solving ability. Fluency, flexibility, and the ability to elaborate also seemed important. However, problem solving and creative thinking are not always identical. Many investigators have felt that a study of emotional instability and neuroticism might throw light on the creative process, but no definite conclusions have been reached. Psychoanalysts are particularly divided on this question: Ernst Kris, for example, believes that neuroticism is a positive factor in the artistic field, but Lawrence Kubie is convinced that artists are no more neurotic than other people, and that neurosis is a handicap wherever it occurs.

Some investigators have found that creative people often have immature personality traits, such as dependency, defiance of convention or authority, a feeling of destiny or omnipotence, and gullibility (Jones, 1957). The last of these qualities may be the most surprising, but biographies of Copernicus, Goethe, Darwin, Newton, and Freud all give evidence of extreme credulousness in certain areas—for example, Copernicus accepted the Greek idea that the circular motions of the planets reflected the perfection of the Creator, and Freud became deeply involved in some aspects of numerology in the middle of his career. It may be that their gullibility grew out of the same receptivity to novel ideas that made them geniuses.

Psychologists, then, have made some progress in describing the process of creative thinking, but they are the first to admit that they have not found the touchstone for creativity, if there is one, nor can they offer a set of rules for discovering original ideas. The evidence does indicate, however, that training, knowledge, and hard work are absolutely essential, and an opportunity to mull over ideas and let them "percolate" by themselves is highly useful. But even though these procedures are religiously followed, no one can predict whether they will produce truly creative solutions. See INSIGHT, CREATIVITY TESTS, MANAGEMENT DEVELOPMENT, ESTHETICS.

CREATIVITY TESTS. Tests designed to identify creative talent.

In recent years a number of psychologists have turned their attention to the subject of creativity, for two major reasons: first, they have recognized that creative ability is not the same as academic intelligence, but involves nonintellectual factors such as receptivity to novel ideas and relaxed attention to problems; second, they felt that creativity research might help to meet the demand for new ideas in science, technology, and social affairs as well as in the arts.

A number of investigations have been made of the factors involved in creativity, notably by Guilford and his associates in their work for the Office of Naval Research (Guilford, 1954). In this project many new tests were developed and administered to students and military personnel. When the results were analyzed, three factors appeared to be most closely associated with creativity, or "divergent thinking": fluency, flexibility, and originality. A few sample items from Guilford's Southern California Tests of Divergent Production will be given to illustrate the type of tests used to measure these factors.

Word Fluency. Within an allotted time, the subject writes as many words as he can containing a given letter, or beginning with a certain prefix, or rhyming with a given word. Performance on these tests has been found to correlate fairly well with achievement in science and art courses.

Ideational Fluency. Naming things that belong in a certain class, such as solids that will not burn; or listing different uses for a common object such as a ruler.

Associational Fluency. Listing as many words as possible that are similar in meaning to a given word such as "excellent"; or inserting an adjective to complete a simile: for example "as———as a firecracker."

Expressional Fluency. The subject is given a series of four letters and is required to make as many sentences as possible using them as first letters of words: "M-A-T-S" (Mothers are too serious, etc.).

Flexibility. Several tests are used, including Hidden Pictures (finding concealed faces), Hidden Figures (finding a geometric figure embedded in a more complex pattern); and Match Problems (removing a given number of matchsticks to leave a given number of squares or triangles).

Originality. One of the items is a Free Association Test in which the subject gives the first word that occurs to him in response to a stimulus word. The responses are scored on the basis of uncommonness. A study by Licht (1947) has shown that scientists, engineers, artists, musicians, and writers tend to give more original associations than executives, politicians, teachers, or salesmen. A second item is the Consequences Test, which calls for listing as many different consequences of a specified

event as possible—for example, "What would happen if every telephone went dead at the same time?" This test yields a score for ideational fluency based on the number of obvious responses, and a score for originality based on the number of remote responses. Moderately high correlations (.30 to .55) have been found between the originality scores and teachers' ratings of the creativity of their students in art and science. Approximately the same correlations were found between scores on the ingenuity test in the FACT battery and criteria of originality in high school art and English classes. *See* APTITUDE TESTS (Multiple).

Many other types of items are used in creativity tests by different authors. Among them are "fable endings"—for example, writing a moralistic, a humorous, and a sad ending for a story about a mischievous dog that bites people without warning (Getzels and Jackson); "pattern meanings"—naming possible objects suggested by abstract geometrical patterns (Wallach and Kogan); "remote associations"—finding a fourth word associated with three other words, such as "rat—blue—cottage" (Mednick); and "ingenuity"—solving a practical problem, such as how to restore transmission after a high wind has destroyed a television tower in a small town on a flat prairie (Flanagan). The Torrance Tests of Creative Thinking present a variety of word and picture items. The battery entitled Thinking Creatively with Words contains such "activities" as: presenting an intriguing picture and asking the subject to write questions he would ask to find out what is happening, and listing possible causes and consequences of the action depicted; suggesting ways of improving a given toy; listing unusual uses for a common object and asking unusual questions about it. A second battery, Thinking Creatively with Pictures, consists of drawing an interesting picture that incorporates a given brightly colored curved shape; completing an unusual picture from a few given lines; and producing as many pictures as possible from pairs of short parallel lines or circles.

The Torrance Tests were developed as part of a research program focused on experiences that foster creativity in the classroom. Other creativity tests have been specifically designed for use with engineers: the AC Test of Creative Ability, the Owens Creativity Test for Machine Design, and the Purdue Creativity Test.

Undoubtedly many new instruments will be devised in the near future, and it may well be that factors other than fluency, flexibility and originality or ingenuity will be stressed. In fact, Guilford and others have already indicated that tests of reasoning and evaluation are particularly important in creative scientific achievement, to counterbalance the emphasis on free divergent thinking. Among the tests employed for these purposes are the Ship Destination Test, Logical Reasoning, Pertinent Questions, and the Watson-Glaser Critical Thinking Appraisal. In addition, it is now recognized that special factors of a visual, auditory and kinesthetic nature may be essential in the arts, although many of these factors have yet to be identified.

Applications of creativity and problem-solving tests have produced many provocative findings. Several studies have indicated that exceptional problem solving ability is frequently associated with the trait of nonconformity (Nakamura, 1958). High school students who score high on creativity tests tend to prefer the more unconventional careers and admire personal characteristics which differ from those they think their teachers prefer (Getzels and Jackson, 1962). These investigators have also found that top scorers on creativity tests average 23 IQ points less than the top scorers in intelligence tests, and were frequently unable to solve problems that required rigid, systematic,

"convergent" thinking. Various studies have shown that the more creative children tend to be less anxious, more easygoing, more sociable, more self-dependent, and more aware of unconscious motives than other children. They also tend to come from families that permit risk-taking and recognize divergent ideas and interests.

One especially interesting effect of the current investigations is that creativity is becoming a meeting ground for the two general areas of art and science. As Anastasi remarks (1961), "Investigations of scientific talent are becoming increasingly concerned with creative ability. Interest has shifted from the individual who is merely a cautious, accurate and critical thinker to the one who also displays ingenuity, originality, and inventiveness. Thus creativity, long regarded as the prime quality in artistic production, is coming more and more to be recognized as a basis for scientific achievement as well." As greater weight is attached to creativity, the intelligence tests of the future will probably include productive thinking in addition to their traditional emphasis on understanding and recall. *See* ESTHETICS, CREATIVE THINKING.

CRETINISM. A metabolic disorder in which both mental and physical development are retarded as a result of deficiency in thyroid secretion during fetal life or infancy.

Defects in the thyroid gland are most frequently due to lack of iodine in the diet, but they may also result from birth injuries or infectious diseases such as measles, whooping cough or diphtheria in childhood. Recent studies indicate that genetic defects may also lead to low thyroid production in some cases.

If a deficiency of thyroid secretion occurs in the prenatal or early postnatal periods, the brain may be damaged and gross physical and mental defects may result. The typical cretin is short, heavy-set, with a protruding abdomen and stubby legs. He has wiry hair; thick eyelids, lips, and tongue; a broad nose; and dry, cold skin. His basal metabolism is extremely low and he is sexually immature, bland, and phlegmatic, and either moderately or severely mentally retarded. *See* MENTAL RETARDATION (CAUSES).

In recent years the number of cases of cretinism has been reduced to less than 5 per cent of the institutionalized mentally retarded as a result of the widespread use of iodized salt and the early detection and treatment of thyroid deficiency. About half the victims of severe cretinism can be brought up to nearly average intelligence if treated with thyroid extract before six months of age. The rate of success is generally higher for those who have acquired the disorder after birth, provided treatment is not delayed for a long period. Striking improvement is often achieved in both the physical and intellectual condition of these children, and many of them can attain normal or near-normal levels of functioning. But it is essential to keep them on regular doses of thyroxin in order to prevent backsliding. For hypothyroidism in older persons, *see* MYXEDEMA.

CRIME AND CRIMINALS. Psychology and psychiatry have made many contributions to the problem of adult criminality. Among the most significant have been (1) delineation of many basic personality patterns and emotional disturbances associated with crime, (2) a study of various internal motives and environmental factors that lead to antisocial behavior, (3) recognition of the emerging types of criminals whose behavior is, at least in part, a response to the tensions of our time, and (4) methods of integrating psychotherapy and other psychological techniques into the rehabilitation of criminals. Representative examples of each of these contributions will now be given.

Personality. Diagnostic tests and case studies have demonstrated that there is no single "criminal personality." Rather, there are a number of widely different patterns. A recent study (Gaietaniello, 1963) conducted at Sing Sing prison divided the inmates into four major categories: (a) dyssocial individuals, who have adopted a distorted sense of values, usually as a result of faulty home life and membership in a neighborhood gang (31 per cent); (b) antisocial (psychopathic) personalities, who are basically egocentric, impulsive, aggressive, and unethical, but who do not form close relationships even with a gang (35 per cent); (c) psychoneurotics and alcoholics: in contrast to the first two groups, these offenders are immature, anxious, or otherwise emotionally disturbed (20 per cent); (d) borderline schizophrenics, who tend to be hostile, suspicious, and paranoid (13 per cent). The remaining 1 per cent were diagnosed as psychotic. Some inmates, of course, fell into more than one category.

Some investigators believe there are only two major types of adult criminals. The "primary sociopaths," comprising the dyssocial and antisocial types, are characterized by a low anxiety level and an underdeveloped conscience. These individuals engage in criminal activity as a way of life or as a form of rebellious, self-centered behavior. The "neurotic sociopaths," on the other hand, have a high anxiety level and an overdeveloped or misdirected conscience. They are subject to persistent feelings of guilt and apprehension. When these feelings become too intense for them to handle, they do not repress them or transform them into the usual neurotic symptoms, but seek to ward them off through outward activity that all too often takes the form of stealing, sexual promiscuity, or some other form of antisocial behavior.

Many investigations have indicated that certain kinds of persons are prone to commit certain kinds of crimes.

Among sex offenders, voyeurs and exhibitionists are frequently inhibited neurotics or isolated, socially inadequate schizophrenics; while rapists and sadists tend to be hostile psychopaths. Embezzlers and forgers are psychopathic in their lack of scruples and their tendency to be lone operators. They rarely commit crimes of violence.

In spite of these observations, several types of crimes are committed by a wide variety of personality types. Shoplifters have been found to fall into at least eighteen different categories, among them drug addicts, alcholics, neurotics, psychopathic personalities, schizophrenics, and victims of senile brain degeneration. And although homicide is the most extreme of crimes, one cannot simply assume that the murderer is deranged. In a study of 175 murderers, Guttmacher (1960) found that only fifty-three were psychotic, that seventeen had other serious abnormalities, but most of the others represented a variety of types, such as dyssocial personalities, antisocial personalities, and alcoholics.

On another level, evidence has recently come to light that certain chromosomal defects may be associated with highly aggressive tendencies. Two cases in point are Daniel Hugon, a self-confessed French murderer, and Richard F. Speck, the convicted killer of eight nurses. A test known as karyotyping revealed that these men were born with an extra male chromosome (XYY instead of XY). This defect is believed not only to be associated with aggressive tendencies in many cases, but with dull intelligence, acne, tallness and a bizarre sexual history—most of which apply to both Speck and Hugon. Studies of inmates of penal institutions have shown that this genetic abnormality is sixty times as prevalent in men convicted of violent crimes as in the general population—although men with chromosomal aberrations actually make up only 3 per cent of all convicts. Some authorities attribute their aggressive tendencies directly to an excess of male hormones; others maintain that they do not become antisocial because of any specific genetic tendency, but because of difficulties in social and emotional adjustment arising from their excessive height and early maturation. Further research is needed in this entire area.

Causal Factors. In view of the wide variety of personalities that commit crimes, it should not be surprising that adult criminal behavior stems from many different factors. Most of these factors have been mentioned in the discussions of antisocial and dyssocial personalities, as well as under the topic of juvenile delinquency. The majority of adult criminals come from crowded, deprived neighborhoods where lawless behavior is an everyday occurrence. Alcoholics, drug addicts, pickpockets, and prostitutes are part of the landscape, and the major recreational centers are dives, poolrooms, and corner bars. The boy who comes from a broken family or disorganized home has little to protect him from the influences of such a neighborhood, and little to motivate him to make the most of his educational or occupational opportunities. A common pattern today is for the boy to become a high school dropout and then find that he cannot get or cannot keep a job. In time he may turn to petty crime for cash and kicks, and gradually develop into a hardened adult criminal. It should be recognized, however, that not all adult criminals have been juvenile delinquents. In many cases the antisocial or neurotic tendencies which lead to criminality do not fully express themselves until the problems of adult life have to be faced.

Emerging Types. Recent investigators, particularly Yablonsky (1963), have contrasted the "new" criminal of today with the "professional" criminal described in the early studies of social psychologists and sociologists. The earlier type of criminal regarded crime simply as a way of making a living. He received regular training in a gang that specialized in one or another type of crime, but developed techniques of his own which he pridefully regarded as the marks of a "real pro." Class distinctions were common among these criminals, and those who lived by their wits—the embezzlers and con men, for example—considered themselves infinitely superior to the burglars and pickpockets who were more dependent on physical skills. Yet practically all criminals had three things in common: they worked hard to develop their methods of operation, they planned and rehearsed their "jobs" with minute care, and they attempted to avoid violence since it would increase their personal risk and the chances of detection—and in some cases because it violated their professional code of ethics.

The professional criminal is still with us, but a completely different type of offender has recently come to the fore. This new criminal does not belong to a class of experts on thievery or forgery, but to a hoodlum gang committed to violence. The primary motives for his antisocial activities are relief from boredom, release of tension, and status in the gang. He wants money, but mainly as a means of obtaining more kicks, not to help him live in style. He rarely plans in advance; instead, he chooses the nearest or easiest victim and commits his crime on the spur of the moment. His greatest ambition is to prove that he is a cold, brutal, tough guy who will not hesitate to beat or even kill his victim. This, he believes, will gain him the deepest respect among the members of his gang and perhaps even in the world outside. It is obvious that this type of criminal is an extremely dangerous individual—although he may not be as "new" as Yablonsky asserts, for violent gangs were common in London and New York in the nineteenth century.

Rehabilitation. It is almost a truism today that adult crime can be reduced only by handling the problem from every angle at once. It is viewed as an illness of society, not merely an illness of the individual; it reflects a distortion of values in our culture as well as personal maladjustment. It is too large a problem for any single group to cope with. Sociologists, psychiatrists, psychologists, city planners, clergymen, educators, and lawmakers must collaborate in finding a solution. At the same time, each discipline must make efforts to perfect its own approach. What, then, have psychology and psychiatry contributed in recent years? The following are perhaps their most far reaching emphases:

(a) recognition that criminal behavior is an expression of personality maladjustment, and that more exact descriptions must be made of the personalities of criminals, such as those mentioned above;

(b) recognition that the prevention and treatment of criminal behavior should be based on the same general types of approaches that are used in dealing with all pathological behavior: family guidance, correction of unhealthy environmental conditions, early diagnosis, counseling for young people, vocational guidance—and in addition, psychotherapy, medical therapy, and hospitalization when necessary;

(c) emphasis on rehabilitation in the hospital or prison, as opposed to the present preoccupation with punishment —this means greater opportunity for occupational training, development of hobbies and interests, social readjustment, and constructive work experiences. A promising example of retraining is the course in computer programming given to selected inmates of Sing Sing prison—practically all of whom were able to get jobs in industry as soon as they were paroled;

(d) development of new therapeutic techniques: group discussion sessions, group psychotherapy, self-government in the institution, and the "therapeutic community" concept in which offenders learn to live harmoniously in a small society that acts as a bridge to the wider community;

(e) strong recommendations that society take an interest in the criminal after he has been released, by helping him find suitable work, advising him on personal problems, and providing additional psychotherapy or sociotherapy where needed, so that he will lead a more satisfying life and not become one of the 50 per cent or more who now return to criminal behavior after their stay in prison. *See* REHABILITATION, MILIEU THERAPY, LEGAL PSYCHOLOGY, LEGAL PSYCHIATRY, SEXUAL DEVIATIONS (GENERAL), DRUG ADDICTION, ALCOHOLIC ADDICTION, ANTISOCIAL REACTION, DYSSOCIAL REACTION, BORDERLINE DISORDERS, JUVENILE DELINQUENCY.

CRITICAL PERIOD. A stage of development in which an organism is particularly amenable to certain influences, such as physical conditions or learning experiences, which may bring about significant and lasting changes in behavior. It is believed to be difficult or impossible to produce these effects before, and in some cases after, this pivotal period.

The concept of the critical period has been applied to both biological and psychological development. An example in the physical sphere is the effect of German measles on the developing organism. If the mother contracts this disease during the first fifteen weeks of pregnancy, there is a high probability that the child will be defective. This article will confine itself, however, to the various aspects of psychological behavior to which the idea of the critical period has been applied.

The first is *socialization*. The critical period starts when the behavioral mechanisms of the child or animal have developed up to a point where he can maintain social contacts with members of his own kind. Among dogs, the first signs are tail-wagging and playful fighting; among monkeys, clinging to the mother; among human beings, visual investigation of the environment and smiling in response to others. The mother must, however, respond to these advances if socialization is to proceed normally. If she is cold and distant, development may be delayed or distorted. At one time it was thought that animals and children become attached to their mothers only because they receive "rewards" of food from her. Newer experiments and observations, however, indicate that emotional factors are at least equally important. This theory holds that the social bond is largely due to the fact that the mother (or mother figure) alleviates the anxiety of the helpless infant.

Studies of imprinting (Hess, 1959; Lorenz, 1937) as well as experiments on monkeys by Harlow (1959, 1962) and others are frequently cited as evidence that the first signs of *emotional response* to other creatures occur early in life of animals, and investigations of emotional deprivation by Spitz (1945, 1948) and others appear to support this interpretation for human beings. According to Spitz (1947), the critical period begins within the first few weeks of life, when the mother can successfully dissipate the child's anxiety simply by holding or caressing him, and it ends when the typical "eight months anxiety" sets in. During the latter period (which may actually start anywhere between the fifth and twelfth month) the child develops a pronounced fear of strangers and strange situations, and mere contact with the mother is insufficient to allay his anxiety because his tendency is now to escape rather than to seek refuge. However, if his relationship with his mother and others in the family has been a warm one during the first few months of life, he will not be damaged by these new fears, and will in time learn how to overcome them. *See* AFFECTIONAL DRIVE, IMPRINTING, MOTHERING.

Other observations tend to confirm the idea of a critical period for emotional response. When rats are given an ample opportunity to explore their environment early in their lives, they show few signs of upset in tests of emotionality given later on. On the "open-field" test (being placed in a large, unfamiliar compartment) they adapt to the strange environment with less than the usual amount of urination and defecation, which are indicative of fear; and when they are placed under the stress of hunger and thirst, they survive longer than rats that have not had the exploratory experience. There is evidence that the early experiences result in an increase in the size of the adrenal glands, since they play an active role in meeting emergencies (Schaffer, 1958; Levine et al., 1957).

Human infants also need opportunities to explore their environment and adapt to different situations in order to awaken their emotional as well as their sensory responses. However, they can only handle mild, benign "doses" of these experiences. Drastically new situations tend to be traumatic; especially when they occur at certain periods. Scott (1962) puts the critical interval for maximum emotional disturbance in children at about seven months of age (i.e., at the end of the period for primary socialization), and Caldwell (1961) has shown that infants exhibit increasingly severe emotional reactions to adoption between three and twelve months of age. Similarly, Bowlby (1951) has found that a large proportion of juvenile delinquents were separated from their mothers in early infancy. Later on, when the child's emotional security and relationships to people outside the family are better established, these changes are less traumatic. *See* EMOTIONAL DEVELOPMENT, MATERNAL DEPRIVATION.

There also appear to be critical periods for *learning*. Tests show that rats benefit most when they are given opportunities for spontaneous learning at approximately twenty to thirty days after weaning; similar opportunities have little effect when they have reached adulthood (Forgays, 1962). Certain birds, such as the chaffinch, will learn the song of their species only within a fixed period. Among human beings there is evidence of a critical period for learning the sex role at around three years of age. A study of hermaphroditic children reared as members of one sex and then changed to the other indicated that emotional disturbance was minimal if the change was made before two and a half years of age. (Money, Hampson, and Hampson, 1957)

There is also evidence of critical periods for the acquisition of intellectual and motor skills. Studies show, however, that this is no simple matter, since readiness for climbing, toilet training, bicycle riding, reading, writing, and other activities depends not only on maturation of the nervous and muscular systems, but on emotional and experiential factors as well. *See* READINESS TESTS, TOILET TRAINING, MOTOR DEVELOPMENT.

Scott (1962), one of the major investigators of critical periods, views them largely from a maturational point of view, holding that they occur when the organism reaches a stage of development at which an active process of reorganization takes place. He therefore interprets critical periods as "landmarks" during which profound and often lasting behavior changes occur. Schneirla and Rosenblatt (1963) challenge this interpretation, contending that Scott's critical periods are artificially separated from ongoing behavior, and that all periods are critical in the sense that behavior is continually being organized and reorganized as a result of the interaction between the individual and his environment. In this process the changes that occur result from a combination of growth, or maturational factors, with stimulation or experiential factors. These investigators claim that learning does not suddenly take place when a special stage of maturation is reached, but may within certain bounds actually affect the maturational process itself.

Scott (1963) has answered that he did not intend to imply that no development occurs before the critical period, but only that the rate of reorganization

of behavior patterns is most rapid and conspicuous at that time. This more modest point of view does not imply that all will be lost if the individual does not receive exactly the right amount of experience at exactly the right time. Nevertheless it does suggest that there are periods during which the right kind of experience can have an optimum effect.

CULTURE-FAIR TESTS. Tests of mental ability based on common human

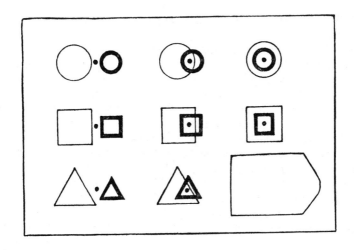

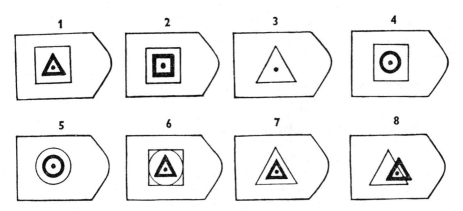

Fig. 13. An example from the Standard Progressive Matrices, used experimentally as a "culture fair" intelligence test. The subject selects one of the eight items to complete the series.

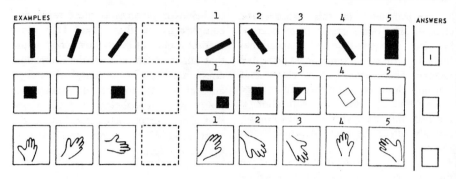

Fig. 14. Examples from the Cattell Culture Fair Intelligence Test. The subject selects the item that completes the series.

experience and relatively free of special cultural influences.

The conviction that standard intelligence tests reflect middle-class values, experience, and information and are therefore unfair when administered to children or adults from other environments has led to widespread interest in culture-fair tests. Theoretically, a truly culture-fair test could be applied across social lines to provide equal opportunity to all individuals examined. Such a universal test would also permit fair comparisons to be made between people from different cultures (*Fig. 13, Fig. 14*).

The need for a culture-fair test has been supported by many observations and experiments. One example, from Cronbach (1960), can be used to typify these findings. Two groups, one from a higher and the other from a lower socioeconomic level, were given the following problem: "A symphony is to a composer as a book is to what?—Paper, sculptor, author, musician, man." Eight-one per cent of the higher level and only 51 per cent of the lower level group gave the correct response. They were then given this problem: "A baker goes with bread like a carpenter goes with what?—A saw, a house, a spoon, a nail, a man." This time 50 per cent of each group answered correctly—indicating that the problem was fairer,

at least for these two groups of subjects.

Analysis of current tests revealed many items of the same general character as the first one given above, particularly among the verbal problems. Psychologists then began to experiment with culture-fair tests, and Davis and Havighurst (1948) suggested three important guides: (1) choose problems that are equally common and equally motivating to all socioeconomic groups and express them in ways that are culturally common; (2) sample a far wider range of mental activities than current tests, and emphasize useful and practical abilities as well as academic items; (3) find other ways of testing and validating the items than their relation to school work.

A number of different techniques have been used in attempting to design tests which rule out language, knowledge and skills that are specific to any given culture. The Leiter International Performance Scale, originally developed through application to different ethnic groups in Hawaii, almost completely eliminates instructions by presenting samples of each task and treating the comprehension of the task as part of the test. The items involve choosing printed cards and inserting them in a frame in order to solve such problems as copying a block design, completing a picture or series, matching identical forms or pictures, and selecting correct analogies. The Culture Fair Intelligence Test, developed by R. B. Cattell, is of the pencil and paper type, and contains such problems as selecting a design which completes a given series, marking a geometrical figure that does not belong with a number of others, and marking a design that correctly completes a given matrix or pattern. The Raven Progressive Matrices presents sixty matrices, or designs, of increasing difficulty, from each of which a part has been removed. The subject chooses the missing insert from several given alternatives. The Goodenough-Harris Drawing Test requires the subject to draw a picture of a man, a woman, and himself; the drawings are then scored for the inclusion of seventy-three items such as individual body parts, clothing details, perspective, and proportion.

These and other attempts to create culture-fair tests have run into a number of difficulties. Various investigations have shown that a truly universal test cannot be constructed. Every test seemed to call for attitudes, skills, or information which were more dependent on one type of experience than another. Verbal tests were soon abandoned as a whole because of the wide differences in vocabulary from society to society. Moreover, the concepts expressed by words were found to vary immensely from culture to culture. But even performance tests have given trouble. On one of these tests, children from a primitive African tribe scored much lower than European children on practically all items except one that required the assembly of colored mosaics. It was later found that their games and ceremonies made extensive use of color and gave them a great deal of experience in examining patterns and shapes. Along the same lines, David Wechsler (1966), creator of the Wechsler-Bellevue Tests, points out that non-verbal tests may be as culture-bound as verbal tests, and that they are also too limited in range to serve by themselves as adequate measures of intelligence. He states: "Culture-free tests fail to attain their end because, in the first place, the items usually employed are themselves subject to particular environmental experiences. A circle in one place may be associated with the sun, in another with a copper coin, in still another with a wheel. In some places a dog is a pet, in others a detested animal. Pictures, in the long run, are just symbols, and these may be as difficult to understand and recognize as words; they have to be interpreted, as anyone who has attempted to learn sign language knows." *See* LANGUAGE, CONCEPT FORMATION.

Attitude and motivation have been found to affect test performance as much as training and experience—and these also vary widely from culture to culture. Children in the educated classes and children from "higher" cultures are usually brought up to place a high value on intellectual ability, and are often prodded and given special rewards for competitive achievement. On the other hand, there is very little impetus to solve problems in environments where intellectual skill is not highly prized. Moreover, the attitude toward the test situation may itself be an important factor. The Zuñi Indian society in Southwest America cultivates cooperation and frowns upon any kind of competition. As a result, when school children were sent to the blackboard to do arithmetic problems, they hesitated to finish them before all the others had completed the work. *See* COMPETITION.

Observations of this kind have led psychologists to abandon the idea of a single test for everyone. Some, however, have concentrated on constructing tests that would be fair to all levels of their own society. Unfortunately even these efforts have met with setbacks. Experience with the Davis-Eells Games seems to be typical. This test presents a series of problems that are not limited to the experience of any social level—for example, the child is asked to choose between drawings that show three ways of carrying packages home from the grocery store. Recent studies indicate that this test has no advantage over others so far as cultural fairness is concerned, since it showed the same differences between socioeconomic groups as were shown on conventional tests. (Drake, 1959)

It may well be that we have underestimated the cultural differences which are actually operative in our own society. New studies related to Head Start and the Poverty Program indicate that there are wide variations not only in basic vocabulary, but in fundamental motor skills and even perceptual ability in different cultural environments. Moreover, extreme variations in the attitude toward testing occur not only between different societies but within our own. The average child on a low-income level has been shown to approach any kind of test negatively since he believes that it will only expose his shortcomings and remind him that he is at the end of the procession. To shorten the period of discomfort, he usually spends little time on difficult items and makes haphazard guesses instead of thinking things through. The middle-class child, on the other hand, has been taught to do his best on all tests and is accustomed to meeting the challenge with all the mental equipment he has at his command.

In short, the problem of designing culture-fair tests is an extremely complex one and far from solution. The attempt to create them, however, has had important effects. It has enlarged our understanding of the vast differences in knowledge, attitude, and behavior that exist from society to society. It has increased our appreciation of the value of cultural diversity as opposed to uniformity. And, perhaps above all, it has led to greater aware-ness of the drastic effects of cultural deprivation, social and economic discrimination, and unequal educational opportunity not only in other societies but in large segments of our own as well. *See* INTELLIGENCE TESTS.

CURIOSITY DRIVE. The urge to investigate the environment, particularly when it is novel or unusual; a general drive which includes or overlaps with the exploratory drive and the manipulative drive.

Curiosity is generally considered an inherent, unlearned response, since it appears spontaneously in both animals and young children. Cats, rats, dogs, and other animals invariably sniff, paw, and search about when they are placed in a new situation. Infants begin to show an interest in objects, such as a ring, even before they are one month old; by three months they actively investigate an object with their hands, and by six months they engage in "sustained inspection" (Bayley, 1933). As he grows, the child exhibits three major methods of investigation: (1) sensory exploration—attempting to taste, smell, feel, mouth, observe, and listen to practically everything in his immediate environment; (2) motor manipulation—squeezing, banging, stroking, biting objects, and moving about to discover how his own body behaves; and (3) asking questions from the nursery school period onward. *See* CHILDREN'S QUESTIONS.

Curiosity was first recognized as a basic drive in consequence of observations and experiments on animals. As early as 1881 Romanes observed that monkeys tirelessly investigated their cages and manipulated new objects without receiving any reward. Later, Thorndike (1898) noted that a monkey repeatedly struck a taut wire and concluded that the animal was intrigued by novel stimulation. Similar behavior was later observed in other animals, but the full recognition of curiosity as a basic drive was delayed by the fact that it did not fit into the theory of motivation which was dominant at the time. This was the "drive reduction" theory, which holds that organisms are goaded into activity only to alleviate unpleasant sensations accompanying physiological needs, such as hunger or thirst. No such psychological need could be demonstrated in the case of persistent exploration and novel stimulation. *See* DRIVE REDUCTION THEORY.

Additional investigations have convinced most psychologists that exploratory behavior can be rewarding in itself. In one experiment, monkeys were placed in an opaque cage and repeatedly opened the door simply to observe the outside of the world (Butler and Alexander, 1955). Another investigator showed that chimpanzees will not only investigate a novel situation but show the same waning of interest that is frequently observed in human beings. He placed various objects in front of them, such as a chain, lights that could be turned on and off, and pieces of wood of different shapes. These objects were invariably examined and manipulated. However, if the same objects were offered for several days, the animals' level of interest gradually declined. (Welker, 1956)

Experiments and observations of this kind have led many psychologists to postulate an inborn curiosity drive. In its simplest form, in animals and children, this drive is primarily expressed through exploration and manipulation (PLATE 2). Some observers believe the three tendencies are aspects of a single drive, but others argue that exploratory behavior may be used for other purposes than the satisfaction of curiosity— for example, the search for food—and manipulation may also have other satisfactions, such as the pleasure of sheer activity. The question is therefore a moot one, but perhaps it is not too vital, since today there is less interest in cataloguing our drives than in show-ing how they can be cultivated and combined to make them more effective.

The question of developing the curiosity drive is a particularly critical one in child psychology. Some parents and even teachers find the child's exploratory urge a burden and an inconvenience. They adopt a "hands-off" policy, give curt answers to the child's questions, and limit his experience for fear he might go "too far too fast." Others, happily, do all in their power not only to satisfy expressed curiosity but to stimulate the child to seek new experiences and raise new questions about the world of people and things. They do this by giving the child toys and games that excite an interest in electricity or chemistry, by exposing him to films and television programs on vital subjects, and by having him visit stimulating people and places. The importance of maintaining active curiosity cannot be overstressed. It is one of the basic keys to the growth of personality and the discovery of new satisfactions in life.

The basic character of this drive can be best appreciated by denying it altogether. This has been done in part in recent experiments in which sensory stimulation was extremely reduced. Subjects were placed in isolated rooms with their eyes, ears, and hands shielded, so that their opportunities to explore, investigate, and manipulate their environment were practically eliminated. What were the effects? Many subjects turned inward and sought satisfaction in the play of ideas—but in a few hours their thinking became incoherent and they were beset by strange fantasies (Solomon et al., 1961; Heron et al., 1956). Not long afterward, many of the subjects found the state of "noxious nothing" so distressing that they could no longer tolerate it, and pressed the "panic button" which released them from the situation. These experiments leave no doubt that the human being has a basic need for exploration and manipulation if he is to continue to function normally. *See* SENSORY DEPRIVATION, SOCIAL ISOLATION.

CUSHING'S SYNDROME. An endocrine disorder due to excessive secretion of cortisone resulting from overgrowth or tumor in the cortex of the adrenal gland or a tumor of the pituitary gland. The condition may also be induced by long-term administration of adrenal-corticosteroids in the treatment of other diseases.

The typical physical symptoms are marked weakness, easy fatigability, reduced sexual drive and purple skin streaks. Patients also become overweight, particularly due to pads of fat in the face, neck, and trunk, producing a moon-face appearance and a lumped posture. Women are more frequently affected than men. They cease to menstruate and develop masculine characteristics, including a deep voice, enlarged clitoris, and growth of body hair. The bearded ladies of the circus are victims of Cushing's syndrome.

These physical changes, especially when they are grossly disfiguring, almost inevitably lead to emotional symptoms. The particular nature of the symptoms, however, depends largely on the basic personality, life situation, and general adjustment of the patient. Most frequent is a reactive depression, with frequent crying spells. Some patients also become anxious, agitated, or irritable, and a small number develop schizophrenic or other psychotic reactions. Treatment consists of surgical removal or resection of the adrenal gland. The prognosis is favorable but may take time, and the personality disorder might persist if severe disfigurement has already taken place. *See* ADRENAL GLANDS, PITUITARY GLAND, VIRILISM.

CYBERNETICS. The science of communication and control as applied to machines and living organisms.

The term is based on a Greek word meaning steersman or helmsman, and is etymologically related to the word "governor," an automatic regulating mechanism first described by James C. Maxwell in 1868. It was coined by Norbert Wiener in 1948 to bring together a group of phenomena belonging to several different disciplines. The most important are information theory, communication engineering, automation, computing and memory mechanisms, and the operation of the nervous system. Our emphasis will be on the application of cybernetic principles to brain functions. *See* INFORMATION THEORY.

The cybernetic approach can be illustrated by the principle of the servomechanism, which is defined by Rosenblueth, Wiener, and Bigelow (1943) as a machine that is goal-seeking or intrinsically purposeful. Its major characteristic is self-regulation. A good example is the thermostat, which responds to stimuli in such a way that it corrects any deviation from its appointed task of maintaining a certain temperature. Self-regulating mechanisms of this kind are contrasted with regulated mechanisms which do not monitor their own performance—a gasoline engine, for example.

The sensitivity of the servomechanism to stimulation, and its ability to change its functioning in accordance with changes in the environment, is termed error-sensitive ability, or feedback. The principle is employed in torpedoes and guided missiles. In moving through the water, the torpedo keeps itself "on beam" by utilizing stimuli, or "input," coming from the target, as well as information from its own output. The term positive feedback is applied to the enhancement of activities already in progress and negative feedback to their inhibition.

Feedback is one of the major characteristics of human behavior, since it enables us to adjust our performance and improve our efficiency. This process takes place largely on an unconscious level. We are usually unaware, for example, of the continuous feedback of information involved in the apparently simple activity of reaching for an object. In this process, light rays from the object and kinesthetic stimulation from our arm must be continuously integrated and reintegrated as we move our hand closer and closer to its objective. A similar process occurs in activities performed with our legs, such as walking, jumping, or dancing. In victims of tabes dorsalis, a degenerative disease of the spinal cord, the individual's gait is seriously distorted even though he has nothing wrong with the muscles of his legs. The reason for this distortion is that the kinesthetic information from the legs cannot be fed back into the system due to destruction of nerve tissue. Such a person must look at his legs or tap his cane loudly in order to provide clues that one leg has moved and now it is the other's turn.

Cyberneticians, then, apply the concept of the servomechanism to the basic operation of the nervous system. In discussing this process, Cofer and Appley (1965) state, "The operation of feedback in relation to behavior might be summarized as follows: reacting to disturbance (i.e. stimulation) the system responds, its response affects the environment in some particular way, at the same time 'reporting back' what has been done. The central regulatory apparatus then computes the discrepancy between performed and intended actions and the succeeding response is 'corrected for error.' Such a sequence is repeated until the residual error is so small as to lie within the range of the target—or, in other words, until a stable equilibrium has been secured."

This general theory has been supported by evidence that neurophysiological feedback circuits exist in the nervous system. Experiments have shown that surgical insult to certain parts of the higher centers of animals such as cuttlefish, cats, rats, and monkeys disrupts the balance between excitation and inhibition. Bailey and Davis (1942) report, for example, that when such operations are performed on the brain stems of cats, they walk forward continually, and if they meet an obstacle, they persist in this "syndrome of obstinate progression" until the hair is rubbed off their heads and their scalps become macerated. The walking continues until they become exhausted and die.

In addition, the concepts of "self-re-exciting chains," reverberating circuits and feedback loops—all of which mean much the same thing—have been developed to explain the control of behavior. In fact, cyberneticians now account for form perception, memory, and learning by postulating interconnecting communication channels, or nerve nets, through which nervous impulses pass and re-pass. Although the existence of these nets has not yet been fully substantiated anatomically, there may be evidence for their existence in the retraining of aphasic and ataxic patients. The recovery of these patients is believed to be due to the substitution of new circuits in the nervous system in place of channels that have been destroyed or damaged. *See* MEMORY STORAGE.

Authorities on cybernetics have constructed some remarkable machines which they believe to be useful in studying the way the human nervous system functions. W. R. Ashby (1952) has designed a homeostat which can simulate many of the activities of the animal nervous system, such as returning to equilibrium when disturbed; and Walter (1953) has devised a "machina docilis" capable of conditioning, motility, and problem solving. The tortoise-like mechanism roams the environment, avoids obstacles, approaches moderate light, obeys a whistle, and appears to be "attracted" by its own kind and mirror image. When it needs recharging, it stops its roaming and returns to home base. Others have constructed automatic machines which run mazes, eliminate errors, take shortcuts, and even "choose" between goals.

As Cofer and Appley point out, these machines, amazing as they are, only illustrate the *general* types of functions found in the nervous system. At the present time it would require a unit at least as large as the Empire State Building to contain all the circuitry of a single human brain, not to mention the fact that the principles on which the brain operates appear to be much more complex than any machine can duplicate. Many investigators, therefore, argue that the proper study of nervous tissue is nervous tissue, not models which are thought to be analogous to the nervous system.

The basic question is whether *new* principles can be discovered through machine operation rather than brain study. Wiener believed that this may be possible. He suggested, for example, that psychoses represent a situation analogous to a "traffic jam" in telephone circuitry. In such a situation, many messages have to be transmitted simultaneously but not enough pathways are available. On this theory, lobotomy is assumed to eliminate the jam by cutting some of the "wires," while electroshock is believed to bypass the jam by bringing other circuits into play. This type of analogy is provocative and might well lead to constructive experimentation. *See* PSYCHOSURGERY, ELECTRO-SHOCK THERAPY.

CYCLOTHYMIC PERSONALITY (Cycloid Personality).

A personality pattern disturbance characterized by frequently alternating moods of elation and dejection.

The cyclothymic (or cycloid) individual tends to be extraversive, responsive, and socially dependent. It is sometimes possible to trace his changes of mood

to acceptance or rejection by other people; but more often these fluctuations appear to occur spontaneously and cannot be related to outside events. They are apparently associated with feelings and attitudes which are deeply embedded in the individual's emotional life.

The cyclothyme's mood changes are likely to be frequent and rapid. At one time he is cheerful, vivacious, and euphoric, but he soon swings unaccountably to a state of sadness or mild depression. The tempo of his entire behavior changes with his mood, and he is therefore lively and active during one period and slow and ponderous during the other. The pendulum, however, rarely swings all the way, for the cyclothymic personality does not usually reach the pathological extremes of exaltation with hyperactivity on the one hand, and despair with psychomotor retardation on the other. In other words, in spite of the fact that the cyclothymic individual's moods are frequently exaggerated, he is still an integrated personality and can meet the demands of life more or less effectively. However, if he is subjected to extreme and prolonged stress, his personality may become disorganized, and he may develop a manic-depressive psychosis.

Some cyclothymes persist in one phase of the cycle and develop the characteristic personality pattern of that phase to an especially high degree. The euphoric type is termed hypomanic personality; the depressed type is the melancholic personality. *See* these topics.

Illustrative Case: CYCLOTHYMIC PERSONALITY

This patient, a businessman of forty-three, sought psychiatric help while during a depressed phase in which he felt his entire life was a miserable failure. As the history developed it became clear that all of his friends recognized him as being an extremely changeable individual who was apt to be either elated or depressed for periods of several weeks at a time. When "feeling good," as he put it, he preferred to play cards, entertain extensively, seek out all possible outside social contacts, and spend a great deal of energy on his business. Such a phase, however, would come to an end for no reason of which he was aware. He would then spend a few weeks in which his mood change was remarkable. He found going to work a drudgery. He felt that his thriving business could not possibly continue to be a success, he condemned himself for some of the business deals that he had made, and felt that his product was inferior and could not be made into anything acceptable. He gave up his social activities, snubbed his friends, and was generally irritable and cantankerous with his own family. It was difficult to draw him into a conversation and he seemed to be distant, withdrawn, and uninterested in social contacts.

Therapy with this patient primarily involved attempts to give him an understanding of some of the mechanisms which precipitated his wide mood changes. He had a rather severe superego from which he periodically escaped into an elated phase and which then caught up with him and again forced him into a self-depreciatory phase. As he gradually learned some of the un-realistic aspects of his rigid conscience, he began to blame himself less punitively for his activities. As a result it was possible for him to feel some renewed interest in his business, his friends, and his family. At the same time this made it unnecessary for him to "run" into his elated phase in order to escape his severe conscience. This patient essentially had many of the dynamics of a compulsive patient and his therapy was somewhat similar, although he presented no overt neurotic symptoms but instead a personality problem primarily illustrated by his remarkable mood swings. (English and Finch, 1964)

CYTOMEGALIC INCLUSION BODY DISEASE. A mild virus infection in the mother which may cause brain damage in the fetus, together with enlargement of the liver and the spleen (hepatosplenomegaly), jaundice, and erythroblastosis (yellow baby disease). The disorder is recognized by the presence of inclusion bodies in the urine, cerebrospinal fluid, and other tissues. It is one of the rarer causes of severe mental retardation. *See* MENTAL RETARDATION (CAUSES).

D

DANCE THERAPY. The use of various forms of rhythmic movement—folk dancing, ballroom dancing, exercises to music—as a supportive and adjunctive measure with psychiatric patients.

A constantly growing number of mental hospitals are including dance in their therapeutic program, and an organization, the National Association for Dance Therapy, has recently been formed to promote its use and set professional standards. The pioneer in this movement is St. Elizabeth's Hospital, in Washington, where dance techniques have been employed by Marian Chace since 1942. With the co-operation of the hospital's director, Dr. Winfred Overholser, she began by experimenting with dance as a means of reaching schizophrenic patients, and soon found that this form of activity not only aroused many of them from listlessness and apathy but often dissolved the barriers which were keeping them isolated from other people.

Miss Chace later discovered that rhythmic response to music could also be used effectively to quiet the manic, arouse the depressed, and stimulate the stuporous. As Edith Stern has put it (1957), "To break through the invisible walls with which all psychotics surround themselves to keep people away, she used primitive means of communication that go deeper than words —rhythm, movement and touch. Old and fundamental as humanity itself, simple and universal as mothers crooning and rocking their babies in their arms, these catch patients off guard, painlessly crumble their defenses, make them susceptible to other approaches. Over and over again she demonstrates that there is more strength in the mentally ill than most of us realize."

Dance therapy does not, of course, cure these patients by itself, but it frequently does serve as a bridge to other people and other activities. After a dance session a mute woman may begin to speak, a withdrawn man may abandon his solitaire and play cards with others. When such patients begin to "open up," they usually become more amenable to group or individual psychotherapy. As Marian Chace points out, the dance affords these patients an opportunity to express their feelings in movement and gesture when they cannot put them in words. This enables them to drain off some of their hatred, anger, and tension, and begin to relate themselves to other people in a more normal and healthy manner.

There is no set procedure in dance therapy. It must be an open and flexible affair in which the dance specialist takes her cues at all times from the patients themselves. At St. Elizabeth's, the therapist does not call a group together, but merely enters the room with a phonograph and records, and waits until one of the patients asks to hear some music. Experience has shown that a waltz is usually most effective at the beginning, since it is nonthreatening and evokes a response from the majority of patients. While some may dance together, others take tentative steps alone or with the dance therapist or nurse. Still others simply listen and nod their heads, often with the shadow of an unaccustomed smile on their lips. After about five minutes of waltzing, a circle is formed and the patients are encouraged to make free movements such as swinging their legs, shaking their wrists, stretching their arms, or following simple steps. None of the movements requires previous training; the emphasis is on unison of rhythmic action for the purpose of feeling relaxed together. When relaxation has been achieved, the music is gradually speeded up and the session usually ends with simple polkas and square dances in which everyone can participate.

This is the general procedure adopted for the more withdrawn patients. In the wards where most of the patients are excitable and unpredictable, the therapist usually starts with rapid music and movement. The nurses and aides participate, and this helps them establish closer relations with the patients. No formation lasts more than a few minutes, since these patients have an extremely short span of concentration. As the session goes on, the rhythms become slower and the group tapers off into quieter activity. The hour ends with the patients in restful postures listening to soft, rhythmic music such as a Bach passacaglia. It is an interesting fact that these dance sessions seldom lead to unrestrained "acting-out" even among the most volatile patients. Instead, they release their energies in an orderly manner. Moreover, these patients, as well as the phlegmatic, usually become more accessible to psychotherapy after the dance sessions.

Undoubtedly some of these benefits can be gained simply by having the nurses or attendants arrange regular periods in which the patients can engage in free movement to music. However, if the dance is to be a truly effective form of therapy, a trained dance therapist is needed. She should first of all be a dancer herself, not only because she will be an inspiration to the patients, but because her training will help her detect muscular movements and tensions that have emotional significance. But even though she is a professional, she must be able to keep her technical skill in the background and adapt herself to the spontaneous movements of others. In addition, she must make a study of behavior patterns and acquire clinical experience in a hospital setting. Finally, she must have a genuine feeling for people, and an ability to accept and respect them as they are. *See* MUSIC THERAPY.

DARK ADAPTATION. The ability of the eye to adjust to darkness or reduced illumination through an increased sensitivity to light.

Dark adaptation is commonly experienced in a darkened motion picture theater or in a forest at night. At first we may be almost totally blind, but in time our eyes become accustomed to the dark and we begin to distinguish many details. This process takes about a half hour to reach completion, and during this time the sensitivity of our eyes increases a thousandfold for longer wavelengths to one hundred thousandfold for shorter wavelengths. At its maximum we can see when the illumination is only seven billionths as strong as ordinary daylight—but contrary to popular opinion, no eye, not even a cat's, can see in total darkness.

Dark adaptation is due to changes both in the pupil and the retina. In dim illumination the pupil enlarges to as much as sixteen times its area under bright conditions in order to admit more light. This change, however, accounts for only a small part of the eye's increased sensitivity under low illumination. Two types of retinal changes are much more important. First, a substance called iodopsin found in the cones, or color-sensitive cells, regenerates during the first seven to ten minutes of darkness. This increases sensitivity to light one hundred to two hundred times. During this period and for about twenty minutes longer, a second photochemical substance, called visual purple or rhodopsin, also regenerates. This substance is found in the rod cells of the retina and accounts for most of the increased sensitivity of the eye during darkness.

These phenomena explain other ordinary experiences as well. Most of us have noticed that we cannot see colors at night even though we can make out shapes rather clearly. The reason is that the cones are not sensitive enough to function under low illumination, and therefore color is not registered. We may also have noticed that at night faint objects such as stars can be distinguished only when we do not look directly at them. Here the reason is that the sensitive rods are found predominantly in the periphery of the retina, and we can focus light most directly on them by looking out of the corner of our eye.

We occasionally come across people who are deficient in dark adaptation. The common term for this defect is night blindness, and the technical term is hemeralopia. In some cases this condition is congenital and permanent, in others vitamin A may bring some improvement. This vitamin, which is found in carrots, helps in the synthesis of visual purple. In one experiment a number of subjects who were given food deficient in vitamin A showed a hundredfold loss in dark adaptation within thirty-five days (Hecht and Mandelbaum, 1938). In consequence of this finding, all the night fighters in the English air force were given tremendous quantities of carrots—but this proved to be wasted effort in most cases since a surplus of the vitamin does not produce any better vision than a bare minimum. It is interesting that the Egyptians used raw liver, one of the richest sources of vitamin A, as a remedy for night blindness.

Although it takes about a half hour to reach the maximum of dark adaptation, this condition can be completely eliminated in a few minutes of bright illumination. This fact is particularly important in work that requires a constant shift between light and dark. Night fliers, for example, must be able to keep an eye on their instruments and yet watch for dark objects outside the plane. It has been found that they can remain dark-adapted by wearing special tight-fitting red goggles, since dark-adapted rods are negligibly affected by red light. Instrument panels and darkrooms are sometimes illuminated with red light for the same reason, and sailors sometimes wear red goggles or stay in red-illuminated compartments before going on the night watch. This reduces the time it takes for their eyes to become adapted to the dark.

DARWIN, CHARLES ROBERT
(1809–82). Darwin, whose theory of evolution has had a profound influence on psychology, was born in Shrewsbury, England, the son of a doctor and grandson of the celebrated Erasmus Darwin, a poet, physician, and philosopher. He entered Cambridge in 1827, and after three years of study for the ministry became disinterested in this field and began to devote himself to the study of botany and zoology. Soon after graduating, in 1831, he took a position as naturalist aboard a ship, the *Beagle,* and made a five-year scientific cruise around the world. In the course of the trip, he made innumerable observations and collected a large number of plant and animal specimens. Two years after his return Darwin became secretary of the Geological Society in London, and a year later published *The Journal of a Naturalist.* This was followed by *Zoology*

of the Voyage of the Beagle (1840) and *The Structure and Distribution of Coral Reefs* (1842).

Darwin was not a healthy man, and retired to the country in an effort to regain his health. There he devoted himself to the intensive study of several living species, with one major question in mind: "Why were animals so well adapted to their environment and what force eliminated those that were not as fit to survive?" In attempting to answer this double-barreled question, he was influenced by evolutionary ideas which had been recurrent in Western thought ever since the Greeks, but which had gathered force during the preceding fifty years. Goethe had made use of this concept in his studies of botany in 1790, and in his suggestion that the vertebrate skull is nothing more than a modified and developed spinal column. His own grandfather, Erasmus Darwin, had sought to account for the multiplicity of species by suggesting a theory of transmutation. Laplace had applied an evolutionary explanation to the development of the planetary system from a single nebula. Lyell, whom Darwin knew, had described the orderly geological changes through which the earth itself evolved, and had also studied extinct fossil organisms found at different strata, indicating that they therefore stemmed from different eras. Lamarck had suggested that animal forms are modified by their attempts to deal with the environment, and had developed the theory that these acquired changes were passed on to the offspring.

All these ideas, then, were "in the air" at the time of Darwin—but it was a specialist in quite a different field who helped to provide the key to his problem: the great economist Malthus. In his *Essay on the Principle of Population* he had pointed out that improvement in food production increases food output arithmetically, while population increases geometrically. This process, he held, inevitably leads to overpopulation, which is eliminated in part by starvation, war, and disease. When Darwin read this book, he felt that the concept of struggle for existence was basic to the entire process. From this idea he developed the biological theory that since an excess of offspring is produced among animals, only the fittest survive—that is, only those adapted to their particular environment in terms of getting food and resisting their enemies. He also theorized that the fitness itself was based on a process of natural selection. Due to variations in the hereditary process, some animals developed characteristics that helped them adapt to the environment, while others fell by the wayside. The ones that survived passed their characteristics on to new generations and eventually produced a new species.

Darwin collected a huge amount of evidence in support of his views, and in 1859 published his monumental work, *The Origin of Species: By Natural Selection; or the Preservation of Favored Races in the Struggle for Life.* All 1250 copies of the first edition were sold out on the day of publication, and the impact on the scientific community, as well as the religious community, was immediate and immense.

One of the sciences most affected by Darwin's theory was psychology. At least five general trends can be traced to its influence. First, functionalism, which looked upon mental processes as adaptive measures, became the dominant approach, and structuralism, with its emphasis on analysis of the contents of consciousness, receded into the background. Second, comparative psychology, with its study of animal behavior, came to the fore, not only because of Darwin's recognition of the biological continuities between men and animals, but also because he noted similarities between the reasoning processes

of men and those of the higher vertebrates. Third, studies of expressive behavior were stimulated by Darwin's book *Expression of Emotion in Man and Animals* (1872), in which he showed, for example, that the hair tends to stand on end during displays of anger, probably to make the body seem larger and thereby frighten off enemies. Fourth, genetic psychology received a strong impetus from the evolutionary doctrine, and as a result many studies of the development of the individual from infancy to old age were made. Fifth, the concept of survival of the fittest focused attention on individual differences and stimulated the study of hereditary tendencies, genius, and the measurement of human capacities through psychological tests. *See* EXPRESSIVE BEHAVIOR, FUNCTIONALISM, DIFFERENTIAL PSYCHOLOGY, GENIUS, INTELLIGENCE TESTS.

DAYDREAMING (Fantasy). A waking fantasy or reverie; the free play of thought or imagination.

Daydreaming is classed as a form of autistic thinking, since the individual's imagination is controlled primarily by his inner desires and not by outer reality. It is a normal feature of childhood behavior and especially prevalent during adolescence. In most instances it tends to subside in early adulthood when the individual becomes absorbed in realistic activities or finds other ways of exercising his imagination. Some people, however, revert to this form of fantasy when they are frustrated or under stress. A few retreat from reality and appear to live in a dream world, and in these cases it is taken as a sign of underlying emotional disturbance.

Two general kinds of daydreaming are frequently mentioned. In the "conquering hero" type, the child or adult overcomes all odds and destroys all opposition to reach a goal that gives him status and recognition. This type of fantasy frequently occurs after frustration or disappointment, providing an outlet for aggressive urges which these experiences arouse. In the "suffering hero" type, the individual imagines he is the target of undeserved abuse, the victim of a horrible affliction, or a martyr for all mankind. But in spite of the handicaps imposed upon him, he performs feats of daring and resourcefulness that gain him recognition in his own eyes if not in the eyes of others. This type of daydream is considered less healthy than the conquering hero type, since it expresses feelings of inferiority, revenge, self-pity, and a tendency to project blame on others. It is also less effective as a morale booster, and tends to build up antisocial attitudes that intensify existing tendencies to poor adjustment.

Systematic studies indicate that these two types do not account for all daydreams, nor do they express all the motivations involved in fantasy. Jersild et al. (1933), found that only about 19 per cent of children between five and twelve reported daydreams of self-glorification; more often their fantasies dealt with amusements, play, or specific objects which they desired. Many older children also used daydreaming as a "rehearsal for life"—that is, they pictured themselves in realistic occupations as opposed to romanticized situations. The daydreams of adolescents, as might be expected, often focused on social relationships, love, and sexual activities. In studies of undergraduates (average age twenty-one) and graduate students (average age twenty-eight) carried out by Shaffer and Shoben (1956), all but 3 per cent reported recent daydreams. Among the most frequent themes were vocational success, money or possessions, and sex conquests; somewhat less frequent were fantasies about mental feats, worries, and physical attractiveness (twice as many women as men had this type of daydream). The majority reported that at one time they had daydreams of grandeur, homage, martyrdom, display, and physical feats (men more than women), but their recent daydreams rarely centered around these themes.

Daydreaming provides the child, and the adult, with an undemanding form of activity which yields considerable ego satisfaction. In moderate amounts it is considered a healthy stimulant for imagination and a healthy outlet for emotion. As Peller (1959) has pointed out, a well-adjusted child usually daydreams only when he cannot engage in other forms of play, but a poorly adjusted child substitutes daydreaming for constructive play or activities with other children. If the daydreaming is carried to excess, it may become an unhealthy form of escape, and in some cases fantasy may begin to take precedence over the world of reality. But this will not occur if the child receives a reasonable amount of love and attention and has an opportunity to engage in activities that develop his skills and give him personal satisfaction. See AUTISM, DEREISTIC THINKING, IMAGINARY COMPANION.

DAY HOSPITAL (Day Care Program). A mental hospital program organized on a daytime basis. The patients come to the hospital in the morning, receive practically all the care and treatment ordinarily provided, and return to their homes in the late afternoon or evening.

The day hospital concept was first outlined by D. Ewen Cameron in 1947 and is now widely utilized to counteract the seclusion of the mental institution and to keep patients in contact with their families and social groups. During the day patients receive individual or group psychotherapy and engage in the hospital's activity program according to their needs and interests, but during the evening they are cared for by their family or foster family. In some institutions the program is set up in conjunction with an outpatient clinic or as a separate center; in others, the day patients receive care and treatment along with the residential patients. Those who require rehabilitation rather than definitive treatment often engage in such a program on a day-care basis, since remaining in the hospital overnight might tend to overemphasize their sickness or handicap.

Day care has a number of advantages. It gives the family a respite during the day. It reduces the costs of hospital treatment. It enables the staff to observe the behavior of patients within the hospital environment in a way that is not possible with outpatients. It can serve as a gradual transition from the community to the hospital, enabling the patient to become acquainted with the staff and to overcome the fear of hospitalization. Or, after a hospital stay, it can be used to facilitate the transition to full-time community life, since it helps the patient to gain self-confidence at his own pace.

When patients return home every night the staff is given an additional opportunity to study the effects of the family environment upon them. And when the family transports the patient to and from the hospital every day, they have a chance to get acquainted with the personnel, to learn about hospital activities, and to discover how they can collaborate in the treatment process. They are also likely to be drawn into hospital social events and thereby help to bring the "outside world" into the institution and thus bridge the gap between the hospital and the community.

The day program also helps to prevent the dependent patient from using the hospital as a refuge from life. When he goes back to the home or community at night, he comes to regard the hospital as merely a center for temporary treatment rather than permanent care. This helps to maintain his morale and in many cases keeps him from becoming a residential patient. Moreover, he will not have to learn to "readjust" to the community because he has not left it in the first place.

A promising variation on the day hospital approach has been developed in Africa. Since 1953, Dr. Thomas A. Lambo, a Nigerian psychiatrist trained in America and Britain, has conducted an experimental program in which psychotic as well as neurotic patients are placed in homes near a modern mental hospital built by the government (Lambo, 1968). In each case a member of the patient's own family takes care of him, markets for him, cooks his food, and escorts him to the hospital for treatment every morning and afternoon. All modern therapeutic procedures are used—drug therapy, electroshock therapy, group therapy—but in addition two native healers are also used, since they are directly acquainted with the culture and philosophy of the people, and are especially adept at interpreting the patient's dreams.

This combination of traditional with modern treatment, and of day care with home living, has been remarkably successful. A two-year study conducted by the National Institute of Mental Health has compared the village plan with ordinary hospitalization: fifteen times as many patients were treated on the village plan, at roughly fifteen times less cost; four out of five were discharged after six months, as contrasted with two out of five; and only one out of twenty had to be returned for treatment within a year of discharge, as contrasted with three out of seven of the hospitalized patients. Though skeptical at first, the villagers gradually came to accept their sick neighbors, and no cases were reported of patients involved in violence of any kind. The treatment plan, which recalls the family care system used in

Gheel, Belgium, is now spreading to many other points in Africa. *See* FAMILY CARE, SOCIAL BREAKDOWN SYNDROME, MENTAL HOSPITAL.

DEAFNESS. There are two general varieties of organic deafness. The totally deaf, or "anacusic," cannot respond to any sounds; the partially deaf, hard of hearing, or "hypacusic," can hear certain frequencies but not others. A third category is sometimes used, the "dysacusic," applied to individuals whose hearing is distorted.

In addition to organic deafness there is a functional, psychogenic type in which the individual experiences a partial or complete loss of hearing due to emotional conflicts or tensions. Tests indicate that the hearing mechanism is intact, and that it may function selectively to screen out some types of stimuli more than others. Deafness of this kind is classified as a hysterical, or conversion, symptom. It usually represents an unconscious attempt to escape from a painful or threatening situation and in some cases to elicit sympathy or help. The case at the end of this article illustrates the psychogenic type of deafness. *See* CONVERSION REACTION.

Organic deafness comprises two major types, conduction deafness and perceptual or nerve deafness. These will be briefly described before considering the effects of deafness on the personality.

In conduction deafness the vibrations which reach the ear are disrupted due to a broken eardrum, a stopped-up canal, or damage to the three small connected bones, called ossicles, which transmit them to the spiral mechanism that contains the receptor cells (*Fig. 28*). The effect can be compared to stuffing cotton in one's ears, since the hearing loss is the same at all frequencies. The most common cause of conduction deafness is chronic middle ear infection, particularly in young peo-

ple. Over 40 per cent of these cases are due to scarlet fever; other cases are due to such disorders as sinusitis, tonsillitis, and sore throat. Another cause is prolonged exposure to loud sounds; machinists, boilermakers, pilots, and the men who man large guns in wartime are some of the major victims. Tests conducted at a Denver high school have recently shown that 75 per cent of the students suffered hearing losses due to repeated exposure to overamplified "hard rock" music in the school cafeteria and elsewhere. Exposure deafness is often permanent, and may be accompanied by a ringing in the ears termed tinnitus. The condition can usually be prevented by wearing earplugs. It is important to recognize that sensitivity to high frequencies generally decreases progressively starting at age twenty-five, due to changes in the conduction mechanism.

Since the primary problem in conduction deafness is one of sound intensity, mild cases can be overcome by using a telephone amplifier or by having people raise their voices. More severe cases require a hearing aid. Three major kinds of surgical correction are effective in many cases: (1) the stapes, or stirrup, ossicle can be replaced with a plastic device (stapedectomy); (2) the connection between the stapes and the cochlea (the snail-like mechanism that contains the nerve endings) can be loosened; or (3) an artificial window can be cut into the cochlea (fenestration operation).

The second type, nerve or perceptual deafness, is due to damage to the neural pathways of the inner ear or brain resulting from injury, degeneration, or infectious disease. There may be a loss of sensitivity to a restricted range of frequencies (tonal gaps), but more often there is an extensive loss in the high frequency range alone. This defect is common over the age of sixty. The name perceptual or perceptive deafness is used because the high-tone loss makes it extremely hard to understand speech. In talking to a person with this defect it is more important to speak distinctly than to speak loudly. The voice of the conduction-deaf individual is usually normal, since he can control its volume through bone conduction; but the voice of the nerve-deaf person is likely to be either too loud or too soft. There is no satisfactory treatment or operation for perceptual deafness, but a hearing aid is frequently helpful.

In addition to these primary types of deafness, there are many cases of distorted or disordered hearing (dysacusis, paracusis). Révész (1954), for example, recognizes four distinct types of paracusis and attributes them to diseases of the ear. In diplacusis binauralis echotica, a given sound is first heard in the healthy ear, then in the diseased ear at a slightly higher or lower pitch. In diplacusis monauralis echotica, the diseased ear hears the same sound twice in succession, the second sounding like an echo of the first. In diplacusis binauralis disharmonia, the diseased ear hears certain notes as higher or lower than the normal ear but simultaneously. In diplacusis qualitas, the diseased ear hears a certain range of notes in the right pitch but with a different tonal quality or timbre.

Hearing aids are of no use to the totally deaf. Fortunately there are few of these extreme cases, and many so-called deaf children have been found to have some degree of hearing. The totally deaf and severely handicapped are taught to read other people's lips, and can learn to speak through special training procedures that utilize electronic apparatus which greatly amplifies sound without distortion. Experiments are also being conducted on teaching them to read pictures of words made out of sound waves registered on an electronic device. *See* AUDIOGRAM.

Hearing loss is usually a progressive affair, and many cases are not discovered until they are far advanced. Too often parents label a child stupid or stubborn because they fail to recognize that he does not hear well enough to understand what is being said. Adults frequently develop a 25 to 50 per cent loss before they do anything about it, and many of them are too self-conscious or obstinate to wear hearing aids. The development of small devices to be worn in the ear or attached to eyeglasses is making hearing aids more acceptable, but some people still wear them at work but not in social life where they are needed just as much.

Every attempt should be made to overcome hearing loss because of its profound effect on personal and social adjustment. Hearing is more essential for communication than any other sense. Long before he can understand either oral or printed words, the child learns what to do and what to avoid by responding to the modulation of his parents' voices. As he grows older, he is inducted into the customs of the group and becomes a socialized human being largely through verbal communication. The person who has a total hearing loss will live in an isolated, lonely world unless every effort is made to compensate for this defect.

Even a partial hearing loss can have pervasive effects. Comparisons between normal and hard-of-hearing children have shown that the partially deaf usually lack social competence and tend to be more shy and much less aggressive and assertive than children who hear normally (Madden, 1931). These difficulties are rarely outgrown, and hard-of-hearing adults have been found to be "significantly more emotional, more introverted and less dominant than the average of their hearing friends" (Welles, 1932). These characteristics were found to persist even when they attained occupational and social positions equal to those of their friends.

Loss of hearing, then, is not an isolated characteristic. Its potential effect on the total personality must always be considered. Studies have shown that an effective way to prevent serious harm is to help the deaf or hard-of-hearing person to live a useful life. In recent years many firms have been hiring these people for regular jobs, and it has even been found that a hearing loss can be an advantage. Deaf typists are sometimes used in "typing pools", because they are not distracted or annoyed by the clatter of the machines. The armed forces are also employing deaf people to work with equipment such as jets that emit noises which would be intolerable to people with normal hearing. As with other handicapped individuals, the deaf have been shown to be responsible employees with excellent work records.

Illustrative Case: FUNCTIONAL DEAFNESS

Mrs. C.D., aged forty-three years, was referred from the department of otolaryngology for partial deafness, which had no determinable organic basis. When the patient entered the consulting room, she spoke in a normal-toned voice, and yet would not hear unless the examiner raised his voice almost to the shouting stage. The patient told of her husband's death some three years ago, and of her struggle for existence. She had two children, aged three and four and a half, and worked in a factory earning a very meager wage. She lived with her sister, who was married and had a small, crowded apartment. Not only was the physical standard of living very low, but there was intense dissatisfaction between the two sisters. When the patient returned home from work, the sister would begin to nag and complain. The constant whining, the fault-finding, the seeming hopelessness of her position discouraged the patient to the point of brooding and frequent tears. One day while preoccupied, the patient did not hear what her sister said, and the sister caustically remarked, "You must be getting deaf." From then on the patient heard less and less in the house, though she managed to make

her way about at work and away from home with no difficulty. When the examiner spoke to her, it was necessary almost to shout to be understood, but as the patient began to unfold her story more and more, it was possible to reduce the loudness of the voice to a conversational tone. However, when her story was finished, and she was being given various suggestions, it became necessary to raise the tone again. (Kraines, 1948)

DEATH INSTINCT. A universal unconscious drive for destruction and self-destruction, according to some psychoanalytic theorists.

The concept of the death instinct was one of the last contributions of Freud, and arose from many sources: "Impressed by the destructiveness of World War I, by the cruelty of many aspects of human behavior, and by the sadism and masochism evident in all neuroses, Freud in 1920 suggested that all humans, in common with all other animals, were driven by an instinct for destruction and death" (Ostow, 1958).

According to this theory, which the majority of analysts do not accept, the death instinct operates in opposition to the equally basic life instinct, which has the constructive goal of self-preservation, social unity and perpetuation of the species. The death instinct (aggressive instinct, "destrudo") operates under control of the repetition-compulsion principle, a blind impulse to repeat earlier experiences and ultimately to return to the stability of the inorganic state (the Nirvana principle). The life instinct (erotic instinct, libido) is under the control of the pleasure-unpleasure principle. To give these two forces dramatic and classical flavor, Freud referred to them as Thanatos and Eros, and pictured human life as a theater of operations in which these two ultimate forces battle for supremacy.

Freud did not elaborate on the death instinct, nor show its operation in detail. His followers, however, applied the concept to many areas of behavior.

Karl Menninger (1938), for example, has found evidence for the theory not only in cases of actual suicide, but in the slow, "chronic suicide" of the alcoholic who gradually destroys himself and his family, the martyr who invites torture, the ascetic who renounces life for no positive reason, the criminal who unconsciously seeks punishment, the neurotic who enjoys his invalidism, and the psychotic who surrenders reality itself. He also finds evidence for the death instinct in the "focal suicide" of patients in whom the self-destructive impulse takes the form of impotence or frigidity, self-mutilation, and a series of purposive accidents or unnecessary operations. The difference between cases of actual suicide and cases of the chronic and focal type is simply that in the latter types destructive impulses have been partially neutralized by constructive urges stemming from the life instinct.

Menninger believes that cases of full or partial suicide are so numerous that the death instinct must be put on an equal footing with the life instinct as a "law of life." These cases have many common denominators which seem to him indicative of a basic drive—especially a strong aggressive urge which gradually turns into self-destructive tendencies, and a need for punishment that arises from a sense of guilt. These factors are all prominent in the illustrative case at the end of this article.

Critics of the theory of the death instinct (and many psychoanalysts are among them) claim that the idea of a single destructive urge is vague and fanciful, since unlike other instincts it does not have a foundation in the physiology of the organism. They also argue that the hypothesis is superfluous in our attempts to explain actual cases of self-destruction, since more specific causal factors can almost always be found. Other critics deny the existence of the death instinct as an ultimate, universal force on a par with the life

instinct, since we do not seek destruction for its own sake—and when we are aggressive, as in the case of war or competition, we may be acting in the service of life rather than death.

Nevertheless, the concept of the death instinct has served to focus attention on the hostile and masochistic drives that still beset mankind. And there seems to be rather general agreement on these points: that we should make every effort to prevent self-punitive drives from gaining a foothold early in life, and that we should redirect our hostile urges, whatever their source, into positive channels through greater emphasis on our humane and creative impulses. *See* AGGRESSION, HOSTILITY, MASOCHISM, SADISM.

Illustrative Case: SELF-DESTRUCTIVE HOSTILITY

A twenty-three-year-old housewife sought treatment ostensibly because she remained sexually frigid after three years of married life. She also revealed that nothing aroused her interest or gave her pleasure, that she suffered from constant headaches and depression and sometimes wept continually for weeks. Nevertheless she was a devoted slave to her family and always consulted her mother and sister before making any decision about everyday matters. One of her major complaints was that her husband failed to assign her any daily jobs or keep her at her duties.

The case history showed that the patient had been sent to a Catholic convent school until the age of eighteen, even though she was Protestant by faith, since there were no good public schools in her community. She became extremely pious and often slept on a bare floor. Although she wished to become a nun, she could not bring herself to confess earlier errors, which included sexual play with playmates and an older brother, as well as seduction by an uncle. To atone for these sins, she had taken an oath never to have sexual relations with any man.

During therapeutic sessions, the patient revealed that she had feelings of anger and resentment toward every member of her family. She hated her sister for having been held up as a model, had strong death wishes toward her mother, whom she blamed for her unhappy marriage, and criticized her father for being unfaithful. Her hostility, however, was most fully directed toward her husband. She would periodically squander his money on unnecessary purchases, then throw the articles away; and in spite of solemn promises would soon repeat this performance. More indirect expressions of hostility took the form of extreme dependence and demand for attention, fantasies about other men, frigidity, and constant complaining. She also refused to take care of her child because he made her nervous, and at times she had an urge to strike or kill him.

Psychoanalytic interviews revealed that the woman was unconsciously using extreme submissiveness and devotion to the family as an infantile way of atoning for her inward hate and dissatisfaction. At the same time her frigidity served the triple purpose of self-punishment, atonement, and aggression against her husband. Treatment was successful and in time she was able to move away from her parents and enjoy life with her husband. (Condensed from Stekel, 1929)

DEFENSE MECHANISM (Ego Defense Mechanism). An adjustive reaction, typically habitual and unconscious, employed to protect oneself from anxiety, guilt, or loss of self-esteem.

In the course of his development, every individual gradually acquires a set of defensive reactions, dynamisms or, as Karen Horney calls them, "safety devices," which are automatically called into play when he finds himself in situations that threaten his ego. These reactions serve many purposes. They reduce emotional conflict, protect the self against its own dangerous impulses, alleviate the effects of traumatic experiences, soften failure or disappointment, eliminate clashes between attitudes and reality ("cognitive dissonance"), and in general help the individual maintain his sense of adequacy and personal worth.

The theory of defense mechanisms was developed by Sigmund Freud and elaborated by his daughter Anna Freud in her work *The Ego and the Mechanisms of Defence* (1937). The im-

portance of these reactions is now widely recognized by Freudians and non-Freudians alike. Among the most common types are refusal to admit the truth (denial of reality), escape into a satisfying world of fantasy (daydreaming), giving false but socially approved reasons to justify questionable behavior (rationalization), blaming others for personal shortcomings or attributing to others our own unacceptable impulses or desires (projection), excluding painful or dangerous thoughts from consciousness (repression), gaining sympathy or avoiding problems by retreating to infantile behavior (regression), denying faulty impulses by going to the opposite extreme (reaction formation), avoiding hurt through apathy or detachment (emotional insulation), and increasing feelings of worth by identifying with important people or institutions (identification). *See* these topics, and DISPLACEMENT, UNDOING, INTELLECTUALIZATION, SUBLIMATION, SYMPATHISM, COMPENSATION, INTROJECTION, DISSOCIATION, SYMBOLIZATION, SUBSTITUTION, INCORPORATION, IDEALIZATION, and FLIGHT INTO REALITY.

Although these mechanisms are based upon normal tendencies and are employed in the interest of adjustment, they cannot be considered an ideal method of coping with the problems of life. It would be far better to face our difficulties directly and deal with them rationally than to erect an artificial system of defense or escape. Such a system is bound to involve a high degree of self-deception and distortion of reality. The person who denies obvious facts is likely to create more problems than he solves, and the individual who habitually rationalizes away his mistakes or blames them on others is not likely to profit from his experience.

Moreover, many defense mechanisms interfere with our relationships with other people and in the end aggravate our interpersonal problems. The woman who continually discharges pent-up emotions on innocent scapegoats (displacement) is bound to be disliked and accused of unfairness, and the man who is a pillar of the church on Sunday but a ruthless businessman all the rest of the week (dissociation) can hardly be expected to command the genuine respect of people who get to know him.

Most individuals are unaware of their defensive behavior, and have little, if any, realization of the anxiety and "ego threat" that lie behind it. Counselors and psychotherapists usually devote considerable time to bringing these mechanisms into the open since this is an important means of increasing the individual's insight into himself. However, it is not always easy to distinguish defensive from non-defensive behavior, and, as Rosen and Gregory (1965) point out, "It is as false to call all behavior defensive—e.g. to explain all generosity as a reaction-formation against stinginess, all reasoning as rationalization and all criticisms of others as projection— as it is naive to take all behavior at its face value and overlook its defensive components." One major mark of defensive behavior is the intensity of the response. The defensive person is overemphatic and protests too much—he hammers on the table as he denies he is angry.

It is also not easy to distinguish between a normal and a pathological use of defenses without examining the total personality. But in general neurotic defenses tend to be more rigid and extreme than normal defenses. One or a small group of defense mechanisms usually predominates and plays a central role in the neurotic individual's life— for example, the hysteric overuses repression and denial of reality while the obsessive-compulsive constantly resorts to reaction-formation and undoing (performing expiatory acts). And in spite of their intensity, neurotic defenses are less successful than normal defenses in staving off anxiety and banishing unacceptable impulses—for this reason the unconscious forces often express themselves in pathological symptoms such as bodily ailments, insomnia, rituals, anxiety attacks, and phobias.

DEHYDRATION REACTION. A disturbance in behavior resulting from an insufficiency of water, classified as a metabolic disorder.

In addition to intense thirst sensations, dehydration produces widespread cellular changes which may have severe mental as well as physical effects.

When the supply of water falls far below the body's normal quota, cells in all parts of the body, including the brain, give up their water, and disturbances in function result. The most pronounced dehydration symptoms are found in patients suffering from cholera and third-degree burns, as well as survivors of shipwrecks and persons lost in the desert. Dehydration is also a danger in postconcussion disorders and certain senile conditions.

Early symptoms are apathy, irritability, and drowsiness. These are followed by inability to concentrate and changes in temperament in which habitual characteristics tend to be exaggerated. The worrisome become anxious, the pessimistic become morose, the lively become overvivacious. As intense feelings of thirst develop, they dominate all mental activity even to the exclusion of hunger, pain, and fatigue.

If dehydration develops to a point where 10 per cent of body weight is lost, more serious symptoms appear: delirium, spasticity, and inability to walk. After that, perception grows increasingly defective, blindness and deafness may develop, and in the last stages before death, stupor and unconsciousness set in.

Illustrative Case: DEHYDRATION REACTION

The following classic account was written by the great flier Antoine de Saint-Exupéry, whose plane had crashed in the North African desert:

I went on, finally, and the time came when, along with my weariness, something in me began to change. If those were not mirages, I was inventing them.

"Hi! Hi, there!"

I shouted and waved my arms, but the man I had seen waving at me turned out to be a black rock. Everything in the desert had grown animate. I stooped to waken a sleeping Bedouin and he turned into the trunk of a black tree. A tree trunk? Here in the desert? I was amazed and bent over to lift a broken bough. It was solid marble.

Straightening up I looked round and saw more black marble. An antediluvian forest littered the ground with its broken treetops. How many thousand years ago, under what hurricane of the time of Genesis, had this cathedral of wood crumbled in this spot? Countless centuries had rolled these fragments of giant pillars at my feet, polished them like steel, petrified and vitrified them and indued them with the color of jet. . . .

Since yesterday I had walked nearly fifty miles. This dizziness that I felt came doubtless from my thirst. Or from the sun. It glittered on these hulks until they shone as if smeared with oil. It blazed down on this universal carapace. Sand and fox had no life here. This world was a gigantic anvil upon which the sun beat down. I strode across this anvil and at my temples I could feel the hammer strokes of the sun.

"Hi! Hi, there!" I called out.

"There is nothing there," I told myself. "Take it easy. You are delirious."

I had to talk to myself aloud, had to bring myself to reason. It was hard for me to reject what I was seeing, hard not to run toward that caravan plodding on the horizon. "There! Do you see it?"

"Fool! You know very well that you are inventing it."

"You mean that nothing in the world is real?" . . .

I had been walking two hours when I saw the flames of the bonfire that Prévot, frightened by my long absence, had sent up. They mattered very little to me now.

Another hour of trudging. Five hundred yards away. A hundred yards. Fifty yards.

"Good Lord!"

Amazement stopped me in my tracks. Joy surged up and filled my heart with its violence. In the firelight stood Prévot, talking to two Arabs who were leaning against the motor. He had not noticed me, for he was too full of his own joy. If only I had sat still and waited with him! I should have been saved already. Exultantly I called out:

"Hi! Hi!"

The two Bedouins gave a start and stared at me. Prévot left them standing and came forward to meet me. I opened my arms to him. He caught me by the elbow. Did he think I was keeling over? I said:

"At last, eh?"

"What do you mean?"

"The Arabs!"

"What Arabs?"

"Those Arabs there, with you."

Prévot looked at me queerly, and when he spoke I felt as if he was very reluctantly confiding a great secret to me: "There are no Arabs here."

This time I know I am going to cry. (Saint-Exupéry, 1939)

DELAYED REACTION. An experimental technique for determining whether an animal or young child can remember the solution to a problem after a lapse of time. The method is used in studying thinking processes and learning ability.

Adult human beings can learn any number of tasks that involve delays of short or even long duration. They can respond to the command "Forward . . . March!" where the reaction is only slightly delayed, and they can find a letter which they put away a year before. But how early in life are we capable of such delayed reactions? And do any animals possess this ability? Psychologists have felt that the answers to these questions might throw light on thinking and learning ability, since some kind of mental process, such as language, memory traces, or other symbolic activity, seems to be needed to bridge the gap when reactions are delayed. This idea has led to a number of revealing experiments.

In a typical setup, a young child is shown how to obtain an object which he has seen the experimenter hide. He is then seated in front of three small boxes, and watches while the experimenter places a toy in one of the boxes and closes the lid. The child is then turned around, or his eyes are covered for a period, and after that he is asked to find the toy. Hunter (1917) found that thirteen-month-old children performed correctly 80 per cent of the time with delays up to fifteen seconds. This ability increased with age and mastery of language, and many five-year-olds were consistently accurate after intervals of a month or more. It was found that these children frequently verbalized during the first observation, "It's under the middle box," and when they were tested after the delay, they would say something like "Oh, yes, I saw it under the middle box." Hunter's experiments indicated that delayed reaction is possible without the use of language, but that language greatly expands this ability.

The first experiments with animals seemed to indicate that chimpanzees and dogs could only make correct choices if they remained oriented toward a cup under which food had been placed. Modifications in the apparatus later proved that delayed responses could be made by some animals without this orienting posture. The period of delay did not approach that of adult human beings, but in some cases it amounted to many minutes or even days. Further experiments demonstrated that monkeys were capable of a particularly advanced form of delayed reaction. Their favorite food, a banana, was placed under a cup, and after a delay they were allowed to retrieve it. Then a piece of lettuce (not a favorite food) was placed over the banana and this time they refused to take the reward, and some even had a typical temper tantrum. However, they remained in the vicinity as if they were waiting for the banana (Tinklepaugh, 1928). This experiment, together with the previous studies, showed that many animals are capable of using some form of "symbolic activity"—that is, thinking—even though they do not have language to aid them.

Although these experiments have shown that some animals use thinking processes similar to those of human beings, they have also helped to distinguish between men and animals. It was found that chimpanzees cannot use color as a cue even though they have good color vision. Children, on the other hand, used position alone until they were a year of age, but color became the dominant cue when they grew older (Miller, 1934). Moreover, the time interval was strictly limited for all animals, while older children and adults were able to make correct responses even after a period of months or even years. Language is believed to be the prime factor in accounting for this difference.

Delayed-reaction experiments have been used to good advantage in brain research. It had long been suspected that the forwardmost part of the brain, the prefrontal area, is extremely important in higher learning and especially in thinking that is directed to the future. This theory has received support from the fact that when the prefrontal lobes of monkeys were removed, they usually failed in the delayed-reaction task if the interval was more than a few seconds. They also seemed unable to concentrate on the task, although they became more docile and calm.

These findings have an interesting sequel. When they were mentioned during a professional convention, a neurosurgeon, J. W. Watts, conceived the idea that deeply disturbed human beings might become calmer and less concerned about their problems if the prefrontal area was eliminated. As a result, this operation was performed on many mental patients who seemed to be otherwise incurable. Although it has effectively alleviated emotional disturbance in many cases, it has usually reduced the patient's ability to think and plan, and for this reason is now used only as a last resort. *See* PSYCHOSURGERY.

DELIRIUM. A mental state, or "acute brain syndrome," characterized primarily by confusion and disorientation, and in some cases accompanied by fear, apprehension, illusions, and hallucinations. Electroencephalographic (EEG) changes are usually found, with a shift toward slower frequency. These changes indicate an impairment of brain functioning due to lowered blood supply or other conditions causing "cerebral insufficiency." The most common factors that produce delirium are infectious diseases, toxic conditions, and head injury.

Delirium is ordinarily most marked at night when external stimulation is reduced. It is often preceded by drowsiness, disturbed sleep, and impaired attention. The first signs are usually difficulty in concentration, interference with thinking processes, increasing bewilderment, and disturbance of time orientation. These symptoms are usually followed by pronounced fluctuations in rationality, mood, and activity. The patient may be reasonable, calm, and only mildly restless at one moment, but highly unreasonable, irritable, and overactive at the next. If the delirium progresses, he may become disoriented for place as well as for time, incoherent in both thought and expression, and increasingly unco-ordinated in motor control. He may have terrifying dreams and fantasies, followed by distorted perception and vivid hallucinations. The content of the fantasies and hallucinations may sometimes be traced to wishes, fears, or internal conflicts. If the course of the delirium continues without arrest, it may reach the final stage of stupor and coma.

Delirium is usually a transient condition, but in rare cases it may persist for more than a month. After it subsides, the patient usually has only a dreamlike recollection of the episode; but if there has been a considerable clouding of consciousness during the delirious state, he may have only a patchy memory or no recollection at all of what occurred. The condition clears up without residual symptoms or brain damage. *See* POSTOPERATIVE DISORDERS (ILLUSTRATIVE CASE).

It has been found that some individuals are more susceptible to delirium than others, probably for both physical and psychological reasons. In these vulnerable individuals a slight fever may produce delirium, but in others, particularly well-integrated personalities, even a high fever will fail to have this effect.

Delirium may occur in a wide variety of disorders. The most prominent are infectious diseases (diphtheria, pneumonia, etc.), metabolic disturbances (pernicious anemia, pellagra, dehydration), toxic states (alcoholic, barbiturate, or bromide intoxication, lead poisoning, etc.), head injury, cardiac breakdown, senile psychosis, postoperative conditions, exhaustion states, puerperal disorders, and manic-depressive reaction (delirious mania). *See* Index for topics.

DELIRIUM TREMENS. An acute psychotic reaction occurring in chronic alcoholics following a prolonged drinking bout. The disturbance may also occur after a sudden withdrawal of alcohol or in connection with head injury or infection incurred during a period of abstinence.

The cause of the delirium is probably a combination of physiological and psychological factors. It is believed to result from an emotional crisis produced by the fears, anxieties, and tensions associated with excessive drinking, plus metabolic disturbances due to impairment of liver function, acidosis, dehydration, and nutritional deficiency. The condition rarely occurs before the age of thirty, and follows at least a three- or four-year history of alcoholism. The delirium is generally preceded by a period of restlessness, irritability, aversion to food, and disturbed sleep with nightmares. During the DTs, the patient experiences several types of symptoms: (1) mental confusion and disorientation: he fails to recognize relatives, mistakes the doctor for an old friend or the hospital for a jail; (2) terrifying hallucinations: the wallpaper comes to life with menacing creatures; imaginary insects crawl over his skin; a foul-smelling gas makes him gasp for breath; (3) extreme suggestibility: he imagines he sees any animals mentioned to him, and uses any suggested way of trying to destroy them; (4) coarse tremors (deliriums *tremens*) of the hands, tongue, and lips; (5) rapid or irregular pulse, perspiration, fever, and coated tongue.

The acute symptoms last from three to ten days and are followed by deep and prolonged sleep. Treatment includes confinement to bed, gradual withdrawal of alcohol, constant supervision and reassurance to avoid injury or suicide, tranquilizing drugs, high enemas, vitamins, enriched soft diet, and large amounts of orange juice and milk. In spite of precautions, the death rate averages 10 per cent due to complications such as heart failure, pneumonia, or liver disease.

In cases where there is a predisposition to psychosis, a persistent mental illness may be precipitated by the alcoholic episode. But most frequently the patient recovers from the delirium and has only the vaguest memory of what occurred. He is usually apologetic and remorseful for the trouble he has caused, but in all likelihood will resume his drinking and return to the hospital with another delirious attack within a few months. *See* ACUTE ALCOHOLIC HALLUCINOSIS, DELIRIUM, ALCOHOLIC ADDICTION.

Illustrative Case: DELIRIUM TREMENS

The patient was brought forcibly to the psychiatric ward of a general hospital when he fired his shotgun at 3:30 A.M. while "trying to repel an invasion of cockroaches." On admission he was confused and disoriented and had terrifying hallucinations involving "millions and millions" of invading cockroaches. He leaped from his bed and cowered in terror against the wall, screaming for help and kicking and hitting frantically at his imaginary assailants. When an attendant came to his aid, he screamed for him to get back out of danger or he would be killed too. Before the attendant could reach him he dived headlong on his head, apparently trying to kill himself.

The patient's delirium lasted for a period of three and a half days, after which he returned to a state of apparent normality, apologized profusely for the trouble he had caused everyone, stated he would never touch another drop, and was discharged. However, on his way home he stopped at a bar, had too much to drink, and on emerging from the bar collapsed on the street. This time he sobered up in jail, again apologized for the trouble he had caused, was extremely remorseful, and was released with a small fine. His subsequent career is unknown. (Coleman, 1964)

DELUSION. A false, irrational belief arising out of unconscious emotional needs and maintained in spite of logical absurdity or proof to the contrary.

Delusions may be fragmentary, as in delirium; or highly systematized, coherent, and superficially convincing, as in paranoid states. Most of them fall into the area between these extremes. Some delusions are strongly held convictions, while others are more tenuous and may be in the process of formation. In a psychiatric examination, great tact must be used so that the patient will feel free to talk about his beliefs. The examiner must be careful neither to endorse nor to criticize the delusions he hears expressed.

The tendency toward delusions reflects the universal human need for emotional support, reassurance, and relief of anxiety, as well as the common human tendency to use defense mechanisms to protect the ego and cope with problems. Normal individuals keep these mechanisms within bounds and limit themselves to occasional rationalizations, prejudices, wishful thinking, and the like. With the acutely disturbed individual, on the other hand, the pressure of deep-seated emotional needs may become so overwhelming that he may alter reality itself to make it conform to his frustrated desires or feelings of guilt, rejection, or inadequacy. The patient then develops persistent delusions as a means of solving his own special problems. Delusions can therefore be interpreted as an attempt to achieve adjustment—but in adopting them, the patient inevitably loses touch with the actual world and becomes more maladjusted than ever.

Delusions tend to fall into the following nine categories. Not infrequently two or three types may be exhibited in the same case:

(1) *Delusions of grandeur.* Grandiose ideas arising from feelings of inferiority, insecurity, or guilt. The individual reacts by going to the opposite extreme, believing he is a brilliant scientist, a powerful military leader, or perhaps the savior of all mankind. Most frequently he identifies himself with the prevailing hero or other important personages of his time: the Kaiser, Henry IV, the Prince of Wales, a fighter pilot. *See* GRANDIOSE DELUSIONS.

(2) *Delusions of persecution.* The individual feels that others are threatening him, discriminating against him, or conspiring to bring about his downfall. The reaction originates in the patient's inner resentments and self-dissatisfactions. He denies and disowns these feelings by shifting them to others. Delusions of persecution and delusions of grandeur are frequently found in the same patient; both reactions serve the same purposes of relieving anxiety and maintaining self-esteem.

(3) *Delusions of sin and guilt.* Delusions in which an individual believes he is extremely wicked and has committed unpardonable sins. He may see himself as the incarnation of all evil and feel that he is to blame for wars, depressions, famines, and other catastrophes. These delusions are exaggerations of vague feelings of guilt which in some cases originate in hostile attitudes and the wish to see others harmed or destroyed. Delusions of sin and guilt are often accompanied by an intense fear of punishment or damnation.

(4) *Delusions of reference.* The individual believes that other people are talking about him, drawing pictures of him, or referring to him in plays and films. He feels that most of these references are derogatory. The sources of this delusion are similar to the preceding two types.

(5) *Delusions of influence.* The patient is convinced that other people are controlling his thoughts and actions—for example, that a doctor is treating him by radar, or that enemies are "pouring filth" into his mind. These beliefs are often associated with delusions of persecution.

(6) *Hypochondriacal delusions.* The patient believes he is afflicted with a dread disease which is poisoning his brain, rotting his liver, or eating away his stomach. The delusion may be based upon a half-conscious feeling of physical deterioration (as in old people), or it may represent punishment for deeply buried feelings of guilt or hostility. *See* HYPOCHONDRIASIS.

(7) *Delusions of impoverishment.* The patient has a false conviction that his money has run out and that he will soon be sent away to the poorhouse. The delusion probably originates in the feeling that he has lost his social and personal worth; it may also be associated with delusions of guilt.

(8) *Nihilistic delusions.* The patient believes that he has no right arm, or no brain, or no sensations. He may be convinced that he died years ago or that he is now living in a realm of spirits. The source of these delusions seems to lie in the feeling that changes have

taken place in his own personality. They may also originate in vague feelings of unreality and depersonalization. *See* DEPERSONALIZATION, COTARD'S SYNDROME, NIHILISM.

(9) *Erotic delusions.* In one type, the individual may believe that he is loved by another person—often a stage, screen, or political figure—who does not avow his love but indicates it in many small (and imagined) ways. He may deluge this person with letters or even threaten police action. In another type, the individual has a fixed delusional jealousy that may lead to great embarrassment or even violence. He rejects all evidence that would contradict his delusion, and is constantly on the alert for even the most minute and trivial indications that will confirm it. *See* EROTOMANIA.

Delusions of grandeur, persecution, reference, and influence are most frequently found in paranoid schizophrenia, alcoholic psychosis, senile psychosis, and general paresis. Delusions of sin and guilt are most prevalent in affective disorders of the depressive type, although they may also be found in schizophrenia. Hypochondriacal, nihilistic, and impoverishment delusions are often found in senile psychosis. Erotic delusions occur primarily in paranoid states. Other disorders in which delusions occur are Addison's disease, psychosis with cerebral arteriosclerosis, and delirium caused by infection, exhaustion, alcohol, or head trauma. *See* these topics.

DEMENTIA. This term was originally applied to "insanity" or "madness" in general, and mentally ill persons were frequently described as "demented." Today it is reserved exclusively for a permanent loss of intellectual ability due to structural disturbance or degeneration of the brain.

The deterioration may be slight or severe. Milder cases involve impairment of the ability to make fine distinctions, perceive shades of meaning, use abstract ideas, or make sound judgments or decisions on personal or moral issues. As deterioration progresses, practically all mental abilities are increasingly affected. The patient narrows his span of interest and concern, and has more and more difficulty in learning, understanding others, making decisions, and profiting from experience. The flow of thought and imagination slows down, memory becomes defective, and emotional response is blunted. This general impoverishment of thought and affect is sometimes accompanied by mental confusion and disorientation as to time, place, and person.

The degeneration of the brain which produces dementia can be due to a number of different factors. The most common are brain atrophy occurring in old age (senile dementia), vascular disturbances of the brain caused by cerebral arteriosclerosis or hypertension, and brain inflammations due particularly to syphilis and epidemic encephalitis. Less common are the degenerative brain diseases (Alzheimer's disease, Pick's disease, Huntington's chorea), the deficiency diseases (Korsakoff's syndrome, Wernicke's syndrome, pellagra), as well as brain tumor and head injury disorders. *See* these topics.

DEMONOLOGY. Even before Greek and Roman civilization collapsed under the impact of the barbarian onslaught in the fifth century, the Dark Ages in psychiatric history had already begun. The scientific approach to mental disorder which Galen had advocated at the end of the second century had gradually been abandoned, and physicians had returned to the primitive superstitions which had dominated man's mind before the classical era. Abnormal behavior was divorced from medicine and associated once again with the supernatural and the magical. Demonology, which had been rife in primitive society, reappeared in full force, modified only slightly to conform with the theology of the time. The mind of man was pictured as a theater of war in which invisible spirits fought to gain possession of the soul, and treatment of the mentally ill was once again put in the hands of priests instead of physicians.

During the early part of the medieval period victims of mental disorder were usually confined in monasteries. Generally speaking, they were handled in a kindly manner, and treatment consisted of prayers, holy water, sanctified ointments, the breath or spittle of priests, touching of relics, and visits to holy places. In some monasteries and shrines the priests sought to exorcise the demons by the gentle "laying on of hands." These procedures were often mingled with crude naturalistic ideas derived from Galen and Hippocrates. For example, one of the unpalatable prescriptions read: "For a fiend-sick man: when the devil possesses a man or controls him from within with disease, a spew-drink of lupin, bishopswort, henbane, garlic. Pound these together, add ale and holy water." And here is one of the incantations that recalls Hippocrates' theory of hysteria: "I conjure thee, oh womb, in the name of the Holy Trinity, to come back to the place from which thou shouldst neither move nor turn away without further molestation, and to return, without anger, to the place where the Lord has put thee originally."

These relatively mild procedures were gradually replaced by more and more violent measures. The priests became convinced that incantations and laying on of hands were not powerful enough to exorcise the devil. Believing that it was Satan's pride which originally led to his downfall, they tried to strike back by hurling at him the foulest epithets and most obscene curses they could devise: "May all the devils that are thy foes rush forth upon thee, and drag thee down to hell! . . . May God

set a nail to your skull, and pound it in with a hammer, as Jael did unto Sisera! . . . May God hang thee in a hellish yoke, as seven men were hanged by the sons of Saul" (From *Thesaurus Exorcismorum*). Treatment of this kind was apparently successful in many cases, probably because the patients were highly suggestible and believed so implicitly in demonology that they gave up their most obvious symptoms. A striking example of the suggestibility of the age can be found in the "psychic epidemics" which took place from about the tenth century on. The two major forms of this "mass madness," dancing mania and lycanthropy, are described under another topic, MASS HYSTERIA.

Unfortunately those who "treated" the mentally disturbed did not limit themselves to verbal attacks on the devil. The theologians of the time came to believe that demons could be driven out only by administering physical punishment. They therefore used every conceivable torture to make the bodies of "madmen" so uninhabitable that not even a demon would want to reside in them. They flogged, starved, chained, and branded them mercilessly, adding physical suffering to their mental anguish until their condition became so hopeless that they pleaded with God to release them through death.

The era came to a tragic climax in the fifteenth and sixteenth centuries, partly as a result of the doctrine of demoniacal possession and partly as a reaction to the ravages of a series of storms, pestilences, floods, and especially the Black Death, which destroyed millions of lives and disrupted the entire fabric of society. The populace attributed all these terrible catastrophes to supernatural causes and sought to root out the spirit of Satan which had invaded the land. They came to believe—with the theologians—that demonic possession took two forms: some victims were unwillingly seized by the devil as divine punishment for sins, while others were actually in league with the devil. The latter group were supposed to have signed a pact with Satan which gave them supernatural powers of many kinds. They could cause famines, floods, impotence, and sterility. They could ride through the air, drive their enemies mad, and turn themselves into animals at will. At first the group who were unwillingly seized by the devil were considered mentally disturbed and were subjected to the practices of exorcism. However, by the end of the fifteenth century mental illness had itself been equated with sin (especially sexual sin), and both groups were considered heretics and witches.

Witches were blamed for every personal and social calamity that occurred, and in 1484 Pope Innocent VIII issued a bull in which he exhorted the clergy of Europe to use every means of detecting them. Ten years later two Dominican friars named Johann Sprenger and Heinrich Kraemer were authorized to root out the evil in northern Germany. To assist them in this work, they issued a manual entitled *Malleus Maleficarum* (The Witches' Hammer) which became the "bible" for witch-hunters for two and a half centuries. The first part of the book asserted the existence of witches: "True faith teaches us certain angels fell from heaven and are now devils." The second part described the signs to be used in detecting them, such as pigment spots or areas of anesthesia on the skin, which were supposed to have been left there by the "devil's claw" as proof that he had sealed a pact with them. The third part dealt with the legal procedures to be applied in examining and sentencing the witches.

In accordance with the *Malleus,* special assistants tested suspected witches by pricking all parts of their bodies in order to find insensitive areas. Another method was to shout biblical passages in the ears of women undergoing convulsions. If they responded in any way, this was taken as a sign that they were possessed, since the demon was indicating that he had been frightened by the word of the Lord. Even delusions were taken as proof of possession, since they were believed to result from a pact with the devil: "The devil has extraordinary power over the minds of those who have given themselves up to him, so that what they do in pure imagination they believe they have actually and really done in the body" (from the *Malleus*).

The work of the devil usually took a sexual form. Invisible demons called *incubi* were believed to have intercourse with women, and others called *succubi* seduced men. Women, however, were thought to be the chief offenders: "All witchcraft comes from carnal lust, which is in women insatiable . . . wherefore for the sake of fulfilling their lusts they consort even with devils" (from the *Malleus*). Once they were apprehended, they were subjected to the most agonizing tortures to elicit a confession. This was the accepted way of obtaining sure proof of witchcraft. Many of the victims could not endure the pain inflicted on them and confessed to anything the inquisitors sought to prove —and if they were forced to name accomplices, these unfortunate individuals were tortured until they also confessed to misdeeds. Every confession, no matter how outlandish, was accepted by the learned judges. James I of England, for example, sought to prove that witches were to blame for the tempests that beset his bride on her voyage from Denmark. In the course of the investigation, a Doctor Fian was apprehended and, after wedges had been driven under his fingernails and his legs had been crushed in the "boots," he finally confessed that more than a hundred witches had put to sea in a sieve to produce the storms. (A. D. White, 1896)

The belief in witchcraft was reinforced by the fact that the victims were frequently mentally ill, or became mentally ill as a result of the inhumane treatment they received. The prevailing attitude toward "madness" was one of fear, and many of these disturbed individuals had been turned out by their families. Reduced to wandering about the countryside in rags, their unkempt appearance and haunted look fed the suspicions that were directed against them. Many of them were afflicted with hysteria, and were so suggestible that they accepted the symptoms of this disorder—the anesthesias—as evidence that they were actually in league with the devil, and as a result some of them freely claimed the extraordinary powers attributed to them. Those who suffered from severe depression or involutional melancholia became afflicted with delusions of sin and sought relief from their burden of fancied guilt by elaborating on their evil doings. Stone (1937) cites this example in point:

"A certain woman was taken and finally burned, who for six years had an incubus devil even when she was lying in bed at the side of her husband. . . . The homage she has given to the devil was of such a sort that she was bound to dedicate herself body and soul to him forever, after seven years. But God provided mercifully for she was taken in the sixth year and condemned to the fire, and having truly and completely confessed is believed to have obtained pardon from God. For she went most willingly to her death, saying that she would gladly suffer an even more terrible death if only she would be set free and escape the power of the devil."

About fifty women were brought before the judges for every man. At their trials they were stripped of their clothes, their torture marks were exposed, their hair was shaven so that no devils could hide in it, and they were brought into court backward lest they cast an evil eye on the judges. If they were convicted, they were executed in one of three ways. Some were beheaded or strangled and then burned, some were mutilated before being burned, and others were burned directly at the stake.

An appalling number of people were put to death during the fifteenth and sixteenth centuries when witchcraft rose to its peak. Both the Roman and Reformed churches carried out this practice, in Europe and in the American colonies as well. The executions were rationalized as an act of mercy that freed the victim from the clutches of the devil. The extent of this man-made holocaust is indicated by this statement from Bromberg (1937):

"A French judge boasted that he had burned 800 women in 16 years on the bench; 600 were burned during the administration of a bishop in Bamberg. The Inquisition, originally started by the Church of Rome, was carried along by Protestant churches in Great Britain and Germany. In Protestant Geneva 500 persons were burned in the year 1515. In Trèves some 7,000 people were reported burned during a period of several years."

Although the execution of witches continued until near the end of the eighteenth century, voices began to be raised against demonology during the sixteenth century. In Switzerland Paracelsus rejected the doctrine and maintained that the dancing mania was due to a diseased condition which should be treated. In France Montaigne asserted that witches were more deranged than guilty. In Spain Juan Luis Vives insisted that attempts should be made to understand the emotions of the mentally ill, and that they should be treated with understanding and compassion. In Germany Johann Weyer, a physician, published a book in which he claimed that most witches were sick in body or mind, and that their afflictions were due to "natural causes." In England Reginald Scot devoted his life to exposing the "erroneous novelties and imaginary conceptions" of demonology. In his book *Discovery of Witchcraft* (1584) he pointed out, "These women are but diseased wretches suffering from melancholy and their words, actions, reasoning and gestures show that sickness has affected their brain and impaired their powers of judgment."

The writings of these men were placed on the *Index Expurgatorius,* and their books were publicly seized and burned. But gradually the churchmen themselves joined the critics. One of the great theologians who led the way was St. Vincent de Paul (1576–1660), who risked his life to declare; "Mental disease is no different to bodily disease and Christianity demands of the humane and powerful to protect, and the skilful to relieve the one as well as the other." Within a century after this courageous and insightful utterance, demonology was clearly on the wane and the modern era of psychiatry had begun. *See* GALEN, HIPPOCRATES, WEYER, MASS HYSTERIA.

DEMYELINATING   DISORDERS. These diseases, which include multiple sclerosis and diffuse sclerosis, are due to the degeneration of the insulating (myelin) sheath around nerve fibers, and its replacement by scar tissue. The cause of this degeneration is unknown.

Although these disorders are structural and neurological, they are included in the American Psychiatric Association's Diagnostic and Statistical Manual (1952) under "Chronic Brain Syndromes associated with diseases of unknown or uncertain cause," since they are frequently accompanied by personality disturbance. The psychiatric symptoms may, in fact, be so pronounced as to mask the organic picture and make correct diagnosis difficult.

In multiple sclerosis there is no characteristic psychiatric syndrome; the symptoms depend largely on the basic personality of the individual patient. Frequently there is an accentuation of pre-illness trends. One of the more common symptoms is an exaggerated cheer-

fulness or even euphoria, which is doubtless a compensatory reaction to the destructive effects of the disease. Another common symptom is marked irritability, and a third is emotional instability. In cases where nerve destruction has progressed to a marked degree, emotional control may become so impaired that the patient may have a sudden compulsion to laugh or cry, without experiencing the feelings that usually go with these reactions. There may also be some intellectual impairment. In addition, paranoid, hypomanic, and depressive reactions are occasionally found in multiple sclerotic patients.

In diffuse sclerosis, particularly Schilder's disease, extensive demyelinization occurs in the cerebral hemispheres. Since different areas may be affected in different cases, the major features of the disease vary widely. Neurological symptoms may include cortical blindness, hemianopsia (half vision in each eye), optic atrophy, and all varieties of motor and sensory disturbances. These symptoms are frequently accompanied by headache, vomiting, vertigo, and convulsions. Sometimes the clinical picture is similar to that in brain tumor; and early in the course of the disease diffuse sclerosis may be confused with hysterical and schizophrenic reactions. Common psychological symptoms are memory defect, apathy or irritability, personality changes, and, in some cases, confusion, disorientation, and general mental deterioration.

Diffuse sclerosis runs a rapid course, although remissions occasionally occur. The terminal stages are characterized by dementia and paralysis of all the limbs. No effective treatment has been found for this disorder.

Illustrative Case: DEMYELINATING DISORDERS, MULTIPLE SCLEROSIS

This thirty-five-year-old male was admitted to the hospital with a complaint of numbness and weakness in the right arm and leg and left hand for a period of two years. Physical examination revealed some spasticity of the involved extremities with irregular sensory disturbances. Reflexes were increased unequally. There was a positive Babinski on the right, absence of abdominal reflexes, and no co-ordination in movements of the upper extremities. The patient had a hypotonic neurogenic bladder.

Laboratory studies were essentially negative, including studies of spinal fluid. Diagnosis of multiple sclerosis was made.

This patient seemed, when interviewed, comparatively unconcerned about his physical incapacitation. He was quite happy and at times almost euphoric, claiming that he loved to be in the hospital. He seemed neither worried nor depressed about his condition. He stated on occasions that his tongue was "growing" and therefore got in his way when he tried to talk. His speech was often of a scanning type. His memory was relatively clear. His first symptoms had appeared about eighteen months prior to his admission when he had difficulty walking and would sometimes fall because his knees gave way. This was soon followed by the presenting complaints, and he finally reached the stage where he was not ambulatory at all. This also gave him little apparent worry. He felt that all of his trouble were caused by "too much aggravation from being unemployed."

When left alone this patient sometimes became noisy, obstreperous, and tried to get out of bed. He was somewhat irritable and unpredictable with the other patients. At times it became necessary to restrain him. At such periods he seemed rather confused and disoriented but subsequently his sensorium would clear up. Whenever interviewed he usually presented a picture of contentment, satisfaction, and lack of concern, in spite of the gradual progression of his symptoms, difficulty with constipation, and some physical wasting. (English and Finch, 1964)

DENIAL OF REALITY (DENIAL). The unconscious defense mechanism of denying the existence of painful facts.

This technique enables an individual to escape from intolerable thoughts, wishes, actions, or events and the anxiety which they produce. In denying

their existence he is not lying or malingering, nor does he deliberately repudiate the ideas or consciously dismiss them from mind. He simply fails to perceive that they exist.

There are many forms of denial. An individual may become totally unaware that he has feelings of hostility or homosexual urges or that he has actually committed a crime. Parents fail to see physical or mental defects in their children though they are obvious to everyone else. Prisoners in solitary confinement sometimes lose their sense of reality and feel "This isn't happening to me." Some amputees lose sight of the fact that they have lost a limb and act as if it still existed. In hysterical paralysis and other conversion reactions, defensive denial frequently takes the form of cheerful unconcern. In depressive reactions the patient may deny facts he cannot face, and in catatonic schizophrenia the patient may deny his own existence or the whole of reality. See BELLE INDIFFERENCE, GRIEF (ILLUSTRATIVE CASE), NIHILISM, COTARD'S SYNDROME.

Although the term denial is usually reserved for an unconscious mechanism, it shades almost imperceptibly into a conscious or half-conscious process in which we screen out unpleasant thoughts and disagreeable realities by a variety of devices. We postpone decisions we do not want to make, ignore problems we do not wish to face, suddenly become intensely preoccupied when disagreeable topics arise. Through these devices we do not deny the existence of problems, but we deny them our attention. This may sometimes help to protect us from stress, or give us time for making decisions—but as a regular pattern of behavior, denial is bound to interfere with our adjustment since it is a way of dodging difficulties instead of facing them. See ANOSOGNOSIA.

DEPENDENCY NEEDS. Basic needs which must be satisfied by other people, particularly the need for mothering, love, affection, shelter, protection, security, physical care, food, and warmth.

Today psychologists emphasize the fact that every child starts out in life as a completely dependent individual who has as vital a need for emotional as for physical nurturance. The need for emotional dependence continues beyond infancy, although sometimes in covert forms. It is now recognized that normal adults, including men, have deep needs for emotional support in the form of approval, reassurance, and devotion. Sometimes these needs may be hidden or denied by a rough exterior or an air of complete independence, but they are believed to exist nevertheless. One of the prime purposes of friendship and especially of marriage is to gratify them. Such needs are particularly intense in situations of stress or disappointment, and husbands and wives, or friends for that matter, should not be ashamed of seeking each other's support or even crying on each other's shoulder.

Dependency needs, however, may be exaggerated to a point where they are unhealthy. This often happens among immature persons who regress to infantile behavior under stress. Instead of requiring emotional warmth as part of the general climate of life, or emotional support to help them over difficult situations, these people constantly lean on others and look to them for a solution to their problems. In consequence they fail to develop traits of self-confidence, decisiveness, and self-reliance. The clearest example of this character disorder is found in the passive-dependent personality. Excessive dependency needs are also found to underlie certain neurotic disorders. They are most common in hysterical (or conversion) reaction and are found in some psychosomatic disturbances, such as gastric ulcer. See PASSIVE-AGGRESSIVE PERSONALITY, MOTHERING.

DEPERSONALIZATION. A disturbing feeling of unreality concerning the self or the outside world, or both.

In this reaction, sometimes termed "depersonalization syndrome," the sense of personal identity is lost and the body feels like an automaton. The patient, however, does not feel that he is or is becoming someone else. Instead, he feels estranged from himself and alienated from the world as a whole. Nothing he does, says, or experiences has the full ring of reality. People and objects have a distant and unfamiliar air; thoughts, feelings and emotions have a cold and colorless character. He may report that everything happens "as if in a dream," or, in extreme cases, that his brain has gone dead.

Most people have transient feelings of unreality at times, and it has been found that sensitive, imaginative, and introverted individuals are more inclined than others to experience this reaction in intensified form. It is most likely to occur after a severe emotional shock or long period of stress. Women are more prone to the reaction than men.

Some degree of depersonalization is frequently experienced in both neurotic and psychotic disorders, such as hypochondria, depression, hysteria, obsessional states, and early schizophrenia. It is interpreted as a defensive reaction expressing an unconscious need to escape from unbearable or threatening situations. The patient withdraws from reality by feeling that reality has withdrawn from him. For extreme depersonalization, *see* NIHILISM, COTARD'S SYNDROME.

Illustrative Case: DEPERSONALIZATION

I don't recognize my body. The other day, I lay in bed, and I actually felt petrified. My head feels like wood. When I strike my head, it seems feelingless—I have to feel myself to know it's me. I have no illusions, but everything seems so unreal. In the beginning, I had different sensations go through my head but now it's a blank. It feels like a vacuum. Sometimes in bed, I raise my leg and look at it. Yes, it's me, but it doesn't seem like me. At times, I wish I had some anxiety, so that at least I could "feel" something that was normal. It may seem funny to you, but I am happy when I sneeze; it's something real. I'm even envious of people who have headaches, because those are real.

Only my dreams seem real to me. I dream of business deals, of people I meet, and they seem real to me, in my dreams—so it seems when I awake—but when I'm awake the real world seems unreal.

I look at people and they seem so small, so insignificant. I went to church and people were like shriveled-up little creatures. And I couldn't pray as I used to, with fervor. Now my prayers are just the repetition of words; I have no feeling in them. Then at times, my brother-in-law looks so large and powerful to me, because he can get up in the morning and go to work, and all I can do is lie there in bed, and feel like wood. When I try to have intercourse with my wife, she seems so immense, so big and strong, and I feel so weak and puny. (The patient was six feet tall and weighed 210 pounds—his wife, five feet, two inches, weighed 122 pounds.) The world seems so big, and the people so small. (Kraines, 1948)

DEPRESSION. An emotional state of morbid dejection and sadness, ranging from mild discouragement and downheartedness to feelings of utter hopelessness and despair.

Depression is probably the most common complaint of psychiatric patients. In its *mild* form, the patient is quiet, unhappy, pessimistic, and inhibited. He feels listless and inadequate, finding it hard to think, concentrate, and make decisions. He tends to be preoccupied with his own problems and may become irritable and quarrelsome. Mild depressions frequently progress to a *moderate* stage, in which patients suffer from persistent feelings of unpleasant tension, anguish, and "psychic pain." They find conversation difficult and become totally absorbed in melancholic ruminations on a limited number of topics. Their entire manner is dejected and dispirited, and they are inclined to project their pessimistic attitudes to others, complaining that they are unwanted, unloved, and unappreciated. Other common complaints are inability to think, bewilderment, feelings of unreality, and various somatic disturbances such as tightness in the head, insomnia, fatigue, loss of appetite, and constipation.

In *deep* depressions, the facial expression is hopeless, the mouth sags, and the eyes are directed downward. All initiative is lost, and questions are answered in a halting, monosyllabic manner. These patients become preoccupied with ideas of guilt, unworthiness, and self-accusation, often recounting their faults and exaggerating the peccadilloes of their past. Delusions of sin are common, and suicidal thoughts are frequently entertained.

Depressions may be classified into *agitated* and *retarded* types. In agitated depression the patient wears an anguished look, with deep furrows between the eyebrows; he wrings his hands and paces restlessly about, bemoaning his lot. The retarded patient wears a despondent look, sits with bowed head, speaks slowly in a toneless voice, executes all movements with apparent difficulty, and may sink into a state of stupor, becoming totally mute and immobile. Both types, but especially the retarded, are frequently accompanied by loss of appetite and weight, a coated tongue, and foul breath.

Depressions are also classified according to the source of the condition. A *reactive* depression is primarily a response to overt situations such as death of a loved one, failure in business, jilting, or social rejection. It is more likely to be of the retarded than of the agitated type, and is of relatively short duration, especially if the external situation changes for the better.

Endogenous depressions, on the other hand, have their roots within the individual, particularly in the unconscious effects of past behavior and interpersonal relationships—"perhaps," as Noyes and Kolb (1963) state, "from unconscious ambivalence and hostility with resentful and aggressive impulses directed toward persons who are the objects of an undesired obligation (a mother whose dependency prevents her daughter's desired marriage) or toward persons on whom one is dependent for security. The hostile impulses originally directed against other persons become directed against one's own self." Feelings of remorse, guilt, and sin are more common in endogenous than in reactive depressions, although they sometimes occur in the latter type when the individual blames himself for his business difficulties, or when he has entertained hostile feelings against a person who has died, or when rejection is accompanied by an acute sense of shame.

Depression is by no means confined to psychiatric disorders. In fact, it is one of the most widespread emotional reactions occurring in normal life. In these cases it is usually traceable to specific, outward causes such as disappointment, loneliness, setbacks in school or business or social life, inability to find goals or interests, and loss of perspective due to fatigue or stress. Such depressions are generally transient, either subsiding spontaneously or as a result of short-term therapy. Some individuals, however, develop more persistent "personality pattern disturbances" involving depression: the melancholic personality or the cyclothymic personality. *See* these topics.

Depressive syndromes may be either neurotic or psychotic in nature. The neurotic form is termed neurotic depressive reaction, or reactive depression; the psychotic forms include psychotic depressive reaction, involutional psychotic reaction (depressive type), and manic-depressive reaction (depressive phase, circular type, and mixed type). Depressions also occur in many other severe disorders, such as general paresis, postpartum psychosis, brain tumor, Huntington's chorea, and senile psychosis. *See* all these topics; also ANACLITIC DEPRESSION.

Illustrative Case: DEPRESSION

Everything seems to be contradictory. I don't seem to know what else to tell you, but that I am tearful and sad—and no kick out of Christmas. And I used to get such a boot out of it. . . . It's an awful feeling. . . . I don't get a bit of a kick out of anything. Everything seems to get so sort of full of despair. . . . I can't get interested in other people. I only seem to be interested in my own self. Can you offer me any advice in any way? . . .

Sometimes you seem to have a load of friends and yet nobody you really love. . . . You feel awful lonesome. . . . You just feel low . . . not a laugh nor a kick out of anything. . . . It's all so sort of vague and hollow—nothing behind it. . . . I hear and see everybody who comes to work so full of smiles and laughter and happiness. With me it's not like that at all. And why is it that every once in a while I feel it's all going to end in disaster?

I feel so sort of what I call "empty"—nothing in back of you like when you're feeling yourself. . . . You go to bed and you dread each day when you feel low like that. . . . And I try to keep saying to myself, like you say, that I haven't been that bad that I should have to punish myself. Yet my thinking doesn't get cheerful. When it doesn't get cheerful it makes you wonder will it all end in suicide sometime. . . .

I don't seem to have much feeling to want to go places—to concerts like I used to, and back to work. There just doesn't seem to be anything perking. Do you think I've improved at all?

I don't know why I don't get some help from praying. I ask God to help me through. I suppose it's my trial—guess I deserted the Lord for a long time. . . . When you feel low like this it all seems so hopeless. You dread the holiday and the long weekend. . . . This low feeling is so horrible.

I cried terribly when the family left Sun-

day. If only I could be like they are—
healthy, be one of them. The old fight
seems to be gone. . . . I can't seem to say
that I'm going to get well with any real conviction. It all seems so shallow. (Nemiah,
1961)

DEPTH PERCEPTION. The ability to
view the world in three dimensions.

One of the most important adjustments we make to our physical environment is learning to perceive the
size, location, and physical qualities of
objects in three-dimensional space.
When we look at a parked car we
see it as a 3-D object of a specific
size and shape located in a specific
place. The amazing thing about this
ability is that the receptor cells that
respond to light are embedded in a
curved 2-D surface, the retina of the
eye. This surface can only register images in an up-down and right-left
orientation, yet we perceive the world
with the added dimension of depth.

Three-dimensional perception comes
about because our brain is able to
utilize various cues to depth. When an
image falls on the retina, certain nerve
endings are activated and neural impulses are transmitted to the brain. The
brain therefore receives different patterns of nerve impulses, not miniature
copies of the object we see. Nevertheless it is able to put together these
cues in such a way as to give us
not only a flat picture of these objects, like a mosaic, but a solid picture
with the added dimension of depth.
Full depth perception is the result
of a long learning process. The baby's
first sense of depth and distance probably arises from reaching for objects
he wants. At first he misjudges the
distance of a rattle, but gradually he
becomes more accurate. Even a two-
year-old child who has learned a good
deal about the nature of his environment may lack accurate depth perception. Many a toddler asks his father

to lift him up so that he can pull
down the moon.

The cues to depth are of two general types, *monocular* and *binocular*.
The monocular cues, six in all, function
when only one eye is used. The ancient
Greeks first discovered them and they
were widely used by Renaissance
painters to give their work a three-
dimensional quality. First, *linear perspective:* objects farther away appear
smaller and closer together than nearby
objects (PLATE 14). The tracks of a
railroad appear to converge on the horizon, and uniformly spaced telephone
poles appear smaller and closer together as they recede in the distance.

Second, clearness or *atmospheric perspective:* nearer objects are sharper and
clearer than those farther away. The
dust and smoke in the air tend to
make distant objects appear blurred,
and the farther they are, the more
indistinct they become. This cue helps
us estimate distance, but it can lead
to difficulty when the clarity of the
air changes. A person who has lived
all his life in a smoky city will greatly
underestimate distances of faraway objects seen through clear air.

Third, interposition or *relative position:* if two objects are in the same
line of vision, the nearer one will be
fully in view and will partly cover the
farther one.

Fourth, light and shadow or *chiar-
oscuro:* when light strikes any irregular
surface, some parts of the object will
be bright while others will be cast in
shadow. These shadows lengthen as
distance from the light source increases. Where the transition from a
light part of a figure to a dark one
is gradual, a gently curved surface is
seen; when the change is abrupt, we
perceive a corner or an edge. These
cues help us interpret shape as well
as distance—for instance, we learn,
without realizing it, that one pattern
of light and shadow means "depression"
and another means "mound," as in

PLATE 15. The artist uses shading for the same purpose.

Fifth, *movement:* when we move our head, the objects we are looking at move relative to ourselves and to each other, a phenomenon known as "motion parallax." Nearby objects, however, move in the direction opposite to the viewer while those in the distance move in the same direction. Nearer objects also appear to move more rapidly than those farther away; an airplane in the distance hardly seems to move at all. Movement cues also help us estimate the relative distance of objects.

Sixth, *accommodation:* the lens of the eye changes shape according to the distance of the object. The ciliary muscles which are attached to the lens make it bulge when objects are close, and thin out when they are farther away. The feeling of contraction or relaxation of these muscles gives us a cue to distance, but one that can only be effective up to twenty feet, since beyond this point accommodation is very slight. There is some question as to the importance of this kinesthetic feedback for depth perception.

Binocular cues, the other general type, depend on the use of both eyes simultaneously. *Retinal disparity*—that is, differences in retinal images—is the most effective of all the cues to depth. It results from the fact that the two eyes are separated from each other by a distance of about two and a half inches, and therefore receive slightly different images of any solid object. This can easily be tested by looking at a fixed object with one eye and then, without moving the head, looking at it with the other eye. The difference in the two images is greatest when the object fixated is close, and decreases as it is moved farther away. The importance of this cue can be shown by trying to thread a needle with only one eye open. Some people look at paintings in museums with one eye only, since by eliminating retinal disparity, they can better appreciate the cues to tri-dimensionality the artist has put into his work.

This cue is also utilized in stereoscopic color slides. Here, two pictures are taken simultaneously by two cameras with lenses set slightly apart. If each of these pictures is separately viewed, one by each eye, a 3-D picture is produced. The same principle has been used in detecting camouflage. Two photos taken from a plane at points above one hundred feet apart are combined in a stereoscope. The relief of the terrain, which is barely observable in a single photo, will be clearly brought out. A cannon roofed over by foliage will be readily detected by this method.

A second binocular cue, *convergence,* is of more questionable value. It is a kinesthetic response arising from the muscles which turn and point the eyes at an object. Up to a distance of seventy feet, the closer the object the greater the amount of convergence, and the greater the amount of muscular tension required to produce it. The degree of muscular tension is believed to give us some idea of the distance of the object from our eyes.

Most of our experience of depth is achieved through vision, but we sometimes obtain cues through other senses such as touch, smell, heat, cold, and especially hearing. When we listen to voices, music, or noise, the sound waves that reach the two ears are somewhat different in frequency, amplitude, phase, and time of arrival. These differences, slight as they are, provide cues to the distance and direction of the sound source. In stereo recording, two microphones are placed some distance apart in order to capture these differences. They become the ears of the system, and each one records its own sound track. The sound from these separate tracks is then individually amplified and emitted through two speakers. If the listener can arrange the speakers so that they are in different parts of the room, the impression of depth will be striking. It can be as different from monophonic sound as a real scene from a photograph. See AUDITORY SPACE PERCEPTION, VISUAL CLIFF.

DEPTH PSYCHOLOGY. A general approach in psychology and psychotherapy focused on the relationship between unconscious and conscious experience.

Depth psychology is based upon the belief that abnormal behavior, as well as a good deal of normal behavior, can be explained only be delving beneath the surface of the mind. We are constantly being affected for good or ill by hidden memories, repressed impulses, and buried feelings. The aim of the depth approach is to uncover and illuminate these unconscious influences.

In general, depth psychology holds that the only way to bring about lasting changes in personality and adjustment is to trace emotional disturbances to their roots. This is not an intellectual exercise for the therapist—rather, the patient himself must become aware of the unconscious forces that are causing his symptoms. The more insight he achieves, the greater the likelihood he will be able to alter his faulty reaction patterns.

There are many varieties of depth psychology. The classic example is Freudian psychoanalysis, but other analytic schools, such as those originated by Horney and Sullivan, recognize that unconscious mental processes play a major role in our reactions. Jung's analytic psychology, with its emphasis on the collective unconscious, is an example of depth psychology, as is Adler's individual psychology with its recognition of compensatory drives and the unconscious creation of a unique style of life. Recently developed techniques for exploring the unconscious, such as hypnoanalysis and narcosynthesis, are

further variations on the theme of depth psychology. All these approaches contrast sharply with psychologies and therapeutic methods which focus on conscious factors and the use of learning and reconditioning techniques in changing behavior. See PSYCHOANALYSIS (THEORY), HORNEY, SULLIVAN, JUNG, ADLER, CLIENT-CENTERED THERAPY, BEHAVIOR THERAPY.

DEREISTIC THINKING. Mental activity which is not in accord with reality, experience and logic.

Daydreams frequently fall into this category, but the most striking examples are found in the irrational fantasies of schizophrenics—for example, a patient may think he is the Messiah or that he can cure illness by a gesture. Dereistic and autistic thinking are similar terms. See AUTISM, DAYDREAMING, SCHIZOPHRENIC REACTIONS (GENERAL).

DERMO-OPTICAL   PERCEPTION (DOP). Perception through the skin; cutaneous vision.

During the past few years a number of investigations have been made of individuals who appeared to be able to "see with their fingers." The phenomenon came to the attention of American psychologists through a report of a Soviet woman, Rosa Kuleshova published in *Soviet Psychology and Psychiatry*, Fall 1963. According to a physician, I. M. Goldberg, she was able to discriminate colored paper and plastic, identify colored lights, and read ordinary letter-press print with her fingers. A neurologist, N. D. Nyuberg, who examined her, stated that she undoubtedly had photosensitive substances in the skin similar to those in the retina, and reported that after special training she was able to distinguish between black and white with her toes. Goldberg suggested that the ability might be attributed to sensitivity to minute differences in surface texture due to a pathological condition of the nervous system, and supported this theory with observations of rheumatic and epileptic patients who appeared to show DOP ability. Russian scientists are attempting to develop finger vision in blind and near-blind individuals as a partial compensation for their defect.

Cases of skin perception have been reported before. One example is Margaret McAvoy, a Liverpool woman born in 1800, who became blind at the age of sixteen. According to Edith Sitwell's account in her book *English Eccentrics,* this woman was able to distinguish colors with her fingers, but lost the ability "when her hands were cold" or when she had made "long and unremitting efforts." A second example is Sophia M-Va, whose case was reported by a Russian psychiatrist, A. N. Khovrin, in an article entitled "A Rare Form of Hyperesthesia of Higher Sensory Organs," which appeared in a St. Petersburg journal in 1898. Working in the dark, Sophia was apparently able to identify the colors of paper and of raw silk and wool threads concealed under a heavy blanket.

In this country DOP has been systematically investigated by R. P. Youtz (1963, 1968). His principal subject was a Michigan housewife, Mrs. Patricia Stanley, who had apparently shown the ability to identify colors with her fingers during her high school years. In the summer of 1963 Youtz subjected Mrs. Stanley to over fifty-five hours of testing, using a sleep-mask blindfold and a light-tight experimental box. During the experiment she inserted her hands through armholes, with her forearms covered with velveteen sleeves to exclude all outside light and all visual cues. The interior of the box could be illuminated but most of the experiments were performed in the dark. Preliminary tests showed that she was unable to distinguish between colors of wooden or sponge rubber objects, but seemed to distinguish the color of paper and plastic cards. Most of the experiments were performed with stimulus cards covered with a neutral gelatin filter or a piece of thin clear plastic to eliminate the possibility of texture cues. In a typical trial she was presented with three cards, two of the same color and one different, and was asked to put together the two that seemed similar.

The long series of tests yielded the following major findings. First, Mrs. Stanley was able not only to separate the cards correctly, but to identify red and blue materials correctly 85 to 95 per cent of the time when they were covered with a filter down to 13 per cent transmittance, or plastic up to .01 inch in thickness and glass up to .003 inch in thickness. Second, when the filter blocked more than 87 per cent of visible wavelengths or when the glass was one-sixteenth inch thick, judgments were no better than guesswork. Third, when her finger temperature was below 75 degrees or when the objects were immersed in water at 90 degrees, she also did no better than chance. Fourth, telepathy was ruled out by performing "double-blind" experiments which showed that results were the same when the experimenter himself did not know the color of the cards being used. Fifth, when tests were performed during the winter when her hands were colder than usual, Mrs. Stanley was less successful though still above the chance level, and during the following summer, in 1964, at a time when she was fatigued and distracted, her accuracy did not exceed chance. Apparently two of the factors mentioned in the case of Margaret McAvoy—fatigue and cold—actually work against this ability.

A large number of Barnard College students were also tested. Among the subjects who seemed successful, one girl scored above chance for ten days but later fell to chance. A second did significantly better than chance on red and blue cards but not on red and white or on blue and white; a third distinguished all three types of cards with 40 per cent accuracy, and was correct 67 per cent of the time with blue and white cards. The fact that the latter subject performed best in separating the dark (blue) from the light (white) cards suggested that the major factor in making these discriminations might be temperature differences, for dark colors absorb more heat than light colors. It is interesting that this subject as well as others stated that the cards seemed to be of different temperatures. Youtz has pointed out, however, "It is important not to overlook the fact that skin as well as colored cards will radiate heat, or infrared rays . . . Perhaps the heat radiated by my subjects' hands was differently reflected by the different-colored stimulus cards, and this difference was what the subjects detected" (1968). Reflected radiation from Mrs. Stanley's hands may account for the fact that she could discriminate correctly when the box was dark. It may also account for the fact that her performance was better when her hands were warm than when they were cold.

So far, tests of the temperature theory have not yielded conclusive results, but the possibility is still a live one. There is also the possibility that the phenomenon may be due, in some cases at least, to sensitivity of the skin to light. Studies of animals indicate that skin photosensitivity is common in aquatic animals with non-waterproof skin, less common in terrestrial anthropoids, but rare in amniotes, which include human beings. In a series of experiments performed on a twenty-one-year-old girl, using essentially the same type of apparatus as that used by Youtz, J. Z. Jacobson and his colleagues (1966) found that his subjects' judgments were significantly correct when light was shining on the colored paper but were no better than chance when the light was turned off. Although no conclusions can be drawn at present, it may be that some subjects discriminate primarily on the basis of temperature differences and others on the basis of different patterns of wavelengths absorbed or emitted by objects.

DESCARTES, RENE (1596–1650). Though primarily a philosopher and mathematician, Descartes nevertheless had a profound influence on the development of psychology. Born in La Hague, he attended a Jesuit school where he studied both theology and science. He went on to receive a law degree at the University of Poitiers, but did not practice this profession. Instead, he became a gentleman soldier, applying his scientific knowledge to military engineering, and later to problems of meteorology and glacier formation. During this period he had a prophetic dream which suggested that all science should be interrelated, and that physics can be reduced to geometry.

After traveling extensively in Europe, Descartes returned to Paris to write, but found that his views conflicted with Church doctrine. For this reason he went to live in Holland, where he was assured of greater intellectual freedom than in France.

Descartes was largely responsible for the mechanistic viewpoint in French psychological thought. However, he arrived at his mechanism through a circuitous route, since his view was based on a dualistic conception of substance. In his *Discourse on Method* he adopted a universal "methodical doubt" in an attempt to discover at least one indubitable idea on which to base all knowledge. This he found in the *"Cogito, ergo sum* (I think, therefore I am)" —that is, to him the only certainty was the existence of the self or soul as a thinking being. On this foundation he based his proof of the existence of

God and his recognition of the existence of matter.

Since the self was, by definition, an unextended, incorporeal mental substance (*res cogitans*), it contrasted sharply with the material or extended substance (*res extensa*) which geometry describes. This brought up two problems: first, since mind and body are essentially different, how does each of them operate? And second, since they are not only distinct but together, how do they interact?

Descartes attempted to solve the first problem by showing that the rational acts of the soul and the mechanical activities of the body can be approached and studied in their own right. His account of the soul is closely allied with scholastic thought, for he viewed it as an indivisible, "unitary substance" which nevertheless contained innate ideas of God, geometrical maxims, etc. which could be accepted by reason because they were "clear and distinct." He also held that the six elementary "passions de l'âme" (passions of the soul)—wonder, love, hate, desire, joy, sadness—are rationally motivated. These philosophical doctrines had little direct effect on psychology, although the view of McDougall that behavior is governed by a set of innate tendencies or instincts, and the Gestalt emphasis on basic organizing principles of the mind, are sometimes traced back to Descartes' general position.

Descartes' handling of "corporeal substance," however, had a more direct influence on psychological investigations. Since mind and body were essentially different, he proposed that the body could be freely studied as a thoroughly mechanical phenomenon, an automaton—a view that received its impetus from the Galilean theories of mechanics, which were beginning to be accepted at the time. This theory helped to establish a milieu for the development of the scientific approach to man in general, and the field of physiological psychology in particular.

Descartes himself made a number of contributions to the study of emotions, vision, the senses, and nerve conduction. Although he characterized emotions as passions of the soul, he nevertheless treated them almost as mechanical events, explaining them in terms of motions in the brain, blood, and vital organs. He described the functioning of the normal and diseased eye, and demonstrated that the crystalline body is a lens through which light waves form an image on the retina. He was aware that muscles operate in opposing pairs, and recognized that both nerve and muscle responses follow from stimulation of the sense organs. Though he pictured the nerves themselves as hollow tubes conducting "animal spirits" in either direction between the muscles and sense organs, he nevertheless offered a "pathway" theory of the peripheral nervous system, and came close to the modern concept of the reflex arc (Boring, 1950).

Descartes took the position that the mechanical approach could be fully applied to animals, since they do not have a soul, but man is partly physical and partly spiritual in nature. This left him the problem of the relationship between the "substances." He recognized that in spite of their essential differences, mind acts upon body and body upon mind, and proposed that the locus for this activity is in the tiny pineal body, naming the point of contact the "conarium" (which, according to Hinsie and Campbell, 1960, became Freud's id). The reason for choosing this site was that the pineal body is located at the center of the brain, and was apparently the only part of the brain which was unitary and not duplicated. According to Descartes, its primary purpose is to direct the animal spirits to one or another part of the body, making possible mental activities like recognition and imagination, as well as physical activities such as move- ment. Though crude, this theory intro- duced the idea of interaction, and when psychology eventually divorced itself from theology, it helped to give rise to a holistic approach to the human being. *See* PINEAL GLAND.

DESCRIPTIVE PSYCHIATRY. A sys- tematic approach to psychiatry based upon the observation, study, and clas- sification of directly observable symp- toms and clinical patterns. It con- trasts with the dynamic approach, which puts the emphasis on the con- scious and unconscious forces that pro- duce symptoms and disorders.

The leading figure in modern de- scriptive psychiatry was Emil Kraepe- lin, who gave an exhaustive account of manic-depressive psychosis, schizo- phrenia ("dementia praecox") and all other major mental disorders, based upon the case histories of thousands of patients. His classification was so com- prehensive and factual that it is the principal basis for the standard system of psychiatric classification in use to- day.

In general, descriptive psychiatry takes the position that certain groups of symptoms occur together with such regularity that they can be regarded as specific diseases, in much the same way that we think of pneumonia and typhoid fever as distinct ailments. With Kraepelin this approach led to the con- viction that each type of mental ill- ness is separate and distinct from all others, and that the course and out- come of these illnesses was as pre- dictable as any physical illness. In fact, Kraepelin believed that mental illness does not basically differ from physical illness since he held that it is caused by brain pathology. His work launched an entire "descriptive era" in which description and classification were greatly furthered by Golgi, Broca, Head, Alzheimer, and many others, all of whom also championed the organic

point of view. They succeeded both in describing the symptoms and un- covering the pathological basis of such disorders as general paresis, cerebral arteriosclerosis, senile psychosis, toxic psychosis, and certain types of mental retardation. *See* ORGANICISM.

The development of descriptive psy- chiatry is still continuing—in fact, the American Psychiatric Association has included a number of new clinical entities in its revised classification of psychiatric disorders (1952). Among these are Transient Situational Person- ality Disorders, Personality Pattern Dis- turbances, and Personality Trait Dis- turbances. Also, psychosomatic dis- orders have been renamed Psychophys- iologic Autonomic and Visceral Dis- orders. Nevertheless, the primary em- phasis has shifted from descriptive to dynamic psychiatry, and today most psychiatrists are far more concerned with the motivational forces that pro- duce better or worse adjustment than with the classification of symptoms and syndromes. *See* DYNAMIC APPROACH, KRAEPELIN.

DETECTION THEORY. An explana- tion of the way signals are perceived against a background of noise.

The psychological study of signal de- tection is an extension of work per- formed by engineers on the detection of targets by radar in World War II. Investigators (Smith and Wilson, 1953; Tanner and Swets, 1954) found that any signal from the environment is su- perimposed on both internal and ex- ternal noise and must be distinguished from this noise. Internal or "neural" noise is produced by the workings of the individual's body—for example, breathing sounds or sounds produced by changes in posture. It has even been found that some subjects become aware of the sound of their own blood circulating when they are in a sound- proofed room. External noise, on the other hand, is any sound from the environment that interferes with the reception of a signal. Even in a sound-proof room the subject may hear a high-pitched noise, the so-called "noise of silence." When a signal is emitted, the subject must detect it against the background of both types of noise.

Research has shown that the individual does not merely *receive* the signal, but makes a decision as to its presence. When the signal is extremely faint or when there is considerable interference, or both, this decision is not based on absolute knowledge but on probabilities (Carterette and Cole, 1962). Each individual sets up a criterion value against which he checks the sensory input. However, different subjects have been found to differ in the criteria they use in spite of the fact that they are presumably receiving the same stimuli. A cautious person will only claim to detect a signal when it is strong or when any background noise is faint. Personality factors therefore enter into this decision.

Experiments show that the decision is also affected by motivational factors. In one investigation, one group of subjects was given a reward of ten cents for guessing correctly that the signal had been presented and were penalized five cents for guessing incorrectly, while another group was rewarded and penalized only one cent. The first group was found to venture positive guesses more often than the second because they had a chance of winning more money. In addition, it was found that when the subject is told in advance that the signal will be presented nine out of ten times, he will practically always guess "signal presented" •in uncertain cases, since the schedule favors this strategy. He also does better when he is told he is right or wrong.

These observations have shed new light on the problems of detection. In the early days of psychology it was assumed that a subject is a "passive receptor" who simply reacts to stimuli

in the same way that a galvanometer reacts to changes in voltage. The new findings, however, suggest that the process is not nearly so automatic and mechanical. Even in a situation as simple as the detection of signals there is an element of strategy. Detection is a "game" which the individual tries to win. It is therefore more than a sensory experience, since a person uses all relevant information in making his decision and tries to adjust his behavior to maximize his returns. In doing so, he compares signal-plus-noise to noise value alone, and does so within a personality and motivational matrix. Like a computer, he integrates his data and arrives at a decision on this basis. In a word, the process is far more complex than was recognized fifty years ago. *See* SUBLIMINAL PERCEPTION.

DETERIORATION (Mental Deterioration). In psychiatry, deterioration denotes a progressive impairment or decline of intellectual and personality functions such as memory, reasoning, concentration, communication, and emotional response.

The deteriorated patient gradually loses his ability to think clearly, express himself coherently, recall events (especially recent events), make decisions, and solve problems. His condition may degenerate into severe dementia, in which he becomes confused and disoriented. Along with the loss of intellectual functions there is usually an emotional deterioration, characterized by such symptoms as apathy, shallowness of affect, lability (emotional instability), and inappropriate response.

Mental deterioration may be due to brain pathology, as in cerebral arteriosclerosis, toxic conditions, senile brain disease, and cerebral tumors. It may also be functional in origin, as it is believed to be in chronic, advanced schizophrenia. The term "deteriorative psychosis" is sometimes applied to disorders in which progressive impairment of mental functions takes place. In many cases, particularly the organic conditions, the deterioration is considered permanent. Recent studies, however, have indicated that irreversible changes occur less frequently in deteriorated schizophrenics than had been assumed. In reports by Foulds and Dixon, Lubin et al., and Griffith et al., published in 1962, there was no definite evidence of permanent deterioration among schizophrenic patients when they were given standardized psychological tests. *See* DEMENTIA, SOCIAL BREAKDOWN SYNDROME.

DETERMINISM. The doctrine that every event has a cause. Nothing occurs by chance alone; nothing "just happens."

The deterministic point of view is essential to science, which is basically the study of the causes of phenomena and the laws that govern these causes. The idea that every event has a cause applies to psychology and psychiatry as well as the physical sciences. This means that nothing in the individual's mental or emotional life occurs spontaneously; every thought, feeling, and wish, and every mental or physical symptom has its antecedents. Given complete knowledge of conditions, we would have complete knowledge of how a person will behave. Put in another way, determinism holds that even when men act freely and make their own choices there are always reasons for their behavior, even though they may be hard to fathom.

In modern psychology, determinism is linked with naturalism, since the study of behavior is concerned with natural as opposed to supernatural events. This contrasts with an earlier era in which human thoughts and activities, and particularly mental illnesses, were attributed to spirits and demons. At the beginning of modern psychiatry the emphasis was largely on organic causes, particularly brain pa-

thology. Griesinger, Kraepelin, and Head are three of the names associated with this point of view. During the earlier part of the twentieth century, psychological causes came to the fore, due to the work of Janet, Freud, James, and many others. More recently, social and cultural causes have also been emphasized as a result of the work of sociologists, anthropologists, and social psychologists.

Today all three kinds of behavior determinants are recognized, the organic, the psychological, and the social. Psychological determinants include drives, impulses, attitudes (both conscious and unconscious), childhood influences, interpersonal relations, emotional stresses, and traumatic experiences. Biological determinants include heredity, constitution, congenital characteristics, and the influence of the glandular and other bodily systems as well as physical illness and defect. Some of the more important sociocultural determinants are socioeconomic class, specific customs and conventions, social tensions and stresses. Although one or another type of determinant may be predominant in a given instance, all three are regarded as significant, particularly by those investigators who subscribe to a comprehensive, holistic point of view. *See* HOLISM, DEMONOLOGY, ETIOLOGY.

DEVELOPMENTAL TASKS. The basic tasks which must be mastered at each stage of life if the individual is to achieve normal development and healthy adjustment. Failure to perform any of these tasks may hamper development in succeeding stages.

The tasks group themselves around several poles: physical skills, intellectual advancement, emotional adjustment, social relationships, attitudes toward the self, attitudes toward reality, formation of standards and values. To meet these requirements successfully, the individual needs to develop not only constantly increasing competence and understanding, but a sense of responsibility, a realistic outlook, and a capacity for self-direction. Here is an outline of these "pathways to maturity" for each major stage in life, based on Havighurst (1951) and Erikson (1950):

Age 0–6 (Infancy and Early Childhood). Learning to take solid foods, walk, talk, control elimination. Developing trust in one's self and others, as well as respect for rules and authority. Exploring the immediate environment and developing skills through play. Learning to identify with one's own sex and relate to parents, siblings, other children, and adults. Learning to control emotions and distinguish right from wrong. Acquiring simple concepts of time, space, and safety. *See* TOILET TRAINING, PLAY, CONCEPT FORMATION.

Age 6–12 (Middle Childhood). Expanding knowledge and understanding of the physical and social world. Adopting a masculine or feminine role, and building attitudes of confidence and self-esteem. Developing conscience, a scale of values, and the ability to take responsibility. Acquiring academic skills, reasoning, judgment. Learning physical and social skills through group activities and by trying different hobbies and interests. Achieving increasing independence and self-reliance. *See* SEX ROLE, SOCIAL DEVELOPMENT, CHARACTER DEVELOPMENT.

Age 12–18 (Adolescence). Developing self-assurance and a sense of identity. Discovering and accepting personal limitations as well as strengths, and adjusting to bodily changes. Developing sexual interest and more mature relations with peers. Achieving emotional independence from parents, as well as social and ethical values that reach beyond the self. Exploring interests and abilities; deciding on an occupation. Preparing for marriage, parenthood, and participation in the wider world.

See ADOLESCENCE, ADOLESCENCE (THEORIES).

Age 18–35 (Early Adulthood). Completing formal education and embarking on an occupation. Finding and learning to live with a mate. Developing a home, and providing for the material and emotional needs of children. Finding a congenial social group and participating in civic affairs. Developing a basic philosophy of life. *See* MARITAL ADJUSTMENT, VOCATIONAL COUNSELING.

Age 35–60 (Middle Age). Taking greater social responsibility. Developing a fuller life and helping one's mate do the same—including adult leisure time activities pursued together as well as separately. Establishing a standard of living and building financial security for the remaining years. Helping one's teen-age children become effective and stable adults. Adjusting to aging parents, and accepting the physiological changes of middle age.

Later Life. Adjusting to increasing physical limitations, reduced income, the loss of friends or spouse. Accepting retirement as a way of life, and finding adequate living arrangements. Affiliating with one's own age group, and maintaining active interests beyond the self. Meeting social and civic obligations within one's ability and circumstances. *See* AGING.

DEWEY, JOHN (1859–1952). Dewey, who was to become pre-eminent in three fields—philosophy, psychology, and education—was born in Vermont, and graduated from the state university at the age of twenty. His interest in education was aroused when he taught school while studying for his Ph.D. in philosophy at the Johns Hopkins University. After serving as instructor in philosophy at the University of Michigan (1884–94), he took a position at the University of Chicago, where he organized the Laboratory School in 1896 and became director of its new School of Education in 1902. In 1904 he was appointed professor in philosophy at Columbia University, remaining there until his retirement in 1930. In these years he made many visits abroad, during which he taught at Cambridge and at the University of Peking, studied educational facilities in the U.S.S.R., Mexico, Turkey, and other countries, and made many suggestions for improvement in their academic procedures. He also helped to organize the American Association of University Professors, and served as president not only of that organization but of the American Philosophical Association and the American Psychological Association as well.

Dewey's earliest book, entitled *Psychology* (1886), was the first text on the subject written by an American. It was designed to introduce the new scientific findings on psychophysics, memory, thinking processes, and other topics, and it contained a strong plea that philosophical assumptions on such subjects as will, morality, and the nature of the mind be spelled out and understood—a plea that is as relevant today as it was at that time. As his position crystallized, he contributed heavily to the development of the functionalist point of view, along with such men as William James, James M. Cattell, George T. Ladd and James R. Angell. This movement defined psychology as the study of adjustment to the environment, and emphasized the co-ordinated activity of the total organism and the use of the mind as an instrument in meeting the practical problems of life.

The functional approach became the theme of the so-called Chicago School, which "officially" dates from 1896, the year in which Dewey published a paper entitled "The Reflex Arc Concept of Psychology" in the *Psychological Review*. In it he argued against the current overemphasis on elementary aspects of behavior, such as the reflex arc, and proposed that psychologists view behavior in terms of integrated, purposeful adaptations. In taking this stand,

he not only opposed the structuralist's attempt to explain behavior in terms of elementary, isolated units, in imitation of the physical sciences, but also anticipated both the Gestalt position and that of dynamic psychology. *See* FUNCTIONALISM, WUNDT, INTROSPECTION, GESTALT PSYCHOLOGY, DYNAMIC PSYCHOLOGY.

Dewey applied his functionalist, or "instrumentalist," point of view at the Laboratory School of the University of Chicago, which was, in his words, devoted to "the problem of viewing the education of the child in the light of the principles of mental activity and processes of growth made known by modern psychology." In his presidential address before the American Psychological Association in 1900, he called for the scientific study of education, and his own ideas on methodology have been heralded as the start of the progressive education movement. He insisted that (1) the curriculum should be brought into relation with the child's interests, and therefore be student-centered instead of subject-centered; (2) the school atmosphere should be democratic; (3) tasks should be related to the child's own experience and undertaken when he is ready for them; (4) learning occurs most effectively when the pupil sees a problem *as* a problem, when he wants to clear up his own perplexity and uneasiness, and when he actively participates in the process; and (5) the school experience should not be concerned only with academic performance, but should imbue the student with the spirit of inquiry and at the same time prepare him for active participation in the larger setting of the community itself.

Dewey was keenly aware of the changes being wrought by the Industrial Revolution, and felt that education must be adapted to the new social aims and needs it was bound to introduce. He stressed especially the importance of the thinking process and the need for expanding the teaching of science, which he viewed as the best means of promoting social progress. In his book *How We Think* (1910) he linked these two together by showing that the most effective procedure for solving any kind of problem is to go through the same steps that are applied in scientific method—that is, defining and delimiting the problem, constructing and developing hypotheses, and testing them empirically. This pragmatic, or "experimentalist," point of view was a protest against the a priori, deductive logic and the doctrine of immutable ideas which had dominated much of philosophy. Instead, he advocated the inductive method in which truth is viewed as relative and constantly modifiable as new discoveries are made.

Dewey's views were more fully expressed in other works which had a profound influence not only on psychology and education, but on social thought as well. They include *The Child and the Curriculum* (1902), *Democracy and Education* (1916), *Reconstruction in Philosophy* (1920), *Human Nature and Conduct* (1922), *Experience and Nature* (1925), *The Public and Its Problems* (1927), *The Quest for Certainty* (1929), *Art as Experience* (1934), *Logic, the Theory of Inquiry* (1938), and *Freedom and Culture* (1939). In general, these works provide a philosophical point of view which supports a functionalist, experimentalist position, although they do not attempt to offer new data of a specific nature. This general position can probably best be expressed in his own words: "Philosophy recovers itself when it ceases to be a device for dealing with the problems of philosophers and becomes a method, cultivated by philosophers, for dealing with the problems of man."

DIABETIC REACTIONS. The weakness, excessive thirst, loss of weight, and other symptoms characterizing diabetes mellitus are due to low sugar metabolism resulting from a deficiency of insulin. Although the basic cause is physical, and usually constitutional, the onset and course of the disease are known to be greatly influenced by personality and emotional factors. Psychiatry therefore has much to contribute to the problem of treatment and management of diabetics.

Psychophysiologic (psychosomatic) investigations have shown that the blood sugar level of diabetics rises during periods of emotional stress. Many attempts have been made to find a common denominator among these situations, but there is no universal agreement on this question. Nor is there agreement on a basic personality structure of diabetic patients. Some studies, however, indicate that they tend to be passive, somewhat immature individuals who need an unusual amount of attention and affection. When these needs are frustrated, they feel anxious and depressed, and at this point diabetes may set in or become exacerbated. Sometimes the precipitating event is a feeling of abandonment due to loss of a person on whom the patient is dependent, through separation, jilting, or divorce.

Although the management of diabetes is the responsibility of the physician, there are many areas where psychiatric assistance can be helpful. Some patients are precipitated into dangerous states of acidosis or insulin coma by acute but transient emotional disturbances. Severely depressed men and women sometimes act out suicidal drives by giving up their diets or neglecting to take insulin. Many adults have sexual difficulties that interfere with their adjustment: diabetic men are often impotent, and diabetic women may be deeply concerned about having children. If a child is born to a diabetic woman with a dependent personality, her need for attention and care may be accentuated to a point where the child becomes a rival. If an immature diabetic husband is made to feel neglected, he may go off his diet and medication, or he may feel so resentful and anxious that his metabolic balance becomes disturbed and his blood sugar level elevates.

Many diabetic children present psychiatric problems. Some have difficulty adapting to the strict diet because their parents have let them eat whatever they wanted in the past. Others feel rejected when deprived of foods they want because of an unconscious connection between food and love, or because their parents have used candy as a reward. The problem of diet sometimes becomes a focus of other tensions between the child and the parent. As a result, the parents may be oversevere and perfectionistic in keeping the child to the diet, and the child may react by either refusing to eat at all or by violating the diet and lying about it. A psychiatrist may be called upon to help the parents understand the child's problem and mitigate the conflict between them; he may also be needed to interpret the child's reaction to the internist. In some cases, too, he may suggest modifications of the diet and insulin regimen that will be more acceptable and workable. *See* PSYCHOPHYSIOLOGIC DISORDERS (GENERAL).

DIAGNOSTIC TESTS IN EDUCATION. In contrast to achievement tests, diagnostic tests are designed to analyze individual performance and identify special disabilities. Most of these tests are concerned with reading, but a few have to do with mathematical skills. The reading tests range from group tests for rapid but superficial checking to individual tests of an intensive clinical nature. The latter usually provide detailed check lists of errors, and frequently utilize a tachistoscope, ophthalmoscope, or other apparatus. The following are representative samples of both types of tests:

Iowa Silent Reading Tests. This short, widely used group test consists of an elementary battery (grades 4–8) and an advanced battery for high school and college. Both cover rate of reading, vocabulary, sentence comprehension, paragraph comprehension, use of an index, as well as a test of "directed reading" in which the subject identifies parts of a paragraph that answer given questions.

Nelson-Denny Reading Test. A test for high school, college, and adult groups, yielding separate scores on vocabulary, reading comprehension, and reading rate, with norms based on a large nationwide sample.

Diagnostic Reading Tests. A more intensive series, for grades 7–13, containing (a) a survey section for an entire class, testing vocabulary and ability to read and comprehend story and textbook material; and (b) a diagnostic battery from which tests can be selected according to difficulties revealed on the survey test. This battery measures vocabulary from various subjects, comprehension of textbook material (silent and auditory), rate of reading of different types of material, and word attack, both oral and silent.

Durrell Analysis of Reading Difficulty, for grades 1–6. Designed for intensive individual testing, this battery measures rate and comprehension of oral and silent reading, word and letter recognition, word pronunciation, with supplementary tests of written spelling and speed of handwriting. It also includes tests for non-readers on visual memory, rate of learning words, and learning comprehension. A check list is provided, based on reading errors gathered from a study of 4000 children.

Other diagnostic reading tests are: the Gates-McKillop Reading Diagnostic Tests (grades 1 to 8), the Gilmore Oral Reading Test (grades 1 to 8), the Group Diagnostic Aptitude and Achievement Test (grades 3 to 9), the Roswell-Chall Diagnostic Reading Test (grades 2 to 6), and the Diagnostic Reading Scales. The most recent instrument is the Stanford Diagnostic Reading Test (1967), a reliable group test for grades

2.5 to 4.5 and grades 4.5 to 8.5. This test was standardized on over 12,000 students in six school systems, and yields separate scores on such skills as comprehension, vocabulary, blending, syllabication, sound discrimination and, in the later grades, rate of reading.

The Compass Diagnostic Test in Arithmetic is a comprehensive group test for grades 2 to 8, consisting of twenty subjects covering different types of arithmetic operations and problems. The *Diagnostic Chart for Fundamental Processes in Arithmetic,* for grades 2 to 8, is an example of a thorough test for individual administration. Since the problems have to be solved orally, the examiner can observe not only errors but methods of attack. A checklist of errors and faulty work habits is included. No time limits, no norms or total scores are given, since the test is designed for qualitative rather than quantitative analysis. Two other important tests in this area are the *Diagnostic Tests and Self-Helps in Arithmetic* and the new *Stanford Diagnostic Arithmetic Test* (1967) which, like the Stanford Diagnostic Reading Test, is available in two equivalent forms, at Level I (grades 2.5 to 4.5) and Level II (grades 4.5 to 8.5).

DIFFERENTIAL DIAGNOSIS. The process of identifying a disorder and distinguishing it from other disorders.

Differential diagnosis is a particularly difficult problem in psychiatry for several reasons: (1) different disorders frequently share many of the same symptoms; (2) most syndromes (symptom patterns) tend to vary to some degree from patient to patient; (3) the same patient may exhibit different symptoms at different times; (4) there are many mixed cases and cases on the border line between two or more disorders. In view of these facts, it is widely recognized that a diagnosis can be made only on the basis of the predominant symptom pattern at a given time, and

that many cases cannot be rigidly fitted into the standard classification scheme.

The reasons just given help to account for the fact that diagnoses made by different specialists do not always agree. This occurs far more often in functional cases than in organic disorders, since the symptom picture is usually more varied in functional cases, and different diagnosticians may focus on different symptoms. Also, organic disorders, such as paresis and epilepsy, can usually be identified by the use of medical tests. In 1928 Elkind and Doering compared the diagnoses of a group of patients at Boston Psychopathic Hospital with diagnoses of the same patients made in various state hospitals, and found that they agreed in only 58 per cent of the cases, including both organic and functional types. In 1959 Norris made a similar study in England and arrived at practically the same over-all results. Both studies showed far more agreement on organic than on functional disorders.

A few examples will indicate the types of problem involved in differential diagnosis. Infantile autism is sometimes hard to distinguish from mental retardation, since in both cases the child may be unresponsive and may engage in repetitive activities. The delirium that occurs in acute organic disorders may be confused with schizophrenic excitement until a specific cause, such as a toxic or infectious condition, can be found. Hysterical seizures may be misdiagnosed as epileptic convulsions, especially when the EEG findings are inconclusive. The differentiation of organic from psychogenic forms of amnesia may be difficult when there are no clear signs of head injury and no clear indications of psychological conflict.

In recent years a number of investigators have pointed out that the process of labeling and pigeonholing cases tends to emphasize common denominators and direct attention away from the unique characteristics of individual patients. But while it is essential to recognize these characteristics, it is also important to put the patient in one or another diagnostic category in order to know what type of treatment to apply. Even though diagnoses are not completely reliable, they cannot be wholly avoided. We know, for instance, that electroshock therapy is more effective with depressives than with chronic schizophrenics, and that psychoactive drugs are frequently helpful with schizophrenics when convulsive therapy fails to bring improvement. Moreover, if one disorder is confused with another, months of valuable time may be lost, and the condition may become fixed and hard to reverse. Likewise, a child may be relegated to an institution for the mentally retarded when he is actually suffering from childhood schizophrenia or learning disorder. This would not occur if a thorough differential diagnosis were carried out.

DIFFERENTIAL PSYCHOLOGY (Individual Differences). An area of psychology concerned with behavioral differences between individuals and groups of individuals—including, among others, sex, race, nationality, cultural and socioeconomic differences.

The importance of individual differences has long been recognized. Anthropological studies show that many positions in preliterate cultures—the tribal chief, the priest, the medicine man —are based on special talents. Plato described an ideal republic in which the citizens would be tested early in life and educated for positions in the state according to their capacities. As society became increasingly complex, and the idea of division of labor took hold, it became more and more necessary to appraise and classify individuals on the basis of ability, interest, and personality, for this was the only way to help them realize their potential and be of maximum service to the community. In ad-

dition, as the techniques of communication and transportation became more highly developed, nationalities, races, and social groups were brought into closer contact with each other, and this focused attention on the problem of group as well as individual differences.

These historical developments constitute the general background for differential psychology, but more specific events shaped it into a scientific discipline. Darwin showed that species differ widely in the ways they adapt to the environment, and that some individuals have unique characteristics which enable them to compete and survive. Galton made some of the first studies of individual variations in skill and ability, measuring visual discrimination with the Galton bar and the range of hearing with the Galton whistle. Experimental psychologists turned their attention to quantitative investigations of sensory thresholds and motor abilities, and also helped to develop useful statistical concepts, such as average, deviation, and correlation. In about 1890, Cattell designed tests to measure differences in memory and reaction time, and in 1905 Binet created the first intelligence test. From that point onward, tests for practically every trait and ability were developed, and a wide range of human differences and similarities were investigated. *See* DARWIN, GALTON, CATTELL.

These investigations have increased our appreciation of the uniqueness of the individual and the differences both within groups and between groups of all kinds. We now realize that many of the distinctions between the races, nationalities, and sexes have been too sharp, for there is considerable overlap between groups on practically any characteristic that can be named, and the variations within these groups are always greater than the differences between them. The exploration of differences has also led to continuous refinement in the crude classifications of

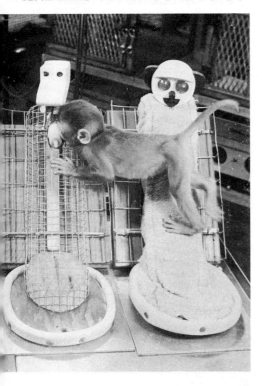

1. The artificial mother. Raised in isolation from its true mother, this monkey clings to a warm terry-cloth "mother surrogate," even when it can obtain food only from a cold wire "mother." *See* AFFECTIONAL DRIVE, MOTHERING.

2. Is manipulation a basic drive? Like children, monkeys take things apart without any apparent reward other than the "monkeying" itself. *See* CURIOSITY DRIVE, MANIPULATION DRIVE.

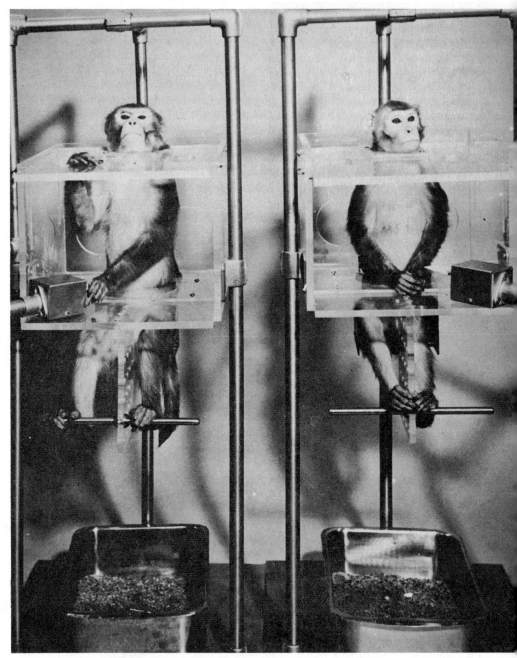

3. Decisions, decisions, decisions. The monkey at the left has the responsibility of pressing a lever at intervals so that both may escape a mild electric shock. The lever at the right is not connected, and is soon ignored. The monkey at the left gets an ulcer—but not the one at the right. *See* EXPERIMENTAL NEUROSIS, GENERAL ADAPTATION SYNDROME, PEPTIC ULCER.

4. Can animals think? This duck has been trained to distinguish a triangle from other figures. *See* CONCEPT FORMATION.

5. The Chimpomat. Chimpanzees not only learn to insert a poker chip to get a grape, but work for the chips themselves, hoarding them like money until they have a chance to spend them. *See* REINFORCEMENT.

6. and **7.** A monkey can learn the concept of "oddity." He pushes aside the odd object, no matter where it is placed, to get the food beneath it. *See* ODDITY METHOD.

humanity which held sway for many years—for instance, the old division of the "feeble-minded" into idiot, imbecile, and moron has given way to less rigid classifications and the recognition of the wide variations within each category. Similarly, there is a growing realization that the differences between various mental disorders are not so fixed as we once believed, and that a large number of cases present a mixed diagnosis. Explorations of the normal personality also indicate that few individuals can be "typecast," since people seldom conform to the rigid specifications laid down by the classifiers. For this reason many investigators now feel that intensive studies of individual cases, normal as well as abnormal, can yield information that is bound to escape those who limit themselves to a statistical approach. See FIELD THEORY, PERSONALITY TRAIT THEORY (ALLPORT).

The study of individual differences, then, has brought to light the infinite gradations of human behavior. Even characteristics that were once believed to be poles apart are now pictured as extremes on a continuum. It is therefore not a question of possessing or lacking abilities, but whether we have a large or a small amount of them. It was once thought that people were either color-sensitive or color-blind, but we now know there are many degrees and types of color blindness. The same is true of musical ability, mathematical ability, memory, introversion and extroversion, and even masculinity and femininity. In other words, individual differences tend to be quantitative rather than qualitative, a difference of degree rather than a difference of kind. This means that few if any of us are doomed to be totally unmusical or unmathematical. Rather, we probably have latent or weaker capacities that can be developed—and this puts the responsibility where it belongs, on education, stimulation, and experience.

The differences between *groups* of individuals, such as races and nationalities, also tend to be differences of degree rather than kind. Studies show that there are probably no inherently superior or inferior races or nationalities as a whole, since the differences that exist are due mainly to environmental rather than hereditary factors. This, too, puts the emphasis on education and opportunity.

The fact that differences between individuals and groups are not so fixed and unalterable as we once believed should not be taken as meaning that all people are fundamentally the same. Needless to say, any group has its own distinctive characteristics, and every individual is unique. The point is that these differences—some hereditary, some environmental, some a combination of the two—should be recognized and put to use where they help most. Without these differences life would be a dull affair and we would not be able to call upon either talent or genius to solve our problems. For this reason differential psychologists are continuing to explore and describe these differences, and other psychologists are attempting to identify individual needs and abilities through tests and interviews, and to guide their clients into schools, colleges, and occupations where they can develop their individual potential and apply their individual skills in the most effective way. See RACE DIFFERENCES, SEX DIFFERENCES, CONSTITUTIONAL TYPES, TEMPERAMENT.

DIPSOMANIA. The compulsion to consume alcohol to excess. The term is sometimes used for a recurrent craving, generally at relatively long intervals, as opposed to chronic alcoholism.

Dipsomania is usually a symptom of personality disorder, and the treatment of choice is psychotherapy. Some epileptic patients revert to episodes of drinking to relieve their tensions; this is extremely likely to activate an attack and should be avoided. The term is not applied to cases of alcoholic psychosis, such as Korsakoff's syndrome, which is due to long-continued rather than spasmodic drinking. *See* ALCOHOLIC ADDICTION.

Illustrative Case: DIPSOMANIA

A gifted and fairly successful writer had periods when he drank heavily. They would occur anywhere from every three to every eight months and would last from two weeks to a month. He would get into trouble. He would wander away from the house and turn up in a hospital with a fractured rib, without knowing how he broke it. He would neglect his work, fail to keep appointments and to live up to his contract. He would become belligerent, get into fights, and be beaten up. Several times he attempted to forge checks, but they were not accepted.

The patient's drinking bouts occurred after a disappointment, either with a friend or with his work. During his free periods, he worked quickly and wrote voluminously; he had a good market for his material. After many years of drinking, his work began to deteriorate, the periods of drinking grew much longer, his hands trembled, and he showed signs of chronic alcoholism. He would spend the money that he earned on drinking, and then would beg his friends for money to buy food for his wife and child. Frequently, when he was drinking at home, he shouted abuse to men whom he heard talking and who he said called him obscene names. He accused his wife of infidelity and threatened to kill both her and his child. He refused all psychotherapy and nothing could be done for him. (Maslow and Nittelmann, 1951)

DIRECT ANALYSIS. A therapeutic approach developed by John Rosen, in which an attempt is made to understand and communicate directly with the unconscious of psychotic patients. The method utilizes psychoanalytic theories as well as techniques which are ordinarily applied only to patients with neuroses.

Rosen's approach is based on the theory that the behavior of the psychotic patient, no matter how bizarre it may appear, is actually an attempt to communicate. If the therapist understands the logic of the unconscious and studies the meaning behind the patient's idiomatic verbalizations, he will be able to enter into an interchange with him on both a verbal and emotional level, and thereby lay the foundation for effective psychotherapy. Rosen maintains that this can be accomplished with every patient, no matter how regressed, unreachable, or incurable others believe him to be. (Rosen, 1953)

Rosen believes that every functional psychosis is due to severe emotional deprivation during the oral stage of development. The patient's condition is, as McKinnon puts it (1959), "analogous to the state of a helpless infant in terror of starvation in this early period of life." The therapist must therefore provide the affection and understanding which the patient missed as an infant. In fact, he must accept the patient as a member of his own family, and act as a loving parent who is deeply involved in his welfare and who will be unhappy until he is at peace with himself. In carrying out this form of therapy, the patient actually lives in a home with Rosen's assistants, and Rosen treats him in the presence of this "psychological family."

In essence, the treatment consists of having the patient relive early traumatic experiences with the mother. In this process the original image of the mother is destroyed in order to induce him to give up the delusions and fantasies he has developed as a reaction to emotional deprivation. At the same time Rosen and the psychological family give the patient the "emotional nutriment" he needs for a more healthy development.

In direct analysis the therapist makes a head-on attack on the patient's delusions. He actually participates in the patient's world of fantasy, and shows him that he has nothing to fear from the voices or visions which frighten him. If the patient says he would like to go to the sun, Rosen replies that he was going to visit it that afternoon and would take him on the next trip. If the patient claims he is God, Rosen says, "Prove it!" He may even tell patients who deny their psychosis that he was himself psychotic and had the identical symptoms, but was cured—a device he uses to remove the secrecy of illness and to indicate that cure is possible. When patients have improved to some extent and their resistances have begun to dissolve, he may use direct reciprocation by answering curse with curse or silent treatment with silent treatment. On the other hand, with patients who have regressed so far that words have lost their meaning, he may shout or slap to capture their attention and awaken them to reality. Or he might squeeze the hand of a mute patient to get her to scream, and then use this as evidence that she feels real pain. These drastic measures are employed not only to shock patients into reality but to show them that a truly loving "parent" can be powerful, and yet use his power to protect and not to harm them. Rosen claims that they accept this treatment because of their strong positive transference to the therapist and their feeling that he is acting in their best interests.

According to Rosen, the duration of the treatment depends upon the length of time the patient has suffered from the psychosis and the type of prior treatment which has been used, not on the degree of deterioration or the type of psychotic reaction. He claims to have freed patients from a psychosis in a period of weeks, especially when it is of recent onset and shock therapy or other organic treatment has not been applied. When the patients have given up their psychotic symptoms, they develop neurotic symptoms (a "neoneurosis," as he calls it), but this phase can be overcome by close foster parent guidance.

Rosen has reported a high percentage of recoveries, but the great majority of psychiatrists are skeptical about his methods and their effectiveness. An Institute for Direct Analysis has been established at Temple University Medical Center to evaluate this technique and determine whether it can be formulated for teaching purposes.

DIRECTIONAL CONFUSION. A term applied to difficulty in distinguishing left from right, and in some cases other directions as well, such as uptown from downtown.

Some directional confusion is to be expected in children up to age six or seven. It is usually manifested in reversals in reading, but may also appear in spelling, written numbers, and typing. Although it may be found in any pattern of lateral dominance, it is most likely to occur in cases of mixed dominance, that is, cases where the dominant eye and the dominant hand are on opposite sides of the body. The Harris Tests of Lateral Dominance (1958) include tests for directional confusion.

About 25 per cent of reading disability cases show directional confusion, and many authorities believe that severe cases may be due to faulty neurological development. Some, of these cases seem to be the result of minimal brain damage acquired before or during birth, while others appear to reflect a family pattern. Conversion of a naturally left-handed child to the right hand during the beginning stages of reading may also cause serious directional difficulty. A few cases may be due to emotional disturbance. The condition can usually be improved through classroom instruction or remedial reading and writing techniques. *See* LATERAL DOMINANCE, READING DISABILITY, HANDEDNESS.

DIRECTIVE PSYCHOTHERAPY. An eclectic procedure developed by Frederick C. Thorne, in which the therapist provides the type of treatment needed at each stage of the process.

This approach originated as a reaction to what Thorne believed to be an overemphasis on nondirective techniques and a neglect of traditional methods, due to the sudden popularity of the methods of Carl Rogers. He holds that we cannot rely exclusively on a nondirective approach, for "the need for direction is inversely correlated with the person's potentialities for effective self-regulation" (Thorne, 1955). Since most patients do not have this capacity at the beginning of therapy, the more "passive" techniques cannot be used. However, if they develop the ability to regulate themselves, nondirective techniques may later be introduced.

In selecting the most appropriate type of therapy for a given patient, Thorne utilizes the concept of distributive analysis developed by Adolph Meyer. This involves a thorough case study in which every function of the individual is investigated (physical, emotional, social, intellectual) and trends of greatest etiological significance are noted. The course of therapy is directed along the lines determined by this psychobiological approach. The treatment process itself is viewed as an educational or reeducational process during which the patient gradually learns to utilize his own capacities to regulate his behavior effectively. Thorne believes this must be achieved largely on an intellectual level: "The goal of therapy is to replace emotional-impulsive behavior with deliberate rational-adaptive behavior based on the highest utilization of intellectual resources."

In placing great stress on rational methods of control and adjustment, Thorne differs somewhat from the common-sense therapy of Meyer. His approach is based on the psychology of learning and involves two general steps: (a) the establishment of suitable conditions for learning, using psychoanalysis and nondirective techniques to establish rapport, release repressions, and produce insight into traumatic experiences; and (b) the provision of appropriate training situations based upon the patient's history and diagnosis. Thorne maintains that the first approach helps the patient to gain insight; but he must go through the second, or reconditioning, process before he can master a new style of life. The process is not a mechanical affair, but an exercise in problem-solving during which the patient improves his mental health by focusing his intellect on his life situation. The therapist is viewed as a master educator who takes over from the forces which have produced unhealthy behavior—i.e. the patient's family, social environment, education and experiences, as well as his own personality. As an educator, he uses scientific knowledge to reveal the illogical premises on which the patient's faulty behavior is based, and to bring him to a point where he will adopt a new approach. During this procedure, the patient's morale is maintained by the therapist's interest in his history and by assurances that his condition is not unusual or dangerous.

In their book *Six Approaches to Psychotherapy,* McCary and Sheer (1955) summarize the directive approach by pointing out that the therapist assumes responsibility "for conducting all details of case handling according to the highest ethical and professional standards," including (a) adequate diagnostic studies involving not only a complete case history but clinical examinations, psychometric and projective studies, laboratory procedures (EEG, etc.); (b) formulation of the psychodynamics of the case, including etiology, clinical status, personality resources, and prognosis; (c) outline of a plan of therapy related to the needs of the individual patient; (d) a genuinely eclectic approach utilizing all resources, either directive or nondirective; (e) utilization of experimentally established principles at all levels of case handling. Thorne believes that the short-cut therapies and purely nondirective approaches of our day tend to oversimplify the therapeutic process and bypass a scientific approach to psychodiagnosis and therapy.

DISCIPLINE (literally, "to learn"). Discipline is the process of learning to adapt one's behavior to the requirements of society. It "arises from the need to bring about balance between what the individual wants to do, what he wants of others, and the limitations and restrictions demanded by the society in which he lives or by the hazards in the physical environment." (Jersild, 1960)

The child cannot be counted on to teach himself to curb his impulses and to conform to rules and regulations. He has to be taught by others. This teaching, however, satisfies many of his own inner needs. It helps him learn what is expected of him, it protects him from his own destructive urges, and it gives him a sense of security by letting him know how far he can go and what he must do to win the approval of others.

There is considerable agreement among psychologists on the question of good versus poor disciplinary techniques. In general, good discipline cultivates inner growth, understanding and self-discipline. It is scaled to the child's level of maturity and encourages him to seek desirable behavior because it is satisfying and not merely because it's required. Poor discipline, on the other hand, rests entirely on external authority and restraint. It utilizes disapproval more than approval and coercion more than education. This contrast can best be clarified by outlining three quite different approaches to discipline: the authoritarian, the permissive, and the democratic.

Authoritarian discipline is characterized by strict rules and regulations enforced by severe punishment. Some of the restraints imposed on the child are reasonable, others are arbitrary and oppressive. But in either case the restraints are issued as commands and little if any attempt is made to explain or justify them. The emphasis, therefore, is almost entirely on obedience. In families where authoritarianism is most extreme parents seldom relax their control or abandon corporal punishment as their children grow older. In less rigid authoritarian families, older children remain subject to the parents' decision, but their own wishes are not wholly ignored and the number of irrational restrictions diminishes.

The permissive approach can hardly be called discipline at all since the parents make little attempt to set limits to the child's behavior: "Some parents see in their relationship with their children only the necessity to make them happy as each day goes by, not recognizing that this treatment may deprive the children of the strength that comes from wise restriction, and that it is likely to give them a false idea of what to expect from life outside the home. . . . They give him a minimum of guidance, and may even consider guidance as domination of the child's personality" (Vincent and Martin, 1961). Mothers are considerably more likely to use this approach than fathers since they feel more guilty about restricting or punishing their children, and more often give in when the children call them "mean" (Rosenthal, 1962). The avowed purpose of permissiveness is to encourage the child to assume responsibility for his own behavior and to avoid the psychological damage which some psychoanalysts have attributed to inhibition and repression.

Those who favor democratic techniques approach discipline from an educational point of view. They make use of explanation, discussion, and reasoning to help the child understand why he is expected to conduct himself in certain ways. Good behavior is generously rewarded with praise and encouragement, and bad behavior is punished only when it is willful. The punishment, however, is never harsh, and usually takes the form of scolding, deprivation, or a quick slap. Some democratic parents tend to be more lenient than others, but even these parents do not follow an extreme laissez faire policy. The aim of this approach is to encourage self-discipline by showing the child that there are good reasons for controlling his behavior, and that he will win approval if he does so.

A number of studies have been made of the effects of the three methods of discipline. The authoritarian approach produces outward conformity but gives rise to rankling resentments. If discipline is harsh and punitive, one child will become timid, resigned, or apathetic, while another will be rebellious and hostile—but in either case the world is likely to be viewed as a threatening place. The timid children tend to express their resentments in fantasies; the hostile children may become bullies or, in extreme cases, juvenile delinquents. Both types are likely to lack genuine self-confidence and security.

Overpermissiveness also leads to feelings of insecurity and resentment—but in this case these reactions arise out of too little guidance instead of too much. The insecurity arises from feelings of anxiety and uncertainty due to the fact that the child does not know what he is supposed to do or how to cope with situations that are difficult for him. The resentment arises from the feeling that his parents do not care enough about him to give him the attention and guidance he needs. Moreover, he takes advantage of their leniency and becomes extremely egocentric and self-assertive. As a result the child feels that he can do exactly what he wants outside the home as well as inside, and he soon becomes labeled as a spoiled brat or a little monster. This makes him resentful toward other children, but even more resentful against his parents for causing him to have such a hard time (Henry, 1961).

Democratic discipline provides guidance without domination and freedom without laxity. When the child is respected as an individual and is encouraged to develop internal control, the outcome is more favorable both at school and in the home than with the permissive or authoritarian approach. He is more co-operative, friendly, resourceful, and self-controlled, and on the whole is better adjusted both personally and socially. He also tends to feel more secure, to have a healthy, confident attitude toward himself, and to be more active, spontaneous, and outgoing than children whose discipline has been too strict or too lenient (Geisel, 1951; Mussen and Kagan, 1958).

Now for a brief look at three specific questions that arise in almost every discussion of discipline: How important is consistency? Is punishment necessary? How far should rewards be used?

The need for consistency is stressed by almost all child psychologists. If the child is given different directions at different times or by different individuals, he becomes confused and fails to learn to control his own behavior. Moreover, he loses respect for parents or teachers who are unsure of themselves, plays one off against the other, or acts as he pleases because he does not know what is expected of him. In general, mothers—especially young, inexperienced, middle-class mothers—tend to be more inconsistent than fathers. They are frequently ambivalent toward their children, tender at one moment and annoyed at another, and consequently they will threaten but not carry out their threats, slap and then hug the child, impose restrictions and then apologize, or punish for a misdeed at one time while overlooking it entirely at another. The most destructive type of inconsistency, however, is open disagreement between the parents, since it tends to undermine discipline completely. Parents do not have to agree on every detail—and with older children they can explain their differences—but they should avoid criticizing each other in front of the child, and should resolve their differences in private and support each other wherever possible.

It is impossible to raise children without resorting to punishment of some kind and on some occasions. Even though punishment does not itself show them the right way to act, or alter the impulse that motivated the misdeed, it can often curb unacceptable behavior. It is therefore more effective as a deterrent than as a corrective. There is also evidence that children do not feel right if their misbehavior is persistently overlooked. They develop a feeling of guilt and sometimes invite punishment in order to relieve it.

The most effective and reasonable punishment is the kind that is directly related to the misbehavior: isolating a child who fights with his playmates is more sensible than putting him to bed without supper. Since punishment should be appropriate to the situation, there probably is no single "best kind." In so far as possible it should also be appropriate to the child—that is, one child will be more responsive to a stern warning, another to scolding, and another to deprivation. Finally, there are two *worst* kinds of punishments: first, harsh and repeated corporal punishment, since this is a form of brutality that either breaks a child's spirit or makes him resentful and defiant; and second, any form of humiliation and rejection such as sarcasm, belittling, general disapproval, or withdrawal of love, since these will corrode the child's self-esteem and belief in himself. But in any case punishment should not be given without letting the child know why it is necessary, otherwise it will have little if any educational value.

The parent who gets into the habit of using punishment is likely to lose sight of the value of approval in disciplining the child. Many experiments and observations have proven that approval is a more constructive instrument than disapproval and that praise is more effective than reproof. These approaches not only build up pleasant associations with the desired act, but build up the child as well. Moreover, positive motivation has greater educational value than punishment because it shows the child what is right, not simply what is wrong. And at the same time it helps him satisfy his desire for recognition. Generally speaking, encouragement and praise should be enough, although an occasional free gift might be given as a token of admiration or appreciation rather than as a bribe. Naturally praise should be given judiciously, not indiscriminately, but it is probably better to err on the side of giving too much than giving too little.

DISCRIMINATION LEARNING. Learning to detect and respond to differences among stimuli.

In the course of our development we all must learn to perceive both similarities and differences. Without this ability we could not adequately deal with things or people, nor could we develop the concepts that are needed for thinking and communication. The child has to learn that oranges and lemons both belong under the concept "fruit," but he also has to learn that one is sweet and the other sour. On the whole it seems to be easier to detect likenesses than differences, and therefore discrimination is usually considered a more advanced form of learning than generalization. The young child, for example, tends to lump all small animals together, treating them all alike and calling them all "bow-wow," before he learns to react in one way to a cat and another way to a dog.

The standard way of teaching a child to make discriminations is to point out differences, correct his errors, and reward him with "Good" or "My smart boy!" when he responds correctly. Punishment does not advance the process, since it shows him where he is wrong but not why he is wrong. It also interferes with the learning process by making the child fearful, tense, and resentful. *See* DISCIPLINE.

Experiments with animals show that they can be taught to discriminate in much the same way as children. In the classical conditioning technique, a dog is first conditioned to salivate to a bell by sounding it repeatedly when he is shown food. He then tends to "generalize" this response and salivate to any bell he hears, no matter what pitch. If his response is reinforced (that is, if he is rewarded with food) when he salivates to one particular pitch but not to others, he soon learns to discriminate between them up to a point. In instrumental conditioning, animals are rewarded and reinforced when they make correct responses such as pressing a lever. Through this technique rats have learned to discriminate between black and white, a square and a triangle, and a circle and an ellipse. *See* CONDITIONING.

Discrimination learning is not all a question of deliberate teaching and conditioning. We often underestimate the ability of children to notice differences by themselves. What they need most is an ample opportunity to explore and experiment. If they are given a full chance, they will acquire an enormous amount of information about soft and hard, rough and smooth, agreeable and disagreeable, and a multitude of other differences simply through the process of touching, smelling, tasting, and banging everything around them. A child will learn the difference between a lemon and an orange much more effectively by tasting them than by being told that one is sweet and the other sour. The Montessori method of education is based largely on the philosophy of giving small children the greatest possible opportunity to learn through direct experience. *See* CONCEPT FORMATION.

DISORIENTATION. Impaired ability to identify time, place, or persons, accompanied by bewilderment and confusion.

The disoriented individual cannot fully comprehend what day or year it is, where he is, why he is there, or what kind of person he is talking to. He is not necessarily disoriented in all these ways at once. He may have an approximate or confused idea about himself and his environment, or, on the other hand, he may believe he is a different person existing in another century and in a totally different situation.

Disorientation is one of the major indications of profound psychosis, both of the functional and the organic type. It may occur in any mental disorder where there is extensive impairment of the patient's memory, attention, and perceptual ability. Among the functional psychoses it is most often found in advanced schizophrenic reactions; it is far less common in affective disorders such as manic-depressive and involutional reactions. It is a particularly significant and frequent symptom in organic brain syndromes of both the acute and chronic type—especially in delirious states, toxic psychosis, advanced senile brain disease, and cerebral arteriosclerosis.

Temporary disorientation sometimes occurs in situations of acute stress such as fires, earthquakes, or air raids. It is one of the panic reactions that take place during these catastrophes. It may also result from acute psychological conflicts, intense emotional experiences, or extreme distractibility. *See* CIVILIAN CATASTROPHE REACTIONS, PANIC.

DISPLACEMENT. The unconscious defense mechanism of transferring emotional reactions from one object to another.

This is the common human tendency of "taking it out" on an innocent party. The spanked child does not dare to strike his mother, but kicks his little brother or breaks a toy instead. The worker criticizes his wife's cooking instead of telling the boss what he thinks of him.

The mechanism does not involve merely relieving emotion and getting it out of one's system; rather, an outlet must be found that arouses little or no anxiety. We might feel like beating a business rival over the head, but we settle for beating him at golf. The first reaction would provoke fear of retaliation or punishment, the second would be perfectly acceptable and even admirable. Similarly, the child gradually learns that even though kicking his little brother or breaking a toy may provoke less anxiety than kicking his mother, it is still better to kick a football. The mechanism of displacement can therefore have some value if it helps us discharge our tensions in acceptable ways.

This reaction, however, may take far from benign forms. The child who succeeds in repressing all resentment against his parents may come to hate his teachers or, in extreme cases, rebel against all authority. In Nazi Germany, party members were encouraged to direct all their feelings of frustration and hostility toward Jews and communists, with appalling results. The mechanism may also be instrumental in producing irrational fears and compulsive actions. In one such case a man who harbored repressed murderous impulses became morbidly afraid of any death-dealing instruments, including not only guns but knives and rocks. This displaced fear kept him away from these instruments and therefore protected him from giving vent to his dangerous impulses. In another case, a woman came to a psychiatrist complaining that she had to wash her hands so many times during the day that she had no time for anything else. During treatment the therapist discovered that she had developed a severe and unwarranted feeling of guilt

when she was a child. This feeling had been unconsciously repressed, and now she was displacing it and redirecting it to a symbol of guilt: dirt. *See* PHOBIC REACTION, OBSESSIVE-COMPULSIVE REACTION, SCHIZOPHRENIA (PARANOID TYPE), TRANSFERENCE.

DISSOCIATION. The unconscious defense mechanism of keeping conflicting attitudes and impulses apart.

This is the common human tendency of not letting the left hand know what the right hand is doing. We may assert a belief in co-operation but behave competitively, protest love but act with hate, proclaim good will but practice discrimination—without being aware of our inconsistency. The reason for this lack of awareness is that it is the only way we can satisfy two opposing urges and still maintain our sense of integrity and self-esteem. Even if our inconsistency is directly pointed out to us, we can still deny it by using another mechanism of defense—rationalization—which provides us with poor excuses and distorted reasons designed to soften the conflict and justify our actions.

Dissociation, then, goes beyond mere social expediency, in which we adjust our attitudes and behavior to different situations. When it functions as a defensive technique, we actually isolate one set of ideas or impulses, or one part of our personality, from another because it would cause us emotional distress to bring them together. This tendency may take unusual or pathological forms. A recent first-person account of a nymphomaniac contains this passage: "I was such a good little girl, everybody expected me to be, and when I wasn't, like when I kissed, or other things, I started blaming it on something inside, a bad me, *she* made me do it. I really got to believing that, so I didn't lie when I kept quiet or said I hadn't done it."

In some cases, a fragment of the

ego may temporarily break away and gain control. In obedience to hidden impulses, a person may not only walk in his sleep but perform some outlandish act. In response to unconscious forces, an individual may spontaneously enter a dissociated state in which his hand writes by itself, without conscious control. A woman using the name Patience Worth wrote entire novels in this way. The phenomenon of "automatic writing," as it is called, can also be used as a psychiatric technique. The process of dissociation may go even further in certain poorly integrated personalities, where it may take the extreme form of loss of personal identity, or a splitting into two or more contrasting personalities. See DISSOCIATIVE REACTION, SOMNAMBULISM, AUTOMATIC WRITING AND DRAWING, FUGUE STATE, MULTIPLE PERSONALITY, AMNESIA (DISSOCIATIVE TYPE).

DISSOCIATIVE REACTION. A psychoneurotic reaction in which a portion of experience is split off, or isolated, from conscious awareness.

As a neurotic reaction, dissociation is an unconscious attempt either (1) to protect the self from distressing and threatening impulses and events; or (2) to gain expression for forbidden desires without paying the penalty of guilt or anxiety. Dissociative reactions were at one time classified as one type of hysteria, the other being conversion reactions, in which emotional conflicts are expressed as bodily symptoms. Although the dynamics of the two disorders are similar, they are classified separately today.

There are four primary kinds of dissociative reactions: amnesia, fugue, dual personality, and somnambulism. In some types of amnesia, the individual protects himself from distasteful experiences by an unconscious process of repression, or forgetting. In the fugue state, he obeys an unconscious urge to flee from a distressing situation,

and afterward has no recollection of what he did during the episode. In dual or multiple personality, he gives expression to repressed urges by unconsciously assuming more than one identity. In somnambulism he expresses forbidden impulses and feelings through actions carried out during sleep.

All these reactions are unconscious attempts to solve problems with a divided mind which keeps conflicting ideas and impulses apart. Aside from somnambulism, dissociative reactions comprise less than 5 per cent of psychoneurotic disorders today. See AMNESIA (DISSOCIATIVE TYPE), FUGUE STATE, MULTIPLE PERSONALITY, SOMNAMBULISM.

DISTORTION. In psychoanalysis, an unconscious or half-conscious modification of forbidden or unacceptable thoughts, images, or experiences which makes them more acceptable to the ego.

Distortion is believed to be a basic mental mechanism which aids in the repression of dangerous ideas but at the same time allows them some expression in disguised form. This enables them to pass the censor set up by the superego. The most highly developed example of this process is found in Freud's account of the translation of unconscious wishes and impulses (the latent content) into the images and events (the manifest content) of a dream. The distortions involve such processes as symbolization and condensation, which effectively disguise the latent content while giving it partial expression. See DREAM INTERPRETATION (MODERN).

Distortion is a common device found in both normal and abnormal behavior. Many people give a twisted version of an experience which puts them in a bad light, often without realizing that they are doing so. Distortion of this kind helps them maintain their self-respect and avoid criticism or conflict with social convention.

Neurotics frequently use this mechanism as a means of warding off anxiety and maintaining their emotional security or social acceptability. In its extreme form it may be a major feature of psychotic reactions. Any type of behavior or mental process can be distorted. Delusions are intellectual distortions; hallucinations and illusions are distortions of perception; feelings of unreality, depersonalization, and inappropriate affect are among the many distortions of emotions; verbigeration, neologisms, and word salad are distortions of expression and communication. In some cases these psychotic distortions can be shown to serve dynamic, defensive purposes; in others, they may be so extreme or garbled that no rationale can be discovered. *See* DELUSION, HALLUCINATION, ILLUSION, DEPERSONALIZATION, AFFECT, VERBIGERATION, NEOLOGISM, WORD SALAD.

DIX, DOROTHEA LYNDE (1802–87). Dorothea Dix was the most effective advocate of humanitarian reform in American mental institutions during the nineteenth century. Born in Maine, she lived in an unhappy home until the age of ten. At that time she showed the same initiative that characterized her later work by moving to her grandmother's, and by fourteen she had already started on a teaching career as a means of achieving further independence. Within a few years she established a school for young girls, Dix Mansion, in Boston, in which the major emphasis was placed on character building and natural science. Chronic lung trouble forced her to retire from the school in 1833 and live as an invalid until 1841.

In 1841 a more or less chance incident occurred which was to change the face of American psychiatry. Miss Dix was instructing a Sunday school class at a house of correction in East Cambridge when she noticed that several so-called "lunatics" were confined with the prisoners but had no stoves to keep them warm. When she asked the reason, a jailer told her that lunatics do not need heat because they are insensitive to cold. This was the stock answer at the time, since the attitude toward the mentally ill had "progressed" to a point where they were no longer believed to be possessed by the devil, but instead were regarded as a lower form of life, a species of wild beast.

Outraged by the cruel and inhumane treatment she witnessed, Miss Dix started to make a further investigation on her own. During the next two years she visited almshouses, jails, and houses of correction throughout the state. Then she wrote a clear, well-documented account of her findings, and presented it in the form of a memorandum to the Massachusetts Legislature under this title: "The Present State of Insane Persons Within This Commonwealth, in Cages, Closets, Cellars, Stalls, Pens! Chained, Naked, Beaten with Rods, and Lashed into Obedience!"

With these words Dorothea Dix launched a relentless, indefatigable campaign that was to have a remarkable effect on the mental institutions not only in this country but in Europe as well. Her Memorandum to the Legislature was followed by letters to the press in an effort to arouse public interest. Although many people greeted her revelations with scorn and disbelief, her zeal and spirit led to the passage of a bill that helped to correct the overcrowded conditions in the Worcester State Lunatic Hospital.

Encouraged by this "break-through," Miss Dix then traveled from state to state with the same plan of attack—a personal investigation, use of the press to arouse the public, and presentation of indisputable evidence to government officials. By 1847 the record showed that she had visited five hundred almshouses, three hundred houses of detention, and eighteen penitentiaries, in addition to innumerable hospitals and asylums. Everywhere she had to combat the prevailing attitudes of fear and ignorance toward the mentally ill, as well as prejudice against a woman who did not limit herself to the role assigned to her sex at the time. These difficulties were compounded by poor transportation facilities and her chronic lung condition. In spite of these obstacles, she was responsible for the introduction of legislative reforms that humanized the treatment of mental patients in many states, and through her personal efforts no less than thirty-two mental hospitals were either constructed or modernized.

Between 1854 and 1857 Miss Dix extended her crusade abroad, visiting England, Scotland, France, Italy, Scandinavia, Holland, Turkey, and Russia. In all these areas she not only examined conditions in the institutions, but presented herself to public authorities in an effort to achieve reforms. Among the fruits of these three short years were a new mental hospital in Rome, another on the island of Jersey, and an investigation of treatment of the insane in Scotland by a Royal Commission appointed by Queen Victoria. Upon her return from this trip she found that the state asylums she had been instrumental in founding were successfully replacing the almshouses, penitentiaries, and jails where the mentally ill had been confined before she began her campaign. She continued her humanitarian work by raising money for hospitals, inspecting them, and advising on personnel, both before and after the Civil War, taking time out only to perform an outstanding job as Superintendent of Women Nurses under the Surgeon General.

In their *History of Medical Psychology* (1941) Zilboorg and Henry pay tribute to this amazing woman in these words: "The history of medical psychology during the 19th century is the history of the American Psychiatric Association and the life of Dorothea Dix."

DOMINANCE RELATIONSHIP. A pattern of social organization in which some individuals assert a higher rank than others.

Dominance relationships are frequently observed in animals as well as human beings. A familiar example is the "pecking order" of barnyard hens. The top-ranking hen has the "right" to peck all the others, and each lower hen in the hierarchy can peck those below her but not those above her, with the bottom-ranking hen pecked by all the rest but unable to peck in return. A similar process occurs in groups of small children in a sandbox. The dominant child will direct the others in their work, keeping the most interesting tools and activities for himself. Occasionally the lower members of the group may attempt to usurp the place of the higher members or perhaps test their strength, but the general tendency among children—and among older people as well —is to accept their place in the scheme of things as "natural" and "right."

The drive for dominance takes many forms. Among animals it is primarily if not wholly a physical struggle for food, sex, mastery, or territory, or a combination of these drives. The same motives are basic in primitive human societies, but symbols of rank and prestige also come to play a major role. Among these symbols are special titles, forms of dress, and status in the tribe's councils and ceremonials. Such symbols of power not only command respect in themselves, but are endowed with a special aura that helps the individual maintain his status. Prestige symbols continue to play an important role in more sophisticated societies. The titles, rites, and ceremonies of lodges and other secret societies are remarkably similar to those of the primitives, and many of the practices in industry are merely a further extension of the same tendency. In some companies certain individuals are given the title of vice-president solely for status purposes (only a v.p. can deal with a v.p.), but the "lower" v.p.'s may not be given the golden key to the washroom that signifies genuine rank. There is a story that a non-v.p. was to be moved to a v.p.'s office when this man was given new quarters—but before he was allowed to occupy the room a workman was sent in to cut a foot-wide strip from the periphery of the wall-to-wall carpeting.

Dominance relationships are so prevalent that some psychologists have suggested that they may have an instinctual basis. The fact that physiological factors are usually involved, at least in animals, would seem to bolster this point of view. In the case of sex, this has been proven by both observation and experiment. Among chimps it has been found that a female in heat will become dominant in food-getting behavior, and an ordinarily dominant male who would usually grab most of the food will become submissive and wait impatiently until she finishes eating (Yerkes, 1940). Changes in the hierarchy have also been induced artificially. Low-ranking hens, for example, can be made more dominant through injection of male hormones (Allee, Collins, and Lutherman, 1939). But even though dominant behavior is under physiological control in animals, it is a highly variable quantity and not a fixed pattern of response like, for example, the nest-building instinct in wasps. Among human beings it is even more variable and it is also dependent on cultural factors. In certain societies, such as the Zuñi Indians, there are practically no dominance relationships —but where they are highly developed, as among the Kwakiutl Indians or middle-class Americans, it can readily be shown that the tendency is not in-herent or instinctive, but due to cultural influences.

A strong argument against the instinct theory is that dominance relationships are the result of actual learning experiences rather than innate tendency. If a group of rats are placed in a pen, the larger and stronger animals soon learn that they can get a bigger share of the food by defeating the weaker ones, and the weaker animals learn to be submissive and take what they can get when the stronger ones have had their fill. Observations have also shown that the social hierarchy is perpetuated by other learning experiences—for example, if the offspring of the submissive rats wander into the territory of the dominant rats, the females teach them a lesson by drubbing them with their paws without inflicting actual injury. Moreover, the lesson is frequently reinforced since the dominant rats are constantly on the alert, and bare their teeth or move aggressively the moment other rats threaten to tread on their territory. Similar behavior can be found among other species such as baboons, chimpanzees, pigeons, and wolves. It is even present among certain species of fish. The strongest set up a territory of their own, while the weakest are chased from place to place in the tank like a man without a country.

Human beings, too, learn that one way of getting what they want is to appropriate and defend a territory of their own. The strongest child captures the sandbox and claims it as his own (the right of "eminent domain"). The street gang may claim that an entire public block is its "turf," and even fight to the death to defend it. Many children's games, such as King of the Mountain, are based on territoriality. (For further examples, see *The Territorial Imperative* by Robert Ardrey, 1966.)

Dominance relationships in human and animal societies, then, have much in common. Yet there are important differences. Animal dominance is based largely on physical strength, though in some cases cunning and alertness may also play a part. Among humans physical strength is rarely the major factor, except among school children, and even then many weaker children learn that they can successfully assert their supremacy by becoming cleverer or more skillful than their stronger playmates. As they grow up there is even more emphasis on abilities and personality characteristics; at the same time they learn that certain signs of status are recognized by the society in which they live. If their parents or companions put a premium on status symbols, they too may seek to attain them. This is no hard and fast rule, however, for many young people develop their own standards and remain relatively unconcerned about status and rank.

Dominance, then, is a drive which some people develop and other people do not. It is not universal or instinctual. Yet how do we account for the fact that it *is* so prevalent, that so much of society is organized along hierarchical lines? Psychologists have no positive answer to this question, but three points appear to be highly relevant. First, many individuals and groups find that they can obtain a high degree of ego satisfaction as well as special rights and privileges by maintaining superiority over others. They therefore use every available means of asserting themselves. If they succeed, they remain dominant; if they do not, they lose "face" and status. Second, assertive tendencies are supported and reinforced by the fact that a great many people do not want to exert themselves, or have no confidence in their own ability, or feel more secure when they are in the hands of the strong or the elite. Third, it seems true that organized society usually functions more effectively and survives longer than unorganized society, and organization implies dominance re-

lationships of some kind. The question, of course, is not whether these relationships exist, but what form they take —whether they are based on sheer force, divine right, status-striving, hereditary aristocracy, or, hopefully, on competence and concern for the group as a whole. *See* LEADERSHIP, COMPETITION.

DREAM INTERPRETATION (Historical).

The belief that dreams have a special significance is practically universal. They have been an object of curiosity in all cultures and all times, and have been variously interpreted as portents of the future, the handiwork of gods or demons, guides to the solution of problems, the wandering of the soul in the spirit world—and, most recently, a key to the unconscious, an instrument in psychotherapy, and a basic contributor to mental health.

Dream interpretation, or "oneirology," has had such a long and varied history that we will only be able to note a few of the highlights from earlier periods as a preface to modern theories. There is evidence that dreams were recorded as soon as man developed a written language. The first known "dream book," the Chester Beatty papyrus, contains material dating back to 2000 B.C., and indicates that dreams played an important part in the magic, religion, and government of the early Egyptians. There is evidence that their beliefs were borrowed from the Assyrians and Mesopotamians; at any rate, in all three of these societies dreams were viewed as manifestations of either gods or demons, and as revelations of an invisible world which cannot be experienced in the waking state.

The two hundred dreams contained in the papyrus are interpreted as warnings of future events, advice on the treatment of illness, and guidance on affairs of state, success in love, and other ventures—for example, sawing wood predicts the defeat of an enemy, and dreaming of a funeral is an omen of long life (an example of the "law of contrast" later applied by Freud). The papyrus also contains rituals and incantations to ward off the effects of threatening dreams produced by demons, as well as prescriptions for potions to be used in overcoming infertility. The priests of the time took over the ritual aspects of dreaming, and one sect utilized "incubation," a practice in which sick persons slept on a temple floor in order to learn, through dreams, what treatments would be most effective.

The early Hebrews followed the same pattern, except for their monotheistic belief that God alone is the source of revelations occurring in dreams—for example, the prophecy of the flight from Egypt. Later, the Talmud held that dreams occurring just before waking are particularly vivid and significant, and when they occur in a series, later dreams can be used to interpret earlier ones. Both of these points are emphasized in recent studies of the dream state. In common with all these early cultures and religions, Mohammedanism recognized the divine source of certain dreams, and the use of ritual to induce them and of holy prophets to interpret them. The Mohammedans, however, were especially insistent that some dreams have a purely physiological origin, such as those provoked by wine or salty food, while others have divine significance. They also recognized that dreams are symbolic, and that the same symbol could mean different things to different people depending on their character and age—for instance, the dream of having one's hands tied signified final damnation for an evil man, but aversion from sin for a just man. See DREAM-STATE.

The Greeks borrowed the practice of incubation from the Egyptians and Babylonians, and it is said that the cult of Aesculapius had over three hundred centers devoted to temple sleep. Typically, the patient was anointed with purifying oils, then sleep was induced by drugs, potions, poor ventilation, or hypnosis. The priest or oracle then "interpreted" the individual's dreams and administered the therapy supposedly prescribed in them. This approach was first used for the cure of sterility, but was later applied to other disorders, including the use of suggestion and autosuggestion in the removal of apparently hysterical symptoms. Early Christianity adopted much of this mystique, with saints replacing priests, prayer replacing the Aesculapian rituals, and a broader concept of divine inspiration replacing the emphasis on dream inspiration. It is interesting, however, that inspiration continued to be associated with healing in certain sacred places such as Lourdes—and sleeping in church after fasting was practiced for many centuries.

Characteristically, the Greek philosophers introduced a rational approach to dreams and attempted to divorce them from their aura of mystery and magic (oneiromancy). Heraclitus viewed them as a carry-over of the cares and intentions of waking life. Democritus explained them in terms of physical emanations from persons and objects which penetrate the body and enter the consciousness of the dreamer. Plato believed that some dreams are divinely inspired, but also anticipated the Freudian view that repressed impulses are released in sleep: "In all of us, even in good men, there is a lawless wild-beast nature which peers out in sleep." Aristotle advanced the theory that dreams are a continuation of sense activity during sleep, especially when we are under emotional stress. Though he rejected the idea of prophetic dreams, he suggested that fantasies occurring in dreams appear so vivid and real that they may influence our waking behavior. This appears to be a recognition of the power of the unconscious.

In the second century, Artemidorus

drew upon Greek, Assyrian, and Egyptian sources in writing the most important dream "bible" of ancient times, the *Oneirocritica.* In contrast to the prevailing approach of today, he stressed the associations the dream evokes in the mind of the interpreter rather than in the mind of the dreamer. He was "modern," however, in recognizing the importance of certain fundamental symbols, and in warning that each dream has to be interpreted in the context of the dreamer's personality and the conditions under which it took place. He further recognized that recurrent dreams have particular significance for the individual, especially when they evoke intense emotion; and that wordplays and puns in dreams should be analyzed. He also anticipated Jung in making a distinction between "insomnium" dreams, which reflect the current state of the individual's mind and body, and "somnium" dreams, which arise from deeper, more mysterious sources and may predict future events.

Both the Hindu and Buddhist religions held that dreams reflect the soul's experiences as it wanders from the body during sleep. The Chinese explained not only dreams but trances, fits, and visions as separations of the soul from the body, and, as in Egypt, judges and other officials fasted and performed rituals in order to induce dreams that would guide them in their affairs. Though the older Indian philosophers adhered to the view that the soul leaves the body, the Yoga practitioners of more recent times believed that dreams represent the highest degree of self-knowledge, in which the illusions of waking life are eliminated and our innermost feelings and aspirations are revealed. This, too, was an anticipation of current Western thinking.

The Middle Ages did little more than reiterate older themes with a religious and moral emphasis. Christian writers, influenced by biblical dreams, believed that some dreams are prophetic and divinely inspired, but had great difficulty separating the true from the false, the good from the wicked, and those due to deity from those due to digestion. Gregory of Nyssa (fourth century) held that an individual's passions expressed themselves in dreams, and that his type of personality can be gauged from their content. (It has been suggested that gargoyles are demonic dream symbols representing the repressions of the time.) Thomas Aquinas distinguished between dreams as divine revelations, as demonic messages, and as reflections of the body or soul of the dreamer himself. Luther and Calvin were particularly troubled by the problem of distinguishing demonic messages from those of divine origin. Augustinian monks practiced "sensory deprivation" in order to obtain a vision. They fasted for seven days, then placed themselves upright in a coffin for two days, and, if they lived, related their prophetic visions. There is evidence, too, that medieval Europe used a wide variety of hallucinogenic drugs to induce fantasies.

By the end of the fifteenth century, occultism, numerology, and clairvoyance were dominant, and dream interpretation reflected far more superstition than genuine insight. Ancient rituals and magic were revived, and dream books, such as that of Raphael the Astrologer, became the vogue. In America the first such books were *The New Book of Knowledge,* appearing in Boston in 1767, and *The Universal Interpreter of Dreams and Visions,* published in 1795. These and other volumes discussed divine dreams, somnambulism, the nature of sleep, and also presented interpretations from a variety of sources, along with material on palmistry, cards, and lucky numbers. (Similar books, updated only in language, are still widely available.)

The association of dreams with superstition turned many nineteenth-century intellectuals against the whole field of dream study. Some of the rationalist and associationist philosophers, however, developed ideas that directly or indirectly led to modern points of view. In Germany, Fichte and Schelling recognized the existence of the unconscious, and others suggested that insight into the problems and passions of the individual could be gleaned from the study of dreams. Philosophers of the English school focused on the stimulation of dreams, and also suggested that dreams reflect not only the images and ideas of waking life, but the deeper, less organized thoughts that emerge when logical controls are set aside. Robert McNish (1841) cited, as stimulators, illness, indigestion, and two other factors later emphasized by Freud —namely, the experience of the previous day, and sensory impressions received during sleep. John Abercrombie anticipated the psychoanalytic technique in using associationist methods to show how buried memories are fused with present behavior, and in suggesting that anxieties are the motivating forces behind many of our dreams.

During the latter part of the nineteenth century, anthropological studies of preliterate societies revealed the universality of dream symbols, a close relation between myths and dreams, and the fact that primitive men often used dreams as guides for their personal affairs and tribal decisions—all of which suggested that a study of dreams would throw light on human behavior. The psychology and physiology of dream experience were also investigated. Experiments performed by the French psychologist Alfred Maury and others showed that stimuli such as bright lights and touch sensations evoke dreams—for instance, grasping the hand of a sleeper might instigate a dream about touching a dead body. Havelock Ellis held that sensations from the stomach arouse dreams, but also

recognized that the images of the dream may be determined by deeper levels of the mind which do not come to light in the waking state. In addition, Ellis cited a wide variety of possible explanations for dreams, suggesting, for example, that dreams of flying might stem from an instinctive recollection of man's ancestry, the movements of early maritime creatures or even the child in the womb, changes in the respiratory muscles, or loss of internal equilibrium due to the horizontal sleep position.

Finally, the dynamic character of the unconscious was suggested but not fully developed by a number of authors. The philosopher Bergson held that visual sensations produced by internal changes in the organism are responsible for the images we see in dreams, but that memories push their way into the "relaxed consciousness" of the sleeper and are woven into his fantasies. De Quincey vividly described the effect of opium on fantasy, and made the important point that in the dream experience one immediately recognizes images and feelings from childhood that would not be acknowledged in waking life.

Many nineteenth-century writers were struck by the fact that the imagination is given freer rein in dreams. Poe and Coleridge claimed that their dreams were frequently a source of creative ideas. Stevenson remembered most of his dreams, and referred to his waking self as merely an agent which recorded insights and themes that came to him during sleep. But most significantly, the motif of his story *The Strange Case of Dr. Jekyll and Mr. Hyde* came to him in a dream and is believed to represent a raging conflict between the instinctual, destructive urges that dominated his unconscious and the civilized behavior of his conscious life. It was but a short step from this notion to the Freudian theory that latent, unacceptable impulses are given expression

in our dream life. *See* DREAM INTER-
PRETATION (MODERN).

DREAM INTERPRETATION (Modern).

As the preceding topic indicates,
many provocative ideas on dreams were
"in the air" at the turn of the twentieth
century. Individual writers, and in some
instances whole schools, had suggested
that (1) dreams can be clues to the
"problems and passions" of life; (2)
deeper levels of the mind come to the
surface during the "relaxed consciousness" of sleep; (3) dreams are often
aroused by the experiences of the previous day; (4) immediate sensory impressions might also act as stimulators;
(5) different people, even different races,
tend to have the same type of dreams
and use the same dream symbols; and
(6) dreams may release both unacceptable impulses and creative ideas. These
notions were widely scattered, and no
comprehensive, systematic theory of
dreams was presented until Sigmund
Freud made his contribution.

Freud. Freud's *Interpretation of
Dreams,* dated 1900, is regarded as
his magnum opus. However, the volume was almost completely ignored by
his colleagues, and it took years to
exhaust the first edition of six hundred
copies. The insights it contains are
largely the result of the study of his
own dreams—the principal technique
he used in his self-analysis, undertaken
after the death of his father in 1896.
He had also discovered that when he
applied the method of free association
with his patients, they frequently related revealing dreams.

The investigation of his own dreams
and those of his patients led Freud
to the following ideas: (1) lost memories
of childhood can be recaptured by associating to dream contents; (2) many
of these memories involve painful
thoughts and feelings, suggesting that
they had been expelled, or "repressed,"
from consciousness and stored in the
unconscious; (3) dreams appear to be
patterned after infantile, prelogical experience, since dream fantasies do not
obey the usual laws of reality; (4) the
motive force for dreams appears to
stem from instinctive and predominantly
sexual drives; and (5) dreams always
represent the fulfillment of hidden
wishes in disguised form. The last point
was the most important, since it meant
that dreams had meaning and could
be interpreted.

In developing his theory further,
Freud made several other important
suggestions. First, dreams are stimulated
by the "day's residues," usually consisting of incidental details and minor
incidents that touch upon unconscious
impulses and memories during waking
activity. Second, the reason why this
unconscious material appears in disguise is that the censor—that is, our
moral code or conscience—is still operative during sleep, though in attenuated form. Third, the disguises enable the individual to express his unacceptable impulses and desires, but at
the same time prevent him from expressing them in such a blatant form
that he would have to wake up and
defend himself. In this sense the dream
can be described as "the guardian of
sleep."

The study of the wishes expressed
in dreams and the various disguises
they take gave rise to a distinction
between manifest and latent content.
The manifest content is the series of
images and events that constitute the
dream itself just as it appears to the
dreamer. The latent content is the underlying meaning of the dream—the repressed wishes and impulses seeking to
break through and find expression. The
process by which the latent content is
transformed into the manifest content
is called the dream work. Three basic
mechanisms are involved in this work:
(a) in *condensation,* several meanings
are fused together or combined into
a single image, word, or event—e.g.
dreaming of the death of a parent may

stem from the patient's childhood fear that this parent will abandon him, and at the same time reflect a guilt-laden wish that the parent will go away (death usually means simply departure to the young child); (b) in *displacement,* feelings or attitudes are redirected from their true object to a substitute—e.g. a child in a dream might express his hostility toward his father by breaking a male doll; (c) in *symbolization,* the unconscious expresses itself in symbols—a king and queen may stand for the dreamer's parents; climbing a ladder may represent the sexual act; a pair of sisters may stand for breasts; a snake, sword, steeple, or tree may represent a penis; a purse, ravine, or book may stand for a vagina. In addition, a fourth mechanism, *secondary elaboration,* comes into play when the patient revises and distorts his dream in recalling and relating it.

The object of dream interpretation is to penetrate beneath the manifest content to the latent content and thereby uncover some aspects of the patient's unconscious wishes and impulses. The basic technique here, as in other phases of psychoanalysis, is free association—that is, the patient narrates his dream and then brings forth whatever it calls to mind. This process usually gives the analyst clues to its meaning. However, he must also interpret these clues in the light of the four mechanisms, noting where two or more meanings may be telescoped into one image, discovering possible substitutions and displacements, identifying distortions which might reveal unconscious tendencies that influence recollection and narration, and deciphering the symbolic language of the dream. Freud placed special emphasis on the mechanism of symbolization, but recognized that even though some types of symbols tend to be more universal than others, *every* symbol must be interpreted in the light of the individual's personality,

experience, and unconscious tendencies as revealed by free association.

As this brief account indicates, Freudian dream interpretation is no simple matter. The patient makes free associations based on every detail—every image, idea, turn of phrase—so that gradually the full meaning of the dream is revealed. This meaning must then be integrated with other insights gathered in the ongoing process of psychoanalysis. *See* PSYCHOANALYSIS (THERAPY).

Jung, Carl Gustav. Jung's conception of dreams had a considerably wider scope than Freud's. He saw them as an expression of many other drives and impulses than sex alone; as a source of creative ideas and intuitions, not merely a "royal road" to repressed material that tended to produce pathological reactions; as an expression of the collective unconscious of the race as well as the personal unconscious of the individual; and as a guide to future thought and action, not just a reflection of unsolved personal problems of the past.

For Jung, then, the study of dreams is not directed primarily to clearing away infantile impulses that hamper the personality; it is more concerned with revealing constructive forces and positive ideas that might broaden and deepen the individual's insight into life. In his own words (1928), "Dreams may give expression to ineluctable truths, to philosophical pronouncements, illusions, wild fantasies . . . anticipations, irrational experiences, even telepathic visions and heaven knows what besides." These new insights will often enable us to reach a level of self-understanding we could not ordinarily attain in waking life: "Within each of us there is another we do not know. He speaks to us in dreams and tells us how differently *he* sees us from how *we* see ourselves. When we find ourselves in an insolubly difficult situation, this stranger in us can sometimes show us a light which is more suited than anything else to change our attitude fundamentally; namely, just that attitude which has led us into the difficult situation."

Jung's approach to dream interpretation differed from Freud's on several other counts. First, he believed that Freud made too sharp a distinction between manifest and latent content, and insisted that the dream as it stands has meaning: "The dream is its own interpretation." Second, since the dream reflects present difficulties, the interpretation deals primarily with present attitudes, not childhood patterns. Third, though single dreams may be revealing, it is more helpful to focus on recurring themes and whole series of dreams, since later dreams will often comment on prior ones and even provide interpretations of them. Fourth, the free association technique, with its emphasis on every detail, may "miss the forest for the trees"; it is better to work the dream over as a whole and view the symbols in the total context of the dreamer's present life. Fifth, the symbols may be interpreted not merely as disguised representations of the individual's life, but as "archetypes" that express the collective unconscious and evoke the "wisdom of the ages."

The difference between Freud's and Jung's interpretation of dream symbols has been illustrated by MacKenzie in his recent book, *Dreams and Dreaming* (1965). He suggests that even though both authors believed that symbols cannot be detached from the dreamer, a Freudian would be likely to view a serpent and a lighthouse as sexual symbols, while a Jungian might regard the serpent as an archetypical symbol of medicine and the lighthouse as a guiding beam over the stormy sea of life. MacKenzie also quotes a contrast made by Jung himself between his interpretation and a Freudian interpretation of a young man's dream: "I was going up a flight of stairs with my mother and sister. When we reached the top I was told my sister was going to have a child." In the Freudian interpretation, a flight of stairs would be a censored version of sexual intercourse; the mother and sister would represent an incestuous wish; and the expected child would stand for either a displacement of sexual feeling from the mother to the sister, or an expression of the brother's desire for his sister.

Jung, on the other hand, makes the following comment: "If I say that the stairs are a symbol for the sexual act, where do I obtain the right to regard the mother, the sister, and the child as concrete, that is, as not symbolic?" He then notes that the dreamer was a young man with homosexual inclinations who had finished his studies but had not been able to choose an occupation, and that in associating to his mother, he had remarked, "I haven't seen her for a long time, a very long time. I really ought to reproach myself for this. It is wrong of me to neglect her so." This suggested to Jung that "mother" actually stood for something inexcusably neglected, and when he asked what it might be, the young man answered with embarrassment, "My work." In associating to his sister, the young man said he longed to see her because he felt genuine affection for her, and she had helped him understand "what love for a woman can mean." For Jung this simply meant that the sister represented love for a woman. The stairs and the child led to associations that were almost as direct. The stairs suggested "climbing upward; getting to the top; making a success of life; being grown up"; and the child suggested "newborn; a revival; a regeneration; becoming a new man." Jung concludes: "One has only to hear this material in order to understand at once that the patient's dream is not so much the fulfillment of infantile desires, as it is the expression of biological duties which he has hitherto neglected because of his infantilism." *See* JUNG.

Adler. Unlike Freud and Jung, Alfred Adler found little use for dreams in the therapeutic process, since he felt that whatever they revealed could be more easily inferred from the patient's conscious attitudes and behavior. He believed they did not differ materially from our thought processes in the waking state, since they are concerned with hopes, fears, plans, and possible courses of action. However, dreams frequently present aspects of life situations that are too threatening to face in the waking state, and the distortions of dream images represent an attempt to cushion the ego against these threats. But most significant in the light of his theory as a whole is his suggestion that some dreams—especially heroic fantasies—are attempts at compensating for failures in actual life, while others are experiments or "dress rehearsals" in which we envisage new solutions to our problems or new styles of life. *See* ADLER.

Stekel and others. Wilhelm Stekel placed even more emphasis on dreams than Freud, viewing them as "the signposts which show the way to the life-conflict." Like many other analysts, he held that the first dream presented by the patient was a summary of his problem and an anticipation of the course of treatment. His major emphasis in dream interpretation was on deciphering symbols. However, in attempting to discover their meaning, he depended far less than Freud on the patient's associations, for he felt that they were unreliable. Instead, he developed a catalogue of symbols which would enable him to cut quickly through to the essential conflict the neurotic was attempting to solve in his dream. As an example, water may stand for birth; a stormy sea, for a troubled life; a flood, for unsatisfied instinctual cravings; bathing, for the psychotherapeutic process

and its cathartic effect; and "dark waters," for the mysterious unconscious as a whole. Interpretation of this type become the core of Emil Gutheil's "brief psychoanalysis," as outlined in his book *The Handbook of Dream Analysis* (1951).

We can only sample the suggestions of other authors. Rivers (1923) viewed dreams as attempted solutions of conflicts, and claimed that the patient in therapy experiences a drop in anxiety level as his dreams move toward healthy resolutions. Hall (1953) holds that the dream is both an expression (often metaphorical) of the way the mind formulates problems and the way the unconscious attempts to find a solution. Erich Fromm (1951) extended Jung's emphasis on serial dreams by showing that they reflect progress in therapy. French and Erika Fromm (1964) argue that even though dreams do not follow the ordinary laws of logic, they are nevertheless congruent with the personality of the dreamer and reflect his basic problems. At the present time it appears that many investigators are moving away from the Freudian view that dreams are fulfillments of infantile wishes, and toward the view that they are attempts to solve problems. *See* NIGHTMARE, PRODROME.

DREAM-STATE (D-STATE, REM-STATE). A state of the organism that occurs during dreaming, recently found to be physiologically distinct from both the ordinary sleep state (S-State) and the waking state (W-State).

During an average night's sleep, the individual goes through four or five periods in which rapid conjugate eye movements can be detected (REM) and EEG, or brain wave patterns, resemble those of wakefulness (Aserinsky and Kleitman, 1953). People who are awakened during these periods almost invariably report that they were dreaming. It also appears that dreaming takes place *only* during these states. Ordinarily these periods first appear about fifty to ninety minutes after the onset of sleeping, occur periodically throughout the night, and occupy a total of about ninety minutes (PLATE 16).

Many indices show that the organism is more active during the D-State than the S-State: increased pulse and respiratory rate, irregularity in these functions as well as in blood pressure, full or partial erection in 90 per cent of male subjects, an increase in brain temperature and oxygen intake, greater blood flow in the cortex, and especially sporadic brain wave patterns similar to those occurring when an object is followed with the eyes during the waking state. *See* BRAIN WAVES.

The D-State has been reported in all mammals fully tested, including sheep, dogs, cats, rabbits, and monkeys, but it has not been found in reptiles. The time spent in the D-State varies greatly. It occupies 20–60 per cent of the total sleep time in adult cats and only about 2 per cent in sheep (Jouvet et al., 1960; Jouvet and Valatx, 1962). The reasons for the variations are unknown, although there is evidence that species that live longer and have a lower metabolic rate have longer D-State periods. In human beings the average length is fourteen minutes, the longest of any species so far investigated. The total amount of time spent in the D-State, however, depends on the age of the organism. Studies made on cats, sheep, and men have shown that the young spend more time in the D-State that the adults (Jouvet et al., 1961; Roffwarg et al., 1964). In human beings, the total time spent in the D-State amounts to 45 to 65 per cent of the sleeping time among newborn infants, 20 to 25 per cent among eighteen- to twenty-year-olds, and 13 to 18 per cent among fifty- to seventy-year-olds. These figures seem to indicate that the D-State is more primitive than the W-State or the S-State.

How essential is the D-State? To answer this question, Dement (1960) made a classic study of "dream state deprivation" in which human subjects were awakened every night for five nights as soon as the REM-State began. After this, the subjects were allowed five "recovery" nights of uninterrupted sleep. The experiment demonstrated that (1) only four to five interruptions were required to eliminate the D-State on the first night, but this number increased to twenty to thirty on the fifth night; (2) on the recovery night D-State activity comprised 30 to 40 per cent of the total S-Time, as if to make up for the lost D-Time; (3) even though the subjects obtained six to seven hours of sleep during the deprivation nights, they tended to be irritable and tense during the following day, as if they had gotten too little sleep.

In a control study the same subjects were awakened the same amount of time from S-Sleep rather than D-Sleep, and they failed to show these emotional reactions the following day. As a further test, Dement extended the D-deprivation to fifteen days in three subjects (1963), and obtained the same results as above, but in exaggerated form. Toward the end of the experiment, it became almost impossible to awaken the subjects, and Dexedrine had to be administered. During the recovery period the time spent in the D-State rose to 60 per cent of the S-Time. Moreover, two of the subjects underwent distinct personality changes during the day, one of them giggling constantly and the other showing paranoid symptoms.

Dement's studies indicate that there is a basic need for the D-State, and probably for the psychological experience of dreaming itself, since it takes place during some and perhaps all of the D-State. It may well be that our physiological and mental health are both dependent upon it.

The investigation of the effects of D-State deprivation on the personality has recently been extended to mentally disturbed patients.

In spite of the fact that many specialists have noted that schizophrenics appear to be living in a dream, studies have shown that their waking state is physiologically similar to that of normal individuals, and their D-State during sleep occupies a normal amount of time. However, as Hartmann (1966) points out, their D-Periods are less sharply demarcated than among normals. He has also found that D-State deprivation may be involved in the onset of the psychosis, since these patients often report that they cannot sleep or that they sleep poorly during this period. The lack of sleep cuts down on the D-State time and leads to waking state difficulties—a situation that may produce a vicious cycle. What is needed, Hartmann suggests, is a drug that will induce sleep without interfering with D-Time. There is also evidence that borderline patients spend more time than usual in the D-State (Fisher and Dement, 1963), and there appears to be a significant correlation between D-State time and anxiety scores among college students (Rechtschaffen et al., 1964).

Studies of the D-State have thrown new light on the nature of dreaming. Rechtschaffen et al. (1963) report that dreams occurring nearer to morning are more vivid and bizarre than dreams occurring earlier. Offenkrantz and Rechtschaffen (1963) found that successive dreams on the same night tend to express the same material in an increasingly clear and undisguised manner. External stimulation such as light or sound will become incorporated in a dream during the D-State, but will not induce a dream during S-Sleep (Dement and Wolpert, 1958). It has also been found that people who ordinarily do not recall their dreams will usually recall them if awakened during the D-State (Goodenough et al., 1959). A relationship between eye movements and the actual scene dreamed about has likewise been reported—when the scene was one in which a great deal of movement occurred, the eye movements tended to change more rapidly than in dreams involving little activity. Moreover, the muscle potentials recorded during dreaming appear to be an attenuated form of those occurring in actual behavior.

Finally, considerable progress has been made on the physiological aspects of the dream-state. Through surgical intervention on animals, Jouvet and others have localized the pons (a structure in the brain stem) as the area most involved, and for this reason the D-State is often referred to as pontine sleep. The exact control center and specific circuits involved, however, have yet to be identified. The effects of drugs on the D-State is another area of physiological investigation. Barbiturates have been found to increase D-State time; alcohol, tranquilizers, and hypnogenic drugs decrease it. Murio et al. (1964), have shown that LSD may increase the length of the single D-Period but not increase total D-Time. As Hartmann (1966) suggests, it would be useful to have a drug that will increase total D-Time because of its importance in maintaining our psychological equilibrium. However, no such drug is presently available. *See* SLEEP.

DRIVE REDUCTION THEORY. The theory that learning is dependent on the alleviation or satisfaction of a drive; more specifically, that an organism will acquire new responses only when it is motivated by a need and receives a reward that meets that need.

This principle was first proposed by the psychologist Clark Hull in 1943 to explain the conditions under which learning takes place. If we want to teach a dog to stand up when we hold up our hand, we first make sure he is hungry by not feeding him for some time, then we hold a piece of food high enough so that he has to stand up to look at it, and finally we drop it into his mouth while he is standing up. By repeating this process a number of times he will learn to associate the hand signal with standing and will eventually stand when we hold up our hand even though he is no longer rewarded with food. The theory holds that this association is firmly established and reinforced by repeatedly giving him a reward that reduces (i.e. satisfies) his hunger drive.

The central idea of the theory is that no learning can take place unless the organism (animal or human being) is goaded by a drive that makes it tense and uncomfortable, and receives a reward of some kind that relieves this discomfort. The drive reduction hypothesis has inspired a great deal of experimentation since it permits the conditions for learning to be carefully regulated. Hunger, thirst, sex, and other drives can be increased or reduced to see how these changes affect the speed of learning—for example, when rats were kept thirsty for six hours they were found to learn more rapidly than when they were deprived of water for two hours. This technique is also used in attempting to discover the effects of rewards on physiological processes, and the changes that occur in an organism when learning takes place. Studies of hunger and thirst have contributed a limited amount of information on this aspect of the problem.

Recent research indicates that the Hullian theory does not fully explain the learning process. Both animals and human beings have been shown to acquire new responses when there appears to be little possibility of drive reduction. Rats, for instance, will learn when the only "reward" is an increase in illumination (Roberts, Marx, Collier, 1958), and monkeys learn when the

only reward is the opportunity to look at another monkey or to hear a colony of monkeys (Butler, 1953, 1957). Other animals have acquired new responses when they were merely given an opportunity to explore a maze (Montgomery, 1954). Electrode implantation experiments have shown that animals will learn to press levers and perform other operations when correct responses are followed only by electrical stimulation of certain areas of their brain (Olds, 1958). See LIMBIC SYSTEM.

All these experiments show that learning can apparently occur in animals without involving the satisfaction of physiological needs. This is even more true of human learning. Many people engage in study and research because of the intrinsic satisfaction that learning itself brings, and not because of drives that make them tense or uncomfortable. We even acquire information without realizing we are doing so and without having a problem to solve, a phenomenon called incidental or latent learning. See INCIDENTAL LEARNING, LEARNING (GENERAL), LIMBIC SYSTEM, PLEASURE PRINCIPLE.

DRUG ADDICTION. Compulsive dependence on the use of narcotic drugs.

Drug addiction is characterized not merely by persistent use of a drug, but by (a) an inner compulsion or overpowering urge to use it; (b) a tendency to increase the dose due to increasing tolerance; and (c) both physiological and psychological dependence on its effects. Addiction should be distinguished (although sometimes it is not) from habituation. In habituation there is persistent use and desire for a drug because of its psychological effects, but the elements of compulsion and physical dependence are lacking, and there is little or no tendency to increase the dosage.

The problem of drug addiction today centers around the opiates (opium and its derivatives, morphine, heroin, pare-

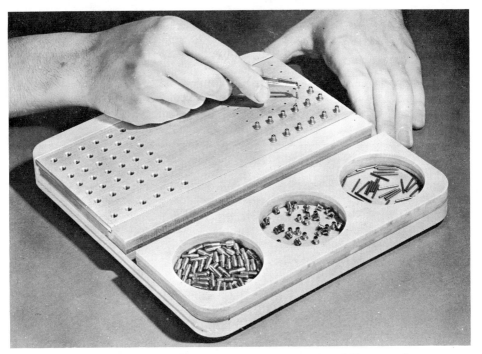

8. The Crawford Small Parts Dexterity Test, used in assessing ability to perform jobs requiring manual dexterity. *See* APTITUDE TESTS (Special), PERSONNEL TESTS.

9. Which version is artistically superior? One of many items on the Meier Art Judgment Test. *See* ART TESTS.

VARIOUS TYPES OF TESTS AND APPARATUS

Brain wave (electroencephalograph) tracings from selected lobes of the cerebral cortex. *See* BRAIN WAVES, EPILEPSY (Symptoms and Types), *Plate 19.*

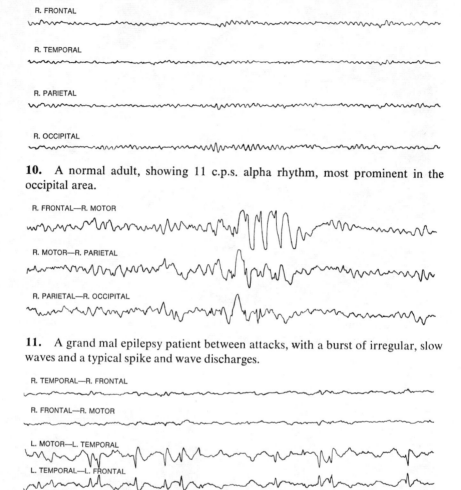

R. FRONTAL

R. TEMPORAL

R. PARIETAL

R. OCCIPITAL

10. A normal adult, showing 11 c.p.s. alpha rhythm, most prominent in the occipital area.

R. FRONTAL—R. MOTOR

R. MOTOR—R. PARIETAL

R. PARIETAL—R. OCCIPITAL

11. A grand mal epilepsy patient between attacks, with a burst of irregular, slow waves and a typical spike and wave discharges.

R. TEMPORAL—R. FRONTAL

R. FRONTAL—R. MOTOR

L. MOTOR—L. TEMPORAL

L. TEMPORAL—L. FRONTAL

12. A patient subject to psychomotor seizures of temporal lobe origin, showing spike discharges from the left anterior lobe between attacks. Contrast the left and right areas.

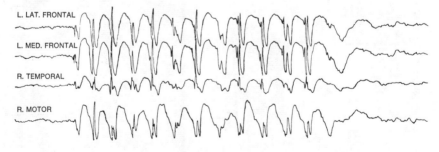

L. LAT. FRONTAL

L. MED. FRONTAL

R. TEMPORAL

R. MOTOR

13. A short petit mal epilepsy attack with 3 c.p.s. spike and wave discharges beginning and ending abruptly.

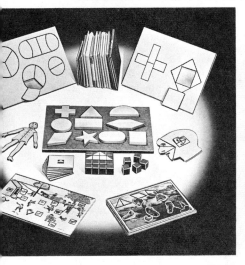 

14. *(Left)* The Arthur Point Scale of Performance Test, an intelligence test not requiring the use of language. The Seguin Form Board, one of the earliest intelligence test items, is in the center. *See* INTELLIGENCE TESTS. **15.** *(Right)* The Hanfmann-Kasanin Test, used in studying concept formation and diagnosing mental impairment. The blocks are turned over to conceal the names, and the subject tries to sort them into four groups having certain characteristics of color, shape or size in common. If he succeeds in discovering the correct principles of classification, the blocks in each group will have the same name on the bottom. *See* CONCEPT FORMATION, MENTAL IMPAIRMENT TESTS, VIGOTSKY TEST. **16.** *(Below)* A finger maze, used in studying human learning and problem-solving. *See* MAZE.

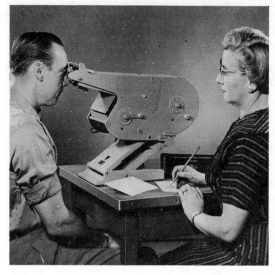

17. The Ortho-Rater, used in testing visual functions: near and far acuity, depth perception, color discrimination, eye balance. *See* APTITUDE TESTS (Special), PERSONNEL TESTS, VISUAL ACUITY.

18. A memory drum, used in studying verbal learning and memory span. The experimenter can control the amount and rate of exposure of material on the rotating drum. *See* NONSENSE SYLLABLE, PAIRED ASSOCIATES LEARNING, REMEMBERING.

19. An electroencephalograph records brain wave patterns from different parts of the cerebral cortex during sleep. *See* BRAIN WAVES, DREAM-STATE, SLEEP DRIVE.

goric, and codeine), and the barbiturates. The problem of habituation involves the use of marijuana, the amphetamines (Benzedrine, Methedrine, and other "pep pills"), as well as cocaine. This article will deal with the addiction problem in general and the opiates in particular. (Discussion of the other drugs will be found under separate topics.)

The problem of drug addiction is a conspicuous one in the United States because of its relationship to crime and mental health, and because it involves so many of our young people. The rate of addiction has actually dropped materially since the beginning of this century when opiates were used in many patent medicines sold without prescription. Nevertheless there are now about 100,000 addicts in this country and the number does not appear to be decreasing. Males outnumber females by four to one, and the great majority come from the lower socioeconomic levels, although the number from the upper levels appears to be on the rise, as in the "hippie" movement. Psychoses associated with addiction account for about 1 per cent of first admissions to mental hospitals each year.

Narcotic addiction rarely starts after the age of fifty. The most vulnerable group in our population are high school dropouts and young adults, especially in crowded, decaying urban areas where drugs of various kinds are readily available and their use is tolerated or even approved. There is usually a history of delinquency prior to the use of drugs, and criminal behavior generally continues after addiction. Addicts rarely commit violent crimes and do not fall into the standard pattern of professional criminals, since they usually steal, prostitute themselves, or peddle narcotics only for the purpose of maintaining their drug supply. A few habitual criminals, however, use cocaine or other drugs to reinforce themselves before committing offenses.

Psychologically speaking, the largest group of addicts consists of immature, inadequate individuals with "passive-aggressive" personalities. Generally they come from families in which the father is weak and shiftless or totally absent, and the mother is a tense, unhappy person who resents her children and tends to frustrate, dominate, or overprotect them. These people are often lured into taking their first dose as a result of a dare, or out of defiance, curiosity, desire for adventure, or pressure to conform to the group mores.

A few teen-age drug users, sometimes called the "reactive" type, or "joy-poppers," do not become physiologically dependent since they take small amounts only on weekends "for kicks." Those who become full addicts are the maladjusted individuals with deep-seated personality problems, who have a compelling urge to seek relief from tension or anxiety, and to escape from reality. Most of them have never developed healthy or constructive outlets for their energies, and have progressed to the opiates through the use of other tension-relievers, such as alcohol, marijuana, or barbiturates.

As time goes on, these immature individuals center their lives more and more around the blissful world of narcotics. The result is that they restrict their associations to drug users and gradually abandon any aspirations and ambitions they may have had, including all interest in school, work, sex, and marriage. They live only for the moments when they are "out of this world." If they continue the "habit" for long periods, their social and moral standards deteriorate to a point where they become social outcasts, drifters, petty criminals, or "pushers." In a word, their original immaturity and inadequacy are increased, not diminished, by the continued use of drugs.

There are several smaller groups of

addicts. A few neurotics resort to drugs for relief of anxiety and tension, particularly when a pattern of escape has already been established and the individual comes in close contact with narcotics users. Occasionally psychotics are also lured into addiction. In isolated cases, patients who are given morphine for an extended period to counteract pain may become addicted. This form of addiction, however, is usually broken by gradual withdrawal of the drug—unless there is a prior susceptibility due to personality defect. A small and diminishing amount of addiction is found among doctors, nurses, and others who have easy access to drugs and take them out of curiosity or to gain relief from stressful situations.

The effects of the opiates are both psychological and physical, and one reason why addiction occurs is that these effects are both immediate and intense. Within a few seconds after an injection of morphine or heroin (or after smoking or eating these drugs), feelings of tension and anxiety drop away and are replaced by a warm, glowing sensation that gradually permeates the entire being. This sensation is followed by feelings of euphoria and relaxation which make the addict feel supremely contented, regardless of how distressed or poorly adjusted he may be in everyday life. Pain, hunger, and sexual urgency subside. Although he feels drowsy, his mind is clear and he enters a state of reverie, daydreaming, and strange but pleasant perceptual distortion: space is expanded to infinite heights and depths, and time stretches out to cover years and even centuries in a single night.

These pleasurable effects last for four to six hours, and are followed by gradually increasing uneasiness and depression, which produce a stronger and stronger craving for another dose. If the drug is available and the procedure is repeated day after day, the user

may find that he is "hooked" within a month or so, and has become both psychologically and physiologically dependent on the drug. Moreover, he will require constantly increased doses to obtain the desired effects, since tolerance for these drugs builds up with repeated use.

If the opiates are suddenly unavailable, withdrawal symptoms are experienced in a regular sequence of mounting severity. The first symptoms appear within twelve hours: yawning, sneezing, perspiring, followed by anorexia (loss of appetite), dilated pupils, tremor, and goose flesh. Within twenty-four hours the addict becomes weak, restless, irritable, and apprehensive, and there is a rise in pulse, blood pressure, and respiration rate. Soon after, his muscles begin to twitch uncontrollably and excruciating cramps attack his legs, abdomen, and back. At this stage he is subject to insomnia, violent vomiting, and diarrhea attacks, and as a result he loses weight and becomes dehydrated. These reactions, plus alternating attacks of flushing and chilliness, wear him down physically and psychologically—yet he may use all his remaining energy in cursing, shouting, and attempting to "climb up the walls." Many authorities feel that these reactions may be deliberately dramatized by the addict. As evidence, they point out that withdrawal in isolation tends to be less severe than when it takes place in a group where he can complain to others.

The withdrawal symptoms reach their peak in seventy-two to ninety-six hours, and are such a severe drain on the heart and other internal organs that there is danger of collapse and even death. By the fifth day, however, they begin to subside, and by the eighth have usually disappeared entirely. The patient then begins to take normal amounts of food and drink and gradually regains his strength and weight. The withdrawal period has, however, decreased his tolerance, and if he has access to drugs and takes his usual large doses the result may be fatal due to rapid congestion of the lungs.

In view of the torture experienced in sudden withdrawal, and the dangers involved, most specialists extend the process over a period of ten to twenty days. The morphine or heroin is gradually reduced, and a milder narcotic, methadone, may be substituted to suppress the withdrawal symptoms as fully as possible. Sometimes a tranquilizer is also used to reduce the tension that accompanies withdrawal.

After this procedure, the patient is generally kept in the hospital for several months, during which intensive efforts are made to rehabilitate him physically, psychologically, and socially. The physical rehabilitation is necessitated by impairment to health brought about by an inadequate diet and poor living habits rather than by the morphine or heroin, since it has been found that these drugs do not produce physical damage by themselves. Social rehabilitation is aimed at developing occupational skills, interests, and relationships which have been grossly neglected during the period of addiction. Psychological rehabilitation usually consists of individual psychotherapy designed to help the patient revise the faulty attitudes and emotional patterns that led to addiction in the first place, and to counteract the personality deterioration which has taken place as a result of the life he has been leading.

On the whole, the prognosis in drug addiction cannot be called favorable, although a few recent approaches appear promising. While some addicts "mature out" of the need for heroin by the age of thirty to thirty-five, most of them continue to seek this form of escape and a great many lapse back into the habit after undergoing treatment. Follow-up studies of patients who have completed the hospital program in Lexington, Kentucky, have revealed that over 90 per cent become addicted again, practically all within six months. There may, however, be a latent effect, since less than 50 per cent have been found to be addicted after a period of five years—particularly those who were over thirty years of age at the time of discharge. A number of these former addicts have found reinforcement in Narcotics Anonymous, a mutual support organization modeled after Alcoholics Anonymous.

In view of the difficulties encountered in curing addiction and its close association with crime, some authorities have advocated medical dispensation of drugs in minimum maintenance doses to registered addicts. This approach has not aroused widespread support, since the narcotics addict is legally classified as a criminal in this country and would therefore be unlikely to register. In recent years it has been tried in Britain, but the experiment has not been a success and stricter control of narcotics is now being planned.

Three of the newer approaches to the problem are civil commitment for treatment and rehabilitation, methadone treatment, and group-community therapy. The civil commitment program in New York State has been described by Louria (1967) as follows: "Until this year, the New York program was largely voluntary. Now, if the user is arrested, he can choose either to stand trial or to sign up for rehabilitation—with a three-year follow up period. If he chooses to go to trial and is found guilty, he is likely to be put in the rehabilitation program anyway. Previously, after-care was voluntary, and more than 80 per cent of discharged patients disappeared within a month. Now, after-care is compulsory—authoritarian but benign. New York's program —with its emphasis on education, job rehabilitation and careful follow-up— seems to me to be potentially the most effective of any yet undertaken."

The New York State program is

based largely on the success of the pioneer California Rehabilitation Program, dating from 1961. There, too, practically all patients (97 per cent) are committed to a large-scale "therapeutic community" by court order. Withdrawal from drugs takes place in a jail or hospital while the addict is waiting for admission, and the program itself is a form of milieu therapy which emphasizes the development of social feeling through group living in dormitories, varied sports and recreational activities, work assignments on the grounds, elementary or high school classes under the Corona school system, and vocational training to develop marketable skills. All these ingredients of the "total living" program are regarded as therapeutic, since they are aimed at altering the pattern of the patient's life and preparing him for a normal, constructive existence. The focus of therapy, however, is on daily group therapy sessions, both large and small, in which the patients gradually recognize why they used drugs, and learn to take responsibility for their lives instead of blaming their addiction on childhood neglect or the shortcomings of others. By scrutinizing and criticizing each other, they arrive at greater self-understanding, and through the exercise of "peer group pressure" they attain greater self-control and a fuller sense of responsibility for each other. An equally important part of the therapy is the outpatient program in which patients are paroled after about a year, often living in half-way houses until they are ready to function completely on their own. In most cases they are not paroled until a job is waiting for them, and therapy continues in the form of weekly group sessions and support from a parole agent. Formal discharge is not granted until they have achieved three years of drug-free life.

The second approach, the methadone blockade, is based on the fact that drugs of the opiate class produce a state of tolerance, and that tolerance induced by one drug in the group extends to others. Accordingly, the addict is given daily doses of the synthetic narcotic methadone, since this drug has been found to block the euphorigenic (euphoria-producing effects) of heroin and other opiates without producing abstinence symptoms or toxic effects, and without interfering with behavior in work or social life. Carefully controlled tests of the "double blind" type (in which neither the physician nor the subject knows whether the actual drug or a placebo is being given) have shown that even if heroin is taken while the patient is undergoing methadone treatment, the methadone will effectively block its euphoric action without itself producing euphoria or other narcotic effects.

In a pilot study reported by Dole, Nyswander, and Kreek (1966) and Dole and Nyswander, (1966), a group of over one hundred confirmed "mainline" addicts who had been unsuccessfully treated by all the usual methods were subjected to a three-step rehabilitation program based on the use of methadone. In phase one, the patients were hospitalized for six weeks and given small but increasing doses in an orange-flavored juice two or three times a day until a stable blocking dose was reached. In phase two, they were discharged to an outpatient clinic for a period of transition during which they continued to receive the drug while developing job skills and readjusting to society. During this phase they received group support from older addicts but without psychotherapy or group sessions. In phase three, the subjects reached a point where they could hold a steady job and live a responsible social life, while still taking maintenance doses of the drug.

A review conducted two and one fourth years after the start of the test showed that 11 per cent of the addicts had been discharged from treatment for psychopathic behavior unrelated to narcotics, but that treatment was highly successful with the remaining 89 per cent. All of these patients had lost their craving for heroin, side effects were minimal, sensitivity to pain remained normal, crime related to narcotic use was eliminated, and the great majority were holding regular jobs or going to school. More widespread applications of this treatment are now in progress in New York State (1968).

The third approach, group therapy in a community of addicts, is an intensive program of discipline, work, group therapy, and community living carried on by ex-addicts on the principle that only those who have experienced addiction can understand and help an addict. The original community, Synanon, was established by an ex-alcoholic, C. E. Dederich, in California as an outgrowth of discussions in his own home, which indicated that addicts have an intense need to verbalize their feelings and frustrations, and that communication with others who have similar problems can reduce dependency on drugs. The core of the communication process in Synanon is the aggressive group therapy session held several times a week, in which an ex-addict leader "leans heavily on his own insight into his own problems of personality in trying to help others find themselves, and will use the weapons of ridicule, crossexamination, and hostile attack as it becomes necessary" (Dederich). (The term Synanon is derived from a confused addict's mispronunciation of "seminar.") The basic therapeutic force of Synanon, however, is the community itself, which treats the addict as a member not an inmate, imposes rigid rules against violence and use of drugs and alcohol, and gives each member the chance to achieve status and recognition through hard work that contributes to the life of the entire group. One of the criticisms of Synanon is that practically all of the addicts remain in the close-knit community. One of the offshoots of Synanon, however—Daytop Village, on Staten Island, New York—makes it a practice to return the ex-addict to life in the outside world. The results of this approach are considered promising but still experimental.

Illustrative Case: DRUG ADDICTION, SYNANON

As a youth, Frankie had been a member of the violent Egyptian King gang. He became addicted in his early teens, and his pattern of life included armed robbery, pimping, and "pushing" heroin. Before the age of twenty-five, he had served time in two penitentiaries. His crime partner, a girl, once remarked: "Frankie would never use a knife; unless he had to. Mostly with his fists he would beat a guy down and try to kill him right there."

After a session in the Bellevue Hospital psychiatric ward, Frankie's family gave him a plane ticket to Los Angeles and told him to "straighten out or drop dead." On arriving, he tried to continue his customary way of life but had trouble getting a good drug connection and stealing enough money to supply his habit. On an impulse he decided to try Synanon "to get cleaned up a little." There he met "lots of hip people"—that is, criminals, addicts, and con men, but he soon found himself treated like a "young punk" instead of an admired operator. When he tried to assert himself by picking a fight with some of the members they refused and told him that if he insisted on fighting he would have to leave.

But Frankie stayed because "Synanon was better than anything else I could do at the time." The ostensible reason was that he had an opportunity to swim and dance and the meals were good. But perhaps the real reasons he remained were that he inwardly respected people he could not "con" and that he felt he was a member of a "family" which he could accept. Moreover, he could also make a name and a place for himself without being punished or locked up. He even found that he could become a director of Synanon itself, and this gave him a feeling of pride because the organization was already in the national spotlight. Frankie did not accept the Synanon way of life at once. He tried to make deals in his usual way, but was immediately given a "haircut" (a verbal dressing down) by men who were determined to protect the organization that had given them a new life. In the Synanon sessions, held three nights a week, he found that he could not "con" anyone, as he had been able to do with the group therapists in prison, where "I said what I thought they wanted to hear so I could hit the street sooner." In these sessions, he began to identify with the thoughts and feelings of others, and he also began to care about what happened to them.

Frankie's first job was in the kitchen, washing dishes, but he soon moved up to serving food at the counter. After several months, he was allowed to work on a truck which collected food donations from the neighborhood. While on a job, he and two others decided that "one shot wouldn't hurt," but the group was only able to obtain some sedative pills. They took them and when they returned, they were immediately spotted by the others. A general meeting was called, and their behavior was exposed and mercilessly condemned. On another occasion, Frankie was censured for failing to report that a Synanon member suggested that they take a drink. This was the first time he had ever been criticized for *not* "squealing."

Through these experiences, Frankie gradually realized that the group's life depended on keeping each other "straight"—exactly the opposite of his customary ethics. As he learned to express himself on a nonviolent, verbal level, he gave up his usual pattern of assaulting others, for he found that "talking to someone in the right way makes them do more things than belting them." He also lost his feeling that "work is for squares," and in time rose to the position of supervisor of one of Synanon's buildings. (Condensed from Yablonsky, 1962)

DRUG INTOXICATION. A number of medical drugs have been found to produce mental symptoms when taken in excessive doses over long periods. Large doses of thiocyanate, a drug which is sometimes used in the treatment of high blood pressure, occasionally causes cyanide poisoning. The symptoms are incoherent speech, confusion, disorientation, hallucinations, and convulsions. Belladonna, chloral hydrate, and paraldehyde have also been found to produce an acute delirious state in some patients. Excessive use of sulfa drugs (sulfonamides) may induce not only headaches and dizziness, but also confusion, inability to concentrate, and hallucinosis. Isoniazid, now widely used in the treatment of tuberculosis, occasionally causes such psychotic reactions as disorientation and auditory or visual hallucinations.

Mental disturbances have also been observed in some patients who have been given heavy doses of cortisone or ACTH. In these cases the reactions seem to depend largely on the personality of the patient, and include such widely diversified symptoms as excessive joviality, hypomania, apathy, depression, feelings of depersonalization, and flight of ideas. Some patients also experience illusions, delusions, and hallucinations. These symptoms usually disappear rapidly when the drug is discontinued.

DWARFISM. A severe congenital abnormality characterized by short stature and an appearance of premature senility due to the fact that the facial features are wizened, the hair sparse, and the skin wrinkled. Intelligence rarely develops above the severely retarded level, and the average life expectancy is less than twenty years. The condition is probably caused by multiple genetic defects.

In dwarfism of the achondroplastic type, the trunk is of normal size but the long bones of the arms and legs are foreshortened, and there are frequently other deformities such as a large head, sunken nose, and twisted spine. Mild forms of this defect may remain undiagnosed. Mental deficiency is not the rule, though some degree of mental impairment may occur. *See* MENTAL RETARDATION (CAUSES).

DYNAMIC APPROACH. Dynamic psychology and psychiatry approach the study of human behavior by examining underlying forces of motivation. This approach contrasts with the descriptive approach, which concentrates on the study of readily observable events such as the symptoms of disorders, the contents of consciousness, and the objective facts of behavior.

The descriptive approach is more concerned with naming, classifying, and diagnosing; the dynamic, with tracing behavior to its origins in prior experience. The dynamic approach is therefore concerned with the development of the individual and the events which have molded his personality, as well as the unconscious factors that are now influencing his attitudes and adjustment. A personality characteristic, a significant act or attitude, a symptom or syndrome—all these are viewed as products of many forces interacting within the individual. Among these forces are the basic physical drives, emotional needs, personal aspirations and ideals, self-concept, moral code, and defense measures that govern his behavior.

In a word, the dynamic approach is an inquiry into the whys and wherefores of the individual's adaptation to life. To carry it out it is necessary to explore past relationships with parents and siblings, early crises and how they were handled, present interpersonal relations, anxieties and reactions to anxiety, basic conflicts, and the unconscious motivations that influence adjustment. A descriptive approach merely notes that the individual is highly prejudiced or extremely competitive, or has chronic headaches or inhibiting fears; the dynamic approach probes beneath the surface to discover the reasons for these phenomena.

In the dynamic point of view, which dominates most of psychiatry today, the human being is conceived as active, changing, constantly adjusting and readjusting to the demands of life. In the history of psychiatry, Charcot, Janet, and particularly Freud laid the groundwork for this approach, and Adler, Jung, Sullivan, Horney, and many others have developed it in their own ways. In the field of psychology the dynamic approach is equally dominant, as evidenced by the vast amount of observation and experimentation devoted to the subject of motivation. See MOTIVATION, MOTIVATION RESEARCH, PSYCHOANALYSIS (THEORY), ADLER, JUNG, HORNEY, SULLIVAN, JANET, CHARCOT.

DYNAMIC PSYCHOLOGY. An eclectic approach developed by Robert S. Woodworth, which focuses on the motivating forces that underlie human behavior.

Woodworth's objective was not to create a new viewpoint in opposition to existing theories, but to bring together a variety of constructive approaches that were already in existence (Woodworth, 1958; Woodworth and Sheehan, 1964). He believed that behaviorism, Gestalt psychology, functionalism, and structuralism tended to investigate different aspects or levels of experience, and that each of them had much to contribute to the understanding of the mind. Likewise he recognized the importance of the early studies made at Columbia University, where he was a professor of psychology—particularly Cattell's work on individual differences in visual acuity, reaction time, etc., and Thorndike's studies of animal learning, transfer of training, and educational measurement.

Woodworth himself believed that psychology should take reactions as a starting point, and then proceed to study the conditions which determine them. Such an approach would open the way to an exploration of both consciousness and behavior, and the utilization of both introspectionist and behaviorist methods. He insisted that this dual approach is essential if we are to trace the entire chain of behavior from its inception to its conclusion.

An investigation of the causes of our reactions also involves both mechanisms and drives. A study of drives reveals *why* we behave as we do; a study of mechanisms explains *how* we behave. To take a simple example, the mechanisms involved in pitching a baseball are such factors as aim, distance, and co-ordination; an investigation of this behavior from the drive point of view would involve such questions as why the man became a pitcher instead of a fielder, why he pitches better to some batters than to others, and why he performs more effectively on sunny than on cloudy days. Woodworth believed that the state of the organism's internal drives plays an important part in determining whether a reaction will occur. The old formula was simply S-R, as if a magical tie existed between stimulus and response. Woodworth "put the organism back into the picture" and changed the formula to S-O-R, since he held that the drive state of the organism determines which stimuli will arouse a reaction. We do not eat if we are not hungry; we do not strive for advancement if we have a low level of aspiration. Our inner motives therefore inhibit some reactions and promote others.

The distinction between drive and mechanism is not an absolute one. A drive such as hunger or thirst is itself a mechanism, since it is a response of a living organism. On the other hand, a mechanism can have drive qualities since it may determine the character of the response—that is, even if the hunger drive of a cat and a human being were the same, the fact that these two species have different neural and muscular systems would lead to different types of behavior aimed at satisfying the hunger. Moreover, highly developed mechanisms tend to run on their own drives—for example, reading may be viewed as a mechanism, but once we develop our level of skill, it may demand its own expression. Simi-

larly, a businessman may be so accustomed to his daily activities that he feels miserable when he is forced to retire and cannot satisfy his work drive. This idea that mechanisms generate their own motive power is a forerunner of Allport's concept of functional autonomy.

Drives, then, occupy the central position in dynamic psychology. This view recalls the theory developed by McDougall, who also emphasized the importance of motivating forces. However, there are basic differences between the two theories. McDougall listed a limited number of instinctual drives and believed they were sufficient to account for the whole range of human behavior. He also conceived of the organism as an inert structure which these powerful forces act upon. Woodworth, on the contrary, felt that the organism is dynamic to the core, since its inner mechanisms determine the way drives are expressed and themselves become motivating forces. Moreover, he did not set any limit to the number or nature of these forces. He believed that human beings are not motivated simply by a few universal drives or instincts, but that each person possesses his own unique spectrum of natural capacities, needs, wishes, purposes, and emotions which set his personality in motion. The only way to do justice to these dynamic forces is to investigate people as individuals in order to discover why they behave the way they do. *See* FUNCTIONAL AUTONOMY, DYNAMIC APPROACH, MCDOUGALL.

DYNAMICS (PSYCHODYNAMICS). The force or pattern of forces which gives rise to a particular psychological event or condition, such as an act, attitude, symptom, or disorder. Psychodynamic forces consist of drives, wishes, emotions, and ego defense mechanisms acquired in the course of our development and experience. They also include basic biological urges, termed instincts in the Freudian theory. Psychological events are usually due to an interaction of many of these forces, some on a conscious and some on an unconscious level. *See* DYNAMIC APPROACH.

DYNAMISM (Mental Dynamism). A psychological device used to protect the ego; a defense mechanism, such as compensation or rationalization.

Defense mechanism is the more widely used term, but some theorists, such as H. S. Sullivan, prefer dynamism because it stresses the idea of active forces bringing about changes in our adaptive behavior, and mechanism seems to imply automatic, machinelike reactions. Many other terms are also used, such as adjustment devices, ego defense reactions, defense processes or strategies, behavior mechanisms, and coping mechanisms. The distinctions among these terms are largely on a verbal level, since they refer to the same types of reaction. They all denote techniques which people use in attempting to maintain their emotional security and self-esteem when confronted with difficulties which threaten their ego and arouse anxiety.

These patterns are acquired early in life as a means of coping with frustrations and conflicts, and are considered essentially normal and even necessary for personal adjustment. Some are more effective and some are more socially acceptable than others, but all of them tend to become important components of the personality and not just transient expedients. As Thorpe, Katz and Lewis (1961) remind us, "Since they are dynamic in nature, they may become habitual and persist long after the original threats have been removed or overcome." And since they are so closely involved in adjustment and are such an integral part of the self, any full description of an individual's personality should include the dynamisms—or mechanisms—he characteristically utilizes. *See* DEFENSE MECHANISM, MECHANISM, SULLIVAN.

DYSARTHRIA. Distorted speech usually due to disorders of the central nervous system, and less often to defective or damaged speech organs.

These neural and muscular defects interfere with the co-ordination needed for speech, impairing articulation in varying degrees. The tongue may move clumsily, the lips may flutter, jaw movements may be wrongly timed or disorganized, the larynx may be wrenched out of place, the chest may expand and produce inhalation while the individual is trying to talk (Van Riper, 1963). Some cerebral palsy patients cannot control speech muscles well enough to speak at all; others may be taught to utter understandable sounds even though their arms and legs make jerking movements and their face is contorted with effort.

Dysarthria is frequently due to congenital brain defect, as in cerebral palsy. The motor region in the frontal lobe is affected. It is also observed in patients who have suffered cortical damage due to severe head injury, brain tumor, Parkinson's disease, encephalitis lethargica, general paresis, chronic alcoholism, Huntington's chorea, and barbiturate poisoning.

DYSAUTONOMIA (Familial Dysautonomia). Dysfunction of the autonomic nervous system, believed to result from an obscure brain defect. The condition tends to run in families and is sometimes confused with childhood schizophrenia and mental retardation.

The dysautonomic child is tense, irritable, cannot adapt to change, and has difficulty performing complex motor or perceptual tasks. He is also likely to be emotionally unstable and to manifest a variety of physical disorders such as inability to shed tears, fluctuation of temperature, relative insensitivity to pain, and hyperhidrosis (excessive sweating). Barbiturate sedatives are effective in alleviating the physical symptoms in some cases, especially those in which the sympathetic portion of the auto-

nomic system is overactive. *See* AUTO-
NOMIC NERVOUS SYSTEM.

In a recent study by Sak et al. (1967)
the performance of twenty-five dysautonomic children referred by the Dysautonomia Association was compared
with that of a control group of ten
normal children on four tests: the
Wechsler Scales (five verbal, five nonverbal subtests), the Bender-Gestalt
(copying nine figures and reproducing
them from memory), the Goodenough
Draw-A-Person Test (drawing a figure,
then another of the opposite sex, and
telling a story about them), and the
Benton Left-Right Discrimination Test
(performing some simple tasks that indicate a preference for one eye, hand,
or leg).

On the full scale Wechsler, the dysautonomic children scored in the low
average range (averaging 86.4 versus
118 for the controls), with the most
pronounced retardation in nonverbal
skills. They usually (particularly the
older children) scored best on the similarities subtest, indicating an ability to
think abstractly, and worst on the object assembly human figure test, indicating a distorted self-image. The Bender-
Gestalt figures were copied and recalled
with great difficulty and many distortions (*Fig. 15*), with twenty-four of the

twenty-five subjects falling below their
age level, suggesting organic brain disorder.

Performance on the Draw-A-Person-
Test was considerably below the I.Q.
on the Wechsler test, probably reflecting
the generally poor scores on nonverbal
subtests. Moreover, from a clinical point
of view, the drawings were not only
extremely immature but bizarre, and
suggested a disturbance in self-image
typical of emotionally disturbed and so-

Fig. 16. The Goodenough Draw-A-Person
Test, as used in a study of dysautonomia.
Both subjects were fifteen years old and in
the average range of intelligence.

cially isolated individuals (*Fig. 16*). This
result tied up with their performance
on the face assembly subtest of the
Wechsler and was also demonstrated on
the Left-Right Discrimination Test.
They were usually unable to identify
right and left on the examiner, could
not identify parts of their own bodies,
and 65 per cent showed mixed dominance as compared with about 5 per
cent among unselected boys and girls.
In addition, a school survey of nineteen
of the twenty-five dysautonomic children
revealed that only two were able to
maintain a normal position; the rest
were either in special classes or had
repeated at least one grade.

In interpreting these findings, the authors suggest that the widespread sen-

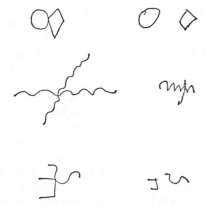

Fig. 15. The Bender-Gestalt Test, as used
in a study of dysautonomia. The subject
being tested is asked to reproduce the figure
on the left.

sory defects characteristic of this disease, as well as the highly emotional environment in which the children develop, both contribute to their poor performance. They believe there are indications of a central (brain) defect as well as a peripheral defect, and point out that recent evidence suggests that both types of deficit may be due in part at least to deficiencies in neurotransmission. *See* NERVE CONDUCTION, MINIMAL BRAIN DYSFUNCTION.

DYSLALIA. Disorders of articulation not due to overt defects of the central nervous system or speech mechanism. *See* DYSARTHRIA.

These disorders constitute the largest single group of speech problems in childhood, and include lisping, "baby talk," and other forms of infantile speech. In general, such conditions are due to (a) "maturational lag" in the development of sensory or motor functions involved in speech; (b) poor language patterns in the home, often aggravated by punitive or overindulgent attitudes of parents toward normal speech difficulties; or (c) insufficient stimulation and practice. Arnold (1957) states that "the child with functional dyslalia needs a longer period to acquire certain abilities which normal-speaking children master in average time. Such abilities as auditory discrimination and various motor skills are delayed in developing, and hence articulation, which depends on these abilities, is similarly delayed." If the dyslalia involves not only delayed speech but the prolonged use of infantile speech and grammar, with reading and spelling difficulties, it may be one aspect of a condition sometimes called "general language disability," which probably stems from minimal brain damage.

The term "baby talk" is frequently applied to immature speech in which sounds are either omitted (ittle for little), distorted (thum for some), or others substituted (tandy for candy). Lisping is usually but not always involved in baby talk. Errors of this kind are to be expected during the first years of speech and arise out of normal difficulties in articulating certain consonants, especially those requiring delicate and exact use of the tongue. These patterns are generally outgrown by five or six years of age if the parents set a good example, give the child ample opportunity to practice speaking, and pronounce difficult words clearly without actively correcting the child. But if baby talk persists beyond these ages, it is usually due to one or more of the following factors. First, the parents may be encouraging the child to speak like a baby because they think it is "cute," or they may set a pattern by using baby talk themselves. Second, by pressuring the child to grow up they may create an overcritical or rejecting atmosphere, and the resulting tensions may aggravate the child's natural speech difficulties. If these faulty approaches are modified and the child is encouraged but not prodded to become more mature in all respects, the baby talk will usually subside. Third, there may be an organic basis for the faulty articulation. In persistent cases therapy is indicated because the speech defect is bound to interfere with the child's social and emotional adjustment.

Speech correction is rarely recommended before the age of four or five, and must be preceded by a thorough examination and diagnostic evaluation, including tests of auditory discrimination, auditory memory, general motor co-ordination, co-ordination of the speech musculature, as well as a medical examination of the ears, mouth, teeth, and vocal cords. When speech therapy is undertaken, it usually follows a fairly regular course, for the therapist knows that certain sounds—l, r, k, g, v, th, and s—are generally hardest for a child to master. He determines which sounds the child can correct most easily and works on these first.

If the child makes no progress with

a certain sound, such as l, for two or three lessons, the therapist usually drops it for the time being and concentrates on others. In general, only one sound is worked on at a time, and the child is taught to produce it in isolation first, then in words, then sentences, and finally in practice conversation. All pressure is avoided, and the therapist usually limits himself to practice words which the child already knows. The lessons are kept on a "fun" level—for example, the child pastes colorful pictures in a book and learns word games which he can play with the teacher or a parent, brother, or sister. The teaching is usually supplemented by short home practice sessions, but parents are urged to refrain from correcting the child's speech at other times.

For infantile speech as a psychiatric symptom, *See* REGRESSION.

DYSSOCIAL REACTION. A "sociopathic" personality disorder in which the individual adopts a delinquent or criminal way of life as a result of distorted moral and social influences.

Studies indicate that about 10 per cent of children brought before children's courts are confirmed delinquents of this type. Most gangsters, racketeers, and other "public enemies" who make a career of criminal activity can also be classified as dyssocial personalities. In contrast to the psychopathic or antisocial personality, the dyssocial individual is not predominantly egocentric and impulsive, but is capable of strong loyalty and warm feeling for others. He is generally a well-integrated personality who can control his behavior and operate effectively within his own group —that is, within the "delinquent subculture." For this reason dyssocial reaction is sometimes termed "adaptive delinquency," as opposed to "maladaptive delinquency."

Typically, dyssocial individuals have acquired their distorted goals and behavior patterns by identifying with juvenile gangs or adult criminal models in the neighborhood. A large number of them, probably 50 per cent, come from broken homes, and in practically all cases their family life is characterized by neglect, disinterest, extremely harsh or extremely lax discipline, absence of affection, and general disorganization. Few of them, however, develop mental disorders of either a neurotic or psychotic character, probably because they tend to express their tensions in action, are single-minded and not in conflict about the pursuit of their goals, and are accepted and approved in their own social group. The following excerpt from *The Jack-Roller,* by C. R. Shaw, is a classic illustration of the development of the dyssocial reaction:

Illustrative Case: DYSSOCIAL REACTION

When I started to play in the alleys around my home I first heard about a bunch of older boys called the "Pirates." My oldest brother was in this gang and so I went around with them. There were about ten boys in this gang and the youngest one was eleven and the oldest one was about fifteen. . . .

Toni, Sollie, and my brother John were the big guys in the gang. Toni was fifteen and was short and heavy. He was a good fighter and the young guys were afraid of him because he hit them and beat them up. . . . My brother was fifteen and was bigger than Toni and was a good fighter. He could beat any guy in the gang by fighting, so he was a good leader and everybody looked up to him as a big guy. I looked up to him as a big guy and was proud to be his brother. . . .

When I started hanging out with the Pirates I first learned about robbin [sic]. The guys would talk about robbin and stealing and went out on "jobs" every night. When I was eight I started to go out robbin with my brother's gang. We first robbed junk from a junkyard and sometimes from the peddlar. Sometimes we robbed stores. We would go to a store, and while one guy asked to buy something the other guys would rob anything like candy and cigarettes and then run. We did this every day. . . .

The gang had a hangout in an alley and we would meet there every night and would smoke and tell stories and plan for robbin. I was little and so I only listened. . . . When I was ten the gang started to robbin stores and homes. We would jimmy the door open and rob the place. I always stayed outside and gave jiggers. The big guys went in and raided the place. They showed me how to pick locks, jimmy doors, cut glass and use skeleton keys and everything to get into stores and houses. Every guy had to keep everything a secret and not tell anybody or he would be beat up and razzed. The police were enemies and not to be trusted. When we would get caught by the police we had to keep mum and not tell a word even in the third degree. . . . A stool-pigeon was looked down on and razzed and could not stay in the gang. . . .

The guys stuck together and helped each other out of trouble. They were real good pals and would stick up for each other. (Shaw, 1930)

E

EARLY INFANTILE AUTISM. A psychotic disorder of infancy characterized by stereotyped behavior and a total lack of response or relationship to other people.

The condition, which is considered the most severe mental disorder of childhood, occurs more frequently in boys than in girls, and usually becomes apparent before the end of the first year (Kanner, 1944). These children cannot form emotional ties of any kind and develop an "impenetrable aloneness." The mothers consistently report that they cannot reach their baby: "He never smiled at me," "The minute she could walk, she ran away from me," "She never liked to be cuddled and kissed," "He never cried or even noticed when I left the room."

The behavior patterns of these children indicate that they are enclosing themselves in a restricted world of their own. Hour after hour they play with the same toy, go through the same motions, repeat the same phrases, use strange metaphorical expressions, or appear to talk irrelevantly and nonsensically if they talk at all. They become addicted to such activities as twirling, jumping, hand-clapping, turning light switches on and off, and cannot tolerate any change in daily routine, furniture arrangement or other surroundings. In this way they limit reality to something they can manage, for the ordinary world of sensory impressions and particularly of people is apparently too complex and threatening for them to cope with. They are contented only when they are left alone.

The psychoanalytic explanation of these behavior patterns is that these children have failed to establish a bridgehead to reality through their mother's love and the normal sensory experiences of babyhood. They have also failed to go through the regular sequence of psychosexual development (oral to anal satisfaction) which helps children develop a feeling for their own bodies. Instead, they adopt "autoaggressive" activities, such as biting themselves or knocking their heads, in an attempt to become aware of themselves and develop a sense of identity. Interestingly, they may refer to themselves as "you" and to another person as "I." Their confusion about their own ego leads them to relate to things but not to people.

Because of their limited responsiveness and stereotyped behavior, autistic children are sometimes thought to be mentally retarded. Usually, however, they are found to have average or superior intellectual capacity, and their facial expressions are generally intelligent though serious. More often than not, they come from superior homes, but in many cases the parents are preoccupied with their own interests and treat the child in a cold mechanical fashion: the "Frigidaire atmosphere." On the other hand, it must be recognized that many autistic children have warm, accepting parents, and that their other children may be quite normal. For this reason, researchers have sought other explanations for this condition. Recently, Rimland (1964) has attributed it to a single, highly specific cognitive defect stemming from a neurological disorder. There is also the possibility that it may be, as Redlich and Freedman (1966) suggest, "A collection of different etiologically determined diseases having very similar symptomatological manifestations," for "to date, researchers have implicated parental etiological factors, inborn constitutional factors, factors of brain damage, maturational lag, and factors of familial interaction."

In treating these children, the therapist encourages them to live through early stages of development, so that they may become aware of themselves and form an integrated ego. To enable them to relive the anal stage, for example, they are given clay and finger paint to play with and may even be permitted to soil. Though warm and permissive, the therapist shows them that they must not harm themselves or their surroundings. At the same time the children are lured out of their inner world through music and rhythmic activities, and are taught basic concepts of time and space which they missed because of their lack of communication with others. Follow-up studies show that between one third and one half of these children achieve a satisfactory social adjustment.

Illustrative Case: EARLY INFANTILE AUTISM

The girl was first admitted to a child psychiatry ward of a general hospital at the age of nine years. Her history was one of lifelong developmental retardation and deviant behavior that, hitherto, had been attributed to mental subnormality. The parents reported that during the first year of life she had been quiet, passive, and unresponsive to the parents and older sister. She did not sit up by herself until the age of nine months and only started to crawl when she was fifteen months old. She was able to stand alone at eighteen months but did not walk by herself until she was thirty months old. At this time she was tested psychologically and obtained a Cattell Infant Intelligence Scale I.Q. of 58.

When she was three years old the only words she spoke were "Mommie" and "Daddy," but at the age of five she suddenly began speaking whole sentences. A Stanford-Binet test administered at the time showed her I.Q. to be 77. On this basis, she was still considered to be mentally subnormal and was placed in special classes in the public school system for several years. At the age of eight she obtained a Stanford-Binet I.Q. of 85 and her teachers became increasingly concerned about her complete preoccupation with self-directed activity and with her inability to participate in any group activities. When she was nine she was able to do the work in the basic first-level reader and workbook, despite inattentiveness during reading instruction. Her workbook exercises were sometimes completed accurately, and sometimes the page was decorated with scrolls, curves, pictures, or drawings of bugs. She appeared happiest when looking through books on or pictures of science, birds, animals, or insects. She had a remarkable memory for details which was demonstrated in a most unusual ability to cut out freehand any bird or animal in a matter of minutes.

When she was admitted to the hospital, her two outstanding characteristics were self-isolation and an extreme need for sameness. Other deviant behavior that was observed or reported included: not talking aloud anywhere except in her home setting; refusing to exit through a door unless someone else opened it, and refusing to enter through a door unless she herself opened it; refusing baths because of a fear of water; fear of television, which had kept her parents from buying a set until recently; standing in one place and insisting that she was unable to move; negativism, which resulted in her doing the opposite of what was requested; responding to any physical contact with people by touching or hitting them; complete egocentricity or narcissism, with disregard for the feelings or wishes of others; interpreting any accidental hurt or discipline as a withdrawal of love; compulsive behavior, such as touching things or jumping off the last step when descending stairs; obsessional preoccupation with the letter K (with which she replaced her middle name) and the number 8; restricted interest patterns involving animals, birds, flowers, masculinity, femininity and pregnancy; enuresis, habitual at night and occasional during the day.

The patient was the second of four children; she had an older sister and two younger brothers. Her parents maintained that the pregnancy was planned and she was wanted, but it appeared that they might have preferred having had a boy and that the patient experienced some rejection following the birth of the older son. Psychological testing of the parents showed defensiveness but no gross personality disorder, and the only abnormal behavior identified in interviews with them was their excessive compliance with the patient's demands and their inability to set limits or reward her for more normal behavior.

In the hospital her deviant behavior was discouraged by ignoring it, whenever possible; every slight manifestation of social participation was reinforced and rewarded with increased attention and other means. For example, she was given second helpings of food at mealtimes only when she asked for them out loud; within three months she was talking out loud most of the time. Gradually, she learned that human relationships could be satisfying but could not always be obtained on her own terms.

About four months after admission she obtained a Stanford-Binet I.Q. of 95, and a few weeks later obtained a full scale I.Q. of 116 on the Wechsler Intelligence Scale for Children (verbal score 104 and performance scale 127). She was now ready to participate far more fully in school classes held in the hospital, and worked at a grade-three

level. After a little more than eight months in the hospital she was discharged to her parents but continued to attend a special class in public school for the remainder of the academic year. She and her mother also continued to see a child pyschiatrist at approximately monthly intervals. During the next two years both academic performance and social participation improved. She remained at a disadvantage in her relations with other children, however, as they were inclined to tease her and ridicule her behavior. Continuing difficulties were anticipated for her during adolescence and adult life. (Rosen and Gregory, 1965)

EBBINGHAUS, HERMANN (1850–1909).

Ebbinghaus, noted for his lasting contributions to the psychology of learning, was born in Barmen, Germany, studied at the University of Bonn and obtained his Ph.D. in philosophy in 1873. During the years that followed, in which he devoted himself to independent study, he came across Fechner's classic work, *Elements of Psychophysics*. While reading it, he realized that psychophysical methods had not as yet been applied to the study of memory. He therefore began to carry out a series of experiments in which he used himself as subject. When he was appointed instructor at the University of Berlin, he extended this experimental work to other subjects, and in 1885 published the celebrated monograph *On Memory*, which represents the first quantitative approach to the higher mental processes.

In his work on memory, Ebbinghaus suggested many principles and methods that have been incorporated in modern psychology. He invented the nonsense syllable, which advanced experimentation by eliminating already-formed associations, in this way equalizing the task for all subjects. He made the first systematic measurements of memory span, showing that seven to eight nonsense syllables could be learned at one reading. He introduced the concept of overlearning, and used the "savings method" to measure its effect. He quantified the process of forgetting, and constructed a standard curve which showed a large initial drop—that is, we forget most rapidly immediately after the learning has taken place. He demonstrated that meaningful material (stanzas from Byron's *Don Juan*) could be memorized in one ninth the time of nonsense syllables of equal length, and used the method of relearning to show that the effects of the original learning were still in evidence twenty-two years later.

In addition, Ebbinghaus proved that spaced learning is generally superior to massed learning and therefore study periods should usually be broken up, at least for highly factual material. And he showed that when we memorize a series of items, we establish backward as well as forward associations—for example, in A-B-C-D (the hyphens are associations), not only is A linked with B, but B with A, and the same for the other items in the series.

As Murphy (1949) has pointed out, Ebbinghaus' memory experiments were "one of the greatest triumphs of original genius in experimental psychology," and "set a new direction for psychology as dramatically and as clearly as did anything in this area." They brought him great acclaim which resulted in an appointment to a professorship at Berlin and later at Breslau and Halle. Between 1890 and his premature death in 1909, he opened up a number of other avenues of research, and presented his results in a lucid, personal style that has been compared with that of William James. While at Berlin, Ebbinghaus collaborated with Arthur König in founding the first German journal of general psychology (1890). He also performed experiments on brightness contrast, which he incorporated in a theory of color vision published in 1893. At Breslau he made a number of contributions to mental testing. The most noteworthy was the Ebbinghaus Completion Test which consisted of sen-

tences with missing words to be filled in by the subject—for example, "The . . . rises . . . . . . morning and . . . . . . night." By applying this test, which is still used, he showed that bright students did better than poor students and older children better than younger. These investigations, carried out in 1897, anticipated the more systematic work of Binet in 1903.

Ebbinghaus' final book, *Foundations of Psychology* (1902) was a highly successful and influential text. He was engaged in revising it at the time of his sudden death in 1909, a loss that was deeply felt by the academic community. In evaluating his contributions, Boring (1950) suggests that his importance lies not merely in his specific discoveries, but in helping to free psychology from its philosophical heritage and in stimulating others to investigate problems that cannot be solved by philosophical methods. In commenting on the fact that problems in learning and memory had rarely been approached scientifically, Ebbinghaus himself coined the apt and oft-quoted remark, "Psychology has a long past, but only a short history." *See* NONSENSE SYLLABLE, REMEMBERING, FORGETTING, LEARNING TECHNIQUES.

ECHOLALIA. A pathological reaction in which the patient mechanically repeats words or phrases uttered by another individual.

Echolalia is a form of automatic obedience due to heightened suggestibility, and appears to be related to "command automatism." In some cases it may represent a regression to mocking behavior in childhood, and an undercurrent of hostility is therefore suspected. The symptom is often observed in the catatonic form of schizophrenia. It is also found in latah, and in disorders involving brain damage and aphasia such as Pick's disease, Alzheimer's disease and diffuse sclerosis. *See* AUTOMATISM, EXOTIC PSYCHOSES,

PICK'S DISEASE, ALZHEIMER'S DISEASE, APHASIA.

ECHOPRAXIA. A pathological reaction in which the patient automatically imitates actions or gestures of another individual. If this person raises his arm, the patient will raise his arm; if he walks around in circles, the patient follows suit.

Echopraxia is a common symptom in catatonic schizophrenia. It may be accompanied by echolalia, which undoubtedly stems from the same sources. *See* AUTOMATISM, ECHOLALIA.

ECOLOGICAL STUDIES. Ecology is the scientific study of the mutual relations between organisms and their environment.

Ecological research on animals and plants focuses on their geographic distribution and the ways they adapt to a particular environment. It includes the study of seasonal cycles in plants and such animal behavior as eating habits, formation of groups, and the building of shelters of different kinds as a response to the particular climate, terrain, or materials found in the environment. Human ecology studies the way the physical characteristics of the environment affect social, economic, and political behavior. An example is the way individuals form a social structure that will enable them to adapt and survive in their particular environment: the close-knit family of the Eskimo contrasts sharply with the looser social groupings of migratory workers or occupants of trailer camps. Similarly, the fact that a group of people live in a mountainous terrain or close to a river may determine their whole way of life.

An increasing number of ecological studies have been made in the field of psychiatry and abnormal psychology. They include research on geographical distribution of mental disorders, urban-rural comparisons and the effects of special environments. A recent example is the Midtown Manhattan study of Srole and others (1962) which revealed that 9 per cent of the upper class, 18 per cent of the middle class and 28 per cent of the lower class living in the same area of New York City were afflicted with severe mental and emotional disturbances. (The incidence of individual disorders is reported in this book under each major reaction type.)

A number of ecological studies have also been made in the field of social psychology. One area of research is the geographical distribution of voting patterns on different economic levels and in various parts of the country. Sectional loyalty such as the "solid South," and minority group behavior such as "the Negro vote" are being re-examined today. Another example is the study of Wilner et al. (1952), who found that Negro and white families living in close proximity had more interaction and showed more respect for each other than others living widely apart—but this is by no means a universal finding. Moreover, mere physical distance cannot be easily separated from psychological circumstances such as the character of a housing development, its social climate, and the auspices under which it functions.

Other studies have investigated the interactions between children in the same cabins at summer camps, people living in the same housing development (or even in the same court), and in the same resettlement project. Loomis and Beegle (1950) found that in such situations the mere geographical proximity has considerable effect on newly formed relationships, but as time goes on people become sorted out according to such psychological factors as interests, personality, nationality and social attitudes. In the resettlement communities, for example, ranchers tended to visit ranchers and farmers visited farmers. Barker and Wright coined the term "behavior setting" for such situations, and use the term "psychological ecology" for the influence of environment on attitudes, personality, and behavior. An example is the fact that we act differently in a doctor's office, a classroom, and on a fishing trip. Note, however, that in these cases the environment is both physical and social.

Ecological considerations are found in a wide variety of other investigations. The classic Western Electric study of factory workers engaged in wiring components indicated that the positions in the front of the room had higher status than positions in the rear; also, cliques were formed on the basis of proximity of workers and work of the same type (Roethlisberger and Dickson, 1939). Seating positions in a factory cafeteria have also been found to follow geographical lines: office workers, plant workers, and supervisory personnel usually sit in separate groups and form their friendships accordingly. Investigations of primitive tribes, such as the Jibaro Indians, show that their hostility toward other tribes is often in direct proportion to the distance from them (Danielsson, 1949). On the other hand, Steinzor (1949) found that in discussion groups, the "social distance" was greater for people next to each other than for people on opposite sides of the circle—in other words, people sitting opposite each other interacted more than people sitting next to each other.

For other ecological studies, *see* PSYCHONEUROTIC DISORDERS, PSYCHOPHYSIOLOGIC DISORDERS (GENERAL), SCHIZOPHRENIC REACTIONS (ETIOLOGY), PSYCHOTIC DISORDERS, SUICIDE.

ECSTASY. An exalted feeling of rapture.

In sexual relations ecstasy is the climactic experience of pleasure, release, and unity that occurs in full orgasm. In religion it is the attainment of a sense of union with the power and perfection of the cosmos—a trancelike, metaphysical sensation that lifts the believer to another plane of being where he experiences a "peace that passeth understanding." In psychiatry it is an affective disturbance in which the patient feels a similar detachment from everyday reality accompanied by a sense of identification with cosmic power and the achievement of utter tranquility. The experience may be short-lived, but the patient has a vivid recollection of the episode, and may carry away from it a sense of having been reborn.

The psychiatric form of ecstasy is occasionally experienced in dissociative, schizophrenic, epileptic, and hypomanic reactions.

EDUCATIONAL PSYCHOLOGY. An area of applied psychology which includes the activities of school psychologists and educational psychologists.

These two groups have much in common, but their functions are distinct enough to warrant separate divisions in the American Psychological Association. The activities of the school psychologist include: observing, testing, and diagnosing learning and behavior problems of individual pupils; conferences with parents; organization and administration of the school's group testing program; participation in curriculum development; and in-service training of teachers with regard to test interpretation and problems of mental health. The educational psychologist serves on the faculty of a school of education or works in an educational research bureau. He is primarily concerned with teacher training, learning theory, and development of learning aids. Since all these subjects except teacher training and educational research are presented under separate topics, this article will be confined to some of the contributions of psychologists in these two fields. See SCHOOL PSYCHOLOGY.

The psychologist does not approach the problem of teacher training from the point of view of specific techniques or formulae. His emphasis is on the need for background material that will enable the teacher to understand how pupils think and behave, as well as the conditions under which they learn most effectively. Courses in educational psychology therefore include such subjects as child development, personality adjustment, learning processes, individual and group differences, and psychological testing. In these courses the prospective teacher does not learn how to present specific subjects, but acquires the kind of information he will need in approaching different classroom situations, in adapting his procedures to different requirements, and in dealing with different kinds of children and the problems they are likely to present. Hopefully, too, he learns to make full use of his own characteristics and to create a comfortable and stimulating classroom climate.

Many psychologists feel that the standard education courses tend to fall back on time-honored concepts and draw too little upon recent research. A few examples will be used to illustrate some of the more active fields of investigation. There is evidence that transfer of training is most effective when the task is learned in a variety of contexts and when the learner himself works out the principles (Haslerud and Myers, 1958). The old idea that praise is more effective than blame has been refined in a Swedish investigation which showed that the relative influence of praise and blame vary with the child's initial level of performance, attitude toward the teacher, anxiety level and type of task (Johannesson, 1962). Studies of children in deprived environments have shown that learning readiness is not only dependent on sensorimotor development but on the level of verbal communication and play opportunities in the home and neighborhood. Sarason and others (1960) have shown that anxiety which is barely observable on the surface may have a disruptive effect on children who appear to be working close to capacity. Studies of creativity by Guilford, Gallagher and others have suggested many ways of eliciting creative thinking among schoolchildren, such as asking them to think of unusual uses for tin cans and other common objects. *See* CREATIVITY TESTS, TRANSFER OF TRAINING.

At one time educational research was identified with the gathering of statistics on class size, attendance, teacher salaries etc.; today it is concerned with far more psychological problems, such as tests and measurements, thinking processes, and teacher characteristics. The construction and validation of tests is the primary concern of many educational psychologists, and two major publications are devoted to their findings, the *Journal of Educational Psychology* and *Educational and Psychological Measurement*. The schools of today are using, and in some cases overusing, a huge quantity of test material. The major types—readiness tests, intelligence tests, achievement tests, academic aptitude tests—are described elsewhere in this volume; here it should be noted that psychologists are not concerned merely with the development and administration of tests, but with such problems as the influence of practice and coaching on test scores and the effect of the child's emotional state upon his performance. *See* PSYCHOLOGICAL TESTING.

Considerable research has been done on the thinking processes utilized by the child in solving problems. Rimoldi (1960) has analyzed the questions which subjects ask in attacking problems, noting their number, sequence and effectiveness. On the basis of his findings he has set up training sessions in which they are given assistance in studying and improving their procedures for dealing with mathematical problems. This approach has proven effective and will probably be used more widely not only for training purposes but for the development of new approaches to teaching.

Research on teacher characteristics is another promising field. The difficulty here is that there is probably no single "good teacher," since the goals of education are complex and one teacher will be more effective in one situation and another in another. It is also difficult if not impossible to measure the actual effect of teaching on pupils since many factors other than teaching enter into pupil achievement. Nevertheless, some recent studies have been highly suggestive. In a six-year investigation conducted by American Council on Education, 6000 elementary and high school teachers were rated by trained observers, and analysis of their ratings revealed three major dimensions: (1) warm, understanding, friendly vs. aloof, egocentric and restricted; (2) responsible, businesslike, systematic vs. evading, unplanned, slipshod; (3) stimulating and imaginative vs. dull and routine (Ryans, 1960). An intensive investigation of fifty-five elementary school teachers made by Heil and others (1960) showed that the classes in which pupils made the greatest gains in achievement and friendliness were taught by teachers who were warm and understanding, but who at the same time emphasized planning and order. In other words, the first two dimensions of the A.C.E. dimensions were found to apply. Moreover, these results struck a blow against the free and easy, unplanned approach which some teachers identify with "permissiveness." *See* PROGRAMMED LEARNING, LEARNING TECHNIQUES, LEARNING AIDS, UNDERACHIEVER, OVERACHIEVER, SCHOOL PHOBIA, LEARNING (GENERAL), INTELLIGENCE TESTS, ACHIEVEMENT TESTS, SCHOLASTIC APTITUDE TESTS.

EFFECTORS. The organs of response and adjustment.

Effectors are the mechanisms by which organisms react to their environment. Effector cells were the first cells to be differentiated in the course of evolution, and in primitive species such as the sponge they combine the two functions of irritability and contractability—that is, they both receive and respond to stimuli. In time a further differentiation occurred, and certain cells or groups of cells became receptor mechanisms—the eye, for example—while others became response mechanisms or effectors. In man and other animals effectors consist of highly developed muscles and glands.

There are three kinds of muscles in the human body. The striated or striped muscles, made up of bands called fibrillae, enable the body to move or hold itself rigid. The smooth muscles, which are more primitive and spindle-shaped, control the movements involved in digestion as well as the expansion and contraction of blood vessels. The cardiac muscle is a special network of striated muscle cells found only in the heart. It performs its cycle of contraction and relaxation about eighty times a minute throughout life. This muscle and the smooth muscles are termed involuntary, while the striated muscles are termed voluntary, even though they frequently operate by automatic, reflex activity.

The glands are classed as effectors because most but not all of them are innervated by effector neurons of the nervous system. The duct or exocrine glands secrete directly into the cavities of the body or onto its surface. They consist of the salivary glands, the tear glands, the sweat glands, the mucous glands, the liver, the kidneys, the mammary glands, the sebaceous glands, and the many glands in the stomach and intestines that produce substances aiding in digestion.

The ductless or endocrine glands discharge their secretions, called hormones, directly into the blood stream. Six of these glands are particularly important in psychology and psychiatry because of their effects on behavior as well as on the internal environment of the organism. These are (1) the pituitary: the anterior portion regulates growth and acts as a master gland, influencing the thyroid, pancreas, adrenals and gonads, while the posterior portion controls water metabolism; (2) the thyroid, regulating metabolic rate and thereby affecting activity level, fatigue, and body weight; (3) the parathyroids, controlling calcium metabolism and the excitability of the nervous system; (4) the pancreas, regulating sugar metabolism by means of secretion of insulin; (5) the adrenals: the cortex maintains life processes as well as salt and carbohydrate metabolism, while the medulla governs physiological changes in emotion; and (6) the gonads, which determine secondary sexual characteristics and maintain the functioning of the reproductive apparatus in both male and female. Others are the thymus, lying behind the breastbone, which is large in infancy and gradually shrinks: it is believed to play a role in building immunity and possibly in regulating growth and maturity; and the pineal gland, situated between the cerebral hemispheres, whose functions are still in doubt, although tumors in this gland are one of the causes of precocious sexual development. *See* PITUITARY GLAND, ADRENAL GLANDS, GONADS, THYROID GLAND, PARATHYROID GLANDS, PINEAL GLAND.

EGO. A psychoanalytic term denoting the part of the personality which carries on relationships with the external world.

The ego is conceived as a group of functions that enable us to perceive, reason, make judgments, store knowledge, and solve problems. It has been called the executive agency of the personality, and its many functions enable us to modify our instinctual impulses (the id), make compromises with demands of the superego (conscience, ideals), and in general deal rationally and effectively with reality. It operates largely but not entirely on a conscious level, and in a mature person is guided less often by the pleasure principle than by the reality principle—that is, the practical demands of life. It may, however, be torn between these two opposing forces.

The ego, unlike the id, is not ready-made at birth. It develops slowly as the child learns to master his impulses, know what behavior the world requires, and use intelligence in meeting difficulties. A person who develops a "strong ego" successfully integrates the demands of the id, superego, and reality. He therefore does not have to resort to rigid defenses or escape mechanisms in handling the stresses of life. An individual with a "weak ego" is dominated by unconscious impulses and may disintegrate under strain, with the result that mental symptoms or character defects are likely to develop. *See* ID, SUPEREGO, PSYCHOANALYSIS (THEORY).

EGO IDEAL. The image of the self we would like to be or think we ought to become.

The ego ideal comprises our aspirations and goals, as well as our ideals of character and conduct. In the Freudian theory it is an aspect of the superego, or conscience, which is composed of our standards of good and bad, right and wrong.

In some individuals, the ego ideal is vague and half-formed; in others it is conscious and clearly formulated. In any case it is an essential and revealing aspect of our personality and helps to define the kind of person we are or wish to become. It has been found that outside observers may be better able to describe our ego ideal than we can, since many of us tend to deceive ourselves about our real values and goals.

The ego ideal is primarily the result of our tendency to emulate people or ways of life we admire. Society offers us an unlimited variety of models, beginning with our parents and gradually broadening out to include other relatives, teachers, companions, or persons we read or hear about. These models may range in character from the thoroughly pedestrian to the flamboyant and heroic, and from the most upright to the most irresponsible. But whatever its source or content, our ego ideal is a potent force in determining our behavior and style of life. *See* EGO, SUPEREGO, IDENTIFICATION, PSYCHOANALYSIS (THEORY).

EGO-INVOLVEMENT. The perception of a situation in terms of its relation to our purposes and satisfactions. Sherif and Sherif, who have developed the concept, define it more explicitly as "circumstances in which attitudes relative to the person himself and his possessions, the people, groups, values and institutions with which he is involved are engaged" (1956).

We do not react to all situations with the same degree of effort or concern. If our favorite tennis star loses, we are not likely to take it seriously; if we ourselves are defeated by an inferior player, we are somewhat more upset; and if we are dismissed from a job or lose the respect of a friend, we will probably feel extremely disturbed. As these examples indicate, the more deeply our goals or self-esteem are concerned—that is, the more ego-involved we are—the more intense our reactions. In this connection Cofer and Appley (1965) point out that situations in which we are ego-involved have the capacity of bringing about a state of arousal or stress. In fact, these situations may produce so much discomfort or suffering that we call one or another defense mechanism into play, such as rationalizing our failures, blaming our shortcomings on others, or insisting that "it doesn't really matter."

Ego-involvement is a broad concept that brings together many aspects of experience. It helps to account for our inner conflicts, our self-concept, and the feelings of frustration we so often experience. As Coleman (1964) suggests, the mobilization of our energy and our activity level are largely determined by ego-involvement: "The individual who is strongly ego involved in becoming a physician is willing to make more sacrifices and devote more energy and effort to his studies than the individual who is going into medicine because his parents want him to do so." The concept is also put to practical use in the commercial and industrial world. Large firms use many devices, such as company newspapers, suggestion boxes and films to raise the level of involvement of their employees. Advertisers often take the public "behind the scenes" to show how the product is made, the problems involved in manufacturing, and the concern of the company for the welfare of the customer. Surveys conducted by market research organizations also keep this end in view.

The concept of ego-involvement has led to many psychological experiments. Most of them are based on "the possibility of interference with or deprivation of the need to enhance or to maintain one's feeling of self-esteem" (Iverson and Reuder, 1956). A common technique is to tell a group of students that the test they are about to take will become a part of their permanent record, and then to note their reactions when they are told they have done poorly or well. The information about success or failure may be true or false, and, as Cofer and Appley point out, much depends on the credulity of the subjects. (Also, the procedure is only likely to have an effect in a culture like that of middle-class America, where intellectual achievement is highly rewarded.) One rather consistent finding is that subjects rated low in anxiety and/or high in need for achievement on separate tests tend to improve their scores on subsequent tests when they are told they have done poorly, but subjects with a low need for achievement and a high anxiety level do less well. Alper (1946) has also shown that ego-involved subjects retain memorized material longer than control groups. Conversely it has been found that when two memory tasks are presented consecutively and the subject is told he has done poorly on the second, retention of the first is adversely affected—an apparent case of retroactive inhibition due to the feeling of failure. Rosenthal (1944) and Zeller (1950, 1951) have shown that in such cases both hypnosis and later success can lead to the recovery of the material. *See* FORGETTING.

Another general finding is that when failure is induced, subjects tend to remember completed tasks better than uncompleted tasks (Rosenzweig, 1943; Glixman, 1949). The more the subject feels threatened by failure, the more this is true (Eriksen, 1954). This is the reverse of the usual finding in such experiments, probably because our self-esteem is more involved in tasks we have completed than in tasks that have been interrupted by others. Experiments by Edwards (1942) also showed that subjects tended to remember more statements about the New Deal that agreed with their own views than statements that disagreed with their position. Similarly Cofer and Appley report that many other investigators "have found that recall is superior for material that agreed with the subject's attitudes, values or beliefs, for materials favorable to his sex or color, for materials produced by the subject, such as associations, and for story titles labelled normal rather than abnormal." However, they also point out that in practically all experiments on ego-involvement there are large individual differences in response. *See* ZEIGARNIK EFFECT.

EGOMANIA. Morbid preoccupation with one's self; the tendency to be totally self-centered, or egocentric.

The egomaniac is extremely selfish, callous to the needs of other people, and often conceited and egotistical. Egocentricity is one of the more general characteristics of neurotics, and it may sometimes be extreme enough to be called egomania. Neurotics tend to be painfully aware of themselves, over-concerned about their own feelings, wishes and ambitions. As a consequence, they may become insensitive to the rights or interests of other people, make unrealistic demands on their associates, and eventually antagonize them.

Psychopathic or antisocial individuals also tend to be highly self-centered, but in a somewhat different sense. Unlike the neurotic, who is self-concerned because he is anxious and insecure, these people are out to get what they want without consideration of others, placing immediate gratification of their own impulses and desires above all other goals. *See* NARCISSISM, ANTISOCIAL REACTION.

EGO PSYCHOTHERAPY. A therapeutic approach developed by Paul Federn and his disciple Edoardo Weiss, based upon the theory that mental disturbance involves a blurring of the boundaries between the ego and outer reality or between the ego and the id. The approach is applicable primarily to psychotic and schizoid disorders.

Though Federn was an associate of Freud, he created a theory of the ego and a treatment technique which differed sharply from those of classical psychoanalysis. In contrast to Freud, who conceived the ego in terms of consciousness and "executive functions," Federn defined it as "the feeling of unity in continuity, contiguity and causality in the experience of an individual" (1952). The ego is therefore equated with ego *feeling,* which can remain unified even though the contents of experience are constantly changing. The experience of "I" is generated by what he called the "ego-cathecting" of mental contents, a process in which energy arising from body metabolism is used as an integrating force. The stronger the "binding capacity," or integrating ability, of the ego, the better it can endure frustration, give acceptable expression to id impulses (sex, aggression etc.), and maintain a clear boundary between the ego and the outside world.

In Federn's view, the healthy ego not only has boundaries which separate it from external reality, but boundaries which separate it from the id. There are, then, basically two kinds of "ego states." "Reality" is sensed when energy from the id or from the outside world crosses these boundaries. But if the boundaries are disturbed, profound mental disorder sets in. Where the boundary between the ego and the id has been weakened, primitive id material may break through and be experienced as hallucinations; where the boundary between the ego and external reality is blurred, the patient often experiences feelings of estrangement and depersonalization. These feelings—the sense of being in an alien world and the sense of unreality—are steps on the way to loss of contact with the outside world. They are due to "loss of the ego's inner firmness" (Weiss, 1952), or loss of the ability of the "ego nucleus" to integrate new experiences with old ones and to relate them to already acquired knowledge in terms of time, place, and causality—a process to which Federn applies the old term "apperception."

Therapy is largely a question of redirecting the "ego cathexis," or integrating force, so that the patient can exert control over his id and distinguish himself and his mental contents from external reality. It attempts (a) to bring about a better balance in the expenditure of the ego energy, so that it will be utilized more effectively in dealing with impulses and relationships with the outside world; (b) to increase the "reality testing" ability of the patient by helping him understand the process by which he "misperceives" reality and by encouraging him to check his subjective thoughts, feelings, and impulses ("inner mentality") against objective fact or "external reality"; and (c) to bring about repression of the id, in contradistinction from Freud, who sought to release its contents. See CATHEXIS.

Federn introduced a number of therapeutic approaches in the treatment of psychoses which were at variance with the psychoanalytic school. He eliminated the anamnesis or autobiographical history of the patient on the ground that the memories of former psychotic episodes would release the id and lead to a relapse. He felt that the patient needs the continual support of the therapist outside as well as inside the analytic sessions, and recommended that treatment be interrupted if a negative transference takes place. He did not, however, encourage the development of a transference neurosis, which is an integral part of the Freudian technique, since this would become a transference psychosis. (A transference neurosis is an intense attachment or antagonism toward the therapist stemming from childhood attitudes toward the parents). He advocated reinforcing rather than removing resistance to disclosure of unconscious material, since he believed the psychotic process was already producing too much of this material. He dispensed with the couch and the recumbent position of the patient, since this not only encouraged the production of unconscious material but also because he thought the patient would make more normal associations while sitting up. He felt that a moderate amount of sexual gratification would promote recovery. (Freud insisted on celibacy during analysis because he felt that the energy of the libido would help to release unconscious impulses.) He believed in working with the family and environment of the patient in order to help him solve current problems of adjustment. And finally he insisted that treatment could not be successful without the help of a skilled woman, on the premise that the mother is the original source of support of the patient's ego. *See* TRANSFERENCE.

In carrying out his procedures, Federn held that a successful transference could be established with schizophrenic patients even when they were severely deteriorated and were considered "unreachable." He insisted that the boundaries between the mental world and the real world could be re-established if the therapist confines himself to simple explanations, reality testing, and emotional support while the patient is in the psychotic state, using only very small doses of typical analysis.

EGO STRENGTH. A term used by psychoanalysts and others for the ability of the ego, or conscious self, to maintain an effective balance between inner impulses and the demands of outer reality. In Freudian phraseology, it is the capacity of the ego to mediate between the id, and superego and reality—that is, between instinctual impulses, conscience, and the situations of life.

A person with a strong ego has high frustration tolerance and is able to control his impulses and modify his selfish desires and "primitive urges" to conform to socially acceptable patterns. He shows flexibility in handling the stresses of life and does not resort to rigid defenses or inflexible behavior. A person with a weak ego is dominated by unconscious feelings and impulses and has poor tolerance for frustration, disappointment, and other forms of stress. When confronted with psychological problems he suffers from conflicts and anxieties, makes excessive use of defense mechanisms, and may develop character defects or psychiatric symptoms. Neurotics to some extent, and

psychotics to a greater extent, are lacking in adequate ego strength.

One of the major aspects of personality development can be put in terms of ego strength. The small child tends to be dominated by his impulses of the moment, and must gradually develop the power to manage his urges, emotions and actions. A temper tantrum is a good example of ego weakness. In the course of growing up the child must also learn to endure failure and defeat, and to react constructively to situations of stress. In other words, he must build frustration tolerance and stress tolerance. He must also learn to adapt to social and moral requirements without sacrificing his own individuality. This problem becomes particularly acute during adolescence. A club or group of peers may help to solve it, since it often provides the kind of group support and adolescent needs in his search for ways to express himself and at the same time keeps him from feeling that he is simply surrendering to the demands of the adult world.

Ego strength is an important concept not only in assessing personality health and growth, but in the therapeutic process. One important goal of psychotherapy and social work is to find ways of increasing ego strength. Supportive measures such as encouragement, reassurance and friendliness are often effective. Sometimes the patient has to live on borrowed ego strength for a time until he can build up his own.

The whole process and aim of psychoanalysis has been put in terms of this concept. At the start of the therapy, the analyst must appraise the patient's ego strength to see whether the analytic approach is possible. As Greenson (1959) has pointed out, he must have "a relatively strong ego in areas relatively free of neurotic conflict . . . so that he can work effectively with the interpretations." In the course of the therapy the analyst must also assess the strength of the patient's ego to see whether he can confront his own dangerous impulses and the painful feelings he is bound to experience as he gains insight. This will determine the "dosage and timing of interpretation." Finally the termination of the treatment depends largely on the amount of increase in the patient's ego strength—that is, whether he has developed a "more reasonable and tolerant superego" and can express his id impulses on a more mature level, in keeping with the requirements of external reality. "The analyst's goal is to provide insight to the patient so that he may himself resolve his neurotic conflicts—thus effecting permanent changes in his ego, id, and superego, and thereby extending the power and sovereignty of his ego." (Greenson) See EGO.

EGO SYNTONIC. A term used largely by psychoanalysts to describe impulses, values or behavior that are acceptable to or consonant with the aims of the ego, the portion of the personality which directs our actions and mediates between our inner needs and outer reality. Attitudes and actions that are repugnant to or at variance with the ego are termed ego dystonic. To illustrate: the irresponsible, egocentric behavior of psychopathic, or antisocial, individuals is extremely hard to modify because it is not in conflict with their basic personality—that is, it is ego syntonic. Homosexual behavior, on the other hand, is sometimes repulsive to the homosexual himself, and therefore ego dystonic. Similarly, hallucinations brought about by such drugs as mescaline and LSD may be completely foreign to the individual, while hallucinations that occur in schizophrenia are believed to express the patient's emotional needs, and are therefore ego syntonic. See EGO.

EIDETIC IMAGERY (Photographic Memory). Mental imagery, usually visual, which closely resembles actual perception.

Some people are able to look at a drawing or page of print for a short time and later see it in their "mind's eye" with amazing vividness. They appear to "project" the image on a mental screen and are able to describe every detail as if they were still looking at the object itself. Some "Eidetikers" claim they can even enlarge portions of the mental picture in order to see them more clearly.

Eidetic imagery is found in 5 to 10 per cent of children, but usually disappears before adolescence. The few adults who retain this ability can often perform feats of "photographic memory," such as repeating the entire content of a newspaper page after looking at it for only a few minutes. Some "lightning calculators" are Eidetikers who are able to keep one part of a long problem on their "mental blackboard" while working on another. In addition, adults occasionally experience a form of eidetic imagery for a short time after engaging in fatiguing activity of a monotonous nature, such as playing cards or closely studying blueprints. The images are so vivid and realistic that they are sometimes momentarily mistaken for the actual objects. A similar if not identical phenomenon is occasionally found in patients with tetany and Basedow's disease (hyperthyroidism).

A common test for eidetic imagery is to ask a subject to look briefly at a picture containing many details, including, say, a twelve-digit figure, or a long word in a language he does not know. If he is a genuine Eidetiker, he will be able to describe every detail and repeat the number or the letters of the word forward and backward. An even simpler test is to show him a comb for a moment, then ask him how many teeth it contained. A true Eidetiker will summon up the image and count the teeth even after several minutes or even hours have elapsed. Occasionally one comes across an acoustic, or auditory, Eidetiker. Here the test is to read aloud a long list of digits and ask the subject to repeat them. An Eidetiker will be able to repeat three or four times as many as the average individual.

ELATION. A mood of exaggerated well-being and joyous excitement accompanied by restless energy and a confident, optimistic attitude.

The most typical psychiatric manifestation of elation is found in acute mania. The patient has an air of overriding cheerfulness, and proposes unrealistic schemes that will work wonders without fail—if only he can put them before the proper authorities. He brushes aside all objections and brooks no criticism. When his activities are opposed or curbed, the elevated mood may abruptly change to irritability and anger.

Periods of elation are also observed in general paresis, psychosis with brain tumor, and schizophrenic excitement. *See* MANIC-DEPRESSIVE REACTION (MANIC PHASE), EUPHORIA, ECSTASY.

Illustrative Case: ELATION (MANIC-DEPRESSIVE REACTION)

"There is absolutely nothing the matter. Everything is perfect, all is peace and love. I feel fine—perfect. Everything is hotsy-totsy now. My only complaint is Patsy isn't here. I have never been sick. I have always been good or else God couldn't have lifted me up. Now Adam made a mistake and he's doing time now. I never did. I was perfect and I see the light and love. He sent my mother and father down here as the best in order to have me. They were perfect when they had me—I've always been clean." (Muncie, 1939)

ELECTROSHOCK THERAPY (Electroconvulsive Therapy; EST, ECT). Convulsive therapy was originated by the Hungarian psychiatrist, Ladislaus J. Meduna in 1935, after he had noted that epilepsy and schizophrenia rarely occur together, and that psychotic symptoms may temporarily disappear after

spontaneous convulsions. Reasoning that a "biological antagonism" existed between epilepsy and schizophrenia, he began to induce convulsions by using, first, injections of camphor and oil, and later the drug metrazol. This treatment was later abandoned as "barbaric" as a result of the high incidence of fatalities and fractures and of the intense feelings of fear and apprehension experienced by the patients during the few moments between receiving the injection and losing consciousness. The idea of inducing convulsive seizures, however, was not abandoned, and in 1938 Ugo Cerletti and L. Bini introduced electroconvulsive therapy in Italy.

In the ECT procedure the patient is placed on a well-padded bed with a rubber gag between his teeth to prevent injury to the tongue. Today succinylcholine (Anectine) or other muscle relaxants are administered to "soften" the seizure, and virtually eliminate any danger of dislocations or fractures. Electrodes are lightly clamped to the temples and a current ranging from 70 to 130 volts is applied for .1 to .5 seconds. Since the electric current travels faster than the nerve impulse, the patient loses consciousness before he can feel any pain. He immediately goes into a brief two-stage convulsion: in the tonic phase the muscles become rigid for about ten seconds; and in the clonic phase spasmodic, quivering contractions occur throughout the body for about thirty to forty seconds. When these contractions have subsided, the patient remains unconscious for another ten to thirty minutes. After awakening he appears drowsy and confused for an hour or so, and cannot remember the shock or the events immediately preceding it.

Electroshock treatment is usually contraindicated or postponed with patients who have had recent heart attacks, but is considered safe for practically all other patients, including the pregnant and the aged, when proper precautions are applied. Though some patients readily accept the treatment, others are apprehensive and may be given drugs to allay their anxiety. Treatments are generally administered two to three times a week, with depressives requiring five to ten treatments and schizophrenics twenty or more. A variation known as regressive shock therapy, in which the patient receives two or three treatments per day has also been tried. Electroshock treatment practically always produces some amnesia, which disappears in a few hours, but the regressive technique results in extensive amnesia, confusion, and reversion to infantile behavior for a period of weeks. It is said to be helpful with antisocial personalities, highly resistant cases of schizophrenia, and pseudoneurotic schizophrenia, but is still considered experimental. Other variations, such as applying the current only to the nondominant lobe of the brain (Cannicott, 1963), and electronarcosis, in which a shock is applied for thirty seconds instead of less than one second, are also under study.

ECT is remarkably effectual with affective disorders. A short course of treatments produces dramatic improvement, often amounting to full recovery in at least 90 per cent of involutional melancholics and manic-depressives in the depressed phase. It is somewhat less effective with manic reactions, for even though the symptoms may often be alleviated after three or four treatments, the improvement tends to be unstable. Recovery rates as high as 68 per cent for catatonic schizophrenia have been reported (Kalinowsky and Hoch, 1961). The treatment is less successful with paranoid schizophrenics, and of limited value with simple and hebephrenic types. It is considered ineffective for neurotic patients, with the exception of neurotic depressive reactions. In general, ECT produces its best results where (a) the disorder is of recent and rapid onset, (b) the premorbid personality was relatively stable, (c) the patient is emotionally responsive, and (d) external stresses play a greater role than internal, or "endogenous" factors in precipitating a breakdown. These points apply to other forms of treatment as well.

During the years following the introduction of tranquilizers and antidepressants there was a strong trend toward replacing ECT with drug therapy except in acute, urgent cases—but recently the use of ECT has increased. In reviewing the comparative value of the two procedures, Kalinowsky (1964) makes the following points. First, though antidepressants bring improvement in a fairly high percentage of depressives, ECT leads to far more full recoveries—and if drug treatments are used first, and prove insufficient, private patients often cannot afford the extra expense of ECT. Second, depressive patients quickly lose their suicidal tendencies under ECT, but the drug patient recovers more slowly and may retain his suicidal impulses even after he has gained enough initiative to act on them.

Third, various investigators (Hoffet, 1962; Flynn and Hirsch, 1962) report only about 50 to 55 per cent success in treating pure depressions with drugs, as compared with 90 to 95 per cent with ECT. Some studies have also shown that ECT is successful in practically all pure depressions where drugs have failed to produce results. However, ECT is less effective than drugs with milder depressions, those of the reactive and psychoneurotic type—but there is no need to use it in these cases since there is less danger of suicide. Drugs may also be administered to patients who show incomplete recovery after ECT; as a preventive measure in recurrent depressions; and with older patients who are chronically depressed.

Fourth, in schizophrenic reactions, ECT is generally effective only in the first year or two of illness, but drugs tend to remain efficacious no matter how long the disease has lasted. In addition, they also render many patients accessible to psychotherapy. In acute cases both types of treatment may successfully remove symptoms, but ECT usually produces more dramatic results and leads to fewer difficulties with patients who have physical complications. In less acute cases pharmacotherapy is generally justified, though remission tends to be "longer lasting and of better quality" among shock-treated patients than among those treated with drugs. As to other conditions, drug treatment is recommended over ECT for cases showing a mixture of schizophrenic, depressive, and neurotic symptoms, addiction withdrawal symptoms, psychotic episodes in chronic organic brain disease, and psychoses associated with postoperative, toxic, and infectious disorders.

There is little agreement on the reasons for the effectiveness of ECT, but there is no dearth of theories, both psychological and physiological. Psychologically, its effectiveness has been attributed to the attention given the patient, reorganization of thinking processes during the amnesic episode, unconscious interpretation of the shock as an expiation for sins, and mobilization of the patient's "vital instincts" as he faces the sudden threat of death in losing consciousness. None of these explanations is sufficient, for attention to the patient does not in itself effect a cure, the treatment is beneficial even when amnesia does not occur, patients who do not have guilt feelings often recover; and many patients experience no fear of the treatment and no feelings that it threatens their life.

The physiological theories are equally inadequate. Meduna's theory of an antagonism between schizophrenia and epileptic convulsions does not hold, since the two are actually found together more often than he believed—and besides, convulsive therapy is even more effective with depressive than with schizophrenic disorders. The theory has also been advanced that the temporary anoxia produced by ECT accounts for its effectiveness. No satisfactory explanation has been given as to how or why this occurs and, moreover, reduced oxygenation is only a short-lived effect and may be entirely avoided by the use of Anectine. Cerletti, the co-originator of the technique, has suggested that the electric current acts as a stressor that releases a defensive substance which has a stimulating effect on the nervous system—but he was unable to isolate this substance, if it exists at all. So far, then, ECT remains in the realm of empirical medicine, along with many other treatments of undoubted value.

ELIMINATION DRIVES. The physical and developmental facts about urination and defecation are simple and clear-cut as compared to the amount of theory and emotional concern these processes have generated. The healthy infant eliminates without showing any very noticeable reactions during the first month of life, but during the second month the bowel function is accompanied by flushing, leg tensions, and breathing changes. Defecation usually occurs after feeding and may be stimulated by warmth and cuddling. Tension and "nervousness" apparently interfere with the process, as shown by the fact that infants who receive little or no mothering at home or in an institution are usually constipated (Ribble, 1944). In most cases, however, children respond readily to the muscular pressure patterns that signalize a "need." They also come to assume the postural pattern of urination associated with their sex. Among human beings this is probably the result of imitative learning or direct teaching rather than constitutional differences, but Berg (1944) has found that among male and female dogs the differences in posture are due in part at least to the sex hormones.

On the average, bowel control is achieved with occasional relapses by the time the child is ten to twelve months of age, and bladder control by the age two or two and a half. Gentle reminders that help the child become aware of his own needs are far more effective than nagging, threats, or overemphasis on cleanliness. Any form of pressure may arouse tensions and resentments which hold back the learning process. *See* TOILET TRAINING.

Many psychologists and psychiatrists believe the child experiences his first feelings of power and productivity during elimination. This helps to account for the pride he takes in his own "products," and also his desire to handle the material he has produced as well as similar materials such as clay, mud, and finger paint. The eliminative process also stimulates normal curiosity which can usually be satisfied by touching the feces once or twice. This curiosity usually extends to the toilet itself, but once the child is shown how it works he will no longer be particularly interested in it. However, it is important to avoid the suggestion that he might fall into it or be flushed away, since this would lead to emotional tension and interfere with the rather delicate process of learning bowel and bladder control.

Some theorists, especially of the psychoanalytic school, go much farther in this direction and hold that touching the feces is such a basic expression of curiosity that the child may become generally inhibited if it is not gratified. This school of thought also maintains that the eliminative processes are one of the fundamental expressions of the libido, and therefore provide erotic pleasure. At the same time the child finds that he can exert power over others by "holding back." If he does not adequately "work through" both these phases of the "anal stage," he may become overconcerned with "bathroom jokes" and anal forms of sexual expression, or he may develop a rigid or sadistic "anal character." The analytic school also points to certain cases

of advanced schizophrenia in which patients devour their own waste products. This school explains such behavior on the ground that (a) the patients are reverting to the infantile stage in which the child does not differentiate between himself and what comes out of himself, and (b) they consume their own wastes for fear that they are losing a part of themselves. *See* ANAL CHARACTER, COPROPHILIA, PSYCHOSEXUAL DEVELOPMENT.

The eliminative system is intimately associated with emotional expression through the activity of the autonomic nervous system. Tension, such as stage fright, usually leads to frequent urination or defecation, and intense fright may precipitate an involuntary voiding of the bladder and intestines. This is supported by a study of Shaffer (1947), who found that 5 per cent of war pilots experienced this reaction during or shortly after flying a combat mission. Other emotional upheavals can also produce the same effect, as shown by the fact that many people urinate involuntarily during a fit of laughter. *See* ENCOPRESIS.

Finally, the eliminative functions are surrounded by a special emotional aura in our society. Though the attitudes of families may differ, the general tendency, especially on the middle and upper economic levels, is to associate these processes with negative feelings such as shame, disgust and guilt. As Jersild points out, "The tendency to regard the process of elimination and the organs connected with elimination as obscene is so strong that even the children whose parents are least prudish and rather free and outspoken at home pick up some of the prevailing attitudes in the community . . . The attitudes of disgust that some children acquire extend far beyond what is required or justified on practical counts of cleanliness or on moral grounds" (1960).

The difficulty, however, is not so much that children come to feel that the excreta themselves are dirty, but that this feeling extends and generalizes to other areas as well. This accounts in large part for our great emphasis on antiseptic purity and cleanliness, as well as the excessive pressure we exert in toilet training. Moreover, children easily detect their parents' anxiety about the process of elimination, and soon find they can use it as an aggressive weapon or a way of forcing their parents to cajole or reward them. Finally, the feelings of disgust and shame become associated with the entire nether region of the body, and almost inevitably spread to sexual functions. Too often, they generate tensions, anxiety and guilt that stand in the way of natural, healthy relationships between men and women.

EMERGENCY PSYCHOTHERAPY. Active psychological treatment undertaken while the patient is in a state of panic. According to Rosenthal (1965), "Emergency psychotherapy is advisable in any instance in which any untoward occurrence—critical surgery, accident, shocking news, or other events inducing panic—creates an acute psychical disturbance of an individual."

The concept of emergency psychotherapy was introduced by the Dutch psychiatrist, Joost Meerloo (1956) as a result of his work with combat patients during World War II. He found that the most common feature of panic reactions was a regression to infantile behavior: the soldier would "freeze up" and be "scared stiff" like a frightened child, or experience a temper tantrum in which he would "go berserk" and shoot wildly at his own troops. The usual treatment for such conditions was sedation, but Meerloo found drugs ineffective since they did not counteract the psychological reactions. They were also too risky because they often produced paradoxical or allergic responses. He therefore introduced an approach based primarily on the fact that the in-

dividual reverts to infancy during panic and needs a parental figure to guide him through the danger and to allow him to give vent to fear and hostility before these emotions have a chance to produce neurotic effects.

Meerloo's technique was largely a three-stage affair. The psychiatrist, representing a strong but accepting parent (as well as the "magic" of the medical profession), gives the patient a cigarette and hot soup or coffee while he is in the midst of his acute fright. Experiments showed that more could be accomplished during the initial contact by giving the patient this "oral satisfaction" than by administering a narcotic. (Before these measures were used, however, it was sometimes necessary to bring the patient out of a state of catatonic rigidity by giving him a few whiffs of eau de cologne or ammonia.) To relax him further, the psychiatrist had the patient lie down in a darkened room. This was followed by a hypnotic procedure which Meerloo has termed hypnocatharsis. In response to suggestion, the patient was induced to "relive" the traumatic experience, but at the same time to see it from a distance. After this, hypnotic suggestion was used to make him relax and sleep for a half hour. He found that the hypnosis not only brought about cathartic relief, but deepened the rapport with the therapist and lowered the patient's resistance to bringing forth unconscious fears and impulses. This process opened the way to a prolonged interview or series of interviews in which Meerloo did not obey the usual custom of the fifty-minute hour, since he found that by taking full and immediate advantage of his therapeutic opportunities he could frequently "trigger off" a cure.

Meerloo found the technique highly effective and believed it could be adapted to civilian cases arising out of such traumas as highway accidents, train wrecks, floods, earthquakes, the death of a relative, acute psychosomatic reactions, or extended labor. Unfortunately, as he pointed out, most of these cases are now left for time to heal, or are put in the hands of individuals who are unaware of their psychological implications and not prepared to apply psychological techniques.

Rosenthal points out that the traditional "comforting" approach often prompts the panic-stricken person to try to suppress rather than express his disturbing emotions. Moreover, the comforter himself responds to the individual's anxiety by becoming anxious, and this creates a vicious cycle. She proposes a psychoanalytic approach, based on Freud and Fenichel, in which the patient is encouraged not only to discharge emotions created by the trauma, but to try to understand its symbolic meaning. This technique, she believes, will prevent the formation of neurotic or psychotic symptoms that may arise if the patient uses his defensive energies to put aside the effects of the trauma, or if he generalizes his reactions so that previously neutral situations will become traumatic. There is a danger, too, that these reactions will produce psychological disabilities or psychosomatic symptoms which will persist because they provide "secondary gains"— that is, they enable the patient to gain attention or control over others.

If the patient is given no outlet for his original reaction, and no effort is made to help him understand it, two things may happen. First, the normal, appropriate reactions to catastrophe may become intensified to a point where they interfere with the individual's functioning—for example, after an accident, an athlete may become so worried about his ability to play again that he will not even try to return to the game. Second, the panic reactions may produce symbolic symptoms by activating earlier repressed fears, guilt feelings, or other unconscious processes. One of Rosenthal's examples here is the boy who maintained a hunched-

over position after the bombing of London, muttering "Father! Father!" In a psychotherapeutic session she found that the boy had felt extremely hostile toward his father, but the hostility had gone unpunished, and he was afraid his father would retaliate at a later date. In his mind the explosion represented the final reckoning in which the father would "throw him out," and his hunched-over position was a symbolic pronunciation of guilt. When he was brought to an understanding of the connection between his posture and his feelings, he quickly straightened up and accepted his physical injuries without neurotic consequences.

Rosenthal's technique involves the following steps. First, attempt to "reach" the patient while he is still in a state of shock—before sedatives can decrease his awareness and accessibility, and before his defenses and associations to prior traumatic experiences can take over. Second, give him the kind of attention and reassurance that will alleviate his sense of desperation. Third, make an immediate attempt to examine and understand any intense anxieties as they are developing, and before they can be repressed. Fourth, be aware of nonverbal communications—gestures, posture changes—even more than usually. Fifth, accept as valid any interpretation of the connection between the present trauma and past events which the patient offers, and use only "gentle questions" to elicit material. Sixth, record all details because of their possible importance if future psychotherapy is needed. Seventh, help to allay anxiety by mentioning the reactions of other people in similar circumstances: "At a time like this everybody feels tense and upset." Eighth, whenever possible, and as soon as possible, discuss the patient's future plans so that he will realize that the present crisis will end, that his world is not going to fall apart, and that he will "make it" on his own again. Finally, it is important throughout to recognize that the psychological, symbolic meaning of the event is more crucial and may be more threatening than the event itself.

Rosenthal, like Meerloo, believes that emergency psychotherapy should be carried out wherever possible by specially trained therapists. Such therapists should be on call, either in clinics and other institutions, or in private practice. At the same time, the public and the medical profession in general should be made aware of such services and their value in providing immediate relief and preventing future complications. *See* PANIC, CIVILIAN CATASTROPHE REACTIONS, HYPNOTHERAPY.

EMOTION (General). Emotions are intense "stirred up" feelings, usually directed toward a specific person or event, and involving widespread visceral and skeletal changes.

The feelings involved in emotion are extremely elusive and hard to describe. Any attempt at introspection tends to defeat itself since the intellectual attitude modifies or dispels the emotion being experienced. It is a well-known fact that when we closely observe ourselves during anger, we feel the emotion much less acutely. For this reason it has been said that such introspective experiments "die by their own description."

On the other hand, Nafe (1924) has found that milder affective states such as pleasant sensations produced by drawing fur gently across the neck could be adequately described without destroying the feeling in the process. The same was found for unpleasant stimulation, as in smelling glue or decayed flowers. Interestingly, both of these feeling states involve pressure sensations. When pleasure could be localized, it was felt most often as a bright, diffuse pressure in the neck and shoulder regions; unpleasantness appeared to be a dull or heavy pressure in the abdomen or lower trunk. It is probable that these pressure reactions are basically muscular in nature.

The subjective descriptions of feelings and emotions have yielded very few concrete, verifiable results; and since the introspective method is no longer popular, psychologists have adopted more objective procedures. One technique is to note the overt changes that occur in different emotions—for example, speech changes due to the dry mouth experienced during stage fright, dilation of the pupils when we encounter a surprising or shocking scene, and the "drooping" posture of a person suffering from grief or depression. Other attempts to understand emotion through outward behavior are discussed under the topic EXPRESSIVE MOVEMENT.

Another objective technique is to measure the internal, physiological changes that occur during emotion. Some of the major instruments used for this purpose are (a) the psychogalvanometer, a sensitive piece of apparatus which records involuntary changes in the electrical resistance of the skin (the galvanic skin response, or GSR) caused by sweating and possibly by muscular contractions occurring during intense emotion; (b) the electrocardiograph (EKG), which records the electrical activity of the heart—reliable in measuring the "pounding heart" that occurs in strong emotions, but unreliable for weak emotions; (c) the electroencephalograph (EEG), which generally shows a shift from the longer, slower Alpharhythms to shorter, more rapid "brain waves" under emotion; (d) the sphygmomanometer, used to measure blood-pressure changes in intense emotion; and (e) the polygraph, which measures the breathing pattern (inspiration/expiration ratio), blood pressure and GSR. *See* LIE DETECTION.

The physiological basis of emotion was recognized by folklore and language long before scientists applied these instruments. The visceral areas are most often implicated, as in the expression "butterflies in the stomach," the description of love as an "affair of the heart," and the Scriptural assertion that the bowels are the seat of compassion. But the skeletal area is also involved: when we are tense, we are "tied in knots." Although some of these expressions appear to localize the physiological changes, the current opinion is that they are extremely widespread and that there are more similarities than dissimilarities among the strong emotional states. In fact, physiologists and psychologists have all but despaired of finding exact patterns of physiological changes which differentiate the major emotions. Recently, however, there has been some evidence that anger is primarily controlled by epinephrine (adrenalin), which raises blood pressure by increasing the pumping of the heart; and that fear is the result of norepinephrine (noradrenalin) secretion, which raises blood pressure by constricting the blood vessels.

Most of the physiological changes that take place during strong emotion are produced by the sympathetic nervous system. They generally have the effect of putting the organism on an emergency footing. Among the circulatory changes are: increase in heart rate; rise in blood pressure and pulse rate (though sometimes there may be a sudden and dangerous fall); constriction of the blood vessels in the gut, causing more blood to flow to the brain and muscle; increase in red corpuscles (making more oxygen available); rapid change of glycogen into blood sugar (releasing energy); and increase in blood-clotting time. The gastrointestinal and urinary changes include: reduced flow of saliva; inhibition of stomach movement, secretion of gastric juices, and peristalsis (slowing down digestion); inhibition of colon and bladder functions (often resulting in constipation) except in some cases of sudden stress, in which involuntary defecation and urination may occur.

Other sympathetic effects are: increased sweating (to eliminate wastes and dissipate heat); goose pimples; gasping and panting under sudden stress, and deep breathing under prolonged exertion; dilation of the bronchioles (accelerating exchange of oxygen and carbon dioxide); dilation of pupils of the eye (apparently to see better). Glandular changes, primarily in the adrenals, also play an important role: adrenalin (epinephrine) reinforces the effects of the sympathetic nervous system; and norepinephrine contracts small blood vessels on the surface of the skin, which increases blood supply to the vital organs and also makes us look "white as a sheet." In prolonged emotion the adrenal cortex is also stimulated, and this may eventually bring about psychosomatic effects such as hypertension. *See* AUTONOMIC NERVOUS SYSTEM, PSYCHOPHYSIOLOGIC DISORDERS (GENERAL), EMOTION (THEORIES).

Finally, it is important to recognize that the physiological responses which occur under intense emotion may be either a help or a hindrance. A dry throat can keep us from speaking, or speaking clearly, just when we need our voice most. A "lump in the stomach" can be distracting and may also deplete our energy. Involuntary elimination can be embarrassing to a child and a danger to life on the battlefield. Muscles that become rigid in fright are worse than useless. On the other hand, by far the greatest number of changes that take place help us mobilize our energies and facilitate our handling of stressful situations. Perhaps the best evidence for this can be found in well-authenticated examples of people who perform astonishing feats under emotional circumstances—for example, the football player who plays a good part of a game with a dislocated knee, the frail mother who picks up the front end of her car to release her child pinned beneath it, the mountain climber who carries an injured companion down a treacherous slope during a raging snowstorm. In practically every one of these cases, the individual collapses when the ordeal is over, but emotion has carried him through. In most instances the emergencies are temporary and short-lived. As Hans Selye has pointed out, the human organism cannot remain overmobilized for extended periods without incurring tissue damage, especially to the vital internal organs. *See* GENERAL ADAPTATION SYNDROME, AFFECTIONAL DRIVE, LOVE, ANGER, HOSTILITY, JEALOUSY, PLEASURE.

EMOTION (Theories). There appear to be three general aspects of emotional response. First, the perceptual or cortical aspect: the recognition of a situation as threatening, fearful, surprising, etc.; second, the physiological aspect: the pattern of changes in the respiratory, circulatory, muscular, and other body systems; third, the sensory aspect: the feeling-tone associated with the specific emotions of fear, anger, horror, etc. While there is general agreement on these aspects, there has been considerable disagreement as to the sequence of events in emotional response and the centers which control the process. Let us look at the leading theories.

James-Lange Theory. In 1884 William James, and one year later the Danish physiologist Karl G. Lange, independently proposed a theory which conflicted with the common view of emotion. The accepted sequence of events was that we encounter a fierce-looking dog, feel frightened, and then leave with a beating heart. James and Lange, however, held that the correct order is (a) we meet the dog, (b) we experience the physiological reactions including the urge to run, and (c) these reactions generate the feeling of fright. These investigators maintained that our physical responses are the core of the emotion—or, as James put it, "We are afraid because we run; we do not run because we are afraid." All these phys-

ical responses, visceral and skeletal alike, are mediated by the autonomic nervous system, and the feelings of the muscular tension (or relaxation), and especially the changes in our stomach and other internal organs, constitute the full emotion. Without them the emotion would not exist: "A disembodied emotion is a sheer nonentity."

The James-Lange theory led to a great deal of heated debate and, more importantly, to considerable research which has raised a number of crucial questions about it. First, it was found that the visceral organs are relatively insensitive to stimulation, and when they do respond, they react too slowly to account for the quickly occurring feelings of fear, anger, etc. Second, the few differences that can be found in the visceral patterns are insufficient to account for the wide variety of emotions we experience. Third, if visceral changes are artificially induced, for instance, through adrenalin injections, a full-blown emotion is not experienced; the subject simply feels that an emotion is coming on, but it never actually arrives. These findings have led many investigators to believe that there must be some central control of emotion, since the visceral and other peripheral factors do not tell the whole story.

The Cannon-Bard Theory. A second major theory, proposed by Walter B. Cannon (1927) and elaborated by his pupil, Philip Bard, appeared to supply the "missing link." It is sometimes referred to as the thalamic theory and sometimes as the hypothalamic theory, since it involves both of these structures. The hypothalamus is primarily concerned with the direct expression of emotion—for example, stimulation of this area in a cat has been found to produce rage reactions in the absence of any rage-producing situation. Moreover, cats showed emotional responses when the sympathetic nervous system was cut along the whole length of the spinal cord, thus depriving them of the usual autonomic responses. Cannon and Bard believed, further, that the thalamus controlled the *experience* of emotion, since it was the station on the way to the cortex. When external stimulation occurs, *both* of these centers, the hypothalamus and thalamus, become active at the same time, one accounting for emotional behavior and the other for emotional feeling or experience.

Geldard (1962) points out that the Cannon-Bard theory arose from studies of lower animals whose feelings cannot be directly observed, while the James-Lange theory was created to explain precisely those feelings in man. He suggests that the two theories are concerned with different phenomena, or different aspects of the same process, and therefore neither one is a substitute for the other. The view that the hypothalamus is deeply involved with emotion has received strong support from many types of experiments. There is also evidence that portions of the thalamus are concerned with emotional reactions, and probably emotional experience as well, including anxiety, anger, and fear. However, as the following two theories indicate, the thalamus is by no means solely responsible for the experience of emotion. *See* HYPOTHALAMUS, THALAMUS.

Lindsley's Activity Theory was proposed shortly after the influence of the reticular formation on the arousal of the organism was demonstrated (1951). He accepted the view that the hypothalamus was the organizer of expressive behavior, but held that the reticular formation must be active before such behavior is at all possible. In other words, the organism must be tense and excited if it is to show the usual fear or anger responses—and if this structure is not aroused, it will be apathetic and unemotional. This has been demonstrated by studies of animals with damaged reticular systems. It has also been experimentally proved through the use of drugs that affect this structure. Schachter and Wheeler (1962), for

example, gave groups of subjects placebos, adrenalin, and chlorpromazine. After this, they were shown an amusing film. The experimenters found that the group that had been given adrenalin, which activates the reticular formation, reacted boisterously, while the group given the placebo showed less reaction, and the group which had received the tranquilizer hardly reacted at all. *See* RETICULAR FORMATION.

The Lindsley theory recognizes that the hypothalamus, visceral and autonomic activities, cerebral cortex, and recticular formation are all involved in emotion. But its chief contribution, as Morgan (1965) puts it, is that it "integrates the reticular system, and the behavioral arousal accompanying its activity into the picture of brain mechanisms and emotion." However, the theory may actually overemphasize the role of this system, since the hypothalamus has recently been found to have its own activating function through both the cerebral cortex and the autonomic nervous system, and has the effect of arousing the reticular formation itself (Gellhorn, 1961).

Papez-MacLean Theory. Originally proposed in 1937 by Papez, this theory brings another whole set of structures into the picture—that is, the hippocampus, fornix, mammillary bodies of the hypothalamus, and cingulate gyrus. These structures are all grouped together at the base of the brain, and were at one time thought to be concerned with the sense of smell. Papez, however, made the startling suggestion that they are all involved in emotion, and subsequent investigators have shown that they constitute a single system, which has become known as the limbic ("border") system.

Later, MacLean (1949, 1958) performed a number of experiments that seemed to support Papez' theory, indicating that the limbic system may be the organizing center responsible for both emotional expression and emotional experience. It does not eliminate the hypothalamus, the autonomic nervous system, the reticular formation, or the cortex, but is believed to integrate all their activities. Many of the details of its function are still obscure, but in the opinion of Morgan as well as others, "the Papez-MacLean Theory is now much more than a theory. It is a general description of what experiment has established."

For a brief account of some of the evidence supporting this view, *see* LIMBIC SYSTEM, AMYGDALA, SEPTAL AREA, THALAMUS, HIPPOCAMPUS, CINGULATE GYRUS.

EMOTIONAL DEVELOPMENT. The emotions play a number of major roles in life. They lend zest and color to experience. They are intimately involved in personal adjustment and mental health. And they act as motivating forces in meeting the problems and challenges that face us. Without them life would be dull, static, and mechanical.

A person can attain a full emotional life only if he develops his capacity to experience every type of affect, including both the pleasant emotions of delight, happiness and affection, and the unpleasant emotions of fear, anger, anxiety and jealousy. However, if his emotional life is to be not only full but healthy and happy, the pleasant emotions must be clearly predominant over the unpleasant; and this is likely to happen only if he has a full opportunity to experience love, approval and happiness right from the beginning of life. If he does not, he will be emotionally deprived or even emotionally starved, and it will be difficult if not impossible for him to achieve normal personality development as he grows. *See* MATERNAL DEPRIVATION.

Emotional capacity is part of the natural endowment of every individual: "The ability to respond emotionally is present in the newborn as part of the developmental process and does not have to be learned" (Bakwin, 1949). As a matter of fact it is present long before the normal term, since premature infants are capable of emotional reactions. In any case, the first visible manifestation of emotion is a diffuse excitement which the infant shows in response to strong stimulation such as a sudden bright light or loss of support. Typically, he cries loudly, squirms, kicks, and waves his arms—a characteristic form of the "mass activity" which is present at birth. There is no evidence of clear-cut emotional patterns at the beginning of life, but within a few weeks it is usually possible to distinguish between responses that suggest pleasure and displeasure. The pleasant reactions are first expressed by a general relaxation of the body elicited by sucking, being rocked, caressed and held snugly. Unpleasant responses are expressed by crying and mass activity, provoked by wet diapers, cold objects on the skin, sudden loud noises, abrupt change of position, or hampered movements.

Emotional expression develops rapidly. The baby's first smiles and frowns appear within six to eight weeks. By the end of his first half year he can express delight, fear, anger and disgust in much the same way as adults. During the latter half of his first year he is especially wary of strangers and shows his fear by tensing up, hiding his head or crying. Between one and two years of age he begins to show feelings of affection and jealousy, and during this period there is also a rapid increase in curiosity. A little later he shows definite signs of satisfaction in his own accomplishments such as building a high block tower or riding a tricycle.

All through this early period the young child acquires increasingly effective responses to people, objects, and situations. Instead of simply crying and making random, chaotic movements, he comes to express displeasure by throwing things, stiffening his body, running away, hiding and shouting—and instead of merely relaxing his body, he shows his pleasure by hugging, babbling happily, humming, or shouting "nice" or "ta-ta." *See* FEAR, AFFECTIONAL DRIVE, SYMPATHY, ANGER, JEALOUSY, CURIOSITY, ANXIETY, LOVE, STARTLE REACTION.

Even though the child has an inborn tendency to express his feelings, the course of his emotional development is determined by learning as well as by maturation. The two forces, however, are so closely intertwined that it is often hard to assess their relative effects. Nevertheless we will try to outline the areas where maturation plays the major role, and then do the same for learning.

The ability to react to situations and express emotions is based largely upon the maturation of the nervous system. The development of the cortex, and especially the frontal lobes which are involved in understanding, is a gradual affair. In the early years of life the child lacks the capacity to control his emotions because the upper areas of the brain are not yet fully operative. He also has little experience to draw upon, and is therefore limited in his comprehension of such emotion-provoking situations as death, disease, or divorce. One study has shown that children do not fully appreciate the significance of death until they reach adolescence (Alexander and Adlerstein, 1958). Other investigations have shown that the fear of snakes and many other common fears develop only when the child has reached an intellectual level where he can understand potential dangers. The full meaning of the violence and crime presented on television and in the movies cannot be comprehended until later childhood, although some younger children become upset just *because* they find it hard to understand what they see and to distinguish between fiction and reality. *See* TELEVISION EFFECTS.

Emotional development is also dependent on the maturation of the endocrine glands. The adrenal glands, which play a major role in emotional expression, actually decrease in size directly after birth so that the new-born child is not capable of sustaining emotional expression. Within a few months, however, these glands begin to increase in size. Their growth reaches a high level at five years of age, then slows down between five and eleven, and speeds up again at puberty. These changes have a pronounced effect on the child's emotions and help to account for the peaks of emotionality that occur around five years and in early adolescence.

The other major influence on emotional development—learning—operates in many ways. The child's emotional responses are greatly affected by the way he is treated, the kind of behavior that elicits help or approval or reproach from others, and the general climate of the home and neighborhood. A cheerful home will foster a cheerful temperament, an anxious mother will engender apprehensive reactions, an overindulgent father will—without realizing it—teach his child to be petulant and willful, and a cold home atmosphere will usually restrict free expression and lead to emotional flatness. Similarly, rigid training and harsh treatment arouse intense fear and resentments, while excessively high standards and an overemphasis on gratitude for "advantages" often give rise to strong feelings of guilt and anxiety. It has also been found that parents who encourage their children to give voice to their feelings and discuss them openly have greater success in teaching them to manage their own emotions than parents who turn a deaf ear to their children's inner life.

Two specific types of learning are involved in emotional development: conditioning and imitation. Conditioning is particularly effective during the first years of life since it is an automatic affair that does not involve reasoning and judgment. All that is usually required is association and repetition. In the classic experiment of Watson and Rayner (1920), a nine-month-old child, who had not displayed any fear of objects or animals up to that time, was conditioned to fear a white rat simply by the process of sounding a loud noise whenever he reached for it. Moreover, this fear spread, or "generalized," to a rabbit, a dog, a sealskin coat, and cotton wool. The fear of men in white coats often originates with an inoculation, and many other negative reactions are learned in the same manner. Positive as well as negative emotional reactions may arise from conditioning—for example, the young child associates his mother with personal care and attention, and therefore often displays more affection toward her than toward his father. *See* CONDITIONING, BEHAVIORISM.

The second method of learning—imitation—is largely carried out through observation of other people's reactions. Children are remarkably sensitive to the emotional state of others almost from the beginning of life. A three-week-old infant will react negatively to breast feeding if the mother is tense or feels disgusted by the process. A mother who becomes "tied in knots" at the first sign of a storm will usually transmit this anxiety to her child; on the other hand, if she remains calm and cheerful, the child will not be alarmed. And anyone who watches the dramatic play of young children is bound to be impressed with their ability to imitate the manner and tone of voice of adults. Playing house or playing policeman are really practice sessions for the expression of their own emotions. *See* IMITATION, EMPATHY.

One of the best ways of gauging the developmental changes that occur through the years is to compare the emotional reactions of the child with those of the adult. Even though children differ widely in the expression of emotion, because of differences in basic constitution, speed of maturation and learning opportunities, nevertheless a number of common characteristics can be found. First, children's emotional reactions are usually brief and quickly forgotten; adolescents and adults are less subject to momentary outbursts and are more prone to longer-lasting moods. Second, children's emotions tend to be more frequent and more intense than adult emotions. The child has not learned to control his reactions and is less "civilized" in the way he expresses himself. He therefore displays emotion whenever he feels like it, even when the situation does not seem to warrant it. He also shows fewer gradations in his responses than the adult; all his emotions tend to be equally intense. Third, children's emotional reactions show rapid shifts from anger to pleasure, from laughter to tears, or from jealousy to affection—partly because they get them out of their system quickly and partly because their attention span and understanding are limited. Fourth, children's feelings are closer to the surface and more clearly detectable than adult feelings. Children have not learned to conceal their reactions, and when they are disturbed they show it in a variety of ways: by fidgeting, frequent urination, nail-biting, thumbsucking, daydreaming, eye blinking, hysterical outbursts, crying, and speech difficulties.

A full recognition of these differences is essential if we are to give our children the kind of understanding and guidance they need. It is reassuring to know that their emotional storms blow over quickly and that they show their inner feelings by outward signs. But it is also important to take these signs seriously and help them over the emotional hurdles they are bound to face on the way to maturity. The interest and attention we show in their early years, while their personalities are still plastic, can save them a great deal of difficulty later on.

EMOTIONAL INSULATION. The unconscious defense mechanism of indifference and detachment.

Nearly all of us learn early in life that disappointments and frustrations are inevitable, and that if we get too excited, too enthusiastic or too involved, we lay ourselves open for possible hurt. We therefore begin to hold our hopes and aspirations within bounds, and we keep in reserve such expressions as "I really didn't want to," and "I wasn't sure I liked him anyway," in case events don't live up to expectations.

These common protective devices serve well enough for ordinary situations. But people who have highly sensitive personalities, or who are subjected to a series of psychological body blows develop more extreme forms of emotional insulation. The boy who has been rejected by girl after girl may become aloof and detached: "Who needs people?" The girl who fails "to make the grade" socially may surround herself with a protective shell of indifference or cynicism: "Nothing really matters anyway." These young people may develop a thoroughly defeatist attitude toward life. Many victims of chronic unemployment become so apathetic and beaten that they cannot apply for a new job or job training for fear of disappointment.

In one situation at least, apathy has been found to serve a positive purpose. In prisoner of war camps and concentration camps, many inmates have at least partially insulated themselves from inhuman conditions by retreating behind a curtain of indifference.

Emotional insulation can, however, take pathological forms. In cases of chronic depression the patient may detach himself so completely that he loses the power to react even to fortunate events. In schizophrenia, apathy may become so complete that the patient withdraws into a stuporous state. *See* WITHDRAWAL, ISOLATION.

EMOTIONALLY UNSTABLE PERSONALITY. A personality-trait disturbance characterized by immaturity and lack of control over emotional reactions.

In unstable persons minor obstacles or irritations produce major outbursts of anger, obstinacy, and general excitement, and they may shout, threaten, or assault others. At all other times, however, they may be amiable and pleasant.

Most of these individuals show poor tolerance for frustration and defeat; they tend to sulk like children, lapse into despair, threaten or even attempt suicide. Their relationships with other people are constantly interrupted by displays of temper, jealousy, and quarrelsomeness. Under stress their judgment is undependable and their actions unpredictable.

Behavior patterns of emotionally unstable personalities are outward attempts to compensate for inner weaknesses. If they are continually faced with situations they cannot cope with, they usually do not retreat into psychosis, but regress to more pronounced infantile reactions along the same lines they have always followed. They simply become more excitable, more stubborn, more aggressive, and the periods of amiability become shorter and shorter. *See* PERSONALITY TRAIT DISTURBANCE.

Illustrative Case: EMOTIONALLY UNSTABLE PERSONALITY

Rosemary C., an eighteen-year-old single girl, was taken to her family doctor after having taken many aspirin tablets in an impulsive suicidal gesture. She was treated and referred to a psychiatrist because of the pattern of unstable behavior she had displayed over the few preceding years.

Rosemary, an only child, lived with her father and stepmother, her own mother having died at the time Rosemary was born.

Her first five years, until her father remarried, were spent with her father in the home of her paternal grandparents, elderly people who indulged her greatly. When she was five, Rosemary's father married her stepmother and established a home for them. From the outset Rosemary resented the intrusion of her new mother on the relationship she had with her father, a man described as being quiet but steady and understanding. Rosemary's stepmother did not make things easy for the youngster, because she was a finicky person who lived according to a fixed routine which failed to make room for an active child. When things did not work out as she planned them, she tended to become highly emotional and required special attention. Crises were very upsetting for her and on many occasions Rosemary saw her stepmother become completely helpless in the face of such stresses. Because of this situation Rosemary found little real companionship in the home and frequently returned to her grandmother for the attention and affection she needed. Her grandmother's death when Rosemary was twelve was therefore an inconsolable loss and marked the beginning of a very unstable and rebellious existence for her.

At school Rosemary was able to do well when she applied herself, but more often than not she shirked her homework in open rebellion against the authority of her teachers. She was in frequent conflict with other girls over the attentions of favored boys in the school and was not above becoming engaged in physical conflict at times. She persisted in dating boys of poor reputation and, when rebuked by her parents, often responded with such an attack of hysterics and screaming that they were all disturbed for days. When she was sixteen, Rosemary decided to leave school, after having been chided by a teacher for smoking in the rest room. All efforts by her family to dissuade her failed, and she took a job as a salesgirl.

Rosemary's work history from the time she left school to the time she was sent to a psychiatrist was a checkered one. She failed to stay at a job for more than a few months, and she either left in fury or was fired for having committed gross errors of judgment when faced with relatively minor pressures.

The incident leading up to Rosemary's psychiatric referral involved a young man she had been seeing steadily for some months. Her parents had tried to discourage the relationship because of the young man's unsavory reputation and because they feared Rosemary might consider marrying him. When their more oblique efforts to break the couple up failed, they confronted Rosemary directly with their concerns and insisted that she stop seeing the boy. A stormy scene followed, climaxed by Rosemary's abortive attempt at suicide.

When she was interviewed by the psychiatrist to whom she was referred, Rosemary was tense and hesitant initially, but as she grew to feel that she would not be punished or rebuked she relaxed considerably. After two sessions she was able to talk freely and openly. Without displaying any deep insight, she showed some awareness of her difficulties and sincerely seemed to desire help in finding a way out of them. It was felt that she was an immature, impulse-ridden girl who had used the suicide attempt to punish her parents and to extort attention and affection from them. It was also felt that she might respond well to a warm, supportive figure and that her parents too might profit from counseling with respect to developing a better understanding of Rosemary's needs and the effects their relationships had on her.

Rosemary was seen in weekly therapy sessions for a period of about nine months. During this time she decided to give up the boy friend about whom she and her parents had quarreled. Furthermore, she met a more acceptable man, and they were considering marriage at the time treatment ended. The relationship with her parents also improved greatly over the course of treatment which was concluded at the mutual agreement of Rosemary and her therapist. (Zax and Stricker, 1963)

EMPATHY. An awareness of the thoughts and feelings of another person; the capacity to understand and in some measure share another person's state of mind.

When we "empathize" with someone, we identify with him to such an extent that we can project ourselves into his thoughts and can usually assure him that we know how he feels. Some people have a far greater capacity for empathy than others. They tend to be warm, understanding, insightful individuals who are basically interested in others.

A good parent or teacher has this capacity in high degree. Some investigators also regard empathy as an important quality of leadership, especially in dealing with small groups. It is essential in any form of psychotherapy, whether individual or group. In psychoanalysis, as Greenson (1959) has pointed out, it is the most important factor in determining how much insight a patient's ego can bear and how far he can be confronted with his dangerous impulses: "The dosage and timing of interpretation are primarily accomplished by the capacity of the analyst to empathize with the situation of his patient." The feeling on the part of the patient himself that the therapist empathizes with him is considered an important factor in treatment, since it gives him emotional support, encourages him to express his deepest feelings, and increases his confidence in the therapist.

The experience of empathy takes many forms. When we can "feel along" with the actors of the stage, we achieve a greater understanding and enjoyment of the play. In watching a football game, we identify with the action to such an extent that we tense our muscles and grit our teeth, move forward or back as the players move, and feel elated or disappointed with them. We also experience emphatic reactions from things as well as people: we identify ourselves with the speeding car on the race track, or feel overwhelmed by the height of a skyscraper.

Empathy can probably not be taught in an academic way, but undoubtedly sensitive people such as poets, artists, and personal counselors can help to make us more aware of the feelings and reactions of others. There is also little doubt that experiences in helping others, and in dramatics, psychodrama

and role-playing will often increase our capacity for empathy. See PSYCHO-DRAMA.

ENCOPRESIS (Enchopresis). Involuntary defecation not caused by organic defect or illness.

In our culture inability to control bowel function after the age of two is an indication of faulty training, or, in some cases, retarded development or psychiatric disorder. In a review of seventy cases among children, Shirley (1938) found that thirty-seven had an I.Q. of less than 80, and in many instances there was evidence of an exceptionally poor home environment or parental oversolicitude. Persistent soiling is generally considered a much more severe symptom of emotional disorder than enuresis. It may also lead to disturbances of the colon, and for this reason a thorough physical examination is necessary. As English and Finch (1964) point out, "The child of grade-school age who continues to soil usually represents a more seriously disturbed child than one who has chosen a less primitive way of showing his problems." These authors state that more often than not the child has shown great resistance to toilet training and is reacting to parental inconsistency or over-discipline: "For a variety of reasons the child has retained unconsciously the magical concept that defecation has both sexual and aggressive connotations, and may involuntarily soil himself when sexually excited or angry." Similarly, Redlich and Freedman (1966) state, "In the case of encopresis, a mixture of infantile sexual pleasure and rebellion and revenge against the parents coexist." The disorder usually requires intensive psychotherapy.

END SPURT. The burst of effort that often occurs at the end of a period of work or other exertion, usually resulting in a rise in performance.

In both factory and office work the end of the day frequently brings with it a final release of energy that dramatically increases production. There are several reasons for this upward turn in the work curve. The prospect of going home keys us up; we find ourselves faced with a "mountain of work" that should not be put off; and we feel guilty or worried about the lag that often occurs in the afternoon. For these reasons we make an added effort in the last few minutes.

The end spurt also occurs in athletic events. Boxers often fight harder in the last round than in any previous round, and long distance runners put forth a final burst of speed as they approach the finish line. When the end is in sight they are willing to use up all the energy they have left, since they do not need to spare themselves for further effort. In some cases they deliberately save their energy for the last stretch.

Sometimes a worker hits his peak production only during the end spurt. This is revealing evidence that he has not been making a full effort all along. The end spurt should show an increase of production over the period immediately preceding it, but it should not show peak production unless the worker starts to "put out" in order to make his record look good.

An analogous burst of effort is often observed at the start of a job. This "beginning spurt" takes place because we are fresh and enthusiastic when we first tackle the task and therefore go "all out." After we realize it is going to take quite a while—or simply to save our energy—we settle down to a slower pace geared to the long haul. The beginning spurt occurs more often in new tasks than old ones, and it is more frequently observed among inexperienced than among seasoned workers. *See* WORK CURVE.

ENERGIZER (Antidepressant). A stimulating, mood-elevating drug used primarily in combating depressions.

Two types of energizers, or "psychoanaleptics," are in use today: MAO inhibitors, which have a largely indirect stimulating effect by suppressing the action of the enzyme monoamine oxidase; and non-MAO inhibitors, which appear to have a more direct effect on the central nervous system. Both have the advantage of long-term action with minimal side effects, in contrast to such stimulants as amphetamines (Benzedrine, Dexedrine, Desoxyn), which have only transient effects and produce anorexia (loss of appetite) and insomnia. *See* AMPHETAMINES.

MAO inhibitors are the outgrowth of experiments with iproniazid (Marsilid) in the treatment of tuberculosis. This drug was found to have a euphoric effect on patients, making them gay, optimistic and lively. As a result, Nathan S. Kline tried the drug on depressive patients and found it effective. Unfortunately it had dangerous side effects—particularly toxic hepatitis—but within a short time several chemical analogues were developed with similar antidepressant properties but which could be administered with safety. The most widely used are isocarboxazid (Marplan), phenelzine (Nardil) and the somewhat less effective nialamide (Niamid).

These drugs have relatively mild and readily controlled side effects, such as constipation, insomnia, headache, tremors, dry mouth, lowered blood pressure, and, if given in large doses, hypomanic (excited) states. Frequently a tranquilizer is given along with the antidepressant to prevent excitement and overactivity. Good to excellent results have been achieved within a few days in 70 to 90 per cent of depressions of both the neurotic and psychotic types. Preliminary studies have indicated that a newer MAO inhibitor, MO-109, is also effective with schizo-affective patients who manifest autism and flatness of affect as well as depression.

Several non-MAO inhibitors are also in wide use. Imipramine (Tofranil), introduced in 1957, has proved effective in 70 to 80 per cent of clear-cut depressions, particularly of the retarded type. It is less effective with agitated depressions, though it may be combined with a tranquilizer of the phenothiazine type in these cases. It has limited use in depressions complicated by schizophrenic or organic brain disorder, and in neurotic depressions and hypochondriacal states. Similar results are achieved with amitriptyline, marketed as Elavil, but sometimes one of these drugs works when the other does not. Side effects are slight with both drugs; the most common are dry mouth, perspiration, difficulty in focusing the eyes, and insomnia when first given. Two related drugs are desmethylimipramine (Pertofrane) and desmethylamitriptyline (Nortriptyline). Another important drug of the non-MAO group is chlorprothixene (Taractan), which has both tranquilizing and alerting effects.

In addition to these drugs, there are a number of minor antidepressants rarely prescribed for severe depressions. Small doses of amphetamines are occasionally used as mood-elevators, since these drugs can help in overcoming mild depression and apathy, and in restoring self-confidence. Continuous use, however, may result in addiction, and large amounts may produce weakness, depression, gastrointestinal disturbances, tremors and in some cases symptomatic psychoses. Combination drugs, such as the stimulant dextroamphetamine plus the sedative amobarbital (Dexamyl) are also used in combating depression. Other psychomotor stimulants used for mild depressions are methylphenidate (Ritalin), pipradol (Meratran), and deanol (Deaner). Like the amphetamines, they are more often prescribed for fatigue and for maintaining wakefulness in extreme situations, and are also recommended in organic cases of narcolepsy. The tranquilizer chlordiazepoxide (Librium) may also be prescribed for mild depressions accompanied by marked anxiety.

Finally, there is a "bimodal" group of drugs, combining amphetamine-like stimulation of the central nervous system with a slower-acting effect resulting from the inhibition of monoamine oxidase. Among them are tranylcypromine (Parnate), etryptamine (Monase), and pargyline (Eutonyl). These drugs produce the rapid but sustained action needed in cases of non-agitated neurotic and psychotic depression as well as depressed forms of schizophrenia. They are safe with respect to the liver but may have side effects such as overstimulation, insomnia, headache, and lowered blood pressure.

Antidepressant drugs have not replaced electroshock therapy in the treatment of severe depressions, but they have reduced the need for it, particularly when the threat of suicide is not acute and improvement can be somewhat delayed. After initial improvement, patients are usually kept on maintenance doses for several weeks, and the medication is then gradually withdrawn. For energizers combined with tranquilizers, *see* TRANQUILIZER. *Also see* ELECTROSHOCK THERAPY, CHEMOTHERAPY.

ENGINEERING PSYCHOLOGY (Human Engineering). A field of applied psychology devoted to technical aspects of the work process, particularly the improvement of methods of work, the working environment, the problem of fatigue, and the design of equipment used by the worker. Although some psychologists restrict the field to equipment design, the current trend in America is to include all these areas. A number of other names have been applied to the field, however, chiefly human engineering, human factors research, applied experimental psychology, ergonomics, biomechanics, and biotechnology.

The engineering psychologist works in close collaboration with engineers in developing procedures, equipment and environmental conditions that lead to greater efficiency and satisfaction. As a psychologist, his major contributions stem from his knowledge of human behavior and his experience with experimental methods and techniques. The specific subjects of investigation can be grouped into three categories: (1) *working conditions* (illumination, ventilation, noise, music); (2) *working procedures* (fatigue effects, work schedules, time and motion studies, monotony, accident prevention); (3) *equipment design* (man-machine systems, spatial layout, displays, controls).

Although these topics are primarily associated with industrial psychology, many of the investigations apply to other fields as well. Studies of lighting, music, ventilation, and noise have found many applications not only in factories, offices, and stores, but in schools, libraries, and waiting rooms. Considerable research has also been done on extreme environmental conditions, particularly in space travel, underwater exploration, and polar expeditions. Many of the studies of safety and accident-proneness apply not only to accidents in industry but in the home and on the highway as well. Research on equipment design has been extended to the design of military equipment, space vehicles, telephone dials, road signs, traffic lights, and many consumer products such as kitchen appliances.

The rapid expansion in industrial and military technology in recent years has brought with it an ever-increasing interest in engineering psychology. The growth of the field is indicated by the fact that there is a special division of the American Psychological Association, the Society of Engineering Psychologists, devoted to this field. Current research is reported in the Association's *Journal of Applied Psychology. See* ILLUMINATION CONDITIONS, VENTILATION CONDITIONS, NOISE CONDITIONS, FATIGUE, MONOTONY, MUSIC AND WORK, WORK HOURS, TIME MOTION STUDY, SAFETY PSYCHOLOGY, EQUIPMENT DESIGN.

ENTROPY (literally "turning toward or turning inward"). A diminished capacity for spontaneous change; the inability to translate psychic or physical energy into a new form.

In its psychiatric use the term is roughly equivalent to rigidity or stodginess, and is sometimes applied by psychoanalysts to an incapacity to form new attachments or make any kind of change in life. This often occurs among aged persons, who insist on wearing the same clothes, eating the same food, or taking the same walks even though other opportunities are offered to them. They become set in their ways not only because they lack the physical energy to make a change, but because they have a profound emotional investment in their habitual way of life. Any change would therefore arouse feelings of uncertainty and put a strain on their reduced powers of adaptation. Entropy, however, varies greatly. Some people lose their "mental plasticity" at a relatively early age, others extremely late in life.

In sociology, the term "social entropy" applies to the doctrine that every social change reduces the energy available for further progress, and therefore every society has a tendency to become static in time. This usage, like the first, is derived by analogy from thermodynamics, in which entropy is the measure of the amount of the energy in a system which cannot be taken out and is therefore not available for doing work. In this sense, the total available energy decreases in old age, and therefore the capacity for making changes is diminished.

ENURESIS   (Bed-wetting). Persistent involuntary discharge of urine, usually during sleep, after the age of three. Bed-wetting may occur every night, several times a week, or only in reaction to stress.

An estimated two million children and a large but unknown number of adults are afflicted with enuresis in the United States. It is more common among males than females and was one of the most frequent causes of neuropsychiatric discharge from recruitment training during the last war. The incidence declines sharply with age and is relatively low among persons over thirty.

Many causal factors and combinations of factors appear to be responsible for enuresis. Some cases are clearly due to organic conditions. Slight anatomical defects and persistent low-grade infections of the genitourinary system are most frequent; brain pathology and damage to the nerves in the spinal cord that control bladder function are infrequent and usually occur only in adults. A recent study by Muellner (1960) suggests that restricted bladder capacity may have greater significance than is now recognized, since he found that this condition was particularly common among enuretic children.

Today the great majority of cases are believed to be psychogenic, although psychological and physical factors may collaborate in some instances. Most psychologists and psychiatrists emphasize emotional tension and disturbances in family relationships, particularly when these lead to repressed resentments and persistent feelings of anxiety. A neglected child may wet his bed not only to attract his parents' attention but to force them to take care of him. An angry child may unconsciously use this indirect means of getting even with his parents, since he realizes that bed-wetting will irritate them. A child who has had his parents to himself may regress to bed-wetting when a new baby appears on the scene, both to express his anger and to recapture his parents' attention. Even the normal stresses of life may make an anxious,

insecure child so tense that he will lose control over his bladder during the day as well as at night.

In many cases, then, enuresis seems to be related to emotional difficulties. Yet there are other cases where no special problems of adjustment can be detected. It may well be that some children are born with sensitive urinary systems that are thrown out of gear even by ordinary, everyday frustrations and tensions.

The relationship between enuresis and emotional disturbance is probably even closer among adult than among child enuretics, because structural defects or infections tend to be outgrown or corrected before maturity is reached. Several American investigations, and also an extensive study carried out in Sweden (Hallgren, 1956), indicate that emotional disorders can be found in over 80 per cent of adult cases. These disorders are primarily neurotic in character and often involve emotional immaturity. Enuresis also tends to occur among mental retardates, in proportion to the severity of the defect. About 4 per cent of mild retardates have been found to be enuretic as compared to 13 per cent of moderate and 84 per cent of severe cases.

Many techniques are used in treating enuresis. Different forms of punishment have been tried, among them an electrical device which shocks the child when he urinates in bed. This technique has been found more effective than forcing the child to wash his own sheets since the punishment immediately follows the bed-wetting—and, more important, it conditions the child to wake up and go to the bathroom whenever his bladder is full. However, several studies have shown that this technique may bring on other problems in children who are easily upset or who have a restricted bladder capacity. A more humane device rings an alarm instead of shocking the child, and has been found to correct or greatly improve the condition in at least 75 per cent of cases. Relapses occur rather frequently, but the treatment can be successfully repeated. The common practice of restricting fluids during the latter part of the day is effective only in a minority of cases. The opposite technique of having the bed wetter take extra fluids for a time in order to increase bladder capacity seems to be far more successful, especially when it is accompanied with practice in holding urine during the day as a means of achieving better control at night.

Tranquilizers and other drugs which inhibit the bladder reflex are sometimes used as auxiliary measures, particularly when childhood enuresis has been reactivated by special stresses in adult life. Psychotherapy designed to relieve the child's tensions and anxieties, and sociotherapy directed to reducing the pressures and stresses in the family life, are considered essential by many therapists. Adults who have regressed to enuresis as a result of recruitment or combat stress usually respond to briefer psychotherapy. The prognosis is less favorable for chronic adult enuretics who have been clearly maladjusted since childhood or adolescence.

Illustrative Case: ENURESIS

Vivian was a six-year-old child referred to the psychiatric clinic from the pediatric clinic, where her mother had brought her with the chief complaint of bed-wetting. Physical studies had been entirely negative. Her mother stated initially that her only complaint about the child was the fact that she had wet the bed ever since infancy. Upon further questioning, it developed that the youngster had various other neurotic traits. However, these had not been particularly bothersome to the mother, and, therefore, she had paid little attention to them. The child suffered from frequent nightmares, bit her nails badly, and was a fearful and timid child who played poorly with other youngsters. She was reported by the teacher to be somewhat slow in her work, although her intelligence was found to be above average.

Vivian was an only child. Her mother was a dominating, authoritative person who ran the family. The father was a hard-working, sincere, conscientious, but quite passive individual who bowed to all of his wife's demands. He was extremely fond of his daughter, but played little part in her upbringing. All the rules and regulations in the house were made by the mother. As the psychiatric interview progressed, it developed that the mother had begun toilet-training her child at four months. She was proud of the fact that she had accomplished toilet training, with the exception of enuresis, by the time the child was ten months of age. Wetting had continued in spite of all her punitive attempts to suppress it. The mother was particularly disturbed by the messiness involved and by the fact that she herself had to change the sheets as well as wash them. The child adopted a passive attitude about her wetting, as if there was nothing she could do about it. She was an obedient if timid child who obeyed all the commands given to her by her parents and as far as the mother was concerned, measured up adequately with the one exception of her wetting. The child, according to the mother, had been particularly stubborn in this area.

It was obvious that this child resented her mother's strict approach and, although submitting to it, had allowed herself the one passive outlet of wetting the bed, which she knew was extremely disturbing to her mother, although she was not conscious of its rebellious nature.

This child had struggled with a problem common to so many children in her particular situation. She was extremely attached to her mother in a dependent and immature way and yet was resentful of her mother's dominating, authoritative attitude. Her rigid upbringing prevented the release of hostile impulses toward her mother—originally by her mother's prohibition and then by her own developing conscience. The result was that she had to express her unconscious infantile wishes in terms of a passive-regressive type of behavior which, while not overtly aggressive, represented hostile feelings toward the mother. As therapy proceeded, a more flexible atmosphere was provided in which Vivian could live out, without guilt or criticism, her dependent childish wishes, which allowed her to feel sufficiently secure to attain more emotional maturity.

The cessation of the enuresis was in a way the by-product of the intrapsychic changes which took place. There was no longer any reason for the girl to express her hostility and her infantilism by means of this regressive symptom. She subsequently became able to express resentment toward her mother in situations where she felt it and yet developed a much healthier positive relationship toward the mother. Her own conscience was made less severe and her mother's restrictions made equally less severe. Eventually when the youngster had worked out a more satisfactory relationship with her mother, the enuresis began to diminish, and finally after approximately a year of treatment during which she was seen once a week, the symptom disappeared. (English and Finch, 1964)

EPIDEMIC ENCEPHALITIS. An inflammation of brain tissue caused by a filterable virus, and sometimes associated with systemic infections such as measles, mumps, and hepatitis.

The disease reached epidemic proportions following World War I, when it was known as encephalitis lethargica, or sleeping sickness. Today it is seldom seen and comprises only .1 per cent of first admissions to mental hospitals. There are two acute forms. In the "hypersomnic" form, the patient is drowsy, intellectually slow, sleeps excessively, and is subject to visual disturbances. The "hyperkinetic" form, which may follow a stuporous state, is characterized by insomnia, restlessness, agitation, irritability, and choreiform (jerky, uncontrolled) movements. These symptoms are sometimes followed by delirium, disorientation, and convulsions.

In adults the aftereffects of encephalitis include parkinsonism, muscle twitching, tremors, oculogyric crisis (eyes suddenly turning upward), loss of the blink reflex, and a masklike facial expression. In most cases there is no serious impairment of intelligence or psychological adjustment. A few patients react with agitated depression or withdrawal, and others may become impulsive and aggressive. The aggressive

patients are often aware of their dangerous urges but are powerless to control them. *See* PARKINSON'S DISEASE.

In children the aftereffects of encephalitis present a special problem. They tend to be restless, hyperactive, irritable and impulsive—and in many cases they lose all self-control and become cruel, destructive and generally unmanageable. Hospitalization is frequently necessary because of violent, aggressive and sexually deviant behavior. Other common symptoms are a peculiar bent posture, an expressionless face, and poor co-ordination. If the disease strikes before they are five years of age, they may become severely retarded. *See* MENTAL RETARDATION (CAUSES).

Today most investigators ascribe the poorly controlled hyperactive behavior of postencephalitic children to residual brain damage. Recent research has pointed to special perceptual defects which make it hard or impossible for them to organize and interpret what they see and hear, hence they cannot effectively use observation in controlling behavior. As a result, they become anxious, and try desperately to bring their world into some sort of order. This helps to explain their characteristic hyperactivity. It is probably due in large part to constant "reality testing"—that is, in attempting to adjust to the environment, control their bodies and get a perceptual hold on reality, they try one response after another in what seems to other people haphazard and disorganized activity. Their irritability and violence are, in part at least, the result of painful feelings of frustration and inadequacy experienced when they fail in these attempts—and these feelings are aggravated in many cases by the ridicule of other children.

Today epidemic encephalitis can generally be arrested by antibiotics; in some cases, however, treatment is delayed and chronic symptoms set in. Atropine and other drugs may relieve

Parkinson symptoms, and benzedrine sulfate has recently been used successfully in reducing hyperactivity and aggressiveness in child patients. Special educational procedures developed for brain damaged children can sometimes be applied effectively, and many of these children gradually learn to do academic work. *See* MINIMAL BRAIN DYSFUNCTION, NARCOLEPSY.

Illustrative Case: EPIDEMIC ENCEPHALITIS

"Harold is a boy of fifteen years whose behavior is so unpredictably and dangerously impulsive that his family cannot keep him at home. He must always live in an institution.

"He presents a strange, almost uncannily freakish appearance. He is short and squat in stature and has a short squarish head that is oversized for his body. He walks with an awkward shambling gait, a little like a monkey. As you watch him, he sidles toward another child in a gingerly apparently affectionate manner. Suddenly he grasps the child's finger and bends it backward mercilessly; then he slinks impishly away, laughing and chuckling. In a moment he raises his bitten nails to his mouth and stares at the cloudless sky as though abruptly transported, and mutters some incoherent remark about a 'terrible storm coming that will break all the limbs of the trees.' A few minutes later with tears streaming from his eyes he presents an appearance of genuine remorse. He puts his arms around the same child's neck and suddenly chokes the child painfully with a tremendous hug. When a teacher pries him away he tries to bite her hand. He murmurs to the teacher: 'I hurt you, didn't I? Can you whip? Whip me.' Perhaps a while later he may be seen to shuffle stealthily toward the same teacher and whisper to her in a childlike manner: 'I like you.' Then quick as a flash he may poke his finger into her eye and cry again. 'Can you whip? Whip me.'

"He did not thrive well in his childhood, for he was beset with many illnesses. His physical and mental development was markedly retarded. He failed to adjust himself to school and at home became uncontrollably provocative and destructive. Very much distraught, the parents resorted to beatings to discipline him, but they were of no avail.

"His mental age is about eight years (I.Q. 60). Emotionally he is very unstable; often he unaccountably bursts into tears. The most striking aspects of his behavior are his uncontrolled impulsive cruelties and his perverted craving to suffer pain himself. Like the rest of us, he wants love and affection, but he seeks it in a strange way. He torments and hurts others so they may do the same to him. He appears to derive an erotic pleasure from the pain which he provokes from others in lieu of love. To such injuries he adds those which he inflicts upon himself.

"This is a strange boy indeed. His disordered behavior is the consequence of an inflammatory illness of the brain, encephalitis, which complicated a contagious disease in infancy." (Menninger, 1945)

EPILEPSY (Etiology and Therapy). The primary symptoms of epilepsy, alterations of consciousness in association with convulsive movements, are produced by disturbances in the electrical discharges of the brain cells. The abnormal firing of neurons is indicated by electroencephalographic (EEG) recordings which show not only unusual brain waves for epilepsy in general, but distinctive wave patterns for the four different types of seizures. The exact mechanisms which cause these electrical charges are still unknown, but they are believed to be biochemical changes which increase the excitability of the neurons and lead to irregular, explosive patterns of discharge.

Even though new diagnostic techniques (including the implantation of electrodes) have succeeded in identifying brain pathology in the majority of cases, we know little about these important processes. The pathological condition may be due to a variety of causes: inflammations, fever, tumor, vascular disturbances, structural abnormality, and degenerative disease or brain injuries occurring before, during or after birth. Where brain damage can be found, the epilepsy is termed "symptomatic"; where it cannot be found, it is termed "idiopathic"—that is, of unknown origin. Even in these cases there is believed to be a defect in brain cells, since the EEG patterns are abnormal, showing a diffuse rather than a focal cerebral dysrhythmia (irregularity). In addition, about 10 per cent of the general population show brain wave abnormalities. Although these individuals do not suffer from epilepsy they are believed to be more susceptible than others to seizures.

Most authorities agree that there is a hereditary predisposition to epilepsy in the majority of cases of idiopathic epilepsy and a minority of symptomatic cases—particularly when the seizures start early in life. Grand mal seizures have been found to occur three times more frequently in near relatives of idiopathic epileptics than in the general population, and the chances that they will occur in both identical twins are eight times greater than among fraternal twins. But even where there is a predisposition to epilepsy, there is usually a precipitating factor which irritates the unstable, hypersensitive nerve cells and leads to their abnormal discharge. Stimuli which provoke seizures in one individual may not do so in another. They include sudden sounds or certain musical notes (musicogenic epilepsy), flickering lights (photic or photogenic seizures), menstruation, emotional stress, or a heavy intellectual burden.

The frequency of seizures varies greatly and in many cases seems to be closely related to the life adjustment of the patient. An individual who is subject to persistent conflicts, frustrations and tensions generally has more seizures than one who is rarely upset and leads a relatively satisfying, productive life. A recent theory holds that psychomotor seizures may serve the purpose of reducing tension, since some patients feel relieved after they have had an attack.

In the past some investigators have claimed there is a specific "epileptic personality," but more recent observers have discarded this idea. There is, however, a higher than average incidence of maladjustment among epileptics, due primarily to social rejection, insecurity, and job difficulties caused largely by the attitudes of employer or co-workers toward the disorder. Institutionalized patients sometimes react to their frustrations, and probably to the brain damage directly, by becoming irritable, rigid, self-centered and resentful. Significantly, office patients who live with their families do not exhibit undesirable traits nearly so often.

Children who suffer from symptomatic epilepsy frequently show the same personality characteristics as many other brain injured children: hyperactivity, aggressiveness, and irritability. Those who suffer from idiopathic epilepsy tend to be especially self-conscious and uncomfortable in social situations. Frequently their feelings of inadequacy and insecurity are aggravated by parental overprotection or rejection, as well as by difficulties in competing with other children at school or on the playground. These reactions do not, however, constitute a specific epileptic personality pattern.

The basic treatment for epilepsy today consists of medications which control the explosive activity of the nerve cells of the brain. Bromide salts (especially sodium bromide) were the major anticonvulsants from the middle of the nineteenth century to early in this century but have been almost completely discarded in view of their side effects and the danger of bromide intoxication. Phenylethyl barbituric acid (Phenobarbital), introduced in 1912, has proved to be a more successful drug and is still widely used for grand mal seizures as well as psychic equivalents, psychomotor seizures, and myoclonic attacks. It tends to produce drowsiness when first taken, but this effect diminishes if usage is prolonged. Though addiction is rare, dosages must be carefully controlled to avoid barbiturate poisoning.

Sodium diphenyl hydantoinate (Dilantin Sodium), introduced in 1937, has less sedative effect than the barbiturates though it may produce such side effects as unstable gait, tremor, gastric upset, and skin eruptions. Many physicians have found it more effective than barbiturates in controlling seizures, both grand mal and psychomotor. In some cases it also leads to improvement in co-operation, alertness, and general attitude.

Another anticonvulsant, methyl hydantoin (Mesantoin), has fewer side effects and is also widely used for grand mal, sometimes in combination with Dilantin, Phenobarbital, or related drugs such as Methobarbital and Mebaral. Three more recently developed drugs, phenylacetyl urea (Phenurone), primidone (Mysoline), and phenyl hydantoin (Peganone) are also administered both in grand mal and psychomotor cases, although special care must be exercised with Phenurone because of the possibility of liver damage and undesirable personality changes.

The first important drug for the treatment of petit mal was trimethadione (Tridione), which came into use in 1945. Since that time other effective drugs, particularly paramethadione (Paradione) and phensuximide (Milontin) have been developed. The dangerous condition known as status epilepticus, in which one seizure rapidly follows another, is treated with massive intravenous injections of sodium phenobarbital, and if that fails, the physician tries a general anesthetic such as ether, chloroform, or sodium pentothal.

Taken as a whole, the majority of epileptic patients must continue on medication indefinitely. Drugs can be discontinued in only about one-third of cases, after seizures have been eliminated for at least two years. There is no standard dosage for anticonvulsants. The physician must determine the most effective amount of the drug for each patient by experiment, and administer it under continuing supervision in order to avoid harmful side effects.

Where patients do not respond to drugs and where a tumor or focal brain lesion on one side of the brain can be operated on without special hazard, surgery may be employed. The number of persons who can be surgically treated is not large—only 1 to 2 per cent of all patients. The operation abolishes seizures in about 5 per cent of these cases and worthwhile improvement is achieved in another 25 per cent. New drugs and new surgical techniques are constantly under investigation.

The treatment of epilepsy must be based on an inclusive approach. Although drug therapy is the keystone, specialists find it important to maintain the general good health of the patient through a nutritious diet, regular exercise, and sustained activity. Excessive use of alcohol, undue fatigue, and long periods without food are to be avoided. Equally important is the solution of occupational, marital and educational problems, as well as provision for an active social life. A regular existence with a minimum of special stress has been found to be effective insurance against frequent seizures.

Many investigations have indicated that epileptics are, as a whole, capable of normal work performance, academic success, and social adjustment. Although some hazardous occupations must be avoided, the general accident record of epileptics is at least as good as average. In some states, such as Ohio and Wisconsin, they are permitted to drive, provided a doctor certifies that the seizures are under control. In these states their safety record has been far better than the average.

The prognosis for epilepsy has strikingly improved within the past generation. Seizures can be completely controlled in 50 to 60 per cent of cases, and the number and severity of attacks can be markedly reduced in another 30 per cent. Grand mal and petit mal respond best, then Jacksonian, while only about one-third of psychomotor patients become seizure-free. An increasing number of patients show such complete recovery that they can discontinue medication even after it has been given for years. An estimated 80 per cent of all adult epileptics are capable of regular employment. The fact that business and industry are giving epileptics a greater chance to work is one of the most hopeful signs for the future. In the past, society has been as great an enemy as the disease itself.

Preventive measures have yet to be discovered. Early detection and prompt treatment, however, can often forestall the development of a serious condition, especially when the stress of life is reduced while medication is being taken. In view of the possibility of hereditary predisposition, many specialists advise against having children if both husband and wife show epileptic brain waves, even if they have never experienced seizures. The chances that an overt epileptic will transmit the disease are minimal if he has no family history of epilepsy and if he has developed the condition after childhood or in an acquired form. Every case, however, requires individual investigation before advice on having children can be given.

Illustrative Case: EPILEPSY (PSYCHOTHERAPY)

Many epileptics are in need of individual psychotherapy in addition to medical treatment. Twenty-year-old Ray, who had been suffering from grand mal epilepsy for many years, is a case in point. The doctor who diagnosed Ray's condition found that he had a brain tumor, and recommended surgery. The young man, however, persistently refused to submit to an operation. In the course of discussion, the doctor was led to suspect that Ray might be unconsciously using his organic defect as a crutch.

When Ray was brought in for psychologi-

cal testing, the psychologist noticed that his mother dominated him and that he accepted this domination good-naturedly. He scored in the high average range on the intelligence test, but showed considerable uncertainty in giving his answers even when he knew them. On the "Draw a Person" test he had great difficulty completing an entire figure. When he finally finished it, the face had a stylized quality that suggested controlled emotion, and the young man displayed a hostile attitude in discussing it.

Social service records showed that Ray's father had left for the service when the boy was eight years of age. He had reacted by becoming insecure and withdrawn, and even after his father returned, remained fearful that he would leave again. At twenty he still shied away from social contact, and in his report the psychologist described him as "an alert, sensitive, intelligent boy who was unable to develop adequate social interest because of his unacceptable self-image, stemming from the organ inferiority" (that is, his epilepsy). Psychotherapy was strongly recommended.

Ray refused psychotherapy but finally agreed to see a social worker in the clinic. At the beginning of the sessions, his attitude toward himself was consistently self-deprecating, and his attitude toward all adults was mistrustful and hostile, although these feelings were somewhat disguised by a jocular attitude.

Ray soon revealed that he longed to work and be "free," but he was certain that he would fail on any job. Similarly, he wanted to date and engage in normal sexual behavior, but was afraid of his own impulses and was convinced that he would be rejected. He revealed that his father was highly critical of him and pressured him about getting a job and going out with girls. At the same time, his mother and three older sisters had been pampering him for years. His mother supplied him with an ample allowance which he spent at the local pool hall. The social worker felt that the original diagnosis of inferiority feelings with infantile dependence was fully confirmed.

The sessions with the social worker brought Ray to an awareness for his need for psychotherapy. Weekly sessions with a psychologist followed, during which a full study was made of his early recollections. He disclosed that he had always been helped because he was considered "different," and at the same time he had frequent dreams and fantasies in which he saw himself as an athletic champion. During these sessions he achieved considerable emotional insight, and as a result the therapist encouraged him to apply for a job.

Ray failed the first test he took, "because I was thinking of my mother"; but he recognized this reaction as an example of his defensive pattern. A few weeks later, he visited a government rehabilitation agency and was given an opportunity to register at a business school. While waiting for an opening at the school he took his first full-time job. The day he received his first pay check, he proudly informed his mother that he would no longer need an allowance. She seemed unimpressed and objected to giving up the allowance, and Ray at last realized that his mother had contributed to his neurosis by keeping him dependent.

Ray began to rebel at his mother's overprotection, and his father began to accept him as a son. Finally, after many sessions with the psychologist, he ceased to use his physical defect for defensive purposes. He began to take fuller responsibility for his own life, and showed greater vitality and confidence by joining a recreational center and dating girls. At this point he declared that he was willing to undergo surgery, and psychotherapy was discontinued by mutual consent. (Adopted from Angers, 1962)

EPILEPSY (Symptoms and Types).

Epilepsy comprises a group of disorders characterized by transient, recurrent episodes of clouding or loss of consciousness, sometimes with convulsive movements or automatic behavior. These symptoms, often referred to as "seizures," are associated with disturbances in the electrical discharges of the brain —that is, cerebral dysrhythmia.

Epilepsy is said to have the longest medical history of any disease. The word itself is derived from the Greek word for "seize," and in ancient times it was called the sacred disease, since it was believed to be due to divine visitation. Hippocrates, however, wrote prophetically, "Surely it too has its nature and causes whence it originates, just like other diseases, and is curable by means comparable to their cure."

Many historical figures have been subject to seizures—among them Caesar, Mohammed, Napoleon, Lord Byron, de Maupassant and Van Gogh. The present incidence of epilepsy in the United States has been estimated at between one and a half and two million. All races, and both sexes, are about equally subject to the disorder. Although it may have its onset at any age, over half of known cases appear before age fifteen. Thanks to the newer drugs, relatively few cases require institutional care today, and psychoses associated with convulsive disorders constitute only about 1.4 per cent of first admissions to mental hospitals.

Epileptic seizures take innumerable forms, depending on the precipitating cause, region of the brain affected, and character of the electrical discharge. They can be grouped, however, into four main types, each of which has its characteristic electroencephalograph or brain wave record (PLATES 10, 11, 12, and 13).

1. The most common and dramatic form of epilepsy, occurring in 60 per cent of cases, is *grand mal,* or "great illness." The typical brain wave pattern for this form of the disorder is a series of rapid sharp spikes. About half of these seizures start with a momentary warning "aura," usually too brief to permit the individual to prepare himself. The aura varies with the brain area involved, and may consist of stomach distress, numbness, unpleasant smells, noises, flashes of light or twitching muscles. This opening phase is immediately followed by the "tonic" phase in which consciousness is suddenly and completely lost, the arms and legs rigidly contract, and the patient falls and may injure himself. In this phase breathing is suspended, the face turns pale, the pupils dilate, the bladder usually empties, and contracting chest and

laryngeal muscles may produce a peculiar "epileptic cry." *See* AURA.

After ten to twenty seconds the "clonic" phase sets in, and for about a minute there are acute muscle spasms. The head strikes the ground, the legs jerk up and down, and the jaws open and shut so forcefully that a foamy mixture of air and saliva is generated. At this point there is danger of biting the tongue, and an object such as a pen should be thrust between the teeth on one side of the mouth. Within a few moments the convulsive movements begin to subside, and the patient either returns to consciousness or falls into a deep post-convulsive "coma" characterized by stertorous breathing, facial congestion, and absence of tendon reflexes. This is followed by a deep sleep of an hour or two. On awakening, the patient is usually bewildered and complains of headache and fatigue.

Some patients have grand mal attacks during sleep or just as they are falling asleep. A few suffer from *status epilepticus* in which one seizure follows another without intervening recovery of consciousness. This is a dangerous condition, but it can be arrested by medical means.

2. In *petit mal* or small illness epilepsy, consciousness is suddenly disturbed or interrupted without warning. In the most common form the patient does not fall, but stops whatever he is doing and sits for a few seconds with staring eyes and expressionless face. There is often a rhythmic twitching of the eyes, and he will probably drop anything he is holding. Immediately afterward he resumes his activities and may not even be aware of his momentary "absence."

Petit mal occasionally takes other forms. One type is the "akinetic" seizure in which there is a sudden muscular collapse accompanied by head nodding or falling. Another is the "myoclonic" seizure, during which the arm muscles contract but consciousness is usually retained.

Petit mal seizures tend to be frequent, varying from one or two to several dozen attacks a day. The illness usually starts between the ages of four and eight, but it may have its onset during adolescence. These smaller attacks sometimes develop into grand mal seizures, and occasionally the two types exist together. The typical electroencephalograph record shows wave-and-spike patterns.

3. *Jacksonian* epilepsy, named after the British neurologist J. Hughlings Jackson, resembles grand mal but starts with muscle twitching, numbness, tingling, or burning sensations in one region of the body. The disturbances then spread to the other side of the body and often terminate in a generalized convulsion with loss of consciousness. This type of attack rarely occurs in childhood, and is believed to result from focal lesions sustained early in life or later on. The most characteristic EEG pattern is a focal spike discharge, usually in the temporal lobe.

4. The major feature of *psychomotor* epilepsy is a trancelike state usually accompanied by some form of activity. The attacks vary considerably from case to case, but typically last for a minute or two and are associated with chewing and swallowing movements and incoherent speech. Some patients continue to perform routine activities automatically, although consciousness is clouded; others are briefly overwhelmed by feelings of terror, alarm, rage, depression, or ill humor. Delusions and auditory or visual hallucinations may occur, sometimes of a vague and ill-defined nature; in some cases the patient hears clear voices emanating from the abdomen or from the environment. A small minority, probably fewer than one out of a hundred, perform bizarre, senseless acts. During an episode of this kind the artist Van Gogh cut off one of his ears and sent it to a prostitute. A

few psychomotor patients have been known to commit crimes of a particularly brutal and revolting nature. In these cases the attack, or "furor" may last for several minutes, several hours or even days, and is followed by total amnesia for the episode. *See* FUROR, AUTOMATISM.

Psychomotor attacks occur in about 10 per cent of children and 30 per cent of adults who are afflicted with seizures. The confusional state is sometimes misdiagnosed as schizophrenia, but an electroencephalograph record will distinguish the two, since it shows characteristic spike discharges focusing in the anterior temporal lobe. Some specialists use the term *temporal lobe* epilepsy as a synonym for the psychomotor type.

Other forms of epilepsy are sometimes observed. In *epilepsia cursiva* ("running fit") the seizure takes the form of sudden running. This may be a variation of the psychomotor type, and occasionally follows a grand mal seizure. The running episode is brief, and consciousness is clouded to a variable degree. *Autonomic seizures* are characterized by recurrent attacks of heart palpitation, vomiting, sweating or abdominal pain. Some authorities hesitate to include these attacks among the "true" epilepsies. The sudden irresistible sleep attacks known as *narcolepsy* are sometimes considered variants of epilepsy, as is the sudden collapse of all voluntary muscles known as *cataplexy*. Hysteric patients sometimes have seizures, but these attacks are distinguished from true epilepsy by several factors: the electroencephalogram is usually normal; the convulsion always occurs in the presence of others and is likely to be theatrical and attention-getting; the usual "march" of phases (tonic, clonic etc.) is lacking; the patient rarely injures himself; and the episode is not followed by a period of unconsciousness. *See* CONVERSION REACTION, NARCOLEPSY, CATAPLEXY.

An estimated 25 to 40 per cent of epileptic patients experience more than one type of seizure. The combination of grand mal with petit mal is most common, although grand mal is sometimes associated with the Jacksonian type. Even where seizures are frequent very few patients suffer permanent mental or physical damage. In the rare case where a psychosis develops, it seems to be a reaction to the affliction rather than implicit in the disorder itself. In any type of epilepsy the patient's reactions may be complicated by the attitudes of the family and the community toward the disorder. *See* ILLUSTRATIVE CASE, *under* EPILEPSY (ETIOLOGY AND THERAPY).

Some children who have epilepsy also suffer from cerebral palsy, mental retardation, or anomalies of brain structure. Such children may have an almost insupportable psychological and physical burden to carry. A few adults and some children with severe epilepsy become mentally deteriorated, particularly after long institutionalization. In these cases seizures started early in life and are usually frequent; response to medication is poor; and there is evidence of both focal and generalized encephalographic abnormality. Deteriorated patients show a narrowing of interest, poverty of ideas, blunting of emotional response, and impairment of memory and comprehension. In extreme cases they lose all relationship to the environment and sink to a vegetative level.

Illustrative Case: EPILEPSY

Eddie F., is a twenty-seven-year-old single man who has a history of grand mal, petit mal, and psychomotor seizures. The petit mal condition was noticed first when the patient was ten years old. Since that time he has shown various other forms of convulsive disorder, and has been on continuous medication.

He was referred to a psychiatric hospital when he was twenty-two years old because of uncontrollable seizures involving both legs. The condition cleared spontaneously soon after hospitalization. After six months in the hospital, the patient was discharged. Two months later, he was admitted to the city hospital in a dirty, unshaven, confused state. He appeared to be having auditory hallucinations, and had the delusion that someone was trying to kill him. He was referred to the psychiatric hospital where a diagnosis was made of chronic brain syndrome associated with a convulsive disorder. Within several days the patient's condition improved, although there was a loss of memory for the entire episode.

The patient was sickly as a child, and frequently ran high fevers without apparent cause. He was a feeding problem throughout his early years. When he entered school, he had trouble concentrating and did poor academic work. His teachers described him as a "dreamy" individual. However, intelligence tests showed that he was of well above average intelligence. The first convulsive seizures were noted when he was twelve years old. He was working as a caddy at a golf course and his companion noticed that he had brief blackout periods. The mother recalled instances in which she had seen him blink his eyes and seem dazed for a few seconds at a time when he was younger. Eventually neurological examinations were undertaken, and a diagnosis of convulsive disorder was established. As he grew older, Eddie showed various behavior problems and adjustment difficulties. On one occasion he ran away from home, on another he stole an automobile, and he had an extremely poor work record. There is also a history of heterosexual promiscuity and homosexual prostitution.

When seen at the hospital, the patient was a neat, pleasant, and co-operative young man who appeared eager to talk about his problems. While there was some irrelevancy, there were no signs of disorientation, delusions, hallucinations, or other psychopathology. His judgment appeared good, and there was some degree of insight. (Kisker, 1964)

EQUILIBRIUM (Labyrinthine Sense; Vestibular Sense). The sense of balance and position.

Two sets of receptors in the inner ear, or "labyrinth," are responsible for our senses of balance and position (see *Fig. 28*, p. 543). The first of these consists of three semicircular canals which respond mainly when the head is rotated. They are in the form of hair-lined tubes oriented at right angles to each other: up-down, right-left, and backward-forward. The hairs contain sensitive nerve endings which are bent and activated by a watery liquid which flows one way or another when there is an acceleration or deceleration in the rate of rotation. The second set consists of the vestibular sac receptors (utricle and saccule) which contain the otolith ("ear stone") organs that respond to the static force of gravity as well as to the straight-line motion. Pressure of the stones, or granules, on hair cells in the sacs produces nerve impulses that inform the brain of the upright position or tilt of the head.

The equilibrium mechanism is largely automatic and works closely with our sense of movement (kinesthesis). When we are thrown off balance, sensory impulses from the inner ear set off reflex motor adjustments which enable us to regain our equilibrium. A good illustration of these adjustments is the cat's ability to land on all fours after being turned upside down and dropped from a height. The head is twisted into a normal position first, followed by a reflex twisting of the trunk and body. Parachutists make similar movements during the free fall before the parachute is opened.

The vestibular sense is involved in "motion sickness," an ailment which is totally absent in people whose vestibular mechanisms are not functioning. At present there is no adequate explanation for the fact that some people become motion-sick when traveling in planes, autos and ships while others do not. However, we do know that this unpleasant feeling of nausea is caused by both physiological and psychological factors. The physiological effects appear to be due to reflex actions in the alimentary tract. Among the psychological factors are suggestion, emotional conditioning and past experience. Many people become ill because they expect to, and therefore pay excessive attention to slight discomfort. Nausea can also result from an inconsistent set of sensations, particularly in an airplane. If the plane is flying smoothly, and if we close our eyes or keep them focused on its interior, we do not usually experience vestibular sensations. But if we look out of the window, the combination of the unfamiliar sight of the earth or clouds moving rapidly by, plus the absence of a sensation of movement, may make us dizzy or sick to our stomach.

Vestibular sensations may be counteracted by drugs such as Dramamine and Bonamine, or by lying down with the eyes closed. It is also possible to reduce or prevent motion sickness by becoming habituated to the stimuli and by anticipating the regularly recurring motions. The latter method of adjustment is utilized by acrobats, figure skaters, and ballet dancers. These performers learn to ignore vestibular sensations and rely on other senses during their complicated routines. One trick is to keep the head as motionless as possible while spinning around. This can be done by fixating on a stationary object. After a time the rapid eye movements (nystagmus) that accompany head rotation, one of the primary reasons for dizziness, become very slight.

Candidates for commercial aviation, airborne military service and space flight must go through rigorous tests of equilibrium as well as long hours of practice in flight trainers. The object of their training is not merely to overcome any tendency to motion sickness, but to teach them to disregard misleading vestibular sensations and rely instead on their instruments when engaged in climbing, diving, or other maneuvers. *See* VERTIGO.

EQUIPMENT DESIGN. Equipment design is an area of human engineering

or engineering psychology devoted to the arrangement of the work space, the design of information devices or "displays," and the design of control devices. In a broader sense, equipment design extends beyond these areas to include the design of military equipment and space vehicles, road signs, traffic lights and highways, and consumer articles such as radios or kitchen ranges.

The study of equipment began with F. W. Taylor's efforts to design the most effective shovels for men working in steel plants (1898), and F. B. Gilbreth's attempt to design a work chair and a work space that would minimize strain and fatigue (1916). The field was further advanced by the Great Britain Industrial Fatigue Research Board, which introduced the idea that "the worker and the machine form a single system" (1926), and which recommended the redesign of machines in such fields as laundering, leather working, and textiles in order to make them easier to use. During World War II, engineering psychology became a separate discipline, since airplanes, rockets, radios, and other instruments became so complex that they taxed human capacities to an extreme degree. This led to the development of design principles which have been applied throughout civilian as well as military industry. The whole field is a rapidly expanding one today, and has already made significant contributions to our basic psychological knowledge.

Man-Machine Systems. The specific details of equipment design can best be understood when projected on the broad background of a man-machine system. This is defined as a co-ordinated whole in which the human being and the machine play interacting parts. The major components of such a system are input, mechanism, displays, operator, controls, output, and work environment. In driving a car, as Smith (1964) has pointed out, oil and gas are inputs, the battery and motor are mechanisms, the speed and oil gauges are displays, the driver is the operator, the accelerator, steering wheel and brakes are controls, the speed and power of the car are outputs, and the temperature and noise inside the car are the work environment. Each of these must be coordinated with all the others for the most efficient operation, and it must be possible for the driver to adjust and readjust the components as traffic conditions, road conditions or his own desires dictate. In more technical terms, the input and output of the parts of the machine must be matched, the speed of each must be adapted to the others (time constants), and no part of the system must be overloaded. This same analysis can be readily applied to industrial systems in which the worker is involved with machines of greater or lesser complexity.

The psychologist enters the picture as a "human engineer" who provides information on the man component so that the industrial engineer can design the total system and its parts with human behavior and human limitations in mind. In the most general sense, human beings perform three functions in the system: information receiving (seeing, hearing, etc.), information processing (making judgments, data processing, making decisions), and action (operating controls, using tools, communicating). The two aspects of this process that are most concerned with equipment design are receiving information through the meters and other "displays" and controlling operations through dials and other "controls." But since these operations take place in a particular environment, the "work space" also has to be considered.

Work Space. Early time-motion analysts recognized the importance of spatial arrangement and designed the work space so that (1) the worker would not cross and recross his line of motion in reaching for materials;

(2) he would not have to search for articles because each would have its place; and (3) tools such as screw drivers were "pre-positioned" so that they could be grasped in the position in which they were to be used.

More recently the entire work area has been redesigned in accordance with the dimensions and movement characteristics of the worker. One design places the bins containing parts to be assembled in a semicircular layout in order to avoid excessive reaching. In some designs two different areas are used: a "normal" area in front of the worker, determined by using his elbow as a pivot, and a "maximum area" which includes positions farther out on the sides, determined by rotating the full arm with the shoulder as pivot. Careful design of the space is especially important for repetitive operations such as collating papers, stuffing envelopes, and small assembly jobs. One radio company saved 34,000 hours a year by shortening the reach to supply bins by six inches!

Studies for the Navy have resulted in a modification of the traditional semicircular work space (*Fig. 17*). The circle was somewhat flattened, and the right and left corners were chopped off because it was found that the elbow does not remain in a fixed position but moves out and away from the body during work activities. This finding has been useful in designing not only a flat working surface, but also control panels and vertical working areas.

Research has also shown that the standard typewriter layout makes inefficient use of the fingers, since it overloads smaller and weaker fingers and the left hand as a whole, while it underloads the stronger and more efficient fingers. A totally different keyboard has been designed on the basis of tapping and strength tests, and studies have shown that it requires less learning time, increases typing speed, decreases errors, and produces

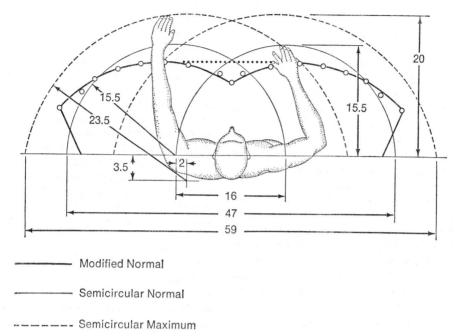

——————— Modified Normal

——————— Semicircular Normal

– – – – – – - Semicircular Maximum

Fig. 17. Where should work and materials be placed for greatest efficiency? A Navy study has shown that the area enclosed by the solid line is superior to the traditional semicircular areas. The area is flattened at the center for a vertical work space, as indicated by the dotted line.

less fatigue than the standard keyboard. However, in the thirty years since the new arrangement was first suggested, it has not been adopted by typewriter manufacturers. For other details on the work environment *see* ILLUMINATION CONDITIONS, MUSIC AND WORK, VENTILATION CONDITIONS.

Displays. Fast-moving vehicles and machinery have made the problem of displays a crucial one not only for efficient operation but for safety and comfort as well. The constantly growing complexity of modern apparatus has increased the need for meters and indicators to a point where the human being is often overloaded. Five major approaches are employed in solving this problem today. First, *eliminating unnecessary displays:* a study of the goals of the entire system may reveal, for example, that a revolutions-per-minute dial may be unnecessary when

the operator of the machine is not an engineer. Second, *nonvisual displays* may be substituted for visual displays, since the eyes are often overworked. Auditory indicators (bells, buzzers) are the most common alternative, although vibrators that touch the skin are also in use. Third, *qualitative displays* are sufficiently accurate for some operations, and are quicker to read than quantitative instruments—for example, a high-medium-low temperature gauge may be substituted for a dial and pointer. Fourth, *check displays* can often be used in place of numerical or quantitative indicators—for instance, a red light that glows if the oil pressure of the car is low. If several check and qualitative displays are used, the panel itself will be simplified and the danger of overloading will be reduced.

Fifth, *indicator design* can often be improved. Tests show, for instance, that counter displays like the mileage indicator on a car can often be read more quickly and accurately than dial displays such as the speedometer (Weldon and Peterson, 1957). In an airplane, however, an altimeter that combines a dial with a counter has been found superior to either one alone. The counter shows units of 1000 feet, and the dial shows units of 100 feet—for example, if the altitude is 7300, the counter shows 7 and the arrow of the dial points to 3. When dials are required, the nearer they are to counters the better. Tests have shown that open window dials showing about three numbers are most easily read, with round dials, semicircular dials, horizontal, and finally vertical dials following in that order (Sleight, 1948) (*Fig. 18*). Studies have also been made of the specific characteristics of dials. A three-inch diameter with numbers one-half inch apart and progressing in a clockwise direction has been found best for most purposes (Chapanis et al., 1949). Finally, dials should be arranged in a simple, definite pattern, with the normal reading in the twelve o'clock position,

and with special prominence given to the most important indicators.

Controls. Many of the above principles can be applied to controls. In some cases the number can be reduced by redesigning the apparatus—for example, it has been possible to eliminate the stick shifts in automobiles and the many knobs on the older radio and television sets. On-off controls (light switches for example) are the simplest type. Next in simplicity is the position control, which can sometimes be substituted for the more complex continuous control. An example of the position control is the three-position (low, medium, high) control used for heating pads and some stoves. In some cases it is also possible to substitute stick controls, which require the use of only one hand, for wheel controls which require two hands. Foot and knee controls are also used on some machines to relieve the hands and thereby increase the safety of the operation.

Natural controls (turning right to go right) are best, although they cannot always be used. Rotor controls are most easily managed when they turn in a clockwise direction; a good ex-

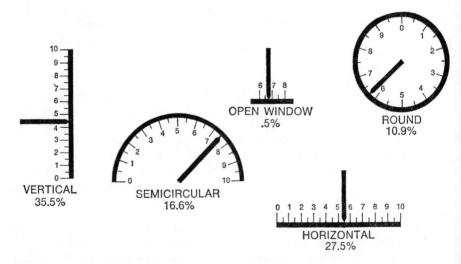

Fig. 18. Which dial is easiest to read? The percentage of errors is indicated under each type.

ample is the telephone dial. Tests of the all-numeral system of telephone dialing show that it is 10 per cent faster and slightly more accurate than the combination of letters with numbers. Memory studies show that the two methods are about equal for short-term memory, but the combination method is slightly superior for long-term memory, although this is relatively unimportant because we usually look up numbers we have not used for some time. A survey made ten weeks after installation of the new system showed that 43 per cent favored it, 24 per cent had no preference, and 33 per cent preferred the older system.

Efficiency in the use of controls can also be improved by using shape, size, color, and position coding. In experiments with controls of sixteen different shapes, Green and Anderson (1955) found that operators successfully distinguished between controls with small and large handles, and made very few errors in judging different shapes by touch alone. There is less confusion when controls are far apart than when they are close together, but this is not always feasible. The positions should also be standardized wherever possible. Many accidents have been traced to the fact that gear positions are different in different cars, and that controls are placed in different positions in different airplanes. Reaching for a control that isn't there has proved fatal in more than one case.

EROTIC. An adjective applied to any person, object, or experience that is consciously or unconsciously charged with sexual feeling.

In psychoanalytic theory all sexual energy is believed to stem from a single instinctual source, the libido. A great many activities, ideas and parts of the body may become "eroticized," or "libidinized." Dancing is an obviously erotic activity. The pursuit of ideas is less obvious but is regarded as an ex-

pression of the same basic instinct. Some psychoanalytic theorists trace scientific curiosity to voyeurism, others simply remind us of phrases like "the love of knowledge." In fact, in this theory anything we "love" to do or to be has been eroticized and can be traced to the libido. *See* LIBIDO.

EROTOGENIC ZONE (Erogenous Zone). An area of the body that is particularly susceptible to erotic stimulation. Three of these zones are considered primary: the oral, anal, and genital. In addition, the breasts and especially the nipples, in women (and to a lesser degree in men), the region surrounding the genital organs, and the other orifices of the body (nose, ears) are also invested with sexual feeling. The entire surface of the skin, particularly in regions close to the three primary zones, is also considered erogenous, as indicated by the pleasurable sensations experienced while being caressed or lightly stroked.

EROTOMANIA. Pathological preoccupation with erotic thoughts and fantasies; also used for compulsive sexual activity with the opposite sex. This compulsion takes two primary forms: nymphomania, which is an insatiable sex drive in females; and satyriasis, an insatiable sex drive in males.

People who manifest erotomania constantly think and talk about sexual activity to the exclusion of almost any other subject. The popular explanation is that they are physically "oversexed," but studies indicate that this is generally untrue. Another common idea is that the tendency to be preoccupied with sex is due to sexual frustration and deprivation. This theory can often be used to explain a normal preoccupation with this subject but not the extreme, morbid reaction that is termed erotomania.

In true erotomania there are believed to be deeper sources than either frustration or excessive physical drive. The two sources most frequently mentioned are unrecognized doubts about sexual adequacy, and latent homosexual tendencies.

A psychotic form of erotomania is sometimes found in paranoia and paranoid schizophrenia. Here it takes the form of an erotic delusion in which the patient believes he is sexually loved by an individual he does not personally know. In many cases this individual is a public figure. The patient falsely interprets statements made by this person, even in the press, as proof of his love, and may pester him with letters or telephone calls. The French use the term "psychose passionelle," or Clérambault's syndrome, for this condition, and some American psychiatrists call it "pure erotomania." Arieti and Meth (1959) cite this case: "One patient, the wife of a successful storekeeper, considered the business success of her husband as proof of another man's love for her. Because of his love, he was directing many customers to the husband's store, so that the husband would make a lot of money. Any gift the husband bought for the patient was interpreted by the patient as an indirect gift from the other man." Psychoanalysts stress three points in interpreting this type of delusion. It may be a projection of self-love onto another person; a defensive maneuver substituting heterosexual attachment for unconscious homosexual desires which the patient is seeking to deny; or an attempt to cling frantically to a love-object, especially when the patient fears he will be rejected by a person he loves. See NYMPHOMANIA, SATYRIASIS.

ESCAPE LEARNING. Acquisition of patterns of response that lead to escape from a dangerous or unpleasant situation.

Escape learning is highly important in both animal and human life. To avoid injury, birds scatter at the sight of hunters, and people seek shelter from sun, rain and wind. Human beings have the benefit of verbal instruction and admonition from others, and are more capable of utilizing reasoning and past experiences than animals. Nevertheless, our first attempts to get out of undesirable situations are often of a simple trial-and-error variety. This is particularly true when we are suddenly faced with a fire, earthquake, or other disaster that involves a threat to life. See CIVILIAN CATASTROPHE REACTIONS, PROBLEM-SOLVING.

Laboratory studies of escape learning have usually been carried out on animals. In a typical experiment, a rat was placed in a specially constructed box with a metal grid on the floor and a wheel that would turn an electric current off. In one procedure, the current was turned on full force and the rat received a painful shock from the grid. On the first trial most rats became extremely agitated, squealing and jumping about; but in thirty to forty seconds they usually turned the wheel by accident and cut off the shock. This response occurred more and more promptly in subsequent trials, until they learned to escape the shock within a fraction of a second after its onset.

The same apparatus was used in a second procedure, except that the shock was gradually increased from zero to maximal intensity. In this experiment rats reacted to the shock about sixty seconds after the electricity was turned on, and only chanced upon the escape wheel three to six minutes later. After about ten trials they were able to escape the shock as soon as they began to feel it. The slower reaction enabled the investigators to observe more closely how the emotional response to the shock stimulus developed. The experiment also showed that rats can learn to use a weak stimulus as a signal to turn the wheel and avoid a more intense and painful shock. Responding to a signal is regarded as a relatively advanced ability, somewhat comparable to the behavior of human beings who seek shelter as soon as they see storm clouds in the sky.

Further experiments have demonstrated that the rat is capable of still another variety of escape learning. In this case the first procedure was used. After the animal had learned the wheel-turning response, a light bulb was turned on just before the onset of the shock, and when the animal turned the wheel both the light and the shock went off. After about thirty to fifty pairings of light and shock, the rat learned to turn the wheel as soon as the light was turned on, and thus avoided the shock. Avoidance learning of this kind is considered even more complex than the first two types, since the signal is not directly connected with the painful stimulus. The experiment helps to explain how some of our common fears are acquired. A child might try to hide from all white-coated men because the doctor who hurt him wore a white coat. In this case the coat acts as a signal that elicits the fear associated with the doctor. See AVOIDANCE LEARNING.

ESQUIROL, JEAN (1772–1840). Esquirol, an early exponent of the functional point of view and of humane treatment in psychiatry, was born in Toulouse, France. After studying medicine at the University of Toulouse and Montpellier, he served as public health officer in the army. In 1794 he became Philippe Pinel's assistant at Salpétrière, taking over as director in 1811. His first published work was his doctoral thesis, in which he proposed that emotional conditions were the source of many mental illnesses, a revolutionary concept in view of the prevailing opinion among doctors that insanity was caused by organic disorders, and among laymen that it resulted from possession by the devil.

At Salpétrière Esquirol continued Pinel's humane approach and made systematic studies of his patients. In 1817 he established the first teaching clinic in psychiatry, and was probably the first investigator to use a statistical approach to the types and causes of mental illness. His studies revealed that a large percentage of his patients had been subjected to disturbing experiences, among which he mentioned monetary problems, unhappy love life, loss of position, and conflict with the mores of society. These statistics buttressed his theory that mental illness was primarily due to psychological factors.

As a result of his clinical studies, Esquirol classified all psychoses into five categories, in contrast to the current tendency to give a different Latin name to every new symptom, a practice that produced more confusion than understanding. The five categories were mania, dementia, idiocy, lypemania, and monomania. He applied the term lypemania to melancholia with delusions, a condition that is now classified as depression. He also introduced the term hallucination, clearly differentiating it from delusion or false perception. His category of monomania applied to persons who were dominated by a single idea, a condition which is now recognized as paranoid schizophrenia. In addition, he anticipated the modern view that some disturbances of intelligence may be due to emotional disturbances rather than brain lesions.

Esquirol left the Salpétrière in 1826 to become director of the Royal Sanitarium at Charenton, a semiprivate institution of the highest reputation. During the years that followed he had a profound influence on the practice of psychiatry in France. He drafted the Law of 1838, which legally established humane treatment for mental patients. He insisted that criminals were sick people suffering from monomania, and should therefore be treated like any other patient. He sent a *mémoire* to the Minister of the Interior, stating how an institution should be run—a document which Zilboorg and Henry (1941) have called "one of the ablest and most influential in the history of administrative psychology." On a trip to Italy he convinced the king that a newly built hospital was unfit for patients, and as a result it was turned into an armory, and a new structure was built according to Esquirol's plans. In his own country he was responsible for the construction of ten new mental hospitals.

Esquirol's final work, published two years before his death, *Les Maladies Mentales Considérées sous Les Rapports Médicales, Hygiéniques et Médico-Légales,* (*Mental Disorders Considered in Their Medical, Hygienic and Medico-Legal Relationships*) summarizing his lifelong teaching, has been called the first modern treatise on clinical psychiatry (Bromberg, 1959). In attempting to evaluate Esquirol, it would be hard to determine whether he made greater contributions on a practical or on a theoretical level to the development of modern psychiatry.

ESTHETICS. The study of the nature of art and the art experience.

Ever since Plato esthetics has been a province of philosophy, but from the time of Fechner, it has also been approached from a psychological point of view. Though the two approaches overlap, they tend to differ in both objectives and methodology. The philosophy of art utilizes the methods of direct observation and intellectual analysis, and is primarily concerned with the definition of art, standards to be used in judging works of art, and the esthetic experience as a human value. The psychology of art is based on systematic observation, measurement, and experimental method; it is aimed at describing the sources of the creative impulse and the way we perceive, understand and react to works of art. The following is a summary of recent psychological findings based largely on a review by Irvin L. Child (1967).

Understanding of Art. Psychology has made a number of contributions to the study of the meaning of art. First, it has focused attention on the esthetic experience itself, and has shown that individuals differ widely in their reactions to the same work. In other words, instead of possessing a single "true" meaning, a painting or poem or piece of music appears to have many meanings. One of the reasons for this diversity is that different individuals bring different backgrounds of experience and different levels of understanding to the act of contemplation—but another is that there are varied *kinds* of meaning involved in the experience itself, and an observer may respond to one kind more fully than to another.

Many attempts have been made to identify the different kinds of meaning; Child offers a particularly comprehensive classification, based on the distinction between "referential" and "expectational" types. Referential meaning includes (a) conventional reference—for example, a dove in a medieval painting signifies the Holy Spirit; (b) iconic or configurational representation, as when a portrait directly represents the subject, or an actor is made up to look as well as act like Mark Twain; (c) exemplary reference, as when certain patterns and colors in abstract paintings, or certain tones and melodies in music represent emotional states without resembling them iconically. Expectational meaning includes (a) syntactical expectation: the syntax or structure of poetry leads us to expect a certain rhythm or rhyme, and the syntax of music leads us to expect the resolution of chords in a certain way; (b) causal expectation: the images in a work of art may reveal something about the unconscious wishes or conflicts that led the artist to produce it; and (c) pragmatic expectation: the architecture of an office building can be understood, in part at least, in terms of expectations about what it would be like to work in it. All these types of meaning contribute to our understanding of works of art.

Many studies have been made of the meanings experienced in the individual arts. In the field of music, Meyer (1956) bases the perception of meaning on the arousal and resolution of an ever-changing series of expectations about the next note, alterations in rhythm, melody, and other components. The trained viewer may experience these "embodied meanings" more technically and the untrained more emotionally. Cooke (1959) believes emotions are essential to the perception of *all* meaning in music, and Pratt (1954) states that "music sounds the way the emotions feel."

As to the specific emotions experienced, tests have shown that groups of students agree substantially on the emotional meaning attributed to many musical passages; and when changes are made in specific passages (such as raising the pitch or altering the tempo), they exert a marked effect on the judgment of emotional meaning (Hevner 1937). Other experiments have shown that listeners tend to make the same type of drawings in response to single notes sounded in crescendo or in diminuendo (Karwoski, Odbert, Osgood, 1942), and it has also been found that college students tend to select the same sensory metaphors that critics use in characterizing operatic voices (Brown, Leiter, and Hildum, 1957). Many studies have also shown that musically educated and musically uneducated people tend to agree closely on both the emotional and sensory meanings they ascribe to musical passages. There is also some evidence of agreement across cultural lines in studies of folk music made by Gundlach (1932), and Lomax (1962), though more research of the intercultural, comparative type is needed.

In the field of visual art, experimental psychology has concentrated largely on the meaning of specific elements rather than entire works, although Arnheim (1962) has made a start in the latter direction in his study of the evolution of Picasso's Guernica mural. Several investigators have found considerable agreement between the emotional meanings ascribed by college students and by critics to colors and forms in abstract paintings (Child, 1962; Springbett, 1960). Research has also shown that the same adjectives are often applied to individual details (Poffenberger and Barrows, 1924); and that many people draw similar lines to fit specific mood terms like "gay" and "sad" (Scheerer and Lyons, 1957). People also tend to agree in their reactions to different colors. Wright and Rainwater (1962) have sampled the entire population of West Germany, and found marked agreement in the emotional and sensory meanings which adults associate with different colors. However, none of these studies has resulted in complete consensus, and hence there is room for individual interpretation. *See* COLOR REACTIONS.

In the field of literature, various studies have shown that the meaning of poetry, as opposed to prose, is largely dependent on sound. Hevner (1937), for example, performed experiments with nonsense syllables and found that different emotional meanings were attributed to harsh and smooth consonants, front and back vowels. Not enough research has been done, however, to indicate whether similar sounds have universal meaning in poetry or in language as a whole. Hymes (1960) has found some evidence that the meaning of individual poems may be dependent on a repetition of key words having special sound patterns, somewhat parallel to the leitmotifs in Wagner's music.

A totally different approach to meaning is suggested by psychoanalytic theory, which interprets literature as well as other art forms as objectifications of unconscious mental processes, in the same way that dream fantasies express forbidden desires. Though it is not easy to prove that these meanings are operative, the "depth" approach gives the critic an additional tool for interpretation and helps to show the extent to which art may be an expression of universal human conflicts.

Psychological Reactions to Works of Art. The investigations here have been confined largely to immediate reactions rather than long-term effects of art experiences on values, character and way of life. On the problem of judgment, several experimenters have shown that college students tend to be strongly influenced by the judgments of others. Farnsworth and Beaumont (1929), for example, found that unfamiliar paintings were rated more attractive when accompanied by comments suggesting that they were highly regarded by experts and by the social élite; and Sherif (1935) found that when a prose quotation was falsely attributed to a well-known author, a student's judgment tended to conform to his evaluation of that author. A number of more recent experiments, however, have indicated that the effect of prestige suggestion may be relatively slight, especially in poetry and drama (Michael, Rosenthal, DeCamp, 1949; Francès, 1963).

Attempts have also been made to discover what effect training in the arts has on judgment. A comparison between ratings of pictures of oriental rugs has indicated that although the judgments of experts differ considerably among themselves, they show little agreement with judgments of nonexperts (Gordon, 1923). By reworking Gordon's statistics, Child has shown that the experts tended to agree with each other somewhat more closely than the nonexperts; and in a study of his own, he found marked differences between student preferences and connoisseur preferences for the same group of pictures (1962). Others, however, have found less agreement among connoisseurs than among non-connoisseurs (Francès and Voillaume, 1964; Gordon, 1956).

A number of crosscultural studies also relate to the problem of art judgment. Some of them indicate that in spite of the fact that art products in primitive societies must usually conform to ritual and practical requirements, there is often considerable interest in their esthetic qualities on the part of both producers and spectators. But the question whether the judgments of connoisseurs would agree across cultural boundaries is still unsettled. Empirical studies are hard to carry out, since cultural backgrounds and symbolic meanings differ so widely. Nevertheless, a start has been made in the visual arts by Gerbrands (1957) and Child and Siroto (1965), who have found some agreement in judgments of primitive masks made by individuals in more advanced and less advanced cultures.

What are the bases on which connoisseurs and non-connoisseurs judge works of art? Peel (1944) has found that nonexperts tend to judge paintings by naturalness, and experts by good composition; Pickford (1948) has concluded that subjects from both groups respond primarily to harmony between emotional expression and form or design. Many investigators agree that artists as a whole place far less emphasis than nonartists on faithfulness of representation. There is also evidence that artists tend to prefer complex and asymmetrical designs, while nonartists prefer simple, symmetrical designs (Barron and Welsh, 1952; Munsinger and Kessen, 1964).

Other investigations have indicated that preference for deviation from regularity may be shared by connoisseurs and non-connoisseurs, such as a preference for vibrato over pure tone (Seashore, 1947), variability in sound patterns in poetry (Schramm, 1935), novelty and surprise in paintings judged excellent by experts (Springbett, 1960).

On the other hand, Berlyne (1966) and others have concluded that observers prefer *either* a very low or a fairly high degree of complexity, with connoisseurs preferring complexity more than non-connoisseurs.

Studies made by Williams (1960) and Burt (1960) have shown that subjects who scored high on art judgment tests in one field of art were likely to score high in other fields of art—an indication of the existence of a general esthetic sensitivity. Child (1962, 1965) has found that students whose evaluations of paintings agreed with those of connoisseurs tend to have certain personality characteristics in common, particularly independence of judgment and tolerance of complexity.

As to agreement among nonexperts, various studies indicate that although correlations *within* student groups are low, correlations between the averages of different student groups tend to be high. Comparison between judgments of the same works of art in different nations are inconclusive; some show substantial agreement, others little or none. As to sensory preferences, studies in this country show a high degree of uniformity in reaction to colors, with blues usually given the highest preference rating, followed closely by certain reds and greens, and with yellows generally appearing at the low end of the scale (Guilford, 1939; Helson and Lansford, 1966). The latter experimenters also found a pronounced general preference for high saturation in figure colors and low saturation in background colors, as well as a consistent preference for warm colors among men and cool colors among women.

Finally, another step toward relating preferences to personality characteristics has been taken by Knapp (1964), who found that a special interest in abstract expressionist painting correlated highly with freedom of emotional expression; interest in representational painting with a practical, matter-of-fact approach; and

interest in geometric abstract painting with intellectualism and withdrawal.

Creator and Creativity. Application of creativity tests indicates that originality in art is sometimes, but not always, positively correlated with originality in nonartistic activities such as unusual responses on word association items (MacKinnon, 1962). MacKinnon (1965) has also found that creative individuals tend to be confident and self-accepting, and to set their own standards instead of being preoccupied with the impression they make on others or the demands of others. Similarities in background have been found among architects as well as among school children who score high on creativity tests. In both groups, the mother has usually led an active life outside the home, and both parents have stressed independence, integrity, and self-determination, rather than conformity and obedience. *See* CREATIVITY TESTS.

A start has also been made on the problem of relating the personality of the creator to the characteristics of his work. Freud emphasized the artist's ability to mold material in such a way that it expresses his fantasies faithfully and at the same time opens the way for others to obtain "comfort and consolation" from their own unconscious sources of pleasure. He believed it was possible to infer the artist's personality from his art productions, as he himself attempted to do with Leonardo da Vinci. Others have followed this approach with Shakespeare, Jonson, Marlowe, and Melville. Some interpreters stress the embodiment of manifest personality characteristics in art productions, while others follow Freud in stressing latent characteristics. Another avenue of research as suggested by Wallach and Gahm (1960), who found a correlation between personality characteristics and the production of abstract designs and doodles by nonartists—for example, a tendency toward expansive drawings among extroverted women with a low anxiety level and introverted women with a high anxiety level.

ETIOLOGY. Causation; the systematic study of the causes of mental and physical disorders. This article will deal with the causes of mental disorders.

The causes of mental disorders can be roughly divided into predisposing and precipitating factors. Predisposing factors take the form of either constitutional tendencies or faulty development, or both together. These factors render the individual vulnerable to disorder by weakening his capacity to adjust or by lowering his tolerance for stress. Precipitating factors consist of stresses that overburden the individual's adjustive resources and produce an overt condition. In most cases both types of factors play important parts. In some instances, however—toxic conditions or disaster reactions, for example—extreme stress plays the major role; while in others, as in the gradual formation of a character or neurotic disorder, the major responsibility lies with faulty personality development.

Both predisposing and precipitating factors tend to fall into three general categories: the biological (organic or biogenic), the psychological (functional, or psychogenic), and the sociological (sociogenic). Here again one or another type of factor may play the dominant role. In one case a physiological condition such as cerebral arteriosclerosis may be the major factor; in another a psychological factor, such as internal conflicts; and in a third a sociological factor such as a pathogenic home and neighborhood. In many cases all three types of determinants contribute in some degree. Moreover, they do not operate in isolation, but in dynamic interaction, and for this reason the term "dynamics" is frequently used instead of etiology or causation. As an example, alcoholic psychosis may be traced to (a) the cumulative toxic effects of excessive alcohol, (b) personality deficiencies which prompted the patient to drink excessively and (c) social factors, such as a highly competitive job and the cultural pattern of using alcohol as a source of satisfaction and an outlet for tension.

Since the etiology of each type of mental disorder is discussed under an individual topic, we will confine ourselves here to a bare enumeration of the major predisposing and precipitating factors involved in abnormal behavior as a whole. These will be presented under the three headings—biological, psychological, and sociological—following Coleman's general outline (1964).

Biological Determinants. Predisposing causes include: (1) *hereditary factors:* chromosomal aberrations producing such anomalies as mongolism and Turner's syndrome; defective or mutant genes probably causing biochemical disorders such as phenylketonuria and degenerative diseases such as Huntington's chorea; the possibility of inherited predisposition to schizophrenic, manic-depressive, and other reactions usually regarded as functional; (2) *constitutional factors:* the possibility that specific types of physique contribute to the development of specific types of personality and favor the development of specific types of disorder; the possibility that physiological differences in body organs and systems contribute to specific reaction tendencies and susceptibilities— for instance a constitutional tendency toward vascular rather than muscular reactions, or toward gastrointestinal rather than circulatory reactions may render the individual prone to a specific type of psychophysiologic (psychosomatic) condition—or a tendency to discharge tension through fantasy rather than physical activity may help to determine the specific type of neurotic or psychotic reaction; (3) *congenital and acquired defects:* persons born with hearing, visual, orthopedic, perceptual, and other defects frequently have great difficulty in educational, social and vocational adjustment and may therefore be vulnerable to emotional and personality disorders; those who suffer from acquired handicapping defects, such as loss of a limb or blindness are also more vulnerable than intact individuals, although the attitude toward the disability rather than the disability itself is usually considered the major determining factor.

Precipitating biological stresses include: excessive fatigue, prolonged loss of sleep, dietary deficiencies, incapacitating accidents, painful or debilitating disease, toxic conditions produced by infections or ingestion of drugs or metals, sustained overmobilization of the autonomic nervous system under conditions of prolonged pressure, frustration, and tension.

Psychological Determinants. Predisposing factors include: (1) *early deprivation:* separation from the mother or lack of mothering in the home; an impoverished or frustrating environment that stunts psychological growth; (2) *pathogenic family patterns:* parental rejection, maternal (or paternal) overprotection, overindulgence, perfectionistic demands, rigid or unrealistic standards of behavior, excessively harsh, lenient, or inconsistent discipline, encouragement of sibling jealousy and rivalry, faulty parental models, marital conflict and broken home, maladjusted parents who make contradictory demands on the children and foster tensions and hostilities in the home; (3) *early psychic traumas,* such as sexual assault, frightening experiences with animals, beatings by parents or peers, discovery of adoption under adverse circumstances; (4) *inadequate preparation for adolescence and adulthood:* insufficient attention to development of independence, responsibility, and sex role; poor physical condition affecting the individual's self-image and competence in facing difficulties; poor adult models, lack of guidance in handling such emotions as fear, worry, anger and guilt; lack of training

in social skills, resulting in inability to fulfill normal social roles and establish constructive interpersonal relationships; insufficient development of the ability to think clearly and solve problems realistically; (5) *defective frame of reference:* faulty assumptions that distort the individual's picture of the world and undermine his belief in the worth and meaningfulness of life—for example, the conviction that the world is a dangerous "jungle" or that sex is evil; (6) *lack of personal identity:* a confused self-image, inability to "be one's self," achieve self-direction, know one's values and purposes, and form an integrated personality.

Precipitating psychological stresses include: (1) *frustrations leading to loss of self-esteem:* feelings of failure due to mistakes or inadequacies; death or illness of a loved person; social rejection; severe financial setback; status comparisons and fantasies, such as "keeping up with the Joneses"; intense guilt over selfishness, cowardice, feelings of hostility toward loved ones, early sexual activities, or wasted opportunities; acute feelings of isolation, loneliness, and alienation; (2) *disruptive conflicts:* conflicts between avoiding and facing reality, between dependence and self-direction, between fear and positive action, between sexual desires and restraints; conflicts among basic values and goals; (3) *pressures:* stresses arising out of competitive activities; educational, occupational and marital demands; and the general complexity and pace of modern living which tends to overload and overmobilize the organism.

Sociological determinants: predisposing factors operating in the sociocultural setting which tend to weaken the individual's ability to adjust and meet the stresses of life—for example, crowded home conditions; an impoverished environment; pathological family conditions created by a lack of family cohesiveness and family ties; or a subculture that makes delinquency acceptable and even laudable in some neighborhoods. Precipitating sociocultural factors include stresses arising out of: (1) *war* (and *threat of war*), with its catastrophic anxiety, separation from loved ones, privations, grief, and mutilation; (2) *occupational difficulties and economic fluctuations:* unemployment, unsatisfying work, dislocations due to automation, recessions and depressions, retirement without preparation; (3) *marital and family problems:* the high divorce rate and higher "unhappiness rate," the mobility and instability of many of today's families; (4) *racial discrimination* which leads to open and covert conflict, self-devaluation, and interference with educational, economic, and personality development; (5) *rapid social change,* bringing with it confusion and bewilderment concerning traditions, values, morality, and the meaning and purpose of life.

EUPHORIA. An exaggerated feeling of physical and emotional well-being and contentment; a pervasive mood of happiness.

The individual in a euphoric state feels confident, optimistic and exhilarated, even though these reactions may not be warranted by actual events. In psychiatric practice, euphoria is most frequently observed in hypomanic states, general paresis (expansive type), opium and cocaine addiction, and in frontal lobe tumors, particularly in their advanced stage. Euphoric reactions also occur with senile dementia, multiple sclerosis and head injury (including punch-drunk fighters), and occasionally in Pick's and Alzheimer's diseases. In addition, temporary states of euphoria may be experienced while smoking marijuana and after taking mood-elevating drugs, such as amphetamines, as well as sedatives that relax tension and anxiety. The hallucinogens, mescaline and LSD, may produce transient states of euphoria and elation, though their effects are highly unpredictable. *See* all these topics; also ELATION, ECSTASY.

EXHAUSTION DELIRIUM. An acute psychological reaction arising out of the physical prostration and toxicity that accompany extreme overexertion.

Delirium is particularly apt to occur when a state of exhaustion is coupled with prolonged insomnia, starvation, loneliness, or excessive heat or cold. Mountain climbers, explorers, and individuals lost in remote regions are the most frequent victims. The condition is also observed in patients suffering from chronic debilitating diseases such as cancer.

Initial symptoms are usually mild confusion, vague fears, restlessness, insomnia, perceptual distortion, fleeting hallucinations, and changing delusions. As the disorder deepens, impairment of perception becomes more severe, disorientation sets in, and the individual may hallucinate an oasis, a rescue team, or a table loaded with food. These visions soon dissolve into dreamlike unreality, and he lapses into bewildered confusion. In some cases this state of "mental fog" may alternate with brief periods of lucidity.

The patient who succeeds in getting sufficient food and rest usually recovers rapidly. If, however, the conditions that cause the exhaustion are not corrected, the delirious state may last for several weeks and eventuate in death. *See* DELIRIUM.

EXHIBITIONISM. A sexual deviation in which pleasure is achieved through exposure of the genitals to members of the opposite sex or to children of either sex.

The act is usually performed in a public place, often near a school or bus stop. It frequently follows a pattern—for example, one patient exhibited himself repeatedly at the top of an escalator in a large department store. Exhibitionists are practically always male adults, and are found in all occupational and educational groups. They usually feel restless and apprehensive prior to exposure, and may fight the impulse until the tension becomes overwhelming. In most cases they merely exhibit themselves, but sometimes the exposure is accompanied by suggestive gestures or masturbation. After the act they are likely to feel depressed and remorseful, particularly if they have reached orgasm.

Exhibitionists constitute the largest single group apprehended for sexual offenses, but they are usually put on probation rather than imprisoned. In most cases they are quiet, insecure, puritanical individuals who come from strict homes. Frequently they are excessively attached to domineering mothers. They are too strongly inhibited and emotionally immature to have any relations with the opposite sex, and cannot use masturbation as an effective outlet except under the special excitement of exposing themselves. Exhibitionism is considered by many authorities to be a regressive type of sexual behavior, since over 99 per cent of children who engage in sex play have been found to exhibit themselves.

Exhibitionism is thought to serve a purpose beyond that of sexual satisfaction. Because of their attachment to their mothers, these men are usually assailed with doubts about their masculinity, and as a consequence have an impulse to exhibit themselves as proof of potency. Even though half of all exhibitionists have been married, their marriages were often a result of family pressure, and in practically all cases they have failed to achieve satisfactory sexual relations with their wives. (Psychoanalysts ascribe this failure to incestuous wishes directed toward the mother, and explain exhibitionism as a form of reassurance against castration by the father.)

Some cases of exhibitionism, however, arise out of more serious conditions. One study of fifty-one cases revealed that eight were psychotic, ten mentally retarded, four chronically alcoholic, and three psychopathic, while the remainder were classified as emotionally immature (Henninger, 1941). In all these conditions there is a common denominator of weakened control over behavior.

Psychotherapy is usually highly effective in helping the emotionally immature exhibitionist abandon his exhibitionism for a healthier sexual relationship. Behavior therapy has also been successfully applied in a limited number of cases. See BEHAVIOR THERAPY, SEXUAL DEVIATIONS (GENERAL).

Illustrative Case: EXHIBITIONISM

A twenty-four-year-old married man was hospitalized for evaluation after his third arrest for indecent exposure. He was the son of an alcoholic who had worked irregularly, spent all his money on drinking parties, and been inconsistent and, at times, cruel to his children. (There were three older sisters.) The patient's mother, on the other hand, was described as good, kind, long-suffering, and easy to get along with. There was a great deal of open discord between the parents.

The patient's physical development was normal. He was a well behaved, overtly conforming boy who left school to be trained as an electrician. As a boy he had always been emotionally immature and shy, and avoided participation in athletic or social activities. He obtained little sexual information in childhood, but at fourteen began to expose his genitals to girls in his age group and sometimes to masturbate in front of them. However, his behavior did not result in arrest until at age twenty he exposed himself in front of a mature woman. He was beaten up by her brother, arrested, and fined. Nevertheless, he continued to exhibit himself frequently and at twenty-three was arrested again for exposure before an adolescent girl. This time he spent a month in jail.

Shortly afterward he met a pregnant woman who soon gave birth to an illegitimate child. The child was immediately adopted. The patient and the woman—

clearly a mother-figure for him—were married. Their sexual relationship was at first satisfactory to him and his exhibitionism ceased. However, he soon began to manifest a pattern of behavior in which any trivial conflict with his wife caused him to feel childishly hurt and resentful and to refuse to have sexual relations with her even if she approached him. She soon became pregnant and he regressed to his former pattern of exhibiting himself; he picked up a woman in his car, began to masturbate, and once again was arrested. As is common with married exhibitionists, he had successfully concealed his deviant impulses from his wife, and his arrest and the subsequent revelations came as a complete surprise to her.

He was a quiet, mousy-appearing, self-effacing, and tense young man. He was introverted and ridden by strong feelings of inadequacy. On a sentence completion test, two of his responses were, "When I was a child I always ran away or didn't fight back," and "My greatest mistake was running away from everything." The only trace of exhibitionism in his makeup was in his sexual behavior. His I.Q. was 118, he was not severely depressed, and there was no reality distortion, that is, he was neither retarded nor psychotic.

The patient withheld from the hospital personnel as much information as he could about his sexual deviation and admitted to far fewer incidents than had actually occurred. (In general, exhibitionists withhold information about their sexual histories.) However, he reported that beginning at age fourteen, the age at which his exhibitionistic behavior had started, he had had frequent migraine headaches associated with blurred vision, numbness on one side of the head, buzzing in one ear, and frequent nausea or vomiting. He felt that these attacks occurred when he was under emotional stress or tension; the same emotional factors apparently precipitated his exhibitionism. His regression when his wife became pregnant was a reaction to the frustration he anticipated because of her impending sexual unavailability. Furthermore, the child would be a rival for the attentions of his wife. At a deeper level, it is possible that one of the origins of his sexual pattern was castration fear at the hands of his sometimes cruel father, although there was no direct evidence for this hypothesis.

Diagnostically, the patient could be considered as a case of either neurotic anxiety with sexual deviation, or psychophysiologic reaction (cardiovascular) with sexual deviation. Medication in the hospital relieved his headaches and psychotherapy resulted in considerable insight into the dynamics underlying his sexual behavior. It is not known, however, whether his exhibitionism recurred after discharge from the hospital. (Rosen and Gregory, 1965)

EXISTENTIALISM. A psychological (and philosophical) approach which views each individual from the standpoint of self-discovery and self-realization.

Existentialism focuses on the inner core of man, as opposed to the emphasis on outer adjustment which is found in so much of contemporary psychology. The essential problem of existence is that of finding oneself, being oneself and actualizing oneself—in a word, it is a "quest for identity." If this problem is solved, the individual will make his contribution and meet his responsibilities in his own way. Moreover, he will be most likely to think and act in a creative and effective manner, because his behavior will stem from his own existence, his own "being-in-the-world," and not from the dictates of others or the necessities of circumstance.

But how can we solve the problem of our own existence? The existentialists say, "Only by drawing upon the uniqueness of your own experience, only by becoming aware of the pattern of your own potentialities, and only by preserving your freedom of decision as to the kind of life you want to lead."

Existentialism derives from a number of sources. In its emphasis on direct, individual experience, it draws heavily from the phenomenology of Edmund Husserl. This philosopher believed that before we can understand reality we must be aware of what is *there,* what we actually experience, instead of starting with concepts or theories and sifting reality through a preformed screen. If we want to understand the reality which is *ourselves,* we must also abandon preconceptions and see ourselves as we really are.

Another root of existentialism lies in the literary work of men like Dostoyevski, Kafka and Camus, who attribute modern man's anxiety and confusion to the fact that he has become alienated from himself. They claim that we are dimly aware that there is an area of "being" within ourselves, yet we ignore it and focus our attention on "nonbeing"—that is, we forget our own identity, sacrifice our inner self, and devote ourselves solely to keeping busy or to satisfying our physical senses and drives. To put it in the German terms used by some existentialists, we become enveloped in the Umwelt, the biological world; or in the Mitwelt, the world of relationships with our fellow men, and we neglect the Eigenwelt, the world of our own inner consciousness. If we are at all aware of our alienation from our own being, we are beset by "existential guilt," the haunting sense that we are not realizing our full potential, that we have chosen "not to be" instead of "to be."

According to this philosophy, being is not a static affair. Though it is important to recognize what we are and are not at any given moment, our true being lies in what we can *become,* or, put in a different way, what we *are* is our emerging, evolving self. Time, growth, and inner striving are the essence of existence. This puts the emphasis where it properly belongs, on the potential which we can either realize and utilize, or waste and cast away.

The emphasis on being and becoming determines the general character of existential therapy. It is not an attempt to trace conflicts and symptoms to roots in the past, for existentialism does not view the individual merely as a product of psychological and biological forces. Its objective is not to bring about more socially acceptable behavior or even to eliminate anxiety, for this type of "cure" will only submerge individuality and lead to outer conformity. Rather, the emphasis of "Dasein Analysis" ("The One Analysis") as Heidegger termed it, is on the future rather than the past, on the potential rather than the actual, on being oneself rather than adapting to others.

In carrying out this therapy, existentialists do not prescribe special techniques, but only suggest an over-all approach. First, they attempt to understand the patient as a being-in-the-world, and they do this by coming to know him directly, and not simply knowing *about* him. To accomplish this, the therapist adopts a phenomenalistic attitude in which he puts aside all hypotheses, analyses, and classifications, and in their place, listens to his patient, communicates with him, and attempts to enter into his world. This approach requires a different level of awareness from the usual social interaction, and is similar to living along with the character in a play we see or a novel we read. It is a matter of empathy and rapport, not of interpretation or suggestion. Second, the therapist helps the patient—by a comment here and a gesture there—to recognize and experience his own existence. Here the emphasis is on the patient's discovery of his basic personality needs, the values that are truly a part of himself and not taken over from others, as well as the goals that will fulfill his own unique existence.

But even though the patient may come to recognize his objectives and his potential, he may still find the way blocked by forces inside or outside himself. The third task of the therapist is therefore to help him free himself from the fears and conflicts that are holding him back. Again the emphasis is not so much on understanding the sources of his inner obstacles as on releasing the energy and will required for overcoming them. Recognition of the power of will is extremely important in this therapy, for it means that the patient, aided by the encouragement and understanding of the therapist, will be responsible for his improvement. By making his own decisions and choices he will gradually begin to realize his potential and affirm his own existence.

Existentialism has been criticized for belaboring the obvious and for inventing new phrases that carry "surplus implications" which make well-known ideas appear novel. It has also been criticized for failing to define its postulates adequately, although this criticism is met by the retort that they are basically indefinable. In spite of these criticisms it is an undeniable fact that many people have at times experienced the world in an existential manner. We do occasionally attain glimpses of what we really are and what we could become. Moreover, we live at a time when many of us feel estranged not only from other people but from ourselves as well, and any psychology that helps us to be ourselves and create a meaningful existence would seem to have special relevance today. *See* PHENOMENOLOGY, LOGOTHERAPY.

EXOTIC PSYCHOSES. Severe psychiatric disorders found in primitive cultures but not in Western society. The term is usually applied to functional conditions such as amok, latah, koro, witigo, and voodoo death.

Amok, or "running amok," is a sudden homicidal mania first discovered in Malaya, but also found in other areas, including the Philippines, Africa, and Tierra del Fuego. It appears to be similar to the Viking disorder known as "going berserk." While there were many cases in Malaya and the Philippines at the beginning of this century,

the number has greatly diminished since modern medical care and improved education have been instituted.

The disorder occurs in males with schizoid personalities. In the brief prodromal phase they become more withdrawn and brooding than usual, then suddenly leap to their feet with a blood-curdling scream, pull out their dagger and rush wildly about stabbing anyone or anything they encounter. After killing or wounding all the people and animals within reach, they are usually killed by others or end up by mutilating or killing themselves. The few who escape death claim they cannot remember the episode, or state that the world suddenly went black and that they tried to slash their way out of the darkness.

Running amok can usually be distinguished from violent episodes that occasionally occur in other disorders. The paranoid or catatonic schizophrenic experiences delusions or hallucinations and can usually remember the episode; neither of these facts applies to amok. Another condition, known as pseudoamok, has also been compared to it. In this case an excited patient brandishes a weapon but avoids harming anyone, and when he is cornered, he meekly gives himself up. This is probably a hysterical disorder and not true amok, since in the latter condition the patient actually commits violence and will never surrender.

The explanation of amok is largely a matter of conjecture. Kraepelin believed it could result from a variety of organic conditions, among which he mentioned malaria, epilepsy, and schizophrenia. Arieti and Meth (1959) employ a "sociopsychodynamic" interpretation, in which they suggest that it is a sudden expression of repressed rage in accordance with the accepted behavior of the society—and when this cultural acceptance disappears as a result of Western influence, the disorder also disappears. They suggest, too, that among the Bantu the belief that a person can escape death by killing another individual may be a contributing factor. Release of repressed rage may also explain the rare schizoid individual in Western countries who suddenly "goes berserk" and kills everyone around him.

Juramentado (Spanish for cursed person). This acute disturbance is believed to be limited to Mohammedan men ethnologically related to the Malays and Moros, although a similar disorder has been reported in India and Siberia. As in amok, the individual is suddenly overwhelmed by a state of frenzy during which he rushes into the street stabbing everyone he encounters. After the attack—if he has not been killed by others—he lapses into a stuporous sleep, from which he awakens in a disagreeable state of mind but with a complete amnesia for the homicidal episode.

The causes of this disorder are none too clear, but in many cases the sudden seizure appears to be precipitated by the excitement of religious rites involving music, dancing, and incantations. The attack may also be preceded by a devastating emotional experience such as the death of a loved one, infidelity on the part of the wife, fear of disgrace, or an accusation of cowardice. In some cases the afflicted individual had been depressed for a long period, and had given up all work and lost all interest in life.

A number of similar but less violent conditions have also been observed. The Philippine disorder, *delahara,* is more prevalent among women than men; the African disorders, *tropenkohler* and *misala,* afflict young males primarily. As Kisker (1964) notes: "Victims of these disorders start quarrels and rapidly work themselves up to a frenzy of speech and gesticulation, without apparent object or cause. The attack, which may last anywhere from a few minutes to a few hours, is followed by utter exhaustion."

Latah. This syndrome was also first discovered in Malaya, but was later found under different names in other societies, including Siberia, Siam, Burma, northern Japan, Nyasaland, the Philippines, and the Congo. In Malaya it is considered an eccentricity rather than a disease, and occurs primarily in middle-aged and elderly women, sometimes in epidemic form. In other parts of the world it may occur among men with equal frequency.

The disorder usually develops in dull, submissive individuals, often as a result of a sudden fright such as stepping on a snake. The first symptom other than fearfulness is echolalia: the patient repeats his own words and phrases many times, then begins to repeat the utterances of other people, especially persons in authority. Later on echopraxia appears, and the patient compulsively pantomimes the gestures and actions of others, or does exactly the opposite of what they do. The next symptom is coprolalia (literally, "fecal speech"), which begins with incomprehensible mutterings and ends with obscenities and curse words the patient has never before used. All these symptoms are uncontrollable, and when he is teased and ridiculed, the patient tearfully pleads to be left alone—but if the teasing persists, he may become violent.

Latah is sometimes interpreted as the attempt of a self-abnegating individual to resolve his conflicts. He first attempts to relieve his anxiety by yielding completely to others, imitating everything they say and do, just as a frightened child may unconsciously seek security by mimicking people who are stronger than himself. But when the patient finds that he cannot allay his anxiety by self-surrender, he begins to vent his rage by uttering obscene and profane expressions. This theory is supported by the fact that the condition is particularly prevalent among women in Malay society, where the female is usually confined to the home and lives a submissive, colorless life. The latah reaction is believed to stem from her inability to cope with a threatening, anxiety-provoking situation.

Koro. A phobia occurring in the East Indies and southern China. The disorder consists of a sudden fear that the penis will disappear into the abdomen and lead to death. To keep this from happening, the patient grasps his penis, and when he tires, calls upon his wife, relatives, and friends to help him. The wife may succeed in stemming the phobia by practicing fellatio immediately after it starts, but in many cases the condition lasts for days or even weeks. Koro—or *shook yong,* as they call it—is common enough for the Chinese to make a special clasp to hold the organ mechanically. They also administer a medicine belonging to the "male factor," Yan (e.g. powdered rhinoceros horn) because they attribute the disorder to an excess of the "female factor," Yin.

A female form of koro has been found in Borneo, in which the patient feels that her breasts are shrinking and her labia are being sucked inward. In either case, male or female, the individual develops a morbid fear of being deprived of organs associated with sexuality. The psychoanalytic interpretation would be in terms of castration fear, or at least the fear of inadequacy in sexual or other activities.

Witigo. A psychosis occurring primarily among the Cree Eskimos in the southern Hudson Bay area. It is also found among the Ojibwa Indians of southeastern Ontario, where it is known as *windigo.* The first symptoms are usually anorexia, nausea, vomiting and diarrhea, accompanied by the brooding fear of being possessed by a witigo, or witch, who craves human flesh. This supernatural figure is pictured as a giant skeleton made of ice which devours human beings. The patient becomes increasingly depressed and withdrawn, and cannot eat or sleep. The family calls in

a "good" shaman to cast out the bad shaman's spell by magic and incantations. But if a good shaman cannot be found, the patient may yield to his cannibalistic impulses and proceed to kill and eat one or more members of his household.

Witigo is based on a phobia that is indigenous to the Eskimo culture, and is believed to represent the fear of being reduced by starvation to a point where cannibalism is the only means of survival. The phobia develops into a psychosis when the patient actually goes to this extreme. Arieti and Meth (1959) offer this psychodynamic interpretation of the disorder: "If cannibalism can be life saving in an emergency (extreme famine), then it can also save the life of the patient who is suffering from an emotional emergency."

Voodoo Death. This strange psychosis, technically termed thanatomania (preoccupation with death), is found in many primitive societies. In some cases an individual who seems healthy in every respect becomes convinced that he has transgressed a taboo, and as a result withdraws from the world and dies within a few days. In other cases the same thing occurs except that the patient becomes convinced that he has fallen under the spell of a sorcerer who wishes to eliminate him. Van der Hoeven (1956) relates the case of a New Guinea sorcerer who had been offended by a young man. Taking revenge, he told the young man that on the day before he had placed an object poisoned by witchcraft in his path. The youth fell ill immediately, and was dead within two days. Interestingly, the Dutch government tried the sorcerer and imprisoned him for bringing about the young man's death.

We can only speculate about the mechanisms through which fear or expectancy can lead to death. It may be that autosuggestion or autohypnosis is involved, for we know that these processes can be used in some cases to affect the activities of the autonomic nervous system and, through this system, control the functions of the heart and other vital organs. Many people today accept the Hindu claim that they can achieve "suspended animation" through this means. Yet this process is said to take years of training, while the voodoo effect—which leads to actual death—can apparently be produced in a matter of hours and with no training at all.

A number of other tribal disorders deserve brief mention. A condition known as *arctic hysteria* was first observed among the Chukchee of northern Siberia early in this century. Its most outstanding symptom was extreme suggestibility, during which the patient imitated the movements and actions of other people (echopraxia). Another disorder, *pibloktoq*, was observed during Admiral Peary's expedition. The victims were Eskimo women who experienced attacks of uncontrollable excitement, during which they would shriek, sing at the top of their lungs, rush about and tear off their clothing until they collapsed into unconsciousness. The disorder was believed to be a long-pent-up response to the insecurities and frustrations endured by these women, who were considered the property of the male and who could therefore be bought, sold, or exchanged at will.

Similar disorders have been observed in other arctic areas, such as Iceland, the Faroe Islands, the Kamchatka Peninsula, the Kirghiz Steppes of Russia, and among the Samoyeds, Yakuts, and other Siberian tribes.

Another set of disorders has been found among the Diegueno Indians of lower California: *kimilue* and *echul*. The tribal medicine men regard both these disorders as sexual disturbances. In kimilue the victim becomes apathetic and disinterested in life, loses his appetite, and has vivid sexual dreams. Echul is somewhat similar but may involve convulsive seizures. The dis-order appears to be precipitated by crises such as the loss or death of a wife, husband, or child. *See* GILLES DE LA TOURETTE SYNDROME.

EXPERIENTIAL THERAPY. A form of depth psychotherapy developed by Karl A. Whitaker and Thomas P. Malone (1953), in which the patient achieves greater maturity largely through sharing fundamental emotional experiences with the therapist.

The experiential approach is based on the psychoanalytic distinction between id psychology and ego psychology. Id psychology has to do with primitive biological drives—the blind, impersonal instincts of sex and hostility from which all behavior is believed to spring. Ego psychology, on the other hand, deals with that part of the psyche, the ego, which mediates between the id and the external environment, and which controls our relationships with other people. Early psychoanalysis focused on the id, and experiential psychotherapy returns to this emphasis. It is a form of "id level therapy" which attempts to promote the basic growth and maturity of the patient by reaching the deepest strata of the unconscious. The authors of the system maintain that this is necessary before the individual can free his basic energies from conflict and achieve greater adequacy in his interpersonal relations.

In attempting to achieve this goal, the therapist operates on an emotional level rather than on the level of analysis. To get to the roots of the patient's experience, he must see the patient as his *own* child-self and therefore deal with him as a projection of himself. The patient is encouraged to express his fantasies, and the therapist seeks to share them with him. The more they share these experiences, the more deeply they become emotionally involved in the therapeutic experience, until the two, patient and therapist, are responding directly to each other's unconscious. In other words, they go through the therapeutic experience together, and "the therapist, seeing the patient as part of himself and the experience as a means of satisfying his own deeper integrative needs, has a feeling of growing significance and urgency to accelerate the growth of the patient" (Harper, 1959).

But how do patient and therapist descend to the id level and come in contact with each other's unconscious? How do they achieve a "joint fantasy experience"? Although Whitaker and Malone do not present a set of specific procedures, they suggest several ways of facilitating this process. One is to eliminate the world of external reality as much as possible by refraining from talking with the patient's family or physician and from discussing his real life problems. The telephone is cut off and in general the therapeutic experience is isolated from every possible intrusion. Another procedure is to use materials such as clay and rubber knives to stimulate fantasy and symbolic expression, as in the play therapy technique. A third is for both patient and therapist to sleep and dream during the therapeutic session, and then to relate their dreams to each other. In some cases, too, the patient is allowed to become aggressive and to come into physical contact with the therapist. Through these and other means they become involved with each other in an "intrapsychic society."

How, then, does the therapist accelerate the growth of the patient? The answer, according to Whitaker and Malone, is that the therapist not only sees the patient as his own child-image, but also presents himself in the role of a good parent who brings his own constructive experiences to bear on the patient. At the start he shows the patient that he understands the inner symbolic meaning of what he does and says by maintaining an understanding silence. This is believed to encourage the patient to penetrate below the surface of his own words and actions and arrive at a deeper, unconscious meaning through experience.

The therapist gives the patient approval and encouragement by showing that he is aware of his maturities as well as his immaturities. At the same time he reassures him by revealing his *own* limitations and immaturities, but without permitting the patient to capitalize on his deficiencies. He also enables the patient to act out his unconscious fantasies and release the energy which has been bound up in them. Later on, in the "ending phase," the therapist encourages the patient to test his more mature reactions by gradually rejecting the therapist as the symbolic parent and by moving toward autonomy and independence.

Experiential therapy has been severely criticized, notably by Wolf and Schwartz (1958–59), who claim that in adopting this procedure the therapist cuts himself and the patient off from reality and becomes deeply involved in the patient's pathological reactions. The technique also assumes that the therapist can actually descend not only to a level where he is in touch with his own instinctual unconscious, but that he can achieve an unspoken communication with the patient's id impulses as well. As Harper points out, "Such activities by their very nature tend to rule out the application of the rational tools of science. We must, however, add a further factor. It is quite apparent that much of the work undertaken by Whitaker and Malone is with very sick persons, for the most part psychotics. A rational realistic approach is considerably less effective with a person who has renounced rationality and has escaped from reality than with a neurotic who is simply exhibiting various self-defeating patterns of reality. Understood in this sense, experiential therapy may be a necessary therapeutic departure from rationality for the purpose of meeting and helping the psychotic in his own world of unreality." *See* DIRECT ANALYSIS, BLEULER.

EXPERIMENTAL NEUROSIS. A behavior disorder produced for research purposes, usually by subjecting an animal to a situation involving a difficult discrimination or choice.

The experimental study of neurosis originated with Ivan Pavlov in 1914. One of his students had conditioned a dog to distinguish between a circle and an ellipse by giving him a food reward each time the circle was shown, and withholding it when an ellipse was presented. To test the dog's powers of discrimination he gradually altered the shape of the ellipse to make it resemble a circle. In the course of the experiment Pavlov noted that when the dog could no longer distinguish between the two his whole behavior changed: he began to squeal and squirm, and tried to tear off the experimental apparatus. When further attempts were made, the dog barked and struggled violently, and his previously established ability to discriminate on simpler tests was found to be grossly impaired. Even after a period of rest he became agitated and disorganized as soon as he was put in the experimental harness. Pavlov interpreted this behavior as the equivalent of an acute neurosis.

Following this lead a number of investigators have performed similar experiments on sheep, cats, rats, pigs, monkeys, and chimpanzees. In one series Liddell (1952, 1954, 1960) found that sheep and goats developed a chronic state of agitation when the usual number of conditioned-response tests was doubled. The added pressure induced disturbed behavior such as rapid and irregular breathing, frequent urination and defecation, and restlessness—and this condition remained unchanged even after three years away from the laboratory.

In another crucial experiment Brady (1958) demonstrated the stressful effects of prolonged vigilance by placing two monkeys side by side in specially designed chairs, and setting up a situation in which mild electric shocks were administered every twenty seconds unless one of the monkeys—the "executive"—pressed a nearby switch (PLATE 3). A number of the executive monkeys developed ulcers, and several of them died, whereas the control monkeys, who were not required to make the decision, suffered no ill effects. *See* PSYCHOPHYSIOLOGIC DISORDERS (ETIOLOGY AND THERAPY).

A series of experiments carried out by Masserman (1961) on cats and monkeys produced still other emotional disturbances. As a first step he conditioned the animals to respond to a signal—a light, bell, or odor—by pressing a treadle that opened a plastic food box. When this behavior was fully learned, an element of conflict was introduced by subjecting the cats to a brief electric shock or a strong puff of air whenever they tried to reach the food; likewise, he exposed the monkeys to a toy snake (which they feared) under the same circumstances. These stimuli faced the animals with the choice of resisting their fear and obtaining the food, or avoiding the fear-provoking situation by withdrawing and remaining hungry.

This conflict produced a wide variety of neurotic reactions. The cats showed typical anxiety symptoms, such as trembling, crouching, dilation of pupils, hair standing on end, rapid breathing and pulse, increase in blood pressure, intense startle reactions, and phobic aversion to lights, sounds, or closed spaces. The monkeys displayed similar reactions plus more severe symptoms, including motor dysfunctions, diarrhea, intestinal upsets resulting in rickets and weakness. Some of them engaged in stereotyped activities such as pacing back and forth, while others lapsed into complete immobility or slept for prolonged periods of time. Many sexual deviations were also observed, including homosexuality, excessive autoerotic activity and absence of sexual drive. As Masserman has pointed out, every one of these responses is commonly found in human neuroses, but they are particularly prominent in situations, such as combat, in which motivational conflict is severe. *See* COMBAT REACTIONS.

All these experimental findings have lent support to the theory that neurosis may be the result of excessive stress produced by insoluble conflicts and situations that force the individual beyond his capacity to adjust.

EXPLORATORY DRIVE. The urge to explore novel objects or a new environment; regarded as a general drive not clearly distinguishable from the manipulative and curiosity drives.

Most psychologists believe these three drives (which may be basically one) are part of the natural endowment of both animals and human beings. They are forces that motivate behavior just as hunger prompts the organism to seek food. But they differ from this drive on two major counts. They do not have an apparent physiological basis, and they do not depend on material rewards such as food (Hunt, 1960).

There is little doubt that the act of exploration brings its own rewards. Cats, dogs, monkeys, and even cockroaches engage in this type of behavior even when their physiological needs have apparently been satisfied. This is even more evident in small children. When they are given a new toy, their first impulse is to shake it, bite it, drop it, etc.; and when they find themselves in a new environment such as an unfamiliar house or play yard, they usually rush about to explore it. Unfortunately many parents discourage such activities and even threaten punishment if the child touches or upsets anything. Some limitations are of course necessary, but these parents do not seem to realize that children are forced to satisfy their

curiosity just as they are forced to show that they are hungry. Nor do they recognize how important these explorations are in helping them know their world and feel comfortable in strange situations.

In his thorough study of this drive, Berlyne (1960) has classified exploratory behavior into three types: orienting responses, locomotor exploration, and investigatory responses. *Orienting responses* consist of the changes of posture and other adjustments which the human or animal organism makes when a novel situation or arresting stimulus is encountered. These responses have the effect of attuning the receptor organs to facilitate exploration. If you give a child a new toy, he will become animated and open his eyes more widely so that he can move rapidly and see better. Pavlov (1927) applied the term reflex to these responses and suggested that they have great biological value, since they keep the organism in constant, efficient touch with changes in the environment.

Studies show that both animal and human infants orient themselves primarily to stimuli that are novel, incongruous and complex—for example, human infants of three to nine months of age were found to orient themselves toward a checkerboard rather than toward simpler patterns. Also, older children and adults have been found to fixate longer on strange pictures, such as an animal with the body of a lion and the head of an elephant, than to ordinary figures. Intense, contrasting and colorful stimuli are especially likely to elicit orienting responses. However, they are not indefinitely effective, since the excitement of novelty wears off rather quickly. Advertisers are well aware of this fact and spend millions each year to hold the "excited attention" of the public.

The second reaction, *locomotor exploration*, is the tendency to move about a new environment or to manipulate a novel object in order to make a full investigation. Here, too, novelty and complexity are important. Children tend to explore unfamiliar things more actively than familiar things, unless they are inhibited or frightened. Even rats have been shown to expend more effort exploring a new pattern than one they have encountered before (Thompson and Solomon, 1954). Rats were also found to have a greater tendency to explore an enclosed area that contained five irregularly shaped objects than an area that contained five cubes that were exactly alike (Welker, 1957).

Investigative responses are the specific activities performed in the process of exploration. They are usually of a manipulative nature and therefore limited to primates: picking up an object, tearing it apart, dropping it, etc. The tendency of children to inspect and manipulate materials has been thoroughly studied by Piaget (1936), but more recently Berlyne used a new technique for studying investigatory behavior in both children and adults. He placed them in a darkened room and gave them an opportunity to press a key which would expose pictures on a screen as many times as they wished. They soon tired of simple patterns and normal photographs, but pressed the key repeatedly when the pictures contained complex, incongruous, or surprising elements. Their only reward was the intrinsic satisfaction of investigation.

These studies leave little doubt that exploratory behavior stems from a drive that is not only fundamental but extremely powerful. It apparently gratifies the animal's need for activity and new sensations, and probably has survival value since it helps him get acquainted with his surroundings. It has similar values for human beings, but in addition it can stimulate a desire for further knowledge and experience, particularly if it is carefully cultivated and channeled in constructive directions. *See* CURIOSITY DRIVE, MANIPULATIVE DRIVE.

EXPRESSIVE BEHAVIOR. This term is used for "those aspects of movement which are distinctive enough to differentiate one individual from another" (Allport and Vernon, 1933). They include gesture, handwriting, facial expression, gait, posture, voice, and linguistic patterns. The studies in the field have focused on two basic questions: How much consistency is there between different expressive movements? and, How well do these movements express emotions and personality characteristics?

There is considerable evidence for consistency among various expressive movements. Enke (1930) has shown that there are consistent differences among Kretschmer's personality types in vastly different activities, such as reacting to music, writing with a pen, and carrying a glass of water. Wolff (1930) found that judges could match records of the same individual's handwriting, vocal expression, manner of retelling a story, and facial profile with considerable accuracy. Arnheim (1928) demonstrated that personality sketches could be matched with handwriting; quotations of authors, with their photographs; and silhouettes with descriptive terms—all somewhat above chance. *See* CONSTITUTIONAL TYPES.

In their experimental studies, Allport and Vernon gave a series of thirty motor tests to large groups of subjects, including writing, tapping, walking, reaching, and drawing simple figures, and then scored each test objectively in terms of such characteristics as pressure of movement, speed, size etc. Analysis of these performances revealed that (a) gesture patterns are stable characteristics of individuals; (b) the same task tends to be performed in the same way by different muscle groups (e.g. by right and left hand); (c) different tasks are also performed in much the same way by different muscle groups. After reviewing their own experiments and those of other investigators, these authors conclude that "Fundamentally our results lend support to the personalistic contentions that there is some degree of unity in personality, that this unity is reflected in expression, and that, for this reason, acts and habits of expression show a certain consistency among themselves."

The Allport and Vernon studies have shown, however, that the unities and consistencies have to be defined with great care. They did not find evidence for a general speed factor, or uniform "psychic tempo," but discovered three independent speed factors, one for drawing, another for verbal expression, and a third for rhythmic movements. Similarly, they did not uncover a general psychomotor power or energy factor, but found evidence that some individuals express themselves more emphatically than others as a result of what they termed "psychic pressure." There was also evidence that some people are more "expansive" than others in all their movements, such as walking stride and handwriting. Others were found to be especially free and impulsive in their movements. These two tendencies, termed "areal" and "centrifugal," were found to be relatively independent of each other.

It is interesting that subjective assessments of personality closely agreed with these objective measurements. The authors therefore contend that "There are degrees of uniformity in movement, just as there are degrees of unity in mental life and in personality. It is surely not unreasonable to assume that in so far as personality is organized, expressive movement is harmonious and self-consistent, and in so far as personality is unintegrated, expressive movement is self-contradictory." Now let us look at some of the details.

Voice. Studies by Wolff (1943) have indicated that voices can be matched to personality sketches with fair success. Allport and Vernon have shown that listeners can describe the general characteristics of persons heard over the

radio with over 50 per cent accuracy. Carp (1945) has shown, interestingly, that the ability to match voice and personality is not significantly changed by having the individual present.

Hands. Subjects were found to match hand positions with other forms of expression with good accuracy. They also constructed fairly valid personality sketches on the basis of their observations of hand movements (Wolff, 1943). A study by Duffy (1940) showed that muscular tension in hands was consistent for several different manual operations.

The symbolic and cultural aspects of hand gestures have also been investigated. Catatonic schizophrenics sometimes reveal their private fantasies through hand movements; one woman with a religious obsession spread her ten fingers apart to indicate the Ten Commandments, clasped her hands together to represent brotherhood, pulled her clenched fists apart to symbolize power, and opened her hands in a receptive gesture when she felt the spirit of God approaching. Variations among gestures in different cultures are almost too obvious to mention—for example, the South American gesture for "Come here" is practically identical with the North American gesture for "Go away."

A careful comparative study has shown that the gestures of Italian immigrants tend to be sweeping, symmetrical, bilateral, and emotionally expressive; while those of traditional Eastern Jews in America were found to be more cramped, intricate, unilateral, and ideographic. However, among assimilated or "Americanized" Jews and Italians the gesture patterns resembled those of the particular social and economic stratum with which they were identified. Moreover, traditional Jews living among Italians and traditional Italians living among Jews also tended to adopt the gestures of the particular group they lived with, and those who were simultaneously exposed to both of these subgroups showed hybrid gesture patterns (Efron and Foley, 1937).

Gait. Anders (1928) analyzed the gait patterns of many persons and found that each of them had a movement rhythm peculiar to himself, possibly related to pulse and breathing rates. Wolff (1943) demonstrated that personality sketches made by different judges on the basis of gait tended to agree with each other. He also found that subjects were surprisingly accurate in recognizing themselves by their gait when they wore special clothing that disguised their other features. As a whole, they did far better on the gait test than on other tests of self-identification, such as those involving silhouettes and voice recordings.

Paintings and Drawings. Waehner (1942, 1946) successfully distinguished between various psychiatric classifications of eight- to eleven-year-old hospitalized children on the basis of their drawings, and also showed that an analysis of the paintings of fifty-five girls closely agreed with Rorschach findings. Wolff (1946, 1948) found that the paintings of American children showed consistent proportions which differed from those of African children. He also found that paintings of blind children exhibited different proportions from those of epileptic children.

Literary Style. In one of his experiments, Wolff (1943) read a story to a group of subjects and had them retell it. He then found that the style of the retold stories could be effectively matched to other types of expression. A study by Balken and Masserman (1940) has shown that patients in different psychiatric categories tend to use different patterns of syntax.

Face. Wolff has performed a provocative series of experiments in which he cut pictures of subjects horizontally and vertically. By combining the photos in various ways, he showed that the lower half of the face tends to be more expressive than the upper half, and the right half is usually more expressive than the left. He also combined halves of pictures taken at different ages, and discovered a startling congruence of expression between pictures taken at age four and at age thirty-eight (1943).

A huge number of studies have been made of facial expressions in emotion. Historically speaking, the anatomist Charles Bell (1806, 1844) held that most facial movements are practical rather than expressive—that is, the angry dog opens his mouth to make respiration easier. But he also suggested that certain muscles found in apes and men, such as the corrugators that knit the brow, function only to express finer shades of feeling. Darwin, on the other hand, felt that the human tendency to open the mouth and show the teeth is a remnant of the teeth-baring that occurs in simian combat. The German anatomist, Piderit (1872), held that facial expression has a present utility in terms of assisting or impeding our sensory experience—for example, the tongue is pressed against the lips in savoring a substance, but is withdrawn to minimize a bitter taste. Similarly, interest and attention are expressed by opening the eyes widely, and indifference by keeping them half shut. These and other points were supported by pictures of facial expressions associated with various emotions.

Boring and Titchener (1923) made compound pictures out of the mouths, brows, noses and eyes taken from the Piderit pictures and showed that almost any combination, even those including contradictory components, would be accepted by some subjects as genuine expressions of certain emotions. Buzby (1924) and Fernberger (1928) presented the full Piderit faces to subjects along with a list of emotions, and found little agreement in their judgments. This suggested that either the face does not effectively communicate emotions to others, or that the subjects were particularly unskilled in reading emotions from facial expression. By giving "false" names to the facial expressions, and asking whether they expressed the designated emotions well or poorly, Fernberger showed that his subjects were often greatly influenced by suggestion. This result indicated that in everyday life the situation, or context, may play a large part in suggesting what the facial expression means.

Many experiments have lent support to this view. In one study, facial pictures of athletes gasping for air at the finish of a hundred-yard dash were shown to a large group of subjects. They named a wide variety of emotions, few of them close to the mark. Similarly, Geldard (1962) cites an experiment in which the *same close-up* of an actor's face was combined with three different pictures, one showing a plate of soup, another a dead woman in a coffin, and the third a little girl playing with an amusing toy bear. When all three photos were shown to the *same* audience, they commented enthusiastically about the actor's ability to express appropriate emotional responses! Other experiments have revealed considerable disagreement among observers who were asked to identify posed expressions of experienced actors (Langfeld, 1918). Kanner (1931) has presented evidence that posed expressions of the more overt emotions, such as surprise, fear, rage, and horror, can be correctly identified by more than 50 per cent of judges, but the average score was less than 25 per cent on posed expressions of the more subtle emotions such as pity and suspicion (PLATES 26 AND 27).

A number of experiments have been performed in which photos were taken of individuals placed in situations designed to elicit various emotions. Landis (1924) had his subjects inspect pornographic pictures, smell ammonia after reading the false label "Syrup of Lemon," put their hand in a bucket of live frogs, examine colored photographs of horrible skin diseases, and so on. Photos of their spontaneous expressions were taken with a hidden camera, and then shown to groups of college students. Only 31 per cent of their judgments agreed with the introspective reports of the subjects who had gone through the experiences. Moreover, a careful analysis of the expressions themselves revealed no significant correspondence either with the situations or with the emotions reported by the subjects. In fact, many subjects used characteristic expressions or mannerisms, such as wrinkling the brow or pursing the lips, for *all* emotions.

These results strongly suggest that there may be no universal facial expressions by which we can distinguish different emotions. As Crafts and others (1938) state, in commenting on Landis' results, "What happens in most cases of so-called 'reading emotion from the face' is that we observe, not only the facial expression of an individual, but also many other perceptual aspects of his behavior (e.g. verbal, gestural, and postural signs), and especially important, we observe, as well, the situation which is stimulating him." They also point out that we can read the emotions of friends and relatives with some accuracy by using subtle cues which we come to know through long and intimate association. *See* GRAPHOLOGY.

EXTRASENSORY   PERCEPTION (ESP). Perception which supposedly takes place outside of the known sensory channels.

The term is applied to: (1) mental telepathy, or thought transference, the sending of messages from one person to another by extrasensory means; (2) clairvoyance, the perception of external objects or events without sensory stimulation; (3) precognition, the perception of future events; and, more loosely, (4) psychokinesis (PK), the ability to control external events through thought, or "mind over matter," such as making dice roll a certain number through the "power" of concentration. A monthly periodical, the *Journal of Parapsychology,* is devoted largely to research on ESP.

According to a series of surveys made between 1938 and 1955, and summarized by Warner (1955), only a small percentage of American psychologists consider ESP an established fact. On the other hand, few psychologists rule it out as an impossibility; the rest maintain it is simply unproven at present. Interestingly, the attitude of psychologists toward ESP has become somewhat more positive over the years. A comparison between the survey of 1938, conducted among full members of the American Psychological Association, with a survey of younger associates in 1955 showed a shift in percentages from 1.4 to 4.0 who thought ESP an established fact; 7.4 to 27.8, a likely possibility; 36.4 to 32.0, a remote possibility; 14.5 to 6.5, an impossibility; and 40.3 to 29.7, merely an unknown.

This article will deal primarily with telepathy and clairvoyance. The largest group of experiments has been conducted by J. B. Rhine and his associates, usually with specially prepared playing cards. The standard ESP deck consists of five sets of five cards, each imprinted with a square, a circle, plus-sign, triangle, or wavy lines. The twenty-five cards are shuffled, usually by a mechanical device, and a person called a "receiver" then tries to "read" the symbols without looking at them. In trials of clairvoyance the receiver usually goes through the whole deck placed face downward; in telepathy experiments, a "sender," seated behind a screen or at a distance, looks at each card and attempts to transmit a thought message to the receiver. If the receiver does significantly better than chance, which would average five correct out of twenty-five, on a sufficient number of trials to meet statistical standards,

his performance is considered positive evidence for ESP.

In trials of this kind some receivers have occasionally made high scores of 10 to 20 out of twenty-five, but long-term scores of successful subjects seldom reach a level of seven hits. As an example, Mrs. Gloria Stewart, who was studied over a long period in England, showed telepathy results above the chance level in 11 out of 13 runs of 200 trials each, with an average score of 6.8 hits. Her score on clairvoyance trials, however, did not exceed chance —a fact that may either argue for the existence of specific ESP abilities, or suggest that the results on the telepathy trials were somehow contaminated. Proponents of ESP also point out that some ESP phenomena appear to be subject to systematic variations resulting from experimental control, for several investigators have reported that early trials are more successful than later ones, and that an attitude favorable to ESP leads to positive results while an unfavorable attitude leads to scores below chance levels. These findings appear to indicate that factors other than chance are operative in some cases.

These positive indications have not, however, had much effect on the generally negative attitude toward ESP among scientists. There are several reasons for this. First, ESP is associated in the minds of many people with claims of other phenomena, such as the Loch Ness Monster, talking with the dead through mediums, and encounters with ghosts or poltergeists, which either have never been established or have been proven fraudulent. Second, scores reported in the early days of ESP investigation were on the whole far better than scores reported today when experimental conditions are more rigidly controlled; the same applies to experiments with PK. Third, statistical methods employed by investigators have been attacked by many mathematicians, who claim that special problems arise when very large numbers of trials are used to establish the significance of small differences. Fourth, studies indicate that the results may in some cases be contaminated by extraneous factors. One investigation revealed that recorders who believed in ESP sometimes made unconscious errors that supported their belief. Another showed that certain "receivers" were unconsciously reading the symbols from the backs of the cards, since they showed through very slightly due to the heavy embossing process. In still another case it was demonstrated that the sender unconsciously changed the tone of his voice according to the type of symbol he was trying to transmit, and the receiver apparently picked up these cues without realizing it. Fifth, no plausible theory has been developed to explain thought transference or other forms of ESP. Any hypothesis, such as brain waves, breaks down almost as soon as it is proposed, and scientists are loath to accept vague, mystical explanations.

ESP experimenters have made genuine attempts at controlled investigation and scientific validation. In quite another category are the popular beliefs in ghosts and other "supernatural" phenomena. To a psychologist, the persistence of such ideas is not only a commentary on human gullibility, but on the desire to escape from mundane reality. It may also be an indication of the prevalence of hallucinations, as well as widespread ignorance of science. One measure of scientific ignorance is the fact that there are about 25,000 "water witches," or "dowsers," operating in the United States today. These people insist that they can discover water by extrasensory techniques. They walk over an area with a forked stick in their hands and claim that this "divining rod" automatically dips down at the exact spot where water can be found. Sometimes they are successful, but not necessarily for the reasons they suggest. It may be that they obtain some indi-

cation from studying the nature of the terrain, or they may merely be lucky. Recently, however, some dowsers have eliminated any possible sensory cues. They practice long-distance dowsing by placing the rod over a *map* of the given area!

Many people are still exploited by mediums who claim to communicate with the dead. Most of these practitioners resist investigation, but if critics are present they invariably claim that the spirit does not move them in an antagonistic atmosphere. Those who have been investigated have been readily exposed. They usually work in collusion with "stooges" who move tables, tap on walls or speak in a hollow, "other-worldly" voice. It is interesting, however, that many people persist in their belief in mediums like the famous Eusapia Palladino even after they have been exposed.

People who read palms often use more subtle techniques. If the client's palm perspires or his pulse rate quickens, the palmist concludes that she has touched on an interesting topic or is moving in a significant direction. She also watches the reactions of the rest of the client's body, such as sudden shifts in posture, unconscious tensing of muscles, or sudden enlargement of the pupils of the eyes. She has usually been trained to attend to these "minimal cues," which have been shown to be fairly reliable on psychological tests. Such cues do not, of course, predict the future course of events, but they often indicate what the client is interested in and what he wants to hear. *See* PSYCHICAL RESEARCH, TELEPATHY IN PSYCHOTHERAPY.

EXTRAVERSION (Extroversion) (literally, "a turning outward"). The tendency to direct one's interests and energies toward the outer world of people and things as opposed to the inner world of the self and subjective experience.

Extraversion figures prominently in Carl Jung's psychology, since he considered the extravert as one of the two basic personality types, correlative with the introvert. Individuals with strong extraversive tendencies are outgoing, sociable, energetic, and more interested in action and practical realities than in abstract ideas. They tend to be emotionally responsive, self-confident, and express their feelings freely and naturally, but usually without the sensitivity of introversive individuals.

Jung made a distinction between four subtypes of extravert, according to the predominance of one or another fundamental psychological process. The subtypes include extraverted thinking, extraverted feeling, extraverted sensation and extraverted intuitive individuals. He divided introversion in the same manner. Freud also used the terms introversion and extraversion, but did not regard them as the basis for personality types. Jung and Freud both defined these characteristics in terms of the direction in which the libido expresses itself, whether inwardly or outwardly. However, Freud defines this basic energy in erotic, pleasure-seeking terms, while Jung defines it in terms of a general vital energy. *See* INTROVERSION, JUNG.

F

FACTOR THEORY OF PERSONALITY. An approach to personality in which basic components are isolated through the statistical analysis of performance on tests.

The object of factor theory is to account for the consistencies and the complexities we commonly observe in behavior. Instead of attempting to identify personality characteristics by the usual intuitive methods, it applies objective, rational techniques similar to those used in measuring intellectual ability. This approach, known as factor analysis, begins with a study of quantitative scores made on a variety of tests by a large number of subjects. The scores may come from many sources, including questionnaires, situational tests and ratings, covering different aspects of behavior. The object of the analysis is to discover underlying factors which determine the variations in these indices. The fundamental factors are isolated by noting which of them crop up most often—or, in statistical terms, the minimum number of different factors that account for the distribution of test scores. When these basic factors are isolated, the next step is usually to devise tests which tap these facets of the personality more effectively than the original tests.

The aim of factor analysis of personality is to discover and measure basic components comparable to those emphasized in personality theories (such as style of life or Oedipus complex); but its uniqueness lies in its statistical approach. An example of this technique is H. J. Eysenck's attempt to synthesize psychometric procedures with clinical insights. He holds that most personality theories are based on unspecified variables which are impossible to measure, but that factor analysis remedies this situation by first isolating the dimensions of personality and then developing the tests for measuring them. His basic idea is that personality is composed of acts and dispositions which can be arranged in a hierarchical order from least to most general: first, specific, transient responses occurring only once; second, habitual responses; third, traits, which consist of habitual responses or "constellations of action tendencies" related to each other; and fourth, types which comprise traits as component parts and constitute the most generalized organizations of behavior. These different levels correspond to the four types of factors which can be isolated through factor analysis.

Eysenck's entire research program is directed toward identifying primary dimensions of personality to be used in establishing a typology or set of basic personality types. In one typical investigation, 700 soldiers classified as neurotic were rated on a large number of traits by the attending psychiatrist on the basis of their life history. Two underlying factors were found to account for most of the ratings and classification differences: neuroticism and introversion-extraversion. Other studies were then undertaken in an attempt to characterize these dimensions more accurately—for example, individuals who rated high in neuroticism and low in neuroticism were given independent tests and assessments, and the situations on which they varied were then used to document the differences more fully. From studies of this kind, Eysenck found that he could make broad descriptive statements as to differences between, for example, neurotic introverts and neurotic extraverts (1947). Thus his method is to find groups that differ widely on one factor, and then give them extra tests to find other measures on which they also vary. Such measures include, among others, intelligence, body build, aspiration level, certain types of symptoms, and esthetic preferences. The ultimate outcome is a rich description of people who differ in the dimension under study, based on objective measurement rather than anecdotes or general observation.

Eysenck's investigations have led him to believe that the introversion-extraversion dimension is a general factor in

emotional behavior, while neuroticism is a general factor in the area of motivation or striving. In 1953 he showed that certain predictions could be made from this formulation—for instance, that the emotional factor of introversion-extraversion would be important in determining the ease with which conditioned responses could be established in human beings, but that the neuroticism dimension could not be used for this purpose. This has proved to be the case. By comparing normal individuals with mental hospital patients he has also uncovered a third fundamental dimension, psychoticism, which can be described in terms that are quite different from those applying to either introversion-extraversion or neuroticism. He suggests that the three dimensions may be used as a basis for a human typology.

Factor analysis has certain recognized advantages. It forces the investigator to test any proposed personality dimensions empirically, and to develop operational rather than intuitive or unspecified concepts. One of its principal uses is to test variables that have arisen in a clinical setting, to see if they actually bear on the case at hand. Too often clinical concepts have not been subjected to any statistical study.

But the method also has its limitations. As Allport points out, it is of little help in describing individual behavior because it only isolates average tendencies that fit the average personality. Moreover, the introduction of quantitative methods too early in the process limits the kind of data to be dealt with, since it favors characteristics that can be readily measured. Finally, although the method of factor analysis has been developed to an impressive degree, the findings it has produced fall short of what is needed to establish it as a widely accepted technique.

FACULTY PSYCHOLOGY. The theory that the mind is composed of a number of separate powers or faculties such as will, feeling, intellect and memory.

The roots of faculty psychology reach back to ancient Greek philosophy. Plato divided the classes in his ideal republic according to three types of "mind": intellectual, volitional and appetitive. In the first work specifically devoted to psychology, *De Anima,* Aristotle categorized mental abilities into remembering, willing, sensation, abstract and concrete intellect. The descriptive terms for these capacities were translated into Latin as powers or faculties which *enable* us to remember, will, and so on. Even though this change did not actually add any new meaning to these concepts, the new terms were taken as *explanations* rather than as *descriptions* of different types of mental function. As a result, the question how an individual remembers was answered merely by saying that he remembers because he possesses the faculty of memory. In other words, a term that was originally meant only as a label became distorted into a process responsible for the behavior it designated.

The faculty viewpoint was crystallized by Thomas Reid (1710–96) and his chief popularizer, Dugald Stewart (1753–1828), both members of the so-called Scottish school of psychology. Reid listed 24 "active powers" of the mind, including among others self-esteem, gratitude, and self-preservation, as well as six "intellectual powers" such as moral taste, conception, perception, judgment, and memory. The approach caught on and became one of the leading schools of the nineteenth century. Franz Joseph Gall (1758–1828) and Johann Kaspar Spurzheim (1776–1832) applied it to phrenology and sought to localize the various functions enumerated by Reid in specific regions of the brain. It was also applied to education, and is largely responsible for the belief that the general faculty of memory can be strengthened through practice. Educators of the time therefore gave their students poems and lists of words to memorize on the theory that this would prepare them for the memory functions needed in law, business, or any other enterprise. Similarly, they believed that reasoning power could be developed by training in geometry and that this general faculty could then be more effectively applied to public affairs, science and other areas.

The theory, then, assumed that each of these operations, memory, reasoning, and so on, is controlled by a single broad power or faculty which could be developed by training in the same way that individual sets of muscles can be strengthened through exercise.

This claim of faculty psychology has been disproved. Systematic studies carried out by Thorndike and Woodworth in 1901 showed that there is no automatic, wholesale transfer from one task to another. The nature of the material is the key. Memorizing Latin and Greek vocabulary will not advance our study of geography except where it involves names of cities or countries derived from these languages. On the other hand, a study of Latin and Greek will be of considerable help with Spanish or French because they contribute many words to these languages. Thorndike and others therefore emphasized the fact that transfer takes place only when there is a similarity of components or the application of the same general principle. *See* TRANSFER OF TRAINING.

The knowledge gained in the course of testing the validity of faculty psychology has been of considerable use. Studies of transfer of training have helped educational psychologists develop more efficient curricula; also, investigations of the areas devoted to different functions in the brain have expanded our understanding of many of its control centers as well as the integration of many of its areas. Faculty psychology has therefore made its contribution to psychology and psychiatry in a negative way. *See* PHRENOLOGY, CEREBRAL CORTEX.

FALSE PREGNANCY (Hysterical Pregnancy, Pseudocyesis). A rare condition in which a woman shows all the usual signs of pregnancy even though conception has not taken place.

In simulated pregnancy, the abdomen becomes distended, the breasts enlarge, weight increases, "morning sickness" occurs—and the patient may even demand pickles in the middle of the night. In other words, everything is there except the baby. The reaction is viewed as a hysterical, or conversion, symptom, though it is sometimes classified as a psychophysiologic reaction of the genitourinary type. It usually occurs in immature women who experience intense unconscious conflicts over childbearing. Therese Benedek (1959) gives this explanation for the condition: "These women are usually infertile. Being unconsciously afraid of pregnancy and guilty because of hostile wishes (toward mother and children), they clamor for motherhood, and, during the period of pseudocyesis, they enjoy gratifications which only pregnancy justifies." She points out that the opposite can also occur—that some women may remain unaware of their pregnancy even when it is far advanced. They may even insistently deny that they are pregnant, convinced that "what should not be, cannot be." *See* AEROPHAGIA.

Illustrative Case: FALSE PREGNANCY

A twenty-one-year-old girl was referred from a prenatal clinic with a note that, whereas they had been unable to detect any signs of pregnancy, the patient not only insisted that she was pregnant, but also attributed her anorexia, vomiting, amenorrhea, abdominal pains, and general irritability to this condition. Physical examination showed only a gaunt, markedly undernourished girl who affected a posture and mode of abdominal relaxation that gave her the appearance of early pregnancy. There were, however, no other physical signs of this, and as previously the Ashheim-Zondek and Rana pipiens tests were negative.

The history and mental status examinations revealed a wealth of neurotic and borderline psychotic patterns, which need not be detailed here. One of particular psychosomatic interest was the following:

The patient's father, an irresponsible, alcoholic psychopath, had seduced the girl into sex play at an early age, and had begun to attempt intercourse with her when she was about 12. This had failed primarily because the patient's genitalia remained infantile, but the two continued the practice of mutual masturbation. At 18 the patient became jealous of a younger sister whom the father had begun to prefer, eloped to another city with a young man who, after a single frustraneous sexual relationship with her, "did the right thing" and married her. The patient, however, was unhappy in her own home; intercourse with her husband again proved impossible and after a few months he lost patience and brought her back to her parents. There the patient discovered that her sister was illegitimately pregnant and immediately suspected her father—a suspicion soon confirmed by the sister. The patient missed her next menstrual period, began to believe herself pregnant by her own husband, and thereafter rapidly developed the pseudocyetic abdominal enlargement, vomiting, dietary idiosyncrasies, and emotional instability that brought her to the clinic.

Course Under Therapy. Under Amytal narcosis administered as part of the initial sedation for her insomnia and her restlessness, the patient furnished additional material which indicated that her unconscious desires to be pregnant were compounded of the following: a jealous identification with the sister together with aggressively tinged wishes to reveal her own incestuous relationships with the father; a longing to force her way back into the family circle as a prospective mother forsaken and requiring prenatal care; a similar wish to regain her husband in a protective, nonsexual relationship—or finally, failing all these, a regressive pre-emptive flight to the haven of a maternity hospital.

The patient showed initial improvement under routine care and was fairly easily induced to relinquish her fantasies of being pregnant. However, she became increasingly demanding of special foods, individual hours of visiting and other indulgences, developed uncompromising animosities to student nurses and other sister surrogates on quite fanciful pretexts, and finally became exceedingly uncooperative. During the later periods distortions of affect and ideation became apparent; for instance, the patient, with a peculiarly remote equanimity, stated that an elderly ward janitor had been hypnotizing her. Commitment was therefore recommended, but the family refused and took her home. There she ate very little, began vomiting frequently and finally became so cachectic [emaciated] that the possibility of Simmond's disease [a pituitary disorder] was seriously considered. She died in a sanatorium a short time later. (Masserman, 1955)

FAMILY CARE (Foster-Family Care). An after-care service which provides mental patients with temporary or permanent placement in a foster family.

The object of family care is to provide for patients who no longer need the specialized services of a hospital but still require some treatment, supervision or care. When relatives or friends are unwilling or unable to take care of the patient, family care is given in private homes selected, supervised and subsidized by the hospital or other treatment agency. The service is available to many kinds of patients: elderly people with chronic, irreversible mental disorders, long-term patients who must learn to adjust to life outside an institution, younger patients who need help in making the transition to independent life but who cannot get it from their own family. In some areas the service is also available to the mentally retarded and victims of convulsive disorders. The primary benefit for all these patients is the opportunity to live in a warm, friendly home with close ties to the community. In addition, they receive special care adapted to their individual needs—for example, regular medication, psychotherapy at the hospital or clinic, a chance to follow hobbies or other recreational interests, and the opportunity to do part-time work outside the home.

Foster-family care has an interesting history. It can be traced back to medieval times when, according to legend, an Irish princess fled to Belgium to escape the incestuous advances of her mad father. There he overtook her and put her to death near a shrine at Gheel. The girl was later re-incarnated as St. Dymphna, who dedicated herself to the care of the insane. By the fifteenth century so many pilgrims came to the shrine seeking a cure that families in town began to care for them as a religious duty. The number continued to increase, and by the middle of the nineteenth century family care itself was recognized as an important factor in rehabilitating the mentally ill. As a result the Belgian government built a small hospital to serve as a reception center for patients sent by mental institutions for family-care placement. In time the entire area became a colony for mental patients, with as many as 3500 living with families at one time—and, interestingly, mental illness in general became known as "St. Dymphna's disease."

The family-care concept spread from Belgium to many other European countries. In America the first program was established by the State of Massachusetts in 1885, but the technique did not begin to arouse wide-spread interest until the 1930s and 1940s. At the present time twenty-four states and a majority of Veterans Administration hospitals have active family-care programs, serving about 12,000 patients in all.

In developing a program, a search must first be made for suitable homes. Prospective families, or "caretakers," are thoroughly interviewed by social workers. If they are accepted, they then receive group instruction in the care of patients and their own working relationship with the hospital. The patients themselves must be carefully prepared and oriented, and the homes must be assigned, where possible, not only with their needs but their preferences in mind. Where advisable, arrangements are made for hospital services such as occupational therapy to be given in the home. In many cases it is also necessary to obtain the co-operation of social agencies in providing vocational rehabilitation, employment opportunities or special family services.

A well-run family care program offers many benefits. It helps to release hospital beds for the acutely ill. It enables the community to assume responsibility for patients, and spreads the idea that people who have recovered from mental illness can take part in everyday activities. It gives the families an opportunity to be of valuable service and to receive some financial return. But most important of all, it gives the patients themselves a chance to live as normal a life as possible.

FAMILY SIZE. The size of the family has important psychological implications. It helps to determine the relationships or "interactional systems" in which the members are embedded, and it has a pronounced effect on the total character and climate of the home. The number of "interactions" multiplies rapidly as families grow larger. According to a formula developed by Bossard and Boll (1960), in a family of three members, there are five such relationships; a second child raises that number to eleven, a third to 26, and a fourth to 57. Moreover, the nature of these relationships is contingent on many individual factors: the age and sex of each member; their interests, needs and demands; their attitudes and personal characteristics; and the special role they play in the family. In some cases not only grandparents but domestics and roomers play a significant part in the family group, but in general it has been found that the "nuclear family" (parents and children only) is more crucial—especially for the development of the children—than the enlarged or "elongated" family.

The effects of the one-child family on the character and growth of the child are discussed under a separate topic, ONLY CHILDREN. The present article will contrast small families (two-three children) with large families (six or more children) from the psychological point of view. Studies show that the small American family has generally been planned with regard to the number and spacing of children, and the parents devote a great deal of attention to the study of child care and to the children's education. They are likely to be "wrapped up" in their offspring, eager to do their best for them, and anxious to have the children do *their* best in school and other activities. The mother is in charge of everyday discipline, but calls upon the father in emergencies. Both, however, make the children the center of attention, and the children, in turn, may come to expect special treatment not only from their parents but from other people as well. They are far more likely to be overprotected, indulged, and dependent than children in a larger family.

The small family is often better off financially than the large family, and the children are therefore likely to have educational, recreational, and health advantages. Studies show that in physical and social adjustment they are usually somewhat superior to children from a very large family. Nevertheless, broken homes are more frequent in small families, and crises have a particularly devastating effect because there are so few members to share them. When death or illness occurs in a large family the child has the benefit of greater group support.

The large family has a number of other advantages over the small family. The parents are far less likely to overprotect, overindulge, or pressure their children, and the children develop qualities of independence, responsibility, and maturity at an earlier age. They learn to work with others and do their share. The first-born girl is usually assigned the role of mother's helper, and the first-born boy becomes the father's right-hand man, and can usually take over if something happens to the father. The other children contribute according to their abilities, except perhaps for the youngest, who tends to be spoiled.

But there is another side to the coin. The older children are often required to do too much household work, and may therefore feel resentful toward the parents and toward the younger children who are put in their charge. They also tend to be underachievers at school, partly because they have too little time to study and partly because of their rebellious feelings.

Generally speaking, it has been found that children from large families are less prone to emotional disturbance and problem behavior than children from small families. But maladjustments do occur, especially in the first-born and the last-born, and more frequently among the girls than the boys. The extent of these difficulties, however, depends greatly on two factors: the relationships within the family and its financial status (Bossard and Boll, 1960). If the parents are harsh and autocratic, and also live under constant economic strain, the children tend to be poorly adjusted. But if a spirit of kindness and co-operation prevails, and financial problems are not severe, many of the adverse effects can be avoided.

Finally, there are indications that medium-sized families, with three or even four children, do not have the disadvantages found in very small and very large families. These families tend to be superior to either extreme in terms of stability and harmony as well as wholesome child development. *See* BIRTH ORDER.

FAMILY THERAPY. A form of group psychotherapy in which the family is the therapeutic unit; its object is to alter the home influences that contribute to the disorder of one or more members.

As Ackerman (1966) points out, family therapy is the only form of psychological treatment that focuses on a "natural" group, as opposed to an isolated individual or an artificial grouping. He contends that since the family is the "matrix" out of which all human interactions develop, it is the logical locus for therapeutic intervention. Treating the family as a whole provides the therapist with a unique opportunity for working with basic, ongoing relationships not merely to improve adjustment but to create a more effective way of living.

Family therapy stems from three major sources: the group therapy approach, the current emphasis on social factors in the etiology of mental disorder, and the increased understanding of family influences resulting from studies of child development and child psychiatry. It rests on the theory that a healthy family is the fundamental source of the individual's sense of identity and emotional stability—and if a breakdown occurs, this will in many cases indicate that there is a disabling conflict in the home. In fact, Ackerman contends, an individual is not usually referred for treatment until the balance in the family is upset by his problem. He suggests, too, that frequently several, and sometimes all, members of the family are disturbed to some degree, not just the patient who comes for help. In 1958 he stated that the "primary patient" is often "an emissary in disguise of an emotionally warped family group," and may not himself be the most disturbed member of the family.

Midelfort (1957) also finds that the entire family tends to be disturbed, but points out that the members tend to counterbalance each other's disturbances —for example, if some members are rigid and compulsive, others may react to them by adopting impulsive "acting out" behavior. In a case of this kind the contrasting members become a threat to each other and create a vicious circle. The therapist's job is to break through this circle and help them moderate their extreme responses. This is done by first getting them to realize that they actually have the opposite tendencies within them, and then by helping them bring these tendencies into the open. The rigid family members are therefore encouraged to express their impulses spontaneously and the impulsive members to exercise greater control. This helps to restore the equilibrium of the family and of the individuals as well—and when this occurs, the family achieves a new sense of unity, and the members are able to meet their problems in a more objective and co-operative spirit.

Ackerman suggests that the process start with a family interview in which problems are aired together, rather than with separate interviews with the members. This enables the therapist to gauge the roles of the various members and the interaction patterns that prevail among them. Ideally, the diagnosis should be made by a team consisting of a psychiatrist, who conducts the interview; a psychologist, who administers tests; and a social worker, who not only gathers data about the family but assesses the emotional climate of the home.

In the therapeutic process, the psychiatrist plays the role of participant-observer, but with the emphasis on participation. He moves directly into the family conflict, helping the members pinpoint their problems and become aware of their distorted reactions. But instead of merely encouraging them to work through their problems on an analytical level, he attempts to exert a direct influence on their interactions. This involves establishing rapport and empathy with each of the members, then directly intervening to point out, for example, that the group is using one of the members as a scapegoat—that

one or another member is overworking certain defensive reactions, such as rationalization, denial, or displacement—or that they are expressing their internal conflicts through their attitudes and behavior. In carrying out this process, the therapist plays the role of an understanding and protective parental figure. As he challenges the pathological defenses of the family members, he helps them discover what they really want from each other, how they can communicate more meaningfully, and how they can handle their difficulties more constructively. And as the therapy proceeds, he encourages them to test out healthier attitudes and behavior patterns in their day-to-day family life.

Ackerman maintains that family therapy is applicable to a variety of disorders, including character disorders (especially of the "acting out" type), neuroses, and psychoses—but it is uniquely effective with cases of marital discord, and with problems involving the relation of a child or adolescent with his family. He also sees it as a valuable adjunct to individual psychotherapy, particularly in helping to break through a period of resistance or an impasse based on secondary gains (clinging to symptoms because they arouse sympathy or attention). In addition, it can be used in reintegrating a patient with his family after he has undergone individual psychological treatment. It is usually contraindicated when communication has completely broken down; when one or both parents cannot be emotionally honest; when a key member is destructive or criminal, malignantly paranoid, or organically psychotic; or when the family is strongly prejudiced against any intervention in its private affairs.

FATIGUE. A feeling of lassitude due to loss of sleep or heavy exertion, usually reflected in impaired performance or reduced output.

Since fatigue is closely related to human efficiency, most of the investigations have been carried out by industrial psychologists. Their findings will be summarized under a number of different headings:

Measurement. Subjective estimates of fatigue are usually too variable and indefinite to be useful, and various objective measurements have therefore been proposed. One index is reduction in output—for example, a decrease in typing speed toward the end of the working day. Another is increase in the number of errors—in one study, telegraphers were found to make three to four times as many errors in the third hour of continuous work as in the first hour. The attitude and set of the worker may determine whether decrease in speed or increase in errors should be used as an index of fatigue. If he is instructed to work for speed, output will usually remain high for a long period but more and more errors will be made; if told to work for accuracy, he will cut down on output as he becomes fatigued in order to avoid making errors.

Physiological changes resulting from continued activity are also measured. These include increases in blood pressure, heart-rate, muscle tension, and oxygen consumption. These changes apply not only to physical activity but, in lesser degree, to mental efforts. So-called mental fatigue is generally a physical effect resulting from postural tensions and contractions in the arms, hands, and other parts of the body— and in many cases physiological changes accompanying emotional tension may also be involved.

Tiredness and Fatigue. The relation between feelings of tiredness and measured fatigue is not a simple one. We may feel extremely tired and yet show no change in performance, particularly when we are engaged in a hobby or task we enjoy. Moreover, physiological changes indicative of fatigue can frequently be found before our output is changed or feelings of tiredness develop.

This is often the case in sports or rescue work: "By all rights I should be tired but I feel great." On the other hand, output may decline long before measurable physiological changes occur, as often happens when we are engaged in tasks we dislike. In such cases we get tired almost as soon as we start, probably because we are tired of *them.*

Motivation. The examples just given show that motivation has a great deal to do with feelings of fatigue. Most of us are capable of working much harder than we do, and we also have hidden reserves that we do not usually call upon. But we often lose our motivation before we lose our energy. Even when we actually become fatigued we can often perform just about as well as before *if* we throw ourselves into the work. This can, however, be overdone. Some people push themselves to the limit or beyond, and some employers introduce incentives which motivate their employees to overwork and exhaust themselves.

The importance of motivation is also shown by the fact that we may feel tired to death on one task, but have a sudden burst of energy when we turn to work that is fresh and interesting. A change by itself has motivation value. Bills (1943) has shown that introducing variety into physical tasks relieves fatigue, and the more variety there is, the less fatigue.

Safety. Many accidents in industry and on the highway stem from fatigue. They are often due to the reduced muscle tone, increased reaction time, or faulty concentration that occurs when the worker or driver is tired. But recent studies show psychological factors of a subtler character may also be involved. It has been found, for example, that a man who has been driving for a long period tends to change his standards of safety. He loses sight of what the situation requires and begins to take chances he would not take when he is fresh. Driving tests show that his ability to perform may not change, but he becomes less vigilant. These changes in vigilance can be used as tests for the effects of fatigue, since they often appear before any of the usual physiological or behavioral signs show themselves, especially in continuous work that requires precise timing, including flying a plane as well as driving a car. We are ordinarily unaware of these changes in attitude and tendencies toward carelessness, but it is extremely important to become alert to them.

Prevention. Many people resort to stimulants such as caffeine or amphetamine compounds, but these drugs often produce tensions, prolonged sleeplessness, or strange and unexpected reactions. There is only one recommended way of preventing or overcoming fatigue, and that is to rest. Many experiments have been performed on rest periods, and there is considerable agreement on a number of points. First, rest periods should be distributed during work periods and should be so spaced that they occur before the worker becomes thoroughly fatigued. The reason is that it takes relatively longer to recover from overfatigue than from moderate fatigue. Studies show that over-all efficiency is increased by shorter work periods, and that the employees also have a better attitude toward the work and take fewer unauthorized rest periods. Second, scheduled rest periods are superior to unscheduled periods, since workers can better adjust themselves to the amount of work to be done if they know that a rest period will occur at a certain time. Third, the type of work should determine both the frequency and the length of the rest periods. Heavy manual labor and trying mental work require longer and more frequent breaks than light sedentary work. *See* EXHAUSTION DELIRIUM.

FEAR. A reaction to a recognized threat, characterized by a feeling of dis-

agreeable tension and an impulse to escape the danger.

This reaction contrasts with anxiety, which consists of vague feelings of impending disaster arising from indefinable threats. Fear is usually more temporary and more directly related to external events than anxiety; anxiety is likely to be more persistent and to stem primarily from internal problems involving feelings of inadequacy or guilty impulses. The two reactions, however, are frequently found together, especially in situations of pervasive danger such as combat. *See* ANXIETY.

The physiology of fear has been studied extensively and new centers of control have been found not only in the hypothalamus but in the limbic system as well. The principal feature of the reaction, however, is the arousal of the sympathetic nervous system. When a person finds himself in a threatening situation, large quantities of adrenalin are secreted, quickening the heartbeat, sending blood to the brain and muscles, and in general mobilizing the organism for "fight or flight." Although these reactions usually have the positive effect of alerting the individual to meet the emergency, there are situations, especially in panic, where the body becomes overmobilized and behavior becomes disorganized. Moreover, if the state of arousal continues for a long period of time, the continual drain may result in psychosomatic disorders. *See* PANIC, GENERAL ADAPTATION SYNDROME, HYPOTHALAMUS, LIMBIC SYSTEM.

Fear, then, can be either stimulating or paralyzing, either constructive or destructive. Since no one's life is entirely free of threat, it is a normal, understandable reaction in many situations. Small, manageable amounts help to keep us sensitive to danger, release the energy we need to meet crises, and remind us that discretion is more sensible than recklessness. Studies of men in combat zones have shown that it is healthier to admit one's fear than to suppress it; the "strong, silent man" is more likely to break down than the man who verbalizes his feelings. However, mere talk about fears is usually not enough; it is more effective to try to understand them and to put them in perspective.

In some cases our fears are quite proportionate to the threat, and we can keep them in control by developing skill and competence and by forcing ourselves to take action instead of "stewing." We can also try to identify the situations in which we are particularly vulnerable and either avoid them or prepare to meet them. On the other hand, some people develop irrational, exaggerated reactions unrelated to any apparent danger. Such fears, better known as phobias, arise from hidden sources in the personality and frequently symbolize threats that cannot be recognized without help. See PHOBIA, PHOBIC REACTION.

A good part of the history of life can be written in terms of fear—both the common fears that most of us experience in greater or lesser degree, and the unique fears we develop as individuals. Both types of fear are now considered to be acquired rather than innate. The common fears develop in a fairly orderly progression, probably due to the fact that most people undergo the same general kinds of experiences as they mature. Bridges' careful observations (1932) have shown that newborn infants react with generalized excitement to disturbing stimulation (hunger, wet diapers, restriction of movement), and by three months show clear signs of distress. The first responses that can be definitely identified as fear do not emerge until about seven months of age. At this time the infant does not simply cry or thrash about, but withdraws from almost any sudden strong stimulation such as loud noises, very hot or cold water, unexpected movements of an animal, a toy abruptly thrust in front of his face, or even a large person in the bizarre costume of Santa Claus. Fear reactions can also be elicited by holding the infant up and suddenly dropping him, although "loss of support" is not such a universal cause as John B. Watson thought it to be. It depends largely on—how it is done. If the child is dropped in a spirit of fun, he may laugh and enjoy himself; but if the person who drops him is tense and serious he will usually cry.

Fear of strangers and strange places commonly occurs around eight months of age and is not, as some parents believe, an early sign of emotional instability or an attempt to embarrass them. Rather, it is merely an indication that the child recognizes and feels threatened by the unfamiliar. Like the adult, he apparently feels more secure with people and places he knows, especially when he has formed close relationships with them. Spitz (1945) has shown that infants brought up in hospitals or orphanages without personal attention do not usually withdraw from strangers. Since they have not had as much opportunity to form close relationships in the first place, the stranger is not particularly threatening. These observations indicate that the fear of strangers does not come about "spontaneously" and without reason, as some investigators have contended, but arises from the fact that a child has learned that novel stimuli of any kind tend to be disturbing. The same idea applies to fear of darkness, which is ordinarily exhibited at about three years of age. This reaction is probably associated with feelings of helplessness arising from the fact that in the dark (a) people and things look unfamiliar, (b) he cannot see what he is doing, and (c) he is reminded of feelings of discomfort which have caused him to wake up in the middle of the night.

The early fears of noise, strangeness, and falling tend to diminish between the ages of three and four, possibly because the child has learned that they are usually groundless (Jersild, Markey, and Jersild, 1933). During this period, however, he may (or may not) acquire a fear of snakes or other animals, especially if adults around him show their own fear or constantly warn him about being hurt. Before the age of four, the child's fears are aroused by concrete objects and situations; after that time his increasing ability to understand language brings with it the fear of the possible and the imaginary. Parents often instil or aggravate these fears by telling fairy tales or horror stories just before bedtime, and a camp counselor may frighten the members of his bunk into doing his bidding by referring to "the monster that lives in the lake." Even though ghost stories and fairy tales are supposed to take place "long, long ago," they may have a vivid and immediate reality for the child, since his concept of time and space are quite different from those of the adult.

During the school years the child's fears are often associated with ideas of right and wrong. He may be admonished and threatened so much that he acquires a fear of punishment, and may be criticized so frequently that he becomes afraid that there is something wrong with him. Such fears may be intensified by feelings of guilt over masturbation, sexual thoughts or, possibly, Oedipal urges. Most children, however, do not develop an active fear of punishment or the notion that something might be wrong with them. In our society, particularly in the middle class, they are more likely to be afraid of not being able to hold their own in competition or to live up to the standards set for them. *See* CASTRATION COMPLEX.

Before the age of nine or ten the child has no adequate concept of death and shows little fear of it; from then on this fear slowly increases (Nagy, 1948). During the preadolescent years the child also becomes concerned over the impression he makes on others.

In early adolescence this concern generally takes the form of worry over social incompetence or inability to gain acceptance from the peer group. As a result many young people between the ages of eleven and sixteen develop a whole set of social fears: fear of ridicule, fear of being left out of the group, fear of making a *faux pas* and fear of talking with "new" people. Fears in later adolescence, particularly among college students, center around both social and academic success. A study of college girls has shown that their fears most frequently involve school work (40%) and loss of prestige (30%), while fears of illness and physical danger were relatively minor (17%) (Anastasi, Cohen and Spatz, 1948). Again, these are primarily "middle-class fears," and are not so likely to occur on other socioeconomic levels.

The common fears of adulthood are closely related to the demands of mature life. Both men and women fear death and illness not only as a personal threat but as a threat to others who depend upon them. In other words, adult fear takes the form of worry over fulfilling social responsibility, and is often aggravated by concern over personal inadequacy, job insecurity, health, and status. In old age the fear of dependency gradually takes over, and the individual worries that his family, or an institution, will have to take care of him. Studies have shown, however, that the elderly are usually much less concerned about death than they are about their inability to earn a living and the possibility of extended illness. It has been suggested that the decline in the fear of death may be one reason why older people frequently lose their will to recover from illnesses.

These, then, are some of the common fears we experience. In addition, each individual develops his own fear pattern which is dependent on three major factors: the behavior of people whom he imitates or identifies with, the way he has been conditioned by people and events, and the traumatic experiences he has gone through. These will be described only briefly, since they are discussed more fully under other topics. First, children acquire many of their fears from parents, nurses, or others with whom they are closely asssociated. Sometimes, too, they take on the fears of other children, particularly those whom they admire. Imitation—often reinforced by warnings and punishments —may account for a child's fear of germs, cats, toads, thunderstorms, or flying in an airplane. He may also be afflicted by the out-and-out phobias of a parent or other family member—for example, a phobia about pointed objects, heights, open spaces, or even crossing the street.

Second, many fears are learned through conditioning and spread from one situation to another by a process known as stimulus generalization. If a child is repeatedly put in a closet as punishment, he may not only hesitate to enter a closet by himself, but his fear may spread, or "generalize," to any small enclosure such as a tunnel, a cave, a tent, or an elevator. Fears often transfer from one object to another by a chain of conditioning, and there is little doubt that we could explain some of the odd "unaccountable" fears and aversions of adults if we could trace the chain back to its first link. See GENERALIZATION.

Third, some fears originate in traumatic experiences. A fall from a ladder may lead to a fear of heights, a near-drowning to fear of water, a cat's scratch to fear of cats (and possibly all feline creatures). Actually traumatic experiences of this kind are simply a disturbing form of conditioning, one that involves a threat to life or health. An even more potent type of traumatic experience is the one that involves a threat to self-esteem or moral worth. Experiences of this kind are at the root of some of the most intense and ir-

rational fears that haunt men and women, as the following example will show:

A woman of about thirty years old became so panic-stricken every time she attempted to light the gas stove that she finally developed a hatred of cooking and gave it up altogether. But her problem did not stop there. The fear became generalized and spread to lighting a cigarette as well, and she soon gave that up, too, asserting that it was a dangerous and unsanitary habit. Somewhat later, during psychoanalysis, she suddenly recalled that many years before she had been jealous of her baby sister and had tried to destroy her by setting fire to the house. To protect herself from feelings of guilt, she had unconsciously repressed the entire event. The memory, however, had remained active and had been preventing her from performing any actions that resembled the original misdeed. See POST-OPERATIVE DISORDERS.

FECHNER, GUSTAV THEODOR

(1801–87). Fechner, one of the great pioneers in experimental psychology, was a native of Germany. After receiving a medical degree at the University of Leipzig at the age of twenty-one, he immediately began to write satires on the mechanistic approach in the sciences under the pseudonym "Dr. Mises." Nevertheless he continued his scientific studies, specializing in mathematics and physics, and by 1824 had obtained a lectureship at the university. He first came into prominence in 1831 when he published an important paper confirming Ohm's Law. In 1834 he was appointed to a professorship and soon after took up the study of sensory physiology. His first paper in this field was on after-images, but his research on this subject nearly cost him his sight, for it involved looking at the sun repeatedly through colored filters. As a result he suffered from violent headaches and became partially blind. A short time later he developed a "nervous breakdown," and in 1839 was forced to resign his post at the university.

Within three years, however, Fechner made a seemingly miraculous recovery. This deepened his opposition to mechanism and confirmed his belief in a panpsychic philosophy, the theory that consciousness pervades the whole of nature from the smallest atom to the largest galaxy. Between 1838 and 1879 he developed this point of view in seven works, among them (in translation) *The Little Book of Life after Death* and *The Day View as Opposed to the Night View* (terms he used to designate the spiritual versus the material point of view).

Fechner's work in psychophysics, for which he is best known in the scientific community, is a mere by-product of his philosophic mission. He set out to prove that mental processes must be related to material events since they are simply different aspects of "soul-substance." To accomplish this, he sought to find a mathematical relationship between the qualitative aspects of experience and quantities that could be manipulated in the physical world. This view was first outlined in one of his philosophical works, *Zend Avesta, or the Things of Heaven and the Life to Come* (1851), and later presented in textbook form in *Elements of Psychophysics* (1860) which in his words, established "the exact science of the functional relations or relations of dependence between body and mind."

The *"Elements"* is regarded as the first important book in experimental psychology. It led to many psychophysical investigations not only on the subject of sensation, which Fechner stressed, but on feeling, attention, and perception. Much of his work had to do with "just noticeable differences" which he arrived at by increasing or decreasing the strength of stimuli. This concept had been proposed by Ernst Weber, but Fechner showed that it

applied to all senses according to a principle he named Weber's Law. *See* JUST NOTICEABLE DIFFERENCE, PSYCHOPHYSICS.

After the publication of the *Elements,* Fechner abandoned the subject of psychophysics except for one series of papers published in 1877 and an answer to his critics in 1882. However, he did turn his attention to another psychological problem, that of esthetics. He was the first to approach this subject experimentally, by presenting rectangles of different proportions to his subjects and asking them to choose the most pleasing. He also made use of a controversy that was raging over a claim that Holbein had painted two different Madonnas. When the two works were displayed together, Fechner attempted to determine their relative merit by having the public answer a questionnaire. While only a small percentage of the viewers answered his questions, this technique is regarded as the first application of the so-called "method of impressions" to the study of esthetics.

Fechner's work on esthetics appeared in book form in 1876 under the title *Introduction to Esthetics.* He then put this interest aside and returned to his philosophic writing which, incidentally, was poorly received by most of his contemporaries. But though he did not attract many followers to the cause of panpsychism, he did succeed in founding two important areas of study, psychophysics and experimental esthetics, more by chance than by design.

FEEDING BEHAVIOR. The feeding behavior of the growing child follows a regular but obstacle-ridden course. The regularity is due to the fact that there is a natural sequence in the development of his needs and skills. The obstacles are due to his difficulty in managing his movements and conforming to the requirements of civilized life. As Jersild has pointed out (1960), the more the process is geared to his changing wants and capacities, the smoother it will be.

Feeding behavior begins with the impulse to suckle. Some infants need help in starting this process, but most of them are capable of taking food from either the breast or the bottle from the beginning of life. The swallowing reflex is also well-developed, although the child may have some trouble co-ordinating it with sucking and keeping from swallowing air along with his food. Apparently the sucking impulse needs extra exercise, and also yields additional satisfactions beyond nutrition, since the baby constantly puts his fingers and practically everything else in his mouth. Biting does not usually appear until about the fourth month, although it may occur before that time. Chewing movements are often made even before the child has teeth and before he is given solid foods. He practices by chewing on milk or apple sauce as if in anticipation of future needs. *See* THUMBSUCKING.

Child psychologists have become deeply involved in the question of breast versus bottle feeding, and scheduled versus self-demand feeding. The choice of breast or bottle usually rests on practical considerations such as pressures of time, scheduling convenience, the flow of milk, or the mother's health. The prevailing fashion in child-rearing also has much to do with the choice. One of the most significant psychological findings is that mothers who show strong feelings of disgust or discomfort about sex are more likely to prefer bottle to breast feeding, (Sears, Maccoby and Levin, 1957). No detectable differences in personality and adjustment have been found between children who were breast fed and children who were bottle fed.

The issue of scheduled versus self-demand feeding is still controversial, and there is no conclusive evidence supporting either practice. Parents who put their children on self-demand usually find that while there is considerable vari-

ation in the number of feedings demanded in the first few days of life, the infant gradually reduces the number and falls into a fairly regular pattern. The same holds true of the amount of food he requires. Many mothers finds that this type of feeding is more psychologically satisfying to the infant than a fixed schedule. On the other hand, regular feeding is, of course, more convenient for the mother and there is no evidence that it is harmful. Possibly the best all-around plan is to start the child on self-demand and carefully adjust the formula so that he can go longer and longer without food, and then nudge him into a regular pattern. For studies on self-selection of diet, *see* CAFETERIA FEEDING.

In learning to eat by himself the child needs very little teaching but a great deal of patience from his parents. When he insists on trying to feed himself with his fingers, it is well to remember that he is also testing out his own abilities and learning to assert himself. Learning to use utensils is a gradual affair, but it follows a fairly regular sequence. At about twelve weeks the average child notices a cup but does not grasp it, at 16 weeks he touches it, at 20 weeks he "corrals" it with both hands, at 28 weeks he lifts it, at 32 weeks he grasps the handle, and at 36 weeks he brings it to his mouth with both hands—but it takes another 30 weeks before he can fully master the art of drinking from it. As to other utensils, the average child makes crude use of a spoon at about 18 months, a blunt fork between 2 and 3 years, a blunt knife between 3 and 5, and a knife for cutting at about 5 or 6. These figures are not offered as a rigid timetable, since there are wide individual differences among normal children. (Gesell and Ilg, 1937)

FERENCZI, SANDOR (1873–1933). An associate and follower of Freud, Ferenczi was chiefly noted for his experiments with an active form of therapy and his later emphasis on love and permissiveness in the therapist's relationship to his patient. Though these practices were departures from classical psychoanalysis, he did not offer a separate theory and was careful not to bring about an open rift with Freud.

Freud recognized that his own psychoanalytic procedures were primarily directed toward anxiety hysteria and obsessional neurosis, and that different kinds of methods might be required in handling other types of illness and in cases where his type of analysis failed to make progress. Accordingly, in 1915 Ferenczi began to experiment with methods focusing primarily on the character structure of the patient, as contrasted with the usual Freudian emphasis on id impulses. His techniques, which he called "active therapy," were not proposed as a radical alteration of the classic approach but as a modification to be introduced when obstacles to free association were encountered and the resistance situation defied analysis. The therapist was to abandon the active approach and return to the standard passive-receptive attitude after that resistance had been overcome. See RESISTANCE.

This approach of Ferenczi's was basically an extension of the Freudian "privation philosophy," which prescribed sexual abstinence so that the energy of the dammed-up libido would be available for the release of early emotional experiences. The theory held that these experiences would be stronger, deeper and more therapeutic if they were energized by a greater amount of libido. Building on this idea, Ferenczi held that abstention from other biologically pleasurable acts—all of which were conceived as expressions of the libido—would direct even more of this basic energy into the therapeutic process. These activities included eating, drinking, defecation and urination as well as direct sexual outlets. He did not, of course, require his patients to abstain completely, but only to keep these activities at an absolute minimum. Furthermore, he did not expect a given patient to cut down on all of them, but viewed each activity in the light of the dynamics of the particular illness, selecting those that most directly applied in the particular case. He theorized that these privations would bring to light and crystallize pathological character defenses which the patient had hidden from himself, and analysis would help him see how infantile and foolish they were. Ferenczi felt that then, instead of handling them by repression, the patient would direct his conscious ego against them and actively engage in his own self-education. (Ferenczi, 1925)

That was, in essence, the theory. But in practice, Ferenczi's harsh treatment had a far different effect. It caused so much suffering that many patients could not endure it. It also aroused intense hostility, especially when a strong positive transference (attachment to the therapist) had not been formed. At first Ferenczi believed the patient's outbursts were releasing unconscious hostility and therefore would have a salutary effect. However, he soon realized that these aggressive reactions were solely due to the privations he had introduced. He then tried putting the schedule on a voluntary basis, but in time became convinced that the entire procedure did not benefit his patients either by releasing hostility or by bringing early memories into consciousness.

In 1927 Ferenczi made an about-face and adopted a new technique based upon the principle of permissiveness rather than privation. He came to believe that the typical neurotic patient had been deprived of love, attention and freedom in his childhood. The therapist must therefore repair this deficiency by setting himself up as a "good" parent, in direct opposition to the "bad" parent of the patient's childhood. To counterbalance the rejection which the patient had experienced, and which had given rise to the neurosis, the therapist must create a loving, permissive environment which would allow emotional release and foster new emotional attitudes. At times Ferenczi deliberately encouraged his patients to act out childhood events, and would even take them in his arms or hold them on his lap as they expressed their need for tenderness. Although most psychiatrists would probably say that Ferenczi went too far in the direction of emotional involvement with his patients, he nevertheless helped to bring to attention the fact that love is a fundamental human need and that an atmosphere of acceptance can have a healing effect on neurotic disorders.

Ferenczi's permissive approach was a distinct deviation from the traditional analytic procedure, but even more radical was his view that the therapist, in acting the part of the good parent, should openly admit his own weaknesses, shortcomings and blind spots. This, he believed, would place him in even greater opposition to the typical self-righteous parent who deliberately sets himself up as perfect. As Harper (1959) points out, such admissions might also have a wholesome effect upon analysts who are oversensitive to criticism: "Ferenczi did much to bring to the attention of at least some analysts that they are imperfect human beings and that it is possible that the criticism of the patient is reality-oriented. Many contemporary analysts would hold to the view that their admission of mistakes can assist, not necessarily disrupt, an analysis, but that such admission of mistakes must be done judiciously and in great moderation so that the patient will not be encouraged to make hostile and defensive diversion of the analysis to the therapist's, rather than his own, problems."

FETISHISM. A sexual deviation in which excitement or gratification is obtained from a part of the body or an inanimate object. The body parts are, most commonly, breasts, buttocks, thighs, legs, feet, hair, and ears; and the inanimate objects include underclothing, shoes, handkerchiefs, gloves, furs and stockings.

Fetishism occurs more frequently in males than in females. It is an exaggeration of a normal tendency to attach special significance to parts of the anatomy and objects associated with the opposite sex—as witness the practice of saving locks of hair and the "panty raids" that occur in many colleges. The true fetishist, however, goes farther than merely collecting symbols and mementoes. He actually achieves sexual excitement and even satisfaction from kissing, fondling, tasting, smelling or licking the objects, or from examining photographs of women's feet, breasts or other parts of the body. In many cases this type of sexual activity is the preferred or even the only source of sexual satisfaction. An example is gratification obtained from female shoes, a symptom termed "rétifism" after a famous French educator Rétif de la Bretonne (1734–1806), who was known for this deviation. For him, and for many others, the shoe represented the female genital organs.

Many fetishists develop a compulsive urge to obtain the cherished articles, and will go to any lengths to get them. Young men steal dozens of stockings from shops or burglarize homes in search of female underwear. Some of them achieve orgasm through the symbolic act of entering through a window; others get their satisfaction from putting on the stolen articles or masturbating while examining them. The risk and excitement involved in stealing usually increases the sexual excitation.

Kleptomania is often considered a form of fetishism, since the stolen objects are practically always associated with sexual stimulation. Pyromania has been given a similar interpretation, since fire is associated with passion and the fire-setter usually experiences orgasm as he watches the flames. See these two topics.

Fetishism appears to develop from two major sources. First, it is based on a conditioning process in which objects acquire sexual significance through association with individuals who are sexually attractive. This is a normal reaction and explains the tendency of many men to become fond of a particular perfume or hair style. Second, if the man is immature and develops a fear of rejection by the opposite sex, he may fall back on the significant object as a substitute for the real object of his affection. At this point it may become "generalized" and *any* perfume or *any* lock of hair will do. He therefore begins collecting these objects and finds that this activity affords him sexual excitement or gratification without risk of failure or humiliation from the other sex. His original natural interest has now become a deviation.

Fetishists, including kleptomaniacs and pyromaniacs, frequently fight against their impulses, but find them irresistible. Most of them are not consciously aware of the connection between their activities and sexual stimulation, and if this association is suggested they may become remorseful and ashamed.

Behavior therapy has proved successful in counteracting the fetishistic pattern through reconditioning procedures. The standard treatment, however, is psychotherapy aimed at helping the patient alter his reactions through insight and understanding. Where the pattern is relatively superficial or recently acquired, this approach is often effective in a fairly short time, but where it is symptomatic of a deep and pervasive personality disturbance, long-term treatment is usually required. *See* BEHAVIOR THERAPY.

Illustrative Case: FETISHISM

At the age of thirty-five I can look back over many years of experience with sex fetishism. I can remember an interest in women's shoes as early as my fourth year, and that this interest continued during my grade-school days. I remember fantasies of women wearing high-heeled slippers of dainty design. There were also secret periods of play with my sister's and mother's shoes in the clothes closets. Shoes had no sexual meaning at this time. I don't know why I felt that secrecy was necessary.

. . . I masturbated at age nine, and I am positive that I thought of women's shoes during the act. I remember too when I first discovered the type of shoes, in an illustration in a book, that excited me most. At age ten or thereabouts I recall staying with my aunt. I was allowed to sleep with her because I was troubled with nightmares. I once went through her dresser drawers looking for hidden Christmas presents when I found a pair of high-heeled shoes. I got very excited, as if I had found a treasure. That night when she came home I persuaded her to put them on by saying I thought they must be too small for her. She did so and then I tried to get her to take a few steps, but she refused, saying it was silly. I was very excited during all this, though I do not recall that it was sexual. However, I do remember having an erection when I saw her putting her hose on one morning.

. . . There were other examples during my teens when I became excited over a girl's shoes, especially when she had shapely legs. In my seventeenth year I met a girl who attracted me strongly at once. Although I was conscious of her figure, neither her shoes nor her legs aroused more than a slight interest. My passion was essentially mental and free from any conscious sex disturbance. Demonstrations of affection were limited to goodnight kisses infinitely tender. I loved her with intense emotion entirely devoid of any lustful thoughts or desires. The romance ended when she went away to college, and I suffered painfully intense heartbreak over it.

Soon after this I secured employment and managed to recover from my depression by heavy physical labor. For several years I had little interest in women and rarely masturbated. I put all my energies into work.

Sometime around my twenty-fifth year my interest in shoes regained its strength. I began to frequent the waiting rooms of railroad stations. Sitting opposite a woman I would concentrate on her shoes and legs. In the earlier stages of this practice I would masturbate through my pocket, concealing this by holding a newspaper over my crossed legs. At a later stage I obtained satisfaction without mechanical means, the effect of looking at the shoes and legs being enough in itself to produce orgasm. What excited me most was patent leather pumps with French heels, of simple design and free of decorations like straps and bows. At times the nervous tension became so great as to cause visible trembling in a kind of ecstasy. Shoes alone were not enough, however. In addition I needed shapely ankles and sheer hose, preferably darker shades. The effect was much increased by movements of the foot. No part of the leg above the knee held any interest for me.

I have never experienced the intense nervous excitation, in anticipating normal sexual intercourse, comparable with the effect of an opportunity to see legs I consider especially beautiful, and provided circumstances are such that I am free of feelings of anxiety. I have noticed that, in watching a woman's legs in a public place, if there is a chance I may lose sight of her I become overeager and anxious, and this sometimes makes me impotent. If I can manage to relax and concentrate on the sheer enjoyment without an interruption, I then experience rising excitement and climax much more quickly. At the period when my fetish passion is most active, the effect of shapely legs, even when glimpsed for only a moment, is enough to set me on fire. The effect is not localized in my genitals, but seems to spread over my entire body. There is a heat sensation, as if my blood has been warmed.

I have suffered a great deal of anxiety during my visits to public places where it is easy to watch women's shoes and legs. In addition to the feeling of guilt which I still feel at times, there is the danger of detection. Plainclothesmen have haunted me, and more than once I have been questioned on suspicion of loitering. (Grant, 1953)

FIELD THEORY. The application of certain Gestalt principles to the study of personality and social relationships, an approach originated by Kurt Lewin.

Field theory arises from two interrelated views: the belief that psychological studies should focus on the individual, and the conviction that the only way to describe and predict behavior with any degree of accuracy is to view the individual in a field of dynamic relationships.

Lewin maintained that psychology has been overconcerned with statistical averages and underconcerned with uniqueness. In fact, the tendency, he claimed, is to disregard individuals who deviate too much from the average. Learning curves, for example, show us how a fictitious "average person" performs, but do not describe the way any individual learns. And even when we describe an individual job applicant as honest and outgoing, we overlook the fact that these trait names are only generalizations with many exceptions, since no one is completely honest or outgoing in every situation. We could not therefore be certain how he would fit into a particular job with its unique demands, surroundings and fellow workers.

In contrast to this emphasis on averages and frequency of occurrence, Lewin insisted that events can be lawful even if they occur only once, and that a thoroughgoing study of a single, well-controlled case can be more fruitful than a statistical analysis of many. In fact, he suggested that instead of disregarding the exceptions, we should subject them to a particularly intensive scrutiny, since this would probably yield more knowledge than all the rest of the investigation. With this philosophy in mind, he went on to propose a special method of studying individual behavior in individual situations.

Lewin's method was based on the Gestalt point of view which views experience in terms of patterns, configurations, and totalities. He therefore believed the study of behavior must be broadened to show the total situation, social and physical, in which the individual is embedded (Lewin, 1951). The only way we can understand and predict what a person will think or do is to see him in the context or "field" of experience, just as the behavior of an electron can be determined only by taking into account the activity of other electrons, the influence of the particles of the nucleus, the space through which it travels and so on.

To depict the forces, or vectors, that act upon the individual, Lewin (1936) invented a diagrammatic scheme. He pictured the individual's situation at any one moment as his "life space." This is a psychological representation of his immediate environment and the alternatives which are open to him. Each person's life space is unique, since there is a unique interaction between his environment and himself. This is particularly true of the person's social environment, since he is caught in a complicated network of interpersonal relationships. But it is also true of his physical surroundings. If the outward environment of two people is the same, its psychological meaning can be vastly different for each of them—for example, the living quarters of a small child and an adult are outwardly alike, but they present quite different possibilities for action and self-expression.

Within his total life space, any individual is constantly responding to needs which produce inner tensions and emotional disequilibrium. The tensions motivate him to achieve goals that are available to him. Objects in the life space that are capable of satisfying his needs are said to have a positive valence, and are designated by a plus sign; while those that threaten or repel have a negative valence and are given a minus sign. These valences differ in degree as well as kind, since an object may vary in the strength of its attraction or repulsion: a person's favorite food is more attractive to him when he is hungry than at the end of a meal. Values of varying strength are diagrammatically represented by vector lines in the Lewin scheme. These lines vividly show what happens in a conflict situation. For instance, a child wants to go out and play with his friends but at the same time feels obligated to practice the piano. If the two vectors are equal, he will vacillate between one alternative and the other; but if the desire to go out becomes slightly predominant, he may compromise by walking around outside without playing with his friends. See VA-LENCE.

The final component of the scheme is the depiction of barriers to the individual's movement toward a goal. These may be in the form of other people, social codes, physical objects, or anything else that stands in his way. They take on a negative valence as they are approached, and usually provoke exploratory behavior aimed at testing their strength and determining if they can be circumvented. If not, they may be directly attacked. An example of such a barrier is the mother who comes into the room to see whether her child is practicing. Other barriers are the child's conscience, and the reminders or threats of punishment he may have received in the past. Like the other components of Lewin's system, each of these obstacles represents a unique psychological meaning for the particular individual, and may have a different meaning for someone else.

In addition to these factors, both past and future events help to predict an individual's movements in his life space. Happy or unhappy experiences in learning a foreign language may determine whether a person will be eager to continue to study later on in life, and whether he will have a strong desire to go abroad. The specific nature of these past experiences will also help to determine whether he will set high or low goals in his future efforts. These dimensions are also diagramed in the Lewin scheme, since they show how the individual might attack present problems and deal with present conflicts. *See* LEVEL OF ASPIRATION.

Lewin has also devised a diagrammatical representation of the "structure" of the individual. It is composed of an outer layer, representing motor and perceptual regions which interact with the environment, and an inner personal core. These areas are divided by boundaries that are more easily penetrated by some people than by others. In a young child they are not insulated from each other and there is less differentiation between the self and outer reality, but the two regions are more sharply separated in a normal adult. Recognition of this fact helps to show why a child's behavior is different from an adult's—for example, it explains why a disturbance in one aspect of a child's behavior frequently spills over into all aspects. A tense home atmosphere will probably affect the way he learns to control elimination, speak, and establish confident relations with other children. Since the boundaries in the adult personality are more definite and the inner region of the self is more structured, he will be more likely to departmentalize his disturbances and keep them from interfering with his functioning in other areas. *See* ADOLESCENCE (THEORIES).

Field theory is particularly well adapted to the study of social relationships, and has led to a number of revealing experiments. As one example thirty 2- to 5-year-old children were allowed to play with certain incomplete toys—for example, floating toys with no water and an ironing board without an iron. The experimenters rated the children's constructiveness in terms of mental age, judging by their ability to make up for the missing parts by using their imagination. Next, they were given another set of toys which were complete and much more attractive than the first group. Finally, they were put back into the first situation with the incomplete toys, but with the attractive toys visible through a wire screen. The experimenters observed their behavior in all these situations and arrived at two significant findings. First, in the final situation the "constructive age" of the children declined an average of seventeen months; and second, a study of the individual behavior of the children showed that those who were most disturbed at the barrier (the wire screen), crying or attempting to reach the attractive toys, also regressed most in their play activities (Barker, Dembo, and Lewin, 1941).

In general, Lewin's theory is of particular value in depicting the field of forces that play upon an individual at any given moment. It is also a healthy reminder that these forces differ widely from individual to individual, so that a statistical approach cannot do full justice to the unique character of the behavior of different individuals.

FIGURAL AFTEREFFECTS. There are two principal types of aftereffect: the apparent distortion of a figure following prolonged inspection, and the effect of inspection of one figure on the perception of a subsequent figure. A single experiment will illustrate both of these phenomena. If you stare at a curved line for several moments it will tend to appear less curved than it was at first; and if you look at a straight line immediately afterward, it will appear to be curved in the direction opposite to the original curved line (Gibson, 1933).

The extent of figural aftereffects increases with the amount of exposure to the first figure, beginning with an exposure of two to five seconds and reaching a maximum after about one minute. Under certain conditions the effects of prolonged exposure to the first stimulus have lasted for several months.

Figural aftereffects are not easy to explain. One theory holds that the brain area which deals with the original stimulus becomes "satiated" or "fatigued" through prolonged inspection, and another area comes into play. The figure then appears to be different because a different part of the brain decodes the message. There is conclusive evidence that figural aftereffects are a function of a brain mechanism rather than a product of activity occurring in the retina: when the first figure is viewed by one eye and the second viewed by the other, the effect is still obtained.

Aftereffects have been demonstrated in sense modalities other than vision. If you pass your hand over a curved surface a number of times and then stroke a straight surface it will appear to be curved in the opposite direction. This is termed tactile-kinesthetic aftereffect.

FIGURE DRAWING TEST. A projective personality test based on the interpretation of drawings of the human figure.

The test is based on the assumption that these figures and the way they are executed will be a revealing reflection of the subject's personality, including his self-image, his attitudes toward other people, and his conscious or unconscious reaction patterns. Studies show that the effectiveness of the test is not limited by age, artistic skill or intelligence, and that it can be applied to illiterates and foreigners who do not know the language. Administration is easy, and the task is ambiguous enough to make it hard for the subject to sham.

The general procedure is to provide a soft pencil and a pile of typewriter paper so that the subject can select a leaf and place it in any orientation he chooses. Adequate room, a comfortable environment and a relaxed atmosphere are important. The subject is asked to draw a person. If he objects that he cannot draw or asks what kind of person it should be, he is told that artistic ability is unimportant and that he should draw whatever he likes and in any way he likes, except that it should be a complete figure and not just a head (*see Fig. 16,* p. 364). Abstract, stereotyped cartoons or stick figures are not acceptable.

After the first figure is drawn, the examiner identifies its sex and asks for a drawing of the opposite sex. The subject's verbalizations, sequence of drawing, bodily gestures and other behavior are noted, as well as his manner (confident, cautious, impulsive etc.), his need for more directions and anything else that indicates how he copes with the task.

There is no single way of interpreting the drawings. Some psychologists use graphological analysis, others apply psychoanalytic concepts such as self-image and ego ideal. Most examiners, however, employ a comprehensive, nondogmatic approach based on individual clinical experience. Levy (1950) believes it is helpful to examine the drawings as a whole in order to note the attitudes and feeling tone they convey, and then look for subtle cues in specific aspects of each figure. As an example of this approach, he interpreted one set of drawings in this way: "Female: this is a very small dowdy woman with a prominent nose and receding chin; she seems to be self-conscious," and "Male: this is a grim, tight-mouthed man wearing a high hat, formal attire and carrying a cane." An interview with the subject indicated that these figures represented herself and her father, who always dressed meticulously and sadistically criticized other people. Moreover, her self-drawing (the female) was not the way she actually looked, but the way the taunting father made her feel she looked (Abt and Bellak, 1950).

The following are some of the more significant features of the drawings, but the interpretations given here are presented merely as illustrations of the method and should not be taken as a set of rules:

Figure sequence. In a study of five thousand subjects, 87 per cent drew their own sex first; 13 out of 16 overt homosexuals drew the opposite sex first. There are, however, other reasons for drawing the opposite sex first, such as strong attachment to or dependence on a member of the opposite sex, or confusion of sex identity.

Comparison of figures. In most cases the male and female figures are drawn differently, and are helpful in revealing psychosexual attitudes. For example, the man may be small, have his hands in his pockets and look passive and introverted, while the woman may be larger, moving and vibrant. The overall impression in such a case may be that the male subject who drew the picture is a sensitive, non-participating individual who wants support from a maternal figure.

Location of drawing. Drawings in the center of the page suggest a self-centered, self-directed personality. Drawings in the upper half suggest that the individual is unsure of himself and "up in the air"; but if the figures are drawn at the bottom, they usually suggest a calm, stable person who has his "feet on the ground." Children who draw on the upper half of the page are usually found to have a higher than average aspiration level.

Movement. The drawings of restless, nervous, hypomanic individuals suggest extreme movement. Subjects with deep-seated conflicts who feel they must control themselves completely tend to draw rigid figures. If there is no feeling of motion whatever, psychosis is suggested. Seated or reclining figures are believed

to be indicative of low energy level, lack of drive, or emotional exhaustion.

Distortions and omissions of any part of the figure suggest conflicts—for instance, leg amputees frequently omit the lower parts of the body, and individuals with sexual conflicts omit or distort the genital area. Shadings, erasures, reinforcement and remarks about these areas are also indicative.

Head area. This is usually drawn first and is believed to show the subject's self-concept. A big head might indicate aggressive tendencies or intellectual aspirations or migraine attacks, depending on the individual. Specific features are also important: very large ears may imply an impairment of hearing, an open mouth which shows the teeth may indicate hostility or sadistic tendencies, a beard or moustache may suggest virility-striving, a long neck may mean a schizophrenic tendency to disorganization since it separates the brain from the body and its physical drives. The treatment of the hair is often revealing. A girl in puberty may give extra attention to the hair on the head because she is concerned with hair on less exposed parts of the body, and people who are upset or angry often show the hair standing on end. Infantile and regressed adults also show special concern for the hair. Voyeurs often omit or close the eyes, either as an unconscious denial of this tendency or as symbolic protection of these organs due to feelings of guilt or fear of possible harm. Many schizophrenics draw bizarre figures or show the internal anatomy.

Articles of clothing. Most figures are drawn with clothing. Ties are particularly important in male drawings since they are believed to be phallic symbols. Small ties indicate organ inferiority; fancy, carefully drawn ties may suggest homosexuality. Pipes and canes are taken as symbols of a striving for virility.

Lines and Shadings. The rhythm,

pressure, and angularity of lines are frequently used in interpretation. Firm, heavy lines may show drive and ambition; fluctuating pressures may be indicative of unstable, impulsive or cyclothymic (mood-swing) tendencies. A preference for vertical strokes suggests determination and self-assertion, while a preference for the horizontal suggests weakness and lack of ambition. Shading indicates anxiety and is perhaps an unconscious attempt to hide a part of the body.

There are a number of variations on basic figure-drawing technique. Karen Machover (1951), a leader in the field, uses a procedure much like the one outlined above in her Draw-A-Person test (D-A-P), although she puts special emphasis on the body image, a reflection of the way the subject actually feels about himself or what he wishes he could be. She originally took the Goodenough Draw-A-Man test as her point of departure. In administering this test, which is designed for estimating the I.Q., she found that the child's spontaneous comments and associations were highly revealing. This suggested the use of figure drawing as a projective method.

As an optional technique, she found it helpful to ask the subject to create a story based on drawings, making believe the person depicted is a participant in a novel or play. Levy (1950) developed a similar approach, the Draw-and-Tell-a-Story technique, in which the subject draws two figures of his own sex and one of the opposite sex, and tells a story about them. This triangle situation often touches on Oedipal and sibling rivalry reactions. In the Rosenberg Draw-a-Person technique, the subject draws a figure and then is asked what that person is like; after this, he is asked to redraw the figure and, if there are any changes, a further inquiry is made. The examiner then interprets the psychodynamics that

appear to lie behind the alteration. *See* DYSAUTONOMIA, BODY IMAGE.

FIGURE-GROUND   PERCEPTION. Perception of objects or events as standing out clearly from a background; for example, pictures on a wall, words on a page, or an airplane against the sky.

The separation of a figure from its background is considered a basic, primitive tendency. It occurs so quickly and spontaneously that it is often overlooked or taken for granted. Every time we shift our glance we automatically set up a new figure-ground relationship. This occurs not only in visual perception but in other sense modalities as well: train whistles and musical themes are heard as figures against a background of other sounds, and an intense smell or taste stands out from other flavor sensations when we eat a meal.

Artists have long used technical devices to make features of their work stand out, but it was not until 1915 that figure-ground relationships were systematically investigated. At that time the Danish psychologist Edgar Rubin noted that the figure appears to have a solid, substantial character, a definite contour and surface texture, and a specific location in the third dimension. The figure is also more impressive, better remembered and more apt to suggest meaning than the ground. On the other hand, the ground is experienced as loose and "filmy," and usually appears to lie farther back in space and to extend behind the figure.

The fact that figure-ground perception is a natural, primitive tendency is fairly well proved by observations of people who have been born blind but who have gained their sight as a result of surgery. When they see for the first time, they immediately perceive figures against a background, even though they cannot identify what they are at the outset. Brain-injured individuals, however, often have great difficulty distinguishing figure from ground, and figure-ground problems can be used in diagnosing this condition (*Fig. 19*).

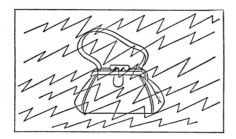

Fig. 19. A figure-ground problem used in distinguishing brain-injured from retarded children. The brain-injured usually cannot separate the figure from the background, due to defective perception.

Although the tendency to organize perception into figure and ground appears to be basic, the particular relationship is not always fixed and unalterable. If we look at a highly patterned wallpaper, we sometimes find that what was originally seen as figure becomes ground and vice versa. This has led psychologists to experiment with "reversible figures," such as those in Figures 20 and 21. You may not

Fig. 20. Stare at the center of this figure and see what happens. Note that as figure and ground reverse themselves, the figure stands out and the background recedes.

Fig. 21. An ambiguous figure. Do you see an old woman or a young one? Or does it shift from one to the other?

even realize at first that Figure 20 can be seen in two ways, since the way a figure looks the first time we perceive it has a tendency to persist. (*See also Fig. 26*, page 507: you will probably find that if you stare at the center of the figure it will reverse itself rhythmically and with increasing frequency.)

The drawing in Fig. 21 is also ambiguous. If certain parts are seen as the figure, it looks like a young woman; if other parts stand out, it appears to be an old hag. This picture has been used to illustrate the influence of "set" on perception. If you were to show a group of people a photograph of the young woman, and then show them the drawing, they would see the drawing as a young woman; and if you showed another group a photograph of the old hag, practically all of them would see the drawing in this way. This experiment, originally performed by Leeper in 1935, has been used to demonstrate the importance of prior experience and suggestion in propaganda and prejudice. It clearly indicates that most people tend to interpret ambiguous events in terms of their emotional and mental set. *See* GESTALT PSYCHOLOGY, SET.

FIXATION. The arrest of one or more phases of development at a childhood or adolescent level.

We normally develop progressively in all respects—intellectually, emotionally, socially, sexually. Even though this process is not always a smooth one, our personality grows as a whole, and we become increasingly capable of meeting different types of situations. In some cases, however, an individual fails to develop in one major respect; this feature of his personality remains "fixated" at an early stage. Usually the lag is in some phase of emotional or sexual growth, and it may be important enough to affect the individual's entire personality and adjustment to life.

Fixations may occur at any stage of child development. A small child may remain so emotionally dependent on his mother that he feels uncomfortable without her and cannot enter nursery school or kindergarten when the time comes. Persistent baby-talk, thumbsucking, and temper tantrums are further examples of early fixation. In older children, such character traits as indecisiveness, submissiveness, and a tendency to sulk or cry when faced with problems are common results of fixation. The development of conscience may also be arrested, and as a consequence the older child or adult may be inwardly trying to obey the behests of his parents instead of developing his own standards of behavior. Similarly, sexual development can be blocked, and the growing child may be so firmly fixed at the stage of masturbation that he cannot establish relationships with the opposite sex. Likewise the young man (or young woman) who engages in promiscuous behavior before marriage may be unable to give it up afterward. *See* SCHOOL PHOBIA, DYSLALIA, THUMBSUCKING, TEMPER TANTRUM, MASTURBATION, PROMISCUITY.

In the Freudian approach, the term fixation is reserved for an arrest at an early stage of "psychosexual development." The theory holds that the growth of the entire personality is governed by various expressions of basic sexual energy, the libido. The individual ordinarily goes through an infantile oral stage in which mouth satisfactions predominate; then follow the anal, latency, and homosexual stages until he finally reaches adult heterosexuality. Failure to work through one or more of the stages results in the development of special character traits and faulty behavior patterns. For example, the child who refuses to "let go" of his feces at the anal stage may later become a stingy person who cannot let go of his money; a person who failed to obtain the full satisfactions of the oral stage may later develop a drive to overeat. *See* ANAL CHARACTER, ORAL CHARACTER, PSYCHOSEXUAL DEVELOPMENT, OBESITY.

Why do fixations occur? There are undoubtedly many possible causes, and several may be operative at once. Some parents consciously or unconsciously encourage their children to remain at an immature stage of development because it is "cute" or because they do not want to feel the children—or themselves—are growing older. Such parents usually keep their children dependent on themselves and give them too little practice in independent thinking and action. It has also been found that children who are overcriticized or overprotected frequently feel too insecure to venture into more mature behavior. Others fail to develop in one or more respects because they meet failure or defeat at play or in school. Parents may also instill active fear, disgust, or guilt feelings which inhibit development in the sexual sphere.

Fixations produce immature, defective character traits and special vulnerability in the areas where the individual has failed to develop. Such a person is not fully equipped to meet the normal stresses of life and is quite likely to develop maladjustive behavior patterns.

FLIGHT INTO REALITY. The tendency to become overinvolved in activity as a defense mechanism.

To avoid threatening or unpleasant situations, or to escape from painful feelings and thoughts, some people become extremely busy and preoccupied with overt activities. The term flight *into* reality, is often used for this reaction, in contrast to flight *from* reality, in which there is a retreat into inactivity, detachment or fantasy. Both mechanisms, however, serve similar defense and escape functions.

As a defense mechanism, flight into reality operates on a basically unconscious level. The individual does not realize that his overactivity is a protection against anxiety. Frequently the nature of the activity itself gives this fact away. It is likely to be trivial in character, but may be inflated to great importance as a means of unconsciously denying that it is a defensive measure. Its purpose is to avoid stress, not conquer it.

On the other hand, "keeping busy" may be a completely conscious and deliberately chosen course of action. It is often recommended by personal counselors as a means of taking one's mind off grief or other misfortunes. They generally suggest, however, that the sufferer avoid involving himself in mere "busywork," and look instead for constructive activities which contribute to a sense of personal worth and usefulness. *See* DEFENSE MECHANISM.

FLIGHT OF IDEAS. A disturbance of thinking characterized by a rapid succession of disconnected, fragmentary ideas.

The flow of thought is a constant series of digressions which have no common theme and lead to no conclusion. The only thread that can be found consists of superficial associations arising from the sounds of words, their initial letters, or some passing event that happens to attract attention. There is therefore no genuine continuity of thought whatever.

Flight of ideas is observed in manic states in which the patient is responding to an inner "pressure of activity" accompanied by an inability to sustain attention and direct the flow of thought toward a single goal. It is also found in some cases of schizophrenia. In distinguishing these forms of "topical flight," as he calls it, Cameron (1947) states: "The manic makes rapid shifts from topic to topic, but the alert, attentive listener can keep up with the changes because they do not differ fundamentally from the changes in subject a normal elated person might make. The shifts in schizophrenic talk . . . are confused by the indiscriminate overinclusion of material belonging to both shared social and private fantasy contexts." Instead of keeping to "social trails," the schizophrenic "makes his own trail as he goes."

The following excerpt (sic) from a fifty-page autobiography written by a hypomanic patient illustrates many of the typical features of flight of ideas. Note especially the headlong pace, the abrupt shifts of attention, the garrulous good humor, the clang (sound) associations, and the pun on the word "issues." *See* CLANG ASSOCIATIONS, MANIC-DEPRESSIVE REACTION (MANIC PHASE).

Illustrative case: FLIGHT OF IDEAS.
The Life and "Pedigree" of George Fox

Published by	Edited by
So Long & Co.	the "Big Chief"
N. Y. City—N.Y.	(himself)
	GEORGE FOX

Well on a Balmy and Clear Day in the month of December, to be Exact, Dec. 10, 1894, I selected for my dear old Mother, Mrs. Barbara Fox, whose maiden name was

"Wilson" (that's all) a wee bit of Scotish methinks in her parents, probably born in Old Scotland, England,—perhaps thats where I Inherit my so styled "Pins" or "Buns"—some original—mostly "Antiques" but Dressed in Kilties or a new "Calico Wrapper" they sound new to some—it's strange how "Illiterate" many of us are!

My father, not having an authenticated Data of my ancestry, I'll just say from memory, was born in the state of Virginia, where our Revered First in War, First in Peace, and First in the Hearts of His Countrymen and (the "First," but not *"Least"*) President of these Wealthy if not the Wealthiest (in *"Natural* Resources") at least "Nation" on the "Face of the Globe" or in other words—The World—named "The United States of America"—America Right," "America Wrong"—"America Forever" or as said in the "Star Spangled Banner" May her Flag *Ever Wave* for the *Brave* and the *Free,* or United we *"Stand"* but Divided we "Fall" and as Rome "Fell" we trust God will Keep us by his "Almighty Help" from Ever Falling either by His Hands, "Earthquakes" "Floods," "Whirl Winds" "World Wars" or other *"Calamaties"* or *"Catastrophies"* Since we are not writing the "End of the World" or The History of the United States, we might wisely return to our subject, the life of the writer George Fox.

Well, I was born, as I said, one of the most unpleasant things imaginable, especially for the mother of 1894, before the "Twilight Series" and other ISSUES were published (et cetera, et cetera, et cetera). (Pronko, 1963).

FOLIE À DEUX. A functional psychotic reaction in which two persons who have long been intimately associated come to share the same delusions.

The first hospital case was reported in 1860, and the name was suggested by Ernest Charles Lasègue and Jean Pierre Falret in 1877. The dominant member of the pair develops paranoid delusions, usually of a persecutory nature, and talks so much and so persuasively about his false ideas that they come to be accepted by the more dependent, submissive, and suggestible member. The transfer of delusions from one to the other is due largely to the fact that they are both poorly adjusted individuals who live together in comparative seclusion, have a narrow range of interests, and face the same stresses. In some cases there is evidence that the closeness of relationship stems not only from a similarity in pre-psychotic personality but also from an unconscious homosexual bond.

One study of over a hundred cases revealed the following combinations: two sisters, 40; husband and wife, 26; mother and child, 24; two brothers, 11; brother and sister, 6; father and child, 2. The investigator, Gralnick (1942), attributed the greater incidence among women to the fact that in our society they are more frequently required to play a passive role and have a narrower range of interests and activities than men. The fact that such a large proportion of patients were husband and wife would seem to rule out hereditary or constitutional factors. If the two individuals are separated and independently treated, the more dependent member of the pair tends to abandon his delusions sooner than the more dominant one who provoked them.

Illustrative Case: FOLIE À DEUX

The daughter was twenty-eight years old and the mother sixty-five at the time of their admission to a mental hospital from the women's jail of a large city in Canada. Both they and the girl's father had been born abroad and had come to Canada when the daughter was a child. They were quite poor and neither the mother nor daughter had much education. Six months before their admission to the hospital, the father was admitted to an old people's home. Even before this, the mother and daughter had worked, eaten, and slept together for many years.

On arrival at the hospital, the daughter stated that six years previously she had developed a nasal obstruction and a plastic surgeon in the United States had performed an operation on her nose. Soon after, she was involved in an automobile accident on her way to the doctor's office and was thrown against the windshield of the car. She complained that ever since she suffered from excruciating pains in her nose, face, and neck. She had attempted to sue the doctor for half a million dollars but no lawyer would take the case. Subsequently, she and her mother entered the doctor's house and refused to leave until he paid. They were arrested, jailed and deported to Canada. On five occasions after this the two entered the United States and attempted to sue the doctor. Finally, the United States immigration officer in Canada refused to issue visas to them. They decided that the doctor was paying the immigration officer to keep them out of the United States and therefore tried to collect the half million dollars from the immigration officer. For several weeks they waited in his office every day until they were arrested and taken to jail from which they were transferred to the hospital.

In addition to her primary delusions, the daughter reported that she and her mother had a great deal of trouble in rooming houses during the preceding months because other people were after their money. The mother told exactly the same story as the daughter and felt that all of the daughter's claims were well founded. She was very anxious for the daughter to marry and looked forward to living with her and the hypothetical son-in-law, but she believed that it would be impossible for the girl to find a husband unless her nose was healed. Both wished to be released as soon as possible in order to return to the United States and collect their money from the doctor.

Shortly after admission, they were separated from each other for three months while the daughter underwent an intensive program of ECT and insulin coma treatment. Initially, her delusional system changed and she began to believe that the doctor wished to pay her the half million dollars but was being prevented from doing so by her relatives. Soon, however, she reverted to her former beliefs and thereafter these remained unshakable. During the period of separation, the mother first became severely depressed and then, as often happens with separation in folie à deux, lost her faith in the daughter's delusional system. Nevertheless, she could not accept the fact that her daughter was ill and remained anxious for the two of them to leave the hospital. When treatment of the daughter was terminated as useless, she was reunited with her mother and they remained inseparable companions in a chronic ward of the hospital. (Rosen and Gregory, 1965)

FORCED CHOICE. A testing technique that requires the subject to make a choice between two or more favorable or unfavorable alternatives.

This technique was developed as a means of eliciting fuller information from a subject about his likes, dislikes, attitudes, interests or personality traits. He is required to give a definite answer instead of checking noncommittal responses such as "I" for indifferent, "DK" for don't know, or "NP" no preference. The test itself has to be carefully constructed to offer equally plausible alternatives, otherwise it would not give a true indication of the individual's preferences or attitudes. A forced choice test would therefore avoid offering a choice between attending a dance and doing homework, since for most people these alternatives would be weighted in favor of attending the dance. A choice between attending a dance and visiting an art museum would be far more revealing.

The Edwards Personal Preference Schedule and the Kuder interest test are representative examples of this technique. It is also used in rating scales for employment or college entrance. One form of the test offers four favorable alternatives from which *two* are to be selected—for example, a rating scale might include this set: "is well informed in the field," "can apply his knowledge to practical situations," "creates confidence in others," "explains the reasons for his suggestions." In another form, two favorable and two unfavorable items are given and the rater must choose the one that is most applicable and the one that is least applicable to the individual. In both cases, some statements are closer than others to the attributes required for the particular job or educational institution. The method therefore helps to pinpoint the ratings. It also helps to make the rating scale more objective. However, as Freeman (1962) has pointed out, it has its disadvantages. Some raters find it too restrictive since none of the statements within certain sets may really apply to the person being rated. They also contend that the usual graphic, numerical and percentage ratings give them greater independence in making their own judgments. *See* PERSONALITY INVENTORIES, INTEREST TESTS.

The forced choice method is also used in certain experimental investigations. In the standard studies of absolute threshold—that is the minimal detectable level of stimulation—the subject is presented with a stimulus and asked to say whether he detected it or not. In the forced choice method he is told that a faint sound, for example, will be presented during one of four time intervals, and he is required to indicate or guess the period in which it occurs. This technique has resulted in lower threshold levels than the classical method. In other words, many of the so-called "guesses" are correct even when the sounds are below the accepted minimum intensity. This indicates that human beings are more sensitive than psychologists had previously realized—or, put in another way, we encode more information than we can usually express verbally. There is an interesting application of this idea in taking multiple choice examinations: our first choice is often the correct one, though we may later change it. Apparently we remember more than we realize, and our "antenna" captures this knowledge before we start to dissect and analyze the alternatives. *See* DETECTION THEORY, ABSOLUTE THRESHOLD.

FORGETTING. Forgetting is sometimes defined as failure to *recall* and sometimes as failure to *retain* previously learned material. The two definitions are probably meant to refer to the same process. It is worth noting, however, that some of the material that we cannot now recall or recollect may still be stored, or retained, in some way, since we may be able to recall it at some other time or by using special techniques.

The time course of forgetting was first documented by Hermann Ebbinghaus in 1885. He showed that forgetting of nonsense syllables is most rapid immediately after the initial learning, and then declines at a more gradual rate until it ceases entirely. He found that about 47 per cent of the learned material was lost after only twenty minutes, and only 79 per cent after thirty-one days. Similar results were later obtained with other types of rote material. The curve for meaningful material is quite similar, although the general level of retention is much greater throughout. *See* EBBINGHAUS.

The rate of forgetting depends not only on the type of material but on the amount of "overlearning"—that is, studying or repeating the material beyond the point where it can be accurately reproduced once or twice. The greater the overlearning, the slower the forgetting. This means that since we forget most rapidly right after the original learning process, it is best to start reviewing the material immediately instead of putting it off until later. The value of overlearning is clearly illustrated in motor learning. One reason we remember how to ride a bicycle, roller skate or play jacks long after we forget the poems we learned at school is that we have practiced—that is, overlearned—these skills far more thoroughly.

There are at least four major explanations of forgetting. Some psychologists claim that learning produces a physiological change in the nervous system, a so-called "memory trace" which can later be revived or reactivated. The first theory holds that this trace fades or decays through disuse just as a muscle atrophies when it is not exercised. As time goes on, the trace disintegrates until it completely disappears, and the curve of forgetting is believed to mirror this process. There is no direct physical evidence to support this theory, and a number of facts tend to contradict it. Childhood memories supposedly lost forever are often revived in old age, and delirious patients sometimes speak a language they have not used for fifty years. The recovery of forgotten or repressed material in psychoanalysis and hypnosis also argues against the theory of decay. Finally, the neurologist, Wilder Penfield (1959), has proved the same point through direct stimulation of the brain. *See* HYPERMNESIA, REMEMBERING.

A second theory holds that the memory trace does not decay but becomes distorted through the normal metabolic processes of the brain. These changes are believed to explain why we cannot accurately reproduce either verbal information or visual forms even after a short period of time. Years ago Wulf (1922) showed that we have a tendency to alter visual figures (line drawings) in three ways when reproducing them from memory: we make them more regular and symmetrical by leaving out details ("leveling"); we accentuate impressive features ("sharpening"), and we make them resemble real objects ("assimilating") (*Fig. 22*).

The distortion theory is also illustrated by experiments employing the method of "chain reproduction," which is similar to the popular game of Gossip (Bartlett, 1932). One subject looked at a line drawing that vaguely represented either an owl or a cat, then drew it on a sheet of paper. After this he showed his reproduction to another person, who made his own drawing and showed it to the next, and so on. The end product in one group was an almost perfect owl, and in another group a nearly perfect cat (*Fig. 23*). In other words, the process of remembering and forgetting is influenced by individual interpretation: what we *think* we see or hear shapes the way we reproduce it.

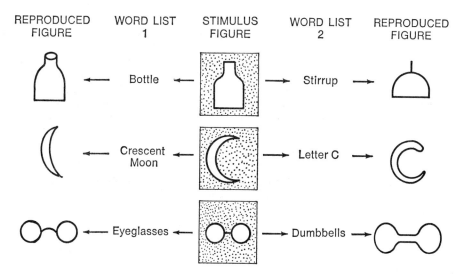

| REPRODUCED FIGURE | WORD LIST 1 | STIMULUS FIGURE | WORD LIST 2 | REPRODUCED FIGURE |

Bottle ← → Stirrup

Crescent Moon ← → Letter C

Eyeglasses ← → Dumbbells

Fig. 22. Memory plays tricks: The stimulus figures in the center were presented along with the words in either list 1 or list 2, and the figures were later reproduced accordingly.

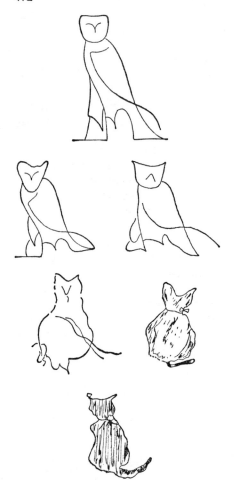

Fig. 23. Distortion breeds distortion. A "chain reproduction" experiment, in which each person sees only the drawing of the person preceding him. Some chains ended with a cat instead of an owl. Similar distortions occur in memory and rumor.

A similar process occurs in passing stories from person to person. *See* RUMOR.

The question is, are these distortions and differences in interpretation due primarily to metabolic processes in the brain or to some other factor? Many experiments have indicated that the basic distortion takes place when the material is *first* seen—that is, we perceive it with a specific frame of reference, just as a prejudiced person hears what he is inclined to hear. This interpretation argues against the idea that the distortion is based on changes in the memory trace. It suggests that forgetting is determined by perception and motivation—and this leads to the third theory.

This theory holds that motivation is the key to forgetting—or, more simply, we forget because we want to forget. This process usually operates on an unconscious level. Many studies have shown that we tend to forget unpleasant experiences, as well as facts or ideas that contradict our basic beliefs. We also have trouble remembering distasteful tasks or the names of people we dislike. Forgetting of this kind is an example of what Freud called "the psychopathology of everyday life."

Of far greater psychological significance is our tendency to "repress" highly disturbing, traumatic events, and early memories associated with feelings of guilt or anxiety. An extreme form of motivated forgetting occurs in cases of amnesia, in which the individual unconsciously attempts to escape from emotional conflict by forgetting his own identity. There are, then, many compelling illustrations of this theory, although very few psychologists believe that *all* forgetting is motivated. *See* REPRESSION, AMNESIA, SCREEN MEMORY.

The fourth theory attributes forgetting to interference of two kinds: "retroactive inhibition," in which new material interferes with previously learned material, and "proactive inhibition," in which prior learning interferes with new learning. There is extensive evidence for both types. In testing for retroactive inhibition, an experimental group learns one task, then a second task, and is later retested on the first. This retest is compared with a retest of a control group which did not engage in the second task. Proactive inhibition is tested by having subjects learn two tasks, one after the other, and then having them try to recall the *second* task. Results are compared with a control group that does not learn the first task. In one test, a subject who had been memorizing many lists of nonsense syllables was able to recall only 25 per cent of a new list after an interval of twenty-four hours, while a fresh subject recalled 74 per cent.

Tests of this kind have uncovered a number of significant facts about forgetting. First, the greater similarity between the two tasks, the greater the amount of interference; second, the quicker the succession the greater the interference; third, meaningful material is less affected than purely factual or nonsense material; fourth, overlearning reduces the inhibitory effect; fifth, retention is greater when learning is followed by sleep than when it is followed by everyday activities, provided we are alert and wide awake during the learning process. These findings have practical implications. To avoid both proactive and retroactive inhibition, two similar subjects, such as Latin and French, should not be studied in succession. When important material has to be learned, it should, if possible, be followed by an entirely different activity or by a rest period. Close attention should be paid to the meaning of any material we study, and even verbatim material such as series of facts or terms should be related wherever possible to previously acquired knowledge. And finally, it is best to review the material periodically because of the value of overlearning. *See* MEMORY IMPROVEMENT, LEARNING TECHNIQUES.

What is the status of these four theories? At the moment all we can say is that each of them appears to account for some important feature of forgetting, but none is adequate to explain the entire process by itself. We simply do not have the tools as yet to decide between them or to combine them into a single theory. Above all, we need to know more about what takes place in the nervous system when we learn; and we must find ways of relating that knowledge to the psychological processes we now call repression, interference and distortion. It is quite possible that this information will give rise to a new explanation that will supersede the four which have so far been advanced.

FORMICATION (From the Latin word for ant). A sensation of ants or other insects crawling on the skin.

In psychiatry, formication is a tactile or "haptic" hallucination which occurs most frequently in delirium. The sensation is acutely distressing to the patient, often producing intense fear and anxiety. The delirium may be the result of infection of the central nervous system, as in meningitis or encephalitis; or it may be caused by systemic infections such as rheumatic fever, scarlet fever, diphtheria and influenza. The formication symptom is particularly common in acute alcoholic hallucinosis, narcotic addiction, and cocaine habituation, where it is often called "the cocaine bug."

FRANZ, SHEPHERD IVORY (1874–1933). Chiefly noted for his studies of brain functions, Franz did his undergraduate and graduate work at Columbia University, except for a year of study with Wilhelm Wundt in Leipzig. He received his Ph.D. under Cattell in 1899, assisting him in the development of the psychological laboratory. He then spent two years as assistant in physiology, after which he taught that subject at the Dartmouth Medical College (1901–1904) and at George Washington University (1906–1924). From 1907 on he was also scientific director and later laboratory research director of the government hospital now known as St. Elizabeth's. From 1924 until his death he served as professor of psychology at the University of California and head of the psychological and educational clinic of the Children's Hospital in Hollywood.

Franz' most lasting contributions were made in the study of brain functions. The background against which he worked is highly important. During the nineteenth century most investigators, under the influence of faculty psychology and the doctrine of phrenology, sought to discover specific brain centers for specific intellectual, emotional and motor functions. The chief opponent of this point of view was Pierre Flourens, a French anatomist who removed different parts of a pigeon's brain and showed that although certain functions were lost, they could also be reacquired. He therefore concluded that the nervous system characteristically acts as a unit ("action commune"), and that intact tissue might come into play as a means of regaining lost functions.

Other investigators, however, turned the tide against these views. In 1861 Paul Broca performed an autopsy on a man who had not been able to talk, but who did not appear to be paralyzed or retarded in any other way. When he found a lesion in the frontal lobe of the left hemisphere, he concluded that the speech center was located in that area. In addition, two German surgeons, G. Fritsch and E. Hitzig, studied the reactions of soldiers who suffered head wounds during the Franco-Prussian War, and also applied weak electric currents to various parts of the motor cortex of animals. Their studies showed that stimulation of different areas produced different bodily reactions; and when they published their results in 1870, the race to find specific centers was on.

When Franz entered upon the study of brain functions, he focused his attention on an area that had been largely neglected, the frontal lobes. Some investigators had termed them "silent areas" since they did not seem to have a function. Others suggested that they mediated associations, simply because this function was the only one not assigned a locus in the brain. However,

the famous case of Phineas Gage who had a crowbar driven through his left frontal lobe by an explosion, suggested that damage to this area interfered with complex mental activities but not with simple functions. Franz attacked this problem and showed that (1) lobotomy of both lobes of monkeys and cats did not cause a loss of old habits, such as eating or scratching, but interfered with more recent ones, since these animals forgot how to escape from a problem box; (2) lost habits could be relearned without tissue restoration; (3) destruction of only one lobe did not eliminate habits but only reduced efficiency of performance. These findings were first recorded in a paper published in 1902.

Franz found further evidence against a strict localization theory in performing autopsies, discovering that when cerebral atrophy had occurred, neither the location nor severity of the tissue loss could be closely related to the specific symptomatology. He also mapped the motor areas of the monkey brain, showing that stimulation at the same point in the cortex produced different effects in different animals. These and other findings led him to the conclusion "that the paths of reactions are not simple anatomical unities which have commonly been believed in but that these paths are diffuse and that anatomically as well as physiologically they are complex."

In his later work, Franz continued to oppose "the new phrenology" as he called it. One of his major contributions was the development of re-educational programs for persons with brain lesions, based on his discovery that lower animals were able to relearn activities which had been lost after brain extirpation. He combined a psychological with a physiological approach by including games as incentives, by introducing friendly competition, and by devising apparatus that permitted the patient to see how much he was improving. When he found large individual differences in the rate of improvement for different patients, he called for individualized rehabilitation programs, a point that is stressed today. As a result of his efforts, a large number of paralyzed and crippled patients recovered a surprising amount of mobility, and many aphasic patients whose condition was caused by brain injury were greatly helped.

Franz was elected president of the American Psychological Association in 1920, and served as editor of the *Psychological Bulletin* from 1912 to 1924, and of Psychological Monographs from 1924 to 1927. In addition to numerous journal articles, he published the *Handbook of Mental Examination Methods* (1912), *Nervous and Mental Re-education* (1923), and *Persons One and Three* (1933). His work in the field of brain functions was carried on and expanded by his colleague, Karl S. Lashley. *See* LASHLEY.

FREE-FLOATING ANXIETY. A diffuse, chronic sense of uneasiness and apprehension that is not attached to any specific situation or cause.

The individual suffers from generalized anxiety, but does not recognize its source because it arises from repressed impulses and unconscious conflicts. He is haunted by the feeling that something disagreeable or catastrophic is going to happen, and attaches this dread to almost anything he does or any situation he encounters, whether it is actually threatening or not. According to Freud (1924–25) free-floating anxiety is the outstanding mark of anxiety-neurosis: "Anxious expectation is the nuclear symptom of this neurosis; it clearly reveals, too, something of the theory of it. We may perhaps say there is a *quantum of anxiety in a free-floating condition,* which in any state of expectation controls the selection of ideas, and is ever ready to attach itself to any suitable ideational content."

Though particularly prominent in anxiety-neurosis, some degree of free-floating anxiety is found in all types of psychoneurosis and may be converted into bodily symptoms, obsessive thoughts, compulsive acts, or specific phobias. *See* ANXIETY, ANXIETY REACTION.

FREUD, SIGMUND (1856–1939). Freud was born in Freiburg but lived in Vienna from age four to the last year of his life, when he went to London to escape the Nazi terror. After receiving his medical degree at the University of Vienna in 1881, he became resident physician at the Vienna General Hospital, where he studied with the physiologist Ernst Brücke and the brain anatomist Theodore Meynert. In 1886 he went into practice as a neurologist, marrying Martha Bernays the same year. The youngest of their six children, Anna, became an outstanding analyst.

Freud made a number of noteworthy contributions to neurology during the years when his interest in that field was at its height. He discovered the analgesic properties of cocaine, showed that the spinal ganglia cells are identical in lower and higher animals, differentiated various tracts of the nervous system, found that the sensory nuclei of the spinal cord and cranial nerves were homologous, and investigated the roots of the acoustic nerve. For a few years he was associated with a children's clinic, and on the basis of his observations published a major volume on cerebral paralysis and another on aphasia in children. In 1902 he was appointed professor of neuropathology at the University of Vienna, a nonteaching position that he held until 1938.

During the years at the Vienna General Hospital, in 1885–86, Freud spent four months in Paris, where he attended Charcot's demonstrations of hypnosis and studied various aspects of hysteria. His biographer, Ernest Jones, regards this period as a turning point in his life, since it aroused his interest in studying mental illness from a psychological rather than a physiological standpoint. He also carried away Charcot's rather offhand suggestion that sexual factors were always involved in hysteria.

Even before his visit to Paris, Freud had been using hypnosis (as well as massage, baths, rest and electrical stimulation) with hysterical patients, and he continued to apply hypnosis on his return. However, he became dissatisfied with this technique, since many patients could not be easily hypnotized; and even when symptoms were successfully removed they were often replaced by others. Moreover, he found that many patients became dependent on posthypnotic suggestion and could only function under this influence. A visit with Bernheim during which both specialists failed to bring about a deep somnambulistic state in one of Freud's patients further convinced him of the shortcomings of hypnosis.

Freud continued to use this method for a time, but gradually turned it in new directions. He was particularly impressed by the case of "Anna O.," brought to his attention by Josef Breuer, in which a young woman experienced a catharsis while reliving painful experiences under hypnosis. As a result of this case and his own observations, he began to use this technique for two basic purposes: first, to trace the history of the patient to a traumatic event which was presumed to have caused the illness, and second, to induce him to re-experience this event in order to dissipate the energy that was producing the symptoms.

In applying hypnosis, Freud became aware that the most important aspect of the treatment situation was the relationship between analyst and patient. This realization, plus his dissatisfaction with the technique, gradually led him to develop the method of free associa-

tion between 1892 and 1895. Through this procedure he not only successfully helped the patient to resurrect forgotten material, but discovered that at the core of this material were unacceptable wishes—an insight that led him to the concept of repression and later to the theory of defense mechanisms. In 1895 Freud, in collaboration with Breuer, published the epoch-making *Studies in Hysteria,* in which these findings were presented. From that time on, the concepts of the unconscious and repression, and the method of free association, became the cornerstones of a new discipline which he called psychoanalysis.

The new approach contained one more crucial element: Freud had become convinced that the unconscious conflicts which produced psychoneurosis were always of a sexual nature. This view alienated not only Breuer but most of the scientific community. As a result, his theories were poorly received and he was labeled a crank and a pervert.

Freud continued his work, and in 1900 published *The Interpretation of Dreams,* which showed that dreams are not random events but disguised expressions of wishes emanating from unconscious sources. This work, usually considered his greatest, contains many of his other contributions as well, including the concept of psychic determinism, the distinction between the primary and secondary systems of the mind, and the description of unconscious content in terms of infantile hostile and sexual feelings directed toward the parents. Students of Freud's life have pointed out that he was motivated to undertake an investigation of dreams by the realization that his own dreams indicated that a part of his psyche was "happy" over the death of his father. Through the study of these personal dreams he performed the outstanding feat of conducting his own self-analysis, while at the same time developing principles and procedures which he applied to his patients.

The Interpretation of Dreams received scant attention. For several years afterwards Freud wrote little but devoted himself to the development of his psychoanalytic discipline. In 1902 he invited several pupils and colleagues, including Wilhelm Stekel and Alfred Adler, to discuss his new theories. Together they formed the "Wednesday Psychological Group," which later evolved into the Vienna Psycho-Analytical Society. In 1904 he published *The Psychopathology of Everyday Life,* which documents the concept of psychic determinism by showing that accidents, slips of the pen and tongue, forgetting, and losing things are all brought about by unconscious factors. This book was probably the most widely accepted of all his works. It was followed, however, by another work, *Three Essays on the Theory of Sexuality* (1905) that aroused a storm of protest. In it he developed his theory of infantile sexuality, and argued that adult perversions are distortions of infantile sexual expressions. As Ernest Jones points out, these views made Freud the most unpopular member of the scientific community in Germany and aroused criticism of the most abusive kind.

Two other books also appeared in 1905: *Wit and Its Relation to the Unconscious,* showing how jokes can be used to express unconscious sexual and aggressive impulses; and *The Dora Analysis,* which illustrated the use of dream interpretation in psychoanalytic treatment. At about the same time a small group of disciples began forming around Freud, including not only Viennese psychiatrists but Ernest Jones of England, and Carl Jung and Eugene Bleuler of Switzerland. By 1908 Freud's following had grown to a point where 42 men were attracted to the First International Psycho-Analytic Congress, held in Salzburg; and in 1910 the first Psycho-Analytic Association was established.

Between these two events, Freud accepted an invitation from G. Stanley Hall to visit Clark University. This was the first official recognition of the psychoanalytic movement.

Between 1911 and 1914, three important colleagues, Adler, Stekel, and Jung, left the Freudian camp over personal and theoretical differences. Jones, however, remained loyal and formed a small group called the "Committee" which helped Freud with the practical problems of publishing journals and training disciples.

Motivated by the defections of many of his disciples, Freud published *The History of the Psychoanalytic Movement* (1914), in defense of his doctrines. To disseminate his views more widely, he founded an international firm which between 1919 and 1938 published a total of 150 books and five journals on the subject of psychoanalysis. Instead of limiting the theory to psychiatric problems, these publications widened its scope by applying it to analysis of the creative process in works on Leonardo da Vinci and Wilhelm Jensen, and to cultural anthropology in *Totem and Taboo* (1913). In the latter work Freud attempted to show that the same psychosexual concepts can be applied to the childhood of the race as to the childhood of the individual—concepts of ambivalence, Oedipus complex, incestuous wishes, for example. But he went even further by tracing morality, religion, and culture to the act of parricide and reactions to it in primitive man. Though many scientists and laymen were intrigued with his interpretations of the symbols of primitive cultures, his general approach met with disfavor outside the analytic school.

Freud's only book on current problems, *Thoughts for the Times on War and Death* (1915) was a commentary on World War I. In it he suggested that the war was a reflection of the level which man had reached in his effort to live peacefully with his fellows.

He also claimed that we feel discouraged only because we have an illusion that we have progressed farther than we have in actuality. In his correspondence with Albert Einstein, which began in 1933 at the suggestion of the League of Nations, he emphasized the obstacles involved in attempting to abolish war.

During the war period, Freud began to reformulate his position. Partly as a result of world events, he introduced the concept of the death instinct in his *Beyond the Pleasure Principle* (1920). Up to this time he had maintained that man is governed by the pleasure principle primarily, but in this work he put forth the notion of the repetition-compulsion, the tendency to repeat instinctual gratifications and therefore to restore a *previous* state of affairs. This view was carried to the extreme in his contention that the ultimate objective of existence is to reduce the living to the pre-vital, inorganic, tensionless state of nature. In this view, he apparently accepted Schopenhauer's statement that "death is the goal of life." Human existence was now interpreted as a battlefield on which two opposing forces, Eros, the life instinct, and Thanatos, the death instinct, engage in mortal combat. He also attributed man's inhumanity to man to the expression of the instinct for hostility and aggression which he viewed as an integral part of the death instinct.

This new philosophic formulation was rejected by most of Freud's disciples. It was followed by other revisions of his original thought. In *Group Psychology and The Analysis of the Ego* (1920), and *The Ego and the Id* (1923), he presented the foundations for ego psychology and also changed the structural picture of the mind from his earlier division into unconscious, pre-conscious and conscious to the id, ego, and superego. One reason for the change was his realization that some ego processes, especially those surrounding the "ego ideal," were themselves unconscious. As a result, he expanded the ego ideal into an agency, the superego, representing the demands of the parents which the individual unconsciously accepts (or "introjects") and out of which he creates his conscience.

Other later works of Freud include: *Inhibitions, Symptoms and Anxiety*, (1923), dealing with the origins of fear and anxiety; his *Autobiography* (1926), in which he strongly defended lay analysis in the hope that psychoanalysis would not remain an adjunct of medicine; and *The Future of an Illusion* (1927), in which he attributed religious beliefs such as immortality and God to such psychological forces as fears and wishes. The work was highly unpopular because it denied the actual existence of God. Equally unpopular was *Civilization and Its Discontents* (1929), which dealt with the basic weaknesses of society and the nature of the bonds which drive men together. His last book, *Moses and Monotheism* (1938), written during the Nazi persecution, brought him disfavor in Jewish circles since it revived the legend that Moses was an Egyptian who borrowed the idea of monotheism from the Pharaoh Ikhnaton. He held that the Jews resisted this doctrine, and that Moses was killed in an uprising. Reverting to his earlier anthropological views, Freud explained this uprising on the basis of inborn parricidal wishes which he believed to constitute a part of man's inheritance.

Freud was stricken with cancer of the jaw in 1923 and suffered through thirty-three operations. In 1938 he fled to London to escape the Nazis, and died there the following year. Despite sixteen years of agonizing pain he worked until one month before his death.

FRIGIDITY. A female sexual disorder consisting of impairment of desire or inability to achieve full gratification; usually classified as a psychophysiologic disorder of the genitourinary system.

There are many forms, degrees, and causes of frigidity, or sexual anesthesia, as it is also termed. It is far more common than impotence in the male; an estimated one-third of all women rarely or never experience orgasm. The condition has a wide range, including mild disinterest in sexual relations, sexual interest without orgasm, and active aversion. Some women who accept a passive role or a reduced level of gratification attain considerable satisfaction without being fully aroused. On the other hand, aversion can be so intense that sexual relations are actually painful (dyspareunia) or spasms of the vaginal tract (vaginismus) may occur. In rare instances the vagina contracts so powerfully during intercourse that relaxant drugs or anesthesia have to be used to free the male organ. This condition is known as penis captiva.

Although it is recognized that some women have a weaker sex drive than others for constitutional reasons, the great majority of cases of persistent frigidity are believed to be due to psychological factors. In these women sexual desire is blocked or inhibited, not merely low or lacking. Probably the single most prevalent factor in such cases is faulty attitudes acquired early in life. In some instances these women were taught actively or by innuendo that sex is ugly, disgusting, or sinful; in others, they were negatively conditioned to marriage as a whole by observing constant scenes of bickering or abuse between their parents. A background of this kind frequently prepares the way for frigidity.

Several other factors are known to contribute to the disorder. First, many women find it difficult or impossible to overcome the effects of early sex experiences which have been painful, disappointing, or accompanied by a fear of pregnancy or a sense of guilt. Sometimes these experiences instill such a lasting sense of inadequacy or such strong feelings of hostility toward men in general that they interfere with sexual response later on. Second, some husbands are clumsy, hasty, or self-centered in their approach to the sex act, and the entire relationship becomes so unpleasant and disappointing for the woman that frigidity develops. Third, the husband may be afflicted with premature ejaculation; it has been found that in these cases the wife may in time suppress her own response because her desires only lead to frustration. Fourth, occasionally women suppress their response because they are startled by their own unexpectedly intense reactions. This is most likely to occur when early training has made them feel guilty about "letting themselves go" and having such "unladylike" feelings.

Some psychoanalysts ascribe frigidity to unconscious hostility toward the male sex. Such hostility is believed to stem either from penis envy during childhood or from anger and fear toward an overbearing, punitive father. Other therapists attribute the disorder to strained relations between husband and wife, arising out of such situations as the husband's interest in other women, his preoccupation with work, or his inability to provide for the family. It is a well-recognized fact that tension is the enemy of sexual response, particularly for women.

Although psychoanalytic treatment has been used with success in cases of frigidity, "deep therapy" is often unnecessary. Briefer psychotherapy is usually sufficient to help a woman overcome the effects of early training and experiences. Discussions with the husband are frequently useful, particularly when they help him understand his wife's reactions, the differences between male and female response, and the importance of schooling himself so that he can arouse his wife at her own pace. But none of these approaches will be fully effective unless the couple establishes a warm and loving relationship in which each partner understands and respects the other.

In some cases anxiety and guilt are so deeply ingrained, or feelings of hostility are so strong, that the pattern of frigidity cannot be changed. In many instances, too, a woman may be unalterably frigid with one man but not with another.

Illustrative Case: FRIGIDITY

A twenty-seven-year-old woman came for treatment because of "fear spells," depression of spirits, irritability, and headaches. She had been married three years and was childless. Her symptoms had become troublesome one and one-half years after marriage. She had been a lonely girl during her teens and had never become very popular socially. She had looked for the sexual relation in marriage to bring more pleasure and to have more meaning than proved to be the case. Her husband was potent and while she enjoyed intercourse during the first year in the sense that she liked being close to her husband and to feel that he wanted her, the vaginal pleasure was minimal and intercourse often left her restless and sleepless. After her symptoms began she tried to avoid coitus; she did not "want to be bothered with it."

The family history brought out that the patient's mother was a cold, selfish woman, cruel to her husband and children. She nagged and belittled her husband's efforts to earn a living until he finally gave up in despair and perhaps in retaliation lived a life of almost complete idleness after the age of forty.

The patient had no direct sexual instruction and never dared to ask any questions. She used to hear her mother complaining once in a while about the way men "imposed upon their wives sexually." Her mother always discouraged her from associating with boys but grudgingly permitted her to have a few dates and attend an occasional dance. The mother had always shown a great tendency to criticize our patient, ostensibly in order to prevent her from becoming vain. Actually the excessive criticism on the part of the mother could only be due to hatred and jealousy. As a young child the patient was frequently told how ungrateful she was, and that if her aunts and uncles only knew what a bad child she was they could never like her. When she tried to be friendly with her father she was shamed and scolded and made to feel there was something wicked in her desire to be near her father or sit upon his knee. In her adolescent years the mother told her how unbecomingly she was dressed and commented that she "couldn't see what a boy would want of her." When the girl tried to choose bright and attractive clothes, the mother would denounce her as behaving like a hussy and would make her take them back for something more subdued. The patient often hoped that her father would come to her rescue but he seemed to fear his wife's sharp tongue too much.

Treatment sessions resolved themselves into a discussion of the following problems: (1) the patient's unsatisfied craving for affection, (2) her hostility toward both women and men, (3) her inability to give feeling. After about six sessions she said, "I guess I looked for my marriage to bring me all the things I had missed at home but of course that was impossible. My father and mother certainly provided a poor example of a happily married couple. I suppose my mother did not have a happy childhood either but that wasn't my fault. I needed someone to do better for me. I guess I hate father for being so spineless. Why didn't he give me some security and friendship in spite of mother's cruelty and jealousy? I feel as if I now had nothing to give my husband in the sexual relationship. There was a little feeling of love in me in the beginning but it soon gave out. I feel so lonely and helpless at times. That's just the way I felt as a child."

For many months the same complaints went on. She spent much time describing her loneliness, irritability, and depression of spirits. She said, "I'm like a whining child. I don't see how you stand it. Why don't you scold me?" We pointed out that it was our function to understand people who had unfulfilled emotional needs and to be trained to accept their demands, since this was the medicine they need most, i.e., friendship. She began to appreciate and utilize the friendly attitude toward her emotional needs, and after a few more discussions, said, "I seem to get something from you. I must cheer up and give more to my husband and everyone else." She began to find that to be interested in someone else and to want to do something for that person made her less lonely and less depressed. At the same time her feelings about sexual matters underwent a change. She said, "I once thought everything my mother said about sex was the truth but I know now it wasn't. Just because mother couldn't be happy doesn't mean that I cannot be. Just because she was sexually frigid doesn't mean that I have to be. Mother wasn't generous and could give very little of herself. I know my husband wants me to feel sexual desire; he wants me to experience pleasure and I now feel I can. It's queer how a person can just tighten up and hold everything in when one's dreams do not come true. I had my dreams but didn't have enough love and good will in me to make them real."

The patient was seen four times weekly and the treatment period lasted ten months. As she related her family history and past experiences, the lack of love in the family background and the resulting emotional emptiness became clear to the patient. The unconscious hostility which had been so damaging to her personality became less pronounced. A friendly and understanding person to work with made it possible for her to reach out and absorb from the people in her environment the love and good will she had missed. At the same time her symptoms began to disappear it became possible for her to experience sexual pleasure with orgasm. (Weiss and English, 1949)

FROHLICH'S SYNDROME (Adiposogenital Dystrophy). A disorder produced by underfunctioning of the anterior lobe of the pituitary gland (hypopituitarism) and lesions in the adjacent diencephalic center of the brain; first described in 1901 by the Viennese neurologist Alfred Fröhlich (1871–1953). *See* CEREBRAL CORTEX, PITUITARY GLAND.

The major symptoms of this disorder are obesity, underdeveloped genital organs and secondary sex characteristics, general sluggishness and "poverty of drive." Boys who are afflicted with this condition tend to be timid and passive, usually prefer to play with girls and smaller children. In some cases they fail to develop ordinary skills and are mildly retarded.

Some of the symptoms of Fröhlich's syndrome are also found in the Laurence-Moon-Biedl syndrome, another form of pituitary deficiency. In this disorder, patients are not only afflicted with obesity and genital dystrophy, but also with clear-cut and progressive mental deficiency, diabetes insipidus, polydactylism (excess number of fingers), and pigmentary retinitis (inflammation of the retina). The cause is unknown, although there appears to be some evidence of genetic defect. *See* MENTAL RETARDATION (CAUSES).

The following case shows the interlocking of physical and psychological factors in Fröhlich's syndrome.

Illustrative Case: FRÖHLICH'S SYNDROME

The patient was a stout boy with small genitals. His basal metabolism was −20. His mother was overprotective, strict, and dominant. He tried to play with other boys of his own age (about five), but was unable to compete with them effectively in sports. After a period of distress, he gave up further attempts and instead played with his sister, with other girls, and with smaller boys. He was peaceful and never fought with other children. When he was ten years old, his classmates, some of them nearing puberty, became increasingly rough and teased him about his stoutness and about his playing with girls. About the same time, while in the shower room, some other boys remarked about the smallness of his genitals. He felt bitter and inferior about this. His behavior soon underwent a considerable change. He became disobedient and abusive toward his mother; he beat his sister; he fought with the boys if they called him "sissy"; and started to play games with his classmates, picking quarrels with them frequently.

The treatment of the patient at the age of thirteen consisted of the administration of thyroid gland tissue to raise his metabolism to normal, and the injection of a pituitarylike substance. He began to develop normally and lost his stoutness. Both he and his mother needed psychotherapy in addition. The patient's behavior grew normal in about six months' time.

The factors that influenced this boy's be-

havior at various times were these: His
metabolism was always low; hence he had
a constant "general poverty of drive." His
mother was always oversolicitous. Both of
these factors made him inclined to be passive, as did also his difficulty in competing
with other boys. When he was five years old,
the most painless and gratifying solution was
to find pleasure and consolation in playing
with girls and with younger children. His
experiences at the age of ten—the attitude
of the other boys in connection with his
body and his passive mode of behavior—
hurt his self-esteem deeply. His reaction to
this hurt was overaggressiveness, in spite of
his "poverty of drive." Thus we see that this
patient's problems were caused partly by the
direct influence of his disturbed metabolism
and partly by the reaction of his total personality to his deficiencies. (Maslow and
Mittelmann, 1951)

FROMM, ERICH (1900–) Fromm received training in psychology, sociology,
and psychoanalysis in Germany before
coming to the United States in 1933.
In his widely read books—*Escape from
Freedom* (1941), *Man for Himself*
(1947), *The Sane Society* (1955), *The
Art of Loving* (1956)—he has infused
the psychoanalytic approach of Freud
with the cultural point of view of
Horney and Sullivan and the historical
materialism of Marx. Yet, though he
has drawn liberally from others, he has
developed a unique emphasis which has
struck a responsive chord among social
scientists, religionists, and the general
public. His major thesis is that modern
life has lost much of its meaning because men have sacrificed themselves
to the machine and the superstate—
and we must therefore find new ways
of establishing more personal and productive relationships with our fellow
men. The prime features of Fromm's
approach will be summarized under five
headings: character, individuality, marketing orientation, productive orientation, and love.

Character. Human nature is built
upon two equally basic, inherent needs:
the need for self-preservation (hunger,

thirst, etc.) and the need to belong
and avoid loneliness. The way we attempt to satisfy these needs molds our
character and determines our actions.
In this process, socioeconomic factors
play the most important part. Our relationship to society, however, is a twofold one. Social processes shape our
character, and we also shape the social
processes, as illustrated in the Protestant ethic which motivated men to
crave work, and this in turn furthered
the development of capitalism.

Fromm views character as a human
substitute for instinct, since it is a
structure which fosters consistent behavior. It can best be viewed as the
way man relates to the world, and
has two aspects: an "individual character" which sets us apart from others,
and a "social character" which helps
direct our energies toward the further-
ance of a particular society. The first
important agency that affects character
formation is the family; somewhat later
the school exerts its influence, and still
later the mass media. In adult life
our character is affected by political,
religious, and educational influences, but
for Fromm the greatest weight by far
is given to economic forces. These
forces impinge most directly on us in
the type of job we perform, for this
requires us to adapt to social conditions which we can do little to change.
Different jobs require different types of
personality, and in a sense we grow
into a job, and are changed and molded
to fit its specific requirements.

Individuality. Freedom and individuality have evolved slowly. Early in
man's history he was part of a tribe
or clan bound together by blood, and
this tie made him more of a group
than a person, since he could not make
his own decisions and group survival
took precedence over his dimly felt
individuality. The group orientation,
however, had its advantages, since it
gave him a place in the sun, assigned
him a job to do, and prevented him

from being threatened by feelings of loneliness, doubt, and uncertainty. Genuine individuality emerged gradually in society, just as it does in the individual, and modern man is still struggling to achieve independence.

The reward of individuality is freedom, but this reward always arouses ambivalent reactions. When he first tries to go it alone and be free, the young child finds himself beset with anxiety, doubt, and feelings of helplessness. He therefore oscillates between the safety and security of his parents' dictates and his desire to strike out on his own. He wants his freedom but at the same time he is afraid to take it. Similarly, many adults desire freedom but cannot give up the comfort of groups in which their roles are guaranteed by others. They, too, regress and retreat and try to "escape from freedom." They allow themselves to become enveloped by rigid institutions—educational, political, economic, religious—which tell them what to do and how to think, giving them little opportunity for the development and expression of their own individuality. The most extreme form of this escape from freedom is found in identifying with an all-powerful organization like the Nazi party in which people surrender not only their individuality but their integrity and humanity as well.

The Marketing Orientation. The urge to escape from freedom expresses itself in a number of specific orientations to the world. According to Fromm, these orientations take two general forms, the "process of assimilation," which means the way we relate to things; and the "process of socialization," the way we relate to ourselves and to others. All our feelings, attitudes, perceptions, and thoughts are rooted in these two types of orientation. Together they determine our character and our acquired reactions, as contrasted with our temperament, which merely consists of our inborn

tendency to react quickly or slowly, strongly or weakly.

In Fromm's opinion, there are a number of dominant modes of nonproductive character constellations within each of these two orientations. In assimilation these are: (a) receiving, (b) exploiting, (c) hoarding, (d) marketing. These correspond, respectively, to the four under socialization: (a) masochistic, (b) sadistic, (c) destructive, and (d) indifferent. As Mullahy has pointed out in the *Handbook of Clinical Psychology* (1965), this division tends to be redundant and misleading. While a person who "receives" may, in a sense, be called "masochistic," and one who "exploits" is apt to be "sadistic," the two sets of terms seem to say much the same thing. Moreover, it is hard to see how hoarding is related to destructiveness.

At any rate, Fromm placed most of his emphasis on the "marketing-indifferent" form of the nonproductive orientation, since he believed it to be the most characteristic of our present economic and social life. In the modern system where barter is no longer practiced, the market value of goods is determined by impersonal factors rather than face-to-face exchange. This situation applies to work as well as goods, and as a result people now look upon themselves as commodities to be bought and sold. They also attempt to develop the kind of personality pattern that is best fitted for the type of market in which they find themselves. Personal knowledge and ability to communicate ideas become secondary to playing the proper game at the proper time, and salability is developed at the expense of ability to feel, think, will, or imagine. The marketing person judges his own worth and that of others only in terms of sales success, and he lives in constant fear that others will not accept him or recognize his efforts. As a consequence, his relationships with other people are superficial and depersonalized, and he finds himself "alone, afraid to fail, eager to please."

Closely related to the marketing orientation is the view that modern man is an "automaton," a mere cog in a vast industrial machine. Working on one small portion of a product, he is cut off not only from the ultimate article he is producing, but from his own potentialities as a human being. He accepts the niche in the social structure assigned to him by the powers that be, and conforms as best he can to alleviate the fear that he will not be accepted. Out of this situation arises the "socialization orientation" which is inevitably coupled with the marketing orientation—that is, a feeling of basic indifference to society, and an acceptance of the meaninglessness of life.

The productive orientation. This is a key concept in Fromm's thinking, his alternative to the marketing-indifferent and other nonproductive orientations. In his view, a person is productive when he is realizing the powers which are essential aspects of human nature, and a well-developed science of man would enumerate the nature, type, and number of uniquely human powers. So far we have only gleaned a little knowledge here, since human nature can never be fully realized in any society at any given time. Nevertheless, the outlines of this orientation are fairly clear. In terms of our relation to things ("assimilation") we need to replace the marketing orientation, as well as hoarding, exploiting, and receiving, with meaningful work that does not reduce the worker to the status of appendage to a machine. There are some promising models for this new orientation in co-operative communities that combine living with working, since they provide opportunities for integrating productivity with social life, educational improvement, and the development of the whole human being.

Love. The other aspect of the productive orientation lies in our relation-ship to people ("socialization"). Here the two major concepts are reasoning—the free use of the mind—and loving. Both of these must be linked with working, in the institutions of the future, if we are ever to develop a "sane society." For Fromm, love has a special meaning. It cannot be reduced to sexual expression or feelings of dependency. It is viewed as an activity, a passion that keeps humanity from disintegrating, a way of giving that involves sharing the entire spectrum of life—joy, interests, understanding, sadness, humor. The practice of love is a "unique attempt at interpersonal fusion" through which human beings can deal with their greatest problem and challenge—their separateness. It is not a simple matter, for at its core are respect, care, knowledge, and responsibility, and these require competence in many areas of life. The development of the ability to love is therefore an "art," and if it is ever fully achieved it is bound to bring the highest expression of individuality and the greatest guarantee of mental health. *See* HOARDING, LOVE.

FROTTAGE. A sexual deviation in which excitement or gratification is repeatedly obtained by men through pressing or rubbing against women in elevators, subways, or other crowded places.

Frottage (French for "rubbing") often passes unnoticed and is therefore more common than is usually recognized, particularly among young men. It is based on acts involved in ordinary sexual relations, and is considered a perversion only when frotteur does not or cannot obtain sexual satisfaction through coitus. Little is known about the dynamics of this behavior pattern since frotteurs rarely seek treatment. However, some investigators believe it is due to a persistence of infantile pleasure in being cuddled and rubbed; and Freud suggested that it has an instinctual, biological basis since cats apparently enjoy rubbing against people's legs, and many other animals seem to derive pleasure from being stroked. It may be that the frotteur adopts this secret, unthreatening form of stimulation because he feels inadequate and insecure, and is unable to face the challenge of mature sexual relations—an explanation that also applies to many cases of exhibitionism, voyeurism, pedophilia, and other deviations. See SEXUAL DEVIATIONS (GENERAL).

FRUCTOSURIA. A rare familial disease involving the metabolism of fructose (fruit sugar) and resulting in mental retardation. The disorder is probably transmitted by a single recessive gene. See MENTAL RETARDATION (CAUSES).

FUGUE STATE. An amnesic dissociated state characterized by physical flight from an unbearable situation.

A fugue is a more extreme form of escape than the more common types of amnesia, since the patient not only loses his identity but actually leaves his normal surroundings for days, weeks or even years. In fugues of short duration he is likely to wander aimlessly about in a highly emotional state, and to be confused and agitated when found. In some cases he may perform wish-fulfilling activities such as going on a fishing trip or attending four movies a day. Episodes of this general type may be recurrent.

Although long-repressed desires may be acted out during these periods of fugue, crimes are rarely committed. The claim of amnesia during criminal prosecution should, therefore, be regarded with suspicion.

During the more extended fugues, the individual may travel widely, assume the name and identity of an admired person, take up an occupation he always wanted to pursue, get married, and raise a family. Although his past is a complete blank, he usually appears normal in all other respects during these episodes. He unconsciously avoids communities or situations where his identity might be revealed, and he may fabricate a story about his past if he is questioned.

The psychodynamics of the fugue state are the same as for other dissociative reactions. In some cases a history of lying and hysterical reactions can be found. Some studies suggest that the purpose of the fugue is to ward off a depression. Most authorities, however, believe these states arise out of an unconscious desire to escape a threatening or intensely distasteful life situation.

When the fugue state is terminated either spontaneously or through hypnosis or sodium amytal techniques, the patient regains either a full or a partial memory for the period before the episode. In some cases he becomes amnesic for the fugue period itself, but in others he can gradually recall and integrate the episode with his total life. Interviews under hypnosis or sodium amytal may be helpful not only in restoring the memory, but in revealing the emotional factors which led to this escape reaction. These findings are useful in initiating a program of psychotherapy when it is considered necessary. See DISSOCIATIVE REACTION.

Illustrative Case: FUGUE STATE

I was sitting at a bar having a beer when the juke box began belting out the tune "Because." That music certainly snapped me out of it. It happened to be the melody that they played at my wedding. In that instant, I recalled that I had a wife and two daughters in San Antonio! But what was I doing in this bar when I had never frequented bars before (at least not since my college days)? I had many puzzling questions to ask of the group of tavern habitués who were equally puzzled about my bizarre behavior. What town was this? And how did I ever get to St. Louis? Why was I so suntanned and why were my hands so calloused? And where had I been for fifteen months? Soon

I was in telephone contact with my jubilant wife and, in two hours more, I was on a plane bound for San Antonio to resume my life after that mystifying, troublesome, blank gap of over a year. The joyous reunion with my family at the airport permitted a temporary postponement of such nagging worries.

Once more, my life fell into the routine that I had formerly known so well, with its familiar faces, places, and duties. I was installed again as president of a chemical company and took up my life where I had interrupted it. Lucky fellow!

Things went well, my business prospered, and I went back to my duties as Sunday School superintendent again. Within six months I could even relax for long weekends with my family, in order to get reacquainted with them and to make up for lost time. The leisure and rest that I enjoyed were a luxury but not an unmixed blessing, by any means, because now the problem of the gap in my life began to press upon me and insinuated itself into my moments of pleasure and fun with my beloved wife and children.

Here's where Dr. X stepped in with his help. Over many weeks, we had long sessions with and without hypnosis. At first, with great difficulty, but soon with increasing facility, hypnosis helped one thought to attract another until eventually they tumbled over each other, and I was able to recall many aspects of my fifteen-month fugue. Furthermore, I was able to retain them in the posthypnotic condition as well.

Retracing my steps hypnotically convinced me that my fugue was an unwitting attempt to run away from certain problems and conflicts. I recalled the uneasiness and guilt that I frequently felt as I would walk through my chemical plant and observe men, not as fortunately situated as I, doing menial work. After all, what right did I have to a cushy job that I had merely inherited from my father-in-law? Another problem centered in my married life. The tenderness and passion that Marjorie and I constantly expressed for each other for several years had gradually burned itself out. Our marriage seemed on the verge of bankruptcy. Then, one night, a violent argument developed and lasted until 2:30 in the morning. My fugue occurred the very next day.

What had I done in the intervening fifteen months? Under hypnosis I learned that I had gone to St. Louis and worked as a laborer at a chemical plant there. In fact, it was the same job I had held summers when I worked my way through the university. It was here, too, that I had led a frivolous, unrestrained Bohemian life in my younger days, frequenting bars and cocktail lounges. Apparently, I had returned to the scene of the crime and tasted once more a bit of the fast life. Some of the incidents of my fugue that I recalled caused the Sunday School superintendent to blush. (Dorcus and Shaffer, 1945)

FUNCTIONAL AUTONOMY. The theory that motives may become independent of the biological need from which they originally stemmed, and operate on their own.

The theory of functional autonomy is based on the idea that our behavior is governed by certain primary physiological needs such as hunger, thirst, and sex—yet even after these needs are physically satisfied, they still seem to govern our behavior. The man who originally worked to meet the physical needs of his family and himself still works hard after he has amassed wealth that far exceeds any material need. The gourmet, who started by eating to live, now lives to eat. The miser who began to save because of a deprived youth continues to put money away even though he no longer needs to be thrifty. Older men and women remain interested in sex even though they are not primarily motivated by physical need. In all these cases the drives appear to have a life of their own.

The term functional autonomy was invented by Gordon Allport (1937) for behavior that appeared to develop its own motive power. He found that activities which were initially undertaken to satisfy primary needs developed new, secondary goals of their own. The millionaire continues to work in order to meet such needs as companionship, prestige, pride, or a feeling of responsibility toward his enterprise and his associates. Allport believed that the concept of functional autonomy applied to these cases much better than other theories of motivation, such as Freud's, which trace all behavior to biological or infantile origins. He maintained that present interests are sufficient to explain present motivation.

The theory has been criticized as more descriptive than explanatory, because it does not show how motives become autonomous. Moreover, other psychologists have suggested that many of the drives which Allport considered secondary, such as curiosity, activity, and affection, are actually as fundamental as the physiological drives. They motivate our behavior practically from the beginning of life, but often come into special prominence after our physical needs have been satisfied. This view may make a special theory of functional autonomy unnecessary. *See* CURIOSITY DRIVE, ACTIVITY DRIVE, AFFECTIONAL DRIVE, PERSONALITY TRAIT THEORY (ALLPORT).

FUNCTIONAL DISORDER. Any disorder or abnormality of behavior for which there is no known organic or structural basis.

Functional disorders are considered to be psychogenic since physical changes do not appear to be causal factors and psychological (that is, emotional) factors can usually be demonstrated. The two terms, functional disorder and psychogenic disorder, are often used interchangeably, although "psychogenic" specifies that the disorder is emotional in origin and can be attributed to events in the individual's psychological history.

Some writers (English and English, 1958) distinguish between two meanings of functional. In the first, impaired performance cannot be related to any pathological change in organic structure; hysterical, or dissociative, amnesia would be an example. In the second, it is definitely known that the disorder is not due to organ or tissue pathology. An example of this type of functional disorder is glove anesthesia, since it can be positively proved that the nerves and sense organs that control sensation in the hand are not structurally impaired. *See* CONVERSION REACTION.

All psychoneuroses are considered functional disorders. Stress reactions and psychosomatic (psychophysiologic) disorders are likewise classed as functional, since the primary causal factors are emotional and the physical changes are the result of these factors. Psychoses may be either functional or organic. Schizophrenic, manic-depressive and psychotic depressive reactions are classified as functional, although many investigations of possible biochemical factors are now in progress. In contrast, general paresis, toxic psychoses, and psychoses associated with brain inflammation or tumor are classed as organic, since structural impairment can be clearly demonstrated.

FUNCTIONALISM. A general psychological approach that views behavior in terms of active adaptation to the environment.

The functionalist point of view was initially developed by John Dewey, James R. Angell, and William James in opposition to structuralism, which limited psychology to the dissection of states of consciousness. Functionalism focused attention on mental activities rather than mental contents, and its objective was to show how judging, perceiving, feeling, willing, and other activities help us meet the problems and situations we encounter in life. This interpretation of consciousness as a dynamic force was in sharp contrast to the static, descriptive approach of the structuralists. It was also directly in line with the American temperament in its emphasis on action and utility. In addition, it was in accord with the Darwinian theory not only because it stressed the interaction of the human being with his environment and the survival value of mental activity, but because it proposed to show how we can use our resources in improving human life. *See* WUNDT, INTROSPECTION, DARWIN.

The functionalist movement was anticipated to some degree by Franz Brentano's act psychology, Binet's concept of intelligence as the ability to solve problems, and Harold Höffding's interpretation of psychological processes in terms of activity. However, the "official" start of the movement dates from Dewey's 1896 paper on reflexes, in which he objected to the atomistic approach that conceived reflexes as isolated, discrete units, and insisted that behavior is a continuous process of adjustment and readjustment involving many activities at once. Dewey also attacked the dualistic separation of mind and body and put forth the idea that the distinction is only a methodological one since every act has both mental and physical aspects. Moreover, even when we investigate the mental aspects of our experience, we cannot view them in isolation, as structuralism did, but only as part and parcel of ongoing events. Our thoughts, ideas, and concepts can therefore be understood only in terms of the conditions from which they arise and the consequences which they produce.

This approach of Dewey's had a twofold effect. First, the emphasis on causes turned attention to the problem of understanding the antecedents of thought and behavior—that is, to discovering the reasons why we think and act as we do. Only by understanding causes would we be in a position to change and improve our interactions with the environment. And since these causes were to be viewed as psychophysical, the functionalist movement spurred investigations of the physiological as well as the psychological processes which underlie our behavior. Second, the emphasis on consequences meant that ideas

are not good or bad, true or false, in themselves, but can be judged only by what they lead to and how they square with the external world. This put the stress on objective testing of theories in the laboratory and outside, as opposed to the subjective, introspective approach of the structuralist. The new point of view was a major factor in developing psychology as a scientific discipline.

Finally, the functionalist approach was instrumental in opening up the wholly new area of applied psychology. Its entire approach pointed in this direction—its emphasis on mind as a biological tool to be used in meeting the ongoing demands of life, on the power of thinking in producing change, on evolution and the future, and on the practical, observable consequences of ideas. In view of this general approach, plus the emphasis on change and improvement which was characteristic of American democracy, it is not surprising that the functionalists had much to do with the development of such fields as educational psychology, child guidance, and human relations.

Functionalism was never a systematized, well-defined theory of psychology. It can best be viewed as a trend rather than a school. Today that trend no longer exists as a distinct approach in competition with other approaches, because it has been so fully incorporated in the psychology of this country. Its influence has been felt in every major field of the subject—in social, abnormal, physiological as well as applied psychology—for it reminds us that at some point we must ask, What is the practical value of this investigation? Does it help us solve a real problem? Does it contribute to the improvement of human life? *See* DEWEY, JAMES, ACT PSYCHOLOGY.

FUROR (Literally, "rage"). Transitory outbursts of anger or excitement during which the individual becomes totally irrational and may commit violence.

The term "furor epileptika" applies to the enraged behavior that very occasionally follows grand mal or occurs during a psychomotor attack. The term catathymic crisis is sometimes applied to a similar reaction which appears to be precipitated by a state of overwhelming, intolerable tension. Here, too, the patient suddenly commits an isolated, unrepeated act of violence. *See* EPILEPSY (SYMPTOMS AND TYPES), PATHOLOGICAL INTOXICATION.

Illustrative Case: FUROR

Precociously husky and muscular, he was visiting an aunt, twenty-three years old, the mother of two children and pregnant, to watch television. When the young woman complained of feeling unwell and asked the boy to leave, he was overcome by a "sudden urge" as he rose to go. He struck her in the face and when she fell kicked her about the face and head. He struck her again with a soda bottle, brought a metal spray gun from the next room and struck her with that. He then beat her with a lamp, obtained a large knife from the kitchen and stabbed her in the neck. Still in furor, he wound a lamp cord around her neck and was dragging her into the kitchen, intent on stringing her body on a water pipe, when a knock on the door alarmed him and he fled through a window. The boy had a history of two serious head injuries and of black-outs attributable to them. His only previous offense had been car thefts, carried out in frivolous disregard of the likelihood of detection. He was clinically found to be an epileptic as a consequence of brain injury. (Banay, 1961)

G

GALACTOSEMIA. A disorder of carbohydrate metabolism which inhibits physical development and leads to mental retardation unless recognized and treated early in life.

An infant afflicted with congenital galactosemia lacks the enzyme necessary to metabolize lactose and galactose. He appears normal for several days, but soon develops feeding difficulties, vomiting, and sometimes diarrhea. If he continues to be fed milk, galactose and lactose accumulate in the blood and result in jaundice, enlargement of the abdomen, formation of cataracts, and delay in standing, walking, and talking.

The condition can be diagnosed soon after birth through blood tests. If milk is eliminated from the diet and replaced with soybean or other substitutes, the symptoms subside and permanent cerebral damage may be prevented. *See* MENTAL RETARDATION (CAUSES).

GALEN (C. 130–C. 220). Galen was not only the most eminent physician of his time, but influenced the entire course of both physical and mental medicine through the Middle Ages and well into the modern era. Though a Greek, he was appointed physician to Marcus Aurelius, the emperor of Rome, at the age of thirty-three. He is said to have written over 500 treatises, 98 of which are still in existence. In these works he synthesized the entire history of medical thought to date, but added distinctive contributions of his own primarily in the field of anatomy and physiology.

Galen did not make any extensive contributions to the diagnosis or treatment of mental disorders, but he did attempt to approach them from a scientific point of view. In general, he viewed the brain as the center of all motion and sensation, and the seat of mental disease. He recognized both physical and psychological factors in mental illness, citing as causes not only head injuries, alcoholic excess, and menstrual changes, but shock, economic reverses, and disappointment in love. He accepted Hippocrates' theory of the four humors, and thereby recognized the dependence of temperament on variations in physiological and constitutional factors. In his own anatomical investigations, he employed both animal dissection and human vivisection and took an important first step toward the science of neurology. *See* HUMORAL THEORY.

Although many of Galen's general approaches pointed in constructive directions, the details of his medical theory and practice were a crude mixture of science, folklore and religion—and it was these details that became medical dogma for the next 1500 years. At one time he appeared to base his views on careful observation and experimentation; at another he asserted his belief in dreams and portents, primitive remedies, and supernatural intervention. He sought to relate the four humors (yellow bile, black bile, phlegm, and blood) to the four basic elements, earth, air, fire, and water, and attributed differences in disposition to states of dryness or moistness which they produced in the brain. Following Plato, Aristotle, and Hippocrates, he believed that climate was an important determinant of character, but did not make clear its relation to the humors. He appeared to take a step forward in rejecting the prevailing theory that hysteria was due to a wandering uterus, but he resorted to the humoral theory instead, claiming that this disease was produced by engorgement of the uterus with blood.

Although Galen discovered experimentally that the arteries contain blood, he described the nerves as hollow tubes which carry "animal spirits" from the brain to all parts of the body. Mental disease was conceived as a disturbance in animal spirit functioning. He believed that most of the factors mentioned above, such as head injury and shock, could produce conditions of heat, hu-

midity, coldness, etc. in the brain, which in turn brought about mania, melancholia, dementia, or imbecility. In some cases, however, he felt that the impact was more indirect, and developed a theory of "consensus" which held that the various parts of the body work together and can influence each other. An example of this view was his belief that excessive drinking does not affect the brain directly but acts through the heart or liver.

Even though Galen recognized that the brain is the center for sensation and motion, he pictured these processes in purely mechanical terms, putting forth the theory that impressions are stimuli which tap on soft brain tissue like "little hammers," while movement is initiated by striking harder areas. He also held that both the quality and quantity of brain tissue affect mental functioning, that fine tissue is involved in the process of thinking, while firm, stable tissue accounts for memory.

Finally, Galen appears to have applied the same type of treatment to mental as to physical disorders. He believed that the animal spirits flowing from the brain could be influenced by administration of herbals which later became known as galenicals. He put special store by one drug in particular, theriaca, whose principal ingredient was opium. This drug was prescribed for a wide variety of physical and mental ailments, as indicated by the following statement:

"It resists poison and venomous bites, cures inveterate headache, vertigo, deafness, apoplexy, epilepsy, dimness of sight, loss of voice, asthma, coughs of all kinds, spitting of blood, tightness of breath, cholic, the iliac poisons, jaundice, hardness of the spleen, stone, urinary complaints, fevers, dropsies, leprosies, the trouble to which women are subject, melancholy, and all pestilences." Judging from this account, it would appear that the ancients had discovered a miracle drug which was equally effective for mental and physical ailments.

GALTON, FRANCIS (1822–1911). Galton, the first to make a systematic study of individual differences, was a native of Birmingham, England. In view of his later investigations of genius it is interesting that he was himself a true "child prodigy" who was able to read at two and a half, write a letter before he was four, and read both Latin and French by five. He studied medicine at Birmingham University, St. George's General Hospital in London, and later at Cambridge. However, he did not actually enter the medical profession, since his father died and left him a considerable fortune. Instead, he traveled widely in Europe and made a number of expeditions to Africa, for which he received the Gold Medal Award of the Royal Geographic Society. His major objective in these efforts was to study human individuals and races in the light of the evolutionary concepts developed by his half-cousin, Charles Darwin. *See* DARWIN.

Galton's first major work, *Hereditary Genius* (1869), was undertaken to show that eminent men have eminent offspring. By comparing the genealogies of over 1000 British leaders with an equal number of average citizens, he showed that the former group had far more distinguished relatives than the latter, and concluded that the difference was due to heredity. He carried this view even further by claiming that specific types of genius were inherited— for example, a great jurist would tend to have children who became eminent in the field of law. In applying this "pedigree method," Galton ignored the influence of environmental factors and did not question the authenticity of the historical documents on which he based his case. In spite of these obvious deficiencies, the study had the positive effect of stimulating research on in-dividual differences, and of demonstrating the importance of exceptional individuals in the survival of mankind. *See* GENIUS, PRODIGY.

One of Galton's major motives was to carry evolution forward into the future in order to produce a superior species. He therefore embarked upon a survey of human abilities which would determine man's present assets and limitations, and thus point the way to possible improvement of the race. His initial findings are contained in *Inquiries into the Human Faculty and Its Development* (1883), which is regarded as the first scientific study of individual differences, since it reported the first use of tests in assessing human capacities. It is also the first book to advocate a program of eugenics, for Galton believed that man's basic capacities are inherited and the race can be improved only through selective breeding. It is ironic that Galton himself, whose IQ was later rated close to 200 by Lewis Terman, and who became the first president of the Eugenics Education Society, had a childless marriage.

The *Inquiries* contained many original contributions to psychology. Among the most influential were his studies of association and imagery, and his use of standardized tests. In one of his experiments on association he wrote seventy-five words on slips of paper, hid them under a book, and drew them out by one, recording the time it took for him to produce two associations to each word. The experiment yielded two significant results: He found that (1) many of his associations harked back to boyhood and adolescence, a clear demonstration that childhood experiences have an effect on adult thinking; and (2) through a study of his own introspections he found that many of his associative processes occurred on an unconscious level.

In his investigations of mental imagery, Galton made the "first extensive psychological use of the questionnaire" (Murphy, 1949). Subjects were asked to conjure up a mental picture of their breakfast table and to rate the images on a 0 to 100 scale in terms of illumination, definition, and coloring. The individual differences were surprisingly large. Some people, including even well-known painters, were quite deficient in imagery, and women and children appeared to have clearer imagery than men. The results cast doubt on the prevalent notion that thinking processes were dependent upon mental images, since many brilliant scientists were found to be almost completely lacking in visual imagery. Moreover, the experiments suggested that people could be divided into ideational types, since some were found to be dominantly visual, while others were dominantly auditory, kinesthetic, or even olfactory. Once again Galton attributed the differences to heredity, and offered as evidence the fact that brothers and sisters, and especially identical twins, showed a closer resemblance in type of imagery than individuals chosen at random.

Galton not only created the first psychological tests, which he applied in his study of individual differences, but also originated many pieces of apparatus for measuring human capacities—among them the Galton whistle which determined the highest pitch an individual could hear, the Galton bar on which variable amounts could be laid off for testing judgments of visual extent, and a series of weights which subjects were asked to compare. He believed that these and other tests of sensory discrimination could be used in measuring intelligence, a view which was embraced by Cattell but opposed by Binet.

The year after his publication of the *Inquiries,* Galton made the first large-scale anthropometric and psychometric investigation by applying his tests to hundreds of people at the International Health Exhibition of 1884. This program was continued for six additional years at the South Kensington Museum in London, where data on the height, weight, breathing power, strength of pull and squeeze, hearing, vision, color sense, and other capacities of over 9000 people were compiled. Galton's ultimate object was to assess the resources of the entire British population as a first step toward improvement through eugenics. It is an interesting fact that the studies did not reveal any consistent pattern, and did not support his original belief that man is superior to woman in all capacities. *See* CATTELL, BINET.

In the course of his investigations, Galton made many other noteworthy contributions. He was the first to use the method of statistical correlation, a mathematical technique for determining the degree to which two variables, such as weight and strength of grip, are related. In his studies of imagery, he discovered the strange phenomenon of synesthesia (cross sensations, such as seeing colors while hearing music). He originated the "twin study" procedure, which has since been applied to many psychological problems, including the relative influence of heredity and environment on intelligence and mental disorder. He helped to establish the use of fingerprints as a means of identifying individuals, and he devised the "composite portrait," which consisted of a number of superimposed photographs designed to give a generalized picture of races, families, criminals, and even thoroughbred horses. These are only a sample of the products of Galton's fertile mind, but all of them have the common denominator of furthering our knowledge of human similarities and differences. *See* SYNESTHESIA, TWINS, DIFFERENTIAL PSYCHOLOGY.

GALVANIC SKIN RESPONSE (GSR) (Psychogalvanic Response, PGR; Electrodermal Response). A decrease in the electrical resistance of the skin during intense emotion or other forms of stimulation.

The GSR was discovered during investigations of the physiological changes that occur in emotion. It is based on the commonly observed fact that our skin tends to perspire when we are upset, plus the fact that perspiration increases the conductivity of the surface of the skin, particularly in the palms. The changes in skin resistance are measured by a device called a psychogalvanometer. As a result of studies made with this sensitive instrument, the GSR is now used as an index of emotional state and physiological reactions to stress.

GSR measurements are particularly useful because changes in skin conductivity are not under conscious control. This can be illustrated by a simple but striking demonstration. A male subject is brought before a group of people, and the apparatus is attached to the palm of one hand. He is then instructed to recite the letters of the alphabet slowly while thinking of the name of his girl friend. When he reaches the first letter of her name, the needle suddenly jumps. This is believed to be a reflection of his embarrassment or fear of detection. Experiments of this kind have led to the development of a lie detector which uses GSR readings. *See* LIE DETECTOR.

The psychogalvanometer has been widely employed in psychological research. It has been found that any abrupt change in bodily activation is reflected by the instrument. A sudden sharp noise will cause a rapid increase in the GSR within a few seconds, with a return to normal functioning in about half a minute. A loud sound produces greater changes in conductivity than sounds of lesser intensity. Any situation that keys up the organism, from starting a race to tackling a mathematical problem, may produce changes in the GSR. It is therefore used not only as an indicator of emotion but as an index

of preparation for activity. It has also been found that any stimulus which captures attention increases the GSR. This fact has been utilized in determining the reactions of consumers to different advertisements.

Another field in which it is used for research purposes is psychotherapy. In one procedure, psychoanalytic sessions are recorded on tape, with parallel records of skin conductivity. The therapist then correlates the remarks of his patient with the GSR changes. This has proved to be an effective way of uncovering analytic clues, since patients may gloss over material that is emotionally significant, and the instrument may pick up their involuntary reactions. The technique, however, is still considered experimental. Along the same line, it is an interesting fact that palmists have long realized that a slight increase in perspiration can indicate emotional involvement. This cue, plus increased pulse rate and hand tremor, helps to guide them in their readings.

GAMBLING. There are two general types of gambling, the social type and the compulsive type. Social gambling is the kind ordinary individuals occasionally engage in for excitement, social intercourse, and possible financial gain. Some people also derive intellectual satisfaction from attempting to figure the odds or from devising or testing a "system." Social gamblers may find themselves trapped by the thrill of the game and risk more than they can afford— but in general they can "take it or leave it."

Compulsive gamblers, on the other hand, are driven by an irresistible impulse that dominates and often disrupts their lives. Even though they know the odds are against them, they must continue gambling—regardless of their losses and the effects on their family, social, and occupational life. Frequently they will squander their entire savings, borrow heavily, and resort to illegal means for obtaining money, always convinced that their luck is bound to change.

The number of compulsive gamblers in the United States alone has been estimated at six million, and their annual losses are said to run to twenty billion dollars a year. If the estimated number is anywhere near correct, compulsive gambling represents one of the most widespread psychological disturbances in this country. A gambler of this type is rarely a neurotic, since he is not torn by internal conflicts or crippled by anxiety. Instead, he "acts out" his impulses without sufficient regard to consequences. His disturbance is classified by the American Psychiatric Association (1952) as a character or personality disorder in which a single symptom is predominant (a "special symptom reaction").

There has been a limited amount of research on this disorder, but enough to indicate the outstanding personality traits of the compulsive gambler. He tends to be a rebellious and immature individual who dislikes rules, regulations, and responsibilities. His behavior is usually unconventional, and ethical standards of any kind mean little to him. On the surface he appears sociable and engaging, but he seldom forms deep attachments and frequently uses others for his own purposes. If his acquaintances refuse to advance him money, he either becomes resentful or simply crosses them off his list and tries others. He thoroughly rationalizes his gambling activities as a form of business venture, and justifies himself by pointing to the one or two times when he made a big killing in a single evening. Even when he loses, the act of gambling itself seems to bring him intense satisfaction, since he is a person who lives on the stimulants of risk, excitement, action, and a constantly changing situation.

The compulsive gambler has many unrealistic attitudes and illogical beliefs that are extremely resistant to change. He is convinced that his efforts will make him rich and that he will never have to stoop to working for a living. He believes that there is always a loophole in the odds, and that he will be able to take advantage of it. He is prone to "magical thinking," the belief in signs and omens that point toward winning, or the feeling that he can control the dice or cards with his own thoughts. He takes seriously the old fallacy that after many losses one is bound to have not only a winning streak but a big one. Frequently he borrows money from his friends or embezzles funds from businesses on the basis of his irrational beliefs. *See* MAGICAL THINKING.

Little is known about the dynamics of gambling, but there are many theories. Some investigators believe that compulsive gamblers are "passive-dependent" personalities who have been encouraged in childhood to be helpless and indecisive, and to cling to others for support. As grown men, they cannot face the problems of holding a job, and depend upon Lady Luck for support. Others believe they are basically obsessive-compulsive individuals who feel comfortable and secure only when they are repeating the same thoughts and actions. On this theory, gambling becomes a psychological ritual. They are also classed by some writers as psychopaths who are so egocentric, rebellious, and hostile that they have no regard for other people, including their own families. *See* PASSIVE-AGGRESSIVE PERSONALITY, OBSESSIVE-COMPULSIVE REACTION, REPETITION-COMPULSION, ANTISOCIAL REACTION.

Many psychoanalysts, however, have a totally different point of view. They believe that compulsive gamblers are masochistic individuals who have an unconscious desire to lose instead of win. They are driven by an urge to punish themselves for guilty behavior or guilty impulses stemming from childhood.

Since they are unaware of the source of their drive, they continue to appease their sense of guilt not only by losing their money and social position, but by alienating their friends and dragging their families down with them. *See* MASOCHISM.

Psychoanalysis and other forms of psychotherapy have been used in treating compulsive gamblers, and some success has been achieved in helping them gain insight into themselves and adopt more constructive and mature behavior. But too few cases have been treated to permit any general evaluation of results. The organization "Gamblers Anonymous," modeled after Alcoholics Anonymous, has helped a number of gamblers to control their impulse. Through group discussions they share experiences and attain greater understanding of their irrational behavior and its consequences. They also give each other emotional support when they are having trouble controlling their urge to gamble.

GANGLION. A cluster of nerve cell bodies and synapses, usually but not always outside the brain or spinal cord. (A clump of nerve cells within the central nervous system is usually called a nucleus.)

Each of the thirty-one sensory spinal nerves connects with the spinal cord through a ganglion lying just outside the cord. The sympathetic tracts serving the heart, stomach and other internal organs also have ganglia outside the bony case of the spinal cord. The ganglia for the twelve cranial nerves, on the other hand, are found here and there in the recesses of the skull near the entrances and exits for the nerve fibers. Other ganglia are found throughout the body—for example, in the optic nerve.

Another important group of cell bodies, known as the basal ganglia, is located just below the cerebral cortex. From an evolutionary point of view, these ganglia are the oldest structure in the telencephalon, the highest part of the brain. Most of the fibers emanating from these cells connect with various parts of the body through the thalamus, the organism's central switching point. They carry impulses from the receptors (sense organs) up to the brain and downward from the brain to the effectors (muscles and glands). A few of the ganglia appear to have migrated downward from the main group, and are involved in maintaining posture and co-ordination of movement. *See* SPINAL CORD, CRANIAL NERVES, SPINAL NERVES.

GANSER SYNDROME. A relatively rare reaction pattern in which an individual gives approximate, inappropriate answers to questions, as if he were not wholly rational.

The disorder, which is also known as the "syndrome of approximate answers," was first described by the German psychiatrist Sigbert Ganser (1853–1931) in 1898. It occurs primarily in prisoners awaiting criminal trial, and secondarily in patients under examination for commitment to mental institutions. It is not regarded as a deliberate attempt to deceive or malinger, but an unconscious effort to avoid a distasteful situation.

The answers these individuals give are always related to the question, but at the same time are absurd or beside the point ("Vorbeireden" or paralogia). Even the simplest questions are answered in a distorted way. If the questioner, as a test, asks silly questions, he gets even sillier answers. If the patient is shown a pair of scissors, he may say they are knives. A cat may be identified as a dog, a nickel as a half dollar. Ask him what a saw is for, and he may reply, "to hammer a nail." Ask him how many legs a horse has, and he might say, "six." He seems to be playing a game, and yet he appears to have a genuine air of bewilderment and confusion, and may even claim that he does not know who he is or where he comes from.

Authorities disagree as to whether Ganser's syndrome is a psychosis, a psychoneurosis, or the result of low mentality. The reaction does seem to have a psychotic flavor, and some investigators (Weiner and Braiman, 1955) suggest that the loss of rationality is an unconscious attempt to reject the total self and its life history. Yet the answers are often even sillier than those given by schizophrenics of the hebephrenic type, as if a voluntary effort were being made to say something ridiculous. Other specialists classify the condition as a psychoneurosis of the hysteric type, since the patient is unconsciously attempting to avoid a distressing situation. He may also exhibit other hysterical symptoms such as amnesia and analgesia. Still others point out that the reaction usually occurs in people who are of borderline intelligence—but perhaps bright enough to recognize that at times it is to their advantage not to be too smart! In any case, the individual is probably yielding to an impulse, whether conscious or unconscious, to escape from an unpleasant situation by appearing irresponsible and incompetent. See PRISON PSYCHOSIS, PSEUDORETARDATION.

GANZFELD PHENOMENON. Our visual world is usually filled with a myriad of different shapes, colors and forms. Some objects are large, others small; some red, others green or blue; some are regularly, some irregularly shaped. Psychologists have wondered what would happen if the visual field were uniform instead of varied, so that all the stimuli we received would be the same. They have therefore set up a homogeneous field or "Ganzfeld" (literally, "whole field") by placing half a translucent ping-pong ball over each eye of their subject, or by having him look into large white spheres (Dember, 1960).

In either case any light that reaches the eyes comes from a uniform visual field.

The most interesting finding in these experiments is that colors tend to disappear. When a red light is shown on the inside of the spheres it is first seen as a diffuse red fog, but after about three minutes most subjects report that the color vanishes and the spheres appear whitish. The same effect is obtained with green illumination. Later on "inhomogeneity" is gradually introduced into the Ganzfeld in various ways. Figures then start to emerge and certain fundamental properties of the background, such as color and distance, become stabilized.

These experiments indicate that both the registration of color and the visual perception of forms are due to stimulus change, or heterogeneity, in our field of vision. The absence of contrast actually denudes our world and distorts our experience. A similar effect has been noted in sensory deprivation experiments in which all external stimulation—visual, tactual, auditory, etc.—has been reduced to a minimum. See SENSORY DEPRIVATION.

GARGOYLISM (Lipochondrodystrophy; Hurler's Disease). A metabolic disorder in which fatty deposits (lipoids) in various parts of the body produce distorted features and mild to severe mental retardation. The condition is believed to be determined by a single gene, and may be transmitted either as an autosomal recessive character or a sex-linked recessive with only males affected.

The major physical symptoms are an enlarged head, protruding forehead, bushy eyebrows, saddle nose, coarse features, and a stunted body. The result is the grotesque appearance which suggested the term gargoylism. No treatment or preventive measures have been discovered, but the condition is rare.

Most victims do not survive beyond their teens. *See* MENTAL RETARDATION (CAUSES).

GENERAL ADAPTATION SYNDROME. The total mobilization of the organism's resources in meeting situations of excessive stress.

The concept grew out of Hans Selye's research on endocrine secretions in animals subjected to various stress conditions. He found that the body has three levels of defense. In the first stage, which is termed *alarm-reaction,* the body's defense forces are quickly called up by pituitary-adrenal secretions, which produce an increase in heart rate, bood sugar, and muscle tone, as well as general alertness. In the *stage of resistance,* further reactions take place that enable the organism to repair damage and sustain continued stress. These new defenses are brought into play largely by secretions from the adrenal cortex (corticoids). In the final stage of *exhaustion,* the hormone defenses and protective reactions break down, and further exposure to stress may lead to disintegration or death. Selye (1956) believes that many of the human "diseases of adaptation," including hypertension, arthritis, and peptic ulcer, are due to the excessive use of the body's defense system during long-continued stress (PLATE 3). Today this is considered one of the major explanations for psychophysiologic, or psychosomatic, disorders.

The general adaptation syndrome suggests a parallel between psychological and biological defenses. Prolonged psychological stress tends to produce reactions that also follow a three-stage pattern. First comes alarm and mobilization, in which the individual becomes emotionally aroused, tense and alert, and calls upon psychological defense mechanisms and self-control in order to meet the danger. At the same time he may show some failure in adaptation by developing feelings of anxiety, aches and pains, or lowered efficiency. In the second stage, new defenses are brought into play, such as blaming others and denying that the problem exists. If these defenses are inadequate, neurotic patterns may gradually be introduced. He may then develop obsessions, compulsions, conversion symptoms or psychosomatic reactions. In rare cases these defenses may also prove insufficient, and psychotic reactions such as delusions may be adopted in order to reconstruct reality itself to conform to psychological needs. If these psychotic defenses are employed for a long period, he may reach the stage of exhaustion, in which the ego itself disintegrates, and a stage of disorganized activity or stupor sets in (Coleman, 1964).

GENERAL PARESIS. A syphilitic mental disorder caused by the destructive action of the spirochete germ on the brain.

This disease was formerly called general paralysis of the insane, dementia paralytica, or simply paresis. The descriptive term syphilitic meningo-encephalitis is also used to indicate that the germ has invaded the neural tissue of the brain, in contrast to meningo-vascular syphilis, in which the blood system and meninges (brain coverings) are the centers of infection.

The number of cases of general paresis is decreasing, due to reduced incidence and successful treatment of syphilis, and it now accounts for about 1 per cent of all first admissions to mental hospitals. For reasons unknown, only 3 per cent of untreated syphilitics develop this disorder, and it is far more prevalent among men than women, and among whites than Negroes.

There is a lengthy incubation period in general paresis, initial symptoms appearing between five and thirty years after the primary infection. A preclinical period, in which there are spinal fluid findings but no symptoms, may precede the appearance of symptoms. The onset of the disease is insidious, and the first outward signs can easily be overlooked. They consist in an exaggeration of previous personality traits, accompanied by irritability, forgetfulness, fatigue, periods of confusion, disturbed sleep, and headaches. At the same time there is a deterioration in manners, morals, and judgment, leading to a slovenly appearance, mistakes in work, and sexual excesses—all carried out with total unconcern and lack of insight. The early paretic cannot grasp finer shades of meaning, thinks slowly, makes few associations, and fails to react emotionally to situations of joy or sorrow. In addition, he gradually loses his memory and fills in the gaps with fabrications. See CONFABULATION.

As the disease advances, personality deterioration sets in, and one of three major reaction types develops, depending, in part at least, on premorbid personality trends. The distinctions here are somewhat arbitrary, since many patients cannot be readily classified or shift from one category to another. The most common form is the *demented or simple type.* In patients of this type mental deterioration, which occurs in all forms, develops without any special emotional coloring. There is a gradual loss of mental alertness, interest, and memory. The facial expression becomes increasingly vacant, and the patient usually takes on weight. He becomes withdrawn and apathetic, and may have hallucinations or delusions of a simple character.

In the *depressed type,* the patient becomes increasingly discouraged by his failing abilities, and later loses all insight and sinks into despondency. This mental state is usually accompanied by hypochondriacal and nihilistic delusions: he believes his brain or heart or bowels have ceased functioning, and that he is simply a hollow shell. Sometimes the depression takes an agitated form, and

may be accompanied by feelings of guilt and unworthiness. Ineffective suicidal attempts are not uncommon. As deterioration advances, the patient's mood may change to euphoria.

The *expansive type* is characterized by euphoria and grandiose ideas. In the early stages the patient is good-natured and insists that he feels wonderful and everything is perfect. Soon he develops delusions of grandeur and proposes plans and schemes that reach the height of absurdity. He claims that he has untold wealth and power, and offers fantastic solutions to huge problems without the slightest recognition of their unrealistic character. He blithely dismisses any attempt to question his ideas, but if the criticisms are pressed, he is likely to become irritated or even violent.

The paretic patient's mental symptoms are paralleled by a wide range of physical disturbances. The pupils become irregular in size and react sluggishly to light, or in some cases not at all (the Argyll-Robertson pupil or sign). The facial muscles sag and the expression becomes fatuous and vacant (the "ironed out facies"). Speech functions become increasingly disturbed; at first words are merely slurred or clipped, but later they become totally unintelligible. (The standard test is to ask the patient to say "Methodist Episcopal.") The patient's handwriting undergoes a similar deterioration; at first it is simply irregular or minute, but later on letters are omitted, syllables transposed, and finally it is reduced to an unintelligible scrawl. At the same time, motor coordination is affected, resulting in tremors of the tongue, face and fingers, as well as a shuffling, unsteady walk (locomotor ataxia). In time motor control deteriorates to a point where the patient cannot dress himself and becomes so weak that he must be confined to bed. These physical disturbances may be further complicated by sudden fevers, paralysis, and convulsions.

As general paresis enters the terminal period, all mental processes gradually come to a halt and all contact with the environment is lost. The patient can no longer take care of himself and sinks to a vegetative level of existence. Finally, infection sets in or body functions break down of themselves, and death follows. In untreated cases the disease takes from two to three years to run its course from the initial symptoms to death. For treatment, *see* SYPHILIS.

Illustrative Case: GENERAL PARESIS

She was an average pupil at school. At the age of fifteen years she had an illegitimate child before marrying another man when she was aged seventeen. Later she married again. Her work record as a waitress had been satisfactory. She denied any history of venereal infection.

Her relatives had noticed a marked change in her disposition and behavior during the four months previous to her admission to hospital in 1958. She "made silly remarks and did silly things," and told lies. Her gait was unsteady, her appetite voracious. At her brother's shop she had made a nuisance of herself, and on several occasions she had gone, unexpectedly, for long, solitary, motiveless walks; on one occasion the police brought her back from a railway line. In the month before admission she had twice been arrested for soliciting. Two days before admission to a mental hospital she had complained of acute abdominal pain, but examination in a general hospital proved negative. The pain subsided and she explained this by saying that she had had an appendectomy on the previous evening. She was mentally confused, gave a wrong home address, and stated that she had been working until the day before admission, when in fact she had not done outside work for several years.

In hospital she was in a foolish, happy, facile state. She was indifferent to her surroundings and answered questions at random. She announced that she was pregnant and expected a baby in two months; shortly afterward she said she had had a menstrual period one month ago. Asked to name the capital cities of Europe she said that when in Rome she had gone, dressed in ermine and diamanté, to dinner with Mussolini's son, and added, "The Mussolinis did very well during the war." Her memory was faulty, she lacked concentration and was disorientated.

Physically the pupils were unequal, the right was small, irregular, and did not react to light. Her tongue was coarsely tremulous. The Wasserman reaction was positive both in blood and cerebrospinal fluid. The Lange curve was of the paretic type 5555532210; there was no pleocytosis.

The patient was treated with procaine penicillin, 24 million units.

At the time of her discharge she was mentally well, and no organic mental defect could be demonstrated. Her serological abnormalities persisted and arrangements were made so that her condition could be constantly reviewed. (Henderson, Gillespie, and Batchelor, 1962)

GENERAL SEMANTICS. Semantics is the scientific study of the meaning of words and other signs or symbols.

A number of semanticists have been concerned not only with meaning in the technical sense, but also with the psychological and sociological aspects of language, especially the influence of words, signals, and gestures on human behavior. Attempts have been made to apply the study of semantics to psychotherapy, for two main reasons: (1) practically all emotional disturbances involve difficulties in communication of one kind or another, and (2) most of the techniques of psychotherapy depend on communication between therapist and patient. In this connection, D. G. Campbell (1937) has stated: "Upon communicability depends psychotherapy, which has as its first aim the re-establishment of lines of communication, and then, as its final goal the development of the communications-potentials of an individual to their utmost social value. . . . That psychiatrist will be most successful in therapy who has mastered the science and art of communication."

The first point—that specific problems of communication arise in most psychiatric conditions—can readily be illustrated. Conversion hysteria may be interpreted as a failure of communication between the patient and his unconscious drives; the drives then express themselves symbolically in terms of bodily disorders. In the treatment process these symptoms are regarded as "signs which are not only observed and interpreted by the therapist, but are to be read in a certain way" (Spiegel, 1959). This author gives the example of a patient who had a severe and painful cramp in her hand, a symptom which was found to stem from the fact that she had escaped from a train bound for Buchenwald: she was expressing her rage by symbolically strangling the Nazis who had killed her entire family. In extreme depression, retardation may be so great that "imagery stops, the flow of ideas becomes slowed, emotion flattens. There is little giving or receiving of communication. Seemingly, the impulse to communicate is lost." In the manic state, on the other hand, communication, if it can be called such, is a one-way affair: "The manic patient, however, despite his verbal flow, does not relate to others as receiver of their communication, and he tends to impose his verbal communication on others." The greatest outright disorganization of the communication system occurs in schizophrenia. The patient in a catatonic state is wholly severed from the outside world and verbal communication is given up completely (though symbolic gestures or posture and stereotyped expressions, termed verbigeration, sometimes remain). In simple schizophrenia communication is greatly reduced, and in paranoid conditions logic and imagery may both be distorted. In the hebephrenic state of "silliness," only "pseudocommunication" occurs—that is, fragments of words or gestures or sounds. *See* BODY LANGUAGE, VERBIGERATION, FLIGHT OF IDEAS, WORD SALAD.

Ruesch (1959) suggests three ways in which communication between therapist and patient can advance the therapeutic process. First, when the patient has someone to talk to—someone who understands and responds—the exchange, or "interpersonal feedback," gives him a sense of pleasure which encourages him to strive for further improvement. Second, the therapist helps the patient mobilize and organize internal material, material within himself of which he may not even have been aware—just as, in the case above, the psychiatrist helped the patient to see the connection already existing between her hand cramps and her experience during the war. Third, the therapist introduces new information so that the patient can expand his knowledge and compare his own experiences with those of other people. The three processes together help the patient sharpen his self-perception, clarify his emotional reactions, and develop new concepts and modes of expression to be used in modifying his self-image and relationships to other people.

Alfred Korzybski and Wendell Johnson have both attempted to apply the specific approach of semantics—that is, the study of meaning—to psychotherapy. Korzybski maintains that neurotic behavior actually *arises* from a failure to understand the meaning and use of words. In his view emotionally disturbed individuals as a whole are characterized by confusion, distortion, or vagueness in their basic concepts about themselves and other human beings. This he traces to a lack of clarity in the use of words as symbols. Semantic therapy, therefore, consists primarily in helping the patient rectify faulty word habits so that he can think clearly and critically about his aims, values, and relationships. The therapist puts the patient through a training procedure which includes, among other things, (a) actively searching for the meanings of key words he uses, (b) defining them in terms of the objects to which they may be applied, and (c) practicing the formation of clear abstractions from given facts. In this process the patient uncovers his unconscious assumptions and becomes aware of the emotional tones behind the words he has been using. And as the treatment proceeds, he gradually replaces his faulty values and behavior patterns with others that are more in keeping with reality.

Wendell Johnson takes the position that people bring on their own emotional difficulties by harping on distorted ideas about life, unrealistic ideas which carry built-in stress and frustration. He feels that a good part of the patient's problem arises from a failure to think clearly about goals and to consider the significance of the words he uses. He must be taught to improve his use of language and penetrate beneath the surface of words to their true meanings so that he can define his goals and formulate his problems more adequately. As he develops the ability to deal with his own inner thoughts and feelings and learns how to communicate more effectively, the patient acquires enough confidence to handle his relationships with other people more successfully.

GENERALIZATION (Stimulus and Response Generalization). The tendency to make the same response to new but similar stimuli.

Generalization is a basic principle of behavior and our greatest shortcut to learning. We would be totally handicapped if we had to learn everything individually and could not extend our knowledge from one situation to another. If we find a method that will solve one problem, we try it on other problems. If we learn to drive one type of car we usually find it easier to drive another. The same principle applies to a wide variety of experiences, both positive and negative. The child who nearly drowns in the bathtub may develop a fear of wading or swimming, and this fear may spread to water in general. The person who has had an unfortunate experience with a member of a minority may become prejudiced against the entire group. The troubled son of a domineering father may later defy teachers, employers, and others symbolic of authority, and the boy who has learned to live harmoniously with his parents will probably extend his co-operative attitude toward others. Generalization can therefore work for good or for ill.

The generalization process has been extensively studied in the laboratory, and two types have been distinguished. In stimulus generalization, the organism makes the same response to different stimuli that resemble each other—for example, if a dog is conditioned to raise his paw when a particular bell is sounded, he tends to make the same response to bells of any pitch. In response generalization, the dog may be conditioned to lift his left paw when the bell is sounded, but if that paw is held, he will usually lift the other (Bekhterev, 1932). See CONDITIONING.

Generalization is one of the major contributors to over-all adjustment. It gives us the tools to meet a constantly changing environment, and the ability to meet a large set of stimuli with a limited set of responses. If we could not make generalizations about individual people and groups of people, we would not be able to deal with them. If we were unable to transfer what we learn from school to life, there would be very little point in getting an education; and if scientists failed to discover general principles, our studies would have very little value anyway. Imagine the chaos and confusion if we had to learn a new way of reacting every time we met a new situation or a new person—and in fact, *every* situation and *every* person would be new because no two stimuli are absolutely identical!

We can, of course, go too far in the direction of generalization, as we do when we use stereotypes, clichés, and "glittering generalities." The only way to counterbalance the tendency to lump things, and people, together is to pay attention to differences as well as similarities. This process is known as discrimination. It is usually a more advanced and refined ability than the process of generalization, and requires extra effort to develop. The dog automatically reacts to the different bells as if they were the same; it takes extra training and conditioning to teach him to respond only to the bell that sounds a middle C. The child who fears the water must learn to distinguish between water situations that are dangerous and those that are not. And the man or woman who is prejudiced against whole groups of people must learn to judge each person for what he is. *See* DISCRIMINATION LEARNING, PREJUDICE, STEREOTYPE.

GENIUS. An individual who possesses an extreme degree of creative ability, usually demonstrated by exceptional achievement in an important field of endeavor.

Studies of geniuses have been plagued by problems of definition and by confusion with such characteristics as eminence and high IQ. The first systematic treatise on the subject, *Hereditary Genius,* was published by Francis Galton in 1869. Galton undertook to prove that genius is inherited by studying the genealogies of 1000 of Britain's most eminent statesmen, professional men, military and naval leaders. According to his calculations, one would expect to find only four eminent persons among the relatives of 1000 unselected British citizens, but in the family trees of his selected population he found well over 500. Galton believed that this finding established his thesis, but his study has been severely criticized. First, he judged eminence by his own personal standards and not by any objective criteria. And second, although eminence and genius are undoubtedly associated in some cases, there is no necessary connection

between them, since many people attain recognition through political favor, social prestige, or good fortune.

The most telling criticism of Galton's theory was the fact that he completely ignored the role of environment in developing talent. This oversight prompted a Swiss, A. De Candolle, to publish a reply in which he listed a number of influences that fostered creativeness among eminent European scientists. These included wealth, leisure, scientific traditions, educational opportunity, available libraries and laboratories, freedom to express opinion and follow the profession of their choice, and location in a temperate zone. He put so much stress on these environmental ideas that he went to the opposite extreme from Galton and excluded hereditary factors from any consideration. Thirty years later, James M. Cattell lent support to the environmental explanation by showing that more than half of a large group of American scientists came from the most favorably situated 1 per cent of the population. On this basis he also calculated that the son of a professional man was fifty times as likely to become a leading scientist as a son from a nonprofessional family.

Like Galton, Havelock Ellis investigated the background of prominent individuals, and in 1904 reported that they came chiefly from professional families. Although his study had obvious limitations, it contributed several positive findings. In contradistinction to the theory advanced by Cesare Lombroso and others that genius is akin to insanity, Ellis found that less than 2 per cent of his group of over 1000 had either mentally ill parents or offspring. He also discovered that they were often last-born children, who arrived when their parents were, on the average, thirty-seven years old. These findings tend to be verified by other investigations. Another of his conclusions, however, has been widely challenged. He noted that his group of 1000 included far more men than women and attributed the difference to the fact that males tend to extremes more often than females. Other investigators believe that the discrepancy was largely or wholly due to the fact that women were more closely tied to the home, and that social custom allowed them less opportunity to develop their abilities. *See* BIRTH ORDER.

Lewis Terman applied the term "genius" to children with an IQ of 140 or more, the upper 1 per cent. His long-term follow-up study of over 1000 of these children, starting in 1921, has contributed much to our understanding of the intellectually gifted—but it does not shed much light on genius in the accepted sense of the term. The subjects he studied turned out to be exceptionally well adjusted and well rounded, and many have become leaders in their field of work. However, even though they had passed the age of fifty in the last follow-up study, very few of them could be termed geniuses. Leta Hollingworth laid down more stringent requirements. She called children with an IQ of 180 or more *potential* geniuses, and estimated that they had one or two chances in ten of making a contribution that would justify calling them actual geniuses.

Terman's associate, Catharine Cox Miles, shed light on the relation between intelligence and genius by carefully studying the biographies of 300 famous persons, most of whom would be accepted as geniuses by virtue of their achievements. From her data three psychologists estimated that the IQs of these famous men and women averaged around 160. J. S. Mill and Galton, Goethe, Macauley, Pascal, Leibnitz, and Grotius were all assigned IQs over 180. The most interesting aspect of this investigation is not the average but the *range* of IQs, which varied all the way from 100 to 200. Abraham Lincoln scored between 125 and 140, Benjamin Franklin 145, and Napoleon be-

tween 135 and 140. While these are high scores, they are often equaled or exceeded by students, professional persons, and others. What is more, Miles noted that the geniuses she studied had many favorable personality traits, among them persistence, self-discipline, independence, self-confidence, and strength of character—and most of them had other distinct advantages, including able relatives, cultured homes, and good schooling. She concluded that three types of factors usually combine to produce genius: natural ability, personality traits, and environment.

Two leading psychiatrists have attempted to explain genius in terms of personality dynamics. Alfred Adler attributed exceptional achievement to overcompensation for feelings of inferiority. Such feelings may be due to a variety of factors, including low social status, parental criticism, or physical shortcomings (Napoleon's short stature). Adler held that many individuals react to feelings of inferiority by developing their abilities to the utmost, but he also seemed to assume that those who become geniuses must possess outstanding ability in the first place. Freud and other psychoanalysts, on the other hand, believed that geniuses are basically conflicted and frustrated persons who solve their emotional problems by expressing themselves through works of art and science. Although analytic theory attributes genius to the same psychodynamic roots as neurosis and psychosis, it holds that geniuses resolve their difficulties through socially recognized activities, while other disturbed individuals express themselves in more socially unacceptable ways. In other words, the average neurotic or psychotic produces symptoms, while the genius produces positive contributions to society.

Psychoanalytic theories start with the assumption that geniuses are born with exceptional ability, but their psychological conflicts provide the motivating forces that lead them to a full development of their potential. The work of a genius is interpreted as a sublimation of instinctual drives. Since he is in basic conflict with society, this expression is bound to be unconventional, and since he is extremely talented, it is also likely to be constructive. In the realm of art, the sublimations are believed to reflect basic psychosexual phenomena, as shown by the Oedipal situations of Shakespeare's *Hamlet,* Euripides' *Oedipus Rex* and Stendahl's *Le Rouge et le Noir.* Such works are elaborations of fantasy that express the unconscious through the same distortions and disguises that occur in dreams.

According to psychoanalytic theory scientific work is also a form of sublimation, and has artistic value in the elegance of its theories and the uniqueness of its experiments. Sublimations, however, are not fantasies in this case, but represent the scientist's attempt to come to closer grips with reality, and to work through his conflicts in a way that will gain him acceptance and recognition by the world at large.

The psychoanalytic approach has been severely questioned by many studies which indicate that genius does not depend on psychological conflict or abnormality. While a long list of disturbed or frustrated geniuses can be assembled (for example, Dostoevski, Van Gogh, Joan of Arc, Napoleon), an equally impressive list of undeniable geniuses who did not suffer from basic conflicts can be cited (Bach, Einstein, Churchill). Moreover, a carefully conducted study by Juda (1949) has shown that genius does not depend on psychological abnormality; and an investigation of highly creative individuals made by MacKinnon (1962) has disclosed no relationship between creativity and psychopathology. The major characteristics of the subjects in the latter study included not only openness to new experience and richness of per-

sonality, but self-acceptance and lack of defensiveness. It may be that personality studies of this kind—plus recognition of inherent ability—will eventually give us clues to the true nature of genius. *See* GALTON, TERMAN, GIFTED CHILDREN, CATTELL, ADLER, SUBLIMATION.

GESELL, ARNOLD LUCIUS (1880–1961). Gesell, the leading authority on child development, was born in Wisconsin and graduated from the State University. After receiving his Ph.D. degree from Clark University in 1906, he taught psychology at Los Angeles State Normal School. In 1911 he was appointed professor of education at Yale, founding the Yale Psycho-Clinic (later changed to Yale Clinic of Child Development) in the same year. In 1915 he obtained a medical degree at Yale Medical School, and taught child hygiene there until 1948. The Gesell Institute of Child Development was established in his honor in 1915, and he was active as research consultant until 1958. During his long professional career, these centers trained many pediatricians and child psychologists who practiced their profession all over the world.

Gesell's voluminous bibliography contains over 400 items, including among others, papers on cerebral palsy, mongolism, cretinism, visual deviations, and studies of twins. Many of his earlier works dealt with investigations of infancy and the preschool years. His major books in this field are *The Mental Growth of the Preschool Child* (1925), *Infancy and Human Growth* (1928), *Infant Behavior* (1934), *Developmental Diagnosis* (1941) and *Infant and Child in the Culture of Today* (1943). Later he turned his attention to the development of the child during the school years, publishing *The Child from Five to Ten* in 1946 and *Youth: the Years from Ten to Sixteen* in the same year. His last book was *Vision: Its Develop-*

ment in Infant and Child, published in 1949. *See* ADOLESCENCE (THEORIES).

Gesell's major contributions lie in the study of changes in behavior patterns from the fetal period through adolescence. In his opinion, behavior develops in a predictable and measurable sequence, although the exact timing is not identical from child to child. This view is based on a belief that the organism goes through a cycle of "morphogenetic events" that enable it to progress in an orderly way in terms of the activities it can perform. He held that emerging behavior patterns have as much structure as does the growing physical organism. In describing the process of development, he stressed an alternation of ages of flexion and extension, inwardness and outwardness, equilibrium and disequilibrium, which he believed to be in accord with a principle of reciprocal neuromotor activity. Thus the child has more internal tensions at age three than at two, and is more unstable at thirteen than at fourteen or sixteen.

These sequential changes meant that "behavior has shape." He believed this shape is basically determined by internal forces rather than by environmental factors, which in his opinion can only modify, inflect, and support the progressive changes that occur. This emphasis on maturation was not readily accepted, since it was formulated at a time when behaviorism had come to the fore and was taking an extreme environmentalist position on the development of the personality.

Most of Gesell's research on infant development was carried out in a controlled test situation. He placed the infants in a specially contructed dome, and filmed their spontaneous activities as well as their reactions to various objects and stimuli such as a bell or a pellet. He and his associates would make a detailed behavior analysis of the films and other records, comparing the results with findings on other normal subjects. Many of the films were made available to other universities and child study centers for teaching and demonstration purposes. Gesell was also one of the first investigators to make use of one-way screen observations and the "co-twin control" method. The latter technique was used to test the effects of learning versus maturation—for example, he would allow one identical twin to go through a learning experience, such as climbing steps, and a few weeks later compare his performance with that of the other twin to see if maturation took place during those weeks. He later extended his investigations to the less structured situations of the home and schoolroom. *See* TWINS.

Gesell's influence was, and is, extremely pervasive, but it is too early to evaluate its full effect. The Gesell Developmental Tests are given at many clinics, and are especially useful in assessing neurological defect. Another direct effect of his work is the inclusion of a section on the development of infant behavior in the admittance examination of the American Academy of Pediatrics. But the best indication of his influence is the fact that his books have been widely used as texts in colleges and teacher-training schools, as well as by the public itself, and his sequences of development are constantly cited by authorities in psychology and psychiatry, although many investigators put more emphasis on variations and individual differences than did Gesell. Beyond this, we can say that a great many specialists agree with the comment made by the *Yale Register* at the time of his death: "Dr. Gesell was a pioneer, one who traced unchartered paths to chartered conclusions."

GESTALT PSYCHOLOGY. An approach to behavior which emphasizes the organization of experience into patterns or configurations ("Gestalten," plural, in German).

The Gestalt viewpoint was developed as a revolt against two other approaches. First, it opposed the structuralist view that the best way to understand experience is to analyze it into simpler components called sensations, just as a chemist might reduce a complex compound to its elements. The method used by the structuralists was introspection, the systematic analysis of conscious experience. The second approach was that of behaviorism, which abandoned introspection in favor of an objective, quantitative, experimental study of behavior. This theory also held that complex behavior is built up of elementary components, but in this case the "building blocks" were believed to be simple, learned responses to stimuli known as conditioned reflexes.

In contrast to both of these approaches, Gestalt psychologists hold that experience and behavior contain basic patterns and relationships which cannot be reduced to simpler components. Put simply, the whole is greater than the sum of its parts. Moreover, these totalities give our experiences a distinctive and meaningful character, whether we are dealing with insight into a human personality, perception of a geometrical figure, or the dynamic relationships among a group of people. Such phenomena can only be understood by viewing them as a whole instead of dissecting them into bits and pieces.

The Gestalt viewpoint was launched into prominence by a crucial experiment conducted by Max Wertheimer in 1912. He showed that when two lines were flashed successively at an optimal interval, subjects reported that the first appeared to move toward the second—an illusion which is basic to motion pictures. Wertheimer pointed out that the experience of motion was a new characteristic created by the relationships between the lines, a characteristic that would not be recognized by an introspective analysis that reduced the experience to two separate sensations of light. This dramatic example led not only to hundreds of other illustrations of Gestalt principles, but to a new procedure based on the phenomenological approach. It consisted of "naïve inspection" or "pure awareness" of the raw facts of experience, to be reported without elaboration or analysis. This led to the discovery of patterns and configurations that would be overlooked or actually destroyed by artificial fragmentation. *See* PHENOMENOLOGY.

The Gestalt approach has made its greatest contribution in the field of perception, and many important relationships have been discovered. The most fundamental is the principle that all our perceptions are organized into a figure that has a well-defined contour, solidity, and depth, and a background that is less well defined—for example, this book is a figure, and the surrounding room is the background. When we shift our attention to another object such as a picture, the picture becomes the figure and the wall behind it becomes the ground. This tendency to experience the world in terms of figure and ground, like the other Gestalt phenomena, does not depend on learning, but is considered to be a spontaneous, inevitable consequence of man's perceptual apparatus. *See* FIGURE-GROUND PERCEPTION.

SOME PRINCIPLES OF GESTALT PSYCHOLOGY, BASED ON THE PERCEPTION OF PATTERNS

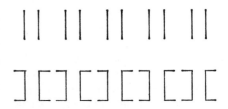

Fig. 24. The top lines are grouped according to the principle of proximity, and the bottom lines according to the principle of closure.

Fig. 25. The lines are organized into a word instead of being viewed separately.

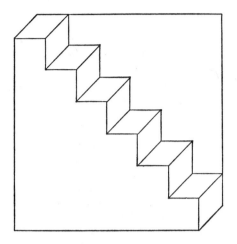

Fig. 26. The staircase changes as a whole when we focus on the near edge of the middle step.

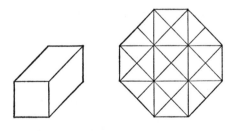

Fig. 27. The pattern at the right is so dominant that we fail to see that it contains the figure at the left—a principle used in camouflage.

Other important "laws of primitive organization" can be readily illustrated. The *law of proximity* states that events experienced close together in time or space will be grouped together: the top lines in Fig. 24 are seen as five pairs, rather than ten separate lines. The *law of similarity* states that similar items tend to be organized into a pattern. The *principle of closure* means that

we read unity into our experiences: Fig. 25 will easily be read as the word "plane," although the letters are not complete. Gestaltists believe that a single general principle underlies all these tendencies, the *principle of Prägnanz* (pregnance). According to this concept, perceptions take on the most stable possible form under the circumstances. We see the separate lines that make up "plane" as a single word because the word resists dismemberment or "fractionation" better than the separate lines and because it appears to be the easiest, most tensionless and most meaningful way of viewing these lines. Moreover, this tendency is not limited to visual perception. We group separate musical notes into melodies, feel two pin pricks near each other on our arm as a single unit, and "round out" a story by supplying missing details or a happy ending.

Gestalt psychologists have also attempted to explain the way the brain organizes the neural impulses it receives from the senses. They hold that the form of our perceptual experience corresponds to, but is not identical with, the form or configuration of the brain excitation in the same way that a topographical map reflects the relationships in a landscape but is not a literal transcription of it. Our "mental map," in other words, is a true representation of the physical world but not a photographic copy of it. It mirrors the world with enough exactitude, however, to allow us to function in it.

This principle, named "isomorphism" (literally, "similar form"), is one of the key concepts of the movement. It holds that all perception depends on activities which take place in the brain. These activities have one major function: they *organize* sensations into balanced, stable patterns in much the same way that the interplay of internal and external forces shape an oil drop into a symmetrical form (Köhler, 1929), or a magnetic field aligns iron filings into a well-defined order (and if we add new filings, it will reorganize them into a new equilibrium).

The theory of isomorphism is far less accepted than the principles of perceptual organization introduced by the Gestalt psychologists. If it were true, any interference with brain activity would obstruct or distort perception, and yet this is not the case. When an electric current was passed through the visual area of the brain of subjects engaged in various mental problems, it did not interfere with their functioning (Thomas and Stewart, 1957). Also, extensive lesions in the visual cortex of monkeys and cats (Lashley, Chow, and Semmes, 1951), as well as the implantation of pieces of gold foil into their brains (Sperry, Miner, and Myers, 1955) did not affect their ability to perceive patterns.

Many of the principles of perceptual organization have also been applied to the investigation of learning and thinking. One major contribution has been the study of insight, the sudden perception of relationships that leads to the solution of a problem. Since the details have been given elsewhere, only one point will be made here. The problem, such as reaching an object that is beyond one's grasp, apparently sets up a state of tension or disequilibrium, and we attempt to resolve this disagreeable state by restructuring our thinking. In so doing, we reorganize what is already there, search for new relationships, or bring in new possibilities. If we are successful, this process makes us perceive the situation in a different light, and the solution abruptly suggests itself. The basic idea, then, is one of organization and reorganization. *See* INSIGHT.

Studies of perception and insight have led to a number of significant contributions to education. In his early experiments with animals, Köhler observed that when chimpanzees solved a problem through insight—for example,

piling up boxes to reach a piece of fruit—they not only retained the solution and quickly applied it to the same problem again, but were able to transfer their insight to other problems of a similar nature. Wertheimer followed these leads in experiments with young children. For instance, he had them learn to solve a mathematical problem by rote memory or "blind repetition," and showed that afterward they were completely lost when they attempted to solve a problem that was only slightly different from the one they learned— nor could they explain why the rote memory solution worked in the first place. However, if they were given insight into the principles on which the solution was based, they understood it better, retained it longer, and applied it more productively. This approach has been substantiated by recent experiments in which elementary school children have been successfully taught not only foreign languages, but the difficult subject of calculus. The key is to emphasize principles and illustrate them with examples from everyday life—in other words, to help the pupil organize his thinking and perceive meaningful relationships. These are the basic features of the Gestalt approach.

Although Gestalt psychology is largely a theory of perception, one noteworthy attempt has been made to apply its principles to psychotherapy. The object of treatment, according to Perls, Hefferline, and Goodman (1951), is to overcome the fragmentation of feeling, thinking, and acting which is so characteristic of our culture, and replace it with a holistic, unitary outlook on life. This can be done, they claim, by encouraging a more flexible relationship between the individual and his environment or, in Gestalt terms, between figure and ground. The attitudes of neurotics and psychotics, they hold, tend to be rigid and fixated—their figure-ground formation is dominated by compulsions, anxieties, and confusion instead of by healthy interest, excitement, and concern. In attempting to overcome emotional disturbance, the Gestalt therapist does not probe for repressed feelings and experiences, as in psychoanalysis, but seeks to discover the repressing forces which the individual is employing, since these forces stand in the way of personality flexibility and growth. By setting up experimental situations, or exercises, the therapist helps the patient to become aware of his blocks and resistances, and eventually arrive at a more creative and elastic adjustment to reality. Therapy is terminated when he reconstructs his self along more organized, effective lines.

GIFTED CHILDREN. The 1 per cent of children with IQs above 135 or 140. Children with IQs above 170 or 180 are usually termed extremely gifted.

At one time it was taken for granted that gifted children were bound to be frail, one-sided, and eccentric. As a result of extensive research, it is now recognized that, taken as a whole, they are more often above than below average in all major characteristics, though particularly outstanding in intellectual ability.

In the early years of life these children show more curiosity, ask more questions, and explore more widely than other children. As they grow, they develop far larger and richer vocabularies, start reading even before entering school (often teaching themselves), and almost immediately acquire a voracious appetite for books of all kinds. In addition, they show superior ability to remember and profit from their experiences, accept more responsibility, and make more mature moral judgments than the average child. These characteristics are generally accompanied by excellent health, superior physical development, and good character, as well as sound emotional ad-

justment and a wider than average range of interests.

This is not to say that gifted children have no problems. Although they usually do superior work in school, there are many exceptions. Some become bored, easygoing, or disenchanted with school—especially when no attempt is made to put them in special classes or involve them in special projects. Others work far below their capacity because they are afraid they will not be popular if they are too far ahead of their classmates. A "sizable minority" have trouble with social relationships, and about 20 per cent have hidden emotional problems, according to a study conducted by Gallagher and Crowder (1957). It has also been found that many of these children have a surprisingly low opinion of themselves, apparently because they cannot live up to their own high standards.

Understandably, the *extremely* gifted are especially subject to these difficulties. These are the children with towering IQs, whose achievements take on legendary proportions—for example, the second grade girl who read seven books at her own age level in a single afternoon so that she could finish *Green Pastures* before bedtime (Dunlap, 1958); or the eight-year-old boy who had already studied geology and astronomy, had achieved a reading knowledge of Latin and Spanish, and could carry on a conversation in French, German and Italian (Hollingworth, 1942). Children of this kind are seldom antisocial or actively maladjusted, but they are frequently asocial and uninterested in their age mates or their activities. They tend to live in a different world from their peers and sometimes from their parents as well.

Studies conducted by Terman and his associates (1925) have given us some remarkably definite answers to questions about both the background and the later development of gifted children. Starting in 1921, data were gathered on 1000 children who had a mean age of ten and a mean IQ of 140. One interesting finding was that the great majority came from the higher socioeconomic levels (with professional or business parents), while only 7 per cent came from the lowest economic level—a fact that can probably be explained by both hereditary and environmental factors. The indications are that their superiority in interest patterns as well as emotional and social adjustment (as mentioned above) are due largely to the stimulating home surroundings. Recently, Laycock and Caylor (1964) found that similar groups of gifted children were above average in physical development, but not physically superior to their intellectually normal brothers and sisters. This suggests that their physical development is also in large part a reflection of a superior home environment.

Do gifted children make good the "promise of youth," or do they burn out as they grow older? Since their initial selection, Terman and his associates have made periodic follow-up studies to see how the 1000 gifted children developed. Reports published by Terman and Oden in 1947 and 1959 revealed that 85 per cent of the girls and 90 per cent of the boys attended college, and took three times their share of honors even though they averaged two years younger than their classmates. A few who did not achieve as well as might be expected were found to live under severe home tensions, or had deliberately neglected their studies in favor of other pursuits. Although they graduated during the depression, less than 1 per cent were unemployed in 1936, and some had already achieved national reputations. About 150 out of the 750 who were contacted were judged very successful by such criteria as holding responsible managerial positions and recognition by Who's Who and American Men of Science. Even though the others had received less public recognition, most of them were rated more success-

ful than people of average intelligence. Studies made of the relatively few who had become school dropouts, criminals, or vocational misfits indicated that personality factors rather than intellectual ability made the difference. These individuals, unlike the great majority, were poorly adjusted emotionally and poorly motivated to achieve success. *See* TERMAN, PRODIGY, GENIUS.

GILLES DE LA TOURETTE SYNDROME. (Tic de Guinon, tic convulsive, multiple tics with coprolalia, imbacco). A rare disorder of unknown etiology found in Asia and Africa; first described by a Paris physician, Georges Gilles de la Tourette, in 1885.

The syndrome has its onset in childhood between the ages of five and fifteen, starting with spasms of the eye muscles, which later spread to other facial muscles, then to the neck, upper extremities, and in some cases the entire body. These involuntary spasms are accompanied by throat noises, animalistic sounds ("aboiement"—"barking"), and ejaculation of phrases and sentences which are often of an obscene nature (coprolalia). As the disease progresses, the dominant symptoms of latah gradually appear, but as Arieti and Meth (1959) state, "It is more than doubtful that Gilles de la Tourette's disease is a special form of the latah syndrome. Perhaps it is a combination of the two conditions." *See* EXOTIC PSYCHOSES.

The disease runs an unpredictable course, and the prognosis is generally unfavorable. In some cases the paroxysms last for weeks or months, then gradually abate; in others the symptoms remain unchanged; and in still others the patient becomes progressively worse and develops a severe obsessive-compulsive neurosis or even a psychosis that resembles schizophrenia.

GLOBUS HYSTERICUS. The distressing feeling of a lump in the throat, sometimes accompanied by choking sensations. When medical examination reveals that there is nothing wrong with the throat, as is usually the case, the condition is diagnosed as globus hystericus—that is, a hysterical, or conversion, reaction in which an acute conflict or threatening impulse is expressed as a physical symptom.

There appear to be two general reasons why the throat is affected. It is not only a sensitive part of the body, but is associated with two basic drives: hunger and communication. Sometimes the difficulty can be traced to "distasteful" situations that seem to be symbolically or metaphorically related to the throat as an organ involved in eating: "I couldn't swallow that kind of treatment." In other cases it is more directly related to communication: "Whenever I try to answer him, my voice gets stuck in my throat."

A full discussion of current personal problems with a therapist will usually lead to increased self-understanding and more effective ways of coping with the situations that precipitated the symptom. In such cases the lump will almost always disappear. Sometimes, however, the globus is an expression of a more deep-seated neurotic pattern, and there may be other conversion symptoms as well. Such cases require more extended psychotherapy. *See* CONVERSION REACTION.

GLUTAMIC ACID. An amino acid which plays an important role in the chemistry of the brain and nervous system.

This protein "building block" is found in large quantities in milk, meat and cereals but is also available in pure form. Since it helps to maintain oxygen uptake in the brain, and therefore appeared to be crucial to nervous system functioning, psychologists began experimenting with it about twenty-five years ago. Albert and Warden (1944) found that when powdered glu-

tamic acid was mixed with food for rats, it seemed to improve their learning ability in problem-box experiments. Large doses were then given to mentally retarded children, and the first results were promising. One group, for example, showed a seven point increase on the Stanford-Binet intelligence test over a six months period of treatment (Zimmerman et al., 1947). However, studies which used better controls failed to repeat these findings (Arbitman, 1952).

In 1960, Astin and Ross reviewed 30 animal and human experiments with glutamic acid. About half of them yielded clearly negative results. The other half were positive but inadequately controlled. The early hope for this substance has therefore not been realized. There is no conclusive evidence that it increases the intelligence of either normal or mentally retarded individuals. It is interesting, however, that certain types of mental retardation, such as phenylketonuria and congenital galactosemia, respond to nutritional treatment of a different type when it is administered early in life. See these topics.

Although glutamic acid cannot be used to raise the intelligence of the retarded, it apparently has a positive effect on patients with senile psychosis: "L-glutavite, a mixture containing L-glutamate plus vitamins (nicotinic acid, pyridoxine, thiamine, etc.), iron, and calcium, has been reported as helpful in rendering the patient more active, more interested in his surroundings, and more inclined to participate in ward activities—reading, playing, attending social functions." (Ferraro, 1959)

GODDARD,   HENRY   HERBERT (1866–1957). A graduate of Haverford College, Goddard became one of the pioneer clinical psychologists in this country. In 1906 he founded the Vineland Training School for Feebleminded Children at Vineland, New Jersey, and served as its director until 1918. During World War I he helped to develop tests used to screen candidates for different branches of the service, and soon after the war was appointed Professor of Psychology at Ohio State University, where he remained until his retirement in 1938. His most influential books were *The Kallikak Family* (1912), *Feeblemindedness, Its Cause and Consequences* (1914), *School Training of Defective Children* (1915), and *The School Training of Gifted Children* (1928).

While at Vineland, Goddard made an important contribution to intelligence testing by translating and modifying the Binet scale for American use. The revised test was employed in the detection of different degrees of feeblemindedness, and one result was the introduction of the "moron" category. He applied this term to adults with a mental age of eight to ten or eleven years and an IQ of 50 to 70, and showed that these individuals were usually capable of holding productive jobs at the level of janitor, laborer, sewing machine operator, and waitress.

The next step in Goddard's study of mental deficiency was prompted by Francis Galton's book, *Hereditary Genius,* which sought to prove that genius was inherited by tracing the ancestry of eminent individuals. Goddard decided to apply this "pedigree method" to mental defectives, and in the course of his work discovered that a pupil at the Vineland Training School and some derelicts in the vicinity had the same last name as a prominent family in the community. Investigations revealed that a soldier in the Revolutionary War was the common ancestor of both of these groups. To keep the family name confidential, Goddard applied the fictitious name Martin Kallikak (Greek for good-bad) to this man, and later published a widely read book entitled *The Kallikak Family* (1912). In it he reported that Martin had fathered an illegitimate male child by a retarded girl, and this individual, known as "old

horror," produced a chain of 480 traceable descendants, of whom 143 were considered defective and only 46 known to be normal. After the war, Martin married a normal woman, and this union produced 496 traceable descendants, only three of whom were known to be defective. The descendants of this line included many eminent citizens—businessmen, doctors, political leaders, etc.—and several New Jersey towns were named after them. Crime, illegitimacy, epilepsy, alcoholism, and mental illness were virtually nonexistent in this branch of the family, while they were extremely prevalent in the other branch.

Goddard believed these findings firmly established heredity as the prime factor in mental defect. In doing so he grossly underestimated the effect of environmental factors, almost entirely ignoring the fact that the "degenerate branch" grew up under conditions of squalor and neglect, while the "eminent branch" were raised in well-to-do and cultivated homes. He apparently assumed that since both families lived in the same geographical locale, they were both subject to the same environmental influences. But in spite of the fact that his conclusions were naïve and one-sided, the investigation is considered a landmark in the attempt to apply a genetic approach to the study of mental deficiency.

Goddard continued his genetic studies, and in his book *Feeblemindedness, Its Cause and Consequences,* he claimed that mental defect is due to a recessive trait and follows the laws of heredity laid down by Mendel. As evidence, he studied the family trees of two people and predicted with considerable accuracy the intellectual ability of their offspring. However, he incorrectly assumed that hereditary mental defect (when it does occur) is produced by a single gene rather than by many interacting genes. His procedure was also vitiated by the fact that he disregarded gradations of ability and arbitrarily grouped his subjects into subgroups of high and low intelligence. As with *The Kallikak Family,* the chief importance of this work lay in stimulating discussion of the problem and suggesting factors that must be taken into account in solving it. *See* GALTON, MENTAL RETARDATION (CAUSES), MENTAL RETARDATION (TYPES).

GONADS. The sex glands, consisting of the testes in the male and the ovaries in the female. These glands serve the double purpose of (1) secreting hormones that influence bodily development and behavior; and (2) producing gametes, or sex cells (sperms or ova), for reproduction.

There are three general classes of gonadal hormones: the estrogens, the androgens, and the progestins. They are all chemically related and are secreted in varying amounts by the ovaries, testes, adrenal cortex and placenta. The two most active androgens, testosterone and androsterone, are principally produced in the testes; the two most active estrogens, estradiol and esterone, are produced in the ovaries and the placenta; and the primary progestin, progesterone, is produced in the ovaries and placenta of the pregnant female.

The gonads secrete small amounts of hormones into the blood stream during childhood, but do not have a pronounced effect on development until the onset of adolescence. This period, which begins at about 10 or 11 in girls and 13 or 14 in boys, is marked by a sharp rise in the output of sex hormones. The gonads become increasingly active, first bringing about the bodily changes that prepare the individual for parenthood, then producing the mature sperm or eggs two to four years later. This marks the beginning of puberty, when reproduction is first possible, but adolescence continues for a few more years until the boy or girl has reached his full stature and maturity.

The bodily changes during adolescence are too well-known to require detailed description. In the male, the testicular androgens, aided by adrenal and thyroid hormones, stimulate muscular and skeletal growth, change of voice, and the maturation of the reproductive organs. They are also responsible for the development of sexual desire, nocturnal emissions, and the aggressive behavior of adolescent boys. In the female, sexual maturation is controlled by both types of hormones secreted by the ovaries. The estrogens stimulate the growth of the internal reproductive organs, and then produce the more obvious changes that occur in adolescence, such as the budding of the breasts, the growth of pubic hair and the widening of the hips. They are also responsible for the menarche, or first stage of menstruation, which ordinarily occurs between eleven and fourteen. Menstruation, however, does not mark the start of puberty in the full sense of the term since pregnancy is not possible until several months later. In the interim, the second female hormone, progestin, becomes active and prepares the uterus for supporting and nourishing a fetus. When this has been accomplished, the girl has reached sexual maturity and ordinarily ceases to grow. The boy, on the other hand, continues to grow for a few years after reaching puberty. *See* SEX DRIVE, MENSTRUAL DISORDERS, ADOLESCENCE.

GRADIENT. As used in the study of motivation, the graduated change in the strength of drives in situations involving conflict—that is, the degree to which we feel pulled in different directions.

Everyone experiences these variations in response. A worker, prodded by his wife, makes up his mind that it is time for a raise. He decides to face the boss directly, but when the fatal moment approaches his resolution begins to waver and he becomes increasingly hesitant. At last he screws up his courage and, after a few more false starts, eventually goes into the boss's office and states his case—or he may at the last minute decide that he is running too great a risk, or that there is no immediate need for the raise.

These graduated changes, or gradients, can be duplicated in any number of situations involving attitudes and decisive action: choosing a career, getting engaged or married, retiring from work. They are based on the fact that we frequently have ambivalent attitudes toward our goals. We find them both desirable and undesirable, attractive but fraught with danger, immediately satisfying but involving questionable consequences. This creates a tug of war, known technically as an "approach-avoidance conflict": we have an urge to achieve the goal, but we also have a counter-urge to avoid it. Moreover, as Miller (1959) has pointed out, both these tendencies vary in relative strength, and we can therefore speak of an "approach gradient" and an "avoidance gradient." See AMBIVALENCE.

In concrete terms, when the worker was at home, his approach gradient was high, his avoidance gradient low, but as he neared the "point of no return"—the boss's office—these gradients came so close to being so equal in strength that he vacillated and temporized. It is important to note that a prolonged period of vacillation actually has the effect of avoidance, since the goal is constantly being put off. Many an opportunity is lost out of pure indecision. It should also be recognized that the strength of the avoidance gradient generally increases more rapidly than the strength of the approach gradient as we get closer to an ambivalent goal. In other words, our hesitation tends to increase as we approach the moment of decision or action. Nevertheless, we can often overcome this hesitation by "accentuating the positive." If this did not occur, the marriage

rate would certainly be far lower than it is.

The Miller studies have also shown that the approach and avoidance gradients can be altered by changes in motivation. If the fearful employee postpones his visit to the boss, his need for money may become so desperate that he will eventually overcome his hesitation. In fact, it can become so strong that it will abolish the conflict altogether, and he will march right into the boss's office without further thought. If, on the other hand, his wife punctures his self-confidence, or if he hears that the boss has fired other men because they asked for a raise, his determination may recede to a point where avoidance wins out.

Many situations involve more than two gradients. The drinker is not merely torn between the pleasant effects of alcohol and the discomfort of a hangover; his decision may also be contingent on his desire to escape responsibility, his responsibility to his family, religious considerations, fear of loss of control, desire for companionship and so on. Situations of this kind complicate the picture, but they can still be described psychologically in terms of gradients.

The study of gradients brings out two outstanding facts about behavior. First, it emphasizes the fact that we are constantly being faced by ambivalent situations, and it is useful to analyze our conflicts in terms of the strength of our positive and negative "pulls." Although we may not be able to measure these pulls with any degree of accuracy, it is important to recognize what they are. Second, it is equally important to realize that goals are frequently attractive at a distance because we lose sight of their negative aspects, but as we approach them and have to grapple with them at close quarters, we find ourselves beset with problems that have to be overcome. If we are aware of this fact, we will be more likely to prepare ourselves in advance to meet those problems. *See* VALENCE.

GRANDIOSE DELUSIONS (Delusions of Grandeur). Delusions of great power, wealth, or self-importance. The patient believes he has a private key to Fort Knox, owns fifty-seven Rolls-Royces, or was descended directly from Genghis Khan.

Grandiose ideas occur in a number of psychoses. In paranoid schizophrenia they are often transient and confused. In "true" paranoia they tend to be well-organized, persistent, and unmodifiable. This type of delusion is also found in cases of general paresis, probably as a form of wish-fulfillment or as a reaction to failing powers. Preoccupation with grandiose, "expansive" ideas or schemes is sometimes referred to as megalomania. *See* DELUSION, SCHIZOPHRENIA (PARANOID TYPE), PARANOIA, GENERAL PARESIS.

GRAPHOLOGY. The investigation of personality through analysis of handwriting.

Handwriting interpretation has been called the oldest projective technique. The Chinese used it as a means of character study as long ago as the eleventh century, and the Abbé Michon invented the name graphology early in the seventeenth century. Theoretically an individual's writing would seem to be an ideal source of information about his personality, since it is a unique personal product that is relatively consistent over a long period of time. It has been shown that no two people make the same movements even when copying the same model. Moreover, since feelings of confidence, inferiority, and other tendencies are known to be reflected in posture, voice, and facial expression, it would seem to follow that handwriting might also be a mirror of the inner man.

Many psychologists would accept this general point of view, but few would agree that an adequate method of handwriting analysis has been discovered. This opinion is shared by most American psychologists, but in Europe graphology is far more accepted and is widely used in personnel selection. The attitude of American psychologists stems largely from a number of experiments that have yielded inconclusive or negative results. In a study conducted in 1919, Hull and Montgomery examined the published works of a number of professional graphologists and selected six character traits which they claimed to be associated with specific handwriting characteristics: ambition and pride were associated with an upward slope of writing, bashfulness with fine writing, force of character with heavy writing and heavy bars on t's, perseverance with long t bars, reserve with the openness of a's and o's. The investigators then asked a group of college students to write the same paragraph, and had their fraternity brothers rate them on the six character traits. Finally, they carefully measured the handwriting and correlated these measurements with the character traits. The results showed no evidence whatever for the graphologists' claims.

Critics of this experiment, notably Allport and Vernon (1933), pointed out that many graphologists have abandoned the idea of relating specific character traits to specific patterns of writing. However, their own attempts to relate general personality characteristics to general handwriting characteristics did not yield impressive results.

In another influential experiment, trained graphologists and college students with no knowledge of graphology were asked to judge personality traits from handwriting samples. Little difference was found in the over-all accuracy of the two groups. They both scored better than chance on some traits, but there were just as many judgments in the wrong direction on others (Guilford, 1959). Other studies have employed the technique of matching handwriting samples with personality sketches. Here, too, the results have not been promising. In one investigation, groups of college students and faculty members scored slightly above chance—but, interestingly, the average score made by seventeen graphologists was not much higher, although seven of them did considerably better than their colleagues (Powers, 1930).

Psychologists who tend to be positively disposed toward graphology believe it is misleading to expect a full and accurate personality diagnosis on the basis of graphic signs alone. But they claim that handwriting analysis can be a valuable tool when used in conjunction with other projective tests, such as the TAT and Rorschach, since it can record individual behavior patterns and expressive movements which other tests do not deal with. A number of systems have therefore been proposed for clinical use, and though they differ in details, there are some fairly common elements. The paper, or "writing field," is held to be symbolic of the external world, and the writing itself is believed to be indicative of the way the individual characteristically interacts with his environment. As many as twenty to twenty-five variables are used in appraising some characteristics—for example, personality control is indicated by the size of small letters, direction of lines, space between words, slant, and pressure. These and other features show whether the writing is overcontrolled, a sign of inhibition; undercontrolled, a sign of impulsivity; a combination of the two, an indication of internal conflict; or rhythmic and well-balanced, a sign of "flexible adaptation and productive co-ordination"—in other words, a healthy, effective personality.

To be more specific, the handwriting is judged to be overcontrolled if (among other things) small letters are narrow, writing slants leftward, and there is equal spacing between words. These characteristics are believed to indicate slow, impeded execution—for example, the backward slant symbolizes the individual's tendency to regard impulsive, "forward" behavior as dangerous. A forward slant, on the other hand, would suggest an impetuous nature, while oscillation between the two would suggest emotional disturbance (Pulver, 1919). These "readings" on personality control are not taken at face value, but are checked against other indicators in the writing. They are also combined with analysis of graphic elements that throw light on additional features of the personality, such as "rational organization," in order to construct a comprehensive picture of the individual. This is not a mechanical procedure, but is believed to require the same kind of intuitive ability as other projective techniques.

The clinical approach to graphology has not yet been fully validated. We do not know to what extent the individual whose writing is highly controlled will also be rigid and inhibited in his daily living, nor does the analysis tell us whether the characteristic is superficial or deep, occasional or constant. Two investigators, Lewinson and Zubin (1942), made a start in this direction by constructing scales for twenty-two different variables—for instance, they attempted to correlate the exact size and form of letters with different degrees of inhibition and impulsiveness. Unfortunately they did not follow up their initial studies, and their scales have never been fully tested. This is a good indication of the present state of graphology. It is still in limbo, and much more work will have to be done before it is put on a firm foundation—or abandoned altogether as a scientific instrument. See EXPRESSIVE BEHAVIOR.

GREGARIOUSNESS. The tendency to associate with others; also the need to live together. Gregariousness is not distinguishable from the affiliative drive.

Early studies emphasized the fact that gregariousness is a universal social motive, since it is found in animals as well as human beings. For this reason the drive was regarded as instinctual—a "herd" or "flock" instinct. The more recent view is that this tendency is acquired during the long period of relative helplessness and dependence which every child goes through. During this time he is continually surrounded by people who tend to his needs, and he therefore becomes increasingly dependent on others for both physical and social satisfactions. As he grows he experiences more and more satisfactions in social life, and his drive to associate expands still further. Among these satisfactions are social approval, status, friendship, mutual assistance, companionship, and a sense of security.

The character of the child's early experiences determines the strength of this need and the general forms it is likely to take. If the family has been at the child's beck and call, he frequently continues to depend on others to meet his needs, and expects to get his way outside the home as well as inside. But if his wishes have been denied, or if his parents have demanded implicit obedience and subservience, he will probably feel hostile toward others and will be prepared to fight for everything he wants. Most children, however, are raised in a middle ground between these two extremes, and as they grow older are able to experience the many benefits of "belonging" without being too aggressive or demanding toward others.

There are any number of ways of demonstrating the power of the gregarious drive. Among the most compelling are the following: (1) the individual who leads a solitary life feels incomplete; (2) castaways, prisoners of war, and religious hermits frequently describe loneliness in terms of anxiety and even physical pain: (3) isolated individuals and subjects of experiments on sensory deprivation often report that they are beset by visions, hallucinations, and other emotional disturbances; (4) people who fail to develop satisfying relationships with others are likely to be afflicted with a sense of alienation, that is, a feeling that they are strangers on earth and have no purpose in life; (5) periods of stress increase our need to be with others, especially those who have given us comfort and safety in the past—hence the acute feelings of homesickness and the psychosomatic illnesses which often afflict men in the armed forces as well as children who are away at summer camp for the first time; (6) practically all people derive satisfaction from signs of social acceptance, such as praise, titles, and prizes, and most of us react strongly to social rejection in the form of snubs, discrimination or ostracism. See AFFILIATIVE DRIVE, SENSORY DEPRIVATION, SOCIALIZATION, SOCIAL ISOLATION, STATUS.

GRIEF. An emotional state of intense sadness resulting from loss of a cherished person.

Grief is normally an appropriate response consisting of such reactions as sighing, sobbing, withdrawal, preoccupation with thoughts about the lost individual, and feelings of regret. Some bereaved persons show more extreme reactions, which can be described as acute anguish or agitation. They pace up and down, wring their hands, wail and moan. Others may become immobilized or apathetic. Spitz and Wolf (1946) have shown that these reactions are not confined to older children and adults, for they found that infants who are separated from their mother may show these signs of grief. The customs of different religious or social groups are often as much involved in the expression of grief as are the individual's own tendencies. In any ordinary case, where neurotic tendencies are not involved, grief reactions are generally self-limiting and gradually subside within a reasonable time.

It is important to make a distinction between grief and depression. Grief is a reaction to an external, consciously recognized loss; depression is primarily the result of internal, unrecognized factors. Even in reactive depression, in which there is actual bereavement or disappointment, the morbid nature of the reaction is due to feelings that are largely, if not wholly, unconscious. These often consist of repressed feelings of guilt toward the lost person, or shame due to repressed hostility harbored toward the deceased. Sometimes there is a haunting feeling of responsibility for his death. It is these unconscious feelings that prolong the reaction and exert an incapacitating effect on the depressed individual. Instead of merely regretting and mourning his loss, he may derogate himself, harbor suicidal thoughts, and become so despondent that he can hardly work or carry on social relationships. In some cases the individual unconsciously resorts to the mechanism of denial of reality and fails to recognize that the person has died. *See* DEPRESSION, MANIC-DEPRESSIVE RE- ACTION, MATERNAL DEPRIVATION, ANA- CLITIC DEPRESSION, DENIAL OF REALITY.

The case that follows illustrates one type of pathological grief reaction. The patient, a thirty-two-year-old woman, had been deeply dependent on her husband—but after six years of marriage he had begun to drink heavily and stay out late with friends she could not accept. She continued to love him, and acceded to his demand to come and go as he pleased—but at the same time developed intense feelings of anger and resentment to the point of wishing he would die and entertaining fantasies of killing him. When he actually died, by his own hand, her feelings of guilt for these thoughts and for failing to help him blocked the normal process of mourning and led to the "defensive maneuver" described in the excerpt.

During therapy she was able to release her anger, become aware of her ingrained tendency to take blame on herself, and achieve a normal expression of grief.

Illustrative Case: GRIEF

At first she began to grieve in what appeared to be an appropriate and normal manner. Then, when she learned that his death was not from natural causes but by suicide, the process of mourning abruptly stopped. From her associations in therapy it became apparent that the fact that he had *chosen* to die caused her almost unbearable mental pain. In the first place it meant that he cared so little for her that he was willing to leave her in this cruel way. It felt to her like a desertion and served to increase her feelings of helplessness and inadequacy. Secondly, his behavior raised her fury to new heights of intensity as she felt spurned by him and permanently deprived of the love she needed. At the same time, her augmented rage only increased her sense of guilt and her feeling that she was responsible for his troubles; it seemed to her that in some magical way her fantasies of killing him had brought this to pass. To admit to herself that he was dead and to face the emotions that this fact aroused in her meant subjecting herself to an insupportable burden of grief, anger, helplessness, and guilt. The saving solution was to feel and act as if he were still alive—to *deny* his death; this was the only way she could protect herself against the pain attached to the loss of him. It meant, however, that she could not complete the process of grieving; although her husband was gone, she could not free herself of him. Bound to him, she was dead to the real world of living people. Her *denial* exacted the price.

The patient's maneuver of denial was not a fully conscious, voluntary, thought-out plan of action. It was an ego defense mechanism, and like all defenses it operated for the most part out of the sphere of her conscious awareness. She felt its effect in her conscious conviction that her husband was not dead, and in her lack of feelings of grief, but these did not appear to her to be the result of her own volition; on the contrary, intellectually she was puzzled by her unusual response. (Nemiah, 1961)

GRIESINGER, WILHELM (1817–68). A German by birth, Griesinger—the first systematic organicist in psychiatry—received his medical degree at Zurich. After studying for two years in a mental hospital, he devoted himself to general practice and research in physiology, specializing in brain disturbances. In the following years he wrote numerous articles, edited a journal on physiological treatment, and at the age of twenty-eight published an influential textbook, *Pathology and Therapy of Psychic Disorders* (1845). Through this book, as well as his subsequent research, teaching, and clinical activities in Berlin, he established himself as the major spokesman for the somatic point of view in psychiatry, which held that all mental illness could be explained on the basis of brain pathology.

Through his great prestige and the power of his intellect, Griesinger helped to counteract the romantic, semitheological orientation which had dominated German psychiatry for centuries. Even though his writings indicated that he was aware of psychodynamics, he ignored this approach entirely in making diagnoses, since in his eyes only organic factors were significant. He characterized psychological reactions as reflex actions, and one type of cause, brain disease, was invoked for all disorders ranging from general paresis to hysteria. Unfortunately he presented few facts to document his position, and often fell back on dogmatic pronouncements instead. To give one example, when a controversy over the etiology of general paresis arose in 1857, he vehemently opposed the suggestion made by Esmarch and Jessen that the disease was caused by syphilitic infection, and asserted that more men than women were afflicted because of their "more frequent excesses in spiritous liquors" and perhaps because of the use of "strong cigars and strong coffee." As far as he was concerned, that settled the matter.

In spite of his limitations, Griesinger had a constructive effect on the psychiatry of his time. He helped to establish the principle of nonrestraint in German mental institutions during a period when it was a subject of heated debate in America as well as Europe. He was instrumental in making these institutions centers for research in which physicians sought to determine the origin, cause, and outcome of mental disease. And even though his somatic approach to mental illness was one-sided, it had the effect of encouraging physicians to see their patients as persons who were ill and to view mental disease as treatable and curable. In short, he helped to bring psychiatry within the field of medical research, and stimulated a course of action which ultimately led to important discoveries in brain pathology and the physical treatment of mental illness, an approach which is very much alive today. *See* ORGANICISM.

GROUP DYNAMICS (Group Processes). The study of the underlying features of group behavior, particularly the interactions that take place within the group and between the group and the surroundings or social field.

The term was introduced by Kurt Lewin to emphasize the dynamic interrelationships that take place in social groups. In his own words, "The essence of a group is not the similarity or dissimilarity of its members, but their interdependence. A group can be characterized as a 'dynamical whole'; this means that a change in the state of any subpart changes the state of any other subpart. The degree of interdependence of the subparts of the group varies all the way from a 'loose' mass to a compact unit" (1948). This article will summarize four types of studies, dealing with interaction process analysis, collective problem-solving, group pressure, and social climate.

Interaction Process Analysis. This is a recently developed technique for determining how individuals interact in a problem situation. The procedure is to have a small group engage in a discussion or do some form of work while trained observers watch through a one-way screen and record their interactions in terms of twelve categories: shows solidarity, shows tension release, shows agreement, gives suggestions, gives opinion, gives information, asks for information, asks for opinion, asks for suggestion, shows disagreement, shows tension, shows antagonism. The record is later analyzed to throw light on the behavior of the individual members and the dynamic processes at work in the group as a whole.

To take a specific example, the first step might be to select the individuals who make up the group, then give each of them an identical written report of the facts of a human relations case. Each person reads the report by himself, without knowing that anyone else is being given the same information. They are then brought together in a meeting room to discuss the case—and their remarks and interactions are recorded, unknown to them, by the observers. Here is a brief excerpt from one of the sessions, with the interaction categories in parentheses:

Member 1: I wonder if we all have the same facts about the problem? (asks for opinion); perhaps we should take some time to find out (gives suggestion) . . .

Member 2: Yes (agrees). We may be able to fill in some gaps in your information (gives opinion). Let's go around the table and each tell what the report said in his case (gives suggestion).

Member 3: Oh, let's get going (shows antagonism). We've all got the same facts (gives opinion).

Member 2: (blushes) (shows tension).

In one study of conferences recorded by this method, Bales (1955) found that about 56 per cent of the total reactions were devoted to problem-solving itself: "gives suggestion," "gives information" and "gives opinion," with "gives opinion" predominating. But more important were the findings on individual leadership. He discovered that three variables were especially prominent: task-ability, likability and talkativeness —but few individuals rated high on all three. This led to a distinction between two major types of leaders, the task specialist who rates high on talkativeness and task-ability and lower on likability; and the social specialist who rates high on likability and relatively low on the other two. However, further study has shown that while a few individuals exhibit the same kind of leadership in differently composed groups, it is more likely that people take the lead in some settings but not in others, or even alternate between the roles of leader and follower as the activities of the group change. In other words, leadership is not a fixed personality attribute but a function of the situation. *See* LEADERSHIP.

Collective Problem-Solving. The question here is not what types of interactions take place in groups but how successfully they solve the problems presented to them. A long series of studies has been conducted on this question, with ambiguous results. Watson's early study (1928) of word derivation (making small words out of large ones) is still sometimes cited: Five subjects working alone produced from 18 to 49 words each, with an average of 32 words within the time limit, for a total of 87 different words—while groups of five working co-operatively derived 75 different words in the same period. In other words, the individuals produced more words per person and a larger total score, but the total output of the group was greater than that of any single individual working alone. Another early investigator (Shaw, 1932) showed that in working on more complex problems, groups were not only more efficient than individuals, as a result of division of labor, but made fewer errors because each member tended to check the others.

More recently, Taylor and Faust (1952) used the Twenty Questions game as a problem-solving situation and found that group performance was superior to individual performance in number of questions needed, number of failures, and elapsed time per problem —but in terms of man-minutes required, the performance of individuals was superior to that of groups. Restle and Davis (1962) found that randomly chosen groups showed little superiority over independent workers, although groups composed of experts who bring different information to bear on the problem are often more effective than individuals. Studies of creative thinking employing the brainstorming technique have not obtained consistent results. Taylor, Berry and Block (1958) found that college students working alone produced more and better ideas than when working together, because the members of the group tended to inhibit each other and also to fall into similar trains of thought. However, college students who received special training in brainstorming techniques improved significantly in problem-solving ability. *See* MANAGEMENT DEVELOPMENT.

Group Pressure. Why do people tend to conform to the behavior of a group? One of the major reasons (as discussed under Social Norms) is fear of social disapproval in the form of criticism, rejection or outright punishment by people we know or people who have the power to enforce the norms. This type of pressure to conform begins in childhood with parental discipline but is later exerted by teachers, the gang, the clique, and the entire subculture or social class. As a result, the desire for social approval becomes so ingrained and so generalized that we may even seek approval from complete strangers. As early as 1924, Floyd Allport demonstrated this fact by showing that subjects tended to give less extreme judgments when in the presence of others than when alone.

Other experiments have shown that we also "go along" with the opinions of other people because we believe these opinions are correct or at least more nearly correct than our own. A number of investigators (Festinger, 1954; Schachter and Singer, 1962) have demonstrated that we are particularly likely to compare our behavior with that of other people when the situation is ambiguous and we do not know exactly what is expected of us—and in these cases we often (though not always) adopt the behavior of another individual or of the group. In a series of classic experiments, Asch (1951) found that even when there is a decided discrepancy between the evidence of an individual's senses and the stand taken by a group, the individual may become convinced that the group is correct. His technique was to set up a relatively clear-cut group situation in which (a) a subject was required to judge the length of three lines when they were presented as "an experiment on visual judgment"; and (b) the other members of the group had been secretly instructed to give the correct judgment on certain trials but to make incorrect judgments on others.

The results were significant. First, very few subjects suspected the nature of the experiment (and in these cases the data were discarded). Second, there were marked individual differences in the reactions of the subjects. In one study of about fifty subjects, only about 25 per cent "stuck to their guns" in the face of the group, and the remainder showed varying degrees of change toward the suggestions of the group. Some were induced to make as many as eleven errors out of a possible twelve. The average number of errors in the entire group was 3.84, as compared to .8 errors made by a control group who gave individual judgments outside the group situation.

Third, most of the subjects who opposed the group opinion did so at considerable cost, since they tended to feel anxious, disturbed and "doubt-ridden." Fourth, many of the subjects who yielded to the group rationalized the change in their judgment by saying that something must be wrong with their eyes. Fifth, in a variation on this experiment, it was found that when one of the group was instructed to agree with the subject, or when two subjects were used instead of one, the influence of the majority was greatly reduced. In other words, they were more likely to stick to their guns if they had some support. Sixth, in a further variation, the subjects were led to believe they could express their judgments anonymously after learning the judgments of the group. In this case very few of the subjects yielded to the majority since the anonymous situation apparently reduced their fear of appearing "different" or of incurring social disapproval. Seventh, a similar study conducted by Tuddenham (1961) showed that children of ten to twelve yielded somewhat more often to the majority than college students, and female subjects in both groups yielded more often than male subjects.

Social Climate. The study of group dynamics has also been advanced by experiments that show the effects of different types of leadership on morale, productivity, and general behavior. The most celebrated investigation is the series of experiments conducted by Lewin et al. (1939) and White and Lippitt (1960) in which carefully equated hobby groups made up of ten-year-old boys were conducted by three different types of trained leaders. In one situation an authoritarian leader selected the projects himself, directed the activities at every step, frequently criticized the members, and refused to listen to their suggestions. In the second situation, a laissez faire leader remained on the sidelines, gave the group complete freedom to choose and carry out projects, and refrained from participating or giving information unless it was requested. In the third situation, a democratic leader encouraged the boys to discuss the project and divide the tasks, suggested but did not dictate procedures, and participated by giving objective, constructive guidance where needed. Each group worked for substantial periods (six weeks) under each of the three types of leaders, one group starting with the laissez faire, another with the authoritarian, and the third with the democratic leader.

The experiments demonstrated that the climate or atmosphere set up by the leader had a significant effect on group behavior. When the groups were under laissez faire leadership, they accomplished very little, were generally bored and at loose ends, and tried to relieve the monotony through horseplay. When the leader went out of the room (by prearrangement), this group fell completely apart and became destructive—and when a graduate student dressed as a janitor came in (also by prearrangement) and asked what they were doing, they simply shrugged their shoulders and said, "Nothing much."

Under autocratic leadership, the groups produced more work, though they rarely showed independence or originality in their activities. However, "When the leader left, the boys stopped working as if glad to be relieved of the task they 'had' to do," and when another person criticized their work, they would not defend it but said, "He told me to do it this way." The autocratic situation also had a substantial effect on the boys' relations with each other: some of the group became passive and apathetic; others became aggressive at the slightest opportunity and tended to pick on a scapegoat when the leader was out of the room.

In the democratic situation a substantial amount of work was accomplished, considerable originality was shown, morale was high, and there was little hostility toward the leader or between the boys. When the leader left the room, they kept right on working, and when the "janitor" came in and heckled them, they rallied together in defense of their efforts. As to preference, in one series of experiments 95 per cent of the boys preferred their democratic leader to their autocratic leader, and 70 per cent liked the laissez faire leader better than the autocratic leader. *See* SOCIAL FACILITATION, SOCIOMETRY, MANAGEMENT DEVELOPMENT, COOPERATION, COMPETITION, SOCIAL CLASS, FIELD THEORY, VALENCE.

GROUP FOR THE ADVANCEMENT OF PSYCHIATRY. An invitational organization with a membership of approximately 185 psychiatrists organized into working committees to study specific problems in psychiatry, mental health, and human relations.

GAP came into being in 1946 largely as a result of psychiatric needs revealed by World War II and, in words of its first president, William Menninger, "the frustration we experienced in attempting to practice psychiatry in the armed forces." The fact that more than two and a half million servicemen were either rejected or discharged because of emotional difficulties brought the problem of mental health to a focus and gave rise to the idea of organizing task forces to deal with special issues. The investigating committees consist of a team of specialists, who usually work in collaboration with consultants from related fields—anthropology, biology, social work, education, statistics, etc. —in collecting and appraising data, re-evaluating old concepts, and developing and testing new ones "on the advancing edge of psychiatry." After studying the problem, they draft an action-oriented report to be reviewed and adopted by the membership as a whole.

At present (1968) twenty-one working committees are in operation, dealing with problems in the following fields: adolescence, aging, the college student, child psychiatry, the family, governmental agencies, international relations, medical education, mental hospital services, mental retardation, preventive psychiatry, psychiatry in industry, psychiatry and law, psychiatry and religion, psychiatry and social work, psychopathology, public education, research, social issues, therapeutic care, and therapy.

The organization's widely circulated and highly influential publications include, to date, not only fifty-eight GAP Reports, but the proceedings of ten symposia on current topics, a regular feature of the semiannual meetings of the membership. Representative examples are Promotion of Mental Health in Primary and Secondary Schools, Mental Retardation—a Family Crisis, Medical Practice and Psychiatry, Psychiatric Aspects of School Segregation, Sex and the College Student, Psychiatric Aspects of the Prevention of Nuclear War, and Psychopathological Disorders in Childhood.

GROUP PSYCHOTHERAPY. In recent years there have been many applications of the group approach in psychotherapy. Some of the major varieties are psychoanalytic group therapy, nondirective group therapy, didactic group therapy, inspirational group therapy, play group therapy, activity group therapy, family group therapy, and psychodrama (PLATE 20).

Although these techniques differ widely among themselves, they are all based upon the principle "that intimate sharing of feelings, ideas, experiences in an atmosphere of mutual respect and understanding enhances self-respect, deepens self-understanding, and helps the person live with others" (J. D.

Frank, 1959). Specific advantages of the group approach include the following: (1) the realization that others are in much the "same boat" reduces the patient's anxiety and gives him courage to express his deeper feelings; (2) listening to others and exchanging ideas with them stimulates the patient to recall and relive experiences that have affected him; (3) the experiences and comments of other members of the group often suggest new ways of approaching and solving problems; (4) by expressing himself in the presence of a sympathetic group, the patient can dissipate some of the feelings of hostility or guilt that may be standing in his way; (5) acceptance by the group gives him the kind of emotional support he needs to put new solutions into practice; (6) since the group itself represents a segment of social reality, the patient has an opportunity to test and reinforce new ways of behaving and new relationships with other people in a practical, realistic way.

Group therapy of the more analytic, depth-oriented type is usually performed by psychiatrists and clinical psychologists. Activity and play groups may be conducted by psychiatric social workers. Groups organized for discussion of attitudes, feelings, and information may be led by marriage counselors, clergymen, penologists, personnel officers, or members of mental health associations. Many groups of ex-mental patients are meeting regularly throughout the country, some with and some without professional leadership. The 10,000 chapters of Alcoholics Anonymous operate on group-therapy principles applied by the members themselves. It is apparent from these examples that the group approach is carried out on a variety of therapeutic levels.

Before reviewing the specific forms of group psychotherapy, it might be well to note some of the historical roots of this approach. As Rosenbaum (1965) points out, among its early pre-cursors are mass religious movements, Greek drama, medieval morality plays, and Mesmer's seances. The first scientific use of the technique is credited to a Boston physician, J. H. Pratt. Beginning in 1905, he brought together groups of tubercular patients, and sought to overcome their feelings of discouragement through lectures on sound health practices. He soon discovered that they gained more strength from the knowledge that they were not alone in their suffering than from the information he gave them. He also found that they developed a spirit of comradeship which transcended differences in religious and ethnic backgrounds.

A few years later German, Austrian, Russian, and Danish psychiatrists utilized group methods, or "collective counseling," with neurotics, stutterers, alcoholics, and patients with sexual problems. Between 1910 and 1914 J. L. Moreno applied the technique to displaced persons, children, and prostitutes in Vienna. Shortly afterward Alfred Adler, who was a socialist, suggested that the group approach might be an effective way of bringing psychotherapy to the masses.

European psychoanalysts were for the most part hostile to group psychotherapy, but the technique took firm root in America. In 1921 Edward W. Lazell began to use a didactic approach (see below) with schizophrenic patients. In 1935 L. C. Marsh, who had been a minister before he became a psychiatrist, developed an inspirational approach that anticipated Alcoholics Anonymous in some respects. In addition to lectures, he held art and dance classes, and encouraged the members of his groups to give each other assistance and support with their emotional problems. Beginning in 1929, Louis Wender (1936) practiced what was probably the first form of group psychotherapy based on psychoanalytic principles, as opposed to what he termed educational and orientative approaches. His groups consisted of borderline psychotics, on the theory that patients who showed no intellectual impairment and little loss of affect would benefit. Along the same lines, Paul Schilder (1939) conducted experimental groups consisting of patients from the outpatient division of Bellevue Hospital in 1934.

During the 1930s S. R. Slavson, (1943), working at the Jewish Board of Guardians in New York, originated an approach that combined psychoanalysis, groupwork, and principles of the progressive education movement. He carried out effective group therapy on different age levels, using play techniques with very young children, hobby groups with older children and adolescents, and verbalization of feelings and experiences with adults. *See* ACTIVITY GROUP THERAPY, ANALYTIC GROUP THERAPY.

World War II accelerated the use of group therapy both as a supportive and a reconstructive technique, largely due to the shortage of trained personnel in the armed services. Shortly after the war a number of therapists began to adapt this technique to the client-centered, or nondirective, approach of Carl Rogers. This and other current approaches will be described in the next few paragraphs, following the general classification suggested by Rosenbaum (1965).

The directive-didactic approach. This method, the earliest form of group therapy to be used in state hospitals, is based on the theory that institutionalized patients will respond most effectively to group situations that are well defined and actively guided by a professional leader. It was first applied to regressed psychotic patients, and later to juvenile offenders, prisoners and paroled convicts. The approach is primarily pedagogical and intellectual, and takes two major forms. In one, the patients bring up the problems, and the therapist leads the discussion, oc-casionally giving his own interpretations; in the other, the therapist structures the situation by presenting a short lecture based on printed material handed out beforehand. The latter technique is particularly appropriate with highly inarticulate patients, especially regressed schizophrenics. The printed material is designed to stimulate them to break through their resistances and express themselves, but at the same time acts as a control over their associations. No pressure is applied to cover a given amount of material, and the class may therefore stop to discuss and associate to any point whatever. Some of the discussions may also be based on autobiographical material presented by the patients. To advance the learning process, the results of previous sessions are often reviewed, and carefully selected books and pamphlets are assigned as reading material. This technique as a whole has proved an effective means of reaching chronic, "backward" patients and drawing them into therapeutic activity. *See* BIBLIO-THERAPY.

The didactic approach is also used in therapeutic social clubs. A good example is Recovery, Inc., founded by a psychiatrist, Abraham Low, for psychoneurotic and post-psychotic patients. The emphasis is on self-help and "will therapy," since the group sessions are designed to call forth the patient's own therapeutic efforts. Each meeting starts with a reading from Low's book (1950), which presents a concrete, directive approach and suggests slogans for the individual to use as guides and reminders. This is followed by a series of testimonials in which members of the group describe specific problems they have encountered, showing how they would have handled them before joining the club and how they handle them now. In discussing these episodes the members gradually adopt a common language and affirm common values. The shared understanding and sense of solidarity that result from this process give them the support they need in combatting their illness and advancing their recovery. *See* MENTAL PATIENT ORGANIZATIONS.

The repressive-inspirational approach. This method is represssive in the sense that it is designed to strengthen the individual's defenses instead of breaking through them to elicit unconscious material; and it is inspirational in that a dynamic leader uses a wide variety of supportive measures to arouse and encourage the group. Corsini and Rosenberg (1955) have listed the measures which are most often used: "Group identification, group status, esprit de corps, friendly environment, communal feelings, unification of the group, group socialization, loss of isolation, emotional acceptance of the group, ego support, social approval, realization that others are in the same boat, testimony and example of others, sharing of mutual experiences, and reassurance."

One of the clearest and most effective examples of this type of group therapy is Alcoholics Anonymous, which utilizes every one of the mechanisms just mentioned and in addition, the recognition of a higher spiritual power. It also combines a didactic with an inspirational approach by presenting factual information on alcoholism as a disease. A second example is Synanon, which combines an emphasis on group identification and support with drastic social controls. In this approach, groups of narcotic addicts not only meet but live together, forming a "supportive subculture" under the energetic leadership of ex-addicts. *See* ALCOHOLICS ANONYMOUS, DRUG ADDICTION.

The Christian Science approach to health is an example of the repressive-inspirational technique on a religious level. Another type is exemplified by groups of mothers who meet with psychologists or other leaders to discuss problems they encounter in raising children. The atmosphere of such groups is usually a permissive one, with the leader playing a supportive and often an active and even directive role. Rosenberg holds that this type of group has "something of the reparative, inspirational, and constructive aspect of psychotherapy."

Nondirective group psychotherapy. In this approach the therapist is not a leader in the directive sense of the term, but a "permissive catalyst" who helps the members achieve self-understanding by confronting them with their own attitudes and reactions. He does little more than repeat their comments and encourage them to elaborate. The object is to stimulate the group to explore and clarify their own feelings rather than to probe into the dynamics that produced them. This approach stresses the value of communication between members of the group and the importance of seeing themselves as others see them.

The nondirective procedure is based on the view that human beings have an inner growth potential and an urge for "self-actualization." The group setting evokes this urge by giving each member an opportunity to examine his conflicts and behavior difficulties in the presence of others. This enables him to discover that he can gain what he needs by developing sounder relationships with other people. The entire process is viewed as a form of self-healing. *See* CLIENT-CENTERED THERAPY.

Psychoanalytic group therapy. This approach is a blend of the group process with psychoanalysis. Rosenbaum characterizes it as "regressive-reconstructive" since it attempts to bring about basic personality changes by eliciting unconscious material. The therapist sees each patient individually and assigns him to a group according to his disorder and special needs. In some cases individual therapy and group therapy run concurrently, each feeding into the other.

The group analyst utilizes an approach that closely resembles psychoanalysis, with the differences due mainly to the presence of more than two persons. In the course of the sessions, past events, particularly those involving the family, are revived and sometimes re-enacted; fantasies, dreams, and delusions are discussed; and the interactions between group members are analyzed.

The early experiments of Wender and Schilder were followed by the development of systematic techniques by Slavson, Wolf, and others. Since Slavson's "group analytic psychotherapy" is discussed under a separate heading, ANALYTIC GROUP THERAPY, we will only make the comment here that he applies practically all the standard Freudian techniques, such as free association and transference, to the group situation. Wolf (1949), motivated by a desire to provide treatment for patients who could not afford individual therapy, has developed a procedure that also utilizes basic analytic principles, but with certain special techniques of his own. His groups meet for one and a half hours twice a week, with at least one "alternate session" without the therapist. The object of the latter session is to move the patients along through experiences with their peers, and to give them an opportunity to discuss their reactions to each other and to the therapist in his absence. Wolf's basic process consists of working through unresolved problems by using the group as a re-creation of the original family. He therefore calls his method psychoanalysis *in* the group rather than *of* the group, stressing that he does not treat the group itself but only the individual in his interactions with others. He feels that the group setting has an advantage over the individual setting since the group serves as a representation of social reality, and most people find their fulfillment in aligning themselves with the common aims of a group, and not in the one-to-one relationship that obtains in individual therapy.

In eliciting material for discussion, Wolf uses a method called "going around," in which each member of the group free-associates about the next member. Mullan and Rosenbaum (1962) offer a modification of this procedure in which each member is asked to comment spontaneously and freely on the *same* member's fantasies, dreams, attitudes, and problems. This method, termed "ice-breaking," encourages the patients to become co-therapists and increases the impact of the group on the individual. It also works as an ego-strengthener, since the members of the group come to realize that they can themselves contribute to the healing process. In addition, the technique enables the therapist to obtain more than one view of the individual's problem. He is then in a better position to utilize the analytic approach, which consists largely in pointing out the symbolic character of the patient's distortions, and helping him trace them back to their origin in past experiences. For other examples of group psychotherapy, *see* FAMILY THERAPY, MULTIPLE THERAPY, PLAY THERAPY, PSYCHODRAMA.

H

HABIT. A long-standing pattern of learned behavior; often contrasted with set, which is a temporary or recently established tendency to act or react in a specific way. *See* SET.

Habit is one of the most pervasive

of all aspects of behavior. We develop habitual ways of thinking, feeling, talking, walking, and perceiving. All our characteristic attitudes, reactions, verbal patterns, gestures, facial expressions, and mannerisms fall into this category. Our mental patterns help us to organize our experience, and our motor patterns enable us to act swiftly and automatically. Habit therefore has the positive value of providing a structure that enables us to cope with reality as it usually presents itself. On the other hand, it may have distinct disadvantages. The tendency to fall back on habitual ways of acting and reacting may blind us to the novel and unique, lull us into sameness, prevent us from adapting to change, and betray us into giving old solutions to new problems.

Habits tend to operate on an unconscious, automatic level. We are usually unaware that we are acquiring them and equally unaware that we are using them. The golfer can rarely tell what started him to slice, and may fail to realize that he is twisting his club as he swings. The speaker who says "as it were" in every other sentence has no idea he does so until his wife points it out. Some of the most striking examples of the automatic in behavior are found in the psychology of perception. The cues we employ in seeing distance—perspective, color, and brightness differences—are so automatic that we do not realize we are using them. The same goes for perceptual constancy, the fact that we see a six-foot man as a six-footer even when the image on our retina is that of a four-footer. The photograph on Plate 20 is a particularly vivid example of habitual perception. We see it as a crater because we are used to certain patterns of light and shadow. If the book is turned upside down, these patterns will change and the crater will look quite different.

How rigid are our perceptual habits? To answer this question, Stratton (1897) performed a classic experiment in which he had subjects wear special lenses which reversed the visual field, both left and right and above and below. Surprisingly, it took only a few days for the subjects to change their deeply ingrained habits and get used to seeing down as up, and to reaching toward the left for things that appeared on the right. In 1940 another experimenter, Foley, not only distorted the visual field of an adult monkey in these two ways, but made him see near as far and far as near. Within eight days the monkey was reaching, climbing, and walking practically as well as ever. It took him three days to readjust to the normal perceptual field when the lenses were removed. A similar experiment was performed by Willey et al. (1937), with hearing, using an apparatus called a pseudophone. He had human subjects wear earphones that delivered sounds from the right side to the left ear and vice versa. This produced confusion at first, but again the subjects soon learned to adapt to the new conditions.

These experiments indicate that some of our most basic habits can be altered—a good thing to remember when we are called upon to adjust to new circumstances. The recruit may never come to like army food, but at least he gets accustomed to it. The student who uses a microscope for the first time is sure he will never see anything more than a blur, but within a week or so he begins to establish different habits of perception that open up a whole new world of understanding. The same thing happens with the medical student as he gradually learns what to listen for when he uses a stethoscope.

Clinical studies have amply demonstrated the effect of early habit training on the child's personality development. Disturbances in childhood and later can often be traced to the period when the child formed behavior patterns associated with sleeping, weaning, speech, and elimination. It is now generally agreed that the attitudes of the parents and the atmosphere of the home are as important as how or when the habit training occurs. Encouragement, approval, and trust not only make it easier for the child to acquire good physical habits, but are instrumental in the establishment of healthy emotional patterns as well. On the other hand, pressure and reproof can generate feelings of anxiety or resentment which corrode his relationships to himself and other people. Though both the healthy and unhealthy patterns tend to be lasting, it is important to recognize that the neurotic tendencies have a peculiar kind of persistence. This is illustrated by the fact that when an individual develops anxiety reactions in his adult life, he tends to revert to earlier habits which have laid a basis for this reaction. As a result, a vicious cycle may set in. Some of the newer behavior therapies, such as Wolpe's technique, are directed toward breaking these habits and forming new ones. See BEHAVIOR THERAPY, REPETITION-COMPULSION.

Some investigators view the learning process in terms of habit formation, since it establishes a connection between a stimulus and a response which did not exist before. Verbal habits are a particularly clear example: we learn to associate an instrument that contains ink with the response "pen." The theory holds that all other activities that involve habit formation, such as the ability to ride a bicycle or the acquisition of emotional reactions and attitudes may also be interpreted in terms of learning appropriate responses to simple or complex stimuli. Opponents of this view argue that it makes learning a mechanical procedure and ignores the role of the cognitive processes. The "cognitive" camp tries to show that new, unpredictable insights can be gained from a knowledge of principles, while the "habit" or "as-sociationist" camp argues that all learning and knowledge can be explained from the single principle of establishing stimulus-response links through either classical or operant conditioning. See CONDITIONING, ASSOCIATIONISM, STIMULUS-RESPONSE ASSOCIATION, STIMULUS-STIMULUS ASSOCIATION.

The study of habit raises three other important questions. How many repetitions are necessary to implant a habit? Once it is acquired, is a habit ever completely lost? What is the best way to break a habit?

There is no single answer to the first question, but two important discoveries have been made. First, each repetition of an act tends to increase habit strength somewhat, but the returns tend to diminish. This means that we learn most rapidly at the very outset, and should therefore be particularly careful to start out on the right foot. In sports, for example, it is advisable to obtain instruction from an expert so that we can begin to form the correct habits at once. This also prevents us from acquiring habits that will have to be replaced later on, when it is extremely hard to change. Second, there is evidence that certain habits can be formed on the basis of single experiences, without any repetition at all. This seems to be especially the case where the emotions are involved, as in traumatic experiences. It probably does not apply to complex motor tasks, although some parts of them, like the habit of resting one's foot on the clutch while driving a car, may be developed during the first trial. See TRAUMA.

The question of the permanence of habits has long been debated. Many psychologists today feel that habits are never completely lost, though they may be overlaid by more recent or stronger habits. There appears to be evidence for this theory in the ease with which we return to old motor habits such as touch typing after an interval of many years—also in the revival of extremely early patterns of behavior in senile patients or in individuals subjected to hypnotic regression. The question can only be argued but not settled at this moment. The study of the mechanism of memory may eventually shed some light on it. *See* MEMORY STORAGE.

Habit-breaking is another question to which no single answer can be given. The following are some of the techniques most commonly discussed by psychologists. First, *incompatible-response:* supplanting the habit with a new behavior pattern that is antagonistic to it. This method is a form of extinction through "counterconditioning"—that is, eliminating the original response by replacing it with a new one. An example is the smoker who gets in the habit of chewing a mint when he feels the desire to smoke. (Sometimes he ends up by smoking and chewing at the same time!) In applying this method as well as others, it is important to follow two maxims first proposed by William James in 1890: "We must take care to launch ourselves with as strong and decided an initiative as possible," and "Never suffer an exception to occur till the new habit is securely rooted in your life."

The second technique is *exhaustion:* forcing the individual to repeat the undesirable behavior until the habit is fatigued. For example, a boy caught smoking might be forced to continue smoking until he becomes, literally, sick of it. When this happens, the desire to smoke will come to elicit a new response, nausea, and this discourages the boy from practicing the habit. A similar technique has been applied to nail-biting. The exhaustion method is closely related to "deterrent therapies," such as the use of Antabuse or hypnotic suggestion in the treatment of alcoholic addiction. Like most habit-breaking techniques, these methods are forms of behavior therapy and do not attempt to alter the motivation that produced the pattern in the first place. *See* HYPNOTHERAPY, ANTABUSE THERAPY, BEHAVIOR THERAPY.

A third method is *toleration:* introducing stimuli that arouse an undesirable habit or reaction in small doses, so that more acceptable responses can be gradually established. As an example, the child who fears grown dogs may react positively to a puppy, and as he and the dog mature, these positive reactions will continue and eventually replace the fear. Similarly a shy person can sometimes overcome his timidity through pleasant social experiences with one or two people, and then gradually widen his acquaintance. In experiments performed on animals, Kimble and Kendall (1953) found that the toleration method was superior to the exhaustion method. It is also likely to be more humane.

A fourth technique is *change of environment:* getting away from the stimuli or situations that produced the bad habit. This is not always feasible—for example, it is hard to get away from smokers entirely, and most people would not abandon their old friends simply because they smoke. A change of scene usually brings only temporary results, though it might sometimes work if at the same time the individual finds new satisfactions to replace those provided by the original habit. This is again a form of counterconditioning. The Alcoholics Anonymous approach is a good example. An important part of the process is to provide new recreational activities and new friends to make it unnecessary for alcoholics to seek the company of other alcoholics or the companionship of the bottle. *See* ALCOHOLICS ANONYMOUS.

Fifth, *punishment* is often used as a method of breaking habits, but it is probably the least effective of all the techniques. At best it merely suppresses the undesirable habit temporarily, and usually only in the presence of the punisher. It does not in itself encourage more desirable behavior and therefore tends to be purely negative. Moreover, it may even strengthen the bad habit, since the punished person may cling to it as a form of retaliation. For habit disturbances, *see* ENURESIS, NAIL BITING, MASTURBATION, TEMPER TANTRUM, THUMBSUCKING, TRANSIENT SITUATIONAL PERSONALITY DISORDERS.

HALFWAY HOUSE. A temporary residence which provides a transition between the mental hospital and life in the community. This type of facility is "based on the assumption that experience in a protected setting can significantly increase the ex-patient's chances of remaining out of the mental hospital, as well as preparing him for more independent living" (Joint Commission on Mental Illness and Health, 1962).

Three types of halfway houses are in use today. First, the *cooperative urban house* limited to a small number of ex-patients of the same sex who need minimum supervision and who are immediately or potentially employable. Second, the somewhat larger *rural work-oriented house,* often called a ranch, farm, or homestead. This facility accepts ex-patients of both sexes, as well as selected individuals with mental disorders who have never been hospitalized. The third type is the *treatment-oriented facility,* which occupies a place midway between the mental hospital and the patient's home. In this facility the residents are still patients and are not required to assume much responsibility or to participate in community life.

The halfway house is becoming more generally accepted, but it has its critics as well as its supporters. The critics argue that the residents are segregated from the community and encouraged to look to the house for their entire social life. They also claim that it may become a static and costly "little mental hospital ward." Some of these critics

suggest that foster-family care avoids these disadvantages and at the same time serves as a more satisfactory bridge to the community. The proponents of the halfway house concept argue that it provides more freedom and privacy than the foster family, and therefore the residents feel more comfortable than if they were living with a family. They also point out that the tendency to become dependent on the house is a problem that would arise in any environment; and that if it is properly managed, the facility will help to achieve early release of patients from the hospital, as well as a lower relapse rate. *See* FAMILY CARE.

HALL, G. (GLANVILLE) STANLEY (1844–1924). Hall, a pioneer in educational psychology, was born in Massachusetts, and graduated from Williams College. He then attended the Union Theological Seminary and the University of Bonn, and after completing his divinity degree, began his professional career by teaching philosophy, modern languages, and English at Antioch College (1872–76). During this period his interest in psychology was aroused by Wilhelm Wundt's *Physiological Psychology,* and he decided to go to Harvard to study under William James. There he received what is believed to be the first Ph.D. in psychology granted in America (1878). During the following two years Hall lived in Germany, studying not only with Wundt but with the physiologist Ludwig and the physicist Helmholtz. Upon returning to the United States, he obtained a position at Johns Hopkins and in 1883 opened the first official psychology laboratory in this country. Four years later he founded the first American psychological periodical, the *American Journal of Psychology.*

During his years at Johns Hopkins (1882–88), Hall established himself as an outstanding critic of education, and published, among other works, *The Con-*

tents of Children's Minds (1883). When Jonas Gilman Clark established Clark University, he was chosen its first president and, after a year in which he examined universities in almost every country in Europe, the new university was opened with a heavy emphasis on research. In the years that followed, Hall founded two other journals, the *Pedagogical Seminary* (1891) (now the *Journal of Genetic Psychology*), the *Journal of Religious Psychology* (1904–14), and the *Journal of Applied Psychology* (1915). He was elected first president of the American Psychological Association when it was established in 1892, and was re-elected in 1924, the year of his death.

Despite his studies with Wundt, Hall felt that the "new psychology" could not do justice to all psychological phenomena because of its exclusive concern with consciousness and introspection. He took the position that the general doctrines of psychoanalysis filled in many of the gaps in the psychology of his day, and therefore invited both Freud and Jung to lecture at Clark in 1909. This event introduced the American public to psychoanalytic theory. In 1920 Hall again gave impetus to the movement by translating Freud's widely read book, *General Introduction to Psychoanalysis.*

Hall's greatest contributions lie in the area of educational psychology. In 1893 he started an extremely fruitful child study movement at the Columbian Exposition in Chicago. Between that date and 1903 he and his associates investigated the child's experience by administering over 102 different questionnaires on such topics as anger, dolls, crying and laughing, fears, prayer and other religious experiences. This technique, which he had come across in Germany, revealed the need for teaching children many things which adults assumed they learned by themselves—for example, he found that 80 per cent of primary school children in Boston knew that

milk came from cows, but only 10 per cent knew that animals are the source of leather. Moreover, 20 per cent of the children had never seen a cow or hen, and a much larger percentage had not seen a crow or a beehive. One result of this type of research was the creation of a department of pedagogy at Clark; it also had the effect of stimulating interest in child guidance among professional educators.

The new area of study was greatly advanced when Hall published his observations on older children in a monumental two volume work, *Adolescence: Its Psychology and Its Relations to Physiology, Anthropology, Sociology, Sex, Crime, Religion and Education* (1904). The book came out at a time when there was widespread hope that psychology would unlock the secrets of a scientific education for all, and an abbreviated addition of the book entitled *Youth, its Education, Regimen and Hygiene* (1906) became a standard text in colleges and normal schools. *See* ADOLESCENCE (THEORIES).

Hall's viewpoint has been termed "synthetic psychology" since it was broadly eclectic in approach. However, he leaned heavily toward biological interpretations, and has been described by Boring (1950) as "a genetic psychologist, that is to say, a psychological evolutionist who was concerned with animal and human development and all the secondary problems of adaptation and development." As Murphy (1949) has pointed out, this biological emphasis led to the outright exclusion of cultural factors. As examples, he believed that the "big-Injun" war play of preadolescent children represented a phase of the child's recapitulation of the history of the race; and he viewed adolescence almost entirely from the standpoint of the organic changes which take place during this period.

Hall wrote a number of other books in the psychological field—among them *Educational Problems* (1911) and

Founders of Modern Psychology (1912). He brought his early interest in religion into relation to psychology in *Jesus, the Christ, in the Light of Psychology* (1917), and stated his views on war in *Morale, the Supreme Standard in Life and Conduct* (1920). He retired from Clark in 1919 at the age of 75, and then addressed himself to the problems of aging, publishing *Senescence: the Last Half of Life,* in 1922.

HALLUCINATION. A false perception occurring without external stimulation: seeing, hearing, tasting, smelling or feeling things that are not there.

Transient hallucinations may occur in healthy persons in the form of dreams, and in the "hypnagogic state" between sleeping and waking. Children who lead a particularly active fantasy life may occasionally think they hear voices or see persons or objects that are not there, especially when they are undergoing emotional difficulties.

Both positive and negative hallucinations can be produced by hypnotic suggestion. In response to command some subjects will see a person who is not present, or fail to see one who is present. Hallucinations may also be experienced by normal individuals when they are subjected to special conditions, such as sensory deprivation, solitary confinement, extreme exhaustion or hallucinogenic drugs. In most of these cases the hallucinations are poorly formed and may lack a full sense of reality. They also have limited significance as expressions of the personality and are not considered symptomatic of persistent or deep-seated mental disorder.

Psychiatric hallucinations may be associated with either psychogenic or organic disorders. In either case the individual accepts these false perceptions as reality, and responds accordingly. If he hears a voice accusing him of sin, he may cower in the corner; if he sees himself as a saint, a beatific expression will spread over his face; if he smells poison in the surrounding air, he may borrow a nurse's mask. Hallucinations of this type are considered by many authorities to be perceptual expressions of underlying wishes, feelings, and needs. They may reflect, for example, a need to escape from reality, to enhance self-esteem, to relieve a sense of guilt, or to fulfill aspirations. Personality needs of this kind may influence the content not only of psychogenic hallucinations, but of hallucinations produced by physiological conditions such as toxic or organic states. Moreover, the type of hallucination itself seems to be determined to some extent by psychological factors. A person who is ridden by guilt generally hears condemnatory voices; one who is beset by fear may have visions of terrifying animals; and a victim of sexual anxieties usually sees himself surrounded by sexual symbols.

Hallucinations fall into six categories, of which the auditory type is by far the most common:

(1) *Auditory hallucinations.* Sometimes the patient hears strange noises, muffled voices, disconnected words, or his own thoughts in speech ("écho des pensées"), but most frequently he clearly hears remarks addressed to him. The voices are usually attributed to particular persons, to God or simply to "enemies." They may appear to come from external objects, such as light fixtures, the heating system, or an imaginary telephone. They may also emanate from various parts of the patient's own body, or from all directions at once. In some cases the remarks are of a pleasant nature, even to the point of assuring the patient that he has been given extraordinary powers or has been appointed by God to save all mankind; but more often he is berated or accused of heinous crimes and unforgivable sins, often in obscene language. Sometimes the patient answers back or conducts a lengthy conversation with an imagined interlocutor. Occasionally the voices may issue commands which lead to at-

tempted suicide or violence against others.

(2) *Visual hallucinations.* Visual images are sometimes of a pleasant nature—angels or circus animals, for example—but in most instances they are disgusting or frightening. The most vivid examples are found in delirium tremens, in which tiny, fast-moving animals terrify the alcoholic patient. These are termed Lilliputian hallucinations. *See* DELIRIUM TREMENS.

(3) *Olfactory hallucinations.* Most hallucinated odors are strongly objectionable or downright repulsive; for example, decaying flesh, garbage, poison gas, carbolic acid. Such hallucinations seem to be associated with unconscious feelings of guilt, and may be accompanied by accusatory voices.

(4) *Gustatory hallucinations.* The patient tastes poison in his food, or complains that his mouth is full of acid or lye. Hallucinations of taste are usually associated with hallucinations of smell.

(5) *Tactile or haptic hallucinations.* The patient feels electric impulses in various parts of his body, or insects crawling on or under his skin ("formication hallucinations"). Sexual sensations are also hallucinated in some cases of schizophrenia. *See* FORMICATION.

(6) *Kinesthetic hallucinations.* Various parts of the body feel as if they are changing their shape, size or movement. In schizophrenic reactions and toxic states, an arm may feel twisted, the legs six feet long, or the inside of the body completely hollow. Hallucinations of nonexistent body parts also occur in patients who have undergone amputation. *See* PHANTOM REACTION.

All types of hallucinations occur in the paranoid form of schizophrenia. The visual type predominates in psychoses associated with acute infectious diseases and toxic disorders produced by alcohol (delirium tremens), barbiturates, and metallic poisoning. The auditory type is found primarily in acute alcoholic hallucinosis, senile psychosis (paranoid type), and affective psychoses (involutional psychotic reaction, and the depressive phase of manic-depressive reaction). Hallucinations also occur in epileptic disorders, psychoses with brain tumor, symbiotic psychosis, syphilitic disorders, cocaine addiction, Pick's disease, and psychosis with cerebral arteriosclerosis.

HALLUCINOGEN. A drug or other substance that is capable of producing hallucinations.

Although hallucinogenic chemicals have been utilized for both experimental and therapeutic purposes in Western psychiatry only since World War II, roots, seeds, and fungi with hallucinogenic properties were known to the ancient world and have long been used in tribal societies. Some of the potions employed in medieval witchcraft contained ingredients that may also be hallucinogenic—for instance, henbane, belladonna, toadskin, and the urine of certain animals.

During the conquest of Central and South America, a number of powerful hallucinogenic substances came to light. The Peruvian Aztecs consumed the "divine" peyot, or peyote, made from dried cactus tops, or "buttons," a natural source of the drug mescaline. Mexican Indians were using more than thirteen different "phantastica" (the botanical name for hallucinatory plants), including sacred mushrooms containing psilocybin, and olilinqui, the Indian name for morning glory. Other Indians in the Amazon basin ate hallucinogenic seeds known as cohoba, and drank caapi, which contained the drug harmine. Explorers also found tribes in the Congo who chewed tabernanthe iboga (ibogaine), inhabitants of Northern Siberia who ate a vision-inducing fungus called fly agaric, and natives of the Pacific Ocean who consumed a mullet known as the "dream fish."

All these drugs were apparently taken to induce fantastic visions and open the "doors of perception," to use William

Blake's expression. In some cases, the experience served ceremonial purposes; in others it provided release for deepseated impulses or relief from oppressive situations. An early account of mushroom-eating, written by Bernardino de Sahagun, who lived among Mexican Indians from 1529 to 1590, shows how much the effects vary from individual to individual, probably reflecting the emotional needs and urges of different personalities: "The mushrooms they ate with honey, and when they began to get heated from them, they began to dance and some sang and some wept, for now they were drunk from the mushrooms. And some cared not to sing but to sit down in their rooms and stay there pensivelike and some saw in a vision that some wild beast was eating them, others saw in a vision that they were taken captives in war, others saw in a vision that they were to be rich, others saw in a vision that they were to own many slaves, others saw in a vision that they were to commit adultery and that their heads were to be bashed in therefore. . . . Then when the drunkenness of the mushrooms passed, they spoke with one another about the visions they had seen."

Mescaline, the hallucinogenic ingredient of the cactus plant, was isolated in 1888, and a short time later Weir Mitchell and Havelock Ellis began experimenting with it. The observations of these and other investigators indicate that the subjects experience (1) distorted perception of time, space, ordinary objects, and their own body image; (2) vivid visual illusions and hallucinations; (3) transformation of everyday things into objects of irridescent beauty; (4) a sense of detachment from all cares and concerns; (5) some degree of intellectual impairment, confusion, and clouded consciousness; (6) paranoid thinking and lack of emotional control; (7) the experience of "double consciousness"—that is, simultaneous awareness

of events in both the inner and outer worlds. *See* MITCHELL.

The term psychedelic has recently been applied to mescaline and other hallucinogenic drugs, such as lysergic acid (LSD) and dimethyltriptamine (DMT), to denote their ability to stimulate the mind and expand perceptual experience. A second term, psychotomimetic, is also used since they produce psychosis-like reactions. However, studies show that they do not reproduce the exact manifestations of naturally occurring psychoses of either the functional or the organic type. Although they produce visual hallucinations, which are common in toxic psychoses, they do not usually produce the gross impairment of memory and orientation that occurs in brain syndromes due to lead poisoning, alcohol, barbiturates, and infectious diseases. Many of the symptoms resemble those found in acute schizophrenia—especially perceptual distortions, paranoid thinking, and visual hallucinations. On the other hand, they do not produce auditory hallucinations, which are frequently observed in schizophrenia. And even though verbal and affective changes may be induced, they are quite different from those occurring in natural forms of schizophrenia. The experimental subject tends to become emotionally excited and talk wildly; the true schizophrenic is more likely to retreat into silence, to use garbled verbiage, and to be emotionally flat and unresponsive.

In spite of these differences, mescaline has been investigated as a possible key to schizophrenia. A number of researchers have suggested that schizophrenic reactions might be associated with malfunction of the adrenal gland, and in 1952 Osmond and Smythies noted similarities between the chemical structure of mescaline and that of epinephrine (adrenalin). This prompted a search for components of epinephrine or substances related to it that would be capable of producing the same symptoms as schizophrenia. A number of such substances, including adrenoxin, were found to induce temporary psychotic states, but none of them has been conclusively proved to be present in higher than normal amounts in natural forms of schizophrenia. However, even though the experimental studies on mescaline have not demonstrated that toxic substances are involved in schizophrenia, the search continues and has recently focused on another hallucinogenic drug, LSD-25. *See* LYSERGIC ACID.

In the following excerpts, compare the reactions of Weir Mitchell to mescaline with the visions experienced by the poet George William Russell (AE) without the use of a drug.

Illustrative Case: HALLUCINOGEN (MESCALINE HALLUCINATIONS)

During these two hours I was generally wide awake. . . . Time passed for me with little sense for me of its passage. I was critically attentive, watchful, interested, and curious, making all the time mental notes for future use. . . .

A white spear of gray stone grew to huge height, and became a tall, richly finished Gothic tower of very elaborate and definite design, with many rather worn statues standing in the doorways or on stone brackets. As I gazed, every projecting angle, cornice, and even the face of the stones at their joinings were by degrees covered or hung with clusters of what seemed to be huge precious stones, but uncut, some being more like masses of transparent fruit. All seemed to possess an interior light, and to give the faintest idea of the perfectly satisfying intensity and purity of these gorgeous color-fruits is quite beyond my power. All the colors I have ever beheld are dull as compared to these . . .

After an endless display of less beautiful marvels I saw that which deeply impressed me. An edge of a huge cliff seemed to project over a gulf of unseen depth. My viewless enchanter set on the brink a huge bird claw of stone. Above, from the stem or leg, hung a fragment of some stuff. This began to unroll and float out to a distance which seemed to me to represent Time as well as immensity of Space. Here were miles of rippled purples, half transparent and of ineffable beauty. Now and then soft golden clouds floated from these folds, or a great shimmer went over the whole of the rolling purples, and things, like green birds, fell from it, fluttering down into the gulf below . . . (Mitchell, 1896)

Illustrative Case: HALLUCINOGEN (DRUGLESS VISIONS)

There was a hall vaster than any cathedral, with pillars that seemed built out of living and trembling opal, or from some starry substance which shone with every color, the colors of eve and dawn. A golden air glowed in this place and high between the pillars were thrones which faded, glow by glow, to the end of the vast hall. On them sat the Divine Kings. They were fire-crested. I saw the crest of the Dragon on one, and there was another plumed with brilliant fires that jetted forth like feathers of flame. They sat shining and starlike, mute as statues, more colossal than Egyptian images of their gods, and at the end of the hall was a higher throne on which sat one greater than the rest. A light like the sun glowed behind him. (George William Russell, 1920)

HALO EFFECT. The tendency to allow one characteristic of an individual to influence our judgment of other characteristics. The halo effect may work positively or negatively. If a person appears outgoing and attractive, we may judge him to be brighter than he is. If he is disagreeable or distasteful, we may judge his intelligence more severely.

The halo effect is a common reaction, and a compelling illustration of the power of suggestion. It is also one of the major sources of personal bias and distortions of judgment. Teachers must guard against the halo effect, since a favorable or unfavorable impression of a child's personality may influence the grades she gives or the way she treats the child in class. Motion-picture producers know that by using a well-known star in a film, they can influence box office receipts out of all proportion to the merits of the production. Politicians realize that personal magnetism can go far toward convincing the public that they will make competent public servants.

The halo effect is of particular importance in personnel selection. The applicant for a job or for admission to a school or college knows that first impressions often mean a great deal; he therefore dresses and comports himself accordingly. The interviewer, however, has usually been trained to put this general impression in its proper perspective and not give it more weight than it deserves. Personnel psychologists have also devised a number of specific procedures to counteract the halo effect. One technique is to use objective rating scales instead of asking the interviewer to write his own description of the applicant. A second is to have two or three interviewers appraise each applicant. A third is the policy of having one personnel officer test the applicant and another interview him. These methods usually reduce personal bias even though they may not eliminate it altogether. *See* PERSONNEL SELECTION.

HANDEDNESS (Dextrality, Sinistrality). The tendency to prefer one hand to the other has long been considered a significant fact of human behavior. Many superstitions, such as throwing salt over the left shoulder for good luck, involve the hands; and the words "dexterous" and "sinister" indicate that the Romans associated skill with the right hand and harm with the left. Within the past thirty years the question of handedness has taken on new meaning because of its relation to reading and emotional problems.

The origin of our preference for one hand over the other is still a mystery. Some authorities believe it is wholly due to heredity; others, that it is entirely acquired through training and social conditioning. The trend today is toward the view that in most cases children have a natural (i.e. congenital)

tendency to favor one hand over the other, whether or not that tendency is inherited. Preference is therefore implicit in the body itself, perhaps because of the dominance of one hemisphere of the brain over the other.

Even though hand preference appears to be based on a natural tendency, it does not begin to manifest itself until the child is about eighteen months old, and it often takes three or four years to become fully established. Moreover, the strength of this tendency varies considerably from child to child. Some children are so strongly left-handed that they resist all attempts to encourage the use of the right hand. Others are only slightly left-handed and will switch over with little difficulty. Right-handed people, too, are seldom exclusively right-handed; one can almost always find some operations which they prefer to perform with the left hand.

The crucial question is whether it is good psychological practice to urge or encourage the child to use one or the other hand. Authorities differ on this question, too. Some strongly advocate letting the child decide for himself, even to the point of handing him objects in the midline of his body. But many child psychologists hold that since we live in a right-handed world, we should deliberately encourage children to use their right hand unless it is difficult or impossible for them to do so. If such encouragement is given, it should be gentle and pressure of any kind should be avoided. We might, for instance, hand toys to the child's right hand, place his spoon to the right of the plate, or show him how to throw a ball with the right hand. An approach of this kind favors the right hand, but permits a strong natural tendency toward left-handedness to assert itself.

It has been found that early development of handedness—right *or* left—contributes to the child's feeling of security and stability, as well as to the development of manual skill. A long delay may lead to uncertainty, awkwardness, and tension and may also cause directional confusion when the child starts to read (as in reading "was" for "saw"). It is therefore a good idea to see that the child has plenty of games, such as darts, that give him practice in hand control.

Though there is some disagreement on the extent to which the child should be encouraged to use the right hand, there is little or none on the question of making the final choice. It should rest with the child himself. It has been found that forcing a naturally left-handed child to use his right hand, or pressuring him to convert from left to right after his basic habits have been formed, almost invariably generates emotional tension—and this tension will frequently express itself in such symptoms as stuttering, nail-biting, and reading difficulties. Parents or teachers who are tempted to do this should remind themselves that the five to ten per cent of our population who are left-handers do not suffer any great degree of discomfort or inconvenience, and certainly not enough to warrant the difficulties that may be produced by a forced changeover.

If the child chooses the left hand, it is never wise to make him feel "different." If others make him self-conscious about it, we can assure him that many of our greatest athletes are "lefties," and point out that there is an unexpected advantage in being left-handed. Since many things are designed for *right* hand use, he will probably acquire the special ability of being able to use *either* hand!

Jersild's comment (1960) on this whole question is an apt one: "Our handedness is not so important in itself that parents should interfere if the child himself shows a strong inclination to lead with his left as he squares off for the battle of life." See DIRECTIONAL CONFUSION, LATERAL DOMINANCE.

HEAD INJURY (ACUTE TRAUMATIC DISORDERS). A temporary impairment of brain functions immediately following a severe blow to the head.

The problem of head injury has been on the increase in recent years due to the huge number of automobile, industrial and home accidents. Fortunately, most cases are minor, even when they involve loss of consciousness, and few victims develop mental disorders severe enough to require hospitalization. At present these cases account for only .6 per cent of first admissions to mental hospitals. This number is small enough to belie the ancient notion that blows on the head are a major cause of mental disorder—a notion that is still widely accepted because it lays the "blame" for mental illness on physical factors rather than on the patient or his family.

But though the number of mental cases due to head injury is small, it is nevertheless constantly increasing. These cases pose special difficulties of a legal nature, for they usually lead to claims for compensation. They also present knotty psychiatric problems, since traumatic injuries involve a mixture of psychogenic and organic factors that is extremely hard to untangle.

Traumatic disorders due to head injury may be either acute or chronic. Acute reactions immediately follow the injury, and are of three types. In *cerebral concussion* the blow to the head disrupts brain functions and causes a momentary clouding or loss of consciousness. The typical case is the football player who meets his opponent head-on, or the boxer who receives a heavy blow to the head. If consciousness is lost, the victim is confused, disoriented, and has a severe headache when he comes to. There is usually a partial or total amnesia for the event, but there are seldom any residual symptoms. In one case a boxer who had received such a blow went down for count of nine, but got up and won his match. When his trainer congratulated him in the locker room, he expressed utter amazement. The blow had partially knocked him out, and he had gone on fighting automatically, but could not remember the end of the bout at all.

In *cerebral contusion* the blow to the head is severe enough to displace the brain and bruise its surface. The period of unconsciousness or coma may last for hours or days, and is followed by restlessness, clouding of consciousness, and often delirium. When the state of confusion clears up, the patient usually complains of severe headaches, nausea, dizziness, weakness, and sensitivity to light and noise. These symptoms usually subside in a few days or weeks, but in some cases there is prolonged irritability and impairment of mental and motor functions.

In *cerebral laceration* there is an actual rupture or lesion of brain tissue, usually due to penetration by pieces of bone, bullets or other objects. The symptoms are similar to those in contusion cases, but they are usually more severe and may be followed by permanent intellectual and motor defects. The coma may last for days or weeks, and if the patient survives he practically always develops a delirious reaction. In its mild form, the delirium is characterized by haziness, restlessness, and irritability, but in some cases the patient becomes acutely bewildered, fearful, noisy, talkative, and violent. These reactions, as well as the residual impairment of function, are dependent not only on the type of brain damage sustained by the patient, but on his basic, or "premorbid," personality. Unstable individuals are far more likely to develop acute delirious states than stable individuals.

Lacerations which cause heavy internal bleeding generally produce more lasting and disastrous effects than those followed by mild bleeding. Repeated blows on the head, however, may cause scattered spots of bleeding called "petechial hemorrhages." Veteran prize-fighters frequently develop these multiple hemorrhages, which accounts for the fact that these men are frequently afflicted with slight mental confusion, uncertain balance, inability to concentrate, and involuntary movements—a chronic condition that is technically termed boxer's traumatic encephalopathy or, in extreme cases, boxer's dementia—and popularly described as "punch drunk." No cure for this disorder has been found. *See also* HEAD INJURY (CHRONIC TRAUMATIC DISORDERS).

Illustrative Case: HEAD INJURY, ACUTE TYPE

A man twenty-eight years old suffered a severe head injury when his car collided with another car. He was taken to a hospital and remained unconscious for two hours. An X-ray examination showed that his skull was fractured; the facial nerve on the right side was paralyzed, and he had difficulty in hearing with one ear; his spinal fluid was bloody. After being drowsy for several days, the patient became rather talkative. He obeyed instructions and stayed in bed, but had to be watched constantly because he would sit up and give everybody advice. He calmed down after several days except that he remained overtalkative; flight of ideas and distractibility developed. He would talk about how well he felt, and say that he had planned a trip; then he would relate his experiences on one of his supposed trips and discuss political policies of the various places he had visited. A few weeks later he began to talk of being secretly commissioned by the government to undertake various engineering projects to improve the condition of the country, and he described several visits to Washington which he had actually never made. He felt that he was in the best of health, although his face was still paralyzed from the accident. His condition remained essentially the same for about eight months, after which he gradually recovered, under ordinary medical treatment and discussions with a psychiatrist. (Maslow and Mittelmann, 1951)

HEAD INJURY (CHRONIC TRAUMATIC DISORDERS). A permanent or relatively permanent impairment in brain functions resulting from a severe blow to the head. Chronic, or "post-traumatic," disorders occur when the blow, or trauma, does lasting damage to the brain.

The damage is usually confined to one area, and produces such symptoms as persistent headaches, dizziness, fatigue, irritability, anxiety, impaired memory, and defective concentration. Extensive damage may result in a general loss of intellectual ability, or produce specific defects, such as paralysis, aphasia or deafness, depending on the site of the destruction. Post-traumatic epilepsy occurs in 2 to 4 per cent of all cases, although some estimates are far higher. Seizures occur most commonly after penetrating wounds, and may take a Jacksonian, petit or grand mal form. The epileptic reactions sometimes occur months or even years after the injury took place. *See* EPILEPSY (SYMPTOMS AND TYPES).

Personality changes are found in a small number of post-traumatic cases, perhaps 2 to 3 per cent. The less severe reactions are sometimes termed *post-concussion syndrome,* and are characterized by anxiety plus such symptoms as headache, oversensitivity to stimuli, vertigo, insomnia, inability to concentrate, and sudden emotional changes. These patients also have a reduced tolerance for alcohol, and frequently develop an intense "head consciousness."

The more severe reactions are sometimes classed as *post-traumatic personality disorder.* Adults who suffer from this condition show marked changes in attitude. Some of these patients become indifferent and withdrawn, but they are more likely to be irascible, petulant, impulsive, extremely selfish, and irresponsible. Older patients and those suffering from frontal lobe damage often show impaired memory with confabulation—that is, they fill in missing details with fictional material. *See* CONFABULATION, KORSAKOFF'S SYNDROME.

Although children withstand head in-

jury better than adults, their behavior is likely to be more disorganized and their reactions more extreme. A small percentage of children who have suffered head injury become disobedient, destructive, quarrelsome, distractible, and cruel. Like some post-encephalitic children, they are constantly restless, disruptive, and show little interest in school work. Many of them show intellectual impairment, and some have to be institutionalized.

It is difficult if not impossible to determine the extent to which the personality changes are due to organic as opposed to psychological factors. Injured children usually suffer from headaches, dizziness, and sensitivity to light and noise. It is also known that brain injury tends to distort perception and to weaken the child's ability to think abstractly, concentrate on problems, and carry out instructions. All these factors are due to organic damage. But they also show psychological reactions to these physical effects. They are deeply affected by the attitude of their parents or teachers to their handicap— for instance, if adults show impatience and lack of understanding, they are bound to feel resentful. They also react to their own feelings of frustration, inadequacy, and anxiety aroused by the sudden loss of key abilities. *See* MINIMAL BRAIN DYSFUNCTION.

Among adults, the personality changes seem to be related to a number of different psychological factors. The most important is the premorbid personality. Post-traumatic disorders are most likely to develop in poorly adjusted or restricted, rigid individuals, even when the injury itself is relatively minor. In these patients the usual sequelae, such as perceptual disturbance, intellectual disability, physical symptoms, and head-consciousness, have a particularly disturbing effect. A number of other factors may also play a part in developing and fixing neurotic symptoms. Among them are family tensions, financial or occupational problems, anxiety about the future, fear of permanent defect, repeated examinations, and a desire for compensation. It is not surprising, therefore, that many people who have suffered head injuries become neurasthenic and hypochondriacal, and that in some instances the combined organic and psychological stresses bring latent psychotic tendencies to the surface.

Treatment of chronic traumatic disorders takes three major forms: medical and surgical care, preventive psychotherapy, and carefully planned rehabilitation. Medical care is given as promptly as possible in order to repair lesions and stem hemorrhaging. Mild cases are released from the hospital and returned to work as soon as practicable. With other patients, preventive psychotherapy is given immediately in order to forestall neurotic reactions. This includes reassurance and emotional support, as well as explanation of the type of injury sustained.

A rehabilitation program is launched as soon as possible. It consists not only of physiotherapy, recreational therapy and occupational therapy, but of re-education of the brain itself, so that new areas will take over lost functions. This is followed by a program of careful psychological testing and retraining aimed at preparing the patient for a return to vocational life. The specific nature of the rehabilitation program depends upon the location and severity of the injury, the patient's motivation for recovery and resumption of work, the stability of his personality, and the possibility of returning to a favorable life situation. If these factors are generally positive, the prognosis will be good. If they are unfavorable or complicated by special factors such as alcoholism, drug addiction, arteriosclerosis, or severe emotional conflicts, it is likely to be poor.

In a recent article (1968) Howard A. Rusk, director of the Institute of Rehabilitation Medicine, New York University Medical Center, summarized the results of a rehabilitation program involving 127 severely brain-injured patients. All were suffering from crippling disabilities due to brain hemorrhages, brain lacerations, contusions, or diffuse edema (swelling) resulting from automobile accidents, industrial accidents, assault, or attempted suicide. On the average, they had spent three weeks in coma and five weeks more in different stages of stupor, and their brain injury disabilities were in most cases compounded by fractures, amputations, lung damage, or other complications.

In spite of the fact that most of these patients were not referred to the Institute until about a year after injury, all but 25 were judged feasible for rehabilitation. The program consisted of individualized training, including mat exercises, muscle re-education, gait training, and hand-eye activities, as well as bowel and bladder training and speech therapy where needed. An integral part of the program was retraining in everyday activities necessary to achieve independence. In addition, prevocational testing was provided to determine their ability to work, and the families were counseled and instructed on the management of the patient at home.

In spite of the severity of the disabilities, the results of this "total approach" were most encouraging. Out of the 102 patients capable of participating, 55 were able to return to reasonably satisfactory and productive lives as housewives, students, executives, or artisans; 43 learned to dress and feed themselves independently; and 30 others required only moderate help. *See* REHABILITATION.

HEARING (AUDITION). Despite the claim that 90 per cent of our information input is visual, hearing is a close second to vision in terms of knowledge about the world. The reason is that the *kind* of information gained through hearing is extremely important, since it provides us with the cues on which social contact and communication are based, the signals that warn us of danger, and the sound of music which gives us so much enjoyment. Centuries ago Aristotle claimed that while vision is important for survival, hearing is more important for intellectual development. This opinion was shared by Helen Keller.

The physical stimulus for hearing consists of waves of molecules generated by the vibration of a physical object. A wave of positive pressure is transmitted through the air at the rate of about 1100 feet per second as molecules push against neighboring molecules. But since vibrating objects move back and forth, this positive pressure is periodically followed by negative pressure—that is, a vacuum. The alternation of positive and negative pressure constitutes a sound wave.

The physical properties of sound waves are frequency, intensity, and complexity. Their psychological counterparts are, roughly speaking, pitch, loudness, and timbre. Frequency is stated in cycles per second, the number of times a wave alternates between positive and negative pressure in a single second. Middle C, for example, has a frequency of 261.6 cps. When frequency is varied we experience changes in the highness or lowness of notes, or pitch. The relationship, however, is not a simple one. A tone of 400 cycles per second is experienced as a little more than twice the pitch of one 100 cps, and one of 20,000 cps is only 50 per cent higher in pitch than one of 4000 cps. It has been found that pitch depends on intensity as well as frequency, since a change in loudness can vary pitch without changing frequency at all. A train whistle sounds much higher as it passes us than at a distance.

The human range for hearing loud tones is approximately 20 to 20,000 cps. The higher frequencies become progressively inaudible in the later years of life. Dogs, cats, rats, and bats have a higher range than man. Bats emit sounds at 30,000–80,000 cps and are guided by their echoes; porpoises hear sounds up to 80,000 cps, four times higher than man. Most of our speech occurs between 300 and 7000 cps, and in this range man's sensitivity to sound is as good as any animal's.

Noise as well as tone (except for the occasional pure tone) is a mixture of sound waves; but in tones the basic vibrations are regular and periodic, while in noise they are aperiodic. Some noise, however, is usually produced along with tones; a whistle, piano, or any other instrument always emits noise of some kind. Noise has little or no tonal quality, and since it lacks a fundamental tone, it has no clearly defined pitch.

The intensity of sound is determined by the height or "amplitude" of the sound-wave curve. This characteristic represents the magnitude of the pressure changes and is measured in decibels on a log scale because the intensity range of the human ear is so great. The most intense sound we can respond to is five million times as loud as the softest. Normal conversation is about 60 decibels above threshold; loud thunder is 120 db. Sounds in the 120–140 db. range are usually painful and can cause "exposure" deafness. Airplanes, a speeding subway train, or very heavy traffic, produce sound greater than 80 db if the hearer is relatively near the source. These sounds can also be painful if the individual is exhausted or under emotional tension.

Intensity is a physical measure; the corresponding psychological dimension is loudness. This characteristic is particularly important in music and the expression of emotion. Gentleness is expressed by sounds of low intensity, as in whispers or lullabies; fear and anger by screams and shouts. Variations in loudness are important in public speaking, but equally important are variations in pitch and rate of speech, the modulations and inflections the speaker uses to convey meaning, emphasis and emotional expression. Together, these qualities constitute the speaker's "dynamic range." Musicians as well as speakers should also remember that very low and very high tones have to be sounded with much more intensity than tones in the middle range to make them audible.

Practically all the sounds we hear are made up of complex waves; we rarely encounter pure tones. In any complex sound, the lowest frequency wave is called the fundamental, and waves which are multiples of this frequency are called harmonics. The psychological counterpart of tonal complexity is timbre, or tonal quality. This dimension enables us to distinguish musical instruments from each other and accounts for the infinite diversity of human voices. Sounds of the same pitch and loudness often have marked timbre differences: the same note sounds quite different when sung by two different singers or when played on a clarinet and a French horn. The reason is that the fundamental tone is accompanied by different harmonics and overtones generated by the structure of the instruments or the singers' vocal apparatus.

The human ear (*Fig. 28*) evolved from structures closely related to the static or equilibrium mechanisms in lower animals. The outer ear, or "pinna," is actually the vestige of an organ that originally helped to collect sounds. It is of little use in man and is important only in animals that can move their ears toward the sound source without turning the head. The

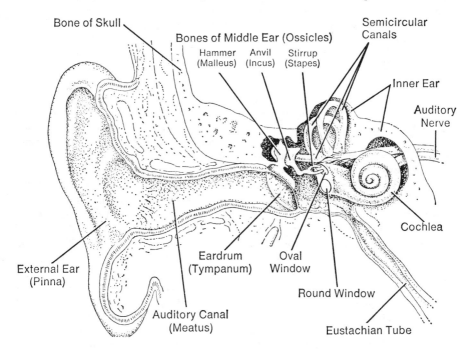

Fig. 28. A cross-section of the human ear. Note that the auditory nerve has two branches, one from the cochlea, which contains cells that respond to auditory vibrations transmitted through the eardrum and ossicles; the other from the semicircular canals, which serve the sense of equilibrium.

sound wave moves through the auditory canal to a thin membrane, the eardrum, which is so sensitive that it responds to wave pressures that move it less than one billionth of an inch. Next, the impulse is conducted from the drum through the middle ear via the ossicles, which consist of three tiny connected bones, the hammer (malleus), anvil (incus), and stirrup (stapes). A membrane called the oval window separates the middle and inner ear, and the impulse is conveyed through it to the cochlea, a structure shaped like a snail.

The cochlea is filled with a fluid which responds to the movement of the ossicles, producing pressure changes that in turn stimulate some of the 24,000 hair cells of the organ of Corti. These cells vary in length like the strings of a harp; some respond to higher, others to lower frequencies. The impulses they generate are then carried to the auditory cortex of the brain, which apparently sorts them out and registers and interprets the different sounds. There is, however, considerable difference of opinion as to whether this process can fully account for the full range of hearing. *See also* HEARING (THEORIES), DEAFNESS.

HEARING (Theories). Theories of hearing must explain both the wide range of pitch—from 20 to 20,000 cycles per second—and the full range of intensity or loudness audible to the human being, from about 15 to 160 decibels. The two outstanding explanations, the place theory and the frequency theory, both accept the fact that the basilar membrane, within the snail-like cochlea of the inner ear, responds to changes transmitted from the outer ear to the oval window—and both recognize that the organ of Corti, situated on this membrane, contains sensitive cells which are activated by deflections of the basilar membrane, and which connect with the auditory nerve that transmits the impulses to the brain. However, the place theory holds that the basilar membrane actually sorts out the different tones, high and low, while the frequency theory holds that it merely transmits the different impulses to the auditory nerve and the sorting out process is done in the brain itself.

Place or Piano Theory. This theory was originated by Helmholtz in the middle of the nineteenth century. He noted that the basilar membrane is wide at one end and narrow at the other, and suggested that fibers in the narrow end respond to high tones and those in the wide end to low tones, just as the strings of a piano or harp vibrate in resonance to differently pitched tones. The nerve fibers connected to different parts of the membrane then transmit stimuli of different frequency to the brain. In this theory, loudness is explained by the amount of the basilar membrane activated by a given sound—that is, a loud sound would activate a wider range of fibers than a soft sound.

The place theory is supported by three types of evidence. First, it has been demonstrated that different portions of the basilar membrane are damaged by prolonged exposure to loud tones of different frequency. Second, electrical and mechanical measurements made within the normal functioning ear show that different portions of the membrane are actually sensitive to tones of different frequency. And third, "mapping" of the temporal lobe of the brain indicates that different regions represent different parts of the cochlea and respond more to one frequency than to another. Recently, however, Békésy (1960), has shown that since the ear is filled with a viscous fluid, the basilar membrane is not free to vibrate like the strings of a piano. While still adhering to the place theory, he has developed the "traveling wave theory," which states that when a sound enters the ear, a wave travels along the basilar membrane and displaces it a maximum amount at a point which corresponds to its frequency. The theory is supported by experiments performed on both animals and human beings.

Frequency or Telephone Theory. According to this interpretation, the basilar membrane is essentially a transmitting instrument, like a telephone or microphone, which vibrates as a whole at the frequency of the incoming sound. These vibrations are then translated into nervous impulses according to their initial frequency, and different portions of the auditory nerve have been found to transmit impulses of different frequencies. This has been proved by amplifying the electrical impulses picked up directly from the auditory nerve of a cat. These impulses will produce a sound which is similar to the sound that is striking the ear of the cat, just as if its ear were behaving as a telephone instrument.

Evidence of this type, however, seems to indicate that the auditory nerve does not respond to frequencies above 4000 to 5000 cycles per second. Moreover, the basilar membrane itself appears to be limited in its capacity to respond to the higher frequencies within the range of human hearing, and it is an accepted fact that a single neuron can transmit no more than 1000 impulses per second. These objections have led Wever (1949) to introduce the "volley" theory, which holds that fibers respond to the higher frequencies by firing in groups or squads. One group may fire at the first condensation of the sound wave, remain in a refractory phase while another group discharges, and then fire again at the third condensation. For a tone of 3000 cps there would be a spurt of activity in the auditory nerve every three thousandth of a second, with different groups of fibers responding each time. Pitch would therefore depend on the frequency of the volleys and not on the

frequency of discharge of individual nerve fibers. Loudness, on the other hand, is believed to depend on the number of impulses that occur in each spurt—that is, intense stimulation activates more fibers than less intense stimulation, and also produces more frequent responses in each fiber. A loud sound would therefore produce more impulses per volley than a soft sound.

At present the tendency is to favor a combination of the two theories. As Hilgard and Atkinson point out (1967), "Even with the help of the volley theory, however, it is difficult to apply the frequency notion to account for frequencies above 5000 cps. Consequently, most experts agree that a two-process theory of pitch is necessary: the frequency principle is used to account for frequencies up to about 5000 cps and a place theory takes over at higher frequencies."

HELMHOLTZ, HERMANN LUDWIG FERDINAND VON (1821–94). This remarkably versatile scientist, who made many pioneering contributions to physiological psychology, was born in Potsdam, Germany, and was educated at the Friedrich-Wilhelm Institute for Medicine and Surgery in Berlin. After completing his studies, Helmholtz served as an army surgeon for seven years (1842–49). His medical dissertation, written at the age of twenty-one, adumbrated the neural theory by showing that ganglionic nerve cells are individually connected to separate nerve fibers. This work helped to gain him admittance to the inner circle of scientists at the University of Berlin, which included H. G. Magnus, the physicist, and Johannes Müller, the greatest physiologist of the time.

In 1845 Helmholtz and three other outstanding scientists, Ludwig, Brücke, and Du Bois-Reymond, formed a pact to fight the doctrine of vitalism, which recognizes other than organic forces as the basis of life. His own support of the mechanistic view took the form of a paper "Uber die Erhaltung der Kraft," which attempted to show that the workings of the body are subject to the law of "conservation of energy."

From 1849 to 1856, Helmholtz served as professor of pathology and physiology at Königsberg. In an early series of experiments he used a device he called a myograph to measure the speed of nerve conduction in a frog. The same technique was then applied to human subjects by varying the point of stimulation (the toes, the thigh, etc), and measuring the time differentials in obtaining a response. From these experiments—which were actually the first studies of reaction time—he calculated the transmission rate for sensory impulses at between 50 and 100 meters per second, with wide differences between subjects and within the same subject at different times.

These experiments had far-reaching effects. They upset the opinions of the experts, some of whom believed the impulses traveled at many times the speed of light, claiming that "we shall probably never obtain the power of measuring the velocity of nerve action, for we have not the opportunity of comparing its propagation through immense space, as we have in the case of light" (Müller, 1843). More significantly Helmholtz's experiments showed that events within the organism, which most people believed to be immeasurable and directed by the soul, could actually be investigated in the laboratory. Boring (1950) makes this comment in his *History of Experimental Psychology:* "In Helmholtz's experiment lay the preparation for all later work of experimental psychology on the chronometry of mental acts and reaction time. The most important effect of the experiment and all the research that followed upon it was, however, that it brought the soul to time, as it were, measured what had been ineffable, actually captured the

essential agent of mind in the toils of science." *See* REACTION TIME, NERVE CONDUCTION.

While at Königsberg, Helmholtz also began to apply himself to the scientific study of vision, inventing the ophthalmoscope and ophthalmograph to aid him in investigating the internal mechanisms of the eye. He continued his work at the University of Heidelberg, where, as professor of physiology, he published the first edition of his *Handbuch der Physiologische Optik* (1867), which is still a fundamental text. This work reviewed all previous studies on optics, brought together recent findings and principles, and presented the results of original experimental investigations on the external muscles and the internal focusing mechanism of the eye.

In the *Optik,* Helmholtz also introduced a theory of color vision which extended the earlier findings of Thomas Young. In addition, he sought to explain perception by applying the concept of "unconscious inference." In essence, this concept meant that we do not directly perceive external objects, but only nervous excitation; however, when certain patterns of excitation are repeatedly associated, we automatically and "irresistibly" infer that they constitute actual objects. *See* COLOR VISION THEORIES.

During the years at Heidelberg, Helmholtz also turned his attention to the study of hearing, publishing his classic volume *Die Lehre von den Tonempfindungen* in 1963. This work was translated into English under the title *Sensations of Tones* in 1875, and is still consulted by students of music, physiology, and psychology. It proposes the resonance, or "place," theory of audition, explains the nature of timbre, beats, discord, harmony, and many other acoustical phenomena. Helmholtz was also greatly interested in the history of music, and traced the dynamics of harmony from Greek times to the more completely integrated relationships of the 19th century. *See* HEARING, HEARING (THEORIES).

In 1871 Helmholtz became professor of physics at the University of Berlin, and was appointed president of the university in 1877. He remained there for the rest of his life, working primarily in the areas of hydrodynamics, meteorological physics, and theories of electricity and electrodynamics. His contributions to these fields are considered as creative and brilliant as his work on nerve conduction, optics, audition, and music.

Helmholtz richly deserves the appraisal of Lindskog (1966), who characterizes him as "One of the last great universalists of science, (who) was able not only to unify the practices and teaching of medicine, physiology, anatomy, and physics, but to relate these sciences significantly to the fine arts."

HEPATOLENTICULAR DEGENERATION (Wilson's Disease).

A rare disorder involving severe damage to the brain and liver due to a deficiency of copper metabolism. It is one of the causes of mental retardation.

If this condition develops in childhood or early adolescence, it may run its course quickly and terminate in death within a few months or years. Afflicted children are excessively childish and emotionally labile (forced laughing and crying). They also have difficulty with swallowing and other voluntary movements. Cases developing later are characterized by cerebral impairment, contractures, hand tremors, and involuntary arm movements which sometimes become violent enough to be known as "wing beating." Treatment is aimed at eliminating the excessive copper in the system through the administration of BAL (British Anti-Lewisite), penicillamine, and Versene. In some cases the motor symptoms can be alleviated, but the mental defect remains. *See* MENTAL RETARDATION (CAUSES).

HIGHER ORDER CONDITIONING.

A process in which a new stimulus is paired with a stimulus to which a response has already been conditioned. The organism then responds to the new stimulus in the same way it responded to the original conditioned stimulus.

Higher order conditioning was originally demonstrated by Pavlov. A dog was conditioned by sounding a metronome and then showing him some food. At first he responded simply by salivating at the sight of the food, but after a number of repetitions, he began to salivate at the sound of the metronome even when the food was not presented. When this conditioning had been well established, a black card was shown just before the metronome was sounded. After a number of trials the dog began to salivate to the black card (the new stimulus) just as he had done to the metronome (the original conditioned stimulus). Pavlov attempted to go on with this process, substituting other stimuli for the black card, but found that he could only occasionally and briefly obtain third and fourth order conditioning.

Human beings are capable of more extended chains of conditioning than animals, and this accounts in large measure for the greater flexibility and range of their learning processes. In learning to speak, we associate a certain sound with a certain object (first order conditioning); when we learn to read, we substitute letters for the sound (second order conditioning); in learning to write, we make certain movements which represent the letters (third order conditioning); and if we study a second language, we substitute new words for those we already know (fourth order conditioning). This illustration, like the black card of Pavlov, is an example of classical conditioning.

A similar process can be carried out in operant or instrumental conditioning, in which the connection between stimulus and response is reinforced by a reward. This process is frequently illustrated in teaching a child a new skill. We may, for example, motivate him to practice piano by offering candy, but as he progresses he will probably respond to praise just as well—and still later he may need no other reward than the intrinsic joy of playing.

Since many stimuli may become rewarding through association with a reward stimulus, the range and complexity of conditioning is greatly increased. A long chain of responses may be built up if there is an important enough goal at the end of the sequence and a series of satisfying subgoals in between. An example is the sequence of promotions in school, each of which is satisfying because it brings the over-all goal of graduation a little closer.

The concept of higher order conditioning applies, then, to a considerable amount of everyday behavior. It can also be used to explain some highly unusual abilities. We have long known that the reflex which reduces the size of the pupils of the eye in bright light (the pupillary reflex) can be conditioned to the sound of a bell, but experiments have also shown that some subjects can achieve a second order conditioning in which the size of the pupil is controlled by their own commands. The discovery that basic reflexes can be self-controlled has been used to explain the fact that Indian fakirs can sometimes be buried alive for long periods of time provided they have a minimal amount of air to breathe. The secret of this amazing ability lies in the fact that they go through a lengthy training procedure which enables them, through conditioning, to cut down on their metabolism by suppressing their heartbeat and reducing their breathing and other vital functions. They literally put themselves into a quasi-vegetative state in which they can survive with a minimum of energy expenditure. *See* CONDITIONING.

HIPPOCAMPUS. A structure situated in the center of the brain below the cortex; a portion of the limbic system. The name, which means "horse's tail," describes its general shape.

The hippocampus is in the oldest part of the cerebral hemisphere, the rhinencephalon or "nose brain," which is entirely devoted to the sense of smell in lower animals. In the course of evolution olfaction became less important, and as a result the hippocampus has come to serve several additional purposes in man and other vertebrates. First, since the nerve fibers from the nostrils end up in this structure, it must still play a part in our reactions to smell, although other parts of the hind brain are also involved. Second, it appears to have an inhibitory effect on sexual behavior, at least in cats and other higher mammals, since lesions in this structure result in increased frequency of sex activity (Kim, 1960). Third, it seems to be involved in emotional response (Isaacson and Wickelgren, 1962). The evidence comes primarily from experiments on rats. Ordinarily these animals are intensely disturbed by electric shocks received while eating, and even after a single shock will refuse to enter a compartment where this punishment is administered. But when the hippocampus was experimentally damaged, they showed only a slight and transient avoidance reaction. *See* LIMBIC SYSTEM.

HIPPOCRATES (c. 460–377 B.C.). According to his biographer, Soranus, the "father of medicine" was born on the Island of Cos and received his early training at one of the ancient temples of health operated by followers of the God Aesculpius. In these temples, always situated near medicinal waters or on high hills, the standard treatment for all physical illness consisted of dietetics, rest, exercise, baths, massage, and a form of suggestion known as incubation. In the latter process the patient was required to lie on the temple floor, and Aesclepius would appear in a dream either to heal the disease outright or to suggest a course of treatment. The priests are believed to have used ventriloquism and possibly hypnosis in this process. They did not attempt to treat mental illness, since it was viewed merely as queer behavior. Another form of the theological or "theurgic" approach was applied, however, since medico-psychological advice was sought from divinely inspired oracles, who were often deeply disturbed themselves.

A second influence helped to shape Hippocrates' approach to medicine: the experimental and scientific movement which had started about a hundred years before. By the sixth century, Alcmaeon had dissected the human body, Empedocles had suggested that the emotions were molecular forces that could alter thought and behavior, and others had attempted to locate the "seat of the soul" in various parts of the body. These attempts, however, had made little headway against theurgic mysticism and the tradition that theology and not medicine had the exclusive right to deal with the human mind. It was in this unfriendly atmosphere that Hippocrates initiated his efforts to divorce medicine from religious influences. These efforts were apparently so successful that they inspired a movement that covered several centuries, for the so-called "Hippocratic collection" comprises about sixty different treatises varying in date from about 500 B.C. to A.D. 250. Although these treatises deal with a wide variety of subjects, including climatology, head wounds, epilepsy, and other mental disorders, they all reflect the heightened curiosity of the Hellenistic age and the assumption that there is a natural order in the universe which can be discovered through investigation.

Typical of this new scientific approach was the Hippocratic comment on epilepsy, which was commonly considered a divine illness. "It thus appears to me to be in no way more divine, nor more sacred than other diseases but has a natural cause from which it originates like other affections." Another example is the careful observation of clinical cases. The collection contains detailed descriptions of psychoses following childbirth, (post-partum psychosis), depression and phobias, as well as states of delirium, confusion, and memory disturbance associated with malaria, tuberculosis, and other infectious diseases. The writings even point out that mental illness is often alleviated when the patient is afflicted with a physical illness such as dropsy or dysentery—an insight that was put to medical use by Wagner-Jauregg in about 1883 when he introduced fever therapy in the treatment of general paresis.

Hippocrates' classification of mental illness contained many terms which are still in use today, although the precise meanings have sometimes changed. Among them are epilepsy, mania, melancholia, and paranoia. His views on etiology were largely physiological, since he held that many disorders were due to brain injury or disease, while others resulted from an imbalance in the bodily "humours" (blood, phlegm, black bile, yellow bile) which were believed to be the basis of temperament. His prescriptions for treating these ills were individualized but not particularly original. They consisted primarily of medicinal herbs and purgatives, as well as bleeding when the patient appeared to be intoxicated due to an engorgement of blood in the head. He viewed hysteria as a bodily dysfunction caused by a wandering uterus, but nevertheless prescribed a nonorganic treatment—marriage—as its best remedy. He also anticipated some aspects of the Freudian theory of dreams by suggesting that they result from the unimpeded expression of inner drives which are held in abeyance during the waking state because we have to meet the demands of reality. *See* HUMORAL THEORY.

Finally, Hippocrates held that feeling, dreaming, thinking and other complex mental processes are mediated by the brain. However, he did not believe that the brain itself was responsible for the psychological aspects of experience, but accepted the widespread doctrine that breath or air taken in through respiration was the actual source of feeling and intelligence, while the brain merely delivered the breath to various parts of the body. Nevertheless he recognized that brain functions were involved in disorders we now term psychiatric, for he ascribed epilepsy to a brain condition, and suggested that one good index of brain injury was a loss of sensation in some part of the body.

Hippocrates remained the dominant influence in Greek medicine for four hundred years—until Galen came on the scene. But Galen himself based many of his ideas about psychology and mental illness on the Hippocratic school. Through his works its influence was extended until the Middle Ages, when society returned to the primitive concepts of demonology. *See* GALEN, DEMONOLOGY.

HOARDING. The drive to save appears to be a dominating characteristic in certain individuals. Such people derive basic satisfaction simply from accumulating money or objects as opposed to putting them to use. The tendency goes far beyond ordinary thriftiness or prudence, and has a compulsive, insatiable, and irrational quality that puts it in the class of personality or character disorders. In addition, hoarding of trash and useless objects is frequently observed in deteriorated schizophrenics and patients with organic brain disorders.

Erich Fromm (1947) considers the "hoarding orientation" to be a major character type. This kind of individual bases his security upon what he can save or own. His attitude toward other people is to possess rather than to love them, and any form of personal intimacy is threatening to him. He is obstinate, rigid, obsessively orderly, and tends to be more concerned about death and destruction than about life and growth. Though many examples of the hoarding orientation can be found today, this character type was far more prevalent in the relatively stable bourgeois economy of the eighteenth and nineteenth centuries.

Fromm's hoarding orientation is clinically similar to the "anal character" described by Freud. According to psychoanalytic theory, interest in the feces, which characterizes the anal period of early childhood, becomes displaced to money and other pleasurable possessions. Saving and hoarding symbolize the sense of power which the individual first experienced when he retained his bodily wastes in defiance of his mother. These drives are therefore believed to be particularly strong in persons who constantly and deliberately withheld the feces as a reaction to their mother's overconcern about elimination. Many of these individuals show a history of constipation in the early years, and this is interpreted as a form of revenge against the mother as well as an attempt to obtain anal-erotic gratification at her hands by forcing her to use enemas or suppositories. In this view, hoarding and miserliness are a continuation of the pattern of anal retention in adult life. *See* PSYCHOSEXUAL DEVELOPMENT, ANAL CHARACTER.

A large number of observations have been made on hoarding in animals, but very few definitive findings have resulted. The most common hoarders are rodents such as squirrels, chipmunks, pack rats, and European hamsters. California woodpeckers have been found to hoard acorns in the holes they drill in trees. Some investigators, such as Morgan (1947), regard hoarding as instinctive; others, such as Marx (1950), believe it is basically learned; while still others, including Bevan and Grotsky (1958), place it somewhere in between, holding that the impulse is derived from the manipulation drive.

In a typical laboratory experiment, rodents are placed in cages with an alleyway leading to a bin containing food pellets. Morgan et al. (1943), found that when rats were kept on a restricted diet for a week or more and then placed in this set-up, they tended to hoard more than well-fed rats, and continued to hoard after they had eaten their fill. However, food deprivation is not the only factor in hoarding, since rats hoard saccharin-flavored foods even when they have had ample food to eat. This indicates that food preference may be a factor. There is also evidence that this drive may in some cases be related to dietary deficiencies, for when lettuce and codliver oil are introduced into the diet, the tendency to hoard is often reduced. On the other hand, hoarding behavior is not affected by injecting rats with glucose before a hoarding test (Stellar, 1943), or by raising them on diets deficient in carbohydrates, fats, or proteins (Bindra, 1947).

Experience may also be a factor. Holland (1954) found that a group of rats given hoarding experiences in the set-up described above tended to hoard more than a group that was only allowed to explore the alley. On the other hand, Smith and Ross (1953) found that mice reared on food pellets which can be readily hoarded did not differ from those reared on liquid diets.

Experiments involving temperature control and brain surgery have also been made. McCleary and Morgan (1946) found that lowering the temperature substantially increases hoarding. This may be an important key to the behavior-pattern. Operations performed on the nervous system indicate that even small lesions made along the midline of the brain have the effect of reducing hoarding (Stamm, 1953). This suggests the possibility that the cingulate gyrus, which is known to be involved in motivation, may have something to do with this activity.

So far these studies have been suggestive rather than conclusive. The only clear indication is that many complex factors are probably involved in this activity.

HOLISM. A general approach to human behavior based on the view that man is a unified organism in whom biological, psychological, and sociocultural aspects are fundamentally integrated. Also an approach to science in general which emphasizes the study of wholes or totalities.

In psychiatry and psychology holism originated as a reaction to the many approaches which fragmentize and segmentalize behavior. These include, among others: (1) faculty psychology, based on separate mental functions such as will, intellect and emotions; (2) the Cartesian dualism of mind and body; (3) the reduction of behavior to a set of reflexes, instincts, conditioned responses or sensory elements. In contrast, the holistic approach maintains that emotions, drives, perceptions, and physical reactions have an essential effect on each other, and the only way to understand any phase of behavior is to view it in its relation to the total organism immersed in its environmental setting. Only through a comprehensive approach can we arrive at a full explanation of behavior and do justice to the integrity and uniqueness of the individual.

The holistic point of view was developed primarily by Adolf Meyer, who created the theory of psychobiology, and Kurt Goldstein, who originated the organismic theory. Their work, however, is part of a general trend based on a great many observations and developments, such as the following: (1) biological theories, including that of Hans Driesch, which view maturation in the light of the total organism; (2) observations in physics and chemistry—for example, the fact that the properties of salt cannot be predicted from those of its ingredients, sodium and chloride; (3) Gestalt psychology, which emphasizes the organism's basic integration of experience into patterns and configurations, and demonstrates that perceptual and other wholes cannot be reduced to a sum of their parts; (4) the gradual rapprochement between the organic and functional approaches in both psychiatry and general medicine as expressed in the idea that every illness is a condition of the total organism and that the doctor should concentrate on the man and not merely on the disease; (5) the development of organic treatments for functional illnesses—for example, electroshock therapy and psychotropic drugs; (6) the observation that the course of physical illness can be influenced by volitional factors such as the will to live; (7) the psychosomatic approach, which shows that emotional factors are often deeply involved in such conditions as peptic ulcers, migraine, and asthma; (8) the observation that the course of severe brain disorders such as general paresis, senile dementia, and cerebral arteriosclerosis can be affected by the patient's attitudes and disposition; (9) the recognition that emotional factors are involved in perhaps fifty per cent of all ailments for which patients seek treatment; (10) studies that show a different incidence of mental disorder on different socioeconomic levels and in different cultural environments; (11) investigations that reveal different types of mental disorder in different societies—for instance, latah and running amok—as well as in different historical periods.

All these factors, and more, have brought the holistic approach to the fore. As a result, science now draws heavily upon a variety of research areas, including physiology, neurology, sociology, anthropology, and psychology in its attempt to understand human behavior and treat mental disorder. The integration of these disciplines is continuing, and there is no doubt that the comprehensive approach of holism is one of the major trends in the contemporary study of man. See GESTALT PSYCHOLOGY, PSYCHOBIOLOGY, ORGANISMIC THEORY, SOMATOPSYCHOLOGY, PSYCHOPHYSIOLOGIC DISORDERS, EXOTIC PSYCHOSES.

HOMEOSTASIS. The process of maintaining constancy or equilibrium in the physiological activities of the organism. The normal functioning of all parts of the body is dependent on this balance; it is essential for both physical survival and psychological well-being.

Two general types of activity are involved in keeping the internal environment within favorable limits: homeostatic mechanisms (Cannon, 1932), and regulatory behavior (Richter, 1942–43). The homeostatic mechanisms are largely automatic processes which maintain constancy of body temperature, blood sugar level, calcium-phosphate balance, salt and water balance, blood pressure, heart rate, and hydrogen-ion (PH) concentration. Practically all the organs and systems of the body participate in these homeostatic processes, and frequently a number of them work together—particularly the lungs, the digestive tract, the kidneys, the liver, the circulatory system, and the nervous system which directly or indirectly regulates all the other mechanisms.

Here are some examples of these activities. If body temperature becomes too high or too low, a "homeostat" located in the hypothalamus initiates certain body activities: we either perspire, and the resultant evaporation cools the body, or we generate heat through stepped-up metabolism and shivering. If our blood-sugar level falls, some endocrine secretions release glucose from our liver, while others regulate the rate at which the intestine absorbs and utilizes carbohydrates.

These "automatic" physiological mechanisms are sometimes insufficient. The body cannot maintain homeostasis for any length of time if it is not getting enough heat, food, water, or air from outside itself. In that case the animal or human being is motivated to meet its needs through overt, regulatory behavior. To maintain warmth, animals roll into a ball or move to a warm area; and to ensure adequate nourishment, they hoard food, increase their intake, or select a diet of high caloric value. Human beings behave in similar ways. We counteract the cold by wearing warm clothing, insulating our houses, or moving south; and we guard against insufficient oxygen at high altitudes by designing pressurized airplane cabins and special masks for astronauts to wear.

In spite of the fact that there are two general approaches to adjustment, homeostatic mechanisms and regulatory behavior, they have a common denominator: they are equally dependent on the co-ordinated functioning of the nervous system. Without this factor it would be impossible to bring together all the activities that are necessary to keep the internal environment within normal limits.

HOMOSEXUALITY (ETIOLOGY AND THERAPY). Erotic relationships between members of the same sex, ranging from sexual fantasies through kissing and mutual masturbation to oral or anal contact.

Today it is a generally accepted fact that human beings cannot be divided into two separate and distinct sexual groups, one composed of a relatively small number of homosexuals and the other a relatively large number of heterosexuals. Rather, there is a continuous line between these two poles, with many individuals sharing both tendencies to a greater or lesser degree. Some investigators believe that all of us are in some degree bisexual, although the homosexual component remains latent in the majority.

At any rate, there is evidence for a widespread potential for homosexual response in Kinsey's estimates (1948, 1953) that 50 per cent of males and 28 per cent of females have engaged in overt homosexual activity at least occasionally. The number of persistent cases—men or women who can be termed active homosexuals—is much smaller. It has been variously estimated at from 2 to 8 per cent of the population.

In recent years there have been two competing approaches to homosexuality, the constitutional and the psychosocial. The constitutional approach emphasizes heredity, chromosomal differences, and hormone balance. Kallmann's twin studies (1953) seemed to give impetus to the hereditary explanation, since he found a concordance rate (both homosexual) of 100 per cent in identical twins, and only 40 per cent among fraternal twins. Yet identical twins usually spend more time together than fraternal twins, and are often subjected to the same experiences—in other words, they probably do not develop their homosexual patterns independently. Similar interpretations may apply in the few cases where homosexuality seems to run through two or more generations. Moreover, some individuals shift from exclusively heterosexual to exclusively homosexual patterns, or vice versa, in the course of their lives, and this shift could hardly be the result of heredity. Genetic factors, therefore, appear to be highly debatable.

The recently suggested hypothesis of chromosomal differences seems to be even more questionable. Although anomalies do occur—for example, a male with two X chromosomes, which is normal for females—they do not necessarily affect sexual behavior. Some early studies seemed to indicate that homosexuality is the result of an abnormal androgen-estrogen ratio, but recent investigations have failed to support these findings. Moreover, hormonal imbalance occurs in many nonhomosexuals, and it is known that people may shift their sexual pattern without a shift in hormone balance. Also, medical treatment with sex hormones does not change the direction of sexual interest. At most all these constitutional factors play an interacting rather than a determining role in homosexuality.

The emphasis today is increasingly on psychological and social explanations. The sexual impulse is somewhat amorphous during the child's early years, and it is quite possible to encourage it to take a homosexual direction even in a predominantly heterosexual society. One of the major influences is *early homosexual experiences*. Bieber and others (1962) have shown that well over twice as many homosexual as heterosexual individuals have had such experiences in childhood. These incidents were usually repeated many times and were reinforced by physical pleasure. In many cases the young person also derived comfort and emotional support from the person with whom he had the experience. This is believed to be an important factor in establishing the homosexual pattern.

A second major influence is *distorted family relationships*. An unhappily married mother may establish a pathologically close relationship with her son, and even act seductively toward "mummy's little lover." A boy also becomes extremely attached to his mother if the father is absent from home, extremely harsh to him, or domineering and yet basically weak (Bender and Paster, 1941). Some authorities believe that attachment to the mother encourages the boy to identify with the feminine role. Others believe that the mother discourages the boy's masculinity in order to suppress his incestuous impulses as well as her own, since these impulses

arouse guilt feelings. Moreover, the boy who feels guilty about his feelings toward his mother may later on avoid all relationships to women because they remind him of the forbidden mother.

Boys who become pathologically attached to their mothers usually fail to learn how to be a man through the normal process of identifying with their father. Frequently the father actually refuses to serve as a model because he rejects the boy as a rival. This, however, is not the only distorted family pattern. In cases where the father shows a marked preference for a daughter, the son may wish he were a girl. Such a wish may remain latent for a long period and later manifest itself as overt homosexuality. In other cases the mother may be so hostile or detached that the boy acquires a dislike or fear of women, and later turns to his own sex for satisfaction.

The end result of these distorted family relationships is that the boys become dependent on their mothers, closely identified with them, and develop traits of timidity and effeminacy that make them shy away from masculine activity of any kind. Bieber found that less than one-fifth of the male homosexuals he studied had participated in typically masculine games. Practically all of them had been humiliated and rejected by other boys. He therefore concluded that "failure in the peer group, and anxieties about a masculine, heterosexual presentation of self, paved the way for the prehomosexual's initiation into the less threatening atmosphere of homosexual society, its values and way of life."

Several other influences have also been stressed. Occasionally a boy becomes identified with femininity because he has actually been raised as a girl in early childhood. Similarly, a girl may want to play a masculine sex role because she has been reared as a boy, or may think that it is better to be a boy than a girl. The attitude of one or both parents may determine that preference. The psychoanalytic theory focuses on "castration anxiety": homosexuals are motivated by unconscious fears associated with losing or being deprived of the penis. The male homosexual therefore avoids women because they remind him that he may be castrated; he can only function with a "woman with a penis." The female homosexual, on the other hand, avoids males because they remind her that she has *already* been castrated; she can only function with women because they do not arouse "penis envy."

Finally, homosexuality may arise from social contact. Both males and females become involved in homosexual behavior in correctional institutions, military service, or boarding schools, where they are in close contact with members of their own sex and at the same time have little or no opportunity for heterosexual relationships. This is sometimes called accidental or pseudohomosexuality, to distinguish it from the type that results from faulty development. These individuals do not consider themselves homosexuals and usually change back to heterosexual behavior when they have an opportunity. Some, however, remain homosexuals, and a few—particularly men who have served a long prison term—have been found to seek out children or adolescents of their own sex after they have been released.

Therapy for homosexuality presents a difficult problem. Most homosexuals believe their tendencies are inborn or the unalterable result of familial influences operating early in life. Many have accepted and fully rationalized their way of life, particularly if they belong to a fairly well organized "homosexual community." They are more likely to seek help because social disapproval and fear of detection have made them anxious or depressed than because they want to change their sexual orientation.

Some homosexuals, however, seek to alter their pattern through psychoanalysis or other forms of psychotherapy, and

25 to 30 per cent of these patients succeed in becoming heterosexual. One promising new approach is the conditioning program designed by Freud (1960). The male patient is given an emetic which makes him vomit, and while he is sick he is shown slides of dressed and nude males. Later on he is given an injection of the male hormone, testosterone, to increase his sex drive, and he is then shown films of nude and semi-nude women. Follow-up studies indicate that the treatment is fully effective in at least 25 per cent of cases.

Not all therapists attempt to alter homosexual patterns. Some believe that it is more practical to help the confirmed homosexual to accept himself as he is, provided his relationships are confined to adults. Others insist that all homosexuals are emotionally disturbed and in need of treatment because they are inevitably haunted by a sense of guilt, although this feeling may be more deeply buried in some than in others. *See* TRANSVESTISM, TRANSSEXUALISM, CASTRATION COMPLEX, PENIS ENVY, BEHAVIOR THERAPY, HOMOSEXUALITY (FEMALE), HOMOSEXUALITY (MALE), SEX ROLE.

HOMOSEXUALITY (Female). Homosexuality is considerably less prevalent among women than among men. In the Kinsey studies (1948, 1953), 28 per cent of women, as contrasted with 50 per cent of men, reported that they had had some type of homosexual experience. In a great majority of cases, however, the relationship was experimental, and only one third had reached the point of orgasm. Among single persons between thirty-six and forty years of age, 10 per cent of women, as compared with 40 per cent of men were found to be currently involved in overt homosexual relationships. Various reports also indicate that female homosexuals generally have far fewer sexual partners than male homosexuals, and do not persist in their activities for as long a time.

Female homosexuality has as long a history as male homosexuality. The practice was widely accepted in later Greece and Rome, and there were prostitutes for women as well as for men. The term Lesbian, often applied to female homosexuals, derives from the Greek island of Lesbos; the less frequently used term Sapphism refers to the Greek poetess, Sappho, who wrote glowing accounts of this type of relationship. Although female homosexuality is considered objectionable in our society it usually arouses less active revulsion and censure than male homosexuality, and relatively few of these women are arrested and convicted.

Female homosexuality is characterized by strong sexual interest between women, but does not always express itself in overt behavior. When it does, sexual activity takes the form either of mutual masturbation or oral-genital contact (cunnilingus). During the latter type of contact, one partner plays the active role, the other the passive role. Sometimes the active member wears an artificial male organ (a "dildo") for purposes of stimulation or penetration. Contrary to the common impression, the sexual roles are not fixed and are frequently interchanged. Likewise, it is a mistake to think that one female homosexual always has masculine personality characteristics while the other has more feminine traits (the so-called "butch" and "femme" types). This is sometimes the case, but it is by no means the rule. Actually the great majority of female homosexuals of today try to make themselves as attractive and feminine as possible, and are indistinguishable from normal women. Some of them claim to feel more feminine than ever in their homosexual relationships. A few female homosexuals, however, have been found to menstruate later than usual, and some have narrow hips, relatively undeveloped breasts and wide shoulders. HOMOSEXUALITY (ETIOLOGY AND THERAPY).

Female homosexuals show many disturbances in attitude and emotion. Many of them are actively repelled by menstruation, possibly because it is a reminder of the reproductive function, which demands heterosexual relations. They have an equal revulsion toward the male genital and frequently state that they are disgusted by the thought of intercourse with a male. (Psychoanalysts believe this reaction to the male organ is a defense that disguises a strong unconscious desire for a penis.) But despite their attitude toward heterosexual relations, many of these women would like to have social relationships with men. Here they are caught in a basic dilemma, since many men will not accept a Platonic friendship. If these women are married—and a good many are—their conflicts over sex are likely to be extremely acute.

The female homosexual is beset by a variety of other problems. If she is working, she must make special efforts to remain undetected for fear of dismissal. If her family does not know about her tendencies, she must maintain secrecy there as well. But perhaps the most disturbing emotional problem of these women is the feeling that they are isolated and outside the mainstream of society. Many of them are afflicted with an almost constant sense of loneliness and rejection. They resent the implication that they are peculiar, almost inhuman creatures; and they feel that an artificial wall has been erected between them and practically the whole of humanity. They cannot understand why the world will not accept their form of sexuality, which seems completely right to them.

Some homosexual women succeed in obtaining a measure of emotional support by joining an informal clique or a more formal organization such as the Daughters of Bilitis. This is a national organization with chapters in many large cities, and is named after a collection of poems by Pierre Louÿs dealing with the women of Lesbos. In general, however, opportunities for group contact seem to be far fewer for female than for male homosexuals, and they have fewer centers like the "gay" bars of the men. For this reason—and probably because they are less interested in transitory gratification—they become more dependent on individual relationships. These partnerships, or "marriages," do not often work out well since so many female homosexuals are unhappy, conflicted people who cannot maintain lasting relationships of any kind. Although many of them feel that their problems would come to an end if society would only recognize and accept them, practically all psychiatrists regard them as sick people in urgent need of treatment. Some specialists, however, feel that the treatment process should be directed toward making them more comfortable in their present role rather than toward changing their sexual orientation.

HOMOSEXUALITY (Male).

Male homosexuality, like female homosexuality, takes a number of forms: the latent type, in which there is an attraction to men but no overt sexual activity; incidental and transient contacts; a mixture of homosexual and heterosexual relationships; and a completely homosexual life in which all sexual gratification is achieved with men.

Overt homosexual behavior generally begins—and often ends—in mutual masturbation, which is widespread among children and adolescents. In some cases it starts with seduction by an older homosexual (pedophilia), in the form of oro-genital or ano-genital intercourse in which the boy is the passive partner. Kinsey and his colleagues (1948) reported that 37 per cent of males admitted having some kind of homosexual experience to the point of orgasm after the onset of adolescence, and 8 per

cent had been engaged exclusively in homosexual activity for at least three years after the age of sixteen. These figures were largely the same in cities, towns, and rural areas throughout the country.

The sex roles of male homosexuals are less fixed than is commonly believed. Although some men play the male or female role exclusively, most of them have been found to alternate from time to time. Similarly, some homosexuals fit the common picture of a "swish" who walks, talks, and gestures in a feminine manner, and confines himself to interests and occupations that are supposed to be female—but contrary to popular opinion, the great majority (some say 85 per cent) cannot be recognized as homosexual either by their appearance, their behavior, or their interest patterns. A few, however, are transvestites—that is, they derive sexual pleasure from wearing feminine clothes and make-up—yet even these men may look and act completely masculine in their ordinary attire. Some male homosexuals do appear more effeminate than others, but contrary to popular expectation these men often play the active role in their sexual relationships while ruggedly masculine homosexuals often prefer the passive role. Actual anatomical differences in secondary sex characteristics—broad hips, narrow shoulders—are found in only a small minority of cases, but even when this occurs there is no difference in the primary sex organs, nor do these individuals always play the feminine role.

Practically all male homosexuals are beset with acute personal problems. They may appear to accept their pattern of behavior quite blandly, and may even flaunt their relationships before the public—nevertheless they are constantly aware that they are outside the pale and keenly feel disapproval of others, even when it is not openly expressed. Many of them agree with the common attitude that they are "queer," and wage a continual but losing battle against their impulses. Such men are in a constant state of internal conflict. Others hotly defend their way of life and their right to behave as they choose. But despite their bravado, these individuals are likely to be insecure and apprehensive, since they live in constant fear of detection, humiliation, or loss of employment.

Homosexuals, then, have a special need for emotional support and reassurance. Many of them become dissatisfied with five-minute contacts with total strangers in washrooms, or one-night stands with casual acquaintances. As a result, they seek a deeper relationship as well as a greater sense of security by living with one other man. But this monogamist arrangement rarely lasts, since one or the other partner is almost bound to stray—and it would be hard to find more intense displays of jealousy or more violent quarrels than the kind that occurs between two homosexuals. If one of these "marriages" fails, the partners usually set up another, and their lives become a continuous series of short-term affairs.

Most male homosexuals, however, live alone and become involved in small cliques which hold "parties" in one or another apartment. These gatherings provide them with social life, sexual gratification, and a change of partners.

Today's homosexuals probably derive their greatest sense of security from the feeling that they belong to a society of their own—a subculture with its own standards, customs, and even language. In large cities, male homosexuals may have their own shops and beaches; but their basic social institution is the "gay" bar where they can meet friends, exchange news about their world, find acceptable partners, learn about the latest police activities, and receive invitations to parties. A homosexual who plans to visit another city usually inquires in advance about these meeting places.

Even though male homosexuals desire relationships that have some degree of security, most of them shy away from emotional involvement and long-term commitments. The following definition of the word "gay," as given by a homosexual, is quite typical. It is followed by a description of the initiation of a new recruit:

To be gay is to go to the bar, to make the scene, to look, and look, and look, to have a one night stand, to never really love or be loved, and to really know this, and to do this night after night, and year after year. . . .

The young man who may have had a few isolated homosexual experiences in adolescence, or indeed none at all, and who is taken to a "gay" bar by a group of friends whose homosexuality he has only vaguely suspected or was unknown to him may find the excitement and opportunities for sexual gratification appealing and thus begin active participation in the community life. Very often, the debut, referred to by homosexuals as "coming out," of a person who believes himself to be homosexual but who has struggled against it, will occur in a bar when he, for the first time, identifies himself publicly as a homosexual in the presence of other homosexuals by his appearance in the situation.

If he has thought of himself as unique, or has thought of homosexuals as a strange and unusual lot, he may be agreeably astonished to discover large numbers of men who are physically attractive, personable, and "masculine" appearing, so that his hesitancy in identifying himself as a homosexual is greatly reduced. Since he may meet a complete cross-section of occupational and socioeconomic levels in the bar, he becomes convinced that far from being a small minority, the "gay" population is very extensive indeed.

Once he has "come out," that is, identified himself as a homosexual to himself and to some others, the process of education proceeds with rapid pace. Eager and willing tutors—especially if he is young and attractive—teach him the special language, ways of recognizing vice-squad officers, varieties of sexual acts and social types. They also assist him in providing justifications for the homosexual way of life as legitimate, and help to reduce his feelings of guilt by providing him with new norms of sexual behavior in which monogamous fidelity to the sexual partner is rare. (Hooker, 1962)

Illustrative Case: HOMOSEXUALITY, MALE

Martin L., a twenty-nine-year-old single male hairdresser, was referred by the court to a state hospital on the Pacific Coast for evaluation in connection with his trial for sexual offense. He had been living alone in a small, neatly furnished apartment in the Los Angeles area.

Martin was the only child born to an elderly midwestern farmer and his much younger and very socially active wife. Martin was very fond of his mother and loved to be with her, but his upbringing was left principally to a female hired hand, in order to free the mother's time for her social activities. Perhaps because of the age of his father, Martin later commented, "I never felt in any way close to my father." He added by way of explanation, "My mother walks all over him and runs the family."

The family lived in a sprawling farm community, so that Martin's only available peer was a boy on the neighboring farm, and the two became inseparable companions. Although Martin was a very bright child he had a difficult time in school, since he never prepared his lessons and his parents never disciplined him about this. To add to his difficulties at school the other children considered him a sissy because he did not participate in team sports. This made him even more dependent on his one friend, and the two spent many hours together in solitary activities like hunting and fishing. Reflecting about his schoolday experiences, Martin said, "Starting at about twelve some boys from school used to masturbate in a group and one boy used to perform fellatio on me frequently. I masturbated at least once daily until I joined the service. I never felt guilty about sex, didn't think anything about the homosexual experiences. I had never even heard of the word until I joined the service."

Martin's sexual activity was richly supplemented by heterosexual experiences. He dated frequently and presumed himself in love with a schoolmate. He impulsively joined the Navy as soon as he was able to do so and while in the service received a letter informing him that his beloved had married someone else. His career in the Navy was not marked by any sexual activity until almost two years had passed, when he began engaging in fellatio as the active partner with a group of teen-age boys. When this was discovered he was immediately discharged and while returning home fell into the company of a group of homosexuals who were going to Los Angeles. He became fascinated by them, joined them, and in Los Angeles met his old neighbor and closest friend, who was a member of the homosexual community. Martin began to frequent the homosexual bars and engaged in much overt homosexual activity, until he spent all his money, when he decided to return home.

However, he shortly returned and resumed his homosexual life, taking a job as a cosmetics salesman to support himself. Besides his sexual activity with his contemporaries, he continued to pick up teenage boys for fellatio, and was arrested on this count when the parents of one of the boys complained. He was given a suspended sentence on the condition that he enter therapy, which he did. His therapist gave him carbon dioxide treatments, which did not do any apparent good. He took a job as a hairdresser, continuing his homosexual adjustment and his behavior with teen-age boys. He also dated girls, attempting unsuccessfully to have intercourse with them on rare occasions, leading his homosexual companions to refer to him as the "fickle one." He was again arrested for fellatio with a teen-ager, and this time his trial was postponed so that he could be placed under observation in the state hospital.

Martin reported for the initial interview dressed in Bermuda shorts. He showed no apparent concern about the proceedings, and was flippant and familiar with the interviewer. During his stay he continually denied belonging in the hospital, saying that he did not wish to have his personality altered and had no desire for treatment. When it was discovered that he was engaged in a homosexual relationship with an attendant, he was discharged as unchanged and returned to court for trial. (Zax and Stricker, 1963)

HORNEY, KAREN (1885–1952). Born in Germany, Karen Horney was trained as a Freudian analyst. She came to this country in the early 1930s, and soon after founded an association and training institute which she headed until her death. Since then, the institute has grown in size and importance, and exponents of the Horney approach are currently found throughout this country as well as abroad.

Horney accepted the general psychodynamic approach of Freud, but drew away from classical psychoanalysis because she felt it overemphasized man's biological endowment and relegated social and cultural factors to a minor role. She rejected Freud's instinct theory, his structural approach to the mind (id, ego, and superego), and his view that an unresolved Oedipal conflict is at the root of all neuroses. Instead of putting the primary emphasis on sex and aggression, she held that the need for emotional security is the underlying determinant of human behavior. In her books, the most important of which are *The Neurotic Personality of Our Time,* (1937), *New Ways in Psychoanalysis* (1939), and especially *Neurosis and Human Growth* (1950), she presented a "correction" of many of Freud's concepts which actually amounted to a reformulation of the entire development, structure, and dynamics of neurosis.

Horney held that neuroses arise out of the "strategies" which the individual adopts in attempting to handle what she terms basic anxiety, which is a feeling of uneasiness, dread, and impending disaster. The major source of anxiety lies in disturbed relations between the child and his parents, such as indifference to the needs of the child, a cold family atmosphere, excessively high standards, and constant, caustic criticism. These relationships make the child feel that he is isolated, helpless, and insecure in a hostile world. They also generate feelings of counterhostility in the child, which become especially powerful when he is prevented from expressing his an-

ger because of guilt, fear, and helplessness. But the more he represses his hostility, the more intense becomes his basic anxiety.

But how does the neurosis itself develop? According to Horney, it is a maladaptive reaction to the basic anxiety. This feeling is so pervasive, devastating, and frightening that when it is not alleviated by positive experiences outside the home, the child will undertake various strategies to counteract it. He may try to placate his parents in order to win their love, or attempt to avenge himself by spiteful behavior. He may seek to compensate for feelings of helplessness by exerting power over others. He might turn his hostility inward and belittle himself, or withdraw into his shell to avoid being hurt by others. All these strategies have one thing in common: they are attempts to cope with a world which he feels is threatening to overpower and crush him.

The unfortunate feature of these strategies is that they start out merely as devices to allay anxiety, but end up as persistent needs which become an integral part of the individual's personality. These needs are termed neurotic for two reasons. First, they are irrational, unrealistic attempts to resolve disturbed relationships. And second, they generate insatiable drives by creating a vicious circle—that is, they produce more problems, and therefore more anxiety, than they alleviate—and to allay this additional anxiety, the individual resorts to these strategies all the more.

Horney enumerates ten of these neurotic needs: the insatiable need for affection and approval, for a partner who will take over ones' life, for restriction of one's life, for power, for exploitation of others, for prestige, for personal admiration, for personal achievement, for self-sufficiency and independence, and for perfection and unassailability. All such needs tend to group themselves into three general categories. First, *moving toward people:* an excessive need for love and a tendency to lean on others. This need arises out of feelings of helplessness. Second, *moving away from people:* an inordinate need for independence and for setting up one's own limited world. This drive arises out of the feeling that one is misunderstood by others or has nothing in common with them. Third, *moving against people:* an inordinate need for power, prestige, or possessions obtained at the expense of others. This need arises out of the conviction that the environment is basically hostile.

These needs are not "unnatural"—in fact, every individual has an urge for affection and dependence, for self-sufficiency and independence, for power and recognition. Moreover, everyone is faced with conflicts in his life. The normal person, however, can integrate the three orientations and is flexible enough to use now one, now another as circumstances require. In so doing, he can satisfactorily resolve his personal conflicts. The neurotic, on the other hand, is dominated by one of the three needs and employs it rigidly, inappropriately, and in the extreme. He tries to solve *every* problem by clinging to others, or by restricting his life, or by exploiting people. To justify and rationalize his one-tracked approach, he unconsciously develops an idealized picture of himself as a self-sacrificing martyr, a self-sufficient recluse, a man of power and glory. He then devotes his energies to living up to this idealized but false image, and in the process destroys his relationships with other people.

Unlike the normal individual, the neurotic can neither resolve his personal conflicts nor the conflicts that stem from the culture itself—such as the emphasis on competition and success versus a religious heritage which stresses humility and brotherly love, or the emphasis on freedom of the individual versus the limitations on freedom imposed by social reality. "These contradictions embedded in our culture are precisely the conflicts which the neurotic struggles to reconcile: his tendencies toward aggressiveness and his tendencies toward yielding; his excessive demands and his fears of never getting anything; his striving toward self-aggrandizement and his feeling of personal helplessness" (Horney, 1939). Since our culture puts its greatest stress on competitiveness and prestige-striving, Horney finds that the "neurotic personality of our time" is more likely to be characterized by an insatiably competitive drive than by the tendency to be submissive or withdrawn.

In the Horney approach, the object of therapy is to help the individual overthrow his idealized self-image and replace it with a "real self" that will release his capacities for personal growth. This requires that the patient go through a "disillusioning process" in which he is made aware of his faulty strategies. Horney believes he must come to realize that these strategies are futile and harmful before he can deal with the reasons for which they were set up. But when he attains some recognition of the defense system he is using, the next step is to help him gain insight into the conflicts that underlie it. In this process, the therapist utilizes many of the Freudian techniques, but in general plays a more direct and active role than the classical analyst.

HOSTILITY. Persistent anger accompanied by an intense urge to retaliate.

Hostility is a common feature of normal behavior but may also be a major factor in mental and emotional disturbance. The line between anger and hostility is not a sharp one, but the term hostility is usually used in the psychological sciences to denote the kind of aggressive anger or rankling resentment that arises from prolonged frustrations or deprivations. Some common sources of hostility are: favoritism toward another child, outright rejection by the parents, harsh and rigid discipline, excessive criticism, unfair treatment in school or on the job, racial or religious discrimination, and a sordid environment.

In most individuals hostile feelings can be kept within bounds by such means as talking them out, draining them off through sports or other "sublimations," or by active attempts to alleviate the frustrating situation. These measures, however, rarely eliminate all hostility, and the excess may seek an outlet in both direct and indirect ways. Children frequently express their anger overtly in tattling, belittling others, dawdling, refusing to eat, soiling, or exhibiting sibling rivalry. Older people tend to express their hostility more covertly through resentful attitudes, prejudice, general irritability, overcompetitiveness, overaggressiveness, and in some cases becoming "angry at the whole world" or engaging in criminal behavior.

Hostility is one of the most troublesome of all emotions. First, it generates intense feelings of guilt, especially when directed against our parents or mate, since we have been taught that hostile attitudes and hostile actions are unethical. Second, vengeance and other attempts to harm people who frustrate us frequently arouse a fear of retaliation. And third, we are afraid we will lose the love and approval of others if we give vent to hateful impulses. For these reasons hostility may become a major source of anxiety and insecurity, and we may use a variety of defensive maneuvers to protect ourselves from these uncomfortable feelings. For example, we might vehemently—too vehemently—deny we are hostile ("denial of reality"), or we might go to the opposite extreme and become overfriendly or oversolicitous toward the person who is standing in our way ("reaction formation").

If an individual's hostile impulses are extremely powerful and persistent, he may overuse defensive measures and develop neurotic symptoms. Coleman (1964) points out that "sometimes hostility . . . may threaten to break through the individual's defenses into consciousness and even into behavior which would lead to serious self-devaluation or would endanger his relationship with others. The handling of hostility is often a very real problem for the neurotic, who typically feels forced to take a compliant, subservient, self-suppressing attitude toward others as the price for security, love, and acceptance." If these defenses do not work, the hostile impulses may suddenly come to the surface and produce an anxiety attack —an acute state of panic.

Feelings of hostility may be a major factor in other neurotic reactions as well. In obsessive-compulsive individuals, they may be covered over by preoccupation with thoughts of brotherly love or may be kept under control by an overrigid conscience. In one case, a businessman felt compelled to call his wife three or four times a day because he felt that she or his children might be in danger; actually, he hated the responsibility of marriage and this was an unconscious attempt to conceal his guilty feelings of hostility toward his family. In a situation of this type another individual might have developed a depressive reaction—that is, he might have felt, unconsciously, that his constant concern about the safety of his family was a sign that he wanted them to come to some harm, and guilt over entertaining such hostile thoughts might have driven him into a depression. This would be particularly likely to occur if a member of the family actually came to some harm.

Hostility is an important factor in many other types of disorder. In the antisocial reaction (psychopathic personality), the individual not only feels hostile but impulsively acts out his hostility, apparently without pangs of conscience or feelings of guilt. Enuresis (persistent bed-wetting) may sometimes be an unconscious means of expressing anger at the parents. In exhibitionism, self-exposure is sometimes interpreted as a manifestation of hostility toward the other sex or a retaliation against society as a whole. In the "simple" form of schizophrenia, the patient frequently has difficulty handling hostility; typically, he is so inhibited and "good" that he cannot express any impulses which he regards as immoral or dangerous—and this is one reason he is so withdrawn. In the paranoid form of this disorder, the patient's hostile impulses take the form of extreme suspiciousness, arrogance, litigiousness, resentfulness or, in some cases, homicidal urges. These impulses frequently give rise to delusions of persecution: "In his effort to control his hostile impulses in which the genesis of his paranoid reaction is often to be found, the patient projects them and experiences them as directed against himself. Filled with hate, he feels and believes that he is the victim of persecutors, who, in fact, are but the objects upon whom he has projected his own hate." (Noyes and Kolb, 1963). See AGGRESSION, ANGER.

HOUSE - TREE - PERSON TECHNIQUE. A projective test based on interpretations of drawings of a house, a tree and a person.

According to J. N. Buck (1948), the psychologist who devised this technique, the renderings of these particular objects reveal personality dynamics with special clarity. The house is believed to represent the subject's conception of his home as the place where his most satisfying and most frustrating relationships have been experienced. It also gives information about his psychosexual adjustment, since the various features of the house (chimney, balconies, doorways) are unconscious sexual symbols. Details close to the ground are believed to represent the level of reality, while details close to the top are a projection of the subject's fantasy life. The tree drawing symbolizes his relationship to his environment and his response to outside pressures. The trunk represents his feeling of basic power, the branch structure depicts the satisfactions he derives from the outside world, and the over-all organization of the tree represents his feeling of inner balance. The subject's drawing of a person also reflects his personality. The dimensions, posture, malformations, or overemphasis on one or another part of the body yield information about interpersonal relationships, sexual role and the way he feels about himself. See FIGURE DRAWING TEST.

In administering the test, the examiner asks his subject to draw the three objects on separate sheets of paper with a lead pencil. He notes the order in which the parts of each figure are drawn, comments made by his subject, pauses in the process, and the time taken for each drawing. He then asks a series of questions about each picture—for example, the sex, age, and identity of the person drawn, as well as what this person is thinking and feeling.

After the test is given, a detailed analysis is made of the drawings and the notes of the examiner. Buck believes this will yield a fairly clear picture of the subject's emotional tone, intelligence, drive level, psychosexual dynamics, major needs, and personality trends. This picture is based not only on the general character of the drawings but on specific details. In one instance, the omission of a chimney on the house suggested a lack of warmth in the subject's home situation, as well as difficulty in playing the masculine role. In another case, thin, leafless branches on the tree suggested that the subject's will was weak and constricted, and that he was not obtaining the kind of satisfaction that would allow him to "bloom." Similarly, a picture of a man with a cigar in his mouth suggested a preoccupation with oral needs. Buck cautions that such interpretations should not be made mechanically, but only in the light of the individual's background. *See* ORAL CHARACTER, PSYCHOSEXUAL DEVELOPMENT.

Estimates of intelligence based on the H-T-P technique correlate well with the Wechsler-Bellevue Intelligence Scale. It undoubtedly yields much valuable information about the subject's reactions, and is considered provocative and interesting. However, its value as a personality technique has still to be substantiated.

HUMOR. Ever since the ancient Greeks, humor has been a subject of endless discussion by writers and philosophers. Most of their theories have been based on general observation and speculation, and only in recent years have there been any systematic investigations of this aspect of behavior. This article will review some of the major findings on the development and expression of the sense of humor from infancy to adulthood, its functions in the psychic economy, and various theories that seek to explain why we laugh.

The child's first smile, which sometimes occurs during the first week of life, is actually a reflex response. Not until he reaches about three months of age will he begin to show pleasure by smiling at other people. By the end of the first year, most children show some appreciation of the comic. They not only laugh when tickled, but also respond to unusual sounds, funny (but not frightening) faces, and action games like peek-a-boo. Throughout the preschool years, humor continues to be largely of a concrete, slapstick variety, but toward the end of this period the child will also enjoy word play, simple jokes, and comic drawings of animals.

As they grow older, children begin to see humor in obvious incongruities (a thin man with a fat wife), defiance of authority (whispering forbidden words), misfortunes of other people (slipping on a banana peel), and situations that release some of their deeper feelings (a clown wheeling a baby carriage that suddenly collapses). They may also get fun out of teasing and embarrassing others, but they are usually unable to take any kind of kidding themselves. Until ten or eleven they are "not very skilled at high-class humor," as Gesell, Ilg and Ames (1956) have put it; they laugh most uproariously at "corny" jokes, "idiot" stories, and obscenities.

In the later years of childhood and in early adulthood young people learn to appreciate witty remarks, humorous commentaries, stories that build to an unexpected climax, and "gallows" humor that takes serious matters lightly. And as the tensions of life increase, some people also develop behavior patterns based on humor reactions—a "nervous" laugh that conceals feelings of insecurity, or "hysterical" laughter that releases pent-up emotion in the same way that genuine humor relieves underlying tensions.

Even though humor follows a general developmental pattern, there are considerable variations from child to child in the appreciation of the comic. Studies have indicated that these differences are due largely to four factors. First, *attitudes of other people:* a happy, relaxed, fun-loving atmosphere at home and at play helps to cultivate a sense of humor, while tensions and antagonisms prevent it from developing. Second, *intelligence:* brighter children can usually see the point of the joke more readily than duller children, and are often better able to empathize with or imagine themselves in the place of characters in a humorous situation. They are also more likely to see the humor in situations that involve themselves. Third, *social pressures:* humor is largely social, and children will laugh at jokes that are accepted by their particular group and frown on humor the group rejects. If the group, for example, ridicules a certain person or a member of a certain race, the child may adopt this pattern in order to gain social acceptance. Humor patterns have also been found to vary with the social level: a "belly laugh" would be considered uncouth among the "upper class." Fourth, *personality needs:* a rebellious child will appreciate jokes about people in authority, and an insecure child will readily laugh at other people's misfortunes but never at his own.

These observations of children and young people—most of which carry over into adulthood—indicate that humor serves many psychological functions. Laughing at the foibles of people in authority enables us to express hostility safely and without fear of retaliation. Laughing *with* others increases our sense of solidarity and social acceptance. Getting the point of a joke, especially if it is a subtle one, enhances our self-acceptance and self-confidence. Taking serious things playfully fortifies our sense of perspective. Observing incongruities reminds us that life is full of surprises. The very act of laughing itself provides a healthy release of pent-up emotional energy, especially when we are beset with tensions and stresses. And laughing at ourselves, or at things that would normally disturb us, proves that we can relax our defenses without being overwhelmed. It also helps us to regain control over situations which have been too much for us to handle.

These psychological functions show that humor is closely tied to deeper feelings and attitudes. For this reason it should not be surprising that a great deal can be learned about an individual's inner dynamics by discovering what he does and what he does not find amusing. In many cases people cannot laugh at certain topics or certain types of jokes because they arouse feelings of anxiety—in fact, they may not even get the point of an obvious story because their psychological guard automatically goes up while it is being told. In this regard, it is an interesting fact that mental patients are usually humorless themselves and cannot enjoy the humor of others—not only because of their psychological defenses but because life itself is so threatening to them. On the other hand, therapists sometimes find that humor can be used to by-pass resistances, since the patient may accept an interpretation if it is suggested in an offhand, joking manner, but not when it is offered seriously.

The observations of children's humor noted above have confirmed many of the concepts suggested by writers and philosophers throughout history. Plato pointed out our tendency to laugh at people or situations which make us feel superior, and Aristotle added the benign comment that we laugh at the misfortunes of others only when they are minor. Hobbes carried this "derision theory" to its extreme by describing laughter as a "sudden glory" which we feel in "observing the imperfections of other men." Bergson asserted that we never laugh at things, but only at people when they behave like things or automata, as they do when they slip and fall. Kant emphasized the element of surprise and anticlimax: "Laughter is an affection arising from the sudden transformation of a strained expectation to nothing." (As an example, he cites the rich merchant who was forced to throw his merchandise overboard during a storm at sea, and "grieved thereat so much that his wig turned gray the same night.") Max Eastman stresses the idea that humor is "playful pain"—that is, we take serious things in fun, and this enables us to triumph over adversity and come to better terms with life.

Freud, in his *"Wit and Its Relation to the Unconscious* (1905), has suggested still another interpretation. According to his theory, wit originates in the nonsensical word play of children, which in itself is not humorous but simply a pleasurable experimentation with sound. Real humor and wit enable us to recapture the freedom of childhood, including freedom from grammar and syntax; but at the same time it gives us another and more important freedom —freedom from the censor, the social sanctions that force us to repress the basic drives or "instincts" of sex and hostility. When we tell a joke, or laugh at a jest, we "let the cat out of the bag"—that is, we give expression to these forbidden drives—and in so doing, the energy we have been using to keep them out of consciousness is suddenly released in the form of a burst of laughter. *See* CENSOR.

Freud's theory helps to explain why so many jokes deal with sexual or hostile subject matter. Laughter is indeed a form of release, and we do utilize it to give vent to tendencies we do not dare to express more directly. Here, then, is one more psychological function performed by humor. It must be recognized, however, that Freud has not given us a theory of humor itself, for he does not explain why jokes not only give us release but appear *comic*. Perhaps the reason is that a good joke, through the sharpness of its wording or action, makes us suddenly appreciate the incongruities that life presents and, by taking them lightly, we relieve ourselves of the tensions they would normally produce.

HUMORAL THEORY. The theory that ascribes personality characteristics to the effects of bodily fluids, or "humors."

The humoral theory is the oldest known typology, or descriptive system, used for classifying all individuals into a limited number of categories. It was originated in about 400 B.C. by Hippocrates, who believed that a predominance of blood was associated with a sanguine (hopeful) character or temperament, black bile with a melancholic (sad) temperament, yellow bile with a choleric (irritable) temperament, and phlegm with a phlegmatic (apathetic) temperament. If, however, all the humors were mixed in proper proportions, they would produce a well-balanced person. Since the Greeks held that man is a mirror of the whole of nature, many of them believed that the four humors corresponded to the four cosmic elements, fire, earth, air, and water, which Empedocles had postulated in about 450 B.C.

As Bromberg (1959) states, "The Hippocratic theory of the four humours, under the dogmatic espousal of Galen, became the guide for all physicians until the Renaissance." Its nearest counterpart in modern science is the view that the hormones are the basis of temperament. There is evidence that the size of glands may differ greatly even among normal individuals, so that thyroid or adrenal tissue in one person may actually weigh three times as much as in another. There is further evidence on this point in studies which indicate that some individuals react with typically sympathetic and others with typically parasympathetic responses to the same situations, and that autonomic responses in the same children tend to be stable over a long period (Wenger and Wellington, 1943).

Some investigators believe they have found a relationship between these autonomic response patterns and personality measurements (Lacey, Bateman, and Van Lehn, 1952), but others have pointed out that these constitutional patterns—granted that they exist—are not the key to the entire personality structure, since acquired habits, attitudes, and reactions must also be taken into account. Moreover, accurate measurement of autonomic functioning has not resulted in the isolation of a few specific types, as the humoral theory suggests, but shows continuous gradations instead.

HUNGER DRIVE. Hunger has been studied more intensively than any other drive, yet its exact mechanism is still in doubt. Newer investigations, however, have added to our knowledge in three major areas. They have shown (1) that the drive does not merely stem from stomach contractions; (2) that it is regulated to a large extent by the brain and particularly the hypothalamus; and (3) that psychological factors are deeply involved in the strength of our appetite and the foods we choose to satisfy it.

Earlier observations suggested that contractions taking place in an empty stomach produced hunger pangs, and these in turn led to awareness of hunger and attempts to find food. The theory received its strongest support from an experiment in which a subject swallowed a balloon which responded to the peristaltic movements. A close correspondence between stomach contractions and conscious sensations of hunger was found (Cannon and Washburn, 1912). Since that time this "local theory" of hunger has been contraverted by many other investigations. Tsang (1938) found that removal of the stomach did not eliminate food-seeking behavior in rats. Morgan and Morgan (1940) obtained the same result when they blocked the sensory connections between the stomach and the brain. Keys et al. (1950), put a number of subjects on a semi-starvation diet for a long period, and discovered that they continued to feel hunger pangs even when they were taken off the diet and given full meals. In other words, the stomach does not seem to be the center, or at least the only center, for hunger sensations.

Where, then, is the center? Present theory holds that certain structures in the brain control the hunger drive by reacting to the chemical state of the blood. This theory was suggested by research conducted by Tschukitschew in 1929 (See Templeton and Quigley, 1930), and verified by Bash in 1939. Bash discovered that well-fed dogs would start looking for food when they were injected with blood from hungry dogs, and the stomach contractions of starving dogs would cease when they received blood from recently fed animals. Further investigation has revealed that the actual brain center which regulates the state of the blood is in the hypothalamus. Electrical stimulation of the lateral part of the structure causes satiated animals to eat (Andersson, Jewell, and Larsson, 1958), and destruction or removal of this area produces loss of appetite, a condition termed aphagia (Anand and Brobeck, 1951). Moreover, a "satiation center" has also been found in the hypothalamus. When this center is stimulated electrically, a hungry animal will stop eating; and when it is removed, the animal will eat ravenously and continuously, a condition known as hyperphagia. It is believed that medications used for curbing the appetite have their effect on this brain area. *See* HYPOTHALAMUS.

At present there are two competing theories concerning the relation between the hypothalamus and the blood. The glucostatic theory holds that this structure contains special "glucoceptors" which respond to variations in available glucose and alert the body when the blood-sugar level runs low (Mayer, 1955). Although the available evidence is ambiguous, the theory seems to be supported by the general observation that when candy is eaten before a meal it will destroy the appetite. A second explanation, known as the thermal theory, rests on the idea that the hypothalamus responds to changes in blood temperature associated with food deprivation and food intake. There is evidence for this view in the fact that animals will not feed when the heat content of the blood is rising; also, protein, which yields the greatest satiety, produces the greatest amount of body heat (Brobeck, 1957).

At the moment there is no way of deciding between these two theories.

Nevertheless they do indicate that both the brain and the blood are involved in the hunger mechanism. This general approach is a fruitful one, but it does not explain one important aspect of hunger, namely the wide variations in appetite and food preference that occur in different individuals. We are not just hungry, we are usually hungry for specific foods at specific times. Some of our cravings are doubtless due to the body's need for certain food elements, and some of our aversions stem from allergies or other physical reactions. Moreover, psychological factors enter into the picture, since our appetite is also governed by social custom and personal taste. Some people are disgusted by the idea of eating snails. Others regard them as a delicacy. Grasshoppers are an accepted food in Japan, but they would turn the stomach of the average American. Such preferences or aversions are acquired, not innate, but they are extremely hard to change because they are surrounded by emotional associations. See SPECIFIC HUNGER.

The time for eating is also dictated by custom. Many nutritionists hold that a five-times-a-day schedule is best, especially for children. Nevertheless we not only adapt ourselves to three meals, but are conditioned to specific hours. The Spanish are accustomed to a nine o'clock dinner, but Americans are adjusted to eating three hours earlier—and if we are so occupied that we let the six o'clock hour slip by, and then discover our error, we suddenly become extremely hungry. Eating behavior is also influenced by "social facilitation." When hens eat in groups of three, they have been found to eat almost twice as much as when they are alone; and a satiated hen will eat an additional 50 per cent when exposed to other hens while they are eating (Bayer, 1929). Human beings are similarly affected. A finicky child will eat everything on his plate at a Scout picnic, and the person on a diet had better

beware of dining with gourmets. Many older people who live alone do not maintain an adequate diet because they eat by themselves. See SOCIAL FACILITATION.

Hunger also has a pronounced effect on perception and emotion. When we have not eaten for some time, we become increasingly aware of everything that has to do with food, such as odors, advertisements, and restaurants. In fact, we may become so selectively attuned to these stimuli that we are inattentive to everything else (Deutsch and Deutsch, 1963). Experiments show that when we are very hungry we have a tendency to interpret vague or ambiguous shapes as articles of food (R. N. Sanford, 1936). The half-starved men in the Keys experiment mentioned above became so preoccupied with food that they were unable to think or talk of anything else, and in some cases planned to change their occupation to dietetics or agriculture. Finally, emotional disturbances have been found to lie at the root of many cases of overweight and loss of appetite. See OBESITY, ANOREXIA NERVOSA, STARVATION REACTIONS, ABULIA, PICA.

HUNTINGTON'S CHOREA. A rare degenerative disease of the central nervous system, characterized by choreiform movements and mental deterioration.

Huntington's chorea was named after the American neurologist, George Huntington, who published a paper on it in 1872. The only psychiatric disorder known to follow a simple Mendelian ratio, this disease is carried by a dominant gene and affects 50 per cent of the children of a gene-carrying parent. In one study, over a thousand cases in the United States were traced to three individuals who came to this country in 1630. However, a few patients have recently been found with no family history of the disease. These cases were apparently due to a mutant gene.

The disease occurs in both men and women between the ages of thirty and fifty. Its overt symptoms are often preceded for several years by a change in personality involving such symptoms as irritability, violence, vagrancy, depression and suicidal attempts. When the disorder becomes apparent, its most conspicuous physical symptoms are involuntary jerking and stretching (choreic) movements which usually begin in the facial muscles and gradually spread to the trunk and limbs. The movements subside during sleep, but are almost continuous during waking life. Most common are grimaces, smacking of lips, indistinct and explosive speech, and a shuffling gait. As these disturbances become more severe and uncontrollable, mental and emotional deterioration increase to a point where attention, memory, and judgment are seriously impaired, and hallucinations and paranoid delusions usually follow.

Huntington's chorea is a progressive disease which runs its course in ten to twenty years. There is no effective treatment, although drugs and surgery are frequently used to alleviate the involuntary movements. Its hereditary basis, however, offers hope for prevention through eugenics. But this hope is qualified by the fact that the disease does not manifest itself until after the normal age for having children. When the exact nature of the genetic effect is determined, it may be possible to develop a test which can be applied to all descendants of its victims. *See* BRAIN DISORDERS.

Illustrative Case: HUNTINGTON'S CHOREA

R.A. was admitted to a mental hospital at the age of fifty-six. The familial incidence of Huntington's chorea was striking. A maternal grandmother, a maternal uncle and his daughter, the patient's mother and four of the patient's siblings exhibited definite symptoms of Huntington's chorea. Two members of the family committed suicide after they had developed the disease. Prior

to her illness the patient was apparently an attractive, well-adjusted person. She was a Girl Scout leader and took part in community affairs. Shortly before she was thirty-five she began to show an insidious change of personality. She discontinued her church, Girl Scout, card club, and other activities; she lost interest in her family and at times wandered away from home, returning at night but giving no information as to where she had been. In this same period she began to drop articles and to show twitching of her hands.

The patient became neglectful of her personal appearance, refused to comb her hair, bathe, or change her clothes. She refused to launder soiled garments and would hide them in closets or corners. The choreiform movements increased in extent, and she occasionally fell. At times she showed temporary alertness and interest in anticipation of a visit from her daughter, but after one or two days she drifted back into her former seclusiveness and deteriorated habits.

On many occasions she threatened and even attacked her husband, sometimes with a knife, and on one occasion inflicted a four-inch scalp wound. She became profane and her favorite term in addressing her husband was, "You G-d fool." She was subject to tantrums in which she would threaten to jump from a window. She came to be known to the children in the neighborhood as "the old witch on the third floor." Finally, the choreiform movements became so extreme that it was difficult for her to go up and down stairs and she often fell.

On arrival at the hospital, her facial expression was vacant and she showed such unco-ordinated and choreiform movements of her legs that she had difficulty in walking without assistance. There were gross choreiform movements of the head and all extremities. Her constant grimacing, blinking of her eyes, and twitching of her fingers were quite striking. The co-ordination of her hands was so poor and the movements of her head were so extreme that she had difficulty in eating. Her speech was explosive and difficult to understand. Although somewhat irritable, demanding, and distrustful, she adjusted to the hospital environment without serious difficulty. (Noyes and Kolb, 1963)

HYDROCEPHALY (Hydrocephalus). An enlargement of the head resulting from excessive accumulation of cerebro-spinal fluid within the ventricles (open spaces) of the brain (internal hydrocephaly) or, less often, between the hemispheres (external hydrocephaly).

In most cases progressive accumulation of fluid produces internal pressure that damages the brain tissue. If the damage is slight, intellectual impairment is not great; if it is extensive, severe, or profound mental retardation may result, sometimes accompanied by convulsions and impairment or loss of sight and hearing. Most hydrocephalics require custodial care. The less severe cases can be trained to care for their physical needs, but where the head is extremely large and heavy they must be confined to bed.

Hydrocephaly may be present at birth, and probably results from prenatal conditions that affect the formation and circulation of the cerebrospinal fluid. In rare cases, known as anencephaly, the fluid completely inhibits the growth of the brain. In some instances the condition develops during infancy and early childhood in connection with intracranial neoplasms (tumors), head injury, or brain inflammations associated with chronic meningitis or congenital syphilis. The rare infectious disease, toxoplasmosis, may also result in hydrocephaly.

Recently developed surgical techniques have been dramatically successful in arresting the condition in its early stages before severe brain damage occurs. These procedures are directed toward reducing the production of cerebrospinal fluid or channeling it past obstructions resulting from congenital malformations or postnatal infections. Some cases, however, develop severe postoperative complications or do not respond to treatment, and the cranium continues to expand until gross deterioration and death occur. *See* MENTAL RETARDATION (CAUSES).

HYDROTHERAPY. The use of water in the treatment of disease.

Hydrotherapy of one kind or another is as old as the history of medicine, dating back to Hippocratic times. Today it is only occasionally used in psychiatry, and then only as an aid or adjuvant in the treatment of such disorders as delirium, involutional psychotic depression and hypochondriasis—particularly when the patient cannot take medications. There are two major types. First, the *continuous tub,* or prolonged neutral bath, which is given for a minimum of an hour. The patient lies in a canvas hammock in an oversized tub, with his head supported by pillows. The water is continually circulated and kept 1 to 3 degrees below body temperature. The treatment is given primarily to control major excitement, tension, and apprehension, but is terminated if the patient becomes agitated or develops dermatitis, fever, or circulatory disorder.

Second, the *cold pack,* or wet sheet pack. Here the patient is wrapped loosely in layers of sheets and blankets which have been wrung out in cold water. A temperature of 48° F is used for vigorous patients, 60° to 70° for the average patient, and 92° to 97° for those who are frail and cold-sensitive. The treatment is never used as a punishment, nor with patients who do not accept it, and is most effective with the young and robust. When first applied, the sudden cold produces a "therapeutic shock," which helps to induce a sedative effect. This effect usually sets in within ten to twenty minutes, but may be delayed if the patient is extremely excited. Sedation may be increased by applying ice packs to the back of the neck, and hot packs to the feet. The treatment is terminated if the sedative effect is not obtained within forty-five minutes, or if the patient shows symptoms of "superheating": rapid pulse, talkativeness, restlessness, flushed face, perspiration. The procedure is contraindicated for aged and emaciated patients, and for those suffering from heart, respiratory, or hyperthyroid disorders.

Other types of hydrotherapy include: hot foot baths for sedation; jet sprays and Scotch douches for their tonic and stimulating effect; and the electric-cabinet bath for reducing agitation and feelings of guilt in depressed patients. A recent innovation is the use of swimming pools and aquatic recreation in mental hospitals.

HYPERMNESIA. Extreme retentiveness of memory, excessive memory activity, or unusual clarity of memory images.

Hypermnesia occasionally occurs in normal individuals who are undergoing great stress or who are faced with death; in mental prodigees and certain individuals who devote excessive time and effort to the cultivation of memory; and in patients suffering from certain mental disorders. A striking example of the first type is what has been called "panoramic memory," the tendency to review one's entire life, particularly while drowning. Menninger (1948) cites the following experience of a young man as he was sinking for the third time: "The course of those thoughts I can even now in great measure retrace . . . the event which had just taken place; the awkwardness which had produced it; the bustle it must have occasioned; the effect it would have on a most affectionate father; the manner in which he would disclose it to the rest of the family; and a thousand other circumstances minutely associated with home, were the first series of reflections that occurred. Then they took a wider range: our last cruise; a former voyage and shipwreck; my school, the progress I had made there, and the time I had misspent, and even all my boyish pursuits and adventures. Thus traveling downward, every past incident of my life seemed to glance across my recollection in retrograde succession; not, however, in mere outline, as you stated, but the picture filled up with every minute and collateral feature. In short, the whole period of my existence seemed to be traced before me in a kind of panoramic review, and each act of it seemed to be accompanied by a consciousness of right or wrong, or by some reflection on its cause or its consequences; indeed, many trifling events which had been long forgotten crowded into my imagination, and with a character of recent familiarity."

Psychologists who have made a special study of geniuses and prodigies report many cases of remarkable memory. Catharine M. Cox (1926) cites, among others, the fact that the German philosopher Fichte could repeat an entire sermon after hearing it once, that Racine could quote entire plays from memory, and that Chateaubriand learned the entire table of logarithms by heart. In the field of music, Mozart was able to write the entire Miserere of Allegri after hearing it played once; and in the field of politics, it is said that Themistocles could address twenty-one thousand Athenian citizens by name. *See* PRODIGY.

As a pathological symptom, hypermnesia occurs most frequently in the manic phase of manic-depressive reaction, particularly in hypomania. It is also observed, though less often, in paranoid reactions and in states of catatonic excitement experienced by some schizophrenic patients. Typically, all these patients not only register and retain minute details of personal experiences, but recall them with striking vividness and clarity. The reaction is usually limited to specific situations in which the patient is emotionally involved. Menninger cites the following samples of the stream of conversation of a twenty-two-year-old manic girl who talked continuously in this vein for months:

"From there we went over to Jane's apartment, 4137 Broadway, telephone Maine 4521-W, second flight up—we went there and she wasn't home, but I said we'd wait, because it was only 3:30—3:27, to be exact—I'm sure it was because I looked at Jane's mantel clock—she has a clock that George got for her in Chicago—at a place on Michigan Avenue—let me see, I ought to remember the name of that store—oh Abt's—that's it—on Michigan Avenue near—well, anyway, it keeps wonderful time but this day it was slow—half an hour slow—and I couldn't believe it was so early yet and so I called Central and asked the time and she wouldn't tell me, but I remembered that Dixon's always . . . are you listening to me? Well, we stayed there until Jane came—about four o'clock— no, it was after four, because I saw Mr. Smelzer go to work, and Jane says he has to be there at five and always leaves at four. He works at the Post Office, you know . . ." *See* CIRCUMSTANTIALITY.

Examples of the type quoted above indicate that the brain retains far more experience than is commonly recognized. It appears that little if anything is lost, once it has been registered, though as yet we do not know much about the registration process itself. This fact has been illustrated experimentally in two major ways. First, it has long been known that hypnotic suggestion can produce a state of hypermnesia. Many hypnotists are able to induce their subjects to recall buried events from the past, recite poems learned in early childhood, or locate articles they have misplaced. Second, direct stimulation of certain regions of the brain itself has been found to resurrect long-forgotten events with the clarity of a film or tape recorder. A classic example is Penfield's account (1954) of experiments performed during brain surgery on epileptic patients. The patients were conscious, since the brain does not contain nerve endings that register pain, and it was therefore possible to test the subject's response to stimulation of various points in the cortex as a means of determining the proper site of the operation:

"A young woman heard music when a certain point in the superior surface of the temporal cortex [on the side of the brain] was stimulated. She said she heard an orchestra playing a song. The same song was forced into her consciousness over and over again by re-stimulation at the same spot. It progressed from verse to chorus at what must have been the tempo of the orchestra when she heard it playing thus. She was quite sure each time that someone had turned on a gramophone in the operating room.

"A South African who was being operated upon cried out in great surprise that he heard his cousins talking, and he explained that he seemed to be there laughing with them although he knew that he was really in the operating room in Montreal."

As Penfield remarked, "It is as though the cortex contained a continuous strip of cinematographic film, a strip that includes the waking record from childhood on."

See MEMORY STORAGE, REMEMBERING, IDIOT SAVANT, GENIUS, MANIC-DEPRESSIVE REACTION (MANIC PHASE).

HYPERTENSION. Hypertension, or persistent high blood pressure, may be purely physical in origin, due to kidney or other disorders. Where the causes are unknown or believed to be emotional, it is termed essential hypertension, and is viewed as a psychophysiologic or psychosomatic disorder of the cardiovascular (heart and circulatory) system. In many cases it appears to be due to a pre-existing tendency toward high blood pressure which is aggravated by emotional stress.

The situations that contribute to hypertension often involve anger against people on whom the patient is extremely dependent. Some authorities believe this pattern originated early in life when the patient was unable to handle his ambivalent impulses toward his parents—that is, he was afraid of expressing his resentment fully and openly because at the same time he loved and depended on them. At any rate these patients get in the habit of repressing their hostility instead of releasing it through speech or action. Their pent-up anger then discharges itself through the vascular system, causing increased blood pressure. Not surprisingly, then, adult hypertensive patients tend to be outwardly calm, controlled, and conforming—but these attitudes conceal inward urges of an aggressive character. When situations occur that arouse their anger and threaten their dependent relationships, their blood pressure tends to rise.

This pattern is found in other psychosomatic reactions, and therefore the idea of a specific "hypertensive personality" has been dropped. As a matter of fact many hypertension patients themselves suffer from other psychosomatic symptoms, such as stomach upsets, headaches, and fatigue. These are not due to the hypertension itself, but to the same emotional tensions that contributed to the raised blood pressure. Once the patient discovers his tendency to high blood pressure, he may also develop a "blood pressure phobia," and this fear may feed back and aggravate the condition.

Psychotherapy focused on the patient's characteristic reactions and life situation will usually improve his emotional adjustment. It is too much to hope, however, that psychological treatment will reduce the blood pressure to normal, since emotional factors are probably not totally responsible for the condition.

Illustrative Case: HYPERTENSION

Mr. K.N., age fifty-three, complained of dizziness, of headache and of "high blood pressure." Examination revealed no pertinent pathology in the cardiovascular system or elsewhere except for a blood pressure reading of 176/104. He stated that he was without any special irritations, "except of course those occurring in business," which was running smoothly. Wife and children were congenial and he could list no emotional difficulties. His son, however, gave some significant information. The patient was in the laundry business with several partners. Financially he was successful; but there was intense rivalry among the various partners as to efficiency, and there was constant fault finding. It had been to their financial advantage to remain together; but "there was constant grief and aggravation." The patient was a conscientious person who "carried his business troubles to bed," and in the last few years he had become exceedingly irritable and had violent temper outbursts. Moreover, he had no outlets and no recreation other than his work. On Sundays and holidays he was restless, not knowing how to relax or what to do. His symptoms were thus the result of his way of living, and of his continuous irritation. (Kraines, 1948)

HYPERVENTILATION SYNDROME.

A psychophysiologic (psychosomatic) disorder of the respiratory system characterized by repeated anxiety attacks accompanied by "overbreathing"—that is, the patient breathes rapidly and deeply even though he may not always realize that he is doing so. If the overbreathing continues for any length of time it usually produces a lightheaded sensation, palpitation, shortness of breath, perspiration, and tingling in the fingers. Prolonged overbreathing may result in loss of consciousness.

The anxiety which produces hyperventilation is generally caused by stress situations which bring unbearable feelings of anger, fear, or sexuality close to the surface. Sometimes the attacks may follow a disturbing dream or a nightmare. In diagnosing these cases, the psychiatrist asks the patient to overbreathe for two minutes to show him that giddiness and other symptoms are bound to result. This procedure sometimes leads to immediate and continuing relief, since the patient becomes aware of the relation between his symptoms and the hyperventilation. Sometimes relaxation and breathing exercises are also prescribed to be carried out under the direction of a physiotherapist. Usually, however, psychotherapy is needed to help the patient understand and handle the problems that are at the root of his anxiety attacks.

Illustrative Case: HYPERVENTILATION SYNDROME

The patient, a fifty-seven-year-old woman had been under medical care for symptoms of menopause beginning at age fifty, but her husband had abruptly terminated this treatment two years previously. He brought her to the psychiatrist's office, stating that he could no longer stand her "huffing and puffing." The attacks occurred every morning and had the effect of delaying his departure for work and keeping his wife from doing her housework.

The two-minute test was used to show the patient that her symptoms could be produced through overbreathing. In discussing her attacks, she revealed that she had been concerned about the possibility of her husband's dying. She also spoke of the recent death of her brother, the fact that her children were grown and no longer needed her, and that the family had threatened to place her in a mental hospital because of her menopausal symptoms. She was a driving, energetic woman who had been completely immersed in her family. Her remarks about death suggested that she harbored buried feelings of resentment toward her husband, who showed little sympathy for her: "It soon seemed apparent that situations arousing repressed hostility toward her husband and family, feelings that were unacceptable to her as a conscientious person, and threats of separation from her family induced the acute anxiety attacks manifested by overbreathing."

Questioning revealed that the patient had given up an excellent job to marry her husband. She had married suddenly after having been jilted—and her own daughter had likewise been jilted six months before the consultation. The husband was self-centered, buried in his work, and had a disparaging attitude toward his wife's activities. He was advised to spend more time with her.

The patient was seen four or five times, and encouraged to ventilate her unacceptable feelings toward her husband—feelings which had culminated when he forbade her to continue treatment for menopause. She was also encouraged to plan activities outside the home in order to be less dependent on the family. This short-term psychotherapy was successful, and within six weeks the patient was completely free of overbreathing attacks. (Adapted from Noyes & Kolb, 1963)

HYPNAGOGIC STATE. The drowsy, trancelike state between sleeping and waking.

During the hypnagogic period some people experience transient, dreamlike fantasies which have been termed hypnagogic hallucinations. Suggestibility is high during this state, and the sleeper may respond to a simple command such as "Raise your left arm," or even mumble answers to questions. Experiments have shown that some individuals can retain vocabulary lists or other data read to them during this period. The increase in suggestibility which occurs in this twilight state seems to account for this ability to learn simple material. *See* LEARNING DURING SLEEP, HYPNOSIS.

HYPNOSIS. A state of heightened suggestibility induced by another person, or, in some cases, by the individual himself, usually attained through bodily relaxation accompanied by concentration on a narrow range of stimuli.

Susceptibility. Various investigations indicate that between 90 per cent and 95 per cent of the population can be hypnotized to some degree, but only about 10 per cent can reach the deepest level of trance. After reviewing a huge body of material, Weitzenhoffer (1953) states that "in sum, it appears that we may say that suggestibility is highest at the ages of seven to eight, that it is somewhat greater for women and girls than for men and boys, and greater for individuals of higher than of lower intelligence. . . . In regard to personality traits no general conclusions can be drawn." Hypnotizability varies in the same individual from time to time, and the hypnotist must therefore take into account his subject's emotional needs and state at the moment. While a positive, expectant attitude appears to favor the process full cooperation with the hypnotist is not always necessary, and a few people can even be hypnotized against their will.

Induction. Different methods of induction are used, depending on the personality and susceptibility of the subject as well as the preferences of the hypnotist. Most of the standard procedures involve these four steps: "(a) limitation of sensory input and motor output; (b) fixation of attention; (c) the repetition of monotonous stimulation; and (D) the setting up of an emotional relationship between the therapist and subject" (Brenman and Gill, 1947). The hypnotist usually begins with a discussion designed to establish rapport, reassure his subject, and correct any misconceptions he may have—such as the idea that susceptibility is a sign of weakness or that he will be deprived of his will or forced to do things against his ethical code.

The standard "sleeping method" is usually carried out with a single patient (though it has been used with groups) in a semidarkened room. The hypnotist may start with a demonstration, followed by suggestibility tests. One common demonstration is to have the patient stand at right angles to a wall, pressing against it with all his strength, and then step away. The arm that was pressed against the wall will usually rise spontaneously, showing what it feels like to yield to an external force (the Kohnstamm test). One of the standard test procedures is to have the subject stand rigidly while the hypnotist gives him suggestions that he will

fall forward or backward. The next step is "ocular fixation": the subject fixates on the hypnotist's eyes or on a light or bright object, while he makes repeated, monotonous suggestions of drowsiness or relaxation: "Look at me and think of nothing but sleep. Your eyelids are beginning to feel heavy. Your eyes are tired and it is hard to keep them open, etc. I want you to relax . . . relax your arms . . . your neck . . . your legs . . . your jaws. Now sleep, sleep, sleep, etc."

To test the effect of the suggestions, the hypnotist may tell the patient to try to raise his arm when he counts to five, "but the harder you try, the more difficult it will be." An admission of some heaviness, if not complete inability to raise the arm, is a cue that the suggestions are working and that he can go on, step by step, to produce a deeper and deeper trance. The total order of suggestions is somewhat as follows: (a) suggestion of inability to open the eyes; (b) suggestion of dulling of sensation to a pinprick (hypesthesia, anesthesia); (c) suggestion of inability to remember words written on a mental blackboard (amnesia), with return of the memory at the hypnotist's suggestion; (d) suggestion of inability to recall, or to recall clearly, what happened during hypnosis after awakening (posthypnotic amnesia); (e) suggestion of actions to be carried out after hypnosis, such as opening all the windows (posthypnotic suggestion); (f) suggestion of positive hallucinations (e.g., seeing a friend enter the room) and negative hallucinations (e.g., inability to recognize the presence of a particular person in a room). It is usually unnecessary, and often impossible, to go through all these steps.

Three other induction techniques are also used. In *drug hypnosis,* sodium amytal, sodium pentothal, or other chemicals are used to induce or help induce a trance state. This method is sometimes more readily accepted by the patient than verbal methods, and may be more effective. It can also be applied by physicians who have not been trained in hypnotic techniques. However, drugs increase suggestibility for only short periods and cannot be repeated too often because of side effects. A drug-induced state may be utilized in many kinds of hypnotherapy, including suppression of symptoms by direct suggestion, prolonged sleep, and the release of repressed material in both the abreaction technique and in hypnoanalysis. See HYPNOTHERAPY.

In *hypnoidization,* the patient is asked to recline, close his eyes, and attend to a stimulus, such as reading or singing or the beat of a metronome. This puts him in a "hypnagogic state" midway between sleep and waking. In this state he experiences a vivid flow of free associations that frequently arouse memories of early emotonal events. As Kubie (1943) points out: "The hypnagogic reverie might be called a dream without distortion. Its immediate business is the day's 'unfinished business,' but like the dream it derives from the more remote 'unfinished business' of an entire lifetime as well . . . (but) the content of the dream can come through with less disguise . . . (and) significant information of the past can be made readily available and directly accessible, without depending upon the interpretations which are requisite in the translation of a dream." See HYPNOGOGIC STATE.

Waking Hypnosis is based on the discovery that all the standard hypnotic responses may be induced without any reference to sleep. Wells (1924) developed a technique in which the subject is first given examples of absent-minded actions—such as our tendency to make spiral motions as we attempt to define the term "spiral"—and is then asked to fix his attention on an object like a ring or pen. The hypnotist urges him to watch it steadily, think of nothing else, and note every

detail. Then he orders the subject to close his eyes as tightly as possible, saying, "I am going to count to seven, and when I reach seven you will find that your eyes are stuck tight, and the harder you try to open them, the tighter they will stick." If this suggestion is successful (several repetitions may be necessary), he goes on to suggestions of muscular contractures, such as clasping the hands so tightly that they cannot be unclasped, and then proceeds to further steps in the hypnotic process. According to Wells, the waking method has several distinct advantages over the sleeping method. It is easier to learn, easier to apply, appears less occult, and a higher percentage of subjects can be hypnotized either individually or in groups.

Levels of Trance. The steps outlined above, under "sleeping method," represent a progressive deepening of the trance. The full procedure usually takes considerably more than an hour, and may be carried out in several sessions. At the end of each session the hypnotist gives his subject a signal which he will use to start the next session where he left off. No attempt is usually made to go through the entire progression, since recent studies have shown that a light trance is actually preferable to a deep trance for psychological treatment (Kline, 1965). Though there is considerable variation from individual to individual on the progression from stage to stage, the Davis Hypnotic Suggestibility Test is often used as a general guide. On this scale, the first, or "hypnoidal" stage is characterized by relaxation, fluttering of eyelids, closing of eyes, and complete physical relaxation, in that order; a "light trance," by inability to open the eyes (eye catalepsy), limb catalepsies, rigid catalepsies (the patient can lie like a board between two chairs), and hand anesthesia; a "medium trance," by partial amnesia, posthypnotic anesthesia, personality changes, simple posthypnotic suggestions, kinesthetic delusions (feelings of movement without moving) and complete amnesia; a "deep trance," by ability to open the eyes without affecting the trance, bizarre posthypnotic suggestions, complete somnambulism, positive posthypnotic visual hallucinations, positive posthypnotic auditory hallucinations, negative auditory hallucinations, negative visual hallucinations, and hyperesthesias (excessive sensitivity to stimuli).

Termination. Arousing the patient from a trance is a simple procedure. In the sleeping method, the subject is told, while under hypnosis, that at a given signal, such as the count of five, he will wake up. He is also assured, particularly during the first few sessions, that he will feel rested and well, as if he had taken a nap. A similar technique is used in the waking method— for example, "When I say the letters from A to G, you will gradually come back to your normal self. At A you will move your feet; at B, your arms, (and so on); and at G you will open your eyes and will feel perfectly normal once again."

"Dangers." Most investigators hold that an individual cannot be induced to perform any act contrary to his moral code under hypnosis. When such suggestions are made, he either refuses to comply or awakens from the trance. A number of ingenious experiments have been performed to test this principle. Rowland (1939) showed subjects the effects of pure sulfuric acid on metal, then ordered them to pick up the beaker and throw the acid in his face. At least one subject, though reluctant, obeyed the command and then covered her face in horror—only to find out that the experimenter was standing behind a sheet of curved invisible glass. Another hypnotized subject tried, on command, to put her hand into a box containing a rattlesnake, but encountered a similar sheet of glass. Wells (1941) succeeded in get-ting subjects to take money from an overcoat pocket by having them hallucinate the coat as their own.

Erickson (1939) used a variety of techniques to get his subjects to perform objectionable social acts, but failed consistently "even though many of the suggested acts were acceptable to them under circumstances of waking consciousness." In one experiment he repeatedly urged a deeply hypnotized student of upright character to read his roommate's mail. The young man fumbled with the envelope, eventually got the letter out, "tried" to read it upside down, then found it "competely illegible." Erickson finally started to point out the words—which were perfectly legible—whereupon the student suddenly went blind (a condition that was quickly cleared up by suggestion).

In commenting on these apparently contradictory findings, Weitzenhoffer (1953) states that "in every instance where investigators have reported obtaining antisocial acts under hypnosis, the suggestions used were such as to alter the subject's awareness of the 'true' situation by means of illusions, hallucinations, and paramnesias created in regard to both the imposed task and the environment in which it was to be carried out . . . In the past there has been general agreement that subjects would carry out antisocial acts if and when they (a) felt protected, (b) had latent criminal tendencies, (c) had an implicit trust in the hypnotist . . . [There is] a fourth possible situation: the subject does not perceive the suggested act as being antisocial in nature."

It is generally accepted that hypnosis does not in itself produce harmful effects such as weakening the subject's will or his capacity to resist propaganda or other suggestions. Wolberg (1959) points out that "instances have been reported of individuals plunged into anxiety as a result of unwise suggestions given them by stage and amateur hypnotists," and "sometimes a patient is not awakened properly and for some hours he may walk around in a daze," but "the dangers residual in hypnotherapy are minimal or absent if it is employed by a responsible and well-trained therapist who knows how to handle the patient's general reactions and resistances to psychotherapy."

Theories. Even though hypnosis has been studied for over 200 years, it still remains a mystery. There is no lack of hypotheses, but to date no theory is comprehensive enough to explain all the phenomena involved. Most of the physiological theories are based on the similarity between hypnosis and sleep, although EEG studies show that it seems closer to light sleep than to either waking or deep sleep (Weitzenhoffer, 1953), and pulse and respiration rates are the same as in the waking state. Pavlov believed it to be a state of brain inhibition related to sleep but limited to inhibition of motor impulses. Others have suggested that certain centers in the hypothalamus are activated by suggestion. The psychological theories seek to explain hypnosis in terms of an expansion of autosuggestion into heterosuggestion, sexual submission to the hypnotist, identification with the hypnotist's omnipotence as a realization of infantile power and magic fantasies; regression to a primitive level of functioning in which the organism is barely differentiated from its surroundings; and as a form of psychological mothering that activates earlier patterns of behavior. There is little concrete evidence for any of these theories as yet. *See* LEARNING UNDER HYPNOSIS, EXPERIMENTAL NEUROSIS, AUTOMATIC WRITING AND DRAWING, MULTIPLE PERSONALITY, AMNESIA (DISSOCIATIVE TYPE), ABREACTION.

HYPNOTHERAPY. The use of hypnosis in psychological treatment, either in short-term therapy aimed at removal of symptoms and modification of behavior patterns, or in long-term reconstructive therapy aimed at personality change.

The history of hypnotherapy dates back to antiquity, where hypnosis was used primarily as a quasi-religious and quasi-magical technique. An example is the practice of "temple sleep" among the Babylonians, Egyptians, and Greeks. The work of Mesmer at the end of the eighteenth century is regarded as the dividing line between the prescientific and scientific uses of hypnosis, in spite of his theory of "animal magnetism," since he was the first to recognize the importance of systematic suggestion and the relationship between hypnotist and subject. Little was done to follow up his work until the latter part of the nineteenth century, when James Braid re-examined "mesmeric phenomena," renamed the process hypnosis (from the Greek word for sleep) and ascribed its effects to psychological rather than physical forces. Shortly after, Charcot, in Paris, claimed to find a close relation between hypnosis and hysteria, mistakenly claimed that only hysterics were hypnotizable, and attempted to explain both states by a theory of nervous energy. The Nancy school of Bernheim and Liébeault, however, opposed these physiological explanations, developed the concepts of suggestion and suggestibility, and applied them successfully in the treatment of hysterics. *See* MESMER, DREAM INTERPRETATION (HISTORICAL), CHARCOT.

Janet attempted to combine the Paris and Nancy approaches by claiming that suggestibility is itself due to dissociation, a split or breakdown of normal mental integration, and by ascribing this process to a physical weakening of "mental synthesis." He did not, however, fully recognize the dynamic effect of split-off material on the emotional life of the individual. It remained for Freud and Breuer to show, through the use of hypnosis, that dissociated material can produce symptoms of disorder—and that these symptoms can be removed by employing hypnotic suggestion in reviving the experiences that produced them and in discharging the emotions they aroused.

Freud went on to explain dissociated memories and impulses in terms of the mechanism of repression, a process in which material is automatically expelled from consciousness because it is unacceptable or threatening. He then found that revival of this material under hypnosis only temporarily removed the symptoms, and did not in itself bring about the basic change in personality which he believed to be necessary for complete recovery. He therefore abandoned hypnosis and developed the free-association technique. This dampened interest in hypnosis until the late twenties and thirties when Clark Hull undertook his experimental work, followed by further explorations and applications by Morton Prince, William McDougall, Boris Sidis, and Paul Schilder. The use of hypnosis was further advanced by the need for short-term therapy during World War II and the discovery that hypnotic techniques could be combined with analytic approaches. We are now in the midst of an ever-widening acceptance of hypnotherapy, though, as Wolberg (1959) points out, it "has never freed itself from the obloquy of its superstitious origins, which compromise its reputation to this day." See FREUD, JANET, PRINCE, SCHILDER.

Before discussing current applications of hypnosis in psychotherapy, it might be well to mention its uses in general medicine. Actually, these uses are well within the scope of psychology and mental health, since emotional factors play a large part in our reactions to organic conditions, as well as in disorders of the psychophysiologic or psychosomatic type. Wolberg mentions the use of hypnosis to induce relaxation and relieve anxiety and stress effects in "cases of hypertension, Raynaud's disease, coronary disorders, paroxysmal tachycardia (heart palpitations), cerebral accidents (strokes), asthma, speech disorders, enuresis, impotence, chronic gastritis, dyspepsia, spastic colitis, ulcerative colitis, dysmenorrhea, amenorrhea, and menorrhagia (menstrual bleeding), as well as in reducing the effects of Parkinson's disease, syringomyelia, muscular dystrophy, multiple sclerosis, and the post-traumatic (head injury) syndrome."

Other medical applications of hypnotic suggestion include alleviating symptoms in chronic skin diseases, diabetes, and peptic ulcers; controlling obesity and insomnia; preparing women for childbirth through breathing and relaxation exercises; eliminating or reducing the need for chemical anesthesia in childbirth; treating spontaneous abortion and functional sterility; relieving intractable pain in such conditions as slipped disc, neuralgia, causalgia, and terminal cancer; and minimizing pain and discomfort in minor surgical and diagnostic procedures. Direct suggestion (hypnosuggestion) may be the "treatment of choice" in such emergencies as combat reactions, panic, hysterical amnesia, fugues, somnambulism; and it may be a "life saving method" in cases of uncontrollable hiccuping and severe undernutrition caused by psychogenic vomiting or anorexia nervosa. In addition, the use of hypnosis in dentistry (hypnodontics) merits special mention, since an estimated fifteen hundred dentists are using this technique as a means of relaxing tense patients, reinforcing or replacing local anesthesia, fostering co-operation in the use of dental appliances, and correcting such habits as nail-biting and bruxism (teeth-grinding).

In outlining the major applications of hypnosis in psychotherapy, we shall use the widely accepted sixfold classification of Brenman and Gill (1947), amplified by M. V. Kline's recent article in the "Handbook of Clinical Psychology" (1965). The six techniques are arranged in order of therapeutic intensity and depth, and culminate in hypnoanalysis.

In *prolonged hypnosis,* the patient is kept under deep hypnosis, sometimes reinforced by small doses of drugs, for a period of several days. No attempt is made to undertake therapeutic suggestions or explorations. The originator of the technique, Wetterstrand (1902) likened its effect to the healing power of sleep, but Schilder and Kauders (1927), suggested that its effects are also due to "the psychic elaboration which the person devotes, during sleep, to his experience." The treatment is effective with certain conditions, such as stubborn tics and acute conversion symptoms (for example, psychogenic vomiting), but is not widely used today because of the practical difficulties involved in maintaining a deep trance and nursing the patient.

In *direct suggestion of symptom disappearance,* the oldest and still widely used technique, a fairly deep trance is induced by sleep suggestions, and the patient is simply told that his symptoms will go away. This is the technique used by Bernheim. There have been many reports of temporary cures, though sometimes the original symptom is replaced by a substitute. Permanent recoveries have also been reported by Janet and others, especially in cases where the disturbance was treated shortly after its onset. Wells (1944) was even able to eliminate a hysterical symptom (a disabling headache) which had affected a student for over five years.

In the older literature claims have been made of successful treatment of practically every functional ailment, including mutism, hysterical amaurosis (blindness), sleepwalking, contractures, and speech disorders, and some specialists have even claimed success with alcoholism and drug addiction. The method has also been effectively applied to a variety of psychosomatic disorders —among them, menstrual disturbance, psoriasis, asthma, constipation, muscular rheumatism, migraine, and seasickness. Phobias, obsessions and compulsions, psychoses, and depression are generally regarded as unsuitable for treatment by direct suggestion.

Direct suggestion was widely used in World War I for various psychiatric casualties, including the recovery of amnesic episodes, but it was not extensively employed in World War II except for occasional symptomatic relief. Though useful on a temporary basis, the technique is limited to suppressing symptoms instead of dealing with their underlying causes.

Direct suggestion of disappearance of attitudes underlying symptoms. In this technique the therapist goes beyond mere suppression of symptoms by command, and attempts to give the patient some awareness of the roots of his difficulty. Though Bernheim pointed out that the character and inclinations of the patient should determine what type of hypnotic suggestions to apply, it was Prince and Sidis who first used suggestion as a form of re-education. Early attempts at inducing "insight" were naïve and crude. In one case, for example, the therapist discovered that a young woman whom he was treating for "psycho-epileptic attacks" had experienced a fright followed by what she called a "delirium," and that people had remarked that she must have acquired epilepsy from her mother. The treatment then consisted in putting her into a deep trance and telling her she did not have epilepsy, and that she "realized and believed" that her fear was unfounded.

More recently, Kraines (1948) applied this technique on a somewhat deeper basis to a case of torticollis (twisted neck or "wry neck"), by giving the usual commands to relax the neck plus suggestions aimed at the emotional basis of the symptom. The disturbance was interpreted as a symbolic representation of the patient's relationship with an overbearing and irritable employer, and the hypnotic suggestions consisted in telling him that he would no longer be angered by the employer and would be able to face him "straightforwardly." As this case indicates, the therapist has to know something about the origin of the symptom before this technique can be fully applied. Specialized training in psychotherapy is therefore necessary; and because of the probing required, the treatment takes more time than direct suggestion. However, as Brenman and Gill suggest, it is "a more reliable and substantial" method because it provides the patient with at least *some* understanding of his problem.

In *abreaction of traumatic experiences,* hypnotic suggestion is used to recover significant disturbing events with their attendant emotions. This "cathartic" technique was used by both Breuer and Janet, and adopted by many therapists who were dissatisfied with direct suggestion. Their use of the method, however, varied considerably. Some believed the original memory should be revived and relived in a highly emotional manner; others felt that a kind of "muted echo" was all that was necessary. Some depended on a mere "ventilation" of the traumatic event, while others made a systematic effort to integrate the newly discovered material with the patient's current life. In any case, the method was most frequently applied with hysterical patients who suffered from functional paralysis, blindness, and other conversion symptoms.

Since these early applications of the technique at the beginning of this century, abreaction has become the treatment of choice for amnesia. It was also widely used in cases of traumatic neurosis during World War I, but in World War II the reliving of harrowing experiences was usually brought about by drugs rather than by hypnosis. Since these methods are discussed in detail under the topics Combat Reactions and Narcosynthesis, we shall confine ourselves here to a general evaluation of the hypnotic abreaction technique. Its major advantages, as noted by Brenman and Gill, are that it is relatively brief; it can be applied by therapists who have not had extensive training in psychotherapy; and yet it is an "uncovering" method that goes to at least one of the sources of disorder. Its limitations lie in the fact that it requires a deep trance (except in cases of war neurosis where the repressed experiences are close to the surface), and is only a symptomatic and relatively shallow treatment when restricted to the abreaction alone. In addition, the technique is limited to cases where a neurotic reaction can be traced to a single traumatic experience. *See* ABREACTION, CATHARSIS, EMERGENCY PSYCHOTHERAPY.

The use of *specialized hypnotic techniques* is considered by Brenman and Gill to be a separate type of therapeutic application, since the various procedures are employed not merely as aids but as the "nucleus of therapeutic leverage." In *automatic writing,* the patient is first put in a trance and instructed to let his hand write "by itself," then the therapist suggests that the hand will give a clue to the experiences that have caused his problem. In *automatic drawing,* the patient is instructed to draw objects or symbols related to his conflict, and to interpret what they mean. In *crystal gazing,* the hypnotist has the patient fix his gaze on a neutral field such as a light bulb, mirror, or glass ball, and then suggests that he will visualize people or events that have to do with his difficulty. In *dream suggestion,* the patient is instructed to dream about his problems or their source either during the hypnotic state or posthypnotically during natural sleep. *See* AUTOMATIC WRITING AND DRAWING, AUTOSUGGESTION.

In *age regression,* the therapist helps the patient recapture a crucial experience by inducing amnesia for the current date, then suggesting that he return, year by year, to the earlier age when the experience occurred (PLATE 33). In the *experimental induction of conflicts,* the therapist brings his patient to an awareness of the relation between his symptoms and his repressed conflicts by artificially implanting a similar conflict through suggestion. In the recently developed technique of *hypnoplasty,* the patient is put into a light trance and given a claylike modeling substance. The therapist encourages him, by suggestion, to give .plastic expression to repressed feelings, and then to verbalize his conflicts.

These technical devices are employed as strategies designed to "outwit the unconscious" of the patient and release material that will be useful in the therapeutic effort. Few attempts have been made to systematize these techniques, and they are therefore dependent on the intuition and ingenuity of the therapist. Though they usually bring about only a "rudimentary insight," they frequently lead to recovery from acute, limited problems such as amnesias, phobias, and hysterical depressions.

In *hypnoanalysis,* the techniques of hypnosis are combined with those of psychoanalysis. In past years the term has been loosely applied to a wide range of procedures, including the classical abreactive method, as above described; but it is now limited to a modified and shortened psychoanalytic treatment carried out with the patient under hypnosis. Simmel is credited with the first extensive application of this technique. During World War I he used a combination of analytic-cathartic hypnosis in which the patient relived battle experiences, and was then engaged in analytical discussions during the waking state. In addition, dream interpretation was carried out both in the waking state and under deep hypnosis (Simmel, 1921). The release of feelings associated with battle trauma were often so violent that Simmel had his patients vent their rage against a dummy dressed in an army uniform. He also directed them, under hypnosis, to discharge their repressions in dreams. Since his time, Kardiner and others successfully applied hypnoanalytic techniques to servicemen suffering acute battle reactions in World War II, and still others have extended the method to civilian neuroses. Some of the newer approaches will be briefly reviewed.

Lindner (1946) developed a three-stage technique. In the first phase, the patient was given intensive training in hypnosis for about a week, with emphasis on ability to enter the trance state immediately, carry out posthypnotic suggestions, and recapture memories through regression and revivification (reliving) techniques. In the second phase, he was directed to choose a starting point and associate "without regard to form or content"; but when resistances were encountered, free association was abandoned, and the therapist sought to undercut the resistances through the use of either regression or revivification. Then, through the use of posthypnotic suggestion, he had the patient abreact during the *waking* state so that his entire personality would share in the benefit. The third phase utilized the transference relationship as the central agent in helping the patient understand his faulty goals and attitudes. The object here was re-education and reorientation of the personality along "more hygienic lines." Posthypnotic suggestion was used to reinforce this process and help the patient to incorporate the new goals and attitudes into his personality.

In hypnoanalysis a wide variety of methods is used to circumvent resistances, fill apparent gaps, and release repressed material. Some investigators find it useful to put the patient into a hypnoidal state through suggestions of relaxation; others induce a state of deep hypnosis and apply special techniques. Among these are: (a) "directed association," in which the patient is told that when the therapist counts to a certain number he will say the first thing that comes to mind in connection with his problem; (b) ordering the patient to dream or complete an unfinished dream, and (c) inducing vivid visual images related to the difficulty. Wolberg (1948, 1959) advocates the use of all the specialized techniques mentioned in the preceding section in releasing repressed material, and emphasizes the value of hypnosis as a means of stimulating the transference process. As in standard psychoanalysis, the patient's original attitudes toward his parents are transferred to the therapist and "worked through." This helps him to arrive at a better understanding of the sources of his problem and enables him to see how his faulty attitudes are disrupting his present life and producing the symptoms that are causing him emotional distress. The resulting insight removes emotional hindrances to the adoption of new attitudes, and therefore has a re-educative effect.

Hypnoanalysis has the advantage of not only uncovering the root of the problem, but of helping to integrate early experiences with the total personality. It requires far more training and takes more time than any other form of hypnotherapy, but its exponents claim, on the whole, more complete and lasting results. It also has its limitations, as Wolberg points out: not all patients can be hypnotized to the necessary depth; it is sometimes hard to integrate material evoked in the trance with the patient's conscious life; the elicited material itself may in some cases be fantasy rather than true memory; and the technique appears to be more effective with conversion reactions and traumatic neuroses than with character disorders.

HYPOCALCEMIA. An endocrine disorder most commonly caused by removal or damage to the parathyroid glands during thyroidectomy. Damage to these glands may also result from accident or disease. The physical consequence is a lowering of the calcium level of the blood, leading to cramps, spasms, and tetany. These effects are usually accompanied by psychological symptoms, and for this reason the disorder is classified by the American Psychiatric Association as an acute brain syndrome associated with metabolic disturbance. The most common psychological symptoms are depression, memory defect, and emotional lability—that is, unstable and shifting moods. Both the physical and mental symptoms can be relieved by the medical administration of calcium salts and vitamin D. *See* PARATHYROID GLANDS.

HYPOCHONDRIASIS (Hypochondria, Hypochondriacal Reaction). Persistent, excessive concern with one's state of health, accompanied by various bodily complaints even though no organic pathology can be found.

The reaction may be focused on either physical or emotional health, but more often the former. Most hypochondriacs make numerous complaints about different organs, and many of them insist that they are incurably diseased. They are acutely aware of sensations which most people disregard, and exaggerate the effects of normal fatigue and the symptoms of ordinary illnesses such as colds and headaches. They are also overconcerned about the everyday functions of the body, particularly digestion and elimination. Physicians must be extremely careful not to suggest new disorders simply by the process of examining them or giving them medical tests. *See* IATROGENIC ILLNESS.

The tendency to hypochondria increases with age and is aggravated by situations that produce physical or emotional stress. When faced with difficulties, the hypochondriac unconsciously resorts to the defense and escape mechanism of "flight into illness," which often brings him "secondary gains" in the form of attention, sympathy, and control over others. In some cases these "gains" may lead to chronic invalidism.

Although this type of reaction is neurotic in nature and was at one time classified as a neurosis in its own right, today it is regarded as a symptom rather than a disorder. The reason is that hypochondria is associated with a variety of syndromes, both neurotic and psychotic. It resembles a phobic reaction in that it involves fear of disease; and it has an obsessive-compulsive character since it involves persistent preoccupation with one idea and may lead to compulsive pill-taking, dieting, handwashing, or surgical operations. In many cases it seems to be a displacement of anxiety onto the body—that is, instead of being concerned about his emotional difficulties, the hypochondriac becomes concerned about his health. It is a common symptom in asthenic (neurasthenic) reactions, neurotic depressive reaction, involutional psychotic reaction, and the mental disorders of old age. As a symptom of these disorders, it tends to disappear or become less intense when they are successfully treated by psychological procedures.

Illustrative Case: HYPOCHONDRIASIS

Luther R., male, thirty-three, divorced. Complains of abdominal pains, low back pains, tightness in head. Fears he has "bad heart." For past three years has refrained from doing any heavy physical work because he feared a heart attack. Unable to carry on with work (shipping clerk) because he is afraid of overexerting himself.

Family History: Patient's father died at thirty-five when the patient was six. He died suddenly, from an illness of five days' duration (pneumonia). He was described as being sociable, intelligent, and well-liked. Had been practicing dentistry for five years at time of death. Mother fifty-seven, living and well, pictured as quiet, methodical, overly cautious. After father's death she went to work as an office clerk in a department store. She never remarried, concentrated efforts on making good home for Luther and caring for his every need. Very devoted mother, took every precaution to safeguard

son's health. Sudden death of father seemed to have made her extremely health-conscious. Any slight symptom of a cold or fever meant a day or more in bed for Luther with mother at his side. Continuous inquiries on how he felt, was he warm enough, was he too cold, was he losing weight. As Luther grew older mother's interest in his health did not diminish. At twelve, he was severely ill with influenza. Mother maintained constant vigil until he was out of danger. Lived with mother until married at twenty-four.

Personal History: Considered self-centered child. Until five had to play by himself because no other children of his age in neighborhood. Not permitted to participate in sports because mother feared he might get injured. Had few friends, became more and more seclusive as he grew up. Always seemed more at ease with adults than with persons of his own age. In adolescence became extremely self-conscious and quite sensitive. Spent most of time at home reading and listening to radio. Always greatly attached to mother.

(1) Medical history: In childhood measles, chicken pox, diphtheria—good recovery in each instance. At twelve, attack of influenza. At sixteen fell while running and fractured right arm. At twenty-one mild case of food poisoning. No significant illnesses since that time.

(2) Educational history: Graduated from high school at eighteen. Repeated part of sixth grade because absent a great deal. During this semester was ill with "flu." Mother did not permit him to go back until six weeks after he was out of bed. Average student in school, got along well with classmates and teachers. However, made very few friends in school.

(3) Vocational history: First job at nineteen repairing books at public library; remained there four years; quit to take a civil service job with city as clerk, still employed. So preoccupied with state of his health that he asked for sick leave.

(4) Social and marriage history: Never at ease with girls, had only a few "dates" in teen years. At twenty-one met girl he married, after six months'

acquaintance. Marriage lasted fifteen months, ended in divorce. Principal difficulty, according to patient, was sexual incompatibility. No children. Patient stated he had been given no sex education. Masturbated during adolescence and was once apprehended by mother. She told him that "it would lead to a diseased body and a diseased mind." Engaged in no heterosexual relations before marriage.

Summary: Hypochondriacal symptoms apparently developed as a result of mother's overemphasis and overconcern about his physical health. Seems probable that complaints are in part a bid for attention based on inferiority feelings. (Thorpe, Katz and Lewis, 1961)

HYPOGLYCEMIA, IDIOPATHIC. A form of hypoglycemia, or low blood-sugar level, that occasionally runs in families.

Children who are afflicted with this disorder not only show the usual hypoglycemic symptoms of weakness, fatigability, apathy, and occasional seizures, but also fail to develop intellectually. It is therefore included among the causes of mental retardation associated with faulty metabolism. The term idiopathic refers to the fact that the hypoglycemia cannot be traced to another disorder. It is believed to be due to a single recessive gene. *See* MENTAL RETARDATION (CAUSES).

HYPOGLYCEMIC STATES. Acute but transitory mental symptoms occasionally associated with a deficiency of blood sugar (hypoglycemia).

There is no single psychological pattern, but rather a wide variety of reactions in different cases. The most frequent are apathy, irritability, anxiety, restlessness, and negativism. In severe cases confusion, disorientation, fugue states, delirium, and stupor may occur. Disturbed speech, hallucinations, and delusions have also been observed. *See* BRAIN DISORDERS.

During a hypoglycemic attack the patient complains of weakness, hunger, and perspiration. He may also suffer from tremor, unsteady gait, double vision (diplopia), and convulsions. The symptoms disappear soon after the administration of sugar and there is no recollection of the attack.

Hypoglycemic states are sometimes experienced by diabetics who have taken too much insulin. The majority of cases, however, are due to spontaneous overproduction of insulin caused by islet cell tumors of the pancreas. A small number appear to be functional or psychosomatic in origin, although the mechanism is obscure. An occasional case is due to self-administration of insulin in an attempt to solve emotional problems.

Illustrative Case: HYPOGLYCEMIC STATE

A hospital nurse suffered from severe hypoglycemic attacks. She was thoroughly examined, but the doctor could not find any organic basis for this reaction. He therefore called in a psychiatric consultant. During a preliminary interview the psychiatrist began to suspect that she had been taking insulin by herself. A search of her room revealed that this was so. When she could not give an adequate explanation of her behavior, he continued his investigation.

The psychiatrist found that a number of causative factors were probably operating, some on a conscious, some on an unconscious level. He discovered that the doctor who had conducted the blood-sugar examination had previously performed a hysterectomy on the nurse, and had at that time informed her of the existence of a pancreatic tumor. He also found that her mother had been a diabetic, that she herself had often administered the drug to patients in the hospital, and that her father had been given insulin to relieve depression shortly before he died of cancer. All these factors had combined to make her particularly aware of hypoglycemia.

But why was she administering insulin to herself? The answer was twofold. First, questioning revealed that not long before her attacks she had gone to a doctor to obtain dispensation from a religious fast. (She had always been a heavy eater and suffered intensely when she fasted.) He said he would grant the dispensation only if she were found to be suffering from hypoglycemia. She therefore took insulin before the examination and naturally the hypoglycemia was found. In taking it she discovered that it made her feel particularly well.

All these reactions were brought into the open in the course of discussions with the psychiatrist, and the result was a complete cessation of the attacks. (Adapted from Noyes and Kolb, 1963)

HYPOMANIC PERSONALITY. A personality pattern disturbance characterized by a mild degree of exhilaration and overactivity.

Hypomanics are enthusiastic, gregarious, lively individuals constantly overflowing with ideas, emotions, and talk. They are usually pleasure-loving, and are almost completely unrestrained and uninhibited in language and action. Though often amusing for a time, their incessant exuberance tends to be wearing.

Most hypomanics are unstable and easily swayed. They are rarely people of sound judgment, since they are so often influenced by the ideas of others and blinded by their own enthusiasm. When faced with a demand for caution, they tend to override objections and bluster through. As a rule they find it hard or impossible to tolerate frustration, subordinate themselves to other people, or accept any criticism that might puncture their confidence. When things go wrong they protect themselves by shifting the blame to other people or by focusing attention on a new scheme of their own making. Under severe stress, these individuals may in some cases develop a manic-depressive psychosis. *See* MANIC-DEPRESSIVE REACTION (GENERAL).

HYPOTHALAMUS. A structure at the base of the brain containing centers for sleep, temperature, thirst, hunger, sexual activity, emotion, and other autonomic functions.

The hypothalamus is one of the principal areas of the diencephelon, a portion of the forebrain just below the cerebral hemispheres. It consists of several groups of nuclei, or clumps of cells, with the pituitary gland and the mammillary bodies protruding from its floor. Two of the main groups of nuclei integrate the autonomic activities of the organism, which are under the control of the medulla and the spinal cord. One group, the posterior and lateral nucleus, organizes the sympathetic functions. Experiments show that if it is electrically stimulated, sympathetic activities are elicited: the pupils dilate, the heart speeds up, blood pressure rises, stomach and intestinal activity cease. Removal of these nuclei has the opposite effect. The other group, the anterior and medial nucleus, organizes the parasympathetic functions. If it is stimulated, the heart slows down and the blood sugar level falls. Destruction of this area puts the sympathetic nerves in charge and leads to the opposite effects.

The hypothalamus performs its primary function of adjusting the internal environment of the organism by receiving impulses from the cerebral cortex and sending messages to the spinal cord and to the centers for respiration, heartbeat, and glandular regulation in the medulla. The hypothalamus also controls certain of the activities of the nearby pituitary gland; through this gland it governs endocrine secretions throughout the body. These secretions play a major part in regulating the metabolism of fat, carbohydrates, and water, as well as sexual activity and emotional behavior.

It was long suspected that the hypothalamus had many functions, but it is only in recent years that they have been explored experimentally. Research is still in progress, but the results to date can be summarized in terms of specific activities:

Sleep. For many years scientists have

known that tumors and inflammations in the general region of the hypothalamus are associated with an abnormal tendency to sleep, but no one knew what specific areas were involved. The next step was to destroy various regions and note the effects on behavior. In 1939 Ranson found that lesions made in the posterior part of the hypothalamus in monkeys produced almost continuous sleep for four to eight days and marked drowsiness for months. In 1946 Nauta substantiated this finding, and also discovered that when an area in the anterior portion was destroyed, rats and other animals stayed awake until they died of exhaustion. These areas are now known as the waking center and the sleeping center. However, experimentation on the reticular formation has indicated that this region also controls waking. See RETICULAR FORMATION.

Temperature. The anterior part of the hypothalamus also contains a center for temperature regulation (Hardy et al., 1962). Changes in temperature in this area have been found to produce circulatory changes throughout the body (Adams, 1963). The specific mechanisms, however, have not been fully determined.

Hunger and Thirst. Destruction of one area of the hypothalamus, the ventromedial nucleus, has been found to lead to overeating and gross overweight in animals, a condition known as hypothalamic hyperphagia. This ties up with previous observations that tumors and lesions of the hypothalamus cause obesity in man and animals. Oddly enough, animals with experimental lesions were less highly motivated to start eating and were also less finicky than normal animals—but once they started to eat, they continued for a long period. This suggested that there is a "satiety center" in the hypothalamus, since destruction of this area interferes with the "stop" mechanism. This theory has been supported by the fact that electrical stimulation of the center immediately inhib-

its eating (Wyrwicka and Dobrzecka, 1960). In addition, there is a stop center for thirst in another part of the hypothalamus, the supraoptic area.

Experiments have also shown that destruction of the lateral area near the satiety center produces aphagia and adipsia—that is, the animal will refuse to eat and drink, and even starve to death unless special measures are taken. This region is now called the feeding system, or center, since it appears to start and control both eating and drinking. Stimulation with electricity and drugs has also confirmed this finding. A further "start" mechanism for thirst has also been found in the limbic system. See HUNGER.

Sexual Behavior. Experimental destruction of various areas of the hypothalamus has established the fact that this structure is crucial for sexual behavior in both male and female animals. However, the exact areas involved are still in doubt, since some studies indicate that mating is abolished by lesions in the anterior portion while other studies implicate the central and sometimes the posterior regions.

Emotional Behavior. "If there is a 'seat of emotion,' it is the hypothalamus. Such a term can be misleading but it points to the fact that the hypothalamus is the principal center in which the various components of emotional reaction are organized into different patterns" (Morgan, 1965). Experiments carried out on dogs and cats (Bard, 1928) have shown that these animals are capable of complete, or practically complete, rage responses only when the hypothalamus is intact. This structure apparently integrates all the autonomic activities involved in this and other emotions, since sections (incisions) made above it, cutting out the cerebral cortex, actually increase the responses while sections made below it result in fragmentary responses. More recent experiments in which electrodes were implanted in the hypothalamus have shown that direct electrical stimulation will produce many emotional reactions, including fear, anxiety behavior, irritation, rage, attack, and something resembling curiosity (De Molina and Hunsperger, 1959; Yasukochi, 1960). There is some indication that the lateral area is associated with attack, the anterior with fear, the middle portion with aggressive behavior, and the posterior with curiosity and alertness. Lesion studies have also helped to locate the specific areas. Posterior lesions make animals stolid and almost completely unemotional, while medial and ventromedial lesions produce savage and enraged behavior.

HYSTERICAL PERSONALITY. A personality trait disturbance characterized by immature, self-centered behavior with frequent emotional outbursts and histrionic display.

Most hysterical personalities are women. Studies indicate that they have usually been overprotected and spoiled in childhood, and their dramatic behavior is more or less consciously adopted to attract attention or get their way.

When faced with frustration, they are likely to throw a temper tantrum or put on a violent scene. And when others ignore or outdo them, they regain the center of stage by having a fainting spell or making a scene in some other way.

Many of these women are provocative and exhibitionistic with men, but their purpose is to make a conquest rather than to establish a deeper (or even a sexual) relationship with them. In some cases they capriciously flit from one superficial affair to another as a means of concealing sexual fears or frigidity. Similar characteristics are found in their male counterpart, the Don Juan, who also seeks to deny or hide his inadequacies by making one conquest after another. These relationships are never fully gratifying; but in the process of making them he derives secondary satisfaction from setting up dramatic situations, outwitting his rivals, and overcoming the lady's hesitations. *See* PERSONALITY TRAIT DISTURBANCE, NYMPHOMANIA, SATYRIASIS.

I

IATROGENIC ILLNESS (literally, physician-originated). A disorder that is induced or aggravated by the physician.

Suggestion plays a part in many psychological conditions, and a therapist may unwittingly produce symptoms through incautious comments or excessive examinations. This probably occurs most frequently in patients with hysteria, or conversion reaction, since this disorder is characterized by a high degree of suggestibility. One investigator, Babinski (1908) has shown that doctors who look for specific signs or "stigmata" of hysteria, such as skin anesthesia or lump in the throat, may actually induce

these symptoms by suggestion. He coined the term pithiatism (Greek for persuasion) to indicate that these symptoms could be cured as well as caused by suggestion. Others have pointed out that information given by the physician may be instrumental in precipitating a neurosis or even a psychosis in individuals who are on the verge of these conditions: "Not entirely unimportant, unfortunately, is the iatrogenic origin of neurotic manifestations. The physician solemnly diagnoses 'enlargement of the heart,' whereupon the patient is frightened and breaks down until the X-ray photograph resorted to by another physician relieves him of his nightmare" (Bleuler, 1930). *See* CONVERSION REACTION, GLOBUS HYSTERICUS, SKIN DISORDERS.

In discussing psychophysiologic reactions of the cardiovascular system, English and Finch (1964) make this comment: "Probably in no other area are iatrogenic illnesses as frequent as in the realm of cardiac difficulties. Many people suffer from functional heart murmurs. Unfortunately a fair percentage of such people have been informed of this fact in a manner that leads them to focus whatever anxiety they may possess upon their hearts. Once an element of doubt has been injected about the healthy status of their cardiac function by even one physician it requires a great deal of effort to eradicate this preoccupation. Patients have an ability to warp and distort through unconscious means the advice and knowledge that is given them to fit their own neurotic needs." Aldrich (1966) makes the additional point that "too much information may make a patient more apprehensive rather than less, especially when it includes serious possibilities and more particularly when no steps are planned at the time to do something about the disturbing possibilities." He offers the following case in point:

Illustrative Case: IATROGENIC ILLNESS

A young woman who complained of headaches had X rays taken. The doctor reassured her that there was no physical cause for her symptoms and attempted to reinforce his reassurance by showing her the films. While looking at them together, he noted an area of increased density and said, "There is a remote possibility that this might be the beginning of a brain tumor; I really don't think you have one, and I wouldn't advise doing anything about it now, but I'd like to check up on it again in a couple of months."

The patient became very agitated, left her job, and returned to her home in another city, convinced that she was going to die. There, a complete examination showed no signs of a brain tumor. (Aldrich, 1966)

ID (Latin for "it"). The collective name applied by Freud to the instinctual, biological drives which supply the psyche with its basic energy or libido, and which together form the most primitive component of personality structure. The other major components are the superego, comprising our conscience and ideals, and the ego, or self, which mediates between the demands of the id, the superego and external reality.

According to Freud, the id resides in the deepest level of the unconscious, far removed from reality. He described it as a "cauldron of seething excitement," which has no inner organization, knows no laws of logic or values, and obeys only the pleasure principle. It comprises the primitive instincts of hunger, thirst, elimination, air hunger, temperature maintenance, aggression, rage, and sex. All these instincts are present at birth, and the infant seeks to satisfy them before he knows anything about morality or reality. His only object is to achieve pleasure through immediate gratification and discharge of tension.

The id and its unbridled, egocentric impulses dominates the early life of the child. As he comes into contact with reality, however, he gradually distinguishes between himself and the outer world, and between his own needs and the demands of others. In this process he develops a conscious self, or ego, which operates in accordance with the reality principle rather than the pleasure principle, and slowly begins to direct his actions under the guidance of the superego which represents social reality. He therefore gains increasing control over his primitive instincts, and becomes more civilized in his behavior.

The id continues to provide the energy for our vital drives even after the development of ego and superego; it is also the source of many strange impulses, weird dreams, and unaccountable feelings that we all experience from time to time. Most individuals are not disturbed by these impulses from the id, but in cases where the ego is poorly developed or impaired, they may gain control and express themselves in the form of distorted fantasies and unbalanced actions. This occurs in immature and psychopathic personalities, but assumes its most extreme form in schizophrenia and other mental disorders in which the individual regresses to a primitive, infantile stage. One of the major objectives of psychoanalysis is to bring material from the id into consciousness through such techniques as free association and dream interpretation. *See* EGO, EGO IDEAL, SUPEREGO, DEATH INSTINCT, PSYCHOANALYSIS (THEORY), PLEASURE PRINCIPLE, REALITY PRINCIPLE.

IDEALIZATION. The defense mechanism of overestimating the character or abilities of another person.

Idealization is usually carried out both on a conscious and an unconscious level, and it serves the double purpose of increasing emotional security and self-esteem. When the child idealizes his parents, he sets up models of perfection and assures himself that he is in the best possible hands. He derives a sense of pride and security from the feeling that "my daddy is the strongest man in the world," or "my mommy is the prettiest lady on the block." During the hero-worship stage in preadolescence and adolescence, young people of both sexes not only admire their idols from a distance but develop a feeling of kinship toward them. They may even take a proprietary interest in their hero, as if in a sense they alone had discovered him and can fully appreciate him. This emotional bond, however fictitious, gives them strength and encouragement.

It is easy enough to see how idealization contributes to a sense of security, but its relation to self-esteem may not be so obvious. There is a strong narcissistic ingredient in this mechanism. The person who exaggerates the virtues of another individual or chooses a hero to worship is unconsciously identifying with that person—as if to say, "See, that's the kind of person *I* admire. *I* couldn't be satisfied with anything short of perfection." There is, in other words, a kind of feedback effect which enhances the individual's self-esteem, and there is also a clear reflection of self-love along with the feedback. This is similar to the self-satisfaction we feel when we choose a winner in a horse race even if the choice may be entirely on a chance basis. We come very close to taking some of the credit for the victory. Even where we do not make a choice, as in idealizing our parents, we capture for ourselves some of the glory of being a member of such a superior family. We exalt ourselves in exalting them. But the fact is that we make doubly sure that the family is a superior one by exaggerating our parents' good qualities!

Like most other defense mechanisms, idealization contains an element of value. It makes us better satisfied with our lot, and it may be a source of inspiration. Nevertheless it can be an emotional trap. We lay ourselves open to disappointment and frustration when we distort reality by exaggerating the good qualities of other people. Moreover, the hero worshiper tends to lead someone else's life instead of his own. His satisfactions are largely vicarious, not the result of his own efforts. This is basically unhealthy and may lead to practical as well as emotional difficulties. *See* IDENTIFICATION, INTROJECTION, DEFENSE MECHANISM.

IDENTIFICATION. The tendency to incorporate or adopt the attitudes and behavior of other individuals or groups. When the purpose of this reaction is to increase one's feelings of strength, security or acceptance by taking on the qualities of others, it can be classified as a defense mechanism. It generally operates on an unconscious or half-conscious level.

Identification is probably the most important factor in shaping the personality and establishing standards and goals. The process begins with the child's admiration for his parents. He considers them superior beings, wishes to gain some of their qualities and abilities for himself, and therefore begins to take over their attitudes and behavior as his own.

As the child develops, he gradually becomes selective and adopts parental characteristics which seem most congenial to him. His conscience and sex role begin to develop largely through this process. The young boy takes on masculine traits by identifying with his father, the girl acquires feminine traits from her mother. Soon group membership begins to exert its influence, and the child identifies not only with the play group or gang as a whole, but with certain individuals within it. New values and new goals must then be integrated with the ones he has absorbed from his family.

During the school years the growing child also identifies in fantasy with the heroes of history, as well as characters in films, stories, and television. He gains vicarious satisfaction from associating himself with these heroes, and uses them as models in constructing his "ego ideal," the self he would like to become. *See* EGO IDEAL, IDEALIZATION.

The process of identification may work for ill as well as for good. Parental models may leave much to be desired. Groups or gangs outside the family may foster distorted values and objectionable behavior. In some environments the child may not have an adequate chance to identify with constructive models at all. In other situations he may reach too high and identify himself with unrealistic or un-

attainable models. Such identifications may distort his picture of himself, or lure him into activities in which he is bound to fail. They are therefore a threat to mental health.

Identification does not cease with childhood. It continues in adolescence and adulthood as new models are presented and new personality needs acquired. In their search for security and approval, adolescents are particularly prone to hero worship. This again may be for good or for ill. One of the most important problems in guiding them is to keep their eyes on positive, inspiring models.

If identification is carried too far, or if faulty models are used, behavior may become warped. An innocuous example is the Shakespearean actor who plays his part off the stage as well as on. A more damaging example is the member of a gang or the follower of a dictator who not only struts and swaggers like his hero, but also bullies other people. Identification can go even farther awry and become a factor in psychiatric disorder. The boy who has not had an opportunity to feel close to his father may identify with his mother instead, and as a result may develop feminine characteristics and, perhaps, homosexual tendencies. Conflicting identifications may be a factor in some cases of multiple personality. The most extreme form of identification, however, occurs in paranoid schizophrenia, where the patient believes he is another person entirely—for example, Napoleon or Hitler—and adopts that person's entire bearing and mannerisms. *See* FOLIE À DEUX.

Illustrative Case: IDENTIFICATION

A clear-cut but not exceptional example of this variety of learning can be seen in the behavior of a young woman of twenty-one, who became unable to complete even the simplest acts. In bathing, dressing, or eating, she had to perform each step over and over, so that she never finished these daily routines. If she tried piano-playing, for which she had outstanding talent, she was forced to turn each page of music again and again, and to repeat each phrase so often that the thread of the composition was lost. She grew progressively ineffectual at her work, could not touch anything for fear it was unclean, and became unable to eat. She explained her behavior by saying that she feared she was sinful; it was not she but God who performed each act for her, which necessitated her repeating every reaction in order to make it her own. It was at this point that she came to a psychiatric clinic for help.

This was the patient's fourth episode of illness. She had first become fearful of sin and dirt when she was seven years old, and again at the ages of eleven and of sixteen she grew temporarily unable to touch things and filled with the conviction that God was everywhere. The background of her concerns lay in life-long social and economic insecurity, in ridicule which she received because of a disfiguring facial scar, and in attitudes of dependency which, by preventing her from making close attachments to her peers, kept her immature and socially unskilled. The patient was strongly attached to her mother, and demonstratively affectionate toward her; she seemed somewhat fearful of her father and said she had not embraced or kissed him since she was one year old. She preferred the company of women to that of men, spoke disparagingly of the opposite sex and, at twenty-one, had gone out with a boy only twice in her life. In this context, it is highly significant for our present purpose that there was a striking parallel between the woman's pathological reactions and those which her mother had earlier developed.

During her own childhood, the patient's mother had suffered from episodes of insistent anxiety which, she said, were the same as those of the patient. While she was pregnant with the patient, the mother again developed fears—this time fear that she would burn her child, that she would commit a sin, that if she touched anything she would become unclean, and that food she prepared might poison others. These reactions persisted and grew worse after the birth of the child, so that our patient was never without a dramatic model of behavior pathology in the person with whom she was most strongly identified. During interviews with the psychiatrist the mother minimized her own "foolish ideas," and rejected the suggestion that her reactions might have contributed to the direction of the daughter's illness. The patient, for her part, denied that she was in any way affected by her mother's behavior. "She can't upset me—I'm used to her," she said. What the patient denied in words, however, she had accepted in her nonverbal behavior, until as a young adult she was a faithful reproduction of the prevailing female pattern in her home. (Cameron and Magaret, 1951)

IDIOT SAVANT ("wise idiot"). A retarded individual who shows unusual ability in one or more specialized activities.

The term is a misnomer. Idiot savants are rarely idiots and never wise in the full sense of the term. The idiot category, which is now abandoned, implies that these individuals have an IQ of less than twenty or twenty-five and can only reach the intellectual and social level of a two-year-old child. The idiot savant is actually of a higher grade, usually on the mildly or moderately retarded level, which are roughly equivalent to the older categories of moron and imbecile. Their "wisdom" is displayed by unexpected and often remarkable skill in a limited area of manual or mental activity, illustrating, as Anastasi (1958) points out, "the extent to which certain intellectual functions may develop independently of others."

One noted idiot savant devoted his life to the construction of ship models that were so accurately reproduced that he received recognition from the King of England. Many others have displayed special aptitude for drawing or music (Anastasi and Levee, 1960) or an amazing memory for detail—for example, one man could not only give the exact dates of all the funerals in his town for many years back, but was able to name every person who marched in the funeral procession. A common feat of idiots savants is to name the day of the week on which any date occurs in any year. They usually give the right answer in a matter of seconds.

Studies of idiots savants indicate that these abilities are not natural gifts but are developed through long and single-minded practice. They probably reach a peak of perfection because they lead simple lives and are not distracted by other activities. Moreover, they are highly motivated by the recognition they receive for their unusual feats. These ideas were recently confirmed in a study of identical twins who not only solved the day-of-the-week and other problems, but usually answered in chorus. *See* PRODIGY.

ILLUMINATION CONDITIONS. Our ability to perform tasks that require visual discrimination is greatly influenced by lighting conditions. But in determining the optimum level of light, the character of the object under observation—its size, and the amount of brightness, contrast, and detail it contains—as well as the time allowed for seeing must be taken into consideration. A small, black-on-gray highway sign requires more illumination than a large, clearly printed black and white sign; and finely detailed articles moving rapidly along an inspection belt must be examined under more intense light than large, crude objects.

Studies show that vision improves sharply when low level illumination is increased, even a small amount, but with further increases the improvement becomes slower and eventually levels off. However, this is merely a general finding since the optimal amount of light differs widely from one type of work to another. The following recommended levels take into account both efficiency and comfort, and are based upon widely accepted research performed by Blackwell (1959). Close inspection requires 500 foot-candles; proofreading, 150; general office work,

100; wrapping and labeling, 50; dish-washing, 30; loading packages, 20; hotel lobby, 10. (A forty-watt lamp produces about 10 foot-candles on a surface two feet away.) A survey made by Tinker in 1939 revealed that many factories were far below the standard for effective illumination. Many industrial operations were being performed under an average illumination of less than 3 foot-candles—and when the level was raised to 11 foot candles, production was found to increase an average of 15 per cent.

Two other considerations are of major importance. First, the general work area should be adequately and uniformly illuminated, and there should be little difference between this level of illumination and the light that falls on the work object. The second principle is related to this point: lights should be positioned in a way that will minimize glare, since glare spots tend to blind and fatigue the eyes.

ILLUSION. A perception that is not in accord with more trustworthy perceptions; a false perception.

Most of the time "seeing is believing"; our visual senses are usually accurate in their representation of the environment. Occasionally, however, we may misjudge the impression we receive, or perceptions based on one sense may not agree with those from another. A common example is the fact that a vertical line appears longer than a horizontal line of the same length. This is so normal and predictable that it is often taken into account in designing buildings. Clothes, too, are sometimes designed and chosen with illusions in mind: a plaid jacket makes the wearer appear larger than a solid color, and vertical clocks on stockings make the legs look longer. Similarly, our eyes tell us that the railroad tracks converge—but our brain tells us that this is an illusion.

The term illusion is often confused

with the terms hallucination and delusion. In illusions we actually perceive something that exists, but perceive it in a distorted way. They are, in other words, misinterpretations of external and real stimuli. Moreover, most illusions, such as those mentioned above, are experienced by practically everyone in the same general manner, and their extent and nature can often be predicted. In some cases, however, they may result from emotional states, hallucinogenic drugs, or mental disorder: a fear-ridden person may interpret the rustling of leaves as a ferocious animal, a delirious patient may perceive a dark shadow as a crouching enemy, a schizophrenic or an individual under the influence of LSD may take a friendly remark as a threat. Hallucinations are private, personal perceptions that have no basis in external reality—for instance hearing accusatory voices or seeing "pink elephants." Experiences of this kind are symptoms of severe mental disturbance resulting from unconscious emotional influences or from overdoses of alcohol, cocaine, or other drugs. Delusions are also manifestations of mental disorder, but are disturbances of thought rather than perception. Instead of seeing something that is not there, as in hallucinations, the patient believes something that is not true—for example, that he is a multimillionaire or an arch criminal. *See* DE-LUSION, HALLUCINATION.

The classic illustration of a visual or optical illusion is the Müller-Lyer figure (*Fig. 29a*). The illusion probably occurs because we cannot view the lines independently of the arrows at each end. Our perception of the first line is "pulled in" and foreshortened because the arrows turn in. Moreover, this figure actually occupies less total space than the second figure, and this probably influences our estimation of the length of the central line. It is interesting that certain natives in the Torres Straits area are less subject to

this illusion than Europeans, perhaps because their use of spears with large heads has in some way made them "immune" to it. On the other hand, cats and other animals trained to feed from the shorter of two lines have been found to select the shorter-appearing line in the Müller-Lyer illusion.

In a striking experiment, A. Ames, Jr., (1946) has shown how much our visual perception may be influenced by assumptions and expectations. He constructed a special room with the left wall considerably longer than the right, the floor slanted down from right to left, and the floor boards converging toward the right side. Two men of equal size were placed in the room, one standing in the far left corner and the other in the far right corner. He then asked his subjects to look into the room with one eye through a peephole. The result is pictured in PLATE 25: the man at the right appears much taller than the man at the left in spite of the fact that their height is actually the same.

How was this illusion created? First, by having the subject view the room with one eye, the experimenter eliminated the binocular cues that would show him that it was slanted, but at the same time retained the monocular cues to depth perception, such as lines of perspective as given by a normal room. Second, since the room appeared rectangular, and since the retinal image of the man at the right was .larger than the retinal image of the man on the left, the observer actually perceived him as taller.

The key to the illusion lies in the fact that both men are assumed to be equidistant from the observer—an assumption that is based not only on the elimination of binocular cues, but on the *expectation* that the walls, ceiling, and floor meet at right angles, as in an ordinary room. In other words, it is more reasonable for the observer to expect one man to be taller than

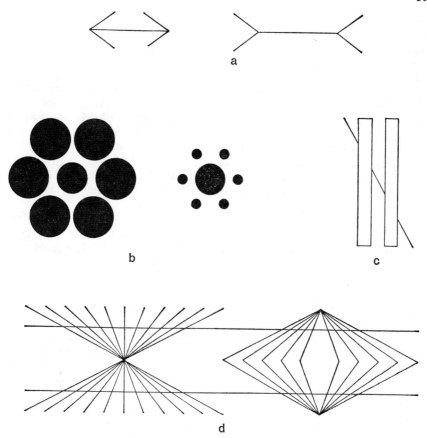

Fig. 29. Some classic illusions. Compare the center lines in *a* and the center dots in *b*. Do the diagonal lines in *c* and the horizontal lines in *d* look straight?

another than to expect a room to be absurdly distorted—in fact, it does not even enter his mind that the room might be distorted. However, if he abandons the peephole and looks directly into the room with both eyes, he will immediately see that the men are of equal size, but that one is actually farther away from the peephole than the other. *See* DEPTH PERCEPTION.

Another experiment, known as the "trapezoidal illusion" (Ames, 1951), has also shown how much our past experience influences our perceptions. A trapezoid window frame—long on one side, short on the other—is slowly rotated. The subject assumes that this window frame is rectangular, like the

others he has experienced in the past. He therefore tends to perceive the longer end as always closer to him, and this makes the window appear to oscillate or sway rather than rotate. This illusion was tried on a group of Zulus, some of whom were urban dwellers while others lived in rural areas. In the rural areas straight lines and square corners are rarely encountered by this tribe, since all their huts and enclosures are round. The urban Zulu environment, on the other hand, contains many rectangular shapes. It was found that twice as many urban as rural Zulus experienced the trapezoidal illusion. This suggests that previous experience with rectangles is important in setting up the type of perceptions on which this illusion is based (Allport and Pettigrew, 1957).

So far we have considered only visual illusions, but there are many other types, such as illusions of smell, taste, temperature, touch, movement, time, and memory. Due to contrast effect, a relatively bland food, such as fish, may appear completely tasteless after eating a peppery dish. Similarly, a fifty-degree day in the middle of a harsh winter will seem to be almost summery. A rough-textured surface usually appears larger than a smooth surface, and a solid representation of the Müller-Lyer illusion will give the same impression to the sense of touch as the linear version to the sense of sight. When we are sitting in a stationary train and the train on the next track begins to move, we are sure our own train is moving because we see through the window what we would see if we were actually moving. *See* APPARENT MOVEMENT, CONTRAST EFFECT.

Time and memory are particularly subject to illusions. When we awaken for a short period in the middle of the night, we may later complain that we were awake all night. When we anxiously wait for an event to occur, it seems to take forever—as witness the father pacing up and down outside the hospital delivery room. Filled time appears shorter than unfilled time, and intervals filled with interesting activities seem to pass more quickly than periods filled with boring activities. Fantasies and attitudes also affect these estimates. If we daydream about exciting events, time usually passes rapidly. If we are afraid sleeplessness will ruin our health or impair our efficiency, our anxiety will help to create the illusion of being awake all night. *See* TIME SENSE.

As for memory, two examples of common illusions are the feeling of having been there before (déjà vu), which is discussed under the topic PARAMNESIA, and retrospective falsifica-tion, the tendency to distort our memory to conform to our wishes or expectations. In the latter process we confuse events we have only read or heard about with events that have actually occurred—or we drop out details that conflict with our preconceptions or show us in a bad light—and we end up with a distorted and illusory view of what happened.

IMAGELESS THOUGHT. Thinking that occurs without the aid of visual images.

During the 1880s and 90s most psychologists believed that thinking always involved images. They held that we must have mental pictures or actual sensory experiences in mind if we are to draw any conclusion or solve any problem. They pointed out, for instance, that when we are in a strange environment, we cannot find our way around until we conjure up a "mental map" of the new environment and visually picture the spatial interrelationships in our new location.

A group of psychologists working in Würzburg, Germany around 1900 were the first to question this view. They asked their subjects to perform extremely simple intellectual tasks and immediately report whatever imagery took place. They found that when the subjects were asked to name a fruit, they responded "apple" or "orange" without picturing these objects in their minds. The fact that tasks of this sort could be performed without the intervention of visual images gave rise to the controversial concept of imageless thought.

The Würzburg experiments pointed up three important aspects of thinking. First, it may not take place wholly on a conscious level. Second, an idea is more like a process than an object. Third, much of our thinking activity seems to go on before specific problems are posed. One example can be used to illustrate all three points. If we are told that we are going to discuss the capitals of the states of the United States, a flourish of mental activity occurs before any questions are asked. As soon as the general category is proposed, we unconsciously begin to run through what we know in that area. Then, when the question is asked, we respond directly (if we know the answer), since the bulk of the thinking has been done before it was actually posed.

The Würzburg investigators called this preparatory activity a "determining tendency," or "set," and defined it as the readiness to respond, or think in a particular, predetermined fashion. Just as the runner sets himself to respond to the starter's gun at the start of a race, so an awareness of a category on which we will be questioned brings that entire area of knowledge to the fore. This process apparently goes on without the use of images.

Another early hint that imagery was not necessary for thinking was Francis Galton's finding that many mathematicians and scientists had much poorer visual imagery than people who were less capable of using abstractions. Also, Alfred Binet found that people with normal visual imagery, such as his own daughters, reported that they did not use imagery in solving mathematical problems. In addition, some people report that they can even dream without the use of images. These and other observations have convinced most psychologists that thinking can be mediated by other kinds of symbols and does not always require "pictures in the mind." *See* BINET, WÜRZBURG SCHOOL, GALTON.

IMAGINARY COMPANION. A fictitious person, animal or object created by a child, usually between the ages of two and a half and four and a half, but often persisting for several years.

Various studies indicate that between 15 per cent and 30 per cent of children have invisible companions of one kind or another, with girls slightly exceeding boys (Hurlock and Burnstein, 1932; Svendsen, 1934; Ames and Learned, 1946). They usually have names and stable personalities and the child talks and plays with them as if they were real. He may also insist that the whole family recognize their existence: "You can't sit in that chair, Bosko is there!" Occasionally it is hard to tell whether the creatures in the child's daydreams are actually imaginary companions or only fictional characters in the stories he makes up.

Imaginary companions are considered a normal expression of childhood fantasy. They are found among children with a wide variety of personality traits —both shy and outgoing, aggressive and withdrawn, emotionally stable and emotionally unstable: "We definitely do not find imaginary companions only in timid or lonely children or in those exhibiting personality difficulties" (Ames and Learned). Adults who recall having these companions show the same wide range of personality (Hurlock and Burnstein). The only general feature of note is that bright children are more likely to create them than dull children. They are also likely to construct more elaborate fantasies, such as an entire family who go through various kinds of adventures during a period of weeks or months.

Even though all kinds of children have imaginary companions, some studies have shown that they are somewhat more frequent when children are lonely or unsociable, or are having difficulties with family relationships (Bender and Vogel, 1941). In these cases they can furnish valuable clues to the child's emotional needs. When all imaginary companions are taken together, however, they are found to serve a variety of purposes. They may represent qualities which the child lacks, such as courage and derring-do. They may provide an outlet for feelings of anger or anxiety or even guilt feelings—and sometimes they are used as scapegoats:

"Bosko made me do it." They may be a means of practicing roles and relationships through dramatic make-believe, as little girls do in playing nurse or little boys in pretending they are bus drivers or policemen. And in many cases they may help to meet a need for intimate friendship—someone with whom to share troubles, pleasures, and confidences.

Each child uses imaginary companions in his own way to satisfy his own particular needs—and as he develops greater social skills, becomes involved in school activities, and finds other ways to meet his emotional needs, he simply outgrows this stage. Usually they fade gradually away, though sometimes they meet a melodramatic end in an accident or an Indian war. But, hopefully, the child's capacity to enjoy fantasy and use imagination in work and play will not disappear with them. See DAY-DREAMING.

IMITATION. Copying the behavior of another person, animal, or object.

Imitation does not receive as much attention in current psychology as it once did, probably because it has been eclipsed by other forms of learning, such as insight and conditioning. Yet it is an extremely important and widespread phenomenon, accounting at least in part for most of our behavior patterns, attitudes, and interests. Even though we add our unique touch to all of our experiences, there is little doubt that we owe our use of language, our manners, motor skills, sex roles and other roles, preferences, prejudices, and aspirations largely to this process. In an even broader context, it is undoubtedly true (as Gabriel Tarde pointed out near the beginning of this century) that the structure and norms of society as a whole, with its lore and laws, customs and codes, can be traced in large part to our tendency to follow behavior prescribed by others.

Imitative behavior begins extremely early in life. As Hurlock (1964) notes, the child begins to imitate facial expressions, especially laughing and crying, around the third month; gestures such as waving bye-bye and throwing a kiss in the sixth month; and simple sounds such as choo-choo and ding-dong as well as actual speech around the twelfth month. She also points out that a child begins to perceive and imitate emotional reactions within the first weeks of life: "Babies less than four weeks old have been found to refuse the breast if the mother was tense." We do not know exactly what cues are used by the infant in making such responses, but they suggest that imitation may be a far more subtle affair than is commonly recognized.

The drive to imitate reaches a peak between the ages of two and three, when the child tries to dress himself, eat by himself, and master the difficult art of speech. He adopts the manners and mannerisms of his parents and others in the household simply by observing them intently and constantly repeating and practicing what he observes. In this way he learns an amazing amount without being actually *taught* by others. A child can be encouraged to make the most of this process if we make it easy for him to imitate us—for example, by speaking distinctly or letting him stand on a chair to watch as we do the dishes, by providing practice materials (for example, a set of plastic dishes), and by reinforcing successful behavior with liberal rewards of praise and approval.

Many psychologists and psychiatrists have attempted to discover the sources of the imitative drive. At the beginning of life it appears to be little more than an automatic, mechanical process, probably closely akin to the process of imprinting. (It is an interesting fact that some deeply disturbed patients who have apparently regressed to infantile behavior automatically imitate the speech or gestures of other people. *See* ECHOLALIA, ECHOPRAXIA.)

After the first few weeks of life, the process ceases to be wholly automatic since we actively encourage the child to imitate us. We show him how to wave or hum or say "mama," and hug him delightedly when he follows our lead. But why is it that the child is so willing to imitate us? And why does imitation continue to play a major part in his life as he grows older?

The reasons imitation plays such an important role in childhood are fairly clear. First, children feel helpless and insecure, and adopt the behavior of others because they are not sure how to conduct themselves in many situations. They not only tend to copy the behavior of adults who appear so knowing and self-confident, but also the behavior of other children who are older, more self-assured or more assertive than themselves. Second, parents and teachers reinforce imitative behavior through the rewards of approval and encouragement, and in some cases through threat of punishment or loss of love. And third, the child has an urge to be "big" and prove that he can handle himself well. The most conspicuous models for acting big are the adults who surround him, and he therefore identifies with them and takes over their behavior. This gives him not only the know-how he needs, but also the vicarious satisfaction of feeling close to the people he most admires. Identification is found throughout early childhood, but takes the form of hero-worship in pre-adolescence and adolescence when the growing boy or girl is anxiously facing new problems and reaching out for help. This tendency can, of course, work for good or ill.

Imitation continues in adulthood for many of the same reasons that it is manifested in childhood—particularly, uncertainty, lack of savoir faire, the desire for social approval, and admiration for successful or prestigious individuals.

These factors all play a part in conformity behavior in which we unthinkingly accept the opinion of the majority, rely upon dubious experts, adopt fads and fashions created primarily for commercial purposes, or follow a self-appointed leader during a crisis. Two additional factors seem to apply to imitative behavior in adulthood. First, we adopt the behavior of others because this is the path of least resistance. This applies particularly to social customs such as the rules of etiquette. The American way of eating, in which we shift the fork from hand to hand, makes little sense, but we don't "fight" it. Second, conformity behavior—whether it is rational or not—lends order to our lives and gives us a sense of belonging. A society in which each person acted uniquely and individually would have no structure or sense or organization—in fact, it could hardly be called a society.

Imitation has both advantages and limitations. It is a highly useful shortcut to learning social behavior and manual skills. Much time and effort is saved when children automatically copy other people's behavior and do not have to be actively taught. Similarly, a worker can get started on a new job simply by observing others or viewing training films; a beginner can learn to correct the way to swing a tennis racket on a "Do as I do" basis; a retarded individual can learn to pull out a nail without knowing anything about the principles of leverage. Imitation is also the basis for the smooth functioning of the social order and for the rituals and customs that serve as a "fly wheel" for society, to use an expression which William James applied to habit.

As to its limitations, we cannot overlook the fact that it is largely an unthinking process which leads to mechanical learning devoid of understanding, and to uncritical acceptance of the opinions and often the prejudices of other people. It also encourages conventional behavior and following the lead of others instead of thinking and acting independently. *See* SOCIAL NORM, SUGGESTION, IDENTIFICATION, FOLIE À DEUX, SOCIAL ROLE.

IMMATURE PERSONALITY. A personality trait disturbance characterized by childish emotional and behavior patterns.

Immature personalities are found at every age. Typically these individuals have little control over their emotions, shifting from laughter to tears or from friendliness to hostility in a matter of minutes. When faced with frustrations and decisions, they are likely either to "fold up" or react impulsively and unthinkingly. They cannot tolerate pressure of any kind and tend to panic in an emergency. If they are unable to solve their problems or gratify their desires, they revert to the tactics of infancy and childhood.

Immature women who cannot get their way invariably sulk, pout, stamp their feet, throw a typical tantrum, or let their household duties slide. Immature men are likely to storm about the house, rush out to the corner bar, blame others for their errors, chase girls, or foist their responsibilities on others. Both tend to be unrealistic in their expectations and spend their money unwisely. As they advance in age they show little capacity to adjust to the changes and stresses that inevitably occur, and their lives become one long series of quarrels, jealousies, accusations of neglect, spiteful actions, and anger outbursts. *See* PERSONALITY TRAIT DISTURBANCE.

The following case illustrates one of the more frequent forms of immaturity in women:

Illustrative Case: IMMATURE PERSONALITY

Jane H. is a seventeen-year-old girl who was referred to the Psychiatric Clinic of the Juvenile Court because of her involvement with a married man. She had been dating this twenty-six-year-old man before she knew he was married and the father of two children. She attended a union party with him, at which time she became drunk and spent the night with him in a hotel room. When the girl returned to her home the next day, the family brought her to the Juvenile Court after she told about what had occurred. The man was arrested, fined, and placed on probation.

When seen at the Clinic, the girl was tense and anxious, and talked hurriedly and with considerable pressure of speech. She spoke intimately and freely about the episode bringing her to the Juvenile Court, and about her relationships with other boyfriends. Her judgment appeared to be undependable under stress, and her relationships with other people were characterized by fluctuating emotional attitudes. There was strong evidence of poorly controlled hostility, guilt, and anxiety. The girl reacted in a primitive and infantile manner, and despite the fact that she was seventeen years old, she behaved much in the manner of a young child. During her examination she alternately laughed and cried, and made free use of dramatic body gestures and facial expressions. (Kisker, 1964)

IMPOTENCE. A male sexual disorder consisting of inability to achieve full gratification. In psychiatry impotence is classified as a psychophysiologic reaction of the genitourinary system.

Impotence is not usually an all-or-nothing matter, but rather an impairment of function that can be expressed in a variety of ways. It may consist of partial or complete failure to achieve erection, periodic failure coupled with limited interest in sex, orgasm without experiencing pleasure, coitus without ejaculation, sexual ability only with prostitutes or in extramarital affairs, or —most frequent of all—premature ejaculation.

There are many causes of impotence. A few cases are due to congenital defect, injury to the genitalia, or diseases of the nervous system. Alcohol reduces potency in some men but increases it in others, probably because it relaxes their inhibitions. In some cases fatigue, business tension, worry, or illness may temporarily decrease potency. On the other hand, when the condition is persistent and not due to organic defect, it is nearly always the result of emotional conflicts. Age is less a factor than is commonly believed: according to the Kinsey report, only 27 per cent of males become impotent by age seventy, and many of these cases, too, are psychological rather than physical.

The conflicts that cause impotence are frequently associated with feelings of fear, guilt, or hostility. Parental warnings against the damaging effects of masturbation may lead to an unconscious fear of injury as a result of intercourse. Fear of detection during early sexual activities may affect later performance. Concern about venereal disease, or even the fear of dying as a result of the excitement of intercourse, also interfere with potency in some cases. So does self-consciousness about exposure of the body. Some men lose their potency because of fear of failure and doubts about their ability to play the male role fully. Psychoanalysts emphasize castration fears stemming from threats made by the father. The tension accompanying these anxieties may produce complete inability in some instances and premature ejaculation in others.

A second group of causes centers around the relationship to the sexual partner. Frequent quarrels, irritations, and tensions between the partners may impair potency. Studies of premature ejaculation indicate that this condition may often originate in feelings of hostility, since the woman is denied her satisfaction. Some women express their own resentment by constantly criticizing their husband or by setting up strict rules about foreplay; as a result, they inhibit the husband's gratification as well as their own. Strong attachment toward another woman, doubts about

the choice of a wife, or conflicts over loss of independence may also have a marked effect. Excessive attachment to the mother may unconsciously arouse feelings of unfaithfulness that interfere with potency.

Latent or overt homosexuality undoubtedly plays a part in some cases. Some men with homosexual inclinations simply become disinterested in women while others have feelings of active revulsion toward them. Still others become sexually inadequate with women because they are using intercourse as a defense against unconscious homosexual fears—in other words, they are trying to force themselves to play the normal male role.

When impotence stems from deeply unconscious sources, the most effective treatment is a penetrating form of psychotherapy. When its source lies closer to the surface, counseling techniques may be successful. A frank discussion of the sexual relation, the difference between the male and female response, and specific fears and inhibitions is often helpful. Where the disorder seems to arise out of a faulty relationship between the couple, the sources of friction and antagonism need to be explored, and it is often best for the therapist to meet the husband and wife together as well as separately. If their relationship improves to a point where they feel affectionate, accepting, and secure with each other, potency is almost certain to return. *See* FRIGIDITY.

Illustrative Case: IMPOTENCE (ANXIETY STATE)

K.Y., aged thirty-four years, complained of pains about the heart and of impotence. He had been married for fourteen years and had two children. For the past three months he had been impotent, although up until that time, sexual relations occurred normally two or three times a week. Six months before, the man had been discharged from his employment and had been unable to find other work. The financial situation became exceedingly acute and the patient, who was proud, put off asking for charity. However, because of the need for his wife and children to eat, he had to go on relief, and it was on the background of these worries that impotence resulted. A different attitude toward his financial state and the partial relief thereof caused the impotence to disappear. (Kraines, 1948)

Illustrative Case: IMPOTENCE (PREMATURE EJACULATION)

A man of twenty-nine, after one month of marriage, came for treatment for premature ejaculation. No other symptoms were evident. He was the third of a family of five. None of the children had been given sexual information and, in fact, the subject was strictly taboo at all times. The mother of the patient was overly religious and although she attended to the ordinary tasks of life she taught her children that religion came before everything else. According to her teaching there were only two important things in life—work and worshiping God. Demonstrations of affection were frowned upon. She kept the patient at arm's length and, in addition, always discouraged his friendships with girls. In spite of this he had numerous sexual fantasies about women. He wished they would surrender themselves to him for sexual pleasure yet he was sure none of them wanted to do so. When he first attempted to kiss a girl he was in great anxiety lest she become angry and scold him. He always expected women to repulse and reproach him. On the one hand he was profoundly grateful to women who would love him and at the same time unconsciously quite hostile to them for the attitude of denial which he felt they all held toward him. When he married he was apprehensive as to whether he could function sexually or not. He was not entirely surprised at his symptom of premature ejaculation. He said, "I can't believe my wife really wants to give herself to me. It seems that I am asking too much. I want sexual pleasure to last longer both for myself and for her but I can't control it."

Inquiry into his daily life revealed that he had always been sensitive to the attentions of both men and women. He craved love and friendship and was easily cast down if disapproved of in any way. He remembered that whenever anyone had shown him much praise or affection, or had given him a present, he would cry. "I was always so ashamed of that. As I grew older and people expected me to be strong emotionally I would be weak. I was ashamed of myself for crying then as I am now about this symptom."

As the treatment interviews went on, the patient more and more related his lack of emotional control in social situations to his lack of ejaculatory control. He said, "When I go to the movies and the hero finally gets what he wants, I cry. I want my wife to give me her body for my pleasure. When she does so I release semen too quickly just as I have always released tears too quickly. It seems to me that I can't stand to get what I want without losing control of myself."

At this point the patient brought out hostility toward his mother. "If my mother had only given me more love and led me to expect more, instead of constantly preaching and making such an ascetic of me! I am inadequate in making love and I cannot make my wife happy. Perhaps I don't want to, insofar as she represents my mother, but at least I must try to accept pleasure for myself and then maybe I'll be able to give it to her."

After the conscious expression of hostility to his mother he was better able to express his feelings without loss of emotional control. At the same time his ability to maintain erection without ejaculation increased to an entirely satisfactory point. (Weiss and English, 1943)

IMPRINTING. A rapid learning process occurring early in the life of some types of animal, and resulting in specific responses to certain objects.

In rural areas we occasionally see chicks or ducks follow a farmer about, as if they were mysteriously responding to signals given by the farmer. We may wonder what magical power he has over these animals, or conclude that he has spent an enormous amount of time training these unintelligent creatures to do such smart things. Actually neither of these surmises is correct. The behavior of the animals is due to a primitive form of learning known as imprinting.

Imprinting was first described in 1873 by an English naturalist, D. A. Spalding, although he did not use the term. He found that newly hatched chicks would follow the first moving object that caught their attention, whether this object was a human being or a member of their own species. As these animals matured they became extremely attached to the object they first followed (the imprinted object). Recent experiments have shown that sexual and other social responses are often made to the imprinted object, no matter how inappropriate they may be. Chicks and ducks sometimes make these responses, including sexual overtures, to a human being, a ball, a cube, or any other type of imprinted object.

Konrad Lorenz (1937), an ethologist (a zoologist interested in animal behavior), coined the term "imprinting" to describe this behavior. He demonstrated that this form of learning will only occur during a critical period early in the life of the animal. The period starts when the animal is first able to move around adequately and ends when it develops fear reactions which cause it to flee from the moving object instead of following it. Lorenz (1937), Hess (1959), and others have observed imprinting not only in chicks and ducks but in insects, fish, sheep, deer, and buffalo.

Some investigators draw an analogy between the smiling response in human infants and imprinting in lower animals. Experiments show that between two weeks and six months of age, infants tend to attend longer to representations of the human face than to other types of figures (Fantz, 1961). They also smile more often at a full face than at a variety of other stimuli (Spitz and Wolf, 1946). The mother's face is held to be the most common releaser of the smiling response of the infant. Many ethologists claim that this first response is instinctive, and that it later becomes associated with pleasurable activities such as playing with toys, animals, or friends because the mother and father smile and nod approval when the child engages in these activities.

Most investigators agree that imprinting is a rapid form of learning that is extremely important for the later social development of animals and possibly of human beings. There is some disagreement, however, as to its dynamics. The ethologists claim that it is an innate, instinctual activity which is released only by moving objects during a critical period in the animal's life. Several American psychologists, however, have demonstrated that imprinting can take place even if neither the animal nor the imprinting object is permitted to move. Claims by the ethologists that imprinting is fixed and irreversible have also been challenged. Experiments have shown that the imprinting response can be extinguished like any other response.

Opponents of the instinct theory of imprinting offer a different explanation of the phenomenon. They contend that all young organisms, including humans, are highly sensitive to their new environment and easily frightened by strange noises, sudden movements and unknown objects. On the other hand, they respond positively to less intense stimulation, and if there is an object in the environment that provides this kind of stimulation they will attend to it. The parent is such a source, and the animal finds that by following this "object" at a fixed distance, it can experience a constant source of mild and pleasant stimulation. The parent soon becomes imprinted through conditioning, and is sought out any time the animal or child feels afraid, since it has found that the presence of the parent has relieved its fear in the past. This process can be compared to concentrating on a pleasant thought or memory when we are in a dangerous, anxiety-filled situation.

Parallel criticisms have also been leveled at the experiments done on smiling infants. It is known that up to six months of age the vision of infants is only 20/400, which means that they could not easily distinguish the human face from other figures. What, then, are they responding to? A reanalysis of Fantz's experiment has shown that the infants preferred figures in the middle range of brightness over figures that were either too intense or too dim. In other words, human infants, like other young organisms, react to stimulation in the comfortable middle range of intensity.

If we accept these newer interpretations, we seem forced to conclude that animals, including humans, become tied to their own species more by association and satisfying contact than by any intrinsic affinity. The parent happens to be around because of the nature of the situation, and the young organism follows it and becomes attached to it because it provides the most constant, reliable, and comfortable stimulation. *See* MOTHERING, CRITICAL PERIOD.

INADEQUATE PERSONALITY. A personality pattern disturbance characterized by failure to adapt to the occupational, social, emotional, and intellectual demands of life.

Although most inadequate individuals have had average educational opportunities and test within normal limits on intelligence examinations, they are not only ineffective in all their dealings, but show attitudes of easy-going unconcern. They are seriously lacking in judgment, ambition, foresight, and stamina. Though often good-natured, their social relationships are almost invariably shallow, and they are too irresponsible and self-centered to work constructively with other people. They tend to live completely in the present, and even when extra effort would bring obvious results in the near future, they fail to carry through.

The majority of shiftless individuals— vagrants, ne'er do wells, and the like—

are inadequate personalities. They may become alcoholics and drug addicts, but they rarely suffer from neuroses since they are relatively insensitive to deep emotional conflict or persistent anxiety. If they are subjected to prolonged physical or social stress, they gradually deteriorate intellectually and emotionally, and in some cases develop psychotic reactions of a schizophrenic type. *See* PERSONALITY PATTERN DISTURBANCE.

Illustrative Case: INADEQUATE PERSONALITY

A single, thirty-eight-year-old male came to the psychiatric clinic at his sister's insistence. She had urged him to seek some advice about his inability to cope with life. He had always been shy and unable to take responsibility. He left school at the eighth grade because he was too incompetent socially to be expected to go to high school. The son of a farmer, he considered himself too inept to plan to learn farming with all its requirements for managing animals and machinery and other farm activity. He left these things to a farmhand who was far less intelligent than he but who had a native capacity for accomplishing things. In addition to the patient's incompetence, he was extremely shy with the opposite sex. He had never had a girl friend and was lacking in confidence and social poise so that he was unable to even consider himself as a suitable companion for a girl. His mother had been a timid person but a good housekeeper. She had had little confidence in herself and had lacked the poise to mix socially. His father was of similar caliber. He would go to town, accomplish his business, but never take part in any community activity, make friends with people, or otherwise join in any social activities.

The patient had been the only boy in a family of four, and it had never been assumed by his parents that he would learn to do the things that other boys and men did. It was as if everything the parents did in terms of effectual living was done at such a cost of anxiety to them that their consciences would not permit them to ask the boy to assume his responsibilities in these directions. He was permitted to grow up afraid of practically every aspect of life from the physical to the social and emotional. As a result he could truly be described as a very inadequate personality. He performed a few simple tasks around the farm under the direction of the hired hand. He did not ask for more to do, nor did he want more. He had no ambition, no envy, and no jealousy. When he was in his late twenties he joined the local peacetime military organization and one summer went on maneuvers for two weeks. This involved traveling two hundred miles away from his home and constituted the biggest event of his life. He continued to discuss it, with what was for him considerable animation, even ten years later.

He lived a simple existence, doing a few chores on the farm, eating his meals, and following the barest outline of current events. His IQ, established by psychological testing, was in the high average group. In spite of this he was not quick at learning new things. He had a lack of physical and emotional stamina and was socially most inept. He had become so fixed in his pattern that it was decided he would not make a good candidate for therapy, even had he wished to undertake it. He had made it fairly clear that he saw no great reason for receiving treatment and that he was not dissatisfied with his own pattern of living. As far as he was concerned, his sister was unnecessarily upset and his own adjustment satisfied him. His sister therefore was advised against further urging him into therapy.

The prognosis of this patient is very guarded as far as improvement is concerned. In all probability he will continue to live out his life on the very limited, inadequate scale which he has set for himself. There is little probability that he will develop a definite mental illness unless he is forced into a traumatic situation with which he is unable to cope, or unless perhaps such changes come on with senility. The patient essentially has very little conflict and is making what he considers to be a satisfactory and acceptable adjustment, so that it is difficult to conceive of his developing sufficient conflict to precipitate a mental illness. (English and Finch, 1964)

INCEST. Sexual activity between persons of closer blood relationship than the culture allows.

The degree of relationship varies considerably from society to society. In some societies marriage between cousins or between uncles and nieces, aunts and nephews is prohibited, in others it is permitted. Privileged groups have been exempted from incest taboos in some cultures—for example, during the Ptolemaic period in Egypt marriage between brother and sister in the royal family was not only permitted but required.

Incest taboos of one kind or another have been found in practically every society. At one time these prohibitions were attributed to the dangers of inbreeding, but today this theory is largely discredited because it applies only when there are latent hereditary defects in the family line. A more widely accepted explanation is that incest creates rivalries that disrupt family life and prevent the society from enlarging and strengthening itself through outside relationships.

The prevalence of incest taboos indicates that the urge to form these relationships must be widespread. In his theory of psychosexual development, Freud held that every child experiences incestuous impulses directed toward the parent of the opposite sex, although during the latency period an "incest barrier" is ordinarily erected, which deflects sexual interest from the parents to other people and activities. Recent investigations, however, tend to favor environmental explanations. It has been found that incestuous relationships occur most frequently where living quarters are crowded, family moral standards lowest, and opportunities for sexual experimentation constantly present themselves. This view is supported by the fact that the practice appears to be most common in the lower socioeconomic groups where brother and sister frequently share the same room and the father lives in close contact with adolescent daughters. Other precipitating factors in father-daughter incest are disturbed marital relationships, death or absence of the wife, and alcoholism. In some cases this form of incest is the result of a lowering of ethical and emotional controls due to psychosis, senile deterioration, manic reaction, or paresis. *See* OEDIPUS COMPLEX.

It is difficult to obtain accurate figures on incest, but the incidence is believed to be relatively low in our society. Mother-son incest is rare, usually occurring only where one or both are psychotic. Brother-sister sex play is not uncommon, but a full incestuous relationship seldom occurs. Father-daughter incest appears to be considerably more common than any other type, and is the most frequent form among men who have been convicted of sexual offenses.

Incest frequently gives rise to emotional disturbance, particularly when it occurs during adolescence rather than earlier. Some young people develop severe conflicts as a result of fantasies centering around incestuous wishes. In cases where girls have been forced into sexual relations with their father or an older brother, the experience is often so traumatic that it leads to intense guilt feelings and a lasting revulsion toward sex. Some girls who have tolerated or accepted the relationship develop feelings of degradation and sin only after they have become more mature. On the other hand, many girls who have had incestuous experiences at home adopt a permanent pattern of promiscuous behavior. *See* PROMISCUITY.

Illustrative Case: INCEST

The patient, a twenty-year-old high-school graduate, had been subjected to incestuous sexual relations by an older brother from about the age of twelve to fifteen. She stated that during this period her family was extremely poor and she and her brother shared the same bedroom. Apparently also the moral level of the family left a great deal to be desired, for from the age of fifteen to seventeen her father forced sexual relations on her as well.

During her last year in high school she took a course in mental hygiene during which the teacher discussed the harmfulness of incestuous relations with considerable emotionality, suggesting that the fathers participating in such activities should be summarily hanged. The patient reported that although she had had severe guilt feelings about her incestuous relationships, it was not until this talk that the full "evilness" of herself and her brother and father was brought home to her. For several days she contemplated suicide but finally gave up this idea.

Following this she could hardly stand the sight of her father—he appeared loathsome to her, "like a snake or something like that." She also stopped going out on dates, stating that she just didn't like men anymore— they all seemed alike to her—and she didn't want to have anything further to do with them. After her graduation at eighteen, she obtained a job as a stenographer and moved into an apartment with an ex-classmate, also a stenographer. Her roommate was not pretty, had few dates, and spent most of her leisure time with the patient. Over a period of several months they became very fond of each other and enjoyed doing things and going places together. The patient stated that she did not know just how it happened, but one night after attending a party where they each had several drinks they found themselves kissing each other. This apparently led to a pattern of homosexual relations which continued over an eighteen-month period.

Then the patient met a homosexual youth at a party and they apparently became quite fond of each other. The patient states that they were good friends and could "feel at home in each other's company without getting involved in sex. Of course in the distant future we may try sexual relations and if this works out even get married." This apparently presented the patient's first attempt to return to a heterosexual pattern. It is interesting that it involved a homosexual partner. However, this first attempt almost failed, for her roommate became extremely jealous and reported to the patient that her boyfriend was planning to get her pregnant as soon as possible so that he could force her to marry him. In the light of her previous relations with men, this news proved extremely traumatic to the patient and she became quite tense and disturbed. The following day she came voluntarily for psychological help. (Coleman, 1964)

INCIDENTAL LEARNING (Latent Learning). The tendency to note and remember things not directly relevant to the activity at hand. Another name for incidental learning is "latent learning," since it takes place without awareness and the information we acquire remains hidden until an occasion for its use arises.

We learn a great deal without making any conscious attempt to learn and without making any kind of overt response. When we are a passenger in an automobile, without responsibility for reaching the destination, we still learn something about the route. Without fully realizing it we notice certain turns, outstanding houses and other landmarks. If we take the same route alone at a later date, we find it easier to get to our destination than if we had never been on the road before. Similarly, we often note that a store sells a certain line of goods we are not shopping for at the moment. If we wish to purchase these goods on another occasion, we will head directly for them.

The existence of this type of learning is accepted by most investigators, but there is some controversy over its origin. Some psychologists contend that no learning whatever can take place unless there is a *motive* to learn. For these investigators, learning is always in response to an interest, an incentive or a need. They therefore conclude that at the very least an exploratory drive must be operating in incidental learning. The person who learns the route even when he is not driving must have a curiosity about the road or a notion that he might need to take the route himself at a later date. Likewise the shopper makes an incidental note of a line of goods because he is already interested in it, even if he does not intend to purchase it at the moment.

Opponents of this interpretation maintain that we acquire a startling amount of information without the slightest intention or motivation. So long as we are awake, and even perhaps when we are asleep, our senses receive constant stimuli, and these are transmitted to the brain whether we wish it or not. Compelling evidence for this view can be found in the quantity of incidental information that can be elicited under hypnosis. Experiments have shown that if you ask a student in his waking state about the color of the shirts of his two nearest neighbors in the preceding class, you will almost certainly draw a blank—but if he is put into a trance and then asked the same question, he will practically always give a correct answer.

Samuel Taylor Coleridge has given us a case that supports the idea of unmotivated incidental learning. A domestic servant he once employed became ill and had to be taken to the hospital. There she developed a delirium, and —though totally illiterate—astonished the doctors by speaking phrases and entire sentences in Latin, Greek, and Hebrew. Subsequent investigation revealed that she had once worked for a learned clergyman who made a practice of walking up and down the corridors of the house declaiming biblical quotations in the three languages.

The idea of incidental learning is frequently used to explain the déjà vu experience. Sometimes new experiences have a familiar ring: we feel we have been in this room before, even though we know we have never seen it. Quite probably we have at one time been in a similar room, and have noted at least its general pattern without realizing it. *See* PARAMNESIA.

INCORPORATION. An unconscious process, sometimes termed a defense mechanism, in which the qualities of another person are taken in, or "ingested," through physical contact, and become part of the self.

According to psychoanalytic theory, incorporation is the most primitive means of recognizing external reality, and the prototype of instinctual satisfaction. It first occurs in the oral stage when the infant feels (or fantasies) that the mother's breast, and perhaps her total being, are becoming a part of himself during the process of nursing. This mechanism is considered the earliest and most basic form of identification and introjection—the first expression of the child's impulse to assimilate the attributes, omnipotence, and later the attitudes of his parents. As he grows, he "swallows them up" psychically just as he did literally during the nursing period.

Incorporation is also considered the earliest expression of sexuality, since it is the first way an instinctual aim is directed toward an object, the mother's breast. As the child grows, the sexual instinct is expressed in other pleasurable oral activities such as sucking, biting, and swallowing objects. When he has reached the stage of genital primacy, or sexual maturity, the oral incorporation impulse is still operative, as indicated by the expression "I love you so much I could eat you up."

Psychoanalytic theory also holds that many of the symptoms of regressed schizophrenic patients, such as voracious eating and "cosmic identification" (identification with the universe), hark back to the infantile incorporation mechanism. See THUMBSUCKING, IDENTIFICATION, INTROJECTION, PSYCHOSEXUAL DEVELOPMENT.

INDIVIDUAL TEST. A psychological test that is given to one subject at a time. The Wechsler Intelligence Scales, the Thematic Apperception Test, and the Stanford-Binet Test are examples of tests designed primarily for individual administration.

Many individual tests require careful oral questioning or close observation of responses. On the Stanford-Binet Test, for example, the verbal part includes direct question and answer exchanges between the examiner and examinee, and the performance part contains items which require observation and timing. On the TAT, a "picture-story" technique, the examiner attempts to gain insight into the subject's personality dynamics by asking questions about the characters, the ending, and where the story came from. These operations could not be carried out on a group basis.

Some individual tests can be sufficiently modified and simplified to be administered to groups. The Rorschach Test may be handled in this way. Ink blots can be projected on a screen, and the subjects asked to write what they see. In contrast to the individual administration of this test, they are not asked what part of each blot they use in each response, nor are they asked a series of questions after the entire group of blots has been shown. Here group administration gains time but loses much valuable information.

Group methods are usually applied when large numbers of people have to be processed in a short period of time. The first important group intelligence test, the Army Alpha, was devised to meet such a need during World War I. Other representative group tests are the Otis Self-Administering Test of Mental Ability, the Kuhlmann-Anderson Intelligence Tests, the Miller Analogies Test, the Raven Progressive Matrices, and the Scholastic Aptitude Test. See THEMATIC APPERCEPTION TEST, STANFORD-BINET TEST, RORSCHACH TEST, INTELLIGENCE TESTS, WECHSLER INTELLIGENCE SCALES.

INFANT AND PRESCHOOL TESTS. Behavior tests given to young children to determine whether development is proceeding normally.

Tests given before the age of two are primarily concerned with sensorimotor development (co-ordination, manipulation, etc.); tests given after that age generally include items that test memory and understanding as well. In no case, however, are they considered intelligence tests in the full sense of the term. Studies show that they are generally unreliable in forecasting the child's IQ at later ages, although the tests given after age two predict future mental level slightly more accurately than those given before that age. There are many reasons for their lack of predictive value: (1) sensori-motor ability does not correlate highly with later intelligence; (2) small children are incapable of solving the kind of problems that are used in an intelligence test; (3) they have a short attention span and show great fluctuation in alertness; (4) they are subject to emotional reactions, such as negativism, that interfere with the testing process; and (5) during the early years of life growth is often uneven, with many spurts and plateaus, and therefore a test given at one time may not be indicative of the child's ability at another.

Sometimes the accuracy of the tests can be improved by including a wider range of items or by giving tests for two or three months and combining the results. Even under these conditions they usually yield only rough estimates, but may be helpful in diagnosing the grosser types of mental and neurological defect. Here are some of the most widely used infant tests:

California First Year Mental Scale (ages 1 month to 18 months). The test covers such features of behavior as postural adjustment, motor activity, attention to persons, sensory perception, vocalization, attention to objects, manipulation of objects, and play behavior. The infant's performance is compared with developmental averages for normal children. The following are a few sample items, with age norms based on Bayley's studies (1933): vertical eye coordination (shown normally at 1.4 months), manipulates table edge (3.6 months), lifts cup by handle (6.6 months), rings bell purposefully (9.9 months), turns pages of book (16.6 months), understands two prepositions (25.0 months), remembers one of four pictures (35.6 months).

Gesell Infant Schedule (4 weeks to 56 weeks). The child is tested in a variety of situations at each level, and evaluated on four characteristics: motor, adaptive, personal-social, and language (including facial expression, postural movements, gestures and words). Each situation is broken into specific sequences of behavior, and the child is scored on each of them—for example, activity with a ball comprises looking at it, moving toward it, reaching for it, grasping it, etc. The inventory at 4 weeks includes analysis of head control, body posture, arm-hand posture, and leg-foot posture. The schedule at 56 weeks includes language and social behavior, manipulation and adaptation, body posture, and progression.

Gesell also devised a Preschool Schedule which extends from 15 months to 6 years, based on the same four categories. The following samples are taken from the 15-month level. *Motor:* walks few steps, creeps up full flight, places pellet in bottle, helps turn pages of a book; *adaptive:* builds tower of two cubes, draws incipient imitation stroke, places round block in formboard; *language:* speaks four to six words, pats picture in book, points to own shoe; *personal-social:* has discarded bottle for feeding, bowel control, says "ta-ta," indicates wants by pointing or vocalizing, shows or offers toy to adult.

Cattell Infant Intelligence Scale (2 months to 30 months). This test attempts to extend the Stanford-Binet Test downward, and is scored in the same way. It presents five items for each month, many of which are borrowed from Gesell—for instance, the items for two months include "attends voice," "inspects environment," "follows ring in horizontal motion," "babbles."

The items at 30 months include "differentiates bridge from tower," "imitates drawing of lines and circles," and "folds paper." Cattell believed that extreme deviations, both above and below the norm, can be detected at 1 year of age (1947), and from 1 year on found a relatively high correlation with the Stanford-Binet Test given at age 3. However, Cavanaugh et al. (1957), found that scores obtained at age 3 correlated poorly with the school age IQ.

In addition, special mention should be made of the *Minnesota Pre-School Intelligence Scales,* consisting of twenty-six tests in the 1½-to-6-year age range, and the *Merrill-Palmer Pre-School Performance Test,* a widely recognized battery consisting of nineteen subtests of nonverbal abilities. Although this test is designed primarily for the evaluation of preschool children, it is applicable in kindergarten and early primary grades, and can also be used for clinical purposes. Escalona has developed an approach to infant testing based on field theory and psychoanalysis. It consists of an impressionistic appraisal of the infant's total social response, frustration tolerance, and attention pattern, as well as management of his body on the Gesell tests. She believes that close observation of the child as a whole will reveal emotional and motivational patterns which are likely to affect the way he will later attack problems of all kinds—for example, a child who seeks immediate motor discharge will have such poor impulse control that he will make a low score on tests involving fine motor co-ordination. So far, not enough critical details on either the observational cues or the theory behind this approach have been presented.

Finally, the *Wechsler Pre-School and Primary Scale of Intelligence* has recently been developed for ages 4 to 6½. This new instrument contains five verbal and five performance tests, some of which are found in the Wechsler Intelligence Scale for Children, but adapted for use at early ages. The test has been standardized on a carefully selected sample controlled for sex, color, father's occupation, geographical region, and urban versus rural residence.

INFECTIOUS DISORDERS: SYSTEMIC TYPE. A number of diseases have been found to produce acute, temporary brain disorders as a result of systemic infections that do not invade the central nervous system. The most important are pneumonia, diphtheria, typhoid fever, uremia, pernicious anemia, influenza, malaria, rheumatic fever, smallpox, scarlet fever, and undulant fever. Brain disorders associated with intracranial infection are discussed under MENINGITIS, SYDENHAM'S CHOREA, EPIDEMIC ENCEPHALITIS, MENINGOVASCULAR SYPHILIS, GENERAL PARESIS, and JUVENILE PARESIS.

The dominant symptom in these cases is a mild to intense delirium. It occasionally appears during the incubation, or pre-febrile, period, but is most acute during the febrile stage and may continue in the post-febrile period. In some instances, however, it sets in after the temperature has dropped to normal. In cases where the patient has suffered prostration and exhaustion, it may take a particularly severe and dangerous form known as "collapse delirium."

The intensity of the delirious state has been found to depend more on the life situation and personality of the patient than on the height of the fever. Well-integrated individuals do not usually develop mental symptoms even in the most severe illnesses, but even a mild fever may bring on delirium in the poorly adjusted.

If the delirium runs its full course it usually shows fairly definite stages. The early symptoms are restlessness, sensitivity to noise and light, and disturbing dreams. This phase may be followed by clouding of consciousness, disorientation for time and later for place and person, impairment of concentration, attention, and understanding. Visual illusions, hallucinations and transient delusions may then set in. These are usually accompanied by apprehensions and fears which may be traceable to the patient's actual worries or repressed urges. If the delirium progresses to the acute stage, the patient becomes increasingly confused and agitated, and may be subject to periods of drowsiness and coma.

Treatment is primarily directed at the infection, but the delirium itself can often be controlled by ice packs, continuous baths or packs, and tranquilizing drugs, accompanied by such psychological measures as reassurance, a quiet and unstimulating environment, and the presence of the patient's family. Disorientation for time, place, and person clears up before the hallucinations disappear, and ordinarily the patient returns to normal a short time after the fever subsides. There is no damage to the brain except in rare cases where the illness has been both severe and prolonged.

INFERIORITY COMPLEX. A term used by Alfred Adler to denote strong feelings of inadequacy and insecurity stemming from real or fancied deficiencies of a physical, mental, or social nature. He believed that such feelings, together with the anxiety, resentment and overcompensatory drives they arouse, are bound to affect the individual's entire adjustment to life.

In Adler's theory, all persons have some feelings of inferiority, arising partly from the helplessness of infancy and partly from a sense of inadequacy in handling significant situations of life. These feelings are the major driving forces which impel normal individuals toward improvement and achievement. They are often manifested with special clarity by the physically handicapped who strive to compensate for their defect by developing special skills or interests.

Some people, however, develop a constellation of deep-seated, exaggerated, and unhealthy inferiority feelings which distort their attitudes and behavior. The special term "inferiority complex" is applied to this group of feelings. They usually exist partially or wholly on an unconscious level, and arise from many sources: an actual "organ inferiority" such as poor eyesight, short stature, defective sex organs; a position in the family or birth order which the individual considers unfavorable; severe parental discipline; excessively high standards imposed by the family; low social status; and, in the case of women, an inferior position in society as compared to men. *See* MASCULINE PROTEST.

According to Adler, many personality disorders result from faulty reactions to the conviction of inferiority. Some individuals react by avoiding competition or by getting sick when they are faced with situations that might expose their inferiority. Others go to the opposite extreme and strive not only to compensate but to *over*compensate for feelings of inadequacy by becoming excessively ambitious, competitive, aggressive, or domineering. All these reactions have a destructive effect on relationships with other people and militate against what Adler called "social interest"—that is, the common good. And if they are persistently expressed, they will eventually militate against the individual as well and give rise to a clear-cut neurosis. *See* ADLER, COMPLEX.

INFERTILITY. Inability to have children, to reproduce; sterility. The term infertile is usually applied to individuals who are relatively unable to have children, but who may (or may not) be able to reproduce after treatment or under different conditions. The term sterile is often reserved for absolute inability to have children, although the two terms are often used interchangeably.

Approximately one marriage in seven is childless, and in most of these cases the couple would like to have a child but are not able to do so. Studies show that pregnancy is achieved within three months in about 60 per cent of couples who wish to have children; if they are unsuccessful for a year, a fertility examination of both husband and wife is usually recommended. Contrary to popular opinion, which assumes that "barrenness" is wholly due to the wife, about 40 per cent of cases are due to the husband—and in some cases the fertility level of both partners may be low. Most of the cases are physical in nature, but there is considerable evidence that psychological factors may also be involved in childlessness, and in these cases infertility may be classified as a psychophysiologic or psychosomatic disorder of the genitourinary system.

Among the most important physical causes and conditions in women are: age—the chances of fertility drop from 96 per cent to 85 per cent between the ages of 20 and 35; infections following induced or spontaneous abortion; infrequent intercourse due to pain (50 per cent of women who suffer from painful intercourse are childless); infrequent intercourse due to unconscious fear of pregnancy; scars or adhesions left by abdominal operations such as appendectomies; inadequately treated venereal disease (gonorrhea or syphilis); glandular disturbance associated with late menstruation or excessive bleeding and pain; and injured or wrongly tilted cervix (the entrance to the uterus). A number of these conditions may interfere with ovulation or produce a blocking of the Fallopian tubes. Common causes in the male are: mumps contracted after puberty; glandular disturbance producing undescended testicles (cryptorchism) in childhood; venereal disease; low sperm production, or an excessive ratio of abnormal sperm.

In many cases—at least 50 per cent —the physical causes of infertility can be corrected. In the woman, ovulation can often be restored and miscarriages prevented by hormone injections; blocked tubes can be reopened with fluid or carbon dioxide (the Rubin procedure); scars and adhesions often respond to heat treatment, infections respond to antibiotics, fibroid tumors and polyps to surgery, and a tilted cervix may be corrected by manipulation or a ring. In men only one in ten infertility cases is found to be totally lacking in sperm production—that is, completely sterile; there is a good chance of overcoming insufficient or faulty sperm production through thyroid treatments, diet, vitamins, and rest; and difficulty in delivery of sperm can sometimes be corrected by surgery.

The psychological aspect of infertility is receiving increased attention today. At present emotional factors appear to apply more clearly to women than to men, and it is an accepted fact that these factors may be involved in both their ability to conceive a child and to carry it to term. In the case of men, the relation between psychological factors and fertility has been less clearly established—yet it is significant that the Margaret Sanger Research Bureau reports that 25 per cent of couples who visit the clinic become fertile while the testing process is going on, and before any specific treatment is undertaken. It appears that the fact that they are openly facing the problem and facing it together reduces the tension, guilt, or anxiety to a point where the physical functions can return to normal. In many cases, too, one or both receive psychotherapy, and this treatment is frequently effective not only in increasing fertility but in overcoming the problem of miscarriage.

Along these lines, English and Finch (1964) state: "Many women who have been childless for years for no demonstrable organic reason have conceived and borne a child after intensive psychotherapeutic measures. The latter has usually been undertaken for some other condition rather than for the infertility. It is also well known that women occasionally, upon assuming sterility after many years of lack of conception, adopt a child only to find themselves subsequently pregnant presumably because of a stirring of what must be called "the maternal instinct" within them. The degree to which this is psychological and endocrinological is debatable, of course, but it certainly would appear that there are strong psychological factors involved." Likewise, Redlich and Freedman (1966) state, "Many infertile couples are fatigued and under stress when they have intercourse, and this may somehow have an untoward effect on fertility. At times, simple clarification may help to correct adverse habits and facilitate impregnation. In some, a more intensive psychotherapeutic effort may help to tackle the sexual difficulties or the unconscious motivation to avoid having children. Unfortunately, there are no controlled studies to demonstrate the role of psychogenic factors in sterility. Fertility after psychotherapy of husband and wife, or either one, has often been observed; whether this is the result of psychotherapy is difficult to establish. An interesting and not infrequent observation concerns previously infertile couples who had children of their own after adopting a child, which presumably produces a better attitude toward parenthood."

Illustrative Case: INFERTILITY

This thirty-two-year-old married woman sought psychiatric treatment because of the presence of constant anxiety. She was uneasy in relationships with her fellow workers, unable to concentrate, and constantly bothered by a feeling that her life was totally lacking in constructiveness. She came to treatment with a reasonable understanding of what psychotherapy involved and willingly entered an intensive treatment program.

Her history revealed that she had been married for eight years and, in spite of a relatively great desire to do so, had never been able to become pregnant. She had never used a contraceptive at any time since marriage. As her treatment proceeded it became evident that her wish to become pregnant was only a halfhearted one and she clung to it in the hope that having a child would give her life some purpose. She had never felt that there was any emotional reason for her apparent sterility and she had not entered psychotherapy with any assumption that this would enhance her procreative ability.

Further history revealed that the patient had been brought up by an extremely tyrannical mother. The latter had ignored her, exploited her, mistreated her, had generally abused her father, and had been deceitful and predatory toward the entire community. The patient's father, on the other hand, had been a gentle, kind, devoted person, particularly fond of his daughter, and the patient had taken over many of the characteristics of her father. However, as might be expected from such a history, she had made an inadequate identification with femininity because of her total lack of experience with a truly maternal figure. Mothers, in her mind, were hostile, exploitive, and cruel. She feared lest she become the same sort of person.

It required several months of therapy for this patient to realize that she did not have to be like her mother, but could be a gentle and affectionate woman. She gave up her halfhearted pursuit of professional interests and felt herself subsequently much more "married." She was no longer ambivalent or halfhearted about her ability or capacity to become a good mother. She already possessed some intellectual understanding of children's psychological life and began to add an emotional conviction to this knowledge. As a result, her desire to become a mother became much more wholehearted. It was during this period in treatment that she became pregnant.

It is impossible, of course, to prove that this patient's pregnancy resulted from her altered psychological structure. However, it is felt that it would be a reasonable assumption, since no other changes had occurred in her life and she had had equal opportunities for pregnancy during the previous eight years. (English and Finch, 1964)

INFORMATION THEORY. A study of the principles involved in communication, with particular reference to the understanding and control of messages carrying information. Information is defined as any message that reduces uncertainty.

There are many systems of communication, some simple, some complex. In one type of system, information passes from person to person, as in conversation, discussion, or lectures; in another, it passes between an object and a person, as between a recording machine and a stenographer; in a third, objects alone are involved, as for example, the keyboard and the paper in a typewriter. Information may be delivered immediately, as when an officer gives orders to his men, or it may be delayed, as it is when a typist transcribes the dictation she received the previous day. Information may also be transmitted in many different ways, such as vocally, in writing, or visually through the use of signal flags or gestures. In the modern world it frequently has to pass through many subsystems before it reaches its final destination.

Although there are many varieties of systems, communication always involves the transfer of information in the form of energy; and the systems are always made up of five basic parts: (1) the source of the message; (2) the encoder or transmitter, which converts the information into transmittable energy in the form of a coded signal (e.g., a telegraph apparatus, or the human voice mechanism which converts ideas into speech sounds); (3) the communication channel, such as a telegraph wire, a piece of paper, or the air which carries sound waves; (4) the receiver, which decodes the message; and (5) the destination (Shannon and Weaver, 1949). These steps apply equally to communication via speech, gesture, writing, and mechanical or electrical devices.

In accordance with the definition of information given above, transmission is viewed as the process of reducing uncertainty. Many of the investigations in this field have therefore been concerned with the amount of information which is needed to reduce uncertainty in different situations. In general, the greater the amount of uncertainty a message reduces, the more information it gives. If we use an obscure word in speech or writing, we reduce uncertainty far less than if we use a clear, well-known word. Moreover, the more alternative meanings the word has, the harder it will be for the person receiving the message to understand, or "decode," what it means. This leads to a general principle: "The greater the number of possible messages, the harder it is to determine what the message is."

Information theorists also point out that messages regarding the occurrence of unlikely events are more informative than messages about very probable events. In technical terms this means that the greater the "surprisal" (surprise value) of the message, the more information it relates. "Man Bites Dog" is therefore more informative than "Dog Bites Man" because it conveys new and unusual information. Similarly, if the letters *th* are followed by *y,* more information is conveyed than if the same letters are followed by *e,* since the latter is the usual sequence. There is very little surprise in *the* because there is an extremely high probability that this combination will occur; *thy* has much greater surprisal because this word is so rarely used today. To express this in the language of information theory: we are much more certain of the *e* than the *y,* and therefore if *th* is followed by *e,* we are given less information than if it is followed by *y* because the letter *e* does not reduce our uncertainty as much as the letter *y.*

There is considerable evidence that human beings (and probably higher animals as well) have a basic need for surprisal—that is, for variety and novelty of information. Most of us have a strong curiosity drive and an intense need to explore and investigate our surroundings. If we find ourselves in the same situation for a long period, we almost inevitably become bored. Put in another way, we experience "stimulus hunger," a desire to receive new and varied information from the environment. Experiments on sensory deprivation strongly suggest that this urge must be satisfied if we are to continue to function in a normal way. *See* SENSORY DEPRIVATION.

Information theorists have attempted to apply mathematical principles to the process of reducing uncertainty. One way of measuring uncertainty is to use a unit called a *bit* (from *b*inary dig*it*), which is defined as the amount of information that reduces the number of remaining alternatives, or uncertainty, by half. Here is an example: Suppose a twenty dollar bill has been placed in one of sixteen identical books standing side by side on a shelf, and our task is to guess which one it is by asking a minimum number of questions that can be answered only with a yes or a no. The best way to proceed would be to begin by asking if the book is to the right or left of center. The answer to this question would provide one "bit" of information since it would cut our uncertainty in half by narrowing the possibilities to eight books. If we proceed in the same way the next question would narrow the possibilities to four, the next to two, and the next one would give us the answer. In other words, four bits of information would be needed to eliminate uncertainty in this case.

If there were thirty-two books (thirty-two alternatives), five bits would be required; and if there were sixty-four, six would be needed. Moreover, since this is a regular progression, the solution for any problem of this type could be readily stated as a mathematical formula. However, such a formula would apply only where the alternatives are equally probable. If they were to differ in probability, the mathematics would be considerably more complex.

The principles of information theory are applicable to many practical problems. First, a study of messages in terms of probabilities for reducing uncertainty has shown that most of them are about 75 per cent redundant—in other words, we could encode them with about 75 per cent fewer words. Similarly, we do not need all the letters we use in the words themselves: *"P wer"* can be easily understood because the other letters give us the information that there must be an *o* in the empty space. By reducing redundancy, we can devise shorthand systems for use in business, or extremely rapid communication techniques for emergency situations.

The information approach is also used to measure "channel capacity"—that is, the capacity of the various senses to receive messages. Many experiments have been performed to determine how successfully we can discriminate between stimuli of different pitch or loudness or size when they are briefly presented. In general, it has been found that we can immediately "absorb" and accurately discriminate only about seven bits of information with any sensory channel (Miller, 1956). This helps to set the limit for the rate at which information can be transmitted to human beings.

Finally, there have been a number of investigations on the importance of "feedback" in communication—that is, must the communicator receive a response in order to transmit his message most effectively? In one experiment, students were required to reproduce abstract geometric patterns according to descriptions given by instructors. Four different conditions of communication were used: (1) zero feedback, in which the instructors were completely separated from the students; (2) a visible audience situation, in which the students could be seen by the instructor but could not speak to him; (3) a yes-

and-no condition in which they could reply yes or no to questions from the instructor; and (4) free feedback in which they could ask questions or interrupt at will. When the reproductions were examined, it was found that the accuracy increased steadily from zero feedback to the free feedback condition, but the time required also increased.

A further experiment was then conducted in which only the zero and free conditions were compared over a longer series of trials. Under free feedback, the accuracy level was high on the first trial and stayed high; under zero feedback accuracy improved considerably, but never reached the level achieved on the very first trial under free feedback. The time required for instruction under zero feedback remained the same throughout, but the time decreased in the later trials under free feedback, although it was always greater than in the zero condition. Another revealing result was that students felt confident under the free condition, but tended to be hostile under the zero feedback condition. The experiment clearly indicated the superior value of two-way communication over one-way communication, even though it did require a little more time. (Leavitt and Mueller, 1951)

INHIBITION. The process of restraining one's impulses or desires.

Inhibition may take place on either a conscious or unconscious level, or on both at once. An individual might deliberately inhibit, or suppress, his urge to strike out or speak out against other people for reasons of expediency. In such cases the reaction is primarily conscious and essentially normal. However, if he is totally unable to stand his own ground or enter into conflict of any kind, the tendency probably stems from unconscious forces and tends to be pathological. The same applies to people who are chronically unable to

give vent to their feelings or to express themselves with any degree of freedom.

Psychoanalytic theory stresses the unconscious roots of inhibition and views it as a mechanism by which the superego controls instinctual or id impulses that would threaten the ego if allowed conscious expression. An example is the neurotic patient who feels no sexual desire whatsoever as a result of unconscious feelings of guilt due to an oversevere conscience acquired in the course of a rigid upbringing. *See* SUPEREGO.

Inhibition must be distinguished from repression. According to the psychoanalytic interpretation, inhibition serves a *preventive* function, since it obviates possible conflict between the ego and id by keeping the impulses from being expressed in the first place. Repression, on the other hand, is called into play *after* the dangerous impulses have been expressed, and consists in forcing them out of consciousness. Hinsie and Campbell (1960) put the difference in these words: "The two processes may be illustrated in a homely way: the locking up (inhibition) of the most rabid or fire-spitting leaders in times of civil strife, in order to anticipate, forestall, or prevent bloodshed and mob violence that will have to be combatted (repression) by armed forces a day or two later." *See* REPRESSION.

A reasonable amount of conscious restraint is required of everyone who lives in society. We cannot express all our impulses and desires with complete freedom and with total disregard of consequences. But too much inhibition is as unhealthy as too little. The compulsive, rigid individual finds it hard to be "human" and give in to normal impulses; the impulsive, disinhibited person, on the other hand, is lacking in self-control and frequently finds himself in trouble with others.

Disorders characterized by an extreme lack of inhibition, or inner control, are sometimes termed "impulse disorders." Two general types are particularly common. One is a behavior disorder that sometimes occurs among brain-injured children, though it is not confined to this category. These children tend to be highly impulsive, overactive, unpredictable, and often aggressive and destructive. The other is a character disorder known as psychopathic or sociopathic personality and found in adolescents and adults. These individuals "act-out" any impulse whatsoever without thought, restraint or feelings of guilt. In addition, the behavior of alcoholics is also characterized by absence of inhibition. In this case the tendency may have a double source: the individual may have a basically impulsive personality; and his lack of inner control may be accentuated by the alcohol itself, since it reduces the inhibitory function of the brain. *See* BEHAVIOR DISORDERS, ANTISOCIAL REACTION, ACTING-OUT.

On a different level, inhibition plays a major role in the theory of conditioning. Here it refers to the fact that a response may be actively blocked or restrained by the subject. In a typical experiment, a dog is trained to delay his conditioned response (salivation) to the stimulus (bell) by withholding the reward or reinforcement (food) for a given length of time—that is, he learns to salivate only after the bell has rung for several seconds. This period of delay has been shown to involve active inhibition rather than passive waiting, for it has been found that the dog remains tense during the entire interval. Probably as a result of this tension it will respond by salivating to practically any extraneous stimulation before the bell is sounded—even a buzzing fly or a strong odor. Such a stimulus is said to "inhibit the inhibition"—that is, it releases the response from its original inhibition, a process that is termed disinhibition.

INSIGHT. An apparently sudden grasp of relationships that leads to the solution of a problem or the achievement of understanding. In psychotherapy, it is the awareness of underlying motives and unconscious sources of personal problems. The therapist gains insight into his patient but, more important, the patient attains insight into himself.

When undertaking a new job or trying to learn a new sport we are faced with novel problems and situations. We usually struggle through the early steps of these activities, trying out first one way to meet the situation and then another. This trial and error process may go on a long time without apparent results—then suddenly, and often dramatically, we "get the hang of it" or "see the point." This abrupt perception, sometimes described as the "aha experience," is termed insight.

Insight is experienced as a completely new event, a novel solution that abruptly dawns on us. In cartoons it is represented by a bulb that suddenly lights up. After it occurs, the problem we are tackling can usually be handled with a minimum of errors. Moreover, we can often transfer our knowledge of the relationships we have learned through insight to other tasks of a similar nature.

Not all problems can be solved by insight. This process would be of little or no use in memorizing a telephone or social security number. The multiplication table, on the other hand, can be learned either by rote or by insight, but insight is superior since it reveals conceptual relationships. Mathematical problems, problems involving the use of tools, and practical problems in general are often efficiently and productively solved through insight. We even apply it in moderate and undramatic degrees to common operations such as filling a pen or putting a battery in a flashlight. It is also helpful in understanding the point of a play, the relevance of a scientific theory, or the structure of an individual's personality.

Much of our knowledge about insight stems from the animal studies of Wolfgang Köhler. In one celebrated experiment he placed a banana outside the cage of a group of chimpanzees, well beyond their reach. A hoe was put inside the cage. After handling the hoe for some time, one of the chimps suddenly seemed to "get an idea" and quickly used it to rake the banana into reach (Köhler, 1925). In other experiments some of the chimps performed even more remarkable feats of insight. They succeeded in reaching a banana by putting a jointed stick together, and they piled up scattered boxes so that they could climb up and get a piece of fruit hanging from the ceiling.

Two facts about these experiments were particularly significant. First, Köhler noted that there was a time lapse between their unsuccessful attempts to reach the prize with their hands alone and their successful use of objects to extend their reach. During this period they usually walked around, looked about, or manipulated the objects, as if searching for a solution. When the "idea" came to them, it probably arose at least in part from this exploratory process. Second, past experience also seemed to contribute to the solution, for it was found that only the chimps that had previously been in contact with sticks or boxes succeeded in solving the problems. In other words, the insight did not simply come "out of the blue."

These facts remove much of the mystery that seems to surround insight. They suggest that it actually consists of applying past knowledge to the requirements of the present situation. In fact, some investigators view insight as coming about through "symbolic trial and error," a process in which one possibility after another is tested internally until one of them "clicks."

These interpretations have been found to apply to insight in human beings as well as animals. Experiments have shown that children go through the same steps as chimpanzees in solving insight problems, but they cannot solve them as early in life as the chimpanzees because they know less about their environment and therefore have less experience to draw on. Richardson (1934) found that children begin to use insight at about two and a half years of age, and the percentage of correct solutions increases with age and contact with the world. Most adults use this process successfully because they have learned that facts and principles they have already mastered can usually be applied to new problems. Moreover, they are highly motivated to develop insight into relationships because they have found it to be the most efficient and least time-consuming method of solving problems.

Insight is one of the keys to effective psychotherapy because it opens the door to self-understanding. This occurs when the patient becomes aware of a relationship between his disturbance and motives or memories that had long been buried in his unconscious. The new insight is usually accompanied by physical signs—a release of body tension, a deep breath, a sigh of relief, an exclamation. Psychiatrists regard these reactions as evidence of progress toward recovery, since they indicate that the patient has become aware of a general principle or a childhood event that brings together and explains various fragments of behavior that have hitherto appeared unrelated.

Can insight be developed or facilitated? The answer appears to be yes, and a number of techniques have been suggested. First, this ability can be improved through practice. Tackling practical as well as theoretical problems—even puzzles and brain-teasers—gets us in the habit of looking for patterns, constructing hypotheses, and observing relationships. It also gets us in the habit of trying different combinations—and the more combinations we try, the more solutions we find. Finally, the value of practice is enhanced by the fact that solving problems in one area frequently helps us solve problems in another, for the same *type* of approach, or the same *type* of solution, often applies to different problems.

Second, an accumulation of knowledge and experience facilitates insight. It gives us a larger reservoir of ideas to draw upon. Most educators, scientists, and businessmen believe this reservoir should be as rich and diverse as possible, since insight often arises from information or experience that does not appear to be relevant to the problem at hand.

Third, insight can often be stimulated either by getting away from the problem or by "sleeping on it," since we tend to fall into a rut when we think too persistently or continuously. Some psychologists believe a "vacation" of this kind gives our unconscious a chance to work on the problem; others contend that we merely approach it from a new and fresh angle when we return to it. Either or both of these ideas can be used to explain the fact that flashes of insight frequently occur when they are least expected or when we stop concentrating and indulge in a period of "free association." *See* PROBLEM-SOLVING, CREATIVE THINKING, PSYCHOTHERAPY (GENERAL).

INSOMNIA. Temporary or chronic loss of sleep. Temporary sleeplessness is usually caused by transient physical conditions or emotional upsets; chronic sleeplessness, by persistent physical disorders or deep-seated psychological difficulties.

As pointed out by McGraw and Oliven (1959), insomnia must be viewed against many factors that affect sleep, including season, climate, social custom, attitude, and occupation. In addition there are large differences among individuals: the so-called monophasic sleeper requires only one long period of sleep, the polyphasic breaks his sleep into short periods and afternoon naps.

There are also large individual differences in toleration of sleeplessness. Many people can function well in spite of a night or two of poor sleep, and a few can actually thrive on prolonged loss of sleep; others, however, quickly react to any substantial sleep loss with such symptoms as poor coordination, inability to concentrate, hyperacuity, loss of appetite, and irritability. It is generally agreed that the seriousness of insomnia should be judged in terms of reactions to the loss of sleep rather than the amount of sleep that is lost.

There are several varieties of insomnia. *Dyssomnia* is poor sleep accompanied by large fluctuations in depth and such disturbances as nightmares, teeth-grinding, and sleep-walking. These reactions can often be traced to emotional problems, but in some cases they may be due to physical disorders such as circulatory conditions, heart palpitation, or in occasional cases, brain damage. In *matutinal* or *terminal insomnia* the individual awakens early, feels unrefreshed, and cannot go back to sleep. This condition is sometimes found in elderly patients with cerebral arteriosclerosis as well as in individuals suffering from moderately severe depression or chronic anxiety. Other victims are individuals who suffer from severe chronic daytime fatigue, and recently widowed or divorced women who sleep alone for the first time in years. In *intermittent insomnia*, the sleeper wakes up many times and cannot easily get back to sleep. Protracted cases of this type are often found among middle-aged or elderly patients suffering from such physical disorders as hypertension and precordial stress (pains in lower chest, not necessarily from the heart). In *initial insomnia*, the individual has trouble falling asleep night after night. The classical "nervous" type of insomnia usually takes this form. It stems from such disturbances as tension states, mild depressions, and anxiety reactions. Included in this category are also the compulsive insomniacs, who feel they might miss something by falling asleep; and the anxiety insomniacs who become so worried about falling asleep and so fearful of the effects of loss of sleep that they are unable to relax.

Conn (1950) has made a special study of the relation between insomnia and psychoneurosis. In an investigation of 857 neurotic patients, he found that over 50 per cent listed insomnia as a major complaint. In his analysis, he makes the point that "insomnia is not sleeplessness, as has often been emphasized, but it is an *attitude* towards sleeplessness." He believes that many neurotics cannot relax and surrender control long enough to invite sleep because they have an unconscious fear of being attacked while in a defenseless position. Some of these patients are also afraid that they will walk in their sleep and attack other people. In either case sleeping will put them in a dangerous situation, and they must therefore remain awake and alert.

Conn also found that many neurotics engage in physical activities to ward off sleep—for example, they hyperventilate and thus increase the blood supply to the brain, instead of decreasing it as is required for normal sleep. Moreover, their state of emotional tension causes a blocking of alpha waves—the brain wave, or electroencephalographic pattern, when the brain is at rest—thus producing an EEG state that stands in the way of sleep. The emotional tension itself may be the result of any number of psychopathological conditions. Some neurotics feel so weak and vulnerable that they are afraid they will die during sleep. Others may be overwhelmed by drives and impulses such as fear, hate, jealousy, guilt, rage, anxiety, frustrated ambition, or preoccupation with murder and death. Still others are harassed by sexual frustration, unconscious guilt feelings, or the compulsive need to perform a complex series of rituals before they can even attempt to sleep.

The treatment of insomnia is dependent on the conditions that give rise to it. Temporary insomnia may be due to noise, light, poor ventilation, an uncomfortable mattress, or other conditions that prevent relaxation. This common type of insomnia can often be overcome by improving these conditions or by applying the stock remedies such as warm baths, milk-based drinks, soothing music, or systematic relaxation of the muscles, as in Jacobson's technique of "progressive relaxation." *See* RELAXATION THERAPY.

Severe and persistent insomnia requires more drastic measures. Hypnotic and tranquilizing drugs are frequently prescribed for cases of dyssomnia. Hypnotics combined with analgesics are employed in some cases of intermittent insomnia caused by physical conditions. Since patients who suffer from chronic initial insomnia are often emotionally disturbed, the treatment of choice is psychotherapy, although barbiturates, hydrotherapy, and other physical treatments may also be utilized for short periods. *See* HYDROTHERAPY.

INSTINCT. An unlearned behavior pattern that appears in fully developed form at a specific point in the growth of the organism.

The term has had a long and varied history. One investigator has listed over 800 separate and distinct meanings. Everyday speech throws little light on the concept because it is loosely used to include widely different ideas, as in "a killer's instinct," "a child instinctively knows his own mother," "he instinctively raised his hand to protect his face." The term has also been applied to the tendency to wage war, engage in competition, and even collect articles such as stamps and coins. This type of usage implies that these tendencies are universal and inevitable, and gives a false impression that calling them instinctive somehow explains their existence. The use of the term reached its peak of absurdity early in this century when almost every type of behavior was claimed to be instinctively motivated, including the impulse to steal fruit from a neighbor's garden and the urge to throw rocks at birds.

Some investigators have become so disabused with this term that they avoid it altogether. Others reserve it for specific technical use. Psychoanalysts apply it to the inborn "primitive" drives that comprise the id, such as hunger, thirst, and sex. Id impulses are unreasoning and operate according to the "pleasure principle"—that is, they create tension and "unpleasure" when not gratified and produce pleasure when gratified. In his later theory Freud distinguished between the life instinct that preserves the individual and propagates the species, and the death instinct that leads to aggression and self-destruction. Human existence was pictured as a theater of operations in which the two are constantly at war with each other. Most psychologists, on the other hand, use the term in a biological sense, applying it to complex patterns of response which are built into the organism and spring forth full-blown when it has reached a certain level of development. See ID, DEATH INSTINCT.

The psychological usage has raised many crucial questions, such as: Exactly how is an instinct expressed in terms of behavior? How many instincts are there? Do human beings have as many instincts as animals? How far do they govern behavior? Recent research has thrown light on some of these questions, but none of them has been answered conclusively.

In its technical sense instinctive behavior is described not only as unlearned, but as (1) automatic and stereotyped, and (2) "species specific." The clearest, and some say the only, conclusive illustration is the maternal behavior of animals. A specific example is the impulse of the rat mother to retrieve and care for her straying offspring. This impulse is believed to be basic and inborn since the rat mother expresses it in fully developed form the first time the baby rat wanders from its nest. Moreover, it is "species specific" because *every* rat mother, regardless of previous experience, exhibits this same behavior.

Some investigators believe that retrieving the young is part of a single maternal instinct that includes nest-building, nursing, cleaning the young, and general protection. They also point out that although the details of the activities differ in different species, the protective impulse of the mother is found in almost all other animals as well. In fact, some psychologists, among them Morgan and Klineberg, maintain that maternal behavior constitutes the most characteristic instinctive pattern in mammals.

Other behavior that is widely accepted as instinctive is nest-building in birds, web-spinning in spiders, pecking in chicks, swimming in tadpoles, and mating patterns in rats and other lower animals. Experiments have shown that these activities appear under appropriate stimulation when the animal has reached a certain level of maturation. The swallow will build its characteristic nest with no prior experience in nest-building, and the trapdoor spider builds his ingenious home without any architectural lessons from his elders.

Some experimenters even question these widely accepted examples. They point out that in every case in which an intensive study of a so-called instinct has been undertaken, the effect of previous learning or conditioning has been uncovered. Kuo (1930) has shown that the "instinctive" enmity of cats and rats is probably mythical. He found that cats do not kill rats unless they have watched a rat being killed, or have, while hungry, accidentally drawn blood from a rat during play. Moreover, when cats were raised with rats, they never attempted to kill one in later life. Kuo (1932) also studied chicks while they were still embryos, and showed that all the elements of the pecking response were established during this period. In other words, the pecking pattern did not spring into use full-blown. Even the maternal drive has been called in question, since it appears to depend on learned responses. When female rats were prevented from handling material of any kind during their early life, they failed to build a nest or adequately retrieve their offspring when full grown.

Human beings may have no instincts at all—at least, if there are any, they become so modified by learning and experience that they cannot be detected. The maternal drive can be extremely strong; and it seems to have a physiological basis in the secretion of prolactin and other hormones. Yet it is also true that many normal women do not have a drive to nurse or care for their children. The sex drive varies widely from person to person, and there is no single, unlearned pattern for satisfying it. Studies conducted a generation ago emphasized the importance of physiological maturation for activities like walking, and experiments were offered as proof of its instinctuality. In one study, two groups of Hopi Indian children were found to start walking at the same age even though the children in one group had been bound to a cradle board carried on the back of the mother, and the others had been allowed complete freedom of movement (Dennis and Dennis, 1940). Yet a more careful investigation showed that the children on the cradle board could actually move their legs and practice certain parts of the total walking pattern. When they were tested, they simply integrated these learned components. This suggests that even though human beings are born with individual reflexes such as withdrawing their legs

when touched, the integration of these simpler activities into more complex behavior patterns is brought about by learning and training.

INSULIN SHOCK THERAPY (Insulin Coma Theraphy).

A treatment for serious mental disorders in which prolonged periods of coma are induced by heavy doses of insulin.

The technique was developed by the Austrian psychiatrist, Manfred Sakel, after he had observed that insulin relieved the manic symptoms of morphine patients during the withdrawal period. He then tried the treatment with excited schizophrenics and discovered that the best results could be obtained when the dosage was large enough to induce a deep coma.

Sakel's original method is still occasionally used today. It is based on the fact that the principal fuel of the brain is a carbohydrate, glucose, and not fat or protein—and insulin reduces the glucose content of the blood, thus depriving the brain of needed fuel. When the doses are large enough, brain cell oxidation decreases to a point where coma takes place.

Sakel discovered that the higher brain centers are affected by hypoglycemia (low blood sugar) before the lower centers. He used this knowledge to establish five stages of insulin coma, and regulated the doses accordingly. The technique, however, requires an exhaustive series of psychiatric, physical, and neurological examinations before it can be undertaken, and constant medical supervision and vigilant nursing are necessary during the treatment and for twenty-four hours afterward in order to avoid "after-shock." It is contraindicated where there is active infection, diabetes, serious heart, liver, or kidney disease, and in ages below sixteen and above forty-five.

Various techniques have been developed for administering insulin, and specialists differ about the optimum depth, length, and frequency of comas. In general, insulin is injected intramuscularly in the morning before food is taken, and several hours later the patient becomes increasingly weak, hungry, and drowsy. As somnolence deepens he goes into a typical shock state with muscular spasms, body tremors, heavy breathing, and mumbling. This is followed by a deep coma. Some therapists use a variation known as "subshock," in which small amounts of insulin are injected and the reaction stops short of coma. This technique is used particularly to quiet anxious or excitable patients, but not for schizophrenia. In severe cases, convulsions are sometimes induced, although extra precautions must be taken. Methods of terminating the coma also vary, but in all cases glucose is used and usually has a rapid effect. The patient is then given a meal rich in carbohydrates. With most patients the treatment is administered five or six times a week for a total of thirty to fifty coma hours.

Insulin shock is limited to cases of schizophrenia and shows best results during the first year of the illness. The prognosis is most favorable when the patient is in his twenties and has shown a relatively stable pre-illness personality, and when the onset of the illness was sudden and acute. It is least favorable in cases of meager personality resources, ingrained schizoid personality, and insidious onset below the age of fifteen or above the age of forty. Paranoid and catatonic patients, and those with affective (emotional) overtones respond considerably better than simple and hebephrenic types. However, the remission rate is rarely higher than 40 to 50 per cent, and often less, and the rate of recurrence tends to be high (Kalinowsky and Hoch, 1961).

Insulin shock therapy has been almost completely replaced by psychoactive drugs and electroshock therapy, since they produce a higher rate of improvement and more lasting results, are less time-consuming, and involve far less danger to the patient. Some psychiatrists, however, resort to it when drug or electroshock treatments fail. It may also be used in combination with electroshock for schizophrenic patients who do not improve or who show insufficient improvement under insulin or electroshock alone, and for patients who are overactive, assaultive, aggressive, suicidal, or in a stuporous state. The two methods may also be alternated. English and Finch (1964) sum up the present status of insulin therapy in these words: "While great results were expected from its use, it gradually became evident that this type of treatment did not produce any lasting beneficial results and its use has been almost entirely discontinued." See ELECTROSHOCK THERAPY.

INTELLECTUALIZATION. The unconscious defense mechanism of concealing feelings through intellectual activity.

Intellectualization takes many forms. One individual may protect himself from guilt feelings by "analyzing away" the difference between right and wrong. Another may sidetrack emotions that cause him distress by becoming totally preoccupied with minute and meaningless details. Still another may work on his emotional problems as if they were problems in accounting—for example, he might try to make decisions by adding up all the "reasons for" in one column, and all the "reasons against" in another. When an approach of this kind is applied to personal problems, such as choosing a mate, it usually indicates that an emotional conflict exists well beneath the level of awareness.

Many healthy individuals resort to intellectualization in coping with difficulties. This is not surprising, since most of us have been exhorted all our lives to "Use your head," "Reason your way out of your problems," and "Don't be swayed by emotion." We may also have discovered that when things get to be too much for us, it helps to lose ourselves in a book, a serious discussion, or an intellectual hobby. These are normal devices which, if used with discretion, usually help rather than hinder adjustment.

But if intellectualization is repeatedly employed as an automatic, unconscious response to inward threats, it is likely to be a pathological reaction. A typical example is the man who occupied himself all day long with making philosophical distinctions between love and hate. Although he struggled against this compulsion, he could not give it up and in time it obsessed his mind so completely that he had to quit his job. He eventually undertook treatment, in the course of which the therapist uncovered a deep conflict which, significantly, involved hateful impulses toward a person he loved. See OBSESSIVE-COMPULSIVE REACTION. For other defense mechanisms that border on intellectualization or overlap with it, see ISOLATION, RATIONALIZATION, DISSOCIATION, EMOTIONAL INSULATION.

INTELLIGENCE. General mental ability, especially the ability to make flexible use of memory, reasoning, and knowledge in learning and in confronting new situations and problems.

There is no universal agreement on any single definition of intelligence, including the one just offered. This definition, however, was designed to embody some of the major aspects of mental ability emphasized by psychologists and the tests they devise: (a) versatility or flexibility, (b) utilization of a variety of mental processes, (c) ability to learn, (d) application of learning and experience to the solution of new problems. The current emphasis on characteristics of this kind implies that intelligence is not a single entity, but a complex, multifaceted set of abilities. It is interesting that the first major attempt to characterize intelligence, that of Alfred

Binet, over sixty years ago, also viewed it as composite in nature and directed to problem-solving. The three characteristics he emphasized were the tendency to take and maintain a direction without being distracted, the ability to adapt means to ends, and the capacity for self-criticism or dissatisfaction with partial solutions. A representative recent definition is: "Intelligence, operationally defined, is the aggregate capacity of the individual to act purposefully, to think rationally, and to deal effectively with his environment" (Wechsler, 1966). See BINET.

Many psychologists have abandoned the attempt to give a formal definition of intelligence and offer a practical definition instead: intelligence is that which an intelligence test measures. As Hilgard and Atkinson (1967) point out, "Although the statement sounds empty it is not, for it takes in all the careful steps that have gone into the construction of the tests. All the tests constructed by different workers distinguish the dull from the bright and lead to scores with high intercorrelations; therefore they are measuring something in common. What they measure in common defines intelligence." Even a cursory examination of these tests indicates that they measure differences in performance on problems, or "items," which are carefully chosen to represent a wide variety of abilities. Among them are mathematical problems requiring numerical reasoning, vocabulary questions that test an understanding of words, perception items requiring accurate observation, as well as problems based on such mental processes as drawing analogies, abstract reasoning, and comprehension of verbal material (Fig. 30).

But the question is, how does the psychologist know which of the many kinds of mental activities are most indicative of intelligence, and what kind of items he should use in measuring intelligence? There are two general ap-

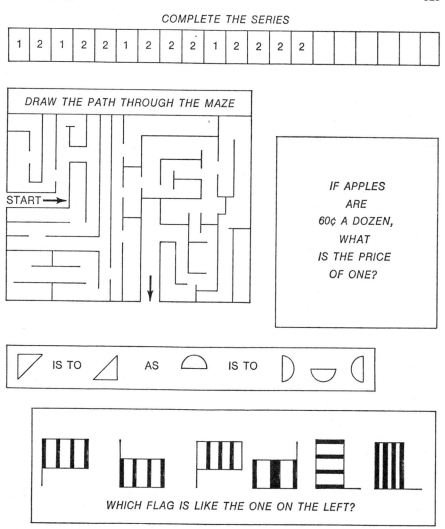

Fig. 30. Items of the kind used on group intelligence tests.

proaches to these questions, the first placing the emphasis on the test items, and the second on the components or factors of intelligence. Item analysis, as it is called, is usually based on Binet's assumption that (a) intelligence can be scaled according to age—that is, a child can ordinarily solve more difficult problems as he grows older; and (b) a bright child will solve problems representing an age level above his own, an average child will in general solve problems only at his age level, and a dull child, below his age level—that is, the subject's mental age (MA) will exceed, equal or fall below his chronological age (CA). The IQ, or intelligence quotient, is the ratio between the MA and CA multiplied by 100 to eliminate decimal points. It was originated by the German psychologist Wilhelm Stern (1871–1938). *See* MENTAL AGE, STANFORD-BINET TEST.

Since intelligence tests are designed

to measure intellectual aptitude or ability, and not knowledge or achievement, it is necessary to find items that do not reflect special training. In general they are of two types: items which should be novel and unfamiliar to both unschooled and schooled individuals, giving them an approximately equal chance; and items which should be familiar to all the subjects tested—that is, items they have had an approximately equal chance to learn to deal with. The term "approximately" is used in both cases because we cannot be certain that an item will be totally unfamiliar or assuredly familiar to every subject. As examples, the designs in Fig. 13, p. 281, are meant to be unfamiliar to all subjects; and the language in the following item is assumed to be understandable to all subjects who can read English: Mark F if the sentence is foolish; mark S if it is sensible. S F. Mrs. Smith has had no children, and I understand that the same was true of her mother. (Thurstone and Thurstone, 1941)

Binet and those who followed him selected a wide variety of items that appeared to test all phases of intelligence—at least those aspects included in their definitions of this ability. This process was not as haphazard as it sounds, for the items themselves were submitted to two kinds of tests. First, the investigators determined what proportion of children answered each item correctly at different ages, and then carefully placed them at the appropriate ages. Second, they determined whether or not the results on each item corresponded to the results on the test as a whole. Through this procedure they collected what appeared to satisfy the two basic requirements of psychological testing, validity and reliability. If an item was solved correctly by an increasing percentage as the age of the subjects increased, it was regarded as valid (or sound) because it distinguished older children from younger ones in the in-

telligence scale; and if the score on this item correlated fairly highly with the total score, it was considered reliable since it appeared to be consistent with the other measures. *See* PSYCHOLOGICAL TESTING.

The second general method of constructing intelligence tests is factor analysis. The object of this procedure is to discover the components of intelligence and base the selection of items on these underlying factors. The first attempt at factor analysis was made by the English psychologist, Charles Spearman, in 1904. His technique was to determine statistically how closely various pairs of tests correlated with each other. If the scores on two tests or test items proved to be positively correlated to a high degree (i.e., the scores corresponded closely), he concluded that they were measuring a common factor which he termed general intelligence, or *g*. He then showed that many types of tests were positively correlated with each other—some to a higher and some to a lower degree—and concluded that they were all "dipping into" this common pool of ability, *g*. But since the correlations were not perfect, he concluded that tests tended also to involve special abilities, or *s*'s, such as mathematical or mechanical ability. More recent psychologists, however, doubt the existence of a general intelligence and claim that *g* can itself be analyzed into a number of different abilities, or factors. One of the major exponents of this point of view was L. L. Thurstone.

In the Thurstone technique, a total of about sixty different tests were given to the same children, each composed of items representing one type of mental process, such as verbal comprehension and reasoning. He then computed the intercorrelations between the scores on all the tests, grouping together the tests that showed high correlations with one another. This exhaustive process yielded seven "primary abilities" which he claimed to represent basic, "unitary" factors of intelligence. He then developed the Primary Mental Abilities Test (1938) on the basis of this analysis.

The following are Thurstone's seven abilities, together with some illustrative items. *Numerical Ability* (N): Mark every number that is exactly three more than the one just before it: 15 19 21 26 29 22 25 5 8 7 11 4; *Word Fluency* (W): Write as many words as you can which end with *tion; Verbal Meaning* (V): Underline the word that means the same as the first word: FETID amusing feverish putrid contagious; *Memory* (M): Learn the following names so well that when the last name is given you can write the first name: John Jones, Mark Lamb etc.; *Reasoning* (R): Three of the following groups of letters are alike in some way: which are they? XURM ABCD MNOP EFGH; *Spatial Relations* (S): Mark the figure which will make a complete square of the first figure:

Perceptual Speed (P): As quickly as possible mark the two which are exactly alike:

The Primary Abilities Tests appear to be as successful in measuring intelligence as the Binet tests, although many psychologists prefer the Wechsler Tests to both types since they offer a performance scale as well as a verbal scale. Moreover, Thurstone's seven abilities have not proved to be the last word in factor analysis, for two reasons: they exclude important factors such as learning ability, and they can be broken down into more specific components. One group of investigators, headed by Guilford, has developed a theoretical model of intellectual ability containing 120 factors, including various kinds of "divergent production," or creativity, and the ability to evaluate, as well as the more commonly recognized components. Guilford's creativity tests are one important result of this analysis. *See* CREATIVITY TESTS, WECHSLER INTELLIGENCE SCALES.

Since the major types of intelligence tests are discussed under INTELLIGENCE TESTS and under separate topics, we will end this article by reporting the findings of psychological research on three important questions: How stable is an individual's IQ as he grows older? At what age does intelligence begin to decline? How much does the environment affect the development of intellectual ability?

Stability. Intelligence is regarded as a basic set of abilities which presumably remain fairly constant over the years. IQ tests, however, do not show much consistency during the preschool period —probably because the tests are predominantly of the sensorimotor variety, and these abilities are known to develop at a highly variable rate. From the early school years on, when verbal abilities are developing rapidly, measured intelligence appears to be quite stable. Changes from test to test rarely average more than 5 points, and these may be largely due to difference in tests, test conditions, and "test anxiety." A study conducted by Brown (1950) is typical: a group of children who were tested in the first grade and retested as college freshmen showed a change of 5 points or less in three quarters of the cases, with a maximum change of only 9 points. In this group there was little change in health, emotional status or educational stimulation—but where any of these factors are drastically altered, changes of as high as 20 to 30 points in IQ may be found. A study conducted by Sontag, Baker, and Nelson (1958) has indicated that children whose IQs tended to increase substantially between the ages of three and six were less emotionally dependent on their parents than other children, while substantial increases among older children appear to be related to high achievement motivation.

Age changes. The question of the upper limit of mental growth has long been debated. There is considerable agreement that individuals with low intelligence reach their limit relatively early in life, and those with high intelligence relatively late. For average individuals the rate of growth appears to be fairly constant between the third or fourth year and the early teens, and after that the yearly increments become relatively small. Although some early studies have indicated that the peak is reached somewhere between age fifteen and twenty, some of the more recent investigations put the peak at about age twenty-five. A number of investigations have shown that mental abilities remain quite constant from the twenties through middle age, but that a marked decline generally occurs in all major categories in later life. There are, however, considerable variations in the rapidity of this decline among different individuals. Moreover, some abilities decline more sharply than others: vocabulary and general information remain at a high level throughout the life span, and numerical ability improves until middle life, while reasoning, speed of response and ability to acquire new learning decline rapidly during middle and old age (Jones and Conrad, 1933; Schaie, 1958). These changes are often counterbalanced by knowledge and experience already acquired.

Environmental effects. Intelligence is based upon innate capacity, but environmental conditions determine the degree to which potential ability is developed. Children from rural areas both in America and Europe have been found to average about 10 IQ points lower than city children. This may be due in part to selective migration—that is, more bright people than dull people move to cities. It may also be partly explained by the fact that intelligence tests tend to include items which are more familiar to city children than to farm children. However, it is also attributable in part to the stimulating effects of city life and city schools, as shown by the fact that the IQs of Southern-born Negro children who moved to Philadelphia increased substantially between the first and ninth grades, while the IQs of Philadelphia-born children remained the same (Lee, 1951). Along the same lines, Skodak and Skeels (1949) have shown that adopted children may gain at least ten IQ points when they are reared in superior homes; and identical twins who have been separated and raised in different environments may come to differ even more substantially. *See* TWINS, RACE DIFFERENCES.

Likewise, the twenty-point difference in average IQ between children whose fathers are unskilled laborers and those whose fathers are in the professions is usually attributed in part to the superior home environment and educational opportunities of the latter group (McNemar, 1942). The differences are even more striking in studies of isolated mountain children in this country, and canal boat children in England, which show that their average IQs are not only low but decline with age. As Munn (1966) points out, "This suggests that, whatever the hereditary background may be, continued residence in an educationally impoverished environment increases the child's handicap in doing mental tests and the handicap becomes greater the older he gets." On the other hand, substantial changes can be made through the educational system, as shown by a study in which improved schooling in an isolated mountain region raised the average IQ of children ten points in ten years (Wheeler, 1942). *See* PSEUDORETARDATION.

INTELLIGENCE TESTS. Tests of general intellectual ability based on the measurement of a variety of mental skills.

The impetus to construct intelligence tests probably had its origins in Darwin's theory of evolution. His research emphasized the ability of different species to meet the challenge of survival, and this turned the attention of psychologists to the scientific measurement of ' individual differences in human beings. In their earliest studies, they focused on specific abilities such as strength of hand-grip, memory for nonsense syllables, sensitivity to pain, etc. These investigations were more effective in developing scientific techniques than in producing significant results. *See* GALTON, EBBINGHAUS, CATTELL, DARWIN.

The French psychologist, Alfred Binet, however, turned his attention to the more general problem of the differences between bright and dull children. Starting around 1890, he tried all kinds of measures: size of cranium, moral judgment, suggestibility, mental addition, graphology, and even palmistry. These tests did not prove promising, and in 1904 he and a physician, Théophile Simon, in response to a request from the French government, began to approach the problem from a new angle. They assembled a large number of simple, everyday problems which required different mental skills, and tried them on children of different ages. This enabled them to select appropriate items for each age—for example, they found that an average seven-year-old could correctly copy a diamond figure, and an average twelve-year-old could unscramble the sentence "at-country-we-for-started-hour-an-the-early." The number of items the child could pass determined his "mental age," which was later used in the Stanford revisions of the test in establishing the child's IQ. *See* STANFORD-BINET TEST, MENTAL AGE.

A second set of tests, the Wechsler Intelligence Scale for Children and Wechsler Adult Intelligence Scales (WISC and WAIS), was developed by David Wechsler between 1939 and 1958. Unlike the Binet test they contain an equal number of performance and verbal subtests. These two parts of the scales can be separately scored, and individual scores can also be calculated for the different types of subtests. These scores and their interrelationships yield a general profile of the individual's performance and not merely a single over-all rating. In addition, the Wechsler scales represent a movement toward the use of intelligence tests as a means of assessing an individual's emotional adjustment to a situation that makes intellectual demands. This approach recognizes that far more than intellect is involved in mental effort. The test reflects, among other things, the subject's self-concept, his ability to work under stress, and his attitude toward the "authority" giving the test. In a word, the Wechsler scales can be used as part of a battery of projective tests as well as for intelligence testing. *See* WECHSLER INTELLIGENCE SCALES.

Many performance tests have been constructed, both before and after the Wechsler scales. They are usually given in pantomime and include such problems as solving a maze, copying a design in blocks, and fitting jigsaw shapes together to form a design or picture. These are three of the items on the WISC tests as well as on the Arthur Point Scale of Performance Tests (1947), which presents tasks that are appropriate from age four and a half to adulthood (PLATE 14). Another important performance test is the Leiter International Performance Scale (Leiter and Stoelting, 1948), which presents memory analogies, perceptual matching and other problems, in the two to eighteen year age range. Quite a different approach is taken by the Goodenough Draw-a-Man Test (1926) which requires children to draw a man as best they can. The drawings are carefully scored according to age norms for certain features, such as eyes, nose, hair, ears, clothing and facial expression, as well as the basic structure of the figure. (*Fig. 16*)

In addition, a number of tests require a pointing or nodding response rather than a verbal response, and are therefore particularly suitable for the severely handicapped, such as the cerebral palsied. They may also be used for rapid screening purposes when a trained examiner is not available. Among these tests are the Peabody Picture Vocabulary Test, the Full Range Picture Vocabulary Test, the Quick Test, and the Columbia Mental Maturity Scale. The Leiter Scale, the Porteus Mazes, and the Stanford-Binet have also been adapted for use with the orthopedically handicapped. The Pintner-Paterson Performance Scale, the Arthur Performance Scale, and the Hiskey-Nebraska Test of Learning Aptitude are frequently employed in testing deaf and hard-of-hearing children. The last-named test was specifically developed and standardized for this purpose. Adaptations of the Stanford-Binet and Wechsler Scales (as well as a number of group tests, such as the Otis and Kuhlmann-Anderson tests) are available for measuring the intelligence of the blind.

Performance tests have a number of special advantages. They are a valuable aid in studying very young children and people of foreign background with little or no knowledge of the language, as well as subnormal and disturbed individuals who have special difficulty with words. Even more important is the fact that they call for knowledge that is required in almost every phase of life, yet is relatively independent of educational background. For this reason they are often more accurate than verbal tests in predicting practical ad-

justment, while verbal tests are better adapted to predicting educational achievement. To use one example, the adjustment of mental retardates in the community was predicted with greater accuracy from their performance on a group of mazes (the Porteus Maze Test) than from their Stanford-Binet scores (Porteus, 1939). Performance tests are also highly useful in the clinic, particularly in detecting the adverse effects of brain damage and emotional disturbance. *See* CULTURE-FAIR TESTS, MENTAL IMPAIRMENT TESTS.

Another variety of intelligence test is the infant development scale. Among the most important are the California First Year Mental Scale (1 month to 18 months), the Gesell Developmental Schedules (4 weeks to six years), the Cattell Infant Intelligence Scale (2 months to 30 months), and the Griffiths Mental Development Scale (0 to 2 years). These tests place heavy emphasis on sensorimotor co-ordination—for example, vertical eye co-ordination (looking upward with both eyes) is normally found at 1.4 months; reaching for a ring at 3.0 months; lifting a cup by the handle at 6.6 months; making a tower of two cubes at 13.5 months; and remembering one of four pictures at 35.6 months (Bayley, 1933). Some of the tests also include social items such as gazing into the examiner's eyes, attending while he is talking, and changing facial expression when he puts on a mask. *See* INFANT AND PRESCHOOL TESTS.

If infant tests could adequately gauge the IQ, they would be extremely valuable in detecting mental deficiency at a time when some cases might be corrected. They would also be helpful in adoption and foster-home placement. But unfortunately when they are given before the age of two they are extremely untrustworthy as predictors of school-age scores on intelligence tests (Bayley, 1949). On the other hand, tests given after the age of three, when children are capable of purposeful problem-solving, are considered good predictors of later intellectual ability (Cronbach, 1960).

Most of the tests mentioned so far are individual tests. They are generally considered more accurate than group tests. Nevertheless, there are situations in which group tests are indispensable, particularly in dealing with masses of subjects in schools, industry, and military recruitment bureaus. The first of these tests, the Army Alpha, was developed by a group of psychologists during World War I in answer to the urgent need for quickly dividing huge numbers of inductees into three groups: officer material, servicemen, and those who were unfit and had to be rejected. The Alpha is a paper-and-pencil test which measures simple reasoning, information, arithmetic, and the ability to follow directions. Another form, the Army Beta, presents nonverbal problems, and was given to illiterates and foreigners who were not proficient in English. During World War II, the Army General Classification Test (AGCT), which measured arithmetic, reasoning, and computation, verbal ability and spatial comprehension, replaced the Army Alpha. Similar tests were developed by the Navy and Air Force, and a total of over ten million men were tested during the Second World War. See INDIVIDUAL TEST.

These tests convinced the nation that mass processing could be used to predict success, and as a result many group tests have been developed in schools and industry in recent years. The Otis Self-Administering Test of Mental Ability (Otis SA), one of the earlier tests, has been widely applied in personnel selection. It stresses verbal ability and reasoning, but the newer tests present a broader variety of items designed to tap many other aspects of intelligence. The Raven Progressive Matrices is a nonverbal series that requires the subject to solve problems presented in abstract figures and designs. Several forms of this test are available, including a children's form, an adult form, and an advanced set for persons of above-average intellectual ability. The Chicago Non-Verbal Examination, standardized for both pantomime and verbal directions, has been designed specifically for children who are handicapped in the use of the English language, such as the deaf, those with reading disabilities, and those brought up in a foreign language environment. The Proverbs Test is used not only in assessing general intelligence but in appraising the abstract verbal functioning of mental patients. In a group form of this test the subject chooses the best of four explanations of common proverbs, and in the individual form the subject freely explains their meaning.

Two other tests are particularly suitable for superior adults: the Miller Analogies Test, which consists of complex analogies drawn from many academic fields, is widely used in the selection of graduate students and high level industrial personnel; and the Concept Mastery Test, consisting of analogies and synonym-antonym items from many fields, originally developed by Terman for his study of the gifted. Other important group tests are the Academic Ability Test, the new Analysis of Learning Potential, the California Test of Mental Maturity, the Culture Fair Intelligence Test, the Goodenough-Harris Drawing Test, the Henmon-Nelson Tests of Mental Ability, the Kuhlmann-Anderson Intelligence Tests, the Cooperative School and College Ability Tests, the Lorge-Thorndike Intelligence Tests, the Ohio State University Psychological Test (forms 21 and 23), the Purdue Non-Language Test, the Quick Word Test, the Pintner General Ability Tests, the SRA Tests of Educational Ability, the SRA Short Test of Educational Ability, and the Terman-McNemar Test of Mental Ability.

Among the most widely used tests for academic purposes is the Cooperative School and College Ability Test (SCAT) which can be given from grade four to college. It yields separate scores for vocabulary, reading comprehension, reasoning, and understanding of arithmetic operations. The Scholastic Aptitude Test (SAT), prepared by the College Entrance Examination Board, also measures a variety of abilities: verbal reasoning, knowledge of high school mathematics, vocabulary, and quantitative reasoning. Other tests, such as the instruments used in selecting applicants for medical, law, or graduate schools, can better be classed as scholastic aptitude tests than as general intelligence tests. *See* APTITUDE TESTS (PROFESSIONS), PERSONNEL TESTS, SCHOLASTIC APTITUDE TESTS.

Group intelligence tests are used not only to determine whether a student is measuring up to his abilities at present, but whether he is capable of more advanced work. They also help the guidance counselor pinpoint trouble areas, such as poor study habits or personal difficulties, that require special attention. In general, however, these tests are not so effective as individual tests for these purposes. Moreover, the examiner is not in a position to note whether the subject is ill, confused by the instructions, or emotionally upset when he takes a group test. Their major value is for mass screening. If we are to do justice to the individual, group tests must be supplemented by more personal procedures such as individual tests, interviews, and biographical material.

In recent years many criticisms have been leveled at intelligence tests, and in a few areas, as in New York City, they have been eliminated from the school system. Some writers have objected to intelligence tests as an invasion of privacy, claiming that schools have no right to assess the child's ability as a whole, but only to test his achievement in academic work. This criticism overlooks the fact that the object of the testing program is to discover what can

be expected of the child and whether he is measuring up to his own potential —both of which are important in appraising his performance in school as well as his potential for the future. Hilgard and Atkinson (1967) make this comment: "The problem of invasion of privacy is of the same order as a physical examination to qualify for participation in athletics. When the purpose is benign and the tests are used to help the individual to plan his own life and avoid failure, it is no different, in principle, than advising the child with a heart ailment not to go in for long-distance running."

The fact that test scores are generally kept secret has also aroused criticism. There are good reasons, however, for the secrecy. Psychologists and educators are afraid that parents will misinterpret the scores or place too high a value on them. There is also a danger that they will make invidious comparisons between children, labeling one child a failure and another a success on the basis of the IQ alone. Similarly, if the score is divulged to the child, he might become arrogant or complacent if it is high, and discouraged or depressed if it is low or even middling. Today some psychologists believe there is too much emphasis on secrecy, claiming that the child is not damaged by the knowledge that he has a low (or high) IQ any more than he is by receiving a poor or excellent report card. This view is supported by a study by Brim (1965), who found that when children were given their scores, they more often raised than lowered their intelligence estimates, probably because they had other means of appraising their ability than the IQ alone.

If parents and children could be convinced that the IQ is not the *key* estimate of ability, and if it were counterbalanced with results on aptitude tests as well as indicators of creativity, social adjustment, common sense, practicality, and other measures of success in life, perhaps they would cease to place an unrealistic value on the IQ. Intelligence test scores could then be revealed as only one of many useful indicators. However, it will take some time before the general attitude toward the IQ can be revised, and it is probably preferable at this time to use such general descriptions as "He is a very superior child," "He is a good average boy," "He is doing about as well as can be expected," or "He is working far below his real ability."

A third objection is that the IQ is accorded undue weight in selecting individuals for school or college. This is not a criticism of intelligence tests but of their interpretation and application. Practically all psychologists—and most admissions officers as well—would agree, again, that the IQ is only one among many factors. Not only must school grades and entrance examinations be taken into consideration, but also extracurricular activities, motivation, personal adjustment, and other non-intellectual factors. Recently a number of psychologists have pointed out that the factors of productive and "divergent" thinking, or creativity, have been overlooked, and many attempts have been made to devise tests which would measure these types of ability. If these attempts succeed, such tests would be important instruments for use in academic as well as job selection. *See* CREATIVITY TESTS.

Finally, intelligence tests have been characterized as unfair to deprived groups in our population. The chief objection is that they have been standardized on middle-class groups and in so doing accept their intellectual skills and experiences as the norm. They therefore do not do justice to individuals from other cultural or socioeconomic groups who may develop and express their mental abilities in quite different ways. More specifically, most intelligence tests stress verbal ability, and for this reason tend to handicap children

from restricted homes and neighborhoods where the stimulation required for full development of verbal ability is lacking.

One answer is to give performance tests as well as verbal tests, or to give a combination of the two as in the Wechsler-Bellevue scales, which yield separate performance and verbal scores. But it must be recognized that individuals from deprived environments do not usually have the toys, games, and experiences of middle- and upper-class children which would help them develop even the performance skills to a high degree. Limiting intelligence testing to the performance items would therefore not solve the problem, especially since, as David Wechsler (1966) points out, these tests do not "measure a sufficient number of abilities that go to make up the total picture of intelligent behavior" and "are poor prognosticators of over-all learning ability as well as school achievement."

A second alternative is the "culture fair" test, designed to present items that are not bound to a particular environment. So far, however, it has not been possible to devise test items either that are free of cultural influences or that reflect a common experience of mankind. Even the idea of taking a test has been found acceptable in some cultures but objectionable or unheard of in others. *See* CULTURE FAIR TESTS.

Since performance on IQ tests is dependent on cultural experience, and especially on verbal and academic information, there is no denying that some groups are bound to be penalized. But, as Wechsler points out, "It is true that the results of intelligence tests, and of others too, are unfair to the disadvantaged, deprived, and various minority groups; but it is not the IQ that has made them so. The culprits are poor housing, broken homes, a lack of basic opportunities, etc., etc." Similarly, Hilgard and Atkinson state, "A point that is overlooked is that ability tests provide objective criteria and, when properly used, may overcome some of the discrimination practiced against minority groups, thus increasing the opportunities of members of minority groups."

Moreover, there are concrete ways of overcoming some of the defects in the present administration of tests. One way is to have all children take at least one *individual* intelligence test, since individual tests are subject to fewer errors than group tests and give the examiner further insight into the child than the score itself reveals. A second is to repeat tests at intervals, since some children are slower in developing than others and a single early test would be a distinct handicap. Also, extraneous influences (ill health, tension, distraction) may have a greater effect at one time than another, and deprived children frequently reveal their potentialities more fully later in school than earlier due to the effects of the stimulating atmosphere and academic experience. A third approach is to offset the limitations of verbal tests by giving greater weight to aptitude tests and tests of ability to solve practical problems of life; and by devoting more attention to the development of performance scales that would reflect a wider range of abilities.

INTERESTS OF CHILDREN. The child's pattern of interests—that is, the activities he undertakes of his own accord—play a number of important roles in his life. They enable him to explore many facets of his world, to exercise his growing powers and capacities, and to fulfill his personal needs, wishes, and aspirations. The child who has a variety of interests, or one consuming interest, leads a happier, more stimulating and more balanced life than the child who constantly has "nothing to do." Moreover, he is preparing himself for the future, for in pursuing his favorite activities he is bound to develop knowl-

edge and skill that will serve him well later in life. One of the major regrets expressed by adults is that they failed to develop enough genuine interests when they were young.

The child's interests develop step by step, and many transient pursuits must be tested before a lasting pattern is developed. His choice of interests may be determined by a number of different factors: physical and mental "readiness" for particular activities such as baseball or music, the activities of his peers, opportunities offered within the home, and the influence of teachers, Scout leaders and camp counselors. However, these factors do not automatically create the child's pattern of interests. They must interact with two internal factors. First, the child's individual skills and abilities; for in general he will become interested in things he does well. And second, his special emotional needs. One child may pursue sports to develop a puny body, another to show off his strength, and a third to build up his ego by winning. Even an interest in stamp collecting may stem from several sources—for example, a need for isolation, an urge for information, or a desire to identify with the father's hobby. In view of these diverse influences, there is little wonder that the interests of children, and of adults as well, are so varied.

The interest pattern of any individual, then, is a unique product which can only be explained by particular forces, both internal and external, that shape his personality. Yet in spite of this fact there are some common interests among American children, and research has uncovered a number of ways in which they are developed and expressed. These will be summarized under the following headings: Play, Mass Media, Reading, School Influences, and Vocational Interests.

Play. The earliest form of play starts during the first two or three months of life when the infant looks at objects around him and tries to touch them. As soon as he is able to control his movements, he begins to explore shape and texture by banging, biting, and manipulating everything within reach. Shortly after he begins to walk, he takes the greatest pleasure in large-muscle activity, pulling and pushing wheel toys or anything else that moves. This starts him on a long period of free, spontaneous play with toys of all kinds—a period that reaches its peak at around six or seven.

Much of the child's early play is exploratory, and much of it is sheer exercise; but beginning at about three years of age he goes through a stage of make-believe and dramatic activity. This helps not only to lengthen his span of interest (from about six minutes at two years to twelve minutes at five), but, more importantly, gives him a chance to express his interest in the world of trains and buses, doctors and nurses. By six, when he enters school, dramatic play is already on the wane, especially among the brighter children, who tend to become realistic at a relatively early age. Play interests now shift over to peer activities, such as tag and other running games. After about two or three years the average youngster gives up these "pick-up" activities and becomes involved in team sports and games with definite rules and schedules (Hartley and Goldenson, 1963).

During the later elementary school years the child also devotes an increasing amount of time to recreational reading, hobbies, movies, television, and spectator sports. By adolescence these less energetic forms of play take over almost completely in some cases, though many others still engage in active sports; also, leisure-time activities become more rigidly divided according to sex. *See* PLAY.

Mass Media. In recent years, television has become "children's most time-consuming activity" (Witty, 1960). In many homes it is used as a "built-in baby sitter" during the preschool years, and from three or four on the average child devotes about a fifth of his waking time to this one medium. Interest (or at least viewing) reaches a peak at about six, and does not decline appreciably until the later elementary school years. Bright children lose interest before dull children; good students spend less time before the TV screen than poor students, and the well-adjusted watch less than the poorly adjusted. There is also less viewing in higher than in lower socioeconomic groups due to greater opportunities for other activities and also a somewhat higher intelligence level.

As to specific television interests, preschool children like cartoons, simple comedy, stories about animals and familiar people; first- and second-graders prefer puppet shows, cowboy stories, and family comedies; third- and fourth-graders are interested in stories about astronauts and skin divers, as well as variety shows, Westerns, detective dramas, and situation comedies. By the fourth grade or even before, most children abandon the strictly children's programs, except perhaps for cartoons, and watch adult programs almost entirely. Boys spend more time at TV than girls, probably because there is so much aggression on the air. Many older children also view news programs and documentaries, especially when they tie in with school work or are suggested by the teachers. *See* TELEVISION EFFECTS.

At one time about 90 per cent of children between eight and thirteen were regular readers of comic books (Witty and Sizemore, 1954), but today the number has greatly diminished, since television apparently satisfies the same interests with more drama and less effort. Most of the comic magazine stories are realistic in tone; many are horror tales, and only a few are truly comic. Boys, on the average, read more comic books and comic strips than girls, and slow learners devote more time to them than rapid learners. The combination of word and picture gives many of these children a boost toward better reading ability, although comic magazines seldom lure them into book reading. Children of preschool age prefer comics about animals acting like human beings; in the early school years boys like action and adventure stories, simple science fiction, and heroes of the superman variety, as well as humorous characters; girls like stories about nurses, children and animals. Older boys are attracted to masculine stories of crime and danger as well as stories about sports and athletics. The older girls sometimes read the same comic books as the boys, but more often prefer stories about dating, romance, and the antics of teen-agers.

Motion pictures rarely appeal to five- or six-year-olds, since they cannot understand what is going on and do not realize that it is make-believe. Many young children are also frightened by noise and shooting on the screen. By seven they begin to enjoy animated cartoons and children's pictures. A little later sex differences start to develop, with boys preferring films about cowboys and Indians, adventure, and war, and girls preferring stories with dancing, singing, and animals. Comedies and cartoons appeal to both boys and girls, but later in childhood girls become vitally interested in love stories while boys think they are silly.

Books. Children start to enjoy picture books around the age of two, and nothing gives them greater pleasure than identifying the people, animals and objects they find on the printed page. They also like to have simple factual stories read to them even before they can understand every word, and the sound of jingles and rhymes appeals to them even more than the meaning. During the preschool and kindergarten years they like to hear about what *might* happen somewhat more than about what *did* happen, since they want reality to be liberally sprinkled with fantasy. Stories like "The Three Bears" and *Mary Pop-*

pins are more enjoyable, and better for them, than fairy stories. Studies have shown that these early reading experiences have a marked influence on both the kind and amount of reading they later undertake.

The reading interests of different children begin to diverge sharply during the primary school years, due to differences in intelligence, available reading material, and stimulation by parents and teachers (Goldenson, 1957). Also, children on the upper economic levels receive more guidance and supervision than children on the lower levels. Nevertheless there are some general patterns. Six- and seven-year-olds prefer stories about animals and nature, especially when they have a plot and an element of surprise (*Winnie the Pooh,* for example). Eight-year-olds also like to read folk tales and even fairy tales, but realism predominates. By seven the reading interests of boys and girls begin to diverge. Girls prefer stories about home life, school life, and children in other lands; a little later they like a dash of romance.

From the fourth to the sixth grades boys are primarily interested in stories of adventure, horror, mystery, or aggressive action, but they also read books about sports and sportsmanship, airplanes, and inventions. As they get into the junior high years many boys and girls become absorbed in stories of history and the biographies of great men and women. There is also considerable interest in humorous books and hobby books. Boys of twelve and thirteen are likely to prefer action stories and science fiction stories far more than girls, and girls show a greater interest in romantic fiction and stories about children and teen-agers (Rudman, 1955).

School interests. The young child looks forward to school with eager anticipation because it is a sign of growing up. During the first two or three grades there is a peak of interest in every aspect of this experience. Studies show, however, that as he continues through the grades interest in academic work progressively declines and rebellion against regulations and homework increases. At the same time the child's interest in nonacademic aspects of school life, such as sports and extracurricular activities, shows a rapid increase. As a result, by the end of the elementary grades, most children have distinctly mixed feelings about school, with about 20 per cent expressing an active dislike. (Jersild and Tasch, 1949)

Many reasons have been given for this disturbing change. Among the most important are: (1) the competition of other interests—as they near adolescence, children become more absorbed in social contacts and status to be gained from participation in sports and other nonacademic activities; (2) they often find the curriculum remote from their increasingly personal concerns; (3) many parents fail to show sufficient interest in their school work, denigrate teaching as a profession, or speak of school as if it were a penal institution; (4) peer attitudes induce many children to adopt unfavorable attitudes because it is the "thing to do," or because they are afraid to be labeled as "brains" or "teacher's pet"; (5) specific antagonisms growing out of academic failure, unpopularity, discrimination against a child who is a member of a minority group, or dislike of teachers who seem bossy or unfair. These are the negative aspects, but it must not be forgotten that interest in school can increase progressively or maintain a high level due to favorable experiences with teachers and classmates, as well as personal satisfactions derived from academic success and expanding knowledge.

The specific pattern of academic interests also changes as the child progresses through school. In the early years there is far more interest in mathematics, art, and English than in science, nature study, geography, and current affairs. Girls remain interested in literature and writing, but their interest in mathematics declines; boys have the opposite tendency. Nature study and natural science reach their peak in the junior high years, and a genuine interest in history also takes hold, especially among boys. The teacher's ability to make the class exciting has been found to influence the students more than the particular value of the subject as a preparation for the future (Estvan and Estvan, 1959). In general, when children. are asked what they like best at school, junior and senior high school students mention academic subjects less often than children in the earlier grades, and more often name sports, industrial arts, vocational preparation, and relationships with their classmates. (Jersild and Tasch, 1949)

Vocational Interests. A child's interest in vocations starts, in a more or less vague way, when he learns about "community helpers" in nursery school or kindergarten, or when he hears his father talk about his job. The oft-repeated question, "What are you going to be when you grow up?" also arouses an interest in work. During the elementary school years the child goes through a period of identification with admired adults, but rarely thinks about work in terms of his own aptitudes or the kind of preparation he will need. In general, he goes through three stages: a period of "fantasy choices," lasting until the tenth or eleventh year, during which his aspirations are completely unreal; a period of "tentative choices" between eleven and seventeen, during which preferences are first based on likes and interests alone but later on aptitudes, and still later on values and ideals; and finally a period of "realistic choices" when actual opportunities for employment and advancement come into the picture. (Ginzberg et al., 1951)

Specific occupational choices usually shift many times before they crystallize.

Some children, however, follow a single *general* line of interest, such as science or service to others. Young people who ultimately go into professional work usually make their decision earlier than those who go into factory work. Early decisions, however, frequently reflect the preferences of other people rather than their own attitudes or aptitudes. Today vocational choice is freer from parental influence than in the past, but the wishes and aspirations of the parents still have a fairly strong effect, at least on the *range* of choice. On the middle and upper economic levels, status and prestige are often overriding considerations; on the lower economic levels parents exert much less pressure and welcome almost any job that earns a living. Other determining factors are the child's heroes, the "sex appropriateness" of certain jobs, and cultural stereotypes such as "mad scientist" or "rich banker." The individual child's personality characteristics and work experiences also have an effect. Timid children prefer "safe" jobs, the more aggressive want something more exciting. Too often, however, young people have little chance to discover their specific skills and abilities before the time of decision arrives. It is an interesting fact that if they have had varied work experiences they tend to be more realistic in their final choice than if they have not held summer or after-school jobs. *See* VOCATIONAL COUNSELING.

INTEREST TESTS. A comprehensive inventory of questions designed to determine interest patterns, particularly as they are related to vocational choice.

Interest tests are of the "self-report" type—that is, the individual states his own likes and dislikes. The approach, however, is an indirect one since the subject is not asked which specific occupations he prefers. Instead, he chooses among a wide variety of activities which have been found to be associated with one or another type of work—

a technique designed to get below the surface. A boy, for example, might state that he wants to be a doctor because he will be able to save lives, but the test may show that he would not be interested in the lengthy study or tedious routine a medical career requires. Another advantage is that the responses can be compared with those of a reference group. The test might show, for instance, that a young man likes only twenty-five out of eighty activities associated with computation—yet this would actually be enough to place him in the eightieth percentile of high school boys, and would therefore indicate a relatively high interest in this field.

The Strong Vocational Interest Blank (SVIB), one of the most widely used tests, is based on the interest patterns of successful members of different occupations. It presents 400 statements on occupations, school subjects, amusements, peculiarities of people and miscellaneous activities found to be associated with one or another type of occupation, and the subject makes a "like, indifferent, dislike" response to each of them. To take a concrete example, a response of "like" to "writing a technical book" and "dislike" to "actor" would both be weighted positively for Engineer because they reflect the attitudes of representative engineers. The test can be scored automatically for over a hundred occupations for men and thirty-two for women. The subject is given an A, B, or C rating, with pluses or minuses, on each of the occupations, to indicate how closely his preferences match the interest patterns of successful representatives.

The Kuder Preference Record is based on trait descriptions associated with ten clusters of interest: mechanical, computational, artistic, clerical, outdoor, scientific, persuasive, literary, musical, and social service. The items are of the forced-choice variety; such as (a)

Develop new varieties of flowers, (b) Conduct advertising campaign, and (c) Take telephone orders in a flower shop. From each group of alternatives the subject chooses the one he likes most and the one he likes least. In the example just given, the (a) choice receives credit under both scientific and artistic, the (b) choice is rated persuasive, and the (c) counts toward the clerical score. The scores on each of the ten areas are converted into percentile ranks, and a profile is constructed to show the subject's pattern of vocational preferences. These preferences fall into general areas containing a number of specific occupations for the subject to consider. Kuder also recognizes that many subjects have strong preferences in more than one area, and he therefore lists occupations which might be of interest to individuals who show such combinations as mechanical-artistic, scientific-social service, and persuasive-literary. *See* FORCED CHOICE.

A number of other interest tests have been developed. The Brainard Occupational Preference Inventory is particularly suited to individuals with limited reading skill and vocational potential. The subject indicates his degree of preference for 120 occupations, which are described in sentence form and divided into the following fields: Commercial, Mechanical, Professional, Esthetic, and Scientific, plus Agricultural for boys and Personal Service for girls. The Minnesota Vocational Interest Inventory yields scores on twenty-one occupational scales for which a college education is not required, by showing the degree of similarity between the subject's expressed interests and those of men employed in various skilled and semiskilled occupations. The Gordon Occupational Check List is also designed for this general group. The Thurstone Interest Schedule yields a profile of preferences for occupations in ten fields (Physical Science, Biolog-

ical Science, Computational, Business, Executive, Persuasive, Linguistic, Humanitarian, Artistic, Musical) through expression of preferences on a paired comparison check list containing one hundred pairs of vocations or job names. The Forer Vocational Survey explores interests, attitudes, and work adjustment of men and women. The Vocational Interest Inventory (G. U. Cleeton), standardized on twenty-three thousand subjects, compares interest patterns with those of basic occupational groups. The Interest Inventory for Elementary Grades (M. Dreese, E. Mooney) identifies all types of interests: hobbies, reading, school subjects, activities, occupations. The Geist Picture Interest Inventory, designed to facilitate counseling of culturally or educationally limited subjects, identifies vocational and avocational interests and explores the motivations behind them. It is also available in a special form for deaf males. Other interest tests are: the Holland Vocational Preference Inventory, which uses vocational likes and dislikes as clues to personality; the Guilford-Zimmerman Interest Inventory, the Kuder General Interest Survey, and the Occupational Interest Inventory.

Interest tests must not be narrowly interpreted, since it has been found that the same general interest pattern may apply to a number of different occupations. The important thing to note is the *direction* in which an individual's preferences point. Moreover, studies show that interests rarely if ever become permanently and rigidly fixed, especially in a society where opportunities are constantly arising. However, the broad lines of preference remain *relatively* stable, though we may narrow down an interest through specialization or introduce different expressions of the same interest.

Research indicates that interest tests are of considerable value in predicting both occupational choice and occupational satisfaction. They are one of the major tools used by the guidance counselor in helping students decide what vocations to consider. However, it must be recognized that interest is not the only factor involved in making these decisions. Such considerations as intelligence level, special aptitudes, values, opportunities, and financial status must be given their due weight. *See* VOCATIONAL COUNSELING, ALLPORT-VERNON-LINDZEY STUDY OF VALUES.

INTROJECTION. The unconscious defense mechanism of adopting other people's attitudes or behavior as one's own.

Introjection is often described as partial identification, since the individual only imitates selected aspects of his model. It is often operative in threatening situations where the underlying purpose is to ward off anxiety. The child, for example, incorporates his parents' standards and values into his personality, not simply as a matter of course or out of admiration for their superior wisdom, but to protect himself from the unpleasant effects of opposing their ideas. In some cases these introjected attitudes may go against the grain, but the child yields, unconsciously demonstrating the philosophy "If you can't beat 'em, join 'em." Similarly, an insecure youth may take on the protective coloring of a gang, and adopt its particular swaggering gait or manner of speech. The reaction may go even further. Studies of prisoners in concentration camps have shown that a few of the older, broken inmates unconsciously adopted the behavior of the Gestapo itself (Bettelheim, 1943).

Introjection is the direct opposite of projection. Instead of attributing our own attitudes to other people, we absorb their attitudes as part of ourselves. In cases where unacceptable or threatening impulses are adopted, the individual may come to dislike or even hate himself. This is one of the more complex, though infrequent, causes of depression and even suicidal attempts.

See IDENTIFICATION, PROJECTION, INCORPORATION.

INTROSPECTION. A form of observation in which an individual directs his attention to the content of his own consciousness.

Introspection is the principal technique used by the structuralist school of psychology. As defined by Edward B. Titchener, it is not a casual process of "looking within," but a highly technical procedure in which a trained person reports events in a specific sector of his experience which he has been set to watch. The activity is designed to be highly scientific, since the conditions under which it takes place are controlled and reproducible, and a report must be made immediately after the observation has occurred. It requires a good deal of training, or "hard, introspective labor," as Titchener called it, since we ordinarily gear ourselves to perceiving and dealing with objects or events, and not to the activities that take place in our own consciousness. An example will illustrate: the ordinary individual simply reports that he sees a table, but the introspectionist reports an immediate experience which consists of gradations of colors and specific shapes and patterns. *See* WUNDT.

The introspectionist, then, claims that he strips away meaning and gets to the core of experience. To him, sensation is the elementary, primitive reality; perception and meaning are secondary elaborations and additions. The Gestaltists are in violent disagreement with this point of view, since they hold that meaning is implicit in our experience. They also contend that we do not first receive sensations and then build perceptions out of them, but rather that we perceive objects, patterns and relationships as a basic, immediate experience. *See* GESTALT PSYCHOLOGY.

In spite of these doctrinal differences, it must be recognized that controlled introspection has given us valuable information on such processes as learning, problem-solving, dreaming, and decision-making. Here are some examples of its use. First, in his experiments on memory, Hermann Ebbinghaus believed that nonsense syllable was linked to nonsense syllable by a mechanical process; Johannes Müller, on the other hand, asked his subjects to make introspective reports of their experiences in memorizing material, and found that they engaged in a very active process in which they grouped items by rhythm, noted similarities and contrasts, and when possible added meaning. Second, in his early studies of thought processes, Alfred Binet assumed that reasoning involves the manipulation of mental images—but when he presented problems to his two daughters, and asked them to observe the way they solved them, he discovered that a great deal of thinking goes on without images—i.e., "imageless thought." Third, various pieces of apparatus have been built which emit different pitches in order to determine the range of the human ear, but we still use introspection—the "method of impression"—in reporting what we hear. This is the basis of the audiometer test that is in wide use today. As a matter of fact, it must be recognized that any test, experiment or research study that involves personal reporting contains an introspective element. The subject who responds to a Rorschach inkblot, the patient who reports his dreams to the analyst, or the individual who tries to describe the process of creative thinking are all using an introspective approach. *See* IMAGELESS THOUGHT.

INTROVERSION (literally "a turning inward"). Preoccupation with one's self and one's inner, subjective world of experience as contrasted with centering attention and interest on the outer world.

Carl Jung described the introvert as an individual who directs his libido, or life energy, toward his own ideas and fantasies rather than toward the surrounding world of people and things. He characterized this "personality type" as contemplative, reserved, and sensitive, often appearing somewhat aloof. Such an individual does not have free and easy social contacts, but though he is not vitally concerned with other people, he is not necessarily selfish and interested exclusively in his own advantage. He tends rather to be impractical, lacking in self-confidence, and anything but a man of action. As a result of his absorption in thought and feeling, he may make contributions to art, science, or philosophy which have great influence on the outer world.

The trend today is to deny the existence of a separate introversive personality type but to recognize introversive tendencies as a significant personality trait. Introversion and extraversion are also regarded by some authorities as poles or dimensions of personality, useful in defining any individual's character. Some people tend to be extremely extraversive and some extremely introversive, but the majority have been found to fall into the middle zone and may therefore be termed ambiverts. Through the use of psychological tests given to neurotic patients Eysenck (1961) found that anxiety states, obsessive reactions, and depressive disorders tend to be associated with a strong introversive pattern, while hysteric reactions and psychopathic character disorders tend to be associated with extraversion. *See* EXTRAVERSION.

INVOLUTIONAL PSYCHOTIC REACTION. A psychotic disorder occurring in late middle life, usually characterized by severe depression, and less often, by paranoid thinking. Until recently the depressed type was known as involutional melancholia, but that term has been abandoned in the latest

American Psychiatric Association nomenclature (1952).

The term involution (literally "turning inward") is the opposite of evolution and refers to the period of gradual biological decline which is believed to take place between forty and fifty-five years of age in women and between fifty and sixty-five in men. *See* MENOPAUSE.

Both the depressed and the paranoid type of involutional psychosis occur most commonly in compulsive individuals who have not had any previous history of either manic or depressive reactions. The salient symptoms of the depressed patient are extreme agitation, dejection, apprehensiveness, and restlessness. Typically, he paces the floor, wrings his hands, bites his nails, pulls at his hair, and tears his clothing. His facial expression is one of acute pain and suffering, and he may express feelings of utter worthlessness, self-condemnation, and despair. Other symptoms are persistent insomnia, loss of appetite, chronic fatigue, severe headaches, and progressive loss of weight.

The paranoid or delusional patient also suffers from agitated depression, anxiety, and apprehensiveness, but in addition manifests delusions that are most frequently persecutory in character. He may be fearful that certain individuals, usually unnamed and unknown, are bent on torturing or murdering him; as a result he becomes secretive and suspicious, and may refuse to eat or drink for fear of being poisoned. In many cases the delusions take a self-condemnatory, hypochondriacal, or nihilistic form. Instead of venting hostility against others, these patients direct it toward themselves. They may berate themselves for committing an unpardonable sin, believe they are poverty-stricken or afflicted with leprosy, insist that they are changing into an animal, or that their insides are rotting away and their brains are drying up. In both the depressed and de-

lusional types of reaction there is a danger of suicide and therefore a need for constant supervision. *See* NIHILISM.

At one time involutional psychoses were attributed primarily to physiological changes, but today these factors are considered only contributory causes. While it is true that there is often some decline in physical strength, mental alertness, and sexual potency in late middle age, it is also true that only a small proportion of men and women react by developing a psychosis. Most psychiatrists are therefore convinced that the disorder is not due to the physical changes alone, but to the psychological reaction to these changes. This view is reinforced by personality studies which indicate that individuals who are most vulnerable to involutional psychosis have long been sensitive, apprehensive, overconscientious, excessively serious, and narrow in their interests. Such people fail to develop a high enough level of security and inner strength to face the normal stresses of middle age, and may give way to anxieties over illness, loneliness, loss of financial security, or decline in personal attractiveness or sexual capacity.

The treatment of choice for involutional psychosis of the depressed type is electroshock therapy. In well over 90 per cent of cases, a course of six to twelve treatments brings dramatic improvement or full recovery within a month. When the depression has lifted enough to make the patient accessible, he is usually given psychotherapy in order to free him from guilt feelings, build up his sense of security and worth, and prevent recurrence of the disorder. The same types of treatment are applied to the paranoid patients, although the prognosis is less favorable in these cases. *See* ELECTROSHOCK THERAPY.

Illustrative Case: INVOLUTIONAL PSYCHOTIC REACTION (DEPRESSED TYPE)

A fifty-three-year-old woman was admitted to a state hospital after several weeks of worry over financial difficulties and loss of ability to eat and sleep. She paced about restlessly day and night, convinced that she had done something dreadful. Efforts by relatives to talk her out of this delusion failed.

The patient was the fourth of six children. Her father had been subject to episodes of mild depression, but there was no history of severe psychopathology in the family. She grew up in marginal economic circumstances and married a farmer at the age of nineteen. When she was thirty-nine her husband developed tuberculosis which gradually worsened. For three years prior to her breakdown he had been in a sanatorium while she remained home with two sons who successfully worked the farm.

The patient's older son described her as overconscientious and a meticulous housekeeper who hated dirt and disorder. Her only interests were home and church. On the very morning of her admission to the hospital she was up at six o'clock to cook breakfast for her sons. She always found something to worry about and for as long as her sons could remember she had had episodes lasting a few days at a time in which she felt low in spirits, but she had never had a major attack of depression.

In the hospital she was completely careless of her appearance. Her hair and clothing were untidy and she used no cosmetics. She paced about restlessly or sat motionless in an attitude of dejection. Her facial expression was one of constant misery and she periodically moaned. From time to time she wrung her hands, pulled her fingers, examined her nails, and picked and scratched at her clothing. She frequently failed to respond to questions about herself, her family, the time, and the place. At other times she answered, "I don't know" and then remarked, "Something went wrong with my head. I don't seem to remember at all. I can't tell you what. There is something wrong with my head. I don't remember."

Within a few days her confusion disappeared, indicating that she did not have brain damage. She began to answer questions appropriately, but her dejection and the delusion that her family was in financial straits persisted. "I just realized what I have done," she said. "I did something I shouldn't have. I made the boys lose the place on account of my worrying. I guess it's too late to do anything about it now." She felt she was worthless and that the future was completely bleak and hopeless.

The patient was given 12 ECT's (electroconvulsive, or electroshock, treatments). A marked improvement in mood and activity level resulted and she was able to return to the farm three months after admission. Follow-up interviews during the next two years indicated no recurrence of symptoms. (Rosen and Gregory, 1965)

Illustrative Case: INVOLUTIONAL PSYCHOTIC REACTION (PARANOID TYPE)

Hilda S., a forty-eight-year-old mother of two children, was committed to a mental hospital by her family. She was a person of European birth who came to this country alone when in her mid-twenties to work on the New England farm of distant relatives. After a few months she left the farm with the hope of earning more money by working in a large city. She lived alone at this time and worked as a domestic, the main focus of her life being her work. Her formal schooling in this country consisted of only a few years of night classes, which provided her with a modicum of facility with the English language. After seven years in this country, while in her early thirties, Hilda met her present husband, and after a relatively brief courtship they were married. Her employment as a domestic terminated permanently at the birth of her first child, one year after marriage. Her husband was a lower middle class farmer.

Before the onset of her illness, Hilda was a rather quiet woman whose life centered about her home. Gardening interested her and provided a hobby to occupy her spare time. She always had a tendency to be easily upset, and in such situations chose to confide in her husband, obtaining some comfort in this way. She had a few friends, but preferred to entertain them in her home rather than to visit theirs. She was a regular churchgoer, but never was preoccupied with religious questions or affairs. The onset of the disabling symptoms which eventuated in hospitalization was said to be relatively acute, beginning at the time three months prior to admission when she experienced her last menstruation (prior to that there had been none for several months). She became restless and seemed continually on the verge of losing her emotional control.

There were expressions of dissatisfaction with her life on the farm and a demand that the family move to the city. About two weeks prior to admission she began complaining of severe headaches which were unrelieved by sedation. During this time it became obvious that she was becoming forgetful and that her remarks lacked logic. These symptoms were accompanied by a difficulty in sleeping, followed within a few days by talk of seeing spies in her home. Hilda began to respond to auditory hallucinations, and became seclusive, refusing to leave her bed. She engaged in much praying accompanied by frequent episodes in which she would rush around the house kissing holy pictures. Immediately before hospitalization she became quarrelsome toward members of her family because they failed to sympathize with her delusions about spies.

At her admitting interview it was found that although this was Hilda's first hospitalization, she had, for several years, been mildly suspicious of people, and this feeling that others might attempt to harm her was seen as being intensified in the current episode. The interview was marked by behavior and verbalizations which bespoke a severely depressed, agitated mood state. Her facial expression depicted suffering, and almost before the interview began she was complaining of a pain in the lower part of her neck. Her agitation was manifested by frequent moving about in her seat, holding her hand, in turn, to her head, her cheek, and her chin, and continually shifting the position of her body. Her remarks were often punctuated by moans and, at times, groans. She was disoriented for time and place, and both recent memory and attention span were poor.

Hilda's delusions took the form of a fear that both she and her family would be destroyed because of an incident in which she had been involved shortly after she came to this country. When asked why she had come to the hospital she cried, "I heard them say they wanted to put me away on account of the baby. I thought they were going to hang me. They were hanging everybody. They put my children away and I got so scared." Further probing revealed that the baby referred to was the child of a family for whom she had worked over twenty years before. Hilda said that once, during her employ-

ment with this family, she had "made the child touch my body." This incident had been a source of guilt ever since.

Shortly after hospitalization Hilda was treated with five electroconvulsive shocks within a period of one mouth. She responded to treatment very well, and when she was free of delusions she was placed on convalescent care at home. For the next year she was treated with tranquilizers, and except for recurrent but mild depressions she achieved a good recovery. (Zax and Stricker, 1963)

ISOLATION (Isolation of Affect). The unconscious defense mechanism of cutting one's self off from painful feelings.

Any number of techniques are used to insulate the self from anxiety and distress. The individual who loses a beloved parent may automatically adopt a stoical attitude and "yield to the inevitable." The prisoner awaiting execution may screen out feelings of terror by insisting that life is silly and meaningless: "So what if I die?" Some people side-step feelings of guilt by engaging in lengthy metaphysical speculations about the ultimate difference between good and evil. Others may recall traumatic events without experiencing any feeling, or "affective cathexis." These examples indicate that isolation is a general reaction which overlaps considerably with other defense mechanisms, particularly rationalization, intellectualization, dissociation, emotional insulation, and denial of reality. *See* these topics.

Extreme and pathological forms of isolation are found in both neurotic and psychotic reaction types. The obsessive neurotic is believed to become preoccupied with repetitious thoughts or actions as an unconscious means of screening out inner tensions. The dissociative patient may find escape from guilt or anxiety in amnesic episodes. The schizophrenic may feel so threatened that the only way he can defend himself is to cut off all contact with reality.

J

JAMES, WILLIAM (1842–1910). James, probably America's most influential psychologist, was born of an eminent family in New York City and studied in Switzerland and Germany. On his return he enrolled in the Lawrence Scientific School of Harvard (1861–64), taking courses in physiology, chemistry and comparative anatomy. He then entered the Harvard Medical School, and after receiving his degree in 1869, accompanied Louis Agassiz on a trip up the Amazon River to collect zoological specimens.

Due to ill health he abandoned his original intention of specializing in physiological research, and in 1872 became an instructor of physiology at Harvard. Three years later he set up a psychology laboratory in connection with one of his courses, preceding Wilhelm Wundt's "official" laboratory in Leipzig by four years.

During his long teaching career, James first served as professor of physiology (1876–80), then as professor of philosophy (1880–89), and later as professor of psychology (1889–97). In the latter year he returned to his post as professor of philosophy after persuading Hugo Münsterberg to take over the psychology laboratory. During his career at Harvard he taught many men who helped to shape the face of early American psychology—among them, Hall, Thorndike, Woodworth, Yerkes, Angell, and Healy. Dewey and McDougall, though not his pupils, were also greatly influenced by him. In addition to his work in the fields of psychology and philosophy, James took a vital interest in psychical research. He helped to establish the American Society for Psychical Research in 1884, and served as president of the English Society from 1894–1905. It was his belief that this line of research would help to uncover unconscious factors in mental life. He himself took an open-minded but speculative view of the phenomena without accepting the usual "explanations."

In 1890 James published his *Principles of Psychology,* the product of twelve years of work. The two volumes "burst upon the world like a volcanic eruption," as Murphy (1949) puts it, having a tremendous influence not only on the psychological community but among the literate public as well. The full work and an abridgement based on it, the *Briefer Course* were used as texts by hundreds of thousands of students. It contained so many provocative insights and so much information that only a sampling can be given here. It introduced the findings of the "new" psychology of Wundt, Helmholtz, and other Europeans to American readers, although James opposed the structuralists' attempts to analyze experience into its elements and suggested instead that behavior is a steady flow, a "stream of thought," that can only artificially be broken up. It stressed the biological value of consciousness and its evolution as a useful instrument for adaptation—a viewpoint which became central in the functional school which James helped to found. It anticipated the behaviorist movement by emphasizing the importance of studying stimulus-response relationships. It dealt with everyday concepts, such as habit, which gives stability to our lives and is therefore the "flywheel of society"; the self, which is not one but many because we adapt to many different situations in different ways; and will, which influences not only what we do but what we believe. *See* FUNCTIONALISM.

The *Principles* introduced the widely discussed theory that emotions are the result of and not the cause of bodily reactions: "We do not run because we are afraid, we are afraid because we run." And, to give one more example, the book took a strong stand against faculty psychology, particularly on the subject of memory, showing that training carried out with one type of material such as poetry does not improve memory in general. *See* FACULTY PSYCHOLOGY, EMOTION (THEORIES).

After publishing the *Principles,* James turned his attention to the growing discipline of educational psychology and wrote his widely read *Talks to Teachers on Psychology, and to Students on Some of Life's Ideals* (1899). He then became interested in the psychology of religion. In his *Varieties of Religious Experience* (1902), he argued that the value of religion is not nullified by pinning the label "abnormal" on people who have mystical experiences. He also suggested that a study of such experiences can uncover facts about man's nature which cannot be reached through other means. Since the book focused on religion as an experience rather than a set of dogma and beliefs, it had the effect not only of opening up new areas of psychological investigation, but of rekindling the faith of many readers. This volume was followed by a series of philosophic works, which included *Pragmatism* (1907), *The Meaning of Truth* (1909), and *A Pluralistic Universe* (1909).

James was one of the most vivid personalities and suggestive writers in the entire history of psychology. Perhaps the essence of the man has best been expressed by his biographer, R. B. Perry (1935): "He always left the impression there was more; that he knew there was more; and that the

more to come might, for all he knew, throw a very different light on the matters under consideration. He respected his universe too much to believe that he could carry it under his own hat. These saving doubts arose from the same source as his tolerance and respect for his fellow man. The universe, like one's neighbor, is never wholly disclosed to the outward view."

JANET, PIERRE MARIE FELIX (1859–1947). Janet, one of the first systematic students of neurosis, was born and raised in Paris, and studied at the University of Paris. There he attracted the attention of Charcot and others by hypnotizing a dissociated young woman who claimed to have psychic powers. Charcot accepted him as a pupil, and a few years later, appointed him director of the psychological clinic at the Salpétrière Hospital. In addition to his activities at the clinic, he taught psychology at the Sorbonne and the Collège de France. Among his published works are *L'Automatisme Psychologique* (1889), *The Mental State of Hystericals* (1892; English translation, 1901), *Neuroses et Idées Fixes* (1898), *Les Obsessions et la Psychasthénie* (1903), *The Major Symptoms of Hysteria* (1907; English translation, 1920), and *Les Débuts de l'Intelligence* (1937). *See* CHARCOT.

Janet turned his attention to the study of hysteria and other neuroses as a result of his association with Charcot. One of his major contributions was a distinction between neurasthenia and psychasthenia, two categories which he differentiated from convulsive and hysterical disorders. Neurasthenia comprised such symptoms as depression, inability to eat, and easy fatigability, and was considered a relatively mild disturbance similar to the familiar "jangled nerves." Psychasthenia, on the other hand, was characterized by phobias, obsessions, and loss of willpower. To Janet this appeared to be a more serious condition since it involved a greater degree of psychological tension and internal conflict than neurasthenia. *See* NEURASTHENIA, PSYCHASTHENIA.

In using concepts of this kind, Janet was suggesting that factors outside of consciousness can affect behavior. Some people have therefore concluded that he recognized the dynamic character of the unconscious. This, however, is a misconception, for instead of attributing psychiatric symptoms to unconscious forces, he offered the theory that parts of the psyche become split off, or dissociated, from consciousness due to *physical* debility. Some individuals, he claimed, are endowed with a weaker nervous system than others. When they are subjected to sexual or emotional trauma or excessive stress, they cannot act in an integrated fashion, and as a result develop feelings of exhaustion, morbid fears, or other disturbances such as paralysis and amnesia.

In adopting this "physical stress" explanation, Janet was greatly influenced by the British neurologist Hughlings Jackson, who had advanced a theory based on levels of nervous activity. In Jackson's view, one of the primary functions of the brain is to inhibit and control the activities of the lower spinal tracts, and when destruction of brain tissue takes place, conscious control is weakened and the reflexes gain the upper hand. Janet applied this idea to mental symptoms, suggesting, in 1882, that ideas which would normally be under conscious control might not only split off but even develop an autonomous system of their own. He called these dissociated ideas "idées fixes," and even spoke of them as "unconscious" in the special sense mentioned above. By 1892 he held that hysteria was a result of the splitting of the personality due to a concentration of consciousness on one set of ideas and active avoidance of another set. The neglected set, however, remained active and expressed itself in symptom formation. In extreme cases, this process might even bring about the coexistence of two or more independent personalities. *See* MULTIPLE PERSONALITY.

Although these concepts have much in common with Freud's theories of repression and symptom formation, it must be recognized that Janet never advanced a psychological explanation of hysteria. Even though he used the term unconscious, he did not employ it in a dynamic sense, but interpreted symptoms as the "automatic" product of a weakened consciousness which could not keep all ideas in harness, with the result that some broke away and sought outlets on their own. His use of the term unconscious was therefore a façon de parler, a descriptive and not a dynamic concept.

Janet was as interested in therapy as he was in theory. He kept reminding his colleagues that mental illness can and must be actively treated, and even went so far as to suggest that quackery should not be frowned upon if it brought the desired results. He was one of the first to make a systematic investigation of the effectiveness of suggestion, and claimed that hypnotic techniques could be used to counteract the idées fixes which were causing the patient's symptoms. But, as Zilboorg and Henry point out (1941), his view that neurosis is based upon degeneration of the nervous system precluded the development of a fully effective psychotherapy.

JARGONAPHASIA. Unintelligible speech in which correct words are intermingled with words that are completely out of context; the use of words that have no relation to the intended meaning. This condition is a form of sensory aphasia—the inability to comprehend meaning—and is found in various disorders, such as Pick's disease, which result from lesions in the left temporo-parietal region of the brain.

It is also observed in certain cases of severe mental retardation. *See* APHASIA.

JEALOUSY. An anxiety reaction stemming from fear of losing the affection of a loved person to a rival.

Jealousy is a complex emotion compounded of feelings of insecurity, apprehension, self-blame, and hostility toward the rival. It frequently (but not inevitably) makes its first appearance in two- or three-year-olds when a new baby arrives. Until this time the child has enjoyed the exclusive care and attention of his parents, and he now feels that his position is threatened by the newcomer. This may make him anxious, uneasy, and resentful toward the baby. His jealousy may give rise to two general types of reaction. First, he may regress to infantile behavior, reverting to thumbsucking, baby talk, wetting the bed, or even soiling. These reactions are usually interpreted as an unconscious wish to return to infancy in order to recapture the full attention of the mother. However, they may also be more directly due to inner tensions which disorganize recently formed habits. Second, he may express hostility toward the new baby in many ways— by hugging him too hard, hurting him "accidentally on purpose," or directly attacking him. He may also sulk, refuse to eat, ignore the baby altogether, or even deny his existence.

It is usually possible to forestall or at least take the edge off jealousy of this kind by taking certain precautions both before and after the baby has arrived. It is considered advisable to make changes in the older child's room well in advance of the baby's arrival, but to postpone telling him that he is going to have a brother or sister until shortly before the birth, since this will help to prevent resentment from building up. It is not wise to talk too much about the newcomer in the child's presence, but when it is done, he should be constantly assured that he is big and important in comparison with the tiny baby. When the infant does arrive, the older child should be allowed to care for him occasionally—but as "mummy's little helper" and not as a slave to the newcomer. At the same time, he should be assured of the interest of his parents by receiving extra attention and special privileges which will make him feel happier and more grown-up.

There are two other common forms of childhood jealousy. A school child frequently becomes jealous when a friend forms new attachments. The jealous child may react by making extra attempts to keep the friendship, by criticizing the rival directly or indirectly, or by denying that he really cares. In some home situations a child may become jealous of the attention paid by one parent to the other. Many psychoanalysts claim that this is a universal phenomenon arising from the Oedipus complex, the strong attachment of the child to the parent of the opposite sex. Others, however, believe this form of jealousy is likely to arise only when the child is made to feel rejected or is excluded from the parents' relationship. These observers point out that most children derive pleasure and security from the fact that their parents express love for each other, especially when this is accompanied by frequent assurances of affection for the child himself.

Jealousy is not only an intense emotion but a powerful motivating force. There is ample evidence for this fact in the triangle theme of literature and the "crimes of passion" that frequently come into the courts. When a husband becomes convinced that another man is stealing his wife's affection, he may require her to account for every minute of her time, and may even keep her under constant surveillance. Even when there is no actual rival, he may guard his wife lest one appear. These reactions are often a reflection of feelings of inadequacy, real or fancied, or a fear of loss of self-esteem. They may also be projections of the husband's own unrecognized desire to "wander." The same mechanisms apply to jealous wives, but in these cases they are sometimes augmented by envy for masculine freedom.

Extreme jealousy sometimes takes psychotic form. Typically, it is a paranoid reaction involving fixed delusions. The victim is constantly on the watch for any indication that his suspicions are justified, and manufactures evidence if he does not find it. He is completely blind to any facts that contravene his rigid beliefs. See EROTOMANIA, PARANOIA.

Illustrative Case: JEALOUSY (PARANOID TYPE)

A thirty-nine-year-old lawyer became convinced that a conspiracy existed between his wife and an obstetrician. His belief was based on the fact that she had insisted on going to the obstetrician instead of to the family doctor during her second pregnancy. Her specialist was a member of the same nationality as the wife, a group to which the husband did not belong. His suspicion gathered force when she seemed especially pleased with her regular visits and praised the doctor highly, and was further intensified when he received a smaller bill than he had expected after the baby was born. Suspicion rose to conviction when he found that the baby looked foreign, like the obstetrician.

The patient was the chronically insecure son of parents who were intensely devoted to appearances, conformity, and status. He had married the daughter of immigrants against their wishes, and in spite of the fact that he himself looked down on his wife's family and friends. At the same time he felt excluded from their closely knit group, and resented his wife's choice of obstetrician as one more close relationship that left him out. His history revealed that he had serious doubts about his potency when he entered marriage; and, partially to reassure himself and partially out of spite, he had had an extramarital affair during his wife's second pregnancy. This affair made him feel extremely guilty and fearful of discovery, and undoubtedly helped to reinforce his suspicions toward his wife through the mechanism of projection. Therapy was effective in helping him recognize the origins and meaning of his jealousy, and he made a fairly good recovery from his paranoid illness. (Adapted from Cameron, 1947)

JOB ANALYSIS. A study of all aspects of a job, covering the operations performed, equipment used, work conditions, hazards, training and qualifications required, rate of pay, opportunities for promotion or transfer, and relation to other jobs.

The purpose of job analysis is to provide a complete job description to be used in a personnel selection program. Job analyses can also be helpful in developing training procedures, performance rating systems and job classifications; in improving work methods; in devising safety measures, redesigning equipment and layout, and adjusting pay rates. In addition, it is a source of valuable occupational information for the vocational counselor and for the educator who is planning a vocational curriculum.

In making his analysis, the industrial psychologist avoids vague generalities and concentrates on specific details which differentiate sharply between the job under study and others in the same category. He must also look for the "critical requirements" of the job—that is, features which differentiate between the successful and unsuccessful worker. In gathering this information he usually employs a combination of techniques and keeps a systematic record of his findings. The most useful sources of information fall into the following seven categories:

First, *published analyses* of similar jobs, which may provide promising leads, but must be used with caution since outwardly similar jobs may actually be quite different. Second, *interviews* with supervisors, instructors, and workers, including those who are unsuccessful as well as those who are successful on the job, as well as those who are in the process of learning.

Third, an *activity log,* or work diary, in which an objective record is made of all duties during a specified period of time. Fourth, *analysis of written records,* including operating manuals, instructional material, performance records and accident reports. Fifth, *"critical incident" data* gathered from supervisors and associates—that is, specific instances of job behavior which are particularly indicative of either satisfactory or unsatisfactory performance. Sixth, *direct observation* of the job, supplemented where necessary with sound recordings, films, or time and motion study. Seventh, *performance of the job,* where feasible, to supplement the other techniques. In addition to these techniques, workers are sometimes asked to fill out questionnaires relating to various aspects of the job.

Job analysis is the key to the personnel selection program, since it provides the information on which job requirements are determined. These requirements constitute the skills, experience, intelligence level, education, attitudes, physical attributes and other characteristics needed for successful performance. A particular job may, for example, require a high degree of visual acuity, finger dexterity, mechanical comprehension, ability to concentrate under distracting conditions, and a minimum of two years of experience. These requirements establish the "personnel specifications" which serve as the basis for construction or selection of tests, questionnaires, rating scales, and other instruments to be used in job placement. These "predictors," as they are called, must be subjected to preliminary tryout and thoroughgoing validation procedures before they can be adopted for use in a personnel selection program. *See* PERSONNEL SELECTION.

JOINT COMMISSION ON MENTAL ILLNESS AND HEALTH. In 1955, Congress passed the Mental Health Study Act, which directed the Joint Commission on Mental Illness and Health to determine the mental health needs of America and make concrete recommendations for a national program that would "approach adequacy." Its final report, published in 1962 under the title "Action for Mental Health," has become a call to arms for an all-out attack on the nation's number one health problem. Here are the highlights of the report:

It is an accepted fact that one out of ten people suffer from emotional or mental disturbance, and more than one out of one hundred (about 2 million persons) are incapacitated by their illness. These seriously ill people are the core of the mental health problem today. In spite of some advance toward humane and effective care, 80 per cent of the country's 277 state hospitals can still be classified as custodial institutions. Typically, they are located far from population centers, and the patients (often the doctors as well) feel like exiles from society. Moreover, these hospitals spend only $4.44 per day on each patient, as compared with $31.16 in community general hospitals—and the proportion of state expenditures for mental patients is actually declining.

The irony in the situation lies in the fact that highly effective treatments for the mentally ill have been developed—and when they are used, between 60 and 80 per cent of schizophrenic and other serious cases improve sufficiently to lead a useful life in the community. Why, then, do we not apply these treatments more widely? The principal obstacle lies in attitudes of indifference and even rejection toward the mentally ill. They are "singularly lacking in appeal" because their strange behavior tends to disturb and offend people instead of arousing sympathy. In fact, the general public tends to think of them not as sick people, but as nuisances to be avoided. Many members of the medical profession share these attitudes, and until they are changed, progress will be slow.

One of our greatest needs, therefore, is a massive campaign of education and enlightenment, designed to disseminate authoritative information about mental illness, and show that it is possible to work with the mentally ill, to treat them as human beings, and to help them recover. Such a campaign would not only produce more friendly and accepting attitudes toward these sick people, it would also bring more workers, more volunteers, and eventually more funds into this neglected field —and at the same time overcome the defeatism that stands in the way of effective treatment.

A second major need is to develop a comprehensive and diversified research program. It is especially necessary to invest a large proportion of funds in basic, long-term research, since this is the only way to achieve major breakthroughs comparable with those in other fields of medicine. To make this possible, the Federal Government should establish mental health research centers and institutes to be operated independently or in collaboration with educational institutions.

Finally, the entire patient-care program in this country needs to be radically revised, and new patterns of treatment must be introduced. All mental health professions should launch a national recruitment and training program, not only for highly professional personnel, but for nonmedical workers as well. Counseling must be made available in the community at the first signs of disturbance; and emergency psychiatric care should be provided at the onset of acute disturbance. Provision must be made for treatment of all major mental illnesses through (a) community mental health clinics operated on an outpatient basis, in order to reduce the need for prolonged and repeated hospitalization; (b) short-term hospitalization in every community general hospital; (c) conversion of small, suitably located state hospitals (1000 beds or less) into intensive treatment centers as rapidly as possible, with gradual conversion of all large state hospitals into centers for long-term care and improvement of persons with chronic diseases, including mental illness; and (d) inclusion of after-care and rehabilitation as essential components of all service to mental patients, since the objective of modern treatment is to save the patient from the debilitating effects of institutionalization, and return him to home and community life as soon as possible.

To implement this entire program of research, training and patient care, federal, state, and local expenditures should be doubled within the next five years and tripled within the next ten. The federal government should also develop a subsidiary program that will not only bear a share of the cost of services, but also encourage state and local governments to take increasing responsibility. All matching grants to states should be awarded according to criteria of merit and incentive formulated by an expert advisory committee appointed by the National Institute of Mental Health. *See* NATIONAL INSTITUTE OF MENTAL HEALTH, COMMUNITY MENTAL HEALTH CENTERS, ATTITUDES TOWARD MENTAL ILLNESS, MENTAL HOSPITAL.

JUNG, CARL GUSTAV (1875–1961). (Analytic Psychology). Born in Kesswil, Switzerland, Jung came from a long line of physicians and theologians. Before concentrating on the study of medicine at the University of Zürich, he explored biology, archeology, philosophy, mythology, and mysticism, laying the basis for the wide-ranging inquiries he conducted throughout his life. His dissertation for the medical degree, "On the Psychology and Pathology of So-called Occult Phenomena" (1902), emphasized the continuity between the conscious and unconscious levels of the mind, a theory that dominated his entire philosophy. His first experimental project, on word association, brought him into contact with Freud, and when he found that Freud's theories of dream interpretation confirmed his own view of the unconscious, he associated himself with the psychoanalytic school.

After five years (in 1912), however, he left the movement, due to basic differences with Freudian theory. He objected to Freud's theory of infantile sexuality, his emphasis on wish fulfillment, his pansexualism, his view of life as an "endless repetition of instinctual themes," his conviction that the unconscious is primarily a source of primitive and often destructive impulses, and his limitation of mental contents to the personal experiences of the individual. In contrast, Jung believed that our personalities are molded not only by the experiences of this life but by the cumulative deposits of racial history; that we can be motivated by moral and religious values even more than by fundamental instincts; and that the purpose of existence is for each individual to achieve his own unique integration of conscious with unconscious experience, as opposed to Freud's emphasis on the attainment of conscious control by the ego and the mature expression of psychosexual drives.

Jung's own point of view began to take definite shape in *Symbols and Transformations of the Libido* (1912), in which he interpreted the thought processes of the schizophrenic in terms of mythological and religious symbolism. The fullest expression of his theories, which he called analytic psychology, is found in his *Psychological Types* (1921). While serving as a professor in Zürich and Basel, he wrote a number of other books, including *Contributions to Analytical Psychology* (1928), *Modern Man in Search of a Soul* (1933), *The Psychology of Dementia Praecox* (1936), *Psychology and Religion* (1938), *The Integration of the Personality* (1939), *Essays on a Science of Mythology,* with C. Kerényi (1949), *Essays on Contemporary Events* (1947), and *The Practice of Psychotherapy* (1954). An English translation of his entire works, edited by Herbert Read, is now available in eighteen volumes.

Following are the major concepts of Jung's system:

The ego. The ego consists of feelings of continuity and identity, the feeling that we are the same person we were yesterday, and that we have a body of experience which belongs to us. Jung does not picture the ego as torn between a set of animal drives (the id) and a set of moral precepts and social customs (the ·superego). Rather, he views it as a developing entity which gradually incorporates all phases of conscious and unconscious activity into a new whole, a process which he terms individuation. A person with a strong, well-developed ego is one who has achieved an effective and productive balance among all aspects and levels of his psyche, and particularly an integration of conscious and unconscious forces.

The personal unconscious. In its process of development the self draws on two sources, the personal unconscious and the collective unconscious. The personal unconscious, like Freud's preconscious, consists of experiences which were once conscious but which have been superseded or forgotten, as well as ideas and wishes which have never been strong enough to make a conscious impression. Some of these memories, thoughts, and feelings may split off from the main body of the psyche, due to traumatic experiences or internal conflicts, and form a constellation or "complex" of their own. If these "psychic fragments" gather enough strength, they may attain independent status in the form of automatic writing or hallucinations. Even when they are not powerful enough to become independent, they may still obsess our consciousness, influence speech and action, and cause disturbances of memory and association. Complexes play such an important role in the psyche that Jung devised the word association test as a means of detecting them. *See* COMPLEX, WORD ASSOCIATION TEST.

The collective unconscious. The collective unconscious exerts an even greater influence than the personal unconscious. It is the residual of the racial history of man and his animal ancestors, implicit in the pathways and structures of the brain itself. This does not mean that it is only a storehouse of unconscious ideas—rather, it is an accumulation of predispositions and potentialities which in its totality forms the frame of reference with which we view the world. Jung calls these structural components "archetypes," although at times he uses such synonyms as images, primordial images, and mythological images. They arise from historical experience and constitute the inherited foundations upon which the whole structure of the personality is built. In a word, each individual's psyche reflects the wisdom and experience of the ages.

How do archetypes originate? Jung's answer is that they arise from experiences that have been repeated for long periods of time. Primitive man, for example, encountered the dangers of darkness and the poisonous bite of snakes, and as a result we have a predisposition to fear both snakes and darkness, a tendency which may be reinforced by our own personal experiences or the stories we hear. Similarly, the effect of the sun on life and growth gave rise to the archetype of a supreme being; and countless experiences with natural forces, such as floods, earthquakes, and lightning have produced an energy archetype. The archetypes, however, do not automatically determine the specific ideas we hold, since these are molded by our own experiences and interpretations. The archetype of a supreme being may therefore express itself in either primitive sun worship or the most sophisticated metaphysics; and preoccupation with energy may be manifested in the child's interest in firecrackers as well as the scientist's effort to split the atom.

Jung spent a lifetime in attempting to uncover these archaic roots of modern man. He viewed the archetypes as motive forces, organizers of experience that help to account for the way we think and act. Some of those he studied most closely were the images of the earth mother, the hero, unity, magic, power, death, rebirth, the demon, and the elder wise man. Others are the creation myth, the fall from Paradise, the Virgin Birth, the Sphinx, Hercules, and Prometheus. He maintained that two or more archetypes may at times fuse into one—for example, Plato's philosopher-king is a combination of hero and wise man, while a satanic leader like Hitler is a combination of hero with demon. He also believed that certain archetypes have evolved further than others, among them the persona and the anima. But he held that the *central* archetype is the self-concept, since it integrates both the conscious and unconscious aspects of the psyche. This again invokes the ideal of individuation and complete realization, which attained its highest expression in Christ and Buddha. *See* PERSONA.

Personality dynamics. Jung viewed the human personality in terms of polarities: conscious values and unconscious values, sublimation and repression, rational and irrational functions, introversion and extraversion. These are not static components of a finished self but dynamic forces or "tension systems" which are constantly exerting an influence on the development and expression of the individual's ego. Their power derives from the libido, which Jung conceived as a finite reservoir of psychic energy which can flow in one direction or another. In the completely realized individual the total energy is evenly distributed throughout the various fully developed systems. The ordinary person, however, does not reach this state of equilibrium, since he develops one side of his personality at the expense of others. This creates a greater or lesser degree of inner strain and tension.

Jung, then, believed that conflict—the "war of opposites"—is a basic fact of life. Some examples of the polarities mentioned above will make this clearer. First, *conscious versus unconscious* values. An individual's conscious values can be assessed by observing the attention he gives to various aspects of life—for example, if he spends more time in reading than in athletics he values reading more. The unconscious values have to be determined by more subtle means, such as the word association test: a person with a militaristic complex will view the world situation in a completely different light from a pacifist.

Second, *sublimation versus repression.* In sublimation, the psychic energy is displaced from a primitive instinctive system to a higher cultural or spiritual system. Jung describes this process as a forward movement toward individuation. Repression, on the other hand, prevents the energy from discharging into constructive channels and adds to the strength of the unconscious. This may give the unconscious strength to break into consciousness and force the individual to behave impulsively or irrationally. In some instances, however, this process may have a positive effect, since it can also result in the release of creative ideas from either the personal or the collective unconscious.

Third, *rational versus irrational processes.* Each person possesses four and only four ways of orienting toward the world: the two rational functions of thinking (recognizing meaning) and feeling (experiencing pleasure and pain); and the two irrational functions of sensation (receiving concrete facts or representations of the world) and intuition (perceiving by means of unconscious and subliminal processes). The irrational functions put us in direct contact with the raw data of existence and may express themselves as fantasy; the rational functions enable us to look for lawfulness in nature by using generalization, abstraction, and judgment. According to Jung, every person is capable of all four functions, but in most individuals some are more fully developed than others.

Fourth, the *analysis into opposites* also applies to attitudes toward life. Jung put special emphasis on two of these attitudes: introversion, which is an orientation toward inner processes; and extraversion, an orientation toward the external world of people and events. Each person possesses both of these tendencies, but one of them is usually dominant and conscious while the other is subordinate and unconscious. As always, the two are in conflict with each other, and the tendency that is not conscious and dominant will be expressed in dreams and fantasies if it is denied expression in reality.

Personality development. Growth of personality is described as a movement toward unity and individuation. The unity is not of the abstract kind, but is a resolution of opposites through their further development. The most important aspect of this process is the gradual integration of greater and greater amounts of the unconscious, both personal and collective, into the conscious life of the individual. Unlike Freud, Jung does not offer a detailed elaboration of stages of development, although he does hold that a radical change often occurs in the late thirties and early forties. During this period the individual becomes less impulsive and extraversive, and more introversive and controlled. In the earlier stages of life basic instincts and extraversive values have been in the ascendant, but in later maturity the energy of the libido can be channeled into the spiritual life and many individuals are able to turn inward to draw new understanding from the reservoir of the unconscious. It is an interesting fact that many of Jung's most ardent followers, and many of his patients as well, have been older people.

Therapy. Jung held that emotional disturbance stems from disharmony within the psyche produced by: (1) conflicts among our outward, social personality (the "persona"), our ego (deeper feelings and attitudes), and the collective unconscious; (2) domination by impulses and feelings arising from the collective unconscious or by defenses against them; or (3) an extreme tendency toward introversion or extraversion, which creates an unbalanced personality. The aim of the treatment process is a better integration of the personality. This is achieved primarily through understanding and facing current difficulties, and through eliciting hidden, unconscious personality resources which will help the individual solve his problems and realize his potential. The therapist does not employ the couch or the method of free association, but may encourage his patient to relate his dreams and produce drawings and paintings that may reveal present concerns as well as latent tendencies. He takes the responsibility for directing the process along significant lines, but gears his approach to the patient's personality type—that is, an introvert requires refined interpretations and full discussion of dynamics, while an extravert responds better to suggested changes in behavior. Both, however, may be encouraged to express submerged aspects of their personalities by taking up a new hobby or trying a different occupation. Many Jungian therapists tend to keep the rather metaphysical theories in the background; others appear to encourage the development of a fantasy life that verges on the mystical. Although Jung's theories have widened the scope of our thinking about man's mind, his effect on therapeutic practice has not been great.

Jung has been vehemently attacked on a number of grounds, especially by Freudian analysts. They claim that archetypes are metaphysical constructs which cannot be proved to exist, and that the idea of the racial inheritance violates known principles of psychology and evolution. He is also criticized for his failure to offer any detailed scheme of personality development, and for resurrecting an outdated concept of the unconscious. Others simply dismiss him as a mystic or ignore his work because he does not offer experimental evidence for his findings.

Jung has a small but staunch group of followers in the United States. Even those who do not count themselves Jungians may be more influenced by his ideas than they realize. The word association test has become one of the standard instruments of clinical psychology. A number of rating scales have been devised for testing the introversion-extraversion dimension of personality. His concept of self-realization has been incorporated into some of the most recognized personality theories. And finally, the comparative studies of mythology, religion, and the occult which he undertook in his search for archetypes have thrown new light on the universal aspects of human experience. *See* INTROVERSION, EXTRAVERSION, SYMBOLIZATION, DREAM INTERPRETATION (MODERN).

JUST NOTICEABLE DIFFERENCE (JND; Differential or Difference Threshold). The smallest difference between two stimuli that can be reliably detected.

The external world comes to us in the form of ever-changing sensations, and we are constantly called upon to react to slight differences in sounds, colors, shapes and sizes. We could not enjoy a great painting, drive a car safely, play a good game of tennis, or do any precision work if we were not able to make fine discriminations. It is important, therefore, to find out just how sensitive we are to differences— that is, what is the least difference in length, or loudness, or brightness that we can detect?

This was probably the first question ever to be answered experimentally in the history of psychology. Early in the nineteenth century the German physicist, Ernst Weber, developed a technique for measuring the JND, or differential threshold, for different senses. In determining the JND for weight, for example, he would ask a subject to heft an unmarked weight of, say, 300 grams repeatedly, and then heft other weights until he found one that was just noticeably heavier than the given weight on 75 per cent of the trials. The result was then stated in fractional form: if the new weight was 306 grams, the "Weber fraction," as it was later called, would be $\frac{6}{300}$, or $\frac{1}{50}$. The experiment was continued with other weights, and he found that if the base weight was 600, the JND weight was 612; and if the base weight was 200, the JND weight was 204. When he determined the fraction in each case, he made the startling discovery that it was exactly the same in every instance—that is, $\frac{1}{50}$!

Weber performed tests on different senses and made the even more astonishing discovery that there was a constant fraction for each of them. He found, for instance, that if he started with 60 lighted candles, it took one additional candle to make a noticeable difference. If he started with 120 candles; it took two, and so on. Here the fraction was $\frac{1}{60}$ in every case. This finding led to Weber's Law, first proposed in 1834: the smallest noticeable difference in perceived intensity is a constant fraction of the original stimulus.

Weber's Law has been found to hold, with some variation, for all senses— but only in the middle range of intensity. This limitation does not greatly diminish its value, since most of our experiences involve stimuli of medium intensity. The most important Weber fractions (or Weber constants) are: vision (for brightness of white light): $\frac{1}{60}$; for kinesthesis (lifted weights): $\frac{1}{50}$; for pain (heat on skin): $\frac{1}{30}$; for hearing (middle pitch, moderate loudness): $\frac{1}{10}$; for pressure (on skin spots): $\frac{1}{7}$; for smell (odor of India rubber): $\frac{1}{4}$; for taste (table salt): $\frac{1}{3}$. Many other fractions have been determined—for example, for visual detection of differences in length ($\frac{1}{100}$)—but fractions for each modality always remain about the same.

These results shed interesting light on our sense experience. They indicate that vision is our most sensitive, and smell and taste our least sensitive modality. Moreover, these sensitivities seem to be roughly proportionate to the importance of the different sense organs, since we depend far more on vision than on taste or smell for survival. The only result that is surprising is our extremely high kinesthetic sensitivity. We use our muscle sense in learning the proper "reaches" on the typewriter or piano, and in acrobatics or dancing, but we seldom use this sense to its fullest advantage.

Animal studies lend support to the evolutionary hypothesis. Weber fractions obtained from discrimination experiments show that fish are extremely sensitive to tastes, dogs and cats to smell, and bats to high-pitched sounds. Each of these senses is of high survival value for the particular animal.

The Weber fractions given above are, of course, only averages, for there are wide individual differences in sensitivity. They would be far smaller for tea and wine tasters or perfume specialists than for the average person. Such individuals can detect, within an incredibly small margin of error whether a batch of a certain product meets a certain standard. Sensitivity of this kind is undoubtedly increased through training, but it may also be due in part to constitutional factors. At any rate it has considerable survival value of the economic kind, since these experts are usually in great demand.

Weber's Law has been applied in a variety of fields, including esthetics, consumer attitudes, and stock-market analysis. Artists can usually perceive differences in color values, shape and size that are imperceptible to the untrained eye, and the layman may actually perceive differences without being fully aware of them. Experiments show that if extremely slight changes are made in a work of art they are likely to make a noticeable difference in our reaction. (An equivalent change in a publicity poster would be completely overlooked.) In practical matters, a five-cent increase in the price of a newspaper will cause a violent reaction, while a one hundred or two hundred dollar increase in the price of a $40,000 house would cause little concern.

Sometimes, however, a series of changes which are close to the differential threshold will go unnoticed until they produce a major shift—for example, fractional increases in the cost of living index may "sneak up" on us until we suddenly have an inflation on our hands. The same idea lies behind warnings against "creeping socialism." It also applies to progressive disorders, such as deafness, schizophrenia and brain tumor, which grow worse at an extremely slow rate. In terms of the JND, each change is so small that it does not reach the threshold of perceptibility, and therefore the condition often goes undetected until it has reached an advanced state. The term "insidious onset" is used to describe this process. *See* DETECTION THEORY, PSYCHOPHYSICS.

JUVENILE DELINQUENCY. Illegal behavior by a minor, usually a boy or girl under the age of eighteen.

At present more than one million juveniles are apprehended and over 600,000 appear before juvenile courts each year. In 1962, these young people accounted for 62 per cent of all arrests for auto theft, 51 per cent for larceny, 49 per cent for burglary, 25 per cent for robbery, 19 per cent for forcible rape, 13 per cent for aggravated assault, and 8 per cent for murder and non-negligent manslaughter. Other juvenile offenses are truancy, vandalism, arson, and use of narcotics. Male delinquents commit crimes against both property and person; females most often commit sexual offenses, run away from home, or are judged "incorrigible." Sixty per cent of juvenile offenders have been found to have prior police records.

Two significant changes are now taking place in the statistical picture of delinquency. First, the rate for girls is clearly on the rise, and many more girls are involved in offenses against property than formerly. Second, the gap between the lower and higher economic levels is closing. In a large-scale study published in 1963, Hathaway and Monachesi found that the rate for boys from professional suburban families was 25 per cent, which is only slightly below the 30 per cent rate in laboring families.

In the past, investigators have tried to discover the single factor that basically accounts for juvenile delinquency: low intelligence, delinquency area, etc. —but today most authorities agree that a combination of factors is at work in practically every case, a theory known as "multiple causation." The most significant factors can, however, be gathered around these three poles:

First, *home environment*. A broken home is considered a major factor in a large percentage of cases. An extensive study by Glueck and Glueck in 1950 showed that 60 per cent of the homes of delinquents had been broken by separation, desertion, death, or prolonged parental absence, as compared to 34 per cent of the homes of nondelinquents from the same area. Barker and Adams found about the same percentage in a Colorado study in 1962. Many of these children were raised by the mother alone; others had had to adjust to one or more stepparents as well as to their original parents.

It has also been found that many parents of delinquents are present in body but absent in spirit; they may be too concerned with their own affairs to give their children the attention and support they need. Recent research on both lower and upper socioeconomic levels has shown that the parents of antisocial boys are less affectionate and "nurturing" than the parents of boys who abide by the law. As a consequence, these boys feel frustrated and rejected, become critical of parental authority, and act out their aggressive urges without inhibition.

The father seems to be the key figure in most cases of delinquency, either directly or indirectly. In one common pattern, he is too busy or too indifferent to do his part and has the mother take over all responsibility for the boy. Since the child lacks an adequate model for masculine behavior, and is at the same time resentful of being neglected by his father, he soon begins to "prove" that he is a man by engaging in antisocial behavior. In some of these cases the mother has weakened the boy's ability to control his impulses by overindulging him. Such overindulgence may be an unconscious attempt to deny or conceal feelings of rejection toward the child. It is a well-known fact that children can usually see through such attempts.

Several other patterns involving the father have been emphasized in recent reports. Some fathers may be so rejecting that they deprive the child of any incentive to behave acceptably; so primitive in their discipline that they arouse intense feelings of resentment and hostility which are later displaced against society; or so inconsistent in handling the child (or inconsistent with the mother's approach) that the boy becomes confused about what he should or should not do. Such a child is easily misled by others.

Finally, Glueck and Glueck and O'Neal et al. (1962) have found a high incidence of definite sociopathic traits in the fathers of delinquent boys. Among them are alcoholism, shiftlessness, brutality, frequent absences from home, and criminal behavior. Their social and sexual standards have also been found to encourage their daughters in the direction of delinquency. Such fathers are, then, poor models for all their children.

A second group of factors centers around *community influences*. These include the deprived area in general, the delinquency gang, and the relatively new group of "social rejects." The highest delinquency rates have been found in deteriorated areas of the large cities where a "delinquent subculture" exists with its own values and patterns of behavior. The classic studies of Shaw and McKay in Chicago (1942) have shown that this culture persists even though the population of the area may change, provided the poverty, poor housing and crowded conditions remain.

However, more recent investigations in both the United States and England indicate that these conditions must operate hand in hand with a faulty home environment if delinquent behavior is to result. In other words, the family within the community probably has a greater influence than the community by itself. This is proved by the fact that even in the so-called delinquency areas the majority of boys and girls do not engage in delinquent behavior.

It has been found that these children come for the most part from warm, stable families in which the parents closely supervise their children, place a premium on education, and are proud of their home and reputation. Another qualification comes from the fact, as pointed out above, that antisocial behavior can be found in areas that are overprivileged as well as underprivileged. The recent rise in the suburban rate of narcotic addiction is specific evidence that harmful environmental influences and parental neglect can operate in nondelinquency as well as delinquency areas. In other words, a new concept of the deprived area is in the making, since we now realize that children can be deprived of sound home and community influences even when they are not deprived of comfort and opportunity.

It has long been recognized that juvenile gangs are an integral part of the culture in depressed and disorganized urban centers. However, contrary to popular opinion, most of these gangs have a constructive influence on their members and do not engage in antisocial activity. They provide social experience, group support, energy outlets, and recreational activities in areas that offer meager opportunities to young people. It must be recognized that delinquency gangs also meet these needs, even though their values are distorted. At the same time, they go a long way toward meeting the *special* needs of neglected, hostile young people. The delinquency gang provides them with a clear-cut, ready-made set of rules and values; a refuge from an unhappy life at home or school; a feeling of acceptance instead of rejection; a sense of identity as a member of a continuing organization; status and approval in a community of peers; and the satisfaction of loyalty to a group. The gang, then, is a source of security and meaning for these deprived youngsters. But this is not all. It also gives them a battle station for expressing resentment and fighting back at a society which they feel has repudiated them.

Vedder (1963) and others have found that adolescent male gangs currently fall into three major categories: a "criminal subculture" engaged in theft, holdups, extortion, etc., primarily as a means of obtaining income; a "conflict subculture," predominantly devoted to violent activity as a means of attaining status and group approval; and a "retreatist subculture," directed toward illicit experiences and "kicks" primarily through drugs and promiscuous sexual activity.

In view of the multiple satisfactions provided by antisocial gangs, there is little wonder that they gain a firm hold on many young people and largely replace both the family and lawful society as major influences during the crucial period before adulthood.

Gangs have been found to inflict lasting damage on girls as well as boys. Gang life serves the same purposes for them, since the gang provides them with a world of their own in which they can find security, recognition and an outlet for defiance. Many of them play subsidiary roles in male gangs, serving as lookouts or decoys, carrying concealed weapons, helping to obtain drugs. Frequently they must prove their loyalty through sexual activity with the male members. One of the most important recent developments, however, is the growth of the all-girl gang, either as a separate organization or as an affiliate of a male gang.

A new type of delinquent has recently appeared on the scene: the "social rejects." These are primarily young men in the sixteen to twenty-one age range who cannot find or hold jobs since society demands more skills and perseverance than they have to offer. They have dropped out of school because of lack of ability or motivation— and frequently because educators have not developed the kind of courses and school atmosphere that are geared to their potentialities and interests. Increasing automation has deprived them of opportunities for manual labor, and the economy cannot at present offer them enough other jobs that appeal to them. They react to this situation by feeling that they are unneeded and unwanted and by spending their time hanging around street corners and places of amusement. Some of them try to find escape in "pep pills," sexual behavior, drinking, or smoking marijuana. These activities are rarely sufficient to ease their inner tensions and afford even less outlet for their feelings of resentment. Many of them therefore go on to seriously delinquent behavior such as vandalism, stealing cars, picking fights, or beating defenseless people "just for kicks."

In addition to these major determinants of delinquency, possible biological factors have also received considerable attention. In one study (O'Neal et al., 1962) 50 per cent of the fathers and 13 per cent of the mothers of delinquents were found to be sociopathic. This finding, however, may argue for environmental influence as strongly as for heredity. Studies of twins are also inconclusive, since delinquency appears in both twins almost as often when they are fraternal as when they are identical. Even though there is little conclusive evidence of hereditary influence, one major study argues strongly for constitutional difference. Glueck and Glueck (1956) found that twice as many delinquent boys had muscular, athletic, "mesomorphic" body builds as nondelinquent boys from the same neighborhood. The investigators felt that such boys, with their high energy level and superior strength, are likely to respond to inner tensions with aggressive, "acting out" behavior. However, it should also be recognized that gangs tend to select their members on the basis of physical strength and skill.

There are many approaches to the treatment and prevention of juvenile delinquency. Most authorities believe it is extremely difficult to treat these offenders successfully within the environment that has fostered the delinquency. Some progress can be made if the neighborhood offers opportunities for constructive activities acceptable to these young people, and if the family agrees to engage in the treatment process. Unfortunately the parents are often indifferent to treatment and the community itself offers little help. Many delinquents are therefore sent to institutions.

The traditional reformatory is gradually giving way to the training school, with its primary emphasis on developing marketable skills and improved social patterns. These schools also provide consistent but nonpunitive discipline that forces the youngster to face the consequences of his actions. Group discussions and group therapy are preferred to individual psychotherapy, largely because the group experience helps to socialize the young offenders and provides motivations often lacking in an individual approach. In these sessions they air their grievances, gain insight into themselves through the experiences of others, and gradually learn how self-defeating their antisocial behavior has been. The therapists are father figures who also develop individual relationships with the boys and give them the approval, encouragement and interest that were so often lacking at home. In some residential centers the boys (or girls) live in small cottages under the guidance of a warm and understanding adult. As they show progress, they are given increasing opportunities to take responsibility and practice the art of co-operative living.

In the past few years a number of psychologists and social workers have attempted to work directly with juvenile gangs. These workers are carefully chosen for their ability to talk the language and understand the customs and attitudes of these groups. They often come from similar environments and are able to open lines of communication that are closed to other therapists. Some of them have managed to win the confidence and respect of the gang members and have been successful in influencing them to call off their "rumbles," make peace with rival gangs, and even develop normal social activities.

Psychologists and psychiatrists recognize, however, that the problem of juvenile delinquency cannot be solved by treatment procedures alone. It is a social problem—a sickness of society, not just of the individual—and only a comprehensive attack will solve it. That attack has to be mounted on at least three levels: the home, the community, and the nation. The findings of Glueck and Glueck have shown how much harm a faulty "under-the-roof culture" can do, and their investigations have also shown that a study of this internal environment can be used to identify potential delinquents below the age of six. Their technique is to compute a "social prediction score" based on such factors as home discipline, family cohesiveness, the child's personality, and parental attitudes—and they have found that such a score will predict delinquency with an accuracy of over 90 per cent. This finding strongly suggests that one of our greatest needs is the development of new approaches to parental counseling, family life education, and the relief of home tensions.

One of the most promising developments is the community-centered approach to delinquency. There is a growing conviction that each community must define its own problem and plan a concerted attack that utilizes every possible agency, facility, and type of personnel. It has already been demonstrated that improved housing will not solve the problem by itself. The same thing is true of stricter law enforcement, special employment centers, training facilities, and increased recreational opportunities. No matter how worthwhile these approaches may be, they can achieve their full effectiveness only when they are co-ordinated with an over-all community plan. The problem of delinquency is too comprehensive for a piecemeal attack.

In large cities, however, it may be most practical to supplement community-wide planning with projects specifically developed for high-delinquency areas. The multiple approach can then be concentrated on a manageable area and geared to its particular needs. An excellent example is Mobilization for Youth, which deals with such problems as school dropouts, juvenile crime, vocational training, and youth employment in the Harlem district of New York City.

Finally, since the problem of juvenile delinquency affects all areas of the country on all levels of society it must also be attacked on a national scale. In recognition of this fact the President's Committee on Juvenile Delinquency and Youth Crime was established in 1961 to co-ordinate the work of all departments of the Federal Government concerned with youth. Its purpose is to institute long-range social planning to attack the basic causes of delinquency. The emphasis is on increased educational opportunities, vocational courses for today's needs, special training projects (for example, forestry camps), youth employment centers, the improvement of slum conditions—all with the ultimate goal of helping these troubled young people find meaningful lives and become constructive members of society. See CRIME AND CRIMINALS.

Illustrative Case: JUVENILE DELINQUENCY.

Billy, age fifteen, was referred for psychological help while being held in custody for the theft of a bicycle and automobile parts. He had a history of previous thefts and other difficulties. He had always been an aggressive child. In the first grade he was sent home from school several times because he disregarded the teacher's requests and frequently hit other children. At the age of twelve he was apprehended in school taking money from some of the girls' purses. No formal charges were made at that time, and he did not get into any further difficulties at school.

There never had been any harmony in Billy's life. His father married his mother because she was expecting a child. Both parents rejected Billy from the start. There was some talk of offering him for adoption. Billy's father was dominating, strict, and unaffectionate. He never took any real interest in his son. The mother was a submissive and nervous person. She cried easily and was moody for long periods. There was constant bickering between the parents. A younger sister was the father's favorite.

As early as age three Billy began to get into trouble. He was defiant and frequently manifested severe temper tantrums. He was often negativistic and was severely punished for his misbehavior. At five he started taking pennies and nickels for ice cream and candy. From time to time he stole articles of one type or another. Later he began stealing bicycles and auto parts and selling them.

A dynamic study of Billy's behavior indicates that he always felt very insecure and inadequate. He showed his resentment by aggressive behavior even in early childhood. On the basis of his feeling of rejection he unconsciously developed the attitude that "nobody is going to hurt me anymore, and I no longer care whom I hurt." His hurts have caused him to become calloused to the feelings and welfare of others. (Katz and Lehner, 1953)

JUVENILE PARESIS. A brain disorder caused by congenital syphilis.

In the juvenile form of paresis the spirochete infection is transmitted from mother to fetus after the fifth month of pregnancy. The incubation period is about the same length as for adult paresis, and the onset of symptoms generally occurs between the fifth and twentieth years, but most frequently between the ages of ten and twelve. Prior to the outbreak of the disorder, however, about one third of these children are somewhat retarded in mental development.

The first signs of juvenile paresis are usually confusion, restlessness, and purposeless behavior. Visual disturbances, motor inco-ordination, and convulsions are also common symptoms. As the disease progresses, memory, judgment, and comprehension are increasingly impaired. Mental and physical deterioration are gradual, and the child has no insight into his condition. The apathetic, depressed, and euphoric personality reactions which characterize adult paresis do not develop in juvenile form.

The course of the disease is longer than in adult paresis, averaging about five years from the appearance of symptoms to the terminal stages in which the child becomes mute, untidy, emaciated, and finally dies. The basic treatment is penicillin, but it is less effective with the child than with the adult form of the disease.

Although juvenile paresis was at one time the major cause of stillbirths, early infant mortality, and congenital blindness, it is now relatively rare in this country. The Wassermann test for pregnant women, and the efficacy of penicillin treatment for syphilis in adults are primarily responsible for this major change. *See* SYPHILIS, GENERAL PARESIS.

Illustrative Case: JUVENILE PARESIS

Kaybee J. was admitted to the psychiatric hospital at age sixteen following a series of convulsive seizures. From that time he presented a serious management problem. The family had been unable to care for him at home, or to understand what he said. When he was taken to the Probate Court, he attempted to take off his clothes. At the hospital it was necessary to restrain him in bed because he attacked the attendants and tried to bite them. He turned his head from side to side, and mumbled unintelligibly. He was incontinent and continually soiled the bed. He did not respond to questions, although he said something about being "crazy." He was completely out of contact with his environment.

After twenty-five years, the patient is practically mute, although he makes sounds when watching television. Sometimes he becomes upset while watching the programs, and gets up and fights; otherwise he sits quietly all day long. The patient has exhibited some homosexual characteristics, and attendants find it necessary to watch him at all times. It is impossible to communicate with him. There is no judgment or insight. Occasionally the patient has convulsive seizures. (Kisker, 1964)

K

KINESTHETIC SENSE (Movement Sense). Kinesthesis, literally "feeling of movement," is the sense that provides the brain with information concerning the contracting and stretching of our muscles. This information enables us to control our movements.

Kinesthetic receptors are located in three different places. Cells in the muscles respond to stretching movements; cells in the tendons are sensitive to muscular contraction; and cells in the lining of the joints report changes in the position and movement of our limbs. Studies of abnormal functioning suggest that our basic kinesthetic cues stem from the joints.

Many people have never heard of this sense, yet it is indispensable for survival, since kinesthetic impulses provide an automatic system for maintaining posture, walking, talking, gesturing, and performing any motor activity. If this system is seriously disrupted, as in tabes dorsalis, an advanced stage of syphilis, speech is usually slurred, facial movements are unco-ordinated, and the patient walks with a stumbling gait (locomotor ataxia).

Kinesthetic cues are also responsible for our ability to distinguish light from heavy objects, to feel that the sidewalk is rough or slippery, and to walk the stairs in total darkness. All active sports and physical work are dependent on our muscle sense since it lets us know how far we are reaching, bending, or stretch-ing. We become so completely adapted to these responses that we realize they exist only when they are absent—for example, when our foot falls asleep and gives no clue to its position. We are equally unaware of the hundreds of muscular reactions that occur every minute during speech. Some speech defects, such as nasality and lisping, are corrected by first analyzing the imperfectly formed sounds and then changing the movements that produce them. A similar technique is sometimes used in overcoming a foreign accent.

Many occupations require great kinesthetic sensitivity. Dentists, pianists, surgeons, watchmakers, jugglers, and acrobats must all possess a highly developed muscle sense. Psychologists have therefore constructed a number of tests of co-ordination and control for use in vocational guidance. *See* APTITUDE TESTS (SPECIAL).

KINETIC DISTURBANCES. Used in this book to denote disturbances of movement found in either organic or functional disorders.

Akinesia is a reduction of voluntary movement ranging from moderate inactivity to total immobility. This condition is frequently observed in organic disorders of the brain, such as Pick's disease and cerebral arteriosclerosis. In a rare brain disorder known as akinetic mutism, the patient lies with closed eyes, seldom moves or eats, and fails to respond to questions or stimuli. Among functional disorders, akinesia is most often observed in catatonic schizophrenia, retarded depression, and involutional psychotic reaction. The reduction in physical activity is usually accompanied by diminished mental activity, although in some involutional and schizophrenic patients there may be a profusion of ideas despite outward appearances. In schizophrenia the symptom may have symbolic significance: a motionless patient who holds one finger aloft for hours may be warning his countrymen of their sins or might even be immobilizing the armies of the world. Somewhat similarly, patients with idiopathic epilepsy may experience a transient "twilight state" in which they assume the role of God and strike a majestic pose. See TWILIGHT STATE.

Hyperkinesia, or more usually hyperkinesis, refers to exaggerated motor activity and excessive restlessness. This symptom is also found in both physical and psychological disorders. It is one of the common effects of epidemic encephalitis. Some children classified as minimally brain damaged became so hyperactive that they are virtually unmanageable at home or in school. As to functional disturbances, children who live in a tense atmosphere often become restless and hyperactive, and in some cases they develop a character or behavior condition known as hyperkinetic impulse disorder, characterized—as the name implies—by extreme impulsiveness and overactivity.

In childhood schizophrenia and catatonic excitement, hyperkinesis tends to take the form of unending repetition of stereotyped actions, such as rocking back and forth. In the manic phase of manic-depressive reaction it usually manifests itself in a ceaseless "pressure of activity." Here the patient talks "a mile a minute," moves restlessly about, writes dozens of letters, and pours forth an endless flow of unrealistic plans and ideas. See EPIDEMIC ENCEPHALITIS, MIN-IMAL BRAIN DYSFUNCTION, MANIC-DE-PRESSIVE REACTION (MANIC PHASE), BE-HAVIOR DISORDERS, SCHIZOPHRENIA (CATA-TONIC TYPE), SCHIZOPHRENIA (CHILD-HOOD TYPE), STEREOTYPY.

The term *dyskinesia* refers to distortions of voluntary movement, a common symptom in cerebral palsy. It is also applied to involuntary muscular activities such as tics, spasms and myoclonus (sudden contraction of a muscle in the limbs, body or face occurring in certain forms of petit mal or grand mal epilepsy).

KIRKBRIDE, THOMAS (1809–83). Kirkbride, a pioneer in American psychiatry, obtained his medical degree from the University of Pennsylvania, then served as physician in several mental institutions for eight years. In 1840 he became physician-in-chief of the Pennsylvania Hospital for the Insane, remaining there for the rest of his life. The period of forty years in which he served has been called "the Renaissance of American psychiatry."

Kirkbride played an important part in this renaissance. A Quaker, he brought to the hospital the same type of "moral treatment" that had been practiced by another member of The Society of Friends, William Tuke, in England around the turn of the century. He opposed the physical procedures which were still prevalent at the time—bloodletting, emetics, restraint—and insisted that the mentally imbalanced were not "wild beasts" to be put away in an asylum, but victims of diseases that should be treated in a hospital setting. He therefore had his patients engage in occupational therapy and attend religious services, lectures, and social gatherings. In contrast to the sadistic "keepers" of the time, his attendants were kindly individuals who awakened them with a cheerful greeting each morning and handled them on a human level throughout the day. Above all, a physician spoke with each patient every day, serving as a "father figure" who treated them with courtesy and understanding but expected full co-operation in return.

Kirkbride was one of the original founders of the Association of Medical Superintendents of American Institutions for the Insane, the forerunner of the American Psychiatric Association. As secretary and later president of the association he collaborated with Isaac Ray on a series of resolutions adopted at annual meetings between 1824 and 1875. Here is a summary of these tenets, which have been termed the Magna Carta of the modern mental hospital:

Insanity is a disease—to which everyone is liable.

Properly and promptly treated it is about as curable as most other serious diseases.

In a great majority of cases it is better and more successfully treated in well-organized institutions than at home.

It is humanity, economy, and expediency for every state to make ample and good provision for all its insane.

The best hospital—best built, best arranged, and best managed—is always cheapest in the end.

A hospital should be plain, in good taste and well ventilated.

A proper classification is indispensable.

Overcrowding is an evil of serious magnitude.

Abundant means for occupation and amusement should be provided.

As little restraint as possible should be used.

The insane should never be kept in almshouses or in penal institutions.

Insane criminals should not be treated in ordinary state hospitals.

There should be a qualified physician in undivided charge of each hospital. He should be responsible to a board of trustees of high personal character and without political motives.

These resolutions focused attention on the need for adequate and efficient institutions for the huge number of mentally ill who were still being herded into county jails and almshouses. Kirkbride himself pioneered in this important field, and between 1847 and 1880 wrote a series of articles on hospital construction. His proposals, published as a book entitled *On Hospitals,* became known as the "Kirkbride Plan," and until recently served as a bible for architects of state institutions.

Kirkbride's object was to "physicalize" the human treatment of patients by providing a maximum amount of fresh air and sunshine, with full attention to plumbing, heating, fireproofing, and kitchen facilities. His general plan, which called for a central building with extended wings, was widely adopted, and his description of details became what has been called a "set of cast-iron rules" to which hospital men rigidly adhered for many decades. While these rules contributed greatly to improvement in living quarters for the mentally ill, they also encouraged construction of huge, impersonal complexes in isolated locations. *See* JOINT COMMISSION ON MENTAL ILLNESS AND HEALTH, COMMUNITY MENTAL HEALTH CENTERS, MENTAL HOSPITAL.

KLEPTOMANIA. The compulsive urge to steal; pathological stealing.

The behavior of kleptomaniacs differs from that of ordinary thieves in many ways. The great majority are women (some estimates run as high as 90 per cent), though some are boys and young men. They tend to be obsessively preoccupied with articles that have direct or indirect erotic significance—compacts, brassières, handbags—and they usually steal the same type of article repeatedly. Unlike ordinary shoplifters, they do not sell or use the stolen goods but generally accumulate them, throw them away, or send them back anonymously. They often come from financially comfortable families, have been carefully brought up, and may be well-known in the community. They do not plan their stealing, but are seized by an overpowering impulse which they usually try in vain to resist. After the stealing has occurred, they are assailed by feelings of humiliation, guilt, and remorse, and are at a complete loss for an explanation of their strange behavior.

In view of the symbolic character of the stolen articles, kleptomania is usually considered an obsessive-compulsive reaction with fetishistic overtones. As with most neurotic behavior, different interpretations may apply to different cases. In many instances the sexual aspect is particularly apparent, not only because of the symbolism, but because the act of stealing itself arouses sexual fantasies or leads to sexual gratification. The danger and excitement associated with the stealing are believed to contribute to the sexual stimulation. An extreme example is the college student William Heirens, who experienced a sexual response as he climbed through windows to steal women's underthings (the window itself is a female sexual symbol). He also collected these articles and put them on as a means of achieving sexual excitement. His deviant behavior eventually led to the sadistic murder of a six-year-old girl. *See* SADISM, FETISHISM.

Many kleptomaniacs, however, do not appear to be sexually stimulated by stealing, or to have a history of sexual difficulty. In these cases the motivation may be traced to harsh treatment or emotional starvation in childhood. The stealing is then interpreted as an act of revenge against specific symbols of parental authority—owners of stores, or the police. It may also be an expression of a more generalized hostility against society and its ethical standards and conventions. Any of these motives—sexual release, rebellion against parental figures, and general aggressiveness—may generate feelings of guilt and a need for punishment. This need, operating on an unconscious level, may explain why many kleptomaniacs are easily apprehended or continue to steal until they are caught.

It also appears that a few kleptomaniacs, like some pyromaniacs, engage in antisocial behavior and "take what they want when they want it" as a result of "poor impulse control" rather than a deeply motivated compulsive need. There may be a physical element in some of these cases, for repeated stealing is known to occur in children who have been afflicted with encephalitis or other brain disorders. It is also interesting that a woman's impulse to steal is frequently strongest during her menstrual period, possibly because of the weakening of emotional control, and possibly because of an unconscious drive to restore the reproductive cell by taking objects with sexual significance.

Illustrative Case: KLEPTOMANIA

A fifteen-year-old girl stole dresses from department stores. Investigation showed that her family was fairly well-to-do, and that it was not necessary for her to steal if she wanted dresses. But a noticeable characteristic of her thefts was that she always stole dresses that were too large for her. She realized this but could not explain it. Further investigation brought out the following facts:

Her family had originally been rather poor, and her father drank. When she was four years old her father deserted her mother, who thereupon became a prostitute. The child was sent first to one and then to another relative. This went on for many years until finally, when she was thirteen years old, an aunt and uncle (with whom she was still living) took her to live with them. They were good to her; they gave her love and affection and bought her things.

Apparently, in stealing these dresses that were too large for her, the girl was unconsciously thinking of her mother and of true "mother love." She felt that she was not getting a proper measure of love and affection; she felt that she was utterly worthless and abandoned and no one could give her the unlimited and almost illusory amount of mother love that she required. This feeling of worthlessness dated back to the time when as a young child she was unhappy at home because of her parents, and later when she was shifted about from one household to another. Now she was defiant, her attitude being: "I was made worthless, therefore I will actually be worthless and steal." Her associations showed that by stealing large-sized dresses she convinced herself that she really had a mother. (Maslow and Mittelmann, 1941)

KLINEFELTER'S SYNDROME. A rare chromosomal anomaly among males, resulting in both mental and physical defects. These individuals have three sex chromosomes, generally two X and one Y, instead of the normal one X and one Y for males and two X for females. They are usually tall and lean, with enlarged breasts, atrophied testes, and no sperm production. These characteristics are usually accompanied by severe mental retardation. *See* MENTAL RETARDATION (CAUSES).

KOFFKA, KURT (1886–1941). Koffka, the major spokesman for Gestalt psychology, received his psychological training at the University of Berlin and obtained his Ph.D. degree in 1908. Two years later he met Wolfgang Köhler in Frankfurt, where the two men were used as subjects by Max Wertheimer in pioneer studies that led to the Gestalt theory. Between 1911 and 1924 he taught at the University of Giessen, and after serving as visiting professor at the University of Wisconsin and at Cornell University, accepted a permanent position at Smith College.

Wertheimer, Koffka and Köhler are considered the co-founders of Gestalt psychology. These three, together with Hans Gruhle and Kurt Goldstein, established the journal *Psychologische Forschung* in 1921, which remained the recognized voice of the movement until publication was discontinued in 1938. Koffka, however, was the most productive of the three men who introduced the theory. Between 1913 and 1921 he published a series of studies, *Beitraege zur Psychologie Gestalt*, reporting his experimental work on per-

ception and its relation to movement. In 1921 he published a book entitled, in translation, *The Growth of the Mind*. His article "Perception: an Introduction to Gestalt Theory," which appeared in the *Psychological Bulletin* in 1932, introduced the movement to American psychologists. During the years that followed, he and Köhler expounded the theory in many universities in this country.

Koffka's contributions to the Gestalt approach culminated in the publication of *Principles of Gestalt Psychology* in 1935. In this volume he not only explained the principles which had been discovered through experiments on perception, but showed that they were applicable to a wide range of phenomena, including memory and the learning process. Boring (1950) characterizes this work as "the only attempt at a complete systematic Gestalt psychology." *See* GESTALT PSYCHOLOGY.

KORSAKOFF'S SYNDROME (Amnesic-Confabulatory Syndrome). An organic psychosis occurring primarily in chronic alcoholics and victims of severe blows on the head (head trauma) but also occasionally observed in patients with prolonged infections, metallic poisoning, and other disorders, such as pellagra and brain tumor, that involve brain damage; first described by the Russian neurologist Sergei Korsakoff (1854–1900) in 1887.

Korsakoff patients are usually older men who have been drinking excessively for many years, and the syndrome generally follows an attack of delirium tremens. In both alcoholic and head injury cases the most striking symptoms are memory defect and confabulation, but alcoholic patients are also likely to suffer from polyneuritis, an inflammation of the nerves, particularly in the legs and wrists.

The memory loss affects recent or present events primarily (anterograde amnesia). The patient may not recall what was just said to him, or recognize pictures and faces he saw a moment before. To fill the gaps in memory, and apparently to protect himself from anxiety produced by this defect, he cheerfully invents (that is, "confabulates") fanciful tales or accepts the stories of others.

G. N. Thompson (1959) cites the case of a fifty-year-old female alcoholic who was examined on a hot summer day in a hospital room that overlooked a courtyard filled with strong-smelling refuse thrown out by other patients. The doctor asked the woman where she was, and she answered, "You are a doctor, aren't you? You must be the ship's doctor." The doctor: "When did you get aboard the ship?" The woman: "Yesterday in San Francisco. See, we are coming into New York harbor now." When asked if she enjoyed the trip, she took a deep breath of the odorous air, and replied, "Oh, yes, isn't this sea breeze refreshing!"

In the alcoholic cases, Korsakoff's syndrome is not due to an excess of alcohol but a severe lack of Vitamin B, since the alcoholic's diet is usually unbalanced. This deficiency causes damage to cerebral and peripheral nerve fibers. Treatment consists of discontinuance of alcohol, liberal injections of Vitamin B, and an enriched diet. If neural damage has not been extensive, improvement occurs within six or eight weeks; but in some instances there are lasting signs of intellectual, emotional, and ethical impairment. *See* CONFABULATION, PELLAGRINOUS PSYCHOSIS, BERI BERI.

Illustrative Case: KORSAKOFF'S SYNDROME

This forty-one-year-old male was admitted to the hospital after having been sent to a convalescent home as a chronic alcoholic, where he had spent approximately one month. On the night of his hospital admission he had apparently unscrewed the light bulb in his room, cut his wrist with it after breaking it, and subsequently wandered out into the street in his nightclothes. He had

been disoriented and hallucinated and had talked about suicide. He was picked up by the police and brought to the hospital.

At the time of admission he was found to be poorly nourished, dehydrated, and extremely weak. His speech was irrelevant and incoherent. His general physical condition was poor and cor pulmonale (heart-lung disease) was diagnosed secondary to emphysema. The patient was so ill that he was put on the critical list. However, he gradually began to improve and in four or five days became oriented as to person but still was disoriented as to time and place. He gave the date four years ahead of its proper time and yet named as President of the United States one who had been in office six years previously. He was unable to tell what hospital he was in and often called it the "medical and clerical hospital." He said that he had been in the hospital for three weeks on one occasion, three months on another occasion, and overnight on still another. He would relate that the previous night he had been out for a walk with his friends. He went on to deny vehemently that he ever drank anything: "I want that understood. I never touch that stuff." From time to time he would count the coins in his empty hand. On two or three occasions he complained that he saw snakes under his bed but said that he "saw no more than anybody else does." He explained at great length that the lacerations of his wrists, which were actually produced by cutting them with a light bulb, were the result of his girl's having rubbed her head against his wrist and scratched him with an ornament in her hair.

For the next few days the patient talked incessantly about someone being after him. He elaborated the idea that he was in prison. From time to time he kept calling for the "housekeeper" or the "waitress." At other times he wanted to know where "Joe" was, particularly at times when he wet or soiled himself. He gave his occupation as engineer, manager of a large automobile company, vice-president of a railroad, and carpenter, along with several other such fabrications. From time to time he became irritated about being kept in the hospital and said, "I'm going to the Supreme Court about this matter."

There were occasional evidences of further visual hallucinations when he saw "little tractors" on the floors and walls. He was capable of identifying simple objects presented to him but often fell asleep during an interview. His attention span was extremely short. When he could be gotten out of bed he showed a marked ataxia and walked with a broad base, pushing his feet along the floor. It was necessary to give him some support in his attempts to walk. Neurological examination revealed positive Babinskis and Oppenheims, (foot reflexes indicative of nerve damage). There was diminished sensory response of his legs and a poor vibratory sense.

Treatment was essentially supportive, nutritional, and tranquilization. It became quite difficult to get him to drink water but he gradually and steadily improved. He grew somewhat more quiet and cheerful. He became continent and revealed a sense of humor that was a little bit too marked, often singing and cajoling the nurses into singing with him. He would answer questions without hesitance, although even several weeks after his admission there persisted very obvious fabrications. He was sent to the state hospital where he continued a marginal adjustment. (English and Finch, 1964)

KRAEPELIN, EMIL (1856–1926). Kraepelin, the great classifier of mental illnesses, was born in Neustrelitz, Germany and studied medicine at Würzburg and Munich. He then went to Leipzig, where he continued his training in Wilhelm Wundt's psychological laboratory. Between 1885 and 1891 he served as professor of psychiatry at the University of Dorpat, then occupied the same position at Heidelberg (1891–1903) and Munich (1903–26). As a result of his efforts, Heidelberg became a world famous psychiatry center, and Munich founded its Research Institute for Psychiatry, which he headed from its inception in 1917.

In his research work, Kraepelin extended the experimental method, which he had learned from Wundt, to the study of psychopathology. In one of his early investigations, he and his assistants induced mild mental disorders through alcohol, fatigue, and hunger, then applied a word association test to study

the effects of these disturbing influences. The results showed an increase in superficial responses which had little or no relation to the stimulus word. Some of Kraepelin's assistants believed this method could be used as a diagnostic tool, but he did not entirely agree. The technique, however, greatly influenced Jung in his application of the test to the study of psychoneurosis. See WORD ASSOCIATION TEST.

Kraepelin did pioneer work on the effects of bromides, formaldehyde, ether and other drugs on mental processes. He also performed experiments on the physiological reactions involved in surprise, expectation and disappointment, as well as on the depth of sleep. In addition, he and his assistants carried out the first studies ever made on fatigue and recovery from fatigue, including the effect of work pauses on mental efficiency. From these investigations, Kraepelin formulated the concept of the work curve and showed how it is related to fatigue and other factors that affect efficiency. See WORK CURVE, FATIGUE.

But Kraepelin is best known for his contributions to the classification of mental illnesses. In fact, medical historians frequently refer to the period in which nosology—that is, naming and classifying diseases—became a major concern in psychiatry as the "Kraepelin era." His first book in this area, published in 1883 at the age of twenty-seven, was *Textbook of Psychiatry*. He revised this work periodically, and by the ninth edition, published a year after his death, it had grown from a brief compendium to a two-volume work of 2425 pages. During this entire period, covering over forty years, Kraepelin sought to apply the techniques of the natural sciences to psychiatry, examining thousands of case studies and grouping together the patients who showed similar symptoms. From these studies he made sweeping generalizations and set up various classifications. In so doing, he virtually ignored individual variations and concentrated almost wholly on the average clinical picture. He rarely concerned himself with ideological factors or with the inner, personal life of the patient, since his sole objective was to fit his cases into one or another category according to their symptomatology.

This emphasis must be viewed in the light of history and in relation to Kraepelin's basic assumptions. From as far back as Hippocrates, the medical profession had to fight its way into the domain of mental illness, an area that had been appropriated by philosophy and theology. Toward the middle of the nineteenth century, the German psychiatrist Wilhelm Griesinger attempted to show that medicine had a right to deal with these disorders since, in his view, they were entirely due to organic brain disease. Kraepelin accepted the somatic viewpoint and sought to establish mental illness even more firmly within the discipline of medicine by compiling detailed descriptions and classifications and by stressing diagnosis and prognosis. His system recognized two major categories, to which he "officially" attached the names dementia praecox and manic-depressive psychosis. Paranoia was considered a separate disease. See HIPPOCRATES, GRIESINGER, DESCRIPTIVE PSYCHIATRY, ORGANICISM.

The various forms of dementia praecox were described in 1893, and were attributed to an organic brain change which arose from within the organism (i.e., endogenous) and resulted in gradual deterioration. This condition, according to Kraepelin, was incurable, and as a consequence hospitals rarely attempted to treat these "hopeless" cases. Many investigators protested against his negative prognosis, but no alternative interpretation of the disease was presented until Eugen Bleuler came on the scene. See BLEULER, SCHIZOPHRENIC REACTIONS (GENERAL).

In his description of manic-depressive reactions, Kraepelin noted that attacks of elation and depression run a cyclical course. In some cases these attacks alternate between elation and depression, in others there is a series of manic or a series of depressed states. He observed that the patient was usually normal between these episodes, and concluded that they must be caused by external (i.e., exogenous) factors. In contrast to dementia praecox, he believed this disorder did not lead to organic deterioration and was therefore curable.

In his attempts to achieve a thoroughgoing organic interpretation of mental disorder, Kraepelin considered personality factors mere by-products of a diseased brain or faulty metabolism. He has therefore been criticized for offering a "depersonalized" approach which systematized the patient himself out of the picture: "It reduced man to a system of organs, and mental disease to a process of predestined course" (Zilboorg and Henry, 1941). This point of view was soon to be challenged by the psychodynamic approach to human personality, which put the emphasis on individual cases and functional interpretations.

KRAFFT-EBING, RICHARD VON (1840–1902). Krafft-Ebing, chiefly noted for his study of sexual pathology, was born in Mannheim, Germany, and studied at Prague, Heidelberg, and Zürich. After serving as assistant physician at the "lunatic asylum" at Illenau, he directed the electrotherapeutic clinic at Baden-Baden and later became professor of psychiatry at the universities of Strasbourg and Graz. He served as director of the National Insane Asylum at Graz between 1873 and 1889, and was then appointed professor of psychiatry at the University of Vienna, later returning to Graz to work in his own private sanatorium.

Among Krafft-Ebing's earlier publications were treatises on forensic psychopathology and criminal psychology, which became standard texts at the time. Four of his other works became available in English translation: *An Experimental Study in the Domain of Hypnotism* (1889), *Psychopathia Sexualis* (1892), *Psychosis Menstrualis* (1892) and *Textbook of Insanity* (1905). His name is primarily associated with the *Psychopathia Sexualis,* in which he presented clinical descriptions of sexual pathology. The work was a revolutionary contribution at the time, for during the strait-laced Victorian age the subject of sexuality was taboo in polite society and had been almost completely ignored by the medical profession as well. Its chief importance, as Zilboorg and Henry (1941) point out, was in protesting against this omission and in drawing attention to the fact that the "lower instincts" of man clamor for an outlet.

Krafft-Ebing's treatises, along with the work of Nacke, Forel, Weininger, and Havelock Ellis, documented the many forms which the sexual drive can take, and their effect on human relationships. At the same time, the literary works of De Maupassant, Zola, Nietzsche, Ibsen, Shaw, and Proust also reflected the growing attempt to break through the rigidity and intolerance of the age, and to explore the inner needs and impulses of the "bête humaine" on both normal and pathological levels.

Krafft-Ebing also did important work on general paralysis, which later became known as general paresis. In his earlier view (1877) he cited a large number of factors as possible causes: hereditary degeneracy, dissipation (wine and sex), cigar-smoking, excessive heat and cold, head trauma, exhaustion, weak nerves, and fright, as well as menopause in the case of women. At that time he did not mention syphilis as a possible cause, although a paper on syphilis and insanity had been published by Esmarch and Jessen in 1857. Later, however, he inoculated general paralytics with syphilis and concluded that they had previously been infected with the disease since they did not react to the inoculation. This important discovery, which anticipated the Wassermann test, led to preventive measures which greatly reduced the incidence of general paresis. He also stimulated research directed toward curing syphilitic infections, which sometimes remain hidden for years and later attack the spinal cord and brain.

It is an interesting fact that Krafft-Ebing began his intellectual life as a "traditional, organically minded and purely descriptive medical psychologist" (Zilboorg and Henry, 1941), but by 1897 he had begun to be influenced by the growing recognition of cultural and psychological determinants. Yet, though he often referred to "our nervous age" as an important factor in mental disorder, he did not go far in developing this viewpoint.

L

LANGUAGE (Psycholinguistics). Language may be defined as a system of symbols with commonly recognized meanings which facilitates our thought processes and enables us to communicate with one another.

An increasing number of psychologists have devoted themselves to the study of language in recent years as a result of growing interest in the entire field of communication. This article will be devoted to (a) the form and structure of language, (b) the measurement of meaning, (c) the relation between language and thought, and (d) competing theories concerning the acquisition of language. Other aspects of psycholinguistics are discussed under INFORMATION THEORY, SPEECH DEVELOPMENT, SPEECH DISORDERS.

Form and Structure. Descriptive linguistics, the scientific study of the structure of language, deals primarily with the analysis of language into phonemes, or units of sound; morphemes, or units of meaning; and grammar, or rules of order. Every language has a basic number of phonemes varying between fifteen and eighty-five; in English there are about forty-five, corresponding roughly to the different ways we pronounce vowels and consonants. Morphemes, the smallest units of meaning, are made up of phonemes, and comprise root words, prefixes, and suffixes. There are over 100,000 morphemes in English, some of which are single ("speak"), some multiple ("unspeakable"). Rules of grammar vary considerably from language to language—for instance, the verb is always placed at the end of the sentence in German, and seldom in English. There are so many grammatical rules in English, so many ways of pronouncing the same letters and letter combinations, and so many different spellings of the same or similar phonemes that it is nothing short of miraculous that by the age of six the average child has already mastered most of the structure of the language and has developed a vocabulary of seven to eight thousand words.

Phonemes have received particularly close attention from psychologists since they are so important in the perception and understanding of speech. Studies show that during the first two months of life an American infant produces "all of the speech sounds that the human vocal system can produce, including French vowels and trills, German umlaut and guttural sounds, and many that are describable only in phonetic symbols" (Osgood, 1953). Even though only about forty-five of the sounds used by adults are considered different enough to be called phonemes, a trained linguist can distinguish more than eighty distinct sounds—"k" in keep and "c" in cool are slightly different but are regarded as different forms, or "allophones," of the same phoneme.

We do not make equal use of the forty-five English phonemes. Nine of them make up more than half of the words we use; "i" as in bit is the most frequent and "z" as in azure the least frequent sound in our language. Altogether we use more consonants than vowels, particularly at the beginning and end of words; and about 60 per cent of all sounds produced in our speech are made up of only twelve consonants. This is important because consonant sounds play a larger part than vowel sounds in understanding speech. *See* PEAK CLIPPING.

Certain combination sounds, such as "zd" and "fw," do not appear at all in English; other combinations, such as "th," are quite common. Linguistic restrictions on phoneme patterns help to prevent errors of interpretation and communication—that is, if we come across the combination fwame, we know at once that this is a typographical error. Studies show that we become so accustomed to the acceptable sequences that when nonsense syllables contain these sequences they are easier to remember than when they are made up of unlawful sequences—thus, tilb is easier to recall than tlib (Brown and Hildum, 1956). Experiments have also shown that even among the acceptable sequences, commonly found combinations are more quickly recognized than uncommon combinations—for example, in tachistoscopic presentations of eight-letter sequences, a combination like vernalit is more quickly perceived than a combination like utyehuld (Miller, Bruner, Postman, 1951).

Phonemic classifications do not tell the whole story. Electronic devices that translate sounds into pictures show that many speech sounds are slurred or distorted. There are therefore more sounds in use than the classifications indicate. Moreover, the same word is pronounced differently in different parts of the country: compare yard or bird in Bostonian and Brooklynese. In spite of these differences, we learn to decipher the different pronunciations, primarily because we are aided by the context in which the words are used.

Meaning. In language, meaning is conveyed through symbols of different types—verbal symbols, or words, which may stand for objects ("boat"), abstractions ("beauty"), or qualities ("red"); and non-verbal symbols, such as gestures (a nod of the head), directional signs, musical notes, or a five-dollar bill. Both types of symbols, verbal and non-verbal, have one thing in common: they convey meaning by reference beyond themselves, by standing for something else. The ability to manipulate symbols is the essence of thinking, since it frees us from the objects so that we can visualize, anticipate, plan, imagine, and work out problems "in our head." Although a choreographer can plan a dance routine with little or no use of language, practically all of our thinking is carried on in verbal symbols.

Most of our disagreements over meaning have to do with *connotative* rather than *denotative* words—that is, words that convey feelings, evaluations, and abstract meanings as opposed to words that merely designate observable acts or objects. Problems of meaning are particularly acute when we deal with emotionally toned words like equality, democracy, and happiness. Words of this type frequently have a profound effect on attitudes, actions, and social relationships, as indicated by the study of loaded words and stereotypes. It has been proposed that psychotherapy itself can be based on the clarification of the special meanings which the patient attaches to crucial

words and expressions. Hayakawa (1959), one of the leaders in the field of semantics—the systematic study of meaning—gives this striking example of a stereotyped expression with emotional overtones: "In spite of the fact that my entire education has been in Canada and the United States and I am unable to read and write Japanese, I am sometimes credited, or accused, of having an 'oriental mind.' Now, since Buddha, Confucius, General Tojo, Mao Tse-tung, Syngman Rhee, Pandit Nehru, and the proprietor of the Golden Pheasant Chop Suey House all have 'oriental minds,' it is hard to imagine what is meant." *See* STEREOTYPE, GENERAL SEMANTICS.

With examples like this in mind, it is hardly necessary to point out the importance of pinning down the meaning of words and, if possible, explicating them in quantitative terms. A step in this direction has been taken by Osgood and his collaborators (1952) in their development of the semantic differential. In this technique the subject is asked to rate a word along a seven-point scale representing different dimensions. Analysis has shown that the meaning of practically any term can be expressed by using three types of factors: activity (fast-slow, excitable-calm, etc.), potency (hard-soft, masculine-feminine, etc.), and evaluation (good-bad, kind-cruel, etc.). Though this method does not embrace every type of nuance of meaning, it is helpful in demonstrating similarities and dissimilarities in conceptions of the same term (*Fig. 31*) and of different terms. It has also been found useful in esthetics and attitude measurement. *See* ESTHETICS, ADVERTISING RESEARCH.

Language, thought, and culture. The semantic differential has proved a promising tool in distinguishing one culture from another—for example, the Hopi and Zuñi Indians, who have much in common, have quite a different conception of words like "coyote" and

CURIOSITY

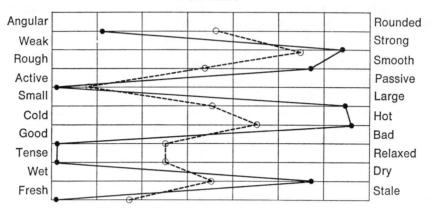

Angular										Rounded
Weak										Strong
Rough										Smooth
Active										Passive
Small										Large
Cold										Hot
Good										Bad
Tense										Relaxed
Wet										Dry
Fresh										Stale

Fig. 31. Profiles of the word curiosity according to the semantic differential, a technique for measuring the meaning of words. Note that the two conceptions differ more in degree than in kind.

"male" than the Navaho, who are culturally dissimilar to them (Maclay and Ware, 1961). This raises two questions: whether the world is conceived differently in societies which have languages of dissimilar structure, and whether the structure of the language itself shapes the way the world is conceived. Whorf (1956) answers both questions in the affirmative on the basis of his discovery that differences among American Indian languages are sometimes so great that it is impossible to translate an idea from one of these languages to another. One language, for example, might make much clearer distinctions than another between past, present, and future, or between nouns and verbs.

Today most psychologists would accept the idea of a relationship between language and ways of conceiving the world, but would hold that the experiences of a particular people determine the linguistic forms they use, and not vice versa. The most frequently cited example is the multitude of different words for different kinds of snow (drifted snow, fallen snow, etc.) among the Eskimos. The theory has also been put to experimental test. It has been found that college students recognize colors that can be named (or "coded") by a single word (red) more rapidly than colors that can only be described by using many words. This was also found to apply to Zuñi Indians, who had difficulty remembering and recognizing colors that were poorly coded in the Zuñi language but well coded in English, and the reverse (Brown and Lenneberg, 1954; Lenneberg and Roberts, 1956). Similarly, Carroll (1964) divided Navaho children living on the same reservation into two matched groups, one made up of children who spoke only English and the other only Navaho. He then found that the Navaho-speaking group tended to sort objects on the basis of shape and form more often than the English-speaking group, presumably because the Navaho language has far more special words for form than does the English language —for example, a single word for round-thin, and another for long-flexible.

Acquisition of language. There are two major ways of explaining the acquisition of language: the learning theory approach and the generative approach. The learning theorists claim that the entire process of learning words and meanings can be explained by the principles of conditioning. They hold that the child learns to apply the word "dog" to a familiar animal by the standard process of classical conditioning described by Pavlov—that is, by hearing the mother repeat the word whenever the child sees that particular animal. Later, the child learns to produce a sound to designate "dog" by a process similar to operant conditioning—that is, the parents reward, or reinforce, his efforts by smiling or patting him when he says the word correctly.

Actually, the child starts out by making a huge variety of sounds, as noted above, but only learns to narrow them down to those used in his native language when the process of reinforcement or "shaping" comes into play, and when he develops the ability to hear and correct his own vocalizations (Skinner, 1957). Deaf children begin with the same ability to produce sounds as children with good hearing, but do not progress because of the lack of "feedback." The hearing child is also in a position to shorten the shaping process by directly imitating the correct production of words, while the deaf child is unable to do this unless he is given special instruction. See CONDITIONING.

A number of psychologists have challenged the Skinner approach on the ground that the process of conditioning cannot account for learning the complexities involved in comprehending and uttering phrases and sentences. They argue that these are not just strings of verbal responses but complex patterns which obey certain grammatical rules—and the child must have some inkling of these rules before he can recognize what other people say or produce meaningful sentences himself. The term "generative" has been applied to this theory because of its emphasis on rules for the production of language, in contrast to the more mechanical process of learning through feedback from the environment. As for choosing between the two theories, Hilgard and Atkinson (1967) comment, "It seems likely that in the long run both approaches may be combined to account for the process of language acquisition. Reinforcement may play the major role not only in the learning of individual words but also in the gradual development of grammatical rules. The child may try out various word forms and sequences, keeping only those that have been reinforced as correct. Once a rule has been learned, however, it can serve to generate a wide variety of responses without the aid of additional reinforcement." See REINFORCEMENT.

LASHLEY, KARL SPENCER (1890–1958). This outstanding physiological psychologist was born in West Virginia and received his Ph.D. in genetics at Johns Hopkins in 1915. He remained there for two additional years, working with the behaviorist John B. Watson and the biologist H. S. Jennings, then accepted a teaching position at the University of Minnesota (1917–26). Afterward he spent three years as research psychologist at the Behavior Research Foundation in Chicago, six years in teaching at the University of Chicago, and twenty years as professor of neuropsychology at Harvard (1935–55). Between 1942 and 1955 he also served as director of the Yerkes Laboratories in Orange Park, Florida. He was elected president of the American Psychological Association in 1929 and president of the Society of American Naturalists in 1947.

Lashley was basically a researcher who applied the behaviorist approach while avoiding the controversies over consciousness in which that school became involved: "To me the essence of behaviorism is the belief that the study of man will reveal nothing except what is adequately describable in the concepts of mechanics and chemistry, and this far outweighs the question of the method by which the study is conducted" (1923). In carrying out his research, however, he departed from the rigid behaviorist orientation by focusing attention on the functioning of the total organism rather than on the measurement of stimuli and responses. In so doing he adopted an approach that was close to the holistic viewpoint of the Gestalt school.

Although Lashley conducted important investigations in the fields of color vision, instinct, sex, heredity, conditioning, and other aspects of animal behavior, he contributed most heavily to the problem of localization of functions in the brain. Prior to the 1900s most of the research had dealt with specific localizations; for example, it had been shown that stimulation of one part of the motor cortex leads to arm movements and stimulation of another part produces leg movements. In 1907, however, S. I. Franz reported new findings that called this theory of specific localization into question. While still at Johns Hopkins, Lashley collaborated with Franz on experiments in which they had white rats go through learning experiences, and then destroyed portions of their cerebral tissue and recorded the effects both on the previously formed habits and on future learning. By this method they discovered that the same function may be mediated by two parts of the brain on different occasions. In 1917 they published a joint paper in which this revolutionary discovery was reported. *See* FRANZ.

During the 1920s Lashley carried this research further by destroying different amounts of the brain tissue and noting the effect on sensory discrimination and intelligence. In one series of experiments he compared a rat's ability to learn before and after extirpation by measuring the time and errors required to learn a maze. For another series he invented a "jumping stand," which consisted of a platform from which the rat jumped at doors on which certain signs, such as a triangle or circle, had been drawn. If the animal jumped at the correct stimulus, the door swung open and it was rewarded with food; if it made a mistake, the door failed to open and it fell into a net. *See* CONCEPT FORMATION.

The results of these experiments were described in numerous monographs and brought together in a book, *Brain Mechanisms and Intelligence,* published in 1929. In it Lashley proposed the principle of equipotentiality, an elaboration of the theory of vicarious functioning which had been anticipated by Flourens about a century before. This view holds that all parts of the nervous system are so closely interrelated that if one part is destroyed, an "equipotential" area can take over its functions. Lashley believed this to be a basic biological principle for activities such as intelligence and motor learning. In one of his experiments he destroyed part of the motor cortex of monkeys and produced a temporary paralysis of the part of the body mediated by that area. According to the earlier theory of specific localization, no recovery of function would be possible, yet Lashley showed that the lost ability actually reappeared in time, although in somewhat less efficient form.

Lashley found that the principle of equipotentiality does not apply to every function. If the visual areas of a rat's brain are destroyed, it loses its pattern vision but not its ability to discriminate brightness, since that function is mediated on a lower level. Human beings, on the other hand, need the visual cortex for both these functions. Lashley further discovered that in lower animals learning and retention depend more on the *amount* of intact cortex than on its particular location. The experiments that led to this discovery were also done on rats. Lashley first gave them an opportunity to learn how to escape from a problem box. Then he destroyed various amounts of cortex in different subjects. Up to about 15 per cent of cortical destruction resulted in no impairment of any motor or sensory task; beyond that point, the more he destroyed, the harder it was for the rats to escape from the box and to relearn the procedure.

Lashley termed the brain activity "mass action," a concept that is closely related to equipotentiality. In essence it means that large amounts of equipotential brain tissue work together in the learning and retention process, so that no matter where the tissue is destroyed, the loss in ability is in proportion to the extent of the damage. The mass action principle, however, applies far more fully to lower animals than to human beings, since there is greater localization of function in the human brain. *See* CEREBRAL CORTEX.

LATERAL DOMINANCE (Laterality). Predominance of one side of the body over the other, resulting in the preferred use and superior functioning of either the left or the right side as a whole.

The concept of laterality arose out of the fact that positive correlations have been found between hand preference, foot preference, and eye preference. These three functions, however, are not equally related: hand and foot dominance are more closely associated than hand and eye dominance.

About one out of three people are right-handed and left-eyed or left-handed and right-eyed. This situation is termed "crossed dominance." Dominance is said to be "incomplete" when no established preference is shown for either side. The term "mixed dominance" includes both crossed and incomplete dominance, and is thought to be one of the causes of both reading disability and stuttering.

Lateral dominance can be tested with readily obtainable materials. In the Harris Tests of Lateral Dominance, hand dominance is determined by ball-throwing, hammering, cutting with scissors, dealing cards, writing, etc.; eye domi-

nance, by looking through a kaleidoscope and sighting a rifle; foot dominance, by kicking or pretending to stamp out a fire. Ear dominance has been found in many cases but is considered relatively unimportant. *See* READING DISABILITY, DIRECTIONAL CONFUSION, HANDEDNESS, STREPHOSYMBOLIA.

LAW OF CONTIGUITY. A principle of learning which states that to establish an association between two events, they must be experienced close together in time and space.

The principle explains how we learn that thunder follows lightning, that fire is hot, or which word follows which in memorizing a poem. It also applies to classical conditioning in which a previously neutral stimulus takes the place of the original stimulus in producing a response. In all these instances two events are repeatedly associated in time, place, or both, and this establishes a connection between them in our minds. As a result, the first becomes a signal for the second—that is, when lightning flashes, we wait to hear the thunder. It is important, however, to emphasize the closeness of the association. If thunder followed lightning after a long interval, we would not readily associate them. Likewise, if the old and new stimuli are more than one half second apart in conditioning the experiment rarely works.

Contiguity is particularly applicable in learning a sequence of any kind (serial learning). When we recite a speech or play a composition on the piano, each response becomes a stimulus for the response that was contiguous with it in the original learning situation. "Four score and" brings to mind "seven," which in turn calls forth "years ago" and so on. We also make practical use of this principle in jogging our memory. If we have mislaid a pair of gloves, we attempt to reconstruct our activities in sequence; and if we cannot remember a historical fact, we try to think of other events that occurred at the same time or place. Sometimes we have to go through a long chain of associations before we succeed in recalling the fact we want. A similar technique is sometimes used in restoring the memory of amnesia victims. *See* AMNESIA (DISSOCIATIVE TYPE).

Although contiguity is undeniably important in explaining the learning process, many investigators believe it does not work by itself. They point out that another factor is required before learning occurs: motivation. Both animals and human beings appear to learn most effectively when their learning is rewarded or "reinforced." A material reward is not always necessary, for a word of approval or even intrinsic satisfaction of curiosity may be sufficient reinforcement. Intention also appears to be a motivating force, particularly in human learning. In meeting a person for the first time, we glance at his face and hear his name, but we may not establish an association unless we have the *intention* of learning his name (and even then we may fail to recall it). This suggests that there is a certain amount of selectivity in establishing associations between contiguous events. On the other hand, some psychologists maintain that we also acquire many incidental facts without any need or motivation. *See* INCIDENTAL LEARNING, CONDITIONING, STIMULUS-RESPONSE ASSOCIATION, STIMULUS-STIMULUS ASSOCIATION, ASSOCIATIONISM, PAIRED ASSOCIATES LEARNING, REINFORCEMENT.

LEADERSHIP. A leader is an individual who plays a key role in mobilizing and directing a group of followers.

Today, as always, society places a high premium on individuals who have the ability to direct businesses, government institutions, political parties, and community services. In fact, more and more effort is being expended on "executive search" and "management development" than ever before. On an-

other level, the importance of leadership is attested by the Communist attempt to brainwash prisoners during the Korean War. One of the first steps in this process was to remove the officers and segregate emergent leaders who arose from the ranks to take their place. Without leaders to give them confidence and support, many of our men found it extremely hard to maintain their morale and keep their perspective. *See* BRAINWASHING, MANAGEMENT DEVELOPMENT, PRISONER OF WAR REACTIONS.

The early psychological studies of leadership made two assumptions. First, the investigators felt that "genuine leaders" possessed a set of personal qualities that gave them a special capacity to lead; and second, they believed that these qualities enabled them to function as leaders in any and all situations. Neither of these assumptions is accepted today. The search for a single set of leadership traits led to little more than arbitrary lists presented by different authors. One would emphasize resourcefulness, initiative, and decisiveness; another would stress persuasiveness, rapport, and verbal facility. The lack of consensus had one positive effect, however. It led to the realization that different types of situations require different approaches—for instance, a leader who is constantly facing new situations must approach his job differently from a leader who is merely carrying on the traditions of an organization. For this reason the search for a single set of leadership traits has been all but abandoned.

As time went on, psychologists and sociologists also began to realize that the emphasis on the personality of the leader gave a one-sided picture of the total process. When they observed different groups in action, they found that the leader did not always initiate activities by himself, and that his effectiveness depended as much on the structure of the group as on his own personal qualities. This did not eliminate the personality of the leader as a factor, but it put the emphasis on the interaction between the leader and his followers instead of viewing them in isolation from each other. As Tannenbaum and Massarik (1957) point out, "The *personality of the follower* (as it manifests itself in a given situation) becomes a key variable with which the leader must deal. The needs, attitudes, values, and feelings of the follower determine the kinds of stimuli produced by the leader to which the follower will respond. The *personality of the leader* (also manifesting itself in a situation) influences his range of perception of follower and situation, his judgment of what is relevant among these perceptions, and hence his sensitivity to the personality of the follower and to the situation. The leader's personality also has impact on his behavioral repertoire (action flexibility) and his skill in selecting appropriate communication behaviors."

Another investigator, Gibb (1954), has also lent support to the view that no consistent pattern of leadership traits has yet been found, though he does not rule out the possibility of finding such a pattern in the future. He makes the point that an individual functions as a leader in a particular situation if he has personality characteristics that make it possible for the *members* of the group to contribute to the achievement of a group goal. Secord and Backman (1964) hold, similarly, that leadership behavior consists in actions that are "functionally related to goal achievement or to the maintenance and strengthening of the group," adding that such behavior is engaged in to a varying degree by *all* members of the group. However, due to the fact that there is "role differentiation" in most groups, certain members initiate more than their share of communication and also direct a larger portion of their comments and efforts to the group as a whole. Since they are therefore in a more directive

capacity, they are recognized by the other members as leaders. While recognizing the existence of leaders, this point of view eradicates the traditionally sharp line between leaders and followers since it emphasizes the important contributions which the followers make to the total process.

Another recent emphasis is the distinction between two types of leadership roles (Bales, 1958). The "task specialist" organizes the group and directs its activities toward the achievement of a specific goal; the "social specialist" maintains group morale and harmony, often helping to release tensions arising from work activities. The task specialist is more emotionally distant from the members of the group, largely because this is necessary for efficient performance of his role as "task master." Ideally the two functions maintain a state of equilibrium which permits the group to pursue its goals effectively.

These two functions may be carried out by the same person or by different persons. They are likely to be allocated to different persons when questions of power, status, values, and communication are unsettled, or where there is a great deal of hostility toward the leader. This makes it necessary for one individual to devote himself fully to the relationships within the organization, while another carries on its activities. On the other hand, the two leadership roles are less ·likely to be divided when the group accepts the leader as legitimate, when either task accomplishment or the problem of human relations is especially important for all members of the groups, or when responsibility and participation in decisions are widely distributed.

Secord and Backman also point out that the balance between the "rewards and costs" involved in leadership determines whether individuals are motivated to perform this function, and the degree to which others allow or invite them to do so. The leader gains rewards from both the satisfaction of the leadership activity itself and from helping to realize group goals; his costs include the extra time and effort he must expend, his heavy burden of responsibility, anxiety over failure, the unpleasantness involved in being the butt of criticism and blame, and, at least in the task role, the necessity of maintaining emotional distance from the group. Rewards of followership include goal achievement, satisfaction of dependency needs, identification with a strong leader, and freedom from extra responsibility and other burdens assumed by the leader. These are balanced against lower status, less control over activities, and the rewards which accrue to the leader. Like the characteristics of leadership itself, all these rewards and costs vary with the situation and with the goals, skills, and personalities of the individuals involved.

Two other points on the nature of leadership are worth noting. First, leadership tends to maintain and perpetuate itself, particularly in successful groups where all members experience rewards. The leader's position tends to be stabilized by the communication, status, and power relationships that develop in such groups. Furthermore, his position gives him an advantage over others because he has special opportunities to improve his leadership skills and perform his functions more effectively. Second, even though no consistent set of leadership traits has been found, there is evidence that leadership has some generality across groups. Studies show that task leaders often do well in a wide variety of groups that require organizing skill and the ability to maintain emotional distance. Social leaders also do well in many different groups where effective functioning depends upon constructive personal relationships between all members. *See* GROUP DYNAMICS.

LEAD POISONING. Lead poisoning is the most frequent type of metallic intoxication, and usually produces the most severe mental symptoms. It is classified by the American Psychiatric Association (1952) under brain syndromes resulting from drug or poison intoxication. Children are more frequently afflicted than adults. Child cases are usually due to chewing on lead-painted toys or eating flakes of paint from walls; adult cases, to inhalation while engaged in paint-spraying, soldering, enameling, or metal salvage operations.

Early symptoms include weakness, listlessness and irritability in all victims, but children are also likely to vomit, cry continuously, and become fearful. Severe intoxication usually results in a sudden and acute delirious state involving confusion, insomnia, tremors, violent outbursts, hallucinations, and convulsions. An episode of this kind may, in some cases, be followed by coma and death. Chronic poisoning produces depression, forgetfulness, confabulation, impaired judgment, loss of self-control, and progressive mental deterioration. Children who survive lead poisoning usually suffer from irreversible brain damage and consequent mental retardation.

There is no known antidote. Therapy is directed at the relief of symptoms and the elimination of lead from the body through medications that increase the output of water. *See* BRAIN DISORDERS.

Illustrative Case: LEAD POISONING

Walter F. is a twenty-six-year-old man who developed normally until age two and a half, at which time he had convulsive seizures, vomiting, and lethargy. He was hospitalized for three months and given a diagnosis of lead encephalopathy. When he returned home, the patient did not talk until he was five years old, although prior to the convulsions he had learned to talk, walk, and had developed other motor skills usual at that age. For some months, the patient showed sudden periods of crying and extreme fear reactions. The child was not admitted to public school because of his deficiencies. He remained home where he was somewhat undependable. Generally he enjoyed being with people but often he was hostile and rebellious. He spent most of his time watching television.

When the patient was twenty-two, he had a series of severe seizures and some months later became increasingly moody, irritable, and difficult to manage. Shortly before his hospitalization, he had a severe seizure during which he injured his head and had to be hospitalized. He was restless, confused, and complained that nothing looked the same to him. At times he seemed incoherent. When he returned home, he showed wide mood swings, became increasingly belligerent and unmanageable, talked to himself, and showed a pressured speech. Since the family could not manage him, he was admitted to the psychiatric hospital.

At the time of the initial examination, the patient was found to be a somewhat disorganized man who appeared younger than his age. When he came into the examining room, he was suspicious, and asked, "Well, what's going to happen now?" During the examination the patient displayed many mannerisms, especially involving his hands. He would stop talking suddenly and scratch the left side of his face, rub the back of his head, stand up, turn around, and rub his buttocks. He was impulsive and unpredictable. For a while he would sit quietly, and then he would get up, pace the floor restlessly, or come close to the examiner and look down in a glowering and challenging way. His gait was awkward, and his face occasionally broke into a frozen, wide-mouthed, toothy smile. (Kisker, 1964)

LEARNING AIDS. In recent years there has been a vast increase in the variety of available materials and techniques designed to enhance the learning process. The traditional blackboard, textbook, workbook, and chart are now being supplemented by films, closed-circuit television, recordings, tapes, slides, film strips, games, and teaching machines.

Though expanding school enrollments and teacher shortages are often given as the prime motivation for wide-scale use of these aids, an even more important reason lies in the more effective application of the principles of learning—principles such as the use of interesting and dramatic materials to increase motivation, reinforcement through repetition of material in different forms, multisensory stimulation, and greater opportunity for active participation by the student.

The development of new learning aids has also been advanced by several other factors: closer collaboration between educational psychologists and technologists such as film producers and electronic experts; the need of the armed forces for quick and efficient instruction; congressional appropriations which enable the schools to acquire new materials; and the growing interest of large companies in this new "industry."

Considerable psychological research has been devoted to the development and assessment of these materials and processes, as exemplified by the following representative studies from the fields of film and television. Though many investigations have shown that carefully chosen films can stimulate learning, it has been found that presentations which elicit active participation and practice are superior to those providing only passive review (May et al., 1947); and when the speaker addresses the viewer directly—as in telling how to tie different kinds of knots —the effectiveness is further enhanced (Zuckerman, 1952). In a study of the effects of different kinds of commentaries (the subject was meteorology) Nelson and Vandermeer (1953) found that technical and numerical data were most successfully learned through a combination of pictures with sound in which the commentator used vivid verbal expressions, repetition, and the device of directing attention to specific aspects of the picture. A study of the effectiveness of animated cartoons as compared to well-written and well-illustrated manuals in conveying information on flexible gunnery has been conducted by the Army Air Force. The results demonstrated that the films taught "fifty percent more facts per person per minute" and were especially effective with the slower learners (Gibson, 1947).

Television presentations have a number of general advantages: students are intrigued by the medium; fuller use can be made of the best teachers and teaching techniques; the change from ordinary classroom activities is stimulating; and quality instruction can be brought to deprived areas. Various investigations have shown that when informational presentations are preceded and followed by discussion and individualized instruction, the over-all results are about the same as with ordinary classroom lectures and demonstrations. *See* TELEVISION EFFECTS.

Though television instruction is carried out primarily in city school systems, a few experiments in college teaching have been conducted. In a study performed at Iowa State University a college credit course on psychology was presented, with the viewers divided into five groups: one group watched at home, another came into the studio, a third watched films of the television talks (kinescopes) followed by twenty minutes of informal discussion, and two campus classes (the control groups) covered the same material in the usual classroom manner. The results showed that the kinescope-discussion group profited most, followed by the TV-at-home group, although the kinescope group felt that the presentations were less personal and interesting than the instructor's live presentation in the classroom. (Husband, 1954)

One of the most promising of the newer teaching methods is "computer-assisted instruction," also called "computer-based learning," which has been used for research purposes at Stanford University. This technique employs an automated-instruction device in teaching such subjects as mathematics and beginning reading. Quite briefly, it consists of a presentation of programmed material of the "branching" variety—but the apparatus is far more complicated than the usual teaching machine. Instead of turning a roll or pressing a button to bring the next frame into view, the student sits in front of a cathode-ray tube wearing earphones, and a computer instructs a microfilm device to project an image on the tube while simultaneously playing an auditory message.

The student responds to the message, which usually consists of a test question, by pressing the keys of an electric typewriter or by touching the surface of the tube with an electronic pencil. This response is fed back into the computer for evaluation. If it is correct, the computer moves on to the next instructional item; if it is incorrect, it automatically evaluates the type of error made and branches into appropriate remedial material. The computer also records both the student's progress and his particular difficulties. If he proves to be slow and halting, he is branched back for review; if he learns rapidly, he is branched ahead at a fast pace or is branched out to special enrichment materials designed to maintain his interest. The result is a flexible system which automatically adjusts itself to the needs of the individual child (Suppes, 1966; Atkinson and Hansen, 1966). *See* PROGRAMMED LEARNING.

A second automated-instruction device is the Edison Responsive Environment (ERE) System, a computer-controlled "talking typewriter" developed by Omar K. Moore and The Thomas A. Edison Research Laboratory. The machine teaches reading by presenting letters, symbols, words, sentences, or pictures on a screen in front of the child, and at the same time pronounces, spells, and explains them. As he sees a particular letter, the child presses the corresponding key symbol on the typewriter (all other keys are automatically blocked) in order to see it typed and hear it spoken. This multisensory activity method has proved effective in the preschool and early school years, as well as with retarded children and youngsters from underprivileged environments.

In a significant test conducted in the Freeport, New York, public schools, an experimental group of twenty five-year-old kindergarten children were carefully matched in intelligence, sex, race, socioeconomic status, and other characteristics with twenty other children who served as a control group. After five months and an average exposure to the instrument of less than thirty hours per child, the self-taught experimental group far outstripped the control group, even though the latter group was taught by exceptionally well-equipped teachers in enriched classrooms. The mean difference between the two groups was 1.7 months at the end of the period. Moreover, children with more limited intelligence advanced at the same relative rate as the brighter children, and the scores of the children from underprivileged environments were indistinguishable from those of the remainder of the group. Other tests have shown that the ERE may be of considerable value in teaching handicapped children, particularly the cerebral-palsied, the hard of hearing, and the autistic.

Finally, a number of special courses and teaching devices have been developed for improving the reading skills of older students and adults. Among them are the Speed Reading Institute Home Study Course devised by Allan Sack and Jack Yourman, the SRA (Science Research Associates) material for school use, and the Rutgers University-Book-of-the-Month Club Reading Skills Program for home study. These courses are aimed at improving reading rate and reading comprehension at the same time, and unlike some highly publicized courses, do far more than increase the student's ability to skim. The average adult reading rate is a hopelessly inadequate 200 to 250 words per minute, little more than the rate of an eighth-grader—but this rate can usually be doubled or even tripled through the practice provided by sound courses. Studies show that even individuals who start at a fairly rapid rate, such as 450 w.p.m., can frequently double their rate—and contrary to popular opinion, these rapid readers usually show greater comprehension than the slow, plodding type.

A comprehensive approach is employed in these courses, involving exercises and self-tests in vocabulary, grasping the main idea and its relation to supporting facts, reading thoughts rather than words, rapid scanning, and spotting specific data. Some use a pacing device which moves a bar down the page at a regulated speed; others find this unnecessary. A major feature of these courses is training in flexibility, the ability to adjust the reading process to different kinds of material and different purposes. Such training helps the student overcome the habit of reading novels or newspapers at the same rate as scientific articles and memos. A second feature is the self-diagnosis of the more common reading defects, such as backtracking and mouthing words, and the use of special exercises designed to alter these habit patterns.

A word must be said about the extravagant claims being made in this field. One course promises the student a reading speed of 2000 to over 6000 words per minute, with complete understanding, based on practice in reading "vertically" rather than "horizontally." A report by Spache (1962), past president of the International Reading Association, cites scientific evidence against this claim. He shows that it is "impossible to read faster than 800 to 900 words per minute," in view of the fact that we can read only when the eye is fixated, the maximum number of words the eye can see at one fixation (2.5 to 3 words), and the total time taken by these fixations plus the sweep or "saccade" to the next fixation and the return sweep to the next line. Studies carried out by Spache have indicated that students trained in so-called vertical reading showed a small average gain but did not achieve exceptional speeds. They averaged 400 to 600 w.p.m., with a maximum of 900 w.p.m.—and when they skimmed at higher rates, their comprehension fell to 50 per cent.

LEARNING CURVE. A graph showing the rate of progress in learning. The curve actually shows changes in

performance after practice, and learning is inferred from these results.

Distances along the base line of the graph represent units of practice, blocks of trials, or intervals of time; distances along the vertical axis show the proficiency of performance. The shape of the curve depends on the behavior studied, the criterion for proficiency, and the subject's initial ability—that is, how much improvement is possible at the start of the experiment.

There are several types of learning curve (*Fig. 32*). In *curves of equal returns,* the upward "curves" are straight lines, indicating that amount of improvement on early and later trials remains the same. Such curves

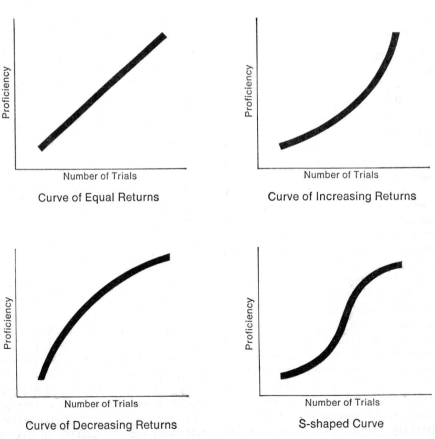

Fig. 32. Common forms of learning curves, showing changes in proficiency due to practice.

are rarely found in lengthy learning procedures, since continued practice seldom results in a steady, regular increase in performance. *Curves of increasing returns,* or "positive acceleration," indicate that each practice trial brings more improvement than the one before it. This often occurs for a short period at the outset, but rarely later on. *Curves of decreasing returns,* or "negative acceleration," apply to most learning procedures. They indicate that the greatest amount of improvement occurs during the early trials; after that the curve shows diminishing returns that continue until a point where further practice ceases to bring improvement.

The three curves often reflect different stages of the same learning situation. In the early stages of a task, when there is great room for improvement, practice will lead to increasing returns. After that there may be a short period of equal returns, and then a curve of diminishing returns can be expected. Since all three types of curve apply, they can often be combined into a *single S-shaped curve* to cover the entire learning process.

The study of learning curves has brought us much useful knowledge about the dynamics of learning. They have demonstrated, for example, that progress in learning is never entirely smooth. Distractions, enthusiasm, fatigue, temporary variations in external and internal environment—all affect performance and result in fluctuations in the learning curve. Lapses are to be expected even in tasks that have almost been mastered. Many adolescents become unduly discouraged in scholastic and social learning when a lapse appears—a poor grade or single unhappy social experience is taken as a crushing defeat. They must learn to expect these "low points in the curve" and take them in stride. Everyone is entitled to a "bad day"; the important

index is the upward trend over the long run.

The curves have also helped to show that no matter how strongly we may be motivated to learn, there is some point beyond which we will not progress even if we apply the most efficient techniques and the most industrious practice. For motor tasks such as typewriting this is called the physiological limit, since it is determined by the speed of nerve conduction and muscle contraction. Each individual has his own physiological limit for each task.

There also appear to be physiological limits for mankind as a whole. Few people have run the mile in under four minutes and no one has run it as fast as three and a half minutes despite determination, effort, and endless practice. Yet we have to be cautious about stating what these limits are. Several years ago the four-minute mile and seventy-foot shot-put were considered "physiologically impossible," yet today they are a reality.

Most of us reach our physiological limits in simple manual or intellectual tasks in a short time, but we must recognize that the more complex skills involved in such activities as mathematics, physics, chemistry, or chess have no apparent limits. Here further learning may even be easier as we continue, since it is based on prior knowledge. The curve may therefore be one of increasing returns.

LEARNING DURING SLEEP. The idea of learning while asleep is of considerable interest to scientists in their exploration of thinking processes. It is also attractive to practical-minded people who see it as an opportunity to utilize this "wasted" one third of life.

Early studies by Leuba and Bateman (1952) appeared to yield positive results, but more recent investigations have been clearly negative. In one of these experiments, EEG electrodes were attached to the heads of the subjects, and when the brain wave impulses indicated that they were deeply asleep, a tape recorder played a list of ten nouns repeatedly. In the morning the subjects were asked to select these nouns from a list of fifty. The same list was shown to a control group who were told that they were participating in an extrasensory perception experiment; they were asked to identify ten nouns which the experimenter had chosen. There was no significant difference in the scores of the two groups (Emmons and Simon, 1956). Two other studies, by Hoyt (1953) and Stampfl (1953), have also yielded negative results.

The discrepancy between these findings and Leuba's original results is believed to be due to the fact that the earlier subjects were only half asleep when the material was read to them. There is good evidence that some material can be acquired during this stage between sleeping and waking. The question is whether a significant amount can be retained. As Munn (1966) points out, "It is perhaps worth noting that the positive results of earlier studies—perhaps of learning while in a state of drowsiness—were for the learning of relatively simple material. There is no doubt, moreover, that a comparable group of wide-awake subjects would exceed the performance of any group attempting to learn while asleep, or while in a state of drowsiness." See HYPNAGOGIC STATE.

LEARNING (GENERAL). A process in which new information, habits, or abilities are acquired; in general, any modification of behavior due to contact with the environment.

Animals and human beings are in constant interaction with their surroundings, but they may be said to learn only when certain criteria are met. The major hallmarks of learning are: (1) the contact with the environment must bring about a change in the way they think, perceive, or re-

spond; (2) this change must come about as a result of observation, practice, study, or other activity, and not by such conditions as fatigue, drugs, illness, or maturation; (3) the modification of behavior must be relatively lasting—a fact or a skill that is forgotten right after it has been acquired is not really learned. At the present time the only way we can know that anything is actually learned is by observing a change in performance—by noting that the person can ride a bicycle or recite a poem better than he could before. We do not as yet know what changes take place in the organism when learning occurs, but this information will probably be acquired as we learn more about the nervous system.

Man is more dependent on learning than the lower animals, partly because his life is more complex and partly because his behavior is less fully determined by reflexes, instincts, and physiological drives. The human being does not come into the world nearly so well equipped as the animal to satisfy his needs and cope with the situations he meets. He has to go through a prolonged infancy and childhood during which he must acquire complex habits, skills, problem-solving ability, and communication patterns which are not needed by any other organism. He even has to learn how to learn. In this whole process he also has a much greater chance than lower animals to acquire undesirable responses, and therefore must go through a great deal of relearning as well.

In spite of present ignorance of the physiological mechanisms involved, the field of learning is one of the most thoroughly studied in the whole of psychology. It covers widely different areas of experience, including motor skills like typing or factory operations; complex activities like piano or chess; attitudes, such as prejudices and feelings about capital punishment or war; social behavior, including customs and occupational or class roles; verbal learning, as in studying literature or memorizing names and dates; and the acquisition of emotional responses, such as sympathy, fear, or resentment. Each of these types will be discussed under separate headings. *See* CATEGORY INDEX.

At present it is not known whether a common set of principles applies to all these forms of learning, or whether there are several different principles. Many psychologists, however, have attempted to find a single basic concept, such as drive reduction or conditioning, which would cover the entire process. At the moment it appears that there are many different techniques for learning.

On the other hand, there is considerable agreement on many of the practical aspects of the learning process. These, too, will be reviewed under separate topics, particularly LEARNING TECHNIQUES and MEMORY IMPROVEMENT, but it might be useful to mention some of the major points in this general article. Motivation is one of the most important keys to learning. It is doubtful if any organism learns unless it is impelled by a need, faced with a problem, or lured by a reward. Moreover, increasing the motivation usually enhances the learning. Practice and repetition are generally needed to advance the learning process and make it "stick." In verbal learning this takes the form of active recitation and periodic review. It has been found that learning periods and practice periods are usually more effective when they are spaced than when they are close together. Also, it is often but not always better to break up complex or lengthy subject matter and work on it piecemeal than to try to learn it all at once. Since there is a danger of "missing the forest for the trees" it is usually best to go through the entire material quickly before studying or practicing the details. This will provide

a frame of reference and give the entire process more meaning—and the more meaningful the material is, the easier it is to learn and the longer it will stay with us.

LEARNING PLATEAU. A flat place in a learning curve, indicating a period of little or no progress (*Fig. 33*).

The occurrence and persistence of a plateau depend on the nature of the task, the motivation, the approach of the learner, and the amount of previous experience he has had. It occurs more often in tasks involving habit formation and routine practice than in complex learning that requires highly organized thought.

There are several reasons for plateaus. First, the skill being acquired may have several distinct stages, each of which must be completed before the next begins. This is particularly true where a "hierarchy of habits" must be mastered, as in studying a musical instrument. The fundamentals of piano-playing are easily learned, but after that a discouragingly long period of little or no progress (the plateau) may be encountered. Once the student gets over this period, he enters a new stage of learning where hands and fingers are integrated and he has the satisfaction of playing actual pieces. A whole series of plateaus occurs in learning to type, since the student must acquire different habits for individual letters, words, phrases, and sentences. There is usually a period of no apparent improvement during the transition from one of these levels to another.

Second, fatigue or distraction may temporarily slow up the learning process. The two often work together because tired students are easily distracted or lapse into daydreaming. Third, a previously learned skill may interfere with the one now being practiced; for example, reading teachers find that children who are used to reading aloud often find it hard to switch to silent

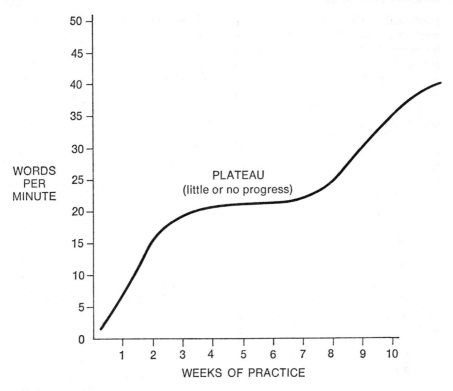

Fig. 33. A typical learning curve for typing, showing the temporary plateau that often occurs after concentrated practice. Plateaus sometimes occur at each stage or level of learning.

reading. A fourth common cause is "forced feeding" of textbooks or lectures. When new concepts are introduced too fast, learning slows down because there is insufficient time to absorb and master one phase of the subject before going on to the next. In such cases special instruction may be needed to help the student overcome the plateau. Fifth, a plateau may also reflect loss of motivation. The learner may become bored, lose interest in the task, and just go through the motions. He may also become discouraged if he is aiming too high.

The teacher who is aware of all these causal factors can usually prevent or at least shorten the plateau. One useful technique is to organize the material into a smooth progression that will minimize the gaps between the

different stages of the subject matter. Another is to anticipate periods of monotony or loss of motivation and be ready to introduce learning aids, incentives, or discussions that will excite new interest. A third strategy is to change the teaching approach or introduce different material that will give the students a rest without wasting time. Finally, it is often a good idea to discuss the slump frankly and openly with the students and give them an opportunity to make constructive suggestions.

LEARNING TECHNIQUES. It is safe to say that no subject in the entire field of psychology has received more attention than the techniques of learning. The reason is probably that many psychologists are educators and see the great need and importance of improved methods of study. Fortunately the many investigations they have conducted have led to some fairly concrete and widely accepted findings. These will be summarized under a few general headings.

Motivation. Although motivation is not itself a technique, it is a basic factor in all learning processes. The best methods in the world will have little value if the student does not have the desire and intention to learn—in fact, increased motivation will usually improve learning even when the procedures themselves remain unchanged. Extrinsic incentives such as report cards, honor rolls, and gold stars are effective with most but not all students; but studies indicate that intrinsic factors, such as interest, meaningfulness, and application to life usually have an even greater and more lasting effect. They also lead to self-motivation, which is generally superior to external motivation. Few students, however, can function in total independence of other people and without some form of external incentive.

In general, both younger and older people react more positively to approval than to disapproval, although the most effective technique is often to couple constructive criticism with encouragement. Outright punishment and caustic criticism are seldom helpful, since they create tensions, resentment, and feelings of discouragement that interfere with the learning process. Rosenthal (1968) has recently shown that academic performance may also be influenced by "teacher expectation." In one experiment, kindergarten through fifth grade pupils were given an intelligence test before the beginning of the school year, and their teachers were told that certain children were found to possess exceptional learning ability—though actually these children have been picked in advance of the test on a thoroughly random basis. A similar test was given at the end of the school

year, and it was found that the allegedly exceptional children were, on the average, considerably ahead of the others in reasoning IQ. The teachers also judged them to be more interesting, curious, appealing, and well-adjusted. These differences were apparently due to the fact that the teachers believed the selected children were brighter, and subtly and often unwittingly communicated their higher expectations to the pupils through their interest and attention, tone of voice, posture, and facial expression. As a result, these pupils came to believe in themselves and expect more of themselves—and were consequently motivated to do better work. The expectations of the teachers therefore became a "self-fulfilling prophecy"—a prediction that brings about the conditions that make it come true.

Expectancy effects apply both positively and negatively—for example, culturally disadvantaged children who are expected to do poorly tend to have a poor self-image and perform below their capacity. On the other hand, those who are expected and encouraged to do well often improve rapidly. The influence of expectation has been demonstrated not only in intellectual development but in many specific areas, such as remedial reading for retarded children, swimming ability of deprived children, classroom behavior of adolescent offenders, and symbol learning of preschool children in a Head Start program.

Instructions. Efficiency in learning can be greatly increased by giving adequate preliminary instructions. Too often students flounder and waste time because they do not know what to look for or how to organize their thinking. This can be obviated by a brief introduction to the material and a preview that will help them to establish a frame of reference and to focus on the important features of the material. A session of this kind will enable them to make better use of specific techniques such as outlining and summarizing. It will also increase motivation by making the task more meaningful.

Involvement. This factor is also closely related to motivation. The active participant learns more than the passive recipient. For this reason, group discussion methods usually prove superior to exclusive emphasis on lecturing. In one experimental study, a department head sought to increase the job-rating skill of one group of industrial supervisors by pointing out their errors, while a second group was asked to analyze their own behavior and decide for themselves where they had made mistakes. The first group failed to increase their skill, while the second improved greatly (Levine and Butler, 1952). Teachers have found many methods of involving their students more fully; among them are class projects, visits to historical sites, and individual research. One of the major principles of programmed learning is active involvement in the learning process. *See* this topic.

Knowledge of results. It has been definitely established that people generally learn faster when they know how well they are doing. Frequent quizzes and self-checks show the student where he needs extra study, and therefore help him use his time more efficiently. They also help him to consolidate and reinforce his correct responses, and keep him from repeating and confirming his mistakes. A long delay between studying and checking one's progress reduces this "psychological feedback," since the student loses the feel of the material and self-correction becomes more difficult. Programmed learning takes full advantage of these principles too.

Practice. Which is more efficient, one long learning period (massed practice) or a number of shorter periods at different times (distributed, or spaced practice)? Tests show that the answer depends primarily on the type of task. In general, massed study is best for complex material that requires considerable effort at understanding—for example, history or philosophy. Moreover, it takes time to "get into" such material; but once we accomplish this, it usually generates its own interest and keeps us involved for a considerable time. On the other hand, spaced learning is usually superior for rote memorization or detailed material—for example, learning poems, vocabulary, or scientific terms. Skills that require muscular co-ordination or great effort should also be practiced in distributed periods. The same often applies to mastering unfamiliar material, such as a new mathematical proof.

It is also advisable to shorten the study period for a particular subject if we find that we are not absorbing it, and to take a brief rest or switch to a different kind of subject matter. When we return to it we usually approach it from a new angle or with a new method of attack. Finally, it has been found that many academic subjects are best handled by massed study at the beginning and distributed learning later on. Longer periods give us the general structure of the material, and distributed practice helps us master the details.

Whole vs. part learning. Should we go through material from beginning to end (the whole method), or break it up into segments and study it piecemeal (the part method)? The whole method is generally superior for complex, meaningful material in which continuity is important; the part method is better for unorganized or rote material that has little intrinsic meaning. Often, however, a combination of the two methods is superior to either one alone. In learning a piece of music, it is usually most effective to go through the entire composition first, then practice the various segments, and finally put it together as a whole. The "preview" gives us the full sweep and movement of the composition, and makes the transitions easier later on; the piece-meal practice enables us to spend most of our time on the difficult portions. A well-organized textbook chapter usually lends itself well to this combination. It is often best to read the summary at the end, then read the chapter as a whole, and after that concentrate on the details that are the hardest to learn.

Overlearning. This means practicing or reviewing beyond the point where we can repeat the material correctly once or twice. Although overlearning takes extra time, it is usually economical in the end, since repeated review promotes lasting retention. The best time to review, however, is immediately after the original study, since forgetting occurs most rapidly at that time. But overlearning can be overdone. In one study, four extra readings of an assignment increased recall by a mere 5 per cent over three extra readings. *See* FORGETTING.

Conditions of study. The basic complaint of students is inability to concentrate—but too often they are studying under conditions that invite distraction: a blaring radio, a cluttered desk, or inner tensions. The cluttered desk is probably the least important of these, except that it is an indicator of a disorganized attitude toward work. The radio can simply be turned off, and perhaps be used as a "reward" for finishing the study. The internal distraction of emotional tension cannot be so readily overcome as external distractions, but a few discussions with an experienced counselor will often help.

The old idea that we learn best when we sit in a ramrod position is probably false; there is no harm in comfort, provided it does not make us drowsy. Much more important is a definite study schedule, since this helps us establish a mental set that is conducive to learning. Many students also find that every hour spent in a secluded corner of the library is worth two spent in their rooms.

LEARNING UNDER HYPNOSIS. Hypnotic learning has not been fully explored, but a number of reported experiments show positive results. The first studies dealt primarily with conditioning during a hypnotic trance—for example, if the hypnotist snapped his fingers while his subject smelled camphor, it was found that the subject would suddenly and mysteriously smell the same odor when the experimenter snapped his fingers after he had been awakened. This occurred without post-hypnotic suggestion. Sears (1955) found that subjects who studied Morse code under hypnosis made fewer errors when they were later tested in the waking state than subjects who were given the same amount of training without hypnosis. Cooper and Rodgin (1952) found that they could increase the learning ability of hypnotized subjects by altering their sense of time, suggesting that seconds would appear like minutes. These subjects were able to memorize word pairs in one quarter of the time it took them to learn equivalent material while awake.

These positive results are believed to be due to the fact that hypnosis is a state of extreme concentration and freedom from distraction. The method has not been widely used for other than research purposes, although a few actors claim that they find it highly effective in helping them learn their lines.

LEGAL PSYCHIATRY (Forensic Psychiatry). There are many points where the provinces of psychiatry and the law impinge on each other. Some of the most important are the problems of hospitalization of the mentally ill, the legal definition of insanity, and the rights of patients with respect to marriage, divorce, wills, and other contracts. Since modern psychiatry looks at man from the viewpoint of the internal dynamics of behavior, and the law is primarily concerned with the external control of behavior, the two fields are sometimes at odds. Yet there is a common meeting ground in their mutual concern for the individual and his relationships to others.

Hospitalization. The question of admission to a mental hospital is a difficult one since the medical right to receive treatment may come into conflict with the legal right to freedom. The mentally ill are frequently too disturbed to enter the hospital of their own free will, and in that case it may be necessary to resort to involuntary hospitalization, or commitment, which by its very nature deprives them of freedom. Moreover, once they are in the hospital, their freedom is further restricted. Not only must they abide by the usual hospital discipline, but—in the older hospitals at least—their freedom may be limited by closed wards, grounds parole, limited outside visits, close supervision of all activities, and even censorship of mail. It must be recalled that mental institutions were originally conceived in terms of protecting society from the insane, and even though we now recognize that the mentally ill are rarely dangerous, these institutions are still, in many cases, bound by outworn restrictions and admissions regulations modeled after criminal procedures.

In view of these facts, it is not easy to establish procedures that look upon the patient simply as a sick person who should be admitted solely on the basis of his need for treatment. Progress in this direction is slowly being made, but wide variations still exist in different jurisdictions. One important approach has been to make it possible for a patient to admit himself voluntarily—which, as Redlich and Freedman (1966) point out, means that we are "progressing on a path from custodial segregation to active treatment in which patients are permitted and encouraged to participate voluntarily." However, since the law usually requires that the individual be deemed mentally competent to make an application, the number of voluntary admissions is still relatively small. A second approach is to provide for temporary commitment in cases of emergency, or certification by one or more physicians. In such cases, the commitment is usually limited to a period of fifteen to thirty days.

In cases where commitment for an indeterminate period is necessary, most states require, first, that a petition be filed with a judicial agency; second, that the patient be notified that a hearing will be held; and third, that he must be examined and certified mentally ill by two physicians. One of these physicians must be a psychiatrist, and neither can be related to the patient or affiliated with the institution to which he is sent. In many states the judge is the committing agent, but in twenty-one states the patient may request a hearing before a jury. A few states, however, permit admission by a superintendent of a mental hospital without a judicial hearing or order, provided a relative or guardian makes a sworn petition, and two physicians find the individual mentally ill and in need of hospital treatment. This method obviates legal procedures which tend to be humiliating to the patient.

A number of states are slowly modifying their admission procedures in the direction of recommendations made by the American Bar Foundation and the "Model Act" developed by the United States Public Health Service. The Model Act proposes easier voluntary admissions, on the basis of the patient's own application or an application by a parent or a guardian if he is under sixteen. Release can be obtained through the patient's (or guardian's) written request, unless the head of the hospital certifies to the court or judge that it would be unsafe to release him at the time. In that event, the act recommends that proceedings for judicial hospitalization must be started within five days. Involuntary commitment—that is, commitment initiated by someone other than the patient—may be carried out without a judicial hearing provided a request for admission is submitted together with certification that two qualified physicians have examined him and believe he should be hospitalized. If, however, the patient refuses hospitalization, a petition for commitment backed by an examining physician is to be filed with the court, and the court appoints two examining physicians of its own and holds a hearing if they recommend commitment.

In addition, the Model Act provides against detention in a jail or other penal facility, except in extreme emergency, pending removal to the hospital. It also provides that during removal to the hospital the patient be accompanied by suitable medical or nursing attendants as well as friends or relatives where practicable. It further guarantees the patient's right to receive visitors, confer with counsel and community agencies, as well as the right to vote, make contracts, and dispose of property, unless he is adjudicated incompetent. Fortunately many states have already put these provisions into effect.

Another area where progress has been made is in the practice of "observation commitment." In certain states an individual indicted for a criminal offense may be legally transported to a hospital for a limited period of observation. If the hospital finds him psychotic or unable to confer with counsel in preparing his defense, the court usually commits him for treatment. As a result of this new approach, many criminal courts in large cities now employ a part-time or full-time psychiatrist.

Confidentiality. Psychiatry also comes into contact with the law on the question of "privileged communications," the right of the physician to withhold medical information unless the patient gives consent. By common law and medical ethics as well, no physician may reveal medical data unless the patient agrees. Psychiatrists hold that confidential communication between doctor and patient is particularly important in their field since a relationship of trust is essential to psychotherapy. In some states, confidentiality is protected by statute—but where it is not, it is incumbent on the doctor to inform the patient that he does not have this legal right. Even where privileged communication is granted by statute, as in Connecticut, it may be withheld if the patient is examined at the court's behest. In some states, the judge may find it in the interest of justice to waive the privilege in civil proceedings in which the patient introduces his mental condition for the purpose of making a claim or a defense. The physician may also be required to reveal the patient's data when a felony has been or is about to be committed.

Legal Capacity. The question of legal capacity is also extremely important. In most cases the right to marry is upheld if the individuals are able to understand the contract and what it entails; if not, annulment will usually be decreed, although this is seldom done. Some states, however, do not permit the mentally ill to marry, on the basis of the questionable idea that the illness may be transmitted to offspring. Concealment of previous commitment is not grounds for an annulment of marriage unless the party actually stated that he had never been in a mental hospital.

Insanity is not a ground for divorce in most states; a few states, however, grant divorce if the individual has been committed for a period of years. Some states specify that the spouse must be "incurably insane," but psychiatrists are reluctant to testify to that effect.

Commitment does not in itself annul the patient's testamentary capacity, that is, his right to make a will. He must, however, "have a sound mind and memory" and, specifically, must (a) know he is making a will, (b) know what he possesses, and (c) know "the natural objects of his bounty"—that is, relatives, friends, or organizations to whom he might feel grateful. The courts will invalidate wills made by senile patients or others who may be suggestible, if there is evidence of deception or undue influence.

In the more advanced states a mental patient is presumed capable of making contracts and carrying out his affairs unless he is proved to be mentally incompetent. If a guardian is needed to take care of the patient's affairs, a hearing is usually required, sometimes before a jury, to consider petitions for the appointment. In a few states this is merely an administrative matter because a patient who is hospitalized for mental illness is ipso facto judged incompetent on civil matters. Where contracts have already been made, they cannot be set aside unless there is specific evidence of mental incapacity at the time they were made.

Criminal Responsibility. The problem of criminal responsibility has long been a particularly knotty one, since psychiatry recognizes partial responsibility, emotional factors, and unconscious motivation, while the law emphasizes conscious intent and intellectual competence or incompetence. But long before this difference came to the fore, Roman law and early English custom held that the mentally ill were not liable for punishment, on the grounds that "madness is punishment enough" (*satis furore ipso punitur*). Moreover, "partial" insanity was recognized as early as the sixteenth century, and in 1723 an English court absolved an accused person of guilt provided he did not know what he was doing "any more than a wild beast." This concept was modified in 1760 to specify that he must not know the difference between right and wrong.

American law stems largely from an English case of 1843 in which a Daniel M'Naghten was tried for the murder of Edward Drummond, the private secretary of Sir Robert Peel. M'Naghten's attorney established that he was suffering from delusions of persecution directed against Peel, but that he had mistaken Drummond for Peel. His plea of "partial insanity" was accepted, and he was declared of unsound mind and committed to an institution for the criminally insane. Shortly afterward the House of Lords established two rules, formulated by the Justices of the Queen's Bench, to be used as a test of responsibility: (a) "To establish a defense on the ground of insanity it must be clearly proved that at the time of committing the act, the party accused was laboring under such a defect of reason, from disease of the mind, as not to know the nature and quality of the act he was doing, or, if he did know it, he did not know he was doing what was wrong"; and (b) "Where a person labors under partial delusions only and is not in other respects insane," and commits an offense in consequence thereof, "he must be considered in the same situation as to responsibility as if the facts with respect to which the delusion exists were real." This formula is still the sole test of responsibility in twenty-eight states, but in nineteen others it is supplemented by the "irresistible impulse test"—that is, an individual is exempt from criminal responsibility if he is acting under an irresistible impulse due to mental illness.

The M'Naghten rules have been severely criticized, and as early as 1869 the Supreme Court of New Hampshire, influenced by the psychiatrist Isaac Ray, set them aside and recognized simply that the accused be acquitted if his act was the result of mental illness, as determined by a psychiatrist. This decision, however, was rendered in a civil case and has seldom been applied to criminal cases in New Hampshire.

Almost a century later, in 1954, the Court of Appeals of the District of Columbia Circuit in the case of Durham *vs.* the United States declared specifically that both the right-wrong test and the irresistible test are inadequate. The court objected to the right-wrong test on the ground that it represents only one symptom of mental disease, and that a person of unsound mind may still know the difference between right and wrong. It objected to the second test on the ground that mentally ill persons may commit offenses as a result of "brooding and reflection" rather than impulse. Instead, the court adopted a rule similar to New Hampshire's, that "an accused is not responsible if his unlawful act was the product of mental disease or mental defect." In 1957 the Vermont legislature adopted a test of insanity that specifies that a person is not criminally responsible if as a result of mental disease or defect (including traumatic and congenital defect) he "lacks an adequate capacity either to appreciate the criminality of his conduct or to conform his conduct to the requirements of law."

If an accused person is found not guilty by reason of insanity, commitment to a mental hospital is mandatory in some states but left to the discretion of the court in others. Upon recovery he usually has to be discharged by the court, although in some states the governor, and in one the legislature, makes the decision.

In 1921, Massachusetts took a long step toward recognition of the need for psychiatric treatment among persons who commit offenses. Its Briggs Law provides that anyone who commits a capital offense or more than one felony, or the same crime twice, must be referred for examination by experts appointed by the State Department of Mental Health. This method obviates a mere "battle of the experts," since juries tend to take the word of the impartial examiner, or "amicus curiae," as against the word of psychiatrists hired by either side. Although the Briggs Law has not worked as well as might be hoped, many psychiatrists believe a procedure of this general kind should be universally adopted.

Fitness for Trial. Another important question is that of competency to stand trial. It is now an established rule that a person who, by reason of mental illness, cannot understand the nature of the proceedings or why he is being tried, or who cannot co-operate with his counsel or plead to the charges, should not be put on trial and should be kept in custody until his mental condition is improved. The criteria for determining mental fitness for trial are quite different from those used in determining lack of responsibility for committing a crime. The judge generally determines fitness for trial, basing his decision on a psychiatric examination made at the jail or during brief commitment to a mental hospital for observation. If a defendant is pronounced mentally unfit for trial, a judge must make a further determination of fitness before he can be put on trial. He does not have to be fully recovered from his illness, but must be able to grasp the situation well enough to make a competent defense.

Current Issues. We will end this article with some brief notes on a few specific issues of our day. Some states and countries have laws permitting compulsory sterilization, but psychiatrists rarely recommend this radical step since few mental diseases are known to be transmitted genetically. Occasionally, however, they may recommend sterilization for the mentally defective, but more often on social than on eugenic grounds. On the question of abortion there appears to be no universal agreement. Some psychiatrists point out that pregnancy and childbirth rarely endanger the life of psychiatric patients or seriously aggravate their disorder; others recommend abortion when they believe the stress of rearing a child is likely to be severely detrimental to the mother and interfere with the favorable development of the child; while some recommend abortion in cases of rape, though usually on social and ethical rather than psychiatric grounds.

Habitual offenders pose another set of knotty problems. In cases where they are judged insane, they are usually sent to a mental hospital for an indeterminate period and have little chance for discharge. However, psychiatrically speaking, the real problem is that most of them receive little or no therapy: "This situation will only change if the public becomes sufficiently interested to provide the necessary funds for such therapy and if psychiatrists will not only talk about therapy of mentally disordered criminals but actually attempt to treat them" (Redlich and Freedman, 1966). The problem of habitual offenders who are not insane is even more difficult. Some psychiatrists regard all recidivists as abnormal (i.e., as sociopaths), and urge that they be treated and rehabilitated. Others distinguish between offenders who might profit from psychiatric treatment and those who can only be segregated to protect society. On the whole, the trend appears to be in the direction of rehabilitation, re-education, and group therapy for an increasing number of criminals. In many states, however, sexual deviates are punished rather than treated, even to the point of life imprisonment for homosexuals. Nevertheless, some of the harsher laws are being moderated and courts are increasingly inclined to recommend psychiatric treatment and place offenders on probation if they do not endanger other persons.

Lastly, it is important to note that our expanding knowledge of human behavior itself gives rise to new legal problems. One example is the recently advanced theory that there may be a relation between certain chromosomal aberrations and violent crime, as suggested in the case of the French murderer, Daniel Hugon. If this relationship is established, it may well raise new questions about criminal motivation and might also lead to the use of genetic chromosomal defect as a legal defense in this country. For details, see CRIME AND CRIMINALS.

LEGAL PSYCHOLOGY (Forensic Psychology). An area of applied psychology traditionally devoted to such problems as testimony, methods of interrogation, and guilt detection.

In recent years the field has been expanded, and psychologists serve many other functions: as expert witness in courts; as diagnostician or therapist in correctional institutions; as a student of antisocial behavior; as a consultant in the development of laws; and as a participant in the formulation of legal policies involving human relations. This article will deal with the contributions of psychology in the courtroom, in prisons and training schools, and in the development of laws. The subjects of lie detection, juvenile delinquency, adult crime, and the antisocial personality are discussed under separate topics.

Psychology in the Courtroom. The first aspect of the law to be investigated by psychologists was the problem of testimony. At the very beginning of this century a number of noted psychologists including Alfred Binet, Hugo Münsterberg, and Wilhelm Stern conducted research and wrote papers and books on this subject. These and other investigators brought together many experimentally verified findings that are important in the evaluation of testimony—for example, facts on visual illusions, light and dark adaptation, localization of sound, incidental memory, and estimation of size, distance, speed, and time intervals. A specific example is the case of a Canadian hunter who was mistaken for a deer and shot to death by his companions (Sommer, 1959). A psychologist was called in as expert witness and testified on two major points. He pointed out that the mental set, or expectation, of the hunters would tend to make them perceive any moving object as a deer; and he showed that they could not have identified the man by his red coveralls, as the prosecution contended, since the accident occurred late on a cloudy day when the human eye perceives the red end of the spectrum as black (the Purkinje phenomenon).

One of Stern's major contributions was the Aussage ("testimony") test, which is still used to impress students with the limitations of testimony. One procedure is to have a class or a lecture unexpectedly interrupted by a stranger who bursts into the room and berates the instructor. After the incident, the students are asked detailed questions about the scene and the participants. Scores on the test show that complete accuracy is extremely rare, and the over-all average is seldom more than 30 per cent correct. What is more, many individuals are found to make the same error—which indicates that the law's emphasis on consensus needs to be questioned. Analysis of the errors reveals that the witness is influenced by many factors: the element of surprise, the power of suggestion, emotional involvement, reactions to the individuals in the situation, mental and physical set, etc. Discussion of the test usually brings out additional factors that are likely to affect reports of accidents or crimes that occur on the street: distance from the scene, angle of vision, interference from other events, social attitudes (e.g., sympathy for the small-car owner), and the tendency to fill in gaps with plausible details.

Experiments on interrogation procedures have shown that (1) free recitals are generally more accurate than reports in which the witness answers questions, especially when he is under cross-examination; (2) leading questions, questions with hidden assumptions, and negative phrasing ("Didn't he have a gun?") encourage false recall; and (3) asking a subject to indicate which facts he would report under oath tends to reduce errors. Other revealing studies have been made on differences in sentences imposed by different judges for the same crime, the tendency of jurors to be affected by social stereotypes and by the personality of the foreman, and the influence of the order in which evidence is presented. On the latter point, most courtroom studies show that the first and last positions ("primacy" and "recency") tend to have equal effect, and a presentation which occupies a middle position between two presentations of the other side is at a particular disadvantage.

Although psychologists were occasionally called to testify as expert witnesses at the time of Wilhelm Stern, it is only in recent years that their testimony has been sought with any degree of regularity. Clinical psychologists are now increasingly called upon to testify in commitment procedures for mental deficiency or mental illness, and in cases involving adoption, contested wills, accidents involving behavioral damage due to brain injury, and determination of legal responsibility for criminal acts. In addition, consumer psychologists are sometimes asked to present scientific data in suits involving misleading advertising or trade name infringements; and an ever larger number of social psychologists are serving as expert witnesses in cases involving racial discrimination and segregation. The trend in many states is to have the psychologist appointed by the court rather than by either side, and in such instances he either serves as an amicus curiae or is paid by both sides. The right of qualified psychologists to serve as a friend and adviser to the court in criminal cases involving the mental condition of the defendant was upheld by the United States Court of Appeals in 1962.

Psychology in Correctional Institu-

tions. In spite of the need for their services, relatively few psychologists are working in correctional settings today. In some cases, however, counseling or clinical psychologists are employed by courts, penitentiaries, probation departments, parole boards, and training schools. They serve on either a full- or part-time basis, or as consultants in individual cases, and they usually function in the role of adviser on diagnosis and treatment, but occasionally as therapists or research workers.

Many juvenile courts as well as a few domestic relations and criminal courts have their own behavior clinics in which psychologists employ interviews and tests in evaluating the intelligence, personality characteristics, attitudes, and motivations of offenders. They may also assess their potential for vocational training, education, and job placement, and help to identify those who need special care due to neurosis, brain damage, mental defect, or psychosis. In some juvenile court clinics they engage in short-term psychotherapy or help to arrange for counseling of parents, remedial instruction, recreational programs, or foster-home placement. These approaches are often effective in salvaging youthful offenders.

Still fewer psychologists are employed in prisons—about one for every three thousand inmates. Again the need is great, but it has often proved difficult for psychologists to function in this setting. In some prisons they are primarily concerned with interviewing and testing new admissions at the prison or at a special center prior to assignment to an institution. The results are then used in placing the inmates in work, educational, or vocational training programs. A similar evaluation procedure is undertaken for parole candidates, with emphasis on their adjustment to life in a community. A few prison psychologists engage in short-term individual or group therapy, sometimes using psychodramatic techniques. They also help to

develop training programs and discussion groups for normal inmates, and recommend the referral of the severely disturbed to special institutions.

So far, only about one half of public training schools for delinquent boys or girls have full-time psychologists on their staff, and many of them do not even employ a part-time psychologist. In the institutions that do utilize their services, the emphasis is primarily on personality diagnosis, psychotherapy, and remedial educational programs. Activity therapy and play therapy may be used, and older children often receive vocational training and counseling.

Psychology and the Law. Many of our laws and legal processes are based upon older conceptions of human behavior, and until recently there has been little attempt to bring them up to date. Today, however, a growing number of judges and legislators are consulting with psychologists and other behavioral scientists on questions that fall within their area of competence. These questions now cover a particularly wide territory due to the increasing emphasis on psychological factors in dealing with such problems as criminal behavior, mistreatment of children, drug addiction, alcoholism, and interracial conflicts.

A few examples will be given to show how psychologists make their contributions to the development of the law. They have appeared before legislative committees to testify against the M'Naghten rule, which applies the inability to distinguish between right and wrong as the single test of insanity. They have been consulted about laws relating to adoption, sex offenses, bilingualism, and the classification and treatment of prisoners. They have brought research data on racial intelligence and the effects of segregation on personality development to the attention of courts dealing with questions of racial discrimination, and they have also submitted data which were cited by the

Supreme Court in its 1954 ruling that state laws requiring or permitting racial segregation in public education are unconstitutional. *See* LEGAL PSYCHIATRY.

Finally, psychologists have begun to play a significant part in problems relating to international relations and international law. The Society for the Psychological Study of Social Issues, which became a division of the American Psychological Association in 1936, has published numerous papers on war and peace in its *Journal of Social Issues.* Symposia on these topics have been held at meetings of the American Psychological Association, and the organization now has a Committee on Psychology in National and International Affairs and an administrative officer for international affairs. Among the topics discussed in the past few years are the cold-war mentality, methods for resolving intergroup conflicts, national differences in personality, tensions affecting international understanding, factors underlying aggression, the value of student exchange programs, international cultural programs, techniques of conflict resolution, disaster reactions, responses to air raid warnings, and the use of simulated situations and political games in the study of conflicting interests.

LEVEL OF ASPIRATION. The level at which a person sets his significant goals; the level of performance to which he aspires.

An individual's aspiration level has an important bearing on his personality and adjustment. It is a basic component of his self-image, the way he appears in his own eyes. Generally speaking, most normal individuals have been found to set their significant goals just a little higher than they are sure of attaining. There may be an element of self-flattery in this tendency, but it is considered healthy since it is a sign of self-acceptance and self-confidence. Relatively high goals also act as a motivating force, since they give us something

to reach for. Nevertheless, the level must remain within reasonable limits, as Coleman has pointed out: "Well-adjusted people tend to have a reasonably accurate evaluation of themselves in relation to their world and hence a fairly realistic level of aspiration. Maladjusted people, on the other hand, tend to be unrealistic—to set their aspirations either too high or too low—leading to inevitable failure or to wasted opportunities and, in either case, to unhappiness." (Coleman, 1964)

Level of aspiration is a universal feature of personality, but it appears to be particularly relevant in a society like our own in which the pressure to achieve is so great and feelings of success and failure so crucial. Too often parents set goals for their children on the basis of their own ambitions, with little regard to the young person's own capabilities or realistic appraisal of himself. They also tend to be overinfluenced by comparisons with other people's children, or interpret too rigidly the "growth gradients" they find in textbooks. Some parents develop feelings of rejection toward their children when they are not measuring up even during infancy or early childhood, and in some environments it is not unusual for a father or mother to warn a third-grader that he won't get into a "good" college unless he studies harder. If the child continues to fall even slightly behind, such parents apply still greater pressure and run the risk of inflicting severe psychological damage on him. Many children cannot do well under constant pressure, and some develop an intense feeling of failure which leads them to set unrealistically low goals for themselves throughout life.

Experiments have thrown a good deal of additional light on aspiration level. Lewin et al. (1944) have shown that a history of repeated success leads to an increased level of aspiration: the more we accomplish, the higher our goals. Experiences of failure, on the other hand, have more complex effects. Infrequent failures tend either to lower the aspiration level or to cause it to rise less rapidly than under conditions of repeated success. Continuous failure motivates the individual either to set his goals so low that success is guaranteed, or so high that his inability to achieve them does not produce a feeling of failure. In either case, the person is setting up a shield against self-exposure, and is deceiving himself about his abilities in order to protect his ego. This situation can usually be prevented if parents and teachers are careful to give children tasks that allow them a distinct possibility of success. Such tasks should be challenging without pushing them beyond their capabilities. An approach of this kind helps them establish a realistic level of aspiration that will carry over to adulthood.

Other studies have shown that group standards have a significant effect on individual levels of aspiration. In one experiment, several groups of college students worked on simple arithmetic problems. The time it took each group to finish a page was publicly announced, and directly afterward each student privately recorded the score he expected to make on the next test—that is, his level of aspiration. It was found that these private levels were influenced by the group's performance. Students who scored above the group average tended to lower their estimates; those who scored below average expected to do better. They were apparently exhibiting a tendency to conform, or at least a "safety in numbers" psychology.

Another important fact is that we carefully select the groups with which we compare ourselves. A good golfer chooses people who shoot in the seventies or eighties as his "reference group"; a duffer compares himself with people who shoot well over a hundred. To test this idea, college students were given intelligence test problems and were later told whether their scores were above or below those of high school, college, or graduate students. Each subject was then asked to estimate his score on a subsequent test. It was found that students who found that their scores were below those of high school students raised their level of aspiration, while those who scored higher than the graduate students lowered their estimates most (Festinger, 1942). These results are further evidence not only of a tendency to conform to one's own group, but also to be influenced by the factor of prestige. *See* SOCIAL NORM, SUGGESTION.

LIBIDO. In Freud, the basic sexual force or energy behind all instinctual, or id, drives, and all pleasure-seeking activity; in Jung, the general life force which provides energy for all types of activities, biological, sexual, social, cultural, and creative.

Freud felt that our pleasure-giving drives are fundamentally sexual, whether or not they appear erotic on the surface. However, he used the term "sexual" in a broad sense, applying it not only to genital sex (intercourse, masturbation, etc.), but also to pleasurable sensations accompanying such activities as chewing, defecation, thumbsucking, and talking, as well as satisfactions associated with intellectual endeavor and esthetic expression.

The theory of psychoanalysis holds that the various expressions of the libido do not all appear at birth, but gradually unfold as we mature. As Otto Fenichel, one of Freud's disciples, put it: "There is but one libido which may be displaced from one erogenous zone to another" (1945). In this process of displacement, or "mobility of libido," the basic energy is first attached to parts of the body, particularly the mouth and anus, that lead to self-preservation. When the tensions involved in the need for food and elimination are relieved, these parts of the body yield what Freud called "organ pleasure." As the individual develops, the libido is gradually focused on the genital organs, which become not only a source of pleasure but ultimately lead to preservation of the race. At the same time, the basic erotic force is gradually directed to persons in the environment who provide pleasure and gratification—first the parents, then members of one's own sex, then members of the opposite sex. This process Freud termed "object finding." See PSYCHOSEXUAL DEVELOPMENT.

The libido provides the energy not only for psychosexual growth, but for all creative activities—for poetry, art, music, science, and any attempts to improve the lot of mankind. These are all interpreted by Freud as transformations or "sublimations" of the original instinctual force. Later in his life he applied the term "life instinct," or "Eros," to this constructive energy and claimed that it is opposed by an equally fundamental counterforce, the "death instinct," or "Thanatos," which he believed to be the source of man's aggressive and destructive drives. He held that "the interaction of the two basic instincts with or against each other gives rise to the whole variegation of the phenomena of life." This "dual instinct" theory has not been widely accepted. See ID, DEATH INSTINCT, PSYCHOANALYSIS (THEORY), CATHEXIS.

The term "libido" was also used by Carl Jung in his theory of analytic psychology. He expanded Freud's original concept, which was based on the energy of psychosexual impulses, and applied it to the entire energy or "life force" of the individual. In his view, sexuality is only one manifestation of this force, which, in the course of life, is first channeled into biological satisfactions, and later into cultural, social, and creative activities.

Jung conceived the development of the individual in terms of the utilization of libidinal energy. In the first phase of life, occupying the first five years, the libido is invested in activities, such as walking and talking, that are essential for survival. After age five it is directed increasingly to sexual aims, which reach their peak in adolescence. (During this earlier period of sexuality, the child may experience incestuous desires, but they do not reach the proportions of the Freudian Oedipus complex unless the child is overprotected.) After adolescence, the libido is expressed in mature love and marriage, as well as in the acceptance of family and vocational responsibility. During this phase of development the individual tends to be energetic, extraversive, and passionate. Later in this period, however, the libido undergoes a radical change in expression, for the mature person gradually becomes more introversive, more spiritual and philosophical in his goals and outlook. The libido now turns from its early biological orientation to its creative orientation, and the individual draws sustenance and inspiration not only from the intuitions, fantasies, and impulses of his own personal unconscious, but from the collective unconscious of the race as well. See JUNG.

LIE DETECTOR. An apparatus designed to detect emotional changes that indicate guilt.

Attempts to detect guilt on the basis of physical and psychological signs appear to be as old as history. The ancient Hindus noted that guilty persons refuse to answer questions, give evasive answers, speak nonsense, shiver, and turn red. The Chinese forced suspects to fill their mouths with dry rice; if they could not swallow it, they were pronounced guilty. Current procedures follow the principle of measuring physiological changes that occur under emotional stress—particularly autonomic changes, since they are not under voluntary control.

The most widely used apparatus is the polygraph (*Fig. 34*), which records changes in respiration (through a chest

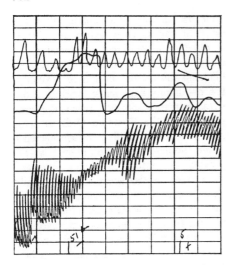

Fig. 34. Portion of a polygraph recording from a lie detector test. The sudden fluctuations in respiration (top line), galvanic skin response (middle line), and pulse and blood pressure (lower line) indicate that the subject lied in answering question 51.

pneumograph), blood pressure (through a cuff plethysmograph or a sphygmomanometer), and the galvanic skin response (through palmar electrodes and a galvanometer). The technique is based on the fact that when a subject experiences apprehension, fear, or emotional excitement—all of which are believed to indicate guilt—his respiration rate, blood pressure, and GSR will sharply increase. The GSR is considered the most accurate of the three indicators; it measures the electrical conductivity of the skin, which increases under emotional stress as a result of secretion of the sweat glands. *See* GALVANIC SKIN RESPONSE.

In giving a lie detector test, a trained operator attaches the apparatus to the suspect's body, then asks a long series of questions, some of which are "neutral" (Did you have breakfast this morning?) and some of which are "critical," since they indicate guilty knowledge (Have you recently had an ax in your hands?). Instead of questions, some operators use a free association

test composed of critical words interspersed among neutral words. Sometimes, too, a third type of question or word is also used, involving emotional responses that have nothing to do with the problem (Do you have a girl friend?). Here the object is to establish a base line for the subject's reactions, since there are wide individual differences even among innocent persons in emotional response to questioning.

After the test, a comparison is made of the responses to the critical, neutral, and emotional stimuli, and a judgment of lying or truth-telling is made. Various surveys indicate that experienced examiners make correct judgments in about 80 per cent of cases, though some have claimed an accuracy of over 90 per cent. Because of the nature of the technique, the errors are usually failures to detect guilt, and it is claimed that innocent persons have rarely if ever been judged guilty by the lie detector.

Today lie detectors are used in a variety of settings—not only police departments and courts, but governmental agencies, such as the Atomic Energy Commission, the military services, banks, retail stores, hotels, and industrial plants, both in personnel selection and periodic examination of employees. In police work the test is employed chiefly in the preliminary examination and screening of suspects, as well as in persuading criminals to confess. Only a few courts admit lie detection data as evidence, and then only when both parties agree to submit to a test administered by a mutually acceptable examiner. In these cases, the findings are presented by the examiner as expert testimony to be considered along with other evidence by the judge or jury.

A professional organization, the Academy for Scientific Interrogation, has been established for improvement of lie detection and other interrogation practices, and training programs for practitioners are now being offered by universities, police departments, and the military services.

Many experiments have been conducted on lie detection, typically with simulated crimes. Kubis (1962) set up a situation in which some students stole money from a coin box attached to a pamphlet rack, while others served as lookouts or innocent suspects. Analysis of the polygraph records by various examiners yielded correct identifications ranging from 73 to 92 per cent, far above the chance expectancy of 33 per cent. Other studies indicate that multiple measures, as on the polygraph, are preferable to single measures, since one subject might show his greatest response to stress through increased sweating, another through blood pressure changes, and a third through respiratory reactions. Lykken (1960), however, has performed an impressive experiment in which only the GSR was used. He first allowed his subjects to practice producing GSRs, and then offered them ten dollars if they could avoid detection. The test consisted of multiple choice questions on such facts as the name of the high school they attended and their mother's first name. The galvanometer tracings indicated with 100 per cent accuracy whether or not they had chosen the correct alternatives.

In spite of these positive results, it has been found that the test cannot be counted on with certain types of individuals—particularly hardened criminals and psychopathic (antisocial) personalities who do not feel guilt or react with fear, as well as retarded individuals who do not appreciate the significance of the situation, highly emotional persons who overreact to nearly all questions, and the false confessor who for unconscious reasons confesses to crimes he did not commit. Moreover, although naïve subjects find it difficult to impossible to "beat the test," it may be possible for some persons to train themselves to control their physiological responses well enough to mislead the examiner. In one case, however, a suspect controlled his breathing so completely that the apparatus did not record any of the normal variations that occur under intensive questioning. When the examiner confronted him with this fact and accused him of trying to cover up, he confessed.

LIGHT ADAPTATION. Adjustment of the eye to light; change in the sensitivity of the eye under different conditions of illumination.

The most familiar example of light adaptation is our reaction to the sudden glare of daylight when we come out of a motion picture theater in the afternoon. A similar experience occurs when we emerge from a long, dark tunnel into sunshine or when we turn on a light in the middle of the night. We are momentarily blinded, then gradually become accustomed to the light. The reaction is based on the fact that we are able to see because light breaks down photochemical substances (rhodopsin and iodopsin) in the retina of our eyes. While we are in the dark these chemicals regenerate, and the resulting increase in concentration makes our eyes more sensitive to light stimulation. This helps us to see in darkness but makes us temporarily oversensitive to bright, glaring light after we have been dark-adapted.

Experiments have shown that the greater the intensity of the illumination, the quicker the adaptation. The process actually takes from one to three minutes (Geldard, 1928; Wallace, 1937). This is far more rapid than the process of dark adaptation, which takes thirty minutes to reach its maximum. In other words, light adaptation is achieved more rapidly than it is lost, and dark adaptation is lost more rapidly than it is acquired. *See* DARK ADAPTATION.

LIMBIC SYSTEM. A complex set of structures extending downward from the cerebral cortex to portions of the mid-brain, and consisting primarily of the cingulate gyrus, septal area, amygdala, and hippocampus. It includes at least three circuits. One has to do with the sense of smell, a second (Limbic System II) is concerned with emotion and motivation, but the function of the third is unknown. *See* SMELL.

The term limbic means "border," and is applied to these structures because they border on both the upper cortical area and the older, subcortical areas (MacLean, 1958). The cortical part of the system is the cingulate gyrus, lying just above the corpus callosum, and extending downward to the subcortical regions including the septal area, the amygdala, and the hippocampus. These structures are all connected with each other and with the hypothalamus and mammillary bodies (*Fig. 35*).

Experiments involving Limbic System II have thrown considerable light on the regulation of emotion. When the cerebral cortex of animals was removed but the limbic system left intact, they became so placid that it was virtually impossible to arouse them to anger (Bard and Mountcastle, 1947). The same investigators showed that lesions in either the cingulate gyrus, the amygdala, or the hippocampus made placid animals ferocious. All these experiments argued that the limbic system has a restraining effect on emotion.

More recent studies have shown that this interpretation was oversimplified. It now appears that one part of the amygdala has a restraining influence while another part has an exciting effect. Moreover, the amygdala, and probably other parts of the limbic system as well, is closely tied up with the lower control center for emotion in the hypothalamus. The exact relationships between these areas are still being worked out, but they seem to be highly complicated. *See* AMYGDALA, HYPOTHALAMUS.

Animal experiments involving direct brain stimulation have thrown further light on the limbic system. When elec-

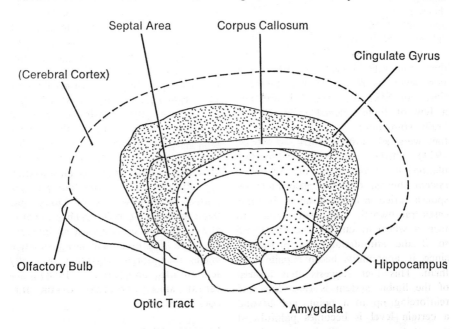

Fig. 35. The limbic system, containing control centers for emotion and motivation deep within the brain. The shaded areas show its major structures in semidiagrammatic form.

trodes were implanted in the septal area of a rat, and the current was turned on for a trial period, the experimenters noticed that it later sniffed around the place where it had received the shock. This seemed to indicate that the brain shock had produced a pleasurable reaction. The experimenters then placed the rats in a Skinner box and trained them to give themselves a brain shock by pressing a lever (*Fig. 36*). It was found

Fig. 36. Self-administered pleasure. An electrode is implanted in the septal area of a rat's brain, and he presses the bar to give himself a mild electric shock up to five thousand times an hour until exhausted, apparently because the shock stimulates a "pleasure center" in the brain.

that some rats pressed the self-stimulation lever as many as five thousand times an hour for several hours, and a few of them seemed to prefer the brain stimulation to food even when they were half-starved (Olds and Milner, 1954). Further experiments with stimulation of various parts of the limbic system showed that the pleasurable response varied in different areas. In some cases rats which had been trained to turn a wheel to cut off the shock did so if the stimulation was prolonged, since it apparently became painful to them. This fact suggests that arousal of the limbic system is rewarding and reinforcing up to a point, but beyond a certain level it becomes painful. At present these newer findings are being worked into a wider theory of motiva-

tion based on the total activity of the nervous system. *See* SKINNER BOX.

The limbic system also appears to be involved in basic learning processes. Both the acquisition and retention of conditioned responses were found to be affected when lesions were made in different parts of this system. Rats acquired avoidance reactions to electric shocks more rapidly when the septal area was partly destroyed, apparently because the lesions increased their emotional response and the shocks therefore had a greater effect on them. Lesions in the amygdala, on the other hand, impaired the ability of wild animals to learn and retain avoidance reactions, since destruction in this area apparently made them more placid and less emotional. Lesions made in one part of the cingulate gyrus reduced the ability to learn active conditioned responses (moving from one compartment of a box to another to avoid shock), and lesions in another part affected the passive type of response (avoiding a part of the box associated with a shock). Passive avoidance reactions were also impaired in rats with hippocampal lesions.

Finally, it has been suggested that all these experiments on the limbic system indicate that it is primarily concerned with "sequential activities"—that is, activities that require a series of movements which enable the animal, and presumably the human being also, to adapt to basic needs such as feeding, attacking, fleeing from danger, and mating (Pribram, 1958). This theory is supported by observations of human patients with limbic lesions. They are usually helpless in carrying out an intended sequence of actions, and any distraction makes them forget what they originally set out to do (Milner, 1958). *See* SEPTAL AREA, CINGULATE GYRUS, HIPPOCAMPUS.

LOCKE, JOHN (1632–1704). Locke, the great empiricist and pioneer in associationist psychology, was born in Somerset, England, studied medicine and science at Oxford, and later became adviser and physician to the Earl of Shaftesbury. His first works were *Essay on a Law of Nature* and controversial writings on political and civil questions, for which he was exiled to Amsterdam for several years. During a discussion with friends in 1671 on a "remote" subject, he became convinced that "difficulties that arose on every side" made it "necessary to examine our own abilities and see what objects our understandings were or were not fitted to deal with." Throughout the following eighteen years he devoted himself to this problem, publishing his conclusions in his most celebrated work, *Essay Concerning Human Understanding* (1690).

Locke returned to England shortly before publishing the *Essay,* taking a position as Commissioner of Appeals in excise cases. In the years that followed he published two other influential works, *Two Treatises on Government* and *A Letter Concerning Toleration,* both of which had a profound effect on the American Constitution. His other major works include *Some Thoughts Concerning Education* (1693), *An Appeal for a Rational Interpretation of the Gospels,* and *Reasonableness of Christianity* (1695).

In his *Essay Concerning Human Understanding,* Locke followed the lead of Hobbes in opposing the doctrine of innate ideas which Descartes had supported. He also developed the theory of association which Hobbes had outlined, and formulated the empirical approach to philosophy and psychology. The key concept of the work is the term "idea," or "object of thinking," which he described as a basic unit of mind or item of knowledge. According to Locke, our conscious, ongoing behavior can be analyzed at any moment into these units, such as man, dog, hardness, and sweetness. In his view the mind is a *tabula rasa* (blank sheet

of paper) at birth, and every one of these ideas—and therefore all our knowledge—derives from sensory experience. This doctrine of empiricism was in direct opposition to the rationalism of Descartes, who held that the mind arrives on the scene already equipped with certain "clear and distinct" ideas.

Locke recognized that ideas were not isolated elements, but combine into totalities of varying degrees of complexity and abstractness. To explain the way they are "held together," he proposed the doctrine of association of ideas. According to this theory, associations are established between ideas primarily by "custom"—that is, by habitually perceiving them together—just as certain configurations of colors, shapes, odors, etc. mean "dog," and a set of abstract concepts combine to form the idea of "autocracy." A basic principle of the associationist philosophy is that ideas may be either simple and unanalyzable (the russet color of a setter, for example), or complex and analyzable into simpler components (for example, government). Locke was not altogether clear about how the process of compounding or "mental chemistry" takes place, but he made a distinction between modes (for instance, different kinds of triangles), substances (dog, house), and relations, which arise when we compare one idea with another (larger, or brighter). These processes were more precisely described by later associationists.

Two other aspects of Locke's doctrines had a particularly strong influence on the development of psychology. First, he traced ideas to two sources, sensation and reflection. In sensation, external bodies impinge on the sense organs, which send messages to the mind, producing perceptions. In reflection, the mind gains knowledge of its own operations through an "inner sense." In this process (similar to introspection), we get ideas about ideas and the manner of their occurrence.

This concept was a forerunner of act psychology, which focuses on the operations of the mind itself.

The other important contribution was Locke's distinction between primary and secondary qualities. Primary qualities are perceived singly by the senses (shape, extent) and are believed to stem directly from objects in the external world. Locke viewed them as presentations of properties inherent in the objects themselves—the shape we see corresponds to the actual shape of the object. Secondary qualities, on the other hand, do not exist in the objects in the form in which they are perceived, but are due to the power of the object to produce the ideas in mind. Examples are colors, sounds, tastes, and smells, all of which are generated by the object but do not resemble it. As Boring (1950) points out, "This distinction between primary and secondary qualities means that the mind is not always a mirror of the external world, but gains much of its knowledge about reality indirectly." Though Locke himself did not describe this process in specific terms, his views are believed to foreshadow both the doctrine of specific energy and the Gestalt theory of isomorphism. *See* ASSOCIATIONISM, SPECIFIC ENERGIES, ACT PSYCHOLOGY, GESTALT PSYCHOLOGY.

LOGORRHEA (Logomania, Hyperlogia, Hyperphrasia). Excessive, uncontrollable talking, often highly incoherent. Logorrhea occurs in states of pathological excitement, particularly in the manic phase of manic-depressive psychosis where one of the major symptoms is "pressure of speech." For examples, see the illustrative cases under MANIC-DEPRESSIVE REACTION (MANIC PHASE).

LOGOTHERAPY. An existential approach developed by Viktor Frankl, based on the arousal of the patient's spiritual drives or "will-to-meaning."

Like other existentialists, Frankl (1955) focuses attention on what has been called the "human predicament," the breakdown of traditional faith and values and the loss of meaning in human existence. The object of therapy is to help the patient overcome what he terms the "existential neurosis," the inability to see meaning in life. He does not propose a definite, systematic procedure, but emphasizes the need for revealing the defects in the patient's system of values and helping him to achieve a more satisfying and constructive approach to life—in Frankl's own words, to find an "authentic existential modality." He believes that it is possible for anyone, no matter how desperate his external condition, to find values that will give meaning to his life.

In this search, the therapist helps the patient examine three sets of values. First, *creative values,* which derive from productive work and achievement; second, *experiential values,* which are discovered by experiencing "the good, the true and the beautiful" in art, science, philosophy, as well as in understanding and loving another person; and third, *attitudinal values,* especially those requiring courage and the ability to face pain and suffering without losing heart. (Frankl himself was a victim of the Nazis and wrote a book entitled *From Death-Camp to Existentialism,* 1959, which he later incorporated in *Man's Search for Meaning,* 1963.) In the therapeutic process, each patient is encouraged to arrive at his own solution to the problem of existence. However, even though that solution may be highly individual, Frankl believes, with other existentialists, that it cannot be egocentric, because man has a basic responsibility to his fellow men and a basic need for positive, mutual relations with other human beings. Therefore if the values which the individual lives by are to have full meaning, they must not only be personally satisfying but socially constructive. *See* EXISTENTIALISM.

LOVE. A complex yet basically unified emotion comprising tenderness, affection, and devotion to the well-being of another person or persons.

In more specific terms, love involves (a) feelings of empathy, the ability to enter into the feelings and share the experiences of the loved one; (b) profound concern for the welfare, happiness, and growth of the loved one; (c) pleasure in actively devoting thought, energy, time, and all other resources to the loved one; and (d) full acceptance of the uniqueness and individuality of the loved one, and his right to be himself (based on Prescott, 1957). To these four components may be added a fifth: "Retaining the separateness and integrity of one's own self. It is an experience of sharing, of communion, which permits the full unfolding of one's inner ability." (Fromm, 1956)

Love takes many forms and has many expressions. In his book, *The Art of Loving* (1956), Erich Fromm delineates five relationships. *Brotherly love,* which is oriented toward all of one's fellow men, includes "the sense of responsibility, care, respect, knowledge of any other human being, the wish to further his life." *Parental love* is a willing, unconditional, and nonpossessive assumption of responsibility for the well-being and growth of one's child, together with an acceptance of the fact that his life is his own. *Erotic love*— "the craving for a complete fusion, for union with one other person. It is by its very nature exclusive and not universal"—involves the greatest possible investment of one's self in the happiness and welfare of another person, as well as the greatest opportunity for growth on the part of both individuals. *Self-love,* is not love of self in the sense of egocentrism and conceit, but is the kind of self-acceptance and self-esteem that give us the confidence to love other people and form social relationships that are both healthy and productive. Finally, *love of God* arises from

man's "need to overcome separateness and to achieve union" with the totality of Being, to identify himself with the highest purposes he can conceive, and thereby fortify himself against anxiety, despair, and meaninglessness.

Of the five types of relationships just outlined, psychologists and other social scientists have focused their attention primarily on two: parental love and erotic love. There are many expressions of parental love, and if the relationship between parent and child is to be healthy and fruitful, these expressions must change as the child grows. In infancy it takes the form of cuddling, physical care, and attention to the child's general well-being. As he develops, it expresses itself in admiration for new skills and encouragement of the child's attempts to test himself and explore his world. During the school years it takes the form of a generally approving attitude (mixed with reproof when necessary), interest in the child's activities, and help in times of difficulty or distress. Later, during adolescence, the emphasis should be on reassurance, respect for privacy, encouragement of independent thought and action, and trust in the young person's basic goodness and ability to profit from experience.

Psychological studies have shown that the ability to give as well as to accept love can develop only if it is nourished during the formative years. This means that positive feelings of affection and approval must clearly predominate, for a person who has lived with attitudes of rejection, suspicion, egocentricity, and hostility is likely to experience great difficulty in forming deep and enduring attachments throughout his life. For such individuals marriage is often a refuge from an unhappy childhood, or a defense against a threatening world. In some cases, however, a predominance of negative feelings in early life at home may be counteracted by outside experiences that restore confidence, assure acceptance by others, and stimulate self-understanding and insight into other people. Such persons may succeed in overcoming their early handicap and become increasingly capable of giving as well as responding to love.

A fruitful way of approaching the question of erotic love is to distinguish the genuine variety from infatuation. The two are not poles apart, for infatuation may ripen into love, and enduring love should retain something of the thrill of infatuation. However, there are a number of points of distinction which H. A. Bowman (1951) has summarized as follows: "Infatuation may come suddenly but love takes time. Infatuation can be based on one or two traits (usually plus sex appeal) whereas love is based on many traits. In infatuation the person is in 'love' with love, whereas in love, the person is in love with another person. In infatuation the other person is thought of as a separate entity and employed for self-gratification, in real love there is a feeling of identity with the other person. Infatuation produces feelings of insecurity and wishful thinking, whereas love produces a sense of security. In infatuation he may suffer loss of ambition and appetite, or be in a daze, whereas in love you work and plan to please the other person. The physical element is much more pronounced in infatuation than in love. Infatuation may change quickly, but love lasts."

As this quotation indicates, infatuation may be a trap leading to hasty and ill-considered marriage, especially between individuals who are dominated by sexual desire or dependency needs, or who are seeking relief from loneliness, insecurity, or unhappiness. Genuine love, on the other hand, grows not only out of a deepening sexual relationship, but out of shared interests, experiences, and aspirations—and, like brotherly love and parental love, it evokes an urge to foster the loved one's well-being and growth as an individual. *See* AFFECTIONAL DRIVE, MARI-TAL ADJUSTMENT, MATERNAL DRIVE, MOTHERING, MATERNAL DEPRIVATION.

LUPUS ERYTHEMATOSUS (literally, wolf-red inflammation). A collagen, or connective tissue, disease of unknown cause affecting small blood vessels in various organs of the body, including the brain; classified by the American Psychiatric Association (1952) as a chronic brain syndrome associated with diseases of unknown or uncertain cause.

Approximately 85 per cent of all cases occur in women. The onset is usually in childhood, but the disease is frequently not recognized until adolescence or early adult life. The early signs are easy fatigability, fever, and migratory joint pains that resemble rheumatic fever or rheumatoid arthritis. In many cases there is a butterfly rash on the bridge of the nose or cheeks. A positive diagnosis is made by identifying certain cells (LE cells) in blood smears.

Mental symptoms occur in the majority of cases. They usually begin with anxiety and exaggeration of previous personality tendencies. Later on about half the patients become delirious or develop schizophrenic reactions, usually of the paranoid type. Phobic and depressive reactions are also found in some cases. These psychological symptoms are believed by some investigators to be due to the use of the steroids cortisone or ACTH, which are the standard treatment for the disease. Others, however, believe they are the direct result of the disease process itself, especially since brain lesions are usually found at autopsy. Treatment requires the collaboration of a psychiatrist with the internist. Remissions sometimes occur, but the disease is usually fatal. *See* BRAIN DISORDERS.

LYING. Lying may take either a normal or pathological form, and will therefore be discussed as (a) a feature of the moral development of the average child, (b) a major characteristic of the character disorder known as antisocial or psychopathic personality, and (c) a symptom of certain brain disorders. Two special forms of lying are treated under separate topics: malingering, or feigning illness; and confabulation, the pathological tendency to fill gaps in memory with false details. *See* these topics.

Children's lies have been classified into seven different types: (1) the playful or make-believe lie: "There's a dragon under my bed!"; (2) the lie of confusion: "The dog was as big as I am"; (3) the lie of vanity: "I got more compliments than anybody"; (4) the lie of revenge: "I saw Johnnie break the window"; (5) the excusive lie, motivated by fear of punishment: "I didn't eat a single cookie"; (6) the selfish lie: "Mommie always lets me eat between meals"; and (7) the loyal lie: "Jimmie didn't do anything wrong." (Jones, 1954)

Studies show that boys lie somewhat more than girls, and peak periods for lying by both sexes occur between five and six and between eight and nine years of age (Macfarlane et al., 1954). Young children's lies are frequently expressions of fantasy rather than attempts to deceive others, though some lies are basically due to misunderstanding or inability to report details accurately. Many children are encouraged to lie by the example of their parents: "Tell Mrs. Jones I'm not in," or "Johnnie is only six—he travels half-fare."

Most childhood lies, however, arise from fear of punishment, disapproval, or ridicule. Children are often frightened into lying because they do not have the inner strength to admit their guilt when stern adults put them "on the carpet." Some children, mainly boys, lie about wrongdoing because the "gang" (and sometimes the parents) assure them that it is all right to break rules if you are clever enough to get away with it. Children under the age of eight think it is wrong to lie because it is forbidden by adults, and only feel guilty if they are punished; older children come to feel that lying is wrong because it violates mutual trust and conflicts with the standards of their parents and of society. This represents a shift from control by rules to control by conscience (Medinnus, 1962). Most psychologists believe the tendency to lie can be overcome more effectively by explaining the need for truthfulness than by applying harsh punishment or labeling the child a liar.

Among adults (and occasionally adolescents), the proverbial "pathological liar" is classed as an antisocial, or psychopathic, personality. This category includes individuals characterized by extreme egocentrism, irresponsibility, impulsiveness, absence of moral standards, and inability to form deep emotional attachments. Typically, they are opportunists, "conmen," impostors— and typically also, they are consummate and convincing liars who make promises with ease and confidence, deny misconduct with utter nonchalance, and even tell solemn lies when detection is virtually certain or when lying serves no purpose whatsoever. Cleckley (1959) gives this example: "A psychopathic husband, already divorced by his wife, wrote in the footnote of a letter to her matter-of-fact instructions about the insurance policies he was sending under separate cover to provide for her and their children. There were no insurance policies and he had never seriously considered providing for his family in this way or in any other. He was well aware that he would soon be found in falsehood about this, and he had nothing to gain materially by such a lie." The lies of psychopaths—particularly the gratuitous lies—have a peculiar quality. These individuals not only have no qualms whatever, but often do not appear to be fully aware that they are lying, and cannot seem to feel or understand the nature of a falsehood: "Perhaps such people mean for the moment to do what they promise so convincingly, but the resolution passes almost as the words are spoken" (Cleckley).

Lying is also a fairly common symptom in brain disorders resulting from severe head injury, alcoholism, congenital syphilis, and encephalitis. In these conditions it is associated with a general loss of intellectual capacity, and in post-encephalitic cases with an "acting-out" syndrome that may include impulsive behavior, stealing and destructiveness as well. *See* KORSAKOFF'S SYNDROME, HEAD INJURY (CHRONIC), LEAD POISONING, SYPHILIS, EPIDEMIC ENCEPHALITIS, LIE DETECTOR.

Illustrative Case: LYING, PATHOLOGICAL TYPE

Some inept social deviants seem to falsify statements so easily, so habitually, and so convincingly, that they have been classified as "pathological liars." The observer who attempts to understand this deviant behavior is struck by the time and effort which a patient may invest in fabricating stories, and in subsequently defending his fabrications. Often the stories are complex rationalizations which elaborate a theme of self-vindication. Sometimes they are so patently wish-fulfilling that we can consider them to be private fantasies translated into communicative speech. Occasionally the fabrications seem to take no consistent direction; a patient misrepresents capriciously, and falsely accuses others or himself without apparent reason.

When fabricating and misrepresenting become autonomous and self-perpetuating activities in adulthood, we may speak of pathological lying. It is clear, however, that what we are then describing is the persistence, into the adult years, of behavior which is more appropriate to childhood. The relative immaturity of pathological lying in adult behavior is illustrated by the following case.

The patient, an eighteen-year-old boy, was brought to the hospital by a solicitous friend. From the age of six, according to his teachers and friends, the boy had been habitually falsifying. As a child, he had lied to escape responsibility for ordinary childish misdeeds, and had told "tall stories" woven around the theme of personal accomplishment and courage. As an adolescent he had impressed his friends with stories of his adventurous life, his social position, and his personal possessions. As a young adult, he was beginning to translate his extravagant tales into reality by stealing large sums of money and expensive cars, by borrowing airplanes and performing dangerous "stunts" in them, and by developing close, dependent relationships with older and more socially prominent persons. The boy was the only child of a widowed mother who told him that she wished he had never been born. She never undertook to make a permanent home for him. During her periodic alcoholic excesses, however, she characteristically appealed to her son for support, embarrassing and frightening him by her behavior. It was clear, from a study of the case, that the patient's "pathological lying" began in the common fancies and rationalizations of childhood, and represented a translation into communicative speech of his compensatory, wish-fulfilling fantasies. The patient himself explained his habitual falsification as an attempt to "build himself up." (Cameron and Magaret, 1951)

LYSERGIC ACID (LSD). A powerful hallucinogenic, "mind-expanding" drug used for experimental and therapeutic purposes.

In its natural form, lysergic acid diethylamide, LSD-25, is a derivative of ergot, a parasitic fungus that grows on rye. It was first isolated in 1938 by a Swiss chemist, Albert Hofmann. In 1943 he reported a peculiar experience involving "fantastic images of extraordinary plasticity," which was traced to inhalation of a small quantity of the substance during laboratory research. Subsequent investigation has demonstrated that LSD is far more potent than other hallucinogens, such as psilocybin and mescaline. When a solution containing a barely visible speck of LSD (one 10,000th of a gram) is injected or swallowed, it produces a full-blown psychedelic, or mind-expanding, experience lasting eight to twelve hours.

A full LSD experience is virtually indescribable, but its outstanding characteristics appear to be these: vivid sensations of sight and sound that produce either transcendent ecstasy or unspeakable horror; the feeling that the personality is disintegrating and "coming apart at the seams"; extreme time distortions, especially the sense that time is standing still and that nothing exists but the present; synesthesia, or crossed perception, in which colors are heard, music smelled, and textures tasted; an illusory feeling of surpassing understanding and speeded-up mental processes; perceptual distortions in which objects, parts of the body, pictures, and people are contracted, expanded, or twisted out of shape (*see* PLATES 24, 25, 26); and a feeling of oneness with all of humanity and the universe at large, resembling a religious experience. As a result of these "mystical" reactions, attempts have been made to form a cult based upon the use of the drug. Many individuals have sought not only an expanded inner life but a meaning for existence in their "trips"—a search that has almost invariably resulted in disappointment.

The drug is nonaddictive, and rarely produces lasting aftereffects when administered in controlled doses to carefully selected patients under medical supervision. However, it is unpredictable in its effects and can be extremely harmful if taken without proper supervision—and for this reason legislation has been enacted to limit its distribution. It is particularly dangerous in the hands of thrill seekers and cultists, since it can produce terrifying reactions and precipitate outright psychoses in unstable persons. Louria (1967), president of the New York State Council on Drug Addiction, has reported that out of 114 cases treated at Bellevue in an eighteen-month period, "13% entered the hospital with overwhelming panic. There was uncontrolled violence in 12%. Nearly 9% had attempted either homicide or suicide. Of the 114, 1 out of 7 had to

be sent to long-term mental hospitalization and half of those had no history of underlying psychiatric disorder." He concludes flatly that "there is no other drug used promiscuously under uncontrolled circumstances that is as dangerous as LSD." We might add that there is some indication that the drug may break down cell chromosomes and even produce congenital defects in children born to LSD users. This possibility is now under active investigation.

Even in stable individuals—as the excerpts at the end of this article indicate —LSD produces "psychotomimetic" effects, particularly symptoms that simulate acute schizophrenic reactions of the paranoid type. (Other psychotomimetic drugs are adrenochrome, harmine, bufotenin, mescaline, and tetrahydrocannabinol.) The discovery of these effects has led to the theory that actual schizophrenia might result from the release of a hallucinogenic chemical in the body. Attempts have therefore been made to use LSD as an investigating tool. It has been suggested that the substance might interfere with the chemistry of one of the adrenal hormones and perhaps release a substance (possibly adrenoxin) that produces the psychotic symptoms. The next step would then be to find a drug that would counteract the noxious effects of this substance. The adrenal gland is known to be involved in mobilizing the body's energy when it encounters situations of stress—and many researchers feel that schizophrenia is a stress disease. So far, however, there is no clearcut evidence for this theory, and the crucial chemical, if there is any, is yet to be discovered. *See* HALLUCINOGEN.

LSD is also used experimentally in psychotherapy, and appears to be of value in a number of ways. Various investigators report that it can help to establish rapport between patient and therapist, facilitate the uncovering and reliving of repressed memories, increase